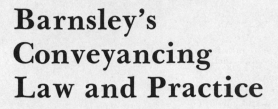
Barnsley's Conveyancing Law and Practice

Second edition

D.G. Barnsley LLM
Solicitor; Professor of Law,
University of Leicester

P.W. Smith MA
of Lincoln's Inn and
the Northern Circuit,
Barrister; Lecturer in Law,
University of Manchester

London
Butterworths
1982

England	Butterworth & Co (Publishers) Ltd 88 Kingsway, London WC2B 6AB
Australia	Butterworths Pty Ltd 271-273 Lane Cove Road, North Ryde, NSW 2113 Also at Melbourne, Brisbane, Adelaide and Perth
Canada	Butterworth & Co (Canada) Ltd 2265 Midland Avenue, Scarborough Ont M1P 451
	Butterworth & Co (Western Canada) Ltd 409 Granville Street, Ste 856, Vancouver, BC V6C 1T2
New Zealand	Butterworths of New Zealand Ltd 33-35 Cumberland Place, Wellington
South Africa	Butterworth & Co (South Africa) (Pty) Ltd 152-154 Gale Street, Durban 4001
United States of America	Mason Publishing Company Finch Bldg, 366 Wacouta Street, St Paul, Minn 55101
	Butterworth (Legal Publishers) Inc 168 Roy Street, Ste 300, Seattle, Wash 98109
	Butterworth (Legal Publishers) Inc 381 Elliot Street, Newton, Upper Falls, Mass 02164

ISBN Hardcover 0 406 55632 6
      Softcover 0 406 55633 4

Typeset by Colset Pte Ltd, Singapore

Printed and bound in Great Britain by
Billing and Sons Limited Worcester

Preface to the Second Edition

'Beginnings are such hard times'

I have not had to face the awesome task of creating a new work; not only have I had the benefit of an existing text of undoubted quality but I have also had the benefit of Professor Barnsley's work on large parts of the text. It was always his intention to undertake the revision of this new edition but he found himself unable to complete the task. I have incorporated almost all his work, which is to be found in Part II and to a lesser extent in Parts III and IV, into this edition. The responsibility for the final version, however, remains mine.

The sections that needed most updating and rewriting were those dealing with Registration of Title and the Contract Stage. To a lesser extent Remedies (Part VI) have also required careful attention. Professor Barnsley, like many another, was a supporter of 'the Cyprian Williams Heresy'. This edition exceeds the last one in extent by approximately fifty pages, reflecting Professor Barnsley's substantial revision of Parts II, III and IV, which have been largely rewritten in the light of the new case law in that area since the last edition. I have added, as an extra appendix, The Law Society Conditions of Sale (1980 Revision). The latest edition of the National Conditions of Sale, which attempts to deal with the decision in *Walker v Boyle*, appeared after the manuscript was delivered and has been incorporated at proof stage. The reader now, therefore, has the text of the general conditions of both the standard forms to hand and I am grateful to The Law Society and the Solicitors' Law Stationery Society Limited for their permission to reproduce them.

I am grateful to Stephen Sauvain, Barrister, who lent his expertise to the chapter on Planning. I should like, too, to thank Professor Barnsley for his contribution. In addition to his work on revising the text he has read the proofs and suggested many stylistic and other improvements which I have been able to incorporate into the text.

On a personal note I will always be grateful to 'P.B.F.' who set me on my way; to the one and only Joe Turner who corrected my course at a very vital stage; and to my wife, Diane, who has tolerated the use of our home as a repository for notes, books, mounted sheets and all the other matters relevant to a task such as this.

I am grateful to the editorial staff of Butterworths for the care and attention they have given me (especially with regard to handwriting!).

The law is generally that as at 1 October 1981 although a number of subsequent developments have been incorporated in the text and footnotes.

Lady Day 1982   P.W.S.
                                                            Manchester.

Preface to the First Edition

'Of making many books there is no end; and
much study is a weariness of the flesh.'

        (Ecclesiastes, Chap. XII, v. 12)

The opening part of this quotation could well be taken as an apt description of the steady stream of new law books currently flowing from the printer's press. Nevertheless I make no apology for adding to this number, for I have long felt there to be a need for a book which explains the mysteries of conveyancing, especially to students who may never have seen the inside of a solicitor's office. At a time when the solicitor's monopoly in conveyancing is being challenged, it is imperative that the aspiring conveyancer is thoroughly versed in the law and practice of his calling. The practical skills, including the art of drafting documents, he can acquire in the office, but he must generally look elsewhere for an understanding of the underlying legal rules and principles. This book, which attempts to discuss the principles of conveyancing in a practical setting, has been written primarily for the undergraduate and the articled clerk, although I cherish the fond hope that the book may be of some value to the qualified practitioner. Suggestions are sometimes made (by the uninformed) that conveyancing requires no special skills or knowledge. The pages of this book should go some way towards demonstrating the falsity of such notions.

I have sought to deal with matters chronologically as they are likely to arise in a normal conveyancing transaction, whether the title to the land is registered or unregistered. Two comments should, perhaps, be made. First, I have departed from this order in one important respect. The drafting of the conveyance (or transfer) must necessarily precede the completion of the transaction. However, it seemed to me to be desirable to have a separate section relating to conveyancing documents, rather than to attempt to slot this important subject into its correct chronological sequence. Secondly, the spread of registration of title renders it necessary to consider in detail the general principles of land registration at an early stage of the book, thus facilitating the consideration of various aspects of registered conveyancing in the subsequent pages. It is to be regretted that registration of title is not a topic which receives satisfactory treatment in real property text books, and the majority of land law courses pay but scant attention to the system. Needless to say, the solicitor of tomorrow requires a thorough understanding of the operation of the Land Registration Act 1925. Unfortunately, the need to consider two separate systems of land transfer has added considerably to the size of the book.

I have assumed that the reader has a basic knowledge of the principles of real property, equity and contract, and in the main I have refrained from covering ground that is adequately dealt with by the standard land law text books. Some overlap has been unavoidable.

Every solicitor involved in a conveyancing transaction should be familiar with the Conditions of Sale regulating the contract of sale. I have, therefore, sought to give due prominence to the terms of the National Conditions of Sale and The Law Society's Conditions of Sale. Partly because of personal preference, partly out of a desire not to confuse the reader unnecessarily, I have concentrated upon the National Conditions of Sale, though in no sense have I attempted to write a commentary on these Conditions. I should like to thank Oyez Publishing Limited, the copyright owners of the National Conditions of Sale, for allowing me to reproduce the front page of their contract form and the Conditions of Sale. I am also grateful to The Law Society for granting permission to quote extracts from their Conditions of Sale.

A wind of change is now blowing over the conveyancing scene, heralding future reforms. The Law Commission are currently looking at various topics in an attempt to simplify the transfer of land. As yet, few of their recommendations have reached the statute book, but the next decade may well see the enactment of several important changes. I have sought to draw the reader's attention to the Commission's tentative proposals, where matters are still under review, though much of the information has, perforce, been relegated to the foot-notes.

I am deeply indebted to my friend and former colleague, Professor M. J. Goodman, who has read the whole of the manuscript; his invaluable comments have saved me from many mistakes. For such errors, inconsistencies and imperfections that remain, I alone am responsible. Thanks are also due to Mr Simon Palk who has kindly read the proofs, to Mrs Barbara Abram and to my wife, both of whom rendered sterling assistance with the typing, and, by no means least, to the publishers who have so patiently endured my dilatory ways.

I have endeavoured to state the law in accordance with the material at my disposal on 30 September 1972. It has been possible, when correcting the proofs, to take account of a number of subsequent developments, mainly in the footnotes.

Finally, I should like to express the hope that, despite the length of this book, those who study its pages will not be afflicted by that 'weariness of the flesh' which seems to have plagued the Preacher of old.

D.G.B.

January 1973

Contents

APPENDICES

Table of statutes

References in this Table to 'Statutes' are to Halsbury's Statutes of England (Third Edition) showing the volume and page at which the annotated text of the Act will be found.

Table of cases

List of Abbreviations

Statutes and Rules

AEA 1925	Administration of Estates Act 1925
CP (VD) A 1981	Compulsory Purchase (Vesting Declarations) Act 1981
LCA 1925	Land Charges Act 1925
LCA 1972	Land Charges Act 1972
LG & P (A) A 1981	Local Government and Planning (Amendment) Act 1981
LPA 1922	Law of Property Act 1922
LPA 1925	Law of Property Act 1925
LP (Am) A 1926	Law of Property (Amendment) Act 1926
LPA 1969	Law of Property Act 1969
LRA 1925	Land Registration Act 1925
LR & LCA 1971	Land Registration and Land Charges Act 1971
LRR 1925	Land Registration Rules 1925
SLA 1925	Settled Land Act 1925
T & CPA 1947	Town and Country Planning Act 1947
T & CPA 1953	Town and Country Planning Act 1953
T & CPA 1968	Town and Country Planning Act 1968
T & CPA 1971	Town and Country Planning Act 1971
T & CP (Am) A 1972	Town and Country Planning (Amendment) Act 1972
T & CP (Am) A 1977	Town and Country Planning (Amendment) Act 1977

Books and Periodicals

Brickdale	Brickdale and Stewart-Wallace, *The Land Registration Act 1925* (4th edn, 1939).
Cheshire	Cheshire, *Modern Law of Real Property* (13th edn, 1982).
CLJ	Cambridge Law Journal.
Co. Litt.	Coke's Commentary on Littleton's *Tenures* (19th edn, 1832, with notes by F. Hargrave and C. Butler).
Conv (NS)	The Conveyancer and Property Lawyer (new series).
Conv Prec	The Conveyancer and Property Lawyer, Precedents for the Conveyancer
Dart	Dart, *Treatise on the Law and Practice Relating to Vendors and Purchasers of Real Estate* (2 vols) (8th edn, 1929).

Emmet	Emmet, *Notes on Perusing Titles and on Practical Conveyancing* (17th edn, 1978).
Ency F & P	Encyclopaedia of Forms and Precedents (23 vols) (4th edn, 1966 – 72).
Farrand	Farrand, *Contract and Conveyance* (3rd edn, 1980).
Gibson	Gibson, *Conveyancing* (21st edn, 1980).
Hallett	Hallett, *Conveyancing Precedents* (1965).
Hayton	Hayton, *Registered Land* (3rd edn, 1981).
JPL	Journal of Planning and Property Law.
K & E	Key and Elphinstone, *Precedents in Conveyancing* (3 vols) (15th edn, 1953 – 54).
LQR	Law Quarterly Review.
LS Gaz	The Law Society's Gazette.
MLR	Modern Law Review.
M & W	Megarry and Wade, *The Law of Real Property* (4th edn, 1975).
NLJ	New Law Journal.
Parker's Precedents	Parker, *Modern Conveyancing Precedents* (1964).
Potter	Potter, *Principles and Practice of Conveyancing under the Land Registration Act 1925* (1934).
Prideaux's Precedents	Prideaux, *Forms and Precedents in Conveyancing* (3 vols) (25th edn, 1958 – 59).
R & R	Ruoff and Roper, *Registered Conveyancing* (4th edn, 1979).
Snell	Snell, *Principles of Equity* (27th edn, 1973).
Sol Jo	Solicitors' Journal.
Walford	Walford, *Contracts and Conditions of Sale of Land* (2nd edn, 1957).
W & C	Wolstenholme and Cherry, *Conveyancing Statutes* (13th edn, 1972).
Williams Title	Williams on Title (4th edn, 1975).
Williams V & P	Williams, *A Treatise on the Law of Vendor and Purchaser* (2 vols) (4th edn, 1936).

Standard Forms of Contract

Con Law CS	Conveyancing Lawyers' Conditions of Sale (1978).
LSC	The Law Society's Conditions of Sale (1980).
NCS	The National Conditions of Sale (20th edn).

Part One

Introduction

Chapter 1

Conveyancing procedures in outline

A Introduction

Compared with other forms of property, land has always occupied a peculiar position in English law. Though not itself the subject of ownership, save in the sense dictated by the doctrine of tenure that all land is owned by the Crown, it is capable of supporting a number of estates and interests which exist quite separately from the land and which are themselves capable of ownership and of being alienated. For centuries land was the most important form of wealth and it has long been necessary to regulate the manner in which land, or rather estates in land, could be acquired. It is not the scheme of this chapter to consider the history of different forms of land transfer, or conveyance[1]. Nor is it our concern to trace the wide divergencies which have existed in our law since the earliest times between the law of real property, or land, and personal property. Suffice it to say that despite the assimilation of realty and personalty effected by the property legislation of 1925[2], several important differences still persist, which render it necessary to distinguish between the transfer of goods and the transfer of land.

Particularly is this true as to the mode of alienation. A contract for the sale of, say, a valuable painting may be negotiated and finalised within a few minutes. Neither the contract nor the transfer of ownership is subject to any special formalities. Physical delivery of the painting to the buyer suffices to transfer the ownership to him. But a contract for the sale of an estate in land cannot be effected so simply. Physical delivery of the subject-matter of the contract, the estate, is not possible. A transfer can only be effected by a document under seal[3]. The contract itself, to be enforceable by action, must at least be

---

1 A brief mention of some of the more important forms is made in Chap. 17, pp. 481–482, post. For a full discussion, see Holdsworth, *A History of English Law*, Vol. iii, 217–56; Vol. vii, 353–87.

2 See Cheshire, 88–93.

3 LPA 1925, s. 52 (1). This has not always been the rule. At common law a feoffment with livery of seisin did not require writing to be valid, though it was not uncommon to execute a charter of feoffment as evidence of the transaction. Writing did not become essential until the Statute of Frauds 1677, s. 1, but by this time the feoffment had been superseded by other more convenient forms of alienation. The system of conveyancing by deeds may be said to have sprung from the Statute of Enrolments 1535. This statute was passed to prevent the Statute of Uses 1535, operating to pass a legal estate by means of an oral bargain and sale, which in equity created a use in favour of the purchaser. It required every bargain and sale of an estate of inheritance to be made by writing, indented, sealed and enrolled in a court of record.

3

evidenced in writing[4]. Furthermore the land may be subject to third-party rights, and unless the purchaser conducts adequate inquiries as to their existence he may find his enjoyment of the land disturbed. The complexities of our land law prompted Baron Pollock to make the following comparison during the course of his opinion delivered to the Lords in the famous case of *Bain v Fothergill*[5] — that whereas a man who sells goods must be taken to know whether they are his or not, no layman can be supposed to know what is the exact nature of his title to real property, or whether it be good against the whole world or not. Whilst this comment should now be read in the light of the simplification of our land law structure effected by the legislation of 1925, it does serve to show the need for a purchaser of land to investigate his vendor's title in order to verify that he is able to convey what he has contracted to convey. An investigation of this nature is not normally considered necessary, nor undertaken, on a sale of goods.

A transfer on sale of an estate in land is divisible into two distinct stages:
(i) the contract stage, ending with the formation of a binding contract for sale,
(ii) the conveyance stage, culminating in the legal title vesting in the purchaser by means of the appropriate instrument under seal. It may be helpful to give a brief survey of the main stages in a typical vendor-purchaser transaction where the parties are represented by different solicitors[6]. It will be left to later chapters of the book to fill in the detail and explain the effects of the various steps in the chain of procedure. The position where the land is unregistered and therefore not affected by the Land Registration Act 1925, will be considered first.

B   Unregistered land

(a) Preparation of contract[7]
Assuming the parties intend to proceed by way of a formal contract, a contract is drafted in duplicate by the vendor's solicitor and forwarded to the purchaser's solicitor for approval. It is frequently prepared on a printed form of contract, which contains a host of terms, known as General Conditions of Sale, which regulate the rights of the parties in relation to the transaction. The two forms in most general use are the National Conditions of Sale (20th edn) (1981) and The Law Society's Conditions of Sale (1980 Revision[8]). Many local law societies also publish their own forms which are widely used by local solicitors. The contract should contain a full description of the land to be sold, the liabilities subject to which it is held and any special terms (Special Conditions of Sale) agreed upon by the parties. The title deeds should be perused and full instructions obtained from the vendor before any attempt is made to draft the contract.

---

4   LPA 1925, s. 40 (1), pp. 101–114, post. In the absence of writing equity may enforce the contract under the doctrine of part performance; see pp. 116–125, post.
5   (1874) LR 7 HL 158, at 173, p. 587, post. See also *Re Spencer and Hauser's Contract* [1928] Ch 598 at 607, per Tomlin J.
6   For a detailed table of the usual procedure on a sale of freehold unregistered land, reference should be made to 18 Ency F & P, 374.
7   See Chap. 6.
8   This Revision makes several amendments, mainly of a minor nature, to The Law Society's Conditions of Sale (1973 edn). See further note 14, p. 139, post.

(b) Approval of contract

It is the responsibility of the purchaser's solicitor to approve the draft contract, subject to such amendments as may be necessary. Strictly, approval is dependent upon the results of certain searches and inquiries that are customarily made[9], as follows:

(i) a search in the register of local land charges to ascertain the existence of any charges affecting the property;

(ii) additional inquiries of local authorities to discover details of matters within their knowledge, which are not registrable as local land charges but are of equal concern to a purchaser;

(iii) preliminary inquiries made of the vendor to elicit information about the property upon matters which the vendor is under no general duty to disclose in the contract.

Approval of the draft contract is signified by returning one copy to the vendor's solicitor. Each solicitor then obtains his client's signature to the contract in his possession.

(c) Exchange of contracts[10]

No binding agreement comes into existence until contracts are exchanged. This is normally effected through the post. The purchaser's solicitor sends to his opposite number the contract signed by the purchaser, accompanied (usually) by a cheque for the deposit which all formal contracts require to be paid. On its receipt by the vendor's solicitor he posts to the purchaser's solicitor the contract signed by the vendor. Exchange of contracts represents the crossing of the legal Rubicon, so to speak, for neither party can as a general rule subsequently withdraw from the transaction without committing a breach of contract, unless the other party consents.

(d) Deducing title[11]

The law does not require a vendor to furnish any evidence of his legal entitlement to the subject-matter of the contract until the parties are in a contractual relationship. After exchange of contracts he must provide the purchaser with a chronological statement of the documents and events by virtue of which he became entitled to the property. Traditionally this duty has been discharged by means of an abstract of title. This document is prepared by the vendor's solicitor and sets out the required information in a special format. It covers a period of time fixed by the contract. Today it is far more common to supply photographic copies of all relevant deeds within the period. In due course the vendor will be called upon to verify the contents of the abstract. This stage in the transaction is generally termed 'deducing title'.

(e) Investigation of title[12]

The purchaser's solicitor bases his assessment of the soundness of the vendor's title on his perusal of the abstract of title, or copy documents, and its, or their, subsequent verification by examination against the original deeds and documents in the vendor's possession. In practice the examination is performed at

9   See Chap. 7.
10   See Chap. 9.
11   See Chap. 10. For the meaning of this word 'title', see pp. 278–279, post.
12   See Chap. 13.

the time of completion (as to which see the next stage). The investigation of title is undertaken to ensure that the vendor has the title which he has agreed to sell. The purchaser's solicitor submits any doubts or inquiries about the state of the title to the vendor's solicitor in the form of requisitions on title which set out the purchaser's requirements for putting the title in order. If he is dissatisfied with the vendor's answers, he may submit further observations on these replies. In practice the Conditions of Sale usually curtail a purchaser's right to raise requisitions and further observations ad infinitum. It is essential to undertake this investigation notwithstanding that the title has recently been investigated on a previous sale. A purchaser should never rely on the investigation conducted on behalf of someone else. Not only might mistakes have been made, but the previous owner might have accepted risks in relation to some matter immaterial to him but perhaps vital to the purchaser.

It is the responsibility of the purchaser's solicitor to prepare the draft conveyance which is submitted in duplicate to the vendor's solicitor normally at the same time as, and subject to, the requisitions. It is also his task to engross (i.e. type) the conveyance, after approval, for execution by the parties[13].

One other point should be mentioned. A few days prior to the completion date, the purchaser's solicitor should obtain an official certificate of search[14] in the register of land charges.

(f) Completion[15]

This is the final step in the transaction. Completion takes place usually at the offices of the vendor's solicitor. In exchange for the balance of the purchase money, the purchaser's solicitor receives the deeds of the property including the conveyance to the purchaser, duly executed (i.e. signed, sealed and delivered) by the vendor. It is this document which operates under s. 52 (1) of the Law of Property Act 1925, to convey the legal estate to the purchaser. After completion various tasks, generally of a minor nature, remain to be performed but specific mention of these need not be made here.

C   Registered conveyancing

1.   Historical development

The system of unregistered conveyancing is self-perpetuating. On a sale of land by a vendor, the purchaser investigates the title in the manner briefly described in the previous section. The same process is repeated when the purchaser comes to sell. Though we have seen that there are valid reasons why a purchaser should not rely on a previous investigation, the work involved is

---

13   Many purchases of residential property are financed with the aid of a mortgage. Where a separate solicitor acts for the mortgagee, he conducts a separate investigation of the title on behalf of the mortgagee. The purchaser's solicitor deduces title and answers any requisitions raised by the mortgagee's solicitor. The latter usually has before him the replies to the purchaser's own requisitions, so that in practice any further requisitions relate to matters solely concerning the mortgage transaction or overlooked by the purchaser's solicitor on his investigation. The mortgagee's solicitor drafts the mortgage deed. Institutional lenders have their own printed forms of mortgage which merely require completing by the insertion of the mortgagor's name and address, details of the loan and a description of the property.

14   See Chap. 14, pp. 400–403, post.

15   See Chap. 15.

largely repetitive and represents a high wastage of man-hours, to say nothing of higher costs to be borne by the public.

Attempts to reform the system of land transfer go back almost one hundred and fifty years. In 1830 the Real Property Commissioners reported that:

> ' The great difficulties which occur in selling estates and obtaining money on real security, the time which usually elapses before the completion of such transactions, and the harassing expenses and disappointments which attend them, are evils universally acknowledged.'

Subsequent reports followed in 1850 and 1857, culminating in the Land Registry Act 1862, whose purpose was, according to its preamble, 'to give certainty to the title to real estate and to facilitate the proof thereof and also to render the dealing with land more simple and economical'. Alas, the effectiveness of its provisions was not matched by the grandeur of its ideals. For reasons that need not detain us, this Act proved to be a total failure and it was replaced by the Land Transfer Act 1875, which was intended to achieve the same objectives. The system established by this Act is basically the same as that operating today, but in practical terms the Act was not particularly effective as adoption of the system was purely voluntary. Compulsory registration was not introduced until the Land Transfer Act 1897[16]. The Acts of 1875 and 1897 were replaced by the Land Registration Act 1925, which also introduced a number of important changes. This Act, together with the Land Registration Rules 1925, made under it, contains the bulk of the relevant law on land registration.

Compulsory registration is extended to a particular area by means of an Order in Council; thereafter certain transactions affecting land within that area lead to first registration of title[17]. At the time of the Act of 1925 it was uncertain whether registration of title was desirable on a widespread scale and so compulsory registration could only be introduced subject to certain safeguards[18]. When in the 1960's the central government committed itself to extending the system throughout the whole of England and Wales, the complicated procedural requirements became unnecessary and were swept away by the Land Registration Act 1966[19]. This Act which also curtailed the power to register land voluntarily was passed as part of an eight-year plan designed to introduce compulsory registration in all built-up areas by 1973. Unfortunately financial stringencies during the period and the increase in conveyancing business have thwarted its implementation[20].

2. Objectives of system

Like its predecessors, the Land Registration Act 1925 has as its principal objective the simplification of land transfer. Its title is somewhat misleading, for it

16   It was first made applicable to parts of the County of London during 1899 and became fully operative throughout the whole of the county on 1 July 1902.
17   LRA 1925, ss. 120 (1), 123 (1), p. 19, post.
18   LRA 1925, ss. 121, 122.
19   Section 1 (1).
20   See the Chief Land Registrar's Report for 1970–71. The Registrar's Report for the year ending 31 March 1972, reveals that on that date there were 3,851, 486 separate registered titles and that during the period under review 225,005 applications for *first* registration were completed. This represented an increase of almost 20 per cent as compared with the previous year, despite the fact that it had not been possible to extend compulsory registration to any new area during the year. The registered system now handles about two-fifths of all conveyancing in England and Wales. For a list of areas where registration is compulsory, see Appendix A.

deals with a system, not of registration of land, but of titles to land. Basically it provides for the registration under separate and distinct titles of freehold estates and certain leasehold estates in land. The essential features of this system are:

1. The establishment of a register of title to freehold and leasehold land containing a more-or-less complete record of all matters relating to each registered title, including the name of the proprietor and the incumbrances and other interests affecting the land.
2. The provision of a facile mode of transfer by eliminating the lengthy investigation of title and simplifying documents of transfer.
3. The introduction of a state indemnity scheme under which compensation is paid to a registered proprietor deprived of his title.

On a transfer of registered land it is unnecessary for the purchaser to delve into the past history of the land in order to discover whether the vendor has a good title. A once-for-all investigation of title has in fact been conducted by the Registry at the time of first registration[1]. All the purchaser need do is satisfy himself that the vendor is the registered proprietor subject only to those third party interests disclosed in the contract. This he can do simply by inspecting a copy of the entries in the register, which the vendor can readily supply. It should be understood that this brief explanation amounts to something of an over-simplification, and the reader will encounter exceptions and qualifications in the subsequent pages.

The advantages of land registration are seen in relation to what has previously been described as the conveyance stage. The procedure leading up to exchange of contracts remains much the same. Ultimately the transaction is completed, but unlike the normal position in unregistered conveyancing the purchaser of registered land does not at this stage acquire the legal title. A further step is necessary — registration.

3. Effect on substantive law

The purpose of the land registration legislation has been to simplify land transfer within the basic framework of the land law. It does not seek to introduce substantive changes applicable solely to registered land. A few examples taken at random may help to demonstrate this vital consideration.

1. The Act provides for the registration of legal estates which are defined to mean 'the estates interests and charges in or over land . . . which are, by the Law of Property Act 1925, authorised to subsist or be created at law.'[2]
2. The register of title is merely intended to be a substitute for title deeds and by and large it does not record any information not revealed in title deeds.
3. Section 82 (1) (g) of the Act permits rectification of the register so as to deprive the proprietor of his title where a legal estate has been registered in the name of a person who if the land had not been registered would not have been the estate owner[3].

---

1 Should the title be defective in some material respect, the proprietor may be registered with an inferior grade of title; see p. 30, post.
2 LRA 1925, ss. 2 (1), 3 (xi). See also pp. 33–34, post, where the view is considered that the Act creates a new statutory estate.
3 See further p. 82, post.

The reader will, however, be mistaken if he imagines that the Act makes no changes in the law of real property as it affects registered land. There are important differences which necessarily flow from the changes made in the machinery of conveyancing. Basic differences exist as to the method of creation of legal rights, their disposition and mode of protection. In particular it should be noted that once a title has been registered, it is registration alone that operates to vest a legal title in the transferee. A duly executed transfer of registered land does not of itself have the same effect as a conveyance of unregistered land[4].

The view has recently been expressed[5] that there has hitherto existed a general failure to appreciate the full import of the changes effected by the Act. This has retarded the development of distinct registration principles, and the judiciary has been chided for their continual resort to general land law concepts in the solution of registration problems, resulting sometimes in a virtual denial of the system. This criticism is by no means entirely justified. The Act of 1925 and its predecessors were founded on existing land law principles and it is hardly surprising that these principles should have permeated the judges' attitude to and interpretation of the Act. Perhaps the time has come for a thorough re-appraisal of the underlying aims and purposes of the system of land registration in this country but this cannot be done satisfactorily within the framework of the present system as laid down by the Land Registration Act 1925.

D Simplification of existing procedures

It may be many years before the extension of land registration totally eclipses the older method of land transfer — time enough to have a good look at existing unregistered procedures with a view to alteration where desirable. The procedure outlined in Section B of the chapter has altered little during the past one hundred years, except that the practice of making preliminary inquiries[6] is of comparatively recent growth, and one which by no means meets with the approval of many practitioners. However as compared with the pre-1926 era, titles to land have become much less complicated and a purchaser's investigation of his vendor's title far less tortuous. The land law reforms effected by the property legislation of 1925 were principally responsible for this improvement. The basis of modern conveyancing is the legal estate and as the reader already knows, only two estates in land are capable of subsisting at law. A purchaser need not as a general rule investigate the title to equitable interests affecting the land. These either operate behind a 'curtain' and are overreached on a conveyance of the legal estate in the proper manner, being transferred to the proceeds of sale, or else require registration as land charges to bind a purchaser of the land.

Today a wind of change blows across the conveyancing scene. More and more practitioners are becoming familiar with the advantages of the system of

4   Yet a purchaser cannot obtain registration without a transfer from the vendor. See pp. 451–455, post.
5   Jackson, 'Registration of Land Interests — The English Version' (1972) 88 LQR 93, 94–97, 136–37.
6   Many of the matters now included within preliminary enquiries were previously, though perhaps improperly, asked as requisitions on title.

registration of title and are beginning to challenge long-established procedures. In particular a school of thought exists which maintains that a purchaser should be furnished with all information necessary to approve the vendor's title (including the abstract of title) before, rather than after, exchange of contracts.

It was only to be expected that the Law Commission would find in land transfer a fruitful topic for study[7] and they are presently engaged in an examination of the whole law relating to the transfer of both registered and unregistered land with a view to its modernisation and simplification. The Commission soon appreciated that neither objective could be achieved without improvements in the substantive law. Accordingly various subjects were earmarked for consideration, as follows[8]: root of title, restrictive covenants, local land charges, purchasers' inquiries, land charges, vendors' duty of disclosure affecting title, standard forms and implied covenants. The Commission's proposals in relation to some of these matters have already been implemented, notably the reduction in the period of investigation of title from thirty years to fifteen years[9], which the Commission considered to be 'a substantial and immediate contribution towards simplifying unregistered conveyancing'[10]. As the Commission's review of the law of land transfer covers many topics which cannot be looked at in total isolation, it may be some years before the full effect of their deliberations and recommendations is felt in day-to-day conveyancing practice. It is to be hoped that any substantial changes will reach the statute book before registered conveyancing becomes so widespread that unregistered conveyancing has become a rarity.

As to land registration the Commission are engaged upon a review of the basic principles of the law in the context of conveyancing. So far they have published three Working Papers for comment[11]. It appears that the Commission are concerned to eliminate defects in the existing system, rather than suggest fundamental changes which 'could only serve to delay the spread of compulsory registration'[12].

7   Item IX of the Commission's First Programme of Law Reform.
8   1st Annual Report, Law Com. No. 4, paras. 70–71.
9   LPA 1969, s. 23 amending the LPA 1925, s. 44 (1), pp. 282–286, post. See the Commission's Interim Report on root of title to freehold land (Law Com. No. 9). The Act of 1969 also implements recommendations made in their Reports on restrictive covenants (Law Com. No. 11) and on land charges affecting unregistered land (Law Com. No. 18).
10   Law Com. No. 9, para. 3.
11   These published Papers deal in the main with leaseholds (Paper No. 32), overriding interests (Paper No. 37), identity and boundaries, and rectification and indemnity (Paper No. 45).
12   See Working Paper No. 32, para. 7. Cf. p. 9, ante.

Part Two

The system of land registration

Chapter 2

General principles of land registration

A   The administrative machinery

The statutes in force relating to registration of title to land are the Land Registration Acts[1] of 1925, 1936 and 1966, the Land Registration and Land Charges Act 1971, Parts I and III, and the Administration of Justice Act 1977, ss. 24–26. The bulk of the relevant law is contained in the Act of 1925, but this is no more than a skeleton of the basic provisions. The detailed rules are left to be worked out by various Land Registration Rules[2] made under section 144 of the parent statute. These have the same force as if they had been enacted in the Act. Unfortunately the drafting of the Act and the Rules leaves something to be desired, and inconsistencies and obscurities are not difficult to find.

1.   The Land Registry

Section 126 (1) of the Act of 1925 provides for the continuance of an office[3] in London to be called Her Majesty's Land Registry, the business of which is to be conducted by a registrar appointed by the Lord Chancellor and known as the Chief Land Registrar.

Section 132 enables district registries to be created for the purposes of registration of titles to land within a particular area. The increase in the volume of business during the past 25 years has resulted in the establishment at periodic intervals of district registries at Birkenhead, Croydon, Durham, Gloucester, Harrow, Lytham, Nottingham, Peterborough, Plymouth, Stevenage, Swansea, Tunbridge Wells and Weymouth[4]. Each district registry is the proper office for the registration of titles to land in its district and for the delivery of any application relating to such land. The headquarters office in London is no longer responsible for any area and applications cannot be accepted there.

There are maintained at the various registries (in relation to land within the areas which they serve) the following:

1   Except where otherwise indicated, references in the text of this chapter and in Chaps. 3 and 4 to 'the Act' or 'the Rules' are references to the LRA 1925, and the LRR 1925, respectively.
2   These being principally the Rules of 1925, 1967, 1976, 1977 and 1978.
3   This is in fact the same office (under a new title) as that originally established by the Land Registry Act 1862, s. 108. It is located at Lincoln's Inn Fields, London, WC2. The Land Registry is a Department of the Civil Service.
4   For the administrative areas covered by each district registry, see the Schedule to the Land Registration (District Registries) Order 1980, S.I. 1980 No. 1499.

 (i)   A register of title to freehold and leasehold land[5]. This comprises the
       sum total of all the registered titles, individual particulars of which are
       maintained on a vast card index system.
 (ii) Index maps, collectively termed the public index map, which show the
       position and extent of every registered estate[6]. As its name suggests, it is
       available for inspection by any member of the public.
(iii) An index of proprietors' names in alphabetical order, showing the
       numbers of the titles, charges, or incumbrances of which the several
       persons mentioned therein are proprietors[7].
(iv)   A list of pending applications, also open to public inspection[8].

The role played by these various documents will be more fully discussed in
this chapter and elsewhere in the book.

2.   The Chief Land Registrar

At the head of this complex system is the Chief Land Registrar, assisted by a
vast array of registrars, assistant registrars, clerks, messengers and servants[9].
He must be a barrister or solicitor of at least ten years' standing[10] and is charged
with the conduct of the whole business of registration under the Act[11]. He is
authorised to formulate such forms and directions as may be requisite, and can
permit necessary alterations or additions to the statutory forms prescribed in
the Schedule to the Rules of 1925. One of the most important powers vested in
him is the jurisdiction to hear and determine disputes affecting registered titles.
A general power is contained in r. 298 (1), which provides:

  'If any question, doubt, dispute, difficulty or complaint arises before the
  Registrar upon any application or during any investigation of title —
  (a) as to the registration of a title, incumbrance or charge,
  (b) as to any dealing with any registered title, incumbrance or charge or
       any matter entered or noted in or omitted from the register, or
  (c) as to the amendment, or withdrawal from the register or production
       to the registrar of any certificate or other document, or
  (d) in any registration or other proceeding in the Registry, or
  (e) as to any claim for indemnity
  . . . the Registrar shall hear and determine the matter and, subject to
  appeal to the court, make such order in the matter as he shall think just.'

He also has ancillary powers to summon witnesses and compel the production
of documents[12]: Extensive though r. 298 is, the Registrar's jurisdiction is
confined to disputes directly or indirectly involving an application for registration. It does not follow that merely because there is an issue concerning

 5 LRA 1925, s. 1.
 6 LRR 1925, r. 8. See p. 203, post.
 7 LRR 1925, r. 9.
 8 LRR 1925, r. 10, as substituted by the LRR 1978, r. 4. There is also a Minor Interests
    Index (see r. 11) which regulates the priority inter se of certain equitable interests affecting
    registered land. This Index is really extraneous to the general scheme of registration of
    title and the Law Commission recommend its abolition: see Published Working Paper
    No. 37, paras. 96–108, but see [1981] Conv 323.
 9 LRA 1925, s. 126 (1).
10 Administration of Justice Act 1956, s. 53, replacing s. 126 (2) of the LRA 1925.
11 LRA 1925, s. 127.
12 LRA 1925, s. 128 (1).

registered land, the Registrar will determine the matter; specific performance suits, actions for breach of covenants and the like come before the courts in the normal way. He only becomes involved in such disputes when a copy of any court order affecting a registered title is served on him so that he can give effect to it by making the necessary entry in the register of title[13]. No procedural rules governing the conduct of hearings before the Registrar are laid down, but this does not appear to create any practical problems[14].

A person aggrieved by the Registrar's order or decision has a right of appeal to the Chancery Division of the High Court[15]. Instead of determining the dispute himself, the Registrar can refer it at any stage to the High Court, a procedure that has been adopted in a few cases recently[16]. The Registrar and those acting under his authority are exonerated from personal liability in respect of acts done or omitted to be done in good faith in the exercise or supposed exercise of their statutory powers[17].

District registrars

As regards the land within the jurisdiction of his registry, each district registrar has the same powers and indemnities as the Chief Land Registrar[18], except that (a) powers and duties personal to the Chief Land Registrar continue to be reserved to and exercised by him and (b) all other powers and duties of a district registrar are exercised and performed under the general direction and authority of the Chief Land Registrar[19].

3. The Lord Chancellor

The making of regulations for the conduct of business at the Land Registry is vested in the Lord Chancellor[20]. He has a wide power to make general rules covering a variety of purposes contained in s. 144 (1) and it is under this provision that the various rules have been made. In the formulation thereof he is assisted by a body of persons known as the Rule Committee, consisting of a judge of the Chancery Division of the High Court, the Chief Land Registrar and three others, one to be chosen by the General Council of the Bar, another by the Ministry of Agriculture and Fisheries and the third by the Council of The Law Society. He is also responsible for the appointment of the Chief Land Registrar himself and, with the concurrence of the Treasury, has established the thirteen district registries.

B Registrable interests

In unregistered land rights in or over land fall into three main groups: (i) legal estates, (ii) legal interests which bind a purchaser of the land affected with or

---

13 See *MEPC Ltd v Christian-Edwards* [1981] AC 205, [1979] 3 All ER 752.
14 See Curtis, 'Hearings before the Chief Land Registrar' (1956) 20 Conv (NS) 194.
15 LRR 1925, r. 299.
16 LRR 1925, rr. 220 (4), 298 (2). See *Re Boyle's Claim* [1961] 1 All ER 620; *Re White Rose Cottage* [1965] Ch 940, [1965] 1 All ER 11, CA; *Barclay's Bank Ltd v Taylor* [1974] Ch 137, [1973] 1 All ER 752, CA; *Myton Ltd v Schwab-Morris* [1974] 1 All ER 326.
17 LRA 1925, s. 131.
18 LRA 1925, s. 133.
19 Land Registration (District Registries) Order 1980, S.I. 1980 No. 1499, para. 2 (3).
20 LRA 1925, s. 126 (6).

without notice[1] and (iii) equitable rights which are either overreached (e.g. interests under a settlement) or binding under the principle of notice. The Act of 1925 has a not-exactly corresponding tripartite division of (i) registrable interests, (ii) overriding interests and (iii) minor interests. Only an interest falling within the first category is capable of being entered on the register of title under its own separate title number. This may conveniently be termed substantive registration. Interests within (ii) and (iii) are protected in the manner provided by the Act in ways to be discussed in the next chapter. This threefold classification is perhaps not entirely accurate. A hybrid group exists, consisting of legal mortgages and legal charges which partake of characteristics of groups (i) and (iii). These are not capable of substantive registration as separate titles, yet the mortgagee receives a certificate (known as a charge certificate) as evidence of his title to the charge in the same way as the proprietor of a registered interest receives a land certificate. The existence of the charge is noted on the mortgagor's register of title, which is a mode of protection applicable to minor interests[2].

As we observed in the previous chapter[3] the Act, despite its title, provides for the registration of titles to land. Section 2 (1) enacts that:

' After the commencement of this Act estates capable of subsisting as legal estates shall be the only interests in land in respect of which a proprietor can be registered and all other interests in registered land (except overriding interests and interests entered on the register at or before such commencement) shall take effect in equity as minor interests. . . .'

Just as there may be several legal estates existing in relation to a particular plot of land, so there may be several registered titles affecting the one plot. The expression 'legal estates' is defined[4] to cover those interests capable of existing as legal interests within the Law of Property Act 1925, s. 1 (2). Section 2 (1) merely limits the boundaries of registrable estates. It does not say that they must be registered; the need to register the title to any particular estate is governed by other provisions.

1. Freehold estates

An estate owner holding a legal estate in fee simple whether entitled beneficially or as limited owner, or a person entitled to require such an estate to be vested in him[5] may apply to be registered in respect of that estate[6]. An estate subject to a subsisting right of redemption and the equitable interest arising under a contract for sale cannot be the subject of any substantive registration. Parts of a house or building, such as a freehold flat, can be separately registered. 'Land' includes mines and minerals whether or not held with the

---

1   Save for puisne mortgages which, though legal, are brought within the scheme of statutory notice by the LCA 1972. This Act consolidates the LCA 1925, and other enactments relating to the registration of land charges, without making any substantive alterations in the law.
2   Mortgages are more fully considered in Chap. 16, pp. 464–469, post. For land certificates, see p. 34, post.
3   Pages 7–8, ante.
4   LRA 1925, s. 3 (xi).
5   E.g. a remainderman who becomes entitled absolutely and beneficially on the death of the life tenant.
6   LRA 1925, s. 4.

surface, so that mines and minerals that have been horizontally severed from the surface can be registered. Registration of a freehold title automatically extends to the mines and minerals under the land (other than coal), unless they have previously been severed, in which case the Registrar is bound to record the fact on the register[7]. An undivided share in land is expressly excluded from the statutory definition of 'land' and is therefore not capable of substantive registration[8].

2. Leasehold estates

The title to a term of years absolute is registrable, except as follows[9]:

(i) *Leasehold land held under a lease containing an absolute prohibition against all dealings therewith inter vivos.* Since registered conveyancing is concerned to simplify land transfers, nothing can be achieved by registering an inalienable estate[10]. The reasoning advocated for this exclusion is suspect since a covenant against assignment does not make an assignment in breach of covenant unlawful or ineffective[11]. The leasor may elect not to enforce his right of re-entry (assuming there is a forfeiture clause), or he may waive it expressly or impliedly by acceptance of rent with knowledge of the breach.

(ii) *A term of years demised by way of mortgage whilst there is a subsisting right of redemption.* A mortgagee by demise cannot register his term of years as a title with its own distinct title number separate from that of the mortgagor's freehold.

(iii) *A lease for a term of which twenty-one years or less are unexpired.* Careful note should be taken of this exception as it is of vital importance, and attention must be paid to the way in which the Act deals with these leases[12]. A lease and a reversionary lease commencing on or within one month of its expiration form one continuous term for the present purposes, if they are vested in the same person in the same right[13]. This exception precludes first registration of any short term lease; it does not affect the need to complete by registration the transfer of an *existing registered* leasehold title with a term of less than 21 years unexpired at the time of the transfer[14].

(iv) *An equitable lease.* Notwithstanding the fact that s. 3 (x) of the Act defines 'lease' as including an agreement for a lease, a person entitled to an equitable lease cannot apply for substantive registration of his lease. An

7 LRR 1925, r. 196.
8 LRA 1925, s. 3 (viii). As to the position where at the commencement of the Act the title to an undivided share in land was registered, see the LRA 1925, s. 78.
9 LRA 1925, s. 8 (1), (2). For the meaning of 'term of years absolute', see s. 3 (xxvii). Leasehold titles are further considered in Chap. 16, pp. 456–464, post.
10 R & R, 453. The Law Commission are of the provisional opinion that this exception should be abolished: Published Working Paper No. 32, para. 27.
11 See *Old Grovebury Manor Farm Ltd v W Seymour Plant Sales and Hire Ltd (No. 2)* [1979] 3 All ER 504, CA.
12 See pp. 22 and 456, post. This category includes leases originally granted for less than 21 years and leases granted for more than 21 years where less than 21 years remain unexpired at the time of application for first registration; see LRA 1925, s. 8 (1) (a).
13 LRR 1925, r. 47.
14 See p. 462, post.

applicant for registration must be the owner of a *legal* estate[15]. Nor does the lessee come within the category mentioned in s. 8 (1) (b) of a person entitled to require a legal leasehold estate, *held* under such a lease, to be vested in him; the word 'held' indicates that the leasehold estate is already in existence. A mere right to require its creation is insufficient[16].

3. Easements

It should be remembered that easements possess a double aspect, as appurtenant to the dominant land and as obligations binding the servient land. Here we are concerned with the rights of the dominant owner. An easement is within the definition of a legal estate for the purposes of s. 2 (1) of the Act[17], but it is not possible for the dominant owner to register his easement separately from the dominant land[18]. Registration of easements as a separate species of property is, of course, unnecessary. They can only exist for the benefit of the dominant land and cannot be dealt with separately from that land. Furthermore, on first registration the Registrar does not automatically register appurtenant easements. This is technically unnecessary, for registration of a person as proprietor of land vests in him the legal estate together with all rights, privileges and appurtenances belonging thereto[19]. This reveals a minor defect in the system since the description of the registered estate appearing in the proprietor's property register[20] may be incomplete, and a purchaser from him can only ascertain the existence of appurtenant easements by making specific inquiries.

It is always open for the applicant for first registration, or any proprietor of a registered estate, to apply in writing for a specific entry to be made on the register of any appurtenant easement, though he will be required to furnish evidence of its existence[1]. Only legal easements can be entered as appurtenant to the registered estate[2]. Entry of the easement as part of the description of the registered land confers a title to it corresponding to the nature of the title granted in respect of the land[3]. This differentiates an easement entered as an appurtenant right from one the benefit of which simply vests in the proprietor by virtue of the general vesting provisions of the Act. Thus, if the dominant land is registered with an absolute title, the proprietor also obtains an absolute title to the appurtenant easement itself, even though under the general law it may have become unenforceable because of abandonment or for some other reason[4]. The easement attracts the indemnity provisions contained in s. 83 of the Act[5], and the proprietor will be entitled to claim compensation should he subsequently lose the benefit of the easement through rectification.

15   LRA 1925, ss. 3 (iv), 4 (1) (a).
16   Brickdale, 87.
17   See p. 16, ante.
18   LRR 1925, r. 257.
19   LRA 1925, ss. 5, 20 (1); LRR 1925, r. 251; *Re Evans's Contract, Evans v Deed* [1970] 1 All ER 1236.
20   See p. 35, post.
 1   LRR 1925, r. 252 (1), (2). But see r. 199. The evidence required is usually evidence of the title of the grantor.
 2   LRR 1925, r. 257.
 3   LRR 1925, r. 254 (1). If the Registrar is not satisfied that the right is appurtenant, he may enter notice of the fact that the proprietor claims it. This usually occurs if the title of the grantor cannot be shown.
 4   Cf. *Riley v Penttila* [1974] VR 547.
 5   See further Chap. 4.

4. Legal rentcharges

The statutory definition of 'land' also includes a rentcharge which if legal is capable of being registered as a separate title. A rentcharge[6] which normally issues out of freehold land and in certain parts of the country is more commonly called a chief rent must be distinguished from a rent service (or ground rent) which is paid by a tenant to his landlord. A rent service is an incident of tenure and its title cannot be registered. By far the largest concentration of rentcharges is in the North West. As a result, the Land Registry at Lytham has developed a considerable expertise in this area.

C Compulsory and voluntary registration

The title to land may be registered either because it has to be, or because the owner has registered it voluntarily. Compulsory registration may occur (a) where the land is situated in an area declared to be an area of compulsory registration of title, or (b) in the case of leasehold titles, because the lessor's title is already registered. A list of areas[7] where compulsory registration operates appears in Appendix A. Section 120 (1) of the Act provides for the making of an Order in Council declaring registration of title to be compulsory within any county or part of a county as from the date specified in the Order. Compulsory registration of title now extends to areas comprising 74 per cent of the population of England and Wales. As at 31 March 1981, the total number of registered titles exceeded 7,200,000[8].

1. Compulsory registration

(a) Land Registration Act 1925, s. 123

Even though registration of title has been made compulsory within a particular area, the registration of actual titles is effected gradually on completion of specified transactions. To require immediate registration of all legal titles within that area would be absolutely impossible. It follows that property within a compulsory area may remain unregistered for many years after the system has become operative in the locality.

Section 123 (1) lists those transactions giving rise to compulsory registration as follows:

(a)   every conveyance on sale of freehold land;
(b)   every grant of a term of years absolute not being less than 40 years from the date of delivery of the grant;
(c)   every assignment on sale of leasehold land held for a term of years absolute having not less than 40 years to run from the date of delivery of the assignment.

Though it is customary to speak of registration being compulsory (as the section itself does), there is no such mandatory requirement. Instead it provides

---

6   See further pp. 342–348, post, and the Rentcharges Act 1977, there discussed, which prohibits the creation of further rentcharges except in certain limited cases; see s. 2 (3).
7   See the Registration of Title Order 1977, S.I. 1977 No. 828, Sch.
8   See the Chief Land Registrar's Report on the Work of H.M. Land Registry for the Year 1980–81.

a sanction against non-registration by enacting that the conveyance, grant or assignment (as the case may be) shall

> 'On the expiration of two months from the date thereof or of any authorised extension of that period, become void so far as regards the grant or conveyance of the legal estate in the freehold or leasehold land comprised in the conveyance, grant or assignment . . . unless the grantee (that is to say, the person who is entitled to be registered as proprietor of the freehold or leasehold land) or his successor in title or assign has in the meantime applied to be registered as proprietor of such land . . .'

The prospective loss of the legal estate is an effective sanction to compel any grantee to apply for registration so that in effect the provisions of s. 123 are mandatory. The Registrar (or the court on an appeal from him) can extend the period if satisfied that an application cannot be made within the time limit, or can only be so made by incurring unreasonable expense, or that some accident or other sufficient cause has prevented an application from being submitted within the period. Apparently the Registrar is always prepared to make the necessary order, provided he is given a reasonable explanation for the delay. The request for an order may be made by letter which should accompany the application for first registration and need not be made in advance of it[9]. Interesting problems arise from a failure to seek registration, which it would not be proper to consider here; they are discussed in a later chapter[10].

In certain special cases Parliament has decreed that s. 123 shall apply to land not situated within an area of compulsory registration. One such instance occurs on the sale of common land which has been registered finally under the Commons Registration Act 1965[11]. The most notable example arises under s. 20 of the Housing Act 1980, which relates to the sale or grant of a lease of a council house under the statutory right to buy provisions of that Act[12]. Where, however, a council house in an unregistered area is conveyed otherwise than in pursuance of the statutory right to buy[13], the transaction does not attract the provisions of s. 123. This may constitute a trap for a purchaser from the original buyer. Unless the initial conveyance recites that the sale was made under the Act's provisions, he will have no means of knowing whether the title ought to have been compulsorily registered on the occasion of that sale.

Compulsory registration of title does not apply to any area of land declared by the Registrar to be subject to a souvenir land scheme[14].

(b) Meaning of 'on sale'

Not every change of estate ownership results in a compulsory registration, only conveyances and certain assignments on sale, and the grant of a legal lease for forty years or more. 'Conveyance on sale' and 'assignment on sale' are defined to

9   See Practice Leaflet No. 5. These leaflets are issued by the Registry for the benefit of solicitors.
10   Page 449, post.
11   See s. 12. For the meaning of common land, see s. 22 (1).
12   Where the title is not already registered, a special streamlined procedure operates: s. 20 (2)–(4).
13   E.g. a conveyance of a council house to a person not qualifying as a secure tenant within s. 1 (1) of the Act.
14   LR & LCA 1971, s. 4; the Land Registration (Souvenir Land) Rules 1972, S.I. 1972 No. 985. For the background to this provision, see Ruoff 'Land Registration: The Recent Act' (1971), 35 Conv (NS) 390.

mean an instrument made on sale by virtue of which there is conferred or completed[15] a title under which an application for first registration may be made[16]. There is no general definition of 'sale'; the exact scope of the section is therefore uncertain. Some transactions are clearly excluded: a gift of property, an assent vesting property in a devisee, the appointment of a new trustee. Other transactions are statutorily exempted from the compulsory provisions[17], including those involving incorporeal hereditaments (such as a conveyance of a legal rentcharge) and mines and minerals apart from the surface. The definition of 'assignment on sale' expressly excludes an assignment on surrender of a lease to the reversioner containing a declaration that the term is to merge; a conveyance or assignment by way of exchange *provided money is paid for equality of exchange* is specifically included[18].

Some commentators[19] take the view, by way of analogy with the fiscal legislation[20], that the word 'sale' is restricted to a sale by a vendor to a purchaser in the popular and commercial sense of money or money's worth, so that (e.g.) a conveyance in consideration of an allotment or transfer of shares would be caught by s. 123. However, to avoid inconsistencies difficult to reconcile, it seems preferable to exclude from the compulsory provisions of s. 123 any transaction the consideration for which is not money, but money's worth. In *Simpson v Connolly*[1], Finnemore J said: 'The general principle of English law is that a sale means the exchanging of property for money', and held that an agreement to extinguish an existing debt did not constitute a sale. Yet the satisfaction of an existing debt amounts to money's worth[2]. Again, the express inclusion within s. 123 of exchanges where equality money is paid infers that an exchange of land for land (money's worth[3]) or an exchange where part of the consideration consists of the transfer of shares is not intended to be within the section.

Doubts exist in relation to an appropriation by a personal representative of real property in satisfaction of a legacy, share of residue, surviving spouse's statutory legacy, and other appropriations. Whatever the stamp duty position might be[4], it would appear preferable to treat all such transactions as falling outside s. 123. It is a matter of some concern that the Act fails to give clear guidance on such a fundamental point. Hopefully the Law Commission will make some positive recommendation to clarify the issue. In the meantime it is unlikely that the Registry will refuse an application for compulsory registration consequent upon a transaction occurring in one of these doubtful situations.

---

15 This prevents evasion of s. 123 by splitting up the conveyance (or assignment) into two stages so expressed that neither of them by itself is within the definition: Brickdale, 277.
16 LRA 1925, s. 123 (3).
17 LRA 1925, s. 120 (1), proviso.
18 LRA 1925, s. 123 (3).
19 Brickdale, 56; R & R, 174. Cf. Farrand, 141.
20 Stamp Act 1891, ss. 54, 55; *J and P Coates Ltd v IRC* [1897] 2 QB 423, CA.
 1 [1953] 2 All ER 474 at 477; *John Foster & Sons Ltd v IRC* [1894] 1 QB 516 at 528, CA, per Lindley LJ.
 2 *Thorndike v Hunt* (1859) 3 De G & J 563.
 3 Cf. *Littlewoods Mail Order Stores Ltd v IRC* [1963] AC 135, [1962] 2 All ER 279, HL (instrument effecting an exchange of freehold land for leasehold property of equal value not a conveyance *on sale* even for fiscal purposes).
 4 See *Jopling v IRC* [1940] 2 KB 282, [1940] 3 All ER 279 (appropriation of stock in satisfaction of pecuniary legacy constituted a conveyance on sale within the Stamp Act 1891, s. 54).

A transaction does not cease to be 'on sale' simply because no money is actually handed over on completion; thus a conveyance of land where the whole of the purchase price is left outstanding on mortgage is caught by the Act. In relation to newly created leases, it will be observed that no reference is made to a grant 'on sale'. The payment of a premium by the lessee or even of rent is not a pre-requisite for attracting the provisions of s. 123.

Finally it must be stressed that s. 123 provides machinery for the *first* registration of titles *hitherto unregistered*. Once a title has been registered after the introduction of compulsory registration, subsequent dealings authorised by the Act must be registered whether the transaction constitutes a sale or not. Thus a donee of registered property must be registered as the proprietor in place of the donor, before the legal title becomes vested in him[5].

(c) Compulsory registration of leases

The registration of leases can become something of a major puzzle unless careful attention is paid to the relevant provisions[6]. As we have just seen a lease of unregistered land for 40 years or more, granted after compulsory registration has been introduced, is caught by s. 123. There are, however, lesser terms requiring registration, even in a non-compulsory area, *if the lessor's title is already registered*. Where the lessor has already registered his freehold title[7], the lessee should register any lease creating a term of *more than 21* years, irrespective of whether the land is or is not within an area of compulsory registration. The reason for this rule is rather complicated to follow. The granting of such a lease by a registered proprietor constitutes a disposition of registered land[8]. The lease giving effect to the disposition remains uncompleted until the Registrar has registered the lessee as proprietor[9]; until substantive registration of the new leasehold title the lessee does not obtain a legal estate. The two months' time limit imposed by s. 123 (1) does not apply to a 'dispositionary' lease[10]. A lessee can ascertain whether his lessor's title is registered by searching the public index map.

Even where the lessor's title is already registered, a lease granted by him for a term not exceeding 21 years is incapable of substantive registration[11]; if granted at a rent without taking a fine (premium) it ranks as an overriding interest[12], otherwise it should be protected by being noted as an incumbrance against the lessor's title. The restrictions excluding from registration inalienable leases and mortgage terms also apply to dispositionary leases.

---

5   LRA 1925, s. 19 (1); see p. 451, post.
6   The Law Commission have made a number of provisional recommendations affecting the registration of leases; see further Chap. 16, p. 462, post.
7   Or in the case of an underlease, if the underlessor's title is registered.
8   LRA 1925, ss. 18 (1) (e), 21 (1) (d) (in relation to underleases).
9   LRA 1925, ss. 19 (2), 22 (2). In addition, the lease requires notation as an incumbrance in the charges register of the lessor's title (LRA 1925, s. 48); see p. 460, post.
10   This expression refers to a lease of land the title to which is already registered, and which is created by a disposition; see the LRA 1925, s. 18 (1) (e), (5). For the non-applicability of s. 123 (1), see pp. 457–458, post.
11   LRA 1925, s. 19 (2), proviso (a).
12   LRA 1925, s. 70 (1) (k), p. 55, post. It also takes effect as a disposition off the Register if possession is taken within one year, ss. 18 (3), 21 (3). This can be particularly devastating, see e.g. *Freer v Unwins Ltd* [1976] Ch 288, [1976] 1 All ER 634.

2.   Voluntary registration

Over the years considerable advantage was taken of the facilities for voluntary registration, especially in the case of building estates and complicated or defective titles. The examination of title, mapping and survey work involved in considering voluntary applications posed a serious threat to the planned extension of compulsory registration, so that a suspension of voluntary registration became necessary and was given statutory effect by the Land Registration Act 1966. Applications under ss. 4 and 8 of the Act of 1925 affecting land *outside* an area of compulsory registration are no longer entertained except in such classes of cases as the Registrar might specify[13].

At the present time, voluntary applications can be submitted in the following cases[14]:

(i)   properties in respect of which the deeds were destroyed by enemy action during World War II[15], or lost or destroyed in their entirety whilst in a solicitor's proper custody;

(ii)   building estates comprising at least 20 houses, provided certain conditions are fulfilled, such as exact compliance with an approved layout plan;

(iii)   sales by local authorities and development corporations of residential properties or of land for such development;

(iv)   by proprietors of registered leasehold titles for the first registration of the title to their immediate reversion where merger is to take place.

The Act merely restricts voluntary applications involving land in non-compulsory areas. It does not affect the registration of dispositionary leases of land in non-compulsory areas, nor interfere with the voluntary registration of transactions relating to land *within* a compulsory area but falling outside the ambit of s. 123.

Once land has been voluntarily registered, subsequent transactions take effect in the normal way, subject only to a power vested in the registered proprietor, with the written consent of persons appearing by the register to be interested in the land (e.g. the proprietor of a registered charge), to remove the land from the register[16].

D   Classes of title

An estate in land may be registered with one of four different classes of title: absolute, possessory, qualified or good leasehold, the latter being as its name indicates confined solely to leasehold estates. It is necessary to consider what is the effect of *first registration* with a particular class of title. This section does not profess to deal with the effect of registration on a transfer of land already registered[17], though the position is similar to that on first registration.

---

13   Section 1 (2).
14   See (1967), 31 Conv (NS) 7; (1977), 41 Conv (NS) 147; Practice Leaflet No. 12.
15   Loss or destruction resulting from a national disaster (e.g. widespread flooding) will be similarly treated.
16   LRA 1925, s. 81.
17   See Chap. 16.

1.   Absolute title

(a) Freehold land

An absolute title cannot be granted unless and until the title submitted by the applicant has been approved by the Registrar[18]. He is invested with a wide discretionary power to approve a title which is open to objection, provided he is satisfied that the owner will not be disturbed in his enjoyment of the estate[19]. In this way he can ignore minor blemishes and defects in title, so conferring on the applicant an absolute title with all its advantages. The Registrar is in effect put in the same position as that of a willing but prudent purchaser under an open contract[20]. In *Dennis v Malcolm*[1] it was held that no appeal lies from his refusal to grant an absolute title. The court has no jurisdiction to make a declaration that a particular title is fit to be registered with an absolute title and unconditionally[2]. Nevertheless once the court has declared that an incumbrance affecting land is no longer enforceable and in consequence a vendor of that land is able to establish a good title to it, the Registrar will, presumably, act on the court's decision and refrain from entering the erstwhile adverse right as an incumbrance against the title when the land is subsequently registered for the first time.

The effect of first registration with an absolute freehold title is set out in s. 5 of the Act which provides:

> ' Where the registered land is a freehold estate, the registration of any person as first proprietor thereof with an absolute title shall vest in the person so registered an estate in fee simple in possession in the land, together with all rights, privileges and appurtenances belonging or appurtenant thereto, subject to the following rights and interests[3] . . . but free from all other estates and interests whatsoever, including estates and interests of His Majesty.'

Normally this vesting which s. 5 effects simply confirms the existing position. The beneficial ownership of the land will already have passed to the applicant by virtue of the conveyance from the vendor, but as will shortly be seen first registration may have a curative effect and achieve what the conveyance could not do. Appurtenant rights such as easements vest in the applicant without express mention on the register of title, even though he cannot adduce satisfactory evidence of their enforceability. Section 72 provides that if before the registration of any freehold land with an absolute title, any easement, right or privilege has been acquired for the benefit thereof, then on registration the easement, etc., shall become appurtenant to the registered land in like manner as if it had been granted to the registered proprietor. On a literal interpretation the section would appear to revive interests previously avoided[4]. The section is presumably intended to preserve enforceable easements only, and it is conceived that the courts will so construe the provision[5].

18   LRA 1925, s. 4.
19   LRA 1925, s. 13 (c). See Emery, 'The Chief Land Registrar's Power to Approve of Good Holding Title' (1976), 40 Conv (NS) 122.
20   Brickdale, 6. For open contracts, see p. 141, post.
 1   [1934] Ch 244.
 2   *MEPC Ltd v Christian-Edwards* [1978] Ch 281, [1978] 3 All ER 795, CA (abandoned contract for sale): affd. [1981] AC 205, [1979] 3 All ER 752, HL.
 3   As to which see p. 25, post.
 4   E.g. an equitable easement formerly appurtenant to the land which has previously become unenforceable against the servient land for want of registration as a land charge.
 5   Cf. *Kitney v MEPC Ltd* [1978] 1 All ER 595, CA, post.

(i) *Adverse rights.* Registration takes effect subject to:

(a) *Incumbrances and other entries appearing on the register.* The drafting here is somewhat elliptical. An entry is not a right or interest, so that para. (a) must be interpreted as meaning subject to rights and interests created by any document or transaction recorded as an entry[6]. This paragraph relates to enforceable third party rights subsisting at the time of registration and noted on the register as part of the registration process, such as restrictive covenants, adverse easements, certain leases, estate contracts. Entry on the register does not have the effect of reviving a right or interest which has ceased to be enforceable prior to first registration of title because of non-registration as a land charge[7], or because it had been released by the grantee or was void ab initio.

(b) *Overriding interests*[8] unless the contrary is expressed on the register.

(c) *Minor interests*[9] but only if the proprietor is not entitled to the land for his own benefit, in which event he takes subject to such minor interests of which he has notice. This restriction will apply to a first proprietor who is, for instance, a tenant for life of settled land. It has been suggested[10] that the words 'not entitled for his own benefit' are wide enough to cover all cases where a person has become a constructive trustee, as where he purchases from his beneficiary, or the purchase price is provided by some third person in circumstances where there is no presumption of advancement or intention of gift.

Section 5 may operate to defeat an incumbrance, e.g. a restrictive covenant, enforceable against the estate prior to first registration, but which, through some error on the part of the Registry, is not noted on the register. The person formerly entitled to the benefit of the covenant may be able to obtain rectification of the register, failing which he would be able to claim an indemnity under the Act[11], but this pecuniary recompense may be inadequate compensation for the loss of his rights. Since the section only refers to 'estates and interests', it does not seem to defeat purely contractual rights, where they exist. Notwithstanding the omission of the covenant from the register, an original covenantee may still be able to enforce a restrictive covenant against the registered proprietor, if *the original covenantor*, even by injunction, since he can rely on his contractual claim without having recourse to any proprietary interest. In practice this situation will rarely occur, since the first registered proprietor will usually be a purchaser from the original covenantor, or from some remoter predecessor in title.

(ii) *Curative effect of registration.* Section 5 is an important and far-reaching provision, the precise effects of which have not yet been fully explored by the

---

6   *Kitney v MEPC Ltd*, supra, at 602, per Goff LJ.
7   *Kitney v MEPC Ltd*, a case involving an unregistered option to renew an underlease. The underlease (but not the option) was noted against the superior title.
8   See pp. 44–65, post.
9   See pp. 65–77, post.
10 Brickdale, 83.
11 LRA 1925, ss. 82 (1) (b), 83 (2), discussed in Chap. 4, post. See *Freer v Unwins Ltd* [1976] Ch 288, [1976] 1 All ER 634, p. 90, post, where, surprisingly, the covenantee obtained rectification despite the proprietor being in possession of the land. However rectification will not necessarily enable the covenantee to enforce the covenant against the registered proprietor; this will depend on the date when rectification becomes effective: *Freer v Unwins Ltd.*

courts. Registration defines the estate vested in the registered proprietor, whether that estate is identical with the estate vested in him before registration or not[12]. In other words first registration operates to cure defects in the title existing prior to first registration, even to the extent of vesting a title which the conveyance itself was not able to transfer. Thus in *Re 139 High Street Deptford, ex p British Transport Commission*[13], V conveyed a freehold shop and annexe to P who was registered as first proprietor with an absolute title. In fact the annexe belonged to X who sought and obtained rectification of the register by excluding the annexe from P's title. However s. 5 had operated to vest in P the freehold estate and he was entitled to receive compensation[14] for his loss, notwithstanding that the conveyance itself did not vest in P any title to the annexe, since V himself had no title. Registration may also be effective to revest in the first proprietor an estate which has been forfeited. This might have occurred in a case where, before the repeal of the mortmain laws, a corporation not authorised to hold land in mortmain had acquired freehold land, thereby incurring liability to forfeiture[15]. The subsequent registration of the corporation as first proprietor with an absolute title would have vested in it the fee simple free from the estate or interest which had accrued to the Crown on forfeiture[16].

Section 5 leaves one vital question tantalisingly unanswered. Registration is stated to vest in the proprietor 'an estate in fee simple in possession in the land'. Is the curative effect of s. 5 limited to vesting in the proprietor the *legal* title[17] to the land but no more in those cases where the conveyance leading to first registration failed for some reason to vest in him the equitable title to land with which he is subsequently registered? This problem occurs, for example, where a vendor has inadvertently conveyed the same plot of land to different purchasers at different times, the second conveyance leading to first registration of title. To take the facts of *Re 139 High Street, Deptford*, discussed above was P's registration as proprietor of the annexe effective to vest in him not only X's legal estate but also his beneficial (i.e. equitable) interest in that land? The difficulty was not raised in this case. In *Epps v Esso Petroleum Co Ltd*, another case

12   *Kitney v MEPC Ltd* [1978] 1 All ER 595, at 606, CA, per Buckley LJ.
13   [1951] Ch 884, [1951] 1 All ER 950.
14   A sum of £1,278 was paid to P (see (1954), 18 Conv (NS) 138). For rectification and indemnity, see Chap. 4, post. See also *Epps v Esso Petroleum Co Ltd* [1973] 2 All ER 465.
15   See the Mortmain and Charitable Uses Act 1888, s. 1 (now repealed by the Charities Act 1960, s. 38 (1)).
16   *Morelle Ltd v Wakeling* [1955] 2 QB 379 at 410, [1955] 1 All ER 708 at 720, per Evershed MR. The House of Lords subsequently held in *A-G v Parsons* [1956] AC 421, [1956] 1 All ER 65, that failure to comply with the Act of 1888 did not work an automatic forfeiture. It seems to follow that s. 5 can operate to vest a legal title in a minor, even though a minor is not an 'estate owner' within s. 3 (iv) of the Act. Contrast R & R, 134, who state that the usual rule of law that the legal estate is vested in the proprietor does not apply here, and that the register will be rectified on discovery of the facts, but without mentioning under what section. Brickdale, 216, cites s. 82 (1) (g) as the enabling provision, the wording of which clearly indicates that the legal estate is vested in the registered proprietor (i.e. the minor). One of the authors encountered such a case where the legal state was 'vested' in the minor for over two years. Whether or not a minor registered as first proprietor obtains the legal estate, a purchaser from him will, on registration, acquire a good title under s. 20 (1) of the Act. For the effect of a purported disposition of land *already* registered *to* a minor, see s. 111 of the LRA 1925.
17   Bearing in mind that the only freehold estate capable of registration under the Act is a legal estate: s. 2 (1), p. 16, ante.

concerning a double conveyance of land, Templeman J took the view that s. 5 merely vests the legal estate in the first proprietor, P, leaving the equitable title undisturbed in the prior owner, X[18]. With respect it is submitted that s. 5 ought not to be construed in these situations as clothing the proprietor with nothing more than the outer cloak of legal ownership. It should be held to vest in him any outstanding equitable interest as well. To exclude from the operation of s. 5 an outstanding equitable interest is plainly inconsistent with the words 'free from all other estates and interest whatsoever'. This expression clearly envisages a comprehensive vesting, subject only to those third party rights falling within paras. (a)–(c) of s. 5, rights that were existing and binding on the proprietor before first registration. It is not the scheme of s. 5 to create by the fact of registration alone adverse rights which become binding on the proprietor. The view adopted by Templeman J, if correct, exposes a flaw in the Act, which goes to the roots of the system[19], and casts into the arena of speculation the reliability of the register of title. Of course it would not be the first and only occasion of speculation[20].

Any notion that s. 5 should be restrictively interpreted in order to preserve X's rights is unfounded. Even though the Act does divest X of his equitable interest in the disputed land, he is in no way debarred from seeking rectification of the register, and the court can uphold his claim by exercising its discretion to order rectification[1]. On the other hand the indemnity provisions of the Act appear to break down should the contrary opinion be well-founded[2]. These are additional grounds for doubting Templeman J's, view.

(iii) *How absolute?* How absolute is this absolute title? A leading work on registered land conveyancing states that an absolute title is without question the most reliable and marketable title that exists, because it is virtually indefeasible and cannot be bettered[3]. Whilst perhaps such a title cannot be bettered, some commentators[4] have grave misgivings as to its indefeasibility. Only if registration confers immunity from attack can the title be said to be indefeasible. However, the proprietor registered with an absolute title is safe only so long as the register is not rectified against him and it will be seen that his

18 [1973] 2 All ER 465, at 468, 472. To dismiss these observations as mere dicta overlooks the fact that in considering at length whether the plaintiff was in actual occupation of the disputed land, the learned judge accepted the proposition that, notwithstanding the conveyance, the plaintiff possessed 'rights' (i.e. an equitable interest in fee simple) capable of protection under s. 70 (1) (g) of the Act by virtue of that alleged occupation. Cf. the somewhat equivocal statement in *Re Sea View Gardens* [1966] 3 All ER 935 at 941, per Pennycuick J, that the effect of registration is 'to displace the true owner with a valid prior title'.
19 Thus, in relation to the disputed land, registration would be no more than an empty act; see Palk, 'First Registration of Title—Just What Does It Do?' (1974) 38 Conv (NS) 236. See also R & R, 64–65, who do not there advert to the problem, though their discussion of the *Deptford* case at 797 suggests that they accept that s. 5 effects a complete vesting. Note their observation that after registration the British Transport Commission (i.e. X in the example in the text) owned *nothing*.
20 Consider *Peffer v Rigg* [1978] 3 All ER 745, [1977] 1 WLR 285; *Williams and Glyn's Bank Ltd v Boland* [1981] AC 48, [1980] 2 All ER 408, post.
1 E.g. under the LRA 1925, s. 82 (1) (b), (g) or (h), pp. 81–82, post. It must be conceded that rectification is difficult against a proprietor in possession.
2 See p. 89, post.
3 R & R, 74.
4 Jackson 'Registration of Land Interests—The English Version' (1972), 88 LQR 93, 126–133. Farrand, 142–144.

title is open to attack on the widest of discretionary grounds[5]. The absoluteness of his title is only relative; he can never be completely sure that an adverse claim against him will not be upheld, as occurred in *Re 139 High Street, Deptford*[6] or in *Bridges v Mees*[7] where the claim of a squatter was upheld. It might be more accurate to say that the strength of an absolute title depends not on its virtual indefeasibility but on the statutory indemnity behind it; and it by no means follows that a proprietor suffering rectification is entitled to claim an indemnity[8]. Furthermore, it is difficult to reconcile the view of Templeman J in *Epps v Esso Petroleum Co Ltd*[9] with the notion of indefeasibility. A registered title which professes to be absolute, and yet may leave the beneficial interest in the land outstanding in some third party, is a contradiction in terms, particularly if no right to compensation arises under the Act when the registered proprietor is deprived through rectification of what the statute does vest in him.

(b) Leasehold land

Under s. 9 of the Act, registration with an absolute leasehold title is deemed to vest in the first proprietor the possession of the leasehold interest with all implied or expressed rights, privileges and appurtenances. The wording of this section differs somewhat from its freehold counterpart, s. 5, but the effect is thought to be similar. Thus registration should operate to vest in the registered lessee the legal and equitable interests in the leasehold term. The word 'deemed' is apparently without significance[10]. The reference to 'vesting the possession' is taken from the Land Transfer Act 1875, s. 13, which was enacted in the heyday of the doctrine of interesse termini, but in view of that doctrine's subsequent abolition[11] there appears to be no justification for the retention of these words. What has previously been said of s. 72 in relation to freehold land applies equally to leasehold titles.

The vesting is subject to the same rights as those affecting freeholds, i.e. incumbrances and other entries on the register, overriding and minor interests, but in addition it is *subject to all implied and express covenants, obligations and liabilities incident to the registered land*; save for these the registered lessee takes free from all other estates and interests. One point peculiar to leaseholds arises in relation to incumbrances and entries on the register. The register referred to is not simply the lessee's own register, but includes the register of any superior title. Thus the lessee takes subject to restrictive covenants registered against the title of any freeholder, even though the lessee has no actual notice thereof[12].

An absolute leasehold title in effect guarantees that the lease has been validly granted. It is not therefore possible for an applicant to be registered with an absolute leasehold title unless the titles to both the freehold and the leasehold

5 See the LRA 1925, ss. 82 (1) (h), (3) (c), pp. 82–85, post.
6 [1951] Ch 884, [1951] 1 All ER 950, p. 26, ante.
7 [1957] Ch 475, [1957] 2 All ER 577, p. 48, post.
8 See pp. 89–94, post.
9 [1973] 2 All ER 465.
10 *Morelle Ltd v Wakeling* [1955] 2 QB 379 at 414, [1955] 1 All ER 708 at 723, per Lord Evershed MR.
11 LPA 1925, s. 149 (1). Under the doctrine a lessee did not acquire a legal estate until actual entry on the land demised. Section 13 vested the legal title in him irrespective of entry into possession.
12 See p. 357, post. In practice covenants affecting the freehold title are normally noted against an absolute leasehold title.

(including intermediate leaseholds) have been approved[13]. Except where the freehold title is already registered (in which case it will have been previously approved), the applicant must deduce title to the freehold, which he will usually be unable to do because of statutory restrictions[14]. Hitherto, absolute leasehold titles have been comparatively uncommon. However, it is now the Registry's practice to consider every application for first registration of a *dispositionary* lease for registration with an absolute leasehold title, provided the lessor himself is registered with an absolute title[15]. This is done notwithstanding that the lessee has applied for no more than a good leasehold title. Apparently the Registry's practice does not extend to applications for compulsory first registration taking effect after an assignment for value of an existing leasehold term, even though the freehold title, unknown to the applicant, has previously been registered with an absolute title, whatever the length of the lease and the lessee's occupation. It is, of course, important to note also that in the area of leasehold conveyancing the theory and the reality of title deduction are often widely divergent.

2.   Good leasehold title

This type of title is confined solely to leasehold estates and is intended to cover the many leasehold titles not supported by any documentary evidence of the freehold title. Where a good leasehold title is required, the leasehold (but, of course, not the freehold) title must be approved by the Registrar[16]. The effect of first registration with this title is the same as for an absolute leasehold, with this important exception that the title does not affect or prejudice the enforcement of any estate, right or interest affecting or in derogation of the lessor's title to grant the lease[17]. Since the Registrar does not see the freehold title he cannot guarantee that the lessor was in a position validly to grant the lease. This is the basic difference between absolute leasehold and good leasehold title. If it turns out that the lessor acquired the freehold title by fraud, or, being a mortgagor, leased the property contrary to the terms of the mortgage, so that a valid third party claim results in the register being rectified against the lessee, he is entitled to be indemnified under the Act if he has an absolute leasehold title, since the Registrar has warranted the lease's validity, but not if he merely has a good leasehold. Despite the significant difference in the scope of the guarantee attaching to a good leasehold title compared with an absolute title, it must not be thought that these good leasehold titles are not sound marketable titles which a purchaser should avoid at all costs. They have their counterparts (lacking, of course, the statutory guarantee) in the unregistered system of land transfer. There are in various parts of the country numerous unregistered long leasehold titles which have been, and will continue to be, freely saleable on the open market, although the vendor does not deduce the freehold title[18].

---

13   LRA 1925, s. 8 (1) proviso (i).
14   See LPA 1925, s. 44, pp. 305−306, post. For deducing title, see Chap. 10.
15   See the Land Registry Report for 1976−77, para. 7. For the meaning of a dispositionary lease, see p. 22, ante.
16   LRA 1925, s. 8 (1) proviso (ii).
17   LRA 1925, s. 10.
18   For the position where the lease is less than fifteen years old and the contract is governed by The Law Society's Conditions of Sale, see p. 683, post.

Nevertheless a rather disquieting trend seems to be developing among some building societies, who are refusing to lend on the security of a good leasehold registered title[19].

3.   Possessory title

A possessory title is granted where the applicant's title is based solely on occupation as a squatter by himself and his predecessors in title, or where he is unable to produce the documents of title which ought to be in his custody. The application must be supported by such evidence of title as is from time to time prescribed[20]. If there are documents of title these must be forwarded; if the applicant relies on adverse possession, a statutory declaration may constitute prima facie evidence of his right to seek registration[1]. If, on an application for registration with possessory title, the Registrar is satisfied as to the title to the estate, he may register it as absolute or good leasehold[2] as the case may be, though conversely an applicant for an absolute title may find he is registered with a possessory title.

First registration with a possessory title has the same effect as registration with a corresponding absolute freehold or leasehold title, except that the title is subject to any estate, right or interest (whether, in the case of leasehold land, in respect of the lessor's title or otherwise) adverse to or in derogation of the first proprietor's title and subsisting or capable of arising at the time of registration[3]. Thus a proprietor of a possessory title takes subject to any enforceable restrictive covenants affecting the land, even though no mention of them can be made on the register[4]. In effect a possessory title gives no guarantee as to the title prior to first registration. The previous owner may be able to upset the title, on the ground that the evidence does not establish that the proprietor's possession was sufficiently adverse to support a possessory title[5]. The proprietor cannot recover any indemnity if the register is rectified to give effect to a superior title or claim.

4.   Qualified title

It may sometimes appear on an application for registration with an absolute freehold title that the title can be established only for a limited period or subject to certain reservations, or in the case of an application in relation to leasehold land (either for absolute or good leasehold titles) that the lessor's title to the reversion or the lessee's title to the leasehold are subject to similar qualifications. On such rare occasions the Registrar may except from the effect of registration any estate, right or interest arising before a specified date, or arising under a specified instrument, or otherwise particularly described in the

19   See (1977) 121 Sol Jo 161. Cf. R & R, 87 ('As a rule a good leasehold title seems to be considered adequate for all ordinary purposes . . .').
20   LRA 1925, s. 4 proviso (ii) (freeholds), s. 8 (1) proviso (iii) (leaseholds).
1   LRR 1925, rr. 37, 38.
2   LRA 1925, ss. 4 proviso (iii), 8 (1) proviso (iv).
3   LRA 1925, s. 6 (freeholds), s. 11 (leaseholds). In relation to s. 11, see *Spectrum Investment Co v Holmes* [1981] 1 All ER 6.
4   It is the practice to enter a note on the register to the effect that the title is subject to such restrictive covenants as may have been imposed on the land prior to the date of first registration so far as they are still legally enforceable; see R & R, 84. For the enforceability of restrictive covenants against a squatter, see *Re Nisbet and Potts' Contract* [1906] 1 Ch 386, CA.
5   *Tester v Harris* (1964) 189 Estates Gazette 337.

register[6]. Though a qualified title cannot in the first instance be applied for, the Registrar cannot grant such a title of his own accord, but only with the consent of the person seeking first registration.

A qualified title might be granted where, for example, the applicant's predecessor in title (being a trustee) acquired the land from his co-trustees in breach of trust. An entry would be made in the register to the effect that the rights and interests of the beneficiaries under the trust were excluded from the effect of registration, the consequence being that should the applicant's title subsequently be upset by the beneficiaries, he could claim no indemnity under the Act. The specific defect of title appears on the face of the register, so differentiating the qualified title from the possessory title which is subject to all adverse estates, rights and interests existing at the time of first registration. Except for the specified defect, registration with a qualified title has the same effect as registration with an absolute title or a good leasehold title, as the case may be. Very few qualified titles have been registered.

5. Cautions against first registration

The effect of first registration with an absolute title or good leasehold title is to vest the estate in the proprietor subject to certain specified incumbrances but free from all other estates or interests. Normally the interests of third party owners are adequately protected by virtue of the Registrar's examination of the applicant's title, resulting in the entry on the register of adverse rights disclosed by such examination. Occasionally a third party may wish to take positive steps to preserve his rights, which may be lost if the applicant becomes registered with an absolute title. An adjoining landowner having the benefit of a restrictive covenant may wish to ensure that his rights are duly protected when the burdened land is registered, or there may be a boundary dispute between adjacent owners one of whom proposes to sell his land.

Under s. 53 (1) of the Act[7] a caution may be lodged, accompanied by a statutory declaration showing the interest which the cautioner claims in the land. The caution ensures that the cautioner will obtain the necessary protection for his right if and when the title to the land is registered. Until then the caution has no formal effect whatever. There exists no obligation on the part of the cautioner or the Registry to notify the owner of the land of the existence of the caution. Nor has he any right to insist that the cautioner should be required to defend the caution, though the Registry may apparently accede to such a request[8]. The cautioner is entitled to receive notice of any application made to register the title. The notice requires him, if he proposes to oppose the application, to enter an appearance before the Registrar by lodging his objection within, usually, a period of 14 days. If no action is taken in response to the notice, the caution is cancelled and the registration completed; otherwise the

---

6 LRA 1925, s. 7 (freeholds), s. 12 (leaseholds).
7 In terms s. 53 is restricted to a person whose consent is necessary to a disposition of the land to be registered—a very limited class of persons, if construed literally. Cf. LRR 1925, Schedule, Form 14 (the form of statutory declaration to be given in support of the caution) which gives as examples of the kind of interest sufficient to support a caution an estate contract, or equitable mortgage under hand. This seems to justify the Registry's view that 'disposition' is to be liberally interpreted as meaning a disposition free from incumbrances: R & R, 247. Consequently almost any person interested can apply.
8 R & R, 249. He is entitled to inspect the caution and its supporting statutory declaration: LRR 1925, r. 70.

Registrar hears the dispute and makes the appropriate order. An appeal lies to the High Court from the Registrar's order[9]. Lodging a caution is not a step to be undertaken frivolously since a caution lodged without reasonable cause renders the cautioner liable in damages to anyone suffering loss as a result thereof[10].

The Law Commission take the view that these cautions serve a useful purpose, that amending legislation should make it clear that the procedure is available to anybody claiming an interest capable of registration or protection on the register, and that the court (but not the Registrar) should be empowered to direct cancellation if the caution is improperly lodged[11].

A caution against first registration must not be confused with a caution against dealings, which is one of the methods available for the protection of a minor interest[12].

6.   Conversion of titles

The superiority of the absolute title over its lesser brethren is easily demonstrated and provision is made for the subsequent upgrading of inferior titles. In some instances upgrading is automatic, in others the Registrar has a discretion.

(a) Compulsory conversion

If satisfied that the proprietor is in possession, the Registrar is bound on application to convert into an absolute title a possessory freehold title that has been registered for 15 years, and into a good leasehold a possessory leasehold title that has been registered for ten years[13]. The application should follow Form 6 prescribed in the Schedule to the Rules of 1925, but need not be accompanied by any documents of title.

(b) Discretionary conversion

Two different situations call for comment.

(i) On a transfer for value the Registrar may register as absolute or good leasehold (as the case may be) a qualified, good leasehold or possessory title[14]. This conversion is dependent on the Registrar's satisfaction as to title. Two points emerge. In the case of a qualified title, the transferee in effect has to satisfy him that the specific defect has been cured or need no longer be regarded as a blot on the title. For this purpose he must lodge such documents, if any, as may relate to the matters previously excepted from the effect of registration. Similarly, in relation to leaseholds, before a good leasehold can be converted into an absolute leasehold, the transferee will have to deduce title to the landlord's freehold reversion. This difficulty is, of course, obviated if the title to the freehold has meanwhile been registered, in which case the upgrading is virtually automatic.

---

 9   LRA 1925, s. 56 (1).
10   LRA 1925, s. 56 (3). An interesting occasion when a caution was lodged and upheld by
       the Registrar is discussed in (1956), 20 Conv (NS) 3.
11   See published Working Paper No. 67, paras. 129–39.
12   See pp. 69–71, post.
13   LRA 1925, s. 77 (3) (b).
14   Section 77 (2).

(ii) If land has been registered with a good leasehold title for at least ten years the Registrar may at the request of the proprietor enter his title as absolute, if satisfied that successive lessees have been in possession during that period[15]. Mere possession during the period is not per se adequate to ensure a conversion; the lessor's entitlement to grant the lease, and other matters, still need to be established[16], unless again the freehold title has been registered.

Usually a specific application for conversion will be made, but in cases falling within (i) above it may be effected at the instance of the Registrar without charge. The conversion of a good leasehold title into absolute after the intervening registration of the freehold title is a typical occasion for the Registrar to act on his own initiative. A caution against conversion can be lodged in the same way and with the same results as a caution against first registration[17]. Any person suffering loss by reason of a conversion of a title is entitled to be indemnified[18].

7. A new estate?

The Land Registration Act 1925, is a statute designed as a simplification of the processes of making and investigating title[19]. However a not inconsiderable body of opinion exists which asserts that the Act goes much further and creates a new estate in land, a statutory or registered estate which on first registration replaces or even destroys the common law legal estate[20]. Support for this theory is derived largely from the Act itself, a passing reference to 'a statutory title' by Lord Hanworth, MR, in a case where the Court of Appeal were dealing with a claim to rectify the register[1], and a sizeable weight of judicial authority from Australia where a somewhat different system of land registration operates. To what extent can this theory be justified?

(a) Some arguments considered
There is no specific provision in the Act purporting to destroy the common law estate; its demise is presumed from a construction of various sections of the Act. Thus s. 5 enacts in relation to freehold land that registration of a person as first proprietor with an absolute title vests in him an estate in fee simple in possession. Seeing that in normal cases he already has vested in him such an

15 Section 77 (4). See LRR 1925, rr. 48, 49.
16 R & R, 256–7. The Law Commission feel that s. 77 (4) should be amended to enable a conversion to be made at any time if the Registrar is satisfied as to the reversionary title: Published Working Paper No. 32, para. 59.
17 LRR 1925, r. 215 (2).
18 LRA 1925, s. 77 (6).
19 *National Provincial Bank Ltd v Hastings Car Mart Ltd* [1964] Ch 665, at 696, [1964] 1 All ER 688, at 701, CA, per Russell, LJ; revsd. sub nom *National Provincial Bank Ltd v Ainsworth* [1965] AC 1175, [1965] 2 All ER 472, HL.
20 The main proponents are Potter, *Principles of Land Registration,* p. 30; Connell 'The Registered Estate' (1947), 11 Conv (NS) 183, 232; Jackson 'Registration of Land Interests—The English Version' (1972), 88 LQR 93. The view has in the past found favour with Registry officials (see Caswell's edn of Professor Potter's book, 3 K & E, 34) but is not adopted by R & R, 68–9. Professor Potter's chief opponent was A. D. Hargreaves; see the Hargreaves-Potter controversy in (1949), 12 MLR 139, 205, 477. See also Farrand, 151–53, who suggests that the problem is appellative rather than substantive.
1   *Chowood Ltd v Lyall (No. 2)* [1930] 2 Ch 156 at 163, [1930] All ER Rep 402, at 403, CA.

estate by the conveyance from the vendor, what is the purpose of the section unless it is to vest in him something different from what he already possesses? The argument fails to account for the curative effect of first registration. The scheme of registration is not to be hindered by technical defects in title. Even assuming the conveyance was ineffective to pass any legal estate on account of some flaw in the title, nevertheless the subsequent registration[2] cures that defect and achieves what the conveyance failed to do. Registration is complete in itself. Under the complementary provisions of s. 69 (1), the proprietor is deemed to have the legal estate vested in him without any conveyance, and he does not have to obtain any further assurance to cure any defect in title before he can be registered. It has been argued[3] that the reference in s. 69 (1) to 'legal estate' and 'registered estate' implies a distinction, justifying the existence of a separate statutory estate. Nevertheless, the respective definitions of these two expressions rather suggest they are one and the same[4].

A further argument advanced in support of the demise of the common law estate is the provision in s. 69 (4) that the estate vested in the proprietor can only be disposed of or dealt with by him in manner authorised by the Act. If the common law estate has been replaced, what is more vital than a definition of the proprietor's powers in relation to this statutory estate? However, the better view is that the draftsman was compelled to specify the powers, not to define or create them, but as a matter of conveyancing machinery to indicate the manner of their exercise[5].

(b)   The judicial view
However attractive might be the arguments advanced by the proponents of the new statutory estate, it has received no direct support from English judges, the tenor of whose judgments clearly indicates that the Act had no such revolutionary effect. Thus in *Lee v Barrey*[6] Lord Evershed MR, spoke of s. 69 as being 'directed to bringing registered land into the general scheme of the property legislation of 1925.' Even more to the point is Harman LJ's judgment in *Re White Rose Cottage*[7] where, after a brief reference to the Land Transfer Acts of 1875 and 1897, he said:

' When the great change in the law of real property was brought about by Lord Birkenhead's Act of 1925, it was of course necessary radically to reform the land registration system to match with the new regime.'

This is not to say that the Act of 1925 has not made important alterations to the law of real property as applied to registered land, but as we noted in the previous chapter[8] these all stem as a necessary consequence from the changes made in conveyancing machinery.

2   Pages 25–26, ante.
3   Connell, loc. cit., 235.
4   LRA 1925, s. 3 (xxiii) defines 'registered estate' to mean '*the legal estate* . . . as respects which a person is for the time being registered as proprietor', and 'legal estates' to mean 'the estates . . . which are by the LPA 1925, authorised to subsist or to be created at law': s. 3 (xi).
5   See (1949), 12 MLR 139, 140 (A. D. Hargreaves). Potter tentatively suggested (see 12 MLR 207) that some 'sort of ghost of a common law estate' might remain for the purposes of enjoyment as distinct from disposition. But see Hargreaves' reply at 12 MLR 477–8.
6   [1957] Ch 251 at 261, [1957] 1 All ER 191, at 195, CA.
7   [1965] Ch 940 at 952, [1965] 1 All ER 11, at 16, CA. This also is the view to which the Law Commission subscribe; see e.g. Published Working Papers No. 45, para. 73, and No. 67, para. 6.
8   Page 9, ante.

E   The register and certificates of title

The term 'register' as used in the Act of 1925, and the Rules, is somewhat mis-leading as it describes three different things. Section 1 of the Act requires the keeping of a register of title to freehold and leasehold land. The register here referred to comprises all registered titles and consists physically of a vast card index upon which are recorded details of each individual title. The register[9] may also denote the record of title of each individual proprietor; this record is itself divided into three parts each known as a register: the property register, the proprietorship register and the charges register. This section is concerned with the individual proprietor's register of title and its component parts. Each registered title has its own separate title number.

This register of title acts as a mirror; it reflects the state of the proprietor's title. In truth this is merely an approximation, for not all matters in which a prospective purchaser will be interested are recorded on the register. Overrid-ing interests constitute the major exception to the mirror principle. At the same time the register operates as a curtain which ensures that a purchaser need not concern himself with trusts and equities that exist behind the curtain. So s. 74 of the Act enacts that no person dealing with a registered estate is to be affected with notice of any trust and references to trusts shall, so far as possible, be excluded from the register. Nevertheless we shall see that even the curtain principle is not inviolate[10]. Occasionally it may be necessary to go behind a registered entry in order to inquire into the validity of some right or interest which the entry purports to protect[11].

1.   Property register

The property register contains a verbal description of the registered property by reference to a plan. A typical description is as follows:

> ' The freehold land shown and edged with red on the plan of the above Title filed at the Registry registered on — known as — .'

The description may include a reference to appurtenant easements, if an application therefor has been made, though, as previously seen, registration vests in the proprietor all appurtenant rights and privileges without express mention. Where mines and minerals have previously been excepted, a note to this effect appears in the property register; exemptions from overriding interests are also mentioned here. If, after first registration, part of the land comprised in the title is transferred, a note is made in the register that the land edged and numbered in green on the plan has been removed from the title and registered under its own title number shown in green on the plan.

In the case of leaseholds, short particulars of the lease (date, parties, term and the date of its commencement) are included, together with a statement (if applicable) excepting all rights arising from unlicensed dealings[12].

2.   Proprietorship register

This states the nature of the title, the name, address and description of the pro-prietor and any entries affecting his right of disposal. For example, if a tenant

9   See e.g. s. 5 of the LRA 1925, p. 24, ante.
10   Page 54, post.
11   See *Kitney v MEPC Ltd* [1978] 1 All ER 595, CA, p. 24, ante.
12   See the LRR 1925, r. 45.

for life is registered as proprietor a statement is appended that no disposition under which capital money arises is to be registered unless the money is paid to the trustees of the settlement or into court[13]. Any caution[14] registered to protect a claim adverse to the proprietor's title appears in this register, and also miscellaneous matters required by the Rules to be entered on the register without any particular part being specified, e.g. a caution against conversion of the title, or any modification of the implied covenants for title. A reference to the price paid on the occasion of a transfer is not now included unless the proprietor so requests[15]. On a change of proprietor consequent upon, for example, a transfer for value, the name of the vendor is deleted and the purchaser's particulars substituted.

3.   Charges register

Details of charges, incumbrances and other obligations adversely affecting the land from time to time appear in the charges register, such as: restrictive covenants, rentcharges, leases (not being overriding interests), and easements. The practice in relation to restrictive covenants varies. In the case of covenants created prior to first registration, short particulars of the deed of creation are entered in the register and a copy of the covenants are set out in a separate schedule. Where they are imposed on a transfer of registered land, the charges register merely records that the transfer contains restrictive covenants and adds a note that a copy of the transfer appears in the land certificate. The practice varies according to the length of the covenants and the availability of documents[16].

Details of a mortgage or charge are also entered in the charges register together with the name and address of the mortgagee, the proprietor of the registered charge. On repayment of the mortgage the entry is cancelled, as also is the entry relating to any lease, rentcharge or other incumbrance that is determined.

4.   Privacy of register

Unlike most other countries where a register of title or of land is maintained, a proprietor's register of title is not open to inspection by the general public. It is private. As a basic rule no-one can inspect the register or any document referred to therein without the written authority of the proprietor or his solicitor[17]. This roughly compares with the position in relation to unregistered land, for an estate owner is not under any general obligation to produce his title deeds the contents of which are private[18]. Thus Government departments and local authorities cannot use the register of title as a basis for assessing or collecting rates and taxes, though the Registrar has a discretion to provide appropriate authorities with such information as they can by law require owners

13   See further pp. 359–360, post.
14   For cautions, see p. 69, post.
15   Land Registration Rules 1976, S.I. 1976 No. 1332, r. 2 (2), amending the LRR 1925, r. 247 (1).
16   For a case where a precautionary entry caused title problems even though the title was registered see *Faruqi v English Real Estates* [1979] 1 WLR 963, p. 349, post.
17   LRA 1925, s. 112.
18   But it is possible to search for possible land charges affecting the land without the owner's consent or knowledge, solely on payment of the fee.

of property to furnish to them direct[19]. The Administration of Justice Act 1977, now provides for the inspection and copying of the register in certain circumstances in connection with criminal proceedings[20].

Several exceptions to the rule that the register is private exist. For example, the property register and filed plan (but not, it will be observed, the whole of the register) may be inspected by any person interested in the land or in adjoining land or in any charge or incumbrance on the land[1]. Notwithstanding its seemingly wide terms, the application of this rule is restricted in practice. A person claiming a right to enforce a restrictive covenant would probably be within its ambit[2]. This right of inspection of the property register must not be confused with the right to inspect the public index map which is open to the public and enables any person to ascertain whether the title to a particular piece of land is registered. The extent to which the register of title should be private is under consideration by the Law Commission[3].

5.   Certificates of title

As evidence of his title, the registered proprietor receives a land certificate which contains replicas of the register of title to which it relates, and a copy of the plan. Any inaccuracy in the plan or the copy entries appearing in the certificate of title entitles a person suffering loss by reason thereof to be indemnified under the Act[4]. An illustration of the contents of a land certificate, showing some typical entries, appears at the end of this chapter. The certificate is itself admissible as evidence of the several matters it contains, without it being necessary to produce the actual records maintained in the Registry[5].

The form of the land certificate is prescribed[6]. It certifies that the land described in the property register is registered with absolute (or qualified, good leasehold or possessory, as the case may be) title at H.M. Land Registry and that copies of the entries in the register and of the map are bound up in it. The certificate bears the official Registry seal and shows the date (which is stamped in one of the panels printed inside the front cover of the certificate) when the certificate was last examined with the register at the Registry. Since the certificate contains copies of the official register, it is preferable that the certificate is kept up to date. The certificate is always made to agree with the register whenever it is produced at the Registry. However, certain entries can be made on the register without production of the proprietor's certificate (as to which see below) so there is no guarantee that at any given time the land certificate corresponds with the official register. The Registrar will on application make it correspond without the payment of a fee.

---

19   LRA 1925, s. 129.
20   Section 25, adding a new s. 112A to the LRA 1925.
 1   LRR 1925, r. 288 (1). Other examples occur in the LRA 1925, ss. 59 (3), 61 (10), which entitle a judgment creditor, the official receiver or trustee in bankruptcy to inspect the register.
 2   See generally, R & R, 669.
 3   Published Working Paper, No. 32, paras. 70–94. Their provisional recommendations indicate that whilst some amendments to the present rule are clearly desirable, a register wholly open to public inspection is not feasible. Cf. (1970), 34 Conv (NS) 373.
 4   LRA 1925, s. 113; see also (1975), 39 Conv (NS) 315–17.
 5   LRA 1925, s. 68.
 6   LRR 1925, r. 261, and Schedule, Form 78.

If the land is subject to a registered mortgage, the mortgagee receives a charge certificate which certifies that a charge for the moneys therein mentioned has been registered at the Registry against the title number referred to. No precise form is prescribed for a charge certificate[7]. To all intents and purposes it is the same as a land certificate, except that the outer cover is different and the original mortgage deed is bound up inside. The land certificate is retained in the Registry during the subsistence of the mortgage[8].

(a) Production of certificates

It has been said that the land certificate relating to an absolute title constitutes conclusive evidence of the registered proprietor's title to the land and replaces the title deeds which he normally holds in unregistered conveyancing[9]. As evidence of title it will be necessary for him to produce this certificate whenever production of the deeds would be required in unregistered conveyancing, such as on a sale. He is required to produce it to the Registrar on a number of specified occasions[10], the most important of these being:

 (i)   a disposition of the registered land such as a transfer of the whole or part only, the grant of an easement, or creation of a mortgage;
 (ii) a transmission relating to the land, such as that occurring on the death of the proprietor;
 (iii) the noting of any estate, right, claim or restriction adversely affecting the land;
 (iv) any rectification of the register unless the Registrar makes an order to the contrary.

Production of the certificate is not required on lodgment of a caution or inhibition, the entry of notice of certain leases or a charge for capital transfer tax[11]. The Law Commission have provisionally advocated various amendments to the rules governing production of land certificates consequent upon their suggested reforms for the protection of third party rights affecting registered land[12]. These are discussed more fully in the following chapter.

In like manner, a mortgagee's charge certificate is roughly equivalent to possession of the deeds in unregistered conveyancing. Production of the certificate is required for dispositions or transmissions of the registered charge, for the entry of notices, restrictions, etc.

(b) Conclusiveness of certificates

Though the theory is that the land certificate should replace the title deeds, it is not to be thought that reference to the deeds is rendered unnecessary when a title is registered, or that it contains all the information ascertainable by perusing the deeds. In the case of leasehold land, the certificate merely gives brief details of the term and the rent; reference to the lease is still essential to

---

7   Though it must contain certain statutory information: LRR 1925, r. 262.
8   LRA 1925, s. 65.
9 · R & R, 23. *Williams and Glyn's Bank Ltd v Bolland* [1981] AC 487 at 504, [1980] 2 All ER 408 at 412, HL, per Lord Wilberforce.
10 LRA 1925, ss. 64 (1), 82 (6).
11 LRA 1925, s. 64 (1) (c), as amended by the Finance Act 1975, s. 52, and Sch. 12, para. 5 (5). For cautions and inhibitions, see pp. 69–71, post. The noting of leases is considered in Chap. 16, pp. 460–461, post.
12 See Published Working Paper No. 67, paras. 93 et seq.

discover what covenants, provisions and conditions affect the property. Furthermore the Land Registry do not give office copies of any lease[13]. Where the title is possessory or qualified, the title deeds are still important in relation to any pre-registration rights or interests excepted from the effect of registration.

It is doubtless in the realm of the absolute title that the certificate comes nearest to a satisfactory replacement of the title deeds. Even here, however, the certificate does not contain all the desired information. Appurtenant easements may not have been entered in the property register at the time of first registration. Moreover, adverse rights taking effect as overriding interests are not usually revealed, though it should be added that these interests mainly concern matters which would not ordinarily be discoverable by a perusal of title deeds relating to unregistered land[14]. Nevertheless it means that the registered land system is no improvement on, as opposed to a replacement of, the system based on deeds.

Positive covenants existing at the time of first registration are not recorded in the register of title of the burdened land. Though a positive covenant not being between landlord and tenant does not bind the covenantor's successors in title[15], it does not follow that they can be ignored. When he later comes to sell the land, the first registered proprietor needs to know of their existence because of the possibility of taking an indemnity covenant from the purchaser, but he must turn to the deeds, not to his land certificate, to ascertain if any exist. This defect is acknowledged and mitigated to some extent by a note printed inside the cover of the land certificate, giving express warning of the need to inquire into the existence of positive covenants. If the matter is sufficiently important to warrant an express warning, it would seem that the proper place to mention them is somewhere in the register rather than on the cover. As a concession, a note is made in the proprietorship register of the existence of positive covenants created *after* the date of first registration and a copy of them is sewn into the certificate of title[16].

The land certificate as a document of title is also defective in that it is not required to record matters of legal consequence contained in a transfer of registered land, which is permanently retained in the Registry and not returned to the transferee with the land certificate. The transfer may assign the benefit of positive or negative covenants[17] but this information does not appear in the land certificate. Nor is it possible to tell from the certificate whether property

13 R & R, 456−7.
14 See p. 45, post.
15 Except in so far as the principle of *Halsall v Brizell* [1957] Ch 169, [1957] 1 All ER 371, might be applicable.
16 See Registered Land Practice Note 21. These Practice Notes, published by The Law Society, are the result of discussions held regularly by the Joint Advisory Committee of The Law Society and the Land Registry. The notes, though without any binding effect, provide helpful guidance on problems likely to arise in practice. The reason given for not noting positive covenants on first registration is the immense task involved in examining all documents lodged to ascertain their existence. Yet a similar task is undertaken to discover restrictive covenants. Furthermore if positive and negative covenants are intermixed, the positive ones are rarely edited out. The problem about the positive covenant is compounded by the use of a transfer pursuant to r. 72 without any mention of the indemnity covenant therein.
17 The problem of the benefit of restrictive covenants is not adequately dealt with in registered land conveyancing; see pp. 477−478, post.

vested in joint tenants is held by them upon the terms of an express or a statutory trust for sale. Again the transfer may contain an express indemnity covenant in relation to existing covenants, whether positive or negative. Neither the Act nor the Rules require the existence of such indemnity to be noted in the register, though as a concession a note of any indemnity covenant is included in the certificate[18]. There is an argument in favour of the transfer (or a copy) being incorporated into the certificate, not as evidence of the proprietor's title, for that is established by the certificate, but as evidence of special matters in the transfer.

6.   Maps and plans

It has previously been seen that the registered property is in part described by reference to an accurately prepared plan. This is one of the obvious advantages of the registered system over its unregistered counterpart, where plans are notoriously inaccurate and often inserted solely for identification purposes. Nevertheless the alleged benefits of Land Registry plans, namely their great clarity and exactitude[19], are not always apparent in reality. Furthermore as the plans are based on a small scale they should not be used when identification of precise boundaries is required[20]. The question of whether the time devoted to plans in the Land Registry is cost effective has been the subject matter of interesting debate[1]. The plan may take the form either of a filed plan or the general map[2]. The general map is prepared from the ordnance map by the plans section of the Registry. It is a composite map relating to numerous registered properties each of which are separately identified by a different number. The land certificate contains a copy of the relevant section of the general map on which the land is tinted pink and the appropriate identifying number shown.

The general map is no longer used for new registrations; it is subject to several considerable disadvantages[3] and has given way to the more flexible filed plan. This is an individual plan prepared by the Registry for use with one particular title; the extent of the registered property is edged thereon with red. On this plan it is possible to indicate matters peculiar to that title, such as the route of a right of way affecting the land which is shown by blue tinting on the plan[4]. Such a detail could not be recorded on the general map since it would have no relevance to the other properties shown on it. The ease with which a filed plan can be altered, without having to call in a host of land or charge certificates in order to alter the general map, is another advantage which it

---

18   Registered Land Practice Note 21. See further p. 475, post.
19   R & R, 43. But see (1980) 130 NLJ 1166.
20   In *Scarfe v Adams* [1981] 1 All ER 843 the Court of Appeal were heavily critical of the use of such a plan when a house was subdivided.
1   See [1979] Conv 316. It is believed the owner of the second property therein mentioned obtained rectification of his title.
2   LRA 1925, s. 76. Exceptionally the parties' own deed plan may be utilised, for example, in the case of a property comprising overlapping floors.
3   R & R, 46−7.
4   Various modes of colouration are used by the Registry as follows: red edging shows the extent of the registered land; green edging indicates land removed from the title and green tinting relates to islands of land within the land edged red not belonging to the proprietor; blue and brown tinting mark the route of an adverse or appurtenant right of way (as the case may be).

enjoys. The filed plan must not be confused with the public index map which shows the position and extent of every registered title. The general map is used for this purpose[5].

The filed plan usually indicates the general boundaries of the plot of land[6]; it does not purport to determine the precise boundary. The Rules do lay down a procedure for defining the exact boundaries of a registered plot but in practice little use is made of it in view of the expense involved. If adopted the plan (or map) is deemed to define accurately the boundaries of the land[7].

7. Form of entries in land certificate

The illustration given on pages 42 and 43 will give the reader some impression of the nature and form of the entries which may appear in a typical land certificate relating to freehold land registered with an absolute title. The names, addresses and documents referred to are, of course, purely fictional.

5 LRR 1925, r. 8. See further p. 203, post.
6 LRR 1925, r. 278; see further p. 518, post.
7 LRR 1925, rr. 276, 277, p. 518, post. See R & R, 58–9. In their review of the subject the Law Commission were of the preliminary opinion that no substantial reform of the law relating to identity and boundaries affecting registered land was necessary: Published Working Paper No. 45, para. 57. But see *Lee v Barrey* [1957] Ch 255, [1957] 1 All ER 199, CA, and the criticism in Hayton, 6.

H.M. LAND REGISTRY

TITLE NUMBER LT9876

This register consists of 2 pages

A.   PROPERTY REGISTER

containing the description of the registered land and the estate comprised in the title

---

COUNTY OR COUNTY BOROUGH	PARISH OR PLACE
LEICESTER	OADBY

THE FREEHOLD land shown and edged with red on the plan of the above Title filed at the Registry registered on 20 May 1960 known as 'Redacres' Blackthorn Lane, together with the rights granted by but subject to the exceptions and reservations contained in the transfer dated 5 May 1960 referred to in Entry No. 1 of the Charges Register.

NOTE: A Conveyance dated 8 April 1951 made between (1) Samuel White and (2) James Black contains the following exception and reservation and this registration takes effect subject thereto: —

'EXCEPT AND RESERVING unto the Vendor all mines and minerals and mineral substances in or under the property hereby conveyed with full power and authority to work and get such mines minerals and mineral substances but by underground workings only including power to let down the surface whether built upon or not proper compensation being paid to the Purchaser and his successors in title for all damage done by subsidence to the surface or any buildings or erections thereon.'

B.   PROPRIETORSHIP REGISTER

stating nature of the Title, name, address and description of the proprietor of the land and any entries affecting the rights of disposal thereof

TITLE ABSOLUTE

Entry Number	Proprietor, etc.	Application Number and Remarks
1.	~~PETER BROWN of 12 Ivy Drive, Leicester, Headmaster, registered on 20 May 1968.~~	~~Price paid £5250~~
2.	HENRY GREEN, Accountant, and ENID GREEN, his wife, both of 'Redacres' Blackthorn Lane, Oadby, registered on 16 January 1969.	Price paid £11,500[8]
3.	RESTRICTION registered on 16 January 1969: No disposition by one proprietor of the land (being the survivor of joint proprietors and not being a trust corporation) under which capital money arises is to be registered except under an order of the registrar or of the court.	

---

8   This information will not normally be recorded now; see p. 36, ante, and note 15.

C. CHARGES REGISTER		
containing charges, incumbrances, etc., adversely affecting the land and registered dealings therewith <div align="center">TITLE NUMBER LT9876</div>		
Entry Number	The date at the beginning of each entry is the date on which the entry was made on this edition of the register	Application Number and Remarks
1.	20 May 1960 — A transfer of the land in this title dated 5 May 1960 by Grey (Estates) Ltd. to Peter Brown contains restrictive covenants.	Copy in Certificate
2. 3.	16 January 1969 — CHARGE dated 4 January 1969 registered on 16 January 1969 to secure the moneys including the further advances therein mentioned. PROPRIETOR — STANFORD BUILDING SOCIETY of High Street, Stanford, registered on 16 January 1969.	123/69

NOTE. This illustration does not show the outer margin on the first page, which is used to record the particular edition of the register[9] and the date when it was opened. The title number is also repeated in the marginal column.

9 See LRR 1925, r. 4.

Chapter 3

Third party rights affecting registered land

In the previous chapter we were principally concerned with those interests which are capable of substantive registration, in what circumstances and with what consequences. Only incidental reference was made to third party rights which may affect a registered title. The student of real property is accustomed to divide such rights into legal and equitable, and to regard the enforceability of the latter as being governed (in the main) by registration as a land charge, which constitutes actual notice under s. 198 (1) of the Law of Property Act 1925. Under the Land Registration Act 1925, third party rights (other than mortgages which form a special group[1]) are classified into (i) overriding interests and (ii) minor interests. Both categories contain interests which are legal and equitable, a fusion which has prompted the suggestion[2] that the Act has tacitly abandoned the distinction between legal and equitable interests as the chief basis of the classification of incumbrances. A detailed examination of the rights falling within these two classes must now be undertaken.

A   Overriding interests

1.   General nature and characteristics

Overriding interests are defined to mean all the incumbrances, interests, rights and powers not entered on the register but subject to which registered dispositions are by the Act to take effect[3]. The main list of interests afforded this exalted status is contained in s. 70 (1) of the Act. As their name indicates these interests do not depend for their enforceability on being noted on the register; they bind a registered proprietor even though he is completely unaware of their existence. To this extent they partake of the character of a legal interest affecting unregistered land. Rights falling within the list of overriding interests may, however, be entered on the register of title[4] in which case, as the definition clause clearly shows, they do not take effect as such in relation to that particular title. They acquire their protection by virtue of being noted on the register.

In *National Provincial Bank Ltd v Hastings Car Mart Ltd*[5] Cross J explained the general nature of overriding interests in these terms:

1 Page 16, ante.
2 Crane, 'Equitable Interests in Registered Land' (1958) 22 Conv (NS) 14, 17.
3 LRA 1925, s. 3 (xvi).
4 See p. 56, post.
5 [1964] Ch 9 at 15, [1963] 2 All ER 204 at 207; rvsd. [1964] Ch 665, [1964] 1 All ER 688,

'Overriding interests are, speaking generally, matters which are not usually shown on title deeds or mentioned in abstracts of title and as to which, in consequence, it is not possible to form a trustworthy record on the register. As to such matters, persons dealing with registered land must obtain information outside the register in the same manner and from the same sources as people dealing with unregistered land would obtain it.'

It must not be imagined that because these interests are designated overriding a vendor of registered land owes no duty to his purchaser in respect thereof. Save where the existence of the interest is apparent, they constitute defects in his title, which require disclosure in the contract of sale[6]. A purchaser who discovers the existence of undisclosed overriding interests prior to completion of the transaction may be entitled to rescind the contract. On registration as proprietor the purchaser takes subject to them, irrespective of his lack of notice, and his rights are limited to suing the vendor on the covenants for title[7].

It has been thought that amongst the conglomeration of rights and interests included within the statutory list there lurk some strange monsters unknown to unregistered conveyancing. That this is not so is demonstrated by the following dictum of Lord Wilberforce[8]:

'The whole frame of section 70 . . . shows that it is made against a background of interests or rights whose nature and whose transmissible character is known, or ascertainable, aliunde, i.e., under other statutes or under the common law.'

It was not the scheme of the Act to create a difference as to the nature of the rights by which a purchaser may be bound, according to whether the land is registered or unregistered, though it will be seen that some rights enjoy a greater (or lesser) measure of protection under one system of conveyancing than the other. It is undoubtedly the case that this has become the result as the case law has developed. It will be seen that in some cases the position is more favourable to third parties, in others the position is worsened[9].

Overriding interests are at present under consideration by the Law Commission[10]. More than likely the next few years will see considerable (and much needed) changes in the categories of qualifying interests. For the moment we must confine our attention to s. 70 (1) as at present enacted, leaving consideration of the Commission's provisional recommendations until later.

CA; on appeal sub nom *National Provincial Bank Ltd v Ainsworth* [1965] AC 1175, [1965] 2 All ER 472, HL.
6 See pp. 146–50, post, as to this duty of disclosure.
7 See further in relation to registered titles, pp. 634–638, post, where it will be shown that the covenants for title in registered land are of reduced value with regard to overriding interests. This is unfortunate in that a registered table is most likely to be adversely affected by such an interest. See further [1981] Conv 32 (P.H. Kenny).
8 *National Provincial Bank Ltd v Ainsworth* [1965] AC 1175 at 1261, [1965] 2 All ER 472 at 503, HL. But see *Blacklocks v J B Developments (Godalming) Ltd* [1981] 3 All ER 392, pp. 50 and 55, post.
9 See [1977] Conv 405 (J.G. Riddall) and consider *Williams & Glyn's Bank Ltd v Boland* [1981] AC 487, [1980] 2 All ER 408, HL, a favourable case, and *Freer v Unwins Ltd* [1976] Ch 288, [1976] 1 All ER 634.
10 See Published Working Paper No. 37 which contains in addition to the Commission's proposals a very useful commentary on s. 70 (1). See also Jackson, 'Registration of Land Interests—The English Version' (1972) 88 LQR 93, 104–120.

Overlapping categories

As the Law Commission point out in their Working Paper[11], it might have been expected that the Act would have drawn a clear distinction between overriding interests, which are protected without being entered on the register, and other interests which are required to be protected by substantive registration or noting on the register. Unfortunately this is not so. Interests strictly falling within the latter two categories are capable of being protected as overriding interests. One specific example will suffice to illustrate the point, though others will be encountered in the ensuing pages. In Chapter 2 we saw that the grant by a registered proprietor of a lease for a term exceeding 21 years ranks as a disposition of registered land and the lessee, to obtain a legal estate, must seek substantive registration of himself as proprietor of the leasehold title. Nevertheless, notwithstanding the failure to register the lease, his interest (which perforce can subsist as an equitable interest only) may still be protected as an overriding interest under s. 70 (1) (g), which protects the rights of persons in actual occupation of the land[12].

2.   Specific heads of overriding interest

Section 70 (1) of the Act lists 12 distinct categories of overriding interest, and subsequent statutes have added to the number. The opening words of the section reiterate what has been stated in general terms in previous sections of the Act, namely, that all registered land is, unless the contrary is expressed on the register, deemed to be subject to such of the following overriding interests *as may be for the time being subsisting in reference thereto*. These italicised words are important. The section secures the continuing enforceability of existing third party rights. It does not purport to revive or resurrect rights that for some reason have already ceased to be enforceable against the land prior to the relevant date for determining what rights are binding on the proprietor. Particular consideration will be given to those groups likely to be encountered in practice.

(a) Rights of common[13], drainage rights, customary rights (until extinguished), public rights, profits à prendre, rights of sheepwalk, rights of way, watercourses, rights of water, and other easements not being equitable easements required to be protected by notice on the register.

A more motley collection of rights can hardly be imagined. Basically para (a) is concerned with easements and profits and various public rights. It is not clear what is comprehended by some of the expressions. For example, it is uncertain whether *customary rights* include rights arising from custom and enjoyed by the inhabitants of a locality[14], or are limited to rights originating in copyhold tenure and temporarily preserved under the property legislation of 1925 but now no longer enforceable, as the parenthetical reference to extinguishment suggests[15]. The major problem of this paragraph revolves around the eligibility of *equitable* easements to rank as overriding interests. Under earlier legislation

---

11 Para.12. See p. 64, post, for the Commission's proposals.
12 Some commentators consider this 'longstop' effect to be an advantage of registered land. See M & W, 1067; cf. Hayton, 88–91.and further, post.
13 See the Commons Registration Act 1965, s. 1 (1), (2).
14 E.g. the right to an oyster fishery (*Goodman v Saltash Corpn* (1882) 7 App Cas 633, HL), or the right to hold an annual fair (*Wyld v Silver* [1963] Ch 243, [1962] 3 All ER 309, CA), both of which might also be protected as public rights.
15 See R & R, 99; cf. 3 K & E, 47.

all easements were overriding[16] and the express reference in para (a) to 'other easements not being equitable easements' suggests that equitable easements were not intended to be within s. 70. The difficulty lies in the fact that there is nothing in the Act which *requires* equitable easements to be protected by notice, save in the sense that they ought to be protected by a notice if they are to bind a registered proprietor[17]. The majority view favours their exclusion from the list of overriding interests[18], though it is hard to see what justification exists for including equitable profits à prendre[19] but excluding equitable easements. If equitable easements are excluded, so, it seems, must rights arising by expenditure or acquiescence, such as the right of access in *E.R. Ives Investments Ltd v High*[20], which was not even accorded the status of an equitable easement by the majority of the Court of Appeal.

Whilst on the subject of easements as overriding interests, mention must be made of r. 258 of the Land Registration Rules 1925, which provides that rights, privileges and appurtenances adversely affecting registered land are overriding interests within s. 70. The object of this rule is to ensure that where on registration the proprietor acquires the benefit of some easement by virtue of the operation of s. 62 of the Law of Property Act 1925[1], the burden of the easement constitutes an overriding interest affecting the vendor's retained land, if the title to that land is also registered.

(b) Liability to repair highways by reason of tenure, quit-rents, crown rents, heriots and other rents and charges (until extinguished) having their origin in tenure.

Most of these tenurial rights are now obsolete and nothing further need be said about them. Liability to repair highways *ratione tenurae* may still survive[2] but it is rarely encountered.

(c) Liability to repair the chancel of any church[3].

(d) Liability in respect of embankments, and sea and river walls.

This paragraph relates to subsisting liabilities arising by reason of tenure or custom. Liability existing under a covenant to repair or maintain is outside this paragraph, otherwise positive covenants, the burden of which does not run with freehold land, would assume a proprietary nature.

---

16   Land Transfer Act 1875, s. 18.
17   LRA 1925, ss. 49 (1) (c), 59 (2).
18   Brickdale, 192; R & R, 96; Emmet, 214. Contra Potter, 11, 268. The view in favour of inclusion makes the last thirteen words of the paragraph redundant.
19   The reference in para (a) is merely to profits generally, whether legal or equitable. For an example of an equitable profit, see *Mason v Clarke* [1955] AC 778, [1955] 1 All ER 914, HL (oral grant of right to catch rabbits, followed by entry upon the land and the setting of traps).
20   [1967] 2 QB 379, [1967] 1 All ER 504, CA. See also *Crabb v Arun District Council* [1976] Ch 179, [1975] 3 All ER 865, CA, and *Western Fish Products Ltd v Penwith District Council* [1981] 2 All ER 204, CA.
 1   See e.g. the LRA 1925, s. 5, p. 24, ante; LRR 1925, r. 251. For s. 62 see pp. 473–474, post.
 2   See Pratt and MacKenzie, *Law of Highways* (21st edn) p. 76.
 3   See generally, 14 Halsbury's Laws (4th edn) 588, para. 1100; *Hauxton Parochial Church Council v Stevens* [1929] P 240.

(e) Land tax, tithe rentcharge, payments in lieu of tithe, and charges or annuities payable for the redemption of tithe rentcharges.
These various financial charges have now been statutorily extinguished. Land tax was abolished by the Finance Act 1963, s. 68. Tithe rentcharges were extinguished by the Tithe Act 1936, and the annuities which replaced them ceased to be payable as from 2 October 1977[4].

(f) Subject to the provisions of this Act, rights acquired or in course of being acquired under the Limitation Acts.
The Limitation Act 1980[5], applies to registered land in the same manner as it applies to unregistered land, with one exception. Section 75 (1) of the Act of 1925 provides that on expiration of the statutory period of adverse possession, the legal estate is deemed to be held by the registered proprietor in trust for the squatter. There is no immediate extinguishment of the proprietor's registered title. The squatter may apply to be registered as proprietor in place of the dispossessed owner[6]. His application, accompanied by an appropriate statutory declaration in support of his claim, should take the form of an application for first registration. Judicial opinions as to the precise meaning and effect of s. 75 (1) are at variance. The suggestion has been made[7] that it achieves through the medium of trustee and beneficiary a parliamentary conveyance, which was denied by the court in *Tichborne v Weir*[8].

The operation of this paragraph is illustrated by *Bridges v Mees*[9].

> In 1936 the plaintiff orally contracted to purchase a strip of land at the rear of his garden from a company for £7. He paid a deposit of £2 and entered into occupation. The following year he paid the balance of £5, but did not take any transfer of the land nor protect his rights by an entry on the register. In 1955 the company went into liquidation. Later the liquidator conveyed the strip of land with other adjoining land to the defendant who was subsequently entered on the register as proprietor with an absolute title.

It was held that the title acquired by the defendant was subject to the plaintiff's rights acquired by virtue of his adverse possession of the land for almost 20 years. The defendant was a trustee of the land for the plaintiff squatter who was entitled to a transfer of the land or to rectification of the register[10]. If the plaintiff's occupation had commenced ten years later, he would not by 1956 have acquired any adverse title, but since para. (f) includes *rights in course of acquisition*, the defendant could not have alleged that the transfer to him

4   Finance Act 1977, s. 56.
5   This Act came into force on 1 May 1981, being a consolidation of the earlier Limitation Acts including the Limitation Amendment Act 1980.
6   LRA 1925, s. 75 (2). See R & R, 648–56. See *Spectrum Investment Co v Holmes* [1981] 1 All ER 6, where such an application was made. A new title was opened in the name of the squatter. A subsequent purported surrender by the old proprietor was held to be ineffective. Cf. the *Fairweather* case, note 7.
7   *Fairweather v St. Marylebone Property Co Ltd* [1963] AC 510 at 542, [1962] 2 All ER 288 at 295, HL, per Lord Radcliffe; cf. Lord Denning, at 548 and 299 respectively, suggesting that the trust device is mere machinery not affecting the substantive law.
8   (1892) 67 LT 735, [1891–94] All ER Rep 449, CA.
9   [1957] Ch 475, [1957] 2 All ER 577; *Chowood Ltd v Lyall (No. 2)* [1930] 2 Ch 156, [1930] All ER Rep 402, CA.
10   The equitable interest arising under the contract of 1936 also constituted an overriding interest within para. (g); see post.

started time running again. The plaintiff would have acquired a title if the defendant had allowed the remainder of the twelve years' period to expire without challenging his occupation.

(g) The rights of every person in actual occupation of the land or in receipt of the rents and profits thereof, save where inquiry is made of such person and the rights are not disclosed.
This is the most extensive and controversial category of overriding interest. It is the counterpart in statutory form of the equitable rule of constructive notice, but somewhat modified[11]. The paragraph also protects the rights of persons in receipt of the rents and profits of the land. Several points arise for discussion.

(i) *Rights.* The section protects the *rights* of the occupant. Occupation is not the right; it is a form of notice of a right[12]. Furthermore the right need not be one in virtue of which the claimant is in occupation. In *Webb v Pollmount Ltd*[13] an occupying tenant's option to purchase the freehold reversion was held to be an overriding interest enforceable against a purchaser of the freehold. In *London and Cheshire Insurance Co Ltd v Laplagrene Property Co Ltd*[14] it was common ground that a vendor who remained in occupation after a sale of registered land as a lessee under a lease-back arrangement could enforce his lien for unpaid purchase money against the purchaser's chargees.

In order to ascertain what rights are within the paragraph one must look outside the Act to see what rights affect purchasers under the general law[15]. It is sometimes said that the right must be 'an interest in land'[16]. However, the opening words of s. 70 (1) speak merely of rights 'subsisting in reference [to the land]', a phrase wider in meaning than 'interest in land'. Thus in *Williams & Glyn's Bank Ltd v Boland*[17] the House of Lords held that the beneficial interest of an occupying tenant in common fell within the paragraph, despite the imposition of the statutory trust for sale under s. 35 of the Law of Property Act 1925. Yet their Lordships refrained from deciding that such an interest was, prior to a sale, an equitable interest in the land itself[18].

In many cases the claimant's interest will clearly come within para. (g) because it constitutes a recognised legal or equitable interest in land; such interests possess the quality of being capable of enduring through different ownerships of the land according to normal conceptions of title to land[19]. On the other hand mere personal rights are outside the scope of the protection. In

11 *Williams and Glyn's Bank Ltd v Boland* [1979] Ch 312 at 335, [1979] 2 All ER 697 at 708, CA, per Ormrod LJ; affd. [1981] AC 487, [1980] 2 All ER 408, HL. For constructive notice, see pp. 380–382, post.
12 *National Provincial Bank Ltd v Hastings Car Mart Ltd* [1964] Ch 665 at 697, [1964] 1 All ER 688 at 702, CA, per Russell LJ.
13 [1966] Ch 584, [1966] 1 All ER 481.
14 [1971] Ch 499, [1971] 1 All ER 766; *Lee-Parker v Izzet* [1971] 3 All ER 1099 (occupying purchaser's lien on deposit).
15 *National Provincial Bank Ltd v Ainsworth* [1965] AC 1175 at 1261, [1965] 2 All ER 472 at 503, HL, per Lord Wilberforce.
16 Ibid, at 1237 and 488, respectively, and adopted by Ungoed-Thomas J in *Webb v Pollmount Ltd* [1966] Ch 584 at 596, [1966] 1 All ER 481 at 485.
17 [1981] AC 487, [1980] 2 All ER 408.
18 See especially Lord Wilberforce at 507 and 415. Even in the Court of Appeal ([1979] Ch 312, [1979] 2 All ER 697) neither Ormrod LJ, nor Browne LJ, was disposed to adopt the view which Lord Denning MR has consistently advocated since *Bull v Bull* [1955] 1 QB 234, [1955] 1 All ER 253, CA.
19 *National Provincial Bank Ltd v Hastings Car Mart Ltd* [1964] Ch 665 at 696, [1964] 1 All ER 688 at 701, CA, per Russell LJ, on appeal, see note 12, ante.

between there exists a variety of equitable rights, sometimes called equities or mere equities, in respect of which it must be regarded as debatable to what extent they can come within para. (g). Thus, an equity which is ancillary to, or dependent on, an equitable interest in land (e.g. an equity to have a deed or contract rectified) may constitute a s. 70 (1) (g) right, but not, according to Lord Upjohn[20], a 'mere equity standing naked and alone'; for under the general law such a right is incapable of binding successors in title. None of the recent crop of cases involving an equity arising from expenditure, acquiescence or estoppel concerned registered land. According to Lord Denning MR[1], the equity of a licensee arising from expenditure on land is an obvious example of a right within the paragraph. This may perhaps be true of the son's occupation in a case such as *Inwards v Baker*[2], or the mistress's rights in *Pascoe v Turner*[3], or where the licensee's right of occupation has previously been upheld by the courts[4]. On the other hand the right of drainage established in *Ward v Kirkland*[5] would not be protected under para. (g) as the claimant was not in occupation of the land.

It seems that the rights of an occupying contractual licensee are capable of coming with the paragraph. The right of occupation conferred by the licence is a right 'subsisting in reference' to the land[6], even though the status of the licence as an equitable interest in land must at present be regarded as unresolved. Strong doubts have been voiced against the validity of this proposition by Lords Upjohn and Wilberforce in *National Provincial Bank Ltd v Ainsworth*[7]. A claim to rectification has been held to fall within the paragraph[7a].

Parliament has expressly enacted that a spouse's statutory rights of occupation under the Matrimonial Homes Act 1967[8], and a tenant's statutory right to

---

20   *National Provincial Bank Ltd v Ainsworth*, note 15, ante, at pp. 1238, 488, respectively. See also *Lee-Parker v Izzet (No. 2)* [1972] 2 All ER 800 at 803, per Goulding J.
1   *National Provincial Bank Ltd v Hastings Car Mart Ltd* note 12, ante, at 689, 697, respectively. Cf. *Lee-Parker v Izzet (No. 2)* [1972] 2 All ER 800, where the point was conceded. Consider also the Court of Appeal decisions in *Greasley v Cooke* [1980] 3 All ER 710, and *Western Fish Products Ltd v Penwith District Council* [1981] 2 All ER 204.
2   [1965] 2 QB 29, [1965] 1 All ER 446, CA.
3   [1979] 2 All ER 945.
4   *Williams v Staite* [1978] 2 All ER 928.
5   [1967] Ch 194, [1966] 1 All ER 609. Could the right be treated as a 'drainage right' within para. (a)? Alternatively if the person asserting the right provided the materials is he in occupation by virtue of such materials?
6   Cf. *Williams & Glyn's Bank Ltd v Boland* [1981] AC 487 at 510, [1980] 2 All ER 408 at 417, per Lord Scarman, speaking with reference to the right of occupation of an equitable tenant in common under a trust for sale. Unfortunately this decision failed to answer the old problem as to the nature of an interest order a trust for sale generally see [1980] 124 Sol Jo 651 and 670 (P.W. Smith). This case has been much written about; see [1980] Conv 85, 311, 361, 427; [1981] Conv 219; (1979) 42 MLR 567; (1980) 43 MLR 692 see further post in section 4.
7   [1965] AC 1175 at 1239–40 and 1251 respectively, [1965] 2 All ER 472 at 489 and 496 respectively; *Tanner v Tanner* [1975] 3 All ER 776, at 780 CA, per Browne LJ. For the rival view championed by Lord Denning MR, see, e.g., *Errington v Errington* [1952] 1 KB 290 at 299, [1952] 1 All ER 149, at 155, CA; *Binions v Evans* [1972] Ch 359 at 367, [1972] 2 All ER 70 at 75, CA, (agreement providing for temporary home, determinable at occupier's will or on death, held binding on purchaser taking with notice); *DHN Food Distributors Ltd v London Borough of Tower Hamlets* [1976] 3 All ER 462 at 468, CA, per Goff LJ; *Re Sharpe* [1980] 1 All ER 198 (aunt lending money for nephew to buy house in return for right to live there).
7a   *Blacklocks v J B Developments (Godalming) Ltd* [1981] 3 All ER 392. It is not easy to see how a claim to rectification being *discretionary* can be said to be a *right* within the paragraph.
8   Section 2 (7).

acquire the freehold or apply for an extended lease[9], do not rank as overriding interests, despite the claimant's actual occupation. These rights require protection by means of a notice or caution entered on the proprietor's register of title.

(ii) *Occupation*. The section protects the rights of the person in *actual occupation*. This is a matter of fact, not of law[10]. The word 'actual' simply emphasises that what is required is physical presence, not some entitlement in law[11]. Mere temporary presence is not enough; there must be some degree of permanence. The presence of furniture on premises, unaccompanied by occupation, does not suffice[12]. But if a person lives in a house, a temporary absence therefrom on the relevant date (e.g. because the claimant is away on holiday or ill in hospital) will not, it is thought, defeat the available protection. A long period of absence may, however, indicate that the claimant has ceased to live there, as might be the situation where an elderly relative in hospital is too ill to return home. The regular parking of a vehicle on an unfenced strip of land has been held not to amount to actual occupation[13].

Attempts have sometimes been made in the past to interpret the expression 'in actual occupation' as connoting occupation by act recognisable as such; see, for example, the decision of Ungoed Thomas J, at first instance in *Hodgson v Marks*[14]. Even the law Commission have suggested that for the purposes of a revised para. (g) the occupation ought to be apparent as well as actual[15]. This view has been decisively rejected by the judiciary. The occupation does not have to be of such a nature as would necessarily put an intending purchaser on notice of a claim adverse to the registered proprietor[16]. Consequently a person may be in actual occupation of land even though a purchaser may have no effective opportunity of discovering his presence there. Moreover, the occupation of a vendor or mortgagor in no way excludes the possibility of occupation by other persons. In *Boland's* case a wife living with her husband in the matrimonial home was held to be in actual occupation; her equitable interest arising from her contribution to the purchase price constituted an overriding interest binding on the mortgagee, to whom the husband, the sole registered proprietor, had charged the property. The position would have been similar had the occupying, but non-owning, contributor been the husband, mother, mother-in-law, mistress or other third party[17]. A person may be in occupation through the medium of another, such as a caretaker or employee.

9   Leasehold Reform Act 1967, ss. 1, 5 (5).
10 *Boland's case* [1979] Ch 312 at 332, [1979] 2 All ER 697 at 705, per Lord Denning MR.
11 *Boland's case* [1981] AC 487 at 505, [1980] 2 All ER 408 at 413, per Lord Wilberforce.
12 *Strand Securities Ltd v Caswell* [1965] Ch 958 at 985, [1965] 1 All ER 820 at 830, CA, per Russell LJ.
13 *Epps v Esso Petroleum Co Ltd* [1973] 2 All ER 465.
14 [1971] Ch 892, [1970] 3 All ER 513; revsd. [1971] Ch 918, [1971] 2 All ER 684, CA (woman in occupation transferring house to lodger but retaining beneficial interest therein; purchaser from lodger took subject to woman's rights). See further (1973) 36 MLR 25 (R.H. Maudsley).
15 Published Working Paper No. 37, para. 73.
16 *Boland's case*, note 11, ante, at 510, 417, respectively, per Lord Scarman.
17 See e.g. *Bull v Bull* [1955] 1 QB 234, [1955] 1 All ER 253, CA (mother); *Hussey v Palmer* [1972] 3 All ER 744, CA (mother-in-law); *Re Sharpe* [1980] 1 All ER 198 (aunt), note 7, ante. The *Boland* case, therefore, effectively extends the protection to the spouse when there was a school of thought that adverse occupiers i.e. non spouses were within the paragraph but spouses were not.

(iii) *Date of occupation.* Despite a lack of judicial unanimity on the point, the relevant date for determining the claimant's occupation has been held to be the date of registration, i.e. when the transferee is registered as proprietor[18] — not the date of completion (when the purchaser hands over the purchase money in exchange for the land certificate), or the date of the grant of a lease. That this is the vital date appears to be dictated by the statutory provisions regulating the effect of registration[19]. Yet this rule is not without its difficulties. A registered proprietor may have to take subject to the rights of a person entering into occupation after the time of completion of the transaction, a problem of particular concern to mortgagees[20]. It also leads to the curious result (compared with the position in unregistered conveyancing) that he may find himself bound by an interest created after *completion*[1]. In these situations it is not immediately apparent how the provisions of para. (g) relating to inquiry are intended to operate because of the usual time for making inquiries compared with the date of lodging of the application[2].

The protection of rights under the paragraph is not dependent on the duration of the occupation. They remain enforceable against the proprietor even though the claimant subsequently ceases to occupy the land[3]. Once he goes out of occupation they will become unenforceable against a *later* transferee unless protected on the register.

(iv) *Rights of other persons.* Not only is the actual occupier protected, but also the person in receipt of the rents and profits. So, failing any inquiry, the occupation of a tenant operates to preserve the rights of the landlord. A person who allowed his step-daughter and her family to occupy a flat on a rent free basis has been held to be outside para. (g)[4]. According to the obiter opinion expressed in

18 *Re Boyle's Claim* [1961] 1 All ER 620; *E S Schwab & Co Ltd v McCarthy* (1975) 31 P & CR 196 at 204, per Oliver J. Contrast *Epps v Esso Petroleum Co Ltd* [1973] 2 All ER 465 at 472, per Templeman J, favouring the date of completion. Registration takes effect retrospectively as of the date when the application for registration is delivered at the Registry: LRR 1925, r. 83 (2), as substituted by the LRR 1978, r. 8 (2).
19 See, e.g., the LRA 1925, ss. 19 (1), 20 (1), 23 (1); LRR 1925, r. 83 (2), note 18, ante.
20 See the discussion on p. 53, post.
1 This can be seen in the case of a short-term lease falling within para. (k), p. 55, post. Suppose that after completion the vendor, being mistaken as to the extent of the land sold to the purchaser, P, grants to T such a lease of part of the land sold to P. This lease, if granted without taking a premium, takes effect as if it were a registered disposition immediately on being granted (LRA 1925, s. 19 (2)). T would appear to take free from P's rights unless P himself is in actual occupation (since under s. 23 (1) T's deemed registered disposition is itself subject to overriding interests) or P has protected his rights by entry of a notice or caution against the vendor's title (s. 18 (3) which makes T's lease subject to interests intended to be protected by any notice or caution). Normally P's official search certificate will preserve priority for his transaction over entries made on the register during the protection period, provided he lodges his application in time, see p. 405, post. The certificate confers no protection in relation to interests which do not require any entry on the register. Furthermore the lease can take effect in possession up to one year later (LRA 1925, s 19 (3)).
2 This is the more so the case with the extension of the priority period for searches which could delay the lodging of an application still further but see row 1981 S.I. No. 1135 effective from 1 October 1981, post, sub. searches. In the case of a first registration the period can be two months; LRA 1925, s. 123/.
3 *London and Cheshire Insurance Co Ltd v Laplagrene Property Co Ltd* [1971] Ch 499, [1971] 1 All ER 766, p. 49, ante.
4 *Strand Securities Ltd v Caswell* [1965] Ch 958, [1965] 1 All ER 820, CA. The payment of a nominal rent of a penny a week would have made all the difference; see Russell LJ at 983, and 829.

E S Schwab & Co Ltd v McCarthy[5], a landlord does not qualify if the rent reserved is not paid, despite his having taken a deposit as security for it. In this case the landlord never received any rent. Though rent has previously been paid by the tenant during the lease, its non-payment for a sufficiently long period prior to the relevant date may disentitle the landlord to protection, unless perhaps he has by that date commenced proceedings to enforce payment of the arrears.

(v) *Inquiry.* A purchaser takes free from any overriding interest where inquiry is made of the occupier and his rights are not disclosed. Yet this may be of little consolation to the purchaser. The fact that the occupier is not a person of whom it is reasonably possible to make inquiries is quite irrelevant. As Russell LJ observed in *Hodgson v Marks*[6], however wise the purchaser may be he may have no ready opportunity to discover the occupant's rights; nevertheless the law will protect the occupier. This case also demonstrates that an occupier cannot be barred from enforcing his rights by conduct other than non-disclosure on inquiry. The court rejected an argument that there existed some principle based on estoppel or postponement of interest which prevented the plaintiff from asserting her beneficial interest.

There appears to be no reported instance where a purchaser or mortgagee has taken free from the occupier's rights because inquiry of him failed to reveal them. It therefore remains uncertain at what time the inquiry ought properly to be raised. Since, presumably, the inquiry is one 'for the purposes of the intended disposition'[7], it should be made no later than the date of completion of the purchase or mortgage. Indeed a purchaser would be well advised to make inquiries before exchange of contracts[8], so that he could, in the event of an inquiry disclosing an adverse right, decide whether or not to proceed with the purchase before legally binding himself to buy. However, on the basis that the date of registration is the relevant date for determining the enforceability of overriding interests, the only foolproof inquiry is one made on that date. Apart from the fact that the purchaser will not know in advance what that date will be, it is manifestly absurd to treat para. (g) as contemplating an inquiry made after he has paid his purchase money, or a mortgagee has advanced the mortgage loan.

As to the form of the inquiry to be raised, this will have to be directed towards ascertaining from the occupier the nature of his rights, if any, in the land. Inquiry of the vendor is not sufficient, though it may be necessary in the first instance to obtain from him the names of any other occupiers. Strictly speaking, to take free from the rights of the person in receipt of rents and profits, inquiry should be made of that person. Yet, since the only way the purchaser can ordinarily discover the existence of such a person is by inquiry of the occupier, an inquiry made of the occupier that fails to reveal his rights will, it is

---

5   (1975) 31 P & CR 196 at 213 and 215, CA.
6   [1971] Ch 892 at 932, [1971] 2 All ER 684 at 688, p. 51, note 14, ante. Inquiry of the proprietor is irrelevant save that it may give rise to a claim against him for misrepresentation for example, see intriguingly [1980] Conv 85–87, 311–312.
7   *London and Cheshire Insurance Co Ltd v Laplagrene Property Co Ltd* [1971] Ch 499 at 505, [1971] 1 All ER 766 at 771–72, per Brightman J.
8   See p. 181, post, discussing the form of inquiry raised by the standard-form pre-contract inquiries. Such an inquiry would not afford protection against a person entering into actual occupation after exchange of contracts. It has to be addressed to the relevant occupier also.

thought, also be effective to free the purchaser from the rights of the person in receipt of the rents.

(vi) *Occupiers within para. (g).* It is now necessary to have a brief look at different occupiers who may come within the paragraph, always remembering that it is the occupier's rights, not merely his occupation, that are protected. A purchaser in occupation under an enforceable contract for sale[9], or a tenant occupying by virtue of an agreement for a lease are within the provision. Similarly para. (g) extends to protect a transferee of registered land, or a lessee of a registrable lease, who fails to apply for substantive registration, provided he enters into actual occupation[10]. Several cases[11] show that a tenancy agreement entered into by a purchaser-mortgagor before completion of the purchase and mortgage may bind the mortgagee, if the tenant is in actual occupation at the time of the mortgage.

The decision in *Hodgson v Marks*[12] clearly established that a beneficiary entitled to the fee simple estate in equity under a bare trust could rely on para. (g) to enforce his rights against a purchaser from the trustee. Following the House of Lords' ruling in *Boland's* case, the position of an occupying beneficiary under a trust for sale is the same. Significantly, however, their Lordships opinion is completely at odds with a recommendation of the Law Commission[13] that beneficial interests under trusts for sale should be statutorily declared not to be overriding interests. The conveyancing implications of *Boland's* case are considered in section 4 below. The general application of s. 70 (1) (g) to beneficiaries under a bare trust or a trust for sale is not curtailed by s. 74 of the Land Registration Act 1925. This section, which provides that no one dealing with a registered estate is to be affected with notice of any trust, express, implied or constructive, does not affect the enforcement of any interest or right existing as an overriding interest[14]. Conversely, a beneficiary in occupation of settled land cannot claim an overriding interest; s. 86 (2) of the Act expressly enacts that interests arising under a settlement take effect as minor interests *and not otherwise.* Presumably this provision will extend to equitable interests under which a licensee has an equity to reside in a house for the rest of his life. However, the courts have yet to resolve the doubt as to whether these cases attract the provisions of the Settled Land Act 1925[15].

One final and important point needs to be stressed. The fact that an overriding interest claimed by an occupier is also capable of being protected on the

9   *Bridges v Mees* [1957] Ch 475, [1957] 2 All ER 577, p. 48, ante.
10   Cf. *Strand Securities Ltd v Caswell* [1965] Ch 958, [1965] 1 All ER 820, note 4, ante.
11   E.g. *Woolwich Equitable Building Society v Marshall* [1952] Ch 1, [1951] 2 All ER 769;
      Grace Rymer Investments Ltd v Waite [1958] Ch 831, [1958] 2 All ER 777, CA. Or even
      afterwards; see *Jessamine Investment Co v Schwaltz* [1978] QB 264, [1976] 3 All ER 521,
      CA; [1977] Conv 197 (P.W. Smith).
12   [1971] Ch 892, [1971] 2 All ER 684, CA; *Bridges v Mees* note 9, ante (the vendor was in
      fact a bare trust for the purchaser who had paid all the purchase money).
13   Third Report on Family Property, Law Com No. 86, para. 1.333. See further p. 63, post.
14   *Boland's* case, [1981] AC 487 at 508, [1980] 2 All ER 408, 415, per Lord Wilberforce.
15   The question is, is there a settlement within the Act? Is the court order establishing the
      equity to be treated as an 'instrument' for the purpose of s. 1 (1)? See *Griffiths v Williams*
      (1977) 248 Estates Gazette 947 at 949, CA, per Goff LJ; *Ivory v Palmer* [1975] ICR 340 at
      347, CA, per Cairns LJ. Contrast *Binions v Evans* [1972] Ch 359, [1972] 2 All ER 70, CA;
      Dodsworth v Dodsworth (1973) 228 Estates Gazette 1115, CA. See further [1978] Conv 229
      (P.W. Smith).

register in the proper manner, which he has failed to do, is quite irrelevant. Several cases involving para. (g), including *Boland's* case, affirm this principle[16]. A right to rectification has been held to be within the paragraph[17].

(h) In the case of a possessory, qualified or good leasehold title, all estates, rights, interests and powers excepted from the effect of registration.
As we saw in the previous chapter[18] registration with less than an absolute title does not prejudice various interests; these take effect as overriding interests.

(i) Rights under local land charges unless and until registered or protected on the register in the prescribed manner.
Local land charges are not generally protected on the register except in the case of a charge securing the payment of money which requires registration before realisation[19]. Consequently the same searches in the registers maintained by local authorities must be undertaken as in unregistered conveyancing[20]. As to what constitute local land charges see the Local Land Charges Act, s. 1, discussed in Chapter 7.

(j) Rights of fishing and sporting, seignorial and manorial rights of all descriptions (until extinguished), and franchises.
This paragraph deals with that very limited class of manorial incidents formerly attaching to copyhold land and indefinitely preserved by the Law of Property Act 1922[1].

(k) Leases for any term or interest not exceeding twenty-one years, granted at a rent without taking a fine[2].
A lease does not have to take effect in possession to be within this paragraph. An agreement for a lease is not, however, protected. The word 'granted' imports the actual creation of a term of years taking effect at law[3]. The same word also implies the express creation of a term by the act of the parties, either by deed, or by signed writing or parol in the case of leases that can be created informally. A lease arising by implication of law does not seem to be within this paragraph. A lease is excluded if a premium (or fine) has been paid. A premium usually represents a cash payment made to the lessor and representing the capital value of the difference between the actual rent and the best rent that might otherwise be obtained[4]. The courts have on several occasions had to consider whether rent paid in advance constitutes a premium, but no definite conclusion has been reached[5]. It would seem to be essential to differentiate cases where the

16 See also *Bridges v Mees*, ante; *Hodgson v Marks*, ante.
17 *Blacklocks v J B Developments (Godalming) Ltd* [1981] 3 All ER 392, p. 50, ante.
18 Pages 29–31, ante.
19 LRA 1925, s. 59 (2); LRR 1925, r. 155.
20 Pages 29–31, ante.
 1 Section 128, Sch. 12, paras. 5 and 6.
 2 See further p. 456, post.
 3 *City Permanent Building Society v Miller* [1952] Ch 840, [1952] 2 All ER 621, CA. The context displaces the statutory definition in s. 3 (x) that lease includes an agreement for a lease.
 4 *King v Earl Cadogan* [1915] 3 KB 485, at 492, CA, per Warrington LJ.
 5 See e.g. *City Permanent Building Society v Miller* [1952] Ch 840, [1952] 2 All ER 621, CA; *Grace Rymer Investments Ltd v Waite* [1958] Ch 831, [1958] 2 All ER 777, CA. In *Hughes v Waite* [1957] 1 All ER 603, Harman J held rent in advance to be a fine for the purposes of the LPA 1925, s. 99 (6).

total sum payable during the currency of the term is paid in advance from those where the first periodical payment is paid in advance, as is quite common in the case of short residential tenancies. A payment of the latter kind hardly constitutes a premium. However the point will become academic for present purposes if a Law Commission proposal to extend paragraph (k) to all leases granted for a term not exceeding 21 years becomes law[6].

Paragraph (k) protects 'leases'. To what extent the lessee's rights (other than that of possession) are similarly protected is not stated. The problem is only likely to be material where the lessee cannot bring himself within para. (g). It seems that para. (k) enables the lessee to enforce all the terms having reference to the subject matter of the lease, but not those that are merely collateral to the relationship of landlord and tenant, e.g. an option to purchase the freehold reversion[7].

A lessee whose lease falls outside this paragraph because a premium has been paid or the term exceeds the statutory period can claim the protection of para. (g), provided he is in actual occupation or in receipt of the rents and profits.

(l) Mines and minerals
This paragraph, the lengthy wording of which has not been reproduced, deals with rights to mines and minerals relating to land registered prior to 1926. Briefly all such rights created before 1898 are overriding interests where the land was first registered between 1876 and 1898; thereafter only mineral rights created before first registration are overriding interests. On first registration after 1925 the proprietor registered with an absolute freehold title obtains title to the mines and minerals (since they are included within the definition of land), unless they have been severed and the Registrar makes a note on the register that they are excepted from the registration[8]. They do not take effect as overriding interests, except in the case of coal and coal mines vested in the National Coal Board[9] and manorial rights to mines and minerals which are protected under para. (j).

3.   Overriding interests on the register

As defined overriding interests do not include matters entered on the register. Once entered on the register protection as an overriding interest becomes superfluous; the entry itself confers protection, for registration always takes effect subject to entries appearing on the register[10].

Rights and interests included within the list of overriding interests may find their way on to the register for a variety of reasons. Those interests which are duly protected by means of a notice, caution or restriction constitute the commonest examples of s. 70 (1) rights entered on the register. In addition, s. 70 (2) of the Act requires adverse easements created by an instrument to be noted on the register at the time of first registration provided they appear on

6   See Published Working Paper No. 32, para. 46.
7   See *Woodall v Clifton* [1905] 2 Ch 257. In *Webb v Pollmount Ltd* [1966] Ch 584, [1966] 1 All ER 481, p. 49, ante, the option was held to be enforceable under s. 70 (1) (g) because the tenant was in actual occupation.
8   LRR 1925, r. 196. See p. 17, ante.
9   Coal Act 1938, s. 41; Coal Industry Nationalisation Act 1946, ss. 5, 8.
10   See e.g. LRA 1925, ss. 5 (a), 9 (b), 20 (1) (a), 23 (1) (b).

the title[11], whilst s. 70 (3) empowers the Registrar to enter notice of any over-riding interest proved to his satisfaction or admitted. This latter provision is not limited to first registrations, and an interested party has an independent right by virtue of r. 197 to apply for notice of an overriding interest to be entered on the register.

An entry may also be made on the register recording the fact that the title is *not* subject to a particular overriding interest, though the view has been judicially expressed that this provision merely enables the cancellation of a previous entry noting the existence of some liability[12].

4. Conveyancing implications of Williams & Glyn's Bank Ltd v Boland

(a) Scope of decision

The Lords' decision in *Boland's* case[13] sent shock waves reverberating through the offices of solicitors, building societies and other institutional lenders. The facts are as follows:

> H purchased a matrimonial home with the aid of a building society mortgage, and he was registered as the sole proprietor. He lived there with his wife, W. She had contributed a substantial sum of her own money towards the purchase, thereby making her an equitable tenant in common to the extent of her contribution. Later, without her knowledge, H created a second mortgage in favour of the Bank who made no inquiries of W. When H defaulted on this mortgage the Bank issued a summons for possession of the house. W claimed that she was entitled to remain in possession by virtue of her beneficial interest, which was enforceable against the Bank by reason of her actual occupation. Her claim succeeded[14].

Though the actual decision concerned a second mortgage, its scope is far wider. Clearly the principle of the case applies to a first mortgage granted on the occasion of a purchase by the mortgagee, and also to a purchase without the aid of any mortgage. Nor yet is it confined to beneficial interests of occupying spouses. The decision is wide enough to embrace an equitable interest existing under a trust for sale and vested in any co-habitor in actual occupation, whether a parent, child, mistress or other occupant, such as (perhaps) a business associate. It does not seem to matter that the interest arises by virtue of an indirect rather than a direct contribution to the purchase, or by making a substantial contribution to the improvement of the property after its purchase[15]. Prior to *Boland's* case it was not considered necessary, on the basis

---

11 Other than those of a trivial or obvious nature: LRR 1925, r. 199. See also r. 41.
12 LRR 1925, r. 197. *Re Dances Way, West Town, Hayling Island* [1962] Ch 490 at 510, [1962] 2 All ER 42, at 53, CA per Diplock LJ. Cf. R & R, 114–15. The covenants for title arguably will not cover an interest within para. (g) as the purchaser will have notice by occupation: LRR 1925, r. 77 (1) b. This puts a purchaser of registered land at a considerable disadvantage. To say anything rarely happens is to miss the point: The possibility of a defect will of course only arise in a small number of cases. The *consequences* of the defect are being considered here.
13 [1981] AC 487, [1980] 2 All ER 408. For the possible effect of the decision on unregistered conveyancing, see pp. 326–328, post.
14 See also pp. 49–54, ante.
15 As to when a contribution suffices to give rise to an equitable interest, see *Gissing v Gissing* [1971] AC 886 especially at 904–10, [1970] 2 All ER 780 at 789–93, HL, per Lord Diplock; *Hazell v Hazell* [1972] 1 All ER 923, CA; *Hussey v Palmer* [1972] 3 All ER 744;

of the decision in *Caunce v Caunce*[16], for a purchaser or mortgagee to concern himself with a beneficial interest claimed by the spouse of the vendor or mortgagor. The occupation of a non-owning wife, for instance, could be said to be merely a shadow of her husband's; alternatively her presence on the land did not constitute actual occupation within para. (g) because it was not inconsistent with the husband's title. Their Lordships decisively rejected such arguments. In consequence a purchaser must now ascertain that any person cohabiting with the vendor claims no equitable interest in the property. Similarly, and from the practical aspect, more importantly, a mortgagee will need to take steps to ensure that a person residing, or intending to reside, with the mortgagor in the mortgaged property is unable to claim an equitable interest binding on the mortgagee.

The conveyancing implications of the *Boland* decision can best be illustrated by discussing two everyday situations involving conveyancers.

(b) Situation 1: Purchase of land—possibility of purchaser being bound by interest of member of vendor's household

(i) *Purchase from sole proprietor.* Unless the purchaser (P) makes inquiries of all persons living with the vendor, he may find himself bound by the equitable interest of a contributing occupier who refuses to vacate the property after completion of the sale. Where, as is usually the position, a mortgage advance is made to finance the purchase, the interests of P and his mortgagee coincide. In this situation the danger is perhaps more theoretical rather than real. A contract for the sale of property for residential purposes normally provides for vacant possession to be given on completion. Ordinarily P will be most anxious to ensure that he does obtain vacant possession, in which event no question can arise of P (or the mortgagee) being bound by any contributor's interest. The contributor will have ceased to be in actual occupation. The only safe way to be sure that vacant possession is given is to effect completion at the property, a counsel of perfection quite impossible to attain in practice. Unfortunately modern conveyancing procedures may well increase the risk of vacant possession not being obtained. Completions frequently take place on the assumption that it will be, or already has been, given. This is particularly true when completion is effected through the post[17], without P's solicitor attending at the offices of the vendor's solicitor to hand over the purchase money in exchange for the land (or charge) certificate. Some building societies are expressly instructing their solicitors (who will in most cases also be acting for the purchaser) not to release the mortgage advance unless and until they are satisfied that vacant possession has been or is to be obtained. It is doubtful whether this will have any real impact on completion procedures[18].

Cowcher v Cowcher [1972] 1 All ER 943; *Kowalczuk v Kowalczuk* [1973] 2 All ER 1042; and *Re Densham* [1975] 3 All ER 726; Matrimonial Proceedings and Property Act 1970, s. 37; Hanbury & Maudsley, *Modern Equity* (11th edn), pp. 324–332.

16   [1969] 1 All ER 722, an unregistered land case, applied by Templeman J to a registered land situation in *Bird v Syme Thomson* [1978] 3 All ER 1027. Adverse comments on *Caunce's* case had already been made in *Hodgson v Marks* [1971] Ch 892 at 934–35, [1971] 2 All ER 684 at 690, CA, per Russell LJ. This latter case led to the view that only the spouse was disadvantaged, a preposterous position really.

17   See further pp. 409–410, post.

18   If P's solicitor did complete in ignorance of the fact that an equitable owner had not moved out of the property, his interest would bind P only if he was still in occupation when

It has been advocated in some quarters[19] that the dangers inherent in a purchase from a sole proprietor when others are jointly in occupation can be avoided altogether by insisting on the appointment of an additional trustee for sale. This will enable title to be made under the trust for sale so as to bring into play the overreaching machinery of the Law of Property Act 1925[20]. This solution is considered to be appropriate only where a prospective purchaser discovers the existence of an occupier who claims a beneficial interest. He would not be justified in insisting upon this procedure merely because he finds out about, or suspects, that others are living in the property with the vendor, at least not when the vendor has contracted to give vacant possession on completion. A purchaser should not experience difficulty in ascertaining the existence of other occupiers; a question to this effect appears in the standard form preliminary inquiries which solicitors are accustomed to raise before exchange of contracts[1].

One other point should not be overlooked. An occupier with an equitable interest may be estopped[2] from enforcing it against the purchaser if, knowing of his rights, he actively assists in the purchase by e.g. showing the purchaser around the house, or leads him to believe that he will be vacating the property along with the vendor on completion.

(ii) *Purchase from joint proprietors.* The Law Lords did not in the *Boland* case consider the effect of the overreaching machinery on beneficial interests under a trust for sale which are capable of taking effect as overriding interests. The Land Registration Act 1925, proceeds on the basis that this machinery does apply to registered land transactions[3]. Therefore no special precautions need be taken in this situation. A transfer by joint proprietors, to whom the purchase money is paid, will operate to overreach all beneficial interests under the trust, including the interest of any occupying equitable tenant in common arising by virtue of a contribution. The contrary suggestion[4], based on the absence of specific overreaching provisions in the Land Registration Act 1925, is not thought to be well founded.

P was registered as proprietor. In practice the adverse occupation would delay P's registration until the dispute had been resolved. To obtain possession P might be obliged to buy out the occupier, failing which an application under s. 30 of the LPA 1925 (p. 32, post) for an order for sale might be necessary. The vendor would also be liable to P in damages for breach of the contractual term to give vacant possession, for what it would be worth. See further [1980] Conv 361.

19 [1980] Conv 313, 316; (1980) 124 Sol Jo 670, 671; (1979) 42 MLR 567, 571. This device is open to the possibility of fraud by e.g. appointing as trustee a stranger rather than the occupying beneficiary.
20 See ss. 2 (1) (ii) and 27 (1), (2), p. 321, post. See also para (ii) below.
1 Pages 181–189, post. Another suggested necessity is registration in the Minor Interest Index; see [1981] Conv 323. In view of the Chief Land Registrar's view (R & R, 126) that the Index is an 'excrescence' this is of doubtful effect!
2 Cf. *Wroth v Tyler* [1974] Ch 30 at 47, [1973] 1 All ER 897 at 910, per Megarry J; *Spiro v Lintern* [1973] 3 All ER 319; *Watts v Spence* [1975] 2 All ER 528.
3 See e.g. the LRA 1925, ss. 3 (xv), 49 (2).
4 Sydenham, 'Overreaching and the Ratio of Boland's Case' [1980] Conv 427, 430–31. Once the property has been sold by the trustees for sale, the beneficiary can no longer assert any interest subsisting in reference to the land. His interest has been actually (and not merely notionally) converted into an interest in the proceeds of sale: see *Boland's* case [1979] Ch 312 at 331, [1979] 2 All ER 697 at 704, per Lord Denning MR. The LRA 1925, s. 70 (1) (g) ceases, therefore, to be applicable. See further [1981] Conv 219 (J. Martin).

(c) Situation 2: Mortgage contemporaneous with purchase—possibility of mortgagee being bound by interest of member of purchaser's household

It is an everyday occurrence for a mortgagee (M) to grant a mortgage contemporaneously with the purchase of the mortgaged property by the purchaser. One aspect of the decision in *Boland's* case, which the Law Lords appear not to have contemplated, is that a mortgagee who finances the acquisition of the property now faces the prospect of being bound by the equitable interest of a person, such as the purchaser's wife, who has contributed directly or indirectly to the purchase of the matrimonial home. It has to be remembered that it is the date of registration when M becomes a legal chargee, not the date of completion of the mortgage advance, that is the relevant time for determining the enforceability of overriding interests[5]. If, therefore, the contributing spouse is in actual occupation at the date of M's registration, she will be able to claim an overriding interest binding on M. The mortgagee cannot make effective inquiries to discover the spouse's rights. An inquiry made before completion of the purchase and mortgage will not suffice. Neither the purchaser nor his wife will ordinarily be in occupation at that time, and s. 70 (1) (g) requires the inquiry to be directed to persons who are in occupation. Inquiry made after the spouse has taken up residence will afford M no possible protection since the mortgage loan has already been advanced. It is extremely doubtful whether M could establish priority over the contributor's interest on purely equitable grounds. The interest of a spouse contributing to the purchase price will normally come into existence at the latest at the time of the conveyance to the purchaser. This momentarily precedes the mortgage advance[6], which operates, pending registration, to create in the mortgagee's favour an equitable mortgage on the property[7].

A mortgagee will not be bound by the equitable interest of a contributor not in actual occupation at the date of registration, nor by the rights of a person then in occupation whose interest does not arise until some later date.

Building societies have reacted in different ways to the problems presented by the *Boland* decision. Some have decided not to take any special steps, accepting the establishment of an adverse claim as a normal business risk. One solution suggested by Ormrod LJ in the Court of Appeal[8] is for the mortgagee to require the spouse or other initial contributor to join in the purchase and mortgage. It is understood that societies are reluctant to impose this as a condition of the grant of a mortgage to a sole intending purchaser. There may be sound reasons for not putting the property in the joint names of the spouses. A husband in business on his own account may prefer his wife to be the sole owner of the house to prevent it being sold to discharge his business debts in the event of bankruptcy. Alternatively the contributor may be an aged relative unwilling to assume joint liability for the mortgage repayments. Where, however, the mortgage is granted to joint proprietors as trustees for sale, the mortgage (which ranks as a conveyance for the purposes of s. 2 (1) of the Law of Property Act 1925) will overreach all equitable interests arising under the trust,

---

5 Page 52, ante.
6 Cf. *Church of England Building Society v Piskor* [1954] Ch 553, [1954] 2 All ER 85, CA.
7 See *Barclays Bank Ltd v Taylor* [1974] Ch 137, [1973] 1 All ER 752, CA. In any event the equitable charge would merge on registration with the legal charge, with a consequent loss of priority: *Capital Finance Co Ltd v Stokes* [1969] 1 Ch 261 at 278, [1968] 3 All ER 625 at 629, CA, per Harman LJ.
8 [1979] Ch 312 at 339, [1979] 2 All ER 697 at 711.

including that of a third party contributor residing in the property. This result will, however, ensue only when the trustees have express power to mortgage the property in order to finance its purchase. They have no statutory power to raise money for such a purpose[9], although that will not be a problem if they are beneficially entitled[10].

As a simple expediency Ormrod LJ thought that a mortgagee need only obtain the consent of the equitable co-owner. The patent flaw in this solution is that many occupiers will be quite unaware of their equitable entitlement. Many building societies are requiring every intending adult occupier (other than the mortgagee) to sign a consent form or undertaking[11] before completion of the mortgage advance, irrespective of whether or not such occupier is making any contribution to the purchase. The requirement covers each potential occupier disclosed by the mortgagor in his application for a loan. It extends, for example, to resident relatives, lodgers, children temporarily away at University, as well as a spouse or mistress. The consent document purports to confer priority for the mortgage over any rights which the occupier has or may acquire in the property, and contains an undertaking by him not to assert against the mortgagee any right, interest or claim in equity or by way of overriding interest or otherwise. The procedure has been designed so as to obviate the need to investigate the beneficial claims of occupiers. Yet the practice of requiring occupiers who have made no contribution to the purchase to postpone non-existent equitable rights is surely open to objection. Moreover the precise legal effect of the consent form is debatable. The document, though intended to be legally binding, does not appear to have contractual force; nor is it under seal[12]. It may operate to estop the signatory from asserting his overriding interest against the mortgagee, provided he was aware[13], when signing the form, that his contribution would give rise to an equitable interest in the

---

9 See further p. 534, post. As to the position of registered titles see R & R, 377 and 768.
10 See Emmet, 342 and 810.
11 Sometimes it takes the form of a signed declaration endorsed on the mortgage deed.
12 If it was there would be an estoppel by deed see the *Taylor case*, note 13 below, at 922.
13 Cf. *Armstrong v Sheppard and Short Ltd* [1959] 2 QB 384, [1959] 2 All ER 651, CA. But see *Taylor Fashions Ltd v Liverpool Victoria Trustees Co Ltd* [1981] 1 All ER 897 at 912–918. This case shows the increasing reluctance of the courts to put any kind of framework on estoppels of any kind. This kind of development has reached the position now that it is almost impossible to predict the result of an estoppel; see e.g. *Brikom Investments Ltd v Carr* [1979] 2 All ER 753, CA, especially at 760, where the proposition is put forward that if an assignee of the reversion on a lease takes subject to the burden of the estoppel then an assignee of the tenant should take subject to the benefit. In the case the landlords were estopped as against a party who knew nothing of their promise. Cf. Roskill LJ, who decided it on waiver. It is quite clear that there are 'estoppels and estoppels' (*Crabb v Arun District Council* [1975] 3 All ER 865, at 871 per Denning MR). It is also quite clear that each successive case on it is opening new doors (see *McIlkenny v Chief Constable of the West Midlands* [1980] 2 All ER 227 at 235 per Denning MR). There is the further suggestion that a detriment is to be presumed unless the *representor* shows otherwise (see *Greasley v Cooke* [1980] 3 All ER 710 at 713, CA). This will put an impossible evidential burden on such a party. The only other case which appears to put some restraint on these developments is *Western Fish Products Ltd v Penwith District Council* [1981] 2 All ER 204, CA. It is not without significance that the case is comparatively old, the estoppel developments judgment having been given in 1978. It would appear that the estoppel is being asserted against non parties to it with success. As it is an equity, presumably lack of notice coupled with purchase of the legal estate will afford a defence. Occupation now will probably constitute notice in unregistered land. In registered land the representor will undoubtedly assert an overriding interest based on occupation. See further [1980] Conv 27 (Rolson and Watchman); [1981] Conv 341 (Todd).

property when purchased. This will not be the usual case. Without such knowledge, the mere explanation to the occupier of the document's supposed legal
effect, which some societies require, will not be sufficient[14]. Had the contributor actually been aware of the nature of his prospective rights in the land, he
might not have signed the document. One secure method of protection is to
obtain an entry on the register of title, based on an express postponement by the
occupier of an acknowledged prior equitable interest, that the mortgagee takes
free from his rights or alternatively to charge any interest the occupier has[15].
This solution is unlikely to be adopted in practice, since it could well entail
detailed investigation into the borrower's financial arrangements and cause
undue delay in completing the transaction. A consent form is not thought to be
capable of being noted on the register. Apparently, those societies which have
adopted this method of protection require the signature of a consent form in all
cases, even when the mortgage is granted to joint proprietors. This is an
unnecessary precaution where the mortgage brings into play the statutory overreaching provisions.

(d) Second mortgage—mortgage not contemporaneous with purchase
A second (or subsequent) mortgagee is in a much better position before
advancing the loan to discover the existence of adverse rights by making appropriate inquiries of existing occupiers, and to require a postponement of any
equitable interest disclosed thereby. The possibility of a contributor entering
into occupation after the making of the loan and before registration may well
be considered sufficiently remote for the mortgagee to chance the risk of this
happening. The problem in the past was the lack of inquiry.

(e) Possible solutions
The *Boland* case illustrates in a neat form the difficulties of striking a satisfactory balance between the need on the one hand to facilitate and simplify
conveyancing transactions and on the other hand to preserve the rights of occupiers. Both in the Court of Appeal and before the House of Lords counsel for
the Bank argued strenuously that the conveyancing consequences of a decision
in favour of the occupying spouse would be far-reaching, even catastrophic.
These arguments fell on deaf ears. Lord Wilberforce admitted that the decision would increase the burdens of purchasers, involving them in inquiries that
might sometimes be troublesome. He was in fact rather inclined to welcome
this, especially if the present 'easy going practice' of dispensing with inquiries
beyond that of the vendor's occupation were to be replaced by a practice
involving a more thorough inquiry as to the fact of occupation and the rights of
occupiers[16]. It is nevertheless open to speculation whether their Lordships
would have listened more readily to such arguments had they been concerned,
not with a second mortgage where the making of appropriate inquiries may not

14 Further the mortgagee will have to be very careful in the manner in which the document is
    put forward. The signatory clearly must have independent advice (that means presumably
    independent of the building society and would ordinarily exclude the solicitor acting for
    them and the purchaser). Otherwise the question of undue influence will undoubtedly be
    raised; see *Lloyds Bank Ltd v Bundy* [1975] QB 326, [1974] 3 All ER 757; *Cresswell v
    Potter* [1978] 1 WLR 255; *Backhouse v Backhouse* [1978] 1 All ER 1158; and [1979] 123
    Sol Jo 193 (P.W. Smith).
15 The fears presented by *Cedar Holdings Ltd v Green* [1979] 3 All ER 117. If they survive
    the *Boland* case can be overcome by draftsmanship.
16 [1981] AC 487 at 508−509, [1980] 2 All ER 408 at 415−16.

prove to be unduly burdensome, but with a first mortgage granted contemporaneously with the purchase of the matrimonial home. They could not have foreseen the elaborate precautions currently being taken by building societies to protect their interests.

One way to mitigate the harshness of s. 70 (1) (g) would be to change the time when occupation becomes effective from the date of registration[17] to the date of completion, but this would run counter to the theoretical structure of the land registration system. The same result could be achieved with less doctrinal objection by enacting that an application for registration should be deemed to be completed as of the day of actual completion, rather than the date of its lodgement at the Registry. Alternatively, and ideally from the conveyancer's standpoint, the contributor's equitable interest could be deprived of its status as an overriding interest and required to be protected on the register in the proper manner. Such a solution was in fact advocated by the Law Commission in their Third Report on Family Property[18]. They may, however, be reluctant to stand by this proposal in view of the seeming judicial dislike[19] of any scheme for the protection of the spouse's rights based on the need to register. The consequences flowing from non-registration are thought by some to be too drastic for a person who might not even be aware of his or her entitlement to an equitable right that requires protection. It is of course to be noted that if mortgagees operated on the assumption of an interest in favour of a non-owning spouse[20] and acted accordingly many of the major contentions would disappear as the problem would be confined to the non-spouse. A practical solution is to urge the property to be in joint names. This is generally acceptable. For the time being the balance is weighted too heavily in favour of the occupier. An acceptable compromise is not readily apparent, and the Law Commission's solution is awaited with considerable interest.

5. Need for reform

The existence of many overriding interests not appearing on the register inevitably means that the register does not contain a complete record of all matters affecting the title to land. A former Chief Land Registrar[1] regarded them as the stumbling block to land registration and he considered that their enforceability rendered an absolute title something of a misnomer. Viewed from a purchaser's standpoint, overriding interests are doubly odious. Not only is he obliged to make inquiries outside the register, he is denied any right of indemnity under the Act if the register is rectified against him in order to give effect to some overriding interest[2] which perhaps he did not, and could not, discover. Yet their existence can be defended. The recording of all interests on the register is thought by some to be impracticable and undesirable. Not only would it make the register too bulky and unwieldy, it might seriously prejudice

17 See p. 52, ante.
18 Law Com No. 86, para. 1.333. Any beneficial interest subsisting under a trust for sale was intended to be caught, whether belonging to a spouse or anybody else.
19 See the comments about the Class F Charge in *Boland's* case [1979] Ch 312 at 328, 339, [1979] 2 All ER 697 at 702, 711, per Lord Denning MR, and Ormrod LJ, respectively.
20 See ibid, at 329 and 703, per Lord Denning MR; and (1980) 124 Sol Jo 671.
 1 Brickdale, 32.
 2 See p. 86, post.

the rights of persons who acquire interests under some informal arrangement without professional assistance and who are unlikely to be aware of the need to protect their rights by registration. In addition there is the doctrinal argument, which some advocates of the registration system would hotly dispute, that the register of title is merely intended as a substitute for title deeds and it ought not to contain matters not normally recorded in the deeds, thereby reducing the scope for improvement of conveyancing.

In compiling any list of overriding interests a just balance must be preserved between the conflicting interests of a purchaser on the one hand and a third party incumbrancer on the other. The present list contained in s. 70 (1) is open to major attack on the ground that it is too widely drawn and permits an inter-pretation which unduly favours the incumbrancer. Nowhere is this more clearly seen than in para. (g) which has consistently been held by the courts to confer protection on an occupier who has failed to protect his interest in the appropriate manner. Various sections of the Act suggest that this was not intended, of which s. 59 (6) may be cited as an example. Under this provision a purchaser acquiring title under a registered disposition is not to be concerned with any matter or claim not protected by a caution or other entry on the register, whether or not he has notice thereof. Similarly it may be doubted whether the draftsman intended a transferee under a registrable disposition to be entitled to protection notwithstanding his omission, perhaps deliberate, to register himself as proprietor. Any provision which tends to discourage regis-tration can hardly promote the effective operation of any system of registration of title.

Some legislative re-drafting of s. 70 (1) is long overdue. The Law Commis-sion have recognised that a reduction in the number of overriding interests will go some way towards the desired simplification of conveyancing, and they have made a number of tentative proposals to this end[3]. Some mention of the main areas of likely reform is called for. Apart from a welcome tidying up of some of the existing categories, it is proposed to exclude from the list of overriding interests any interest capable of being substantively registered or protected on the register by an appropriate entry[4], or which requires to be noted on the title of the burdened land. This will eliminate the overlap between different classes of interests in or affecting registered land and their mode of protection. In relation to equitable interests subsisting behind a trust for sale the Commission, as we have seen, re-affirmed this principle in their draft Bill appended to the Third Report on Family Property. It would be unfortunate if they felt compelled by the ruling in the *Boland* case to revise their original recommen-dation. Few conveyancers would quarrel with the proposed change.

The Commission felt the need to retain para. (g) but to limit its operation to contractual rights to occupy not capable of protection by any other method. If adopted the new paragraph would protect the occupational rights (but not collateral rights) of, amongst others, contractual licensees, lodgers and persons sharing accommodation. This proposal has already evoked justifiable criti-cism, for it is not clear why the holder of a contractual right to occupy merits preferential treatment compared with other persons in occupation by virtue of some other kind of enforceable interest[5]. It may be that the Commission

3   Published Working Paper No. 37, Part D.
4   Options to purchase or renew contained in leases would constitute an exception: see paras. 20−21.
5   Jackson, op. cit., pp. 114−15.

considered, though this is not stated, that it would be undesirable to require such contractual rights which in many cases are of an informal and temporary nature to be protected by entry on the register—hence their need to be protected as overriding interests. Further, this recommendation represents a departure from the fundamental principle, which the Commission have accepted as valid[6], that the Act and its predecessors set out to establish a system of conveyancing and not to alter the substantive land law. But the proposed paragraph will elevate mere contractual rights of occupation (e.g. the rights of a lodger) to the status of proprietary rights, a position which they do not at present occupy under the general law. In the absence of any apparent justification for protecting contractual occupiers in this manner, it is debatable whether there is any need to retain para. (g) at all[7].

The Commission have also made various provisional recommendations relating to the registration and protection of leases. These will be noted where appropriate in Chapter 15.

B Minor interests

In contrast to overriding interests which are binding even though not appearing on the register, numerous third party rights and interests exist which are liable to be defeated on a registered disposition for value of the burdened land unless they are protected by the appropriate entry on the proprietor's register of title. These are known as minor interests, defined by s. 3 (xv) of the Act to mean:

' the interests not capable of being disposed of or created by registered dispositions and capable of being overriden (whether or not a purchaser has notice thereof) by the proprietors unless protected as provided by this Act, and all rights and interests which are not registered or protected on the register and are not overriding interests, and include —

(a) in the case of land held on trust for sale, all interests and powers which are under the Law of Property Act 1925, capable of being overriden by the trustees for sale, whether or not such interests and powers are so protected; and

(b) in the case of settled land, all interests and powers which are under the Settled Land Act 1925, and the Law of Property Act 1925, or either of them, capable of being overriden by the tenant for life or statutory owner, whether or not such interests and powers are so protected as aforesaid.'

Section 2 (1) provides that apart from legal estates which are capable of substantive registration and overriding interests, all other interests in registered land take effect *in equity as minor interests*.

---

6 See especially Published Working Papers No. 45, para. 73; No. 67, para. 6.
7 The Law Commission feel that the position of a person in occupation under some beneficial interest (e.g. an equitable fee simple as in *Hodgson v Marks* [1971] Ch 892, [1971] 2 All ER 684, CA, p. 51, ante) could more satisfactorily be dealt with if the courts had wider powers to order rectification of the register and award indemnity; see Published Working Paper No. 45, paras. 71–74.

1.   Classification of minor interests

This long and obscure definition clause embraces three categories of interests.

(a) Equitable interests under settlements and trusts

Within this group come the beneficial interests existing behind a settlement or trust for sale. These interests are protected by means of an appropriate restriction entered against the registered proprietor, which ensures that a purchaser of the land complies with the overreaching provisions of the Settled Land Act 1925, and the Law of Property Act 1925, so protecting the interests of the beneficiaries[8]. The presence of the restriction on the register warns the purchaser of the existence of the equitable interests, but he takes free from them (as in unregistered conveyancing) provided the restriction is complied with.

(b) Dispositions of registered land

A disposition of registered land, such as the grant of an easement, or the grant of a lease for a term in excess of 21 years, ranks as a minor interest until the disposition is completed by registration in the prescribed manner. In the case of an easement, this entails entering a notice against the grantor's registered title[9]; whereas a dispositionary lease requires substantive registration. So if A, a registered proprietor, grants a lease to B for a term exceeding twenty-one years, B does not obtain a legal lease until the disposition is completed by registration under s. 19 (2) of the Act[10]. Apart from substantive registration, his lease ranks merely as a minor interest, unless he brings himself within s. 70 (1) (g); as a minor interest it will be defeated on a transfer for value of the freehold reversion if not protected in the appropriate way on the register. The status of the lease as a minor interest is in practice temporary only; it ceases to be such on substantive registration as a separate title. The position of a transferee of registered land until he is registered as the new proprietor is similar.

This class of minor interests, comprising what might be termed inchoate legal estates or interests awaiting their full recognition as such by completion of the registration process, has no corresponding counterpart in unregistered conveyancing, where the full legal title passes under the conveyance or lease and nothing further has to be carried out before it vests in the grantee.

(c) Non-registrable interests requiring protection on the register

This group resembles most closely that class of interests known as land charges in unregistered conveyancing[11], e.g. estate contracts and restrictive covenants. These minor interests cannot be registered as separate titles but require to be protected on the register in the appropriate manner, and if not protected they should become unenforceable against a subsequent purchaser for value. To this extent these interests partake of the character of equitable interests in unregistered conveyancing, whose enforceability depends on notice, usually by means of registration under the Land Charges Act 1972.

---

8   See further post, pp. 359–361 (settlements), pp. 361–363 (trusts for sale).
9   See further pp. 473–474, post.
10   Page 457, post. There is no obligation on B's part to register, but the lessee usually does to obtain a legal title.
11   See note 13, post.

2.   Methods of protection

Minor interests can be protected on the register by the entry of a notice, caution, inhibition or restriction[12]. These are not mutually exclusive methods; for example, some interests may be protected by a notice, caution or restriction[13]. And it should not be forgotten that an interest which has not been properly protected on the register as a minor interest may nevertheless be enforceable as an overriding interest by virtue of s. 70 (1) (g)[14]. Subject to this one point, a transferee for valuable consideration of an absolute freehold title takes free from any minor interest not entered on the register[15], even, it seems, an interest to which he is party or privy[16]. Conversely, a transferee otherwise than for value, such as a donee or transferee for a nominal consideration of £1[17], is bound by all minor interests subject to which the transferor held the land[18], even though they are not protected on the register of title.

(a) Notice

(i) *Interests protected.* A notice (or note as it is sometimes termed) is a specific entry on the register of the interest which it protects. It appears in the charges register of the registered proprietor. The Act specifies[19] those interests capable of being protected by notice, the main ones being—leases (other than those qualifying as overriding interests), restrictive covenants, and other land charges until the land charge is registered as a registered charge[20]. An entry protecting restrictive covenants existing at the time of first registration might be as follows:

'21 May 1976—A conveyance of the land in this title dated 16 January 1973 made between (1) X and (2) Y contains restrictive covenants. A copy of these covenants is set out in the schedule annexed.'

Similarly a notice of a contract for the sale of land might read:

'6 April 1978—Contract dated 15 March 1978 for sale to AB for £20,000.'

The date at the beginning of each entry indicates when it was made on the register.

(ii) *Production of land certificate.* So long as the proprietor's land certificate is outstanding a notice protecting a minor interest cannot be entered on the register unless the certificate is lodged at the Registry. This requirement does

12   LRA 1925, s. 101 (3).
13   See R & R, 702–3, for a list of the normal and possible alternative methods of protection of those interests which in unregistered conveyancing constitutes land charges for the purposes of the LCA 1972.
14   See pp. 54 and 64, ante.
15   LRA 1925, ss. 20 (1), 23 (1), (2) (leasehold titles). On the question whether notice of the existence of an unprotected interest affects the position, see p. 72, post.
16   *Orakpo v Manson Investments Ltd* [1977] 1 All ER 666 at 687, CA, per Goff LJ (obiter); affd. on other grounds [1978] AC 95, [1977] 3 All ER 1, HL. Contrast *Jones v Lipman* [1962] 1 All ER 442 (unprotected contract not defeated by sham transaction).
17   *Peffer v Rigg* [1978] 3 All ER 745, p. 72, post.
18   LRA 1925, ss. 20 (4), 23 (5).
19   See ss. 48–51, 59 (2), (5).
20   This being a reference to puisne mortgages which can be registered as substantive charges under s. 26 of the Act; see p. 465, post.

not apply to a notice of (i) a lease at a rent without a fine, (ii) a charge for capital transfer tax[1], or (iii) a spouse's charge in respect of statutory rights of occupation under the Matrimonial Homes Act 1967[2]. The co-operation of the registered proprietor is thus necessary, at least in theory, and having created the interest he will not normally object to the lodgement of the certificate, provided he is able to do so. If, for instance, he has already deposited the certificate with a third party as security for a loan, protection by way of notice is not possible without the chargee's unlikely co-operation. However the Registry do not regard the certificate as being outstanding when it is already there for any reason, even one wholly unconnected with the application to enter the notice. The need for the proprietor's concurrence is, therefore, rendered illusory particularly when the land is subject to a registered charge, since in this situation the land certificate will always be deposited at the Registry[3], thereby facilitating entry of the notice. In practice the Registry take steps to notify the proprietor of the receipt of any application to enter a notice[4], which affords him an opportunity to object. Should the registered proprietor refuse to deposit his certificate because (e.g.) of a dispute relating to the minor interest, the incumbrancer can protect his (alleged) interest by lodging a caution.

An application to register a notice which is not accompanied by an outstanding land certificate will be accepted by the Registry, albeit provisionally, but no entry will be made against the title until the certificate is lodged there. Nevertheless as a result of the Land Registration Rules 1925, r. 83[5], the application has priority as from the date of its delivery at the Registry, even though it was not then in order. The application will be revealed on any search certificate issued by the Registry to e.g. an intending transferee. Where, however, entry of a notice is applied for during the priority period conferred by an official search certificate, the application is temporarily held in abeyance by the Registry to await the outcome of events. Thus, if a dealing with the land (such as a transfer or mortgage) is completed within that priority period and so protected by virtue of the Land Registration (Official Searches) Rules 1981[6], the notice application is re-dated administratively so that it loses its priority to the protected dealing.

(iii) *Effect of entry.* A disposition of registered land takes effect subject to the estate or interest protected by the notice, but only if and so far as such estate or interest may be valid. The entry operates by way of notice only[7]. It does not render enforceable an interest which is unenforceable under the general law.

1   LRA 1925, s. 64 (1) (c), as amended by the Finance Act 1975, s. 52, and Sch. 12. The Law Commission propose that production of the certificate should cease to be essential for entry of a notice; see p. 75, post.
2   Matrimonial Homes and Property Act 1981, s. 4 (1), adding a new subs. (5) to s. 64 of the main Act.
3   Pursuant to the LRA 1925, s. 65.
4   Except a notice protecting the charge arising under the Matrimonial Homes Act 1967 — a procedure that has evoked strong judicial criticism: *Watts v Waller* [1973] QB 153 at 176, [1972] 3 All ER 257 at 269, CA, per Orr LJ; *Wroth v Tyler* [1974] Ch 30 at 39, [1973] 1 All ER 897 at 903, per Megarry J. Somewhat surprisingly the Law Commission advocate no alteration to the rule: Law Com. No. 86, paras. 2.85−86.
5   As substituted by the LRR 1978. S.I. 1978, No. 1601, r. 8. See also *Smith v Morrison* [1974] 1 All ER 957 at 965.
6   S.I. 1981 No. 1135, r. 5 effective from 1 October 1981. See further for official certificates of search, p. 404, post.
7   LRA 1925, s. 52 (1), (2).

Thus notation of a restrictive covenant satisfies one of the requirements which must be established if the burden of the covenant is to pass in equity; to enforce the covenant, the covenantee must still show, for example, that he owns or retains land benefited by the covenant[8]. An entry that land is subject to a positive covenant does not cause that covenant to run with the land[9], any more than a purchaser of unregistered land is bound by a positive covenant of which he has express notice. Similarly entry of a notice does not operate to revive an interest (such as an option to purchase) that has previously become void for want of registration under the Land Charges Act 1972[10].

(b) Caution

(i) *Cautionable interests.* Section 54 (1) of the Act enables any person interested under an unregistered instrument, or as a judgment creditor or otherwise howsoever, in any registered land to lodge a caution to the effect that no dealing with the land by the proprietor is to be registered until notice has been served upon the cautioner, save that a caution cannot be lodged so long as the claimant's interest is already protected by a notice or restriction. The provision facilitates the protection of a variety of rights. Thus the cautioner may be a purchaser under a contract for sale, a lessee under an agreement for a lease, a person having the benefit of a writ or order affecting land, a person claiming an equity arising out of acquiescence — these are merely illustrations. An interest in the proceeds of sale of land held on trust for sale is a minor interest by virtue of the definition in s. 3 (xv) of the Act, so that an equitable tenant in common is entitled to lodge a caution[11]. Non-proprietary rights are not capable of protection, such as a right of pre-emption which on its true construction did not bind the grantor's successors in title[12]. The statutory charge protecting rights of occupation under the Matrimonial Homes Act 1967, can no longer be protected by means of a caution[13].

A caution is recorded in the proprietorship register. Unlike a notice, the entry gives no indication of the claim which the caution has been lodged to protect; it simply says:

'Caution dated 11 January 1978 registered on 15 January 1978 in favour of AB of . . .'

(ii) *Nature of protection afforded.* Production of the proprietor's land certificate is not required, but the cautioner must lodge with his application a statutory declaration giving brief particulars of the interest claimed by him[14]. Lodging a caution secures interim protection for the cautioner who is entitled to receive notice of any intended dealing with the land. This notice warns him

---

8   *LCC v Allen* [1914] 3 KB 642, CA.
9   *Cator v Newton and Bates* [1940] 1 KB 415, [1939] 4 All ER 457.
10 *Kitney v MEPC Ltd* [1978] 1 All ER 595, CA. But consider *Re Stone and Saville's Contract* [1963] 1 All ER 353 where the converse upset the title nevertheless.
11 *Elias v Mitchell* [1972] Ch 652, [1972] 2 All ER 153. For s. 3 (xv), see p. 65, ante.
12 *Williams v Andrews* (1971) 221 Estates Gazette 1158; aliter if the right creates a proprietary interest in land: *Pritchard v Briggs* [1980] Ch 338, [1980] 1 All ER 294, p. 387, post (an unregistered land case). See further, Barnsley, *Land Options*, pp. 157–60.
13 Matrimonial Homes and Property Act 1981, s. 4 (2), but without prejudice to the effectiveness of any caution already registered.
14 LRR 1925, r. 215 (4), Sch., Form 14.

that his caution will cease to have effect on the expiration of a specified period (usually fourteen days) unless he shows cause why the caution should continue to have effect or why the dealing should not be registered[15]. Whether in fact the caution is cancelled, or registration of the dealing is refused or completed subject to the cautioner's interest, depends on the validity of his claim, which is determined at a hearing before the Registrar. If the cautioner takes no further steps after receipt of the 'warning-off' notice, the caution automatically lapses. Thereupon the land may be dealt with in the same manner as if no caution had been lodged[16].

A caution is not transferable. On the assignment of an interest already pro-tected the assignee should lodge a fresh caution. After the death of a cautioner his personal representative may exercise his rights under the caution[17].

According to s. 56 (2) of the Act, a caution has no effect except as is therein mentioned. The protection which it secures is inferior to that afforded to a person who registers a notice. A notice establishes priority and ensures that the interest protected (assuming it is otherwise enforceable) will bind a subsequent transferee without further inquiry. On the other hand a caution simply confers a right to be heard in opposition to an application to register a dealing[18]. It merely warns that some right is claimed. The cautioner will not be able to enforce his interest against a transferee unless he first establishes the validity of his claim at a hearing before the Registrar. Furthermore his right to oppose an intended dealing applies only if the caution is entered on the register. In *Smith v Morrison*[19] a caution was applied for during the priority period conferred by an official search certificate issued to a prospective transferee. He later applied for substantive registration within that period, whereupon the Registry can-celled the cautioner's application without registering his caution. It was held that the cautioner was not entitled to a hearing.

(iii) *Improper cautions.* As production of the proprietor's land certificate is not required, lodging a caution is regarded as a hostile act, though protection by means of a caution instead of a notice does not necessarily indicate that the interest is disputed by the proprietor. The land certificate may be deposited with a third party by way of security, so preventing registration of a notice. Under s. 56 (3) of the Act a person lodging a caution without reasonable cause is liable to compensate any person who thereby sustains damage. In the context of this provision the phrase 'without reasonable cause' does not appear to have been judicially considered. It is thought that it covers a case where a caution is lodged maliciously, or where there are no substantial grounds for supporting it, but not where the cautioner has a genuine belief that an enforceable right or claim exists[20]. Section 56 (3) does not provide an exhaustive remedy; it

15   LRA 1925, s. 55; LRR 1925, r. 219. See generally in relation to cautions against dealings, rr. 215–22.
16   Presumably, however, an interest 'warned-off' under s. 55 (1) may still be enforceable by virtue of s. 70 (1) (g) if the cautioner is in actual occupation.
17   LRA 1925, s. 56 (4): R & R, 733.
18   *Smith v Morrison* [1974] 1 All ER 957 at 978, per Plowman J.
19   *Smith v Morrison*, ante. Compare the position as to notices, p. 68, ante.
20   Cf. *Frobisher Ltd v Canadian Pipelines Ltd* (1960) 21 DLR (2d) 497 at 535, where in a statutory provision of similar import to s. 56 (3) the expression 'wrongfully and without reasonable cause' was construed to mean 'something in the nature of officious intermeddling without colour of right'. See also *Clearbrook Property Holdings Ltd v Verrier* [1973] 3 All ER 614 at 617, per Templeman J. This is better than the system in unregistered land although the courts have effectively found a similar device by undertakings given on motion to vacate see *Tiverton Estates Ltd v Wearwell Ltd* [1974] 1 All ER 209 at 219, 228.

does not, for instance, oust the inherent jurisdiction of the court to vacate improperly lodged cautions[1].

The section speaks only of lodging a caution. No sanction is imposed for unreasonably maintaining a caution, yet this may just as likely cause embarrassment to the registered proprietor as the initial wrongful registration, as where a purchaser of land fails to remove a caution after the vendor has validly terminated the contract for sale. It should also be noted in passing that there is no comparable provision regulating the registration of notices without reasonable cause. Such a provision is strictly not required. The need for the proprietor's consent means, in theory, that entry of a notice can never be unreasonable, but as has been seen his concurrence is rendered something of a myth when the certificate is already at the Registry. The Law Commission have provisionally recommended an alteration to this no-compensation rule for notices[2].

(c) Inhibition
Except in relation to bankruptcy[3] an inhibition, which can only be entered on the register by order of the Registrar or the court, is an unusual form of protection. It prevents the registration of any dealing with the registered land during a specified period or until the occurrence of a specified event[4].

(d) Restriction
A restriction (like an inhibition) does not directly protect third party rights in registered land, but it may have this effect indirectly. It operates to prevent a disposition of the land taking effect without prior conformity to some specified requirement, such as the obtaining of a named person's consent to the transaction[5]. Entry of a restriction requires production of the land certificate if it is not already in the Registry[6]. It may be applied for by the proprietor himself or by a person having sufficient interest in the land[7]. A clause commonly found in some building society mortgages, which seeks to prevent dealings with the equity of redemption without the mortgagee's consent, is sometimes protected by a restriction. It is by means of a restriction that the equitable interests arising under a settlement or trust for sale are normally protected. In certain circumstances the Registrar is obliged to enter a restriction at the time of registration. This occurs, for example, where land is vested in joint proprietors[8], or is held on charitable trusts (including property vested in trustees on behalf of a church or chapel), or for educational purposes[9].

Provided a dealing with registered land is effected in accordance with the terms of the restriction, the transferee will be registered as proprietor in the normal manner. If the restriction is not intended to continue in force he should

---

1 *Clearbrook Property Holdings Ltd v Verrier*, ante.
2 Law Com Working Paper, No. 67, para. 63, p. 76, post.
3 LRA 1925, s. 61.
4 Ibid., s. 57.
5 Ibid., s. 58 (1).
6 Ibid., s. 64 (1) (c).
7 Ibid., s. 58 (5): LRR 1925, r. 236.
8 LRA 1925, s. 58 (3), unless the survivor can give a valid receipt for purchase money. See the example given in entry no. 3 in the proprietorship register appearing on p. 42, ante. See also pp. 361–363, post.
9 LRR 1925, rr. 60–62, 123 (2). See R & R, 772–79 for a detailed list of voluntary and compulsory restrictions and the form of the restriction applicable to each occasion.

ensure that the person whose interest it protects applies for its withdrawal. No statutory provision exists for the automatic cancellation of a restriction on a dealing which complies with its requirements. Obligatory restrictions cannot be withdrawn on the mere application of an interested party[10].

3.   Knowledge of unprotected interest

Actual knowledge or notice of an unprotected minor interest does not affect a purchaser's entitlement to take free from the interest. Section 59 (6) of the Act provides that a purchaser acquiring title under a registered disposition is not to be concerned with any matter or claim (not being an overriding interest) which is not protected on the register, *whether he has or has not notice thereof, express, implied or constructive*. Similarly by virtue of s. 20 (1) a transferee for value under a registered disposition of an absolute freehold title takes free of 'all estates and interests whatsoever' unless they are protected on the register or take effect as overriding interests. So in *De Lusignan v Johnson*[11] a registered chargee took free from an unprotected estate contract of which he had express knowledge. In *Boland's* case[12] Lord Wilberforce asserted categorically that the land registration system is designed to free the purchaser from the hazards of the doctrine of notice; it has no application even by analogy to registered land. The contrary decision of Graham J in *Peffer v Rigg*[13] cannot, it it thought, be sustained. Here, as part of a divorce settlement X transferred a house, which he held on an express trust for himself and Y, to his ex-wife, W, for £1. Y's interest was not protected on the register, nor was he in actual occupation of the house. It was held that since W was aware of Y's beneficial interest, she was bound by it and took the house on trust for herself and Y as beneficial tenants in common. Surprisingly the learned judge did not consider the vital exclusion of the effect of notice contained in s. 59 (6)[14]. To introduce the doctrine of notice further than the Act itself allows[15] will destroy altogether the certainty (albeit not total) which the register of title at present affords; it will also create a fundamental difference in the consequences of non-protection of third party rights as between the registered and the unregistered systems of land transfer[16].

As an alternative ground for his decision Graham J also held that W, knowing that the house was trust property, took it on a new constructive trust according to general equitable principles. Superficially this would appear to be an attractive solution[17] which avoids a seemingly unjust result. It may well be,

---

10   LRA 1925, s. 58 (4).
11   (1973) 230 Estates Gazette 499.
12   [1981] AC 487 at 504, [1980] 2 All ER 408 at 412; *Strand Securities Ltd v Caswell* [1965] Ch 373 at 390, [1964] 2 All ER 956 at 967, per Cross J.
13   [1978] 3 All ER 745.
14   Which makes it clear that notice is not to be equated with lack of good faith, contrary to what Graham J held. On the basis that the nominal sum of £1 was to be treated as the consideration for the transfer (see at 751), W took subject to Y's interest under s. 20 (4) of the Act.
15   E.g. ss. 5 (c), 70 (1) (g). LRR r. 77 (1) (b).
16   See *Midland Bank Trust Co Ltd v Green* [1981] AC 513, [1981] 1 All ER 153, HL (purchaser with notice not bound by unregistered C (iv) land charge).
17   See (1977) 41 Conv (NS) 207; Law Com Working Paper No. 67, para. 50. Contrast *Miles v Bull (No. 2)* [1969] 3 All ER 1585 (constructive trust rejected).

however, that s. 74 of the Act[18] rules out any possibility of effect being given to a constructive trust within the framework of the registered system. It is more easy to apply the notion in unregistered land where the trust interests which gave rise to the constructive trusts are not registerable and are generally enforceable subject to the doctrine of notice, a precondition to liability as a constructive trustee.

4. Priority between minor interests[19]

In section 2 above we looked at what steps should be taken to ensure that a minor interest is enforceable against a transferee under a registered disposition. When it comes to the related question of *priorities* between competing minor interests, the Land Registration Act 1925, affords little clear guidance. Problems of priority arise most commonly in relation to financial charges on land[20], but they also occur in cases involving non-financial interests (e.g. where the contest is between a Class F charge and an estate contract) or between a financial and a non-financial interest. The case of *Barclays Bank Ltd v Taylor*[1] illustrates the latter type of problem.

> X by deed mortgaged his land to the plaintiff bank. The mortgage was not registered nor protected in the then appropriate manner[2]; it therefore took effect only in equity. Later X contracted to sell the land to Y who paid the purchase money without obtaining a transfer. Y lodged a caution against dealings, and when the bank subsequently sought to register its mortgage Y objected.

The Court of Appeal held that as this was a contest between two equitable interests, priority was to be determined by the order of their creation. Where the equities are equal, the first in time prevails[3]. The bank's charge therefore had priority, there being nothing in its conduct to justify postponement of its interest. It was of no consequence that the bank had failed to protect its interest, nor could Y, by lodging a caution, secure priority for his contract.

Priority disputes will often come to light and be determined once the warning-off procedure has come into operation, as happened in the case just discussed. They can also arise in other situations, for example where applications to protect competing minor interests are received at the Registry on the same day. Fortunately, however, potential disputes are normally still-born because of the effect of ss. 20 (1) and 23 (1) of the Act. Similarly the Land Registration (Official Searches) Rules 1981, r. 5, confers priority on a purchaser who applies for substantive registration of his transfer within the

---

18 Page 54, ante. Perhaps the answer lies in a modification of the rectification provisions of the Act. See, however, *Lyus v Prowsa Developments Ltd* (1982) 126 Sol Jo 102. Purchasers from the mortgagee took subject to a caution registered but not binding on the mortgagee. (Clause in contract stating sale 'subject to but with the benefit of' the cautionable interest created a trust in favour of the cautioner.)

19 See generally Robinson, 'The Priority of Interests in Registered Land', (1971) 35 Conv (NS) 100, 168; R.J. Smith, 'The Priority of Competing Minor Interests in Registered Land', (1977) 93 LQR 542; Hayton, *Registered Land* (3rd edn), p. 131.

20 The priority of *registered* charges is determined by the order in which they are entered on the register: LRA 1925, s. 29.

 1 [1974] Ch 137, [1973] 1 All ER 752.

 2 I.e. by a special mortgage caution prescribed by the LRA 1925, s. 106, a mode of protection since abolished by the Administration of Justice Act 1977, s. 26. This was not surprising as it was then considered to be obsolete. The method adopted was more convenient but very nearly fatal.

 3 See also *Strand Securities Ltd v Caswell* [1965] Ch 958 at 991, [1965] 1 All ER 820, at 833, CA, per Russell LJ.

priority period allowed by his official certificate of search. He takes free from any minor interest, an application for entry of which is received at the Registry during such period. The fact that the purchaser's estate contract was not protected as a minor interest has no bearing on the issue of priority. Conversely, if the priority period expires before the purchaser applies to be registered as proprietor, his registration takes effect under s. 20 (1) subject to the minor interest, even though his own contract was protected on the register before that adverse interest.

Whether the principle enuniciated in *Barclays Bank Ltd v Taylor* is of general application is not entirely clear. The argument has been advanced that in the case of some minor interests protected by a notice, priority is governed by the date of entry of the notice[4]. It is doubtful whether the statutory provisions relied upon give support to this contention. *Taylor's* case is accepted by the Law Commission as laying down a general rule; and whilst the rule may not be entirely satisfactory, they are of the view that the balance of convenience is against making any change in the law so far as non-financial charges are concerned[5]. Nevertheless an express statutory enactment enshrining the principle might perhaps be desirable, if only to dispel the existing doubts raised by the Act.

5.   Cancellation of entries

There exists both an inherent and a statutory jurisdiction for the court to vacate entries on the register protecting third party rights. The court has a general power to make orders in personam against parties interested in property or under contracts. This inherent jurisdiction still subsists notwithstanding that s. 82 (1) of the Land Registration Act 1925, also confers a wide jurisdiction to rectify the register. The two jurisdictions cannot be exercised concurrently[6]. As a matter of discretion the court will usually not exercise its inherent jurisdiction if in the particular circumstances of the case the statutory jurisdiction is satisfactory in terms of 'amplitude, speed and convenience'[7]. When acting under its inherent jurisdiction the court may make an order in a personal form, ordering (e.g.) a cautioner to remove his caution[8]. An order in impersonal form, i.e. one that simply requires the entry to be removed, is preferable since this can safely be acted upon by the Registrar without waiting for the cautioner to take steps to give effect to the order[9]. It also obviates any difficulties that might otherwise arise should a personal order be disobeyed by the cautioner. An order under s. 82 of the Act will direct the Registrar to make the necessary alteration to the register.

---

4   Smith, op. cit., pp. 548–50. Cf. Hayton, 141–147. The sections concerned are s. 40 (restrictive covenants), s. 48 (certain leases) and s. 66 (liens created by deposit of the land certificate).

5   Law Com Working Paper No. 67, paras. 103, 106. An unprotected financial charge would be postponed to any interest, whether financial or not, acquired for value and protected on the register: para. 110.

6   *Lester v Burgess* (1973) 26 P & CR 536 at 543, per Goulding J. For s. 82 (1), see pp. 79–88. post.

7   *Calgary and Edmonton Land Co Ltd v Dobinson* [1974] Ch 102 at 110, [1974] 1 All ER 484 at 491, per Megarry J.

8   As in *Rawlplug Co Ltd v Kamvale Properties Ltd* (1968) 20 P & CR 32, where the proprietor sought an order in the personal form.

9   *Calgary and Edmonton Land Co Ltd v Dobinson*, ante; *Lester v Burgess*, ante.

The courts recognise that the presence on the register of a wrongful or erroneous entry (particularly a caution) may well jeopardise a prospective dealing with the land by the proprietor. In a proper case the court will order the entry to be vacated in interlocutory proceedings on motion, without waiting for the dispute between the parties to be finally resolved at the trial of the action. This speedy remedy by way of motion is in general available only where there is no triable issue or arguable point in support of the registration, otherwise the matter must go to trial in the normal way[10]. Examples of the use of this procedure are quite common. In *Tiverton Estates Ltd v Wearwell Ltd*[11] the court on motion ordered a caution to be vacated under s. 82 (1) of the Act because the defendant purchasers had failed to make out a prima facie case that any enforceable contract for sale ever existed. Similarly the courts have vacated cautions protecting contracts for sale that have ceased to be enforceable[12], and cautions lodged by cautioners claiming some right considered by the court not to constitute a cautionable interest[13]. Nevertheless in all such cases the court seeks to maintain a fair balance between the parties in dispute. For, although registration can be a weapon of considerable nuisance value in the cautioner's hands, simply to vacate the caution without more deprives the cautioner of his protection and leaves the proprietor free to act in a way detrimental to his claim. Where, therefore, there is a triable issue, the court may allow the caution to remain, provided the cautioner enters into an undertaking to pay the registered proprietor any damages caused by its presence if it is subsequently held to have been wrongly entered. Alternatively the caution may be vacated. In this event the cautioner is given the opportunity of moving for an interlocutory injunction, restraining the proprietor from dealing with the land in a manner inconsistent with the cautioner's claim, but coupled with the latter's cross-undertaking as to damages which the court exacts as a matter of course when granting such an injunction[14].

6. Proposals for reform[15]

The Law Commission have made a number of sweeping proposals for the reform of the existing law governing the mode of protection of minor interests. In particular they suggest the adoption of a procedure that will permit a clear distinction to be drawn between contentious and non-contentious entries. As a general rule every minor interest should be protectable either by a notice (or restriction where appropriate) or a caution, depending on whether the proprietor disputes the interest or not. The Commission's proposed procedure may be summarised as follows. Initially the applicant[16] would in every case apply for

---

10 *Clearbrook Property Holdings Ltd v Verrier* [1973] 3 All ER 614 at 615, per Templeman J.
11 [1975] Ch 146, [1974] 1 All ER 209, CA.
12 *Rawlplug Co Ltd v Kamvale Properties Ltd*, ante; *Lester v Burgess*, ante; *Clearbrook Property Ltd v Verrier*, ante; *Mayfair London Bank Ltd v Workman* (1972) 225 Estates Gazette 989; *Curragh Investments Ltd v Cook* [1974] 3 All ER 658.
13 *Calgary and Edmonton Land Co Ltd v Dobinson*, ante (creditor of company in liquidation, not being a beneficiary under a trust for sale, has no minor interest in company's land); *Williams v Andrews* (1971) 221 Estates Gazette 1158 (right of pre-emption not creating proprietary interest).
14 *Clearbrook Property Ltd v Verrier*, ante; *Tiverton Estates Ltd v Wearwell Ltd*, note 11, ante, at 172 and 228, per Stamp LJ.
15 Law Com Working Paper No. 67, paras. 58–67.
16 Including a person claiming an equity or estoppel interest of the kind recognised in cases such as *Ives Investments Ltd v High* [1967] 2 QB 379, [1967] 1 All ER 504, CA; see

a notice (or restriction), which would be entered on the register in the following situations: (1) if the proprietor's land certificate accompanied the application or was later lodged at the Registry expressly to meet the application, or (2) if the proprietor's written consent was lodged with the application in those cases where the certificate was already deposited at the Registry (e.g. under s. 65 of the Act). When consent was not indicated in either of these ways, the Registry would notify the proprietor of the application and request production of his certificate. Should he not object to the notice within a prescribed period, consent to its being entered against his title would be *implied*. In the event of an objection being made a caution would be entered with the same effect as a caution under the existing legislation, except that it would be afforded the same priority as a notice would have had. One important consequence flowing from the adoption of such a procedure would be that in almost every case a protective entry on the register could not be made without taking steps to inform the proprietor[17]. This is to be welcomed, despite the difference to be created in this respect between the rule for protecting third party rights in the registered and the unregistered systems. Two detailed points about this proposed scheme can be made. First, it is presumed that where entry of a notice occurs in situations (1) and (2) with the proprietor's express consent, such consent is not to constitute an admission of the validity of the interest. In other words s. 52 (2) of the Act will continue to apply. Secondly, the proposal to imply consent from the proprietor's failure to object would appear to be unfortunate. There may exist a variety of reasons why he does not do so — he may be abroad, or ill in hospital, or the notification may simply never reach him. Since the Commission obviously feel that the proprietor's consent should be a prerequisite to entry of a notice, it is suggested that if situations (1) and (2) do not apply, only a caution should be entered until such time as his written consent is received. It would thus become unnecessary to provide for the payment of compensation for damage sustained by the entry of a notice without reasonable cause. Of course, s. 52 (2) would ensure that where consent was merely implied, entry of the notice would not prejudice the proprietor, but he would nevertheless be obliged to seek rectification of the register to clear his title of the offending entry.

The Commission's scheme is, however, open to the more basic criticism that it creates a repetitive, or potentially repetitive, procedure. It is envisaged that the proprietor shall have the right to object to a notice being entered. Presumably in practice he will do so only when he disputes the applicant's interest. Yet there seems to be little point in cluttering the register of title with entries protecting interests *known* to be disputed. Would it not be simpler to give the Registrar power to require the applicant to substantiate his claim at that point of time, rather than waiting for the warning-off procedure to come into play on some future occasion? If he succeeds, a notice can be entered; if he fails no entry need be made. In this way the caution would disappear entirely as a method of protection.

paras. 64–66. Few will quarrel with this recommendation. But their controversial suggestion that prior to protection on the register a purchaser with notice should be bound will, presumably, be discarded in the light of the rejection of the doctrine of notice in *Boland's* case; see p. 72, ante.

17 Save for a notice protecting a Class F charge, which the Commission continue to feel should be capable of protection without the knowledge or consent of the proprietor spouse: see Law Com No. 86, para. 2.86–2.90.

The adoption of the new scheme would require concomitant alterations in the rules governing the production of land certificates to the Registry. Briefly those proposed are as follows[18]. Production of the certificate should cease to be essential to support an application to enter a notice or restriction protecting a minor interest. The Commission rightly discounted the possibility that this change might make a proprietor's land certificate less informative than at present. Except in the special case where the certificate is in the hands of a prior mortgagee, production would continue to be required for the registration of a transfer and on the creation of any derivative interest required by the Act to be completed by registration[19]. The statutory obligation[20] to produce the certificate should be extended to cover not only a vendor of registered land as at present, but also a lessor, mortgagor and grantor of any derivative interest created for value requiring completion by registration. Should the proprietor fail to comply with this obligation, thus preventing registration, the applicant would be entitled to have a caution entered to protect his rights in the meantime.

18   Working Paper No. 67, paras. 89–97.
19   E.g. an easement, which requires to be noted against the grantor's registered title if it is to take effect as a *legal* easement; see p. 473, post.
20   LRA 1925, s. 110 (6).

Chapter 4

Rectification and indemnity

A Introduction

One of the main advantages of the system of land registration is the curative effect of registration. However defective the grantor's title might be, registration with an absolute title vests in the first proprietor of freehold land the estate in fee simple in possession in the land[1]. Yet there is no guarantee that a proprietor registered with an absolute title will always be entitled to retain what the statute has vested in him, even though there is no suspicion of fraud or improper conduct on his part. His title may be absolute; it is not indefeasible. It may be wrong, unjust or impossible to recognise him as proprietor according to the general law[2], in which event he may be deprived of his title through rectification of the register. Section 82 (1) of the Act lists eight specific instances when rectification may be ordered against him. If he is in possession, so much the better; under s. 82 (3) he is not to suffer rectification unless one or more of certain conditions are satisfied. Though much is made of the curative effects of registration, it is not altogether clear why the potential liability to or immunity from rectification should have been made to depend, not on the nature or quality of the title which the Act vests in the proprietor, but on the additional fact of his possession, whatever this may mean in the context of s. 82 (3). It is interesting to note in passing that successive statutes have progressively widened the scope of rectification[3]. Under the Land Registry Act 1862, it was not contemplated save in relation to entries procured by fraud; rectification was completely foreign to the original system which did not countenance the registration of any title not shown to be perfect. The Land Transfer Act 1875, permitted rectification on certain limited grounds unconnected with fraud but not so as to prejudice estates or rights acquired by registration. Under the present Act, not only is it available for a variety of reasons, but estates and interests acquired or protected by registration are no longer excepted from rectification[4]. This legislative movement away from indefeasibility of title

---

1 LRA 1925, ss. 5, 9 (leaseholds). Registration of a disposition of registered land has a similar effect: ss. 20 (1) (freeholds), 23 (1) leaseholds. Special considerations apply in the case of titles less than absolute; see pp. 29–31, ante.
2 R & R, 787
3 Except the latest alterations perhaps to s. 82 (3) see post.
4 LRA 1925, s. 82 (2). The Act of 1897 did not materially alter its predecessor in this respect.

throws into sharp relief the view of the Chief Land Registrar that an absolute title 'is virtually indefeasible and cannot be bettered'[5].

The second of these two claims would appear to have more foundation. The proprietor of an absolute title can rely on his registered title with greater security than an owner can rely on his unregistered estate. At the most the latter, in the event of a defect in his title being established, can only seek the protection afforded by the covenants for title[6]. The registered proprietor has the benefit of the State guarantee of title. This is not a statutory expression but it satisfactorily explains[7] the scheme of the Act of 1925 to indemnify a registered proprietor in respect of loss suffered consequent upon rectification. It remains to be considered later in this chapter to what extent rectification and indemnity are complementary remedies.

B Rectification

1. What is meant by rectification?

The Act nowhere defines what it means by rectification[8]. It has been explained[9] as denoting any amendment to the register or the plan for the purpose of putting right any substantive error of omission or commission or any legally recognised grievance. It includes for instance the removal of land from a proprietor's title in order to give effect to some adverse claim thereto. Various powers of rectification are conferred upon the Registrar, which appear to be of a somewhat different nature. He is empowered to amend the register to give effect to the transitional provisions of the Law of Property Act 1925[10], to correct clerical and such like errors which can be altered without detriment to any registered interest[11], or to rectify the register where land has been registered in error[12], an apparently unlimited power[13] which entitles the Registrar to effect rectification of his own accord subject to certain safeguards.

2. Grounds for rectification under s. 82 (1)

The opening words of s. 82 (1) are as follows:

> ' The register may be rectified pursuant to an order of the court or by the Registrar, subject to an appeal to the court, in any of the following cases, but subject to the provisions of this section . . .'

5 R & R, 74. Cf. Law Com. Published Working Paper No. 45, para. 64 where the view is expressed that by 1926 Parliament had come to recognise that the principle of indefeasibility had been 'irretrievably lost' and in consequence it was replaced by the concept of insurance (as to which see post).

6 These are not as strong as in unregistered land (see post, Chap. 24).

7 See *Re 139 High Street, Deptford, ex p British Transport Commission* [1951] Ch 884 at 888, [1951] 1 All ER 950 at 952, per Wynn-Parry J.

8 A claim to rectification can be overriding interest with s. 70 (1) g. See *Blacklocks v J B Developments (Godalming) Ltd* [1981] 3 All ER 392, p. 50, ante.

9 R & R, 787.

10 LRA 1925, ss. 78 (undivided shares), 92 (settled land).

11 LRR 1925, r. 13.

12 LRR 1925, r. 14.

13 *Chowood Ltd v Lyall (No. 2)* [1930] 1 Ch 426, at 439, per Luxmoore J; affd. [1930] 2 Ch 156, [1930] All ER Rep 402, CA.

The first point to observe is that rectification is discretionary. A claimant who succeeds in bringing his claim within one (or more) of the statutory cases is not entitled as of right to rectification. Secondly, and this important point has already been touched on in the introductory part of this chapter, s. 82 (2) of the Act provides that the register may be rectified notwithstanding that rectification may affect any estates, rights, charges or interests acquired or protected by registration, or by any entry on the register, or otherwise.

Section 82 (1) lists eight cases when rectification of the register might be ordered. Wide though these grounds are, the Law Commission feel that they might not be sufficiently comprehensive[14]. Of these eight cases rectification under grounds (a) and (b) is available only if the court makes an order to that effect; in the remaining cases either the court or the Registrar may order rectification. Legal proceedings are instituted by means of an originating summons to a single judge of the Chancery Division[15]. No particular form of application to the Registrar for rectification is prescribed; in practice it will be in writing and will set out the grounds on which rectification is sought. These eight grounds on which rectification may be obtained are not mutually exclusive. A claimant may well be able to bring his case within more than one paragraph.

(a) '. . . where a court of competent jurisdiction has decided that any person is entitled to any estate right or interest in or to any registered land or charge, and . . . such court is of opinion that a rectification of the register is required, and makes an order to that effect.'
This paragraph is applicable where, for example, rectification is sought to give effect to an overriding interest, as in *Chowood Ltd v Lyall (No. 2)*[16] where the claimant sought rectification on the grounds that he had acquired title by adverse possession to part of the land registered in the name of the proprietor. It is also applicable in a situation akin to that which arose in *Re Beaney*[17], where a transfer by way of gift was declared void on account of the donor's mental incapacity and the court ordered the register to be rectified. In *Orakpo v Manson Investments Ltd*[18] Buckley LJ indicated obiter that the court has jurisdiction under para. (a) to order rectification against the registered proprietor in favour of a person claiming an adverse interest which, though created by the proprietor, has by virtue of s. 20 (1) of the Act become unenforceable against him for want of protection on the register. This proposition is difficult to follow. The court can hardly decide that the claimant is entitled to an interest, when the statute expressly declares that such interest, being unprotected, is not to bind the proprietor[19]. The precise nature of the claim will determine the particular form which rectification, if ordered, will take. It may result in the disputed land being removed from the proprietor's title, or the plaintiff's name

---

14   Published Working Paper No. 45, para. 70, a view which appears to be based on no greater foundation than that the existing provisions may not in some circumstances enable rectification to give effect to an estoppel interest.
15   RSC Ord 93, r. 10.
16   [1930] 2 Ch 156, CA; *Bridges v Mees* [1957] Ch 475, [1957] 3 All ER 577.
17   [1978] 2 All ER 595. The report does not reveal the particular paragraph of s. 82 (1) on which the claim for rectification was based.
18   [1977] 1 All ER 666, at 678, CA; affd. [1978] AC 95, [1977] 3 All ER 1, HL, but without reference to the rectification point.
19   Unless *entitled* is interpreted as meaning would be entitled if the land were unregistered; but see Jackson, 'Security of Title in Registered Land' (1978) 94 LQR 239, 243; (1977) 41 Conv (NS) 210, 212.

being entered on the proprietorship register in place of the defendant's, or the vacation of a notice or caution which has been improperly registered against the proprietor's title[20].

(b) '. . . where the court, on the application . . . of any person who is aggrieved by any entry made in, or by the omission of any entry from, the register, or by any default being made, or unnecessary delay taking place, in the making of any entry in the register, makes an order for the rectification of the register'
A case would arise within this paragraph where on first registration the Registrar had omitted to enter in the charges register some third party incumbrance, such as a restrictive convenant. The incumbrancer would be a person aggrieved by the omission, for under s. 5 of the Act registration would vest in the proprietor a title free from the restriction. It may be that para. (b) applies not only to mistakes by the Registry, but also to a mistake made or induced by one of the parties to the dispute[1]. Yet it is not thought that an incumbrancer who has failed to protect his interest on the register so that it becomes unenforceable against a subsequent registered proprietor can maintain that he is a person aggrieved by the omission for the purposes of this paragraph[2]. This paragraph overlaps the preceding one in some respects. Thus a caution improperly entered on the register may be ordered to be vacated under para. (b)[3] as well as para. (a).

(c) 'In any case and at any time with the consent of all persons interested'
This calls for no special comment.

(d) 'Where the court or the Registrar is satisfied that any entry in the register has been obtained by fraud'
This paragraph covers a case where registration has been obtained through fraudulent misrepresentation or a forged document of transfer. There is little English authority on the meaning of 'fraud' in this context. The decision in *Re Leighton's Conveyance*[4] where rectification was ordered following registration of a transfer procured by means of the transferee's undue influence, suggests that fraud in the equitable sense suffices. In various Commonwealth enactments similar to para. (d), 'fraud' has been interpreted to mean actual, not constructive or equitable, fraud, though this has been expanded to cover 'personal dishonesty or moral turpitude'[5]. Such a construction if adopted by our courts might enable rectification of the register to be ordered in a case such as *Peffer v Rigg*[6], but dishonesty is not to be assumed solely by reason of knowledge of an unprotected interest[7].

20 *Tiverton Estates Ltd v Wearwell Ltd* [1975] Ch 146, [1974] 1 All ER 209, CA.
1   *Chowood Ltd v Lyall (No. 2)* [1930] 2 Ch 156 at 168–69, CA, per Lawrence LJ, who declined to express a concluded opinion on the point.
2   See (1976) 92 LQR 338, 342. Yet para. (h) might apply, p. 82, post.
3   *Tiverton Estates Ltd v Wearwell Ltd* [1975] Ch 146 at 156, [1974] 1 All ER 209 at 213, CA, per Lord Denning MR; *Price Bros (Somerford) Ltd v J Kelly Homes (Stoke-on-Trent) Ltd* [1975] 3 All ER 369, CA.
4   [1936] 1 All ER 667 (transfer executed by mother in daughter's favour). See also the LRA 1925, s. 114.
5   See e.g. *Assets Co v Mere Roihi* [1905] AC 176 at 210, PC, per Lord Lindley; *Butler v Fairclough* (1917) 23 CLR 78 at 100; *Wicks v Bennet* (1921) 30 CLR 80.
6   [1978] 3 All ER 745, p. 72, ante.
7   See *Waimiha Sawmilling Co Ltd v Waione Timber Co Ltd* [1926] AC 101 at 107, PC, per Lord Buckmaster, a decision on the Land Transfer Act 1915 (NZ).

(e) 'Where two or more persons are, by mistake, registered as proprietors of the same registered estate or of the same charge'
In this unlikely situation[8] it seems that the second or later of the two proprietors will be the one who technically has the legal estate vested in him[9], but whether he will be the one who is ultimately allowed to retain the land may well depend on which of the rival proprietors is in possession for the purposes of s. 82 (3).

(f) 'Where a mortgagee has been registered as proprietor of the land instead of as proprietor of a charge and a right of redemption is subsisting'
This is of no great importance. It covers a case where an attempt is made to create a mortgage in the pre-1926 manner, e.g. by a conveyance of the fee, and consequently the mortgagee has wrongly been registered as proprietor of land. Paragraph (f) enables the proper entries to be made in the register so as to give effect to the provisions of the Law of Property Act 1925[10].

(g) 'Where a legal estate has been registered in the name of a person who if the land had not been registered would not have been the estate owner'
This paragraph apparently has a wide application. Jurisdiction to order rectification was exercised in *Chowood Ltd v Lyall (No. 2)*[11] to give effect to a squatter's title, and in *Re 139 High Street, Deptford*[12] where on first registration land belonging to an adjoining owner was erroneously included in the proprietor's title.

(h) 'In any other case where, by reason of any error or omission in the register, or by reason of any entry made under a mistake, it may be deemed just to rectify the register'
Paragraph (h) confers a discretionary and virtually uncontrollable[13] power to rectify an error or omission in any case not expressly provided for in the preceding grounds. For instance it entitles the Registrar on the application of a registered proprietor to cancel notice of an adverse easement entered on the title[14]. In *Chowood Ltd v Lyall (No. 2)*[15] Lawrence LJ, expressed the view that an error made in derogation of the right of the true owner was an entry made by mistake within the meaning of para. (h). According to Buckley LJ in *Orakpo v Manson Investments Ltd*[16], para. (h) can be relied upon where there is an omission in the register of some entry which ought to be there for the applicant's protection, notwithstanding, apparently, that the omission is due to his failure to ensure that the interest claimed has been properly protected. Wide though this paragraph is, it is doubtful whether it should be given such an extensive operation.

---

8   Apparently it has occurred; see (1956), 20 Conv (NS) 302, 313–14.
9   By virtue of the LRA 1925, ss. 20 (1) (freeholds), 23 (1) (leaseholds).
10   LPA 1925, ss. 85 (2), (3) (freeholds), 86 (2), (3) (leaseholds).
11   [1930] 2 Ch 156, CA.
12   [1951] Ch 884, [1951] 1 All ER 950. Cf. *Epps v Esso Petroleum Co Ltd* [1973] 2 All ER 465.
13   6 W & C, 77.
14   See *Re Dances Way, West Town, Hayling Island* [1962] Ch 490, [1962] 2 All ER 42, CA; *Re Sunnyfield* [1932] 1 Ch 79, (restrictive covenants no longer enforceable).
15   [1930] 2 Ch 156 at 168, CA.
16   [1977] 1 All ER 666 at 679, CA, obiter; see also Goff LJ, at 687. The case concerned on this point an unprotected vendor's lien allegedly subrogated to the mortgagee.

3.   Restrictions upon right to rectify[17]

Rectification of the register under s. 82 (1) of the Act is expressed to be 'subject to the provisions of this section.' This qualification refers to the restriction contained in subs. (3) as amended by the Administration of Justice Act 1977, s. 24[18]. Section 82 (3) now reads as follows:

' The register shall not be rectified, except for the purpose of giving effect to an overriding interest or an order of the court, so as to affect the title of the proprietor who is in possession —

(a) unless the proprietor has caused or substantially contributed to the error or omission by fraud or lack of proper care; or

(c) unless for any other reason, in any particular case, it is considered it would be unjust not to rectify the register against him.'

(a) Possession
The privileged position afforded to the registered proprietor in possession has been said to represent the last vestiges of the concept of indefeasibility of title[19]. Possession is the key that brings s. 82 (3) into operation. Yet apart from the statutory definition[20] that 'possession' includes 'the receipt of rents and profits or the right to receive the same', the Act gives no indication as to what amounts to possession for this purpose. Physical occupation clearly suffices, but it does not seem confined to this[1]. 'Possession' would appear to have a wider meaning than 'actual occupation', the expression employed in s. 70 (1) (g). A dictum of Lord Hanworth MR[2] suggests that a proprietor is in possession if he exercises acts of ownership on the land, though perhaps sporadic or isolated acts of ownership would not be sufficient[3]. The statutory definition of 'possession' ensures that a proprietor who leases his land is not deprived of the protection of the subsection. Though perhaps s. 82 (4) of the Act[4] may point to the contrary, it is not thought that the context of sub-s. (3) requires displacement of the prima facie meaning. This is the view accepted as correct (albeit without argument on the point) by Walton J, in *Freer v Unwins Ltd*[5].

Rectification against the proprietor in possession is confined to four cases, of which two appear in the opening part of the subsection, and the remaining two

17   See Cretney and Dworkin, 'Rectification and Indemnity: Illusion and Reality' (1968) 84 LQR 528.

18   This section was introduced into the Bill at a late stage in its passage through Parliament, seemingly as an after-thought, to give effect to certain uncontroversial (albeit provisional) recommendations of the Law Commission in their Published Working Paper No. 45.

19   Published Working Paper, No. 45, para. 78.

20   LRA 1925, s. 3 (xviii).

1   Cf. R & R, 793 where it suggests that de facto possession is the key issue. It almost equates this with occupation.

2   *Chowood Ltd v Lyall (No. 2)* [1930] 2 Ch 156 at 164, CA; *Epps v Esso Petroleum Co Ltd* [1973] 2 All ER 465 (proprietor treating disputed land in same way as his adjacent premises held to be in possession).

3   Cf. Hayton, 171–172.

4   Which provides that a person in possession in right of a minor interest shall be deemed to be in possession as agent for the proprietor. See Hayton, pp. 171–172. The example given there is a lease but it seems that the possession is more likely intended to cover a beneficiary in possession.

5   [1976] Ch 288 at 294, [1976] 1 All ER 634 at 636–637. See also Brickdale, 217; R & R, 792; contra 6 W & C, 77–78; (1976) 40 Conv (NS) 304, 305.

are provided for by paras. (a) and (c). Section 82 (3) (b) was repealed by the Administration of Justice Act 1977. Paragraphs (a) and (c) will be considered first.

(b) Fraud or lack of proper care: s. 82 (3) (a)

Under the law as originally enacted by para. (a) the proprietor in possession was liable to suffer rectification if he had caused or substantially contributed to the omission or mistake by his act, neglect or default. The courts interpreted these words in a way that effectively deprived the proprietor of the protection which he was intended to have. Thus in three cases[6] a first registered proprietor was held to have contributed to the Registry's mistake by his *act* of lodging a document containing a misleading description of the property, or an inaccurate deed plan, with the result that he was registered as proprietor of land belonging to another. The courts did not inquire whether the proprietor's error was made negligently or not. This construction was felt to be contrary to the spirit of the subsection, and the Law Commission suggested a reformulation of para. (a) along the lines now enacted by s. 24 of the Act of 1977. In effect, therefore, the proprietor has in some way to be at fault, either because of fraud or carelessness. 'Fraud' is to be understood as having the same meaning as 'fraud' in s. 82 (1) (d), though as has been noticed this is a word of uncertain scope. The expression lack of *proper* care[7] (as distinct from reasonable care) is not altogether welcome. As a result of the change of wording a proprietor will not now fall outside para. (a) simply on the ground that he lodged at the Registry a faulty deed plan. However, he may be guilty of lack of proper care if an inspection of the land could have revealed the discrepancy in the area of the land, or the deeds ought to have put him (or his adviser) on inquiry that something might be amiss[8], or where a non-fraudulent failure on first registration to lodge all relevant documents of title results in some third party interest (e.g. a restrictive covenant) being omitted from the register of title. A subsequent transferee will not normally be responsible for the mistake in registration; to this extent he is in a better position than a first registered proprietor[9].

Cases falling within the discarded para. (b), which permitted rectification if the immediate disposition to the proprietor in possession was void, are now likely to be embraced by the new para. (a). On this basis the Law Commission saw no need to retain para. (b)[10]. Thus a person who procures his registration by means of a forged transfer is guilty of fraud within para. (a). Equally a subsequent proprietor who knows of the forgery displays a lack of proper care. On the other hand no such fault can be attributed to a subsequent transferee in possession (whether for value or not[11]) who is unaware of the forgery or other suspicious circumstances surrounding the original registration.

6   See *Chowood Ltd v Lyall (No. 2)* [1930] 1 Ch 426; affd. on other grounds [1930] 2 Ch 156, CA; *Re 139 High Street, Deptford* [1951] Ch 884, [1951] 1 All ER 950, p. 26, ante; *Re Sea View Gardens, Claridge v Tingey* [1966] 3 All ER 935.
7   The phrase is taken from the LR & LCA 1971, s. 3 (1) see LRA s. 83 (5), pp. 91−92, post.
8   Such as the vendor's failure to comply with a covenant to build a wall which, if built, would have indicated the true boundary: see *Epps v Esso Petroleum Co Ltd* [1973] 2 All ER 465, where this was an important factor in determining the application of s. 82 (3) (c). Quaere whether the use of an inadequate plan would suffice, see *Scarfe v Adams* [1981] 1 All ER 843, CA.
9   *Epps v Esso Petroleum Co Ltd*, ante, at 472, per Templeman J.
10 Published Working Paper No. 45, para. 88.
11 Under the old para. (b) a proprietor in possession claiming otherwise than for value was denied protection. The new para. (a) omits this exclusion.

(c) Unjust not to rectify (s. 82 (3) (c))
This paragraph contains a wide discretionary power to order rectification if 'for
any reason in any particular case it is considered that it would be unjust not to
rectify the register' against the proprietor in possession. The awkward double
negative should be noted. The existence of a discretion to rectify[12] contrasts
markedly with the claim[13] that the land registration system gives certainty of
title, and makes the indefeasibility of an absolute title depend in the final
analysis on what is considered just.

Though there appears to be no reported decision where rectification has
been ordered on the basis of s. 82 (3) (c), the provision has been the subject of
judicial consideration. Luxmoore J[14] expressed the view that it would be unjust
not to rectify where the effect of registration had been to deprive an owner of
land without his assent or knowledge. If this alone is considered sufficient to
apply paragraph (c), it renders somewhat illusory the curative effects of first
registration[15]. This interpretation has not found favour with later judges. The
cases indicate that an applicant for rectification is unlikely to succeed under
para. (c) where he is guilty of conduct which the court considers in some way to
be reprehensible. In *Re Sea View Gardens, Claridge v Tingey*[16] Pennyquick J
thought it 'abundantly clear' that it would not be just to order rectification
where the applicant (who claimed to be the owner of a disputed plot of land
prior to registration) had stood by and knowingly allowed the registered
proprietor to do work on the land before he intervened with his application. In
Epps v Esso Petroleum Co Ltd[17] Templeman J declined to order rectification in
favour of a plaintiff who, by failing to make proper inquiries before completion, did not discover the true boundaries of the land he had contracted to buy.
In the circumstances justice lay wholly with the defendant registered
proprietors in whom the disputed strip of land was vested. Furthermore the fact
that the defendants would be entitled to an indemnity on rectification, whereas
the plaintiff would obtain nothing if his claim were to be rejected[18], did not
suffice to tip the scales in his favour. It is perhaps surprising that the question of
compensation, or the lack of it, did not weigh more heavily in the learned
judge's assessment of the competing merits of the case[19]. What the decision does
indicate is that rectification and indemnity are by no means complementary
remedies.

In determining whether it is unjust not to rectify, different considerations
may apply depending upon whether the proprietor in possession is the first
registered proprietor or a subsequent transferee for value. Suppose application
is made for the entry of restrictive covenants inadvertently omitted from the
register on first registration. It may be unjust not to rectify the register against a
first registered proprietor, particularly if he purchased the land knowing that
it was burdened by those restrictions. Conversely it might be unjust to order

12   See also s. 82 (1) (h), p. 82, ante.
13   R & R 783.
14   *Chowood Ltd v Lyall (No. 2)* [1930] 1 Ch 426 at 438. The Court of Appeal held that
     s. 82 (3) was not relevant because the proprietor was not in possession: [1930] 2 Ch 156.
15   Cretney & Dworkin, op. cit., p. 538.
16   [1966] 3 All ER 935 at 941.
17   [1973] 2 All ER 465.
18   Because of the LRA 1925, s. 83 (11), considered p. 92, post.
19   Cf. the approach of Wynn Parry J in *Re 139 High Street, Deptford* [1951] Ch 884 at 892,
     [1951] 1 All ER 950 at 953.

rectification against a transferee who in reliance upon the register purchased the property on the basis that it was not subject to any restrictions[20].

(d) Overriding interests
The opening words of sub-s. (3) provide for rectification against a registered proprietor in possession 'for giving effect to an overriding interest . . . ' This is an important exception, which calls for little further comment. Registration is subject to overriding interests. Rectification to give effect to such an interest merely records on the register what is the true situation; it does not alter the proprietor's position. When the registered proprietor is in possession the applicant for rectification will not normally be able to claim an overriding interest by virute of s. 70 (1) (g) of the Act, since he himself will not be in actual occupation of the land[1]. Nevertheless such a claim is not entirely incompatible with the proprietor's reliance on s. 82 (3). The relevant time for determining the applicant's occupation for the purposes of s. 70 (1) (g) is the date of registration; whereas for s. 82 (3) to apply the proprietor must be in possession at the date of rectification or the date of the trial when court proceedings are brought, and by this time the applicant could have vacated the land without having prejudiced his claim to an overriding interest[2].

(e) Court order
The register may also be rectified against the proprietor in possession in order to give effect to an order of the court. This somewhat puzzling provision, introduced by s. 24 of the Act of 1977, must be understood to refer to a court order other than an order for rectification made pursuant to s. 82 (1)[3]. Unless it is so construed this new ground for rectification against the proprietor in possession would appear to have removed completely the special protection which s. 82 (3) confers on him — a result Parliament can hardly have intended.

(f) Rectification discretionary
Section 82 (3) enacts that: 'The register shall not be rectified . . . ' unless one of the conditions there stated is fulfilled. This provision should not be interpreted as meaning that rectification *must* be ordered when one of these conditions is shown to exist, a point that has sometimes been overlooked in relation to s. 82 (3)[4]. The court's power of rectification given by s. 82 (1) never ceases to be discretionary[5]. Thus, the court may refuse to rectify notwithstanding that the requirements of s. 82 (3) (a) are shown to have been satisfied. Seemingly

---

20 See the comments of Walton J in *Freer v Unwins Ltd* [1976] 1 All ER 634 at 637. The covenant was missed undoubtedly for two common errors made in respect of land charge registration: (a) the particulars of the land given were not precise and (b) it was imposed against a *vendor* on a sale off. Such factors are often overlooked. Also if the name of the estate owner is a common one registration can be overlooked.

1 *Epps v Esso Petroleum Co Ltd*, ante, at 472. This does, however, emphasise the difference between occupation and possession.

2 See p. 52, ante.

3 26 Halsbury's Laws (4th edn) 474, para. 1058, note 2. Examples would include an order under the Bankruptcy Act 1914, s. 42 (avoidance of certain dispositions by debtor); the LPA 1925, s. 172 (fraudulent conveyances); the Matrimonial Causes Act 1973, s. 24 (property adjustment orders); s. 37 (2) (b) (avoidance of dispositions of property to defeat claim for financial relief).

4 See *Re 139 High Street, Deptford* [1951] Ch 884 at 889, [1951] 1 All ER 950 at 952, per Wynn-Parry J.

5 *Epps v Esso Petroleum Co Ltd* [1973] 2 All ER 465 at 472, per Templeman J.

the court has jurisdiction to deny rectification even when it is sought to give effect to an overriding interest. Since registration is always subject to these interests, the dismissal of the claim in this situation means in effect that the court considers that the claimant has forfeited his right to enforce the interest because of his conduct. According to the Law Commission rectification for the purpose of recording overriding interests ought not to be a matter merely of discretion[6].

(g) Proposals for reform
In their Published Working Paper No. 45, the Law Commission took the view that the scope of the jurisdiction to rectify should be consistent with the basic principle that the land registration system is not intended to effect alterations to the substantive law. Very broadly, they suggested that there should be a discretionary jurisdiction to rectify the register where it is proved (a) that it does not accurately reflect the title to the land on the supposition that it was not registered, and *either* (b) that the error in the register was caused or substantially contributed to by the registered proprietor's fraud or lack of proper care *or* (c) that in all the circumstances greater injustice would be caused by not rectifying the register than by rectifying it[7]. Condition (a) would replace s. 82 (1) with its list of eight grounds giving rise to rectification. As we have seen, partial effect has already been given to these recommendations by s. 24 of the Administration of Justice Act 1977. This was considered to be a self-contained point ripe for implementation in advance of their final report. The Law Commission maintain that their proposals will enhance the reliability of the register since they envisage that condition (b) or (c) will have to be satisfied in every case. The proprietor in possession would, however, lose his favoured position. Finally, the proposed retention of condition (c) does nothing to meet the criticism that ultimately the absoluteness of a proprietor's absolute title is made to depend on what is considered just in the particular circumstances of each individual case.

4. Effect of rectification

Section 82 (2) of the Land Registration Act 1925 provides that the register may be rectified notwithstanding that it may affect any estates, rights, charges, or interests acquired or protected by registration, or by any entry on the register. The effect of rectification in any particular case will largely depend on the nature of the order that is made. Thus, where the court orders the removal of the name of the existing proprietor, X, and the substitution of the applicant, Y, rectification operates to vest the legal title in the new proprietor automatically[8]. But from what date does rectification take effect? According to the modified r. 83 (2) of the Land Registration Rules 1925, an application[9] for rectification of the register 'shall be completed by registration' as of the day on which it is deemed to have been delivered at the Registry. This rule does not envisage rectification operating retrospectively as from the date when X was erroneously registered as proprietor. Y's entitlement to recover any rents and

---

6　Published Working Paper No. 45, para. 87.
7　See paras. 73, 86−88.
8　LRA 1925, s. 69 (1).
9　'Application' in r. 83 (2) is defined to mean 'an application for . . . rectifying . . . any entry in the register': LRR 1925, r. 1 (5B), inserted by the LRR 1978, r. 2.

profits of the land received by X, or an occupation rent if X himself has been in possession, is uncertain, save that such loss would not be recoverable by Y under the existing indemnity provisions of the Act. Seemingly r. 83 (2) does not govern any situation where rectification is claimed and ordered in court proceedings not preceded by an application therefor to the Registrar. On this interpretation a court would be free, if it thought fit, to order retrospective rectification; s. 82 (2) of the Act contains nothing to suggest that the effect of rectification must necessarily be limited in the manner laid down by r. 83 (2).

The provisions of the Act produce some interesting anomalies when rectification is ordered to give effect to a restrictive covenant omitted from the register. If X, a registered proprietor of freehold land, suffers rectification by the entry on his register of title of a restrictive covenant, he becomes bound by it. By virtue of s. 50 (2) of the Act where notice of a restrictive covenant is entered on the register *the proprietor* (and persons deriving title under him) are deemed to be affected with notice of the covenant as an incumbrance. But suppose that before rectification is sought X has already leased the land to T for 21 years and T has assigned it to A. This was in effect the situation that occurred in *Freer v Unwins Ltd*[10]. Walton J held that the assignee was not bound. Section 50 (2) also provides that entry of a notice does not affect incumbrancers and other persons who at the time when it is entered may not be bound by the covenant. The words 'other persons' included lessees, and both T and A were within the exception since the rectifying entry on the freehold title was made subsequently to the date of the lease and the assignment to A[11]. In the end result the rectification which the plaintiff-convenantee had obtained in *Freer v Unwins Ltd* assisted him not one iota. He could neither enforce the covenant against A (the defendant) during the remainder of the lease[12], nor yet obtain any indemnity under the Act for his inability to do so[13]. Had rectification been retrospective to the date when the omission first occurred, then presumably A would have been bound, though it has been suggested that the wording of s. 50 (2) rules out the possibility of retrospective rectification, at least in the case of restrictive covenants[14].

In *Freer's* case the lease, not being for a term exceeding 21 years, was not registrable. Had A been the assignee under a registered lease, the result would have been the same, unless the plaintiff-convenantee had also been able to obtain rectification of the leasehold title[15].

---

10   [1976] Ch 288, [1976] 1 All ER 634; noted (1976) 40 Conv (NS) 304, [1976] CLJ 211, (1976) 92 LQR 338; see also R & R, 793–94.

11   See also the LRA 1925, ss. 19 (2), 20 (1), regulating the effect of the grant of a non-registrable lease; p. 457, post.

12   Presumably, however, any assignee from A would be bound (unless all derivative interests out of the lease take free from it), in which event A could claim an indemnity under s. 83 (1) of the Act (p. 89, post) on the ground that rectification had deprived him of the right to assign his estate free from a burdensome restriction.

13   Page 90, post.

14   Hayton, *Registered Land* (3rd edn), p. 182.

15   Except of course the fact that if the lease had been registered dispositions thereof will be registered. In the case of an assignee from A in the *Freer* case there would be no need ordinarily on his part to make enquiries at the Land Registry, (nor could he) as his interest would be acquired by an unregistered form of assignment the earlier grant of which was the only relevant disposition. See LRA 1925, s. 101 (1) (6).

C   Indemnity

1.   Entitlement to indemnity

It is the general scheme of the Land Registration Act 1925, to compensate persons who suffer loss by reason of some error in or omission from the register. It is claimed[16] that rectification and indemnity are complementary remedies, but the Act itself imposes some important qualifications on the principle, which the courts have not been slow to recognise[17]. The main grounds on which a claim for indemnity may be founded are contained in s. 83 of the Act. For details of indemnity claims which the Registry meets, and the grounds on which they are based, reference should be made to the Reports on H.M.Land Registry, submitted annually to the Lord Chancellor by the Chief Land Registrar.

(a) Loss suffered by rectification (s. 83 (1))
A person suffering loss by reason of any rectification of the register is entitled to be indemnified, subject only to certain exceptions to be considered later. Compensation is therefore recoverable by a registered proprietor where land included in error within his title is removed on rectification, a situation illustrated by the *Deptford* case[18]. At first sight it may seem illogical that a person can recover compensation for the loss of land to which he had no title prior to registration. But this result is a necessary consequence of the statutory effect of first registration which operates to vest a title in him[19]. Similarly compensation may be claimed on rectification by the entry of restrictive covenants omitted in error from the register at the time of first registration. In this situation the right to compensation is not limited to a transferee who, relying on the register, purchases the land on the basis that it is free from any restrictions. An indemnity can be claimed by the first registered proprietor, even though the covenants were, to his knowledge, binding upon him prior to registration. The omission of the covenants from the register results in the registered title being freed from the restrictions and rectification denies him this unincumbered title. The right to an indemnity only arises if the proprietor suffers *loss* by reason of the rectification. The significance of this is explained in the next section.

(b) Non-rectification (s. 83 (2))
Subject again to certain exceptions, where an error or omission has occurred in the register, but the register is not rectified, any person suffering *loss* by reason of the error or omission is entitled to be indemnified. This provision covers a variety of claims, as the Registrar's annual Report for 1979–80, para. 26, reveals. For example, an indemnity was payable for loss resulting from the registration of a forged transfer, the omission of a legal charge on first registration, the omission of a notice of restrictive covenants on registration of an absolute leasehold title, the erroneous inclusion of land on first registration, and an error as to the extent of a transfer of part of a registered title.

16   R & R, 783.
17   *Epps v Esso Petroleum Co Ltd* [1973] 2 All ER 465; *Freer v Unwins Ltd* [1976] Ch 288 at 295–96, [1976] 1 All ER 634 at 637, per Walton J.
18   [1951] Ch 884, [1951] 1 All ER 950, p. 26, ante. The registered proprietor was ultimately awarded £1278; see (1954) 18 Conv (NS) 130, 138. If the case arose today, rectification might not be ordered; see p. 84, ante. See also *Re Boyle's Claim* [1961] 1 All ER 620.
19   Page 24, ante.

The right to compensation is not dependent upon the claimant's own title being registered.

(c) Other cases

The Act also provides for the payment of compensation in a number of other situations which can usefully be considered together. Indemnity can be claimed for loss suffered by reason of the destruction or loss of any document lodged at the Registry[20], or because of any error, omission or inaccuracy in an official search[1], filed abstract, copy or extract of a filed document[2], or an office copy of the register or filed plan[3]. A trustee in bankruptcy is entitled to an indemnity where loss is suffered by the estate of a bankrupt proprietor because of the omission to register a creditor's notice or bankruptcy inhibition[4]. A person suffering loss by reason of any entry made in the register on the conversion of a possessory title into absolute or good leasehold can claim an indemnity as if a mistake had been made in the register[5].

2. No indemnity payable

A claimant may be denied an indemnity under the Act for a variety of reasons.

(a) No loss suffered

To be entitled to an indemnity by virtue of s. 83 (1)−(3) of the Act, the claimant must have suffered loss by reason of the rectification, or the error or omission, as the case may be. In this context 'loss' has a special meaning. It has been held that no loss is suffered for the purposes of s. 83 (1) where rectification is ordered to give effect to an overriding interest[6]. As we have seen, in such a case rectification does not alter the proprietor's real position; he cannot, therefore, be said to suffer loss by reason of it. This obviously constitutes an important qualification to the principle of indemnity and serves to illustrate again the difficulties created by overriding interests and weakness of the system. It is expressly provided that a proprietor of registered land claiming in good faith under a forged disposition is deemed, where the register is rectified on account thereof, to have suffered loss by reason of the rectification and to be entitled to be indemnified under the Act[7].

(b) Rectification obtained

No provision is made for the payment of compensation in cases where a claim to rectification has been upheld. Yet the decision in *Freer v Unwins Ltd*[8] demonstrates that rectification by itself may not always be an adequate remedy. This deficiency in the Act had already been recognised by the Law Commission, and

20 LRA 1925, s. 83 (3).
 1 LRA 1925, s. 83 (3); *Parkash v Irani Finance Ltd* [1970] Ch 101, [1969] 1 All ER 930.
 2 LRA 1925, s. 110 (4).
 3 Section 113.
 4 Section 61 (7).
 5 Section 77 (6).
 6 *Re Chowood's Registered Land* [1933] Ch 574. Consider the effect of the following: — V (proprietor) transfers to P as beneficial owner. The next day he grants a lease for 21 years at a rent to T who then moves into possession. Thereafter P is registered subject to the lease with no claim on the covenants for title and no indemnity assuming T to be innocent.
 7 LRA 1925, s. 83 (4), which is expressed to be 'subject as hereinafter provided' — a reference to (inter alia) s. 83 (5), (11).
 8 [1976] Ch 288, [1976] 1 All ER 634, p. 88, ante.

they have proposed that the court should be empowered to award an indemnity in addition to rectification in appropriate circumstances[9]. Any personal action for damages for loss suffered despite rectification is ruled out by the indemnity afforded to registry officials by s. 131 of the Act, except in the unlikely event of bad faith being established.

(c) Statutory exclusions
The Land Registration Act 1925, contains a number of provisions which exclude the right to an indemnity in various cases. The most important of these[10] arises under s. 83 (5) (a) of the Act, as substituted by s. 3 (1) of the Land Registration and Land Charges Act 1971, which enacts that no indemnity is payable —

> ' where the applicant or a person from whom he derives title (otherwise than under a disposition for valuable consideration which is registered or protected on the register) has caused or substantially contributed to the loss by fraud or lack of proper care.'

A claimant is not allowed to profit from his own wrongdoing or carelessness. The words 'fraud or lack of proper care' have been encountered before in s. 82 (3) (a), and they should, of course, be similarly interpreted. A lack of proper care sufficient to justify an order for rectification against a proprietor in possession will automatically deprive him of any indemnity for loss suffered thereby. This statutory exclusion operates howsoever the loss is alleged to have been caused — whether by rectification or non-rectification. For example, in *Epps v Esso Petroleum Co Ltd*[11] where the claim for rectification failed, the plaintiff would probably have been unable to obtain any statutory compensation, even had his claim not been statute-barred, on the ground that his conduct would have brought him within s. 83 (5) (a).

The fraud or lack of proper care need not necessarily be that of the applicant. No indemnity is payable where he is a volunteer who derives title from a person guilty of such conduct. In this respect s. 83 (5) (a) differs from s. 82 (3) (a) which, as was noticed[12], does not make the volunteer vicariously liable for his predecessor's shortcomings. But to conclude that the recent change in the wording of s.82 (3) (a) effects an improvement in a volunteer's position under s. 83 (5) (a) as regards indemnity is a mistake. Suppose X is registered as proprietor of certain land in circumstances where there has been a lack of proper care on his part. X gives the property to Y who is registered as proprietor and enters into possession. Assuming there is no personal lack of care by Y, rectification cannot be awarded against him on the basis of s. 82 (3) (a). It may nevertheless be ordered under s. 82 (3) (c), in which event Y is debarred by s. 83 (5) (a) from recovering any indemnity under the Act. He claims through X whose lack of proper care has (in the circumstances) caused or contributed to the loss.

9 Published Working Paper No. 45, para. 96.
10 For other instances see s. 42 (2) (disclaimer of registered lease by trustee in bankruptcy), s. 60 (2) (company dispositions free from unprotected incumbrances), s. 83 (5) (b) (mines and minerals).
11 [1973] 2 All ER 465 at 474. See also *Freer v Unwins Ltd* [1976] Ch 288 at 293; [1976] 1 All ER 634 at 635—36 (vagueness of D (ii) registration details contributing to omission of covenant from registered title; indemnity unlikely if rectification proceedings had been unsuccessful).
12 Page 84, ante.

A transferee under a disposition for valuable consideration, which is registered[13] or protected on the register is never prejudiced in relation to any indemnity by his predecessor's fraud or lack of care.

A claimant who is caught by s. 83 (5) (a) is wholly disqualified from obtaining statutory compensation. This is as it should be on the present wording of the section. Where the contribution to the loss is less than substantial, the claimant can, it seems, recover the full amount of the indemnity which the Act permits, even though he is partly (albeit not substantially) to blame. Whether he should be able to do so is questionable. A good case can be made for the introduction of a scheme for the apportionment of responsibility, enabling the court to reduce the amount of the indemnity when the applicant is partly to blame[14].

(d) Claim statute—barred

A liability to pay indemnity constitutes a simple contract debt. For the purposes of the Limitation Act 1980, the cause of action is deemed to accrue when the claimant knows, or ought to have known, of the existence of his claim[15]. Where, however, the claim arises in consequence of the registration of an absolute or good leasehold title[16], it must be made within six years of *the date of registration*, whether the claimant knew about the registration or not. A claimant who does not learn about the erroneous registration until more than six years after the date of registration may find himself without any remedy. He is denied any right to indemnity and his claim to rectification may be defeated by s. 82 (3) if the registered proprietor is in possession. This is precisely what occurred in the *Epps* case[17], where the fact that the plaintiff's right to any indemnity would be time-barred was not sufficient to tilt the balance of justice in favour of rectification. The period for claiming indemnity is extended in four special cases[18], one of which deserves passing mention. A claim to indemnity in respect of a breach of a restrictive covenant affecting freehold land is enforceable within six years from the breach of covenant, where it was binding on the first proprietor at the time of first registration. Where the claim to an indemnity arises by reason of rectification pursuant to a court order, time begins to run from the date of the order, not from some earlier date from which the rectification takes effect[19]. There is no express limitation period for claims for rectification.

3.   Claiming compensation

(a) Indemnity fund

Section 21 of the Land Transfer Act 1897, established an insurance fund out of which any indemnity under the Act was to be paid. It was financed by annual

---

13   This will include a lessee under a non-registrable lease, for it takes effect as if it were a registered disposition: LRA 1925, s. 19 (2).

14   See Law Com. Published Working Paper, No. 45, paras. 97−99.

15   LRA 1925, s. 83 (11), as amended by Limitation Act 1980, s. 40 (2) Sch. 3, para. 1.

16   The expression 'absolute . . . title' embraces both absolute freehold and absolute leasehold titles.

17   [1973] 2 All ER 465, p. 85, ante. The Law Reform Committee have suggested that s. 83 (11) should be replaced by providing limitation is only to be available if the 'right' itself would be lost were the title unregistered (Cmnd. 6293, paras. 3.76−79).

18   LRA 1925, s. 83 (11) proviso (a)−(d). The remaining three cases relate to infants, settled land and mortgages.

19   E.g. by virtue of the LRR 1925, r. 83 (2), p. 87, ante.

allocations from the receipts from registration fees. The Act of 1925[20] preserved this fund, though its assets were subsequently fixed at £100,000 by the Land Registration Act 1936[1]. Provision was made for the replenishment of the fund as and when necessary, but this was never implemented so that by 1971 it was almost exhausted[2]. Section 1 of the Land Registration and Land Charges Act 1971, provides for the winding up and abolition of the fund. As from 1 October 1971, any indemnity is payable by the Chief Land Registrar out of moneys provided by Parliament[3].

(b) Determination of claim

By virtue of s. 2 (1) of the Act of 1971, the court decides any question as to a claimant's right to an indemnity, or its amount. The Registrar's power to determine such matters has been abolished[4], but without prejudice to his power to settle claims for indemnity by agreement[5]. It would therefore seem advisable to submit any claim to the Registrar in the first instance[6] and refer the matter to the court only if the Registrar refuses the claim.

(c) Amount of indemnity

Where an indemnity is paid in respect of the loss of an estate or interest in or charge on land the amount paid shall not exceed (a) where the register is not rectified, the value of the estate, interest or charge at the time when the error or omission which caused the loss was made, and (b) where the register is rectified, its value (assuming there had been no rectification) immediately before rectification[7]. This ensures that the proprietor can recover the value of any expenditure on the property which has increased its value. It is uncertain whether a claimant can recover consequential loss, i.e. loss additional to the value of any estate or interest lost as a result of rectification or a refusal to rectify, though the Act does not in terms exclude such loss. Reasonable costs and expenses properly incurred by an applicant in relation to his claim are recoverable, notwithstanding that no other indemnity is payable[8].

A person who has caused or substantially contributed to the loss by his fraud is liable to the Registrar (on behalf of the Crown) for the amount of any indemnity paid in respect of such loss[9]. No right of recovery exists from a person merely contributing to the loss through lack of proper care. In addition the Registrar is entitled to enforce any covenant for title which the person indemnified could have enforced in relation to the matter in respect of which indemnity has been paid[10].

---

20 Section 85 (1).
 1 Section 4 (1). The balance, something in the region of £400,000; was surrendered to the Treasury to be applied towards the redemption of the national debt.
 2 See generally Ruoff and Meehan, 'Land Registration: The Recent Act' (1971) 35 Conv (NS) 390.
 3 It becomes payable out of what is known as the Land Registry Vote.
 4 See the LRA 1925, s. 83 (7), repealed by the LR & LCA 1971, s. 14 (2) (b).
 5 LR & LCA 1971, s. 2 (5).
 6 The most simple, cheap and logical solution: per Ruoff & Meehan, op. cit., p. 395.
 7 LRA 1925, s. 83 (6). The Law Commission provisionally recommend the repeal of this provision on the ground that an arbitrary restriction of the indemnity recoverable may produce hardship, especially in cases where the register is not rectified: see Working Paper No. 45, para. 105.
 8 LRA 1925, s. 83 (8), as substituted by the LR & LCA 1971, s. 2 (4).
 9 LRA 1925, s. 83 (9).
10 LRA 1925, s. 83 (10). The Registrar's Report for 1980–81, para. 17, reveals that £950 was recovered through the exercise of this statutory right of recourse.

It is worth noting that despite the large volume of business conducted by the Land Registry, the annual amounts paid by way of compensation are incredibly small. For the year ending 31 March 1981[11], the indemnity payments (including costs) totalled a mere £143,146, which reflects the high standard of the Registry's work. It would be useful to note also the above mentioned limitation to the right to an indemnity specially that in respect of overriding interests.

11   Annual Report of 1980–81, para: 17.

Part Three
The contract stage

Chapter 5

Formation of the contract of sale

A   Introduction

A contract to create or dispose of an interest in land is made in the same way as any other contract. There must be a concluded agreement between the parties, supported by consideration and intended to create legal relations. This is already familiar to the reader. Contracts for the sale of real property have been said to be distinguishable from other contracts on two grounds: first because there enters into them a question of the equitable doctrine of specific performance and secondly because of the difficulties of title[1]. In addition they are subject to the special requirements of s. 40 of the Law of Property Act 1925, which will be considered later in this chapter. As we have already noticed[2], it is mainly these difficulties of title that produce the differences. Whereas a contract for the sale of pure personalty may be negotiated, completed and the purchaser in full possession of his new acqusition all in a matter of minutes, weeks or months may elapse between the parties' handshake on concluding an oral contract for the sale of land and the subsequent vesting of the legal title in the purchaser.

Not every transfer of freehold or leasehold property is preceded by any contract. In some cases no element of sale is involved, as where property is vested in a donee, or in a devisee under a testator's will, or on the appointment of new trustees. Each of these and other similar transactions may produce conveyancing problems, and will require the preparation and execution of the appropriate document vesting title in the grantee. They are not our concern in this Part of the book. Where a transfer results from a sale, there must of necessity be a contract between the parties. This is usually embodied in a formal contract prepared by the vendor's solicitor and containing the conditions of sale. On a sale by auction, the property is sold under the particulars and conditions of sale appearing in the contract. These are invariably referred to at the time of the sale, prior to which they are usually available for inspection at the offices of the vendor's solicitor and of the auctioneers. However, there is nothing sacrosanct about a formal contract prepared by the parties' legal advisers. A contract for the sale of land can arise in a variety of other ways. It may result from correspondence passing between the vendor and the purchaser, or from the exercise of an option to purchase land. It may take the

---

1   *Sheggia v Gradwell* [1963] 3 All ER 114 at 121, CA, per Harman LJ.
2   See p. 4 ante. For the problems raised by what is known as gazumping, see pp. 241–242, post.

form of a verbal compromise of court proceedings, as occurred in *Steadman v Steadman*[3]. The parties may be content to rely on an informal document prepared by one of them, or by the vendor's estate agent. Parties proceeding on the basis of some informal contract may encounter special dangers not normally arising under a formal contract; these will be considered later in the chapter.

B   Capacity

Before turning to the Law of Property Act 1925, s. 40, whose shadow looms large over every contract for the sale of land, something must be said concerning a person's capacity to acquire or dispose of land. The following will be considered: bankrupts, companies, minors and persons suffering from mental disorder. Disabilities formerly attaching to married women, aliens and convicts are no longer operative.

1.   Bankruptcy

After a debtor has committed an act of bankruptcy[4], his creditors (or he himself) can present a *bankruptcy petition* to the court for the making of a *receiving order* for the protection of the debtor's property. The order brings his estate into the custody and under the control of the court through its officer, the official receiver. The debtor is not officially rendered bankrupt until the court makes an *adjudication order* whereupon the bankrupt's own property vests in the trustee in bankruptcy on his appointment, pending which it vests temporarily in the official receiver[5]. Though his property remains vested in him until adjudication, a bankrupt is to all intents and purposes unable to deal with it, once a receiving order has been made. A contract or conveyance made or executed by a bankrupt *before* the receiving order can in certain cases be set aside by the trustee in bankruptcy[6], but a purchaser dealing with the bankrupt bona fide for valuable consideration may nevertheless be protected if without notice of any available act of bankruptcy[7]. A bankrupt's inability to deal with his own property extends to property acquired at any time after adjudication and before his discharge from bankruptcy. Such property vests in the trustee[8], subject to the qualification that a disposition of after-acquired property in favour of a person dealing with the bankrupt in good faith and for value passes a good title, if completed before the trustee intervenes[9].

Property held by the bankrupt in his capacity as trustee or personal representative does not vest in the trustee. nor does a legal estate in settled land vested

3   [1976] AC 536, [1974] 2 All ER 977, HL, p. 116, post.
4   As to what constitutes an act of bankruptcy, see the Bankruptcy Act 1914, s. 1 (1); the Insolvency Act 1976, ss. 4, 11 (5).
5   There is one interesting catch to note. When property is held by persons as joint tenants in law and equity the adjudication severs the *equitable* interest but cannot vest the legal interest in the trustee because that would be a severance at law. See *Re McCarthy* [1975] 2 All ER 857 at 859, per Goff J.
6   By virtue of the relation back to the act of bankruptcy; see the Bankruptcy Act 1914, s. 37 (1), p. 269, post.
7   Ibid., s. 45. There are special rules for voluntary conveyances or settlements; see s. 42, and Law of Property Act 1925, s. 172.
8   Bankruptcy Act 1914, s. 38.
9   Section 47 (1). This section applies whether or not the party dealing with the bankrupt has knowledge of the bankruptcy: *Dyster v Randall & Sons* [1926] Ch 932 at 940, per Lawrence J, nor does it seem that knowledge constitutes a lack of bona fides.

in the bankrupt as tenant for life. He has full contractual capacity in relation to dealings involving such property.

2. Companies

A company limited under the Companies Acts has power to enter into such transactions as are specifically authorised in its memorandum of association or are incidental or consequential to its main purpose. A company can, therefore, buy or sell land only in accordance with the terms of its memorandum, though it is the practice to include wide powers to purchase, sell or lease land. Likewise it should be ascertained that a company has power to borrow if it is seeking to raise money on a mortgage of its property; in the absence of an express power, a company has an implied power to borrow for purposes incidental to the course and conduct of its business[10].

3. Minors[11]

(a) Legal ownership
Section 1 (6) of the Law of Property Act 1925, enacts that a legal estate is not capable of being held by a minor; consequently he (or she) cannot be a mortgagee[12], trustee[13], personal representative[14], tenant for life[15] or have a legal estate vested in him beneficially. Where a minor is entitled to an equitable fee simple or a term of years absolute, the legal estate will be subject to a settlement[16]. A conveyance of a legal estate to a minor does not pass the estate to him; it operates as an agreement for valuable consideration to execute a settlement by means of a principal vesting deed and a trust instrument in his favour, and in the meantime to hold the land in trust for him[17]. The ineffectiveness of the conveyance to pass the legal estate is not affected by the rebuttable presumption that parties to a conveyance are of full age at the date thereof[18]. If the mistake is not discovered until after the purchaser has attained his majority, the title can be corrected by a simple confirmatory conveyance from the vendor.

Similarly a purported disposition of registered land to a minor does not entitle him to be registered as proprietor until he attains full age. In the meantime it operates as a declaration binding upon the proprietor that the registered land is held in trust to give effect to minor interests[19] in favour of the minor corresponding, as nearly as may be, with the interests which the disposition purports to transfer[20]. However, it would appear that if by mistake a minor were to be registered as proprietor following a transfer to him, the legal title would vest in him[1], subject to the prospect of rectification to give effect to the

10 *General Auction Estate and Monetary Co v Smith* [1891] 3 Ch 432.
11 See the Family Law Reform Act 1969, s. 12.
12 LPA 1925, s. 19 (6).
13 LPA 1925, s. 20.
14 Supreme Court Act 1981, s. 118.
15 SLA 1925, s. 19 (1).
16 SLA 1925, s. 1 (1) (ii) (d).
17 SLA 1925, s. 27 (1); LPA 1925, s. 19 (1). A conveyance to a minor jointly with a person of full age operates to vest the legal estate in the adult on the statutory trusts: LPA 1925, s. 19 (2).
18 LPA 1925, s. 15.
19 For minor interests, see pp. 65–77, ante.
20 LRA 1925, s. 111 (1).
 1 By virtue of the LRA 1925, ss. 20 (1) (freeholds), 23 (1) (leaseholds). This result is contrary to the spirit of s. 111 (1), but the sub-s. is defective in that it does not say what is

statutory position. Should he attain full age without the register being rectified then, unlike the position in unregistered conveyancing, no further step would be necessary to clothe him with the legal title.

A mortgage by a minor to secure the repayment of money lent is void under s. 1 of the Infants' Relief Act 1874. Prima facie, the mortgage loses his security and cannot sue on the covenant for repayment. However, to the extent that the sum loaned is used to pay the vendor the purchase price, the mortgagee, as against the infant-mortgagor, stands in the vendor's shoes and is entitled to an equitable charge on the property[2].

(b) Equitable ownership

The legislation of 1925 has not interfered with the minor's position in equity; he can still acquire and dispose of equitable interests in land. A devise of land to a minor is effective to vest the equitable interest in him[3], as is a purported conveyance, or lease, of a legal estate[4]. But it would seem that a *contract* entered into by a minor for the purchase of land does not of itself vest any equitable interest in him[5].

(c) Repudiation

Contracts and dispositions by, and to, a minor are subject to his rights of repudiation[6]. The Infants' Relief Act 1874, does not apply to contracts for the purchase (or sale) of an interest in land[7]. Such contracts remain binding upon him unless repudiated during infancy or within a reasonable time of attaining majority. Thus, an equitable lease is binding on a minor prior to repudiation; he must pay the rent reserved[8] and observe the covenants in the lease. Repudiation terminates the minor's future liabilities; it is uncertain whether it also extinguishes accrued liabilities. An infant purchaser who repudiates after entering into a contract to buy can recover any deposit paid provided there is a total failure of consideration[9]. Once completion has been effected and possession enjoyed for a period before he elects to repudiate, no recovery of the purchase money seems possible[10].

to happen if a minor is *in fact* registered. For the position on first registration, see p. 26, note 16, ante.

2   *Thurstan v Nottingham Permanent Benefit·Building Society* [1902] 1 Ch 1, CA; affd. sub nom. *Nottingham Permanent Benefit Building Society v Thurstan* [1903] AC 6, HL.

3   Unless the land is sold for administration purposes, the personal representatives should vest it in trustees of the settlement under s. 26 (1) of the SLA 1925, though usually they themselves will be such trustees: ibid., s. 30 (3).

4   This follows from the statutory trust created in his favour by the SLA 1925, s. 27 (1), note 17, ante. And see *Davies v Beynon-Harris* (1931) 47 TLR 424 (lease).

5   *McFarland v Brumby* [1966] NZLR 230 at 234, per Woodhouse J. The existence of an equitable interest arising from a contract stems from the purchaser's potential entitlement to the remedy of specific performance (see pp. 254–256, post), but the statutory restriction on the holding of a legal estate precludes any award of specific performance in favour of a minor.

6   See further Treitel, *Law of Contract* (5th edn) pp. 418–22.

7   *Duncan v Dixon* (1890) 44 Ch D 211.

8   *Ketsey's Case* (1613) Cro Jac 320; *Davies v Beynon-Harris* (1931) 47 TLR 424.

9   *Corpe v Overton* (1833) 10 Bing 252 (deposit paid prior to execution of deed of partnership recoverable).

10 Cf. *Holmes v Blogg* (1818) 8 Taunt 508 (repudiation of lease after taking possession; no recovery of premium paid). And see *McFarland v Brumby*, note 5, ante (agreement to purchase by minor and adult, under which they took possession on payment of deposit by minor; minor not able to recover deposit on repudiation two months later).

A minor can dispose of an equitable interest in property to a purchaser, or assign an equitable lease[11], subject in each case to his right to repudiate the transaction. On avoidance the equitable interest revests in him without any conveyance and, it seems, he is not obliged to refund the purchase money unless there is fraud on his part such as a misrepresentation of age. In this case, if the minor sought to recover possession of the property, the court would restrain the action except on terms of refunding the purchase price[12].

4. Persons suffering from mental disorder

The legal capacity of such persons depends upon whether or not a receiver has been appointed under the Mental Health Act 1959. The appointment of a receiver renders it impossible for the person of unsound mind to exercise any power of disposition inter vivos over his own property, even during a lucid interval. On the making of the order, his property passes out of his control and an attempted disposition by him is null and void[13]. The receiver is statutorily empowered to make or concur in making all requisite dispositions for conveying or creating a legal estate in his name or on his behalf[14]. In the absence of any receiver, a contract entered into by a person of unsound mind is binding upon him if the other party is unaware of the mental disorder, though the latter's knowledge of the incapacity renders the contract voidable at the instance of the person of unsound mind, his receiver, or personal representative[15]. This rule applies not merely to contracts, but also to conveyances of property for valuable consideration[16] and, presumably, other inter vivos dispositions, except that a voluntary conveyance is absolutely void, even where no receiver is in control[17].

C The written memorandum

1. Preliminary observations

Section 40 (1) of the Law of Property Act 1925, enacts that:

' No action may be brought upon any contract for the sale or other disposition of land or any interest in land, unless the agreement upon which such

---

11 Since a lease to a minor is binding on him until repudiation, an infant tenant still remains liable on the covenants in the lease, even after assigning it. Notwithstanding the assignment he retains, it seems, his right to repudiate the lease (as distinct from the assignment); if exercised, the lease terminates and with it the assignee's rights to possession.

12 2 Williams V & P, 861–62. But the rule that on repudiation a minor can recover property transferred by him under a completed disposition has been somewhat jolted by the majority decision in *Chaplin v Leslie Frewin (Publishers) Ltd* [1966] Ch 71, [1965] 3 All ER 764, CA (copyright assigned under voidable contract not recoverable by minor on repudiation of contract).

13 *Re Marshall, Marshall v Whateley* [1920] 1 Ch 284 (equitable charge executed after the appointment of a receiver under the Lunacy Act 1890, held null and void). Deeds executed by a person of unsound mind so found by inquisition were similarly void: *Re Walker* [1905] 1 Ch 160, CA. He can make a will during a lucid period: *Re Walker* (supra).

14 LPA 1925, s. 22 (as substituted by the Mental Health Act 1959, Sch. 7).

15 *Beaver v M'Donnell* (1854) 9 Exch 309 (agreement for purchase of land upheld); *Imperial Loan Co v Stone* [1892] 1 QB 599, CA. In an action of specific performance it is not for the plaintiff to establish that the defendant was in a state of mental health to be able to contract; the onus lies on the person alleging the incapacity: *Broughton v Snook* [1938] Ch 505, [1938] 1 All ER 411.

16 *Selby v Jackson* (1844) 6 Beav 192; *Campbell v Hooper* (1855) 3 Sm & G 153 (mortgage).

17 *Elliot v Ince* (1857) 7 De GM & G 475; *Manning v Gill* (1872) LR 13 Eq 485.

action is brought, or some memorandum or note thereof, is in writing, and signed by the party to be charged or by some other person thereunto by him lawfully authorised.'

This familiar provision, engraven on the hearts of all real property students, reproduces with a few minor linguistic alterations part of s. 4 of the Statute of Frauds 1677, a statute passed for the 'prevention of many fraudulent practices which were commonly endeavoured to be upheld by perjury and subornation of perjury'. The purpose of s. 40 is to avoid parties being held to a contract the terms of which they have not agreed, not to facilitate the escape of a party from a contract the terms of which he has agreed[18]. Nevertheless, it remains true that a man may be able to break his contract with impunity simply because he had the foresight not to write it down with sufficient formality. Over the years, first the Statute, then the Act, have acquired a thick crustation of legal authority and judicial gloss, much of it inconsistent and unsupported by the enactment itself, as the judges have wrestled with its interpretation in a valiant endeavour to enforce the bargain the parties have made. The nature and complexity of English land law are such that it would not be in the interests of the contracting parties to dispense with the need for a written document. Indeed a strong case can be made out for requiring the contract itself to be in writing and containing certain compulsory information, leaving the parties or their solicitors free to add to it where necessary[19]. Pending reforms in this field, s. 40 continues to cast its unwieldly shadow across every property transaction.

Two preliminary matters, often giving rise to popular misconceptions, must be considered before turning to the section in detail. First, s. 40 presupposes the existence of a concluded contract between the parties. The adequacy of any written memorandum does not become a live issue so long as they are still in a state of negotiation. Assuming there is a contract it does *not* have to be in writing. If it is, so much the better. The agreement will be in writing when it is created by an exchange of formal contracts prepared by solicitors. All that the statute requires is the existence of a written note or memorandum *evidencing* the terms of the agreement. It may take this form when the parties enter into an oral contract and later draw up some informal document recording the agreed terms. In one extreme case a memorandum made over fourteen years after the making of the contract was held sufficient[20].

The second point, perhaps a more fundamental one, concerns the effect of non-compliance. The section says: 'No action may be brought . . . unless . . .' Failure to satisfy the Act renders the contract *unenforceable by action*. It does not make it void, though occasionally even members of the bench have fallen into this error[1]. The contract remains perfectly valid and can be enforced in any way[2] except by an action on the contract. For example, a tenant sued by his landlord for arrears of rent can set up by way of defence an oral agreement for the surrender of the lease[3]. Similarly an oral variation of a written contract for

---

18   *Law v Jones* [1974] Ch 112 at 127, [1973] 2 All ER 437 at 447, CA, per Buckley LJ.
19   Consider the suggestions made by The Law Society's Working Party on Conveyancing: Second Interim Report 1966, paras. 8 and 9; (1966) 63 LS Gaz 171. Cf. Unfair Contract Terms Act 1977, s. 1 (2) Sch. 1, para. 1(b).
20   *Barkworth v Young* (1856) 4 Drew 1.
1   See e.g. Bollard B in *Carrington v Roots* (1837) 2 M & W 248 at 259. Parke B saying it is as a void contract.
2   Page 114, post.
3   *Couvel v Hodkisson* (1961) 179 Estates Gazette 497.

the sale of land, supported by consideration, may be a good defence to a purchaser's action for recovery of the deposit[4]. Indeed it is not strictly correct to say that the contract is unenforceable by action; there is nothing innately immoral, illogical or improper in an oral contract relating to land and if one of the parties chooses to have his oral contract specifically enforced, it is enforceable unless the other party pleads the section[5].

2. Contracts within the section

The section speaks of *'any contract for the sale or other disposition of land or any interest in land'*. Clearly the following are caught: contracts for the sale of freehold land, for the grant, assignment or surrender[6] of a lease, and for the grant of a rentcharge, mortgage, easement or profit[7]. An agreement for the letting of furnished rooms is also within the provision[8], but not a contract for lodgings[9], or for a licence to maintain an advertisement hoarding on land, since in neither case is there any interest in land created. Timber and growing crops (*fructus naturales*) are treated as land within the section, unless the contract requires their severance on sale, but not annual crops (*fructus industriales*) such as wheat, corn, hops, etc[10]. A statutory contract for the sale of land arising under a compulsory purchase order does not require compliance with the section[11].

Less obvious contracts required to be evidenced in writing because they involve an interest in land have been held to include contracts relating to:

(i) fixtures, for these are regarded as attached to the land and part of it[12], but not a contract by a tenant to sell tenant's fixtures to his landlord, since in essence it constitutes a renunciation of his right to remove them[13],

(ii) building materials in a house to be demolished by the purchaser[14],

(iii) slag and cinders forming part of the land[15];

(iv) a share in the proceeds of sale of land held on trust for sale, and, apparently, an agreement that regulates the division of the net proceeds resulting from a sale of land[16].

Despite the express exclusion from the statutory definition of 'land' of an undivided share in land, the Court of Appeal in *Cooper v Critchley*[17] held

4 *Wauchope v Maida* (1971) 22 DLR (3d) 142 (reduction in purchase price).
5 *Broughton v Snook* [1938] 1 All ER 411 at 415, per Farwell J. The report at [1938] Ch 505, at 511 reads: 'there is nothing innately objectionable in . . .' Cf. *Re Gonin* [1977] 2 All ER 720 at 730 where amendment was allowed to let the plea be entered.
6 *Smart v Harding* (1855) 15 CB 652.
7 Land is defined to include 'an easement, right, privilege, or benefit, in, over, or derived from land'; see LPA 1925, s. 205 (1) (ix). And see *Webber v Lee* (1882) 9 QBD 315.
8 *Inman v Stamp* (1815) 1 Stark 12.
9 *Wright v Stavert* (1860) 2 E & E 721.
10 See *Marshall v Green* (1875) 1 CPD 35, for a review of the authorities.
11 *Munton v Greater London Council* [1976] 2 All ER 815, CA.
12 *Jarvis v Jarvis* (1893) 63 LJ Ch 10, even when sold separately from the land.
13 *Lee v Gaskell* (1876) 1 QBD 700.
14 *Lavery v Pursell* (1888) 39 Ch D 508.
15 *Morgan v Russell & Sons* [1909] 1 KB 357.
16 *Liddell v Hutchinson* (1974) 233 Estates Gazette 513 (sale of former matrimonial home by ex-husband) Sed quaere. Should such an agreement be construed as a contract for the disposition of an interest in land?
17 [1955] Ch 431, [1955] 1 All ER 520. The Court found that no binding contract had been concluded.

obiter that an agreement by one of two tenants in common in equity to sell his interest to the other fell within s. 40 (1). This ruling is not without its difficulties, but it has subsequently been accepted as correctly stating the law[18].

In *Daulia Ltd v Four Millbank Nominees Ltd*[19] it was held that a unilateral contract to enter into a formal written contract for the sale of land is itself a contract to dispose of an interest in land, and is unenforceable unless evidenced in writing. The unilateral contract is capable of being specifically enforced and gives the purchaser a right to the land in equity. To allow the enforcement of an oral offer to enter into a written contract would be tantamount to taking the main contract out of the statute altogether. The door would then be open for the practical nullification of the section in a large variety of cases[20], which the Court was not prepared to countenance.

As has already been stressed, the section presupposes the existence of a concluded agreement. If the parties are still negotiating, or have merely entered into a tentative agreement 'subject to contract'[1], no contract yet exists to be evidenced in writing, and the problem of compliance with the statute does not arise. A memorandum which contains adequate particulars cannot of itself create a valid contract, should there be no consensus ad idem between the parties. Where, therefore, the parties intended the sale to be the subject of a formal written agreement prepared by their solicitors, it was held that a signed receipt for a deposit, though otherwise sufficient for s. 40 (1), could not be relied upon to found a successful action for specific performance, notwithstanding the receipt did not contain the words 'subject to contract'[2]. But if a binding contract has been reached the section applies, even though it is a composite agreement only one of whose terms involves the disposition of an interest in land[3].

3.   Form of the memorandum

No statutory form is laid down. All that is necessary is that there is in existence before the particular action on the contract is commenced a sufficient written memorandum. Exceptionally the memorandum may precede the contract, as where a written offer containing all necessary terms is accepted orally or in writing[4], but anything less than a definite offer, such as a mere invitation to treat or a statement of terms proposed for consideration, will not suffice. One of the greatest dangers inherent in the section is that the parties may unwittingly bring into existence a written memorandum. No intention of satisfying s. 40 need be present to their minds; the question is not one of the intention of

18   See *Williams and Glyn's Bank Ltd v Boland* [1979] Ch 312 at 331, 340, [1979] 2 All ER 697 at 704, 712, CA, per Lord Denning MR, and Browne LJ, respectively; *Cedar Holdings Ltd v Green* [1981] Ch 129 at 143, [1979] 3 All ER 117 at 125, CA, per Goff LJ. Moreover the Statute of Frauds 1677, s. 4, had been held to apply to a contract for sale of an undivided share in land: *Gray v Smith* (1889) 43 Ch D 208. But see (1955) 71 LQR 177–79.

19   [1978] Ch 231, [1978] 2 All ER 557, CA (oral promise to conclude formal contract if purchaser tendered signed contract and deposit at specified place and time).

20   Per Goff LJ, at 247 and 564, citing *McLachlin v Village of Whitehall* (1906) 99 NY 721 at 722–23, per curiam. It is not clear what the memorandum of the unilateral contract should contain; see [1979] CLJ 31, 32.

1   See p. 126, post.

2   *G.M. Jenkinson (Builders) Ltd v Partridge* (1970) 215 Estates Gazette 1129.

3   See *Steadman v Steadman* [1976] AC 536, [1974] 2 All ER 977, HL.

4   *Reuss v Picksley* (1866) LR 1 Exch 342; *Lever v Koffler* [1901] 1 Ch 543; *Parker v Clark* [1960] 1 All ER 93.

the party who signs the document, but simply one of evidence against him[5]. A receipt for a deposit, a letter written to a solicitor[6], correspondence passing between the parties, are common examples of inadvertent memoranda held to comply with the section, though the cases are replete with more unusual illustrations[7]. In practice the memorandum normally takes the form of a formal contract prepared by the parties' solicitors. Informal memoranda, whether intentionally prepared or not, tend to be the exception rather than the rule.

4. Contents of the memorandum

The memorandum should state all the terms of the contract. It should contain: (a) the·names or description of the parties, (b) a description of the property, (c) a statement of the consideration, (d) a reference to any special terms agreed by the parties, (e) an acknowledgment of the existence of a contract between the parties, though some judicial disagreement exists as to the precise extent of this requirement[8], and (f) the signature of the party to be charged, i.e. the defendant, or his lawfully authorised agent. A memorandum not containing the necessary information is insufficient and, subject to one exception[9], is fatal. Parol evidence may be given to establish the omission so as to show the alleged memorandum is insufficient[10]. A formal contract will normally record all necessary particulars. Problems relating to the adequacy of the written memorandum revolve around informal agreements prepared by the parties themselves.

(a) The parties

The rule as laid down by *Potter v Duffield*[11] is that the memorandum must contain either the names of the contracting parties or such a reasonable description of them that there cannot be any dispute as to their identity. Expressions such as 'proprietor' or 'owner' of a specified property are adequate, although the document does not actually name the vendor. Conversely, descriptions such as 'vendor' or 'client' are too uncertain to suffice[12], unless the memorandum contains other information enabling the 'vendor' or 'client' to be identified[13].

A memorandum is not unenforceable simply because the vendor, being a limited company, is described by the wrong name, provided that it is clear, either from the surrounding circumstances or in the light of known facts, that the name inserted in the document as being that of the vendor is merely an

---

5 *Re Hoyle, Hoyle v Hoyle* [1893] 1 Ch 84 at 99, CA, per Bowen LJ.
6 *Smith-Bird v Blower* [1939] 2 All ER 406. The letter was held not to be privileged from disclosure, since it was not written to obtain legal advice, but merely to supply information.
7 Other examples include: a note endorsed on a rent book (*Hill v Hill* [1947] Ch 231, [1947] 1 All ER 54, CA), a letter repudiating an alleged agreement (*Dewar v Mintoft* [1912] 2 KB 373) a clause in a revoked will (*Johnson v Nova Scotia Trust Co* (1973) 43 DLR (3d) 222), and an admission in a pleading (*Grindell v Bass* [1920] 2 Ch 487); but see *Hardy v Elphick* [1974] Ch 65, [1973] 2 All ER 914, CA. For cases on the topic, see 40 Digest (Repl.) 29−31, 132−60.
8 See p. 107, post.
9 In certain cases, an omitted term may be waived by the plaintiff, see p. 115, post.
10 *Beckett v Nurse* [1948] 1 KB 535, [1948] 1 All ER 81, CA.
11 (1874) LR 18 Eq 4.
12 See *Jarrett v Hunter* (1886) 34 Ch D 182 at 184−85, per Kay J.
13 *Commins v Scott* (1875) LR 20 Eq 11.

inaccurate description[14]. It is not enough that the parties' names appear in the memorandum; it should reveal their capacities, i.e. as vendor or purchaser[15].

There is one exception to the requirement that the contracting parties should be named or identified. In *Davies v Sweet*[16] a memorandum signed by the vendor's agent was held sufficiently to describe the vendor, although the vendor's name nowhere appeared in the memorandum and there was nothing to show that the agent signed as such. It seems rather anamolous that X can support an action for specific performance against Y by producing a document purporting to record a contract for sale between X and Z. The decision is supported by the rule of agency that an agent who contracts in his own name does not cease to be personally liable even though the other party is aware that he was acting as agent. The memorandum therefore identified two parties contractually bound to each other, and this was sufficient to render it enforceable against the principal under normal rules of agency. In situations involving agency, the contract will not bind the principal unless the agent has express or implied authority to contract on his behalf. One spouse does not as a matter of law possess implied authority to enter into a contract for the sale of land owned by the other spouse; however the circumstances may be such that the owner-spouse is estopped from denying the other's want of authority[17]. An agent who purports to contract for a principal, not having authority to do so, is liable in damages for breach of an implied warranty that he had the authority which he held himself as having[18], unless the other contracting party knows, or is taken to have known, that he was without authority[19].

(b) The property
As with the parties, so with the property, which should be described in such a way as to be capable of being identified with certainty. Parol evidence has been admitted to establish the identity of property described as 'Mr Ogilvie's House'[20], and 'twenty-four acres of land, freehold, at Totmonslow'[1]. A reference to 'my house' may be sufficient[2] if the vendor has only one property, but not if he owns more than one, since parol evidence cannot be adduced to establish which of two (or more) properties is the subject of the agreement.

Generally speaking all that is required is a physical description of the property. A memorandum is not insufficient because it fails to specify the precise legal interest which is to be transferred, and, if no interest is mentioned, then prima facie it is implied that the agreement relates to an unincumbered

---

14   *F. Goldsmith (Sicklesmere) Ltd v Baxter* [1970] Ch 85, [1969] 3 All ER 733 (plaintiff company contracting in the name of Goldsmith Coaches (Sicklesmere) Ltd).
15   *Dewar v Mintoff* [1912] 2 KB 373, unless it is clear from surrounding circumstances what positions they respectively occupy: *Carncross v Hamilton* (1890) 9 NZLR 91.
16   [1962] 2 QB 300, [1962] 1 All ER 92, CA; *Basma v Weekes* [1950] AC 441, [1950] 2 All ER 146, PC.
17   See e.g. *Spiro v Lintern* [1973] 2 All ER 319, CA. For the authority of one personal representative to bind his co-executors, see p. 109, post. See generally P.W. Smith, 'Co-owners and Agency' [1980] Conv 191.
18   *Collen v Wright* (1857) 8 E & B 647 (agreement for lease of farm). If the agent is aware of his lack of authority, he may be sued for the tort of deceit: *Polhill v Walter* (1832) 3 B & Ad 114.
19   *Halbot v Lens* [1901] 1 Ch 344.
20   *Ogilvie v Foljambe* (1817) 3 Mer 53; *Bleakley v Smith* (1840) 11 Sim 150 (the property in Cable Street).
1   *Plant v Bourne* [1897] 2 Ch 281, CA.
2   *Cowley v Watts* (1853) 17 Jur 172.

freehold estate[3]. When the memorandum indicates that something less than the vendor's whole interest is to pass, it should state what exact interest the purchaser has agreed to buy. In *Dolling v Evans*[4] an agreement for the grant of an underlease did not specify the length of the term and this was held fatal.

(c) The price
Either the consideration or the means of ascertaining it[5] must be recorded. Thus a memorandum evidencing an agreement for the grant of a lease should refer to the agreed rent. Any special terms of payment must also be included[6]. An agreement that provides for the price to be fixed by a third person, e.g. a valuer, is not void for uncertainty[7]. The parties are bound by a valuation given honestly and in good faith, even if the valuer is mistaken as to the property's true value[8].

(d) Other agreed terms
It is erroneous to assume that a memorandum which refers to the parties, the property and the price must in every case be a sufficient memorandum to satisfy s. 40. If the parties have agreed upon some special term and their written memorandum is silent about it, then the memorandum does not evidence their bargain. It does not fulfil the statutory requirement, even though the other necessary information is present. Oral evidence is admissible to establish that the memorandum does not contain all the agreed terms. An agreement that one party is to pay the other party's legal fees should be noted in the memorandum[9], as should a term for payment of the purchase price by instalments[10], or the agreed date for vacant possession[11]. The memorandum need not contain terms which are implied by law in the contract, such as a term for vacant possession on completion[12]; nor will a memorandum fail if an agreed term which is omitted is identical with one which the law will imply[13].

(e) Recognition of existence of contract
To satisfy the statute the memorandum must contain some indication that the party to be charged thereby acknowledges or recognises the existence of the

3 *Timmins v Moreland Street Property Co Ltd* [1958] Ch 110 at 118–21, [1957] 3 All ER 265 at 269–70, CA, per Jenkins LJ, and the authorities there cited. If the vendor does not possess a freehold estate, or it is subject to incumbrances, the purchaser has various remedies open to him; see pp. 608–611, post.
4 (1867) 36 LJ Ch 474, *Cox v Middleton* (1857) 2 Drew 209. See also *Ram Narayan v Rishad Hussain Shah* [1979] 1 WLR 1349, PC (omission to record chattels to be sold fatal).
5 *Smith v Jones* [1952] 2 All ER 907 (sale at 'the controlled price fixed by the government') *Brown v Gould* [1972] Ch 53, [1971] 2 All ER, 1505.
6 *Neale v Merrett* [1930] WN 189.
7 It appears however that the court in the absence of machinery for fixing the price will not itself fix it see *Courtney and Fairbairn Ltd v Tolaini Bros Ltd* [1975] 1 All ER 716, CA; *Bush-wall Properties Ltd v Vortex Properties Ltd* [1976] 2 All ER 283, CA (method of paying price not set out). See further Farrand, 41; and *Sudbrook Trading Estate Ltd v Eggleton* [1981] 3 All ER 105.
8 *Campbell v Edwards* [1976] 1 All ER 785, CA. A valuer who makes a negligent valuation may be sued by the party injured thereby: *Arenson v Casson Beckman Rutley & Co* [1977] AC 405, [1975] 3 All ER 901, HL.
9 *North v Loomes* [1919] 1 Ch 378. The term may be waived, p. 115, post.
10 *Tweddell v Henderson* [1975] 2 All ER 1096.
11 *Hawkins v Price* [1947] Ch 645, [1947] 1 All ER 689; *Burgess v Cox* [1951] Ch 383, [1950] 2 All ER 1212, *P Preece & Co Ltd v Lewis* (1963) 186 Estates Gazette 113 (term to forego payment of debt omitted).
12 *Farrell v Green* (1974) 232 Estates Gazette 587.
13 Ibid., per Pennycuick, V-C.

contract. A not inconsiderable body of judicial authority[14] can be cited in support of this requirement. Yet in *Law v Jones*[15] Buckley and Orr LJJ held that an admission of the contract was not necessary, except where the memorandum, though setting out the agreed terms, denied liability under the agreement, cases of 'confession and avoidance' as they are sometimes termed. In the later case of *Tiverton Estates Ltd v Wearwell Ltd*[16] a differently composed Court of Appeal declined to follow *Law v Jones*. In their opinion that decision was inconsistent with earlier cases which showed that the need for some recognition of a pre-existing contract was a general rule, not merely an exception confined to the confession and avoidance class of case. Authority apart, and excluding the special case of a written offer orally accepted[17], it is thought that the written note ought on principle to acknowledge the existence of the contract. According to Stamp LJ[18], a memorandum not containing such an admission would not be a memorandum of the contract sued on, but merely of the terms alleged to have been agreed. It would leave the contract to be established by verbal evidence. An express acknowledgment is not, however, vital. Words which by necessary implication recognise the existence of a contract will suffice, for example by referring to a 'sale' effected by one party to the other[19]. On the other hand a document expressed to be 'subject to contract' cannot ordinarily constitute a sufficient memorandum[20], nor can a document that denies the existence of any agreement between the parties[1].

(f) Memoranda relating to leases

A memorandum evidencing a contract to grant a lease raises one or two special problems. Not only must it refer to the parties, the property and the rent (i.e. the consideration), it is necessary to state the duration of the lease and the date of its commencement[2], as well as any express terms of the lease agreed upon. If, of course, the parties have not agreed upon the length of the term or the date of its commencement, the written memorandum, even though it faithfully records what has been agreed, is unenforceable because in law there is no concluded contract to enforce[3]. In the absence of any agreed date for the commencement, the court will not give validity to the agreement by implying that

---

14   See the cases and dicta reviewed by Stamp LJ in *Tiverton Estates Ltd v Wearwell Ltd* [1975] Ch 146 at 164–69, [1974] 1 All ER 209 at 221–25, CA.
15   [1974] Ch 112, [1973] 2 All ER 437, CA, Russell LJ dissenting. The majority still adhere to the opinions expressed by them in this case. See the obiter comments by Buckley LJ, supported by Orr LJ in *Daulia Ltd v Four Millbank Nominees Ltd* [1978] Ch 231 at 249–50, [1978] 2 All ER 557 at 569–70, CA.
16   [1975] Ch 146, [1974] 1 All ER 209, applied in *Tweddell v Henderson* [1975] 2 All ER 1096 ('I have asked [X] to get *the* contract drawn up . . .' held a sufficient recognition). See further (1979) 95 LQR 7.
17   Page 104, ante. For a suggested reconciliation of the 'offer' cases with the general rule, see per Stamp LJ, in *Tiverton's* case, ante, at 166–167 and 223, respectively.
18   *Tiverton's* case, ante, at 165 and 221–22, respectively.
19   *Law v Jones*, ante, at 124 and 444, per Buckley LJ.
20   *Tiverton's* case, ante; but see p. 127, post.
1   *Law v Jones*, ante, at 125 and 445, per Buckley, LJ. Aliter if it merely denies liability under the agreement: *Buxton v Rust* (1872) LR 7 Exch 279; *Thirkell v Cambi* [1919] 2 KB 590, CA. But consider *Dewar v Mintoft* [1912] 2 KB 373 (denial held to provide memorandum) and *Griffiths v Young* [1970] 2 All ER 601, CA, (oral waiver of 'subject to contract').
2   *Dolling v Evans* (1867) 36 LJ Ch 474, note 4, ante.
3   *Cartwright v Miller* (1877) 36 LT 398; *Edwards v Jones* (1921) 124 LT 740, CA.

the term is to begin within a reasonable time or by taking the date of the agreement as the date of commencement[4].

5. The signature

The section merely requires the signature of the party to be charged, that is, the defendant, or his agent. A complete memorandum need not contain the plaintiff's signature, though it must incorporate his name or other sufficient identifying material. Consequently, X, who has not signed any memorandum, can enforce the contract against Y who has signed[5], but not vice versa. Where the defendants are joint tenants, the signatures of both are essential. Specific performance of the agreement cannot be decreed if only one co-tenant has signed, unless he has authority to bind the other, but the one who has signed is liable in damages for his inability to implement the bargain he has entered into[6].

(a) Mode of signature

The word 'signed' has been liberally interpreted. It includes a signature by initials[7], or by way of a rubber stamp[8]. The signature need not appear in any particular place. In *Ogilvie v Foljambe*[9] it was stated that provided the name is inserted in such a manner as to have the effect of authenticating the document, the requirement of the Act with respect to signature is complied with and it does not matter in what part of the document the name appears. An unsigned memorandum in the defendant's handwriting, which contains his name somewhere in the body of the document, suffices, such as an agreement commencing 'I, P, agree'. This is sometimes called the 'authenticated signature fiction'[10]. The fact that the defendant (P) has himself written his own name is clear evidence that he recognises the existence of the contract. It is tantamount to his signature, unless the document contemplates a further formal signature by the defendant. In one case a document was held to be inadequate which read: 'Articles of agreement made between X and Y', and concluded 'As witness our hands' without being followed by any signatures; the parties had shown that they did not intend the insertion of their names in the body of the document to

---

4   *Harvey v Pratt* [1965] 2 All ER 786, CA. In *Jenkins v Harbour View Courts Ltd* [1966] NZLR 1, specific performance was decreed of an agreement for a lease under which possession was taken and which, though not mentioning the date of commencement, did specify the date of *termination*. The date the tenant received the key was taken as the commencement date.

5   As in *Farrell v Green*, p. 107, note 12, ante, unless the intention is that both (or all) contracting parties should sign: *Beck v Box* (1973) 231 Estates Gazette 1295 (document prepared by intermediary not signed by one of purchasers held not enforceable).

6   *Keen v Mear* [1920] 2 Ch 574; *Watts v Spence* [1976] Ch 165, [1975] 2 All ER 528 (liability for misrepresentation), p. 594, post. The legal effectiveness of one co-owner authorising another co-owner to sign a contract as his agent has been called into question: P.W. Smith 'Co-owners and Agency' [1980] Conv 191.

7   *Chichester v Cobbs* (1866) 14 LT 433. Oral evidence is permissible to identify the person signing.

8   *Bennett v Brumfit* (1867) LR 3 CP 28; *Tourret v Cripps* (1879) 48 LJ Ch 567 (printed letter heading).

9   (1817) 3 Mer 53; *Hucklesby v Hook* (1900) 82 LT 117, per Buckley J.

10 *Knight v Cockford* (1794) 1 Esp 190; *Johnson v Dodgson* (1837) 2 M & W 653 ('sold A' held sufficient). In *Pirie v Saunders* (1961) 104 CLR 149 the fiction was held to be inapplicable to a document not recognisable as a memorandum of a concluded agreement, in this case a solicitor's instructions for the preparation of a lease.

operate by way of signature[11]. When the memorandum is not written by the defendant, it must be prepared at his dictation[12].

(b) Subsequent alterations

If a document is altered after it has been signed by the defendant so as to effect or evidence a variation of the terms of a concluded agreement, s. 40 (1) is not satisfied unless he signs the document afresh, or initials the amendment, or expressly revives his existing signature by appropriate words or gestures[13]. Simply to approve the alteration does not suffice. This rule does not apply when there is no variation of a concluded contract after the time of signature, e.g. where a document is altered to correct a mistake in the written statement of an existing agreement[14], or it is altered before the parties are contractually bound[15]. Provided the defendant approves the alteration, his original signature is taken as authenticating the document in its revised form.

(c) Signature by agents

In determining whether an agent has been 'thereunto lawfully authorised', the ordinary rules of agency are to be applied. The authority may be given orally[16], and an unauthorised signature may be subsequently ratified by the principal. Ratification relates back to the time of the contract between the agent and the other party; a withdrawal by the latter is inoperative, even though made prior to the principal's ratification[17]. One party is not permitted to sign for the other[18]; to hold otherwise would create an obvious inducement for fraud, which the Statute was designed to prevent. One person may, however, act as agent for both contracting parties.

The agent must be authorised to sign. The fact that he has no authority to make a contract is immaterial; but authority to enter into a contract includes authority to sign a memorandum[19]. It may be possible to go further and, by applying general principles of agency, say that a signature is effective if made within the scope of the agent's ostensible authority[20]. Should the agent enter into the contract in his own name, or sign the memorandum with his own name, he incurs a personal liability. To avoid this, he should indicate when appending his signature that he is signing 'as agent' for another, or 'for' a named person[1].

11   *Hubert v Treherne* (1842) 3 Man & G 743. Compare *Leeman v Stocks* [1951] Ch 941, [1951] 1 All ER 1043, p. 111, post.

12   *Hucklesby v Hook* (1900) 82 LT 117 (memorandum written by P on note paper bearing V's printed name and containing V's name in body of document held inadequate).

13   *New Hart Builders Ltd v Brindley* [1975] Ch 342, [1975] 1 All ER 1007; *Richards v Creighton Griffiths (Investments) Ltd* (1972) 225 Estates Gazette 2104 (oral extension of time for exercising option to purchase).

14   *Bluck v Gompertz* (1852) 7 Exch 862.

15   *Koenigsblatt v Sweet* [1923] 2 Ch 314, CA (solicitor's unauthorised alteration of contract later ratified by vendor).

16   *Heard v Pilley* (1869) 4 Ch App 548.

17   *Bolton Partners v Lambert* (1889) 41 Ch D 295, CA, doubted in *Fleming v Bank of New Zealand* [1900] AC 577, PC. But not if the acceptance of the offer is made subject to ratification: *Watson v Davies* [1931] 1 Ch 455.

18   *Sharman v Brandt* (1871) LR 6 QB 720.

19   *Rosenbaum v Belson* [1900] 2 Ch 267, (estate agent) but see note 10, p. 111, post.

20   *John Griffiths Cycle Corpn Ltd v Humber & Co Ltd* [1899] 2 QB 414.

1   *Universal Steam Navigation Co v James McKelvie & Co* [1923] AC 492; *Kimber Coal Co v Stone and Rolfe Ltd* [1926] AC 414.

In special cases the law *implies* authority for an agent to sign. As these occasions have special relevance to sales of land, they must be looked at more closely.

(i) *Auctioneers.* Where property is sold by auction, the auctioneer has authority to sign a memorandum on behalf of both vendor and purchaser. So far as the vendor is concerned, authority is derived from the contract between the vendor and the auctioneer for the auctioning of the property. The purchaser's authority is implied from the fact that he made the highest bid for the property[2]. The authority to sign for the purchaser is limited. It must be made during any period within which it can reasonably be held to be part of the transaction of sale[3]. Usually the auctioneer signs in the auction room. A signature made an hour and a half after the sale on return to his offices has been held effective[4], but not one made a week after the auction[5]; nor does his authority extend to a subsequent sale by private treaty if the original auction proves unsuccessful[6].

The auctioneer's authority to sign for the vendor lasts throughout the period during which he has instructions to sell the property. The extent to which he can bind the vendor is shown by the case of *Leeman v Stocks*[7].

> The auctioneer inserted at the beginning of a contract form the vendor's name prior to the auction. After the bidding was over, he added the purchaser's name and obtained his signature. Neither the auctioneer nor the vendor signed the contract, nor was it even produced to the vendor, though he was informed of the sale and expressed no dissatisfaction. The purchaser sued for specific performance.

It was held there was a sufficient memorandum to satisfy s. 40. The auctioneer had authority to present to the purchaser a document containing the vendor's name as that of the party with whom the contract had been made. The absence of any formal signature was not fatal, as the parties never intended that the document should be so signed.

Since an agent cannot delegate his authority, a signature by the auctioneer's clerk is normally ineffective[8]. The parties may, however, expressly confer on a clerk authority to sign, as where the purchaser gave his name and address to the clerk and stood by while the clerk added the particulars to the document[9].

(ii) *Estate agents.* It is not clear to what extent an estate agent has implied authority to sign on behalf of the vendor. Usually the vendor employs an estate agent to find prospective purchasers with whom to negotiate, and this confers no authority to make a contract[10]. According to Lord Greene MR, the making of a contract is no part of an estate agent's business, not even where he is employed to sell at a stated price; only express authority suffices[11]. Although

2 *Emmerson v Heelis* [1809] 2 Taunt 38 at 48, per Lord Mansfield CJ.
3 *Chaney v Maclow* [1929] 1 Ch 461, CA.
4 Ibid.
5 *Bell v Balls* [1897] 1 Ch 663.
6 *Mews v Carr* (1856) 1 H & N 484; *Garnier v Bruntlett* (1974) 236 Estates Gazette 867 (authority to sell by private treaty established).
7 [1951] Ch 941, [1951] 1 All ER 1043.
8 *Bell v Balls* [1897] 1 Ch 663.
9 *Sims v Landray* [1894] 2 Ch 318.
10 *Thuman v Best* (1907) 97 LT 239; *Keen v Mear* [1920] 2 Ch 574 at 579, per Russell J.
11 *Wragg v Lovett* [1948] 2 All ER 968 at 969, obiter.

the cases are not entirely consistent, the weight of legal authority favours Lord Greene's dictum[12]. No implied authority exists to sign on behalf of the purchaser, though sometimes this is circumvented by requiring the purchaser to sign a contract at the time he signifies his intention to buy.

(iii) *Solicitors.* The mere existence of a solicitor-client relationship does not confer on the solicitor any authority to sign a contract[13]. In the ordinary case where a client instructs his solicitor to act in a particular transaction and the solicitors proceed with the drafting and approval of a formal contract, they have no implied authority to sign. He may be expressly authorised to sign, or the way in which the instructions are given may show by implication that he is entitled to bind his client[14]. Instructions to settle the terms of an agreement[15] or to carry out an agreement[16] have sufficed for this purpose. Where a formal contract is signed by a solicitor, or other agent, the other party ought as a pre-cautionary measure to satisfy himself that the necessary authority exists.

Despite the absence of any express authority to sign a memorandum, a solicitor does have implied authority to write letters as the normal and usual method of communication between solicitors having the conduct of the trans-action. Therefore a solicitor's letter, though authorised for quite a different purpose, may in appropriate circumstances constitute an adequate s. 40 memorandum of an already concluded (oral) agreement[17]. It matters not that the client or his solicitor never contemplated that it might do so. The prudent solicitor incorporates the words 'subject to contract' in any letter setting out the terms of the agreement or enclosing a draft contract, so as to avoid the possi-bility of the correspondence creating a statutory memorandum[18].

6.   Joinder of documents

The requirements of the section may be satisfied even though the terms of the agreement are not contained in a single document. To take a simple illustration: suppose P writes to V saying he will pay £30,000 for V's property, Blackacre, and incorporates within his letter all the proposed terms. V replies: 'I accept your offer', or signs a receipt for a deposit, which refers to the purchase of the property[19]. In any action by P against V, P's letter is insufficient by itself because it is not signed by V. The fact that V's name appears in the body of the

---

12   *Thuman v Best* (1907) 97 LT 239; *Lewcock v Bromley* (1920) 127 LT 116. Contra, *Keen v Mear* [1920] 2 Ch 574, at 579, per Russell J. (authority to sign if instructed to sell at a defined price); *Rosenbaum v Belson* [1900] 2 Ch 267 (instructions to sell, as distinct from merely finding a purchaser, gives implied authority). This case was considered without disapproval by Danckwerts LJ, in *Gavaghan v Edwards* [1961] 2 QB 220, at 226, [1961] 2 All ER 477 at 479. CA, See further Emmet, 68–69.
13   *Smith v Webster* (1876) 3 Ch D 49; *Gudgeon v Squires* (1970) 215 Estates Gazette 922.
14   *Gavaghan v Edwards* [1961] 2 QB 220 at 226, [1961] 2 All ER 477 at 479, CA, per Danckwerts LJ (implied authority for solicitor to complete memorandum by noting agreed completion date on carbon copy letter); see also *Griffiths v Young* [1970] Ch 675, [1970] 3 All ER 601, CA.
15   *Jolliffe v Blumberg* (1870) 18 WR 784 (draft agreement signed by solicitors).
16   *North v Loomes* [1919] 1 Ch 378, at 383, per Younger J.
17   *Daniels v Trefusis* [1914] 1 Ch 788, applied by Ungoed-Thomas J, at first instance in *Law v Jones* (1972) 225 Estates Gazette 1370; affd. [1974] Ch 112, [1973] 2 All ER 437, CA.
18   See p. 126, post. A better alternative may be the use of the phrase 'Contract Denied', see Farrand, 37; and [1981] Conv 165.
19   E.g. *Long v Millar* (1879) 4 CPD 450, CA a much misunderstood decision, see note 7, p. 114, post.

document does not assist P, since the letter was not written or dictated by V. However, in certain circumstances the letter or receipt written and signed by V may be read together with P's letter so as to form a complete memorandum. Though the reports are not lacking in illustrations where documents have been joined for the purposes of s. 40 (or its precursor), it has not always been easy to extract the principles involved. The locus classicus on the subject is contained in Jenkins LJ's judgment in *Timmins v Moreland Street Property Co Ltd*[20]. If two (or more) documents which together contain all the necessary terms are to be read together, it is indispensably necessary that:

> ' there should be a document signed by the party to be charged which while not containing in itself all the necessary ingredients of the required memorandum, does contain some reference, express or implied, to some other document or transaction. Where any such reference can be spelt out of a document so signed, then parol evidence may be given to identify the other document referred to, or as the case may be, to explain the other transaction, and to identify any document relating to it.'

In *Timmins'* case it was sought to join P's cheque for the deposit made payable to V's solicitors with a receipt signed by V himself. Here it was V who was suing for P's breach of contract, but his action failed. The cheque (the document signed by the defendant) contained no reference, express or implied, to any other document or transaction other than the order to pay a sum of money constituted by the cheque itself. The cheque gave no indication of the purpose for which payment was made, and the necessary reference could not be spelled out from the mere fact that it must have been made for some purpose[1]. It should not be imagined that this case establishes that a receipt and cheque can never be joined together. Had the purchaser been suing in *Timmins'* case the result would have been different. The receipt given by the vendor obviously referred to another transaction, namely, payment of the deposit. Parol evidence would have been received to ascertain the mode of payment. This would prove to have been by cheque. Thus cheque and receipt (if together containing all necessary terms) could be read as one, so constituting an adequate memorandum[2].

(a) Requirements for operation of rule

In any question involving joinder of documents it is essential to commence with the document signed by the defendant. It is this memorandum that must contain the reference to some other document or transaction. This explains why in *Timmins* case the starting point was the cheque and not the receipt which bore the plaintiff-vendor's own signature. It follows that there cannot be a reference to a document unknown to the writer[3], or to one which was not in existence at the time the defendant signed his[4]. As to the latter point, the Court of Appeal in *Timmins* case held that the precise order of signature is immaterial where the two documents are signed and exchanged at the same meeting as part of the same transaction.

20   [1958] Ch 110 at 130, [1957] 3 All ER 265 at 276, CA.
1   Though Romer LJ refrained from deciding the point (see pp. 134 and 278–79, respectively), the decision would have been the same had the cheque been drawn in favour of V himself; it would still have failed to contain the required reference.
2   *Stokes v Whicher* [1920] 1 Ch 411; applied in *Grime v Bartholomew* [1972] 2 NSWLR 827.
3   *Peirce v Corf* (1874) LR 9 QB 210.
4   *Turnley v Hartley* (1848) 3 New Pract Cas 96.

There must also be a reference to some other document or transaction, though not necessarily an express one. An extreme example is founded in *Pearce v Gardner*[5] where a letter was held to refer to the envelope in which it was sent, thereby enabling 'Dear Sir' to be connected with the addressee's name on the envelope. There is a particular danger in the joinder of a plaintiff's letter with that of a defendant's with the former setting out all the terms[6].

(b) The side by side rule
Until the decision in *Timmins'* case, cogent reasons existed for thinking that joinder of documents was permissible if there existed two documents and, putting them together side by side, it was clear there was some connection between them. Parol evidence could then be given as to the circumstances under which they came into existence, even in the absence of any identifying reference. The principle was adopted by the Court of Appeal in *Sheers v Thimbleby & Sons*[7] and extended by Harman J in *Burgess v Cox*[8]. However, when confronted with this argument in *Timmins'* case, Jenkins LJ thought that the court was being invited to go beyond anything warranted by the cases and stressed that the laying alongside process was still dependent on there being an adequate reference in the document signed by the defendant[9]. It seems dangerous, therefore, to rely on the side by side principle as a separate rule. Where the only documents in existence are both signed by the defendant[10], it makes no difference which rule is applied. If they are so closely connected as to warrant placing them side by side, then it will be impossible not to find a reference in one to some other transaction, or to the other document[11]. It is in cases where only one of the documents has been signed by the defendant that the more stringent doctrine propounded by Jenkins LJ might prevent a joinder of documents which would otherwise have been possible[12].

D   Enforceability of inadequate memorandum

Attention has already been drawn to the point that the section does not avoid a contract not properly evidenced in writing, but merely deprives a party of his

---

5   [1897] 1 QB 688, CA.
6   See *Griffiths v Young* [1970] 2 All ER 601, CA; and *Law v Jones* [1973] 2 All ER 437, CA, post.
7   (1897) 76 LT 709 (two documents both signed by defendant, one a letter guaranteeing certain investments and the other acknowledging receipt of money loaned on the security of the investments). The rule seems to have originated from the judgment of Bramwell LJ in *Long v Millar* (1879) LR 4 CPD 450 at 454, CA, ('. . . it becomes apparent that the agreement alluded to is the agreement signed by the plaintiff so soon as the two documents are placed side by side'). The CA in *Sheers v Thimbleby* took this to be the ratio of *Long v Millar*. But cf. *Stokes v Whicher* [1920] 1 Ch 411 at 418, per Russell J.
8   [1951] Ch 383, [1950] 2 All ER 1212, where only one of the documents was signed by the defendant.
9   [1958] Ch 110 at 130, [1957] 3 All ER 265 at 276, CA. Romer LJ was prepared to assume the validity of the argument, but felt it did not assist the plaintiff; see at 135 and 279.
10   As in *Sheers v Thimbleby* (1879) 76 LT 709.
11   See, for instance, Jenkins LJ's comments on *Sheers v Thimbleby*, ante, ('Both documents contained what were obviously references to the same transactions.'): *Timmins v Moreland Street Property Co Ltd* ante, at 128, 275.
12   The decision in *Burgess v Cox* [1951] Ch 383, [1950] 2 All ER 1212 would still, however, have been the same since of the two documents concerned, the defendant had signed the later one and this contained an obvious reference to some other transaction.

action for breach of contract or his claim for specific performance. In some situations the contract may still be enforceable, though there is no memorandum sufficient to satisfy the section.

1.   Enforcement otherwise than by action

The section only prevents an action on the contract for sale. A plaintiff is quite free to pursue any other cause of action open to him. In *Low v Fry*[13].

V orally agreed to sell his house to P for £800. P gave V a cheque for £450 as part payment of the price, but later he changed his mind and stopped the cheque which was dishonoured. V was held entitled to recover on the cheque the £450 plus interest.

Although there was no written memorandum the vendor was not debarred from pursuing the independent remedy under the Bills of Exchange Act 1882. A similar case is *Monnickendam v Leanse*[14], where it was held that a deposit paid under an oral contract could be forfeited by the vendor on the purchaser's repudiation. Conversely, if it is the vendor who defaults, the purchaser can recover any deposit paid in quasi-contract on a total failure of consideration[15].

2.   Statute must be pleaded

A defendant who wishes to plead the absence of any sufficient memorandum must do so expressly[16], by incorporating within his defence some statement to the effect that there is no memorandum in writing of the alleged contract sufficient to satisfy the Law of Property Act, s. 40. In the absence of any such plea, an oral contract is enforceable — even by action. The non-existence of a sufficient memorandum is not a matter of which the court is bound to take notice. The court will not strike out a statement of claim simply because it merely alleges an oral contract for the sale of land, since it has no knowledge that the defendant will raise the objection which the section affords[17]. Even where by inadvertence the pleader does not rely on the section in his defence, the court may refuse leave at the trial to amend the pleadings[18].

3.   Waiver of omitted term

Where a stipulation which is to the detriment or for the benefit of one of the parties exclusively is omitted from the memorandum, the plaintiff may submit to its performance or waive the benefit of it, as the case may be. Suppose a memorandum for the sale of property fails to record a term that P should pay V's legal fees. Should P default, V can maintain an action against P if he is willing to waive the term as to payment of his fees[19]. If it is V who defaults, P can

---

13   (1931) 152 LT 585; *Jones v Jones* (1840) 6 M & W 84 (action on promissory note).
14   (1923) 39 TLR 445, not following *Casson v Roberts* (1862) 31 Beav 613. For forfeiture of deposits, see p. 596, post. Cf. *Chillingworth v Esche* [1924] 1 Ch 97 where there was no oral contract.
15   *Pulbrook v Lawes* (1876) 1 QBD 284 (recovery of money spent on alterations by lessee prevented from entering into occupation through lessor's default).
16   RSC Ord. 18, r. 8. See *Gerber v Harvey* (1963) 187 Estates Gazette 253 CA (failure to refer specifically to s. 40 not prejudicial). But see *Re Gonin* [1979] Ch 16, [1977] 2 All ER 720.
17   *Fraser v Pape* (1904) 91 LT 340.
18   Amendment was allowed as a matter of discretion in *Re Gonin* [1979] Ch 16, [1977] 2 All ER 720.
19   *North v Loomes* [1919] 1 Ch 378 at 385–86, per Younger J.

enforce the contract by submitting to the performance of the omitted term which benefits the defendant, i.e. by undertaking to pay V's fees[20]. The precise limits of this rule are uncertain. Until recently there existed authority to support the view that it was confined to omitted terms *of no great importance*[1] (whatever this might signify), but in *Scott v Bradley*[2] Plowman J declined to accept this as a valid qualification. A plaintiff cannot waive an omitted term that the defendant has already carried out (though he offers to pay for it); on the other hand it is not thought that the plaintiff's prior performance of the term deprives him of his right to enforce the contract, since this is nothing more than a submission by him in advance. There can be no waiver of a stipulation which benefits both parties, such as a term relating to vacant possession[3].

4.   Sales by the court

A sale under a court order is one of the two statutory exceptions to s. 40 (1). If a transaction is being supervised by the court, there is no possibility of the mischief occurring, which the statute was intended to prevent. Nevertheless, the title to land being what it is, a formal contract is always prepared and it is the general practice for the particulars and conditions of sale to be settled by one of the official conveyancing counsel to the court. Sales under a court order are discussed in a later chapter[4].

5.   Part performance

(a)   Basis of doctrine

An oral contract for the sale of land, or one not adequately evidenced in writing, may be enforced under the doctrine of part performance. This doctrine originally developed by equity[5] has now received statutory recognition in s. 40 (2). The Statute of Frauds was enacted to prevent fraud and perjury, but it did not require a very ingenious mind to discover that its provisions could be utilised in exactly the opposite manner. As Lord Simon explained in *Steadman v Steadman*[6]:

> ' Where . . . a party to a contract unenforceable under the Statute of Frauds stood by while the other party acted to his detriment in perfor-
> mance of his own contractual obligations, the first party would be pre-
> cluded by the Court of Chancery from claiming exoneration, on the
> ground that the contract was unenforceable, from performance of his

---

20   *Scott v Bradley* [1971] Ch 850, [1971] 1 All ER 583, not following *Burgess v Cox* [1951] Ch 383, [1950] 2 All ER 1212; *Martin v Pycroft* (1852) 2 De GM & G 785 (tenant submitting to perform omitted term to pay premium of £200). See (1951) 67 LQR 300.
1   See *Hawkins v Price*, [1947] Ch 645, [1947] 1 All ER 689, adopting *Fry on Specific Performance* (6th edn), p. 243, note 1. Cf. 1 Williams V & P, 5.
2   [1971] Ch 850, [1971] 1 All ER 583. The principle of this case has been held not to apply where the defendant denies the existence of any agreement for sale: *Huttges v Verner* (1975) 64 DLR (3d) 374. See further conditional contracts, p. 131, post; and *Heron Garage Properties Ltd v Moss* [1974] 1 All ER 421.
3   *Hawkins v Price* [1947] Ch 645, [1947] 1 All ER 689.
4   Page 245, post.
5   *Butcher v Stapley* (1686) 1 Vern 363 seems to be the first case where the doctrine was successfully applied. It did not succeed in *Hollis v Edwards* (1683) 1 Vern 159, nor in Anon. (1680) 1 Freem KB 486.
6   [1976] AC 536 at 558, [1974] 2 All ER 977 at 996, HL.

reciprocal obligations; and the court would, if required, decree specific performance of the contract. Equity would not, as it was put, allow the Statute of Frauds "to be used as an engine of fraud". This became known as the doctrine of part performance—the "part" performance being that of the party who had, to the knowledge of the other party, acted to his detriment in carrying out irremediably his own obligations (or some significant part of them) under the otherwise unenforceable contract.'

Whilst the doctrine clearly illustrates equity's reluctance to permit a statute to be used as an instrument for fraud, this summary way of stating the principle tends to obscure the established limits of the doctrine. It does not explain why equity intervenes in some cases, but not in others. The true ground upon which equity enforces the agreement is that the defendant is charged upon the equities resulting from acts done in execution of the contract, not upon the contract itself. Where one party has partly performed his side of the bargain, an equity arises in his favour. In some cases execution of the contract has reached such an advanced stage that this equity cannot be protected (or administered, as the cases say) without having regard to the contract. The defendant is said to be charged upon the equities arising out of the changed position caused by the plaintiff's acts done in performance of the contract. To refuse to give effect to such equities would be to perpetuate an injustice which the statute could not have contemplated[7].

Until recently it was generally acknowledged that the doctrine in its modern form was to be found enshrined in the leading case of *Maddison v Alderson*[8]. This view has been somewhat disturbed by the House of Lords' ruling in *Steadman v Steadman*, a decision which has been variously described by commentators as virtually repealing s. 40 (1), or as necessitating the re-writing of textbooks on the subject[9]. Judicial reaction has been rather more restrained[10]. It cannot be denied that some of the Law Lords, speaking with their now accustomed divergent tongues, expressed opinions that cannot readily be reconciled with earlier established authorities. To this extent the doctrine appears to have been reformulated in some important respects. Nevertheless its impact on the typical vendor-purchaser transaction is not thought to be as fundamental as has been suggested in some quarters.

(b) Requirements for operation of doctrine

Obviously some limits had to be placed on the operation of the rule, otherwise the statute would have been virtually meaningless. In *Chaproniere v Lambert*, Warrington LJ[11], listed four essentials for the application of the doctrine (though not in the same sequence in which they are now discussed). These will be used as a convenient starting point.

(i) *There must be proper parol evidence of the contract.* There must be a binding contract between the parties, the existence of which can be established by parol evidence once adequate acts of part performance are proved to the

---

7 *Maddison v Alderson* (1883) 8 App Cas 467 at 475, HL, per Lord Selborne LC; *Chaproniere v Lambert* [1917] 2 Ch 356 at 359, CA, per Swinfen Eady LJ.
8 (1883) 8 App Cas 467.
9 See (1974) 38 Conv (NS) 388, 390, (1974) 90 LQR 433, 436.
10 See *Elsden v Pick* [1980] 3 All ER 235 at 240, CA, per Shaw LJ; *Re Gonin* [1979] Ch 16, [1977] 2 All ER 720.
11 Ante, note 7, at 361, 1092, respectively, adopting a passage in *Fry on Specific Performance* (5th edn), p. 290.

courts' satisfaction[12]. There can be no part performance of something which the parties have not yet finally concluded, as in *Lockett v Norman-Wright*[13], where a contract was expressed to be 'subject to suitable agreements being arranged between your solicitors and mine', and no agreements were ever finalised. Seemingly, however, the doctrine does not require a contract binding on both parties. It can apply to a unilateral contract. The offeree's acts of part performance will normally constitute performance of the condition imposed by the offeror in order to create a bilateral contract between the parties[14]. Assuming the validity of this argument, it is unlikely that it can be extended to an option to purchase[15]. So long as it remains unexercised the grantee can hardly allege part performance of a contract for sale which as yet is not in existence. In the case of an option it cannot be asserted that the alleged acts operate to create a bilateral contract, for this can result only from the giving of due notice of its exercise.

(ii) *The contract must be such as in its own nature is enforceable by the court.* Equity intervenes, if at all, by decreeing specific performance of the contract. This is a discretionary remedy. The doctrine of part performance becomes irrelevant in any case where this remedy would be refused on account of hardship, or misrepresentation, or because the plaintiff is in breach of his part of the bargain. Similarly it has no part to play where a decree would be in vain since the contract has at the time of the hearing become incapable of specific performance through lapse of time[16], or where there exists a prior enforceable agreement with a third party relating to the same land.

(iii) *The acts of part performance must be such as to render it a fraud in the defendant to take advantage of the contract not being in writing.* The element of fraud renders it essential that the acts of part performance were carried out with his knowledge and consent and known to have been done in pursuance of the contract. The precise status of this requirement is now somewhat problematical. In *Steadman v Steadman*[17] the majority of the House held that the plaintiff's unilateral act in forwarding a transfer to the defendant for execution was a good act of part performance. There was no discussion of the need for the defendant's knowledge, though there are suggestions that such knowledge was to be assumed because the purchaser's sending of a document for execution after the making of the contract is part of normal conveyancing practice[18]. Unless the decision on this point is to be so understood, their Lordships' ruling is, it is submitted with respect, to be treated with considerable caution. The defendant's acquiescence in (or, perhaps, his adoption of) the plaintiff's conduct would appear to be vital to raise the equity on which he is to be charged. It also demonstrates that both the defendant and the plaintiff are

---

12 See p. 124, infra, where this point is elaborated.
13 [1925] 1 Ch 56; *Stimson v Gray* [1929] 1 Ch 629; *Cohen v Nessdale Ltd* [1981] 3 All ER 118; affd. [1982] 2 All ER 97, CA.
14 *Daulia Ltd v Four Millbank Nominees Ltd* [1978] Ch 231, [1978] 2 All ER 557, CA, obiter. See especially at 243, 564, per Goff LJ.
15 See the doubts expressed by Goulding J, in *New Hart Builders Ltd v Brindley* [1975] Ch 342 at 352–53, [1975] 1 All ER 1007 at 1012.
16 *Lavery v Pursell* (1888) 39 Ch D 508.
17 [1976] AC 356, [1974] 2 All ER 977, applied by Goff J in *Re Windle (a bankrupt)* [1975] 3 All ER 987, another case concerning the settlement of a matrimonial dispute.
18 Per Lord Reid at 540 and 980; per Viscount Dilhorne at 554 and 992.

acting in execution of the agreement[19]. If on the contrary one party to an oral contract can render it enforceable by his own unilateral act without the defendant's assent, then it is indeed difficult to resist the conclusion that s. 40 (1) has been judicially repealed, so opening the door wide to the evils it was designed to avoid.

It must be the plaintiff who acts in partial performance of the contract. If it is the defendant who has done the only act of part performance, failure to execute the contract is not a fraud on him, merely a loss[20], unless it has been done by him at the plaintiff's request[1].

(iv) *The acts of part performance must be such as not only to be referable to a contract such as that alleged, but to be referable to no other title.* Subsequent decisions have modified the rigour of this requirement. Put simply the acts relied on as part performance must establish the existence of a contract between the parties. Oral evidence is not admissible to prove that they were in fact performed in execution of a contract. As Lord Reid stated clearly in the *Steadman* case:

> ' You must not first look at the oral contract and then see whether the alleged acts of part performance are consistent with it. You must first look at the alleged acts of part performance and see whether they prove that there must have been a contract and it is only if they do so prove that you can bring in the oral contract.'[2]

Though the acts of part performance must speak for themselves, it does not follow that each act must be considered separately by itself. They may throw light on each other, and 'there is no reason to exclude light'[3].

But to what kind of contract must the acts of part performance point? Some of the older cases required the acts relied on to show the exact terms of the contract which the plaintiff was seeking to enforce, as the words 'referable to no other title' suggest. This view was exploded in *Kingswood Estate Co Ltd v Anderson*[4], but beyond this the authorities do not speak with one voice. In the *Steadman* case two of the Law Lords[5] considered it enough if the acts pointed to *any* contract between the parties. On the other hand Lord Morris[6] (who dissented in the result) and Lord Salmon[7] refused to depart from the rule that the acts must be indicative of *a contract relating to land* — a principle that was clearly recognised in all the speeches in *Maddison v Alderson*. This is conceived to be the proper rule, especially when it is remembered that the whole area of

---

19   *Phillips v Edwards* (1864) 33 Beav 440 at 444, per Romilly MR.
20   *Buckmaster v Harrop* (1802) 7 Ves 341 at 346, per Grant MR.
 1   Cf. *Williams v Evans* (1875) LR 19 Eq 547 (plaintiff's lessee executing alterations with defendant's approval: held good part performance).
 2   [1976] AC 536 at 541, [1974] 2 All ER 977 at 981. The nexus between the acts and the alleged contract cannot be established by õral testimony, but *the acts themselves* may be, and generally are, proved orally: per Lord Simon at 564, 1001, respectively.
 3   Ibid., at 564 and 1001, respectively, per Lord Simon.
 4   [1963] 2 QB 169, [1962] 3 All ER 593, CA.
 5   See per Lord Reid at 541 and 981, and per Viscount Dilhorne at 554−55 and 992−93, respectively. Perhaps they were influenced by the circumstance that they were dealing with a compound agreement, only one of whose terms related to the sale of an interest in land.
 6   At 547 and 986−87, respectively.
 7   At 567−70 and 1003−6, respectively, passages which stoutly defend the orthodox position. The fifth member of the House, Lord Simon, considered it unnecessary to determine the point; see at 563 and 1000, respectively.

the law of part performance concerns contracts for the sale or other disposition of interests in land. More recently in *Re Gonin*[8] Walton J accepted as correct this view which he considered to be consistent with 'long established equitable jurisprudence'.

As to the standard of proof it suffices that on a balance of probabilities the existence of some contract relating to land is more likely than not to be the reason for the plaintiff's conduct[9]. To take what is acknowledged to be the clearest example of part performance, suppose that under an oral contract for the sale of V's land to P, P enters into possession of the land prior to completion with V's consent. Leaving aside the oral contract, evidence of which is not admissible at this stage, the fact of P's possession can be explained on several possible grounds. He may have been allowed into occupation on a temporary basis solely as an act of favour. He may be a trespasser[10]. However the most probable explanation is that there exists a contract between V and P relating to that land. By itself the taking of possession by P establishes a prima facie case that it was done in part performance of a contract concerning land.

(c) What amounts to part performance

(i) *Acts done in execution of the contract.* Only acts done in part performance of the contract are capable of raising the equity on which the doctrine is founded. As Lord Selborne LC explained in *Maddison v Alderson*[11], it is not enough that the act done should be a condition of, or good consideration for, a contract, unless it is, as between the parties, such a *part execution* as to change their relative positions as to the subject matter of the contract. The importance of the words in italics should not be overlooked. Yet the act need not necessarily be the performance of an obligation which the alleged contract imposes; for example the taking of possession, a good act of part performance, constitutes the premature exercise of a right arising under the contract[12]. The mere fact that the plaintiff has acted to his detriment does not of itself establish that his act was in part performance of the alleged contract[13]. The older authorities suggest that the act must also relate to and affect the land the subject of the contract[14], a requirement that ceases to be relevant if all that is required is that the acts must point to the existence of some contract between the parties, not necessarily one relating to land. Nevertheless, where (as is usual) the only term to be fulfilled by the vendor is the transfer of the land, the effective act of part performance will generally indicate the land concerned[15].

From what has been said it follows that acts done in contemplation of entering into a contract do not suffice, such as undertaking a survey and having

8   [1979] Ch 16 at 31, [1977] 2 All ER 720 at 731.
9   *Steadman v Steadman*, ante, at 542, 982, per Lord Reid; at 563–64, 1000–1, per Lord Simon. According to Lord Salmon they need establish merely a prima facie case; see at 566 and 1003, respectively.
10 The court will not, however, presume an illegality: *Broughton v Snook* [1938] Ch 505, at 514, [1938] 1 All ER 411, at 420, per Farwell J.
11 (1883) 8 App Cas 467 at 478, *Elsden v Pick* [1980] 3 All ER 235 at 240, CA, per Shaw LJ.
12 Normally a purchaser does not enter into possession until completion, but the vendor can agree to an earlier date for possession to be taken. See *Regent v Millett* (1976) 133 CLR 679.
13 *Steadman v Steadman*, ante, at 555 and 993, respectively, per Viscount Dilhorne.
14 See e.g. *Maddison v Alderson*, ante, at 491 and 756, respectively, per Lord Fitzgerald; Snell, 587.
15 *Steadman v Steadman*, ante, at 562 and 999, respectively, per Lord Simon.

plans prepared[16], instructing a solicitor to draft a formal contract[17], applying
for a mortgage loan[18], or seeking planning permission to develop the land[19].
Similarly, acts done by the plaintiff in reliance on the existence of a contract
but which are not performed in execution of it are not adequate, e.g. insuring
the property, or registering a protective C(iv) land charge[20]. Acts done in anticipation of the final completion of the contract, e.g. ordering carpets and
having change of address notices printed[1], cannot bring the doctrine into play.
Acts of a type normally performed during the post-contract stage of the transaction, such as sending an abstract of title or forwarding a draft conveyance for
approval, have previously been rejected on the ground that they are acts preparatory to the performance of a term of the contract or its completion[2].
Whether such acts ought now to be discounted for this reason is debatable[3].
They form part of the standard conveyancing procedures undertaken by or on
behalf of the parties after the conclusion of a binding contract for sale. The
vital matter is the proof of the binding contract. If it can be proved there seems
no reason why these matters should not be regarded as part performance.

(ii) *Surrounding circumstances.* In the *Steadman* case a majority of the
Lords held that in order to discover the significance of the alleged acts of part
performance, the circumstances in which they were performed is a vital consideration. Oral evidence is admissible to establish relevant surrounding
circumstances. The facts were as follows:

> Immediately prior to a court hearing before local justices, H and W orally
> agreed to compromise the proceedings on certain terms including (i) that
> H should pay £1,500 for W's interest in the matrimonial home and (ii)
> that he would pay W £100 towards arrears of maintenance, W consenting
> to the remission of the balance of the arrears. This agreement was com-
> municated to the justices, and on W's confirmation of its terms they made
> the appropriate court orders. H later paid the £100 and his solicitors
> sent to W a transfer for execution, which she refused to sign. In an action
> by H to enforce the agreement, W pleaded the absence of a s. 40
> memorandum.

Their Lordships held (Lord Morris dissenting) that H had sufficiently performed the contract to take the case out of the statute. When looked at in the

16 *Le Club (Mayfair) Ltd v RS Properties (London) Ltd* (1969) 210 Estates Gazette 23;
    Pembroke v Thorpe (1740) 3 Swan 482 (measuring land).
17 *Cooke v Tombs* (1794) 2 Anst 420; *Cole v White* (1767) 1 Bro CC 409 (instructions for a
    lease). Compare *Re Windle (a bankrupt)* [1975] 3 All ER 987 (instructions to draft transfer
    sufficient).
18 *Steadman v Steadman* [1974] QB 161 at 172, 179, [1973] 3 All ER 977 at 985, 990, CA,
    per Edmund Davies and Roskill LJJ.
19 *New Hart Builders Ltd v Brindley* [1975] Ch 342, [1975] 1 All ER 1007.
20 These would, in any event, be unilateral acts (see p. 118, ante) done without the
    defendant's cognisance. They may form part of the surrounding circumstances in the light
    of which the acts of part performance are to be viewed. See para. (ii) of the text.
1   *Boutique Balmoral Ltd v Retail Holdings Ltd* [1976] 2 NZLR 222.
2   *Maddison v Alderson*, ante, at 486, 750, per Lord Selborne LC, citing *Whaley v Bagnall*
    (1765) 1 Bro Parl Cas 345 (delivery of abstract insufficient). But according to Lord Simon
    in *Steadman's* case, ante, at 561, 998, further consideration might have to be given to this
    line of authority.
3   The objection that these are unilateral acts could be disregarded if the defendant or his
    solicitor adopted the plaintiff's act by (e.g.) returning the draft conveyance approved as
    would usually be the case.

light of the surrounding circumstances, it was quite apparent that the £100 was paid in part performance of a contract between H and W, even one relating to land in Lord Salmon's view[4]. Additionally the sending of the transfer to W for execution and the statement of the agreement made to the justices by H's solicitor[5] were held to be acts of part performance. It is not easy to see how the Lords could have declined to enforce the agreement. A ruling in W's favour would have constituted the highest judicial approbation of conduct which amounted to open contempt for the administration of justice. Apart from this consideration the facts of the case are clearly very special, far removed from the typical vendor-purchaser transaction which is basically nothing more than a single term contract for the transfer of land. Here there was a composite indivisible agreement, only one of whose terms related to the transfer of an interest in land.

In interpreting the alleged acts of part performance in the light of the surrounding circumstances, or res gestae as they are sometimes called, their Lordships were not formulating any new principle. Perhaps their significance had not always been fully recognised in the past, though examples can be found in the cases where the courts have clearly had regard to such circumstances[6]. They should not, of course, be confused with the alleged acts of part performance. Acts of part performance, if sufficient, give rise to the equities which bring the doctrine into play; the surrounding circumstances help to explain those acts, enabling them to be construed in their immediate context. They must be subsequent to and arising out of the contract. Circumstances antecedent to the making of the alleged contract cannot be considered[7], but they are not confined to circumstances for which the plaintiff alone is responsible. Thus in *Steadman's* case the defendant wife's oral admission of the agreement before the magistrates showed that the payment of £100 by the husband was in part performance of the agreement. The res gestae will vary in each case, with the result that an element of uncertainty, even of elasticity, can be said to pervade the application of the equitable doctrine. The same alleged act of part performance may be adequate in one case but not in another, and its sufficiency in any particular case may turn upon the circumstances surrounding its performance.

(d) Examples of part performance

(i) *Possession.* Taking possession of the vendor's property (assuming it is not wrongfully obtained[8]) has been described as the act of part performance *par excellence*[9]. It is bilateral inasmuch as the vendor vacates the property to enable the purchaser to occupy. A vendor's notice to quit given to occupying

---

4   *Steadman v Steadman* [1976] AC 536 at 572, [1974] 2 All ER 977 at 1007.
5   The bargain between H and W necessitated the justices being informed of what had been agreed as a preliminary to the request to them to implement part of the agreement. The statement to them was part performance of the bargain, and oral evidence was admissible as to what was said: per Lord Simon at 564 and 1001, respectively. Contrast the views of Lords Reid and Morris at 540, 548 and 980, 987, respectively.
6   See the cases cited in note 14, p. 123, post.
7   See generally per Lord Simon at 560–61 and 998, respectively and *Daulia Ltd v Four Millbank Nominees Ltd* [1978] 2 All ER 557 at 564, per Goff LJ and at 570 per Buckley LJ.
8   See *Delaney v T.P. Smith Ltd* [1946] KB 393, [1946] 2 All ER 23, CA (clandestine entry into possession by tenant pursuant to oral agreement for tenancy).
9   *Fry on Specific Performance* (6th edn), p. 286.

tenants at the request of the purchaser has been held to be a sufficient act unequivocally referring to the contract, just as if the purchaser had himself taken possession[10].

Taking possession must be distinguished from continuing in possession. The mere fact that a tenant remains in possession after the expiry of his lease is not of itself sufficient to enforce an oral contract for a new lease, or for the purchase of the reversion. His continued occupation can be explained on several grounds, all equally plausible[11]. But if accompanied by the payment of an increased rent[12], or the execution of substantial alterations, there will be adequate part performance.

(ii) *Alterations.* There are several instances where the making of alterations to or the expenditure of money on property by a purchaser or lessee has been held to be a good act of part performance[13]. The alterations may be accompanied by physical occupation, but this is not essential. Alterations by a plaintiff to his *own* property are prima facie referable to his ownership of the premises. Yet the circumstances may show that they were undertaken by the vendor or lessor at the request of and under the control and supervision of the purchaser or lessee. In this event the alterations suffice as acts of part performance[14].

(iii) *Payment of money.* Until *Steadman's* case it was universally accepted after some initial hesitation[15] that the payment of money, such as rent paid in advance[16] or even the entire purchase price[17], could never be a good act of part performance. Sometimes it was alleged that equity's intervention was not called for, since the money could be recovered by the plaintiff in an action at law[18]. Alternatively the rule was justified on the ground that payment of money was an equivocal act, not of itself indicative of any contract concerning land[19]. In the *Steadman* case the majority declined to accept the proposition in such absolute terms, holding that the payment of £100 arrears of maintenance was a good act of part performance. By itself it was not even marginally more suggestive of the existence of a contract than otherwise; but taken in conjunction with the husband's acts and forbearances in relation to the matrimonial proceedings and the sending of the transfer for execution it became strongly indicative of a contract[20].

10   *Daniels v Trefusis* [1914] 1 Ch 788. Cf. *Whaley v Bagnall* (1765) 1 Bro Parl Cas 345 (vendor's instructions to his tenants to pay rent to purchaser insufficient). See also *Lance v Smith* (1954) 164 Estates Gazette 581 (deposit of manure on land sufficient part performance of contract to buy).

11   'His remaining in possession is a mere continuance of the character which he all along filled': *Brennan v Bolton* (1842) 2 Dr & War 378 at 382, per Sugden LC; *Wills v Stradling* (1797) 3 Ves 378. What if one co-owner agrees to sell to the other and vacates the property?

12   *Miller and Aldworth Ltd v Sharp* [1899] 1 Ch 622.

13   *Farrall v Davenport* (1861) 3 Giff 363; *Phillips v Alderton* (1875) 24 WR 8; *Broughton v Snook* [1938] Ch 505, [1938] 1 All ER 411. Cf. *Brown v Strong* (1907) 122 LT News 367 (delivery of keys to facilitate the making of alterations held inadequate).

14   *Dickinson v Barrow* [1904] 2 Ch 339; *Rawlinson v Ames* [1925] Ch 96.

15   See *Lacon v Mertins* (1743) 3 Atk 1; *Main v Melbourn* (1799) 4 Ves 720.

16   *Chaproniere v Lambert* [1917] 2 Ch 356, CA.

17   *Hughes v Morris* (1852) 2 De GM & G 349 at 356, per Knight Bruce LJ.

18   See *Thursby v Eccles* (1900) 49 WR 281 at 288, per Bigham J, 'Payment of rent in advance raises no equity, except possibly a right to recover it back'.

19   *Maddison v Alderson* (1883) 8 App Cas 467 at 479, per Lord Selborne LC.

20   See [1976] AC 536 at 565, [1974] 2 All ER 977 at 1002, per Lord Simon; see also per Lord Salmon, at 573, 1008.

It is quite wrong to conclude from this decision that the mere payment of a deposit by a purchaser to a vendor suffices to take an oral contract for the sale of land out of the statute[1]. Normally the payment will not point to any preexisting contract, let alone a contract concerning land; it is susceptible of several other equally consistent explanations, e.g. a gift, a loan, or the discharge of some moral obligation. Moreover payment of a deposit will not normally be irreversible unless the vendor in the meantime goes bankrupt[2]. In the *Steadman* case the payment was not made in respect of the purchase price, but its repayment would not have been possible without the parties making an entirely fresh bargain. On the question of the payment of money the ratio of *Steadman v Steadman* appears to be that there exists no rule of law that payment can never be a sufficient act of part performance, but it may do so in special circumstances only[3].

(iv) *Insufficient acts.* Some inadequate acts have already been noted on page 121. In *Maddison v Alderson*[4] the plaintiff's act of continuing to serve as an unpaid housekeeper was insufficient; her conduct could be explained on several possible grounds. Similarly in *Re Gonin*[5] Walton J held that a daughter's act of relinquishing her wartime employment to return home to look after her aged parents was not referable to any contract concerning the house which she alleged her mother had promised to leave to her on her mother's death. With these should be contrasted the decision in *Wakeham v Mackenzie*[6] where the plaintiff gave up her flat to live with an old man so as to be able to look after him and his house, on the strength of his oral promise to leave her the house on his death. He failed to do so, and specific performance of the agreement was decreed against his executor. The conduct of the plaintiff (who was not a relative) in leaving her own flat and moving into the house of somebody else clearly pointed to the fact that there was some contract in relation to the secured occupation by her of that house[7].

(e) Effect of part performance
As we have observed, oral evidence is not admissible to establish that the acts relied upon were done in the performance of the alleged contract. However, the existence of sufficient acts of part performance (themselves proved by oral testimony) lets in parol evidence of the contract itself and of all its terms, including any term omitted from the written memorandum, which prevented that document satisfying the statute. If the court decrees specific performance, it does so of the contract in its entirety. In *Brough v Nettleton*[8], B orally agreed to take a lease of N's house with an option to purchase the property during the term. B took possession and later exercised the option. It was held that evidence

1 Cf. M & W, 567.
2 According to Lord Salmon payment will be adequate if the vendor is unable (because of bankruptcy) or unwilling to repay, but both his illustrations relate to payment of the entire price: *Steadman's* case, ante, at 571 and 1006−7 respectively.
3 *Re Gonin* [1979] Ch 16 at 30, [1977] 2 All ER 720 at 731, per Walton J. But see *Re Windle* [1975] 3 All ER 987 (payment of legal fees sufficient, but not mortgage arrears); *Cohen v Nessdale Ltd* [1981] 3 All ER 118; affd. [1982] 2 All ER 97, CA (obiter held payment of rent part performance).
4 (1883) 8 App Cas 467. In fact the House of Lords held there was no contract.
5 [1979] Ch 16, [1977] 2 All ER 720.
6 [1968] 2 All ER 783; *Kingswood Estate Co Ltd v Anderson* [1963] 2 QB 169, [1962] 3 All ER 593, CA.
7 Consider also *Schaefer v Schuhmann* [1972] 1 All ER 621, PC.
8 [1921] 2 Ch 25.

could be given of the entire contract, including the option. 'The effect of the removal of the barrier set up by the statute . . . is to open the door to parol evidence of the whole agreement.'[9]

Equitable remedy only. Part performance renders the contract enforceable in equity; the appropriate remedy is the equitable and, therefore, discretionary decree of specific performance. A plaintiff may establish a prima facie case for the operation of the doctrine, but it does not follow that specific performance will be ordered in his favour. That will be governed by ordinary principles regulating the award of discretionary remedies. Moreover, though the court has a statutory jurisdiction[10] to grant damages in lieu of specific performance, it will not make such an award in any case where specific performance could not have been ordered[11]. Consequently it is always advisable for a plaintiff to establish a memorandum sufficient for the purposes of s. 40 (1). If he proves his case, he is at least entitled to common law damages for breach of contract, and often a proper case will exist for the award of specific performance.

E Dangers of informal contracts

The point has previously been made that in the majority of cases the parties are content to have their agreement recorded in a formal document prepared by solicitors, so that no enforceable contract comes into existence until some time after they have concluded their negotiations. Occasionally, impatient at the law's delays, the contracting parties are anxious to have some tangible proof of their agreement. The purchaser may be prepared to pay a deposit in the hope of dissuading the vendor from accepting a more favourable offer, or the vendor may insist on a nominal deposit as a token of the purchaser's good faith. It may be pure chance whether any resulting cheque and receipt, or other documents, be it letter or form of agreement prepared by one of the parties, constitute a sufficient written memorandum. If they do, the parties may encounter difficulties they would have avoided had they not been so hasty. The purchaser may discover all too late that the property is subject to a road improvement scheme or scheduled for demolition; such factors will not provide him with any defence if he breaks the contract and is sued by the vendor. Had he waited until his solicitors had made the customary searches and inquiries[12] before signing a contract, he would have been able to resile without incurring any legal liability. Or again, it may just simply be that he is unable to raise a mortgage.

A vendor, too, is not immune from danger when relying on some informal memorandum. It will be unlikely that he will have incorporated into his memorandum details of the tenure of the property and the incumbrances affecting it. Nevertheless he will by law have bound himself to convey an estate in fee simple in possession free from incumbrances, for this is one of the conditions which the law implies in every 'open contract'[13] unless the contrary is expressed. Should

---

9   At 28, per Lawrence J.
10 By virtue of the Supreme Court Act 1981, as to which see p. 583, post.
11 *Lavery v Pursell* (1888) 38 Ch D 508 (contract incapable of specific performance through lapse of time); *H and A Productions Ltd v Taylor* (1955) 105 LJ 681, CA.
12 See Chap. 7, post, unless these matters can be part performance of an existing oral contract, but see ante, p. 121.
13 An open contract arises when the parties have agreed upon the barest essentials,; i.e. the property and the price. The other terms necessary to give business efficacy to the contract are implied by the general law. See pp. 141–142, post.

the property be leasehold, or subject to restrictive covenants, the vendor is unable to sell what he has contracted to sell; the purchaser, if he wishes, can refuse to proceed with the contract and recover his deposit, leaving the vendor to start all over again.

F   Agreements 'subject to contract'

1.   Meaning of 'subject to contract'

Whether or not the parties to a sale and purchase of land intend to bind themselves contractually immediately on concluding their oral negotiations will depend on the circumstances of each case. They frequently negative such intention by making or accepting an offer 'subject to contract'. This phrase makes it clear that the parties intend that 'neither of them is to be contractually bound until a contract is signed in the usual way[14].' Until a formal contract has been settled by the parties' legal advisers, signed and exchanged, the matter remains in a state of negotiation[15]. The parties have a *locus poenitentia*; either of them is free to suggest new terms or to withdraw from the transaction. As there is no concluded bargain the purchaser, if he decides not to proceed, is entitled to the return of any money paid to the vendor[16]. On the other hand if the vendor withdraws, the purchaser cannot recover from him any abortive expenditure incurred in respect of survey or other similar fees[17]. Once inserted the words 'subject to contract' continue throughout all subsequent negotiations, unless the parties expressly agree that they should be expunged or such an agreement is necessarily to be implied[18]. One point to note, however, is that use of the expression does not always prevent the formation of a contract. Whilst this is usually the invariable result, it remains a question of construction in each case whether the words were intended to have that effect. In one case[19] they were rejected as meaningless when inserted in a letter of acceptance of an offer to sell by tender, and where it was never envisaged that a formal contract should be submitted for approval, then signed and exchanged.

Other expressions have been held by the courts to indicate a mere state of negotiation between the parties, such as: 'subject to the preparation by my solicitor of a formal agreement'[20] or, in relation to the grant of a lease, 'provided the terms of the draft lease are reasonable in our estimation'[1].

---

14   *Spottiswoode, Ballantyne & Co Ltd v Doreen Appliances Ltd* [1942] 2 KB 32 at 35, [1942] 2 All ER 65 at 66, CA, per Lord Greene MR.
15   *Keppel v Wheeler* [1927] 1 KB 577 at 584, CA per Bankes LJ. For exchange of contracts, see p. 237, post.
16   *Chillingworth v Esche* [1942] Ch 97, CA.
17   For the problems of gazumping, see pp. 241–242, post.
18   *Sherbrooke v Dipple* (1980) 255 Estates Gazette 1203, CA. See [1981] Conv 165 and *Cohen v Nessdale Ltd* [1981] 3 All ER 118; affd. [1982] 2 All ER 97, CA. In this case the learned judge found that because the correspondence was 'subject to contract' that negatived a contract which could be enforced by part performance (ground rent) sed quaere: on the facts the terms of the lease had yet to be agreed and the correspondence was passing between the contracting parties. The position would be otherwise if the correspondence was between solicitors. Subject to contract then could not be used to deny an oral contract concluded between the parties and enforceable by part performance.
19   *Michael Richards Properties Ltd v Corpn of Wardens of St Saviour's Parish, Southwark* [1975] 3 All ER 416; *Kelly v Park Hall School Ltd* [1979] IR 340. Cf. *Munton v Greater London Council* [1976] 2 All ER 815. See further p. 128, post.
20   *Lloyd v Nowell* [1895] 2 Ch 744; *Chillingworth v Esche* [1924] Ch 97, CA.
1   *Wilcox v Redhead* (1880) 49 LJ Ch 539; *Raingold v Bromley* [1931] 2 Ch 307.

Negotiations subject to contract for the grant of a lease remain in a state of negotiation until exchange of the lease and counterpart, and not even the execution by the parties of the formal documents suffices to bring into existence an enforceable contract in the absence of an exchange of parts[2]. The position, thus far, is not too difficult. When the parties have agreed 'subject to contract' and the later correspondence is protected by subject to contract, prima facie that correspondence cannot be used to provide a memorandum. What happens, however, if the parties are orally agreed? The solicitor surely has no authority by writing, 'subject to contract' to deny the existence of the prior oral contract. In this area the phrase 'subject to contract' then takes on a less apparent role, namely that it prevents the documents being relied on but it does not negative the prior oral contract which is binding, albeit unenforceable[3]. The first initial finding, therefore, is whether there is a concluded binding agreement. If that is found to be the case then that contract can be enforced by, for example, reliance on the doctrine of part performance or by removing in some way the bar on the use of the protected correspondence[4]. On this basis there is no real problem presented by *Law v Jones*[5] that cannot be dealt with by making proper inquiries of the client as to what precisely has happened. The case rang 'alarm bells' in solicitors' offices throughout the land[6]. There is nothing in the case to suggest that the words 'subject to contract' are ineffective for the limited purpose for which they were intended, namely that they prevent the correspondence from being used as a memorandum. Proof of an oral contract is always required if there is no written agreement. In the *Tiverton* case[7] the purchasers failed to show an oral contract in that the vendors denied there was a binding agreement. The majority[8] in that case decided it on the basis of whether the note or memorandum needs to acknowledge the existence of the agreement which is sought to be enforced. To allow the phrase 'subject to contract' inserted by solicitors[9] to override an oral contract agreed between the parties would, it is submitted, go too far[10]. It may be difficult to prove an oral

---

2   *D'Silva v Lister House Developments Ltd* [1971] Ch 7, [1970] 1 All ER 858; *Derby & Co Ltd v. I.T.C. Pension Trust Ltd* [1977] 2 All ER 890. On the grant of a lease it is customary to prepare (or engross) two copies of the deed; on completion the copy executed by the lessor, termed the original, is exchanged for the other executed by the lessee, termed the counterpart. However, the effect of the law relating to the execution of deeds is such that the parties are bound when the lease and counterpart are executed although no exchange takes place; see p. 431, post. Consider the effect of the words 'subject to formal lease' which are commonly used.

3   See Farrand, 37; *Law v Jones* [1974] Ch 112 at 123, per Buckley LJ. As he said, the later written contract supersedes the oral by implication on exchange but not otherwise. Cf. *Cohen v Nessdale Ltd* [1981] 3 All ER 118.

4   See e.g. *Griffiths v Young* [1970] Ch 675 (oral waiver of 'subject to contract').

5   [1974] Ch 112.

6   *Tiverton Estates v Wearwell* [1974] 1 All ER 209 at 217, per Denning MR. The fears, it is submitted, were based on the same problem as shown by the *Boland* case, namely that unthinking obedience to a system of practice should not be used as a basis for justifying that practice.

7   [1974] 1 All ER 209.

8   Scarman and Stamp LLJ. Lord Denning MR also appears to decide the case on that basis but goes wider; see p. 217.

9   One is reminded of the extra keys on the typewriter — 'without prejudice' and 'subject to contract'.

10   Cf. *H Clark Ltd v Wilkinson* [1965] Ch 694 at 702, CA, per Lord Denning MR concerning the converse: — i.e. lack of authority in a solicitor to sign a contract on behalf of a client see further post. Cf. where exchange is contemplated see *Domb v Isoz* [1980] 1 All ER 942 CA, [1980] Conv 227.

contract[11], but once it is, the question then is whether it is enforceable or not. The words 'subject to contract' cannot be used, for example, to prevent enforcement of the contract by virtue of part performance. If there has been any prior binding oral contract concluded the words 'subject to contract' cannot, it is submitted, be anything other than a 'suspensive condition' barring reliance on those documents to provide a memorandum. It will be seen, therefore, that the words can have a differing effect depending on the state of affairs agreed between the parties.

2.   Problems of construction

It does not automatically follow that because the parties contemplate the execution of some other document incorporating the terms of their agreement, there can be no binding contract unless that document is subsequently signed. It is a question of construction

> ' whether the execution of the further contract is a condition or term of the bargain or whether it is a mere expression of the desire of the parties as to the manner in which the transaction already agreed to will in fact go through'[12].

In the latter case there may still be a binding contract, notwithstanding the non-execution of a more formal document. It was held there was a binding contract where a letter of acceptance stated that the writer had requested his solicitors 'to forward the agreement for purchase'[13]. Another example is furnished by the case of *Branca v Cobarro*[14]. Here a written agreement prepared by one of the parties concluded: 'This is a provisional agreement until a fully legalised agreement drawn up by a solicitor and embodying all the conditions herewith stated is signed'. The court held that the agreement constituted a binding contract. The final clause, particularly the word 'until', implied that the agreement was intended to be immediately and fully binding, and to remain so unless and until superseded by a later agreement of the same tenor but expressed in more precise and formal language.

G   Conditional contracts

Care must be taken to distinguish cases. Where there is no contract at all because the parties' preliminary negotiations are made 'subject to contract', from situations where the parties have concluded a conditional contract. They may have entered into an agreement for sale subject to or conditional upon the consent of the Charity Commissioners, or the reversioner's licence to assign being granted, or the purchaser's obtaining planning permission or the grant of a satisfactory mortgage. The precise effect of a condition of this type is a question of construction. The law on this topic is rather complex, and not all of the cases are easy to reconcile. The draftsman is always well advised to make his intentions abundantly clear on this issue i.e. to state how and in what way the

11   See e.g. *Tweddell v Henderson* [1975] 2 All ER 1096 at 1099. See further Emmet, 50.
12   *Von Hatzfeldt-Wildenburg v Alexander* [1912] 1 Ch 284 at 288, per Parker J.
13   *Rossiter v Miller* (1878) 3 App Cas 1124, HL; *Bonnewell v Jenkins* (1878) 8 Ch D 70, CA. ('We have asked V's solicitor to prepare contract.').
14   [1974] KB 854, [1947] 2 All ER 101, CA.; *Bushwall Properties Ltd v Vortex Properties Ltd* [1975] 2 All ER 214; revsd. on other grounds [1976] 2 All ER 283, CA.

contract is affected by these conditions, in particular what is to happen if they
are not satisfied.

(a) Condition precedent to contract

The condition may operate as a condition precedent to the formation of a
contract for sale between the parties. A condition of this type has the same
effect as a 'subject to contract' qualification. No agreement exists between the
parties unless and until the condition is fulfilled; either party is free to withdraw
without awaiting its fulfilment or non-fulfilment. In *Aberfoyle Plantations Ltd
v Cheng*[15] a purchase of land was expressed to be conditional upon the vendor
obtaining a renewal of certain leases. The Judicial Committee of the Privy
Council took the view that until the condition was satisfied no contract for sale
could come into existence. Since the date fixed for completion had passed
without the condition being fulfilled, the purchaser was entitled to the return
of his deposit. Similarly in *Michael Richards Properties Ltd v Corpn of
Wardens of St. Saviour's Parish, Southwark*[16] Goff J held that a condition
requiring the Charity Commissioners' consent to the sale[17] was a true condition
precedent, and the contract became effective only when it was given.

(b) Condition precedent to performance

Alternatively, and more frequently, the condition is held not to prevent the
formation of a binding contract, but its non-fulfilment renders the contract
unenforceable by either party[18], unless the condition (being for the sole benefit
of one of the parties) is waived by that party. The condition takes effect as one
of the terms of the contract; save for its non-fulfilment neither party is entitled
to withdraw from the contract except by consent. Conditions falling into this
category have been held to occur where the contract was made subject to the
vendor arranging a satisfactory mortgage[19], to planning permission[20], to the
reversioner's consent to the assignment of a lease[1], to satisfactory searches and

---

15 [1960]AC 115, [1959] 3 All ER 910, PC, a 'very unusual and special case': *Property and
Bloodstock Ltd v Emerton* [1968] Ch 94 at 115, [1967] 3 All ER 321 at 327, CA, per
Danckwerts LJ. In the *Aberfoyle* case the entire contract was made subject to the
condition, as the opening words of cl. 1 of the agreement showed; yet there was also a
provision for the contract to become null and void on non-fulfilment of the condition. See
further 9 Halsbury's Laws (4th edn), 143–45, para. 264.

16 [1975] 3 All ER 416.

17 As required by the Charities Act 1960, s. 29 (1). In cases where their consent is necessary
an absolute contract made before approval is given is unlawful: *Milner v Staffordshire
Congregational Union (Inc.)* [1956] Ch 275, [1956] 1 All ER 494. For exemptions, see
s. 29 (4) and Sch. 2; the Charities (Religious Premises) Regulations 1962, S.I. 1962
No. 1421, r. 1.

18 Such a condition may variously be termed a condition precedent to the performance of
obligations under the contract, or a condition suspensive of the obligations thereunder. A
condition may also operate as a condition subsequent, i.e. where the contract provides for
liability to cease on the occurrence of some future event.

19 *Lee-Parker v Izzet* [1971] 3 All ER 1099, more fully reported on this point at (1971) 22 P &
CR 1098. Contrast *Lee-Parker v Izzet (No. 2)* [1972] 2 All ER 800.

20 *Batten v White* (1960) 12 P & CR 66. See further p. 131, post.

 1 *Property and Bloodstock Ltd v Emerton*, ante; *Brickwoods Ltd v Butler and Walters*
(1970) 23 P & CR 317 (contract conditional on vendor procuring car parking licence). For
licences to assign, see p. 311, post.

replies to pre-contract enquiries[2], to the purchaser's solicitor approving the lease[3], and to a survey of the property[4].

(c) Time for fulfilment

The agreement may, or may not, provide a date by which the condition is to be fulfilled. The date so fixed must be strictly adhered to without any extension by reference to equitable principles. In the absence of a specified date the condition must be satisfied within a reasonable time, judged by an objective test applicable to both parties[5], and in any event not later than the date fixed for completion[6]. In the case of a condition that is merely precedent to performance, a party who signifies his refusal to continue with the contract before the time for fulfilment has elapsed commits a breach of contract. Thus in *Smith v Butler*[7],

> V contracted to sell to P the lease of a public house which was subject to a mortgage, on condition that M, the mortgagee, consented to transfer the outstanding loan from V to P. V experienced difficulty in procuring M's consent. Before the date fixed for completion P repudiated the contract.

It was held that V had until the completion date to perform the condition so that P, being in breach of contract, could not recover his deposit.

If the condition is not satisfied in time the contract cannot be enforced. Non-fulfilment discharges the parties from their obligations under the contract. So the purchaser can recover his deposit. This principle is subject to an important qualification. Where fulfilment of the condition requires action on the part of one of the parties, that party cannot rely on the non-performance unless he has taken reasonable steps to secure its fulfilment. He cannot take advantage of a state of affairs that his own default has produced[8]. Thus, where the agreement is subject to survey the purchaser is bound to obtain a surveyor's report. Failure to do so within a reasonable (or a specified) time precludes him from resiling from the transaction. Having obtained and considered a report, he must act bona fide in deciding whether or not to proceed with the purchase. If a reasonable man would be satisfied with the report, the purchaser will experience difficulty in persuading a court that his decision to discontinue the contract was bona fide[9].

The contract may expressly regulate the consequences of non-performance. For instance, it may provide for the contract to become null and void, though the use of this formula is not advisable bearing in mind possible difficulties

2   *Mason v Stapleton's Tyre Services Ltd* (1963) 186 Estates Gazette 113; *Aquis Estates Ltd v Minton* [1975] 3 All ER 1043 (property to be free from adverse entry in local land charges register).

3   *Caney v Leith* [1937] 2 All ER 532.

4   *Ee v Kakar* (1979) 40 P & CR 223, not following *Marks v Board* (1930) 46 TLR 424. See [1979] Conv 285 (V. Callender) and [1980] Conv 446, (J.E. Adams).

5   *Re Longlands Farm* [1968] 3 All ER 552 (planning permission not obtained by purchaser more than three years after contract; vendor discharged).

6   *Aberfoyle Plantations Ltd v Cheng* [1960] AC 115, [1959] 3 All ER 910. These rules apply equally to conditions that are precedent to performance; see *Brickwoods Ltd v Butler and Walters* (1969) 21 P & CR 256 at 264, per Megarry J; affd. (1970) 23 P & CR 317, CA.

7   [1900] 1 QB 694, CA; *Batten v White*, ante.

8   See *New Zealand Shipping Co Ltd v Société des Ateliers et Chantiers de France* [1919] AC 1, HL.

9   *Ee v Kakar*, ante, at 228, per Walton J. A 'subject to survey' condition may be construed as a condition precedent to the formation of a contract, as in *Marks v Board* ante, in which event neither vendor nor purchaser is bound.

surrounding the interpretation of the word 'void'. Alternatively, one or both of the parties, may be entitled to serve a notice terminating the contract. Such a clause ought always to specify the period within which the notice is to be given; otherwise it will be ineffective unless served within a reasonable time after the last date for fulfilment of the condition[10].

(d) Waiver

A term or condition which is for the sole benefit of one of the parties may be waived by that party who can then enforce the contract without that term. In *Batten v White*[11] a vendor repudiated a contract for sale subject to planning permission at a time when the purchaser was still seeking permission; it was held that the purchaser could waive the condition and sue for specific performance. According to Brightman J, in *Heron Garage Properties Ltd v Moss*[12], in the absence of any express contractual right, waiver will in general be allowed only where the stipulation (i) is in terms for his exclusive benefit because it is a power or right vested by the contract in him alone, or (ii) is by inevitable implication for his benefit alone[13]. In this case the learned judge refused to allow the purchaser's attempted waiver of a condition relating to planning permission because it was inextricably mixed up with other contractual terms from which it could not be severed. The date for completion was geared to the date by which planning consent was obtained[14]. Furthermore the term could not be said to be for the purchaser's sole benefit, in as much as the contract conferred on the vendor (as well as the purchaser) a right to determine the agreement in the event of planning consent not being obtained within a stated period.

To be valid waiver must be effected before the time fixed for fulfilment of the condition has expired. Once a condition has been duly waived by one of the parties, it is too late for the other party to seek to avoid the contract under an express power on the grounds of non-fulfilment of the condition. The contractual power of termination is operative only so long as the contract is conditional.

It is not competent for either party unilaterally to waive a condition which is precedent to the formation of a contract[15]. Until the condition is satisfied, no contract exists, so that there is no right or term to waive. Moreover, to allow waiver in such circumstances would enable one party to impose on the other party without his assent a binding contract with different terms.

(e) Uncertainty

A condition that is so vague or imprecise that no definite or practical meaning can be given to it avoids the entire contract. Nevertheless the courts are

---

10 *Brickwood Ltd v Butler and Walters*, ante; *Pine View Developments Ltd v Napthan* (1975) 236 Estates Gazette 53.
11 (1960) 12 P & CR 66; *Morrell v Studd and Millington* [1913] 2 Ch 648 (provision for securing balance purchase moneys to vendor's satisfaction).
12 [1974] 1 All ER 421, criticised at (1975) 39 Conv (NS) 251, 255 et seq.
13 For examples see *Bennett v Fowler* (1840) 2 Beav 302 (condition requiring vendor to make a good title); *Usanga v Bishop* (1974) 232 Estates Gazette 835 (house to be vacated by tenants); *Ee v Kakar*, ante.
14 Waiver was similarly disallowed in *Boobyer v Thornville* (1968) 19 P & CR 768 and *Federated Homes Ltd v Turner* (1974) 233 Estates Gazette 845.
15 *Turney v Zhilka* (1959) 18 DLR (2d) 447; 9 Halsbury's Laws (4th edn) 143, para. 264. Contrast *Scott v Rania* [1966] NZLR 527.

reluctant to declare void on the ground of uncertainty an agreement intended to have legal effect; wherever possible they endeavour to find a reasonable interpretation for the offending clause. The issue of certainty has arisen in a number of recent cases involving mortgage conditions. In *Lee-Parker v Izzet (No. 2)*[16] a contract for sale was expressly subject to 'the purchaser obtaining a satisfactory mortgage'. The concept of a satisfactory mortgage was considered to be too indefinite to be given practical meaning; it left at large two most essential matters — the amount of the loan and the terms of repayment. The contract was, therefore, void for uncertainty. Contrast with this the decision in *Janmohamed v Hassam*[17], where the contract provided that if the purchaser did not obtain a mortgage *satisfactory to him*, the contract should thereupon be rescinded. According to Slade J, the italicised words made all the difference. It was possible to import a term by necessary implication that such satisfaction should not be unreasonably withheld. With that further term imported the condition was not so vague that it could not be given a reasonable effect. Since the condition is for the purchaser's benefit, it is one that he will normally be able to waive[18], but not, it seems, when the condition is void for uncertainty[19].

16   [1972] 2 All ER 800; *Re Rich's Will Trusts* (1962) 106 Sol Jo 75.
17   (1976) Times, 10 June. See also the case cited in the next note at 1105.
18   *Lee-Parker v Izzet* [1971] 3 All ER 1099. 'Subject to mortgage' agreements are infrequently encountered in this country because our 'subject to contract' procedure renders them largely otiose. See Coote, 'Agreements Subject to Finance' (1976) 40 Conv (NS) 37, for a consideration of relevant Commonwealth cases, where such agreements are commonplace in some jurisdictions and Emmet, 86.
19   *Grime v Bartholomew* [1972] 2 NSWLR 827 (subject to finance being arranged).

Chapter 6

Contents of formal contracts

A Drafting the contract: introductory points

1. Use of standard form contracts

(a) Sales by private treaty
It is the usual practice for the parties, whenever a transaction by private treaty involves the payment of purchase money[1], to have a formal contract prepared by their legal advisers. The vendor's solicitor drafts the contract which he submits to the purchaser's solicitor for approval. Both solicitors play their respective parts in formulating the terms of the document. The contract is prepared in duplicate. Each party will eventually sign one copy (his 'part' as it is commonly termed), after which the solicitors will exchange[2] the two parts so that each will have the other's signed part. This procedure is adopted irrespective of whether the title to the land is registered or unregistered.

Frequently the vendor's solicitor drafts the contract on a standard form containing a set of general Condition of Sale. The two most widely used forms are the Law Society's Conditions of Sale (1980 edition)[3] and the National Conditions of Sale (20th edition, 1981). To draft the contract the vendor's solicitor has to add the details, including the Special Conditions of Sale[4], appropriate to the particular transaction. Each set of Conditions has its devotees. Some local law societies publish their own forms, which reproduce The Law Society's form, with various printed alterations or additions. A practitioner may prefer to use his own form of contract, which often incorporates by reference either The Law Society's or the National Conditions of Sale so far as such Conditions are not varied by the express terms of the contract[5]. Late in 1978 a new and complex set of Conditions appeared on the market, published by Eagle Forms (GB) Ltd and known as the Conveyancing Lawyers' Conditions

---

1   As in a conveyance of the freehold, or assignment of a long lease. It is not normal to have a formal contract on the grant or assignment of a short lease at a rack rent (i.e. one representing the full value of the land and buildings).
2   For exchange of contracts, see pp. 237–242, post.
3   For comment and criticism of this latest form, see [1980] Conv 404, [1981] Conv 1.
4   See pp. 150–164, post.
5   Care must be exercised so as to avoid a defective incorporation, as occurred in *McKay v Turner* (1975) 240 Estates Gazette 377.

of Sale[6]. It is perhaps too early to assess what impact this new form will have on conveyancers. The majority of practitioners are reasonably satisfied with one or other of the two main forms, despite criticisms of particular clauses which individual solicitors doubtless have. They may well be reluctant to transfer their allegiance to the new Conditions, and any who do will need to study them very carefully prior to using them.

(b) Sales by auction
When property is to be sold by auction the procedure is somewhat different. The contract and conditions of sale are prepared by the vendor's solicitor, but it is not submitted for approval to solicitors acting for intending bidders. The contract is made available for inspection at the offices of the auctioneer and of the vendor's solicitor a week or so before the date of the auction. Immediately before the auction is conducted prospective buyers are normally allowed to ask questions about the property or the contract. At the conclusion of the auction one part of the contract is signed by or on behalf of the successful bidder, who (or whose solicitor) receives in exchange the part signed by or on behalf of the vendor.

(c) Contracts for use by third parties
The Council of The Law Society consider that the practice whereby a vendor's solicitor prepares a form of contract for the vendor's agent (such as the site office staff of an estate developer) to place before prospective buyers for signature does not accord with proper professional conduct[7]. No steps should be taken which would in any way lead or induce an intending purchaser to sign a binding contract to purchase land without his first obtaining legal advice. It is immaterial that the contract allows the purchaser to rescind without penalty during a stated period. Though he does consult a solicitor within that time, he cannot negotiate any desired amendments to its terms should he desire to proceed with the purchase.

2.   Taking instructions

From the vendor's point of view the contract is a most crucial document. It defines his obligations both in relation to the land and the terms upon which it is to be sold. Unfortunately the drafting of the contract does not always receive the attention that its importance deserves. It is not sufficient to adopt the contract used on the occasion of the vendor's purchase, assuming the solicitor acted on that occasion, though he should undoubtedly peruse that contract and the other documents (e.g. preliminary inquiries) relating to that transaction. Before preparing the contract, the solicitor should arm himself with all necessary information. This might seem axiomatic, but it is not always adhered to in practice. Inquiries should be made of the client to ascertain the need for any special terms to be inserted in the contract, the precise identity of the property especially if situated in a rural area, whether fittings are to be included in the price or taken over at a valuation, whether during his period of

6   Besides providing for the usual matters regulated by the existing standard forms (but with significant differences in some cases), this form contains a number of Optional Conditions dealing with problems not covered by them, such as gazumping and the registration of Class F charges by a non-owning spouse. For a general critique see [1981] Conv 38. In this book it is not proposed to comment in detail upon the provisions of this form.
7   *A Guide to the Professional Conduct of Solicitors* (1974), 78, paras. 2:4, 2:5.

ownership he has entered into any agreements affecting the property[8], to mention but a few matters. Where the property is sold subject to existing leases, full details of the tenancies (i.e. whether contractual or statutory) and the tenants, the rents and the properties should be obtained. Unless he acted for the vendor when he acquired the property, or the title is already registered, the solicitor ought to investigate his client's title to discover any defects of title which may require some special clause in the contract. In some cases a visit to the property may be desirable. Unless specifically requested, it is not a solicitor's duty to advise his client whether the transaction he is instructed to carry through is a prudent one from the client's point of view[9].

To be in a position to draft the contract in a case involving unregistered land, a practitioner needs to have the title deeds in his possession. Where the property is in mortgage (e.g. to a building society) he will not normally be able to obtain the deeds without entering into a written undertaking[10] to hold them to the mortgagee's order. On a sale of registered land the information appearing in the land or charge certificate is widely used as the basis for the draft contract. However, since the certificate may not disclose all the entries recorded against the vendor's title[11], it is always prudent to obtain from the Registry office copies of the subsisting entries.

3. Submission for approval and accompanying documents

Once drafted the vendor's solicitor forwards the contract to his opposite number for approval, enclosing with it a letter expressing the sale (or proposed sale) to be 'subject to contract'. The significance of these words has already been considered[12]. To facilitate its approval it is customary to send copies of any restrictive covenants, or details of other adverse rights, disclosed in the contract. On the assignment of leasehold land a copy of the lease is also forwarded.

One important point must be noted. The vendor is not at this juncture legally obliged to furnish documentary evidence that he is able to convey the subject matter of the intended contract. The complexities at one time affecting the title to land demanded that the deduction and investigation of title were formerly always postponed until after a contract for sale had come into being. For many years Conditions of Sale have contained a term requiring a vendor to deliver an abstract of title after exchange of contracts[13]. Today a not inconsiderable body of professional opinion considers that the abstract should accompany the draft contract. The purchaser's solicitor can thus satisfy himself that the title is sound before his client binds himself to buy; this helps reduce the time-lag between exchange of contracts and completion. Indeed, it is not unusual on a sale of registered property to forward with the draft contract copies of the entries in the vendor's register of title, though the tendency is to send photographic copies produced by the vendor's solicitor himself, rather

8 Especially those of which there may be no evidence with the deeds, e.g. an oral licence granted to a neighbour to lay drains, as in *Ward v Kirkland* [1967] Ch 194, [1966] 1 All ER 609.
9 *Bowdage v Harold Michelmore & Co* (1962) 183 Estates Gazette 233 (no duty to advise as to reasonableness of sale price in option agreement).
10 See further as to undertakings, p. 441, post.
11 See p. 45, ante. See *Faruqi v English Real Estates Ltd* [1979] 1 WLR 963.
12 Pages 126–128, ante.
13 See LSC 12 (1); NCS 9 (1), p. 300, post. For abstracts of title, see pp. 219–303, post.

than office copy entries supplied by the Registry, which the purchaser is entitled to require[14].

The principal justification for the retention of the traditional procedure seems to be one of economy. Both parties are spared the expense of time and effort involved in deducing and investigating the title, should negotiations be broken off and an exchange of contracts never occur[15]. As a means of reducing the frustration felt by the contracting parties before exchange of contracts, the Royal Commission on Legal Services advocated that even in unregistered conveyancing it should become standard practice for a vendor's solicitor to annex the abstract to the draft contract[16]. There can be little objection to adopting this procedure whenever the title is relatively straightforward, as it often is on the sale of the typical urban house. Whether a general rule requiring delivery of the abstract with the draft contract in all cases can be supported is debatable. When the title is lengthy or complicated, objections or queries are likely to be raised by the purchaser's solicitor. In these situations early submission of the abstract may delay exchange, as the vendor's solicitor seeks to remedy the alleged defect or satisfy the purchaser's solicitor that the title offered is sound — assuming he is prepared to go this far. In a seller's market the vendor may be tempted to adopt a take-it-as-it-is-or-leave-it attitude. The intending purchaser is then faced with the prospect of having knowingly to accept a suspect, perhaps even a defective, title if the transaction is to proceed. Under the traditional procedure a purchaser who discovers some defect during his post-contract investigation of the title can require the vendor to rectify the matter, failing which he will often be able to terminate the contract and recover his deposit. But a right of termination is of small consolation[17] to a purchaser who has contracted to sell his existing property on the strength of his contract to buy. Therefore, it is urged, it is better for a prospective purchaser to discover that the title is unsound before committing himself to buy and sell.

When a purchaser is supplied with an abstract of the title prior to exchange of contracts, his solicitor will normally investigate the title before exchange. He is not obliged to do so, unless the contract requires this (as sometimes happens on the sale of new houses on a building estate). If he decides to defer the investigation until afterwards, he should make it clear that exchange of contracts is not to be taken as any acceptance of the title by the purchaser[18].

4.   Contract races

A vendor anxious to secure a quick sale may instruct his solicitor to forward draft contracts to the solicitors acting for different prospective purchasers, stating that he will sell to the one who is the first to return a signed contract with the required deposit. The Council of The Law Society have issued a directive

---

14   LRA 1925, s. 110 (1). LSC 12 (1) confirms this entitlement.
15   See The Law Society's evidence to the Royal Commission on Legal Services, Memorandum No. 3, Pt. II, Sec. XII, p. 122, para. 11.
16   Royal Commission Report, Vol. 1, 285, Annex 21.1, para. 11.
17   Moreover the law hardly affords the disappointed buyer an adequate remedy in damages should the vendor fail to deduce a good title; see the rule in *Bain v Fothergill* [1874] LR 7 HL 158, p. 587, post.
18   Emmet, 127. LSC 12 (3) in effect preserves the purchaser's right to object to defects revealed by a post-contract investigation of the title. But ought a purchaser's solicitor to obtain his client's instructions before deciding to defer the investigation? For investigation of the title, see pp. 364–376, post.

setting out the various obligatory steps to adopt in such cases[19]. The vendor's solicitor must immediately disclose his client's decision direct to the solicitor of each intending purchaser. If given orally it must be confirmed in writing. A purchaser is thus warned of his involvement in a contract race, but this does not enable him to recover wasted expenditure if he is not the first past the post. Should the vendor refuse to authorise disclosure, his solicitor must cease to act for him forthwith.

In the light of the decision in *Daulia v Four Millbank Nominees Ltd*[20] a vendor desirous of starting a contract race should be warned of the possible dangers that he faces. An offer or undertaking to exchange contracts with the first to comply with the condition constitutes a unilateral contract, the offer being subject to an implied obligation not to prevent the condition from becoming satisfied. This obligation arises as soon as a potential purchaser starts to perform it[1]. So, if V's solicitor, acting on instructions, sends draft contracts to the solicitors acting for P1, P2 and P3, V cannot revoke his offer to P1 or P2 once each of them has set in motion steps leading to the performance of the condition. For this purpose it is conceived that P1 and P2 embark on performance (at the latest) when they instruct their respective solicitors to apply for the usual local authority searches or to submit pre-contract inquiries[2], or (perhaps) when either of them applies for a mortgage loan. A revocation communicated to P3 before he or his solicitor has commenced performance is effective to withdraw the offer so far as P3 is concerned. By instigating a contract race V has bound himself to sell, without knowing whether a binding contract will ensue and without being able to sell elsewhere at a higher price so long as his offer remains open for acceptance. At the very least it is vital that the vendor is advised to impose a time limit for the tender of a signed contract.

Of course, the unilateral contract made by V is caught by s. 40 (1) of the Law of Property Act 1925[3]. Nevertheless the statutory requirement of writing may well be met by the fulfilment of the duty, insisted upon by The Law Society, to give written notification of V's decision to institute a contract race. The *Daulia* case also suggests that it may not be possible for the vendor, in an attempt to avoid the consequences just described, to deprive his offer of its potentially binding effect by adopting the usual 'subject to contract' formula[4]. In any event the use of this qualifying phrase in the context of a contract race is self-defeating and likely in practice to dissuade possible buyers from entering the contest.

5. Acting for both parties

It is not appropriate in a book of this nature to discuss the ethics of the same solicitor acting for the vendor and the purchaser in the same transaction, an

---

19 (1977) 74 LS Gaz 834, replacing the *Guide to the Professional Conduct of Solicitors*, 78–79, paras. 3:1, 3:2.
20 [1978] Ch 231, [1978] 2 All ER 557, CA, p. 104, ante.
 1 Ibid., at 238–239 and 560–61, respectively, per Goff LJ.
 2 This step will act as notification to V that they intend to perform the condition, though this is not an instance when communication of acceptance is thought to be required to make the contract binding: *Carlill v Carbolic Smoke Ball Co* [1893] 1 QB 256, at 269–70, CA, per Bowen LJ.
 3 *Daulia's* case, ante. See further, p. 104, ante.
 4 Ibid., at 246 and 566–67, respectively, per Buckley LJ.

issue that has long divided the profession. Prior to 1973 solicitors frequently acted for both parties, in most instances without apparent detriment to either side. But the comparatively few cases where a conflict of interest actually occurred, resulting in an allegation of professional negligence, usually ended up before the courts, and the judges were never slow to censure the practice[5]. The present position is governed by the Solicitors' Practice Rules 1936–72. Rule 2 prohibits solicitors acting for both vendor and purchaser or lessor and lessee in a sale or lease for value at arm's length. To this general rule there are several exceptions, the most important being where—

(i)   both parties are established clients, or associated companies,
(ii)   on a transfer of land the consideration is less than £1,000,
(iii)   there are no other solicitors in the vicinity whom the client can reasonably be expected to consult.

Two offices of the same firm may, subject to certain restrictions, act for the parties if the offices are in different localities. The lack of further explanation of expressions such as 'established clients' and 'vicinity' is intentional; according to The Law Society too precise a definition would merely facilitate circumvention. Each exception is subject to a vital overriding proviso—no *conflict of interest* must appear to exist. Immediately such conflict becomes evident the solicitor should ask both clients in their own interests to seek independent advice. In *Nash v Phillips*[6] Foster J considered that a conflict arose in a transaction where the vendor desired an early completion but the purchaser declined to sign a contract to buy until his existing house had been sold. In a contract race a solicitor ought not to accept instructions to act for more than one prospective purchaser.

When a solicitor does act for both parties, it is common practice for him to prepare a single contract form which they both sign. In this event an exchange of contracts does not take place[7], as happens when the parties are separately represented. An exchange of parts is quite possible and frequently occurs where different branch offices of the same firm are acting for different parties[8].

B   Parts of formal contract

A formal contract is in three parts: the particulars, the conditions of sale and the memorandum for the purposes of s. 40 of the Law of Property Act 1925. The proper office of the particulars is to describe the subject-matter of the contract, that of the conditions to state the terms on which it is sold[9]. It is not clear to what extent the division into particulars and conditions is one of substance or mere traditional convenience. In an old case it was held that a misrepresentation in the particulars could not be cured by information given in the conditions of sale, which revealed the proper position[10]. More recently in a case

5   See e.g. *Moody v Cox and Hatt* [1917] 2 Ch 71 at 91, CA, per Scrutton LJ; *Goody v Baring* [1956] 2 All ER 11 at 12–13, per Danckwerts J; *Smith v Mansi* [1962] 3 All ER 857 at 859–60, CA, per Danckwerts LJ; *Nash v Phillips* (1974), 232 Estates Gazette 1219.
6   Ante, a case involving established clients. See also the *Guide to the Professional Conduct of Solicitors*, 9, para. 2 (1), outlining a solicitor's duty in cases of conflict.
7   *Smith v Mansi* [1962] 3 All ER 857.
8   *Earl v Mawson* (1973) 228 Estates Gazette 529; affd. (1974) 232 Estates Gazette 1315, CA.
9   *Torrance v Bolton* (1872) LR 14 Eq 124 at 130, per Malins V-C, arguendo; affd. (1872) LR 8 Ch App 118.
10 *Robins v Evans* (1863) 2 H & C 410.

involving a clause precluding any annulment of the sale on account of any error or omission in the *particulars*, Sargant J refused to construe the clause so narrowly as to exclude from its purview omissions appearing in that part of the contract headed 'Conditions of Sale'[11]. Furthermore, although it was once said that it was not the function of the particulars to deal with the title[12], it is customary, following the recommendations of The Law Society[13], to incorporate within the particulars not merely a physical description of the property, but also suitable reference to the incumbrances affecting it, whether or not they are also mentioned in the conditions.

The conditions of sale themselves may either be special, or general. The former are specially relevant to the contract in question; general conditions are very much common form, applying more or less to all contracts incorporating such terms. Both The Law Society's and the National Conditions of Sale incorporate a number of Special Conditions relevant to most transactions. These are printed on the back page of each form and need to be completed by the draftsman. The remaining part of the contract is the memorandum of agreement required by the statute, which, in the case of The National Conditions of Sale form, appears at the foot of the document, with a space provided for the signature of the contracting party at the bottom of the page. The front page of this form is reproduced overleaf. The names of the parties, particulars of the property to be sold and details of the purchase price have to be added. The two inside pages of the form are devoted to the General Conditions of Sale[14].

Contracts for sale of registered land

The view has been expressed that on a sale of land registered with an absolute title a contract may be unnecessary. Writing in 1939, the editor of Brickdale and Steward-Wallace's *The Land Registration Act 1925* (4th edn) indicated[15] that a transfer between vendor and purchaser could be effected at one interview by the vendor's producing his land certificate to the purchaser who after a satisfactory perusal pays his purchase money at once in exchange for a duly executed transfer and the land certificate. Expeditious though such a transaction might be, this procedure could hardly be adopted in the vast majority of house transactions. Cash purchases are the exception today, rather than the rule, and few vendors are in a position to hand over the land certificate, since this is always deposited in the Registry, if, as is likely to be the case, the property is subject to a mortgage. Furthermore, substantial legal objections exist to this contemporaneous contract-transfer theory. It has been forcibly urged[16] that a purchaser needs to inspect the register rather than the land certificate which may be out of date, and to preserve priority for himself by making an official search. He should also satisfy himself about the possible existence of overriding interests and the usual local authority searches and inquiries need to be made (though it is only proper to observe that in 1939 the incidence of town planning legislation could hardly have been foreseen).

11 *Re Courcier and Harrold's Contract* [1923] 1 Ch 565.
12 *Blaiberg v Keeves* [1906] 2 Ch 175 at 184, per Warrington J.
13 (1952) 49 LS Gaz 29.
14 See Appendix C.
15 Pages 28–29; R & R (3rd edn), 327. Cf. R & R (4th edn), 304.
16 Potter, 318–19. R & R (3rd edn), 327, were not convinced of the validity of these arguments. Cf. 4th edn.

CONTRACT OF SALE
The National Conditions of Sale, Twentieth Edition

Vendor

Purchaser

Registered Land		Purchase price	£	
District Land Registry:		Deposit	£	
Title Number:		Balance payable	£	
Agreed rate of interest:		Price fixed for chattels or valuation money (if any)	£	
		Total	£	

Property and interest therein sold

Vendor sells as   Completion date:

AGREED that the Vendor sells and the Purchaser buys as above, subject to the Special Conditions endorsed hereon and to the National Conditions of Sale Twentieth Edition so far as the latter Conditions are not inconsistent with the Special Conditions.

Signed

Date   19

The truth of the matter is that it is unwise even in the case of registered titles to dispense with a formal contract. The dangers of proceeding on an open contract basis are illustrated by *Re Stone and Saville's Contract*[17], where the vendor under an open contract failed to disclose the existence of a restrictive covenant noted in the charges register and the purchaser was held entitled to recover his deposit[18]. According to the semi-official view, a formal contract can be dispensed with 'in some instances'[19], but the vast majority of practitioners consider it highly desirable for the parties to sign a contract. It should always be remembered that a formal contract incorporating the standard conditions provides for other matters besides those relating simply to the establishment and proof of the vendor's title. It is not in the parties' best interest to dispense with a formal contract, so depriving themselves of recourse to its provisions if need arises, solely on the ground that the title offered is an absolute freehold.

C   General conditions of sale[20]

Before turning our attention to the Particulars of Sale, it will be helpful to say something at this stage about the nature and function of the General Conditions of Sale. An initial question is, why have them? The answer lies in an understanding of English land law, whose complexities are such that in any contract for the sale of land it is essential that the respective rights and duties of the parties are clearly defined. If the parties have not expressly provided for certain important matters, the law will imply terms regulating them. The term 'open contract' has already been mentioned. An enforceable contract can exist although the parties have done nothing more than state the price and identify the property in writing. This constitutes an open contract. Nevertheless, several fundamental questions remain unanswered. For what estate? What proof of title must the vendor adduce and for how long? When can the purchaser demand possession? These and other basic problems are resolved by the law through the medium of implied conditions. Every open contract is subject to a code of implied obligations, unless specific provision is made to the contrary. These open contract conditions impose onerous terms upon the vendor, and over the years the practice has developed of incorporating within the contract express conditions, designed to facilitate the vendor's task and to cut down the purchaser's rights under an open contract. Such conditions have now become fairly stereotyped and sufficiently general in nature to be capable of being incorporated in a standard form. Every formal contract is made subject to General Conditions of Sale. In the case of The Law Society's form they are made applicable by special condition A which states:

> ' The property is sold subject to The Law Society's General Conditions of Sale (1980 Edition) ("general conditions") printed within so far as they are not varied by or inconsistent with these special conditions . . .'

17 [1963] 1 All ER 353, CA. See also *Faruqi v English Real Estates Ltd* [1979] 1 WLR 963.
18 The covenant had in fact been released, but the purchaser was not informed of this until after commencing his action.
19 R & R (3rd edn), 328. Cf. 4th edn, 304. No indication of these instances were given, except a sale to a sitting tenant. Yet this is a peculiarly inapt example, since it is advisable to provide for possible problems arising from the tenant's failure to complete; see *Nightingale v Courtney* [1954] 1 QB 399, [1954] 1 All ER 362, CA.
20 See generally [1982] Conv 85–93 (Ind).

General Conditions range over a variety of matters; there are provisions regulating the parties' rights of rescission, the charging of interest, the preparation and contents of the transfer deed, and the submission of requisitions. Particular clauses deal with problems raised by existing leasehold interests, undisclosed local land charges, the town planning legislation, etc. In reality, General Conditions are incorporated as an insurance measure. Some may be irrelevant to the contract which may be successfully completed without recourse to the majority of them. Many a vendor and purchaser sign their contracts in blissful ignorance of their existence — and it is perhaps as well! Nevertheless they lurk back-stage, ready to play their part should the need arise. Notwithstanding their generality, it is still incumbent upon a solicitor to consider whether the peculiar circumstances of his case are adequately covered by the General Conditions; if not he should frame a suitable special condition. In particular the two major forms are planned primarily for the sale of houses with vacant possession; consequently either form may require adaptation on the sale of building land, or agricultural, industrial or investment property.

The appearance of a third form of contract with its own set of Conditions of Sale[21] suggests that consideration should be given to the desirability of introducing a statutory form of contract and conditions of sale, or perhaps different forms according to whether the property is residential, industrial, and so on, for universal use on every sale of land. Yet even with a statutory form it would not be possible to deprive the parties of their right to add their own special provisions, or exclude any of the statutory terms. In the course of time recognised variations to the statutory conditions would become common practice, and the position might well be much the same as at present. One advantage of a statutory form is that it would, unless the parties expressly varied its terms, apply to every contract of sale of land, including those that would otherwise have taken effect as open contracts. It must not be overlooked that there already exists a statutory code[1] of conditions of sale prescribed by the Lord Chancellor under the Law of Property Act 1925, s. 46, but this is of very limited application. It is confined to contracts by correspondence, a term of uncertain scope and lacking judicial clarification. It seems to cover an exchange of letters by post, provided these constitute an enforceable contract. Similarly, due exercise of an option to purchase, effected by means of a letter, creates a contract for sale and purchase which, in the absence of any express provision regulating the point, is apparently governed by the statutory code[2]. The code may also by express reference be made to apply to other cases, but in practice it is hardly ever resorted to. It contains no provision substantially differing from what may be termed the standard conditions, and many other matters remain unregulated.

A fuller consideration of individual conditions will be postponed until discussion of the particular topic to which each relates. Though it should not be

---

21 Page 133, ante.
1 See SR & O, 1925, No. 779. The code regulates the date and place of completion, possession and apportionment of outgoings, interest, the delivery of the abstract and requisitions, the preparation of the conveyance and the right of the vendor to rescind in certain cases. See also the statutory conditions of sale made applicable to a sale of land to a tenant under the Leasehold Reform Act 1967, by the Leasehold Reform (Enfranchisement and Extension) Regulations 1967, S.I. 1967 No. 1879, p. 163, post.
2 See *Rightside Properties Ltd v Gray* [1975] Ch 72, [1974] 2 All ER 1169. A well drawn option agreement should stipulate for the resulting contract to be governed by the LSC or NCS. See further Barnsley, *Land Options*, pp. 21–22. Cf. *Pips (Leisure Productions) Ltd v Walton* (1980) 260 Estates Gazette 601.

forgotten that basically most of the General Conditions are modifications or negations of some open contract term, it will be the aim of this book to concentrate upon the General Conditions as they appear in the usual forms of contract and, where appropriate, to consider by way of comparison the corresponding position under an open contract.

D   Particulars of sale

1.   Physical description

The particulars should describe the land to be sold with perfect accuracy and not leave it to inference[3]. Failure to observe this cardinal rule may entitle the purchaser to rescind the contract or oblige the vendor to accept an abatement in the purchase price[4]. It is not uncommon for the vendor's solicitor to adopt the description of the property as it appears in the conveyance to the vendor, at least if he is selling the whole of such property. Yet he should always remember that it is not his duty simply to follow the exact terms of the description of the existing title; he ought to make full inquiry into the facts in order that he may be able to describe correctly the property[5]. The contract description should also be checked against the description in the earlier documents of title, as should the accuracy of all measurements and areas mentioned in the particulars.

(a) Plans
There seems a general reluctance to identify the property to be sold by reference to a professionally prepared plan. If a plan is to be attached to the contract, common sense dictates that it should be accurate, yet many plans are hastily prepared by junior members of the office staff, often using as a basis some out-of-date plan endorsed on an early title deed. It is advisable to have a plan wherever the vendor is selling off a portion of his land[6], particularly when the natural boundaries are not obvious. The absence of any plan increases the risk of the parties, or one of them, being mistaken as to the area of land within the contract. Similarly, on the division of a building into separate parts a large scale plan is essential, showing the rooms and dividing walls if necessary, in order to define the precise boundaries of the sub-divided lots[7]. Where the particulars describe the property by reference to a plan attached to some earlier conveyance of the property[8], a copy of the deed plan should be attached to the contract. It should be checked to ascertain that it accurately shows the property at the present time[9]; it is not unknown for adjacent landowners to alter their

3   *Swaisland v Dearsley* (1861) 29 Beav 430.
4   The nature of the purchaser's remedies are fully considered in Part V of this book.
5   Per Lord Kinnear in *Gordon-Cumming v Houldsworth* [1910] AC 537, at 547, HL.
6   See *Lloyd v Stanbury* [1971] 2 All ER 267 at 273, per Brightman J.
7   Cf. *Scarfe v Adams* [1981] 1 All ER 843, CA (map on a scale of 1:2500 attached to transfer of sub-divided part of house described as 'worse than useless').
8   Most suburban houses are described by reference to the plan on the first conveyance of the property as a separate entity.
9   See *Wallington v Townsend* [1939] Ch 588, [1939] 2 All ER 225, where the contract plan, though an exact copy of the plan on the conveyance to the vendor, included a strip of land on which stood part of the adjacent semi-detached property. It had been overlooked that the vendor had previously purchased the adjacent property and had made certain modifications resulting in an alteration of the boundary between the two properties.

boundaries, and it ought always to be ascertained that the vendor has not entered into any boundary agreement with an adjoining owner.

Care should also be taken to ensure that the plan does not mislead the purchaser. The existence of a right of way over the land should be shown; its non-disclosure may entitle the purchaser to rescind, even though an inspection would readily reveal the way, since the purchaser is justified in relying upon the representation contained in the plan[10]. A plan stated to be for identification purposes only entitles the purchaser to a conveyance of the whole of the land coloured on the plan[11].

(b) Boundaries

General Conditions[12] usually discharge the vendor from any obligation to define the ownership of boundary walls, fences and hedges, though it is usual for the purchaser to attempt to establish this before signing the contract by means of a preliminary inquiry. Where the property sold comprises land of different tenures or of different titles, the vendor does not have to identify the different parts (except to the extent that he can do so from information in his possession). The basic rule appears to be the same even in the absence of such a condition[13].

(c) Conditions as to identity

A purchaser is generally precluded from requiring any further evidence of identity other than that afforded by the particulars and the abstract[14]. Such a condition does not absolve the vendor from establishing identity as part of his obligation to show a good title. A complete failure to identify the property at all entitles the purchaser to rescind and recover his deposit[15]. The only independent evidence of identity that a purchaser may contractually require (but at his own expense) is a statutory declaration that the property has been enjoyed according to the title for at least 12 years. A statutory declaration may be necessary where the land sold forms part of a much larger estate, when it is not unusual to obtain a declaration from an estate agent who has collected on behalf of the vendor the rents and profits from the property to be sold for many years. The fact that the minimum period of enjoyment for the declaration is only 12 years is somewhat limited, though the purchaser is free to seek possible declarants whose knowledge extends for a longer time.

(d) Registered land

In a straight forward case registered land can be adequately described by adopting the description contained in the property register. A copy of the filed plan should be sent with the draft contract. The class of title (i.e. whether absolute, possessory, etc.) can be either incorporated within the particulars or separately mentioned in the Special Conditions. The same need to have a plan exists as with unregistered land if the vendor is selling part only of his property.

---

10   *Dykes v Blake* (1838) 4 Bing NC 463; *Denny v Hancock* (1870) 6 Ch App 1.
11   *Re Lindsay and Forder's Contract* (1895) 72 LT 832.
12   LSC 13 (1), NCS 13 (2).
13   *Dawson v Brinckman* (1850) 3 M & G 53.
14   NCS 13, LSC 13.
15   *Flower v Hartopp* (1843) 6 Beav 476; *Re Bramwell's Contract, Bramwell v Ballards Securities Investments Ltd* [1969] 1 WLR 1659.

2. Legal description

A description of the property cannot be considered adequate unless it states the tenure, and makes mention of the benefits and burdens affecting the property. When drafting the particulars it should always be remembered that, unless the contrary appears, the interest to be sold is to be taken as comprising the fee simple in possession free from incumbrances, and a purchaser is entitled to reject any lesser interest[16]. Where the property is not freehold or is freehold subject to incumbrances not to be discharged on or before completion, care must be taken to refer to such matters.

(a) Tenure

The vendor must not mislead the purchaser into thinking he will obtain something different from what the vendor is able to offer. The particulars should make it clear that the property is freehold or leasehold and in the case of the latter whether the term was created by a head lease or underlease. The vendor does not show a good title to underleasehold property if the contract describes the property simply as leasehold[17]. The purchaser is entitled to know that he will be exposed to the risk of forfeiture through acts done by the underlessor. The purchaser cannot complain of the misdescription if he is aware of the true nature of the vendor's interest when he enters into the contract[18], and it ought to follow that an erroneous description should not be fatal if the contract as a whole contains adequate information to notify the purchaser that the property is held under an underlease[19]. Yet Clauson J held in *Re Russ and Brown's Contract*[20] that this does not suffice; the contract must distinctly specify that what is offered for sale is an underlease. It is submitted that this is too strict a rule. For instance, should the contract provide for the title to commence with a certain underlease, it is conceived that the court would hesitate to refuse to uphold the contract merely because the property was described in the particulars as leasehold rather than underleasehold. That a more liberal approach might prevail today is suggested by the later decision in *Becker v Partridge*[1], where it was doubted whether the description of a sub-underlease as an 'underlease' was a sufficient misdescription justifying rescission.

Similarly a purchaser of an underlease is entitled to be told that the head lease comprises more property than is being sold to him; there is the same risk of forfeiture arising from the acts or omissions of persons over whom he will have no control[2]. In *Becker v Patridge*[3] the court considered that a purchaser's

16 *Hone v Gakstatter* (1909) 53 Sol Jo 286; *Timmins v Moreland Street Property Co Ltd* [1958] Ch 110 at 118, [1957] 3 All ER 265 at 269, CA, per Jenkins LJ. But not if he had knowledge to the contrary at the time of making the contract (ibid).
17 *Re Russ and Brown's Contract* [1934] Ch 34, CA; *Re Beyfus and Master's Contract* (1888) 39 Ch D 110, CA.
18 *Flood v Pritchard* (1879) 40 LT 873.
19 See e.g. *Camberwell and South London Building Society v Holloway* (1879) 13 Ch D 754 at 761−62, per Jessel MR.
20 [1934] Ch 34, CA; *Re Beyfus and Master's Contract* (1888) 39 Ch D 110 at 115, per Bowen LJ, doubting the view of Jessel MR, note 19, ante.
1 [1966] 2 QB 155, [1966] 2 All ER 266, CA.
2 *Creswell v Davidson* (1887) 56 LT 811; *Re Lloyds Bank Ltd and Lillington's Contract* [1912] 1 Ch 601. The same holds true of the assignment of part of the property demised by a head lease, though in this event the contract would provide for the rent to be apportioned, or indicate that it was subject to a rent apportioned by a previous assignment, thus notifying the purchaser of the existence of the other property.
3 [1966] 2 QB 155, [1966] 2 All ER 266, CA.

objection to the lack of such notice cannot be maintained where the property sold is part of a house (e.g. a flat) since it is practically obvious that it will almost certainly be the subject of a letting of the whole house.

As to registered land, the exact nature of the registered title must be made known. To describe a possessory freehold title simply as 'registered freehold property' is positively misleading[4]. Likewise, it seems necessary to make it clear whether leasehold property is held under an absolute or good leasehold title.

(b) Benefits

Appurtenant easements or restrictive covenants existing for the benefit of the land sold should be mentioned in the particulars, though their omission is not fatal. The subsequent conveyance will pass all existing easements without express mention, and it is unlikely that a vendor would be unwilling to assign the benefit of restrictive covenants if his refusal to do so might result in his being unable to enforce the contract.

(c) Burdens

(i) *Duty to disclose.* The state of the vendor's title is a matter exclusively within his own knowledge, and the purchaser is generally in the dark. The vendor is, therefore, duty bound to disclose all latent defects in his title. In this context, the word 'defect' bears an extended meaning. He must disclose any flaw in the documentary title which might affect his ownership of the property and, therefore, his right to deal with it. Such matters are dealt with in the Special Conditions. He must also disclose third party rights which prevent him from conveying free from incumbrances, i.e. all outstanding interests or burdens derogating from absolute ownership of the estate. In this sense a defect in title simply means an incumbrance[5] affecting the property. Within this category come the following: restrictive covenants, easements, rentcharges, overriding rentcharges[6], leases, local land charges, mortgages or charges, licences arising from estoppel or acquiescence. A defect is latent if it cannot be discovered by the exercise of reasonable care on an inspection of the property. With the exception of some easements (for instance, rights of way), none of the incumbrances listed are of such a nature as to be capable of being revealed on inspection. No uniformity of practice exists as to the proper place in the contract for the disclosure of burdens; according to the better view it ought to be a matter of no consequence[7], provided they are properly brought to the purchaser's attention. Existing liabilities are commonly referred to in the particulars (extracts from the relevant documents being attached to the contract) and new burdens in the Special Conditions[8]. Express reference to an adverse right,

---

4   *Re Brine and Davies' Contract* [1935] Ch 388.
5   The word 'incumbrance' is commonly used nowadays to mean any adverse third party right or liability; for a recent judicial example of this usage see *MEPC Ltd v Christian-Edwards* [1979] 3 All ER 752, at 756, HL, per Lord Russell speaking of a contract for sale as an incumbrance on the title. Sometimes it is employed in a narrow sense to connote a charge of a financial nature, as in the LPA 1925, s. 205 (1) (vii). See also p. 499, post.
6   A plot of land may be subject to a rentcharge which issues out of a large plot of land, of which the smaller plot forms part. The rent charged upon the larger plot is known as an overriding rentcharge.
7   *Re Courcier and Harrold's Contract* [1923] 1 Ch 565, p. 139, ante.
8   But see p. 155, post.

though clearly preferable, is not vital. In one case land[9] was sold subject to 'the covenants, conditions, restrictions and stipulations contained in and by' a deed of 1899. This deed referred to an indenture of 1898 which disclosed the existence of an underground watercourse. The purchaser did not consult the earlier document. He was held to have constructive notice of its contents, and this precluded him from objecting to the title. The use of a blanket phrase of the type just considered is very common in practice.

Failure by the vendor to discharge his obligation of disclosure may be a sufficient ground for the purchaser to terminate the contract and recover his deposit, or entitle him to seek a reduction in the purchase price[10]. In the case of a fraudulent concealment the court may even set aside the conveyance after completion[11].

(ii) *Contractual circumventions.* This duty of disclosure imposes a heavy burden on the vendor, for it extends to defects of which he has no knowledge. It is not surprising, therefore, that in the past attempts have been made to relieve a vendor of the obligation by means of a condition to the effect that the property was sold subject to all rights and incumbrances, whether disclosed or not. The courts have not allowed such conditions to flourish. To permit reliance on them would have been 'nothing short of a direct encouragement to fraud'[12]. They simply afforded protection to a vendor if it subsequently turned out that the property was subject to some third party right of which he was unaware. Even constructive notice sufficed to bar recourse to the condition[13].

The standard Conditions of Sale uphold the vendor's basic duty of disclosure. Under a contract governed by The Law Society's Conditions[14] the vendor warrants that he has disclosed all easements, rights, privileges and liabilities of which he knows or ought to know, except such as are known to the purchaser at the date of the contract. Registration of a land charge not disclosed in the contract does not count as notice to the purchaser for this purpose[15]. Subject to this, a purchaser cannot object to an undisclosed incumbrance of which he knew when entering into the contract[16], unless the vendor expressly contracts to convey a good title[17] (which is rare today). The exact significance of this warranty given by the vendor is not immediately apparent. Presumably it is not intended to deprive a purchaser of his right to treat the contract as repudiated on a fundamental breach by the vendor of the duty of disclosure.

9 Re Childe and Hodgson's Contract (1905) 50 Sol Jo 59. Cf. Faruqi v English Real Estates Ltd [1979] 1 WLR 963, p. 349, post.
10 See further as to the purchaser's remedies, pp. 587–594, post.
11 See e.g. Hart v Swaine (1877) 7 Ch D 42, p. 641, post.
12 Nottingham Patent Brick and Tile Co v Butler (1885) 15 QBD 261 at 271, per Wills J; affd. (1886) 16 QBD 778, CA.
13 Cf. Heywood v Mallalieu (1883) 25 Ch D 357 (vendor's solicitor knowing of rumoured existence of easement to use kitchen of property sold, but forbearing to make enquiries).
14 Condition 5 (1), 2 (b); NCS 14 ('Without prejudice to the vendor's duty to disclose all latent easements and latent liabilities known to the vendor to affect the property, the property is sold' subject to various stated adverse rights and liabilities). Planning and other local authority matters are the subject of LSC 3, p. 190, post.
15 LPA 1969, s. 24.
16 Timmins v Moreland Street Property Co Ltd [1958] Ch 110, at 118–19, [1957] 3 All ER 265 at 269, CA, per Jenkins LJ. The rule is confined to irremovable incumbrances.
17 Cato v Thompson (1882) 9 QBD 616, CA.

(d) Disclosure of particular burdens

(i) *Easements.* Although the existence of a right of way may be patent, so that a purchaser who fails to inspect the property cannot complain of its non-disclosure in the contract[18], the courts are generally averse to holding that a right of way is patent. Inspection might reveal the existence of a track, but it may be impossible to tell whether it constitutes a public, or a private, right of way, or merely an accommodation track used by the owner of the land. It is not enough that there exists on the land an object of sense that might put the purchaser on inquiry; to be patent, the defect must be visible to the eye or arise by necessary implication from something so visible[19]. All rights of way should be disclosed, as should other easements, such as rights of drainage[20] or rights of light, but not an agreement preventing the acquisition of a right of light by prescription[1], nor, apparently, rights that may at some indefinite future time adversely affect the land[2].

(ii) *Leases.* Existing tenancies should be revealed, for in the absence of any contrary stipulation, the purchaser is entitled to vacant possession on completion. The rent should be correctly stated[3] so that failure to disclose service of a certificate of disrepair resulting in an abatement of the rent may be fatal[4]. The receipt by the vendor of a notice to quit should be disclosed[5].

The standard Conditions of Sale[6] require the vendor to make available to the purchaser copies or full particulars of the leases or tenancies affecting the property. The purchaser is deemed to have notice of and takes subject to the terms of all existing tenancies and the rights of the tenants, whether he inspects the documents or not. This condition does not enable a vendor to impose on the purchaser a lease different from any of those of which copies have been supplied[7].

(iii) *Exceptions and reservations.* These are not necessarily incumbrances but must be revealed. If the vendor has no title to the mines and minerals under the surface because they have been excepted (i.e. retained) by a previous owner (as is not unusual), the contract should so state. A vendor desiring to reserve some right over the property to be sold must expressly stipulate for it in the contract.

---

18   *Oldfield (or Bowles) v Round* (1800) 5 Ves 508.
19   *Yandle & Sons v Sutton* [1922] 2 Ch 199.
20   See *Pemsel and Wilson v Tucker* [1907] 2 Ch 191 (underground sewer vested in local
     authority).
1   *Greenhalgh v Brindley* [1901] 2 Ch 324; *Smith v Colbourne* [1914] 2 Ch 533, CA.
2   *Dormer v Solo Investments Pty Ltd* [1974] 1 NSWLR 428 (no duty to disclose possibility of
     gas pipe line being laid across land).
3   *Wood v Kemp* (1858) 1 F & F 331; *Jones v Rimmer* (1880) 14 Ch D 88, CA (contract failed
     to mention rent of £43 17s 6d).
4   *Re Englefield Holdings Ltd and Sinclair's Contract* [1962] 3 All ER 503 (purchaser entitled
     to abatement in price). But see LSC 6 (3).
5   *Dimmock v Hallett* (1866) 2 Ch App 21. Cf. *Davenport v Charsley* (1886) 54 LT 372
     (informal intimation that tenant proposing to give up tenancy).
6   LSC 5 (2); NCS 18 (1).
7   *Pagebar Properties Ltd v Derby Investments Holdings Ltd* [1973] 1 All ER 65 (purchaser's
     discovery of undisclosed lease at time of completion). The obligation imposed on a vendor
     by LSC 6 (4) to inform the purchaser of changes in the disclosed terms is to be taken as
     relating to existing leases; it does not affect the principle stated in the text.

Normally no easements are implied in favour of a grantor, and it is too late to insist on a reservation once a contract making no provision for it has been concluded[8].

(iv) *Local land charges.* These will be considered in the next chapter.

(v) *Overriding interests.* There seems no reason why these should be treated any differently from third party rights affecting unregistered land. On a sale of registered land all latent overriding interests should be disclosed. Where a minor interest is protected by an entry on the vendor's register of title, he can discharge his duty by supplying the purchaser with a copy of the subsisting entries on the register.

(vi) *Restrictive covenants.* The vendor must disclose every restrictive covenant affecting the property to any substantial extent[9], including those created prior to the proposed root of title[10]. The burden of showing that an adverse restriction does not substantially affect the land rests on the vendor[11].

(vii) *Sales of leasehold property.* Some of the special problems raised by leaseholds have been mentioned[12]. In the absence of an express condition to the contrary, the vendor must disclose all unusual and onerous covenants contained in the lease, either by specifically referring to them in the contract or affording the purchaser an opportunity of inspecting the lease[13]. The vendor's duty is sometimes eased by providing that the purchaser shall be deemed to have bought with full notice of the contents of the lease (or underlease), whether he inspects the document or not[14]. Such a clause does not override a positive misdescription in the particulars. In *Charles Hunt Ltd v Palmer*[15], leasehold shops described as 'valuable business premises' were subject to convenants restricting their use to a very limited class of business; it was held that the purchaser was not bound to complete though the contract incorporated a condition deeming him to have notice of the lease's contents. There may also be a condition precluding any objection by the purchaser that the covenants and conditions in an underlease do not correspond with those in the superior lease[16]. Under an open contract, non-disclosure of this defect amounts to 'a formidable

8   *Simpson v Gilley* (1922) 92 LJ Ch 194. See also p. 525, post.
9   *Hone v Gakstatter* (1909) 53 Sol Jo 286; *Re Stone and Saville's Contract* [1963] 1 All ER 353, CA (non-disclosure of covenant not to use land otherwise than as private house and garden rendering title 'thoroughly bad').
10 *Re Cox and Neve's Contract* [1891] 2 Ch D 109. For the root of title, see pp. 286–291, post.
11 *Re Ebsworth and Tidy's Contract* (1889) 42 Ch D 23 at 51, CA, per Fry LJ; *Re Higgins and Hitchman's Contract* (1882) 21 Ch D 95; *Re Stone and Saville's Contract*, ante.
12 Page 145, ante.
13 *Reeve v Berridge* (1888) 20 QBD 523, CA; *Molyneux v Hawtrey* [1903] 2 KB 487, CA. Whether a particular covenant can be classified as unusual is a question of fact, depending on, e.g. locality: *Flexman v Corbett* [1930] 1 Ch 672, (covenant not to cause inconvenience to neighbours held unusual). The rule is the same on a contract to grant a sub-lease: *Melzak v Lilienfeld* [1926] Ch 480.
14 LSC 8 (2) (b); NCS 11 (2).
15 [1931] 2 Ch 287.
16 NCS 11 (4).

objection' to the vendor's title[17]. Failure to disclose a rent review notice served by the lessor has been held to constitute a latent defect in title[18].

(viii) *Incumbrances not requiring disclosure.* No duty exists to disclose defects in the physical quality of the land[19], or defects which are patent. It has been held that a notice served by a local authority and requiring the execution of private street works need not be disclosed; an inspection of the property would reveal that such a notice might be served at any time[20]. There is no obligation to disclose a latent incumbrance which will not remain binding on the purchaser after completion. Consequently the particulars should not refer to mortgages to be discharged on or before completion. Incumbrances that have ceased to be enforceable do not, strictly speaking, require disclosure, such as a restrictive covenant that has been openly breached for a long period of time[1]. In *MEPC Ltd v Christian-Edwards*[2] a vendor was held to have shown a good title to freehold land, despite not having disclosed the existence of a contract for sale affecting the land entered into some 60 years earlier. The court was satisfied that in the circumstances the contract had been abandoned and was no longer capable of specific performance. However, in the case of any incumbrance of doubtful validity the vendor is best advised to regulate the position by a special condition in the contract, rather than not disclose it in the expectation that if the purchaser later raises an objection the court will uphold the title offered.

The same procedure should be adopted for an equitable interest governed by the old doctrine of notice, e.g. a pre-1926 restrictive covenant, or an estoppel interest, which the vendor claims is not binding on him because he purchased without notice. A purchaser will not be compelled to accept a title depending upon proof of the seller's lack of notice of an incumbrance. Whether the vendor acquired with or without notice is a question of fact and of evidence capable of being disputed and the courts will not compel the purchaser to buy a law-suit[3]. On the other hand there is no need to disclose a third party right statutorily void against the vendor because of non-registration[4]. In this event he can pass a good title free from it[5].

E   Special conditions of sale

As each particular transaction differs so it is necessary for each contract to incorporate special terms appropriate to that transaction. Some special conditions are so basic as to be present in every contract, like the condition regulating the date of completion. The incorporation of other special terms may be necessary because of the type or location of the property, the state of the vendor's

17   *Darlington v Hamilton* (1854) Kay 550.
18   *F and B Entertainments Ltd v Leisure Entertainments Ltd* (1976) 240 Estates Gazette 455. The obligation to disclose such a notice is now covered by LSC 3 (2) (d).
19   Physical defects come within the caveat emptor rule; see p. 168, post.
20   *Re Leyland and Taylor's Contract* [1900] 2 Ch 625. Cf. *Carlish v Salt* [1906] 1 Ch 335. And see *Spooner v Eustace* [1963] NZLR 913 (no duty to disclose that house encroaches over boundary of adjoining property).
1   *Hepworth v Pickles* [1900] 1 Ch 108.
2   [1981] AC 205, [1979] 3 All ER 752, HL.
3   *Nottingham Patent Brick and Tile Co v Butler* (1886) 16 QBD 778 at 787, CA, per Lord Esher MR.
4   See the LCA 1972, s. 4 (5), (6). No dispute as to possible enforceability can arise, since this is determined by the statute.
5   Cf. *Wilkes v Spooner* [1911] 2 KB 473, CA, p. 383, post.

title, or the nature of the bargain between the parties. It is the responsibility of the vendor's solicitor when drafting the contract to consider carefully what special conditions are warranted by the transaction. In the following pages an attempt will be made to discuss some situations, selective only, when additional clauses are, or may be, desirable. Only a perusal of the various precedent books will reveal how numerous and varied special conditions can be.

Both The Law Society's and the National Conditions of Sale contain a number of printed special conditions covering basic terms relevant in the majority of transactions. These relate to such matters as: the date of completion, the capacity in which the vendor is selling the land, the commencement of the title, vacant possession, incumbrances affecting the property and the prescribed rate of interest for various purposes[6]. Any additional special conditions which the draftsman deems desirable should be inserted underneath the printed conditions.

1. Completion date

Both standard contract forms provide for the insertion of the agreed completion date, though in practice it is not usually filled in until exchange of contracts. At the time the contract is first drafted the parties may have formed but a hazy idea of the completion date. In the absence of any date being expressly stated, the position is governed by the General Conditions[7]. Where time is to be of the essence of the contract[8], a clause to this effect should be added.

2. Capacity of vendor

'The vendor shall convey as beneficial owner', or as the case may be. This condition states the capacity in which the vendor is selling the property and defines the extent of the covenants for title which will be implied on his part in the subsequent conveyance by virtue of s. 76 of the Law of Property Act 1925. Normally it is unnecessary to do more than add the appropriate words, whether beneficial owner, mortgagee, trustee, settlor, or personal representative, which will cause the desired covenants to be implied. In a contract relating to registered land, the vendor's capacity should be given as beneficial owner, personal representative, etc., not as registered proprietor as is sometimes suggested. This latter expression gives no indication how he holds the estate. Some elaboration may be required in special cases, as where the vendor is a tenant for life or statutory owner, when the clause might read:

' The vendor is selling and will convey as tenant for life under the Settled Land Act 1925, the trustees for the purposes of that Act joining in the conveyance for the purpose only of acknowledging the receipt of the purchase money.[9]'

6 The NCS regulate some of these matters on the front page of the form, notably, the completion date and the vendor's capacity.
7 LSC 21 (1); NCS 5 (1). See further pp. 410–411, post.
8 See pp. 412–413, post.
9 1 Prideaux's Precedents, 303. The categories of tenant for life, statutory owner and trustees for sale are not technical expressions resulting in the implication of any covenants for title. Such persons should convey as 'trustees'. Covenants for title are considered in detail in Chap. 23.

Special circumstances may necessitate some limitation of the implied covenants for title as where, for example, the vendor has only a possessory title to part of the land. A reference to the deeds is necessary before this condition can be correctly completed, to ascertain in what capacity the vendor holds the land. However, it does not follow that a purchaser will be entitled to object should the vendor contract to convey in the wrong capacity. The condition does not amount to a warranty that the title will be made in that way, but merely indicates the manner in which the vendor intends to make title. Thus where vendors who were personal representatives contracted to sell as trustees although they had not assented to the property vesting in them as such, it was held that the purchaser must take a conveyance from them as personal representatives[10].

3.   Commencement of the title

The contract should contain a special condition stipulating the document which is to commence the purchaser's investigation of the title, thus: 'The abstract of title shall begin with a conveyance on sale dated 16 January, 1963'. This document is termed the root of title. Under an open contract a purchaser can insist on a root of title going back at least fifteen years[11]. With a formal contract the vendor is free to reduce this period, though he runs the risk of the purchaser's refusal to contract on this basis. A purchaser who accepts less than a fifteen years' title is deemed to have constructive notice of any matters which would have been discovered on an investigation of the title for the statutory period[12]. He also deprives himself of his statutory entitlement to compensation for loss due to undisclosed land charges[13].

When specifying the root of title, a vendor's solicitor ought to state the precise nature of the deed, e.g. a conveyance *on sale*. Simply to provide that 'the title shall commence with a conveyance dated . . .' infers that the document was a conveyance on sale, and that consequently the title was on that occasion investigated and approved. When a title for less than the statutory period is offered, the vendor's failure to disclose that the root of title is a voluntary conveyance makes the condition misleading. In this situation the court will not compel the purchaser to accept a title commencing with such a deed[14].

In the case of leasehold estates, the title usually commences with the lease itself and, omitting the intervening title, continues with an assignment or other document at least fifteen years old. The investigation of title to leasehold land is governed by special statutory provisions. These together with other problems relating to roots of title generally will be discussed in greater detail in Chapters 10 and 11.

---

10   *Re Spencer and Hauser's Contract* [1928] Ch 598. Cf. *Green v Whitehead* [1930] 1 Ch 38, CA.
11   LPA 1969, s. 23, reducing the period of 30 years prescribed by the LPA 1925, s. 44 (1).
12   See p. 284, post.
13   LPA 1969, s. 25, considered at p. 396, post.
14   See *Re Marsh and Earl Granville* (1883) 24 Ch D 11 especially at 23, CA, per Baggallay LJ.

Registered titles
The need to provide for a root of title does not arise in the case of land registered with an absolute or good leasehold title[15]. The purchaser is concerned only with the existing, not the past, state of the vendor's title, for he can rely on the State's certificate that the title is vested in the vendor. The Law Society's Conditions simply give details of the vendor's registered title in alternative special condition E, and provide in a general condition for the vendor to supply the documents, particulars and information specified in s. 110 of the Land Registration Act 1925 (which defines the vendor's obligations as to title on a sale of registered land)[15a]. In the case of a possessory or qualified title, an investigation of the pre-registration title will be necessary, though the vendor is free to stipulate (and he normally does) that no evidence of such title will be adduced. In this event the special condition may, in the case of a qualified title, be in some such form as:

> The title is qualified as follows [*insert qualification*] and the purchaser shall not be entitled to any evidence as to the matters mentioned in the qualification as excepted from the effects of registration[16].

4.   Vacant possession

The contract should indicate whether the sale is with vacant possession, i.e. that the property will be conveyed free from any claim of right to possession by the vendor or a third party so that the purchaser can assume actual uninterrupted possession of the whole. This term also entitles the purchaser to enjoyment of the property free from any physical impediment which substantially interferes with his occupation[17]. This includes the right for the purchaser to occupy the property when it is physically vacant but there are other factors which prevent occupation[18]. Under The Law Society's Conditions the property is sold with vacant possession unless the Special Conditions otherwise provide[19]. A contract governed by the National Conditions normally makes express provision for vacant possession in the Special Conditions, if this is intended, though a term to this effect will be implied in any contract disclosing no tenancies and silent as to vacant possession[20]. It follows that the contract should give details of all leases and tenancies affecting the land to be sold. The vendor

---

15   In the case of registered leaseholds, only short particulars of the lease under which the land is held are given in the property register. The vendor should therefore make a copy or abstract of the lease available to the purchaser.
15a Condition 12 (1) (b) (i); NCS 1 (11). In the NCS form details of the vendor's title appear in the particulars on the front page.
16   See 18 Ency F & P, 657–59, Forms 3:B:20C, E–G.
17   *Cumberland Consolidated Holdings Ltd v Ireland* [1946] KB 264, [1946] 1 All ER 284, CA (rubbish left on premises).
18   See *Topfell Ltd v Galley Properties Ltd* [1979] 2 All ER 388. In the case, part of the premises were subject to a protected tenancy, subject to which the property was sold with vacant possession of the rest. However, a notice under the Housing Act 1961, s. 19 had been served on the property (which the purchaser discovered after contract) stating it was to be occupied by one household only. The purchaser obtained specific performance together with an abatement of the price of £3,850 by £1,000. Templeman J also refused to allow the conditions of sale relating to the need to make enquiries of the local authority (the purchaser made some in writing) to override the express term for vacant possession but cf. *Korogluyan v Matheou* (1975) 30 P & CR 309.
19   LSC Special Condition F.
20   *Cook v Taylor* [1942] Ch 349 at 354, [1942] 1 All ER 85 at 87, per Simonds J.

is obliged to supply copies or abstracts of all leases or written agreements and in the case of an oral tenancy such evidence of its nature and terms as he can supply[1]. This term does not merge in the conveyance however[2].

5.   Matrimonial homes[3]

Quite apart from any right of a spouse to occupy the matrimonial home arising out of any beneficial or legal interest she or he may have, the Matrimonial Homes Act 1967 gave a spouse to register a right to occupy in certain circumstances[4]. The right arises at the latest of three dates (a) when the other spouse acquired the interest (b) the date of the marriage or (c) 1 January 1968[5]. There were potential problems if the other spouse had only an equitable interest[6] but these have been dealt with by the Matrimonial Homes and Property Act 1981[7]. This statutory right has been subject to considerable criticism. The main objection is whether it can ever achieve what it intended to do namely give a right of occupation as against third parties. The problem about such a procedure is the consequence of the delay of registration[8]. From the other spouse's point of view the lack of any procedure whereby he or she is informed of the registration can cause problems as the case of *Wroth v Tyler*[9] shows: —

The defendant lived with his wife and grown up daughter. He was the sole registered proprietor of the property. He wished to move to Norfolk; his wife and daughter were unenthusiastic about this. The defendant advertised the property and eventually exchanged contracts for sale with the plaintiffs on 27 May 1971 for completion on 31 October. He also entered into a contract to purchase a property in Norfolk. On 28 May 1971 the defendant's wife unknown to him lodged a caution at the Land Registry. Eventually it was discovered and he attempted to persuade his wife to vacate the charge which she refused to do. He gave notice to the plaintiffs that he could not complete and they issued a writ for specific performance and damages in lieu or in addition thereto. Megarry J held that they were not entitled to specific performance[10] with vacant possession as this would require the defendant to apply to the Court for a

---

1   LSC 6 (2); NCS 18 (1) where, however, nothing is said as to the vendor's obligations in relation to oral tenancies, save that the purchaser cannot object to there being no agreement in writing. LSC 6 (2) is to this extent clearly preferable.

2   *Hissett v Reading Roofing Ltd* [1970] 1 All ER 122. As to merger see Chap. 15, post.

3   See the Matrimonial Homes Act 1967 and the Matrimonial Homes and Property Act 1981, and S.I. 1981 No. 1275.

4   By a Class F land charge if the title is unregistered and by a notice if the title is registered. These rights can be exercised if the property is held by trustees and the other spouse occupies under the trust see generally Matrimonial Homes and Property Act 1981 ss. 1 and 4 amending Matrimonial Homes Act 1967 s. 2 and Land Registration Act 1925 s. 64. Formerly a caution was lodged; now a notice is lodged but the production of the land certificate is not required.

5   Matrimonial Homes Act 1967, s. 2 (1).

6   See Emmet, 425.

7   Section 1 which gives a right of registration as against the trustees Cf. *Miles v Bull (No 2)* [1969] 3 All ER 1585.

8   It is void against any purchaser in unregistered land and a transferee for valuable consideration in registered land being a minor interest and not an overriding one the Matrimonial Homes Act 1967 s. 2 (5) (7); Land Charges Act 1972, s. 4 (2), (5), (8).

9   [1973] 1 All ER 897.

10   As to this aspect of the case see Chapters 21, 22 and 23, post.

termination of his wife's rights[11] and this was not appropriate. Nor were they entitled to specific performance subject to the rights but with an abatement of the purchase price as this would split up the defendant's family. They were however entitled to substantial damages based on the value of the property at the hearing (some £5,500) in substitution of the claim for specific performance.

The defendant was unable to pay this sum otherwise than by selling the property pursuant to his bankruptcy. The land charge is not enforceable against the trustee in bankruptcy[12] with the result that the defendant's wife would lose out in any event. This was pointed out to her by the judge and he adjourned the case to enable her to reconsider her refusal to vacate the registration. She still declined so to do with the probable results above[13].

Although the use of the Class F cannot be used to stultify the property as opposed to protecting rights of occupation[14], it appears to be true to say that: —

> 'Here should be displayed in every conveyancer's office the minatory legend cave uxorem'[15].

It is felt that any comment beyond this case would be entirely superfluous.

6. The deposit

The payment of a deposit on exchange of contracts is a matter regulated by the General Conditions[16] and will be considered in a later chapter.

7. Burdens

Both the standard forms of contract envisage that liabilities or burdens such as restrictive covenants or easements (whether subsisting or to be created) will find their way into the Special Conditions[17]. Leases and tenancies are normally dealt with in a separate condition. It is essential to set out in the contract the precise terms of covenants and easements which the vendor proposes to create or reserve. Care must be taken to ensure that these will be enforceable and effective to protect the vendor's interests[18]. On the sale of a house on a building estate, it is usual to provide that the conveyance or transfer to the purchaser shall be in the form of the specimen document attached to the contract, and in this way the covenants, exceptions and reservations become incorporated within the contract.

---

11 Under the Matrimonial Homes Act 1967, s. 1 (2).
12 The Matrimonial Homes Act 1967, s. 2 (5).
13 See [1973] 1 All ER 897 at 924.
14 *Barnett v Hassett* [1982] 1 All ER 80. On a sale with vacant possession it becomes a term of the contract that the Class F shall be cancelled by the vendor, Matrimonial Homes Act 1967, s. 4.
15 [1973] 1 All ER 897 at 925.
16 LSC 9; NCS 2, both providing for payment of a 10 per cent deposit; see pp. 250–254, post.
17 But see further, p. 146, ante.
18 Cf. *Cordell v Second Clanfield Properties Ltd* [1969] 2 Ch 9, [1968] 3 All ER 746 (reservation of right of way over estate roads for access to vendor's retained land without imposing obligation on developer to construct road giving suitable access). See also *Nickerson v Barraclough* [1981] 2 All ER 369. The Courts are reluctant to allow vendors to shelter behind standard conditions; see e.g. *Faruqi v English Real Estates Ltd* [1979] 1 WLR 963; *Topfell Ltd v Galley Properties Ltd* [1979] 2 All ER 388.

8.   Variations of General Conditions

The General Conditions apply only so far as they are not varied by or inconsistent with the Special Conditions. The rate of interest payable in certain circumstances is frequently raised above the rate specified in the General Conditions. The amount of the deposit may be varied by agreement. Should the purchaser desire to pay less than the required 10 per cent, it is his solicitor's duty to ascertain beforehand that the vendor is willing to accept a smaller amount. Alas, some practitioners adopt the discourteous and unprofessional habit of sending with the purchaser's part of the contract a cheque for a smaller deposit with the request that the vendor accept it in lieu of a full deposit. For the vendor's solicitor to accept less than the prescribed 10 per cent in such circumstances without his client's authority would amount, it seems, to professional negligence[19].

As a converse to variation, some General Conditions are made applicable only if the Special Conditions so provide[20].

9.   Fixtures and fittings

Fixtures[1] are regarded as part of the realty and so form part of the property to be sold. Subject to any contrary provision, once the contract has been signed a vendor cannot remove, e.g. a valuable ornate door[2], or even fruit trees or rose bushes[3]. A purchaser is under no obligation to pay extra for the fixtures passing to him, unless the contract otherwise provides. Articles not constituting fixtures can therefore be taken by the vendor, or if the purchaser wishes to acquire them he can be asked to pay for them. The parties to a contract often prefer to deal with the sale of chattels and fittings themselves. Where such items are numerous or expensive they are well advised to regulate the matter formally, so obviating future disputes, by annexing to the contract an inventory or schedule of the chattels and fittings to be bought by the purchaser at the agreed price. The standard forms of contract contemplate that a separate price will be negotiated for the chattels and fittings forming part of the sale. Provision is made for this figure to be included in the details of the purchase money appearing on the front page of the document[4]. Where there is an indivisible contract with a single price for the land and the chattels, a memorandum that omits the term relating to the chattels does not satisfy s. 40 (1) of the Law of Property Act 1925[5]. The purchaser could, however, waive the term in his favour as to these.

10.   Defects of title

The vendor's solicitor must not assume that his client's title is in apple-pie order, unless perhaps he acted for the vendor when he acquired the property!

---

19   See *Morris v Duke-Cohan & Co* (1975) Times, 22 November.
20   See e.g. LSC 4 (opportunity for purchaser to rescind in certain events).
1   As to the test for deciding whether an object is or is not a fixture, see *Holland v Hodgson* (1872) LR 7 CP 328 at 334, per Blackburn J; *Berkley v Poulett* (1976) 241 Estates Gazette 911, CA. See generally M & W, 711–19.
2   *Phillips v Lamdin* [1949] 2 KB 33, [1949] 1 All ER 770.
3   *Sinclair-Hill v Sothcott* (1973) 26 P & CR 490 at 494, per Graham J. See also the question on the standard form of pre-contract inquiries, post.
4   Page 140, ante.
5   *Ram Narayan v Rishad Hussain Shah* [1979] 1 WLR 1349, PC (a decision on a Fijian Ordinance equivalent to s. 4 of the Statute of Frauds 1677).

There may be some defect which casts doubt on the vendor's ownership of the estate, or renders it uncertain whether he can convey free from certain incumbrances, such as a restrictive covenant believed to have become unenforceable by acquiescence. Or it may be that though the vendor has a good title, he may be unable to give proof of some matter on which the title depends. By taking proper precautions a solicitor can both protect his client's interests and save himself (as well as his client) inconvenience and expense. As Simonds J once remarked:

> ' The vendor can, by appropriate provisions in the contract, enormously safeguard himself against any undue trouble to which he might be put by inquiries about facts which took place some time ago'[6].

Any special condition of this nature must be clearly and unambiguously phrased. Since it operates to curtail the purchaser's rights under an open contract, the contra proferentem rule will apply. Various attempts have been made in the past to cater for specific defects, and with varying measures of success.

(a) Assumptions

A purchaser may be required to assume the truth of something which the vendor is not in a position to establish by legal proof, such as satisfaction of a mortgage. Such a condition is valid, even though it is intended to cover a flaw which goes to the root of the title[7]. A vendor cannot require the purchaser to assume that which the vendor knows to be false[8]. Provided all the facts are fully disclosed, it is not necessary to explain in the condition the specific defect in the title which it is intended to cover[9]. On the other hand a failure to state the legal effect of the assumption may make the condition misleading, as where the vendor frames the condition in such a way as to suggest he has a title to the property, though in fact he has none. The vendor cannot avail himself of the condition in such circumstances[10].

(b) Acceptance of vendor's title

A term, sometimes inserted in contracts for the assignment of leasehold property, that the vendor's title shall be accepted by the purchaser who shall raise no requisition or objection thereon does not absolve the vendor from his obligation to disclose defects of which he knows or ought to know[11]. Where the

---

6 *Re Holmes and Cosmopolitan Press Limited's Contract* [1944] Ch 53 at 57, [1943] 2 All ER 716 at 718. This is equally the case in registered land; see *Re Stone and Savilles Contract* [1963] 1 All ER 353; *Faruqi v English Real Estates Ltd* [1979] 1 WLR 963.
7 *Re Sandbach and Edmondson's Contract* [1891] 1 Ch 99, CA (condition requiring purchaser to assume that a predecessor in title died before a certain date, intestate and without heirs).
8 *Re Banister, Broad v Munton* (1879) 12 Ch D 131, CA.
9 *Smith v Watts* (1858) 4 Drew 338; *Re Sandbach and Edmondson's Contract*, [1891] 1 Ch 99, CA.
10 *Re Cumming to Godbolt* (1884) 1 TLR 21. In the *Faruqi* case, supra, Walton J said the test is whether an 'ordinary purchaser' as opposed to a 'trained equity lawyer' would understand the problem (at 967). The defect in question was an absence of a copy of the deed creating restrictive covenants referred to on the register. The title may perhaps be accepted if office copies are supplied before the contract.
11 *Re Haedicke and Lipski's Contract* [1901] 2 Ch 666 (onerous covenants); *Becker v Partridge* [1966] 2 QB 155, [1966] 2 All ER 266, CA (breaches of covenant of which vendor's solicitors ought to have been aware).

purchaser agrees to buy all the vendor's estate, right and interest (if any) in certain property, he cannot later complain that the title is bad[12], though he is entitled to the best title the vendor can produce[13]. Conditions requiring the purchaser to accept such title as the vendor has are sometimes encountered when the vendor has encroached on waste land adjoining his property[14].

(c) Restriction on right to inquire about earlier title

A condition which precludes the purchaser from inquiring about the title before a certain date may be effective to prevent his objecting to a defect in the title prior to that date. The effect of the condition depends in each case on its precise wording. A condition that merely restricts the purchaser's right to raise requisitions on the title deduced leaves him free to object that the title is bad if he discovers from other sources (aliunde) that it is defective. So he can insist on an objection to the prior title discovered on examination of the deeds[15]. On the other hand a condition that the lessor's title 'will not be shown and shall not be inquired into'[16], or that the title prior to a certain date 'shall not be required, investigated or objected to'[17] requires that the title shall be accepted without obligation. It is now statutorily enacted that a purchaser shall make no requisition, objection or inquiry with respect to the title prior to the date fixed as the commencement of the title, and this provision takes effect as if it were an express stipulation in the contract[18].

Nevertheless stringent conditions of this nature are subject to important limitations. A purchaser is not prevented from objecting to the title on the ground of some undisclosed incumbrance, such as restrictive covenants, even though created before the root of title[19]. The vendor cannot evade his duty of disclosure in such a facile manner. Furthermore the courts will not decree specific performance against the purchaser when its effect would be to compel him to pay his money for nothing because the title offered is so bad that he could be turned out of possession immediately. *Re Scott and Alvarez's Contract, Scott v Alvarez*[20] provides a good illustration of the application of this rule.

> Leasehold property was sold under a condition that the purchaser should not make any objection or requisition in respect of the intermediate title between the granting of the lease and a certain assignment. The purchaser discovered *aliunde* that the intermediate title rested on a forged deed and a conveyance by a trustee purporting to convey as beneficial owner.

12   *Hume v Pocock* (1866) 1 Ch App 379.
13   *Keyse v Hayden* (1853) 20 LTOS 244. Apart from any contrary provision, he must convey such right or interest free from an existing incumbrance (*Goold v Birmingham, Dudley and District Bank* (1888) 58 LT 560). Cf. *Fowler v Willis* [1922] 2 Ch 514.
14   For precedents, see 18 Ency F & P 645–47.
15   *Smith v Robinson* (1879) 13 Ch D 148; *Waddell v Wolfe* (1874) LR 9 QB 515.
16   *Hume v Bentley* (1852) 5 De G & S 520.
17   *Re National Provincial Bank of England and Marsh* [1895] 1 Ch 190.
18   LPA 1925, s. 45 (1), (11), p. 289, post.
19   *Nottingham Patent Brick and Tile Co v Butler* (1886) 16 QBD 776, CA.
20   [1895] 2 Ch 603, CA. Prior to this, the CA had held (see [1895] 1 Ch 596) that it was not sufficient for the purchaser merely to show that the title was doubtful or open to suspicion. It was not until after judgment in the earlier proceedings that the purchaser discovered the forgery and was given leave to re-open the case. See also *MEPC Ltd v Christian Edwards* [1979] 2 All ER 752, HL.

The Court of Appeal refused to award the vendor a decree of specific performance but held that the condition precluded the purchaser from recovering his deposit[1].

(d) Correct procedure

If there is a defect in the title, the wisest course is to set out in the condition all the relevant facts, remembering not to mislead the purchaser, and then to stipulate that the purchaser shall make no requisition or objection on account of the facts stated. A prudent purchaser will endeavour to probe the defect by asking preliminary inquiries. In the last resort the decision to buy must be his, and the more informative the special condition, the quicker the purchaser should be in making up his mind. From the vendor's position, it is far better that the purchaser decides not to proceed before exchanging contracts than that he should rescind afterwards on the ground that the condition is misleading and does not preclude him from objecting to the defect.

The form of the special condition in the case of *Blaiberg v Keeves*[2] serves as a helpful illustration. There the property sold was originally leasehold but enlarged into a fee simple by deed executed under s. 65 of the Conveyancing Act 1881[3]. There were doubts whether this deed was effective. One of the conditions of sale read:

> ' The property was formerly held . . . under an indenture of lease dated January 31, 1672, for a term of 500 years at a yearly rent of 1/-, but the property was assigned in the year 1828 free from the rent which has never been paid by the vendor and the purchaser shall assume that the rent has been released and is not now charged upon the property sold. By a deed poll in 1902 under the Conveyancing Act 1881, the property was expressed to be enlarged by the beneficial owner into a fee simple. It shall be assumed that the deed poll operated as an effectual enlargement according to its tenor.'

The abstracted deeds between 1828 and 1902 still described the property as subject to the 1/- rent and the purchaser objected that the assumption he was required to make was to the vendor's knowledge untrue and he sought rescission. Warrington J held that the circumstances were such that the vendor might reasonably believe the property was freehold; there was no misrepresentation and the purchaser's claim failed.

11.   Missing documents[4]

The mere fact that the vendor has lost or mislaid the title deeds does not release the purchaser from performance of the contract, but the vendor must furnish satisfactory secondary evidence of the contents and execution of the missing documents[5]. Strictly speaking there is no need to disclose in the contract the

---

1   The court will enforce a title which though bad from a technical conveyance point of view, is good from a businessman's point of view (commonly called a good holding title); see p. 282, post. Loss of the deposit is now subject to the discretion vested in the court under the LPA 1925, s. 49 (2); see p. 583, post.
2   [1906] 2 Ch 175.
3   See now the LPA 1925, s. 153.
4   Walford, 'Missing Title Deeds' (1949) 13 Conv (NS) 349.
5   *Re Halifax Commercial Banking Co Ltd and Wood* (1898) 79 LT 536.

fact that they are missing[6]. The vendor must, however, hand over on completion all the deeds relating solely to the land conveyed and he must bear the expense of obtaining them[7], unless the contract provides otherwise.

It is in the vendor's interest to provide for missing documents by way of a special condition, setting out what secondary evidence will be provided. This may take the form of a counterpart, draft, copy, abstract, or a recital if coupled with long uninterrupted possession under the lost document[8]. Where all the deeds have been lost or destroyed, it will be necessary to obtain a statutory declaration explaining the loss and also the best secondary evidence available in the circumstances, such as an abstract of title compiled from draft documents prepared by solicitors who acted on previous transactions. It may well be advisable to obtain a declaration from the solicitor who acted for the vendor on the purchase of the property to the effect that a good and marketable title was deduced by the then vendor, that the documents of title were examined, the conveyance to the purchaser duly executed, stamped and completed, and the deeds handed to the purchaser or forwarded to the mortgagee (as the case may be). The loss of a single deed can be covered by a condition that the purchaser shall be satisfied with the production of a document purporting to be a copy of the missing deed and requiring him to assume the original was duly executed[9]. If a land or charge certificate has been lost, an application can be made for the issue of a new certificate[10]. As between vendor and purchaser, and notwithstanding any stipulation to the contrary, the vendor must pay the costs of proceedings required to enable the Registrar to proceed without it[11].

It sometimes happens that the deeds reveal the existence of restrictive covenants or exceptions and reservations affecting a large area of land, including the property to be sold, but no copies of such matters or extracts from the relevant documents are with the vendor's deeds. The vendor should disclose the existence of these covenants, etc., in the contract. To save him the trouble and expense of obtaining copies, a special condition should be inserted precluding any requisition or objection in respect thereof and exempting the vendor from any obligation to furnish copies or abstracts. Purchasers do not generally object to this condition, especially if the incumbrances have been created or reserved many years beforehand. They may not relate to the land to be sold (otherwise there would usually be a copy with the deeds) or even if they do, they are probably no longer subsisting, though legal proof is not forthcoming. Before accepting such a condition, a purchaser's solicitor should ascertain by means of a preliminary inquiry that no attempt has been made to enforce the incumbrances against the vendor.

---

6   *Re Stuart and Olivant and Seadon's Contract* [1896] 2 Ch 328, at 335, CA, per Kay, LJ.
7   *Re Duthy and Jesson's Contract* [1898] 1 Ch 419.
8   *Moulton v Edmonds* (1859) 1 De G F & J 246.
9   Due execution of missing documents must be proved (*Bryant v Busk* (1827) 4 Russ 1), though due stamping will be presumed (*Hart v Hart* (1841) 1 Hare 1).
10 LRA 1925, s. 67 (2); LRR 1925, r. 271. A statutory declaration explaining the loss and the efforts made to trace the certificate is required and a bond may also be necessary, indemnifying the Chief Land Registrar from any loss sustained by reason of the issue of a new certificate. See Practice Leaflet for Solicitors No. 3.
11 LRA 1925, s. 110 (6).

12.   Sales-off

Special problems arise when a vendor sells part only of his land and retains adjoining property. To take a simple case. V owns a house in a large garden, part of which he proposes to sell to P. It has already been noted that as a general rule no rights will be implied in V's favour over P's adjacent plot. Apart from any express restriction, V cannot restrain P from building on his plot so as to interfere with the light to V's windows. If V decides to sell the house and retain part of the garden for himself, the subsequent conveyance to P may operate to pass to P easements under the rule in *Wheeldon v Burrows*[12] or under the Law of Property Act 1925, s. 62[13] and these may seriously hamper V in his use of the retained land.

The Law Society's Conditions provide[14] that the conveyance shall contain such reservations in favour of the retained land and grants over it as would be implied had there been a simultaneous sale to purchasers of both properties. This is a considerable improvement on the earlier. It is of course still beneficial to the vendor but not to the extent as was formerly the case[15]. This clause does not appear to negative s. 62. It also includes a warranty provision concerning disclosure of easements[16].

13.   Sales to existing tenants

Similar problems may arise when a vendor is selling the freehold to his tenant. Prima facie any right or privilege, capable of existing as an easement, granted to him during the tenancy over the landlord's adjacent land may be enlarged by the conveyance into an easement by virtue of s. 62. Apart from some special provision in the contract, it may be more difficult for a vendor-landlord to establish that no such right has passed for it has to be assumed that the terms of the bargain are intended to be in accordance with the rights or privileges which the tenant has been allowed to enjoy in fact[17]. Where the purchase results from the exercise by the tenant of an option to purchase, its exercise results in the creation of an open contract, unless the landlord has had the foresight when granting the option to stipulate on what conditions he is prepared to convey the freehold.

Prima facie an agreement by the tenant to purchase the demised premises does not operate to surrender his existing tenancy[18]. The terms of the agreement may have this effect as where, for example, it is provided that interest shall be payable from the expiration of a notice exercising an option to

---

12   (1879) 12 Ch D 31, CA.

13   Except in relation to the easement of light (*Broomfield v Williams* [1897] 1 Ch 602, CA) s. 62 does not apply where prior to the conveyance both plots of land have been owned and occupied by the vendor (*Long v Gowlett* [1923] 2 Ch 177,). See further pp. 527–530, post, but the precise limits of the rule are not clear. See *Sovmots Investments Ltd v Secretary of State for the Environment* [1979] AC 144, HL, and [1977] Conv 415 (Harpum); [1978] Conv 449, (P.W. Smith); [1979] Conv 113 (Harpum); and [1979] Conv 311 (P.W. Smith). The author would not wish to say anything at present but will rest content with the above.

14   LSC 5 (3) (b)

15   See [1980] Conv 404 at 408 (H.W. Wilkinson). Cf. NCS 20 introducing in the 20th edition a more draconian provision.

16   See the criticism of the form of the conditions of sale generally [1981] Conv 1.

17   *Goldberg v Edwards* [1950] Ch 247 at 257, CA, per Lord Evershed MR (privilege afforded tenant after taking possession but before execution of formal lease).

18   *Doe d. Gray v Stanion* (1836) 1 M & W 695.

purchase[19]. Under the standard Conditions of Sale[20] rent continues to be payable until the actual date of completion by virtue of the provision that income and outgoings are to be apportioned as at that date. The contract does not therefore operate to determine the tenancy, with the result that the vendor cannot obtain possession if the tenant fails to complete. This can be avoided[1] by providing that the tenancy shall be surrendered on the making of the contract and thereafter the tenant shall remain in occupation as licensee. It may not be in the tenant's interests to agree to such a clause; a change in the character of his occupancy from statutory tenant to licensee results in his losing the protection of the Rent Act 1977[2].

A sale to a sitting tenant is often at a price below that which the property would fetch if sold on the open market with vacant possession. If it is thought the tenant might resell at an increased price and so make a profit, the vendor should reserve a right of pre-emption at a specified price in the event of a resale within a certain period[3].

Leasehold enfranchisement
The Leasehold Reform Act 1967, enables a tenant of a house held on a long lease (basically a tenancy granted for a term of years certain exceeding twenty-one years) at a low rent[4] to acquire on fair terms the freehold or obtain an extension of 50 years to his existing term[5]. This right can only be exercised by a person who as tenant has occupied the whole or part[6] of the property as his residence for a period of three years (or periods amounting to three years in the last ten) at the time when he exercises his right[7], but once exercised the benefit of the rights acquired are transmissible to the tenant's assigns.

A qualified tenant[8] wishing to take advantage of the Act must serve on his landlord a notice[9] which, if valid, creates a contractual relationship between them binding the landlord to make and the tenant to accept a conveyance of the freehold (or a grant of an extended lease as the case may be)[10]. The rights and obligations of the parties arising from the notice

19 *Cockwell v Romford Sanitary Steam Laundry Ltd* [1939] 4 All ER 370, CA; *Turner v Watts* (1928) 97 LJKB 403, CA (interest payable from date of contract).
20 NCS 6 (2); LSC 19.
 1 *Nightingale v Courtney* [1954] 1 QB 399, [1954] 1 All ER 362, CA, a decision on LSC (1953 edn) 6 (2) which expressly provided that there should be no determination, a condition omitted from the 1980 edn.
 2 *Turner v Watts* (1928) 97 LJKB 403, CA.
 3 See further, Emmet, 80–81.
 4 Defined by the Leasehold Reform Act 1967, s. 4. The rent must generally be under two-thirds of the rateable value of the property. The Act does not apply to premises where the rateable value exceeds £750 (£1500 if in Greater London): ibid., s. 1 (1) (a) unless it was a tenancy created after 18 February 1966 when the figures are £1000 and £500 (Housing Act 1974 s. 118).
 5 The existing tenancy is replaced by a new tenancy for a term which terminates 50 years after the expiration date of the existing tenancy: s. 14 (1).
 6 See *Harris v Swick Securities Ltd* [1969] 3 All ER 1131 (tenant occupying part and sub-letting remainder entitled to acquire freehold of entirety). See also *Poland v Cadogan* [1980] 3 All ER 544 dealing with periods of absence.
 7 Section 1 (1) (b). See the Housing Act 1980, s. 141, Sch. 21, para. 1 (1).
 8 For the position where the notice is served by a sub-tenant, see s. 5 (4), Sch. 1.
 9 See the form of notice prescribed by the Leasehold Reform (Notices) Regulations 1967, S.I. 1967 No. 1768, as amended by the Leasehold Reform (Notices) Regulations 1969, S.I. 1969 No. 1481 and the Housing Act 1980 Sch. 21, para. 7; *Lewis v Harries* (1971) 22 P & CR 905.
10 Section 8 (1). The subsequent discussion in the text relates to cases where the tenant desires to acquire the freehold.

' inure for the benefit of and [are] enforceable against them . . . to the like extent (but no further) as rights and obligations arising under a contract for a sale . . . freely entered into between [them]'[11].

This ensures that the ordinary incidents, rights and remedies attaching to a normal contract for the sale of land will apply to the transaction. Rights and obligations arising under the notice may pass to the personal representatives and assigns of either party, but they determine on an assignment of the lease without the benefit of the notice[12]. The notice operates as an estate contract and is registrable as a Class C (iv) land charge or may be the subject of a notice or caution under the Land Registration Act 1925[13]. Failure by the tenant to protect his rights will not normally be fatal, since there is nothing to prevent service of another notice on the purchaser of the freehold reversion, save in those cases where the tenant's notice must be served within a prescribed period[14]. The purchase price is calculated as provided by the Act and is to take account of any defect in the landlord's title which might be expected to result in a deduction of the price on a sale in the open market[15]. The tenant can escape from his contract by serving on the landlord within one month of the determination of the price a written notice of his unwillingness or inability to acquire at that price but he may be obliged to pay compensation to the landlord[16].

Since a binding contract arises on service of a valid notice, it was highly desirable that the parties' contractual obligations should be expressly regulated, otherwise the position would have been the same as under an open contract. Section 10 of the Act regulates the terms of the conveyance to the tenant, in relation to the grant or reservation of easements, the imposition of restrictive covenants, and other related matters[17]. In addition, the then Lord Chancellor, acting under powers vested in him by s. 22 (2) of the Act, made the Leasehold Reform (Enfranchisement and Extension) Regulations 1967[18], which prescribe the conditions of sale applicable to a transaction undertaken to give effect to the tenant's notice. They provide for such matters as payment of a deposit, delivery of proof of the landlord's title, requisitions, completion, apportionment of outgoings, the preparation and contents of the conveyance, and the parties' rights on failure to comply with their respective obligations. Of the matters already discussed in this chapter, it should be noted that the landlord can by written notice require the payment by way of deposit of a sum equal to three times the annual rent payable under the tenancy or £25 (whichever is greater) either to himself or to an agent or stakeholder nominated by him[19]. It is

---

11   Section 5 (1).
12   Section 5 (2).
13   Section 5 (5). The lease itself is not registrable (ibid); it is difficult to see how it could be, since it is the fact of residence for the qualifying period that establishes the right, not the lease itself. Nor do the tenant's rights arising from the notice constitute an overriding interest within the LRA 1925, s. 70 (1).
14   See s. 22 (1) (a), Sch. 3, para. 2; Housing Act 1974, s. 118 (4).
15   Section 9 (1), (2).
16   Section 9 (3). He is also precluded from serving another notice to acquire the freehold within the following three years. See also s. 19 (14).
17   See further, p. 553, post.
18   S.I. 1967, No. 1879.
19   Ibid. See Schedule, Part I, condition 1. Some of the other obligations similarly do not come into operation until service of an appropriate written notice, see e.g. condition 3 (delivery of proof of title).

also provided that rent shall continue to be payable until actual completion, so that the tenant's notice cannot operate as a surrender of his lease[20].

These conditions apply unless the landlord and tenant otherwise agree[1]. However as service of the notice constitutes a binding contract which statutorily incorporates these conditions, it is not possible for one party to insist upon other terms. A vendor-landlord cannot, having received a valid notice from his tenant, submit a draft contract incorporating the National Conditions and then, on the tenant's refusal to sign such a contract, decline to proceed. There is already a binding contract in existence which the tenant can enforce with the statutory conditions. Subject to these conditions and any others incorporated by agreement, the rights of the parties will be the same as under an open contract.

14.   Public sector tenants

Statutory provision affecting public sector tenants have been introduced which give them the right to buy under the Housing Act 1980. The provisions are very detailed and are outside the scope of this book[2].

F   Conditions avoided by statute

Certain conditions are rendered void by statute. Apart from a few isolated provisions dealing with a miscellany of matters[3], these prohibited stipulations fall into two main categories: those relating to the legal estate and those designed to ensure that a purchaser is free to employ his own solicitor.

1.   Conditions relating to legal estate

The basis of post-1925 conveyancing is the legal estate. Equitable interests are to be kept off the legal title and overreached on a conveyance to a purchaser wherever possible. The Law of Property Act 1925 contains certain provisions designed to ensure that a vendor utilises this machinery.

Section 42 (1) renders void a stipulation requiring a purchaser of a legal estate in land to accept a title made with the concurrence of a person entitled to an equitable interest, if a title can be made discharged from the interest without such concurrence, under a trust for sale or under any statute such as the Settled Land Act 1925, or the Law of Property Act 1925[4]. Thus a purchaser from a single trustee for sale cannot by contract be compelled to take a conveyance with the beneficiaries joining in to release their rights. The purchaser can insist upon the appointment of a second trustee[5]. Nevertheless the subsection leaves a purchaser free to accept a title made with the concurrence of equitable

---

20   Ibid., condition 7. Other valid reasons exist why there can be no surrender, such as the tenant's right of withdrawal under s. 9 (3). The other conditions will be considered, where necessary, when the relevant matters are discussed in later parts of the book.
1   S.I. 1967 No. 1879, r. 2.
2   For a detailed treatise see Emmet, 2nd Supplement pp. Ci–Cxiii.
3   E.g. see Stamp Act 1891, s. 117 (p. 442, post; LPA 1925, s. 125 (2), as amended by the LP (Am) A 1926, Schedule (p. 290, post) and the LRA 1925, s. 110 (p. 350, post).
4   Equitable interests may be overreached on a conveyance of the land in any of the situations enumerated in the LPA 1925, s. 2 (1), (2). But see [1980] Conv 427 (Sydenham); [1981] Conv 219 (Martin).
5   See the L.P.A. 1925, s. 27, p. 326, post.

owners, if he wishes[6]. Moreover, under the Law of Property (Amendment) Act 1926, s. 1 (1), land which constitutes settled land by reason only of the fact that it is charged voluntarily with the payment of an annuity, rentcharge for life, etc.[7], can be sold subject to such charge, without the necessity of having to adopt the Settled Land Act machinery.

As a corollary to s. 42 (1), it is provided that a purchaser shall not be required to pay or contribute towards the costs of obtaining any document necessary to bring into operation the appropriate overreaching machinery. A stipulation to the effect that the purchaser must bear the expense of tracing or getting in any outstanding legal estate, or preventing any objection being taken by him on account of an outstanding legal estate is similarly avoided. The enforcement by the purchaser of any right under the section does not entitle the vendor to rescind the contract[8].

Not all equitable interests are capable of being overreached, for some are protected by registration. If the purchaser is entitled to the legal estate discharged from any equitable interest protected by registration, which will not be overreached by the conveyance to him[9], he can require free of expense to himself the registration to be cancelled or the equitable owner to concur in the conveyance. A stipulation to the contrary is void[10].

2.   Employment of own solicitor

Apart from some statutory prohibition, it might be an easy matter for the vendor to foist a bad title upon a purchaser by requiring him to employ the vendor's own solicitor. Section 48 (1) of the Law of Property Act 1925, makes void any stipulation which restricts a purchaser in the selection of a solicitor or requires the conveyance, or the registration of title, to be prepared or carried out at the purchaser's expense by the vendor's solicitor. Similarly any provision in a lease (or underlease) made before or after the Act whereby dealings with the lessee's interest, e.g. by way of assignment, are to be prepared by the lessor or his solicitor is rendered void. In lieu of any such covenant, there is implied an obligation on the lessee's part to register all assignments and devolutions with the lessor or his solicitor at a fee of one guinea[11]. Failure to comply with this covenant enables the lessor to exercise any power of re-entry reserved in the lease. Section 48 does not prevent the voluntary employment by the purchaser of the vendor's solicitor, but as we have seen[12] the occasions when a solicitor can properly act for both parties have been severely curtailed. The section also expressly preserves the right for a vendor to furnish a specimen form of conveyance from which the purchaser can prepare a draft, and to charge a reasonable fee, a procedure which is commonly adopted on the sale of houses on a building estate to ensure uniformity of conveyance. Where a perpetual rentcharge is to be reserved as the only consideration in money or money's

---

6   See *Cole v Rose* [1978] 3 All ER 1121 at 1127, per Mervyn Davies QC.
7   See SLA 1925, s. 1 (1) (v).
8   LPA 1925, s. 42 (2), (3), (8).
9   It will be recalled that in some cases, an annuity, limited owner's charge or general equitable charge may be overreached, notwithstanding registration under the LCA 1972; see M&W, 382.
10   LPA 1925, s. 43 (1).
11   LPA 1925, s. 48 (4). See the Decimal Currency Act 1969, s. 10, and Sch. 1.
12   See pp. 137–138, ante.

worth, the vendor can stipulate that the draft conveyance shall be prepared by his solicitor at the purchaser's expense. The Act does not alter the practice whereby, on the grant of a lease, the lease is prepared by the lessor's solicitor at the lessee's expense[13].

13   LPA 1925, s. 48 (3). This must now be read subject to the Costs of Leases Act 1958, which exempts a tenant from having to pay the landlord's costs, unless the parties otherwise agree in writing, thus abrogating the custom recognised by *Grissel v Robinson* (1836) 3 Bing NC 10.

Chapter 7

The purchaser's inquiries and searches

A Introduction

In the previous chapter it was seen that the law imposes on the vendor a limited duty of disclosure only. Yet a purchaser's decision to proceed with the transaction may depend mainly on information which the vendor is under no duty to disclose, such as the condition of the property, or of which the vendor is not even aware. To protect himself the purchaser needs to have the property surveyed and to make searches and inquiries not only of local authorities but also of the vendor himself. This chapter considers the nature of, and need for, the following:

  (i)   an independent survey of the property,
  (ii)   pre-contract (or preliminary) inquiries,
  (iii) a search in the register of local land charges,
  (iv)   additional local authority inquiries,
  (v)   a search in the land charges register,
  (vi)   a search in the public index map.

There may also be compelling reasons why a purchaser's solicitor ought to inspect the property, not to check its structural condition, but to view the physical features of the land[1]. These could have important legal implications. The existence of paths may be revealed, problems relating to access discovered, projections from adjoining properties spotted, and not the least is the necessity to check the accuracy of any contract plan. The existence of vacant land adjacent to the property should prompt inquiries as to the possible future development of that land, and the enjoyment of light over it[2], but without first viewing the property the practitioner cannot appreciate whether any need exists to raise these matters. An inspection may also disclose third party rights not mentioned in the contract, though a mere external observation is not likely

---

1 Cf. The Law Society's Digest, Opinion No. 127, stating that though it is the solicitor's duty to satisfy himself as to the identity of the property purchased, the method of doing so is a matter for his discretion and a personal inspection of the property is not, as a rule, necessary. But cf. now after *Williams and Glyn's Bank Ltd v Boland* [1980] 2 All ER 408, p. 57, ante.

2 A contract for the sale of a house with windows overlooking land of a third person imports no warranty that the windows are entitled to the access of light over that land: *Greenhalgh v Brindley* [1901] 2 Ch 324 at 328, per Farwell J.

to reveal the existence of occupational rights of third parties[3]. It is not thought that many practitioners do view their clients' properties, even where factors such as distance do not render this impossible. It therefore behoves a solicitor to ascertain as much as he can from his client about the layout of the property, its physical features and the occupation of persons other than the vendor.

B   The caveat emptor rule

1.   Need for independent survey

For many generations the law of this country has been well settled that on a contract for the sale or letting of land there is prima facie no warranty as to the habitability of the property erected on it. It is not the vendor's duty to reveal defects in the physical condition of his property, rather the purchaser's responsibility to discover them for himself[4]. Indeed he does not need to rely on the seller's skill and knowledge. He can view the state of the property and satisfy himself of its condition, if he wishes, and judge its suitability for its intended purpose. Different considerations may arise if the vendor deliberately conceals defects, or volunteers information. In addition the Misrepresentation Act 1967, greatly increases a purchaser's rights. For statements made as to condition, if inaccurate, may have far more serious repercussions than previously, resulting perhaps in the purchaser's obtaining rescission for a non-fraudulent misrepresentation even after completion, or damages in lieu[5].

The problems raised by the caveat emptor rule have been fully considered by the Law Commission[6], and some of their recommendations have been implemented, with modifications, by the Defective Premises Act 1972, which came into operation on 1 January 1974. In relation to the purchase of existing property the Act makes no change in the law governing the contractual position regarding defects of quality[7]. The Law Commission considered that any alteration in the existing law would be undesirable, particularly for purchasers of residential property[8]. Such a purchaser's interests are best served by an independent survey undertaken on his behalf. A right of action against a vendor (who may in the meantime have died or disappeared) for breach of warranty as to structural condition is no real substitute for a thorough inspection of the property by a qualified person before contract. Yet many purchasers do not in fact commission an independent survey. On a purchase of fairly modern property, a purchaser often dispenses with his own survey if he is

3   On the present state of the authorities it is not clear what precise inquiries should be made by or on behalf of the purchaser of persons (other than the vendor) in occupation of the property in order to ensure that the purchaser is not fixed with constructive notice of such persons' rights (if any) on account of his failure to inspect the property or enquire of the occupier. See *Caunce v Caunce* [1969] 1 All ER 722; *Hodgson v Marks* [1971] Ch 892, [1971] 2 All ER 684, CA; *Williams and Glyn's Bank Ltd v Boland* [1980] 2 All ER 408, HL. The problem is further discussed in Chap. 14, pp. 381–382, post.
4   But see [1980] Conv 287 (Eric L. Newsome) as to the erosion of the principle.
5   See further pp. 184–185, post. During the Lords' debates on the Bill, Lord Upjohn opined that the Act would go a long way to removing the caveat emptor rule: H.L. Debates, 17 May 1966, Vol. 274, col. 943.
6   Report on the Civil Liability of Vendors and Lessors for Defective Premises, Law Com. No. 40, 1970.
7   It is not retrospective in effect either: *Alexander v Mercouris* [1979] 3 All ER 305, CA.
8   Law Com. No. 40, paras. 17–19. The problem of newly built houses is considered later, p. 175, post.

obtaining a mortgage, choosing to rely instead on the survey carried out on behalf of the mortgagee, on the basis that if there is anything radically wrong with the property the mortgagee will either refuse a loan or require any major defects to be remedied. The cost of the mortgagee's survey is borne by the purchaser-mortgagor, but the surveyor's report is solely for the mortgagee's purposes. A purchaser has no right of action against a building society in respect of a negligent survey[9]. To confer on the purchaser a statutory right to see the mortgagee's report would be at best only a partial solution to the problem, for its primary purpose is to assess the value of the property as a security rather than to point out specific defects, though these two aspects are often closely related. Nor can a purchaser-mortgagor derive much comfort from s. 30 of the Building Societies Act 1962, whereby a building society is deemed to warrant to a prospective borrower that the purchase price is reasonable; societies generally exercise their statutory right to give the borrower written notification that the making of an advance implies no such warranty, although the practice of disclosing the survey to the purchaser is becoming more prevalent. In principle there is no justification for not doing so as there is no real conflict between the building society requirements and that of the purchaser. The problem however is to the purpose of the survey although it is done to ensure the property is a satisfactory security there may be many things wrong with a property which would concern a purchaser but which would not be revealed by such a survey. This is increasingly the case the lower the amount sought to be borrowed.

A solicitor should point out to his client the desirability of having an independent survey. Failure in this respect does not appear to constitute professional negligence unless he advises a survey by some unqualified person and the purchaser suffers loss by reason of a negligent survey[10]. The proper measure of damages can be the cost of repairs. Further the time for the repairs can be postponed if the claimant cannot afford to execute immediate work[11].

2. Extent of rule

The doctrine confers on the vendor a far-reaching immunity which is not confined merely to the structural condition of buildings[12].

(a) Legal unfitness

The law treats legal unfitness in the same way as physical or structural unfitness. On a demise of property there is no implied condition on the landlord's part that the premises are legally fit for the purpose contemplated by the tenant

---

9   *Odder v Westbourne Park Building Society* (1955) 165 Estates Gazette 261. An action may lie against the negligent surveyor, even under the principle of *Hedley Byrne & Co Ltd v Heller & Partners Ltd* [1964] AC 465, [1963] 2 All ER 575, HL. See *Yianni v Edwin Evans & Sons* [1981] 3 All ER 592, and the statistics given therein concerning the numbers of purchasers who neglected to obtain an independent survey; i.e. less than 10–15 per cent obtained an independent survey; see further [1981] Conv 435 (M.R. Brazier and G.K. Pople).

10 See *Collard v Saunders* (1971) 221 Estates Gazette 795 (liability admitted; plaintiff recovered damages for injury to health). But why should he not be negligent in view of the serious consequences of the failure.

11 *Dodd Properties Ltd v Canterbury City Council* [1980] 1 All ER 928, CA, disapproving a dictum of Denning LJ in *Philips v Ward* [1956] 1 All ER 874.

12 *Cheator v Cator* [1918] 1 KB 247, CA (no liability for death of tenant's mare after eating overhanging branches of tree on landlord's adjoining land).

and known to the landlord. In *Hill v Harris*[13], a sub-lessee was permitted by his sub-lease to use the premises for the business of a confectionery and tobacco retailer. Such user was in fact prohibited by the head lease and the head lessor refused to consent to such use. The sub-lessee was held to have no action against his landlord. Similarly, it appears to be the purchaser's duty to ascertain whether the existing use of the land is an authorised one for the purposes of the Town and Country Planning Acts; the vendor gives no warranty that it is[14].

It does not follow that a purchaser prevented from using the property for the intended purpose is necessarily without redress. Legal unfitness stemming from an undisclosed restrictive covenant may result in a purchaser of freehold land rescinding the contract, or suing after completion for breach of the covenants for title. A purchaser of land described by the vendor as suitable for building may be entitled to rescind the contract if he later discovers the existence of an undisclosed underground culvert which renders the land unsuitable for building[15]. But provided the purchaser is not being forced to take property substantially different from that agreed to be sold, the contract may be enforced against him subject to compensation[16].

(b) Vendor's liability for negligent work[17]

The old cases established that a vendor was immune from liability even in respect of defects in his property rendering it dangerous or unfit for habitation, which he himself had negligently created[18]. This principle was held in *Otto v Bolton*[19] by Atkinson J, at first instance not to have been affected by *M'Alister or Donoghue v Stevenson*[20], so that a builder of a new house was not liable to the purchaser's mother who was injured when the ceiling collapsed. Subsequent cases endeavoured to restrict the scope of the immunity to builders who were also vendors or owners[1]. The Law Commission felt[2] that this immunity, creating as it did distinctions which were capricious and difficult to justify, should be abolished. Effect has been given to this recommendation in s. 3 of the Act which in terms merely provides that a vendor's duty of care in respect of work done on land is not abated by its subsequent disposal. Section 3 is not retrospective; in the case of a sale of property it does not apply in relation to premises where the contract for sale was entered into before the commencement of the

13   [1965] 2 QB 601, [1965] 2 All ER 358, CA, applying a dictum of Devlin J, in *Edler v Auerbach* [1950] 1 KB 359 at 374, [1949] 2 All ER 692 at 699.
14   *Gosling v Anderson* (1971) 220 Estates Gazette 1117; revsd. on other grounds (1972) 223 Estates Gazette 1743, CA. The purchaser's rights are often governed by the General Conditions; see NCS 15; LSC 3.
15   *Re Puckett and Smith's Contract* [1902] 2 Ch 258, [1900–03] All ER Rep 114, CA.
16   *Shepherd v Croft* [1911] 1 Ch 512; *Re Belcham and Gawley's Contract* [1930] 1 Ch 56. For misdescription and non-disclosure, see Chap. 23.
17   See 'Defective Premises Act 1972 – Defective Law and Defective Law Reform' [1974] CLJ 307, [1975] CLJ 48 (J. R. Spencer). Defective Premises: – Negligence Liability of Builders' [1979] Conv 97 (N. P. Gravells) and 'Damage by Subsidence: – the Conveyancing Problem' [1979] Conv 241 (H. Street).
18   *Bottomley v Bannister* [1932] 1 KB 458, CA (negligent installation of gas boiler causing purchaser's death).
19   [1936] 2 KB 46, [1936] 1 All ER 960. As to the purchaser's rights, see p. 172, post.
20   [1932] AC 562, [1932] All ER Rep 1, HL.
 1   *Gallagher v McDowell Ltd* [1961] NI 26; *Sharpe v ET Sweeting & Son Ltd* [1963] 2 All ER 455.
 2   Law Com. No. 40, paras. 38–47.

Act. As it transpires, however, s. 3 may do no more than give statutory recognition to what appears to be the true common law rule, for shortly after the introduction of the Bill in the Commons, a majority of the Court of Appeal held in *Dutton v Bognor Regis United Building Co Ltd*[3] that the vendor's (or builder's) immunity did not in fact survive *Donoghue v Stevenson*. The supposed distinction between liability for chattels and liability for real property was untenable, and *Otto v Bolton* was wrongly decided. This has been extended to non professional builders also[4].

Consequently both at common law and under the Act a vendor who executes any work of construction or repair to his property owes a duty in respect of defects caused by his careless performance of the work. The duty is owed to all persons likely to be affected by such defects, the purchaser, subsequent purchasers, other occupiers and visitors, and seemingly exposes the vendor to the risk of an endless series of claims. One consideration may operate to restrict his liability. By analogy with the manufacturer's duty for defective chattels, an intermediate inspection or opportunity of inspection may suffice to break the relationship between the vendor and a subsequent purchaser[5], save as to hidden defects which a survey would not disclose. On the other hand it was once thought that time (subject to concealed fraud by covering up the foundations) began to run when the work was done[6]. However it has now been decided that time runs from when the damage is actually sustained[7].

No duty of care is owed in respect of defects not created by the vendor, even though he is aware of their existence. The Law Commission did recommend in relation to known structural defects the imposition of a duty to take reasonable care to ensure that the purchaser (and others) were reasonably safe from injury[8]. This proposal attracted considerable criticism and, perhaps as a matter of political expediency, no attempt was made to implement it[9].

3   [1972] 1 QB 373; [1972] 1 All ER 464, CA. This case has now been followed; see *Anns v Merton London Borough Council* [1978] AC 728; and *Batty v Metropolitan Property Realisations* [1978] 2 All ER 445, CA. It appears from these cases that a builder has a common law duty to build a dwelling so as to comply with building regulations and so as not to constitute a hazard or injury to health; see [1978] AC 728 at 760–762, per Lord Wilberforce; and [1978] 2 All ER 445 at 457–458 per Megaw LJ. There is still an arguable difference relative to a qualitative defect (cf. Stamp LJ in *Dutton* and Bridge LJ in *Batty*). The latter is considered a preferable view.
4   See *Hone v Benson* (1978) 248 Estates Gazette 1013 (a 'do it yourself builder').
5   *Dutton v Bognor Regis Building Co Ltd* [1972] 1 QB 373 at 396, [1972] 1 All ER 462 at 474, CA, per Lord Denning MR. But see [1980] Conv 287, 295 et seq and the cases cited there.
6   [1972] 1 QB 373 at 396–97, [1972] 1 All ER 462 at 474–75, adopting *Bagot v Stevens Scanlon & Co* [1966] 1 QB 197 at 203, [1964] 3 All ER 577 at 579, CA, per Diplock LJ. Sachs LJ expressed no concluded view on the limitation point; see pp. 405 and 482, respectively. It is interesting to note that both Lord Denning MR, and Sachs LJ, held that the defective foundations amounted to more than pure economic loss and constituted physical damage to the house.
7   *Anns case* and *Sparham-Souter v Town and Country Development (Essex) Ltd* [1976] QB 858 at 867–8, [1976] 2 All ER 65 at 69–70, CA, per Lord Denning MR. Cf. Defective Premises Act 1972, s. 1(5) where times runs from the date of the completion of the dwelling.
8   Law Com. No. 40, paras. 48–55, Draft Bill, cl. 3.
9   It may well be that much of the criticism was misguided. The duty proposed was not a duty of disclosure, but a duty to ensure reasonable safety, and in normal circumstances a vendor would have been able to discharge this duty by revealing specific defects after completion.

3.   Exceptions to caveat emptor

In some circumstances a purchaser, or lessee, may have a cause of action in respect of defective premises.

(a) Collateral warranty

A purchaser can maintain an action for breach of a collateral warranty, or contract, as to fitness. The difficulty has always been to decide when a representation made during the negotiations preparatory to the contract amounts to an actionable warranty. According to A. L. Smith MR, in *De Lassalle v Guildford*[10]:

> 'To create a warranty, no special form of words is necessary. It must be a collateral undertaking forming part of the contract by agreement express or implied, and must be given during the course of the dealing which leads to the bargain, and should then enter into the bargain as part of it.'

In this case a tenant refused to sign his lease unless the landlord assured him the drains were in good order. The landlord gave the assurance; he was held liable to the tenant in damages when the drains proved to be defective. Collateral warranties have also been held to arise where a purchaser entered into a contract to buy a new house on the strength of the builder's assurance that it was very well built and there was nothing to be afraid of[11], and where the purchaser of a building plot fronting an unmade road was informed that it would be constructed[12]. In these three instances the purchaser was entitled to recover damages after completion. In some cases the law implies a warranty upon which an action can be founded[13].

The changes made by the Misrepresentation Act 1967, in the law relating to innocent misrepresentation will doubtless make it less necessary for a purchaser to try to establish the existence of a collateral warranty. But it is a debatable point whether the Act renders any distinction between them completely otiose, as the Law Reform Committee fondly hoped[14].

(b) Sale of leasehold property

On a sale of leasehold property subject to a leasee's covenant to repair, a purchaser can require the vendor to repair the property in accordance with the covenant as part of his obligation to assign a good title[15]. Assuming the lease contains a forfeiture clause, any outstanding breach of covenant renders the interest defeasible at the lessor's option, and the court will not order specific performance against the purchaser. The purchaser's rights are subject to any condition to the contrary. He will not be entitled to complain if the contract incorporates the National Conditions of Sale, Condition 13 (3) of which states

---

10   [1901] 2 KB 215 at 221, CA; *Buchanan v Kenner* [1952] CPL 180 (assurance that dry rot eliminated).
11   *Otto v Bolton* [1936] 2 KB 46, [1936]1 All ER 960.
12   *Jameson v Kinmell Bay Land Co Ltd* (1931) 47 TLR 593.
13   See p. 178, post.
14   See p. 185, post.
15   *Barnett v Wheeler* (1841) 7 M & W, 364; *Re Highett and Bird's Contract* [1903] 1 Ch 287. The purchaser's knowledge of want of repair is immaterial. As to the obligation to show a good title, see pp. 278–286, post.

that a purchaser is deemed to purchase with full notice of the actual state and condition of the property[16].

(c) Leases
Apart from any express obligations undertaken by a landlord, there is at common law an implied warranty that a furnished house is fit for habitation when let[17], but no obligation exists to keep it habitable[18]. Various statutory provisions afford a measure of protection to tenants in certain cases by implying conditions of fitness or imposing repairing obligations on the landlord[19].

4. Builder's liability in respect of new houses

(a) At common law
Two fundamental reasons exist why the maxim caveat emptor cannot apply on the sale of a house to be erected or in course of erection[20]. First, the house is uncompleted, perhaps not even built; so the purchaser cannot finally inspect it before deciding to buy. Secondly, as there is not merely a contract to sell, but also a contract by the vendor to do building work, it is only natural and proper that there should be an undertaking that the building work should be done properly. This gives rise to the rule that when a purchaser buys a house from a builder who contracts to build it, there is a threefold implied warranty[1]:

  (i)   that the builder will do his work in a good and workmanlike manner,
 (ii)   that he will supply good and proper materials and
(iii)   that it will be reasonably fit for human habitation.

The decision in *Hancock v B. W. Brazier (Anerley) Ltd*[2] is one of several cases recognising this implied warranty.

> A builder sold a house in course of erection to the plaintiff. He agreed to erect the house in a proper and workmanlike manner. The sale was made subject to the National Conditions of Sale (16th Edn.) so that by Condition 12 (3) the purchaser was deemed to buy with full notice of the property's state and condition. The material (hardcore containing sodium sulphate) used in laying the foundation for the concrete floors was unsuitable, causing the floors to crack, though the builder was not negligent in failing to appreciate the dangers in using the hardcore.

The plaintiff recovered damages for breach of the implied warranty of fitness of materials. Several points arose. The express term for completing the house in a proper manner only related to workmanship; it did not operate to

16 LSC 5 (2) (a) is to the same effect. See *Lockharts v Bernard Rosen & Co Ltd* [1922] 1 Ch 433; *Butler v Mountview Estates Ltd* [1951] 2 QB 563, [1951] 1 All ER 693. But see *Hancock v Brazier* [1966] 2 All ER 901, post. The Condition afforded no immunity to the vendor in *Hone v Benson* (1978) 248 Estates Gazette 1013, p. 171, note 4, ante.
17 *Smith v Marrable* (1843) 11 M & W 5.
18 *Sarson v Roberts* [1895] 2 QB 395.
19 Housing Act 1957, s. 6 (1), (2); Housing Act 1961, ss. 32, 33; see further M & W, 680–683. See also the Defective Premises Act 1972, s. 4, which imposes on a landlord a duty to ensure reasonable safety in certain circumstances.
20 *Perry v Sharon Development Co Ltd* [1937] 4 All ER 390 at 395–96, CA, per MacKinnon LJ.
 1 *Hancock v B. W. Brazier (Anerley) Ltd* [1966] 2 All ER 901 at 903, CA, per Lord Denning MR.
 2 [1966] 2 All ER 901; *Lawrence v Cassel* [1930] 2 KB 83; *Miller v Cannon Hill Estates Ltd* [1931] 2 KB 113.

exclude the implied warranty as to materials. Nor did Condition 12 (3) prevent recovery, for it did not apply to the contract to erect the building[3].

Liability for breach of the warranty is contractual and only the original purchaser can sue for its breach. The limitation period will normally run from the date of the breech. In comparison the builder's liability in tort for negligently constructing a house is, as we have noticed, much wider.

(b) Exclusion of implied warranty

It by no means follows that these implied warranties operate whenever a new house or flat is bought. Where the house is complete at the time the contract is entered into, no warranty is implied[4]. The purchaser has every opportunity to have the property fully surveyed before contracting to buy. No room for any implied term of fitness exists where the contract contains an express term as to the way the house is to be built and the builder complies with his contract[5].

In the past builders have not been slow to devise means to exclude the operation of any implied warranty, but it required very clear words to debar the purchaser from exercising his ordinary rights of suing if the work was not properly done in accordance with the contract[6]. Many builders were prepared to assume a contractual liability to remedy major structural defects discovered within a certain period (often six months) after completion. Undertakings of this nature afford the purchaser some limited protection but, so it was once thought, precluded complaints about other defects. However in *Hancock's* case the Court of Appeal, construing a typical defects clause, held that it did not bar the purchaser's rights in respect of defects not discoverable within the contractual period of six months. Even with regard to those discovered within six months, it only required the vendor to make defects good and did not exclude liability in damages. It is interesting to note that the court construed the clause strictly in circumstances not involving negligence on the builder's part.

As from 1 January 1974, builders of new houses became subject to the statutory duties imposed by the Act of 1972, though the common law rules will continue to regulate their liabilities arising under building contracts entered into before that date and contracts afterwards when the Act 1972 has no application.

(c) Statutory liability

The need to protect house purchasers from jerry-building, shoddy workmanship and sub-standard materials has been increasingly recognised over the

---

3   Alternatively, the condition could be regarded as inapplicable to the contract on account of its inconsistency with the express clause, a view favoured by Diplock LJ at first instance; see [1966] 2 All ER 1. See now NCS 13 (3).

4   *Hoskins v Woodham* [1938] 1 All ER 692. Representations as to the qualities of the house may constitute a collateral warranty enabling the purchaser to sue, even where the house is completed: *Birch v Paramount Estates (Liverpool) Ltd* (1956) 168 Estates Gazette 396.

5   *Lynch v Thorne* [1956] 1 All ER 744, CA (rain penetrating 9 in solid brick wall making room uninhabitable); cf. *King v Victor Parsons & Co* [1972] 2 All ER 625; affd. [1973] 1 All ER 206, CA.

6   *Billyack v Leyland Construction Co Ltd* [1968] 1 All ER 783 at 787, CA, per Edmund Davies LJ (provision that habitation certificate to be 'conclusive evidence' of completion of house no bar to complaints of structural defects); *Hancock v B. W. Brazier (Anerley) Ltd* [1966] 2 All ER 901, CA; *Perks v Stern* (1972) 223 Estates Gazette 1441 (clause excluding liability for any form of consequential loss or damage held not to bar claim for damages for failure to complete house in good and workmanlike manner).

years, and this has been accompanied by growing criticism of the law's ineffectiveness in providing a solution. Individual house purchasers were in practice been unable to negotiate better terms for themselves because of the take-it-or-leave-it attitude adopted by many developers. It was left to an independent but Government approved non-profit making organisation, the National House Builders Registration Council, to take the initiative. This Council, comprised of members of the National Federation of Building Trades Employers and other interested organisations, was first established as long ago as 1937 to ensure a high standard of design, workmanship and materials in house-building. It is only during the past few years, however, that the Council's scheme has become widespread, due partly to the support given by the Building Societies Association. During recent years this Association has also played a part in preventing the widespread use of exemption clauses by recommending member societies to refuse to advance money on the security of properties built under agreements which precluded recourse to common law remedies.

In view of the long and loud clamour for adequate consumer protection for purchasers, it is hardly surprising that the Law Commission urged that a builder's duties in relation to the construction of new dwellings should be put on a proper statutory footing. The Defective Premises Act 1972, gives effect to their recommendations[7].

(i) *Nature of duty*. Subject to one basic exception to be considered in the following section, the Act imposes[8] on a builder (and certain other people to be noted in para. (iii) below), a statutory duty equivalent in terms to the implied warranty existing at common law, i.e. a duty to see that his building work is done in a workmanlike manner with proper materials so that when completed the dwelling will be fit for habitation. The duty arises in relation to work done in connection with the *provision of a dwelling* whether the dwelling is provided by the erection, conversion, or enlargement of a building. It is questionable whether a mere enlargement of an existing dwelling is caught by the Act[9], since there is no provision of a dwelling unless the result is to produce two or more separate dwellings where formerly there was only one. This statutory obligation cannot be excluded or restricted[10]. Any cause of action in respect of a breach of duty accrues at the time when the dwelling is completed, not necessarily when the first purchaser acquired his interest therein, save that time starts running again in respect of further work undertaken to rectify work already done[11]. Subject to these special rules other limitation provisions will apply in the normal way, so that in relation to hidden defects, time will not run until their discovery[12]. The Act is not retrospective[13].

Under s. 1 (3) it will be no defence for the builder to prove that he has complied with plans and specifications provided by him and accepted by the

7 Law Com. No. 40, paras. 20–37; Draft Bill, cl. 1. As to the effectiveness see the articles cited in note 17, p. 170, ante.
8 Section 1 (1).
9 E.g. by adding a fourth bedroom to a house with three bedrooms. No statutory duty arises in relation to industrial or commercial premises.
10 Section 6 (3).
11 Section 1 (5). The Law Commission's Draft Bill contained a more elaborate provision which differentiated between cases where the dwelling was built to order and other cases (such as speculative building).
12 *Archer v Moss* [1971] 1 QB 406, [1971] 1 All ER 747, CA.
13 *Alexander v Mercouris* [1979] 3 All ER 305, CA.

purchase if those specifications do not provide for proper materials or the house when finished is not fit for habitation. In effect this provision prevents any repetition of the decision in *Lynch v Thorne*[14]. On the other hand, if the dwelling is to be erected in accordance with plans and specifications supplied by or on behalf of the purchaser, the builder is regarded as having discharged his statutory obligation if he complies with his instructions in a workmanlike manner[15].

(ii) *Persons to whom duty is owed.* The duty imposed is of more than strictly contractual force and is owed not merely to the original purchaser but to every person who acquires an interest, legal or equitable, in the dwelling. Clearly no duty under the Act arises in favour of mere licensees, visitors, or members of a purchaser's or a tenant's family[16] nor, it is submitted, in favour of persons having rights to occupy under some contractual licence or by virtue of an estoppel interest. However these people are not necessarily without redress; the statutory obligation exists in addition to any duty owed by the builder apart from the Act[17] so that liability may be established in tort for damage sustained by the negligent construction of the property[18].

(iii) *Persons on whom duty is imposed.* The duty is imposed on any person 'taking on work for or in connection with the provision of a dwelling'. It includes not only the builder, but sub-contractors, architects and surveyors, suppliers of 'purpose built' components for installation in specific dwellings, developers and local authorities[19] who in the course of a business or in exercise of statutory powers arrange for others to build dwellings on their behalf. Depending upon the circumstances of the case a purchaser may often have a cause of action against more than one person. This is a most far-reaching and controversial aspect of the new statutory obligation. It does not extend to manufacturers of general building materials or mass produced components whose obligations will continue to be governed by the law relating to the sale of goods and to negligence. The exact nature of the obligation will not be the same in every case. An architect who designs houses for a particular estate will not normally be under any duty to use proper materials, but he is required to execute the work 'taken on' in a professional manner and to provide designs, plans and specifications which, if followed by the builder, will result in the necessary standard of habitation[20]. A sub-contractor who undertakes work on the terms that he adopts plans and specifications provided by the builder or main contractor will under s. 1 (2) discharge his duty if he executes the work in accordance therewith, but not if he substitutes sub-standard materials which cause the premises to be defective.

One very compelling reason exists for creating such an extensive duty. Were the purchaser's only remedy limited to the builder with whom he was in a contractual relationship, the statutory provision would prove worthless where

---

14   [1956] 1 All ER 744, CA, note 5, p. 174, ante.
15   Section 2 (2).
16   Other than a spouse whose statutory rights of occupation under the Matrimonial Homes Act 1967, rank as a charge on the estate as if it were an equitable interest: s. 2 (1).
17   Section 6 (2).
18   Page 170, ante.
19   As to whom see s. 1 (4).
20   See further Law Com. No. 40, para. 31.

the builder became bankrupt or where the defect was not attributable to any breach by the builder of his statutory obligation[1].

5.   The National House-Building Council scheme[2]

In a provision having no counterpart in the Law Commission's Draft Bill, s. 2 of the Defective Premises Act 1972, excludes the operation of the statutory obligation where the erection of the dwelling is covered by a scheme, approved by the Secretary of State, which confers rights in respect of defects in the state of the dwelling on persons acquiring an interest therein. The scheme which has been approved is the one contemplated is that operated by the National House-Building Council. Where the approved scheme applies and provided there is also in existence in relation to any particular dwelling an approved document stating that the requirements as to design or construction imposed by the scheme have been complied with, no action can be brought for breach of the duty imposed by s. 1 in relation to that dwelling[3]. The intention is that every purchaser should have the benefit either of the statutory obligation or of an equivalent obligation under the N.H.B.C. scheme, though it will be seen that the two obligations do not correspond in several important respects[4].

The Council maintain a Register of house builders willing to participate in the scheme. Only builders whose previous work has been inspected and found satisfactory are registered. Houses erected by registered builders are inspected during construction; on completion the Council formerly issued to the purchaser a certificate of compliance with their building specifications. The issue of this certificate was a prerequisite for a builder's exemption from the statutory obligations imposed by s. 1 of the Act. Registered builders are required to offer a House Purchaser's Agreement which safeguards purchasers (including lessees) in respect of defective houses. Now changes have been effected in respect of houses registered for inspection after 18 April 1979. The issue of a certificate is now no longer the practice.

(a)   Nature of protection afforded[5]

This Agreement (HB5 as it is termed) contains a fourfold warranty:

(i)   that the dwelling has been or will be built in an efficient and workman-like manner and of proper materials so as to be fit for habitation (an obligation commensurate with the statutory duty),

(ii)   that a standard notice of insurance cover has been or will be issued (Form HB6),

(iii)   that upon signing of the Agreement the policy shall be issued to the purchaser,

(iv)   that upon signing the agreement (or later) the notices of insurance cover shall be delivered to the purchaser.

---

1   Law Com. No. 40, para. 28.
2   See Adams, 'Legal Aspects of the N.H.B.R.C. Scheme' (1967), 117 NLJ 1206, 1232, 1262;
    'The N.H.B.C. Scheme 1971 Revision' (1971), 121 NLJ 144; 'The N.H.B.C.
    Scheme—1972 Amendments' (1972) 122 NLJ 497 and (1979) NLJ 171, 195, 219.
3   Section 2 (1) (a), (b).
4   The position at common law (subject to exclusions) is probably better, see post.
5   See (1980) 130 NLJ 171, 195 and 219 (J.E. Adams).

Normally the proper person to enter into this Agreement will be the vendor of the land on which the house is to be built whether or not he is the actual builder[6]. This warranty, being similar to the common law duty, is in addition to the obligations entered into in respect of the N.H.B.C. agreement set out below. The new provisions, however, have a limitation in them: — after the initial two-year period a claim against the vendor under the warranty (i) above can only be made *after* a claim has been made under the insurance scheme[7]. The protection which a purchaser receives under the scheme may be summarised as follows:

1. The vendor is obliged to make good at his own expense defects arising from non-compliance with the Council's requirements and reported within a period of two years. This does not extend to (i) defects arising from wear and tear gradual deterioration by neglect, normal shrinkage, (ii) defects resulting from faulty design where the purchaser has provided the design or (iii) dampness or condensation. In the case of various items (e.g. central heating systems) the period is one year.

2. After this initial period the Council's insurance scheme provides cover[8] for a further period of eight years against major structural damage. There is a complicated method of calculating the amount payable under this head and the next one[9]. Broadly this part of the scheme is intended to cover such items as subsidence, settlement, collapse or serious distortion of joists or roof structure. Non-structural defects or even minor structural items are not covered, nor is damage caused by normal wear and tear and certain other specified contingencies, such as loss or damage already covered by insurance.

3. The Council undertake to honour any unfulfilled judgment or award obtained against the vendor in consequence of his non-compliance with the obligations under the Agreement except the warranty set out in (a) above. There is a twelve months' time limit after the initial guarantee period during which arbitration or legal proceedings should have been commenced unless liquidation or bankruptcy rendors the prospects of recovery remote.

4. Protection up to a maximum of £5,000 is available in the event of the vendor's bankruptcy, liquidation or fraud before the house is completed, including reimbursment of money paid where building work has not commenced, provided contracts have been exchanged. There is a three month time limit for notification following knowledge of the bankruptcy, winding up or fraud. It has been doubted whether such a strict time limit would be upheld.

---

6   The Agreement is entered into by 'the Developer' who sells the dwelling to the purchaser. Difficulties arise, however, if the conveyance is by a land owning company and the construction is by another company in the same group. One of the writers has encountered a threefold situation with a nominee holding the legal estate for 'the developer'.

7   Clause 5. This seems somewhat otiose if it is a claim clearly outside the ambit of the insurance scheme, see Adams, op. cit., 171. It is clearly a restriction on the old scheme.

8   The Agreement formerly established a contractual relationship between the Council (acting through the vendor as their authorised agent) and the purchaser. Now the Council's duties are set out in the insurance policy, post (HB7). The agency element is still retained however.

9   See Adams, op. cit. The limit is £50,000 or twice the national average purchase price of dwellings at the date of purchase. The actual limit is the actual purchase price now index linked to the date of payment. After payment the outstanding amount is also index linked. In addition there are deductions of 10 per cent of the amount recovered subject to an overriding limit of 2 per cent of the purchase price.

(b) Exclusions

   (i) No payment is made in respect of professional fees, accommodation, removal fees and consequential loss,
  (ii) Gradual deterioration or neglect will bar a claim,
 (iii) Claims must have been made in writing as soon as reasonably practicable[10],
  (iv) In the case of Common Parts no payments are made except in respect of which the purchaser is obliged directly or indirectly to make a contribution.
   (v) The Council's liability is confined to claims consequent upon the negligence of the vendor or his sub-contractor. In those many cases where the vendor is not the builder and the house is erected by a developer under contract with the vendor, no redress is available under the scheme (though liability may arise at common law) for defective work carried out by a sub-contractor employed by the developer.

(c) Persons protected by scheme

As between the Council and a registered vendor, the latter is duty bound to use the standard form Agreement. Failure to do so may result in disciplinary proceedings, but vis-à-vis the purchaser no such obligation exists. Consequently the purchaser's adviser must ensure that the sale or building agreement includes a term binding the vendor to enter into the Agreement. The Council recommend the following clause: 'The vendor undertakes to make an irrevocable offer to enter into the form of Agreement HB5 prescribed by' the N.H.B.C.

The benefits of the Agreement are intended to accrue to subsequent owners, the word 'purchaser' being defined to include successors in title[11], and mortgagees in possession, save that the successor cannot enforce any rights in respect of defects which should have been, but were not, duly reported before the time of acquisition or possession. Considerable uncertainty existed as to the need for an express assignment of the benefit to a subsequent purchaser[12].

The new agreement[13] provides expressly that the purchaser is contracting on behalf of himself, his successors in title and (curiously) mortgagees in possession. The vendor undertakes not to deny liability or the basis of a lack of assignment. It has been suggested[14] that an assignment should be taken, contrary to the views of the N.H.B.C. A simple clause in the contract between the original purchaser (i.e. the seller) and his purchaser will be effective in equity to vest the benefit of the Agreement in the latter[15]. The view that the successor takes the benefit of the Agreement under s. 56 of the Law of Property Act 1925, appears unsound. Not only is there no instrument under seal[16] but the section does not

---

 10 This can penalise a succeeding purchaser if a predecessor failed to claim. The pre-contract inquiries should deal with this carefully.
 11 It has been held that the benefit of the agreement passes under LPA 1925, s. 78; see *Marchants v Caswell and Redgrave Ltd* (1979) 240 Estates Gazette 127.
 12 See Aldridge, 'Taking Over N.H.B.C. Agreements' (1969), 113 Sol Jo 863; see also ibid., 907, 925. In practice the N.H.B.C. prohibited vendors from taking the point.
 13 Clause 10.
 14 Adams, op. cit., 173.
 15 Written notice of assignment to both the registered vendor and the Council is required to effect a legal assignment of the benefit: LPA 1925, s. 136.
 16 See *Beswick v Beswick* [1968] AC 58, [1967] 2 All ER 1197, HL.

confer benefits on persons who are not known and in existence at the time of the Agreement. The benefit of s. 78 also with respect seems somewhat doubtful.

(d) Other remedies

The Agreement does not abrogate the purchaser's common law remedies although it is limited indirectly with regard to the warranty in respect of the construction. His right to damages from the vendor for breach of his contractual obligations (as distinct from the right to have defects rectified) survives the initial two years' guarantee period, except that he must first pursue his remedies against the Council and redress from that source must be allowed in mitigation of damages awarded against the vendor. Similarly an action may still be maintained in tort for the negligent construction of the building and in the case of a defect causing personal injuries a subsequent purchaser's sole remedy is to sue in tort. No action for breach of the statutory obligation imposed by the Act of 1972 will be possible.

(e) N.H.B.C. scheme compared with the statutory obligation

The Law Commission, whilst duly admitting the benefits of the Council's scheme, considered that certain limitations rendered it desirable to impose a statutory duty (of the type already discussed), not to rival, but to complement the scheme. Thus every house purchaser has the benefit of one of two mutually exclusive but not co-extensive forms of protection. The main advantages of the N.H.B.C. scheme can be summarised as follows:

1. It entitles the purchaser to spot checks during building operations and imposes a minimum standard of construction which exceeds the statutory duty to provide a dwelling fit for habitation.

2. Limited protection is given if the builder becomes bankrupt, whereas that event destroys any effective remedy against him under the statute, a disadvantage which is partially offset by the possibility of maintaining actions based on the Act against others who have undertaken building work.

3. Protection lasts for ten years as compared with a period of six years under the Act (Cf. common law liability in tort).

4. Provision is made for honouring unfulfilled judgments.

The statutory obligation can boast the following advantages:

1. It covers a wider range of building operations (e.g. conversions).

2. Liability is unlimited in amount.

3. Liability arises if the house is not fit for habitation. There are no excluded contingencies, though most of those excepted from the Council's scheme relate to minor matters which would not result in any breach of the statutory obligation. In particular damages for personal injuries caused by an actionable defect are recoverable under the Act, but not under the scheme. Where the latter applies, the purchaser's remedy for personal injuries lies in tort.

4. The duty embraces a wide range of persons. Under the Act actions may be maintainable against sub-contractors in circumstances not giving rise to any claim under the Council's scheme[17].

---

17   See p. 179, ante. The existence of an approved scheme precludes any action under s. 1 of the Act even against sub-contractors whose defective work does not fall within the N.H.B.C. scheme.

5. Consequential loss is recoverable.

It remains to be seen whether speculative or indifferent builders use the Act to justify their withdrawal from the scheme or claim exemption from registration. Any widespread development of this practice would be most undesirable, for on balance the purchaser's interests are best served by a scheme which affords protection that is not dependent on the continued existence of the developer[18] or his financial solvency. Whether either the statute or the scheme improved the common law is a matter for debate.

C Pre-contract inquiries

1. Standard form inquiries

To off-set the vendor's rather limited duty of disclosure it has become the practice for a purchaser, before signing the contract, to submit inquiries (termed preliminary or pre-contract inquiries) to the vendor to elicit further information to assist him in deciding whether to proceed with the transaction. The use of such inquiries has gathered momentum during the past 35 years and, doubtless, the passing of the Town and Country Planning Act 1947, played no small part in the establishment of the practice[19]. Today their use in relation to a whole host of matters has become so widespread as to make the pre-contract inquiry as important, perhaps even more so especially in relation to registered land, than the post-contract investigation of title.

Practitioners tend to use a standard printed form of inquiry published by The Solicitors' Law Society Limited. Over the years the standard forms have seen frequent revision, prompted in large measure by the criticism directed at the questions themselves[20]. The latest edition[1], widely used by solicitors, was introduced in 1980 and contains fifteen inquiries of a general nature, and several special inquiries of relevance to leasehold titles, or new properties only.

(a) General inquiries
The printed form requests information concerning the title documents, boundaries, disputes, services, adverse rights, performance of covenants, the fabric of the property, fixtures, fittings, and roads. There is also an involved question relating to planning matters: the past and present use, development during the previous four years, adverse notices or proposals affecting the land and so on. Not all of these inquiries have met with general approval[2]. Some are considered objectionable because they concern matters which the purchaser (or his solicitor) should already know about, or seek information which can be more readily and reliably obtained from other sources. This is especially true of some of the planning inquiries. Fundamental criticism can also be levelled at

---

18 An important consideration when a building company can be formed for the development of a particular estate and then dissolved almost overnight on its completion.
19 And see *Goody v Baring* [1956] 2 All ER 11 at 16, per Danckwerts J.
20 See Wickenden and Edell, 'The Practitioners' Inquisition' (1961) 25 Conv (NS) 336, who, writing of the published form in vogue in 1961, alleged that the practitioner was confronted with four closely printed pages of questions on every conceivable topic and framed in such terms as to be totally unintelligible to his client and probably partially unintelligible to him.
1 Form LM. See [1980] Conv 401 (J.E. Adams).
2 See (1970) 34 Conv (NS) 224.

the unfortunate, though perhaps inevitable, comprehensiveness of some questions which defy any meaningful answer. Few would deny that the majority of the questions seek information on matters about which a purchaser may properly require to be satisfied before signing his contract, but many would question whether they all concern matters which ought suitably to be dealt with by solicitors.

It is not proposed to consider individual inquiries in detail, save to mention one or two that merit some discussion. The inquiry about disputes asks whether the vendor is aware of any disputes regarding boundaries, easements or covenants. This question, though subject to attack from some quarters[3], is one that a purchaser can fairly raise (provided the offending additional phrase 'or other matters' is deleted), especially as regards boundaries which are notorious troublemakers. The suggestion that in the event of subsequent litigation, a purchaser will normally have recourse to the covenants for title is not convincing, for the vendor cannot expect the purchaser to buy a possible law-suit. Another valuable inquiry seeks information concerning rights not apparent on inspection and exercisable over the land by virtue of some informal arrangement or licence. Cases like *Ward v Kirkland*[4] and *E.R. Ives Investments Ltd v High*[5] have spotlighted the problems that can arise from that somewhat nebulous right, the equity arising by estoppel, or out of acquiescence. It is conceived that a preliminary inquiry of this kind may be the only inquiry that can reasonably be made to free the purchaser from the trammels of constructive notice, at least in relation to rights not apparent on inspection (e.g. underground drainage rights). Since rights of this nature frequently result from some informal neighbourly agreement, the chances of there being any record with the vendor's deeds are remote and consequently the contract will not normally disclose them.

Perhaps the most objectionable of all the preliminary inquiries is the one requesting details of flooding, structural or drainage defects, subsidence, woodworm, dry rot, or defective electric wiring. Inquiries of this nature first became fashionable about the time the Misrepresentation Act 1967 became law and were designed, not merely as a blatant attempt to reverse the caveat emptor rule, but to trap the unwary into making representations of fitness capable of grounding a cause of action under the Act if proved inaccurate. As the content of the inquiry is a matter for surveyors, rather than solicitors, many practitioners refuse on principle to give any reply, except to direct the purchaser to rely on his own inspection. Though this appears to be the wisest course to adopt, it by no means represents the universal attitude. Some are prepared to reply on behalf of their clients with a categorical 'No'[6], whilst others reply out of courtesy, adding a qualification that the reply is not to constitute any warranty or representation. A specific inquiry is now to be found concerning adult occupiers and their interests if any[6a].

---

3   See Adams, (1970) 120 NLJ 610, 611. Yet the same commentator acknowledges the desirability of an additional enquiry designed to ascertain whether the physical boundaries differ from those shown on the deed or field plan.
4   [1967] Ch 194, [1966] 1 All ER 609.
5   [1967] 2 QB 379, [1967] 1 All ER 504, CA.
6   Yet even a simple 'no' may be dangerous. A vendor who honestly believes in the truth of his denial may find himself liable under s. 2 (1) of the Misrepresentation Act 1967, if he did not have reasonable grounds to believe the condition was as stated. This inquiry, although no longer reproduced in the form, is still frequently made.
6a   Consequent upon *Williams and Glyn's Bank Ltd v Boland*, p. 53, ante.

(b) Leasehold inquiries
These request details of the nature of the lease, the lessor and any superior lessor (names and addresses only), the existing fire insurance over and the fulfilment of covenants to do work (e.g. to paint). It should, however, be unnecessary to ascertain whether the property is held under a head lease or an under-lease for the contract ought to disclose this information, and the inquiry whether the vendor will obtain any necessary licence to assign should normally be superfluous as the point is commonly regulated by the General Conditions of Sale.

(c) Additional inquiries
The need to raise further inquiries depends on the special circumstances of each individual transaction[7]. It may be necessary to elucidate, or object to, clauses in the draft contract. Additional inquiries should not be raised without good reason, yet judging by the frequency in which the standard forms are used without the addition of other questions, it is felt that solicitors may well be giving insufficient consideration to the need for extra inquiries. The printed form does not profess to be exhaustive, but all too frequently the form is dispatched to the vendor's solicitor simply as a matter of course before the draft contract and accompanying papers have been studied.

(d) Effectiveness of inquiries
Few aspects of modern conveyancing procedure have attracted as much trenchant criticism as the use of preliminary inquiries. It has been alleged that they have got completely out of hand[8]. The indiscriminate use of the printed form as a sort of safeguard against a possible action of negligence is to be totally deprecated, yet a strong feeling exists that in many cases it is the task of a secretary or typist to send out the form. All too frequently irrelevant inquiries remain undeleted (despite the reminder in bold print to strike out those that are inapplicable), and questions are asked the answers to which the solicitor should already know, were he to ask his client or check the contract or accompanying documents. Complaint is often directed at the vague and unhelpful replies that are given, though it is the comprehensive nature of some of the questions that is largely responsible for answers like: 'This inquiry is too wide to admit of any useful reply.' Some practitioners, adopting the philosophy that stereotyped inquiries deserve nothing better than stereotyped answers, do not consult their clients before replying, whilst others advocate that replies might just as well be sent to the purchaser's solicitor with the draft contract, a procedure quite commonly followed on the sale of new property on a building estate.

It is, however, generally accepted even by the most ardent critics of the current practice that relevant and properly worded inquiries have an important role to play in the conveyancing process. It may be that the existence of a printed form is partly responsible for the problem and every practitioner ought to consider the desirability of drafting his own set of questions, seeking to avoid unnecessary and too-widely drawn inquiries. Unless the solicitors of both parties are willing to play their respective parts, the one by limiting his inquiries to those strictly relevant and the other by ensuring that his replies are accurate and informative, the procedure degenerates into nothing more than a meaningless and time-consuming charade. Alas it is to be feared that the recent

---

7   A printed form of inquiry exists for use when tenanted property is being acquired. In the main it seeks details of the nature of the tenancy and the extent to which the landlord or tenant has exercised his various rights, statutory or otherwise.

8   See (1970) 34 Conv (NS) 226.

changes in the law of innocent misrepresentation, far from improving the
position, may tend to worsen it.

2.   Inaccurate replies and the purchaser's remedies[9]

(a) Replies in general

Strictly speaking, the vendor is under no legal duty to reply to the purchaser's
inquiries, but it has become standard conveyancing practice to give replies
to all reasonable inquiries. The vendor's solicitor may refuse to answer those
which he considers are improper, or which are couched in unduly wide
language (as is the case with some of the printed inquiries). He should always
consult the vendor before replying to any inquiry which he cannot answer from
his own knowledge, or from a perusal of the documents of title, though many a
busy practitioner, anticipating his client's likely answer, is tempted to use a
stock reply, such as 'The vendor does not know', without taking proper steps to
ascertain the exact position. It is clearly the responsibility of the purchaser's
solicitor to discuss with the purchaser the answers to all inquiries which may,
affirmatively or negatively, influence the signing of the contract. The general
belief that frequently the replies are never communicated to the purchaser may
in part be responsible for the unhelpful nature of many replies.

In the case of inaccurate replies, a purchaser need only resort to legal
remedies where the falsity is discovered after exchange of contracts. So long as
they have not been exchanged, the purchaser can refuse to proceed or can
stipulate for better terms, if he considers the vendor's replies unsatisfactory, or
erroneous. It will be helpful at this stage to outline the nature of the purchaser's
rights in relation to inaccurate replies; other aspects of misrepresentation are
considered in Part V of this book which deals with remedies generally.

(b) Fraudulent replies

Assuming the fraudulent reply constitutes a representation of fact inducing
the contract, the purchaser can rescind the contract or, if completion has
taken place, have the transaction set aside on the ground of fraud, or claim
damages[10]. It is immaterial whether the falsity is discovered before or after
completion, except that rescission sought after completion may be more likely
to be barred because of the intervention of third party rights[11]. The
Misrepresentation Act 1967, does not affect the law relating to fraudulent
misrepresentation.

(c) Misrepresentation Act 1967

Prior to this Act a purchaser seeking redress for an innocent misrepresentation
contained in replies to preliminary inquiries was entitled to rescind the contract
before completion, but the so-called rule in *Angel v Jay*[12] precluded any remedy
after conveyance. Damages were not recoverable unless either the misrepresentation had become a term of the contract or a collateral warranty could
be established. There does not, however, appear to be any reported decision

---

9   See Adams, 'The Misrepresentation Act and the Conveyancer' (1970) 67 LS Gaz 183, 256
and 318.
10   *London County Freehold and Leasehold Properties Ltd v Berkeley Property and
Investment Co Ltd* [1936] 2 All ER 1039, CA (damages awarded for fraudulent
representation as to promptitude of rent payments).
11   See further p. 656, post.
12   [1911] 1 KB 666.

where a question and answer contained in pre-contract enquiries were held to constitute an actionable warranty[13], which is perhaps not surprising in view of the court's reluctance to enable damages for innocent misrepresentation to be obtained under some other guise.

The main provisions of the Act[14], so far as are here relevant, may be summarised as follows. Under s. 1 performance of the contract is no longer a bar to rescission for innocent misrepresentation. Section 2 (1) in effect creates a new statutory right of action for damages in respect of negligent misrepresentations inducing a contract, unless the representor (i.e. the vendor) or his agent can establish reasonable grounds for believing the facts represented to be true. A purely innocent misrepresentation (one not even made carelessly) may under s. 2 (2) be remedied at the court's discretion by an award of damages[15] in lieu of rescission. This subsection does not confer any *right* to damages. A purchaser who seeks damages as of right must prove that the representation was made fraudulently, or fell within s. 2(1) as being negligent or had become a term of the contract. The court has no power to order rescission and award damages, save that the purchaser would still seem entitled to an indemnity in respect of liabilities necessarily incurred under the contract[16].

The drafting of s. 2 (2) of the Act creates various difficulties. On a literal interpretation the court would appear to have no discretion to award damages in favour of a purchaser who once had the right to rescind but subsequently lost it[17]. Again the court's discretion arises where 'it is claimed, in any proceedings arising out of the contract, that the contract ought to be or has been rescinded.' During the passage of the Bill through the Lords, Lord Upjohn foresaw a 'highly technical' difficulty arising after the execution of the contract which, on completion, merges with the conveyance[18]. He suggested that in relation to contracts for the sale of land, this doctrine of merger might perhaps exclude the court's discretion to award damages on the ground that there ceases to be any proceedings arising out of the *contract*. If this fear proves well founded, there may well continue to exist situations where it is desirable for the purchaser to establish a collateral warranty, which does not merge in the subsequent conveyance[19].

(d) Purchaser's rights under the Act

The Act clearly opens up new horizons for the purchaser who later discovers that the information given to him during preliminary negotiations or in answer

13   Cf. *Mahon v Ainscough* [1952] 1 All ER 337 especially at 340–41, CA, per Jenkins LJ (untrue reply to inquiry concerning war damage); *Terrene Ltd v Nelson* [1937] 3 All ER 739 at 744, per Farwell J; *Gilchester Properties Ltd v Gomm* [1948] 1 All ER 493 (erroneous statement as to receivable rents).

14   For a detailed consideration of the Act and the problems it creates, see Treitel, *The Law of Contract* (5th edn) pp. 243 et seq.; Atiyah and Treitel, 'Misrepresentation Act 1967' (1967) 30 MLR 369.

15   Uncertainty exists as to the measure of damages and whether it is the same as that under s. 2 (1); see Treitel op. cit., pp. 266–270. By sub-s. (3) damages may be awarded under both sub-ss. (1) and (2), but an award under sub-s. (2) must be taken into account in assessing liability under sub-s. (1).

16   *Whittington v Seale-Hayne* (1900) 82 LT 49 (lease of poultry farm rescinded; indemnity recoverable for rent, rates and repairs, but not for loss of profits or poultry stock).

17   This may operate unfairly against the purchaser where the intervention of third party rights bars the right to rescind; Treitel, op. cit., pp. 265–266.

18   H.L. Debates, 17 May 1966, Vol. 274, col. 943. For the doctrine of merger, see p. 444, post.

19   *Lawrence v Cassel* [1930] 2 KB 83, CA.

to some pre-contract enquiry is erroneous. The Act, though enlarging the available remedies, does not supersede the common law requirements that must be satisfied before an action can be maintained. He must still establish a representation of fact; the Act does not extend to mere puffs, representations of law, or representations as to the future. As already noted, answers to preliminary inquiries may often be vague and inconclusive. In one case where the reply was cautiously qualified by the phrase 'so far as the vendor knows', Romer J, was not satisfied that the reply constituted a sufficiently definite statement of fact to amount to a representation[20]. In *Brown v Raphael*[1] the statement, made on the occasion of a sale of a reversionary interest in a trust fund, that an annuitant was 'believed to have no aggregable estate' was held by the Court of Appeal to constitute a representation of a material fact, importing a representation that there existed reasonable grounds for the belief. Mere lawyer's caution in framing replies[2] may not suffice to prevent liability arising, though a statement attached to the replies denying their status as representations may be effective[3].

Assuming there is a representation, the purchaser must establish that he relied on it when entering into the contract[4]. A solicitor ought to inform his client of the replies given to all inquiries which may affect the purchaser's decision to buy. Normally a contracting party cannot allege that he relied on a misrepresentation of which he was unaware. However the purchaser may still be able to maintain an action against the vendor notwithstanding that his solicitor did not disclose the information contained in the reply, at least where his solicitor's advice to sign the contract was influenced by the representation.

(e) Liability of vendor's solicitor to purchaser

The Court of Appeal refused to strike out a claim against a vendor's solicitor by a purchaser for negligence arising out of answers given to a pre-contract enquiry[5] in respect of boundary disputes.

(f) Excluding liability

The Misrepresentation Act 1967, forestalls any attempt to contract out of the Act by enacting in s. 3[6] that a term contained in a contract which would exclude or restrict (a) any liability thereunder by reason of any misrepresenta-

---

20   *Gilchester Properties Ltd v Gomm* [1948] 1 All ER 493 at 495.
1   [1958] Ch 636, [1958] 2 All ER 79, CA.
2   Adams, op. cit., 319.
3   See (1967) 117 NLJ 975.
4   The Court of Appeal in *Gosling v Anderson* (1972) 223 Estates Gazette 1743, awarded damages to a purchaser for the innocent misrepresentation by the vendor's agent that planning permission had been granted for a garage. The purchaser appears to have been somewhat fortunate in this case. From the facts (see (1971) 220 Estates Gazette 1117, where the decision at first instance is reported) it seems that despite the agent's statement, the purchaser was aware when she signed the contract that the planning position was uncertain, for her solicitors were pursuing their own enquiries with the area planning officer. Nevertheless the court felt that the effect of the misrepresentation had not been nullified, and the inference was that she had acted on the representation when signing the contract. See also *Watts v Spence* [1976] Ch 165 (representation that V was owner of property see further, post). *Esso v Mardon* [1976] QB 801, [1976] 2 All ER 5, CA.
5   *Wilson v Bloomfield* (1979) 123 Sol Jo 860. See also *Ross v Caunters* [1980] Ch 297, [1980] Conv 401.
6   As amended by the Unfair Contract Terms Act 1977, s. 8.

tion or (b) any remedy available to another party by reason of such a representation shall be of no effect save in so far as it satisfies the requirement of reasonableness as stated in s. 11(1)[7] of the Unfair Contract Terms Act 1977. The burden is also thrown on those relying on it to show it does. There are two relevant methods which have been attempted:

(i) *Contractual clauses.* Both the main sets of Conditions of Sale contain a clause which prima facie falls foul of s. 3. Condition 17 of the National Conditions provides that no error[8], mis-statement or omission in any preliminary answer concerning the property shall annul the sale nor (save where it relates to a matter materially affecting the property's description or value) shall damages be payable or compensation allowed[9]. The expression 'preliminary answer' is defined to include any statement made by or on behalf of the vendor in answer to formal inquiries or otherwise. This disclaimer does not extend to information *volunteered* by the vendor or his agent. As a result of the decision in *Walker v Boyle*[9a], NCS 17 has been modified in the latest edition by providing it shall not apply to fraudulent or reckless statements. It remains to be seen to what extent the courts will hold this condition fair and reasonable and allow the vendor to rely on it[10].

(ii) *Other forms of disclaimer.* The printed inquiry form itself contains a warning that the replies are believed to be correct (without their accuracy being guaranteed) and do not obviate the need to make appropriate searches, inquiries and inspections[11]. At the most this note might assist the vendor in showing that the purchaser did not rely on his misrepresentation but on the investigations which he himself undertook.

Section 3 may not catch a disclaimer of liability contained in the replies to the inquiries. It is suggested that it may be caught by s. 2 of the Unfair Contract Terms Act 1977[12]. Various devices have additionally been suggested in an

7 I.e. what is a fair and reasonable term having regard to the circumstances which were or ought reasonably to have been shown to or in the contemplation of the parties when the contract was made.

8 See also LSC 7 which contains a statement that the purchaser has not relied on any statement other than an oral one. This is considered to be somewhat harsh, see [1980] Conv 404, 415 (H.W. Wilkinson). This form of NSC Condition 17 has been held to be void on account of s. 3 of the Misrepresentation Act 1967. *Walker v Boyle* [1982] 1 All ER 634, failure to disclose boundary dispute.

9 Section 3 seems prima facie to invalidate the entire condition, including the provisions designed to exclude or restrict other forms of liability, e.g. misdescription (see p. 604, post). Perhaps the courts will permit severance of the non-misrepresentation provisions, thus allowing full effect to be given to them, otherwise they could only operate at the court's discretion.

9a Note 8, ante.

10 See *Djan v Dahorto*, (1978) 6 December, CA, referred to [1980] Conv 401.

11 But see note 4, ante. Since s. 2 (1) of the Act imposes liability for negligent misrepresentations by means of a fiction of fraud, the vendor cannot, it seems, escape liability thereunder simply by warning the purchaser to test the accuracy of the statements: *S. Pearson & Son Ltd v Dublin Corpn* [1907] AC 351. The latest 'warning' is prefaced by a statement that the replies are given 'without responsibility (sic?) on the part of his solicitors, their partners or employees'. See further JEA, op. cit., p. 401. This is intended to alleviate the impact of the *Wilson* case, supra.

12 JCA, op. cit., p. 402 expressing the opinion that the disclosure does not relate to the contract to create an interest in land and therefore not having the benefit of Schedule 1 para. 1 thereof (exemption for such contracts from s. 2). See also *Walker v Boyle* [1982] 1 All ER 634. See also at 640 where Dillon J considered the warning as being unable to prevent them being representations of fact.

attempt to provide vendors with a complete immunity[13]. These may be effective since it is doubtful whether a s. 3 in terms avoids clauses which seek to prevent liability arising by, for example, denying to the replies or information supplied the status of representations or requiring the purchaser to acknowledge that he has not relied on the vendor's pre-contract statements but on his own inquiries and searches[14]. If the courts permit clauses of this nature to flourish, s. 3 will soon pass into oblivion. The Council of The Law Society have strongly deprecated any attempt to secure for vendors a total exclusion of liability[15]. Of course a purchaser confronted by such terms can first threaten not to proceed and then withdraw from the purchase if the vendor (or more likely his solicitor) continues to insist upon the offending terms. But in days of housing shortage the vendor is often in the stronger position and the purchaser is all too easily tempted to take a chance that nothing untoward will occur[16].

Provisions of the type just mentioned, should they ever become widespread which is a distinct possibility if the courts refuse to allow the disclaimer in the General Conditions to be effective, would obviously sound the death-knell of preliminary inquiries in their present form. No useful function would be served by raising questions; for the purchaser would clearly be unwise to rely on information supplied by a vendor immune from liability save for fraud. In a system of conveyancing which places on the vendor only a limited duty of disclosure, this would clearly work to the prejudice of the purchaser, leaving him without effective means of ascertaining essential information which perhaps only the vendor can provide. What is needed is a statutory redefinition of the vendor's duty of disclosure in terms more favourable to the purchaser, which in itself might result in the demise of the printed form of inquiry.

(g) Tortious liability

Recent developments in the law of torts as to liability for loss resulting from negligent statements[17] suggest that a duty of care is owed to a purchaser when answering preliminary inquiries. A duty appears to be owed by the vendor's solicitor, at least in respect of information which he supplies without consulting the vendor. In New Zealand an estate agent acting for a vendor of property has been held to owe a duty of care when providing information about the property

---

13   A clause excluding the authority of the agent has been upheld: *Overbroke Estates Ltd v Glencombe Properties* [1974] 3 All ER 511 but not a statement that the particulars do not form part of the contract *Cremdean Properties v Nash* (1977) 244 Estates Gazette 547. See also *Collins v Howell-Jones* (1980) 259 Estates Gazette 331, CA, [1981] LQR 522 (Murdoch) and [1981] Conv 326 (J.E. Adams). As s. 3 of the Misrepresentation Act 1967 is now limited to contractual terms, attacks on the clause are restricted.

14   A common form of disclaimer printed on estate agents' house particulars reads: 'These particulars do not constitute any part of an offer or contract and any intending purchaser must satisfy himself by inspection or otherwise as to the correctness of each of the statements contained herein. The vendor and his agents make or give no representation or warranty whatever in relation to this property and no responsibility can be taken for the statements contained in these Particulars which are not to be relied upon as statements or representations of fact on the part of either of them.'

15   (1968) 65 LS Gaz 467. But see LSC 7 (5).

16   See Adams, op. cit, 321 who discusses the respective bargaining powers of the parties.

17   *Hedley Byrne & Co Ltd v Heller & Partners Ltd* [1964] AC 464, [1963] 2 All ER 575, HL.

to a prospective purchaser[18]. So have solicitors[19]. The vendor himself may well be under a similar duty of care. He possesses knowledge relevant to the subject matter of the inquiry and knows or ought to know that the purchaser is likely to act in reliance on his statement; he also has a financial interest in the transaction in relation to which the information is given[20]. Liability can be avoided by making the replies 'without responsibility'[1]. The contractual exclusion clause considered on page 187, which denies a purchaser any right to damages in respect of errors in preliminary answers, would not save the vendor from liability for breach of a duty of care when making statements. The clause could not in any event assist the vendor's solicitor if he were sued by the purchaser.

D   Local land charges[2]

1.   Need for search

A search should be made in the register of local land charges maintained by the appropriate local authority. The search is made with the registering authority (District Councils, London Boroughs and the Common Council of the City of London). These authorities have a duty to keep the local land charges register[3].

The purpose of this search is to discover registered matters which do not require disclosure by a vendor because they do not constitute incumbrances. Merely because something is termed a local land charge, it does not automatically follow that it ranks as an incumbrance which a vendor is under a duty to disclose. Some by their very nature do, such as a financial charge in favour of a local authority in respect of street works expenses[4], some do not, such as a resolution to prepare a town planning scheme[5], whilst the status of others is uncertain. It is equally essential to make a search where the title to the land is

---

18   *Barrett v J. R. West Ltd* [1970] NZLR 789 (inaccurate reply given to specific inquiry about drainage); *Bango v Holt* (1971) 21 DLR (3d) 66.

19   See *Wilson v Bloomfield* [1979] 123 Sol Jo 860.

20   The duty to use due care when making statements does not appear to be limited to cases where the representor possesses special skill or competence: see *Ministry of Housing and Local Government v Sharp* [1970] 2 QB 223 at 268–69, [1970] 1 All ER 1009 at 1118–19 CA, per Lord Denning MR. Cf. the more restricted view of the majority of the Privy Council in *Mutual Life and Citizens Assurance Co Ltd v Evatt* [1971] AC 793, [1971] 1 All ER 150 where, however, Lord Diplock did concede that a duty of care might arise where the adviser had a financial interest in the transaction (see at 809 and 161, respectively); *W.B. Anderson & Sons Ltd v Rhodes (Liverpool) Ltd* [1967] 2 All ER 850. See also *Smith v Mattachione* (1970) 13 DLR (3d) 437. See *Esso v Mardon* [1976] QB 801, CA, [1975] 1 All ER 203 (not following the *Evatt* case).

1   But see p. 186, ante, note 5.

2   See generally Garner, *Local Land Charges* (8th edn). The system was altered radically in consequence of the Law Commission Report on Local Land Charges (Law Com No. 62, 1974). This led to the introduction of the Local Land Charges Act 1975 which came into force on 1 August 1977, S.I. 1977 No. 984.

3   Local Land Charges Act 1975, ss. 3 (1), 16 (1).

4   *Stock v Meakin* [1900] 1 Ch 683, CA.

5   *Re Forsey and Hollebone's Contract* [1927] 2 Ch 379, CA, Town planning schemes were replaced by development plans, in turn replaced by structure and local plans under the Town and Country Planning Act 1971. See also *Aquis Estates v Minton* [1975] 3 All ER 1043 (listing of building held adverse entry); cf. *Amalgamated Investments and Property Co Ltd v John Walker & Sons* [1976] 3 All ER 509.

registered. Under the Land Registration Act 1925, s. 70 (1) (i), a local land charge ranks as an overriding interest unless and until registered or protected on the register. It may at any time be protected on the register by means of a notice, though this is unusual, and must, if it constitutes a financial charge, be registered as a charge before realisation[6].

As indicated at the commencement of this chapter local searches are normally made before contracts are exchanged. The need to await the results of the search can delay this exchange and it has in the past been considered desirable to include in the General Conditions some provision enabling exchange of contracts to precede the making of searches, but without prejudice to the position of the purchaser who in such circumstances binds himself to buy without knowing what local land charges affect the land. The National Conditions of Sale[7] formerly contained a provision which, if expressly made applicable by the Special Conditions, entitled the purchaser to rescind the contract should the vendor be unable to cause to be removed or cancelled certain specific matters, including most registered local land charges, affecting the property immediately before the contract is made and not disclosed by him to the purchaser. The range of specific matters is rather limited and did not extend to matters only revealed by additional inquiries. This Condition was rarely resorted to in practice and has now been deleted from the latest edition.

The last edition of The Law Society's Conditions[8], unlike its immediate predecessor, contained no corresponding provision. These Conditions went much further than previous editions by exempting the vendor from any liability to disclose local land charges and related matters. This change evoked criticism as being unduly vendor orientated[9] but has been defended on the ground that it does no more than recognise current conveyancing procedures[10]. Both the National Conditions and the current Law Society conditions include a provision[11] enabling a purchaser to rescind upon discovery of a financial charge unless it was known to him before contract. It is doubtful whether the clause will be much used. Subject to that LSC Condition 3 provides that the property is sold subject to (a) all matters registered with a local authority pursuant to any statute (which is not confined to mere local land charges), (b) all requirements, proposals or requests of such authority and (c) all matters disclosed or reasonably expected to be disclosed as a result of the usual local authority searches and inquiries. The purchaser is bound by all such matters and has no redress against the vendor in relation to any matter not discovered until after exchange of contracts, save in respect of a 'warranty' given by the vendor that he has disclosed all written communication sent to him. Breach of this warranty does not give rise to an opportunity to rescind[12]. Compensation is only payable to the extent that it is not recoverable from a local authority. Should the vendor make an inaccurate statement or representation on any such matter, Condition 3 (3) (b) requires the purchaser to rely on any information obtained or obtainable[13]

6   LRA 1925, ss. 49 (1) (c), 59 (2), proviso.
7   NCS 13 (18th edn).
8   LSC 2 (1973 Revision).
9   (1971) 121 NLJ 5−6, 122.
10   (1971) 121 NLJ 170.
11   LSC 4, NCS 3.
12   LSC 3 (3) a. Cf. Condition 2 (2) of the 1973 revision which gave a purchaser an opportunity of rescission.
13   This at least requires that the local authority are possessed of the relevant facts.

from a local authority in exoneration of the vendor from liability. This clause is clearly caught by s. 3 of the Misrepresentation Act 1967, and might not be upheld by the courts.

2. What is a local land charge?

A charge is a local land charge if it falls within the definition set out in section 1 of the Local Land Charges Act 1975, provided it does not fall within one of the exclusionary categories set out in section 2[14]. They are as follows:

(a) any charge acquired either before or after the commencement of this Act by a local authority, water authority or new town development corporation under the Public Health Acts 1936 and 1937, the Highways Act 1959, the Public Health Act 1961 or the Highways Act 1971, or any similar charge acquired by a local authority under any other Act, whether passed before or after the Act, being a charge that is binding on successive owners of the land affected;

(b) any prohibition of or restriction on the use of land —
(i) imposed by a local authority on or after 1 January 1926 (including any prohibition or restriction embodied in any condition attached to a consent, approval or licence granted by a local authority on or after that date), or
(ii) enforceable by a local authority under any covenant or agreement made with them on or after that date,
being a prohibition or restriction binding on successive owners of the land affected;

(c) any prohibition of or restriction on the use of land —
(i) imposed by a Minister of the Crown or government department on or after the date of the commencement of the Act (including any prohibition or restriction embodied in any condition attached to a consent, approval or licence granted by such a Minister or department on or after that date), or
(ii) enforceable by such a Minister or department under any covenant or agreement made with him or them on or after that date,
being a prohibition or restriction binding on successive owners of the land affected;

(d) any positive obligation affecting land enforceably by a Minister of the Crown, government department or local authority under any covenant or agreement made with him or them on or after the date of the commencement of the Act and binding on successive owners of the land affected;

(e) any charge or other matter which is expressly made a local land charge by any statutory provision.

---

14 These exclusions are: — (a) prohibitions or restrictions between lessor and lessee; (b) positive obligations between lessor and lessee; (c) various restrictions enforceable by the Crown, a government department or local authority which benefit land held by them; (d) restrictions embodied in bye laws; (e) conditions in respect of planning permissions before 1 August 1977; (f) restrictions under the TCPA 1932 and earlier enactments repealed by it; (g) forestry dedication covenants; (h) prohibitions affecting the whole country.

Though in the main local land charges relate to matters enforceable only by local authorities, this is not true of all the categories. Some are enforceable by independent statutory corporations, and in one case by private individuals.

Parts of the register
Provision is made for the register to be divided into twelve numbered parts[15]. It is outside the scope of this book to consider the different parts in detail[16], but reference will be made to each to indicate the type of charge capable of being registered.

Part 1.   General Financial Charges. Registration of such charges is governed by s.6 (2) of the 1975 Act, and enables a local authority, having expended money on e.g. street works, or maintenance of sewers and drains, to register a charge temporarily, pending calculation of the actual sum chargeable in respect of the property concerned, when a Part 2 charge can be registered. A general financial charge gives advance warning that a specific charge for an ascertained sum will in due course be registered.

Part 2. Specific financial charges. Such charges arise under several Acts where a local authority have incurred expenditure for which the owner of the premises is liable, often after he has defaulted in complying with a notice to execute certain works. A charge for street works expenses will be registered here after the final apportionment has been made in respect of the property[17]. Numerous charges of this nature exist under the Public Health Act 1936, such as the cost of providing a fire escape for high buildings[18]. Any entry in Part 2 will reveal (i) the statute, instrument or resolution under which the charge is acquired, (ii) a description of the land affected, (iii) the date of the charge, (iv) the date of its registration and (v) the amount (which will be the final amount, except where interest is payable, in which case the rate of interest is also given).

Part 3. Planning charges. Entries in this part of the register are those most widely met in practice. They include enforcement notices, compensation notices, tree preservation orders and orders revoking or modifying planning permission. The need to obtain planning consent is not itself registrable; this is a statutory restriction, not one imposed by a local authority.

As a result of the decision in *Rose v Leeds Corporation*[19] conditions attached to a planning permission were apparently not registrable. In this case it was argued that a time condition (that is, one limiting the duration of the permission to a specified period) was void against a purchaser of the land on account of non-registration, with the result that the permission became permanent and unconditional. This contention was rejected. The grant of permission is in reality the grant of a right (and in the case of conditional permission, the grant of a conditional right) in alleviation of the statutory prohibition or restriction. Prior to this decision it was the practice to register in Part 3 conditional permissions. Fortunately many clerks to local authorities continued to do so[20]. Now

15   See the Local Land Charges Rules 1977, S.I. 1977 No. 985, especially r. 3.
16   See Garner *Local Land Charges* (8th edn).
17   See further p. 200, post.
18   Section 60; see also s. 75 (cost of providing dustbin).
19   [1964] 3 All ER 618, CA. For the grant of planning permission, see pp. 214–220, post.
20   See further (1965) 29 Conv (NS) 34, 161; Garner, op. cit.

they are registrable in respect of conditions imposed after 1 August 1977. Questions relating to conditional permission appear both in the printed form of preliminary inquiries and in the additional inquiries asked of local authorities, so that a purchaser making these usual inquiries ought to discover the existence of any conditions.

Part 4. Miscellaneous non-planning prohibitions and restrictions. A variety of charges arising under innumerable statutes are registrable here. Demolition and closing orders under the Housing Act 1957, improvement lines under the Highways Act 1980—these are just a few examples. One of the more recent additions to Part 4 registrable charges is the control order which a local authority can make in respect of a house in multiple occupation in certain cases where it is necessary for the protection of the residents[1]. The order in effect operates as a statutory 'assignment' of the property to the authority for the duration of the period specified therein, without vesting in them any interest amounting to an estate in law[2]. This order requires registration as a local land charge[3].

Part 5. Charges for improvement of fenland ways. This relates to charges incurred in relation to the maintenance of private ways in fenlands[4].

Part 6. Land compensation orders. This contains entries relating to certain charges falling within ss. 52 (8) and 8 (4) of the Land Compensation Act 1973.

Part 7. New towns orders. The first important step in the establishment of a new town is the making of an order designating the area as a proposed new town. This designation order and the compulsory purchase orders made pursuant to it are registrable here.

Part 8. Civil aviation orders and directions. In the interests of safety, the Civil Aviation Authority[5] has wide powers to make orders for the demolition of buildings, the creation of easements or other rights over land and other matters, all of which are registrable in Part 8.

Part 9. Opencast coal mining orders. This covers entries relating to compulsory rights orders and compulsory purchase orders under the Opencast Coal Act 1958, whereby the National Coal Board can obtain rights to carry on opencast coal working for a temporary period.

Part 10. Lists of buildings of special architectural or historic interest. Under the Town and Country Planning Act 1971[6], the Secretary of State can compile or approve lists of buildings of special architectural or historic interest. A copy of so much of the list as relates to a registering authority must be deposited with the clerk of the council and the copy becomes registrable in Part 10.

---

1 Housing Act 1964, s. 73. As amended by Local Land Charges Act 1975 Sch. 1 and Rent Act 1977 Sch. 23.
2 Ibid., s. 74 (2).
3 Ibid., s. 73 (5), as amended above.
4 Agriculture (Miscellaneous Provisions) Act 1941, s. 8 (3) (d).
5 See the Civil Aviation Act 1971, ss. 1, 14, 16.
6 Section 54, replacing the T & CPA 1962, s. 32.

Part 11. Light obstruction notices. Readers will already be familiar with the provisions of the Rights of Light Act 1959, and no further comment will be made[7].

Part 12. Land drainage schemes. The Land Drainage Act 1961, empowers certain authorities to prepare a scheme for the improvement of drainage works in certain cases. The scheme becomes registrable in this part of the register.

3.   Mode of searching

(a) Personal search

A search can be effected by the applicant attending the council offices and inspecting the register in person, on payment of the prescribed fee[8]. Personal searches are seldom made for various reasons. Occasionally a personal search is effected when there is insufficient time to make an official one, as where a purchaser wishes to exchange contracts with the minimum of delay, or proposes to buy land at an auction.

(b) Official search

It is enacted[9] that where a person requires a search to be made of the register, he may on payment of the required fee lodge at the registry a requisition on that behalf and thereupon the registrar shall make the search and issue a certificate setting forth the result. It is the invariable practice to request an official search, except in the circumstances already mentioned. The requisition must be in the prescribed form, signed by the applicant or his solicitor, as follows[10]:

> 'An official search is required in [Part of[11]] the register of local land charges kept by the above-named registering authority for subsisting registrations against the land defined in the attached plan and described below . . .'

Unlike land charges, local land charges are registered against the land. The name of the estate owner is not therefore necessary. Normally the correct postal address is adequate to identify the property, otherwise a plan drawn to scale and furnished in duplicate is required.

Having made the search the registrar issues a certificate, signed and dated, that:

> 'It is hereby certified that the search registered above reveals no subsisting registration *or* the registration described in the Schedule hereto[12] up to and including the date of the certificate.'

The entries are in fact revealed in schedules attached to the certificate, there being different forms of schedules laid down by the Rules for different parts of the register.

---

7   See M & W, 864–5.
8   Local Land Charges Act 1975, s. 8.
9   Local Land Charges Act 1975, s. 9 and r. 11.
10   R. 13.
11   Usually a search in the whole of the register is required, so that the words 'Part of' are deleted.
12   The inappropriate words are deleted.

A composite form (known as L.L.C. 1) containing both the requisition and the form of certificate is employed; all that it is necessary for the solicitor and the registrar to do is to complete the respective parts of the form.

4.   Value of search

As will be seen in the next section a search confers no priority in respect of matters that are not unregistered (unlike land charges). The result is that the search is good only for the day that it is made. Further the compensation[13] will not be payable in respect of a charge which comes into existence after the search but *before* the contract. The purchaser will of course normally be bound. It follows therefore that a long period of time between the search and the contract could be fatal. Obviously it will vary depending on the property but it is doubtful whether a search can safely be left for more than four weeks. This also makes the supplemental enquiries even more important[14].

5.   Effect of non-registration

Formerly the position concerning non registration was open to doubt in that some charges were enforceable irrespective of registration whereas others were rendered unenforceable if they were not registered. In the case of a financial charge non registration avoided the charge but left the debt outstanding. Now the position is that failure to register or disclose a charge shall not affect its enforceability. This is then complemented by the compensation system[15].

(a) Enforcement of registered charges

Unless they have in the meantime been discharged or cancelled, the purchaser will on completion take subject to all registered charges revealed by his official search certificate, and to matters registered but not disclosed and as to which the certificate is not conclusive. The mode of enforcement depends in each case on the type of charge. Thus financial charges take effect as if created by a deed of charge by way of legal mortgage[16], so that the local authority can exercise the statutory powers of sale, or appointing a receiver, without having to obtain a court order. The charges thus take effect without prejudice to their priority. This appears to preserve the view that a charge is a charge over the property as opposed to a particular interest therein[17].

Breach of prohibition or restriction is normally punishable by a fine, coupled with powers vested in the appropriate authority to take steps to secure compliance and to recover any expenses incurred.

(b) Discharge between vendor and purchaser

Under the National Conditions of Sale[18] the purchaser must at his own expense comply with any requirement made against the vendor by a local authority in

13   See p. 197, post.
14   A form is agreed between the Law Society and the local Authorities. The current disclaimer limits liability to negligent acts only.
15   Section 10 (1).
16   Section 7 LPA 1925, s. 101.
17   *Westminster City Council v Haymarket Publishing Ltd* [1981] 2 All ER 555, CA; *Paddington Borough Council v Finucane* [1928] Ch 567. This is not the case in respect of Building Societies who are statutorily obliged to lend on a first mortgage only. A local authority charge will not take priority over it; Building Societies Act 1962, s. 32, Sch. 5.
18   General Condition 16. The rule in *Forsey v Hollebone's Contract* still applies to local land charge. See Section F, post.

respect of the property *after* the date of the contract. There is the question of the time between the search and the contract which has been considered already. Failure to search will fix a purchaser with liability in respect of a registered charge.

The Law Society's Conditions, in keeping with their policy of imposing on the purchaser the responsibility of discovering all local authority requirements, stipulate that he must comply with any requirement, notice, order or proposal whether made *before or after* the contract and must indemnify the vendor in respect of any liability thereunder[19].

6.   Compensation

Compensation is available to a purchaser[20] in certain circumstances. In the case of a material personal search it is available if at the relevant time the charge was in existence but not registered. In the case of a material official search, whether the charge was registered or not, compensation is payable if it is not disclosed by the search[1]. The linking of the right to the date of the contract accords with the usual practice of making sale subject thereto. There is no machinery for quantifying compensation which may be difficult in the case of a non-financial charge[2].

7.   Effectiveness of local search certificates

The value of a local search certificate lies not so much in the protection that it affords the purchaser, but in the information which it reveals. The effect of charges can cause problems for the following reasons: —

(i) The search is normally made before *exchange* of contracts and generally speaking few matters are completed immediately with the result of the purchaser taking the risk of later matters being registered.
(ii) Although a second search can quite properly be made before completion, thus giving up to date notice of matters[3], the disclosure of a charge registered after contract does not, where the Standard Conditions of Sale apply, entitle the purchaser to require the vendor to discharge it or give him any right to rescind.

Nevertheless it constitutes professional negligence on a solicitor's part not to effect a local search, or to fail to inform his client of entries revealed by it[4]. The existence of a registered charge may be vital to a purchaser's decision whether or not to proceed and the disclosure of a financial charge may make it necessary for him to re-negotiate the price.

19   LSC 3 (4). This is subject to the warranty as to disclosure p. 190, ante.
20   A person is a purchaser if he acquires an interest in land or proceeds of sale for valuable consideration (s. 10).
1   A search is material if made by or on behalf of the purchaser before the relevant time (usually the contract date).
2   See further on s. 10 [1976] Conv 118.
3   It is not usual to make a second search. The Council of The Law Society are of the opinion that a mortgagee's solicitor is well advised to make further searches before completion of the mortgage (see (1952) 49 LS Gaz 501), but this is not generally done, the mortgagee's solicitor relying on the one made on behalf of the purchaser, except where there is a considerable time-lag.
4   See *Lake v Bushby* [1949] 2 All ER 964 (failure to advise client of lack of planning permission) and *G and K Ladenbau Ltd v Grawley and de Reya* [1978] 1 All ER 682.

E   Additional inquiries

1.   Nature of additional inquiries

Not all the information in which a prospective purchaser may be interested is capable of being entered in the register of local land charges. No logical justification seems to exist for requiring the registration of some matters whilst excluding others. As it is, it is necessary to raise additional inquiries of the local authority at the same time as the requisition for an official search is submitted. A standard form of inquiry, varying according to the particular type of authority consulted[5], has been approved by the Council of The Law Society and the various local government bodies. The object of such inquiries is simply to elicit information — information on matters similar in nature to local land charges, matters in the process of becoming registrable, or matters contained in other public registers maintained by local authorities. No protection akin to that afforded by an official search certificate attaches to the replies, some of which may merely refer to proposals, and it is common knowledge that proposals sometimes never materialise and often change. These inquiries roughly fall into four categories: roads, sewers, planning (which account for about half), and a miscellaneous group covering a variety of matters, such as entries in the register of furnished lettings, kept under the Rent Act 1977, the location of pipe-lines, the making of a smoke control order under the Clean Air Act 1956, or the existence of a resolution bringing into operation the General Rate Act 1967, which empowers rating authorities to levy rates in respect of unoccupied property. Some inquiries are optional (known as Part II inquiries) and will not be answered unless the applicant initials those to which he requires a reply and also pays an additional fee. Supplementary inquiries can be added, which the authority will endeavour to answer, again on payment of a fee, provided they are not unanswerable or unreasonable. The purchaser's liability for road charges is considered later in this chapter; planning inquiries are dealt with in the next chapter.

2.   Liability for incorrect replies

If the authority give an incorrect reply to any inquiry, can the purchaser maintain an action against the authority for loss sustained as a result thereof? A note to the printed form warns that the replies

> ' are furnished after appropriate inquiries, and in the belief that they are in accordance with the information at present available to the officers of the respective councils, but on the distinct understanding that neither the District nor the County Council, nor any officer of either Council is legally responsible therefor, except for negligence'[6].

In *Coats Patons (Retail) Ltd v Birmingham Corpn*[7], Bean J was called upon to consider, for the first time, the effect of a similar exclusion clause[8]. He held that

5   The standard form is known either as Con 29A or D depending on the situation of the property. Con 29A relates to property outside London, Con 29D to property in London. The use of the additional inquiries will vary depending on the property. As to the types of inquiries see Emmet, 31–40.
6   It is further provided that the liability shall extend to a purchaser as defined in the LLC Act 1975, s. 10 (3).
7   (1971) 69 LGR 356 (failure to disclose proposed subway).
8   The inquiry form then in use did not contain the words 'except for negligence'.

the authority were not protected, either in contract or tort, for supplying wrong information in reply to an inquiry. The contract created as a result of the sending in of the inquiry form and the giving of the answers imposed on the authority an obligation to make appropriate inquiries before replying. This was a fundamental term of the contract which the authority had, on the facts, broken, and a breach of that term prevented it from relying on the exemption clause. As to the claim in negligence, there were no clear words excluding tortious liability which was also held to be established on the facts for, as was conceded by counsel for the corporation, the case fell within the principle of *Hedley Bryne & Co Ltd v Heller & Partners Ltd*[9].

Directly as a result of this decision many local authorities began to adopt a much more stringent form of disclaimer, which purported to exclude all liability, whether in tort or contract, for any mistakes or errors arising from inadvertence, negligence or from any other cause whatsoever. Not surprisingly, this new exemption clause caused considerable concern among practitioners, for it was immediately appreciated that a purchaser whose contract was governed by The Law Society's Conditions of Sale was placed in a very vulnerable position. Vis-à-vis his vendor, he was contractually bound to take subject to, and rely on, matters and information which might reasonably be expected to be disclosed by the local authority. Yet if the disclaimer were upheld, no redress was available from the authority in respect of loss caused by relying upon false information. Fortunately, after protracted negotiations between the Council of The Law Society and the appropriate local government bodies, local authorities agreed to withdraw their new form and to rely on the old disclaimer as interpreted in the *Coats Patons* case. Their acceptance of liability, which extends to replies to the inquiries printed in Parts I and II of the form, has now been made clear by the addition of the words 'except for negligence' to the end of the disclaimer. However, in the case of supplementary questions which a solicitor might ask, the authority are free to determine on what basis as regards liability their replies are given[10].

3. Liability for road charges

The first question on the inquiry form asks whether the roadways abutting on the property are maintained at the public expense, i.e., whether the roads have been taken over and adopted by the local authority. A negative reply renders it necessary to consider the potential liability for road charges, since the local authority may resolve to make it up under their statutory powers, particularly those in the Highways Act 1980. A further question asks whether the Council have passed any resolution to make up the road at the cost of the frontagers. The answer merely records the present position and gives no clue as to what might happen in the future[11].

Under the Highways Act 1980, a local highway authority may resolve to make up any private street, defined as 'a street not being a highway

---

9 [1964] AC 465, [1963] 2 All ER 575, HL. Presumably the point was considered to be covered by *Ministry of Housing and Local Government v Sharp* [1970] 2 QB 223, [1970] 1 All ER 1009, CA.

10 See further (1972) 69 LS Gaz 1164.

11 The purchaser may in theory have the benefit of a covenant to make up and maintain the road but it may be worthless if the covenantor is dead, or a company no longer in existence. However this covenant is becoming of increasing use to protect purchasers in the event of there being a dispute between the developer and the local authority.

maintainable at the public expense'. The word 'private' does not signify that the public have no rights over the road but merely that it is not a charge on public funds. The authority adopt a procedure, known as the 'code of 1892'. The authority must prepare plans and specifications and serve notice of a provisional apportionment of costs, followed after execution of the works by a final apportionment, on the owners and occupiers of land fronting, adjoining or abutting the road[12]. On completion, the authority may declare the street to be maintainable at the public expense and must do so if requested by owners of properties which together account for more than half the rateable value in the street[13]. The street is then said to have been 'adopted' and the authority can make no further claims against the frontagers in respect of street works.

(a) Basis of apportionment
The apportionment of expenses is made according to the frontage of the respective premises liable to be charged. The authority have a discretion to have regard to the degree of benefit to be derived by any premises from the proposed works, or to include in the apportionment premises not fronting the street, but which have access thereto (such as an upper maisonette) and which will be benefited by the works[14]. The power of a local authority to charge a land owner who merely has a flank or rear boundary upon a private street poses a very serious threat to such owners. They may derive little or no benefit from the street works, and yet be called upon to pay a disproportionate amount on account of having a long 'frontage', without being able to challenge the basis of the apportionment if the authority refuse to operate the degree of benefit provisions in his favour[15].

(b) Rights of appeal
A frontager may object to the proposed works on specified grounds[16]. One particular ground of objection is that the street is an ancient highway repairable by the inhabitants at large, that is, one dedicated to and used by the public prior to the coming into force of the Highways Act 1835, or dedicated thereafter in accordance with the procedure laid down by that Act[17]. The existence of an ancient highway may be established from ancient maps, evidence of the expenditure of public money on its repair, old deed plans, even a guide-stone on which was carved 'Road to X. No thorough by'[18]. Not all of such matters will necessarily be conclusive by themselves. The burden is on the authority to prove the highway is *not* repairable by the inhabitants at large[19]. If the objection is upheld, the street must be made up out of public funds. It does not constitute a ground of objection that the authority failed to exercise its discretion under section 207[20]. Objection can also be taken to the final apportionment

---

12 Highways Act 1980, ss. 205, 206, and 211. See *Buckinghamshire County Council v Trigg* [1963] 1 All ER 403 (owner of first floor maisonette not a frontager). See further Cross Sauvain '*The Highways Act 1980*' and Hamilton '*The Modern Law of Highways*'.
13 Highways Act 1980, s. 228.
14 Highways Act 1980, s. 207.
15 An appeal may lie under s. 233; see post. The authority are empowered to make a contribution in respect of premises having a rear or flank to the street; see s. 236 (2).
16 Highways Act 1980, s. 208. Objections are determined by the magistrates' court: s. 204.
17 Section 23, now replaced by the Highways Act 1980, s. 37.
18 *Huyton-with-Roby UDC v Hunter* [1955] 2 All ER 398, CA.
19 *Alsager UDC v Barratt* [1965] 2 QB 343, [1965] 1 All ER 889.
20 See note 14, ante. *Hornchurch UDC v Webber* [1938] 1 KB 698, [1938] 1 All ER 309.

on limited grounds, including unreasonable departure from the plans and specifications[1].

An appeal also lies to the Secretary of State within 21 days after receipt of a demand for payment[2]. On appeal a frontager can argue that the authority should have invoked the 'degree of benefit' provisions, or included other premises, or contributed towards the cost of the works. The Secretary has the widest powers on appeal[3].

(c) Recovery of land charges

The sum finally apportioned constitutes a charge on the premises, registrable in Part 2 of the Local Land Charges register. The authority have the same powers as a legal mortgagee[4], including the statutory power of sale[5]. The charge overrides all other proprietary interests existing in the property, such as prior mortgages[6], but it is statutorily provided that it does not rank as a prior mortgage for the purposes of the Building Societies Act 1962, which prohibits a loan by a building society on the security of land subject to a prior mortgage (unless in favour of itself)[7].

Alternatively, the authority may recover the expenses and interest as a simple contract debt. Proceedings must be commenced within six years of the date of the demand for payment, but a fresh cause of action arises against a new owner who can be sued, even though an action against the previous owner is statute-barred[8] or the charge is void against the new owner for want of registration.

(d) The advance payments code[9]

This code (where applicable) is designed to regulate private street works expenses in relation to *new development*. Before any new buildings can be erected in a private street, a sum likely to be needed to cover the street works must be paid to the authority, or security given. When the development has reached a certain stage, the authority can be called upon to execute the street works and adopt the street. Payment or security does not completely discharge liability; any further sum payable after the works are eventually carried out is recoverable from the then owner under the procedure previously discussed. Conversely any excess must be repaid to the owner of the land for the time being, not the person who made the payment, who, in the absence of any contractual right, cannot recover the excess from the recipient[10]. Payment or security is not required in certain cases[11]. One such occasion arises when an agreement is entered into under s. 38 of the Act.

For the purpose of the advance payments code, a private street includes land shown as a proposed street on plans deposited in connection with an

---

1 Highways Act 1980, s. 211.
2 Highways Act 1980, s. 233, unless some other procedure exists for hearing the objection (e.g. under s. 208): ibid., s. 217.
3 See *R v Minister of Housing and Local Government, Ex Finchley Corpn* [1955] 1 All ER 69.
4 Highways Act 1980, s. 212 (3).
5 *Payne v Cardiff RDC* [1932] 1 KB 241.
6 *Paddington Borough Council v Finucane* [1928] Ch 567.
7 Section 32 (1) and Sch. 5.
8 *Dennerley v Prestwich UDC* [1930] 1 KB 334, CA.
9 Highways Act 1980, ss. 219–225. For the operation of this code see s. 201.
10 *Henshall v Fogg* [1964] 2 All ER 868, CA.
11 Highways Act 1980, s. 219.

application for planning permission[12]. Consequently estate developers come within the requirement for depositing or giving security. In practice, they enter into 'a section 40 agreement'[13], under which they agree with the authority to make up the road to the authority's specification and to maintain it for a certain period (usually twelve months), after which the road becomes maintainable at the public expense. A prospective purchaser is adequately protected against the payment of road charges so long only as the developer fulfils his obligations under the agreement. If he defaults, the authority can recover the charges from the purchaser, as frontager[14]. To cover this contingency most agreements are supported by a bond given by a bank or insurance company, whereby the bondsman undertakes to pay to the authority the cost of making up the road should the developer default. Doubts have been expressed whether the authority can recover from the bondsman in the event of default, on the ground that the authority may still proceed against the frontagers and so suffer no loss. The bond, so it is claimed, constitutes a penalty and is irrecoverable[15]. The question of specific performance of the agreement if there is no bondsman is a nice point also. This perhaps overstates the position, and in practice building societies and other mortgagees are prepared to accept a supporting bond, provided it covers the full estimated cost of making up the road. In the absence of any bond, a building society usually makes it a condition of the loan to the purchaser that the builder makes a cash deposit with the society to cover the liability, or it retains an adequate sum out of the mortgage advance, for release when the work is completed. The existence of an agreement under s. 38, and any supporting bond will be revealed in the replies to additional inquiries. It should be carefully scrutinised to show that it is correctly drafted. The size of the bond should also be verified and whether there has been a partial release of it.

(e) Proposals for widening, improving, etc.
Other inquiries on the standard form are directed to ascertaining whether the council have approved any proposals for the improvement, or widening of any road, whether any road or proposed road in the vicinity of the property is to be made a trunk road, or whether there is any resolution to construct a subway, underpass, flyover or elevated road in the vicinity[16]. The existence of any such matters may be important to a prospective purchaser.

F   Land charges search

The Law of Property Act 1969[17], s. 24 (1) enacts that:

---

12 Highways Act 1980, s. 203 (2).
13 So called after s. 40 of the Highways Act 1959. Now presumably they will become known as 'Section 38 Agreements'.
14 Since the price for the house is inclusive of road charges, the purchaser has in effect to pay twice. The contractual remedy under the road making covenant which the builder gives in the conveyance will be valueless in the circumstances, if the vendor is insolvent. Difficulties have arisen lately over receivers in respect of vendors and the arrangements they made with the local authority. Several authorities have had difficulties with the bondsman also.
15 See (1964) 108 Sol Jo 126, 195, 262; cf. ibid., 611.
16 See *Coats Patons (Retail) Ltd v Birmingham Corpn* (1971) 69 LGR 356.
17 Implementing the recommendations of the Law Commission in the Report on Land Charges Affecting Unregistered Land, Law Com. No. 18, para. 29.

' Where under a contract for the sale or other disposition of any estate or interest in land the title to which is not registered under the Land Registration Act 1925 . . . any question arises whether the purchaser[18] had knowledge, at the time of entering into the contract, of a registered land charge, that question shall be determined by reference to his actual knowledge and without regard to the provisions of section 198 of the Law of Property Act 1925. . . .'

This provision reverses the view, founded upon Eve J's much criticised decision in *Re Forsey and Hollebone's Contract*[19], that s. 198 of the Law of Property Act 1925 fixed a purchaser with notice of any land charge registered at the time of the contract, and as a result disentitled him to rescind the contract on the ground of the vendor's non-disclosure thereof. It was therefore advisable to make a land charges search *before* contract to discover registered charges. This he could not do without the names of previous estate owners which could only be ascertained by investigating the vendor's title. But conveyancing practice dictates that a purchaser investigates the title after he has contracted to buy, not before. Not uncommonly the purchaser's rights were preserved by a contractual provision[20] enabling him to rescind if before the making of the contract an irremovable land charge had been registered of which the purchaser had not received notice in writing.

Such a search is now unnecessary. The question of the purchaser's knowledge at the time of making the contract is determined solely by reference to his *actual* knowledge without regard to s. 198. Not even constructive notice[1] (e.g. from possession) will preclude objection to a registered charge not disclosed by the vendor. Knowledge acquired in the course of the transaction by the purchaser's solicitor, counsel or other agent, is treated as the knowledge of the purchaser[2]. Section 24 (2) avoids any contractual provision so far as it purports to exclude the operation of sub-s. (1) or to restrict the purchaser's remedies in respect of registered land charges of which he was unaware at the date of the contract.

The limits of s. 24 must be noted. It does not dispense with the need for a local land charges search. The expression 'registered land charge' does not include any instrument or matter registered in a register of local land charges, and in relation to such registration still constitutes notice. This presents no problem since local land charges are registered against the land, as has been noticed. The section also does not relate to contracts for the sale of registered land, and there is no reason why it should. There is no provision in the Land Registration Act 1925, or the Rules made thereunder, equivalent to the Law of

---

18   Defined to include a lessee, mortgagee or other person acquiring or intending to acquire an estate or interest in land: sub-s. (3).
19   [1927] 2 Ch D 379, CA (resolution to prepare town planning scheme). It is commonly asserted that Eve J's comments regarding s. 198 were merely obiter, but it seems clear that he based his decision on two alternative grounds; see [1927] 2 Ch D 379, at 382–83. The Court of Appeal upheld his decision on the ground that the resolution did not constitute an incumbrance without hearing argument on the notice point. See also *Re Middleton and Young's Contract* [1929] WN 70. For a discussion of the problems created by Eve J's decision, see Wade, 'The Effect of Statutory Notice of Incumbrances' (1954) CLJ 89.
20   See e.g. LSC (1953 edn) 20 (3); NCS (17th edn) 13. Sometimes the vendor was asked by way of preliminary inquiry to supply the names and addresses of estate owners since 1 January 1926, but often he could not go back so far.
1   *Midland Bank Trust Co Ltd v Green* [1981] 1 All ER 153, HL.
2   LPA 1969, s. 24 (4).

Property Act 1925, s. 198. An entry on the register gives notice to 'all persons deriving title from the proprietor[3]. This is borne out by the decision in *Re Stone and Saville's Contract*[4], a case where a purchaser was held entitled to rescind the contract on the ground of the vendor's failure to disclose a restrictive covenant, even though the incumbrance was duly noted in the vendor's charges register at the date of the contract. Finally, and this point hardly needs stressing, the section leaves the operation of s. 198 unaffected for other purposes.

G   Search in the public index map

Rule 286 of the Land Registration Rules 1925, enables any person to obtain free of charge an official search of the index map and parcels index[5]. This certificate of search reveals whether the land the subject of the search is within an area of compulsory registration, whether the title is registered and, if so, whether as freehold or leasehold and under what title number, and if the land is not registered whether it is affected by any caution against first registration[6]. An application for such a search should be made on printed form 96 and where the land is in a compulsory area it need not be accompanied by any identifying plan[7]. Every purchaser of land is well advised to effect this search before exchange of contracts on any purchase of unregistered land which will result in first registration of title. It enables him to check that no part of the land is registered with a title adverse to the vendor's interest (as, for example, might happen if part of the land has previously been sold off). Further if the purchaser makes a specific request therefor the Registrar will, on payment of the fee of £1, issue with the search certificate an official plan defining the extent of the land as shown on the ordnance survey map (which is used as the basis of all the Registry's plans). This official plan can be compared with the contract plan and any discrepancies in the plot boundaries as revealed by the two plans can be clarified with the vendor. Although the parties may be anxious to avoid delay at this stage, it is in the purchaser's interests to resolve the difference before exchanging contracts. Otherwise, if the inaccuracy of the contract plan is not discovered until after completion when the Registry is preparing the filed plan for the property, the purchaser may find that he is ultimately registered with a plot of land smaller in size than the one which he thought he had acquired[8].

---

3   *White v Bijou Mansions Ltd* [1937] Ch 610 at 621, per Simonds J; cf. [1937] 3 All ER 269 at 274; affd. [1938] Ch 351, [1938] 1 All ER 546, CA.
4   [1963] 1 All ER 353, CA. *Farqui v English Real Estates* [1979] 1 WLR 963.
5   These show the position and extent of every registered estate with its title number, and the existence of cautions against first registration: LRR 1925, rr. 8, 274.
6   Page 31, ante.
7   See Registered Land Practice Note 16, which relaxes LRR 1925, r. 286 (2). The current fee is £2; see S.I. 1981 No. 54.
8   See [1979] Conv 316 (Hyde) and the outraged comments therein.

Chapter 8

Planning considerations

A   Introduction

At common law a man was basically free to do what he liked with his own land, provided that in so doing he did not harm his neighbour. However the complexity of modern society has made it necessary to introduce a multiplicity of statutory controls which have largely eroded this principle by subordinating the interests of the individual to those of the community at large. Perhaps the most important form of control affecting landowners, and consequently vendors, purchasers and their advisers, is that imposed by the town and country planning legislation, an ever expanding topic so voluminous that it constitutes a subject in its own right. Besides the basic statute, the Town and Country Planning Act 1971[1], and a mass of detailed subordinate legislation, regulating the general law as to land use, there are special codes governing specific aspects of planning control, such as advertisements and caravan sites.

The present law relating to town planning is still based in large measure on the Town and Country Planning Act 1947[2], which came into operation on 1 July 1948, a date known as the appointed day. This Act made a fresh start by repealing previous town planning legislation and enacting principles entirely new to planning law. As one commentator has put it, the Act contained some of the most drastic and far-reaching provisions ever enacted affecting the ownership of land[3]. It was even argued in some quarters that the Act brought about the demise of the fee simple estate, and that an owner in fee owned merely a fee simple in the existing, or permitted, use of the land[4], a contention which failed to attract any widespread support. It is now accepted that planning control affects the use and enjoyment of land, and not the existence of estates and interests in it. The fee simple estate in land remains unchanged. As it has been graphically explained, the fruits of ownership have become less sweet, but that is nothing new in land law[5].

---

1   As amended by the Town and Country Planning (Amendment) Act 1972, the Local Government Acts 1972 and 1974, the Community Land Act 1975, the Local Government, Planning and Land Act 1980 and the Local Government and Planning (Amendment) Act 1981.

2   The financial provisions of this Act did not survive very long and were repealed by the T & CPA 1953. The more recent attempt made by the Land Commission Act 1967, to impose a similar but not so far reaching financial structure, has proved to be as equally ill-fated. See generally Telling, *Planning Law and Procedure* (6th edn).

3   Heap, *An Outline of Planning Law* (7th edn), p. 13.

4   Potter, 'Caveat Emptor or Conveyancing under the Planning Acts' (1949) 13 Conv (NS) 36.

5   Megarry, *Lectures on the Town and Country Planning Act 1947*, p. 104.

It is impossible within the space of a single chapter to give even the barest outline of the main principles of planning law as laid down by the Act of 1971[6]. The following pages attempt to do no more than consider those aspects most likely to be of relevance to a conveyancing transaction. A purchaser of land is clearly affected by planning control. For instance he needs to satisfy himself that the existing use of the land is authorised by the appropriate planning authority. He should discover the precise terms of any planning permission granted to the vendor or some previous owner since conditions attached to the permission may conflict with his proposals for the land. Should he contemplate building or changing the use of the land, it may be vital to ascertain before signing a contract that permission will be forthcoming for his project. Alternatively he should ensure that the contract incorporates a clause entitling him to terminate the contract if permission is not obtained within a specified period[7]. Planning considerations are of concern to a vendor as well. In particular it will be necessary to consider to what extent planning matters constitute matters of title, so requiring full disclosure in the contract.

B Meaning of development

Section 23 (1) of the Act of 1971 provides that subject to certain exceptions planning permission is required for the carrying out of any development of land. Development undertaken without permission is subject to enforcement control. A purchaser of land should check whether the vendor, or any previous owner, has undertaken development and if so whether permission was obtained. Development is defined to mean[8]:

' the carrying out of building, engineering, mining or other operations in, on, over or under land, or the making of any material change in the use of any buildings or other land.'

Thus there are two separate limbs to the definition, the carrying out of operations, and a material change of use, and they are mutually exclusive.

1. Operations

The expression *building operations* includes rebuilding operations, structural alterations or additions to buildings, and other operations normally undertaken by a builder. It covers the construction of a model village[9], but not the installation of a moveable coal hopper and conveyer. In this latter case[10] it was said that an operation must change the physical characteristics of the land and

---

6 For a detailed study of the subject, reference should be made to Telling, op. cit., Heap, op. cit.; Hamilton, *Guide to Development and Planning* (7th edn); *Encyclopedia of Planning Law and Practice*.

7 Pages 130–131, ante. See also *Guiness v Pearce* (1971) 22 P & CR 998 (price to be reduced if permission refused).

8 T & CPA 1971, s. 22 (1). Several of the expressions used in s. 22 (1) are themselves the subject of specialised definitions in s. 290 (1), e.g. building, building operations, engineering operations, land, use, etc.

9 *Buckinghamshire County Council v Callingham* [1952] 2 QB 515, [1952] 1 All ER 1166, CA.

10 *Cheshire County Council v Woodward* [1962] 2 QB 126, [1962] 1 All ER 517, DC, applied in *James v Brecon County Council* (1963) 15 P & CR 20, DC (swingboats).

in deciding this the whole circumstances, including the degree of permanency, must be considered.

Engineering operations include the formation or laying out of access to highways, and will cover such things as the construction of roads, sewers, water mains, as well as the making of a second access-way from a road to a house.

Mining operations include the extraction of sand and gravel. Within this category each shovelful of material or each cut of the bulldozer will constitute a separate act of development[11].

The exact scope of the category comprised by *other operations* and its relationship with the other three remains uncertain. The phrase cannot be construed ejusdem generis; there is no single genus comprising building, engineering (which are both normally constructive) and mining (which is destructive). Yet the 'other operations' must in some way be restricted by their juxtaposition with the preceding words[12]. The correct approach to the vexed question whether demolition constitutes development was explained by Lord Pearson in *Coleshill and District Investment Co Ltd v Minister of Housing and Local Government* in these terms[13]:

> ' It is not right to say "This is a demolition or removal operation, therefore it cannot be development". Notwithstanding that an operation is a demolition or removal operation one still has to see whether it comes within the scope of development as defined in section [22] assisted by section [290]. It may be within the definition of "building operations", e.g., because it constitutes a structural alteration of a building or because it is such an operation as to be normally undertaken by a person carrying on business as a builder. It may be an engineering operation. Whether it is or is not any of those things depends on the facts of the particular case.'

Applying this test, it may not even be correct to say that demolition of an entire building (unaccompanied by any redevelopment) does not constitute development, as Lord Denning MR, tentatively suggested in the Court of Appeal[14], or as has been stated in a ministerial circular[15].

Statutory exclusions

It is expressly provided by s. 22 (2) that certain operations do not constitute development, as follows:

(i)   internal or external improvements, alterations or maintenance works to any building, not materially affecting its external appearance, other

---

11   *Thomas David (Porthcawl) Ltd v Penybout RDC* [1972] 1 All ER 733, DC; affd. [1972] 3 All ER 1092, CA.

12   *Coleshill and District Investment Co Ltd v Minister of Housing and Local Government* [1969] 2 All ER 525 at 543, HL, per Lord Pearson; *Parkes v Secretary of State for the Environment* [1979] 1 All ER 211, CA.

13   [1969] 2 All ER 525 at 543. In this case their Lordships refused to interfere with the Minister's decision that the removal of embankments and demolition of blast walls of ammunition magazines involved engineering operations. See also *Parkes v Secretary of State for the Environment* [1979] 1 All ER 211, CA.

14   [1968] 1 All ER 945, at 947.

15   Circular 67/49. For comments on this circular, see [1969] 2 All ER 525 at 538, per Lord Wilberforce. The demolition of buildings of special architectural or historic interest is subject to a special form of control; see T & CPA 1971, ss. 54–58; T & CP (Am) A 1972, s. 7.

than works for the alteration of a building by providing additional space below ground;

(ii) road maintenance or improvement works undertaken by a local highway authority[16];

(iii) repair or renewal works effected by a local authority or statutory under-taker to sewers, mains, cables, etc.

2. Change of use

A change of use only constitutes development if it is *material*. 'Use' is defined in a negative way so as not to include the use of land for the carrying out of building or other operations. A non-material change of use accompanied by building, etc., operations requires permission. Apart from a few specific uses that are expressly referred to, the Act wisely does not attempt to explain what is meant by 'material', since this is essentially a question of fact and degree, varying from case to case.

(a) Statutory provisions

For the avoidance of doubt, s. 22 (3) and (4) declares that the following involve a material change of use:

(i) the use of a single house as two or more separate dwellings;

(ii) the deposit of refuse or waste materials, even on an existing tip, unless certain conditions are satisfied;

(iii) the display of advertisements on any external part of a building not normally so used.

The first of these may be of special interest to a purchaser. He will need to know that permission has been obtained if purchasing property which has been converted into self-contained flats. There may be difficulty in particular cases in deciding whether development has taken place. Multiple occupation is not sufficient by itself; the units formed out of the original single dwelling must be separate. This is a question of fact and degree, to be determined by considering factors like the existence or absence of physical reconstruction, and the extent to which the alleged separate parts are self-contained and independent[17].

The following changes of use do not involve development[18].

(i) The use of a building or other land within the curtilage of a dwelling house for any purpose incidental to the enjoyment of the house as such. This will cover the use of an existing shed as a garage or wash-house, but not the conversion of a stable block within the curtilage of a large house into living quarters for persons employed there[19].

(ii) The use of land for agricultural or forestry purposes. Whilst the word 'agricultural' is widely defined to include (inter alia) the use of land for seed growing, breeding and keeping livestock, market gardens and nursery

16 Repairs effected by builders or abutting owners to unadopted roads rank as 'permitted development', for which see p. 213, post.

17 *Ealing Corpn v Ryan* [1965] 2 QB 485, [1965] 1 All ER 137, DC. See also *Birmingham Corpn v Minister of Housing and Local Government* [1964] 1 QB 178, [1963] 3 All ER 668, DC.

18 T & CPA 1971, s. 22 (2) (d), (e) and (f).

19 See [1962] JPL 350.

grounds, it does not cover the breeding and training of horses for show-jumping[20], or the buying and selling of agricultural products[1].

(iii) A change of use from one purpose to another in the same class of use specified in a use classes order. This needs further elaboration. The order at present in force is the Town and Country Planning (Use Classes) Order 1972[2], which classifies into eighteen groups various similar uses. No development is involved if there is merely a change of use within the same class[3].

A few random illustrations may serve to show the scope of this Order. The change of use of a shop (Class I) from e.g. a butcher's to a baker's, is not development[4]. Class II relates to use as an office (including a bank, but not a post office or betting shop) for any purpose. There are several classes devoted to similar types of industrial user. A convalescent home may be converted into a nursing home (Class XIV), or a theatre into a cinema (Class XVII).

Three specific points must be made about this Order. First, though changes of use within the same class do not constitute development, it does not follow that a change of use from one class to another must be development. It will only do so if the change is material, and that problem must be solved by general principles. Second, bearing in mind the statutory definition of 'use', the Order does not apply to changes of use within the same class, if involving building operations. Thirdly, a planning authority can nullify the operation of the Order by the imposition of a planning condition. In *City of London Corpn v Secretary of State for the Environment*[5] permission was granted for the use of premises as an employment agency, subject to a condition that they were to be used for that purpose and no other. It was contended that the condition was invalid in that it prohibited the use of premises for purposes not involving development i.e. a change to some other office use. Talbot J upheld the condition. The imposition of such a condition fell within the scope of a planning authority's power to impose conditions; indeed the power to impose a condition of this kind is necesary to enable planning authorities to meet the varied and particular circumstances of planning a particular area[6].

(b) Test for determining materiality
With cases not falling within the statutory provisions the question whether a change of use is material is one of fact and degree[7]. For the guidance of

20 *Belmont Farm Ltd v Minister of Housing and Local Government* (1963) 13 P & CR 417, DC. See also *Warnock v Secretary of State for the Environment* [1980] JPL 590, DC.
1 *Hidderley v Warwickshire County Council* (1963) 14 P & CR 134, DC (installation of egg vending machine).
2 S.I. 1972 No. 1385.
3 Use classes are, however, to be interpreted restrictively rather than widely; *Tessier v Secretary of State for the Environment* (1975) 31 P & CR 161.
4 Certain shop uses are excluded — a (i) shop for the sale of hot food; (ii) tripe shop; (iii) shop for the sale of pets and birds; (iv) cat's meat shop; (v) shop for the sale of motor vehicles. A change of use from one of these five excepted types to any other kind of shop constitutes permitted developments; see p. 212, post.
5 (1972) 23 P & CR 169.
6 At p. 178, per Talbot J. For the power to impose conditions, see p. 223, post.
7 *East Barnet UDC v British Transport Commission* [1962] 2 QB 484, [1961] 3 All ER 878, DC (change from coal stacking depot to depot for handling and storage of crated vehicles held not to be a material change since, though the commodity differed, the land was still used for storage purposes); *Marshall v Nottingham City Corpn* [1960] 1 All ER 659.

planning authorities a ministerial circular was issued in 1949[8], suggesting relevant considerations. The new use should be substantially different from the previous one; a change in *kind* (e.g. house into offices) will always be material, but a change in degree only if it is very marked. To determine whether a material change of use has taken place, it is also necessary to ascertain the relevant planning unit. In many instances the whole unit occupied by the developer will be the appropriate planning unit, but this may not be so if there occurs within a single unit of occupation two or more physically separate and distinct areas which are occupied for substantially different and unrelated purposes. In such a case each area used for a different main purpose ought to be treated as a separate planning unit[9].

Decided cases are of little value in deciding the question of materiality. Usually it is the Secretary of State for the Environment[10] who makes the initial decision on an appeal to him against enforcement proceedings[11]. As the question is basically one of fact, the courts will not interfere with his decision unless satisfied that he has misdirected himself as to the law when reaching his conclusion. This is clearly illustrated by *Bendles Motors Ltd v Bristol Corporation*[12]. The Minister of Housing and Local Government had decided that the stationing of a free standing egg vending machine on the forecourt of a petrol filling station involved a material change of use since it might attract non-motoring customers. The Divisional Court refused to interfere with this decision. Although on a personal view Lord Parker CJ, was inclined to regard the machine as de minimis, it could not be said that the Minister had erred in law nor was the decision perverse for there was evidence to support it.

(c) Special problems

A purchaser will be concerned to know about the possibility of development occurring if he proposes to resume some use discontinued by the vendor, or intensify an existing use, or commence a second use, whilst retaining the existing use. These constitute particular problems which cannot easily be resolved. Part of the difficulty lies in attempting to define what is meant by 'use'. It is not clear whether under the Planning Acts the word signifies the actual physical use to which the land or building is being put, or whether it incorporates a notional (or mental) element. Can land be said to be 'used' for a purpose (X) within the Acts when its owner, though discontinuing X (its last use) so that the land is not being put to any active use, still retains an intention to revert to X at some time in the future? The courts, without consciously adverting to the problem, appear to favour a notional concept of the use.

---

8 Circular 67/1949. The circular has no legal force.
9 See generally *Burdle v Secretary of State for the Environment* [1972] 3 All ER 240, DC; *Warnock v Secretary of State for the Environment* [1980] JPL 590, DC; *David W. Barling Ltd v Secretary of State for the Environment* [1980] JPL 594, DC; *Jennings Motors Ltd v Secretary of State for the Environment* [1982] 1 All ER 471, CA.
10 Hereafter referred to as the Secretary of State. By the Secretary of State for the Environment Order 1970, S.I. 1970 No. 1681, the functions of the Minister of Housing and Local Government were transferred to the Secretary of State and the Ministry was dissolved. As for Wales and Monmouthshire, planning functions have been vested in the Secretary of State for Wales since 1 April 1965; see S.I. 1965 No. 319.
11 Pages 228–229, post.
12 [1963] 1 All ER 578, DC; *Howell v Sunbury-on-Thames UDC* (1964) 62 LGR 119, CA (grocer's shop to open-air car mart; material); *Ratcliffe v Secretary of State for the Environment* [1975] JPL 728, DC.

(i) *Discontinuance and resumption.* In a recent case, Ashworth J summarised the law as follows[13]:

(1) If the sole use to which land is put is suspended and thereafter resumed without any intervening different use, prima facie the resumption does not constitute development.
(2) There may be cases in which the period of suspension is so long that the original use can properly be said to have been abandoned.
(3) If land is put to more than one use (i.e. a composite use), the cessation of one of the uses does not of itself constitute development.
(4) If one of two composite uses is discontinued and later resumed, it is a question of fact, to be determined in the light of all the relevant circumstances, whether the resumption involves development.

Abandonment depends on the circumstances. It involves a cessation by the occupier of the activities constituting the use, not merely for a temporary period but without any view to their being resumed. It may be that the courts will be more prepared to find as a fact that there has been abandonment of a composite use than of a single use. Where there has been an abandonment, a resumption of the former use even by the same owner requires planning permission. The use of land for residential purposes is dependent on there being a house on the land. If an existing house is demolished or destroyed by fire, the residential use rights automatically cease and do not become attached to the land. Consequently planning consent is required for the erection of a new house, and it is within the powers of the planning authority to refuse permission if the circumstances so warrant, e.g. because the land is situated within the green belt[14] (that is, an area of open and undeveloped land within which new building operations are generally not permitted in order to prevent the spread of adjoining towns).

(ii) *Intensification of use.* It seems clear that an increase or intensification of an existing use is capable in appropriate circumstances of constituting a material change of use[15]. Again it is a question of fact and degree. The word 'intensification' is normally used to describe a situation which arises where land is used throughout the relevant time for the same purpose but the intensity of the activity varies[16].

13   *Hartley v Minister of Housing and Local Government* [1969] 2 QB 46 at 57, [1969] 1 All ER 309 at 315, DC; affd. [1970] 1 QB 413, [1969] 3 All ER 1658, CA (use of part of filling station for sale of cars discontinued and resumed four years later by different owner: resumption constituted development); *Blackpool Borough Council v Secretary of State for the Environment* (1980) 40 P & CR 104, DC (dwellinghouse used during the summer months for holiday letting; not material). See also Mellows, 'The Abandonment of a Use' (1963) 27 Conv (NS) 250.
14   See the Minister's decision reported at [1963] JPL 491; *Sainty v Minister of Housing and Local Government* (1964) 15 P & CR 432, DC; *Larkin v Basildon District Council and the Secretary of State for the Environment* [1980] JPL 407, DC. See also H.C. Debates, 16 June 1971, Vol. 819, col. 421.
15   E.g. using the Oval Cricket ground to provide several cricket pitches for boys to play on contemporaneously during the summer; per Lord Evershed MR, in *Guildford RDC v Penny* [1959] 2 QB 112 at 125, [1959] 2 All ER 111 at 113–14, CA; *Peake v Secretary of State for Wales* (1971) 22 P & CR 889, DC; *Brooks and Burton v Secretary of State for the Environment* [1978] 1 All ER 733, (1977) 76 LGR 53, CA.
16   *Brooks v Gloucestershire County Council* (1968) 19 P & CR 90 at 98, DC, per Widgery J.

(iii) *Dual user*. Land may be used for two (or more) purposes at the same time or for different purposes at different times. The commencement of a second use will not normally amount to a material change of use if it is merely incidental to some primary use, e.g. the occasional display and sale of cars at a repair garage, but will do so if that secondary use is increased so as to become a co-primary use. Similarly a material change may occur where one of two concurrent uses is absorbed by the other which extends to the whole site[17]. Where the land is used for one purpose during the winter (e.g. cattle grazing) and for another during the summer (e.g. camping), the annual change does not amount to a material change[18].

3. Determination of doubtful cases

The question whether a planning proposal involves development, so requiring permission, may often be difficult, if not impossible, for the applicant to · decide. Section 53 of the Act of 1971 provides for an application to the local planning authority to determine the question. An appeal from their decision lies first to the Secretary of State and from him to the High Court on a point of law[19].

A planning authority may make a valid s. 53 determination without a formal written application therefor. In *Wells v Minister of Housing and Local Government*[20] a letter from the authority declining to proceed further with a planning application because the proposed erection could be regarded as permitted development amounted to a valid determination for the purposes of the section. The section gives no jurisdiction to determine whether a purported grant of permission is effective[1]. As an alternative to using s. 53, a declaration from the court can be sought that no development is involved[2].

C   Planning permission

Local planning authorities[3] exercise control over development by the granting or withholding of planning permission. Where a developer's proposals do not

---

17 *Wipperman v Barking London Borough Council* (1966) 17 P & CR 225, DC (land used partly for storage of building materials and partly for car breaking; car breaking discontinued and whole site used for storage purposes), applied in *Brooks v Gloucestershire County Council* (1968) 19 P & CR 90, DC.

18 *Webber v Minister of Housing and Local Government* [1967] 3 All ER 981, CA.

19 T & CPA 1971, s. 53 (2), applying s. 36; s. 247 (2).

20 [1967] 2 All ER 1041, DC; *Lever (Finance) Ltd v Westminster Corpn* [1971] 1 QB 222; [1970] 3 All ER 496, CA. But see *Western Fish Products Ltd v Penwith District Council* [1981] 2 All ER 204, CA; *Norfolk County Council v Secretary of State for the Environment* [1973] 3 All ER 673, DC.

 1 *Edgwarebury Park Investments, Ltd v Minister of Housing and Local Goovernment* [1963] 2 QB 408, [1963] 1 All ER 124, DC.

 2 *Pyx Granite Co Ltd v Minister of Housing and Local Government* [1960] AC 260, [1959] 3 All ER 1, HL.

 3 County councils and district councils constitute the local planning authorities for areas outside London. In the main, planning applications will be made to the district councils although certain matters of strategic importance are reserved to the county planning authorities; see the Local Government Act 1972, s. 182 and Sch. 16, paras.15 and 32, as amended by the Local Government, Planning and Land Act 1980. Within London the London Borough Councils are in general the planning authorities for determining applications but for certain limited purposes the Greater London Council is the appropriate planning authority; see T & CP (Local Planning Authorities in Greater London) Regulations 1980 (S.I. 1980 No. 443).

constitute development, permission need not be obtained. If development is involved, he should obtain permission before carrying out his proposals, otherwise he runs the risk of the planning authority taking enforcement proceedings against him. To this general rule two exceptions exist which require discussion.

1.   Development not requiring express permission

(a) Section 23 development

By virtue of s. 23 of the main Act various changes of use, though technically constituting development, do not require planning permission. The resumption of the previous lawful[4] use of land can be effected without permission in certain circumstances[5], for instance, after the expiry of a permission granted for a limited period, or after service of an enforcement notice relating to unauthorised development. The section also provides for a number of specialised exemptions[6] based on the use of the land on or prior to 1 July 1948 (the appointed day), but these do not merit specific treatment here.

(b) Permission granted by development order

Permission to undertake certain forms of development is automatically available under the Town and Country Planning General Development Order 1977[7]. This is often termed permitted development. The Order lists 23 classes of development which may be undertaken without the need to obtain permission from the local planning authority, provided the limitations attaching to each class are observed. In particular there are two standard conditions, one or both of which affect most of the classes; the effect of these conditions is that the Order does not authorise development (i) involving the formation or material widening of a means of access to major roads, or, (ii) obstructing the view of road users so as to cause them danger.

Those forms of permitted development likely to arise in practice are as follows:

Class I. Development within the curtilage of a dwellinghouse. This permits the enlargement, improvement or alteration of a house, subject to certain conditions, including size and height. The erection of a garage within the same curtilage counts as an enlargement of the house. The demolition and rebuilding of a house is not permitted by Class I which only applies to a dwellinghouse in existence at the time of the alteration[8]. If the owner enlarges by more than the permissible cubic content, the whole extension is unauthorised, not merely the excess over the permissible size[9]. This class also permits the erection or alteration of various kinds of outbuildings such as greenhouses, tool-sheds, sheds for poultry or pets, etc.

---

4   As to which see *LTSS Print and Supply Services Ltd v Hackney London Borough Council* [1976] 1 All ER 311, CA.

5   Section 23 (5), (8), (9).

6   Section 23 (2)–(4), (7); *Kingdon v Minister of Housing and Local Government* [1968] 1 QB 257, [1967] 3 All ER 614, DC.

7   S.I. 1977 No. 289 as amended by the T & CP General Development (Amendment) Orders 1980, S.I. 1980 No. 1946 and 1981, S.I. 1981 No. 245.

8   *Sainty v Minister of Housing and Local Government* (1964) 15 P & CR 432, DC; *C. W. Larkin v Basildon District Council and the Secretary of State for the Environment* [1980] JPL 407.

9   *Garland v Minister of Housing and Local Government* (1968) 20 P & CR 93, CA.

Class II. Sundry minor operations. This permits the erection or construction of gates, fences, walls and other means of enclosure, provided certain height limitations are observed. The external painting of a building is also authorised, provided it is not in the nature of an advertisement[10].

Class IV. Temporary buildings and uses. This covers the erection of buildings, plant and machinery required temporarily in connection with building or engineering operations, such as builders' site huts. Permission merely lasts for the duration of the operations. This class also permits the temporary use of land (other than a building) for any purpose[11] on not more than 28 days in any calendar year. Thus the temporary use of land for shows, fairs, etc., is covered, including the erection of movable structures (such as tents or stalls) on the land in connection therewith.

Class VI. Agricultural buildings, works and uses. This is important to the farmer, for, subject to various conditions, it permits the erection and alteration of all farm buildings (other than dwellings), and the working of minerals required for agricultural purposes of the land, e.g. for fertilisation. In certain areas of natural beauty where the uncontrolled erection of agricultural buildings might create eyesores, 14 days' notice must be given to the planning authority who may require the design and external appearance (but not siting) to be subject to their approval[12]. Class VI relates to building operations; the *use* of land for agriculture does not constitute development at all[13].

Class VIII. Industrial development. This covers a variety of matters: the provision of private roads, railways, sewers, etc., the installation of plant and machinery, the making of limited extensions to industrial buildings, and the deposit of waste materials. The undertaking of these various forms of development is subject to different conditions.

Class IX. Repairs to unadopted streets and private ways. This allows for the maintenance and improvement of unadopted streets or private ways so long as the works are carried out within the boundaries of the street or way.

It must be stressed that all the matters covered by the Order fall within the definition of development[14], and the Order itself grants the permission. This relieves local planning authorities of the need to determine applications of a comparatively minor nature, leaving them free to consider major projects.

A planning authority may make a direction excluding from the category of permitted development any particular class referred to in the Order. Such a direction (which requires secretarial approval) makes it necessary to apply for permission; if refused, the applicant is entitled to claim compensation[15]. The

10 See *Prengate Properties Ltd v Secretary of State for the Environment* (1973) 25 P & CR 311, DC; *Ewen Developments Ltd v Secretary of State for the Environment* [1980] JPL 404, DC.
11 Use as a caravan site is excluded, and governed by Class XXII.
12 Town and Country Planning (Landscape Areas Special Development) Order 1950, S.I. 1950 No. 729.
13 T & CPA 1971, s. 22 (2) (e).
14 This distinguishes it from the T & CP (Use Classes) Order 1972, which excludes changes of use from the definition of development.
15 T & CPA 1971, s. 165 (1).

direction may relate to the whole of an authority's area, a particular locality (e.g. a housing estate) or even a particular plot of land[16]. This procedure has been widely adopted in relation to Class XI (replacement of war damaged buildings). The Order cannot operate so as to permit development contrary to a condition imposed on the grant of planning permission. The grant of permission for the erection of houses is sometimes subject to a condition which has the effect of preventing householders from erecting gates and fences under Class II without seeking express permission. In this way a planning authority can ensure that a housing estate planned on the 'open front' system remains that way.

2.   Obtaining planning permission

Assuming development does not have the benefit of automatic permission, an application for permission must be submitted to the appropriate authority. The method of application is governed by the General Development Order 1977, as amended. It is proposed to give but a brief outline of the procedure for obtaining permission. The application must be made on a form issued by the planning authority and accompanied by plans and drawings sufficient to identify the land and describe the proposed development. The application must incorporate one of certain statutory certificates, without which the authority cannot entertain the application[17]. Applications for certain types of development, particularly industrial and office development, may also have to be accompanied by additional certificates[18]. In the absence of any statutory provision regulating the position, it was held in *Hanily v Minister of Local Government and Planning*[19] that anyone who genuinely hopes to acquire an interest in land can apply for permission. An application can therefore be submitted by a prospective purchaser who is negotiating to buy land[20], but he must give written notice of his application to the fee simple owner and any tenant whose tenancy has at least ten years to run.

In considering the application the planning authority must have regard to the development plan and to other material considerations[1]. The decision itself may take one of three forms: a grant of permission, either unconditionally or subject to conditions, or a refusal of permission[2]. The actual decision may be taken by the planning committee or planning sub-committee of the planning authority[3]. Not infrequently it will be made by an officer of the authority. Section 101 of the Local Government Act 1972 enables local authorities to

---

16   See e.g. *Fryer v Essex County Council* (1960) 11 P & CR 21.

17   T & CPA 1971, s. 27. Thus an applicant who does not own the land (the subject of the application) must certify that he has notified all the owners of the land (as defined by sub-s. (7)) and, where he does not know the names of all owners, that notice of the application has been advertised in a local newspaper. See also the General Development Order 1977, art. 7 and Sch. 4.

18   T & CPA 1971, s. 67 (industrial development certificate, a certificate issued by the Secretary of State that the proposed development can be carried out consistently with the proper distribution of industry): s. 74 (office development permit).

19   [1952] 2 QB 444, [1952] 1 All ER 1293, CA.

20   See note 17, ante, as to the certificates that are required in this case.

1   T & CPA 1971, s. 29 (1). As to what constitutes a development plan, see s. 20; Telling, op. cit. Chap. 4. Failure by a planning authority to comply with the requirements of s. 29, renders a decision refusing permission void: *Stringer v Minister of Housing and Local Government* [1971] 1 All ER 65.

2   T & CPA 1971, s. 29 (1). For conditional permissions, see pp. 223–226, post.

3   See the T & CPA 1971, s. 2, and Sch. 2.

make arrangements for the discharge of their functions through officers. Accordingly this enables a planning authority to delegate the function of determining various applications, including planning applications, to any officer. Where a developer has been informed by a planning officer that he (the officer) has taken a decision which would be within the delegated powers, it appears that the local authority may be estopped from denying the officer's authority to make that decision even where the powers were not in fact delegated[4]. However, there must be some evidence justifying the developer's belief that the officer was speaking for the local authority. Furthermore it may be that the local authority is only estopped where the developer has acted to his detriment[5]. The decision must not in any event constitute an unlawful fetter on the local authority statutory powers nor must it be one which is ultra vires the authority[6].

The planning authority must give written notice of its decision within two months of the date of receipt of the application, or within three months for development affecting a trunk road. These periods may be extended by written agreement[7]. An applicant who is aggrieved by the authority's decision (because e.g. his application has been rejected) can appeal to the Secretary of State within six months, and if a decision is not notified by the local planning authority within the appropriate period, the applicant is also entitled to appeal 'as if' his application had been refused[8]. A grant or refusal of permission out of time is not void[9], though authority exists for saying that it may be voidable[10]. It is not, however, readily apparent what practical benefits can accrue from seeking to avoid a late decision. The true purpose of the time limit would seem to be to fix a period after which an appeal can be lodged in the absence of any decision[11]. There have been a number of recent cases in which the question of what constitutes the planning permission has been considered. In *R v Yeovil Borough Council, ex p Trustees of Elim Pentecostal Church, Yeovil*[12], it was held that there cannot in law be any planning permission unless and until written notice of the decision is given to the applicant. However, cases have arisen where there is a discrepancy between the authority's resolution and the document notifying the applicant of the decision. The present position appears to be that, whereas the resolution cannot be used to construe the permission, reference to it can be made in order to establish whether a permission has in fact been granted[13].

4   See the observations obiter of Lord Denning MR, in *Lever (Finance) Ltd v Westminster Corpn* [1971] 1 QB 222 at 231, [1970] 3 All ER 496 at 501, CA.
5   See *Western Fish Products Ltd v Penwith District Council* [1981] 2 All ER 204, CA; *Norfolk County Council v Secretary of State for the Environment* [1973] 3 All ER 673.
6   *Southend-on-Sea Corpn v Hodgson (Wickford) Ltd* [1962] 1 QB 416; *Howell v Falmouth Boat Construction Ltd* [1951] AC 837.
7   General Development Order 1977, art. 7(6).
8   T & CPA 1971, ss. 36, 37. The Secretary of State deals with the appeal as if the application had been made to him in the first instance: s. 36 (3).
9   *James v Secretary of State for Wales* [1968] AC 409, [1966] 3 All ER 964, HL, disapproving *Edwick v Sunbury-on-Thames UDC* [1962] 3 All ER 10, DC.
10 *James v Ministry of Housing and Local Government* [1965] 3 All ER 602 at 606, CA per Lord Denning MR; *London Ballast Co Ltd v Buckinghamshire County Council* (1966) 18 P & CR 446 at 458, DC per Megaw J.
11 See Telling, op. cit., p. 139.
12 (1972), 23 P & CR 39, DC. See also *Slough Estates Ltd v Slough Borough Council (No. 2)* [1969] 2 Ch 305, CA; affd. [1971] AC 958, HL.
13 *Norfolk County Council v Secretary of State for the Environment* [1973] 3 All ER 673; *A-G ex rel Co-operative Retail Services Ltd v Taff-Ely Borough Council and Tesco* [1979] JPL 466, CA.

Permission once granted prima facie enures for the benefit of the land and all persons for the time being interested therein[14]. A purchaser therefore acquires the benefit of any permission obtained by his vendor or other predecessor in title. A purchaser may well require advice on various ancillary matters relating to the grant of an existing permission such as its effect and construction, or the enforceability of conditions attached to it. These problems are considered later in the chapter.

3.   Outline permission

Article 5 (2) of the General Development Order 1977[15], enables an application to be submitted for outline planning permission. This is a valuable procedure for a builder, enabling him to ascertain before he contracts to buy land that the planning authority has no objection in principle to residential development. If the authority refuse the outline application, he need not proceed with the contract; if it is granted, he incurs no risk in acquiring the land, for the authority are committed to allowing residential development. An outline application need not provide details of siting, design, external appearance, or means of access, but approval of these matters must be obtained before development commences. Whilst the authority can exercise control over all matters expressly reserved in the outline permission for subsequent approval and can reject, for example, the details submitted in relation to external appearance, they cannot revoke the permission in toto except upon payment of compensation, nor can they impose conditions falling outside those matters expressly reserved in the outline permission[16]. An outline permission lapses unless it is acted upon within certain statutorily imposed time limits[17]. Outline planning procedure is not available for applications involving a change of use.

4.   Effect of planning permission

The grant of planning permission is effective only for the purposes of the town and country planning legislation and ensures that development undertaken in accordance with the permission is authorised for the purpose of the Act. It does not operate as carte blanche, entitling the developer to override the rights of third parties. The permission does not afford immunity from liability should the development obstruct a right of way or be in breach of some restrictive covenant. However there is provision for the stopping up or diversion of highways, public footpaths or bridleways if the Secretary of State is satisfied that such action is necessary to enable the development to be carried out[18]. It must also be remembered that the grant of planning permission does not dispense with the need to obtain other consents or licences, particularly approval under the Building Regulations 1976.

(a) Inconsistent planning permissions
The fact that land already has the benefit of an existing unimplemented planning permission does not debar a later applicant, or even the same applicant,

14   T & CPA 1971, s. 33 (1).
15   S.I. 1977 No. 289.
16   See *Shemara Ltd v Luton Corpn* (1967) 18 P & CR 520; *Chelmsford Corpn v Secretary of State for the Environment* (1971) 22 P & CR 880; *Thomas Langley Group Ltd v Warwick District Council* (1974) 73 LGR 171.
17   Page 220, post.
18   T & CPA 1971, ss. 209, 210.

from submitting a subsequent application to undertake some form of development inconsistent with that authorised by the earlier permission, and the granting of the second application does not of itself revoke the first permission. A purchaser of land, finding that he has the benefit of inconsistent permissions, can prima facie elect which to adopt, assuming that neither permission has been abandoned. In *Slough Estates Ltd v Slough Borough Council (No. 2)*[19] the Court of Appeal affirmed the principle of abandonment of a planning permission. However in the House of Lords, Lord Pearson[20] with whom the other Law Lords agreed, expressly reserved the question whether a planning permission can be abandoned. The point cannot be regarded as finally settled, but there appear to be no valid reasons to outlaw this notion of abandonment. Assuming that in law a planning permission can be abandoned, then, in the absence of an express abandonment, it is a question of inference to be drawn from the applicant's conduct. The mere submission of a second application furnishes no evidence on which it is permissible to raise any such inference[1]. But a second application coupled with a claim for and recovery of compensation for loss of development value consequent upon a refusal of permission does constitute an unequivocal abandonment of rights under the first permission[2].

It is not clear to what extent acting on one of two inconsistent permissions operates as an abandonment of the other. The point arose in a neat form in *F. Lucas & Son Ltd v Dorking and Horley RDC*[3].

> X obtained permission to build 28 houses on both sides of a proposed road. Later he obtained permission to develop the same land by erecting six detached houses, two of which were actually built. X then proposed to revert to the first permission by erecting fourteen houses along one side of the proposed road. The court held that the first permission was still valid and effective.

Unfortunately the question of abandonment was never argued but the case is of interest because of the observations of Winn J, on the effect of the first permission. He held it was not a permission for the development of an *estate* of houses, conditional upon completion of the whole contemplated development. Such a view would leave individual owners of separate plots vulnerable to enforcement procedure if the scheme were never finished. In law the permission authorised development of *individual sites* of land as shown on the deposited plans. There is some slight authority for saying that where a developer at different times obtains permission to build a farmhouse on different sites of the same plot of land and subsequently builds the farmhouse on the second site, the first permission does not cease to be entirely effective since it could be invoked to permit the erection of a farmhouse on the earlier site should

19 [1969] 2 Ch 305, [1969] 2 All ER 988.
20 [1971] AC 958 at 971, [1970] 2 All ER 216 at 225. The HL upheld the CA decision on other grounds, without considering the abandonment point.
1 *James v Secretary of State for Wales* [1968] AC 409, [1966] 3 All ER 964, HL (a case relating to site licences for caravans under the Caravan Sites and Control of Development Act 1960).
2 *Slough Estates Ltd v Slough Borough Council (No. 2)* [1969] 2 Ch 305, [1969] 2 All ER 988, CA.
3 (1966) 17 P & CR 111. See also *Pilkington v Secretary of State for the Environment* [1974] 1 All ER 283; *Hoveringham Gravels Ltd v Chiltern District Council* (1977) 35 P & CR 295.

the existing building be destroyed[4]. However it is submitted that if one of two inconsistent permissions is acted upon, in whole or in part, this is adequate conduct from which it can be inferred that the developer has abandoned the other permission. Had abandonment been argued in the *Lucas* case, the decision might well have gone the other way. It is always open for the planning authority to put the matter beyond doubt by attaching to the second permission a condition that it is not to be exercised in addition to or in combination with the earlier permission. The problem of abandonment is not in future likely to be as important in view of the statutory provisions, first introduced by the Town and Country Planning Act 1968, which limited the duration of planning permission[5].

(b) Effect of permission on existing rights

An analogous problem arises in relation to the effect of planning permission on existing use rights, a question of considerable importance where the existing use does not have tbe benefit of an express permission because it was commenced before 1 July 1948 (the appointed day). The point arose in *Petticoat Lane Rentals Ltd v Secretary of State for the Environment*[6] where Widgery LJ, laid down the following principle. Where a single unit or area of land is developed by the erection of a building on the *whole* of the land, the building creates an entirely new planning unit with no previous planning history. By putting the building to a use inconsistent with the land's previous use, the owner abandons his existing use rights, even though the permission does not contain any express condition prohibiting the former use. Some uncertainty exists as to the exact position where the building operations do not extend to the whole site but take place within the curtilage of the land. It may be that in the absence of an express condition excluding the right to continue the former use, the building development does not automatically extinguish the previous rights of use of the land which still remains open[7].

5.   Duration of permission

As has been previously noted[8], s. 33 (1) of the Act of 1971 enacts that prima facie, any grant of planning permission shall enure for the benefit of the land and *of all persons for the time being interested therein*. The benefit of the permission runs with the land and vests in successive owners. The italicised words indicate how wide the subsection is. A lessee has the benefit of a permission obtained by his lessor, though whether he can take advantage of it vis-à-vis the lessor will depend on the terms of the lease. A vendor takes the benefit of any outline permission obtained by the purchaser, should the contract not be performed. Perhaps even licensees in occupation and squatters are within the ambit of the benefit. However a permission may be confined to a particular

---

4 *Ellis v Worcestershire County Council* (1961) 12 P & CR 178, Lands Tribunal, apparently accepted as correctly decided by Winn J, in *Lucas & Sons Ltd v Dorking and Horley RDC* (1966) 17 P & CR 111 at 120.

5 Page 219, post.

6 [1971] 2 All ER 792 at 796, DC.

7 Bridge J and Lord Parker CJ, left this point open; see at 797. Widgery LJ considered it immaterial whether or not the whole site was covered by the development. Cf. *Prossor v Ministry of Housing and Local Government* (1968) 67 LGR 109 (partial redevelopment of site; express condition restraining former use). See also *Newbury District Council v Secretary of State for the Environment* [1980] 1 All ER 731, HL.

8 Page 216, ante.

individual, or limited in its duration to a specified period. On the expiration of that period, the resumption of the previous use (if authorised) does not require planning permission[9].

A planning authority may by order revoke or modify the permission if it appears to them expedient to do so[10]. Compensation may be recovered on revocation or modification in respect of abortive expenditure as well as for loss directly attributable thereto. This power to revoke or modify is only exercisable if development has not been completed. Thereafter action must be taken under s. 51 of the Act, which empowers the making of an order, subject to confirmation by the Secretary of State and to the payment of compensation, requiring the discontinuance of an authorised use or the alteration or removal of authorised buildings.

(a) Spent permissions
Once development authorised by a grant of permission has been undertaken, the permission has spent its force in the sense that it does not authorise the carrying out of the same development at some future time. For example, permission to erect a house does not constitute permission to rebuild it as often as is desired. If the house is totally destroyed, fresh permission must be sought to rebuild. Of course so long as the original building is standing, the permission remains in force to authorise its continued erection and use for residential purposes.

Similarly if a developer obtains permission, which he implements, to use land for purpose X and later he obtains permission to use the same land for purpose Y, he cannot, having used the land for Y, revert to X on the basis that the original permission is still in existence. Though there is no specific provision in the Act of 1971 regulating this point, it seems a proper inference from the Act as a whole[11] that the second permission once acted upon operates to discharge the first permission. Consequently permission to change from Y to X must be obtained, if the change is material[12].

(b) Statutory time limits
The continued existence of a planning permission, without being acted upon, can create considerable embarrassment for the planning authority, who can only revoke the permission on payment of compensation. Moreover, the accumulation of large numbers of unimplemented permissions might lead to a tendency for other applications to be refused to avoid a surfeit of authorised development. A measure of appropriate time control was first introduced by the Act of 1968. The relevant provisions are now contained in the Town and Country Planning Act 1971, ss. 41 to 44.

(i) *New permissions.* Every permission is subject to a condition that the development to which it relates must be begun within a period of five years from the date of the grant, or such other period (whether longer or shorter) as the

---

9 T & CPA 1971, s. 23 (5).
10 T & CPA 1971, ss. 45, 46. The Secretary of State also has power to revoke or modify a planning permission: s. 276.
11 See e.g. s. 23 (5), (8), (9), which expressly provide for the resumption of a former use without permission in certain circumstances; p. 212, ante. See further [1970] JPL 184–85.
12 If the permission authorising use Y is never implemented, the developer can use his land for X without obtaining fresh permission; see p. 217, ante.

authority may specify[13]. Failure to commence the development within the proper period causes the permission to lapse and anything done thereafter in purported reliance thereof constitutes unauthorised development. Certain types of permission are excluded from the operation of the section, including outline permissions (which are separately dealt with), permissions granted by a development order, and permissions granted for a limited period.

(ii) *Outline planning permissions.* These are similarly affected. Every grant of outline permission is subject (either expressly or impliedly) to conditions requiring:

(a)   submission of an application for approval of reserved matters within three years from the grant of the permission,

(b)   commencement of the development before the expiration of (i) five years from the grant or (ii) two years from the final approval of the reserved matters (whichever is the later)[14].

The same consequences flow as those previously discussed, if the conditions are not observed.

(iii) *Completion notices.* Sections 41 and 42 merely impose conditions requiring the commencement of the development within the required period. Section 44 regulates the position where the development has been commenced *but not completed* within the period. In such circumstances and if it appears unlikely that it will be completed within a reasonable period thereafter, the planning authority can serve a completion notice stating that the permission will cease to have effect on a specified date not being earlier than twelve months from when it takes effect. The notice does not become effective until approved by the Secretary of State who may substitute some longer period.

If the notice becomes effective, the permission is invalidated at the expiration of the stated period except in relation to development carried out beforehand. Development undertaken thereafter will not be covered by the permission and will be liable to enforcement proceedings. The authority may withdraw the notice before the date on which the permission expires, but there is nothing in the Act which prevents the service of a second completion notice if, contrary to expectations, completion of the development is still delayed.

(iv) *Commencement of development.* An understanding of when a particular project can be regarded as having been begun is crucial to any application of these provisions. Section 43 of the Act supplies the answer to this problem[15]. Development commences on the date when any of the following operations are first begun:

(a)   any work of construction in the course of erecting a building;

(b)   the digging of a foundation trench;

13   Section 41 (1). If the condition is not expressly imposed, the permission is deemed to be subject to the five years' limitation: sub-s. (2). Section 41 does not apply to permissions granted before 1 April 1969 (the date when the Act of 1968 became operative). Where development authorised by any such permission was not begun before 1968, the permission is deemed to have been granted subject to a condition requiring commencement within five years from 1 April 1969; see T & CPA 1971, Sch. 24, paras. 18–21.

14   Section 42. The authority can substitute other periods for those of three, five or two referred to. For outline permissions in existence on 1 April 1969, see Sch. 24, para. 20.

15   *Spackman v Secretary of State for the Environment* [1977] 1 All ER 257.

(c)   the laying of an underground main or pipe;
(d)   the laying out or construction of a road;
(e)   any change in the use of the land.

Carrying out demolition work in connection with the clearance of a site is not sufficient.

(v) *Renewal of permission.* A developer who for some reason delays the start of his development is at liberty to apply for a renewal. Provision is made for the application in such a case to be submitted in a simplified form. A written request containing sufficient information to enable the previous permission to be identified will suffice[16]. Planning authorities have been instructed[17] that these applications should generally be refused only where —

(a)   there has been a material change of planning circumstances since the original permission;
(b)   continued failure to begin the development will contribute unacceptably to uncertainty about the future pattern of development; or
(c)   the application is premature because the permission still has a reasonable time to run.

It is to be observed that the simplified application procedure only applies where the time limit in the original grant has not expired and development has not yet commenced. A developer, or prospective developer, is not debarred from seeking a renewal if the time limit has expired without any development or the authority has served a completion notice, but he will have to submit an application in the normal way[18]. It is always open to him in the latter event to try and persuade the authority to withdraw the notice, as an alternative to seeking renewed permission.

6.   Construction of planning permissions

The general rule when construing a planning permission is that reference can only be made to the grant itself, including the reasons given for imposing any conditions[19]. Other documents, such as the application or the plan, are irrelevant. In *Miller-Mead v Minister of Housing and Local Government*[20] the Court of Appeal construed a permission for the 'parking of caravans' as authorising the parking of caravans for any purpose, including residential purposes, even though the application related to the parking of caravans for storage. Here the plaintiff was not the original grantee, but a successor in title who obtained the benefit of the permission and was entitled to rely on the actual words of the grant; the court considered he would be prejudiced if, for construction purposes, resort were had to contemporaneous documents to which he would probably not have access. This rule has since been affirmed by the House of Lords in *Slough Estates Ltd v Slough Borough Council (No. 2)*[1]

16   General Development Order 1977, art. 5 (3).
17   Ministry of Housing and Local Government Circular 17/69.
18   See hereon Circular 17/69 and *Peak Park Joint Planning Board v Secretary of State for the Environment* [1979] JPL 618.
19   *Crisp from the Fens Ltd v Rutland County Council* (1950) 1 P & CR 48, CA.
20   [1963] 2 QB 196, [1963] 1 All ER 459, CA.
 1   [1971] AC 958, [1970] 2 All ER 216; see particularly Lord Pearson at 968 and 222 respectively.

where Lord Upjohn[2] observed that the rules of construction for wills and contracts are inapplicable to public documents such as planning permissions. When construing a public document it is not generally permissible to admit evidence of facts known to the maker of the document (the planning authority) but which are not common knowledge to alter or qualify the apparent meaning of words used in it. Similarly it has been said that the contra proferentes rule does not apply to the construction of planning permission; the authority have a duty to protect the interests of the general public[3].

Extrinsic evidence is admissible where the permission is not complete or self-contained on the face of it because it incorporates other documents by reference. In the *Slough* case a discrepancy existed between the applicant's plan which proposed development on land shown coloured on the plan and the subsequent permission which related to uncoloured land. The permission itself referred to 'the plan submitted' and included the reference number allocated to the application. In the circumstances of the case, their Lordships felt able to examine the plan but as this did not sufficiently identify the land to which the application related, they also looked at the correspondence leading to the grant of permission with a view to ascertaining what the application was, how the plan was submitted and what function it was intended to perform[4].

In the *Slough*[5] case at first instance Megarry J expressed the view that a mere reference by number only to the application, without its express incorporation in the body of the permission, was sufficient to enable the application to be looked at when construing the permission. A subsequent purchaser will not be unduly prejudiced, for he is at least put on notice that some other document refers to the land in relation to the permission and if he does not call for and examine the document he only has himself to blame. With respect this tentative opinion may be open to serious doubt, for the recording of the application number on the permission would seem to be nothing more than a simple administrative matter for the convenience of the planning authority. Furthermore a purchaser may experience considerable difficulty in obtaining a copy of the application. Rarely will the vendor have a copy and the existence of a register of planning applications, which local planning authorities are statutorily required to maintain, does not greatly assist a purchaser. Though Part I of this register contains copies of applications which are in course of being dealt with, once the application has been finally disposed of, only particulars (including brief particulars of the development forming the subject of the application) are recorded in Part II of the register and the copy application is removed from Part I[6].

Statutory rule of construction[1]

A grant of permission to erect a building may specify the purposes for which it may be used. This can take the form of a condition limiting the occupation,

---

2   At 962 and 218, respectively; *R v Secretary of State for the Environment, ex p Reinish* (1972) 22 P & CR 1022 at 1029, DC, per Lord Widgery CJ.
3   *Crisp from the Fens Ltd v Rutland County Council* (1950) 1 P & CR 48 at 57, CA, per Singleton LJ.
4   The introduction of this evidence did not in fact assist the plaintiff's case. See also *Wilson v West Sussex County Council* [1963] 2 QB 764, [1963] 1 All ER 751, CA (permission expressly incorporating the plan, application and relevant correspondence).
5   (1967) 19 P & CR 326 at 345.
6   See generally the T & CPA 1971, s. 34; General Development Order 1977, art. 21.
7   T & CPA 1971, s. 33 (2).

e.g. to persons employed in agriculture. A grant of permission for the erection of an 'agricultural cottage' achieves the same result[8]. If no purpose is specified the permission is construed as including permission to use the building for the purpose for which it was designed[9]. Permission to erect a dwellinghouse includes permission to use it for human habitation. The purpose for which a building is designed includes purposes ancillary or incidental to that purpose. Thus domestic premises may be used without permission for some activity in the nature of a hobby and a private garage for the occasional repair and servicing of cars for payment[10].

7. Conditions attached to planning permissions

A local planning authority may grant planning permission subject to such conditions as they think fit[11], and without prejudice to the generality of this provision they are empowered to impose certain specific conditions[12]. These may regulate the development or use of any land under the applicant's *control*. This is a wide power, for it can affect land which is not the subject of the application. The planning authority cannot use this power to suppress existing development on the other land[13]. A condition may have the effect of limiting its duration by requiring the removal of buildings or works, or the discontinuance of any use of land at the end of a specified period.

An applicant who is aggrieved by a conditional grant of permission can appeal against the decision to the Secretary of State[14]. Since he is empowered to deal with the application as if it had been made to him in the first instance, he may impose more onerous conditions or even refuse permission altogether. He can also re-write the conditions if he considers them ambiguous or drafted in uncertain terms.

A purchaser of land not only acquires the benefit of any existing permission, he is also subject to the conditions which it imposes. If he infringes them, he runs the risk of enforcement proceedings. A purchaser who finds his proposed development prohibited by some condition attached to a permission granted to a previous owner will not normally be in a position to appeal to the Secretary of State. His proper course of action is to apply for permission to retain buildings or continue the use of land without complying with the condition[15]. Alternatively he may seek a declaration from the courts that a condition is invalid, a remedy also available to the original applicant, notwithstanding that he could have appealed to the Secretary of State against the conditions.

(a) Challenging the validity of conditions
The power of a planning authority to impose such conditions 'as they think fit' is apparently unlimited. Nevertheless the courts, in the exercise of their

---

8   *Wilson v West Sussex County Council* [1963] 2 QB 764, [1963] 1 All ER 751, CA.
9   I.e. intended to be used: ibid., per Diplock LJ, at 783 and 760 respectively.
10 See *Peake v Secretary of State for Wales* (1971) 22 P & CR 889, DC.
11 T & CPA 1971, s. 29 (1) (a). Reasons for the imposition of the conditions must be given in the written notice of the decision: General Development Order 1977, art. 7.
12 T & CPA 1971, s. 30 (1).
13 See Ministry of Town and Country Planning Bulletin of Selected Appeal Decisions, Case VII/12.
14 See note 8, p. 215, ante.
15 T & CPA 1971, s. 32 (1) (b).

supervisory jurisdiction, have laid down certain requirements for the validity of any planning condition, as follows[16]:

(i) it must serve a proper planning purpose;
(ii) it must not be unreasonable, or ultra vires as being in conflict with some requirement of the Act[17];
(iii) it must not be void for uncertainty[18].

(i) *Planning purpose.* The condition must fairly and reasonably relate to the permitted development[19] or relate to the implementation of planning policy[20]. A condition requiring the occupants of a cottage to be employed in agriculture has been held to be valid, since it would implement the policy of confining the area to green belt by excluding purely residential usage[1].

(ii) *Unreasonableness.* The courts will watch to see whether, in imposing the condition, the authority have exceeded the powers Parliament has confided in it. A leading case is *Hall & Co Ltd v Shoreham-by-Sea UDC*[2].

> Permission was given to an industrial developer subject to a condition requiring him to build a road on his land and (in effect) to dedicate it as a public highway. The Court of Appeal held the condition unreasonable. If the authority required the construction of a public highway, the appropriate course was to proceed under the Highways Act 1959, which would have entitled the plaintiffs to compensation. It could not have been Parliament's intention for the authority to evade that procedure (and therefore avoid paying compensation) by the indirect manner of imposing a condition on a planning permission.

In the *Kent County Council* case[3] the House of Lords by a majority rejected the argument that a condition attached to an outline permission to the effect that the permission would lapse unless detailed plans were submitted and approved within three years was ultra vires because it restricted the applicant's right of appeal in the event of the authority's refusal to approve the plans.

The extent to which a condition in a planning permission can restrict or deprive the applicant of his existing use rights has been considered on several occasions by the courts — with differing conclusions. In *Kingston upon Thames*

---

16 *Newbury District Council v Secretary of State for the Environment* [1980] 1 All ER 731, HL; *R v London Borough of Hillingdon, ex p. Royco Homes Ltd* [1974] 2 All ER 643, DC.
17 See *Kent County Council v Kingsway Investments (Kent) Ltd* [1971] AC 72 at 86–87, [1970] 1 All ER 70 at 73, HL per Lord Reid.
18 *Chertsey UDC v Mixnam's Properties Ltd* [1965] AC 735, HL.
19 *Pyx Granite Co Ltd v Minister of Housing and Local Government* [1958] 1 QB 544 at 572, [1958] 1 All ER 625 at 633, CA, per Denning LJ; rvsd. on other grounds, [1960] AC 260, [1959] 3 All ER 1, HL.
20 *Kent County Council v Kingsway Investments (Kent) Ltd* [1971] AC 72 at 105, [1970] 1 All ER 70 at 88, per Lord Guest; *R v London Borough of Hillingdon, ex p Royco Homes Ltd,* supra.
1 *Fawcett Properties Ltd v Buckingham County Council* [1961] AC 636, [1960] 3 All ER 503, HL.
2 [1964] 1 All ER 1, CA.
3 [1971] AC 72, [1970] 1 All ER 70. The practical implications of this decision have been greatly reduced by the provisions of s. 42 of the Act of 1971 (p. 220, ante) and the reasons for the majority's decision are outside the scope of this chapter.

London Borough Council v Secretary of State for the Environment[4] it was held that such a condition was valid. Earlier decisions to the contrary were doubted[5]. However, in *Newbury District Council v Secretary of State for the Environment*[6] it was suggested that the extinction of existing use rights only arose from the creation of a new planning unit.

(iii) *Uncertainty.* It is a general principle that if a man is to be subject to restrictions on the use of his property, he should know with certainty what they are. In relation to planning conditions, it is sometimes contended that the developer is entitled to know exactly what they involve before deciding whether to proceed with the development. However, where uncertainty is alleged, the true question, according to Willmer LJ[7] is whether the language of the condition makes sense, that is, is capable of a reasonable construction, and he cited the view expressed by Lord Denning in *Fawcett Properties Ltd v Buckingham County Council*[8] that:

'. . . a planning condition is only void for uncertainty if it can be given no meaning or no sensible or ascertainable meaning, and not merely because it is ambiguous or leads to absurd results.'

It is not sufficient that there are difficulties in the understanding of the condition. The courts will resolve any ambiguity if it can be resolved, and, wherever possible, will construe the condition so as to make it valid, as is shown by the *Fawcett* case and *Hall & Co Ltd v Shoreham-by-Sea UDC*[9], in both of which the plea of uncertainty failed, though in neither case were the judgments unanimous.

(b) Effect of condition being invalid
A condition which is defective on any of these grounds is void, and cannot be enforced. However success in the courts may amount to nothing but a Pyrrhic victory. On the authorities as they stand at the moment, if a fundamental condition is declared void, the whole permission fails, since it is assumed that without that condition the permission would never have been granted in the first place[10]. The end result is that the developer finishes up with no permission at all and his development becomes unauthorised, unless the condition is a trivial one[11], or is one that has nothing whatever to do with planning considerations but is only calculated to achieve some ulterior object thought to be in the public interest[12]. In this event the void condition is severable and the permission remains in force shorn of the offending condition.

4 [1974] 1 All ER 193. See also *Prosser v Minister of Housing and Local Government* (1968) 67 LGR 109; *Leighton and Newman Car Sales Ltd v Secretary of State for the Environment* (1976) 32 P & CR 1; *Peak Park Joint Planning Board v Secretary of State for the Environment* [1980] JPL 114.
5 See *Allnatt London Properties Ltd v Middlesex County Council* (1964) 15 P & CR 288.
6 [1980] 1 All ER 731.
7 *Hall & Co Ltd v Shoreham-by-Sea UDC* [1964] 1 All ER 1, at 5, CA.
8 [1961] AC 636 at 678, [1960] 3 All ER 503, at 517, HL.
9 [1964] 1 All ER 1, CA.
10 *Hall & Co Ltd v Shoreham-by-Sea UDC* [1964] 1 All ER 1, CA; *Kent County Council v Kingsway Investments (Kent) Ltd* [1971] AC 72, [1970] 1 All ER 70; *R v London Borough of Hillingdon ex p. Royco Homes* [1974] 2 All ER 643, DC.
11 *Hall & Co Ltd v Shoreham-by-Sea UDC* [1964] 1 All ER 1 at 18, per Pearson LJ.
12 *Kent County Council case* [1971] AC 72 at 90, [1971] 1 All ER 70 at 75, per Lord Reid. See *Allnatt London Properties Ltd v Middlesex County Council* (1964) 15 P & CR 288.

No satisfactory test has as yet been propounded to determine this question of severability[13]. It may well be that it will vary according to the particular condition under scrutiny. In the *Kent County Council* case Winn LJ in the Court of Appeal[14] approached the question of severability as follows:

' . . . if the condition is ultra vires it is void; if it is void it can have no effect on the force of the permission itself; so far as the permission is concerned it was granted by a responsible authority and by their own decision was kept alive from October 1952 until September 1967 and in accordance with the principle ut res magis valeat quam pereat it should survive, notwithstanding the submission that the seeds of its mortality were sown in it by corruption from the condition grafted on it.'

With respect this produces a more just solution. It accords with other branches of real property law, e.g. that a grant of real property does not become inoperative because a condition is attached to it which is repugnant to it and therefore void. It also avoids the difficulty of determining what is fundamental and what is not, and more important for the developer (or his successor) removes the possibility[15] of enforcement action being taken by the planning authority. This last point has not yet been tested in the courts. Lord Denning[16] has dismissed the potential threat of enforcement procedure as 'moonshine', on the ground that the authority would be estopped from saying that the permission was invalid. Whilst it is true that recent cases[17] have indicated a willingness on the part of the courts to uphold a plea of estoppel against local planning authorities in certain circumstances, this point cannot be regarded as resolved[18] and an early ruling on the question would be welcome.

D   Enforcement of planning control

Where unauthorised development has taken place on land the planning authority may take enforcement proceedings against the owner, although he was not the person originally responsible for the development. Hence it is vital for a purchaser to satisfy himself that he will not become liable to such proceedings. The enforcement powers of a local planning authority are contained in Part V of the Town and Country Planning Act 1971 as amended by the Local Government and Planning (Amendment) Act 1981.

1.   Service of enforcement notice

Section 87 (as amended) of the Act empowers the planning authority to issue a notice (termed an enforcement notice) where there has been a breach of

13 It is not therefore surprising that in the *Kent County Council* case opposite conclusions were reached as to the fundamental nature of the condition. Compare the views of Lords Reid and Upjohn with those of the majority.
14 [1969] 2 QB 332 at 374, [1969] 1 All ER 601 at 628 CA.
15 Provided the time limit, if applicable, has not expired; p. 231, post.
16 *Kingsway Investments (Kent) Ltd v Kent County Council* [1969] 2 QB 332 at 355, [1969] 1 All ER 601 at 612 CA.
17 *Wells v Minister of Housing and Local Government* [1967] 2 All ER 1041, CA; *Lever (Finance) Ltd v Westminster Corpn* [1971] 1 QB 222, [1970] 3 All ER 496, CA. Cf. *Western Fish Products Ltd v Penwith District Council* [1981] 2 All ER 204, CA.
18 See *Rhyl UDC v Rhyl Amusements Ltd* [1959] 1 All ER 257 esp. at 265, per Harman J; *Allnatt London Properties Ltd v Middlesex County Council* (1964) 15 P & CR 288 at 302, per Glyn-Jones J; Garner, 'Void Planning Conditions' [1964] JPL 26.

planning control i.e. development without planning permission or failure to comply with some condition or limitation subject to which permission was granted. The authority are not required to commence enforcement proceedings; they have a power to do so if they consider it expedient. A copy of the enforcement notice must be served on (i) the owner, (ii) the occupier and (iii) any other person having an interest in the land which the authority think is materially affected by the notice[19].

(a) Period for service

The notice must be served not later than 28 days after the date on which it is issued and at least 28 days before the date on which it is expressed to take effect[20].

Under s. 45 (2) of the Act of 1962, the notice had to be served within four years of the carrying out of the unauthorised development; thereafter the authority could not serve a notice and the development became immune from enforcement control. Unless a planning authority employed a band of snoopers to ferret out cases of unauthorised development, it was often difficult for them to discover that certain forms of development, in particular changes of use, had taken place. This rule has now been altered. In relation to any unauthorised development carried out *after the end of 1963*, a notice can be served *at any time*, except in four cases where the old four-year rule still operates[1]. These cases are as follows:

(i)   unauthorised building, engineering, mining or other operations;
(ii) non-compliance with a condition or limitation relating to building or other operations;
(iii) change of use of a building to use as a single dwellinghouse;
(iv) non-compliance with a condition which prohibits, or has the effect of preventing, a change of use of a building to use as a single dwelling house.

(b) Certification of established use of land

A change of use effected without permission before the end of 1963 and continued thereafter is said to become an established use and it is exempt from enforcement procedure. Section 94 (2) of the Act of 1971 provides that where a person having an interest in land claims that a particular use of it has become established, he may apply to the local planning authority for an established use certificate, provided the use subsists at the time of the application. If satisfied that the applicant has substantiated his claim, the authority must grant him the certificate, otherwise it will be refused in which event an appeal ties to the Secretary of State[2].

Now that an enforcement notice can be served in respect of unauthorised changes of use (other than (iii) above) at any time in the future, it might be difficult for an owner of land, wishing to challenge the notice at some future time on the ground that the use first commenced before 1964, to establish that

---

19   Section 87 (5). In appropriate circumstances a licensee is capable of being an occupier: *Stevens v London Borough of Bromley* [1972] 1 QB 400, [1972] 1 All ER 712, CA (caravan dweller). The interest referred to in category (iii) is confined to a legal or equitable interest in land: ibid. at 410 and 717 respectively, per Salmon LJ.
20   Section 87 (5).
 1   T & CPA 1971, s. 87 (4), as substituted by the LG & P (A) A 1981, Sch.
 2   T & CPA 1971, ss. 94 (4), 95 (2), as substituted, ante.

the use did so commence. An established use certificate is intended to cater for this situation. If obtained, it is conclusive, as regards matters stated therein, for the purposes of any appeal against an enforcement notice served in respect of the land to which the certificate relates[3].

(c) Form of enforcement notice

The notice must specify[4]:

(i)   the alleged breach of planning control;

(ii)   the steps to be taken to restore the land to its former condition, or to secure compliance with the condition or limitation alleged to have been broken;

(iii) the period (not being less than twenty-eight days) at the expiration of which the notice takes effect;

(iv)   the period during which the steps required in (ii) must be carried out.

A notice not complying with these requirements is a nullity, and a considerable body of case law has developed regulating the content and wording of these notices. However the past decade has witnessed a wind of change blowing over the courts' attitude to this problem of nullity. The older view advocated by Viscount Simonds insisted upon a strict and rigid adherence to formalities, especially as the Planning Acts encroached on private rights[5]. But formalities were being used to defeat the public good; so they are no longer favoured. The courts now reject technicalities and apply a simple test enunciated by Upjohn LJ, in *Miller-Mead v Ministry of Housing and Local Government*[6]—does the notice tell the recipient fairly what he has done wrong and what he must do to remedy it? Provided it does this, it will be upheld by the courts, even though it fails to contain *specific* directions for the restoration of the land to its pre-unauthorised development use, for the owner should well know its previous use[7]. Nevertheless if the notice is clearly a nullity, the courts do not hesitate to declare it bad.

2.   Rights of appeal

Section 88 (as amended) of the Act provides for an appeal against service of the notice to the Secretary of State on several grounds, for example, that the notice was not served timeously, or as otherwise required by the Act. This right of appeal must be exercised before the notice takes effect, that is within the period referred to in requirement (iii) above. The Secretary of State has no jurisdiction to entertain an appeal lodged out of time or extend the time for appealing[8]. He has wide powers when dealing with the appeal[9]. He may quash the notice, vary its terms in the appellant's favour, or grant permission for the development

3   Section 94 (7).
4   T & CPA 1971, s. 87 (6), (7), (8), (13), as substituted by the LG & P (A) A 1981, Sch. See also the Town and Country Planning (Enforcement Notices and Appeals) Regulations 1981 (S.I. 1981 No. 1742).
5   *East Riding County Council v Park Estate (Bridlington) Ltd* [1957] AC 223 at 233, [1956] 2 All ER 669 at 672, HL.
6   [1963] 2 QB 196 at 232, [1963] 1 All ER 459 at 474, CA, applied in *Munnich v Godstone RDC* [1966] 1 All ER 930, CA.
7   *Ormston v Horsham RDC* (1965) 63 LGR 452, CA. A lack of specific directions might be fatal if the notice is served on a successor in title of the original developer. See also *Metallic Protectives Ltd v Secretary of State for the Environment* [1976] JPL 166.
8   *R v Melton and Belvoir Justices, ex p. Tynan* (1977) 33 P & CR 214.
9   T & CPA 1971, s. 88 (6), 88A, 88B added by the LG & P (A) A 1981, Sch.

to which the notice relates. In relation to this last power, it should be noted that where an appeal is brought the appellant is deemed to have made an application for permission[10]. He can also correct any informality, defect or error in the notice, if satisfied that it is immaterial[11]. He cannot by amendment cure a notice that is wholly bad; on proof of the relevant facts it is his duty to quash the notice[12].

In certain cases the validity of an enforcement notice cannot, except by way of appeal to the Secretary of State, be questioned in any other proceedings[13]. However the Act does not interfere with the right to seek a declaration from the courts that the notice is a nullity[14]. As an alternative to seeking a declaration, it seems that if the notice is a nullity, the recipient could sue for trespass should the authority proceed to undertake any of the remedial work specified in it, or could rely on the defence if prosecuted for non-compliance with the notice.

Lodgment of an appeal suspends the enforcement notice which does not take effect until after the appeal is finally determined or withdrawn[15]. By serving what is known as a stop notice, the planning authority can prohibit the carrying out or continuation of specified *operations* which have been alleged in the enforcement notice to be in breach of planning control. Disregard of a stop notice is a criminal offence[16]. Compensation is payable in certain cases to a person adversely affected by the stop notice[17] e.g. because the enforcement notice is subsequently quashed. This provision ensures that planning authorities do not issue stop notices without due consideration of whether they are justified. This procedure cannot be utilised where the alleged unauthorised development consists of a material change of use.

3. Enforcement action by planning authority

Unless the planning authority are empowered to take further steps in the event of non-compliance, the enforcement notice would be so much waste paper. The consequences of non-compliance are as follows.

(a) Prosecution
Failure to carry out the steps required by the notice, or to discontinue a use of land or observe some condition or limitation is a criminal offence, punishable by a fine of £400 on summary conviction, or a fine of unlimited amount on conviction on indictment. Should the failure continue after conviction, the defendant becomes liable in addition to a daily penalty. There is a special defence available to a person ceasing to be the owner if he proves that he took all reasonable steps to secure compliance and that the failure to comply was due to the default of the subsequent owner[18].

10 T & CPA 1971, s. 88B (3), added by the LG & P (A) A 1981, Sch.
11 T & CPA 1971, s. 88A (2), added, ante; *Hammersmith London Borough Council v Secretary of State for the Environment* (1975) 30 P & CR 19.
12 *Miller-Mead v Ministry of Housing and Local Government* [1963] 2 QB 196 at 233, [1963] 1 All ER 459 at 474, CA, per Upjohn LJ.
13 T & CPA 1971, s. 243 (1), (2) (as amended). An appeal lies from his decision to the High Court on a point of law: ibid., s. 246 (1).
14 See e.g. *Stevens v London Borough of Bromley* [1972] 1 QB 400, [1972] 1 All ER 712, CA.
15 T & CPA 1971, s. 88 (10), added; see note 10, supra.
16 T & CPA 1971, s. 90 (1), (3), (5), as substituted by the T & CP(A) A 1977, s. 1.
17 T & CPA 1971, s. 177.
18 T & CPA 1971, s. 89 as amended by the T & CP (A) A 1977, s. 2. For the meaning of 'owner', see s. 290 (1).

(b) Execution of required work

If any steps (other than the discontinuance of a use) are not taken by the end of the required period, the authority can enter upon the land and effect those works. The reasonable expenses incurred are recoverable as a simple contract debt from 'the person who is then the owner of the land', not necessarily the person who originally carried out the unauthorised development[19]. Suppose V undertakes unauthorised development on land which he later conveys to P. The planning authority serve P with an enforcement notice requiring certain steps to be taken. If P does not comply, the authority can do the work and sue P for their expenses. Any sums paid by P are deemed to be for the use and at the request of V, the person by whom the breach of planning control was committed[20], thereby enabling P to recover the amount of the expenses from V.

(c) Continuing force of notice

Compliance with the terms of an enforcement notice does not discharge it[1]. If the unauthorised development to which it refers is recommenced, the notice automatically revives. The planning authority have similar powers of prosecution and entry as for an initial non-compliance with the notice. Should planning permission be granted for the retention of buildings or works, or for the continuance of a use of land, to which an enforcement notice relates, the notice ceases to have effect, but without prejudice to any offence relating to a failure to comply with the notice committed before the grant of permission[2]. Every district planning authority and every council of a London Borough are now under a duty to keep a register of enforcement notices issued and of stop notices served after 27 November, 1981[3].

4.   Legal effect of development without permission

The precise effect in law of development undertaken without permission (where required) has never been satisfactorily resolved[4]. The problem has relevance in fields other than planning. If a lease provides that the tenant shall not do or commit anything unlawful on or in relation to the demised premises, is there a breach of covenant if he undertakes development without obtaining permission? Another example is afforded by *Best v Glenvill*[5]:

> L leased land to T for purposes other than the permitted use, though T undertook to apply for permission, which he did, but the application was refused. T refused to pay the rent and when sued pleaded that the agreement was illegal.

The lease was held not to be illegal per se, nor was there anything in the agreement between L and T to make it unlawful since it was contemplated that permission would be obtained. However Upjohn LJ expressed the view[6] that if neither party took the trouble to take any steps to obtain permission, or if each

---

19   T & CPA 1971, s. 91 (1).
20   T & CPA 1971, s. 91 (2). As to the extent to which P can allege that the notice is a nullity, see p. 229, ante.
1   T & CPA 1971, s. 93.
2   T & CPA 1971, s. 92.
3   T & CPA 1971, s. 92A, inserted by the LG & P (A) A 1981, Sch.
4   See Mellows, 'Something Unlawful' (1962) 26 Conv (NS) 374.
5   [1960]3 All ER 478, CA.
6   At 481.

party knew that no steps were to be taken, it might well be the case, if proved, that there was something unlawful in the agreement.

In so far as any conclusion can be gathered from judicial observations, the tendency seems to be to regard development without permission as being unlawful, though perhaps too much reliance cannot be placed on pronouncements that were made in passing without considered argument on the point. Speaking of section 12 of the Act of 1947, Lord Goddard CJ said in *A-G v Smith*[7] that the sense 'is obvious: it is that development of land carried out without permission is unlawful — it is contrary to the Act'. According to Lord Parker CJ, s. 17 (1) of the same Act (now replaced by s. 53 of the Act of 1971[8]) enabled a proposed developer to ascertain in advance whether he could safely proceed *without committing a criminal offence*[9]. In *Francis v Yiewsley and West Drayton UDC*[10] Jenkins LJ referred to an enforcement notice charging the plaintiff with an offence other than *the offence he had actually committed*.

The problem raised by unauthorised development is not a new one. There have been other statutes prohibiting certain conduct without imposing any penalty for infringement, and the cases in effect decide that the prohibited conduct amounts to a common law crime punishable by fine or imprisonment, unless Parliament has expressed a contrary intention[11]. In relation to development without permission, Parliament has shown a sufficient contrary intention by enabling the service of an enforcement notice. If the mere carrying out of development without permission amounted to a criminal offence, the developer could in effect be punished twice for the same act. It is submitted that, notwithstanding the dicta on the point, the carrying out of development without permission does not constitute a criminal offence. It is unauthorised, and may bring in its wake the consequences provided by the Act; but no criminal offence is committed until the enforcement notice is disobeyed. The fact that service of an enforcement notice is not obligatory, but merely permissive, confirms this view.

Unauthorised development lasting four years

On expiration of the four years' period for service of a notice (in those cases where the limitation applies), the unauthorised development becomes immune from enforcement control, assuming no valid notice has been served within the time limit[12]. The developer acquires a prescriptive or vested right to retain the development and in the case of a change of use occurring before 1964, he can obtain a certificate of established use. Should the planning authority wish to discontinue the use, or require the demolition or alteration of buildings they can only proceed under s. 51 of the Act, subject to the payment of compensation[13]. This is significant. It has been held to be impossible by the commission of

---

7   [1958] 2 QB 173 at 180−1, [1958] 2 All ER 557 at 558, CA, cited with approval by Lord Denning MR in *Gregson v Cyril Lord Ltd* [1962] 3 All ER 907, at 910 and 914; cf. Upjohn LJ, CA.
8   See p. 211, ante.
9   *Edgwarebury Park Investments Ltd v Ministry of Housing and Local Government* [1963] 2 QB 408 at 415, [1963] 1 All ER 124 at 128, DC.
10 [1958] 1 QB 478 at 491, [1957] 3 All ER 529 at 537, CA.
11 See Mellows, op. cit. pp. 383−89.
12 See p. 227, ante.
13 *Cartwright v Sedgley UDC* (1960) 13 P & CR 1, CA. *Hartnell v Ministry of Housing and. Local Government* [1965] AC 1134 at 1163, [1965] 1 All ER 490 at 499, HL, per Lord Evershed.

an offence to acquire a right[14]. If the development were criminal, it is difficult to see how the passage of time could alter the original nature of the act. The fact that compensation becomes payable if the planning authority seek to interfere once the four years have elapsed indicates there was nothing unlawful or criminal in the original act.

E   Purchaser's planning inquiries[15]

Having considered the main aspects of town planning legislation of concern to a purchaser, it is now necessary to see what planning inquiries are normally made on his behalf by his legal adviser.

1.   Inquiries of the vendor

The inquiries which will be made of the vendor or his solicitor will vary greatly according to the type of property. It has been suggested[16] that on the purchase of a house in a residential area, which the purchaser proposes to use as a residence, there is little or no reason for preliminary inquiries on planning matters. However the possibility of the vendor (or some predecessor in title) having altered or extended the property must not be overlooked and a purchaser would need to ascertain whether any such operations involved development and, if so, whether express permission (if required) was obtained. It is therefore unwise to refrain from making planning inquiries even in the case of residential property. Special care should be taken on the purchase of industrial property, property which is not being used for the purpose for which it was originally designed, or land acquired for development.

Standard form inquiries
The standard form of Inquiries Before Contract[17] contains a long and involved question designed to extract the maximum of relevant information affecting planning matters. Many of the sub-questions will not relate to the property and frequently the vendor's solicitor will have to give the stock reply 'not applicable', after first taking his own client's instructions. One question relates specifically to the present use of the land, its date of commencement and the manner of its authorisation. Another seeks details of any buildings erected, or alterations made to existing buildings, within four years. Oddly enough no question asks directly whether permission was obtained for such operations. It is not considered necessary to extend the inquiry beyond the four years' period since unauthorised operations undertaken beyond that period become immune from enforcement control. It has, however, been observed[18] that a purchaser of a house may strictly be concerned to inquire about extensions going back to the appointed day, in order to establish whether they were constructed with express permission or by virtue of the General Development Order 1977[19], or its predecessor. In the latter event, if the extension has used up the permitted

---

14   *Glamorgan County Council v Carter* [1962] 3 All ER 866 (development contravening pre-1948 planning control).
15   See Rowley, 'Planning Enquiries' (1964) 28 Conv (NS) 27, 101.
16   Emmet, 15.
17   See p. 181, ante.
18   Adams, 'Inquiries Before Contract – II' (1970) 120 NLJ 630–1.
19   Page 212, ante.

tolerances under the Order, any subsequent extension will require express permission. The printed inquiries should never be treated as the maximum that need be raised. Particular cases may warrant additional questions. On the purchase of land and a business conducted thereon, it may be desirable to ascertain the previous use.

Not infrequently a vendor will be unable to give replies covering the period prior to his own period of ownership. To this extent his replies may only be of limited value to the purchaser. This problem could be avoided if purchasers' solicitors made it a general practice to put with the title deeds the preliminary inquiries and replies (or a copy) for reference on future transactions.

As the benefit of a planning permission runs with the land, every purchaser should ensure that he sees the permission or a copy. Confirmation that permission has been obtained for the erection of a building will not satisfy a purchaser's curosity; he will want to know of any condition or limitation subject to which it was granted and which might adversely affect his enjoyment of the property. A cottage erected subject to a condition limiting its occupation to a person employed in agriculture will be of no use to a purchaser proposing to live there in retirement[20]. The date of the grant of permission now becomes important in view of its limited duration[1], and a purchaser will need to ascertain whether it has been acted upon. Another standard inquiry asks the vendor to supply copies of various documents, including planning permissions and building regulations consents. In so far as the vendor is unable to provide the desired copies, the purchaser will have to rely on information supplied by the planning authority.

2.   Inquiries of local authority

(a) Local land charges

It will be recalled that Part 3 of the register of local land charges is devoted to planning charges[2]. The official certificate of search will reveal the registration of (inter alia) any (i) enforcement notice, (ii) order revoking or modifying permission, (iii) order discontinuing an existing use, and (iv) conditions attached to a planning permission. Compulsory purchase orders are not generally registrable as local land charges, except for orders where the acquiring authority propose to make a general vesting declaration under the Compulsory Purchase (Vesting Declarations) Act 1981[3].

(b) Local authority inquiries

The need to make these additional inquiries has already been explained[4]. The approved forms of inquiry contain questions relating to the following planning matters (to mention some)—

(1)   The making of an enforcement notice not yet registered.

---

20   See e.g. *Trinder v Sevenoaks RDC* (1967) 204 Estates Gazette 803. Cf. *East Suffolk County Council v Secretary of State for the Environment* (1972) 223 Estates Gazette 2137 (permission given for purpose of accommodating farm worker; no material change of use when property occupied by non-agricultural worker).
1   Page 219, ante.
2   Page 192, ante.
3   Section 3 (4); see p. 249, post.
4   Page 197, ante.

234 Planning considerations

(2)   Entries in the register of planning applications maintained by the authority. This answer will reveal short details of any planning application and the authority's decision, including the imposition of any conditions.

(3)   The existence of any direction made under article 4 of the General Development Order 1977, withdrawing any class of development from the categories of permitted development prescribed by the order[5].

(4)   The passing of any resolution for the making of certain orders e.g. under ss. 45 and 51 of the Act of 1971, relating to the revocation or modification of planning permission, or the discontinuance of a use of land or the removal of buildings or works.

(5)   The making of a compulsory purchase order, or resolution for the acquisition of the property.

The disclosure of any information which is possibly adverse to the purchaser may necessitate further inquiries of the planning authority and of the vendor.

F   Use and title

1.   General position

To what extent is it necessary for a vendor to disclose planning matters in the contract? The significance of this question from a vendor-purchaser angle is demonstrated by this hypothetical case. V contracts to sell to P premises which V has used for office premises and which P also wishes to use as offices. If three years previously V converted the premises from residential use to office use without permission, and P does not discover the true facts until after exchange of contracts, can P rescind the contract, or if he refuses to complete, can V obtain specific performance? Professor Potter maintained that the permitted use of property was a matter of title and that the contract should contain an adequate description of the use, separately from the normal description of the property[6]. But as previously noted[7], his arguments as to the effect of the Act of 1947 have not been accepted by conveyancers.

The extent of the duty of disclosure under an open contract is obscure, and clear English authority on the point is lacking. Bearing in mind the caveat emptor principle, that in the absence of an express warranty it is the purchaser's responsibility to satisfy himself that the premises are fit for the purpose for which he wants to use them, whether that fitness depends on the state of the structure or the state of the law[8], a vendor would appear to be under no duty to disclose the permitted use of the land. This view seems to be supported by the decision in *Mitchell v Beacon Estates (Finsbury Park) Ltd*[9], though little reliance can be placed on this case since it is only reported in note form. More recently Graham J has expressed the view that the absence of planning permission was not in itself a matter affecting the title nor was it apart

5   Pages 213–214, ante. A direction affecting *part* only of an authority's district is registrable in Part III of the local land charges register.
6   Potter, 'Caveat Emptor' (1948) 13 Conv (NS) 36, 44.
7   Page 204, ante.
8   *Edler v Auerbach* [1950] 1 KB 359 at 374, [1949] 2 All ER 692 at 699, per Devlin J.
9   (1950) 1 P & CR 32; cf. *Sidney v Buddery* (1950) 1 P & CR 34. See Emmet, 15.

from special circumstances a latent defect in the property[10]. In the absence of any duty of disclosure, the purchaser in the example given in the preceding paragraph could not rescind the contract, unless the vendor had made a material representation which he had relied upon[11]. On the other hand it seems unlikely that specific performance would be decreed against an innocent purchaser, on the ground that the court will

> ' not compel a man to buy a property which, if he takes no steps to prevent it, will expose him, as owner, to criminal proceedings by reason of its state at the time of sale[12].'

2. Formal contracts

(a) National Conditions of Sale

Basically the National Conditions in substance require the vendor to disclose planning matters known to him. Condition 15 provides, so far as is here relevant, as follows:

> '(4) . . . the property is not to the knowledge of the vendor subject to any charge, notice, order, restriction, agreement or other matter arising under the Planning Acts but . . . the property is sold subject to any such charges, notices, orders, restrictions, agreements and matters affecting the interest sold.
> (5) . . . the purchaser shall be deemed to buy with knowledge in all respects of the authorised use of the property for the purposes of the Planning Acts.'

Prima facie, therefore, it is the purchaser's responsibility to make adequate inquiries and he cannot rescind the contract if he subsequently discovers some adverse planning matter. However the vendor should disclose any matter of which he is aware, otherwise he will be guilty of fraud. Where the Special Conditions express the property to be sold on the footing of a particular authorised use, Condition 15 (3) gives the purchaser a right to rescind the contract if it appears before completion that the specified use is not an authorised used for the purposes of the planning legislation. It will be observed that this clause gives no right of rescission if there has been unauthorised development by building or other operations not involving any change of use.

(b) Law Society's Conditions

These Conditions do not contain any provision specifically relating to planning matters. As we have seen[13], General Condition 3 places on a purchaser the

---

10 *Gosling v Anderson* (1971) 220 Estates Gazette 1117, adopting *Hill v Harris* [1965] 2 QB 601, [1965] 2 All ER 358, CA (p. 170, ante; rvsd. on other grounds not affecting this point (1972), 223 Estates Gazette 1743, CA.

11 Cf. *Gosling v Anderson* (1972) 223 Estates Gazette 1743 (purchaser awarded damages on account of vendor's agent's misrepresentation that permission available for garage). The rule in Canada appears to be different: see *Kolan v Solicitor* (1970) 7 DLR (3d) 481, at 487, per Lacourciere J. See *Laurence v Lexcourt Holdings Ltd* [1978] 2 All ER 810 (purchaser failed to make searches. Vendor misrepresenting current use of property:-rescission ordered).

12 *Hope v Walter* [1900] 1 Ch 257 at 260, CA, per Lindley MR (property used as disorderly house unknown to both parties); *Pottinger v George* (1967) 41 ALJR 85, especially at 88. For specific performance, see Chap. 21.

13 Page 190, ante.

burden of finding out about all local authority matters, including planning matters, subject to the vendor's warranty with regard to written communications received by him.

A purchaser who is concerned about the planning aspects of his purchase is free to negotiate some special stipulation in the contract[14]. If he is obliged to contract on the basis of either the National Conditions or the Law Society's Conditions of Sale, he is well advised to postpone exchanging contracts until he has made all possible inquiries as to the true position.

14   The circumstances may be such as to make it prudent for the vendor to protect himself by Special Condition. For other planning clauses, see 18 Ency F & P, 700−2.

Chapter 9

Exchange of contracts and the parties' rights pending completion

A Exchange of contracts

1. Introduction

It has already been observed in Chapter 6 that where the parties are separately represented, both solicitors have their respective parts to play in the preparation of the contract. The purchaser's solicitor approves the contract on behalf of his client, but not before he is satisfied that the local searches and answers to inquiries reveal nothing adverse. Objections to particular clauses in the draft contract are best dealt with by way of preliminary inquiry; it merely adds to the delay if the vendor's solicitor first learns of these when the draft is returned to him amended. Where the same solicitor acts for both parties there is no formal approval as such, though the same duty to advise as is discussed in the next paragraph still exists.

Having approved the contract, one copy is sent to the vendor's solicitor for signature by the vendor, and the purchaser's solicitor then obtains his own client's signature to the other. It goes without saying that a solicitor should not ask his purchaser-client to sign, without first discussing the contract with him and its legal effect. The purchaser should be made aware of incumbrances affecting the property, entries revealed by the search certificate or information disclosed in answer to preliminary inquiries; covenants affecting the property should be briefly explained, or, in a purchase of leasehold property, the significance of the lessor's rights of re-entry. Failure to advise the client adequately might constitute a breach of duty, entitling him to damages[1]. Similarly on the grant of a lease, a solicitor is under a duty to advise his client of the effect of all unusual covenants in the proposed lease[2].

---

1   *Lake v Bushby* [1949] 2 All ER 964; *Piper v Daybell, Court-Cooper & Co* (1969) 210 Estates Gazette 1047 (purchaser not informed of existence of right of way; damages included sum for loss of privacy). Cf. *Ford v White & Co* [1964] 2 All ER 755 (failure to advise of existence of restrictive covenants, but purchaser suffered no loss). *Midland Bank Trust Co v Hett Stubbs and Kemp* [1978] 3 All ER 571 (failure to register an option) and *Ladenbau (UK) Ltd v Crawley and De Reya* [1978] 1 All ER 682 (failure to search Commons Register) [1981] Conv 361 (Helen Johnson).
2   *Sykes v Midland Bank Executor and Trustee Co Ltd* [1971] 1 QB 113, [1970] 2 All ER 471, CA.

A vendor must satisfy himself before signing the contract that he will be in a position to convey what he has contracted to sell. In *Baines v Tweddle*[3] the vendor signed his contract without ensuring that his mortgagees would concur in the sale. This was held to amount to reckless conduct debarring him from relying on his contractual right to rescind the contract because of the purchaser's refusal to withdraw his object to the title.

2.   Mode of exchange

When both parties have signed their respective parts of the contract, the next step in the transaction is the exchange of contracts. When a client instructs a solicitor to act in a conveyancing transaction, he is assumed to have authorised him to conduct the business in the ordinary way recognised as customary; if the solicitor without authority agrees to a method of making the contract, other than the customary method, by dispensing with exchange, he would be committing a breach of duty[4]. A solicitor is under no duty to ensure that his client has procured a mortgage before exchanging contracts, provided he warns his client of the risk he runs if any mortgage application is rejected[5]. It was once the practice for there to be what has been described as a ceremonial form of exchange[6], a meeting of solicitors at the offices of the vendor's solicitor and the passing of signed contracts over the table. These would be dated, the completion date inserted in the appropriate clause, and a receipt for any deposit paid at the time of exchange endorsed on the part handed to the purchaser's solicitor.

(a) Exchange by post
This ceremonial exchange has virtually fallen into disuse. It is now customary to exchange contracts by post, the purchaser's contract together with a cheque for the deposit (if not already paid) being despatched first. It is highly desirable that the purchaser's solicitor has agreed the completion date with the other side and inserted that date in the contract, before sending off his client's part. This prevents the insertion of some date unacceptable to the purchaser[7]. The dating of the contract (as distinct from the insertion of a completion date) is usually left to the vendor's solicitor who, on receipt of the purchaser's part, sends the vendor's part to the purchaser's solicitor.

Since exchange is the crucial and vital fact which brings the contract into existence[8], it becomes necessary to know at what point of time the exchange is complete. In *Eccles v Bryant*[9] after a solicitor had posted the purchaser's part of

---

3   [1959] Ch 679 [1959] 2 All ER 724, CA. The court left unanswered the question whether the vendor could have relied on the condition had his solicitor recklessly assured him that the consents had been obtained; when they had not. See further p. 615, post.

4   *Eccles v Bryant* [1948] Ch 93 at 102, [1947] 2 All ER 865 at 868, CA per Lord Greene MR.

5   *Buckland v Mackesy* (1968) 112 Sol Jo 841, CA.

6   *Eccles v Bryant* [1948] Ch 93 at 97, [1947] 2 All ER 865 at 866, CA per Lord Green MR.

7   For some of the difficulties raised by this, see a letter published in (1968) 65 LS Gaz 160. Strictly a purchaser is not bound by the date inserted by the vendor's solicitor, unless authority for the latter to fix the date can be inferred from the circumstances, and the mere sending by the purchaser's solicitor of an incomplete contract is not sufficient authority, since this is equally consistent with an intention by the purchaser to be governed by the General Condition regulating the completion date.

8   *Eccles v Bryant* [1948] Ch 93 at 99, [1947] 2 All ER 865 at 867 CA, per Lord Greene MR.

9   [1948] Ch 93, [1947] 2 All ER 865, CA; *Sim v Griffiths* (1963) 186 Estates Gazette 541 (vendor's death before her part sent to purchaser's solicitor; no binding contract). See also

the contract, the vendor who had signed his part changed his mind and his solicitors never sent his part in exchange. The purchaser's action for specific performance was dismissed. Notwithstanding that both parts had been signed, no exchange had taken place so there was no contract of which specific performance could be decreed. This rendered it unnecessary for the court to decide whether exchange is affected when the latter of the two documents (the vendor's part) is put in the post, or when it is received by the purchaser's solicitor. The Law Society's Conditions[10] adopt the former position, following the normal contractual rule applicable to acceptances communicated through the post. The National Conditions now adopt the same position[10a]. Bearing in mind the requirements of s. 40 of the Law of Property Act 1925, there may be sufficient justification not to apply the normal postal rule to contracts for the sale of land intended to be exchanged in parts. As Asquith LJ, observed in *Eccles v Bryant*[11] it seems a plain, though rebuttable presumption, that neither party would normally wish to be bound to the other in the absence of such a vital security as is afforded by physical possession of a copy of the contract signed by the other.

(b) Same solicitor acting

It has already been seen that a solicitor's freedom to act for both parties has been considerably restricted[12]. Where he does so act, there is no physical exchange in the sense in which there is when different solicitors are employed. The point arose in *Smith v Mansi*[13].

> P orally agreed to buy V's property, and they instructed the same solicitor who prepared a written contract for signature. P signed the contract which he took to V who signed and returned it to the solicitor, instructing him to hold the contract until he (V) had re-arranged the completion date with P. A few days later the solicitor mistakenly (so it was alleged) inserted in the contract the completion date originally agreed by the parties. Subsequently V refused to complete and when sued by P for specific performance he alleged that there had been no exchange and that when he signed the contract he did not intend to bind himself contractually.

The Court of Appeal decreed specific performance, holding that no exchange of contracts was necessary[14]. When once a completed contract had

---

Harrison v Battye [1974] 3 All ER 830, CA, (contract returned to purchaser instead of vendor's copy). Blackett-Ord VC at first instance held there was no actual exchange. The Court of Appeal did not approve of this but decided there was no contract. But see *Domb v Isoz* [1980] Ch 548, post, where the parts were not identical. This was disregarded because rectification was available. There appears to be a difference between the position where the parties have agreed but the memorandum is incomplete and that where they have not, but see Emmet, 2nd supplement, p. xiv.

10   LSC 10 (1). Cf. Condition 4 (4) of the 1953 edn (exchange on receipt).

10a NCS 1 (7) (ii). Previously the position was governed by the open contract rule.

11   [1948] Ch 93 at 108, [1947] 2 All ER 865 at 871. Cf. Cohen LJ, at 107 and 865.

12   See pp. 137–138, ante.

13   [1962] 3 All ER 857, CA. For other aspects of this decision, see p. 411, post. See also *Vater v Tarbuck* (1970) 214 Estates Gazette 267 (parties signing separate documents) and *Beck v Box* (1973) 231 Estates Gazette 1295.

14   '. . . the idea of exchange, in my opinion, can only be described as artificial nonsense': per Danckwerts LJ, at 861.

been signed nothing more was required before the parties were contractually bound. V's uncommunicated reservations at the time of signing the contract were ineffective to prevent his being bound. Where only one party, for example, the purchaser, P, has signed the contract, he is free to withdraw at any time before the vendor, V, signs it. In the absence of evidence to the contrary, P's signature is to be taken as conditional upon V's signature. When parties enter into a contract the manner in which it is to be created so as to bind them must be gathered from their intentions, express or implied[15]. In this situation it is unlikely that P intends to bind himself unilaterally, knowing that V is to sign the same (or a similar) document.

(c) Telephone exchange

The current property market situation has meant that the completion of a transaction is often dependent on a large series of similar transactions. These 'chains' can be kept open for a considerable time. The practice is developing of much of the formal conveyancing requirements being done before exchange of contracts. Once the 'chain' moves, exchange and completion then take place very rapidly (usually within days). The Court of Appeal in *Domb v Isoz*[16] have recently held that a constructive exchange of contracts is possible and that such a method of exchange is ordinarily authorised. This is of course a very risky procedure. It is one thing to have a physical exchange to bring a contract into existence, it is another to have the documents exchanged or deemed to be exchanged as a result of a telephone conversation[17]. The Law Society[18] have given guidelines concerning telephone exchanges. The practice is unsatisfactory but in the current climate there seems no other sensible alternative.

(d) Contract races

Another unhappy feature of the present time is the existence of 'races' for exchange of contracts. This occurs for basically the same reasons as those which gave rise to a need for telephone exchanges. More than one draft contract is issued by the Vendor the prize going to the first purchaser to exchange[19]. The Law Society have issued directives[20] and reminders[1] concerning disclosure of this state of affairs. Doubts have been expressed as to the validity and dangers of this practice[2].

3.   Subsequent variation of contract

The parties may subsequently vary their contract, but to be effective the variation itself must be evidenced in writing. After variation, the contract between the parties is not the original contract, but that contract as varied, and there

---

15 *Eccles v Bryant* [1948] Ch 93 at 99, [1947] 2 All ER 865 at 866– 67, CA per Lord Greene MR.
16 [1980] Ch 548.
17 See e.g. *Griffiths v Young* [1970] Ch 675 at 681 as to the problems of a disputed telephone conversation between two solicitors.
18 Law Society Guardian Gazette Vol 77 No. 6 p. 144 and LSC condition 10 (2).
19 One of the writers has actually seen a case with a literal race from solicitors' offices followed by a dispute as to who answered first!
20 Law Society Gazette Vol 74 p. 834.
 1 Law Society Gazette Vol 76 p. 1177.
 2 In view of *Daulia v Four Millbank Nominees Ltd* [1978] Ch 231, ante, see [1978] Conv 86, 178, [1980] Conv 6, 164, [1980] Conv 386.

must be adequate written evidence of the contract as it then stands[3]. A reference to the variation in correspondence between the parties' solicitors will suffice for this purpose. On the other hand a complete discharge of a written agreement may be effected orally. Suppose V and P enter into a formal contract for the sale and purchase of plot A. Later they orally agree to buy and sell plot B instead. Their parol contract will effectively discharge the written contract[4], but as the second one is itself not evidenced in writing, it will be incapable of enforcement by action.

Rectification
If the contract mistakenly fails to record the parties' true agreement, the court has jurisdiction to rectify the contract and to order its specific performance as rectified, notwithstanding the lack of written evidence of the real agreement[5]. Technically this constitutes an exception to the statutory requirements, but it has been justified on the ground that the jurisdiction of the court to rectify is outside the prohibition of the statute[6]. To permit rectification upon oral testimony also constitutes an exception to the fundamental principle that parol evidence is inadmissible to vary or contradict a written contract[7]. Consequently before granting rectification the courts insist upon clear evidence of a mistake common to both parties.

4.   Gazumping

It will have become apparent that in many transactions relating to the sale and purchase of land no binding contract may come into existence until several weeks after the parties have concluded their initial agreement to buy and sell 'subject to contract'. Sachs J once remarked[8] that experience showed that this so-called gentleman's agreement:

> ' is only too often a transaction in which each side hopes the other will act as a gentleman and neither intends so to act if it is against his material interests.'

Until contracts are exchanged the parties are still theoretically in a state of negotiation and either of them is free to withdraw from the transaction. Thus the vendor may 'agree' to sell to another who offers him a higher price. Unless the original purchaser can match or improve upon this offer he stands to lose any expenses by way of legal, surveying or other fees already incurred. As the vendor is not in breach of any contract, the purchaser has no redress against him[9]. In no sense is this a novel predicament facing prospective purchasers but the spiralling of house prices during 1971, accompanied by the availability of

3   *Goss v Lord Nugent* (1833) 5 B & Ad 58; *Morris v Baron & Co* [1918] AC 1 at 31, HL, per Lord Atkinson; *New Hart Builders Ltd v Brindley* [1975] Ch 342 (alterations not initialled—no memorandum).
4   *Morris v Baron & Co* [1918] AC 1.
5   *United States v Motor Trucks Ltd* [1924] AC 196, PC.
6   Ibid., at 201, per Earl of Birkenhead.
7   For a justification of the exception, see Story, *Equity Jurisprudence*, p. 155. See further on rectification, Chap. 25.
8   *Goding v Frazer* [1966] 3 All ER 234 at 239.
9   See *Tevanan v Norman Brett (Builders) Ltd* (1972) 223 Estates Gazette 1945; *Sherbrooke v Dipple* (1980) 225 Estates Gazette, 1203, CA, [1981] Conv 165; *Cohen v Nessdale Ltd* [1981] 3 All ER 118; affd. [1982] 2 All ER 97, CA.

cash, for the first time focused public attention on the problem, resulting in widespread demand for reform of the law and prompting the introduction of a Private Member's Bill designed to protect purchasers against the practice of 'gazumping', as it has been inelegantly termed. The situation was considered sufficiently grave for the Government to refer the matter immediately to the Law Commission.

The problem admits of no ready solution, largely because of the necessity to protect the vendor as well as the purchaser. The fact that vendors are just as likely to be gazumped was frequently ignored in the clamour for reform[10]. Several possible solutions have been put forward. A more extensive use of option agreements has been suggested but this device has obvious disadvantages for both parties. During the option period the vendor would be in a state of limbo, being contractually bound to sell but not having the benefit of a purchaser's corresponding obligation to buy. A purchaser who decided not to proceed with the purchase would be in a worse position than under the existing law; not only would he be unable to recover his expenses he would also lose the consideration for the granting of the option. The solution proposed by the Abolition of Gazumping and Kindred Practices Bill was to give some statutory effect (falling short of contractual effect) to an agreement to sell residential property, by making it unlawful on pain of a fine not exceeding £100 for a vendor to increase the agreed sale price or to sell to another at a higher figure unless he repaid the purchaser's legal and other fees incurred in connection with the prospective purchase[11]. Apart from the fact that a fine of £100 might prove totally inadequate to deter would-be gazumpers, the Bill itself was not happily drafted and left unanswered several legal problems which its provisions would appear to have created. It is, perhaps, just as well that the Bill failed to obtain a second reading. The Law Commission concluded legislation was not the answer.

Under present conveyancing procedures some time-lag is unavoidable. The period between the initial 'agreement' and exchange could be reduced by requiring searches to be made after contracts. By repealing s. 40 of the Law of Property Act 1925, it would be possible to give full contractual effect to the parties' oral agreement, but such a move would be undesirable unless coupled with a statutory right for either party to withdraw (on terms) within a certain period. But the fact still remains that a breathing space is desirable in the parties' own interests. Few vendors or purchasers of houses are in a position to bind themselves to buy and sell at the time of the initial 'agreement'. Most house buyers are involved in chain transactions. A purchaser's contract to buy is frequently dependent on a contract to sell his existing property and it is clearly desirable for him to synchronise as far as possible the exchange of contracts in respect of both properties. The vendor may well be similarly placed, and his vendor likewise — thus creating the chain. Any satisfactory solution must give due consideration to this aspect of the problem. Any change in the law which might result in a purchaser ending up with two houses, or a vendor with no house must be avoided at all costs[12].

10   For a sane appraisal of the problem, see the editorial comment in (1972) 36 Conv (NS) 1−2.
11   A vendor would be free to terminate his 'agreement' with the purchaser unless the latter had delivered his signed part of the contract within four weeks of the date of the original agreement (cl. 5).
12   The Law Commission are of the opinion that the most satisfactory solution may lie in having a form of contract which it would be safe for any vendor or purchaser to sign

B   Special cases

Hitherto we have been considering the position where the usual conveyancing procedure operates. A contractual relationship between vendor and purchaser can, of course, arise in other ways. The parties themselves may have prepared a memorandum sufficient for the purposes of s. 40 of the Law of Property Act 1925. Some other special situations must now be considered.

1.   Options to purchase

An option to purchase constitutes an offer to sell which the grantor is contractually precluded from withdrawing so long as the option remains exercisable[13]. A binding contract to purchase comes into existence when the notice exercising it is given to the grantor[14], provided the terms and conditions on which the option is to be exercised have been completely fulfilled[15]. A similar situation arises when a tenant gives notice of his desire to have the freehold under the Leasehold Reform Act 1967[16].

An option to purchase must be distinguished from a right of pre-emption (a right of 'first refusal') which merely places the grantor under an obligation to offer the property to the grantee, should he desire to sell. The grantee may, however, recover damages from the grantor if he gives the property away without first offering it to the grantee[17].

2.   Sales by public auction

The form and contents of a contract for sale by auction do not differ materially from a contract for sale by private treaty. Since a contract comes into existence when the property is knocked down to the highest bidder, and the contracts are signed at the close of the sale, there is no opportunity for approval of the contract by the purchaser's solicitor. However the particulars of the property and special conditions are read out at the time of the auction, and they can usually be inspected beforehand at the offices of the vendor's solicitor and of the auctioneer. An interested person may effect his own local searches before the auction, but it is commonplace for these to be made on the vendor's behalf and produced at the auction. Alternatively the contract may provide for the searches to be made afterwards, and the purchaser will have a contractual right to rescind if the certificate of search reveals adverse entries not referred to in the contract.

without prior legal advice. Attempts to settle the terms of such a contract have not, so far, been successful, and the Commission are continuing their consultations with The Law Society; see the Commission's Seventh Annual Report 1971–72, Law Com. No. 50, para. 23. However, it seems unlikely under present conveyancing procedures that a contract of the type envisaged, assuming that a suitable form can be devised, will obviate the need for a formal contract regulating the rights of the parties in detail, with the result that two documents will require signature before there is any final agreement for sale.

13   *Beesly v Hallwood Estates Ltd* [1960] 2 All ER 314 at 321, per Buckley J; affd. on other grounds, [1961] Ch 105,[1961] 1 All ER 90, CA; *Mountford v Scott* [1975] Ch 258, CA.

14   *Mills v Haywood* (1877) 6 Ch D 196; *Holwell Securties Ltd v Hughes* [1974] 1 All ER 161.

15   *Wheatley v Burrell Enterprises* (1963), 186 Estates Gazette 259, CA (notice in purported exercise given too late; specific performance refused); *Holwell* case (never received).

16   See further Barnsley, *Land Options*, pp. 11–12, 69–90.

17   *Gardner v Coutts & Co* [1967] 3 All ER 1064; Barnsley, op. cit., Chap. 7.

(a) Conditions regulating conduct of auction

The Law Society's Conditions and the National Conditions of Sale contain provisions relative to the conduct of the auction, some of which are dictated by the Sale of Land by Auction Act 1867.

(i) *Reserve price.* The sale may be either 'without reserve' or subject to a reserve price; this must be clearly stated in the contract[18]. The standard conditions state that the sale is at a reserve price unless otherwise stated[19]. They also enable the vendor or his agent to bid up to that price, a right which by statute must be expressly reserved, in which case the vendor or one peron on his behalf can bid[20]. By reserving this right the vendor is more likely to achieve the reserve price, thus reducing the chances of an abortive auction. If the sale is without reserve, it is not lawful for the vendor to employ a 'puffer', someone to bid on his behalf[1]. It is usual to provide a right for the vendor to withdraw the property from sale during the auction[2]. Doubts have been expressed whether in the absence of any special term the vendor is free to withdraw the property if the sale is without reserve[3].

(ii) *Bidding.* A bid is in the nature of an offer to buy, and the acceptance of a bid by the auctioneer does not result in a binding contract unless the property is knocked down at that price and, in the case of a reserve price, that price has been reached[4]. Subject to this the highest bidder becomes the purchaser[5].

The contract may provide that no bid shall be retracted[6]. The general consensus of opinion is that this clause is unenforceable[7]; being merely an offer, the bid can be retracted at any time before acceptance, i.e. before the fall of the hammer. Though at the time of the bidding the purchaser is not bound by the contractual term since no contract yet exists, it seems clear that Parliament in the Act of 1867 intended the insertion of certain provisions in the conditions of sale (e.g. as to a reserve price) to regulate the conduct of the auction. If some terms are effective to bind a bidder, why not others? It is submitted that the condition ought to be enforceable and that the auctioneer would be justified in refusing to accept any purported retraction, notwithstanding that the condition reverses the normal rule.

If any dispute arises as to the bidding the auctioneer has power either to

---

18   Sale of Land by Auction Act 1867, s. 5.
19   NCS 1 (2); LSC 25 (2).
20   Sale of Land by Auction Act 1867, ss. 5, 6. Contravention of these provisions renders the sale invalid: ibid., s. 4. It is sometimes said on the authority of *Parfitt v Jepson* (1877) 46 LJQB 529, that if the vendor desires to bid more than once it must be so stated: Williams, Title, 122. This case merely decided that a sale will be invalid if the vendor exceeds the number of bids that he has reserved to himself.
1   Sale of Land by Auction Act 1867, s. 5.
2   NCS 1 (4); LSC 25 (3) (c).
3   For a discussion of the conflicting opinions, see Williams, Title, 123.
4   *McManus v Fortescue* [1907] 2 KB 1, CA. Occasionally the auction takes the form of the submission by interested persons of a single bid, or tender, contained in a sealed envelope which is opened on a specified date. Such actions are known as blind auctions.
5   NCS 1 (5); the latest edition of the LSC omits this term.
6   Cf. NCS (19th edn) 2 (2). The latest editions of both forms omit this term.
7   1 Williams, V & P, 21–22; Williams, Title, 124; 1 Dart, 122. But see *Freer v Rimner* (1844) 14 Sim 391 (sale under court decree; retraction disallowed).

determine the dispute or put up the property again at the last undisputed bidding[8].

(b) Auctioneer's authority to sign contract

After the sale the highest bidder is required forthwith to pay the deposit and complete and sign the contract[9]. However the auctioneer (but not his clerk) has implied authority to sign a contract on behalf of both vendor and purchaser[10]. The insertion by the auctioneer of the vendor's name in the contract prior to the sale constitutes a sufficient signature so as to bind the vendor[11]. His authority to sign after the sale and thus bind the vendor is not conditional on receipt of the deposit from the purchaser[12].

3. Sales under order of court[13]

The court has jurisdiction to order a sale of land in various situations, for example, to enforce equitable liens, in redemption or foreclosure actions, or in execution of trusts for sale. The order which operates as a conversion[14] binds the interests of all persons who are parties to or bound by the proceedings in which the order is made. The sale may be either in court, or out of court. In the former case the sale is usually by public auction, though occasionally it is by private treaty if the auction proves abortive, in which case the contract requires the court's confirmation. A sale out of court is by public auction and it is the usual practice for the court to fix the reserve price and to require the purchase-money to be paid into court[15].

Where the sale is in court, every step is taken under the court's direction, and certain additional formalities must be complied with. The particulars and conditions of sale[16] are drafted by the solicitor of the party having the conduct of the sale (usually the plaintiff). These together with the abstract of title are referred to conveyancing counsel for settlement. Once counsel has certified that the sale may proceed, the auction takes place. After the sale the auctioneer and solicitor sign a certificate of the result of the sale which is left at the chambers of the judge ordering the sale. Then follow the formal certificate of the result, signed by the judge or master. It is not until this certificate has been given that the highest bidder becomes the purchaser[17].

4. Compulsory purchase orders

(a) Notice to treat

The power to acquire land compulsorily must always be derived from an Act of Parliament. An acquiring authority wishing to exercise their powers must

---

8 LSC 25 (4); NCS 1 (4) which gives the vendor the option of withdrawing the property or putting it up again for auction. For what constitutes a dispute, see *Richards v Phillips* [1969] 1 Ch 39, [1968] 2 All ER 859, CA.
9 NCS 1 (5); LSC 25 (5).
10 See p. 111, ante.
11 *Leeman v Stocks* [1951] Ch 941, [1951] 1 All ER 1043, p. 111, ante.
12 *Phillips v Butler* [1945] Ch 358, [1945] 2 All ER 258.
13 See RSC Ord 31, rr. 1–8; and the notes to *Supreme Court Practice* 1982, p. 560.
14 *Hyett v Mekin* (1884) 25 Ch D 735.
15 See e.g. *Pitt v White* (1887) 57 LT 650.
16 One of the standard sets of Conditions of Sale is usually adopted with any necessary modifications.
17 RSC Ord 44, rr. 22, 23; *Re Joseph Clayton Ltd, Smith v The Co* [1920] 1 Ch 257 (incorrect reserve price given to auctioneer; certificate refused). This is described now as a virtual 'dead letter' see *Supreme Court Practice* 1982, p. 562.

adopt the appropriate statutory procedure[18], resulting in the making and ultimate confirmation (by the relevant government Minister) of a compulsory purchase order. The effect of this order, on confirmation, is to give the authority power to acquire the land described in the order. The next step in the procedure is the vesting of title in the authority, which is regulated by the Compulsory Purchase Act 1965.

A notice to treat must be served on all persons interested in, or having power to sell and convey or release, the land, so far as known to the acquiring authority after making diligent inquiry[19]. This includes the fee simple owner, mortgagee, lessee for a term of years, grantee of an option to purchase[20], but not a tenant having no greater interest than for a year or from year to year[1] nor a person entitled to an easement over the land[2]. No prescribed form of notice is laid down but the Act provides[3] that it shall contain certain basic information, such as particulars of the land affected. The recipient has twenty-one days to submit his claim for compensation. If he fails to do so, or if the amount of compensation cannot be agreed, the matter is referred to the Lands Tribunal for assessment[4].

Effect of notice to treat. Though some of the consequences which flow from an actual contract also follow upon a notice to treat, service of the notice does not vest any equitable title in the acquiring authority; at this stage the price has not been fixed and the notice does nothing more than establish conditions in which a contract might come into existence[5]. It is not therefore capable of registration as an estate contract[6] When the price is subsequently agreed, or assessed by the Lands Tribunal, the parties are then basically in the same position as under an ordinary contract, which can be enforced by specific performance[7]. In other respects the rights and obligations created by the notice are much greater than under an ordinary contract. Since they are derived from a statute, they rank as legal rights and obligations[8]. After service the landowner

18   Usually the procedure prescribed by the Acquisition of Land Act 1981, ss. 2 (3), 10−15 and Sch. 1. Specific statutes may sometimes prescribe a special procedure, e.g. the Housing Act 1957, Sch. 3. The Highways Act 1980, s. 250; empowers a highway authority to *create* rights over land by means of a compulsory purchase order; Local Government (Miscellaneous Provisions) Act 1976, s. 13, reversing *Sovmets Investments v Secretary of State for the Environment* [1977] 2 All ER 385. For compulsory acquisition generally, reference should be made to Comfield and Carnwath *Compulsory Acquisition and Compensation* and Davies, *the Law of Compulsory Purchase and Compensation* (3rd edn).
19   Compulsory Purchase Act 1965, s. 5.
20   *Oppenheimer v Minister of Transport* [1942] 1 KB 242, [1941] 3 All ER 485.
1   Compulsory Purchase Act 1965, s. 20. This can include apparently a tenancy under a fixed term with less than a year to run at the appropriate time see *Newham London Borough Council v Benjamin* [1968] 1 WLR 694, CA. Sed quaere. If the relevant time is the time the property is required and not the date of the notice to treat, the local authority can, by doing nothing, deprive a tenant ultimately of a right to compensation except for the disturbance payment under the Land Compensation Act 1973, ss. 47, 37 and 38; see Comfield and Carnwath, op. cit., pp. 365−389.
2   *Grimley v Minister of Housing and Local Government* [1971] 2 QB 96, [1971] 2 All ER 431 (easement of support).
3   Section 5 (2).
4   Section 6.
5   *Haynes v Haynes* (1861) 1 Drew & Sm 426, especially at 450, per Kindersley V-C.
6   *Capital Investments Ltd v Wednesbury UDC* [1965] Ch 774, [1964] 1 All ER 655.
7   *Harding v Metropolitan Rly Co* (1872) 7 Ch App 154; but the 'statutory contract' does not fall within the LPA 1925, s. 40; *Munton v Greater London Council* [1976] 2 All ER 815, CA.
8   *Mercer v Liverpool, St. Helens and South Lancashire Rly Co* [1903] 1 KB 652 at 661−62 CA, per Stirling LJ; affd. [1904] AC 461, HL.

is still free to deal with his land by sale, assignment or otherwise, but he can only do so subject to the acquiring authority's rights and he cannot increase their liability as regards compensation[9]. An interest in the property created by the owner after service of the notice cannot be the subject of compensation[10]. Being legal rights which bind all persons with or without notice, no question can arise of the authority's rights being void for lack of registration[11], even after the establishment of a true vendor-purchaser relationship consequent upon the assessment of compensation.

(b) Withdrawal and lapse of notice

Compulsory purchase powers must be exercised within three years from the date on which the order became operative[12]. A notice served after expiration of this period is bad. A notice to treat can be withdrawn with the consent of all interested parties, or by the authority in certain specified circumstances[13].

Though no other time is prescribed for completion of the acquisition procedure, the authority must not act in such a way as to lose its rights to enforce the notice. The question of lapse was fully considered by the House of Lords in *Simpsons Motor Sales (London) Ltd v Hendon Corpn*[14]. The acquiring authority may cease to be entitled to enforce the notice for one of several reasons[15].

(i) *Delay*. The authority must proceed within a reasonable time to acquire the property and pay the compensation. What is a reasonable time depends on the facts and circumstances of each case. Delay will not be regarded as culpable if resulting from economic restrictions imposed by the government coupled with an alteration in the development proposals for the area.

(ii) *Abandonment*. This is something more than delay (though delay may be evidence of abandonment), since it must be communicated to the owner expressly or by implication, such as a letter written to the owner (but not a third party) that they did not intend to proceed[16]. A purported abandonment is wrongful and the owner may either accept it or enforce the notice against the authority. He must make his own position clear within a reasonable time, otherwise he will be deemed to have accepted the abandonment.

(iii) *Ultra vires*. The authority cannot, having once served a notice to treat, proceed to acquire the land for a totally different purpose. In *Grice v Dudley*

---

 9 *Cardiff Corpn v Cook* [1923] 2 Ch 115 (assignment of lease); *Birmingham Corpn v West Midlands Baptist (Trust) Association* [1970] AC 874, at 893, 904. The purchaser takes over the right to compensation.
10 *Re Marylebone (Singo Lane) Improvement Act, ex p Edwards* (1871) LR 12 Eq 389 (grant of lease for three years; tenant not entitled to compensation).
11 See *Mercer's* case (supra, note 8), at 662, per Stirling LJ.
12 Compulsory Purchase Act 1965, s. 4. Non-exercise results in the *order* lapsing.
13 See the Land Compensation Act 1961, s. 31.
14 [1964] AC 1088, [1963] 2 All ER 484, HL.
15 See the analysis of Upjohn LJ, at [1963] Ch 57 at 82–84, [1962] 3 All ER 75 at 81–82, CA, accepted as correct by the House of Lords: see [1964] AC 1088 at 1117, [1963] 2 All ER 484 at 488.
16 [1964] AC 1088, at 1125, [1963] 2 All ER 484, at 492, per Lord Evershed. In *Simpson's* case a letter written to the Central Land Board, the authority responsible at that time for assessing compensation, was held not to constitute an abandonment.

Corpn[17], the compulsory purchase order was made for the acquisition of land for the purposes of road widening and erecting a market hall. It was held that the defendant corporation could not enforce the notice to treat at a time when their development proposals made provision for neither object.

(iv) *Equitable jurisdiction.* According to Lord Evershed in the House of Lords[18] to succeed on this nebulous ground, it is necessary to establish one or both of the following:

'. . . that there had been on the part of the corporation something in the nature of bad faith, some misconduct, some abuse of their powers: that there had been on the part of [the owners] some alteration of their position — something must have been done or not have been done by them upon the faith and in the belief that there would be a speedy acquisition of the site: in other words, that they had in some sense been put in an unfair position because of the long period which had elapsed since the service of the notice to treat.'

(c) Completion of acquisition

For the sake of completeness, it may be appropriate at this stage to refer to the final steps in the acquisition procedure. The purchase is completed in the usual manner; the title is investigated and the vendor executes a conveyance or transfer vesting the legal title in the authority[19]. The compensation paid to the vendor is assessed in accordance with the rules laid down by Part II of the Land Compensation Act 1961.

If the owner neglects to make title or execute a conveyance, the authority can, after paying the compensation into court, execute a deed pool containing a description of the land and declaring the circumstances under which, and the names of the parties to whose credit, the payment was made. On execution the deed vests in the authority absolutely all the estate and interest in the land of the parties for whose use and in respect whereof the compensation was paid into court[20]. The deed pool does not have any curative effect; it does not operate to vest a good title in the authority if the vendor's title is defective[1].

Under the normal rule[2], and in the absence of a contractual right so to do, a purchaser cannot enter into possession until completion. However, after service of a notice to treat an acquiring authority can serve on the owner not less than fourteen days' notice of their intention to enter and take possession of the land, notwithstanding that compensation has not been agreed or assessed so that as yet no true vendor-purchaser relationship exists. Interest on the amount of compensation is payable from the time of entry until the compensation is paid[3].

17   [1958] Ch 329, [1957] 2 All ER 673. In *Simpson's* case the plea of ultra vires failed because, though the actual use to which the site would be put had become vague, the council had not determined upon a use outside the scope of the original purpose to provide housing accommodation.

18   [1964] AC 1088 at 1127, [1963] 2 All ER 484 at 494.

19   A form of conveyance is specified in the Compulsory Purchase Act 1965, Sch. 5, but it is rarely used.

20   Compulsory Purchase Act 1965, s. 9. A deed poll can also be used where the owner is absent abroad or untraced: s. 5 (3), Sch. 2.

1   *Wells v Chelmsford Local Board of Health* (1880), 15 Ch D 108, decided on the similar provisions in the Lands Clauses Consolidation Act 1845, ss. 76, 77.

2   Page 259, post.

3   Compulsory Purchase Act 1965, s. 11, see *Greenwoods Tyre Service v Manchester Corpn* (1971) 23 P & CR 246. Physical entry is required *Burson v Wantage RDC* (1974) 27 P &

If the owner refuses to give up possession the authority can issue a warrant to the sheriff to deliver up possession; the costs involved are deductible from the compensation[4].

(d) Acquisition of land by vesting declaration

The Compulsory Purchase (Vesting Declarations) Act 1981 contains a new, optional and, in comparison with the previous method, revolutionary procedure for acquiring land by means of a general vesting declaration. The procedure applies to any Minister, local or other public authority authorised to acquire land by means of a compulsory purchase order[5]. It had long been felt that a more expeditious procedure was essential to further planning objectives.

The acquiring authority are empowered to execute a *general vesting declaration* not earlier than two months after giving notice to the owner of their intention to utilise this procedure[6]. Notice of the making of the declaration must be served on every occupier (other than short-term tenants) and certain other persons entitled to claim compensation. The declaration does not become effective until the expiration of a specified period which must not be less than twenty-eight days from the date when notice of its making was served on the occupier[7]. At the expiration of this period, two important consequences result. First, a notice to treat is deemed to have been served on the date on which the declaration was made[8]. Secondly, and more significantly, the land specified in the declaration, together with the right to enter and take possession, vests in the authority (but subject to any short-term tenancy) as if the authority had executed a deed poll under the Compulsory Purchase Act 1965[9]. The authority therefore obtain title to the land *without any conveyance and without investigating the title*. Subject to any minor tenancy or long term tenancy about to expire, the unincumbered fee simple will vest in the authority, even though an incumbrancer was not served with notice of the making of the declaration[10]. The declaration will be effective to cure any defect in the title, even where unknown to both parties the title of the supposed vendor is non-existent[11].

The 'vendor' is, of course, entitled to compensation assessed in the usual way and also interest from the date of entry to the date of payment[12]. The acquiring

---

CR 556. But what is the position if the authority permits tenants to stay on thereafter? Is there then a notional entry?

4   Section 13 (1), (3).
5   CP (VD) A 1981, s. 1 (1), (2). It was first made available to acquisitions under the Land Compensation Act 1967, though in large measure it follows the general pattern of the expedited completion procedure under the T & CPA 1962, s. 74 (now repealed).
6   CP (VD) A 1981, ss. 4 (1), 5 (1). For the form of this declaration see the Compulsory Purchase of Land Regulations 1982, S.I. 1982 No. 6, reg. 5 (a), Sch. Form 8.
7   Section 6 (1). For service of preliminary notes see s. 3.
8   Section 7 (1).
9   Section 8 (1).
10   See s. 8 (1). As to the situation where there is a minor tenancy see s. 9.
11   I.e. where the legal estate is in X and the acquiring authority proceed on the basis that Y is the owner. This is because under para. 6, the authority are assumed to have knowledge of X and a notice to treat is deemed to have been served on him. Under para. 7, X's title vests in the authority as if they had duly executed a deed poll. This avoids the difficulty noted earlier that execution of a deed poll does not vest a good title in the authority if the vendor's title is bad, p. 248, ante.
12   CP (VD) A 1981, s. 10 (1).

authority can recover as a simple contract debt any compensation over paid or paid to a person whom it is subsequently shown was not entitled to the interest in question[13].

C   The deposit

1.   Nature of deposit

The purchaser's part of the contract is often accompanied by a cheque for the deposit, unless one has already paid to the vendor (which is unusual[14]) or to the vendor's estate agent (which is more common), or to an auctioneer if the sale was by public auction. Both standard sets of Conditions of Sale stipulate for payment of a deposit of £10 per cent, whether the sale is by private treaty or by auction[15]. The amount of the deposit can be varied by agreement. The deposit is normally paid by cheque. In a case at the turn of the century Cozens-Hardy J held that a vendor was not bound to accept a cheque for the deposit nor did he consider that any custom had been proved to oblige vendors to accept cheques[16]. In view of the universal use of cheques at the present, it is thought that the rule would now be different.

The deposit operates as a security for the completion of the purchase[17]. It is not merely a part payment; it is also an earnest to bind the bargain and creates by the fear of its forfeiture a motive in the payer to perform the rest of the contract[18]. The threat of its loss operates as a very potent incentive for the purchaser not to make a capricious change of mind. A deposit must be distinguished from a part-payment which is simply payment of part of the purchase price and cannot generally be forfeited by the vendor[19].

No adequate justification seems to have been given for equity's reluctance to exercise jurisdiction to grant relief against the forefeiture of a deposit, in a way similar to the granting of relief against a penalty. It is sometimes said that the law as to penalties has not been applied to deposits because they usually bear a reasonable proportion to the inconvenience likely to be suffered by a vendor[20]. It is unlikely that equity will ever intervene in the case of the normal ten per cent deposit[1]. Decided cases on equity's relief jurisdiction in relation to deposits (as distinct from part payments) are lacking, but recent judicial observations have prompted one writer to state the view that the deposit on a sale of land with its potential forfeiture is still open to equitable attack[2].

13   Section 11.
14   Some building firms require payment of the deposit direct to themselves, with obvious dangers to the purchaser if the firm is of doubtful financial stability: see the correspondence at (1971), 68 LS Gaz 329, 427.
15   NCS 2 (1); LSC 9. See *Morris v Duke Cohen & Co* (1975) Times, 22 November (solicitor liable in negligence for failing to obtain a deposit).
16   *Johnston v Boyes* [1899] 2 Ch 73. But see [1979] Conv 90.
17   *Howe v Smith* (1884) 27 Ch D 89 at 98, CA, per Bowen LJ.
18   *Howe v Smith* (supra) at 101 and 208, respectively, per Fry LJ.
19   *Mayson v Clouet* [1924] AC 980, PC.
20   Treitel, *The Law of Contract* (5th edn) p. 743. See generally, pp. 742–745.
 1   But see *Maktoum v Southlodge Flats Ltd* (1980) Times, 22 April, where a 10 per cent deposit of £1¼ million was repaid. (A resale at a profit was possible.)
 2   Farrand, 197–198. See *Stockloser v Johnson* [1954] 1 QB 476 at 490–91, [1954] 1 All ER 630 at 637–38, CA, per Denning LJ, where he indicated that the court would relieve against forfeiture of a deposit of 50 per cent; *Bridge v Campbell Discount Co Ltd* [1962] AC 600 at 624, [1962] 1 All ER 385 at 396 HL, per Lord Radcliffe. For the statutory power to order return of a deposit, see the LPA 1925, s. 49 (2), p. 583, post.

2.   Capacity of deposit-holder

Where the deposit is paid to a third party, it becomes necessary to determine whether he holds it as agent for the vendor, or as a stakeholder. The contract will normally regulate this question. The standard form conditions of sale provide[3] for the deposit to be held by a stakeholder, whether he be the vendor's solicitor or an auctioneer. In the absence of any express capacity, the vendor's solicitor holds a deposit as agent for the vendor[4], and an auctioneer as stakeholder[5]. Receipt of the deposit by the vendor's estate agent raised difficult problems which will be considered later in this section.

A person receiving the deposit as agent for the vendor must on demand pay it to the vendor, or according to his instructions. Consequently, though a solicitor will normally retain any deposit held as agent until completion and then deal with it in various ways, it is perfectly proper for such a deposit to be used even before completion in discharge of a second mortgage, or in payment towards a deposit on other property which the vendor has contracted to buy. If the contract goes off owing to the vendor's default the deposit should be returned to the purchaser but he must sue the vendor, not the agent, for its recovery, even where the money is still in the agent's possession[6].

On the other hand a stakeholder is the agent for both parties, holding the deposit on trust to deal with it in different ways in different contingencies[7] to pay it to the vendor on the purchaser's default, or return it to the purchaser if the vendor breaks the contract. In the normal case where the contract is completed, it becomes payable to the vendor and the purchaser should authorise the stakeholder to release it to him or his solicitor, a formality rarely observed in practice. A novel point arose in *Skinner v Reed's Trustee*[8] where Cross J held that if the balance of the purchase money is insufficient to pay off outstanding incumbrances, the purchaser is entitled to have the deposit utilised towards their discharge in priority to the stakeholder's claim for commission. Where the vendor goes bankrupt (as happened here), the stakeholder will have to prove for his debt (the commission) in the vendor's bankruptcy. The stakeholder assumes personal responsibility for the safe keeping of the deposit. Any improper disposal of it on the instructions of one of the parties renders the stakeholder liable to the other for its loss[9]. A stakeholder, unlike an agent, can retain any profit (by way of interest or otherwise) resulting from the deposit. It is his reward for holding the stake[10] though doubts have recently been cast upon this principle[11].

---

3   See note 15, p. 250, ante.
4   *Ellis v Goulton* [1893] 1 QB 350 at 353, CA, per Bowen LJ.
5   *Harington v Hoggart* (1830) 1 B & Ad 577.
6   *Ellis v Goulton* [1893] 1 QB 350, CA.
7   *Skinner v Trustee of Property of Reed (a Bankrupt)* [1967] Ch 1194 at 1200, [1967] 2 All ER 1286 at 1289, per Cross J.
8   [1967] Ch 1194, [1967] 2 All ER 1286.
9   *Wiggins v Lord* (1841) 4 Beav 30; *Dimurro v Charles Caplin & Co* (1969) 211 Estates Gazette 31 (vendor's solicitors not entitled to pay rent due from purchaser out of deposit held as stakeholder).
10   *Smith v Hamilton* [1951] Ch 174 at 184, [1950] 2 All ER 928 at 935, per Harman J. *Potters v Loppert* [1973] Ch 399 (estate agent holding pre-contract deposit).
11   *Burt v Claude Cousins & Co Ltd* [1971] 2 QB 426 at 449–50, [1971] 2 All ER 611 at 622, per Sachs LJ, suggesting that the older authorities may need review in the light of *Brown v IRC* [1965] AC 244, [1964] 3 All ER 119, HL. But see *Sorrell v Finch* [1977] AC 728, post.

Vendor's solicitor: agent or stakeholder?

Should a purchaser's solicitor object as a matter of principle to a draft contract which provides for the payment of the deposit to the vendor's solicitor as agent? Until recently it has been the general custom for the vendor's solicitor to receive it as stakeholder, but it seems that in various parts of the country the practice of requiring it to be paid to the solicitor as agent is on the increase. To brand this as objectionable[12] ignores the fact that in some respects the purchaser is better protected when the deposit is received by the vendor's agent[13]. The danger is that the vendor may demand payment of the money and, should he subsequently become insolvent, the purchaser may experience difficulty in its recovery if the vendor or his trustee in bankruptcy[14] makes default in completing. Whilst receipt by a stakeholder ensures that the purchaser has not abandoned all control over the money, it is not felt that in normal cases sufficient valid grounds exist for his solicitor to insist that it should be so paid[15]. It must not be forgotten that under an open contract the vendor's solicitor is by law deemed to receive it as agent.

3.   Forfeiture and recovery of deposit

(a) Forfeiture

The vendor is entitled to forfeit the deposit if the purchaser is in breach of contract and the breach is of such a nature to discharge the vendor from the contract[16]. This right of forfeiture does not depend on any express contractual stipulation[17]. It can be exercised notwithstanding that the vendor suffers no loss because e.g. he resells the property for the same price, and, assuming there is a concluded contract, the absence of any written memorandum sufficient to satisfy the statutory requirements is no bar to forfeiture[18]. His right is limited to the deposit actually paid; he cannot recover by action the balance of the deposit which the purchaser ought to have paid under the contract[19].

(b) Recovery

If the sale goes off owing to the vendor's default, the purchaser is entitled to the return of his deposit. It may, for instance, be as a result of the vendor's failure to make a good title in accordance with the contract, or his failure to complete[20]. The contract frequently regulates the right of recovery in particular instances[1]. The purchaser possesses a lien on the vendor's land for the return of the deposit

---

12   See (1968) 65 LS Gaz 160, and the corespondence in (1972) 69 LS Gaz 359, 422, 469.
13   By virtue of the lien that he possesses for its recovery should he become entitled to it; see p. 253, post.
14   Bankruptcy does not discharge the contract, see p. 269, post.
15   For a scheme giving the purchaser maximum protection where his deposit is to be used by the vendor in connection with the latter's purchase of other property, see (1970) 120 NLJ 1128, 1139.
16   See further Chap. 23.
17   *Hall v Burnell* [1911] 2 Ch 551.
18   *Monnickendam v Leanse* (1923) 39 TLR 445, p. 115, ante.
19   *Lowe v Hope* [1970] Ch 94, [1969] 3 All ER 605, p. 596, post. This decision however is inconsistent with the decisions of *Buckland v Farmer and Moody* [1978] 3 All ER 929, CA, and *Johnson v Agnew* [1979] 1 All ER 883, HL, as to the effect of rescission. Accordingly the balance unpaid should be recoverable as damages; see *Dewar v Mintoft* [1912] 2 KB 373, [1979] Conv 85−89 and LSC 9.
20   See further Chap. 23, pp. 608−612, post.
1   E.g. NCS 10 (2); LSC 16 (2) (a) (recission by vendor on failure to withdraw objection to title).

and interest[2], save where it is held by a stakeholder; if the vendor never receives the deposit, the purchaser cannot be regarded as his secured creditor, which is the true basis of the purchaser's right to a lien[3]. On the sale of new houses the practice has developed of demanding from a prospective purchaser payment of an initial reservation fee on terms such that the builder will not offer the house or plot for sale to other interested buyers, provided contracts are exchanged within a specified period, but the fee becomes forfeitable to the builder if the purchaser does not exchange contracts in time or otherwise declines to proceed. An arrangement of this kind which in effect gives the prospective purchaser something akin to a right of pre-emption is binding upon him and he cannot recover the fee if he decides not to buy. However as time is not of the essence of the agreement[4] equity will presumably extend the time for exchange of contracts.

(c) Non payment of deposit

The question of a partial payment of the deposit has been considered above. It has been held[5] that the failure to pay a deposit in accordance with an express term of the contract is either a condition precedent to the contract taking effect or a term so radical that its breach entitles the vendor to repudiate. There are clear difficulties in practice over which is the correct view[6] not the least of which is the professional liability for taking an inadequate deposit[7].

4.   Parties' rights on loss of deposit[8]

In the event of the insolvency of the deposit-holder (not being the vendor holding the deposit personally), who bears the loss, the vendor or the purchaser? In answering this question it will be helpful to distinguish cases where (a) there is a contract between the vendor and purchaser, and (b) no binding contract exists.

(a) Binding contract

It is well settled that the vendor bears the loss, whether the deposit is held as agent or as stakeholder. In the latter case his responsibility is based on the principle that he who nominates the stakeholder must also accept the risk[9]. Where the deposit-holder holds as agent, the purchaser must suffer the loss if the *vendor* becomes bankrupt, for receipt by the agent is equivalent to receipt by

---

2   *Whitebread & Co Ltd v Watt* [1902] 1 Ch 835, CA; *Lee-Parker v Izzet* [1971] 3 All ER 1099.
3   *Combe v Swaythling* [1947] Ch 625, [1947] 1 All ER 838. For his rights as a secured creditor in the event of the vendor's bankruptcy, see *Levy v Stogdon* [1898] 1 Ch 478 at 486–87, per Stirling J.
4   For time clauses generally, see p. 412, post.
5   *Myton v Schwab Morris* [1974] 1 All ER 326.
6   See Emmet, 82.
7   It has been suggested that a banker's draft should be insisted on (see Emmet, 82). LSC 9 provides (except in the case of sale by action) for payment either by draft or a cheque drawn upon a solicitor's bank account. It further provides that in the event of dishonour the vendor can elect to treat such dishonour as a fundamental breach of the purchaser's obligations. For difficulties see [1980] Conv 409 especially with regard to short payment.
8   Macintyre, 'Loss of the Deposit' (1958) 22 Conv (NS) 258; Murdoch, 'The Lost Deposit' (1972), 36 Conv (NS) 5.
9   *Annesley v Muggridge* (1816) 1 Madd 593 at 596, per Plummer V-C; *Rowe v May* (1854) 18 Beav 613. A party suffering loss through the bankruptcy of the vendor's solicitor can obtain redress from the Compensation Fund administered by The Law Society.

the principal. Normally, however, the vendor's bankruptcy will not affect the purchaser who can enforce the contract against the trustee in bankruptcy.

(b) Deposit 'subject to contract'

Any pre-contract deposit will in practice be paid, if at all, to the vendor's estate agent. Such a payment is not strictly a deposit; it does not guarantee due performance of any bargain for as yet there is no bargain. Technically it is 'earnest money' paid by a purchaser as proof of his genuine intention to negotiate, but it is nevertheless returnable to him should no contract subsequently be entered into, even if due to his own capricious change of mind[10]. As the vendor has no right to demand the money it is difficult to see how he should be made liable for default on the part of the deposit holder. Notwithstanding this apparent logic the authorities[11] were to the contrary until the House of Lords in *Sorrell v Finch*[12] decided that an estate agent has no implied or ostensible authority to receive as agent for the vendor a pre-contract deposit from a prospective purchaser. Accordingly as a vendor could not in those circumstances demand the deposit he was under no liability to the prospective purchasers for it. A vendor therefore will only be liable if the agent receives it with his authority.

D   General effect of a contract on parties' position

1.   Doctrine of conversion[13]

It is a settled doctrine of the Court of Equity that the moment there is a valid contract for sale the vendor becomes in equity a trustee for the purchaser of the estate sold, and the beneficial ownership passes to the purchaser[14]. The result of the doctrine of conversion is that in the eyes of equity the purchaser becomes the owner of the land, the vendor the owner of the purchase money. It must not be assumed merely because there is a contract for the sale of land that the doctrine of conversion automatically operates. The doctrine is subject to one obvious qualification — the contract must be one of which the court will in the circumstances decree specific performance[15]. If for some reason equity will not enforce specific performance or if the right to specific performance has been lost by the subsequent conduct of the party in whose favour it might originally have been granted, the vendor either never was, or has ceased to be, a trustee in any sense at all[16].

It is sometimes said that the beneficial ownership passes the moment the

---

10   *Chillingworth v Esche* [1924] Ch 97, CA.
11   For a classic Court of Appeal 'problem' see *Ryan v Pilkington* [1959] 1 All ER 689; *Burt v Claude Cousins & Co* [1971] 2 All ER 611; *Barrington v Lee* [1971] 3 All ER 1231; *Maloney v Hardy and Moorshead* (1970) 216 Estates Gazette 1582 and *Raynor v Paskell and Cann* (1948) 152 Estates Gazette 270.
12   [1977] AC 728 at 749, 753, [1976] 2 All ER 371 at 380, 383, per Lords Edmund Davies and Russell.
13   See Pettit, 'Conversion under a contract for the Sale of Land' (1960) 24 Conv (NS) 47.
14   *Lysaght v Edwards* (1876) 2 Ch D 499 at 506, CA, per Jessel MR.
15   *Cornwall v Henson* [1899] 2 Ch 710 at 714, per Cozens-Hardy J, revsd; [1900] 2 Ch 298, CA, on other grounds. See also *Holroyd v Marshall* (1862) 10 HL Cas 191 at 209–10, per Lord Westbury LC.
16   *Central Trust and Safe Deposit Co v Snider* [1916] 1 AC 266 at 272, PC, per Lord Parker.

contract is entered into[17]. This may be a satisfactory way of applying the doctrine of conversion in a succession case where the contest is between different claimants to a deceased vendor's estate. But it is something of an over-simplification in a vendor-purchaser context. The peculiar post-contract relationship between the parties is subject to the contract being eventually performed; if the contract is not performed the relation is discharged and the vendor is treated as never being a trustee for the purchaser[18]. The true position was stated by James LJ[19], in the following terms:

> ' I agree that it is not accurate to call the relation between vendor and purchaser of an estate under the contract while the contract is in fieri the relation of trustee and cestui que trust. But that is because it is uncertain whether the contract will or will not be performed[20], and the character in which the parties stand to one another remains in suspense as long as the contract is in fieri. But when the contract is performed by actual conveyance . . . then that completion relates back to the contract, and it is thereby ascertained that the relation was throughout that of trustee and cestui que trust.'

(a) No operative conversion

The purchaser is not regarded as owner in equity if specific performance is not available. This may be because of some defect in the vendor's title[1], or some collateral misrepresentation, or delay sufficient to defeat the claim for the equitable remedy[2]. Acceptance by the purchaser of a defective title effects a conversion and its operation will be retrospective so that the relation between the parties is throughout one of trustee and beneficiary. A contract for the sale of land to an infant does not vest any equitable title in the infant[3]. The position on service of a notice to treat has already been considered[4].

Similarly in the case of a contract unenforceable for want of a written memorandum, no equitable interest vests in the purchaser in the absence of sufficient acts of part performance. If the vendor has signed, the contract is enforceable against him, even though the purchaser has not. In this situation the purchaser has an equitable interest[5], for reciprocity of enforcement does not seem to be essential[6]. If V contracts to sell to X and then contracts to convey the same property to Y, the contract in favour of Y does not vest any equitable

---

17 *Lysaght v Edwards* (1876) 2 Ch D 499 at 510, 518, CA, per Jessel MR.
18 *Plews v Samuel* [1904] 1 Ch 464 at 468, per Kekewich J; M & W, 577–578.
19 *Rayner v Preston* (1881) 18 Ch D 1 at 13, CA. See also *Wall v Bright* (1820) 1 Jac & W 494 at 501–2, per Sir Thomas Plummer, criticised by Jessel MR, in *Lysaght v Edwards* (1876) 2 Ch D 499 at 517–18, CA.
20 In succession disputes non-performance of the contract has been held not to cancel out the conversion effected by the contract: *Whittaker v Whittaker* (1792) 4 Bro CC 31; *Re Blake* [1917] 1 Ch 18 (non-performance of option to purchase). This suggests that the courts treat different cases in different ways.
 1 *Re Thomas, Thomas v Howell* (1886) 34 Ch D 166.
 2 See generally, Cozens-Hardy J, in *Cornwall v Henson* [1899] 2 Ch 710 at 714; *Lazard Bros Co Ltd v Fairfield Properties Co (Mayfair) Ltd* (1977) 121 Sol Jo 793 (two years' delay no bar). But see Pettit, loc cit., pp. 60–61.
 3 See p. 100, ante.
 4 Page 246, ante.
 5 Contra, if the purchaser alone signs.
 6 *Price v Strange* [1977] 3 All ER 371, CA (lack of mutuality goes not to jurisdiction but rather discretion). What would the position be if there is delay?

title in Y. He cannot obtain specific performance, for the court will not make a decree if the sale would be in breach of a prior contract with a third party[7]. A conveyance of the land to Y may operate to defeat X's equitable interest, depending upon whether X has taken the appropriate steps to protect his interest[8].

(b) Option to purchase

As we have already seen[9] the grant of an option to purchase does not of itself constitute a contract for purchase of land but rather constitutes an offer to sell which is irrevocable for a specified period. When the offer is accepted a contract for sale is created[10]. Nevertheless an equitable interest vests in the grantee as soon as the option is granted (save where it is created in such a way as to infringe the rule against perpetuities), rather than on its exercise when a contract comes into existence. Though there is some authority for the latter possibility[11], there is considerable support for the former view. The grantee's right to call for a conveyance of the land is an equitable interest; as far as the grantor is concerned, his estate is taken away from him without his consent, and the right to take it away being vested in another, the contract giving the option must give the grantee an interest in the land[12].

The effect of a right of pre-emption is uncertain. In *Manchester Ship Canal Co v Manchester Racecourse Co*[13],

> A agreed with B that if a racecourse should be at any time proposed to be used for dock purposes, A would give B the 'first refusal.' A contracted to sell the land to C.

It was held that the agreement did not create an interest in the land entitling B to enforce his right of pre-emption against C who had notice of B's right. It did, however, involve a negative contract not to part with land to a third person without first offering it to B who was entitled to an injunction restraining A from selling the land to a third party without first offering it to B at the same price that C was offering.

A right of pre-emption does not entitle the grantee to set in motion any machinery for the acquisition of the land; he cannot obtain specific performance to enforce the agreement, only an injunction to restrain an improper sale or damages in the event of a wrongful sale or gift to a third party[14]. It was a matter of some doubt as to whether a right of pre-emption at a fixed or ascertainable price created an interest in land. On the basis of the *Manchester* case[15] it was considered it did not. This appeared to contradict certain statutory provisions which assumed that it did[16]. Section 186 of the Law of Property Act

---

7   *Willmott v Barber* (1880) 15 Ch D 96; *Warmington v Miller* [1973] 2 All ER 372, CA.
8   See p. 257, post.
9   Page 243, ante.
10   *Mountford v Scott* [1975] Ch 258 at 264–5, per Russell LJ.
11   *Woodall v Clifton,* [1905] 2 Ch 257 at 259, per Warrington J; Gray, *Perpetuities* (4th edn) 365; 23 Halsbury's Laws (3rd edn) 471.
12   *London and South Western Rly Co v Gomm* (1882) 20 Ch D 562 at 581, CA per Jessel MR; *Re Button's Lease, Inman v Button* [1964] Ch 263 at 271, [1963] 3 All ER 708 at 713, per Plowman J.
13   [1901] 2 Ch 37, CA.
14   *Gardner v Coutts & Co* [1967] 3 All ER 1064.
15   Supra.
16   See M & W, 578; Emmet, 98–9.

1925, provides that all statutory and other rights of pre-emption affecting a legal estate shall be and be deemed always to have been capable of release, and unless released *shall remain in force as equitable interests only*, and under the Land Charges Act 1972, s. 2, a right of pre-emption comes within the statutory definition of an estate contract for registration purposes.

The better view[17] was that it created an interest in land and this was supported by some first instance authority[18] although there was also some contrary authority[19]. The Court of Appeal[20] has rejected this 'better' view and held that a right of pre-emption does not create an interest in land. In a careful review of the authorities they concluded such a right was not an interest in land before 1925 and that the Law of Property Act 1925[1] cannot have changed the position[2]. As an alternative it was held that if this was wrong the right of pre-emption was not properly exercised. This leaves the situation at least on the basis of the judgment of Goff LJ and possibly Templeman and Stephenson LJ that registration of a right of pre-emption will achieve nothing. The interesting question is whether something registrable as a land charge and enforceable for that reason *necessarily* has to be an interest in land.

(c) Conditional contracts
Where the contract between the parties is subject to some as yet unfulfilled condition, e.g. the obtaining of planning permission, it seems that an equitable interest vests in the purchaser if the condition is solely for his benefit. Being in a position to waive the condition at any time, he can obtain specific performance of the contract[3]. If the condition benefits both parties, the purchaser does not obtain an equitable interest until the condition is either fulfilled, or waived by the vendor.

2.   Registration of the contract

Should the purchaser's solicitor register his client's contract as a land charge? The contract clearly constitutes a class C (iv) land charge within the Land Charges Act 1972, and therefore becomes void against a purchaser of the legal estate for money or money's worth if not registered[4]. Since the majority of

---

17 Emmet, 98; Barnsley, *Land Options*, pp. 157–160.
18 *Pritchard v Briggs* [1978] 1 All ER 866 where Walton J reviews the position.
19 *Murray v Two Stokes Ltd* [1973] 3 All ER 357; *Imperial Chemicals Ltd v Susman* (1976) unreported. In *First National Securities Ltd v Chiltern District Council* [1975] 2 All ER 766 Goulding J held a statutory right of pre-emption under the Housing Act 1957, s. 104 was registrable as a C(iv) (cf. *Murray v Two Stokes Ltd* which the learned judge did not follow concerning a non-statutory right.
20 *Pritchard v Briggs* [1980] 1 All ER 294.
 1 At pp. 312, 322.
 2 At p. 313 per Golf LJ holding that the draftsman of the 1925 legislation had made a mistake as to what the law was. Templeman LJ at 329 held a right of pre-emption only became an interest in land when it was enforceable. Stephenson LJ (at 333) agreed with this whereas Goff LJ was of the opinion that it never became an interest in land.
 3 *Wood Preservation Ltd v Prior* [1968] 2 All ER 849 (a case on the meaning of 'beneficial ownership' within the Finance Act 1954, s. 17); affd. [1969] 1 All ER 364, CA, on slightly different reasoning. See generally pp. 128–132, ante. See also *Property Discount Corpn v Lyon Group* [1980] 1 All ER 334 (CA) (agreement for lease subject to approval of matters by guarantor's surveyor created interest in land).
 4 Section 4(6), replacing the LCA 1925, s. 13(2), proviso. *Midland Bank Trust Co Ltd v Green* [1981] 1 All ER 153, HL. See further on the registration of estate contracts, pp. 386–388, post.

contracts are completed within a comparatively short period, it is not the practice to register the contract, unless completion is likely to be delayed for some time or a dispute arises between the parties. Whatever the practice of the profession might be, a solicitor failing to register the contract which subsequently became void would be liable to his client for professional negligence. It is equally essential to register as land charges options to purchase and rights of pre-emption.

Registered land

The contract should be protected by a notice in the vendor's charges register, which will require the vendor's co-operation in lodging the land certificate at the Registry[5], otherwise the contract can only be protected by a caution. If the vendor's property is subject to a registered charge, the land certificate will already be deposited at the Registry[6] and the purchaser can obtain the entry of a notice in the register without the vendor's concurrence, though the contract will not bind the chargee. It should not be forgotten that the purchaser's occupation under an enforceable contract constitutes an overriding interest and his rights will bind a subsequent purchaser, with or without notice[7].

In the case of registered land protection of the contract on the register of title will not operate to confer priority over some third party interest which is not entered on the register until after the date of the purchaser's search but before his registration as proprietor. Normally the purchaser will not be affected by such an interest since his official certificate of search (which will not disclose the interest) will confer priority, provided his transfer is lodged for registration within the period of protection afforded by the certificate[8]. However, the recent cases of *Elias v Mitchell*[9] and *Watts v Waller*[10] suggest that the significance of this important proviso is not always appreciated. In both cases there was delay in lodging the transfer and by the time the application for registration was lodged an adverse entry had been made in the vendor's register of title. The purchaser would, therefore, take subject to the interest, even though it had been registered before the adverse interest. However, protection of the contract on the register confers priority over a conflicting interest created by the vendor after completion, which does not itself require substantive registration, such as a lease taking effect as an overriding interest[11].

E   The vendor as trustee

The effect of an enforceable contract for sale is to constitute the vendor a trustee for the purchaser, though it should always be remembered that strictly this relationship between the parties is conditional on the contract's performance[11a]. It is a trusteeship of a special kind, variously described as

---

5   LRA 1925, s. 49 (1) (c). See pp. 67–68, ante.
6   LRA 1925, s. 65 p. 68, ante.
7   *Bridges v Mees* [1957] Ch 475, [1957] 2 All ER 577, p. 48, ante.
8   Certificates of search are considered more fully in Chap. 15.
9   [1972] Ch 652, [1972] 2 All ER 153 (caution lodged after completion but before registration).
10   [1972] 3 All ER 257, CA (entry of notice after purchaser's certificate but before completion which was effected on the very date the certificate expired). See further pp. 73–74, ante.
11   For a possible situation see note 1, p. 52, ante. Until the purchaser's registration, the legal title remains in the vendor, p. 453, post.
11a Cf. *Lake v Bayliss* [1974] 2 All ER 1114 and Emmet, 256; (1974) 38 Conv (NS) 357.

'constructive'[12], or 'qualified'[13]. The vendor is more than a bare or dormant trustee; he has a personal and substantial interest in the property, and an active right to protect that interest if anything should be done in derogation of it[14]. His interest is in actually obtaining the purchase money. When he receives it he becomes a mere trustee for the purchaser, assuming there has been no conveyance of the legal estate[15].

1.   The property subject to the trust

He is a trustee only in respect of the property contracted to be sold. In *Re Lyne-Stephens and Scott-Miller's Contract*[16],

> V sold a freehold house to P with vacant possession. After the contract the outgoing tenant paid to V the sum of £2,060 in respect of dilapidations. P was held not entitled to this sum since he had contracted to buy a house with possession, altogether apart from the lease. Had the sale been subject to but with the benefit of an existing lease, the position might well have differed.

The general rule that a trustee must not make any profit out of his trust does not apply to the vendor. He can retain rents and profits accruing before the time fixed for completion. In effect his trusteeship extends only to the subject matter of the contract, physical accretions thereto and accretions in the nature of timber that might fall, or minerals that might be dug otherwise than under some pre-existing contract[17].

2.   Extent of vendor's interest

Pending completion, the vendor's rights are as follows[18]:

(i) He can retain possession of the property until payment of the purchase money, though this right may be varied by the contract.

(ii) He is entitled to a lien on the property for the security of the purchase money, or the balance. This lien arises immediately there is a binding contract[19], and as a general rule remains enforceable by the vendor so long as any part of the purchase money remains outstanding, notwithstanding he has conveyed the property to the purchaser and let him into occupation. If the purchaser is in possession, the court will restrain him from any act, such as felling timber, by which the vendor's security might be lessened[20].

---

12   *Shaw v Foster* (1872) LR 5 HL 321 at 356, per Lord Hathersley C.
13   *Rayner v Preston* (1881) 18 Ch D 1 at 6, CA, per Cotton LJ; cf. Brett LJ, at 10, ('With the greatest deference, it seems wrong to say that the [vendor] is a trustee for the [purchaser]').
14   *Shaw v Foster* (1872) LR 5 HL 321 at 338, per Lord Cairns.
15   'The vendor is not a mere trustee; he is in progress towards it and finally becomes such when the money is paid, and when he is bound to convey': per Plummer MR, in *Wall v Bright* (1820) 1 Jac & W 494 at 503.
16   [1920] 1 Ch 472, CA; *Re Hamilton-Snowball's Conveyance* [1959] Ch 308, [1958] 2 All ER 319 (purchaser not entitled to compensation payable on derequisitioning of property).
17   *Re Hamilton-Snowball's Conveyance* [1959] Ch 308 at 312, [1958] 2 All ER 319 at 321, per Upjohn J.
18   See generally, *Lysaght v Edwards* (1876) 2 Ch D 499 at 506–7, per Jessel MR.
19   *Re Birmingham, Savage v Stannard* [1959] Ch 523, [1958] 2 All ER 397.
20   *Crockford v Alexander* (1808) 15 Ves 138.

(iii) He is entitled to take the rents and profits until the time fixed for completion[1], or in the case of an open contract, until the time when a good title is made out. Once that date has passed without actual completion, he must account for them to the purchaser, not only for what he actually receives, but for what he should have received had he not allowed the property to lie waste[2]. The vendor is not entitled to retain rents received by him after the contractual date for completion, in satisfaction of rents accrued due before that date[3].

(iv) After the time fixed for completion has passed and delay is attributable to the purchaser's default, the vendor can charge interest on the balance of the purchase money. Alternatively the contract may entitle him to retain the rents and profits until actual completion in lieu of charging interest. The rights of the parties in the event of delay in completion are more fully considered in Chapter 15[4].

3.   Vendor's duty to maintain[5]

The law imposes a correlative duty on the vendor to maintain the property. He is liable to the purchaser if he wilfully damages or injures it[6], or even if he merely fails to take reasonable care of it. It has been described as a duty to use reasonable care to preserve the property in a reasonable state of preservation and as it was when the contract was made[7]. Liability arises in respect of the removal by a trespasser of large quantities of surface soil from the property[8], or for damage caused to the property by an outgoing tenant[9]. Broken windows and slates should be replaced; reasonable steps should be taken to ensure that the property does not become frozen-up during winter time, especially if the property is vacant[9a]. The vendor's duty seems to extend even to keeping the garden of residential property in good order[10].

This duty to maintain applies alike to freehold and leasehold property, though in the latter case there is the additional point that the vendor must perform the covenants in the lease up to completion, otherwise the existence of a breach of covenant renders the lease voidable (assuming there is a forfeiture clause) and entitles the purchaser to rescind the contract. However we have seen that it is usual to stipulate that the purchaser is deemed to purchase leasehold property with full notice of its actual state of repair and he is required to take it *as it stands*. This has the effect of exonerating the vendor from liability for deterioration between contract and completion[11].

Where the property is subject to tenancies, the general rule seems to be that as between the parties the powers of the vendor to act as owner and to change

1   *Cuddon v Tite* (1858) 1 Giff 395; NCS 6 (3), LSC 15 (2) (b).
2   *Phillips v Silvester* (1872) 8 Ch App 173.
3   *Plews v Samuel* [1904] 1 Ch 464.
4   Pages 410–417, post.
5   See Adams, 'Property Damage between Contract and Completion' (1971) 68 LS Gaz 224.
6   E.g. by the removal of flowering shrubs, or an ornate door (*Phillips v Lamdin* [1949] 2 KB 33, [1949] 1 All ER 770).
7   *Clarke v Ramuz* [1891] 2 QB 456, CA.
8   *Clarke v Ramuz* (supra).
9   *Royal Bristol Permanent Building Society v Bomash* (1887) 35 Ch D 390, *Ware v Verderber* (1978) 247 Estates Gazette 1081.
9a *Lucie-Smith v Goreman* [1981] SCL 286.
10 *Foster v Deacon* (1818) 3 Madd 394 at 395, per Leach V-C.
11 Page 172, ante. Since the purchaser may not complete, Walford, 126–27, suggests that the vendor should reserve the right to carry out necessary repairs to avoid a possible forfeiture.

tenants or holdings are suspended pending completion; if the vendor determines a tenancy without consulting the purchaser, he is responsible for any
resulting loss[12]. If the tenant determines the tenancy prior to completion, the
vendor, subject to consultation with the purchaser, should re-let the property[13].

(a) Duration of liability
The vendor's duty lasts so long as he retains possession, notwithstanding that
the date fixed for completion has expired due to the purchaser's delay[14]. References in the cases to the vendor's possession are to be understood in the wider
sense of his right to possession. A vendor cannot, simply by vacating the
property after exchange of contracts, divest himself of his responsibility to the
purchaser. He is not liable for deterioration to the property occurring after the
contractual date for completion if the title offered is such that the purchaser
could safely take possession, but refuses to do so[15]. The vendor can discharge
himself from further liability for repairs if he allows the purchaser into possession before actual completion[16].

(b) Vendor's right of indemnity
The vendor must bear the cost of maintenance and cannot normally look to the
purchaser for an indemnity. Since he is entitled to the rents and profits, it is
only reasonable that the burden of repairs should fall on him. Further the
vendor has a personal interest in maintaining the property, since it may enure
for his benefit if the purchaser defaults[17]. Dicta[18] suggesting that the vendor can
recover money spent on maintenance which is entirely unremunerative to him
are thought to be incorrect.

To this general rule there are two limitations: one general and one specific.
The maintenance of the property ranks as a current expense payable out of
rents and profits; their cost must be borne by the vendor only so long as he is
entitled to the rents and profits for his own benefit, and thereafter the expense
must be met by the purchaser. The purchaser must bear the cost of repairs as
from the date a good title is shown under an open contract, or from the date of
completion under a contract incorporating the Law Society conditions[19]. In
such cases it is still the duty of the vendor in possession to maintain the property,
but he is entitled to be given credit for all proper expenditure as against the
rents and profits (including any occupation rent due from the vendor himself)
for which he must account to the purchaser[20].

The special limitation relates to a sale of premises, together with the goodwill
of a business carried on there. In the event of delay in completion owing to the

12 Raffety v Schofield [1897] 1 Ch 937 at 944, per Romer J.
13 Earl Egmont v Smith (1877) 6 Ch D 469; Abdulla v Shah [1959] AC 124 PC (vendor liable
   for diminishing value of property by reletting rent restricted property without purchaser's
   consent).
14 Phillips v Silvester (1872) 8 Ch App 173. As to delay see further post.
15 Minchin v Nance (1841) 4 Beav 332; Phillips v Silvester (1872) 8 Ch App 173 at 178, per
   Lord Selbourne LC.
16 NCS 8; LSC 18 discussed at p. 266, post.
17 Re Watford Corpn's and Ware's Contract [1943] Ch 82 at 85, [1943] 1 All ER 54 at 56, per
   Simonds J (vendor not entitled to recoup war damage contributions).
18 Bolton Partners v Lambert (1889) 41 Ch D 295 at 302, per Kekewich J; affd. (1889) 41
   Ch D 304, CA.
19 LSC 19, save where apportionments are made as at the date fixed for completion; see
   p. 418, post. Cf. NCS 6 which generally apportions as at the date of completion.
20 Phillips v Silvester (1872) 8 Ch App 173 at 176, per Lord Selbourne LC. See post, for
   payment of rent by a vendor.

purchaser's default, the vendor is entitled, subject to any contrary contractual provision, to carry on the business at the purchaser's risk and to be indemnified against losses incurred, provided he notifies the purchaser of what is happening[1].

(c) Improvements

The vendor's duty does not extend to making improvements, and he cannot recover money so spent[2], though there are suggestions that he may be entitled to reimbursement for exceptional outlay on permanent repairs necessary to preserve the property[3].

A somewhat different problem arises where a prospective landlord undertakes improvements or alterations at the request of the tenant, but no lease is ever executed owing to a break down in negotiations. Who pays for the cost of such expenditure? Whilst it is obviously prudent for the landlord to obtain the tenant's agreement to pay for the work, it does not necessarily follow that a landlord obtaining the tenant's agreement will always be able to recover the cost of the outlay. No general rule can be laid down and each case must be judged by its own facts, as the Court of Appeal were at pains to stress in *Brewer Street Investments Ltd v Barclays Woollen Co Ltd*[4], where the landlord recovered the cost. A prospective tenant who commences modernising premises in the expectation of a lease but leaves the work unfinished when negotiations break down may find himself not only unable to recover the sum spent but also liable to the owner for the cost of putting the property in a proper state of habitation[5].

(d) Contractual provisions

Some local law society Conditions of Sale provide that as from the date of the contract the purchaser shall bear and repay to the vendor the cost of repairs properly incurred by the vendor pending actual completion, save for extraordinary repairs (whatever they may be) executed otherwise than in an emergency, which are not treated as having been properly incurred unless previously authorised by the purchaser. Neither The Law Society's nor the National Conditions of Sale make any such provision, except where the purchaser takes possession before completion[6].

F   The purchaser as beneficiary

1.   His equitable interest

As explained earlier in this chapter, an enforceable contract vests an equitable interest in the purchaser. This he can devise by will, charge or sell. In the event

---

1   *Golden Bread Co Ltd v Hemmings* [1922] 1 Ch 163. Cf. *Dakin v Cope* (1827) 2 Russ 170 (purchaser not notified, held not liable for loss).
2   *Monro v Taylor* (1850) 8 Hare 51 at 60, per Wigram V-C.
3   *Phillips v Silvester* (1872) 8 Ch App 173 at 177, per Lord Selbourne LC.
4   [1953] 2 All ER 1330, CA. Cf. *Jennings and Chapman Ltd v Woodman, Matthews & Co* [1952] 2 TLR 409, CA (lessor unable to recover expenditure). In both these cases there was no concluded contract between the parties. Where a contract for the sale or leasing of land exists, wasted expenditure (including pre-contract expenditure) is recoverable if it is within the parties' contemplation as likely to be wasted if the contract were broken; see *Lloyd v Stanbury* [1971] 2 All ER 267, p. 596, post.
5   See *Hindley v Pemberton* (1957) 107 LJ 620 (Cty Crt).
6   As to which see p. 265, post.

of a sub-sale, the purchaser's contract becomes a vital document of title. He can obtain an injunction to restrain the vendor from transferring the property to a third party[7], or from committing acts of voluntary waste which depreciate the property.

(a) Gains
All improvements to and increases in the value of the property are retained by the purchaser, such as a sudden rise in the value of the land attributable to the discovery of minerals in the sub-soil (assuming these have not been excepted on a previous transaction). Where property is sold in consideration of an annuity, the annuitant's death shortly after the contract does not debar the purchaser from obtaining specific performance[8]. As already noticed, the purchaser is limited to physical accretions, and not to financial benefits accruing to the vendor and not forming part of the contract.

(b) Losses
The prospect of losses is likely to be of more concern to the purchaser than the possibility of gain. As from the date of the contract the risk passes to the purchaser, subject to the vendor's duty to take reasonable care to maintain the property. He must bear all loss or damage to the property resulting from earthquake, war hazards or fire[9]. Service of a compulsory purchase order after contract but before completion does not discharge the purchaser; he remains liable to the vendor for the purchase price and is entitled to receive the compensation from the acquiring authority[10]. If without fault on the part of the vendor, the purchased premises collapse and cause damage to adjoining property or to a highway user, the purchaser must indemnify the vendor against damages and expenses incurred in satisfying the injured person's claim[11].

(c) Frustration
The application of the doctrine of frustration to transactions involving land has usually been confined to leases, rather than contracts for sale. It was considered that the doctrine of frustration did not normally apply to contracts for sale of land[12]. However in two recent decisions[13] the Court of Appeal were prepared to consider it could apply but not to those particular cases[14]. The House of Lords[15] has now held that the doctrine of frustration can apply to leases (but once again

---

7 See *Hadley v London Bank of Scotland Ltd* (1865) 3 De GJ & Sm 63 where no injunction was granted on the ground that the purchaser's own right to specific performance was uncertain.
8 *Mortimer v Capper* (1782) 1 Bro CC 156. On the purchase of a reversionary interest, the purchaser retains the benefit accruing from the unexpected death of the life tenant (*ex p Manning* (1727) 2 P Wms 410).
9 *Cass v Rudele* (1693) 2 Vern 280 (earthquake), but see 1 Bro CC 157n, where the case is said to be misreported; *Paine v Meller* (1801) 6 Ves 349 (fire).
10 *Hillingdon Estates Co v Stonefield Estates Ltd* [1952] Ch 627, [1952] 1 All ER 853.
11 *Robertson v Skelton* (1849) 12 Beav 260.
12 *Hillingdon Estates Co v Stonefield Estates Ltd* [1952] Ch 627 at 631, [1952] 1 All ER 853 at p. 856, per Vaisey J.
13 *Amalgamated Investments Ltd v John Walker & Sons Ltd* [1976] 3 All ER 509; *Universal Corpn v Five Ways Properties Ltd* [1979] 1 All ER 552.
14 In the first case the alleged frustrating event was the listing of the building. In the second it was exchange control regulations depriving the purchaser of funds.
15 *National Carriers Ltd v Panalpina (Northern) Ltd* [1981] 1 All ER 161.

not to the particular case). The case contains dicta which suggest the doctrine can apply to contracts ('hardly ever' as opposed to 'never')[16]. The actual circumstances of a successful plea of frustration have yet to be discovered.

(d) Incidence of insurance

If the risk passes to the purchaser as from the date of the contract, it seems but a simple precaution to insure the property, against fire, storm damage and similar risks, remembering that if the property is vacant, certain risks such as burst pipes or malicious damage may not be covered by the normal household policy. It should be standard practice for every solicitor to ensure that the purchaser is adequately protected between contract and completion, though it is doubted whether a solicitor has authority to effect insurance without his client's consent[17]. Some building societies[18] effect insurance on behalf of a prospective borrower on receipt of his signed acceptance of the mortgage offer. However there is no uniformity of practice amongst building societies and a purchaser's solicitor should request the society (or other institutional lender) to arrange insurance cover as from exchange of contracts.

In the absence of any policy effected by the purchaser, he has at common law no rights to any insurance money received by the vendor in default of express provision in the contract[19], nor is the vendor under any general duty to keep up the insurance[20]. But in the case of leasehold property held under a lease containing a lessee's covenant to insure and reinstate, the purchaser can indirectly claim the benefit of the insurance, since the vendor's failure to observe the covenant amounts to a defect in title entitling the purchaser to rescind[1]. As for the vendor, he is entitled to receive the insurance money on the occurrence of an insured risk, notwithstanding the existence of a contract to sell the property[2], but if the purchase is later completed he must repay to the insurers the amount received from them[3]. He cannot make a profit.

(i) *Statutory provisions.* Section 47 of the Law of Property Act 1925, provides, in effect, that the purchaser is to have the benefit of any insurance money payable to the vendor after the date of the contract in respect of any damage to or destruction of the property, provided (a) there is no contrary stipulation in the contract between the parties, (b) the insurers give their consent (though in many household policies this consent is given in general terms, rendering any express request therefore unnecessary) and (c) the purchaser pays a proportionate part of the premium from the date of the contract. In spite of this provision, the advice given in all the books[4] is that the purchaser should insure. The section does not require the vendor to maintain the insurance or to inform the purchaser that it has lapsed. Then again the policy might be voidable at the

16   Pages 168, 176−179 and 185−6.
17   Emmet, 41.
18   Building societies invariably require the insurance to be with a company of their own choice and pay the premiums themselves, debiting the amount to each borrower's account. The borrower is free to insure his furniture and personal belongings with whatever company he chooses. This practice has been a matter of controversy.
19   *Rayner v Preston* (1881) 18 Ch D 1, CA.
20   *Paine v Meller* (1801) 6 Ves 349.
1   *Palmer v Goren* (1856) 25 LJ Ch 841; *Dowson v Solomon* (1859) 1 Drew & Sm 1.
2   *Collingridge v Royal Exchange Assurance Corpn* (1877) 3 QBD 173.
3   *Castellain v Preston* (1883) 11 QBD 380, CA.
4   See e.g. Emmet, 41.

option of the company. In passing, it is not in the vendor's own interest to allow
the insurance to lapse after exchange of contracts; if he does, he has to bear any
loss should the purchaser successfully rescind the contract[5].

Under the Fires Prevention (Metropolis) Act 1774, s. 83, an insurance
company is required, in the case of loss or damage *by fire*, to reinstate the
insured property upon the request of any person interested in or entitled to it,
provided the insurers have not already paid out to the insured. Remaindermen[6]
and mortgagees[7] have been held to be persons 'interested' but there is no
decision on the rights of a purchaser under a contract for sale[8]. It is generally
felt that the section, assuming it extends to purchasers, does not afford adequate protection and, for not very convincing reasons, tends to be ignored by
conveyancers.

(ii) *Contractual provisions.* The usual Conditions of Sale do not significantly
improve the purchaser's position[9]. Apart from giving him a right to require
notice of his interest in the property to be indorsed on the policy, for which
privilege he must pay a proportionate part of the premium, they expressly
relieve the vendor from any duty to maintain the insurance. Both sets of Conditions, however, preserve the position under the general law[10] by requiring him
to keep up any insurance effected pursuant to an obligation to a third party
(such as a lessor). The possibility of the vendor's failing to renew his policy is
only likely to occur where the property is free from mortgage; a mortgagee will
not permit the policy to lapse so long as the mortgage remains undischarged.

2.   Possession before completion

As we have seen the vendor is entitled to retain possession until actual completion. The parties may agree otherwise and the contract itself may expressly
provide for the purchaser to enter into occupation on the terms of a Special
Condition or under the General Conditions. Vendors of residential property,
even when they are in a position to grant possession before completion, are
generally reluctant to do so. The dangers cannot be minimised. The possible
incidence of the Rent Act 1977, must be considered. The purchaser may be less
anxious to complete on the contractual date. In the event of delay, the vendor
has neither actual enjoyment, nor the purchase money unless the purchaser has
been required to pay the balance (or at least part) as a condition of being
allowed into possession. If the vendor sues for specific performance the court
usually gives the purchaser the option of paying the balance with interest into
court as an alternative to giving up possession[11], even where he has made extensive alterations to the property[12].

5   See *Simmonds v Pennington & Son* [1955] 1 All ER 240, CA.
6   *Re Quicke's Trusts, Poltimore v Quicke* [1908] 1 Ch 887.
7   *Sinnott v Bowden* [1912] 2 Ch 414.
8   There is obiter support for the view that a purchaser is included: *Rayner v Preston* (1881)
    18 Ch D 1 at 15, CA, per James LJ.
9   NCS 21; LSC 11. The latter excludes LPA 1925, s. 47 and attempts to deal with the likely
    position of both the vendor and purchaser insuring.
10 See p. 264, ante, and the cases cited in note 1.
11 *Greenwood v Turner* [1891] 2 Ch 144.
12 *Maskell v Ivory* [1970] Ch 502, [1970] 1 All ER 488.

(a) Contractual provisions regarding pre-completion possession
Both the standard Conditions of Sale[13] regulate in more or less similar terms the rights of a purchaser (not being a lessee already in occupation) who is let into possession before actual completion.

While we are considering the provisions of the General Conditions of Sale, it will be helpful to compare the position under an open contract.

(i) *Licensee or tenant?* The purchaser occupies the property as licensee, not as tenant. Thus the protection of the Rent Act 1977, cannot operate in his favour. Under an open contract the purchaser is a tenant at will[14], which suffices to bring him within the Act[15]. But he will be outside its protection if, though let into possession as a tenant at will, he makes weekly payments in discharge of the purchase price and outgoings[16].

The contractual provisions require the purchaser to vacate the premises forthwith if the contract is rescinded or discharged or where the vendor gives notice[17].

(ii) *Liability for repairs and outgoings.* As from the date of taking possession until actual completion or until he vacates the property following rescission of the contract, the purchaser is responsible for repairs and for the discharge of all outgoings by way of rates, rent, insurance, and even non-recurrent outgoings such as the expenses incurred in complying with a dangerous structure notice. He must pay interest on the balance of the purchase money, and is entitled to the rents and profits from any part of the property not physically occupied by him.[18]

These conditions basically confirm the open contract position. The act of taking possession is an implied agreement to pay interest[19] irrespective of whether the purchaser derives any profit from his possession[20]. As already mentioned the vendor's duty to maintain the property lasts only so long as he retains possession.

(iii) *Improvements.* In one respect the standard conditions are defective. They do not restrain the purchaser from making alterations or improvements. Perhaps the general law adequately protects the vendor in this situation. A purchaser in possession who effects substantial improvements cannot recover his expenditure if the sale goes off because of the vendor's breach of contract[1].

---

13 NCS 8; LSC 18. The Statutory Conditions are silent on this point. The following should be noted: (a) such possession will not waive the right to raise requisitions (b) (in the case of LSC) the purchaser is obliged to insure and (c) a purchaser is obliged to pay interest at the contractual rate.
14 *Ball v Cullimore* (1835) 2 Cr M & R 120.
15 *Chamberlain v Farr* [1942] 2 All ER 567, CA.
16 *Dunthorpe and Shore v Wiggins* [1943] 2 All ER 678, CA. Cf. *Francis Jackson Developments Ltd v Stemp* [1943] 2 All ER 601, CA (payments for use and occupation; purchaser entitled to protection). A device used to avoid the Rent Acts but see now Housing Act 1980, s. 88 which gives a county court discretionary powers to regulate these types of devices.
17 NCS 8 (2); LSC 18 (5). See *Hyde v Pearce* [1982] 1 All ER 1029, CA.
18 See NCS 8 (1) (ii)-(iv); LSC 18 (4).
19 *Fludyer v Cocker* (1805) 12 Ves 25 at 27, per Grant MR; *Birch v Joy* (1852) 3 HL Cas 565.
20 *Ballard v Shute* (1880) 15 Ch D 122 (erection of 'For Sale' board constituted possession).
 1 It is not normally to be regarded as in the contemplation of the parties that the purchaser will spend money on improving the property before it has been conveyed to him: per

Should the purchaser himself default and leave the alterations incomplete, the vendor, it seems, can recover the amount necessary to render the premises habitable[2]. Nevertheless it is desirable to regulate this by expressly providing that the purchaser shall forgo any claim against the vendor for money spent on the property.

(iv) *Waiver of title.* The standard conditions[3] stipulate that the taking of possession is not deemed to be an acceptance of the vendor's title, nor a waiver of the purchaser's right to raise requisitions on title. This is an improvement on the open contract position. Here the taking of possession is an equivocal act. There are numerous ancient authorities on this problem, some of which are difficult to reconcile. The cases appear to establish the following general rules. Possession does not of itself constitute acceptance[4] but will do so if the purchaser exercises acts of ownership in relation thereto[5] or makes structural alterations[6]. Where the contract expressly provides that he shall have possession, this is interpreted as meaning beneficial possession and acts of ownership do not constitute a waiver[7]. A purchaser can always safeguard his interests by taking possession subject to outstanding requisitions, provided the vendor will agree to this term.

The standard conditions are confined to the taking of possession. If the purchaser is let into occupation (otherwise than under the contract) and makes structural alterations, the general rule applies and he is deemed to have waived his right to insist on any particular irremovable objections of which he had notice[8]. In this situation the General Conditions do not appear to assist the purchaser.

(b) Sale to sitting tenant
The Conditions just considered do not apply where the purchaser is in occupation under a lease created before the contract. As we have already noticed[9] the contract does not operate to determine the lease and the purchaser is liable for rent until the date of actual completion. Should completion be delayed the standard conditions make no provision for the vendor to charge interest in lieu of rent, for this would be inconsistent with the continuance of the tenancy. Nevertheless where the contract is governed by the conditions laid down by the Leasehold Reform (Enfranchisement and Extension) Regulations 1967[10], the

---

Brightman J in *Lloyd v Stanbury* [1971] 2 All ER 267 at 275, p. 590, post. Cf. note 4, p. 262, ante. See also *Worthington v Warrington* (1849) 8 CB 134 (tenant in possession exercising option to purchase and making alterations); *Lee-Parker v Izzet* [1971] 3 All ER 1099 (tenant-purchaser not entitled to lien for repairs which landlord failed to carry out).

2 Cf. *Crisp v Fox* (1967) 201 Estates Gazette 769 (purchaser in possession before contracts exchanged liable for damage to property when sale fell through).

3 NCS 8 (3); LSC 18 (3).

4 *Simpson v Sadd* (1854) 4 De GM & G 665, unless possession is taken *after* delivery of an abstract revealing defects of title: *Bown v Stenson* (1857) 24 Beav 631.

5 *Re Barrington, ex p Sidebotham* (1834) 3 LJ Bcy 122 (leasing); *Haydon v Bell* (1838) 1 Beav 337 (mortgaging).

6 *Re Gloag and Miller's Contract* (1883) 23 Ch D 320, unless the defects of title are removable.

7 *Stevens v Guppy* (1828) 3 Russ 171.

8 *Re Gloag and Miller's Contract* (1883) 23 Ch D 320 at 329, per Fry J. See NCS 8 (3), 'A purchaser going into occupation before completion shall not be deemed *thereby* to have accepted the vendor's title.' LSC 18 (3) is of like import.

9 See p. 161, ante.

10 S.I. 1967 No. 1879, Schedule, Part I, paras. 7, 8 (1). See p. 163, ante.

landlord can, in the event of delay in completion for which he is not responsible, elect to charge interest instead of receiving rent until actual completion.

If the contract is brought about by the exercise of an option to purchase, the
parties' position subsequent to its exercise depends on the terms of the option. A
provision for payment of interest from the expiration of the notice exercising it
indicates that the relationship of landlord and tenant ceases as from that time
and prevents the recovery by the vendor of any rent thereafter, even though the
purchase falls through[11].

G   The purchaser as trustee

It has been recently held[12] that in some circumstances the purchaser will be
accountable to the vendor through a failure on his part to disclose material
matters which have come to his knowledge. In the case the prospective purchasers applied for planning permission to develop a plot of land owned by the
vendors. They did not inform the vendors of the application[13] which was
granted, thereby enhancing the value of the property unknown to the vendors.
The purchasers were held liable to account to the vendors for the profit thereby
made.

H   Effect of death before completion

The basic rule is that the death of either, or both, of the parties before completion does not avoid a contract for sale of land; it remains enforceable by and
against the deceased's personal representatives[14].

1.   Death of vendor

The precise effect of the vendor's death depends on the capacity in which he is
selling the land.

(i) If he is selling as sole beneficial owner, the legal estate in the land and his
beneficial interest in the purchase money vest in his personal representatives
who should complete the contract.

(ii) If he is one of two or more trustees for sale or personal representatives, the
legal title will devolve on the surviving estate owners.

(iii) If he is himself a sole personal representative, the proper person to complete the contract will depend on whether the chain of representation remains
unbroken[15].

(iv) On the death of a vendor-tenant for life, the contract remains binding on
and enures for the benefit of the settled land, and is enforceable by and against
his successor, subject to the same rights to vary and rescind as the vendor

11   *Cockwell v Romford Sanitary Steam Laundry Ltd* [1939] 4 All ER 370, CA, p. 162, ante.
      See also *Watney v Boardley* [1975] 2 All ER 644.
12   *English v Dedham Vale Properties Ltd* [1978] 1 All ER 382.
13   It was made in the vendors' names and signed 'as agents' for them by the purchasers. The
      local authority therefore did not notify the vendors see TCPA 1971, s. 27 p. 241, ante.
14   *Hoddel v Pugh* (1864) 33 Beav 489.
15   See the AEA 1925, s. 7; Mellows, *The Law of Succession*, (3rd edn) pp.291–292.

possessed[16]. If the land remains settled, the legal title vests in the trustees of the settlement as the deceased's special personal representatives, otherwise the vendor's general representatives should perform the contract[17].

2. Death of purchaser

On the death of the purchaser the vendor can enforce the contract against the deceased purchaser's personal representatives. As between the different persons claiming through the deceased, it is the person entitled to the property who is prima facie responsible to provide the balance of the purchase money. The vendor's lien, attaching to the land at the time of the contract, constitutes a charge on the property within the Adminstration of Estates Act 1925, s. 35 (1), which the land itself must bear in the absence of any contrary intention in the deceased's will[18]. The vendor is not however deprived of his right to enforce payment out of the deceased's other assets[19]. Should it become necessary he can enforce his lien against the devisee after an assent in the beneficiary's favour, though he cannot sue him personally for the price.

I Effect of bankruptcy before completion

The steps by which a person is adjudicated bankrupt have already been noted[20]. When considering the effect of bankruptcy on the parties's rights, it is important to remember that, although on adjudication the bankrupt's property vests first in the official receiver and then in the trustee in bankruptcy on his appointment[1], the title of the trustee relates back to the time of the act of bankruptcy on which the receiving order was made, or if there were several such acts, to the time of the first of them proved to have been committed within three months preceding the presentation of the petition[2]. There is an exception in favour of a conveyance, assignment or contract entered into before the receiving order bona fide entered into for valuable consideration without notice of any available act of bankruptcy[3].

1. Registration of petitions and orders

Before turning to discuss the effect of bankruptcy, mention must be made of the registration provisions relating to bankruptcy proceedings. In the case of unregistered land, both the petition and the receiving order are registrable under the Land Charges Act 1972, in the registers of pending actions, and of writs and orders respectively[4]. Failure to register avoids the trustee's title against a purchaser of the legal estate in good faith for money or money's worth without notice of an available act of bankruptcy[5].

16 SLA 1925, s. 90 (2). And see s. 63.
17 Page 318, post.
18 *Re Birmingham, Savage v Stannard* [1959] Ch 523, [1958] 2 All ER 397.
19 AEA 1925, s. 35 (3).
20 Page 98, ante.
1 Strictly his appointment takes effect from the date of the Board of Trade certificate confirming his appointment; Bankruptcy Act 1914, s. 19 (2), (4).
2 Bankruptcy Act 1914, s. 37 (1).
3 Bankruptcy Act 1914, s. 45, see Emmet, 292.
4 LCA 1972, ss. 5 (1), and 6 (1) (c) which provides for registration of a receiving order whether or not it is known to affect land.
5 LCA 1972, s. 6 (6), replacing the LCA 1925, s. 7 (2).

Registered land

The provisions for registration of bankruptcy proceedings affecting registered land are complicated. In the first instance registration is effected under the Land Charges Act 1972, not to give notice under the system of registered conveyancing but simply to set the machinery in motion, for at this early stage it will not even be known whether the debtor owns any land.

The following paragraphs describe the subsequent procedure when a vendor of registered land becomes bankrupt after the date of the contract. On registration of the bankruptcy petition as a pending action, the Chief Land Registrar[6] must as soon as practicable register a *creditor's notice* against the vendor's title[7]. He has a discretion to refrain from entering a notice when the proprietor's name, address and description on the register do not coincide with the particulars given in the petition[8]. A creditor's notice is registered in the proprietorship register and, once registered, any subsequent disposition affecting the property lodged for registration (the legal title, it is to be recalled, is still in the vendor) will be subject to the claims of the creditors, unless entitled to priority conferred by an official certificate of search.

Registration of a receiving order under the Land Charges Act 1972, is followed by the registration of a *bankruptcy inhibition* against the title. Until this is vacated, no dealing with the registered land can be registered other than the registration of the trustee[9]. The inhibition puts a complete and effective stop on the title to the vendor's land[10].

Consequence of non-registration. By virtue of s. 61 (6) of the Land Registration Act 1925, if no creditor's notice or bankruptcy inhibition appears on the vendor's title, a purchaser in good faith for money or money's worth will on registration of his disposition obtain a good title against the trustee in bankruptcy, but he is not deemed to be in good faith if at the date of execution of the registered disposition[11] he has notice of an available act of bankruptcy, or of the receiving order or adjudication. It must be stressed that what is relevant is *registration under the Land Registration Act 1925*. If no creditor's notice or bankruptcy inhibition has been registered (and this is a distinct possibility if the Registrar is obliged to postpone registering the notice or inhibition)[12], the purchaser does not cease to be in good faith simply because the petition or receiving order is registered in the Land Charges Registry, nor is he under any duty to search there[13]. Registration there is simply a preliminary step in the process whereby the appropriate entries are subsequently made on the vendor's register of title.

---

6   He also controls the Land Charges Department. This is done by the medium of the index of proprietors names, R & R, 613.

7   LRA 1925, s. 61 (1).

8   Ibid., s. 62 (a); LRR 1925, r. 181.

9   LRA 1925, s. 61 (3), (4). Neither a creditor's notice nor an inhibition can be registered against one of two or more joint proprietors. The proper procedure is to apply for a caution or restriction after adjudication; see R & R, 614, 621, see *Re Turner* [1975] 1 All ER 5.

10   R & R, 621.

11   Presumably this means the date of the vendor's execution, since a purchaser frequently does not execute the transfer.

12   See LRA 1925, s. 62, note 8, ante. The trustee in bankruptcy can claim an indemnity from the insurance fund for any loss suffered by reason of the omission to register: ibid., s. 61 (7).

13   LRA 1925, ss. 61 (6). 110 (7).

But suppose he does search, mistakenly[14], and the certificate reveals a bankruptcy petition. It seems that this will fix him with *actual* notice, and so prevent his being in good faith for the purposes of s. 61 (6). This is so despite s. 59 (6) of the same Act. This enacts that a purchaser of registered land shall not be concerned with any pending action (i.e. the petition) or order (i.e. the receiving order) which is not protected on the register of title, whether or not he has *express*, implied or constructive notice thereof. This provision takes effect subject to the provisions of the Act relating to the title of a trustee in bankruptcy, which include s. 61(6)[15].

2. Bankruptcy of vendor

Bankruptcy does not terminate the contract; it alters the rights of the parties somewhat. The appointment of the trustee in bankruptcy, as to which the certificate of the Board of Trade is conclusive evidence[16], vests the bankrupt's property in him without any conveyance or assignment, the certificate of appointment being deemed to be a conveyance or assignment[17]. A purchaser who takes a conveyance from the trustee should ask for production of the certificate of appointment and for proof of the adjudication, such as an office copy of the order. In the case of registered land the statutory provisions operate to vest the title in the trustee without any alteration to the proprietorship register, thus constituting an exception to the cardinal principle of the registered land system that the legal estate is deemed to be vested in the registered proprietor for the time being. The trustee can apply to be registered as proprietor on production of the requisite evidence of his title[18] and will no doubt take this step in the event of the contract being completed.

Specific performance may be enforced against the trustee[19], but the purchaser cannot sue the bankrupt vendor for breach of contract, except with leave of the court[1]; his claim is provable in the bankruptcy. If the vendor is a mere trustee for the purchaser who has paid all the purchase money to him before the commencement of the bankruptcy, the legal estate does not vest in the trustee in bankruptcy[2] and a conveyance should be taken from the vendor.

(a) Disclaimer

The trustee's statutory right to disclaim onerous property[3] does not enable him to disclaim a contract for the sale of land so as to deprive the purchaser of his equitable interest, even where disclaimer would be beneficial to the bankrupt's estate[4]. The purchaser can still obtain specific performance; alternatively he would appear entitled to treat any purported disclaimer as a repudiation of the contract, entitling him to the return of his deposit.

14 It is unlikely that a purchaser, knowing that the vendor's title is registered, will make a search under the LCA 1972.
15 See R & R, 617.
16 Bankruptcy Act 1914, s. 143.
17 Bankruptcy Act 1914, s. 53 (2), (3), (4).
18 LRR 1925, r. 176.
19 *Pearce v Bastable's Trustee in Bankruptcy* [1901] 2 Ch 122.
 1 Bankruptcy Act 1914, s. 7 (1).
 2 Bankruptcy Act 1914, s. 38; *St. Thomas's Hospital (Governors) v Richardson* [1910] 1 KB 271 at 284, CA, per Farwell LJ. See also *Re Turner* [1975] 1 All ER 5.
 3 Bankruptcy Act 1914, s. 54.
 4 *Re Bastable, ex p Trustee* [1901] 2 KB 518, CA (trustee not able to disclaim contract for sale of lease unless disclaiming lease itself). As to the effect of a disclaimer after an assignant of a term of years, see *Warnford Investments Ltd v Duckworth* [1978] 2 All ER 517.

(b) Completion before appointment of trustee
A purchaser wishing to complete before the vendor's adjudication faces difficulties. The legal title is still in the vendor, but it is not prudent to take a conveyance from him. As a result of the doctrine of relation back, the trustee's title
might relate back to some date prior to that of the conveyance, which would
become inoperative. To obtain a valid conveyance from the trustee, the purchaser would have to pay to him the purchase money in full, thus paying twice
for the same property[5]. He would only be safe in taking a conveyance from the
vendor if he had no notice of any available act of bankruptcy[6].
    The commission of an act of bankruptcy constitutes a defect in title. In
Powell v Marshall, Parkes & Co[7]:

> V contracted to sell a public-house to P. Time was of the essence of the
> contract. Before the date fixed for completion V committed an act of
> bankruptcy of which P became aware. It was held that P could refuse to
> complete and was entitled to recover the deposit paid to the defendants as
> stakeholders. ‹

If the purchaser wishes to proceed with the purchase, he should either take
a conveyance from the trustee after his appointment or wait for three months
to elapse after the commission of the act of bankruptcy. If no petition is presented within that period, he is safe in taking a conveyance from the vendor.
Though the vendor might commit another act of bankruptcy after the conveyance, the trustee's title cannot relate back to the first act since three months
have elapsed, but only to the subsequent one. The conveyance cannot therefore
be impeached.
    The possibility of relation back also precludes a vendor who commits an act
of bankruptcy from obtaining specific performance so long as the act is available to found a petition[8], i.e. during the three months' period.

3. Bankruptcy of purchaser

The trustee can elect to complete the contract or disclaim it as unprofitable; in
the latter event the vendor can forfeit the deposit and prove in the bankruptcy
for any loss suffered by the disclaimer[9].
    The vendor cannot initially sue the purchaser's trustee[10]. He should give
written notice to the trustee to elect either to perform the contract or disclaim
it. If the trustee does not disclaim within twenty-eight days (or such extended
time as the court allows) he is deemed to have adopted the contract[11] and the
vendor can pursue his normal remedies.

Position before appointment of trustee
Similar difficulties face a vendor wishing to complete before the purchaser's
adjudication. Unless he completes without notice of an act of bankruptcy and

---

5   *Powell v Marshall, Parkes & Co* [1899] 1 QB 710 at 713, CA, per Collins LJ.
6   Bankruptcy Act 1914, s. 45, provided the conveyance is before the date of the receiving
     order. If after, he only gets a good title where neither the petition nor the order has been
     registered, p. 269, ante.
7   [1899] 1 QB 710, CA; *Lowes v Lush* (1808) 14 Ves 547.
8   *Lowes v Lush* (1808) 14 Ves 547.
9   *Re Parnell, ex p Barrell* (1875) 10 Ch App 512; Bankruptcy Act 1914, s. 54 (8).
10   *Holloway v York* (1877) 25 WR 627.
11   Bankruptcy Act 1914, s. 54 (4).

before the receiving order, in which case s. 45 of the Bankruptcy Act 1914, protects him, he may be liable to refund the purchase money to the trustee if the latter's title relates back to the date of the conveyance[12]. It was held by Harman J, in *Jennings' Trustee v King*[13] that the vendor cannot treat the purchaser's act of bankruptcy as an anticipatory breach of contract entitling him immediately to repudiate, nor is he entitled to rescind the contract on the contractual date for completion, time not being of the essence. His remedy is to await the three months' period to see whether he can safely complete, or to file a petition in bankruptcy himself.

4. Winding up of company[14]

Where a company is being wound up by the court, every disposition of the company's property (such as a conveyance of land by the company) after the presentation of a winding-up petition is *void* unless the court otherwise orders[15]. The commencement of winding-up proceedings therefore effectively sterilises the transaction until such time as a liquidator is appointed. It is his function to get in and realise the company's property, pay outstanding debts, and distribute any surplus among the members. The liquidator can complete the contract and if the other party refuses to complete he can pursue the appropriate remedies, but he requires the sanction of the court to bring an action on behalf of the company. The liquidator also has power to sell the company's real and personal property and to execute in its name and with its seal all necessary documents[16].

On a voluntary winding up, the company's corporate state and powers continue to exist until dissolution but the directors' powers cease on appointment of the liquidator[17] who can exercise all the powers given to a liquidator in a winding up by the court[18].

Unlike the effect of bankruptcy, the company's property does not vest in the liquidator on his appointment[19], unless a court order is made under s. 244 of the Companies Act 1948. It will therefore be the company that conveys the land to the purchaser. Considerable difference of opinion exists as to the need for the liquidator to join in the conveyance. The better view[20] seems to be that it is not necessary for him to be expressed as a conveying party or for him to give a receipt for the purchase money, or even for it to be stated that the company is acting by the liquidator, though he should preferably join in the conveyance to covenant that he has done nothing to prevent the company from conveying, by, for example, exercising his statutory power to sell. On the exercise of this power

---

12 1 Williams V & P, 584. Similarly an available act of bankruptcy deprives the purchaser of his right to specific performance (*Franklin v Lord Brownlow* (1808) 14 Ves 550).

13 [1952] Ch 899, [1952] 2 All ER 608.

14 See generally Pennington, *Company Law* (4th edn) pp. 674–789.

15 Companies Act 1948, s. 227. See Pennington, op. cit., pp. 721–723.

16 Companies Act 1948, s. 245 (1) (a), (2) (a), (b). As to the effect of the appointment of a liquidator see *Ayerst (Inspector of Taxes) v C and K (Construction) Ltd* [1975] 2 All ER 537, 540–541 HL, per Lord Diplock.

17 Companies Act 1948, ss. 281, 285 (2).

18 Companies Act 1948, s. 303 (1) (a), (b).

19 *Ayerst* case supra.

20 See 'Conveyances by Liquidators,' (1970), 67 LS Gaz 329, and the ensuing correspondence at pp. 459, 536, 626, 714; contra Emmet, 369, and compare the precedent at (1953), 17 Conv (NS) 569, Form 18 with those in 19 Ency F & P, 1147–58. See also *Re Wyvern Developments Ltd* [1974] 2 All ER 535 at 539, per Templeman J.

the liquidator should, according to some authorities[1], give the receipt for the purchase money.

In the case of registered land no registration of the liquidator as proprietor is required. He may apply for his appointment to be noted on the register[2] but this is not obligatory.

1　See e.g. Parker's Precedents, 40, note 5.
2　LRR 1925, r. 185.

Part Four

The post-contract stage

Chapter 10

Deducing title

A   Introduction

We now have reached the stage where contracts have been exchanged and the parties are bound in law to complete, subject to the exercise of any rights contractual or otherwise which they have to terminate the agreement. The aim of this part of the book is to discover the various steps in the transaction ultimately leading to the vesting of the legal title in the purchaser. This particular chapter is devoted to the vendor's obligation to establish that he is in a position to transfer what he has contracted to convey, that is, his duty to deduce title as it is termed, and the manner in which he discharges that duty in practice.

It will be apparent from the previous chapters that the vendor is not obliged as a matter of law to establish his ownership of the estate contracted to be sold prior to the formation of a binding contract for sale. Bearing in mind the complexities of English land law and the period of sixty years' investigation of title prescribed by the common law, the evolution of such a rule was hardly surprising; had it been otherwise vendors would have been seriously inconvenienced in the sale of real property. As Fry LJ observed in *Reeve v Berridge*[1]:

> '. . . there is great practical convenience in requiring the vendor, who knows his own title, to disclose all that is necessary to protect himself, rather than in requiring the purchaser to demand an inspection of the vendor's title before entering into a contract, a demand which the owners of property would in some cases be unwilling to concede . . .'

Today different considerations apply, not the least being a simplification in land law rules designed to facilitate transfers of real property. As we have seen[2], it is usual on a sale of registered land for copies of the entries on the vendor's register of title to be sent with the draft contract. In the case of unregistered land, too, some practitioners do enclose with the draft contract sufficient information to enable the purchaser's solicitor to investigate the title, but this is far from a uniform practice. However the constant clamour for speedier conveyancing procedures may, during the next decade, result in a general abandonment of the traditional methods of deducing title. Such a development could well be beneficial in most transactions involving residential property. Whether it would prove to be so in other conveyancing transactions must for the present remain largely conjectural.

The manner of deducing title varies according to the property involved—

1   (1888) 20 QBD 523 at 528, CA.
2   See p. 135, ante.

whether it is registered, or unregistered, freehold or leasehold. This present chapter sets out the position on the sale of an unregistered freehold estate, assuming that the vendor has not furnished evidence of his title until after exchange of contracts. The following chapter deals with leasehold estates and other cases where special considerations arise. Registered titles are considered in Chapter 12.

B   Obligation to show good title

1.   Introduction

Every contract for the sale of land prima facie imports a term that the vendor will show a good title, or, as it is sometimes alternatively expressed, a marketable title, one which may at all times and under all circumstances be forced on the purchaser[3]. The better view is that this obligation operates as an implied term[4], though there is some authority supporting the view that it is a right given by law.

The obligation to show a good title is only likely to apply in its full vigour in an open contract, when the vendor must show he is entitled to the property for a freehold estate in possession free from incumbrances. In practice the terms of the contract between the parties will often operate to modify the duty. The vendor is free to incorporate in the contract a special condition precluding any objection by the purchaser to a particular defect, and provided the condition is not misleading, a purchaser contracting on such a basis is bound thereby[5]. Occasionally the contract may simply be for the sale of such interest, *if any*, as the vendor has in the land, or it may stipulate that no title shall be required beyond the vendor's possession at the time of sale[6]. But, save as the contract restricts the obligation in whole or in part, the purchaser is entitled to a good title and the vendor must establish that he can convey what he has contracted to sell.

2.   What is meant by good title?

The word 'title' is an ambiguous word[7], meaning different things in different contexts. Conveyancers use the word in two main senses — first, to mean ownership, the vendor's right to the property; secondly, the evidence supporting the claim to ownership, i.e. the proof of 'title' in the first sense. In the expression 'good title', the word is used as equivalent to ownership; a vendor must show a title as will enable the purchaser to hold the property against any person who may probably challenge his right to it[8].

3   *Pyrke v Waddingham* (1852) 10 Hare 1 at 8, per Turner V-C; *MEPC Ltd v Christian-Edwards* [1978] Ch 281 at 288, [1978] 3 All ER 795 at 799, CA, per Goff LJ; affd. [1981] AC 205, [1979] 3 All ER 752, HL.
4   See *Ellis v Rogers* (1885) 29 Ch D 661 at 670–1, CA, per Cotton LJ, who reviews the conflicting dicta; *Gosling v Anderson* (1971) 220 Estates Gazette 1117, per Graham J. See further Farrand, 80–82.
5   See pp. 156–159, ante.
6   See in the case of registered land with regard to titles less than absolute Chap. 2, ante.
7   *Felkin v Lord Herbert* (1861) 30 LJ Ch 798 at 799, per Kindersley V-C. And see Rudden, 'The Terminology of Title' (1964) 80 LQR 63.
8   *Jeakes v White* (1851) 6 Exch 873 at 881, per Pollock CB. And see *Re Stirrup's Contract* [1961] 1 All ER 805 at 809, per Wilberforce J. To have a good title to land is to have the essential part of ownership, namely, the right to maintain or recover possession of the land as against all others: *Williams on Real Property* (24th edn) p. 703.

This obligation to make a good title requires the vendor to show that he alone, or with the concurrence of some person or persons whose concurrence he can compel, can convey the whole legal estate and equitable interest in the land sold[9], free from incumbrances except for those disclosed by the contract.

(a) Legal and equitable

Strictly speaking title must be shown to both the legal estate and the equitable interest in the property. Prior to 1926 it was sufficient to show a good equitable title with power to get in the legal estate[10], but this is no longer true now that the legal estate constitutes the basis of post-1925 conveyancing. In practice it will rarely be necessary to do more than establish title to the legal estate. On a sale by a sole beneficial owner, both legal and equitable titles are in him. Even where the titles are split, e.g. under a settlement, or trust for sale, the purchaser need not concern himself with the equitable interests; for if the appropriate procedure is adopted, a conveyance of the legal estate will overreach the equitable interests and give the purchaser a title free from them, without the equitable owners having to join in the conveyance to transfer their interests. What is more in such circumstances the purchaser cannot be compelled to accept a title made with the concurrence of any person entitled to an equitable interest[11].

It is otherwise when the equitable interests are not overreachable. Suppose X purchases property but the conveyance is taken in V's name. Assuming no question of advancement arises, V holds on a resulting trust for X. If V later contracts to sell to P, V will not be able to enforce the contract against P, because of his inability to show title to the equitable interest vested in X. Nor can V compel X to join in a conveyance of the land in order to pass his interest, unless X has requested the sale.

(b) Title in vendor

The legal title must be in the vendor, or in some person whom he can compel to convey. If the vendor (V) can compel a conveyance from some third party (Y), V is always in a position to obtain the legal estate; but the courts will not require Y to convey to V and then V to the purchaser (P), when the very same thing can be accomplished by getting Y to convey direct to P. The case of *Harold Elliott and H. Elliott (Builders) Ltd v Pierson*[12] illustrates this aspect of the rule.

> W Ltd owned freehold property which it leased to V, the sole director. V granted to P an option to purchase the property, which P exercised. P later repudiated the contract on the ground that V, being a mere leaseholder, had no title to the freehold.

It was held that V, being in sole and absolute control of the company, could compel it to convey the freehold to P. Other instances of the application of this rule occur in the case of a sub-sale, where the purchaser can call upon his

---

9 Williams, *Title*, 565.
10 *Camberwell and South London Building Society v Holloway* (1879) 13 Ch D 754 at 763, per Jessel MR.
11 See the LPA 1925, s. 42 (1), p. 164, ante.
12 [1948] Ch 452, [1948] 1 All ER 939; *Re Baker and Selmon's Contract* [1907] 1 Ch 238 (trustee-vendor with no power of sale held entitled to compel concurrence of beneficiaries who had requested sale). See also *Re Spencer and Hauser's Contract* [1928] Ch 598 (vendors contracted to sell as trustees but held as personal representatives: good title shown). See further Emmet, 135.

vendor to convey the property to the sub-purchaser[13], and a sole beneficiary of full age under a bare trust, who need only show a good title in his trustee, for under the rule in *Saunders v Vautier*[14] he can always terminate the trust by calling for the legal title to be vested in him.

The decision in *Re Bryant and Barningham's Contract*[15] should be contrasted with these examples. Vendors contracted to sell as trustees for sale, but in fact no trust for sale arose till after the death of a tenant for life. Though the life tenant was willing to execute a conveyance, the court upheld the purchaser's objection that a good title had not been shown since the vendors could not compel her concurrence. A vendor cannot require his purchaser to accept one contract in substitution for another.

(c) Freedom from incumbrances

The vendor must also show he can convey the property free from incumbrances, except those subject to which the property is stated to be sold. If incumbrances exist which he fails to disclose in the contract[16], he does not show a good title, for the purchaser is entitled to assume that the property is sold free from incumbrances, or subject only to such as are mentioned. The purchaser can, therefore, refuse to complete, but he cannot object to an undisclosed incumbrance of which he was aware when entering into the contract[17]. Knowledge does not preclude his insisting upon a good title where:

  (i)   the contract expressly provides that a marketable title shall be given[18],
 (ii)   he reasonably believes the incumbrance to be no longer enforceable[19],
(iii)   the incumbrance is removable, that is, capable of being discharged, or removed, before completion without the concurrence of the incumbrancer (e.g. a mortgage), as distinct from being irremovable, such as an easement[20].

(d) Matters of conveyance

The obligation to show a good title does not extend to a matter of conveyance, that is some defect which the vendor can remove independently of the concurrence of another. The following constitute matters of conveyance: the discharge of a mortgage affecting the property[1], the concurrence of a mortgagee who is immediately redeemable[2], the appointment of trustees for the purposes of giving a receipt for capital money arising on a sale of settled land[3], and

---

13   Subject to any contrary term in the contract. See further [1979] Conv 1.
14   (1841) Cr & Ph 240.
15   (1890) 44 Ch D 218, CA.
16   Page 146, ante. The duty of disclosure extends to incumbrances created before the commencement of the title.
17   *Timmins v Moreland Street Property Co Ltd* [1958] Ch 110, [1957] 3 All ER 265, CA (purchaser aware of lease not disclosed by informal memorandum).
18   *Cato v Thompson* (1882) 9 QBD 616, CA; *Re Gloag and Miller's Contract* (1883) 23 Ch D 320 at 327, per Fry J.
19   *Ellis v Rogers* (1885) 29 Ch D 661, CA (restrictive covenants thought to have been extinguished).
20   *Ellis v Rogers* (1885) 29 Ch D 661 at 666, per Kay J.
 1   *Re Jackson and Oakshott* (1880) 14 Ch D 851.
 2   *Re Priestley's Contract* [1947] Ch 469 at 477, [1947] 1 All ER 716 at 720, per Romer J.
 3   *Hatten v Russell* (1888) 38 Ch D 334.

perhaps a lessor's licence to assign[4], but not the appointment of a new trustee for sale to replace one of the contracting parties[5].

(e) Time for performance
The vendor fulfils his obligation if he establishes a good title by the contractual date for completion. If he is in a position to convey at the proper time, it is no defence to an action by him for specific performance or damages that he had no title at the time of making the contract[6]. It is equally clear, however, that a purchaser who discovers a fundamental defect of title is not obliged to wait and see if the vendor can perfect his title by the completion date[7]. He can repudiate immediately. The precise legal effect of such a step is somewhat controversial and consideration of the problem must await a later chapter[8]. It is obviously in the vendor's interests to establish a good title by the time he submits the evidence thereof to the purchaser's solicitor.

3.   Gradations of title

Over the years conveyancers and judges have employed various expressions indicating a hierarchy of titles ranging from good to bad, or from white to black through varying shades of grey.

(a) Good title
This is not necessarily a perfect title but, as already noticed, one that in a vendor's action for specific performance the court will enforce against a reluctant purchaser. If the title is such that it can be sold without the necessity of making special conditions of sale restrictive of the purchaser's rights, it is said to be a 'good marketable title'[9]. In a proper case the court will presume the facts on which the title depends. In *MEPC Ltd v Christian-Edwards*[10] the purchaser maintained that a good title had not been deduced because the abstract of title disclosed an outstanding contract for sale entered into as long ago as 1912. The House of Lords held that a good marketable title had been shown and decreed specific performance against the purchaser. In the circumstances the evidence overwhelmingly supported a presumption that the contract had been abandoned. Apart from this the contract, if it were still subsisting, was no longer capable of specific enforcement. Any claim for this remedy by the persons entitled to the benefit of the contract would have been successfully met by a plea of laches.

(b) Doubtful title
This arises where there is some uncertainty whether the vendor can convey what he has contracted to convey; such a title will not be forced upon an unwilling

---

4   See p. 311, post.
5   *Re Priestly's Contract* [1947] Ch 469, [1947] 1 All ER 716 (contracting parties were A and B, whereas legal title in A and C; A could not compel C's retirement from the trust).
6   *Hoggart v Scott* (1830) 1 Rus & M 293; *Thomson v Miles* (1794) 1 Esp 184.
7   *Hoggart v Scott* (1830) 1 Rus & M 293; *Bellamy v Debenham* [1891] 1 Ch 412, CA.
8   Pages 608–611, post.
9   *Re Spollon and Long's Contract* [1936] Ch 713 at 718, [1936] 2 All ER 711 at 716–17, per Luxmoore J.
10   [1981] AC 205, [1979] 3 All ER 752, HL. See Emmet, 269–270 and 2nd Supplement thereof criticising the decision especially from the point of registration of title. See further Chap. 16, post.

purchaser under an open contract. The courts will not compel him to buy a lawsuit to resolve the doubt. In *Nottingham Patent Brick and Tile Co v Butler*[11], the court refused to decree specific performance against a purchaser who discovered the existence of restrictive covenants which the vendor had failed to disclose and which he alleged were not binding upon him through lack of notice. Litigation might well have proved necessary to substantiate this claim. The purchaser cannot, of course, complain if he contracts on the basis of some special condition governing the uncertainty.

(c) Bad title

Where it is clear that the vendor cannot convey what he has contracted to sell, because, for example, title is in some other person or the property is subject to undisclosed incumbrances, the title is bad, and unenforceable[12]. Even where the contract provides that the purchaser shall not object to the title, if he discovers aliunde that it is bad, and not merely doubtful, the court will not award specific performance against him, but will leave the parties to pursue their legal remedies[13].

(d) Good holding title

There are qualities of badness. Lindley LJ once remarked[14]

'. . . there are bad titles and bad titles; bad titles which are good holding titles, although they may be open to objections which are not serious, are bad titles in a conveyancer's point of view, but good in a business man's point of view . . .'

The learned judge had in mind cases involving some technical defect of title which no longer exposed the purchaser to any real threat of eviction. In other words the defect may be cured by undisturbed possession for at least twelve years and such a title, supplemented by a statutory declaration as to possession, may be enforced on the purchaser[15].

4.   Length of title

Having established that the vendor is under an obligation to show a good title, the next question is to ascertain whether the law requires him to establish this over a specified period and, if so, for how long. Whilst his possession of the land contracted to be sold is prima facie evidence of his seisin in fee simple, it is hardly to be expected that a purchaser, in the absence of any contractual stipulation to the contrary, should be required to hand over his purchase money merely on the strength of the vendor's possession[16]. The vendor may be only a lessee, or even just a squatter. Nor yet is it satisfactory for the vendor simply to produce as evidence of his title the document by virtue of which he acquired

11   (1886) 16 QBD 778, CA. See also *Pyrke v Waddingham* (1852) 10 Hare 1.
12   For recent examples see *George Wimpey & Co Ltd v Sohn* [1967] Ch 487, [1966] 1 All ER 232, CA (vendor's failure to procure statutory declaration of 20 years' undisputed possession as contracted); *Faruqi v English Real Estate Ltd* [1979] 1 WLR 963; *Boyle v Walker* (1981) Times, 10 October.
13   *Re Scott and Alvarez's Contract* [1895] 2 Ch 603, CA, p. 158, ante.
14   *Re Scott and Alvarez's Contract* [1895] 2 Ch 603 at 613, CA.
15   *Re Atkinson's and Horsell's Contract* [1912] 2 Ch 1, CA, considered more fully on p. 291, post. Twelve years' possession will not be sufficient in every case; see p. 340, post.
16   'No man in his senses would take an offer of a purchase from a man merely because he stood on the ground': per Lord Erskine in *Hiern v Mill* (1806) 13 Ves 114 at 122.

that title[17], at least not where he has owned the estate for a short time only. Production of that document and nothing more affords no guarantee that the title was sound when the vendor acquired it. Mistakes could have been made, or the vendor may have knowingly accepted a title defective in certain matters, possibly of no concern to him, but perhaps important to a purchaser. The very complexity of our land law structure renders these considerations of no small consequence.

A title may be good, or bad. The law never speaks of a perfect title. The possibility always exists that some person may claim an adverse estate or interest[18]. There can be no mathematical certainty of a good title. However if the vendor can give proof of the exercise of acts of ownership by himself and his predecessors over a period of time, this reduces the possibility of adverse claims existing — and the more extended the period of research the greater is the assurance of safety[19]. The vendor must therefore give a convincing historical account of how the property came to be owned by him[20]. It is the purchaser's responsibility to investigate this account to check that the vendor can convey the subject-matter of the contract.

The period of research, or investigation, which the law has stipulated has been progressively reduced from sixty years, the period which conveyancing practice had customarily established, to forty years[1], then to thirty years, and finally to fifteen years. Section 23 of the Law of Property Act 1969, provides as follows:

' Section 44 (1) of the Law of Property Act 1925, (under which the period of commencement of title which may be required under a contract expressing no contrary intention is thirty years except in certain cases) shall have effect, in its application to contracts made after the commencement of this Act, as if it specified fifteen years instead of thirty years as the period of commencement of title which may be so required.'

This reduction relates to contracts made on or after 1 January 1970. Two points must be stressed. This statutory period only applies to *open* contracts. The parties are free to stipulate for a shorter or longer period, though in practice the statutory period is often used as a safe yard-stick by the vendor's solicitor when drafting the contract. Secondly, we are concerned here solely with the sale of freehold land. In relation to other classes of property, different periods apply[2].

This latest alteration was not sanctioned until the Law Commission had, after due consideration, advocated the shorter period[3]. In justification of their recommendation they relied heavily on the fact that conveyancers were already accepting less than the then statutory period[4] without apparent disadvantage

---

17   For the insurance-backed Title Certificate Scheme at one time proposed by the Non-Contentious Business Committee of The Law Society, and promptly rejected by the Law Commission.

18   See e.g. *Wyld v Silver* [1963] Ch 243, [1962] 3 All ER 309, CA (purchaser of land without notice subject to right of inhabitants to hold annual fair established by private Act of 1799, though last recorded occasion of its occurrence was in 1875).

19   Hayes, *Introduction to Conveyancing* (5th edn) (1840), p. 282.

20   Farrand, 83.

1   Vendor and Purchaser Act 1874, s. 1.

2   Principally in the case of leaseholds; see pp. 304–307, post.

3   Transfer of Land, Interim Report on Root of Title to Freehold Land: Law Com. No. 9.

4   Cf. (1966) 30 Conv (NS) 158 where it was doubted whether the acceptance of a title of much less than 30 years without a good title was very common.

to purchasers. The reduction was conceived as a 'useful step towards the simpli-fication of conveyancing'[5]. Whilst it certainly saves solicitors a certain amount of routine work (and this should be reflected in lower conveyancing charges), the actual process of investigation remains unaltered. The Commission accepted that a reduction would increase the risks of certain defects not coming to light[6], yet they perhaps failed to identify the kind of defects commonly arising in practice today[7], such as defects arising from faulty plans, inadequate descriptions of the property, or from double conveyancing[8]. These defects may often give rise to an adverse claim to a portion of the land in question, rather than to its entirety, but a matter of a few feet can be very important in days of high density development. Reducing the period of investigation may now deprive a purchaser of the opportunity of discovering mistakes by a comparison of plans or property descriptions in earlier deeds. Nevertheless the past decade has not witnessed any significant increase in the number of titles accepted under the new regime being upset in subsequent litigation. To this extent the shortening of the statutory period of title can be accorded a qualified welcome at least.

(a) Earlier title
Complementary to the provision limiting the period of the purchaser's investi-gation of title is a rule exonerating him from notice of any matter of which he might have had notice had he investigated the title prior to the period of com-mencement fixed by statute, unless he actually makes such investigation[9]. If under an open contract the title commences, for example, in 1963, a purchaser is not deemed to have notice of any equitable interest which he could only have discovered by investigating the earlier title, unless he actually investigates such a title or the interest, being a land charge, has been registered[10]. He will be deemed to have notice of any matter or interest discoverable on inspection of the property, unless it is capable of registration as a land charge and it is void against him for want of registration[11].

(b) Contractual provisions
A formal contract normally provides for the title to commence with a specified document. The vendor may stipulate that less than a fifteen years' title shall be deduced. What risks does the purchaser run by accepting such a condition? His position is as follows.

(i) He will be bound by any equitable interest which he would have discovered had he contracted for the full statutory period. In the words of Romer LJ[12],

5   Law Com. No. 9, para. 36.
6   Ibid., paras. 23 (mainly in relation to the Limitation Act 1939, ss. 6 (1), 7 (2)–(4)), 34–36.
7   See Cretney, 'Land Law and Conveyancing Reforms' (1969) 32 MLR 477, 495; Hallett and Nugee, 'Root of Title' (1966) 110 Sol Jo 179, 201.
8   For recent examples of this occurrence, see *Re Sea View Gardens, Claridge v Tingey* [1966] 3 All ER 935, p. 85, ante; *Bligh v Martin* [1968] 1 All ER 1157; *Epps v Esso Petroleum Co Ltd* [1973] 2 All ER 465, p. 85, ante.
9   LPA 1925, s. 44 (8).
10   By virtue of the LPA 1925, s. 198; see p. 396, post.
11   LPA 1925, s. 199 (1) (i).
12   *Re Nisbet and Potts' Contract* [1906] 1 Ch 386 at 408; LPA 1925, s. 199 (1) (ii) (a). Cf. *Hudston v Viney* [1921] 1 Ch 98 (legal mortgagee not making full investigation not bound by prior equitable charge), p. 375, post.

'. . . if a purchaser chooses, by agreement with his vendor or otherwise, to take less than a [fifteen] years' title, he cannot by so restricting his investigation, and by not inquiring into the title for the full period of [fifteen years], say that he is not affected with notice of such equities affecting the land as he would have ascertained by reasonable inquiries into the title for the earlier part of the [fifteen] years.'

(ii) Where this equitable interest takes the form of a registered land charge he cannot claim compensation under s. 25 of the Law of Property Act 1969. In broad terms, this section enables a purchaser in certain circumstances to claim compensation from public funds in respect of loss caused by a land charge which only comes to light after completion and which he has no means of discovering because it was registered

'against the name of an owner of an estate in the land who was not as owner of any such estate a party to any transaction, or concerned in any event, comprised in the relevant title'[13].

The expression 'the relevant title' is a key phrase in the understanding of the operation of s. 25. It is so defined that whatever title the purchaser accepts he cannot claim compensation in respect of a land charge which he should have discovered had he investigated the full title which he could have required under an open contract[14]. This should ensure that in the future purchasers' solicitors will advise their clients not to accept less than the full statutory period. The wording of s. 25 needs to be noted carefully. It does not provide that compensation cannot be recovered merely on the ground that a purchaser has not investigated the relevant title. As the extract from the section indicates, what is vital is whether the charge has been registered against the name of an estate owner appearing as such within the period comprising the relevant title; for if it has not, then a search could not have been made against his name. Therefore, accepting less than the relevant title will not, it seems, debar a claim for compensation if the registered charge could not have been discovered even on an investigation of the title for the statutory period[15].

(iii) He cannot normally insist on seeing any documents relating to the earlier title, nor raise objections to it[16]. If before completion he discovers the existence of an incumbrance by other means (aliunde), he can object to the title on account of the vendor's failure to disclose it[17], as he can where he has contracted for a fifteen years' title.

(iv) If on the other hand he contracts for a title for the full statutory period but does not discover the existence of a registered land charge until after completion, the charge remains binding upon him, but he may be able to claim

13 Section 25 (1) (c). If the estate owner's name appears as such within the relevant title, the purchaser can search against his name and thereby discover the existence of any registered charge. Section 25 of the LPA 1969, gives effect to the recommendations of the Law Commission contained in their Report on Land Charges Affecting Unregistered Land, Law Com. No. 18. See further on this right to compensation, Chap. 14, pp. 396–397, post.
14 See s. 25 (10) which in relation to a disposition of land made under a contract defines 'relevant title' to mean 'the title which the purchaser was, apart from any acceptance by him (by agreement or otherwise) of a shorter or an imperfect title, entitled to require.'
15 What if the registration is incorrect eg under the wrong name?
16 See the LPA 1925, s. 45 (1), discussed at p. 289, post.
17 Re Cox and Neve's Contract [1891] 2 Ch 102.

compensation under the Act of 1969. He cannot contend that he takes free from the charge under s. 44 (8) of the Law of Property Act 1925, which deems him not to have notice of any matter only discoverable by investigating the earlier title. It is generally assumed that s. 198 of this Act (under which registration constitutes *actual* notice) overrides the terms of s. 44 (8)[18]. Indeed the compensation provisions of the Law of Property Act 1969, presuppose that he remains bound.

C   Root of title

1.   The need for a root of title

Though the statutory provisions speak of fifteen years' title, in practice it will be longer. In *Re Cox and Neve's Contract*[19], North J explained the position in the following manner:

> ' And, when I say a [fifteen] years' title, I mean a title deduced for [fifteen] years and for so much longer as it is necessary to go back in order to arrive at a point at which the title can properly commence. A title cannot commence in nubibus at the exact point which is represented by 365 days multiplied by [fifteen]. It must commence at or before the [fifteen] years with something which is in itself, or which is agreed shall be, a proper root of title.'

The title must commence with a document at least fifteen years old, known as the *root of title*, though it is not absolutely essential that the title should commence with any instrument at all[20]. Under an open contract the document must constitute a *good root of title*. In a formal contract the vendor stipulates the root of title by such a clause as: The title shall commence with a conveyance on sale dated . . . and made between . . .[1] He may stipulate for a root of title which is not a good root. What constitutes a good root of title under an open contract has assumed a greater importance in view of s. 25 of the Law of Property Act 1969. Though the purchaser accepts more than a fifteen years' title, if it does not commence with a good root of title, sufficient under an open contract, he has not investigated *the relevant title*. It is by no means unknown even today, especially in the case of older properties located in rural areas, for the title to be deduced for a period well in excess of 30 years[2].

2.   Good root of title

(a) Accepted definition
A good root of title is not defined by statute, nor, apparently, has any member of the bench hazarded any definition. The Law Commission considered the

18   Law Com. No. 9, para. 23 (c). And see *White v Bijou Mansions Ltd* [1937] Ch 610 at 621, [1937] 3 All ER 269 at 273, per Simonds J; on appeal [1938] 1 All ER 546, CA. Strictly there is no conflict between s. 44 (8) and s. 198 if the former is construed to mean that a purchaser is not affected with *constructive* notice of matters he is prevented by statute from investigating.
19   [1891] 2 Ch 102 at 118.
20   See *Cottrell v Watkins* (1839) 1 Beav 361 at 365, per Lord Langdale MR.
1   See p. 152, ante.
2   One of the authors recalls a purchase in which he was involved in 1973 where the title commenced with an indenture dated 11 June 1900, at a time when the property was held in copyhold tenure. Doubtless the seasoned practitioner will encounter even more unusual examples.

possibility of a statutory definition but accepted the view that this might do more harm than good by introducing undesirable rigidity. Practitioners should continue to have complete freedom to negotiate the root according to the particular circumstances of each case[3]. In keeping with many commentators, the Law Commission were happy to accept the description given in *Williams on Vendor and Purchaser*[4] that a good root of title:

> ' must be an instrument of disposition dealing with or proving on the face of it, without the aid of extrinsic evidence, the ownership of the whole legal and equitable estate in the property sold, containing a description by which the property can be identified and showing nothing to cast any doubt on the title of the disposing parties.'

(i) *Legal and equitable estate.* Because of the overreaching provisions of the 1925 property legislation, it will rarely be necessary for the root of title to have to deal with the equitable title. A post-1925 conveyance on trust for sale is a good root of title, even though it does not deal with the equitable interests. The following do not under an open contract rank as good roots: (1) a pre-1926 conveyance subject to a mortgage, since the legal estate was not vested in the mortgagor; (2) an equitable mortgage; (3) a lease; (4) a post-1925 will or disentailing deed, since both only operate in equity.

(ii) *Adequate description*[5]. Examples of dispositions failing this test are a general devise in a pre-1926 will (e.g. I devise all my realty to X) since extrinsic evidence would be required to show that the property sold belonged to the testator at death,[6], or an assent which merely described the property by reference to the conveyance under which the testator acquired title. An assent may be disqualified on other additional grounds. It may fail to specify the estate assented to, simply vesting the property for all the estate or interest of the deceased at the time of his death; it is also necessary to check the assentor's title to make the assent against the grant of probate. Similarly a conveyance on sale which describes the land conveyed by reference to a full description contained in the parcels clause of an earlier conveyance (a far from infrequent modern practice[7]) will not constitute a good root.

(iii) *No doubt.* A document does not constitute a good root of title if it contains recitals which throw reasonable doubt upon the earlier title. A document is regarded as casting a doubt on the vendor's title if it depends for its effect on some earlier instrument, as where, for example, it is executed in exercise of some power[8]; the purchaser is entitled to know (in the absence of a

---

3 Law Com. No. 9, para. 40.
4 4th edn, p. 124. See Prichard, 'Roots of Title Today' [1975] CLP 125.
5 See *Re Bramwell's Contract, Bramwell v Ballards Securities Investments Ltd* [1969] 1 WLR 1659 (description of land in root of title not identifiable with that agreed to be sold).
6 *Parr v Lovegrove* (1858) 4 Drew 170. Contra, a specific devise of a person dying after 1897; Emmet, 142. Cf. *Gateway Developments Property Ltd v Grech* (1970) 92 WN (NSW) 845, noted at (1971) 45 ALJ 375.
7 Prichard, op. cit., p. 146. Often the following up of earlier deeds referred to in the root conveyance can throw up several deeds creating covenants or easements affecting the property.
8 *Re Copelin's Contract* [1937] 4 All ER 447 (power of attorney); *Re W. and R. Holmes and Cosmopolitan Press Ltd's Contract* [1944] Ch 53, [1943] 2 All ER 716 (pre-1926 power of sale); *Gateway Developments Property Ltd v Grech*, note 6, ante (instrument exercising power of appointment).

condition to the contrary) that the power still subsisted at the time of its purported exercise, which the subsequent document does not show. Some doubts exist as to whether a conveyance in execution of a trust for sale is a good root because of the need, possibly, to go back to the deed creating the trust[9]. In practice such a conveyance is invariably accepted without question by solicitors under an express contractual provision.

(b) Good roots of title

The best root of title and the one most commonly encountered in practice is a conveyance on sale; this constitutes the 'best' root since a transaction on sale raises a strong inference that the title was investigated and approved. Strictly speaking a post-1925 mortgage does not rank as a good root; not taking effect as a conveyance of the fee simple, the mortgage does not deal with the whole legal estate. Nevertheless it is considered by many that a mortgage is a better root than a conveyance on sale since a mortgagee is less likely to accept a doubtful title than a purchaser[10]. Its acceptability may, however, be suspect in a particular case since the description of the property is abbreviated by referring merely to the conveyance to the mortgagor; in consequence there is no adequate description of the property, nor any reference to restrictive covenants or other adverse rights affecting the property. A voluntary conveyance if at least fifteen years old may be a good root, even under an open contract[11].

(c) Contractual provisions

Usually the root of title is provided for in the contract. The vendor may stipulate for the title to commence with something less than a good root, leaving the purchaser to decide whether to accept such a document. But certain rules must be observed. Any stipulation inserted in a contract for the purpose of limiting the period for which a title shall be shown must give a perfectly fair description of the nature of the document forming the root of title[12]. Any stipulation for *less* than the statutory title must be accompanied by a clear statement of the nature of the document forming the root. If it is a voluntary conveyance, the condition should say so, otherwise the court will regard it as misleading and will not force the title upon the purchaser[13].

If the root of title is at least fifteen years old, it is not clear to what extent the vendor is under a duty to specify its nature. However, as the Law of Property Act 1969, lays so much emphasis on the title which a purchaser could demand under an open contract[14], it seems that the vendor ought not to be entitled to conceal that the contractual root would not be a good root under an open contract, for then he would be depriving the purchaser of any opportunity of deciding whether to run the risk of being outside the ambit of the recent Act.

In relation to freehold land both the standard forms of Conditions of Sale leave the vendor to stipulate both the length and root of title. General Condition 6 (1) of the Conveyancing Lawyers' Conditions of Sale provides that the title shall commence with a good root of title at least fifteen years old at the date

9   See Williams, Title, 575; Law Com. No. 9, para. 39 (b); contra, Prichard, op. cit., p. 140.
10   Emmet, 141. Cf. 1 Williams V & P 124, suggesting that it is a proper root if it recites the mortgagor's seisin. But a recital of seisin is not generally regarded as adequate; *Re Wallis and Grout's Contract* [1906] 2 Ch 206; M & W, 580n.
11   *Re Marsh and Earl Granville* (1883) 24 Ch D 11 at 24, per Cotton LJ.
12   *Re Marsh and Earl Granville* (1883) 24 Ch D 11 at 22, per Baggallay LJ.
13   *Re Marsh and Earl Granville* (1883) 24 Ch D 11.
14   Page 285, ante.

of the contract. Unlike the other two standard forms these Conditions do not require a vendor to specify in the contract the document which is to constitute the root of title. He is free to do so if he wishes. The specification of a root of title will override the terms of Condition 6 (1), without any amendment being made to it[15]. Therefore, even though the root selected is not, or may not be, a good root of title, there can be no argument that the Condition operates as a warranty that it is a good root.

3. Pre-Root of title documents

(a) The statutory limitation
The fixing of a root of title limits the extent of a purchaser's investigation and absolves a vendor from establishing the title from any earlier date[16]. By virtue of the Law of Property Act 1925, s. 45 (1), a purchaser is precluded (i) from requiring the production or any abstract or copy, of any document dated prior to the root of title, and (ii) from making any requisition, objection or enquiry with respect to the earlier title, even though the prior title is agreed to be produced. These provisions must be read in conjunction with sub-s. (11), which reads:

> ' Nothing in this section shall be construed as binding a purchaser to complete his purchase in any case where, on a contract made independently of this section and containing stipulations similar to the provisions of this section . . . specific performance of the contract would not be enforced against him by the court.'

The restrictions imposed by sub-s. (1) are construed as if they were express terms of the contract, and they have practically the same effect as those conditions precluding inquiry into the earlier title, which were prevalent prior to the Conveyancing Act 1881, s. 3 (3) (the forerunner of s. 45 (1)). It appears to have been assumed that the Act of 1881 was not intended to constitute a legislative repeal of well-established doctrines[17]. A purchaser is, therefore, not debarred from showing aliunde that the pre-root title is defective, or that there are incumbrances created by a pre-root of title document, which the vendor has not disclosed. He may discover the defect as a result of inquiries made of a third person with reference to another transaction[18], or because the vendor accidently produces the earlier documents for inspection[19]. The courts will not compel the purchaser to take a clearly bad title[20].

(b) Exceptions
Subsection (1) entitles a purchaser to require the production of a pre-root of title document (or an abstract or copy) in three cases.

---

15 Special Condition 5. In the event of any conflict the Special Conditions prevail over the General Conditions.
16 *Re Atkinson and Horsell's Contract* [1912] 2 Ch 1 at 19, CA, per Buckley LJ.
17 *Nottingham Patent Brick and Tile Co v Butler* (1885) 15 QBD 261 at 272, per North J; on appeal (1886) 16 QBD 778, CA.
18 *Re Cox and Neve's Contract* [1891] 2 Ch 109 (undisclosed restrictive covenant).
19 *Smith v Robinson* (1879) 13 Ch D 148; *Waddell v Wolfe* (1874) LR 9 QB 515 (express condition); cf. Walford, 73–76. See *Faruqi v English Real Estates Ltd* [1979] 1 WLR 963 (registered land).
20 *Re Scott and Alvarez's Contract* [1895] 2 Ch 603, p. 158, ante.

(i) A power of attorney[1] under which any abstracted document is executed. In *Re Copelin's Contract*[2] the root of title which was over thirty years old was executed under a power of attorney; the purchaser was held entitled to a copy or abstract of the power, even though it was a pre-root of title document. The purchaser is entitled to a copy or abstract of any power of attorney affecting the title, *notwithstanding any stipulation to the contrary*[3].

(ii) A document creating or disposing of an interest, power or obligation which is not shown to have ceased or expired, and subject to which any part of the property is disposed of by an abstracted document. It seems that this exception was intended to relate primarily to pre-root leases and mortgages, but it is wide enough to cover a document which creates subsisting covenants, or a plan on a pre-root deed, which is incorporated by reference in the subsequent description of the property[4].

(iii) A document creating any limitation or trust by reference to which any part of the property is disposed of by an abstracted document. The purchaser is not, of course, affected by any trust that will be overreached by the conveyance to him[5].

(c) Contractual provisions
A purchaser's right to a pre-root document of title falling within exception (ii) or (iii) can be excluded by an express contractual provision. Under the National Conditions[6], the vendor must supply a copy of any plan material to the description of the property, or any pre-root of title document containing covenants, provided the plan or earlier document is in his possession or power[7], or that of his mortgagee or trustee. It seems, however, that he must make available a copy of restrictive covenants subject to which the property is sold, notwithstanding there is no copy with the deeds[8]. Subject to this, the vendor cannot be required under the National Conditions to procure the production of any document not in his possession, and not in that of his mortgagee or trustee, nor to trace or state who has possession. The Law Society's Conditions[9] regulate the vendor's obligations in relation to the production and delivery of any document forming part of the title which ought properly to be in his possession, or that of his mortgagee or trustee, but the language of the condition is not wide enough to exclude a purchaser's statutory right under s. 45 (1) to an *abstract or copy* of earlier documents of title.

4.   The subsequent title

Having fixed the root of title, the vendor must, subject to any contractual provision to the contrary, trace all the links in the chain of title from that document

1   A power of attorney arises when one person empowers another to act in his stead for certain purposes, e.g. to sell land, to execute a deed. See further, pp. 436–444, post.
2   [1937] 4 All ER 447.
3   LPA 1925, s. 125 (2), as amended by the LP (Am) A 1926.
4   Emmet, 148.
5   See *Williams and Glyn's Bank Ltd v Boland* [1980] 2 All ER 408 and [1980] Conv 427 (Sydenhan); and [1981] Conv 219 (Jill Martin).
6   NCS 12 (1).
7   This word covers the case where the vendor has the benefit of an acknowledgment for production of the earlier document.
8   See NCS 12 (2). This situation calls for a Special Condition; see *Faruqi v English Real Estates Ltd* [1979] 1 WLR 963.
9   LSC 12 (2). The provision makes reference to production of the relevant documents of title.

to the document or event by which the ownership became vested in him. As we have seen[10], the final link must show that the legal title is in himself or in some person whom he can compel to convey.

If the intervening title is shown to be bad on investigation, the vendor fails to establish a good title and the purchaser can rescind the contract. But a title will be forced upon a purchaser, notwithstanding some intermediate defect if that defect has been cured by adverse possession. The case of *Re Atkinson and Horsell's Contract*[11] is highly instructive in showing the relationship between the root of title and the subsequent title.

> V agreed to sell land under a contract providing for the title to commence with a devise in 1842. In fact V derived title from S who in 1874, under a mutual mistake as to the effect of a will, was allowed by the true owner (who was under no disability) to take possession. S and those claiming under her down to V remained in uninterrupted possession to the date of the contract. No mention that the title was partly possessory was made in the contract as the mistake had not then been realised.

The purchaser argued that V had not shown a good title according to the contract, i.e. a title commencing with the root and passing through a chain of deeds and documents to the vendor's deed. A majority of the Court of Appeal rejected this argument, holding that V had shown a good title. According to Buckley LJ[12] the root of title does not mean that the document named as such is the root in the sense that it is an essential factor in establishing the title ultimately to be accepted. This does not mean that the title prior to the date when adverse possession commenced is irrelevant. In particular it may establish that at that date there was no person under a disability who could now defeat the title by possession.

One consequence of the majority's reasoning, as the dissenting judge, Fletcher Moulton LJ observed[13], is that the vendor can in theory force upon the purchaser a title with any number of interruptions filled up by possessory titles. Yet it is not easy to see how the majority could have reached any other conclusion. The vendor's obligation was to show a good title. This he had done. There was no possibility of any dispute as to the title, so the purchaser could not be prejudiced. He should therefore be compelled to take the property.

In short, the root of title need not necessarily have any direct connection with the title actually offered.

D   Deducing title

1.   The abstract of title

It now remains to consider how in practice the vendor discharges his obligation to make title. It is his duty to deliver to the purchaser an abstract of title[14], which may be described as a summary of the documents by which any

10   Page 279, ante.
11   [1912] 2 Ch 1, CA.
12   [1912] 2 Ch 1 at 19, CA, per Buckley LJ.
13   [1912] 2 Ch 1 at 16, CA.
14   In relation to registered titles, the vendor's obligations are quite different; see
      pp. 350–352, post. A delivery of an abstract may amount to a warranty as to title; see
      Errington v Martell-Wilson (1980) 130 NLJ 545, (1975) 39 Conv (NS) 381 and [1981] Conv
      167.

dispositions of the property have been made during the period for which title has to be shown, and of all facts, such as births, marriages, deaths or other matters, affecting the devolution of the title during the same period[15]. It is by perusing the abstract (and subsequently verifying it) that the purchaser's solicitor forms his opinion as to the title. It has to contain in full everything necessary to enable him to make his decision; such parts of the relevant documents as are immaterial for this purpose are mentioned in the abstract in an abbreviated form, or omitted altogether. The process of delivering an abstract of title, and its subsequent verification, is known in practice as deducing title[16].

Production of deeds or copies

Without at this stage knowing anything about the form of an abstract, it will be apparent that it is a document specially prepared by the vendor's solicitor. This raises the question why the deeds themselves are not used to this end.

At one time it appeared that the title-deeds were delivered to the purchaser. As it was customary for the title to be approved by conveyancing counsel, it was the practice to facilitate his task by preparing an abstract of the contents of the deeds; but this was done by the purchaser's solicitor at the purchaser's expense. In course of time it became established that the vendor should prepare the abstract at his own expense. Once this became the rule, it was held that delivery of the deeds was not sufficient[17]. The purchaser was entitled to insist on an abstract; he was not bound to 'wade through the deeds'[18].

Today, very practical considerations prevent the forwarding of the deeds to the purchaser's solicitor. In many cases the deeds are not in the vendor's possession, but with his mortgagee, and a mortgagee can hardly be expected to release them so that they may be forwarded to a purchaser's solicitor[19].

However the advent of sophisticated photocopying techniques now means that photographic copies of all relevant deeds and documents can be supplied in place of an abstract in the traditional form[20]. Clearly there is much to be said in favour of copies rather than abstracts. A copy can be prepared far more quickly and accurately. The risk of error in abstracting is virtually eliminated; the time spent in examining the copy against the original is greatly reduced. Theoretically the objection that the purchaser has to wade through the deeds still remains, but this can hardly be a valid argument against their use,

---

15   34 Halsbury's Laws (3rd edn), 274. For a judicial description, see Kindersley V-C, in *Oakden v Pike* (1865) 34 LJ Ch 620 at 622 (a document which contains with sufficient clearness and sufficient fullness the effect of every instrument which constitutes part of the vendor's title).

16   According to Kindersley V-C, the use of the expression 'deducing title' as meaning the delivery of an abstract is not strictly correct: see *Oakden v Pike* (1865) 34 LJ Ch 620 at 622.

17   *Horne v Wingfield* (1841) 3 Man & G 33.

18   *Sugden on Vendors and Purchasers* (14th edn) (1862), p. 406. It has been observed that the rule obliging a vendor to deliver an abstract at his own expense appears to have been first evolved by Sugden out of the usual conveyancing practice; see Williams, *The Contract of Sale of Land*, p. xvii, note 20.

19   It is commonplace for the mortgagee to forward the deeds to the *vendor's* solicitor at the commencement of the transaction, to enable him to prepare the contract and, later, the abstract. But he usually holds them as agent for the mortgagee and on the terms that they will be returned on demand. Cf. the plea made in (1970) 67 LS Gaz 386.

20   The Council of The Law Society did not give official blessing to the practice until 1969; see Emmet, 149–151. Of course wading through photocopies (on one side only) is often worse than merely wading through the deeds, (1969) 66 LS Gaz 492–93.

especially when the basis of modern conveyancing is the legal estate and the period of investigation has now been reduced to fifteen years.

Where copies are supplied in lieu of an abstract, they should be accompanied by an *epitome of title* listing in chronological order all material documents, events and matters normally appearing in an abstract, stating the date and nature of each and the names of parties to documents. In addition the mode of deducing title (whether by copy or abstract) should be indicated and against each copy it should be shown whether the original will be handed over on completion[1]. Sometimes the title will comprise an event or matter of record of which no copy document is offered as evidence; it may be a probate, or death certificate. In this event relevant particulars should be set out, not in the epitome itself, but on a separate sheet as in a traditional abstract, and supplied with the copy documents. The epitome is not the evidence of title, merely an index.

Though it is now standard practice to provide photographic copies whenever possible[2], it will be some years before the abstract in traditional form disappears completely from the conveyancing scene. It is not customary to produce facsimile copies of deeds already abstracted, but to utilise the existing abstracts prepared on some earlier occasion. Sometimes a vendor is unable to supply photographic copies, for the simple reason that the original deeds are not in his possession and his only evidence is an abstract. Some practitioners prefer to receive a traditional abstract in transactions where the original deeds will not be handed to the purchaser on completion. For these reasons it is necessary to consider the form and content of an abstract.

2. Form of abstract

The abstract usually follows a stereotyped pattern, being typed on brief sized paper[3] and the relevant documents summarised in narrative form, using the past tense and the passive voice. By way of an introductory heading, the abstract contains the vendor's name, a short description of the property and the tenure. The various parts of a deed are abstracted in different margins or columns; this enables the reader to discover more easily any particular part of the document to which he needs to refer. These margins act as starting points. Once the relevant column has been selected, the information is continued across the paper, extending to the extreme right hand side. Working from left to right, the different margins governing the commencement of the various sections of the abstracted document are as follows:

outer (or first) margin: the date of the deed and stamp duty;
second margin: the nature of the deed, the names, addresses and descriptions of the parties, the testatum[4], covenants, conditions, agreements and declarations, powers, privisoes, acknowledgments of the right to production of deeds, certificates for value;
third margin: recitals, the habendum (i.e. to hold) clause, the reddendum (i.e. the 'yielding and paying' clause in a lease);

1 See (1969) 66 LS Gaz, loc. cit. For an example, see 18 Ency F & P, 780−1. The delivery of an epitome is frequently omitted in practice.
2 Very few typists working in solicitors' offices today will know how to prepare an abstract in the correct form.
3 Brief paper measures approximately 13 ins × 17 ins.
4 I.e. that part of the deed commencing 'Now this Deed witnesseth . . .'

fourth margin: uses, trusts[5];
inside all the margins: the heading, the parcels, the execution and attestation.

Events affecting the title, such as deaths or marriages, are commenced in the second margin, as are certificates of search. When an abstract has been checked against the original documents, a signed and dated record of the fact is endorsed in the outer margin by the person undertaking the examination in words such as: 'Original produced at the offices of Messrs . . . and examined by . . .' Such an abstract is commonly known as an examined, or marked, abstract[6].

(a) Typical example of an abstract of a conveyance

All the material parts of the conveyance must be incorporated within the abstract. Subject to the use of the past tense and passive voice, the exact wording should be adopted, though to reduce the length of the abstract and the time spent in its preparation (reading it is another matter, except for those well versed in the art), many of the words appear in abbreviated form[7]. For the inexperienced this adds to the confusion and merely serves to prolong its reading. In cases where a photographic copy of a document cannot be supplied, The Law Society's Working Party on Conveyancing[8] have advocated that the vendor's solicitor should produce full copies of each document or material parts of documents, typed on paper of a size suitable for facsimile copying without first turning the language into the past tense and passive voice.

Notwithstanding this obvious rejection of the abstract in the traditional form, a typical non-abbreviated example of an abstract of a conveyance is set out on the following page[9]. The names of the parties and the properties appearing in this illustration are, of course, fictitious.

> ABSTRACT OF THE TITLE of David Large[10] to freehold property known as 'Fairhaven' Mead Road Oadby in the County of Leicester

10 May 1969   OFFICIAL CERTIFICATE[11] of search in H.M. Land Charges Register No. 637112 against Abel Small revealing no subsisting entries

21 May 1969   BY CONVEYANCE of this date made between the said ABEL
Stamp £34   SMALL[12] of 'Fairhaven' Mead Road Oadby in the County of Leicester
P.D. Stamp[13]   (thereinafter called 'the vendor') of the one part and DAVID LARGE of

---

5   See *Moore on Title* (6th edn), p. 15. Where no uses or trusts are declared (as is frequently the case today) it is the modern practice to abstract the habendum and reddendum in the fourth margin, leaving the third margin exclusively for recitals.
6   See p. 372, post. See LSC 12 (2) requiring the production of an abstract duly marked.
7   E.g. 'vdr' stands for 'vendor', 'prems' for 'premises', 'or' for 'other', 'tree' for 'trustee'. Other more misleading illustrations will be encountered in practice by those readers not already accustomed to this strange guessing game. For a list of the more commonly used abbreviations, see Cosway, *Abstracting and Deducing Title*, pp. 8–9.
8   Second Interim Report, 1966, paras. 40–43.
9   See also 18 Ency F & P, 740–79.
10   In practice the abstract would be prepared on the occasion of a sale or mortgage by David Large, and for this reason it is stated to be an abstract of his title.
11   For the abstracting of search certificates, see p. 297, post.
12   This will often appear as 'the said A. Small' if he has been a party to an earlier abstracted deed or transaction.
13   'P.D.' stands for 'Particulars delivered'. For the significance of this stamp, see p. 444, post.

32 Church Lane in the City of Leicester (thereinafter called 'the purchaser') of the other part

> RECITING seisin of the vendor and agreement for sale

IT WAS WITNESSED as follows:
1. IN pursuance of the said agreement and in consideration of the sum of £6800 paid to the vendor by the purchaser (the receipt etc[14]) the vendor as beneficial owner thereby conveyed unto the purchaser

> ALL THAT plot of land fronting to Mead Road Oadby aforesaid containing in the whole 811 square yards and delineated and described in the plan annexed to the before abstracted Conveyance (hereinafter called 'the Conveyance') of 16 January 1960[15] and thereon edged red AND ALSO ALL THAT dwellinghouse erected thereon and known as 'Fairhaven' Mead Road Oadby aforesaid TOGETHER with the full benefit and advantage of the right of way granted by the Conveyance over and along the road shown coloured brown on the said plan
> TO HOLD unto the purchaser in fee simple SUBJECT to the covenants on the part of the grantee and the conditions contained in the Conveyance

2. COVENANT by the purchaser with the vendor to observe and perform the said covenants and conditions and to indemnify[16]
3. CERTIFICATE for value

> EXECUTED[17] by both parties and ATTESTED

(b) Some additional points

Some further points must be mentioned which it is not possible to incorporate in the illustration.

(i) *Recitals.* As seen in the example, the recitals can be confined to a bare minimum where they merely refer to the vendor's seisin and the contract for sale. Recitals of material facts affecting the title, such as deaths, marriages, grants of probate, must be abstracted. Since such matters will often have been previously abstracted in their own right, it is sufficient to state: 'Reciting the death of XY as before abstracted'. Similarly where the recital sets out the terms of some previously abstracted deed, a reference to the date of the deed is all that is required. A point that is sometimes overlooked is that recitals in the deed constituting the root of title should be abstracted fully (if they affect the property), even though the purchaser is precluded from raising objections or requisitions upon the prior title.

(ii) *Parcels.* The basic rule is that the description of the property should be abstracted in full, except where that description is repeated in subsequent deeds when it is permissible to refer to the property as 'the before abstracted premises'. A copy of any plan forming part of an abstracted deed should be

---

14 This is an adequate summary of the clause acknowledging receipt of the consideration.
15 There is no need to mention the parties to this deed, if it has previously been abstracted.
16 Indemnity covenants of this nature normally follow a set pattern; all that need be shown is that such a covenant was entered into.
17 It is incorrect to add 'duly' before 'executed', as is commonly done. The purchaser should decide the question of due execution.

attached to the abstract, though whether this rule is of general application or relates solely to a plan material to the description of the land is uncertain[18]. Perhaps there is no need, strictly speaking, to supply a copy of a plan stated to be 'for identification purposes only'. Such a plan cannot ordinarily control the parcels in the body of the conveyance, and so may be treated as a non-material part of the document[19]. Solicitors are not accustomed to taking this point in practice.

(iii) *Execution.* It is sufficient to state that the deed was executed by all parties if that was the case, but any variation between the name of a party appearing in the deed and the signature in the execution should be noted. Where an attorney has executed, that circumstance should be mentioned.

3.   Contents of the abstract

The abstract must contain all the documents and events material to the vendor's title, commencing with the root of title and ending with the transaction or event by virtue of which the vendor claims title. Pre-root documents must be included where necessary. Relevant documents and events are abstracted in chronological order, unless the property is or has been held under different titles, in which case each title is kept separate until there is unity of ownership. Each deed forming a link in the chain is abstracted in chief, i.e. as a separate document. The fact that a document is referred to in a recital of some subsequent deed is no justification for not abstracting the earlier deed[20]. The omission to abstract a document in chief may proceed from a desire to avoid revealing matters of a suspicious character not noticed in the recital[1]. The purchaser is entitled to judge for himself the effect of the earlier deed, and not merely obliged to accept the opinion of the person who drafted the recital of it.

In practice the abstract of title supplied may consist of two or more separate abstracts. Suppose that on a sale of land from A to B, A's solicitor prepared an abstract of A's title. Later when B sells to C, B's solicitor will utilise the abstract previously prepared by A's solicitor and will himself draw up an abstract, often termed a supplemental or continuation abstract, (or prepare copies) of all deeds and documents relating to subsequent transactions not covered by the existing abstract. This will frequently entail abstracting no more than the certificate of search made on the occasion of the A – B conveyance, the A – B conveyance and any mortgage created by B.

Where the vendor's solicitor supplies copies in lieu of abstracts, he must provide copies of all deeds which it would have been necessary to abstract in chief had he deduced title in the traditional manner.

(a) Documents requiring to be abstracted or copied
These documents forming part of the title need to be abstracted or copied — conveyances, mortgages, subsisting leases, surrendered leases (but not expired

---

18   Compare *Blackburn v Smith* (1848) 2 Exch 783 at 792, per Parke B, with the Law Society's Digest, Opinion No. 77 (which dates from 1886).
19   Emmet, 528–29, (1977) 41 Conv (NS) 298. This now appears to be the case only if there is no doubt as to the parcels. If there is a doubt the plan can be looked at notwithstanding the limiting words. See *Wigginton and Milner Ltd v Winster Engineering Ltd* [1978] 3 All ER 436, CA and *Scarfe v Adams* [1981] 1 All ER 843, CA.
20   *Re Stamford, Spalding and Boston Banking Co and Knight's Contract* [1900] 1 Ch 287.
1   Ibid., at 289, per North J.

ones), assents, releases, grants of probate, letters of administration, vesting instruments, pre-1926 wills and appointments of new trustees (but in relation to settled land, the purchaser is only concerned with the deed of declaration[2]). Births, marriages and deaths[3] must be recorded, as also should court proceedings and orders, e.g. foreclosure proceedings or a judgment in ejectment[4].

(i) *Mortgages.* Both subsisting and discharged mortgages should be abstracted. In relation to the latter a purchaser is entitled to see that it has been properly discharged or that the receipt has not operated as a transfer on the ground that payment was made by a person not entitled to the immediate equity of redemption[5].

Where the mortgagee is selling in exercise of his statutory power of sale, it should be shown that the mortgage money has become due[6].

(ii) *Equitable charges.* The general practice is to omit such charges from the abstract, though this is at variance with the slender authority on the point. In *Drummond v Tracy*[7] where a letter creating an equitable charge which was intended to be paid off out of the purchase money had been suppressed, Wood V-C considered this course to be incorrect. This view has been roundly criticised as creating a source of difficulty and expense[8]. An equitable chargee will not normally be able to exercise any powers in relation to the legal estate[9], so that if the charge has been repaid, or is to be repaid on completion, the purchaser cannot be prejudiced provided the document is handed over on completion. However it is thought advisable to abstract the charge if it has been registered under the Land Charges Act 1972; as it will be disclosed on the purchaser's official certificate of search, it is preferable to give him notice of its existence when sending the abstract, rather than having inquiries raised about it just before completion.

(iii) *Equitable interests.* It will not normally be necessary to abstract equitable interests, for they will not generally concern a purchaser of the *legal* estate. In certain situations equitable interests will require abstracting and examples will be given later.

(iv) *Certificates of search*[10]. No obligation to include search certificates in the abstract seems to exist but it is the general practice to do so. Indeed, if they are omitted, the purchaser's solicitor will usually ask whether one was made. Their inclusion is particularly helpful in ascertaining whether existing restrictive

---

2   SLA 1925, s. 35, p. 319, post.
3   But see p. 298, post.
4   See Moore, op. cit., p. 48; *Re Heaysman's and Tweedy's Contract* (1893) 69 LT 89, CA.
5   LPA 1925, s. 115 (2). Mortgages have normally been abstracted in a very abbreviated form, recording simply the date, parties, amount advanced, (a brief statement of the property charged) and in the case of a discharged mortgage the fact of repayment.
6   See LPA 1925, s. 101 (1) (i). See further pp. 298, and 336–340, post.
7   (1860) John 608, adopted as correct in *Sugden on Vendors and Purchaser* (14th edn) p. 411.
8   1 Dart, 298.
9   For the position of the equitable chargee, see M & W, 925.
10 It is advisable for a purchaser to ascertain the names of all estate owners to 1926 (if possible). See further Chap. 14.

covenants have ceased to be binding on account of non-registration. It is not customary to abstract certificates of searches in local land charges registers.

(b) Documents which need not be abstracted or copied

(i) *Wills.* Where an estate owner dies after 1925, the correct procedure is simply to abstract the grant of probate or the letters of administration. The will should not be abstracted since it operates only in equity[11]; the legal title vests in the personal representatives[12], and the grant of representation constitutes the sole link in the chain of title. It is not strictly essential to abstract the death, though this is frequently done. The abstract should contain a note of any endorsement on the probate or letters of administration.

(ii) *Acts of Parliament.* Public statutes are not abstracted, notwithstanding that their provisions affect the devolution of the legal estate, an obvious example being the transitional provisions of the Law of Property Act 1925. Private Acts, such as a local inclosure Act, should be abstracted[13].

(iii) *Interests to be overreached.* The Law of Property Act 1925, s. 10 (1) contains an important qualification to the general rule governing the contents of an abstract by providing that where title is shown to a legal estate, it is not necessary or even proper to include in the abstract an instrument relating only to some interest or power which will be overreached by the conveyance of the legal estate. This section fits in with the general scheme of the property legislation of 1925 to keep the equitable interests off the legal title. Therefore on a sale by a tenant for life in exercise of his statutory power of sale, or by trustees for sale or personal representatives, the equitable interests arising under the settlement, trust, or will, need not be abstracted. They are not the purchaser's concern[14]. Where overreaching powers exist, a purchaser cannot be compelled to accept a title made with the concurrence of the equitable owners[15].

Section 10 (1) is not exclusively confined to equitable interests. If A mortgages to B, and then mortgages the same property to C, a conveyance by B in exercise of his statutory power of sale vests in the purchaser A's legal estate, freed from C's mortgage[16]. The abstract should not disclose C's mortgage even though it has been registered as a land charge. It should abstract the circumstances under which the power of sale arose. Strictly this is not a case of overreaching, a term reserved for interests which remain in existence but are

---

11 It is sometimes stated (e.g. 18 Ency F & P 228; Williams, *Title*, p. 581) that it is not necessary to abstract a will further than to give the date, the testator's name and description and the appointment of the executors, but even an abstract limited to these particulars is strictly unnecessary. See the specimen epitomes of abstracts found in the LPA 1925, Sch. 6. Although exceptionally a will may require abstracting (see Emmet, 158) it is generally unwise to give a purchaser notice of the contents of a will, whether in the abstract or in a subsequent assent; see *Re Duce and Boots Cash Chemists (Southern) Ltd's Contract* [1937] Ch 642, [1937] 3 All ER 788, considered at p. 335, post. Compare the common case of an abstracted will followed by an assent 'upon the trusts declared by the will' leaving the purchaser unsure as to what the trusts are.
12 AEA 1925, ss. 1, 3.
13 See Moore, op. cit., p. 49; LPA 1925, Sch. 6, Specimen abstract No. 1.
14 See further Chap. 11
15 LPA 1925, s. 42 (1), p. 164, ante.
16 LPA 1925, s. 104 (1), p. 339, post.

transferred to the proceeds of sale, for in this case C's estate is destroyed altogether. Yet this situation is clearly within the spirit of the section.

The subsection does not obviate the need to abstract any instrument creating or affecting an equitable interest which will not be overreached. Thus if A holds property on trust for B[17] who assigns his equitable interest to C, A can only vest a good title in a purchaser if C concurs in the sale and this will entail showing the devolution of C's title in equity.

It may also be essential to bring equitable interests on to the title to show that a surviving trustee for sale is entitled to sell as beneficial owner consequent upon the determination of the trust. A rather involved example which the author encountered recently may serve as an illustration. X and Y held a legal estate upon trust for sale as tenants in common in equity. They made similar wills whereby each left her respective share in equity to the other for life with remainder to Z absolutely. X died and Y appointed Z as a new trustee of the legal estate held on trust for sale. On the subsequent death of Y, Z became sole owner in equity and the trust for sale terminated. When Z came to convey the legal estate as beneficial owner, he had to show that the trust for sale had come to an end[18]. This entailed abstracting the wills of X and Y dealing with their equitable interests. Alternatively Z could, by appointing a new trustee, have kept the trust for sale alive, and the purchaser by paying his purchase money to the trustees would have acquired a good title without being concerned with the trusts affecting the proceeds of sale[19]. This alternative method is recommended as advisable to offset the difficulties caused by bringing the equitable interests on to the title, but the problems of satisfying the client of the advantages of this artificial procedure may in practice prove to be unsurmountable.

(c) Fraudulent concealment

Under the Law of Property Act 1925, s. 183, a vendor or his solicitor who, with intent to defraud, conceals from the purchaser any instrument or incumbrance material to the title is guilty of a criminal offence punishable by fine or imprisonment. The purchaser (or persons deriving title under him) can maintain an action for damages in respect of loss (including money spent on improvements) sustained by reason of the concealment. Neither civil nor criminal liability arises unless there is an intention to defraud[20]. It would seem that this provision is wide enough to cover concealment of a pre-root of title incumbrance[1]. It is material to the title since it is within the ambit of the vendor's duty of disclosure; and where loss can be established the measure of damages awarded under the section may, depending on the circumstances, be greater than those recoverable under the covenants for title[2].

---

17   There may be a resulting, or constructive, trust in B's favour.
18   This was not a situation where title could be made by Z under the Law of Property (Joint Tenants) Act 1964, p. 328, post. See further P.W. Smith, 'The Chains of Trusteeship' [1978] Conv 423.
19   LPA 1925, s. 27, p. 326, post.
20   *District Bank Ltd v Luigi Grill Ltd* [1943] Ch 78, [1943] 1 All ER 136; and see p. 369, post.
1   1 W & C (13th edn), 340. In *Smith v Robinson* (1879) 13 Ch D 148 at 151, Fry J referring to the Law of Property Amendment Act 1859, s. 24, queried whether this was so.
2   See Chap. 24.

E   The vendor's obligations

1.   Duty to supply

The vendor's obligation to prepare and deliver to the purchaser an abstract of his title is confirmed by the standard Conditions of Sale. Sometimes the vendor's solicitor forwards the abstract on the terms that it is to be held to his order (i.e. returnable on demand) pending completion. This restriction is inconsistent with the unqualified nature of the obligation as stated in the contract, and has been disapproved of by the Council of The Law Society[3]. Where the solicitor acts for both vendor and purchaser he should prepare and put with the deeds a proper abstract[4], a practice that is not always observed.

In the absence of any contrary agreement, the vendor must bear the expense of preparing the abstract, including costs incurred in obtaining documents not in his possession, which are needed for this purpose[5].

2.   Time for delivery

In a formal contract the date for delivery is governed by the General Conditions of Sale. The Law Society's Conditions provide[6] for delivery of the abstract with the vendor's part of the contract when contracts are exchanged. This recognises what is a common, but by no means universal, practice. The abstract may already have been supplied prior to exchange of contracts. The Conveyancing Lawyers' Conditions of Sale expressly provide that such delivery shall be treated as being in or toward performance of the vendor's contractual duties in relation to deducing the title[7]. Under an open contract the abstract must be delivered within a reasonable time[8].

Effect of delay
Time is not of the essence with regard to the delivery of the abstract under either an open contract[9] or one governed by the standard Conditions. The general rules relating to time clauses[10] will determine the consequences of the vendor's delay. Assuming the usual case where time is not of the essence, if the vendor fails to deliver the abstract by the due date (or within a reasonable time, if no date is specified), the purchaser should notify the vendor that unless the abstract is sent within a specified period, the contract is at an end[11]. Difficulties have arisen in respect of defective abstracts. The position is that the time does not run against a purchaser for raising requisitions with regard to those missing parts until they are delivered; it is accordingly not the position that the vendor is absolutely protected by delivery of any abstract nor that the purchaser need

---

3   Law Society's Digest (Third (Cumulative) Supplement), Opinion No. 95 (b).
4   Law Society's Digest, Opinion No. 78.
5   *Re Johnson and Tustin* (1885) 30 Ch D 42.
6   LSC 12 (1); cf. NCS 9 (1) (delivery 11 working days after contract date).
7   See General Condition 6 (1) (delivery within 7 days from date of contract), and (7).
8   *Compton v Bagley* [1892] 1 Ch 313, where Romer J indicated (at 321) that 14 days is about the time usually required for delivery.
9   *Roberts v Berry* (1853) 3 De GM & G 291.
10   See pp. 412–417, post, for the application of these principles when there is a delay in completion.
11   *Compton v Bagley* [1892] 1 Ch 313. The vendor's delay does not entitle the purchaser to repudiate without first serving a notice requiring delivery; his own inactivity will be treated as a waiver of the time clause: *Jones v Price* (1797) 3 Anst 724.

do nothing until all abstracts are delivered[12]. A repudiation after the termination of this period will be effective, even though the date for completion has not arrived, or the vendor subsequently forwards an abstract, though in this event the purchaser should take the precaution of returning the abstract on its receipt[13].

The vendor should always remember that if delivery of the abstract is delayed, the time-table for raising requisitions will be put back and to the extent to which this causes a delay in completion, the vendor may be unable to charge interest in respect thereof[14].

3. Verification of abstract

Not only must a vendor deliver to the purchaser an abstract showing how, during the appropriate period, the title has devolved on him, he has also to furnish satisfactory evidence of all matters included in it. It is the purchaser's duty to verify the abstract by examining[15] it against the evidence which is produced; the vendor's duty is to produce the evidence for examination. The important question of expense will be considered at the end of this section.

(a) Production of deeds

Abstracted deeds or copies are proved by production of the originals. Technically, this is not adequate proof. The original may be a forgery, and how can the vendor establish otherwise? Only by proving it was duly executed. However, he does not normally have to undertake this task. In the absence of suspicious circumstances, a deed is presumed to have been duly executed if produced from the proper custody, that is, if it comes from a place where it might reasonably be expected to be found[16]. In practice the deeds are usually produced by the vendor's solicitor, or the mortgagee's solicitor, and it is not customary to inquire from what source they were obtained.

A deed at least twenty years old is said to prove itself and in the absence of any suspicious circumstances the purchaser must presume it was duly executed according to its tenor[17]. Though authority is lacking, it seems that proof of execution cannot be required even where the deed is less than twenty years old[18] and it is not the practice so to do unless there are suspicious circumstances. For example, a purchaser would be entitled to an explanation (at his own expense[19]) of the marked difference in the vendor's signature of the conveyance to him and the conveyance by him[20] or of suspicious alterations.

12   See *Ogilvy v Hope-Davies* [1976] 1 All ER 683. As a result of this case LSC condition 15 (4) has been drafted to reflect this decision; see Emmet, 156. See also NCS 9 (5).
13   *Hipwell v Knight* (1835) 1 Y & C Ex 401 (waiver inferred from subsequent communications as to title); *Compton v Bagley* [1892] 1 Ch 313.
14   For the raising of requisitions, see p. 365, post; for the vendor's right to interest in the event of delay, see pp. 418–419, post.
15   For the time of conducting such examinations, see p. 373, post.
16   *Croughton v Blake* (1843) 12 M & W 205 at 208, per Parke B.
17   Evidence Act 1938, s. 4, reducing the common law presumption from 30 to 20 years. See *Re Airey, Airey v Stapleton* [1897] 1 Ch 164 (execution by attorney presumed, but not the existence of any authority to execute).
18   See 1 Dart, 309; Williams, *Title*, 658; cf. Farrand, 125, but see [1978] Conv 249 considering *Re Beaney* [1978] 2 All ER 595.
19   See LPA 1925, s. 45 (4), p. 303, post.
20   An actual case encountered by one of the authors.

(i) *Marked abstracts.* A vendor may not have all the original deeds in his possession—a frequent occurrence on a sale of property on a building estate. Individual house owners will not have the deeds of the builder's title, only an abstract (or copies) which will have been marked as examined against the originals at the time of the first sale. Nevertheless the purchaser's solicitor should, strictly speaking, locate and examine the original deeds; but since the purchaser must bear the expense of obtaining the deeds for the purpose of verifying the abstract, it is the usual practice to accept the vendor's examined abstract. In this way a marked abstract becomes a form of secondary evidence. The Council of The Law Society have, however, refused to approve this practice officially 'having regard to the possible issue of negligence involved'[1].

(ii) *Lost deeds.* Normally the problem of missing documents is covered by some express clause in the contract[2]. Even if this is not so, failure to produce an original document which should be in the vendor's possession does not afford the purchaser any ground of rescission, provided the vendor can satisfactorily explain the loss (a statutory declaration will suffice) and can also produce adequate secondary evidence, such as a completed copy or draft. In the case of a missing document, its execution has to be proved[3].

(b) Proof of events
Events such as marriages or deaths are sufficiently proved by production of the appropriate certificate, though grants of representation are commonly accepted as evidence of death, save in Chancery proceedings where the proof of title is involved[4]. A change of street name or house number is proved by a certified copy of the order made by the local authority[5].

(c) Presumptions
A purchaser may be obliged to accept as proof nothing more concrete than a presumption which the law makes. As between vendor and purchaser it has been said that a presumption must be accepted if it would be the duty of a judge to give a clear direction to the jury in favour of the fact, but not if he ought to leave it to them to pronounce upon the effect of the evidence[6]. A purchaser is more likely to be concerned with the statutory presumptions under the Law of Property Act 1925. By virtue of s. 45 (6):

> ' Recitals, statements and descriptions of facts, matters, and parties contained in deeds, instruments, Acts of Parliament, or statutory declarations, twenty years old at the date of the contract, shall, unless and except so far as they may be proved to be inaccurate, be taken to be sufficient evidence of the truth of such facts, matters and descriptions.'

Suppose a deed of appointment of new trustees recites the death of X, a previous trustee. X's death should be abstracted in chief; if the deed is twenty

1 See the correspondence at (1969) 66 LS Gaz 96. The problem ceases to exist when a vendor can commence his title with the conveyance from the developer to the first purchaser.
2 Page 159, ante.
3 *Bryant v Busk* (1827) 4 Russ 1, though it may be presumed in the case of very old documents: *Moulton v Edmonds* (1859) 1 De GF & J 246.
4 See the *Practice Direction* at [1970] 1 All ER 671. For proof of other matters, see Williams, *Title*, 668–83.
5 In practice a letter from the local authority is usually accepted.
6 *Emery v Grocock* (1821) 6 Madd 54 at 57, per Leach V-C.

years old, the fact of death is sufficiently proved by the recital. If the deed is not of that age, the death should be proved by production of X's death certificate.

This statutory presumption is likely to fall into comparative disuse consequent upon the reduction in the period of investigation of title to fifteen years. The Law Commission felt there was much to be said for its abolition but, not having the courage of their convictions, they declined to recommend any change[7].

(d) Expenses of verification

Section 45 (4) of the Law of Property Act 1925, throws the cost of verification on to the purchaser, except in relation to documents or evidence in the possession of the vendor, his mortgagee or trustee. This covers the expenses of the production and inspection of deeds, wills, probates, etc., and the expenses of all journeys incidental thereto, and also expenses incurred in searching for, procuring, making, verifying and producing certificates, declarations, evidences and information, save as above mentioned. For example, if in the situation considered on page 302, the purchaser is not content to rely on the marked abstract, but requires to inspect the original deeds, all expenses involving their production must be borne by him[8]. This subsection does not absolve the vendor from his obligation to procure the production of the appropriate documentary evidence, whether in his possession or not; it merely relieves him of the burden of the *expenses* involved. It is left to the standard Conditions of Sale to lessen the vendor's duty of production[9].

Sub-section (4) proceeds on the assumption that the vendor has delivered a proper abstract. The cost of preparing the abstract, including expenses incurred in obtaining copies or abstracts of relevant documents not in his possession, falls on him[10]. He must also bear the cost of obtaining the deeds for the purpose of handing them over on completion[11], though not if his inability to obtain them is because of some defect in title which under the contract he is absolved from having to cure.

(e) Place of production

Section 45 says nothing about the proper place for production by the vendor. This is governed by the general law. Modern conveyancing practice dictates that this is at the offices of the vendor's solicitor, or his mortgagee's solicitor, though this is at variance with the common law rule as stated by leading authorities[12]. Should a vendor be so eccentric as to produce documents in his possession at some place other than a proper place, any extra expense incurred by the purchaser must be borne by the vendor[13].

---

7   Law Com. No. 9, paras. 42–45. It now becomes unnecessary to consider the much criticised decision of Malins V-C, in *Bolton v London School Board* (1878) 7 Ch D 766, that a conveyance of the appropriate age and containing a recital of seisin in fee constituted a good root of title and precluded a purchaser from requiring a title for the full statutory period.

8   *Re Stuart and Olivant and Seadon's Contract* [1896] 2 Ch 328, CA (root of title not in vendor's possession).

9   See p. 290, ante.

10   *Re Johnson and Tustin* (1885) 30 Ch D 42, CA.

11   *Re Duthy and Jesson's Contract* [1898] 1 Ch 419 (deeds in possession of deceased mortgagee's solicitors who, though debt repaid, refused to hand the deeds over without authority from the mortgagees' representatives).

12   See 1 Dart, 415; 1 Williams V & P, 164, where the rule is stated to be that production should be either at the vendor's own residence, or upon or near the property, or in London, as the vendor shall select.

13   *Hughes v Wynne* (1836) 8 Sim 85; affd. (1837) 1 Jur 720.

Chapter 11

Deducing title II: particular cases

A   Leaseholds

1.   Title to be deduced

The rules governing the title to be offered on the grant of a lease or sale of an existing lease under *an open contract* are contained in the Law of Property Act 1925, s. 44 (2) – (4), the provisions of which may loosely be summarised as follows: an intending lessee or a purchaser of an existing lease is entitled to call for the lease under which the other contracting party holds, but not the freehold or other superior title. The effect of the relevant subsections can best be seen against the background of specific illustrations.

(i) A contracts to grant a lease to B. B is not entitled to call for any deduction of the freehold title: sub-s. (2).
(ii) B contracts to assign the lease to C. C is entitled to call for the A – B lease (the head lease), but not the freehold title: sub-s. (2).
(iii) C contracts to grant an underlease to D. D can call for the A – B lease[1], and the B – C assignment, but no more.
(iv) D contracts to assign the underlease to E. E can call for the underlease, but not the title to the leasehold reversion: sub-s. (3), that is, he cannot investigate the head lease, or the B – C assignment. This puts E, a purchaser of an underlease, in a position inferior to that of the original underlessee, D, in situation (iii). There is some slight authority for the view that on the sale of an existing underlease, the purchaser can call for the title of the headlease, but the generally accepted opinion is to the contrary[2]. E's rights may be enlarged by express contractual provisions[3].
(v) E agrees to grant a sub-underlease to F. F is limited to the underlease and the assignment to E. Sub-section (4) precludes investigation of the title to the headlease.

These statutory restrictions do not prevent a lessee or purchaser from showing aliunde that the superior title is bad[4], nor do they affect the vendor's duty to

1   *Gosling v Woolf* [1893] 1 QB 39, more fully reported at (1893) 68 LT 89.
2   Walford, 118; Emmet, 171; *Becker v Partridge* [1966] 2 QB 155 at 169, [1966] 2 All ER 266 at 269, CA, per Danckwerts LJ. The minority view consists of a dictum of Romer LJ, in *Drive Yourself Hire Co (London) Ltd v Strutt* [1954] 1 QB 250 at 263, [1953] 2 All ER 1475 at 1485, CA, based on *Gosling v Woolf* [1893] 1 QB 39.
3   See further p. 306, post.
4   *Jones v Watts* (1890) 43 Ch D 574, CA, but vague allegations that the property is subject to restrictive covenants do not suffice.

disclose defects of title of which he is aware, such as a breach of a covenant in a superior lease[5]. He must also disclose onerous covenants and reveal that the covenants in the headlease are more stringent than those in the underlease (if such be the case)[6]. Though on the sale of an existing leasehold interest the title must commence with the lease (or underlease), it is not essential to show a complete chain of transactions ending with the assignment to the vendor, provided the title is deduced for a period of at least fifteen years prior to the contract[7].

2. Contractual variations of statutory provisions

These statutory provisions regulate the position under an open contract, and apply only if and so far as a contrary intention is not expressed in the contract[8]. In practice it is the lessee or purchaser who seeks to enlarge the grantor's obligations, depending on the subject-matter of the contract.

(a) Grant of new lease

It is not customary to insist upon an investigation of any superior title in the case of short leases at a rack rent (a rent representing the full annual value of the land and buildings). The parties frequently dispense with a formal contract in these situations. On the grant of a long lease at a ground rent (i.e. a rent representing the annual value of the land only) the position is very different. In some parts of the country developers sell their houses by way of long leases for 99 or 999 years at a ground rent plus a premium which represents the price of the house. In theory no purchaser ought to proceed unless he peruses the freehold title, for by accepting the lease without such investigation he exposes himself to the risk that the lessor's title to grant the lease is defective. His need to obtain the freehold title is all the more urgent if, as is the usual case, he is obtaining a mortgage. The mortgagee is not bound by the terms of the contract between the lessor and the lessee-mortgagor who may find himself considerably embarrassed if, having accepted the open contract position, his mortgagee requires the freehold title to be deduced. It is the common, but by no means universal, practice on the grant of a long term of years for the contract to provide for an abstract of the freehold title to be supplied (often at the buyer's expense!) but the lessee's right to raise objections is expressly excluded. Alternatively the abstract may be delivered with the draft contract so that the lessee's solicitor has the opportunity to peruse the freehold title before his client contracts to take a lease. On the grant of an underlease the underlessee is entitled under the general law to an abstract or copy of the head lease.

Neither the National Conditions nor The Law Society's Conditions require the lessor to deduce his freehold title on the *grant* of a lease. Unless the contract contains a Special Condition regulating the lessee's rights, he must negotiate the best terms he can obtain. The position can hardly be said to be satisfactory. The Law Commission have made certain recommendations to improve the lessee's position, which are considered at the end of this section[9]. However, as their proposals are part of the intended codification of the law of landlord and

5 *Becker v Partridge* [1966] 2 QB 155, [1966] 2 All ER 266, CA.
6 See pp. 144–150, ante.
7 *Williams v Spargo* [1893] WN 100. This assumes that the lease is at least fifteen years old.
8 LPA 1925, s. 44 (11); *Re Pursell and Deakin's Contract* [1893] WN 152.
9 See pp. 314–316, post.

tenant, it will be some time before their reforms are clothed in statutory form, and these could, of course, undergo revision before reaching the statute book.

Duty of solicitor. A solicitor acting for a proposed lessee or purchaser of an existing lease is not to be deemed guilty of neglect or breach of duty by reason of his omitting, in good faith, to negative in the contract the application of the statutory provisions or to insert others in their place[10]. Failure to insist on a right for his client to investigate a superior title does not, it seems, constitute professional negligence[11]. On the other hand where a right to inspect a superior lease exists, a solicitor failing to do so is guilty of negligence[12], as he would also appear to be if he allowed his client to sign a contract without advising him of the dangers involved in being unable to investigate a superior title.

(b) Sale of existing lease
The latest edition of The Law Society's form retains the condition, introduced in 1970, which purports to give effect to the current practice of requiring production of the freehold title on the acquisition of recently granted leases[13]. On the sale of a lease or underlease dated not more than fifteen years before the date of the contract, the vendor is required to deduce the freehold title and all other titles superior to the lease or underlease for at least fifteen years prior to the contract. This provision only operates where the lease or underlease, the subject of the contract, is for *a term exceeding twenty-one years.* If the vendor cannot comply with this obligation a Special Condition is necessary to negative the operation of the General Condition. Practitioners will need to be alive to the need to contract out of this condition. Regrettably this condition is drafted in such condensed terms that it is not always apparent what the purchaser can demand. On the sale of a recently granted lease, its effect is tolerably clear; it entitles the purchaser to investigate a title which is partly freehold and partly leasehold for at least fifteen years. Thus if on 1 January 1982, for example, V contracts to assign to P the unexpired residue of a term of 99 years granted by L in 1973, V must under the condition deduce L's freehold title commencing with a good root of title dated prior to 1967. He does not have to deduce the devolution of the freehold title after the grant of the lease in 1973. On the sale of an underlease the position is somewhat confused. The clause clearly envisages that the purchaser of an underlease can call for production of both the freehold and leasehold titles, but its provisions become difficult to operate when the leasehold title out of which the underlease is created is itself more than fifteen years old[14].

Condition 8 (2) (a) of the same Conditions of Sale stipulates that in all cases the immediate title to the interest sold shall commence with the lease or underlease. The subsequent title will be deduced according to the general law; intermediate dealings can be ignored provided the title recommences with an assignment (or other suitable transaction) at least fifteen years old at the date of

---

10 LPA 1925, s. 182 (1).
11 Farrand, 133; cf. Walford, 113.
12 *Hill v Harris* [1965] 2 QB 601 at 618, [1965] 2 All ER 358 at 363, CA, per Russell LJ, criticised at (1965) 29 Conv (NS) 162–63.
13 LSC 8 (2) (a). The NCS leave the matter to be regulated by the Special Conditions, failing which the open contract rules apply.
14 Is it intended that the purchaser should also have a right to investigate the freehold title for fifteen years prior to the lease? It would seem desirable to regulate the respective rights of purchasers of leases, and purchasers of underleases, in separate clauses.

the contract. A purchaser can now no longer require the vendor, under Condition 8, to supply (at the vendor's expense) an abstract or copy of the immediately superior lease in all cases, even when the contract did not entitle him to require that superior title to be deduced (because e.g. the underlease was for less than twenty-one years).

The Conveyancing Lawyers' Conditions of Sale contain a provision similar in terms to Condition 8 (2) (a) just discussed. Similarly where the land is held under an underlease the vendor cannot be required to deduce the title to the superior leasehold title unless an abstract or copy thereof is in his possession or that of his mortgagee. As to the freehold title, these Conditions impose on the vendor or leasehold property a duty to deduce the freehold title only if the Special Conditions of Sale so provide. See in particular General Condition 6 (4) and (5).

3. Notice

This statutory restriction on the lessee's right to investigate the superior title raises important problems in the field of notice. Prior to 1926 under the rule in *Patman v Harland*[15] an intending lessee or assign was fixed with constructive notice of matters or defects which he would have discovered had he investigated the superior title, notwithstanding that he was statutorily precluded from calling for such title. He was held to have accepted the consequences of not contracting out of the statute.

This rather illogical rule has been abrogated by s. 44 (5) of the Law of Property Act 1925, which enacts that an intending lessee or assign who, by virtue of the statutory restrictions, is unable to call for the superior title, is not

> 'deemed to be affected with notice of any matter or thing of which, if he had contracted that such title should be furnished, he might have had notice.'

Whilst securing a measure of protection for lessees, this rule has been said to provide a remedy worse than the disease by creating insecurity of property[16]; it may result in the destruction of third party rights leaving the third party without any effective means of protection. Suppose X, the owner of a freehold property subject to a pre-1926 covenant prohibiting its use for any purpose other than as a private dwellinghouse, leases the property to Y for seven years. Y opens an art school on the premises[17]. Under s. 44 (5) Y's inability to investigate X's freehold title does not fix him with constructive notice of the covenant and, assuming he has no actual notice, he takes free from it. Thus the person entitled to the benefit of the covenant ceases, through no fault of his own, to be able to enforce it against Y and his successors. Y would be bound if he had *actual* notice of the restriction; the burden of establishing notice lies on the person seeking to enforce the covenant[18].

---

15 (1881) 17 Ch D 353, (decided on the Vendor and Purchaser Act 1874, s. 2 (1)); *Imray v Oakshette* [1897] 2 QB 218, CA.
16 M & W, 707.
17 These are basically the facts of *Patman v Harland* (1881) 17 Ch D 353, where the covenantee obtained an injunction against Y. As to the position where a post-1925 restriction is concerned, see p. 308, post.
18 *Shears v Wells* [1936] 1 All ER 832.

Depending on the wording of the covenant, the covenantee may not even have any remedy against X. A person under a covenant not to use property in a particular way cannot commit a breach thereof except by his own act or that of his agent and the lessee, Y, is not X's agent[19]. Furthermore if X is a successor from the original covenantor, he is not bound at law, for the burden does not pass. Equity will not grant any injunction against X who is not in possession, and since he is only bound on the principle of *Tulk v Moxhay*[20] the court will not compel him to do anything which will involve him in expense (in the present context bringing an action against Y)[1].

(a) Limitations on s. 44 (5)

The protection afforded by the subsection is not as comprehensive as appears at first sight. It does not relieve a lessee from constructive notice of any matter or thing discoverable on inspection of the property, or by investigating such title as he is entitled to call for either by virtue of the statute or under the contract. Thus an intending underlessee who fails to inspect the head lease cannot shelter behind sub-s. (5).

In particular, and this is the most serious limitation on its operation, s. 44 (5), notwithstanding its unqualified language, must be read subject to s. 198 (1) of the same Act, so that a lessee is affected with notice of all land charges registered under the Land Charges Act 1972[2]. In relation to registered incumbrances (e.g. a post-1925 restrictive covenant), the protection afforded by sub-s. (5) is illusory. An effective search can only be made if the lessee investigates the freehold title, which the statute forbids in the absence of any contractual provision to the contrary. He may therefore be bound by a registered charge which he has no means of discovering. Thus the old rule in *Patman v Harland* still lives on[3].

(b) Law of Property Act 1969

This Act, though providing for compensation in certain cases for loss due to undisclosed registered land charges, does not apply to any charge affecting a reversionary title (freehold or leasehold) which a lessee or assignee is *precluded by statute from investigating*[4]. The Law Commission felt that the present hardship stemmed from a general rule of long standing, rather than from the inadequacies of the registration system established by the Land Charges Act 1925[5]. Yet there appears little justification for excluding a right to compensation in cases where the superior title is actually investigated under a contractual right[6].

---

19   *Wilson v Twamley* [1904] 2 KB 99, CA; *Berton v Alliance Economic Investment Co Ltd* [1922] 1 KB 742 at 759, CA, per Atkin LJ.
20   (1848) 2 Ph 774.
1   *Hall v Ewin* (1887) 37 Ch D 74, CA; *Atkin v Rose* [1923] 1 Ch 522 at 534, per Lawrence J.
2   *White v Bijou Mansions Ltd* [1937] Ch 610 at 621, [1937] 3 All ER 269 at 273, per Simonds J (a case on registered land, see p. 351, post; affd on other grounds, [1938] Ch 351, [1938] 1 All ER 546, CA. This dictum appears to be the sole authority on the point, but it is accepted as correct by almost all commentators: M & W, 707; Emmet, 192; Williams, *Title*, 569, note 7; contra (1938) 3 Conv (NS) 116.
3   The effect of the Law Commission's recent proposals, if implemented, would be to give the lessee a remedy against his lessor if he failed to disclose to him the existence of the registered charge. See p. 316, post.
4   See s. 25 (9) and the meaning ascribed to 'registered charge' in sub-s. (10). For the Act generally, see p. 285, ante, and p. 396, post.
5   Law Com. No. 18 (note 13, p. 285, ante), para. 37. But see note 3, above.
6   Cretney, 'Land Law and Conveyancing Reforms' (1969) 32 MLR 477, 485.

The Act does enable compensation to be claimed for loss occasioned by an undisclosed land charge registered against a title which the claimant is statutorily entitled to, and does in fact, investigate. Thus in appropriate circumstances an original underlessee[7] is covered in respect of some charge registered against the immediate leasehold interest, as is an assignee of a lease as regards a charge registered against a previous owner of the term.

(c) Restrictive covenants between lessor and lessee
The difficulties created by s. 198 (1) do not apply to restrictions between landlord and tenant, which are not capable of registration as land charges[8]. On the grant of an underlease, an underlessee who refrains from inspecting the head lease is deemed to have constructive notice of the covenants in it[9], but not a subsequent purchaser of the underlease, save where he fails to exercise a contractual right of inspection. An injunction may be awarded against an underlessee in breach of a negative covenant in the head lease, but not against the purchaser (save as above). When granting an underlease the underlessor should ensure that it contains covenants at least as stringent as those binding upon him, or obtain a covenant by the underlessee to observe and perform the covenants in the head lease and for indemnity[10].

4. Statutory assumptions

A vendor of property held under a lease does not discharge his obligation to show a good title if the lease has become forfeitable because of existing breaches of covenant, and the purchaser can rescind the contract[11]. In the absence of any contrary stipulation, the purchaser is entitled to be satisfied that all covenants have been performed to the date of completion. In what way can the vendor satisfy the purchaser on this point? The Law of Property Act 1925, s. 45 (2) enacts that on a sale of land held by lease (other than an underlease) the purchaser shall assume that the lease was duly granted and that, on production of the receipt for the last payment of rent due before completion, all covenants and provisions of the lease have been duly observed and performed up to the date of actual completion of the purchase[12]. On the sale of an underlease, similar assumptions apply under sub-s. (3), which extend to every superior lease. The presumption that the head lease was duly granted is a corollary of the rule precluding investigation of the freehold title[13].

(a) Rebuttable presumptions
These presumptions do not operate where the contrary appears. A purchaser discovering the existence of breaches of covenant by other means can object to

7 The grant of a lease derived out of a leasehold interest is a disposition expressly within the Act: s. 25 (9) (b).
8 LCA 1972, s. 2 (5) (ii), p. 391, post.
9 See *Becker v Partridge* [1966] 2 QB 155, [1966] 2 All ER 266, CA.
10 This is equally true on the grant of a lease by a freeholder. No statutory indemnity covenant is implied under the LPA 1925, s. 77, on a demise of land.
11 *Palmer v Goren* (1856) 25 LJ Ch 841 (breach of covenant to insure); *Becker v Partridge* [1966] 2 QB 155, [1966] 2 All ER 266, CA (covenant not to under-let without consent); *Pips (Leisure Productions) Ltd v Walton* (1980) 260 Estates Gazette 601 (writ for forfeiture issued) contract rescindible immediately.
12 That a purchaser of an underlease must assume the validity of the underlease is another argument against the view (see note 2, p. 304, ante) that he can call for the headlease.
13 *Becker v Partridge* [1966] 2 QB 155 at 169, [1966] 2 All ER 266 at 268, CA, per Danckwerts LJ. It is common to provide the last receipt is *conclusive*, post.

the title, unless prohibited from raising objection thereto by a bona fide and clear special condition. Even knowledge of the existence of a breach when entering into the contract was held in *Re Highett and Bird's Contract*[14] not to debar the purchaser's objection. Doubts have been cast upon the scope of this decision by the subsequent observations of one of the judges in that case, who sought to limit its application to cases where there was an express contract to make a good title[15]. Notwithstanding this gloss, the better view[16] is that a breach of covenant constitutes a removable[17] defect in title. The purchaser's notice does not constitute a waiver of his right to a good title, since he is entitled to assume that the vendor will remedy the breach before completion. A purchaser's right of objection is subject to any contractual provision to the contrary[18].

(b) Conclusive evidence

A condition requiring the purchaser to accept the last receipt for rent as *conclusive* evidence[19] of compliance with the covenants precludes objection to the title on account of breaches of covenant committed prior to the contract, or of continuing breaches[20]. It does not protect the vendor in relation to a breach of covenant committed subsequently to the contract, otherwise the purchaser might lose the property by the vendor's inadvertence or neglect[1]. A further limitation appears from *Beyfus v Lodge*[2] where the court refused to permit a vendor who knew about the breaches to rely on the condition. This illustrates the principle already encountered that a vendor cannot by his contract require the purchaser to assume the truth of something known to be false[3]. If the vendor is aware of the existence of a breach of covenant, he should disclose it and either bar any objection thereto or stipulate for its waiver to be assumed, though, again, the latter clause will only assist him if he has good reason for believing it to have been waived.

(c) Title of person giving receipt

Under the National Conditions of Sale[4] the purchaser must assume without proof that the person giving the receipt, though not the original lessor, is the

---

14 [1903] 1 Ch 287, CA, applying *Barnett v Wheeler* (1841) 7 M & W 364.
15 *Re Allen and Driscoll's Contract* [1904] 2 Ch 226 at 231, CA, per Romer LJ.
16 Walford, 124–25; 1 Prideaux's Precedents 274, note 72; Farrand, 136. Contra Williams, *Title*, 557 note 3, citing *Clarke v Coleman* [1895] WN 114, CA, a decision too briefly reported to be of much value. Cf. *Lockharts v Bernard Rosen & Co Ltd* [1922] 1 Ch 433 at 439, per Astbury J.
17 Not all breaches of covenant are susceptible of being remedied; e.g. a covenant not to use for illegal or immoral purposes: *Rugby School (Governors) v Tannahill* [1935] 1 KB 87, CA.
18 E.g. NCS 13 (3) and LSC 5 (2) are particularly relevant when breach of a repairing covenant is concerned. See further p. 172, ante. For the need to modify the vendor's statutory covenants for title if the property is out of repair, see p. 623, post.
19 Under contracts governed by the NCS, LSC, and Con Law CS, the statutory presumptions are left to regulate the parties' rights.
20 *Lawrie v Lees* (1880) 14 Ch D 249, CA; affd. (1881) 7 App Cas 19, HL. But the possibility of a forfeiture the day after completion might induce the court not to grant specific performance; see (1880) 14 Ch D 249 at 261, per Bramwell LJ.
 1 *Howell v Kightley* (1856) 21 Beav 331 at 336, per Romilly MR (possession deemed conclusive evidence of due performance). The contract may provide otherwise.
 2 [1925] Ch 350. The vendor was refused specific performance but was entitled to forfeit the deposit. But see now the LPA 1925, s. 49 (2), p. 583, post.
 3 Page 157, ante.
 4 Condition 11 (3). Similarly Con Law CS 8 (5) (a) and the LSC 8 (6).

reversioner expectant on the lease or underlease, or his authorised agent. This does not preclude objection if the reversioner's title is shown to be bad aliunde. Even in the absence of any such clause, it seems unlikely[5] that in normal cases the purchaser can insist on the reversionary title being traced from the original lessor to the person giving the receipt, for this would be in flat contradiction of the restrictions contained in s. 44. Exceptionally he can require deduction of the title to the reversion if the vendor alleges waiver of a breach of covenant[6], or where the purchaser establishes clear uncertainty as to the entitlement to the reversion[7].

5.   Licence to assign

Many leases for short terms are subject to a covenant not to assign, underlet or part with possession without the lessor's consent, such consent not to be unreasonably withheld[8]. On any sale of the lease, the problem of the lessor's consent arises. Depending on the circumstances it may be necessary to obtain more than one licence, e.g. on the sale of an underlease both the consent of the head lessor and of the immediate lessor may be required. A covenant against parting with possession without consent, which does not in express terms restrict an assignment, nevertheless requires consent to be obtained prior to any assignment (or subletting) of the premises[9]. However, provided the tenant retains the legal possession of the property, no breach of this covenant occurs merely by allowing another person to occupy[10].

(a) General points
Before considering the respective rights and obligations of the parties to the contract, it will assist to note a few general points.

(i) An assignment by the existing tenant (T) without the consent of the lessor (L) is effective to vest the residue of the leasehold term in a purchaser (P), but subject to the risk of forfeiture proceedings by L where the lease contains the usual forfeiture clause[11].

(ii) If T seeks consent but it is reasonably withheld, P is not safe in taking an assignment from T. Since an assignment in these circumstances will constitute a breach of covenant rendering the lease defeasible, T is unable to show a good title to the property. A refusal of consent on the ground that the proposed assignee might eventually be eligible to acquire the freehold of the demised premises ·under the Leasehold Reform Act 1967, has been held to be reasonable[12].

5   The point is not free from doubt. The conflicting authorities are considered by Walford, 120–21.
6   1 Dart, 172.
7   *Pegler v White* (1864) 33 Beav 403.
8   See the Landlord and Tenant Act 1927, s. 19 (1) which makes all covenants against assignment subject to this proviso, other than those expressed in absolute terms. Covenants against assignment were considered by the Law Commission in their Published Working Paper No. 25.
9   *Marks v Warren* [1979] 1 All ER 29; *Russell v Beecham* [1924] 1 KB 525.
10   *Jackson v Simons* [1923] 1 Ch 373.
11   See *Old Grovebury Manor Farm Ltd v W. Seymour Plant Sales and Hire Ltd (No. 2)* [1979] 3 All ER 504, CA. The statutory notice required by the LPA 1925, s. 146, should be served on P (the assignee), not on T.
12   *Norfolk Capital Group Ltd v Kitway Ltd* [1977] QB 506, [1976] 3 All ER 787, CA; *Bickel v Duke of Westminster* [1977] QB 517, [1976] 3 All ER 801, CA; *West Layton Ltd v Ford*

(iii) The vendor's (i.e. T's) execution of a declaration of trust of the premises in P's favour does not breach the covenant against assigning without consent[13], even if P enters into occupation. This device cannot be recommended as a satisfactory means of avoiding the necessity for L's consent. In the absence of any contractual stipulation to the contrary[14], T could never compel P to accept such a declaration in lieu of an assignment of the term.

(iv) If L unreasonably refuses consent, an assignment by T to P does not constitute a breach of covenant. Nevertheless specific performance will not normally be decreed against an unwilling purchaser.[15] P himself may obtain specific performance if the grounds of refusal are so unreasonable that T can clearly assign without consent[16]. In cases of wrongful refusal, the vendor's proper course is to obtain a declaration of unreasonableness from the court then launch specific performance proceedings[17].

(v) Section 19 (1) (b) of the Landlord and Tenant Act 1927, renders it unnecessary to obtain the landlord's consent where the lease is for more than forty years and is made in consideration of the erection or improvement of buildings, provided the assignment is effected more than seven years before the end of the term. Instead notice of every assignment must be given within six months.

(b) Vendor's duty to obtain licence
In the absence of contractual provisions, the vendor is under a duty to use his best endeavours to obtain the lessor's licence, but that is all. If having sought consent, it is refused, he is not obliged to risk legal proceedings to enforce consent[18], or allow the purchaser an opportunity of obtaining it[19]. The terms on which the licence is granted are not the purchaser's concern so long as they do not prejudice him. He cannot object on the ground that the vendor is required to deposit with the lessor a sum of money as security for dilapidations as a condition of obtaining the licence, though the vendor cannot require the purchaser to provide the security[20]. Under an open contract the purchaser must assist the vendor in the securing of the licence by using his best endeavours to satisfy the lessor's reasonable requirements, e.g. by providing adequate references[1]. This is made an express term in contracts governed by the standard Conditions of Sale.

[1979] 2 All ER 657, CA (proposed assignee entitled to statutory security of tenure). As to the reasonableness or otherwise of the refusal, see M & W, 695–97; see also the Sex Discrimination Act 1975, s. 31 (1), and the Race Relations Act 1976, s. 24 (1).

13   *Gentle v Faulkner* [1900] 2 QB 267, CA (trust for benefit of creditors).
14   As to which see *Pincott v Moorstons Ltd* [1937] 1 All ER 513.
15   *Re Marshall and Salt's Contract* [1900] 2 Ch 202. Cf. *White v Hay* (1895) 72 LT 281 (consent in modified form given to assignment to respectable undertenant; specific performance granted to underlessor since no risk of tenant's title being impeached).
16   *Curtis Moffat Ltd v Wheeler* [1929] 2 Ch 224 at 236, per Maugham J.
17   Cf. *Theodorou v Bloom* [1964] 2 All ER 399 (declaration obtained by purchaser). There is no claim to damages as against the landlord: *Rendall v Roberts and Stacey Ltd* (1959) 175 Estates Gazette 265.
18   *Lehmann v McArthur* (1868) 3 Ch App 496.
19   *Lipmans Wallpaper Ltd v Mason and Hodghton Ltd* [1969] 1 Ch 20 at 35, [1968] 1 All ER 1123 at 1129, per Goff J.
20   *Re Davies' Agreement, Davies v Fagarazzi* (1970) 21 P & CR 328.
1   *Sheggia v Gradwell* [1963] 3 All ER 114, at 121, CA, per Harman LJ.

(c) Failure to obtain licence

Considerable uncertainty exists as to whether the procuration of a licence to assign ranks is a matter of title or of conveyance[2]. Failure to obtain a licence constitutes a defect of title which the vendor cannot remove of his own volition; to this extent it is a matter of title. Yet it is generally agreed that it is not essential to procure the licence until the time for completion has arrived[3]. If it is not then available the purchaser can terminate the contract, recovering his deposit with interest and the costs of investigating the title[4]. The well known rule in *Bain v Fothergill*[5] precludes any recovery of damages for loss of the bargain, unless the vendor makes no attempt to obtain consent or himself actively induces its refusal[6]. As to the vendor's rights, *Lehmann v McArthur*[7] shows that once the completion date has passed he can treat the contract at an end and resist the purchaser's claim for specific performance, subject to his refunding the deposit with interest and costs.

The vendor's failure to obtain a licence is not a defect of title which the purchaser can waive in the expectation of being able to insist upon an assignment without consent[8]. A court of equity will not decree specific performance if it involves the vendor in breaking a pre-existing contract, nor is it within the purchaser's competence to waive a term which partially benefits the vendor[9].

(d) General Conditions

Both standard sets of General Conditions maintain the open contract position by requiring the vendor to use his best endeavours to obtain the licence at his own expense, the purchaser supplying such information and references as may reasonably be required[10]. This does not impose on a purchaser an absolute obligation to supply information, etc., that will satisfy the lessor[11], nor can the vendor require the purchaser to submit to an interview with the lessor's agents[12] or to provide a guarantee for payment of the rent[13].

The General Conditions also regulate the rights of the parties in the event of a failure to obtain the licence. The Law Society's Conditions enable *either* party to rescind the contract should it not be granted at least five days before the date of completion[14]. A purchaser who enters into occupation knowing that

2 See e.g. *Property and Bloodstock Ltd v Emerton* [1968] Ch 94 at 118, [1967] 3 All ER 321 at 329, CA, per Danckwerts LJ; *Ellis v Lawrence* (1969) 210 Estates Gazette 215, per Stamp J.
3 *Ellis v Rogers* (1885) 29 Ch D 661; *Day v Singleton* [1899] 2 Ch 320 at 327, CA, per Lindley MR; *Smith v Butler* [1900] 1 QB 694 at 699, CA, per Romer LJ.
4 *Re Marshall and Salt's Contract* [1900] 2 Ch 202. For the dangers of a premature rescission, see *Smith v Butler* [1900] 1 QB 694, CA.
5 (1874) LR 7 HL 158, p. 581, post.
6 *Day v Singleton* [1899] 2 Ch 330, CA.
7 (1868) 3 Ch App 496.
8 *Lipmans Wallpaper Ltd v Mason and Hodghton Ltd* [1969] 1 Ch 20, [1968] 1 All ER 1123.
9 *Warmington v Miller* [1973] 2 All ER 372 (specific performance of agreement to grant underlease refused where the covenant against assigning was absolute).
10 NCS 11 (5): LSC 8 (3). See also Con Law CS 9.
11 *Shires v Brock* (1977) 247 Estates Gazette 127, CA.
12 *Elfer v Beynon-Lewis* (1972) 222 Estates Gazette 1955.
13 *Butler v Croft* (1973) 27 P & CR 1.
14 Cf. the complicated procedure in Con Law CS 9 (3), (4) (service by either party after completion date of a notice that if licence is not forthcoming within fourteen days the contract may be rescinded by server within a further seven days' period). Under LSC 16 (2) the purchaser is limited to recovering his deposit with interest if there is four days' delay in repayment until repayment.

the licence has not yet been granted will not thereby be deemed to have waived the contractual right to rescind[15]; for possession would normally be taken on the assumption that the licence could, and would in due course, be obtained.

Under the National Conditions no date is specified. Moreover the right to rescind is confined to the vendor[16], who appears able to exercise his right even before the completion date, provided his best endeavours have already proved abortive and there are circumstances justifying him in treating the lessor's refusal as final. As for the purchaser he can serve a special notice to complete under Condition 22[17], once the completion date has passed without the licence being granted. This step is not strictly necessary. It is to be observed that the National Conditions provide that 'the sale is subject to the reversioner's licence being obtained, where necessary'. This clause does not make the contract conditional in the sense of preventing the formation of a vendor-purchaser relationship between the parties. But if despite the due performance by the parties of their respective obligations the necessary licence is not timeously obtained, the contract is discharged without either party being in breach[18]. The purchaser is entitled, therefore, to recover his deposit without having to take any steps under Condition 22 or otherwise to terminate the contract.

6.   Law Commission reforms

As we have seen the general law confers no right on an intending lessee to investigate the freehold title when a lease is granted by a fee simple owner. In effect he has to accept the lease blindly, unless the lessor agrees to make his title available for perusal. In theory this defect is offset to a limited degree by the lessor's covenant for quiet enjoyment. In reality this covenant (whether express or implied) provides little protection, far less than that afforded by a beneficial owner's covenants for title on a sale of freehold land (and, of course, a purchaser invariably investigates his vendor's title). Not surprisingly the Law Commission considered the present position to be far from satisfactory. In their Report on Obligations of Landlords and Tenants they put forward 'a recommendation for radical reform'. Every lease or tenancy should imply a new enlarged covenant for quiet enjoyment, which would have effect notwithstanding anything to the contrary in the lease[19].

Under the terms of this proposed covenant the lessee (T) would be entitled peacefully to hold and enjoy the demised premises for the purposes of the lease without interruption or disturbance by the lessor (L), or by any person lawfully asserting or enforcing a title or right whether derived from or superior to L's title. It would not extend to an interruption or disturbance by someone other than L in consequence of a 'defect in the title of the landlord' of which L had no notice or of which T did have notice at the time the lease was granted. The

15   *Butler v Croft* (1973) 27 P & CR 1.
16   NCS 11 (5), which applies Condition 10 (2). Notice of rescission under cl. 11 (5) can be validly given without first having to serve the ten days' notice required by cl. 10 (2): *Lipmans Wallpaper Ltd v Mason and Hodghton Ltd* [1969] 1 Ch 20, [1968] 1 All ER 1123 (a decision on similar clauses in the 17th edn). Like the LSC, NCS 10 (2) restricts the purchaser to recovery of his deposit, but without interest or costs of investigating the title. Cf. LSC 16 (2), note 14, p. 313, ante.
17   See p. 415, post.
18   *Shires v Brock* (1977) 247 Estates Gazette 127, CA; *Property and Bloodstock Ltd v Emerton* [1968] Ch 94 at 118, 124, [1967] 3 All ER 321 at 329, 333, CA, per Danckwerts and Sellers LJJ.
19   Law Com. No. 67, para. 62 and Draft Bill, cl. 5. For the effect of their recommendations when the land is registered, see p. 357, post.

expression 'defect in the title of the landlord' would be statutorily defined to include, for example, lack of title, lack of power to grant the lease (e.g. because of a covenant in a mortgage affecting the freehold), or a restriction affecting the use of the premises for the purpose of the lease[20]. Similarly 'notice' would be defined to exclude constructive or statutory notice in circumstances where L or T could not reasonably be expected to discover what it was of which he would otherwise be deemed to have notice. Compared with the present common law covenant, the suggested statutory covenant would afford much greater protection. In particular it would extend to the lawful acts of persons usually excluded from the scope of the common law covenant, such as persons acting under a title paramount[1].

This recommendation of the Law Commission merits more detailed comment. It will immediately be apparent that they do not propose a statutory right for T to investigate L's freehold title. Their aim is to encourage L to disclose his title in order to enable T to discover possible statutory defects in L's title, though with what consequence if T were to learn of a defect is not clear. He would not be affected with constructive notice of defects in L's title except in such title as L expressly contracted with T to furnish. This investigation would serve a different purpose from that undertaken on a sale of freehold land[2]. On such occasion the vendor deduces his title to establish that he owns, and is therefore able to convey, what he has contracted to sell. On the grant of a lease, however, L would furnish his title to protect himself from potential liability under the covenant to be implied in the lease. The Commission deliberately refrained from specifying what title L should make available to T. Their decision was prompted by the circumstance that the covenant would apply to every tenancy, and the majority of these would be of a kind which would not justify the trouble and expense of investigating the title. The Commission's Draft Bill talks about the landlord furnishing his title; see cl. 5 (4) (c). But what title would he be expected to furnish? Such title as would enable T to discover any defects in L's title. The point to note is this. L may not necessarily be able fully to protect himself from liability, simply by deducing his title for the statutory period laid down by s. 23 of the Law of Property Act 1969. This could put him in a difficult position. How much further back ought he to go? The Commission's Report affords no guidance. It is thought that the Draft Bill should contain a proviso limiting L's liability under the covenant to defects of title discoverable on an investigation of the relevant title as defined by s. 25 (10) of the Act of 1969[3], but of which T had no notice at the time of the lease.

The Draft Bill says nothing as to the manner in which L ought to furnish his title. It would not be necessary for his solicitor to submit an abstract of title or copies of relevant documents. Simply to make the title available for

20 Thus abrogating the decision in *Hill v Harris* [1965] 2 QB 601, [1965] 2 All ER 358, CA, p. 170, ante. See also *Stokes v Mixconcrete (Holdings) Ltd* (1978) 38 P & CR 488, CA.
1 On the grant of a sublease by T to S, T's covenant would prima facie cover disturbance by the assertion of a title superior to his own, e.g. by L. But unless T was able (but failed) to furnish S with L's title, he would not be deemed to have notice of any defect in L's title and consequently would not be liable to S, provided he (T) had no actual notice of it; see cl. 5 (2) (b) of the Draft Bill.
2 Law Com. No. 67, para. 45.
3 See note 14, p. 285, ante.

investigation at his offices would suffice. Nor would L be under any duty to reply to T's observations or requisitions on title, as the object of the exercise would merely be to enable T to acquire notice.

The Report does not deal with the question of remedies[4]. It is not clear, therefore, what T's precise rights would be if, on investigating the title, he discovered prior to the grant of the lease the existence of a statutory defect in title. In the absence of any new remedy created for T's benefit he could not repudiate the agreement for the lease, because the defect would not under the present law constitute a breach of any term of that agreement. Nor could he require L to remove the defect. Yet it seems unlikely that a court would decree specific performance against an intending lessee who found a defect and declined to proceed with the transaction, especially as T's notice would, if the lease were granted, debar a claim for damages for breach of covenant in the event of his enjoyment being disturbed as a result thereof. This consideration points to the need for the introduction of a new remedy, enabling T to repudiate the agreement, but without L being liable for damages or costs.

Finally, it is uncertain how the definition of 'notice' in the Draft Bill interrelates with the provisions of s. 25 of the Law of Property Act 1969. According to cl. 5 (4) (a) of the Bill, a person is not to be affected with notice by virtue of s. 198 of the Law of Property Act 1925, of any matter or thing registered under the Land Charges Act 1972, against the name of an estate owner of any estate superior to his own. The explanatory notes to this clause reveal that it is designed to prevent a person from being deemed to have statutory notice of anything which he could not discover because of his inability to search in the register, not having the names of the relevant estate owners. But this provision will not protect a freeholder who grants a lease. He will still have actual notice of any matter registered against his freehold title, as there will be no estate superior to his own. It will be immaterial that the land charge was registered against the name of some estate owner not appearing in the relevant title when he investigated the title at the time of his purchase. The lessee will not be deemed to have such notice, since the charge would affect an estate superior to his newly created leasehold estate. He could, therefore, recover damages for breach of the implied covenant, should his enjoyment be disturbed when the owner of the land charge enforces his rights. It is difficult to follow the Commission's thinking on this issue. It does not appear easily reconcilable with their views contained in an earlier Report[5], which recognised the deficiencies of the Land Charges Act 1925, and advocated changes now incorporated in s. 25 of the Act of 1969.

It is unlikely, as was suggested on page 306, that the Commission's recommendations will be implemented in the near future.

B Settlements

1. General scheme for settled land

The reader will already be conversant with the machinery and operation of the Settled Land Act 1925. It is not proposed to repeat in detail material that is

---

4 Save to state (para. 30) that until their proposals for new and reformed remedies take effect, breach of all the new implied covenants put forward in their Report would entitle the tenant to remedies which the law currently provides for breach of a covenant.

5 Law Com. No. 18.

fully covered in standard real property textbooks[6]. However certain aspects of this machinery are clearly relevant to conveyancing and they must be discussed.

It will be recalled that it is the policy of the Act that a purchaser of settled land should not concern himself with the beneficial interests arising under the settlement. To achieve this end the Act requires all post-1925 settlements to be created according to the statutory pattern and provides that a conveyance by the tenant for life (or statutory owner) operates to overreach the beneficial interests, thus giving the purchaser a title free from them, provided — and this is vital — the purchase money is paid to or by the direction of the trustees of the settlement or into court[7]. As to the mode of creation, two documents are necessary: a vesting deed and a trust instrument (or in the case of a testamentary settlement, the will). If effected in any other way the instrument does 'not operate to transfer or create a legal estate'[8].

(a) Vesting deed

The purchaser's main pre-occupation is with the vesting deed which contains all the information which he requires. It describes[9] the settled land, declares in whom the legal estate is vested and summarises those parts of the trust instrument of concern to him, such as naming the trustees of the settlement. As a general rule, so long as the land remains settled, the existence of a vesting deed is vital. Under s. 13 of the Settled Land Act 1925[10], no disposition of the legal estate can be effective until the execution of a vesting deed. The section expressly excludes from its application a disposition in favour of a purchaser without notice of the existence of a settlement, and a disposition by a personal representation, such as a sale by him of the land in the course of administration[11]. Moreover the purchaser must assume that the statements and particulars in the vesting deed are correct. He cannot call for production of the trust instrument to verify the accuracy of the information in the vesting deed[12]. Exceptionally the Act does permit the purchaser to peep behind the curtain to see the trust instrument[13]. But these are all abnormal situations, rarely encountered today, where for one reason or another no proper vesting deed is executed in the course of creating the settlement[14].

6 See M & W, Chap. 6; Cheshire, 165–193.
7 SLA 1925, ss. 18 (1) (b), 72 (2).
8 SLA 1925, s. 4 (1). It may constitute a trust instrument under s. 9 (1).
9 See SLA 1925, s. 5 (1).
10 As amended by the LP (Am) A 1926, Schedule.
11 See p. 336, post. Section 13 also does not apply to a conveyance made by virtue of the LP (Am) A 1926, s. 1, which in certain limited situations enables settled land to be dealt with as if it were not settled; see M & W, 319.
12 SLA 1925, s. 110 (2). For certain theoretical difficulties regarding this provision, see Emmet, 740–41; M & W, 307–08.
13 SLA 1925, s. 110 (2), proviso (a) – (d).
14 Examples may occur where the settlement comes into existence by virtue of some informal agreement (*Bannister v Bannister* [1948] 2 All ER 133, CA; *Binions v Evans* [1972] 1 Ch 359, [1972] 2 All ER 70, CA), or a court order in divorce proceedings (*Bacon v Bacon* [1947] P 151, [1947] 2 All ER 327; *Martin v Martin* [1978] Fam 12, [1977] 3 All ER 762, CA) or one made to give effect to an estoppel interest (*Griffiths v Williams* (1977) 248 Estates Gazette 947 at 949–50, per Goff LJ). This is an uncertain and rather confused area of law; see *Ivory v Palmer* [1975] ICR 340 at 347 CA, per Cairns LJ; Hornby, 'Tenancy for Life or Licence' (1977) 93 LQR 561; P.W. Smith 'Caveat Settled Land' [1978] Conv 229.

(b) Provisions for protection of purchaser

A sale of the settled land by the tenant for life must be made for the best consideration in money that can reasonably be obtained[15]. Any purported disposition of the land which is not authorised by the Act or by any additional powers in the settlement is void as a transfer of the legal estate in the land[16]. This provision apparently operates to avoid an unauthorised transaction even though the other party is unaware that the land is settled[17]. However considerable protection is conferred on a purchaser of settled land by s. 110 (1) of the Act[18]. This enacts that on a sale a purchaser dealing in good faith with a tenant for life or statutory owner is to be conclusively taken to have given the best consideration that could reasonably be obtained, and to have complied with all the requisitions of the Act. Provided he acts in good faith, he can claim this protection whether or not he knows that he is dealing with a tenant for life[19]. In this context good faith means, or at least involves, a belief that all is being regularly and properly done. The fact that he acquires the land at an undervalue is not, by itself, evidence of bad faith[20]. In the absence of good faith a transaction which does not comply with the requirements of the Act can be upset by the beneficiaries under the settlement, even though the land has subsequently become vested in a purchaser without notice of the defect[1].

2. Devolution of settled land

In tracing the devolution of settled land, and thereby indicating what documents should be abstracted, it will be helpful to discuss two typical situations. It will be assumed (unless the contrary is stated) that all appropriate steps have been taken and documents executed, so far as concerns a purchaser.

Illustration 1. Suppose T (a testator) dies leaving realty to A for life remainder to C absolutely. On a sale of the property by C after A's death, the following should be abstracted (together with earlier deeds to complete a proper chain of title).

(i) *Grant of Probate to T's personal representatives.* As previously noted, neither T's will nor the fact of his death should be abstracted, though the latter often is.

(ii) *Vesting assent by the personal representatives in favour of A.* This assent will contain the particulars required by the Settled Land Act 1925, s. 5. Thus the purchaser has notice of the existence of a settlement.

(iii) *Grant of Probate (or Letters of Administration) to A's estate.* On A's death the land ceases to be settled. The legal title vests in A's general personal

---

15 SLA 1925, s. 39 (1).
16 Ibid., s. 18 (1) (a).
17 *Weston v Henshaw* [1950] Ch 510 (mortgage). But see the next note.
18 *Re Morgan's Lease, Jones v Norsesowicz* [1972] Ch 1, [1971] 2 All ER 235, applying *Mogridge v Clapp* [1892] 3 Ch 382, CA, in preference to *Weston v Henshaw*, supra.
19 Per Kay LJ, in *Mogridge v Clapp*, supra, at 401 (a decision on the SLA 1882, s. 54). See e.g. *Chandler v Bradley* [1897] 1 Ch 315 (bribe paid to life tenant as inducement to grant lease; lessee not in good faith).
20 *Hurrell v Littlejohn* [1904] 1 Ch 689.
1   *Re Handman and Wilcox's Contract* [1902] 1 Ch 599, per Buckley J (assignment of lease not granted at best rent). The CA left this point open, but declined to force the title on an unwilling purchaser.

representatives[2] who must, after obtaining probate, vest it in the person next entitled i.e. C[3].

(iv) *Assent (or conveyance) to C.* As the settlement has now terminated, this document will make no mention of the trustees of the settlement. The purchaser must assume that the person in whom the land is thereby vested is entitled absolutely and beneficially to the land free from all limitations, powers and charges taking effect under the settlement[4]. In other words he must accept that the settlement is at an end and that he can safely pay his money to C.

Illustration 2. If the limitations in T's will were to A for life, remainder to B for life, remainder to C absolutely, the main difference in the devolution of the title would occur on A's death. Where land remains settled on the death of a life tenant[5], he is deemed, in the absence of any express appointment in their favour, to have appointed the trustees of the settlement as his special executors[6]. They should, therefore, take out a grant of probate to A's estate, limited to settled land, and then by means of a *vesting* assent (containing the relevant s. 5 particulars) transfer the legal estate to B. The subsequent links in the chain follow (iii) and (iv) of the previous illustration (B being substituted for A).

Failure to adopt the correct procedure on the death of A may not be fatal. A purchaser is entitled to rely on an order of the court (such as a grant of probate) even if made without jurisdiction[7]. A grant to the deceased life tenant's general personal representatives, instead of to the trustees of the settlement, does not constitute a defect in title provided the grant extends to settled land[8]. On the other hand a grant 'save and except settled land' does not vest the title of land remaining settled in the deceased's general representatives[9].

Should at any stage it have been necessary to appoint fresh trustees of the settlement, the deed of declaration should be abstracted, but not the deed of appointment which does not concern the purchaser. The deed of declaration merely declares who are the trustees consequent upon the appointment[10]. The purchaser must assume the truth of the particulars contained in it[11].

3. Termination of settlements

The purchaser, being ignorant of the beneficial interests, has no means of knowing whether the settlement has terminated. He lacks any assurance whether it is safe to deal with a person claiming to be absolutely entitled to land which, according to the purchaser's knowledge, is still settled. The Settled Land Act 1925, resolves this difficulty by requiring the trustees on request to

2 *Re Bridgett and Hayes' Contract* [1928] Ch 163.
3 SLA 1925, s. 7 (5).
4 SLA 1925, s. 110 (5).
5 Land continues to be settled where it ceases to be so under one settlement and immediately on the death in question becomes subject to another: *Re Taylor* [1929] P 260.
6 AEA 1925, s. 22. The grant to A's general representatives would be 'save and except settled land'.
7 LPA 1925, s. 204, applied in *Re Bridgett and Hayes' Contract* [1928] Ch 163, [1927] All ER Rep 191.
8 A purchaser from a person in whose favour the general representatives make a simple assent would appear to get a good title, notwithstanding the land remains settled.
9 See e.g. *Re Powell* [1935] P 114.
10 SLA 1925, s. 35.
11 SLA 1925, s. 110 (2) (d).

execute a deed of discharge declaring they are discharged from the trusts, whenever the settled land vests in a person free from all equitable interests and powers under the trust instrument[12]. Suppose X owns land subject only to a family charge in favour of Y. The land is settled by virtue of s. 1 (1) (v), and X has the legal estate vested in him[13]. On Y's death X becomes solely entitled, but a purchaser from him could only discover the termination of the settlement from the deed of discharge.

In two situations no deed of discharge is required. One occasion has already been encountered, the simple assent or conveyance not naming any settlement trustees. The other arises where land ceases to be settled before any vesting instrument is executed[14]; it is pointless to inform the purchaser of the termination of something the existence of which he is unaware.

C   Trusts for sale[15]

A trust for sale may exist by virtue of (i) some statutory provision, as in the case of beneficial co-ownership[16] and intestacies[17], or (ii) an express trust which may arise under a will or be created by a conveyance in circumstances where there would otherwise be a statutory trust. At common law a body corporate could not be a joint tenant[18]. By virtue of s. 1 (1) of the Bodies Corporate (Joint Tenancy) Act 1899, land can be conveyed to an individual and a body corporate, e.g. a limited company, as trustees for sale for themselves as joint tenants. On the dissolution of the company the property devolves on the surviving joint tenant.

1.   Conveyance by all trustees necessary

The essence of a trust for sale is that the trustees are under a *duty* to sell, though a statutory power to postpone sale exists unless a contrary intention appears[19]. Accordingly, whereas one trustee can call on his co-trustees to perform the duty and sell[20], all of them must be agreed if they are to exercise their power to postpone. In the case of a *statutory* trust for sale this principle must be read subject to s. 26 (3) of the Law of Property Act 1925. This subsection requires the trustees, so far as practicable, to consult with the beneficiaries and, so far as is consistent with the general interest of the rust, to give effect to their wishes. In the event of a dispute the wishes of the majority (according to the value of their combined interests) are to prevail. Thus a majority of beneficiaries who are also trustees for sale will normally[1] be able to insist on a postponement of the sale.

---

12   SLA 1925, s. 17.
13   SLA 1925, s. 20 (1), (ix).
14   Cf. *Re Alefounder's Will Trusts, Adnams v Alefounder* [1927] 1 Ch 360 (tenant in tail barring entail and disposing of fee simple).
15   For the Law Commission 's recommendations for co-ownership of the matrimonial home, see their 3rd Report on Family Property, Law Com. No. 86.
16   LPA 1925. s. 36 (1) (joint tenancy); SLA 1925, s. 36 (4) (tenancy in common). And see *Bull v Bull* [1955] 1 QB 234, [1955] 1 All ER 253, CA.
17   AEA 1925, s. 33.
18   *Law Guarantee and Trust Society Ltd v Bank of England* (1890) 24 QBD 406. A body corporate could be a tenant in common.
19   LPA 1925, s. 25 (1).
20   *Re Mayo, Mayo v Mayo* [1943] Ch 302. [1943] 2 All ER 440.
1   But see *Smith v Smith and Smith* (1975) 120 Sol Jo 100, post; *Jones v Jones* [1977] 2 All ER 231, CA.

Similarly a beneficial tenant in common (not being a trustee for sale) who is entitled to the larger share in the beneficial entitlement can effectively override the wishes of his co-tenant as to a sale[2]. The necessity to consult the beneficiaries arises not only when the trustees intend to sell, but also on the exercise of any statutory or extended power vested in them[3]. A purchaser is not concerned to see that the provisions of sub-s. (3) have been observed.

Section 26 (3) does not apply to an *express* trust for sale unless the contrary appears in the document of creation. It is not the practice to adopt sub-s. (3) into express trusts.

(a) Refusal to sell

One trustee for sale cannot convey trust land without the concurrence of his co-trustees, nor has he any implied authority on behalf of the others to enter into a binding contract to sell the property[4]. The Law of Property Act 1925, s. 30, provides a solution to the troublesome situation that arises when one trustee declines to agree to a proposed sale. It enacts that

'If the trustees for sale refuse to sell or to exercise any of the powers conferred by [ss. 28 or 29] . . . any person interested may apply to the court for a vesting or other order for giving effect to the proposed transaction . . . and the court may make such order as it thinks fit.'

In the exercise of its statutory discretion the court looks at all the circumstances to decide whether it would be inequitable to order a sale. This discretion is not fettered by s. 26 (3) of the Act[5]. When the property has been acquired for some specific purpose, e.g. to provide a home, which is still capable of being achieved, the court will not usually allow that purpose to be defeated by ordering a sale. This principle[6] has frequently been applied in disputes between spouses on the breakdown of the marriage (as to which see part (c) below). Disputes do, of course, arise in other situations. In *Re Buchanan-Wollaston's Conveyance*[7]

'A, B, C and D, each of whom owned separate but neighbouring properties, purchased a plot of land which they desired to retain as an open space. This land was conveyed to them as joint tenants, and they covenanted inter se to preserve the land as an open space. A later sold his own property and applied, against the opposition of B, C and D, to have the land sold. His application was rejected by the court. It was clearly inequitable to allow the voice of a trustee in breach of his obligation to prevail.'

2 See e.g. *Bull v Bull* [1955] 1 QB 234, [1955] 1 All ER 253, CA. If a sale is threatened he must seek an injunction to restrain a breach of trust; *Waller v Waller* [1967] 1 All ER 305 (sale of matrimonial home by single trustee restrained by wife who had contributed to its purchase). But see *Jones v Jones*, note 1, supra.
3 *Re Jones, Jones v Cusack-Smith* [1931] 1 Ch 375.
4 See *Keen v Mear* [1920] 2 Ch 574; *Watts v Spence* [1976] Ch 165; [1975] 2 All ER 528. See further P.W. Smith 'Co-Owners and Agency' [1980] Conv 191; *Malhotra v Choudhury* [1979] 1 All ER 186; *Cedar Holdings Ltd v Green* [1979] 3 All ER 117.
5 *Smith v Smith and Smith*, note 1, ante.
6 Which is equally applicable where the title to the land is registered.
7 [1939] Ch 738, [1939] 2 All ER 302; *Re Hyde's Conveyance* (1952) 102 L Jo 58; *Re Holliday (bankrupt)* [1980] 3 All ER 385, CA; *Re Evers Trust* [1980] 3 All ER 399, CA; *Dennis v McDonald* [1982] 1 All ER 590, CA; *Re Lowrie (a bankrupt)* [1981] 3 All ER 353.

Another not uncommon occasion for dispute arises when members of a family combine together to purchase a house as a residence for themselves. Should the house sharing arrangement not work satisfactorily so that one of the co-owners is forced to leave, the other who remains in occupation not unnaturally declines to concur in any sale of the house. Since the purpose of the trust has come to an end, the courts will generally order a sale. Thus in *Smith v Smith and Smith*[8] a house was bought as a home by and for a sister, her brother and his wife. After a family squabble for which the brother and his wife were more to blame, the sister left and sought an order for sale, which Goff J granted. It was not consistent with the general interests of the trust for two of the co-owners to insist on the house remaining unsold when it was not producing any income and was therefore of no benefit to the sister. To order a sale in such circumstances was not inequitable. Where appropriate the court will exercise its discretion in a manner that will facilitate the purchase of the property by the co-owner in occupation[9] or to pay rent[10]. Nevertheless, each case depends on its own special facts. In *Charlton v Lester*[11] the judge refused an order for sale on the application of two trustees, because the third (the mother of one of the applicants) had agreed to the purchase only on the basis of a clear understanding that she would always be allowed to keep the house as her home where she had lived as a protected tenant prior to its purchase.

(b) Form of order
Under s. 30 the court can make 'such order as it thinks fit'. The usual form of order is for the property to be sold with vacant possession coupled with an order for the reluctant trustee to concur in the sale. Should the defendant trustee be in occupation (as will often be the case) the court can require him to deliver up possession by a certain date[12]. This works more unfavourably towards an occupying trustee, because it results in his having to move out earlier than if he had simply been ordered to concur in the sale. An order of this type may be necessary to facilitate the sale if there is any likelihood that the trustee might be obstructive. In *Re John's Assignments Trusts*[13] Goff J included in his order an authority for the defendant, notwithstanding that he was a trustee, to take a tenancy of the property on such terms as might be agreed between him and his ex-wife who wanted the sale.

(c) Disputes between spouses[14]
On the breakdown of a marriage the courts have in several cases ordered a sale of the matrimonial home vested in the spouses as trustees for sale[15]. Yet the fact

---

8   (1975) 120 Sol Jo 100; *Mudge v Gibbon* (1962) 181 Estate Gazette 275 (sale ordered; express agreement for sale in the event of dispute).
9   See *Ali v Hussein* (1974) 231 Estates Gazette 372; *Pariser v Wilson* (1973) 229 Estates Gazette 786 (option to purchase included in order by consent).
10 *Dennis v McDonald* [1982] 1 All ER 590, CA; cf. *Jones v Jones*, note 11, infra.
11 (1976) 238 Estates Gazette 115; *Jones (AE) v F W Jones* [1977] 2 All ER 231, (father providing three quarters of purchase price and buying house in own name for son and his family to live in; person entitled to house on father's death refused order for sale).
12 *Re McCarthy (a bankrupt)* [1975] 2 All ER 857.
13 [1970] 2 All ER 210.
14 See Miller, 'Sale of the Matrimonial Home' [1978] Conv 301.
15 *Jones v Challenger* [1961] 1 QB 176, [1960] 1 All ER 785, CA; *Rawlings v Rawlings* [1964] P 398, [1964] 2 All ER 804, CA; *Jackson v Jackson* [1971] 3 All ER 774, CA. See *Ward v Ward and Greene* [1980] 1 All ER 176, CA; and Matrimonial Causes Act 1973, s. 24A added by Matrimonial Homes and Property Act 1981.

that a house, jointly owned, has ceased to be the matrimonial home because the spouses have separated or are divorced does not always point to a failure of the purpose of the trust, justifying a sale. In *Bedson v Bedson*[16] a wife's application for sale was rejected because the property was not only the home but also the husband's business premises; to order a sale in such circumstances would destroy his means of livelihood and support of his family. Similarly an order for sale has been refused because of the necessity to preserve the house as a home for the children[17]. Nowadays in cases where a sale is sought after a divorce, the welfare of the family as a whole, particularly the children, is considered to be the primary factor in determining the issue[18]. A rather novel view was propounded in *Hayward v Hayward*[19]. According to Walton J, when one party to a marriage provided all the purchase money and arranged for the house to be conveyed into the names of the spouses as beneficial joint tenants[20], it could be inferred that individual as well as collective provision of a home was intended. Therefore, should either spouse walk out, that party could not ask for execution of the trusts so long as the other wished to remain in occupation.

(i) *Alternative proceedings.* Instead of proceeding under s. 30, the spouses can take advantage of s. 17 of the Married Women's Property Act 1882. By virtue of this any question between husband and wife as to the title to or possession of property may be summarily referred by either of them to a judge, who may make such order respecting the property as he thinks fit, including an order for its sale[1]. Section 17 is a procedural provision only. The court has no power to alter, merely to declare, property rights[2]. But having declared the spouses' respective shares in the property the court can, in the event of a divorce, order one party to transfer his or her share to the other at the price defined by the declared value of the transferor's share[3]. The s. 17 procedure has been made applicable[4] to property disputes between betrothed persons, provided proceedings are instituted within three years of the termination of the agreement to marry. It cannot, of course, be used to resolve disputes affecting property owned jointly by a man and his mistress. Any disagreement as to the sale of such property must be determined under s. 30 of the Law of Property Act 1925.

(ii) *Sale sought in divorce proceedings.* Almost invariably in practice when a sale of the matrimonial home is desired by one only of the spouses, it will, *and*

---

16 [1965] 2 QB 666, [1965] 3 All ER 307, CA. See also *P v P* [1978] 3 All ER 70.
17 *Brown v Brown* (1974) 119 Sol Jo 166, CA; *Rawlings v Rawlings*, note 15 ante, at 419 and 814, per Salmon LJ. Cf. *Burke v Burke* [1974] 2 All ER 944, CA, on the purely property aspect of the problem; *Re Holliday* [1980] 3 All ER 385, CA, and *Re Evers Trust* [1980] 3 All ER 399, CA. These last two cases laid down clear guidelines for exercising the discretion.
18 *Williams v Williams* [1976] Ch 278, [1977] 1 All ER 28, CA, p. 324, post. In *Re Holliday* and *Re Evers Trust*, supra, the application was refused with regard to an immediate sale. In the former it was postponed until the children reached seventeen with liberty to apply. In the latter it was dismissed with the hint of re-application later if circumstances altered. *Re Holliday* has been described as 'exceptional'. See *Re Lowrie* [1981] 3 All ER 353.
19 (1974) 237 Estates Gazette 577.
20 Contra, if the trusts were for the spouses as beneficial tenants in common, when the inferred purpose would be restricted to that of providing a matrimonial home only.
1   See the Matrimonial Causes (Property and Maintenance) Act 1958, s. 7 (7).
2   *Pettitt v Pettitt* [1970] AC 777, [1969] 2 All ER 385, HL.
3   *Bothe v Amos* [1976] Fam 46, [1975] 2 All ER 321, CA.
4   By the Law Reform (Miscellaneous Provisions) Act 1970, s. 2.

should[5], be sought in divorce proceedings in conjunction with an application for matrimonial relief under ss. 23 and 24 of the Matrimonial Causes Act 1973. These sections confer powers on the court to order financial provision and the adjustment of property rights on divorce, nullity and judicial separation. No express power to order a sale was included. Despite this the Court of Appeal has indicated in *Ward v Ward and Greene*[6] that when the court is dealing with a claim for relief under ss. 23 and 24, it can order a sale where the circumstances justify it, without the need for a separate application being made under either s. 17 of the Act of 1882 or s. 30. In deciding whether or not to order a sale the court must take account of the wide powers of transfer and adjustment available under the matrimonial property regime now enshrined in the Act of 1973. Very considerable weight is attached to the fact that the matrimonial home was bought as a home where the family was to be reared. It is not simply property to be sold, or an investment to be realised for cash. The court will endeavour to preserve it as a home for the remaining partner and the children, seeking at the same time to give the out-going partner such compensation by way of a charge or of being bought out as is reasonable in the circumstances[7]. Indeed, where the only available asset is the matrimonial home, it has been urged that the most important factor to be taken into account is the need for both parties to have a home in which to live[8]. Thus, if the spouse seeking a sale is living elsewhere in secure accommodation, the court may well decline to order a sale, even though there are no children of the marriage. The court now has a statutory power to order sale on divorce[9].

Exceptionally there may still occur situations when a spouse has to initiate proceedings under either s. 30 or s. 17, e.g. where the parties separate but have no intention of obtaining a divorce or judicial separation, or because the spouse seeking a sale has remarried before applying for relief under ss. 23 and 24 of the Matrimonial Causes Act 1973[10].

(d) Bankruptcy of spouse

On the bankruptcy of one of the spouses in whom property is vested as beneficial co-owners, the trustee in bankruptcy as a 'person interested' can apply for an order for sale under s. 30 of the Law of Property Act 1925. No rule of law exists that the court must exercise its discretion in his favour. Usually it will do so. The trustee has a statutory duty to realise the bankrupt's assets for the benefit of his creditors, and his voice will prevail in equity[11]. The approach adopted by the courts is the same whether the marriage is still subsisting or not.

---

5   See *Williams v Williams* [1976] Ch 278, [1977] 1 All ER 28, CA; *Fielding v Fielding* [1978] 1 All ER 267, CA. But see *Re Holliday* [1980] 3 All ER 385, CA, where it was stated that the case should be transferred to the Family Division if no proceedings were contemplated thereon.

6   [1980] 1 All ER 176 (note) per Ormrod LJ. See (1979) 76 LS Gaz 1060, 1285.

7   *Williams v Williams*, note 5, ante, at 285 and 30, per Lord Denning MR.

8   *Martin v Martin* [1977] 3 All ER 762 at 765, CA, per Stamp LJ.

9   Matrimonial Causes Act 1973, s. 24A added by Matrimonial Homes and Property Act 1981 (in effect from 1 October 1981).

10   Matrimonial Causes Act 1973, s. 28 (3). The application must be initiated (though not necessarily determined) before re-marriage: *Jackson v Jackson* [1973] Fam 99, [1973] 2 All ER 395. Cf. *Kowalczuk v Kowalczuk* [1973] 2 All ER 1042, CA.

11   *Re Turner (a bankrupt)* [1975] 1 All ER 5; *Re McCarthy (a bankrupt)* [1975] 2 All ER 857. A judgment creditor in whose favour the court imposes a charging order on the debtor's interest under a trust for sale (see the Charging Orders Act 1979, s. 2 (1) (a) (ii)) may be a 'person interested' within the LPA 1925, s. 30. If so, he can seek an order for the sale of the land itself (as distinct from the debtor's beneficial interest). Unlike a trustee in

Unlike cases when a sale is sought following divorce, the welfare of any children of the marriage is not such a vital consideration in deciding whether the home should be sold[12]. Nevertheless the creditors rights to realisation are not absolute and in appropriate circumstances the application for sale can be postponed as in any other matrimonial case[13]. The court is not bound to consider the power to transfer under the Matrimonial Causes Act 1973[14] but could take into consideration the 'usual' matrimonial factors. On a sale of the property the bankrupt's spouse is prima facie entitled to her (or his) share of the proceeds of sale, subject always to the operation of s. 42 of the Bankruptcy Act 1914, where relevant[15]. Similar considerations now will apply as between man and mistress[16].

(e) Trusts for sale created by will
A trust for sale not infrequently arises under the terms of a will. A testator may leave land on trust for sale and provide for the proceeds to be divided between certain beneficiaries. Here the prima facie object of the trust is the sale of the property. An occupying beneficiary under the trust cannot restrain a sale by the trustees, who are entitled to an order of possession against him[17]. The position is different when the beneficiary (e.g. the deceased's widow) has the right to occupy under a residence clause in the will, which directs that the property is not to be sold during her lifetime (or widowhood) without her written consent. Should a proposed sale by the trustees be opposed by the widow, resort must be had to s. 30 of the Law of Property Act 1925[18]. The widow cannot, however, prevent a sale if the executors require to dispose of the property for the payment of debts, i.e. for administration purposes[19].

2.   Statutory provisions protecting purchasers

(a) Generally
Various statutory provisions exist for the protection of a purchaser buying from trustees for sale. The trust is deemed to be subsisting until the land has been conveyed to or under the direction of the beneficiaries[20]. The purchaser can therefore rely on the trust notwithstanding notice that the proceeds of sale have become absolutely vested in a sole beneficiary of full age. But when the entire legal and equitable interests have become vested in a single person, the trust for sale ceases to exist[1]. As we have seen[2], in the case of a statutory trust for sale the

bankruptcy, a judgment creditor owes no duty to the general body of creditors. Accordingly he may well have no better right to defeat the underlying purpose of the trust than the debtor might have. See Law Com. No. 74, Charging Orders, paras. 71–72. Section 2 (1) (a) (ii) abrogates the decision in *Irani Finance Ltd v Singh* [1971] Ch 59, [1970] 3 All ER 199, CA.

12   *Re Bailey (a bankrupt)* [1977] 2 All ER 26.
13   *Re Holliday* [1980] 3 All ER 385, CA.
14   Section 24.
15   For examples, see *Re Densham (a bankrupt)* [1975] 3 All ER 726; *Re Windle (a bankrupt)* [1975] 3 All ER 987.
16   See *Re Evers Trust* [1980] 3 All ER 399.
17   *Barclay v Barclay* [1970] 2 QB 677, [1970] 2 All ER 676, CA.
18   Cf. *Newcomb v Miller* (1962) 186 Estates Gazette 331 (provision for occupation pending execution of trust; sale decreed).
19   See p. 330, post.
20   LPA 1925, s. 23.
 1   *Re Cook, Beck v Grant* [1948] Ch 212, [1948] 1 All ER 231.
 2   See p. 321, ante. See *National Westminster Bank Ltd v Stockman* [1981] 1 All ER 800.

purchaser is not concerned to see that the sale by the trustees accords with the beneficiaries' wishes. If consents are made requisite to the execution of a trust for sale, the consent of any two persons is deemed sufficient[3].

(b) Overreaching[4]

A purchaser of a legal estate from trustees for sale is not concerned with the trusts affecting the proceeds of sale[5], even though he has express notice of them because they are declared by the instrument creating the trust for sale[6]. As a matter of strict conveyancing practice it may be better to have two deeds, but this counsel of perfection is virtually ignored today and it is commonplace to declare the beneficial interests in the conveyance of the land to the trustees, at least where they hold for themselves in equity[7].

A conveyance in execution of the trust for sale overreaches all equitable interests arising thereunder, provided the proceeds of sale are 'paid to or applied by the direction of [not] fewer than two persons as trustees for sale' or a trust corporation[8]. A purchaser who, knowing of the existence of the trust, fails to comply with this requirement does not obtain a good title and takes subject to the rights of the beneficiaries. There is no power to overreach *prior* legal rights, nor, it seems, prior equitable rights, notwithstanding that trustees for sale have all the powers of a tenant for life under the Settled Land Act 1925[9]. A sole trustee for sale can pass a good title in a transaction where no capital money arises. He can grant a valid lease provided no fine is taken, or effect an exchange of land where no equality money is received.

When an appointment of a new trustee becomes necessary so as to comply with s. 27 (2), the appointment ought preferably to be contained in a separate deed, and not incorporated in the conveyance to the purchaser, particularly when the trust for sale relates to other land. A sound case can be made for effecting the appointment by a separate deed in every case, though it is common practice to include it in the purchase deed[10].

3.   Sale by sole trustee for sale

The safeguard of having at least two trustees or a trust corporation for the receipt of capital money has been called a fairly obvious reform[11]. A purchaser cognisant of the trust for sale will always insist on compliance with the statutory requirement, unless the Law of Property (Joint Tenants) Act 1964, which is considered in the next section is applicable. But many situations arise where a

3   LPA 1925, s. 26 (1).
4   See in this context [1980] Conv 427 (Sydenham) and [1981] Conv 219 (Jill Martin).
5   LPA 1925, s. 27 (1).
6   Emmet, 803.
7   See p. 532, post.
8   LPA 1925, ss. 2 (1) (ii), 27 (2), as amended by the LP (Am) A 1926, Schedule. Strictly the beneficiaries interests are overreachable ab initio without the aid of any statute for under the doctrine of conversion their rights attach to the proceeds, not to the land. See M & W, 379; *Irani Finance Ltd v Singh* [1971] Ch 59 at 79–80, [1970] 3 All ER 199 at 203, CA, per Cross LJ; *Cedar Holdings Ltd v Green* [1979] 3 All ER 117, CA. The last case was however disapproved in *Williams and Glyn's Bank Ltd v Boland* [1980] 2 All ER 408 at 415, HL, per Lord Wilberforce.
9   LPA 1925, s. 28 (1); *Re Ryder and Steadman's Contract* [1927] 2 Ch 62 at 82, per Sargant LJ. Cf. LPA 1925, s. 2 (2) (ad hoc trust for sale).
10   See the correspondence in (1979) 123 Sol Jo 14, 30, 62, 77.
11   1 W & C (12th edn) 268. For the right of a sole personal representative to give a valid receipt, see p. 336, post.

trust for sale exists, of which a purchaser is completely unaware. An apparent sole owner may in fact be a trustee for sale because e.g. his spouse has contributed to the purchase price[12], or to the making of substantial improvements to the property[13]. The application of s. 27 (2) of the Law of Property Act 1925, to this kind of situation has never been directly before the courts. It is significant that no paralysing provision[14] exists to render ineffective a conveyance not complying with s. 27 (2). The generally accepted view is that a conveyance of land by a sole trustee for sale does vest the legal title in the purchaser. But should he have notice, actual or constructive, of the equitable interests existing behind the trust, he will take subject to those interests[15]. What constitutes notice in this situation is somewhat problematical, and is fully considered in Chapter 14. A brief mention of the nature of the difficulty will not, however, be amiss at this point.

The main problem in the case of unregistered land concerns the extent to which a purchaser is to be deemed to have constructive notice of the beneficiary's interest because the latter is in occupation of the property, albeit jointly with the vendor. In *Caunce v Caunce*[16] Stamp J held that a purchaser (or mortgagee) from an occupying vendor (or mortgagor) is not affected with notice of the equitable interests of any other person[17] who may be resident on the property and whose presence is wholly consistent with the title offered. If the vendor who is himself in occupation contracts to sell the land with vacant possession on completion (the usual case), then the mere presence on the land of some other person implies nothing to negative the title offered and demands no explanation. Unfortunately the correctness of this eminently sensible decision has been seriously doubted, wrongly it is conceived[18], by the Court of Appeal in *Hodgson v Marks*[19] and in *Williams and Glyn's Bank Ltd v Boland*[20], two cases involving registered land. If it is indeed the law that occupation fixes a purchaser with constructive notice of the beneficiary's rights, the purchaser can discover their existence only by asking what may often prove to be delicate and embarrassing inquiries of both the vendor and the other occupier. Yet the House of Lords (in a husband and wife context) has exempted a purchaser from any duty to make inquiries of this nature[1]. Moreover a purchaser who is obliged

---

12 *Waller v Waller* [1967] 1 All ER 306; *Bull v Bull* [1955] 1 QB 234, [1955] 1 All ER 253, CA (mother and son).

13 See the Matrimonial Proceedings and Property Act 1970, s. 37. See also *Hussey v Palmer* [1972] 3 All ER 744, CA (mother-in-law paying for extension to house owned by son-in-law).

14 Cf. SLA 1925, s. 18 (1) (a). But see *Taylor v Taylor* [1968] 1 All ER 843 at 847, CA, per Danckwerts LJ.

15 *Williams and Glyn's Bank Ltd v Boland* [1979] Ch 312 at 331, [1979] 2 All ER 697 at 708, CA, per Lord Denning MR; *Caunce v Caunce,* [1969] 1 All ER 722; Garner, 'A Single Trustee for Sale' (1969) 33 Conv (NS) 240. If the purchaser has notice, he will hold the land on trust for sale for himself and the beneficiary.

16 [1969] 1 All ER 722 (non-inquiring mortgagee not bound by spouse's equitable interest). It is doubtful whether this case can survive the *Boland* case, infra.

17 Whether the vendor's spouse, his 'father, Uncle Harry or Aunt Matilda': per Stamp J, at 728.

18 For full reasons, see p. 57, ante.

19 [1971] Ch 892, [1971] 2 All ER 684, CA, p. 51, ante.

20 Note 15, ante. In the House of Lords the speeches expressly confined themselves to the registered land position leaving the unregistered land position in a somewhat difficult state. See (1980) Sol Jo 124 (P.W. Smith) and [1980] Conv 361 at 363–367 (Jill Martin).

1 *National Provincial Bank Ltd v Ainsworth* [1965] AC 1175, [1965] 2 All ER 472, especially at 1235, 1250, and 486, 496, per Lords Upjohn and Wilberforce.

to inquire of the occupier in circumstances such as these has, in effect, to investigate the equitable title to the land — a consequence in direct conflict with one of the prime objectives of the 1925 property legislation. Unless the principle of *Caunce's* case is upheld by a superior court, a purchaser from a single vendor in occupation of the land can never safely rely on his investigation of the documentary title, which will not, of course, reveal the existence of any trust for sale. To be certain of obtaining a good title from the vendor, he must in every case go beyond the documentary evidence and by means of additional inquiries must satisfy himself that no trust for sale exists. This can hardly have been what the framers of our legislation had in mind. It is otherwise when the vendor is not in occupation, as *Caunce's* case recognised. Then the general rule as to constructive notice applies and the purchaser ignores the occupier's presence at his peril[2]. The question of what to do if the purchaser is satisfied a trust for sale exists then arises[3]. A purchaser could not be forced to take a conveyance from the sole trustee with a third party joining in[4]. He should insist on the appointment of a further trustee to obtain[5] a good receipt and an overreaching conveyance.

4.   Sale by surviving trustee for sale

Once the legal estate and the equitable interests existing under a trust for sale have become vested in one and the same person in the same right, the trust for sale determines[6]. The Law of Property (Amendment) Act 1926, catered for this situation by adding to s. 36 (2) of the main Act a proviso that nothing in the Act should affect the right of a survivor of joint tenants, who was *solely and beneficially* interested, to deal with the legal estate as if it were not held on trust for sale[7]. However a purchaser could never be sure that the vendor was solely and beneficially interested; there might have been a severance in equity, unknown to the surviving joint tenant, and notwithstanding the Act it became the practice to preserve the trust for sale by appointing a new trustee.

(a) Law of Property (Joint Tenants) Act 1964[8]
This procedure need no longer be adopted. The Law of Property (Joint Tenants) Act 1964, s. 1, enacts that in favour of a purchaser of a legal estate a survivor of two or more joint tenants shall 'be *deemed* to be solely and beneficially interested if he conveys as beneficial owner or the conveyance includes a statement that he is so interested'. If the survivor has himself died, his personal representative can include in the conveyance a statement of the survivor's beneficial entitlement[9]. The Act is retrospective, being deemed to have come into operation on 1 January 1926[10].

2   [1969] 1 All ER 722 at 728.
3   In the case of possible registered land difficulties see the articles cited at note 4, p. 326, ante with regard to overreaching of overriding interests.
4   LPA 1925, s. 42.
5   Preferably the other beneficiary to show the consent of that beneficiary. If this is not done the purchaser may become involved in proceedings restraining the sale.
6   *Re Cook, Beck v Grant* [1948] Ch 212, [1948] 1 All ER 231.
7   According to Harman J, in *Re Cook, Beck v Grant* [1948] Ch 212 at 214, [1948] 1 All ER 231 at 232, this sentence was an afterthought introduced ex cautela because of some danger, real or imaginary, thought to exist after the Act of 1925 had come into force.
8   See P.W. Smith 'The Chains of Trusteeship' (1977) 41 Conv (NS) 423.
9   See s. 1 (2). This does not enable him to convey as beneficial owner.
10   Section 2.

The Act does not apply in the following situations:

(i)   if a memorandum of severance has been endorsed on or annexed to the conveyance to the joint tenants—this notifies the purchaser that the survivor is not solely and beneficially interested and reminds him of the need to have another trustee appointed;

(ii)   if a bankruptcy petition or receiving order has been registered under the Land Charges Act 1972[11];

(iii) where the title to the land is registered[12].

The existence of a severance in equity will not prevent a purchaser obtaining a good title from a surviving joint tenant conveyancing as beneficial owner, provided no notice of severance is annexed to the conveyance. The Act was not intended to be applicable where there never was a joint tenancy in equity[13]. Thus, suppose land has been conveyed to A and B, and the conveyance expressly declares that they hold the land as tenants in common in equity. On A's death B cannot make a good title under the Act, for the conveyance discloses that he and A held as tenants in common. Should B wish to sell as a beneficial owner, he will have to establish his right to do so. He may, for example, show that he has succeeded to A's share under the terms of A's will. On the other hand, if the conveyance to A and B is silent as to their beneficial entitlement, B can (it seems) utilise the Act, though this is not what Parliament envisaged. This point is elaborated in the next paragraph.

(b) Difficulties raised by the Act
Though laudably brief, the Act is hardly a model of good draftsmanship[14]. It creates several problems. It is uncertain whether a purchaser can safely rely on the Act where no memorandum is endorsed, but he has express notice of severance from other sources. Perhaps the better view[15] is that the Act affords no protection in these circumstances. Its purpose was to remove a difficulty where no evidence of severance was forthcoming, and it can hardly be intended to operate when the purchaser knows the survivor is not so entitled.

A defect of far greater consequence is that the Act may tend to increase fraud at the expense of the beneficiaries—in marked contrast to the provisions of s. 27 (2) of the Law of Property Act 1925, which were designed to minimise fraud and mistake. The Act of 1964 can be used, it seems, in cases where originally the legal joint tenants were tenants in common in equity, or where they had no equitable interest but held on trust for others. Take the example given at the end of para. (*a*) above. Suppose that A dies, leaving his share in the property to a third party, C. B then contracts to convey the land to P 'as beneficial owner'. The curtain principle ensures that P has no means of knowing that B really holds on trust for himself and C. Since the conveyance to A and B says nothing as to B's entitlement in equity, P must assume that B is solely and beneficially interested and able to deal with the legal title as if it were not held on trust for sale. The Act may have remedied a constant nuisance in

---

11   See p. 390, post. Bankruptcy effects an involuntary severance.
12   Section 3. For the position on a sale of registered land, see p. 362, post.
13   27 Halsbury's Statutes (3rd edn), 725n.
14   (1964) 28 Conv (NS) 329, 330. See also Jackson, 'Joint Tenants, Notice and Statute' (1966), 30 Conv (NS) 27.
15   Contra, M & W, 414. It is, however, significant that the Act says the survivor is *deemed* entitled, not that the statement in the deed is to be taken as *sufficient evidence* of his entitlement; cf. AEA 1925, s. 36 (7), p. 335, post.

conveyancing[16] but the expense of exposing the beneficiaries to a greater risk of fraud. Previously cautious conveyancing practice, by insisting upon the appointment of a second trustee, did at least pay lip-service to s. 27 (2) and in so doing reduced the prospect of malpractice. Nowadays a surviving trustee can cheerfully disregard such restrictions, unless the purchaser knows the true position. Bringing the equitable interests on to the title seems the only safe antidote to prevent abuse of the Act.

One other difficulty arising under the Act warrants discussion. Again an illustration will help. Suppose the land is conveyed to A and B as beneficial joint tenants. A dies without severing the joint tenancy in equity. B then dies, leaving the property to C absolutely. B's executor assents to the property vesting in C. Subsequently C contracts 'as beneficial owner' to sell the land to P. How can C satisfy P that B was solely and beneficially entitled at the time of his death? The assent to C may contain a statement that B was so entitled[17]. Though this will be of no assistance to C, who is not a purchaser, the declaration may avail P, notwithstanding that P was not a party to the document in which it was contained. The validity of this point is uncertain, however[18]. More than likely the assent will not include any statement of B's entitlement, in which case it would appear to be sufficient for B's executor to join in the C-P conveyance for the sole purpose of declaring that B was solely and beneficially interested. Failing this, the only safe way is for C to insert in the contract for sale a special condition requiring P to assume that B was so entitled at the time of his death.

D   Transactions by personal representatives

1.   Devolution on death and power to act generally

On death the deceased's real estate devolves on his personal representative[19], and he possesses in relation to both realty and personalty a statutory power of sale for administration purposes[20]. The difference between the legal position of an executor appointed by will and that of an administrator must not be overlooked. The former derives his title from the testator's will, whereas the latter derives his title from the grant of letters of administration. This has important consequences.

(a) Executor
Even prior to obtaining a grant of probate an executor has power to do all the acts which are incident to his office, except such as necessitate production of a grant in order to prove his title[1]. For instance, he can exercise the statutory

16   M & W, 413.
17   The Act is to be construed as one with the LPA 1925; see s. 4 (1). Accordingly 'conveyance' includes an assent.
18   Cf. P.W. Smith, op. cit., 425–426.
19   AEA 1925, s. 1 (1). For this purpose 'real estate' includes leaseholds: s. 3 (1) (i). At common law only the personal estate (including leaseholds) devolved on him.
20   Ibid., s. 39 (1) (iii), giving all the statutory powers conferred on trustees for sale by the LPA 1925, s. 28 (1), as amended. Further, he has the same common law power of sale as was exercisable by a personal representative before 1926 in relation to the deceased's leaseholds: AEA 1925, s. 2 (1).
1   Re Stevens, Cooke v Stevens [1897] 1 Ch 422 at 429, per North J; affd. [1898] 1 Ch 162, CA.

power of appointing a new trustee[2], exercise an option to purchase vested in the deceased[3], serve a notice to quit, or enter into a binding contract to sell land forming part of the deceased's estate[4]. However, neither he nor a successor in title would be able in court to establish or rely on his title to act without producing a grant of representation. Whilst in theory a conveyance of land executed before a grant would vest the legal title in the purchaser, in practice no purchaser would complete the transaction until a grant had been obtained, and the executor could never compel the purchaser to accept the title without first taking out a grant. The death of an executor before he obtains probate does not invalidate acts done by him prior to his death[5].

One of two (or more) executors can enter into a binding contract to sell the deceased's freehold land[6]. For this rule to apply the executor must contract on his own account. Suppose T appoints X and Y as his executors, and after T's death X contracts on behalf of himself and Y to sell T's land to P. In this situation X purports to contract with the concurrence of his co-executor. Should Y refuse to ratify X's act, there is no enforceable contract, and P is left to his remedy against X for damages for breach of warranty of authority[7]. Assuming that Y ratifies the contract, both X and Y must execute the conveyance to P, since a conveyance of real estate devolving on personal representatives cannot be made without the concurrence of all proving executors[8]. If Y had renounced probate, the administration of T's estate would devolve as if he had not been appointed[9].

(b) Administrator

A person entitled to a grant of administration has no power to act qua administrator before a grant is made to him. When granted letters of administration relate back to the date of the deceased's death, enabling him (e.g.) to sue for trespass to land or for breach of covenant committed during the interval between death and the grant[10]. This doctrine of relation back does not operate to validate acts, such as issuing a writ[11] or making a contract for sale, done at a time when he lacked the authority to act. It is uncertain whether on appointment one administrator can, without the concurrence of his co-administrator, enter into a binding contract to sell land forming part of the estate[12].

2   Under the Trustee Act 1925, s. 36 (1); *Re Crowhurst Park, Sims-Hilditch v Simmons* [1974] 1 All ER 991.
3   Barnsley, *Land Options*, p. 72; cf. *Kelsey v Kelsey* (1922) 91 LJ Ch 382 (notice validly served *on* executors before grant).
4   See (1977) 41 Conv (NS) 300.
5   *Re Stevens, Cooke v Stevens*, note 1, ante. If a sole executor were involved, production of a grant of administration with the will annexed, which would establish that he was named as executor in the will, would suffice to prove his title to act.
6   *Fountain Forestry Ltd v Edwards* [1975] Ch 1 at 11–12, [1974] 2 All ER 280, at 283, per Brightman J. For leaseholds the rule was established as early as 1536: *Anon.* 1 Dyer 23b. Cf. Trustees; see [1980] Conv 191 (P.W. Smith).
7   *Sneesby v Thorne* (1855) 7 De GM & G 399; *Fountain Forestry Ltd v Edwards*, supra, a case involving administrators.
8   AEA 1925, s. 2 (2). Conveyance includes an assent: s. 55 (1) (iii).
9   Ibid., s. 5. An executor cannot renounce after intermeddling with the estate: *Re Badenach* (1864) 3 Sw & Tr 465; *Re Stevens, Cooke v Stevens*. But see *Re Biggs* [1966] 1 All ER 358.
10 *R v Inhabitants of Horsley* (1807) 8 East 405 (trespass to land); *Re Pryse* [1904] P 301 at 305, CA, per Stirling LJ.
11 *Ingall v Moran* [1944] KB 160, [1944] 1 All ER 97, CA.
12 See the authorities reviewed by Brightman J, in *Fountain Forestry Ltd v Edwards*, note 6, ante.

2.   Power to assent

Section 36 (1) of the Administration of Estates Act 1925, empowers a personal representative to assent to the vesting of a legal estate in the beneficiary or other person entitled thereto. This power is confined to estates which have *devolved* upon the representative. The consequence is as follows. Suppose that B, a beneficiary under T's will, survives T but dies before the property is vested in him, and that T's personal representatives assent to the property vesting in B's own representatives. When the latter come to vest the property in the person entitled under B's will or intestacy, they should, strictly speaking, do so by way of a conveyance under seal. Technically s. 36 (1) does not apply for the legal title did not devolve on B's representatives; it was vested in them. However it was held in *Re Stirrup's Contract*[13] that if in such circumstances B's representatives execute an assent under seal, that document is effectual to pass the legal title to the ultimate beneficiary, and a purchaser from him has no right to have the formal defect rectified. An assent under hand would probably not have been effective[14].

3.   Form of assent

To be operative, s. 36 (4) requires the assent to be in writing, signed by the personal representative, and to name the person in whose favour it is given[15]. An assent therefore constitutes an exception to the basic rule which demands a deed to convey a legal estate[16]. Prima facie it relates back to the deceased's death and the statutory covenants for title may be implied in it as in a conveyance by deed[17]. All proving executors must execute the assent.

(a) Implied assents

A written assent is necessary *to pass* a legal estate. For many years practitioners had acted on the assumption, though without clear supporting authority[18], that a written assent was unnecessary where there was no 'passing' of the legal estate, but merely a change in the capacity in which the estate was held. An assent could be implied from the circumstances[19]. However this implied assent myth has been exploded for the time being by Pennycuick J, in *Re King's Will Trusts, Assheton v Boyne*[20], where in the space of one judgment the learned judge cast into the melting pot of uncertainty many titles that had previously been accepted as sound on the basis that no assent was necessary. The decision has not been welcomed by conveyancers[1], who need to be alive to its implications. Two important situations where it may create problems require discussion.

---

13   [1961] 1 All ER 805, applying the LPA 1925, ss. 63 (1), 205 (1) (ii).
14   Contra, Elphinstone, 'Assent to the Vesting of a Legal Estate' (1961), 25 Conv (NS) 491.
15   There are suggestions that the beneficiary should be named and not merely described as 'the beneficiary' or more alarming by 'myself'. These suggestions are not considered to be sound. See Emmet, 465.
16   LPA 1925, s. 52 (1), (2) (a).
17   AEA 1925, s. 36 (2), (3).
18   *Re Yerburgh, Yerburgh v Yerburgh* [1928] WN 208, per Romer J; *Re Hodge, Hodge v Griffiths* [1940] Ch 260 at 264–65, per Farwell J.
19   As was the position before 1926; see *Wise v Whitburn* [1924] 1 Ch 460.
20   [1964] Ch 542, [1964] 1 All ER 833.
 1   Emmet, 471; Garner, 'Assents Today' (1964) 28 Conv (NS) 298. See also Ryder, 'Re King's Will Trusts, A Reassessment' [1976] CLP 60.

(i) *Executor and beneficiary the same person.* An illustration will assist. T (a testator) devises realty to B and appoints B as his executor. B proves the will after T's death. Whilst it was clearly desirable (and recognised to be so) for B to execute an assent in his own favour so as to furnish documentary evidence of the change of capacity, it was not considered fatal if no assent was executed. B already had the legal estate qua executor; there was no 'passing' within s. 36 (4), merely a change of character from personal representative to beneficial owner. On completion of his administrative duties B came to hold the legal estate as beneficial owner without any written assent. Pennycuick J dismissed this argument rather summarily. In his view sub-s. (4) contemplates that a person may by assent vest an estate in himself in another capacity; this vesting necessarily implies a divesting of the estate in the original capacity[2]. A written assent is therefore essential. Yet, with respect, the words 'vesting' and 'pass' envisage rather a situation where the personal representative and the assentee are different persons.

The difficulties and inconveniences created by this decision readily become apparent when considering how title should be made on B's death intestate. In the absence of any assent the legal estate is at the time of B's death vested in B as T's executor. Technically T's estate is unadministered and before title can be made a grant of administration de bonis non to T's estate is required. If this had not been appreciated and, for instance, B's own administrator had conveyed the property to C, C would not obtain a good legal title[3]. No problem arises if B dies testate, leaving an executor who proves B's will. This executor becomes T's executor by representation[4] in relation to T's unadministered estate (i.e. the outstanding legal estate), and a conveyance by B's executor will pass the legal estate to C. Similarly if during his lifetime but without executing any assent in his own favour, B conveys the property to C as 'beneficial owner', this conveyance will be effective to vest in C a good title to both the legal and the equitable interests. By virtue of s. 63 (1) of the Law of Property Act 1925, B's conveyance is effectual to pass to C all the estate, right and title which B has in the property, including the legal estate vested in him as personal representative.

(ii) *Personal representative and trustee.* The actual decision in *Re King's Will Trusts*[5] concerned the effectiveness of a deed of appointment of an additional trustee, executed by a surviving executor who had not executed any assent in his own favour. Pennycuick J held that no legal estate vested in the appointee, and he rejected an argument that the appointment itself operated as an assent[6].

2 [1964] Ch 542 at 549, [1964] 1 All ER 833 at 836.
3 To remedy the defect it would be necessary to trace the person entitled to take out a grant of representation to T's estate in accordance with the Non-Contentious Probate Rules 1954, r. 19 (as amended) — an exercise possibly resulting in expense and delay. The technical defect in C's title would be cured by his possession of the land for 12 years. Arguably, once B has discharged all T's debts and liabilities, he comes to hold the legal estate qua trustee for himself without any assent (written or otherwise). The legal and equitable titles will thereupon merge, with the result that B will hold the legal estate as beneficial owner. See Ryder, op. cit., p. 73, citing *Re Ponder* [1921] 2 Ch 59. On this view C would need to be satisfied that B had duly cleared T's estate before B had himself died. Cf. Parry & Clarke, *The Law of Succession* (7th edn), pp. 379–80.
4 See the AEA 1925, s. 7.
5 [1964] Ch 542, [1964] 1 All ER 833.
6 On the basis of the vesting declaration implied in the appointment by s. 40 (1) (b) of the Trustee Act 1925. It is sometimes asserted that the legal title ought to have been held to

This decision may usefully be contrasted with *Re Cockburn's Will Trusts, Cockburn v Lewis*[7]. Here it was held that personal representatives, having completed their administrative duties, became trustees and were empowered by s. 36 of the Trustee Act 1925, to appoint new trustees of the will, and such appointment was effective, apparently without any assent, to confer on the new trustees the powers and discretions contained in the will. Now, because of the decision in *Re King's Wills Trusts*, they are without power to deal with the legal estate in land forming part of the trust until an assent is executed in their favour.

If the decision is to be regarded as wrongly decided the effect is that in the case of a title made by an implied assent the curtain of the grant to the estate will not operate because otherwise a purchaser should insist on the will or the details of the deceased's next of kin being produced in order to satisfy himself that an implied assent is possible[8]. The decision therefore is logically correct. It means that an assent is required as stated above in the case of land[9]. It is another case of conveyancers' outrage at the upsetting of an established but wrong practice.

(b) Assent of share of proceeds of sale

Some uncertainty exists as to the appropriate form of assent in favour of a surviving tenant in common. Suppose that land is conveyed to A and B in trust for themselves as tenants in common in equal shares. A dies leaving his share to B. This is not an infrequent occurrence. How ought A's executor to vest A's share in B, bearing in mind that eventually B may decide to sell the land? Clearly s. 36 (4) does not apply. So, according to one authority, a verbal assent or even the mere letting of B into entire possession of the property suffices, though when title to the land is being deduced (e.g. on a sale by B) a declaration (which can be incorporated in the conveyance) that B holds the entirety of the property beneficially free from the trust for sale is recommended[10]. This may not satisfy a prudent purchaser. What is preferable is an assent in written form[11] by A's executor in favour of B, and containing a statement that the executor has paid or provided for all debts and capital transfer tax. Such a statement would enable the subsequent purchaser to assume, in the absence of anything to the contrary, that the assent was in proper form, provided he also investigated the terms of A's will to verify that B was the person entitled[12]. The

have vested in the additional trustee under the LPA 1925, s. 63 (1) (cf. *Re Stirrup's Contract* [1961] 1 All ER 805, p. 332, ante, which was not cited to Pennycuick J), but it is arguable that s. 63 (1) cannot conveniently be applied where X wishes to vest an estate in X and Y, as distinct from Y alone.

7   [1957] Ch 438, [1957] 2 All ER 522.

8   The decision was not challenged in *Re Edward's Wills Trust* [1981] 2 All ER 941, CA. Cf. *Beebe v Mason* (1980) 254 Estates Gazette 987, CA, where a landlord was held entitled to rely on the resident landlord provisions without the assent in favour of himself (the sole beneficiary) being executed.

9   The problems really arose because of a trust for sale with some of the funds being personalty and the rest being realty. The shortening of the period of investigation may cause this problem to recede but on the other hand this may not be the case where there are successive deeds of appointment in respect of an estate going back several decades. These should have been sorted out by now but often they are not. Cf. Ryder, op. cit., note 56, p. 72.

10   *Kelly's Draftsman* (14th edn), pp. 42–43, Form No. 22, notes (8), (10).

11   To satisfy the LPA 1925, s. 53 (1) (c).

12   Unlike a purchaser of the legal estate (see the AEA 1925, s. 36 (7), post), he is not entitled to assume this.

purchaser could, therefore, maintain that he was in good faith and so safe from the claim of any unpaid creditor to follow the property[13]. Alternatively, if B contemplated a sale of the land in the near future, the appropriate course would be for him to appoint a new trustee in order to make a title under the trust for sale.

4.   Statutory provisions protecting purchasers

Since 1925 a will no longer constitutes a document of title and a purchaser is not concerned with the beneficial interests arising thereunder. Where the executor has assented to the vesting of the testator's property in a beneficiary, the assent will be abstracted but not the will. How then can a purchaser from that beneficiary be sure the assent was made in favour of the proper person? The Administration of Estates Act 1925, s. 36 (7), enacts that in favour of a purchaser the assent shall be taken as sufficient evidence that the person in whose favour it is made is the person entitled to have the legal estate conveyed to him, unless notice of a previous assent or conveyance affecting the legal estate has been annexed to or endorsed on the grant.

(a) Sufficient evidence

This provision does not debar objection to the title, if a defect is otherwise discovered. 'Sufficient' is not to be interpreted as 'conclusive'. In *Re Duce and Boots Cash Chemists (Southern) Ltd's Contract*[14], the land was in fact settled and a recital in the assent showed this, but the operative part of the document purported to vest the property in a beneficiary absolutely. It was held that a purchaser was not precluded from objecting to the title. In practice it may not be very difficult to check that the beneficiary is entitled. The grant of probate incorporates a copy of the will and a purchaser is entitled to inspect the probate for endorsements. Clearly he is not intended to peep inside the grant[15], but what if he does and a discrepancy is discovered? It seems difficult to resist the conclusion that the courts would not enforce the contract on the purchaser if the title was clearly bad. The vendor's solicitor should curb the purchaser's curiosity, or rather that of his solicitor, by ensuring that he sees no more than he is entitled to[16].

Somewhat curiously, an assent relating to land formerly settled is rendered unchallengeable; if it does not name any trustees of the settlement, a purchaser is *bound and entitled* to assume that the assentee is entitled absolutely and beneficially[17]. Why other assents are to be regarded merely as 'sufficient evidence' is not apparent.

---

13 Ibid., s. 38 (1). See Prichard, 'Assents and Assignments to a Tenant in Common of a Remaining Share' (1973) 37 Conv (NS) 42, and for a precedent, see Conv Prec, 6015, Form 12–3. The argument therein that an administrator can only assent under AEA 1925, s. 36 and cannot therefore take advantage of an implied assent seems convincing (an assignment is required). See further Emmet, 463. Cf. *Re Edward's Wills Trust* [1981] 2 All ER 941, CA, where there appear to be suggestions that an implied assent by an administrator was possible (at 949 per Buckley LJ). See [1982] Conv 9 (P.W. Smith).
14 [1937] Ch 642, [1937] 3 All ER 788.
15 Endorsements are normally made on the outside of the back cover of the grant.
16 Cf. *Smith v Robinson* (1879) 13 Ch D 148 (purchaser entitled to object to pre-root of title defect discovered when vendor's solicitor inadvertently produced the earlier documents for inspection).
17 SLA 1925, s. 110 (5), p. 319, ante.

(b) Endorsements

A person in whose favour an assent or conveyance of a legal estate is made by a personal representative may require that notice thereof be endorsed on or annexed to the grant[18]. Every assentee should take this simple precaution, otherwise he runs the risk of losing his estate to a subsequent purchaser[19] to whom the personal representative states in writing that he has not given or made any previous assent. The purchaser is entitled to rely on this statement, though false, as sufficient evidence that no assent has been given, unless there is an endorsement[20]. On a conveyance by personal representatives to a purchaser it is customary to endorse a suitable notice, though failure to do so is not prejudicial as it might be for a volunteer. Whenever the title comprises a dealing with the land by personal representatives, a subsequent purchaser will always be concerned to check the existence of endorsements. For this reason it is that the grant of probate or administration has become since 1925 a document of title[1].

5.   Conveyance to purchaser

A personal representative possesses a statutory power of sale[2] in relation to the deceased's property, as we have previously noticed. Various provisions exist for the purchaser's protection. He is not concerned to inquire why the property is being sold[3], nor is the purchase invalidated by reason only that he has notice that all the debts and other liabilities have been discharged[4].

A sole personal representative *as such* can give a valid receipt for purchase money, even though he may hold on trust for sale (e.g. on an intestacy)[5]. But the limitations on this power must be noted. He must be acting *as such*, i.e. in his capacity as personal representative. Suppose A and B hold land on trust for sale for C and D in equity. A dies, then B. X, B's sole proving executor, could not pass a good title by himself. A sale by him would not be qua executor of B but qua trustee, executing the trust for sale on the instructions of C and D. His conveyance would vest the legal title in the purchaser, but it would not overreach the rights of the beneficiaries. X should therefore appoint another trustee[6].

E   Mortgages

1.   Sale by legal mortgagee

By virtue of s. 101 (1) of the Law of Property Act 1925, every legal mortgagee has a statutory power of sale when the mortgage money has become due, i.e.

---

18   AEA 1925, s. 36 (5). See also Practice Direction (Family Provision: consent orders) [1978] 3 All ER 1032 concerning the endorsement of consent orders on the grant.

19   This can occur quite frequently, though inadvertently, when land vested in the beneficiary is in error later conveyed to a purchaser. Cf. *Bligh v Martin* [1968] 1 All ER 1157.

20   AEA 1925, s. 36 (6).

1   *Re Miller and Pickersgill's Contract* [1931] 1 Ch 511, p. 426, post.

2   AEA 1925, s. 39 (1) (iii), p. 330, ante.

3   Trustee Act 1925, s. 17. 'Trustee' includes 'personal representative': ibid., s. 68 (17).

4   AEA 1925, s. 36 (8).

5   LPA 1925, s. 27 (2).

6   Cf. *Re Myhill, Hull v Myhill* [1928] Ch 100. See also the Trustee Act 1925, s. 18 (2), (3), which expressly makes X's right to exercise any power or trust vested in the surviving trustee, B, subject to the restrictions imposed in regard to receipts by a sole trustee not being a trust corporation. See further (1977) 41 Conv (NS), 423 (P.W. Smith).

when the legal date of redemption has passed. However this power does not become properly exercisable unless and until one of the conditions laid down by s. 103 of the Act has been satisfied, namely:

(i)   notice requiring payment of the mortgage money has been served on the mortgagor who has defaulted in payment for three months after its service; or

(ii) some interest under the mortgage is in arrear at least two months; or

(iii) there has been a breach by the mortgagor of some provision in the Act or in the mortgage (other than the covenant for payment of principal and interest).

In practice most mortgagees are content to rely on their statutory power of sale but it is commonplace to extend or modify the circumstances when it can be exercised. Many building societies expressly reserve a right to sell if the mortgagor commits an act of bankruptcy. The mortgagee is authorised to sell by public auction or private contract, subject to such conditions respecting title or other matters as he thinks fit, with power to vary or rescind the contract and to re-sell, without being answerable for loss occasioned thereby[7]. He is perfectly entitled to sell under conditions of sale in common use[8], and may leave the whole of the purchase price outstanding on mortgage[9]. The court will not inquire into the mortgagee's motive in exercising the power of sale[10]. There must, however, be a genuine sale. It has long been the rule that the mortgagee cannot sell to himself, either alone or with others, neither to a trustee for himself, nor to a person employed in the conduct of the sale[11].

Though a mortgagee is not a trustee of the power of sale for the mortgagor, his duty is not simply to act in good faith, that is, honestly and without reckless disregard for the mortgagor's interest; he must take reasonable care to obtain whatever is the property's true market value at the time when he chooses to sell. In a recent case mortgages were held liable to their mortgagor for failing to advertise the mortgaged property as having the benefit of planning permission for development with flats with the consequence that the price ultimately realised was appreciably less than if such information had been disclosed in the

---

7   LPA 1925, s. 101 (1) (i); *Wright v New Zealand Farmers' Co-operative Association of Canterbury Ltd* [1939] AC 439, [1939] 2 All ER 701, PC (rescission on purchaser's default and re-sale at a loss; mortgagee not accountable for difference).

8   *Falkner v Equitable Reversionary Society* (1858) 4 Drew 352 (condition empowering rescission on ground of objectionable requisition upheld).

9   *Northern Developments (Holdings) Ltd v UDT Securities Ltd* (1976) 32 P & CR 376 at 380, per Megarry J.

10 *Nash v Eads* (1880) 25 Sol Jo 95, CA (mortgagee selling out of spite).

11 *Farrar v Farrars Ltd* (1888) 40 Ch D 395 at 409, CA, per Lindley LJ; *Martinson v Clowes* (1882) 21 Ch D 857 (purchase by secretary of mortgagees). But see s. 112 (2) of the Housing Act 1980, which permits a local authority mortgagee in certain cases (see s. 112 (1)) to vest the property in itself instead of exercising its power of sale. This was not possible under the previous law (*Williams v Wellingborough Borough Council* [1975] 3 All ER 462, CA) in the absence of an express enabling power in the mortgage, which there rarely was. Section 112 (2) does not apply to public sector houses sold and mortgaged by the authority under Pt. 1, Chap. 1, of the 1980 Act with the result that such mortgages are subject to the ordinary prohibition on purchase. They do not have a statutory right of pre-emption (cf. under the *Williams* case) but the prohibition effectively prevents such property coming back into the public sector (unless the authority seek judgment on the covenant and sell to themselves as judgment creditors: see Fisher & Lightwood, p. 371.) The combination of a forced sale in the first five years together with the discount repayment on such a sale may mean a mortgage or being liable for both and a short fall on the sale and a repayment of the discount he obtained on purchase.

particulars of sale[12]. A building society is statutorily obliged to sell at the best price reasonably obtainable[13]. The making of a contract for sale in exercise of the statutory power bars the mortgagor's right to redeem so long as the contract subsists[14], provided the sale is not tainted with any irregularity.

(a) Protection of purchaser

On the exercise of the statutory power of sale a purchaser is not concerned to inquire whether any case has arisen to authorise the sale, or due notice has been given, or the power is otherwise properly and regularly exercised, and the conveyance is deemed to have been made in exercise of the statutory power unless a contrary intention appears[15]. A purchaser from a mortgagee who abstains from inquiry as to the exercisability of the power of sale is not deemed to have constructive notice of any irregularity. But he must otherwise be in good faith[16]. The fact that a sale is made at an undervalue does not per se show that the purchaser is in bad faith[17], unless the price is so low as to be itself evidence of fraud[18]. If on the other hand he has *actual* notice of some impropriety the cases indicate that he cannot invoke the statutory protection[19]. It is also enacted that the purchaser's title shall not be impeached on the ground that the sale is irregular or improper[20]. This provision is of limited application; it operates only where *a conveyance is made* in exercise of a power of sale. It is conceived that the court could, at the suit of the mortgagor, restrain the mortgagee from completing an irregular sale, irrespective of the purchaser's lack of knowledge of the impropriety as between the mortgagor and mortgagee[1]. Even after completion the court has power to intervene in a proper case to set aside the conveyance to the purchaser if the parties have been guilty of fraud or collusion, or the purchaser had actual knowledge of some irregularity[2]. The conveyance would not be completely devoid of effect, for equity would treat the purchaser as having taken a transfer of the mortgage[3]. In effect he would acquire the property subject to the mortgagor's right of redemption.

---

12   *Cuckmere Brick Co Ltd v Mutual Finance Ltd* [1971] Ch 949, [1971] 2 All ER 633, CA, where the older authorities are considered; *Palmer v Barclays Bank Ltd* (1971) 23 P & CR 30 (mortgagee's breach of duty not made out). But see *Barclays Bank Ltd v Thienel* (1978) 247 Estates Gazette 385 (duty not owed to guarantor of mortgage debt). See also *Bank of Cyprus (London) Ltd v Gill* [1980] 2 Lloyd's Rep 51, CA (negligence not found; no duty to wait for a favourable market, nor to keep the hotel open nor to refrain from informing purchasers they were selling as mortgagees).
13   Building Societies Act 1962, s. 36.
14   *Property and Bloodstock Ltd v Emerton* [1968] Ch 94, [1967] 3 All ER 321, CA.
15   LPA 1925, s. 104 (2), (3).
16   'Purchaser' means 'a purchaser in good faith . . .': LPA 1925, s. 205 (1) (xxi).
17   *Lord Waring v London and Manchester Assurance Co Ltd* [1935] Ch 310.
18   *Warner v Jacob* (1882) 20 Ch D 220 at 224, per Kay J.
19   *Bailey v Barnes* [1894] 1 Ch 25 at 30, per Stirling J; *Lord Waring v London and Manchester Assurance Co Ltd*, ante, at 310 per Crossman J; M & W, 910–11.
20   LPA s. 104 (2). See also s. 112 (5) of the Housing Act 1980 (unimpeachability of title of purchaser buying from local authority after execution of vesting deed).
 1   See on a similarly worded statutory provision *Forsyth v Blundell* (1973) 129 CLR 477 (mortgagee acting with calculated indifference to mortgagor's interests).
 2   See *Jenkins v Jones* (1860) 2 Giff 99; *Selwyn v Garfitt* (1888) 38 Ch D 273, CA, both cases involving express powers of sale. See also the authorities cited in note 19, ante.
 3   *Selwyn v Garfitt* (1888) 38 Ch D 273, CA.

(b) Consumer Credit Act 1974

As and when the Consumer Credit Act 1974, is brought into full effect, a mortgage regulated by the Act will be enforceable on an order of the court only[4]. No specific sanction is prescribed for breach of this requirement. It is expressly enacted[5] that nothing in the Act is to affect the operation of the provisions of s. 104 of the Law of Property Act 1925, considered in the preceding paragraph. Seemingly, therefore, a purchaser will be able to acquire a good title to the land despite the lack of a court order. He will not, it is thought, be under a duty to ascertain that the necessary order has been granted; but if the failure to obtain one were to come to his notice, he could properly object to the title which the court would not enforce against him in its absence. The Act of 1974 excludes from its scope mortgages granted by building societies, local authorities, or by certain exempted institutional lenders, e.g. insurance companies[6].

(c) Effect of conveyance

At the most the mortgagee possesses a term of years absolute in the mortgagor's land, and where the mortgage is created by way of legal charge his interest ranks merely as a legal interest. Nevertheless in both cases a conveyance by the mortgagee in exercise of his statutory power of sale operates to vest in the purchaser the mortgagor's fee simple estate, subject to any legal mortgage having priority, but free from all subsequent mortgages and the mortgagor's equity of redemption[7]. In *Duke v Robson*[8] a contract for sale entered into by a mortgagee in exercise of his power of sale was held to override a prior contract for sale of the mortgaged property made by the mortgagor, notwithstanding that the prior contract had been registered as a C (iv) land charge. The court declined to restrain the mortgagee from performing his contract.

In the case of leasehold property the assignment is similarly effectual to pass to the assignee the unexpired residue of the mortgagor's term of years[9], creating privity of estate between the lessor and the assignee and rendering the covenants in the lease enforceable against the latter.

2. Equitable mortgages

The statutory power of sale exists whenever the mortgage is made by deed; it therefore extends to an equitable mortgage by deposit of deeds accompanied by a memorandum of deposit under seal, or to an equitable charge contained in a deed. The difficulty facing an equitable mortgagee is that he has no statutory power to convey the mortgagor's *legal* estate[10], unless his power to sell has been extended by means of one or other of the usual devices[11]: either (i) a

---

4   Consumer Credit Act 1974, s. 126 (not yet in force).
5   Ibid., s. 177 (2).
6   Ibid., s. 16 (1).
7   LPA 1925, ss. 88 (1), 104 (1).
8   [1973] 1 All ER 481, CA.
9   LPA 1925, s. 89 (1): *Rust v Goodale* [1957] Ch 33, [1956] 3 All ER 373.
10 *Re Hodson and Howe's Contract* (1887) 35 Ch D 668, CA. In *Re White Rose Cottage* [1965] Ch 940 at 951, [1965] 1 All ER 11 at 15, CA, Lord Denning MR suggested obiter that the LPA 1925, s. 104, empowered an equitable mortgagee to convey the legal estate, and that *Re Hodson and Howe's Contract* was not authoritative on s. 104. The validity of this opinion awaits further judicial confirmation. It is thought that the view is difficult to reconcile with the LPA 1925, ss. 88 and 89; see (1965), 29 Conv (NS) 222, and Emmet, 884.
11 See Fisher and Lightwood's, *Law of Mortgage* (9th edn) pp. 49–51.

declaration of trust by the mortgagor that he holds the mortgaged property on trust for the mortgagee, or (ii) the creation of a power of attorney in the mortgagee's favour enabling him to vest the legal estate in the purchaser. By virtue of this power of attorney the mortgagee can convey the legal estate to a purchaser without first having to call for the execution by the mortgagor of a legal mortgage[12]. To ensure that the conveyance operates under the statute to give the purchaser a title free from subsequent charges, it is essential that the mortgagee is expressed to *convey* as mortgagee in exercise of his statutory power of sale. If he merely *releases* unto the purchaser the land discharged from his mortgage, the conveyance will be construed as an ordinary sale by the mortgagor (acting albeit by the mortgagee-attorney) with the concurrence of his mortgagee, and the purchaser will only acquire the same title as the mortgagor has, freed from the mortgagee's mortgage but subject to any subsequent charges[13].

Where the mortgage is not made by deed the mortgagee can only enforce a sale, in the absence of the mortgagor's concurrence, under an order of the court. On the mortgagee's application the court may direct a sale on such terms as it thinks fit[14] and it may make a vesting order in favour of a purchaser or appoint a person to convey to him, or vest in the mortgagee a legal term of years absolute to enable him to effect a sale[15] and make title out of court.

F   Title by adverse possession

1.   Open contracts

A title resting solely on the vendor's possession (or that of his predecessors) for at least twelve years, though supported by statutory declarations, does not suffice to establish a good title under an open contract. Statements that a good title is shown by proving possession for thirty years, this being the maximum period under the Limitation Act 1980, for the recovery of land in cases of disability, are misleading[16]. For all the purchaser knows the land may be subject to a settlement in which case time may not begin to run against the remainderman until his interest (even though equitable) falls into possession[17]. In this situation possession for thirty years may not suffice to bar all rightful claimants. Yet it may, depending on the circumstances, but of these the purchaser has no knowledge. The vendor must under an open contract establish that the possession has been sufficient to extinguish the interests of all claimants to the original title. This entails tracing the title from a good root to the point when the previous owner was dispossessed; thereafter possession for at least twelve

---

12   *Re White Rose Cottage* [1965] Ch 940 at 956, [1965] 1 All ER 11 at 18, CA, per Harman LJ. It is usual for the memorandum of deposit to contain an undertaking by the mortgagor to execute a legal mortgage when called upon, although this is implied from the mere fact of deposit: *Pryce v Bury* (1853) 2 Drew 41.
13   *Re White Rose Cottage* [1965] Ch 940, [1965] 1 All ER 11, CA. For a precedent, see 19 Ency F & P, 1347, Form 7:K:31. As to sale by a receiver see (1977) Conv (NS) 83 (P.J. Millett); [1977] Conv 443; and *Sowman v David Samuel Trust Ltd* [1978] 1 All ER 616.
14   LPA 1925, s. 91 (2).
15   LPA 1925, s. 90 (1). The vesting order has the same effect as a conveyance by the mortgagor: ibid., s. 9 (1).
16   See e.g. Williams, *Title*, 570–72; 18 Ency F & P, 645, note 12.
17   Limitation Act 1980, s. 15 and Sch. 1, para. 4.

years may, depending on the facts, constitute a good title, if verified by sufficient evidence.

2. Formal contracts

Where it is appreciated that the vendor's title is wholly dependent on the Limitation Act 1980, a formal contract should provide that the vendor shall convey such title as he has in the property and shall offer in support a statutory declaration that he has been in undisturbed possession of the property or of the rents and profits for so many years without acknowledging the right of any person. Where only a small plot of land is involved the contract may simply stipulate that no title shall be required beyond the vendor's possession[18]. The vendor must ensure he is in a position to procure the preferred declaration. In *George Wimpey & Co Ltd v Sohn*[19]:

> vendors contracted to convey all such right title and interest as they had in certain property and in support they agreed to make or procure a declaration of undisputed possession for 20 years.

This condition was held to constitute a warranty[20] as to the evidence to be furnished in support of their title, and their failure to fulfil that obligation exactly entitled the purchaser to rescind. Even had the vendors established twelve years' adverse possession, the purchaser could still have declined to accept the title. As Harman LJ explained, a vendor who offers only such right as he has must abide by a condition which obliges him to support it in a certain way, and cannot affect to perform his contract by an assertion of a different right and the production of different evidence[1].

(a) Title part documentary, part possessory

The decision in *Re Atkinson and Horsell's Contract*[2], considered in the previous chapter, shows that if at some point in the title offered there is a defect but thereafter the vendor can establish a good possessory title, the title can be forced on the purchaser — even in the absence of any contractual provision. According to *Games v Bonner*[3] the vendor can enforce the contract if his possessory title has accrued before the commencement of his action, even though he did not have a good title at the contractual date for completion, provided the purchaser has not in the meantime effectively rescinded the contract for want of title.

In the absence of any contractual provision, the purchaser is entitled to have the possessory title verified by proper evidence. At least twelve years' uninterrupted adverse possession without any acknowledgment of the disseisee's title must be proved. Such possession following a defect occurring more than twelve years previously will suffice if the disseisee was a sole beneficial owner[4] but not necessarily if he was merely a limited owner. Thus, where the land is subject to a

---

18 For specimen clauses see 18 Ency F & P, 645–47.
19 [1967] Ch 487, [1966] 1 All ER 232, CA.
20 Cf. *Re Spencer and Hauser's Contract* [1928] Ch 598.
 1 At 505 and 237, respectively. *Re Atkinson and Horsell's Contract* [1912] 2 Ch 1, CA, was distinguished on the ground that there the vendor's title could not be questioned.
 2 [1912] 2 Ch 1, CA, p. 291, ante.
 3 (1885) 54 LJ Ch 517, CA.
 4 Even if he dies during the relevant twelve years and is succeeded by a person under a disability, time does not stop running: Limitation Act 1980, s. 28 (2).

settlement, twelve years' adverse possession against the life tenant, though sufficient to bar his equitable title, does not extinguish his legal estate which remains vested in him until all the beneficiaries under the settlement have been barred[5]. As for the ultimate remainderman his title is not extinguished unless he fails to take action within twelve years of the actual dispossession *or* within six years of his own interest falling into possession, whichever is the longer period[6].

One consequence of the reduction in the period of investigation of title will be to increase the risk of defects remaining undiscovered, particularly where dispossession of a trustee occurred before the root of title and the beneficiaries' rights remain unbarred[7]. It also follows that if the purchaser discovers a defect during his investigation, it is less likely to have been cured by adverse possession than previously when 30 years was the statutory period[8].

(b) Implied licence

The implied licence theory which prevented the establishment of a title by adverse possession when the court considered the possession was to be regarded as consensual[9] as opposed to adverse has now been statutorily reversed by the Limitation Act 1980[10] which provides that an assumption of a licence should not be made unless such a finding is justified on the facts of the case.

G   Rentcharges[11]

1.   Nature of rentcharges

To conveyancers unfamiliar with their mysteries, rentcharges are something of a scourge. A rentcharge is an annual sum of money charged upon land (usually freehold), secured by a right of distress and existing independently of any landlord-tenant relationship. A rentcharge in possession issuing out of or charged on land being either perpetual or for a term of years absolute ranks as a legal interest[12]. It will be equitable only if it is to endure until the happening of a certain event. The incidence of rentcharges is largely confined to two main parts of the country — Bristol and Bath, and Manchester[13] and the surrounding area. In these parts they have been for many years a common feature of modern estate development where, in addition to the full market price for the land and dwelling, the purchaser has been required to pay a perpetual rentcharge. At

5   Limitation Act 1980, s. 18 (2).
6   Limitation Act 1980, s.15 (2).
7   The Law Commission were unable to suggest any solution to the question whether the loss should fall on the purchaser or the beneficiaries; Law Com. No. 9, para. 46 (2).
8   For the position when title deeds are lost, see pp. 159–160, ante.
9   See *Wallis's Cayton Bay Holiday Camp v Shell-Mex and B.P. Ltd* [1975] QB 94; *Treloar v Nute* [1977] 1 All ER 230, CA; and Emmet, 175–176. On the other hand, a purchaser in possession under a contract which has not been repudiated cannot be said to be in *adverse* possession: *Hyde v Pearce* [1982] 1 All ER 1029, CA.
10   Limitation Act 1980, Sch. 1, para. 8 (4).
11   See Easton, *Law of Rentcharges* (2nd edn). See also the informative survey of the rentcharge system in the Law Commission's Report on Rentcharges, Law Com. No. 68, paras. 9–23.
12   LPA 1925, s. 1 (2) (b). Rentcharges may be created for a term of years or issue out of *leasehold* land, but these are not frequently encountered, as an underlease could achieve the same result.
13   Rentcharges are known locally as chief rents (Manchester) or ground rents (Bristol). In the Bristol and Manchester areas up to 80 per cent of owner-occupied residential property is thought to be subject to rentcharges: Law Com. No. 68, para. 16.

one time they were employed as a means of financing estate development. Builders bought land, paying no capital sum, but agreeing to pay a rentcharge in perpetuity. Since World War II they have in the main been created simply as a 'perk' for the developer. In theory the creation of a rentcharge on the sale of a new house should have reduced its capital cost, but there is no real evidence to suggest that they have had this effect.

2. Rentcharges Act 1977

Rentcharges have been branded as a land tenure anomaly, repugnant to the concept of freehold ownership. Now surprisingly the Law Commission, which spent several years investigating the rentcharge system, concluded that there was little to justify its retention (save for certain limited exceptions). The Rentcharges Act 1977, in large measure implements the recommendations contained in their Report on Rentcharges (Law Com. No. 68).

(a) Prohibition and extinguishment

As from 22 August 1977, s. 2 (1) prohibits the creation of new rentcharges[14], subject to exceptions mentioned in para. (b) below. As from this date any instrument is void to the extent that it purports to create a prohibited rentcharge (s. 2 (2)). The precise effect of this avoidance is unclear, especially in relation to any covenants created by the document as security for the rentcharge. The Act expressly preserves a rentcharge created in pursuance of an agreement made before the *passing* of the Act[15].

Section 3 (1) enacts (again subject to exceptions) that every rentcharge shall be extinguished (unless it has previously ceased to have effect) at the expiry of sixty years from (i) the passing of the Act, or (ii) the date on which the rentcharge first became payable, whichever is the later. In the case of a variable rentcharge, the period does not commence until the date when it ceases to be variable (s. 3 (4)). A rentcharge is variable if its amount varies in accordance with the provisions of the instrument under which it is payable, e.g. because it is expressly linked to some fluctuating index. On extinguishment the land out of which it issues is discharged and freed from the rentcharge (s. 3 (1)). Beyond this the Act does not deal with the consequences of extinguishment. On general principles a covenant taken solely for the security of the rentcharge (such as a covenant to repair or insure the property) will cease to be enforceable, but it is not always possible to tell whether a particular covenant falls within this category especially when the ownership of the adjoining land is divorced from the rent owner. The Law Commission declined to propose the introduction of statutory presumptions to regulate this position[16].

(b) Permitted rentcharges

Certain rentcharges, which for present purposes may be termed *permitted rentcharges*, are excepted from the ban on creation by s. 2 (3) (a)-(e), viz. a rentcharge —

14 There exists a risk, fully appreciated by the Law Commission, that developers, finding themselves deprived of an easy source of revenue, will simply sell their houses on long leases subject to a small ground rent. It is unlikely that this system will be widely adopted in view of the prospect of enfranchisement under the Leasehold Reform Act 1967, p. 162, ante.

15 Section 17 (3). The wording should be noted. A rentcharge created after 21 August 1977, in pursuance of an agreement made on or after 22 July 1977 (the date the Act was passed) is caught by s. 2 (1).

16 See para. 91 of their Report.

(i)   created voluntarily, or in consideration of marriage or by way of family settlement, i.e. 'family' rentcharges which make the land charged settled land[17], or would do so but for the fact that the land is held on trust for sale: paras. (a) and (b);

(ii)   which is an estate rentcharge, a novel concept explained below: para. (c);

(iii) created by or under certain statutory provisions[18]; para. (d);

(iv)   created by or in accordance with courts orders: para. (e).

As to estate rentcharges, the Law Commission recognised that in the past rentcharges have played a positive role in relation to freehold flats and freehold housing schemes[19]. Sometimes rentcharges, usually of a nominal amount, are created as a conveyancing device to secure the enforceability of positive covenants designed to preserve the development as a unit. At other times they are reserved for the express purpose of providing a fund for the maintenance of services and amenities for the common benefit of the properties out of which they issue. This type of rentcharge, termed by the Act an estate rentcharge, has been very properly excluded from the general prohibition on creation.

All permitted rentcharges, whenever created, are excepted from the extinguishment provisions of the Act by s. 3 (3).

(c) Redemption and apportionment

The Act contains improved procedures for the redemption and apportionment of rentcharges, and a new formula for the calculation of redemption prices[20]. It is not possible to apply to redeem certain rentcharges, including permitted rentcharges: s. 8 (4).

3.   Sale of land subject to rentcharge

Apart from permitted rentcharges and variable rentcharges, all rentcharges will be extinguished by mid-2037 at the latest. But the relentless march of inflation will have ensured that long before this time many rentcharges of small amounts will have ceased to be collected. Once twelve years have elapsed from the date of the last payment, they will become extinguished by virtue of the Limitation Act 1980[1]. Subject to these considerations rentcharges will continue to bedevil freehold conveyancing, albeit in limited parts of the country, for

---

17   By virtue of the SLA 1925, s.1 (1) (v).

18   These are rentcharges created in connection with the execution of various works on land, such as improvement or repair works. See, e.g. the Public Health Act 1936, s. 295; Law Com. No. 68, para. 53.

19   See *Beachway Management Ltd v Wisewell* [1971] Ch 610, [1971] 1 All ER 1 (rentcharge payable until estate roads adopted). The positive covenants can be made to run by virtue of the right of security which being annexed to a rentcharge is legal. See LPA 1925, s. 1 (a) (e) and *Shiloh Spinners v Harding* [1973] AC 691. Problems can also occur if the covenants are mixed as to whether they are annexed to the rentcharge or merely restrictive covenants. In either case a right of re-entry is usually reserved and in the case of the restrictive covenants it will annex to the adjoining benefited land under LPA 1925, s. 78. See *Federated Homes v Mill Lodge Properties Ltd* [1980] 1 All ER 371, CA. Alternatively the benefit of the right of re-entry can be assigned: LPA 1925, s. 4, M & W, 81–82.

20   See ss. 4–7 (apportionment), ss. 8–10 (redemption). For apportionment, see s. 4 (c) infra, p. 346.

1   Sections 15, 38 and Schedule 1. Presumably the covenants and rights of re-entry arising on breach will still be enforceable with the cause of action accruing on the breach: Limitation Act 1980, Sch. 1, para. 7.

years to come. The standard form Conditions of Sale make no attempt to regulate transactions involving rentcharges, so that special conditions need to be added to the contract. In areas where they are common the Conditions of Sale published by local law societies contain appropriate special clauses. The title to land subject to an existing rentcharge is deduced in the same way as a normal freehold. If the root of title commences after the creation of the rentcharge, the purchaser is entitled to a copy or abstract of the rentcharge deed under the Law of Property Act 1925, s. 45 (1). Alternatively the title can be commenced with the deed of creation, and re-commenced with the earliest document at least 15 years old, the intervening title being omitted. The purchaser will usually seek confirmation that the covenants imposed for the security of the rentcharge at the time of its creation have been performed. The contract should therefore provide that production of the receipt for the last payment due before completion shall be evidence of due compliance[2]. It is not necessary to stipulate for any indemnity covenant, which is statutorily implied in every conveyance for valuable consideration[3].

4. Sale of land affected by overriding or apportioned rentcharge

A plot of land may be subject to an overriding rentcharge or an apportioned rentcharge. The former occurs where a rentcharge has been created out of a large plot of land later sub-divided into smaller lots, each lot being subject to a newly created rentcharge, termed a second (or improved) rent, as where A, the owner of land subject to a rentcharge of £50 in favour of B, has built ten houses on the land and on each sale has created a new rent of £10. In this situation the rent of £50 is termed an overriding rentcharge. Alternatively, a rentcharge may be subsequently apportioned between the various owners of individual plots. For instance in the previous illustration, the rentcharge of £50 might have been apportioned between the ten houses as and when each was conveyed, so that each purchaser took subject to an apportioned part of £5. An apportionment of this nature was invariably informal, that is, not binding on the rentcharge owner, B. A rentcharge binds every part of the land out of which it issues. B can, therefore, call upon any purchaser of a sub-divided lot to pay the entire £50, irrespective of whether it has been informally apportioned or second rents have been reserved. In practice the purchaser of the last of the ten houses to be sold will be expected to undertake this responsibility[4].

The creation of second or improved rents is now prohibited by s. 2 (1) of the Act, and they do not fall within any of the categories of permitted rentcharges. The Act does not forbid an informal (or equitable, as it is sometimes termed) apportionment of a pre-Act rentcharge, but there is little to be gained today by this procedure since s. 4 (1) gives a statutory right to apply for a legal apportionment. Any attempt by contract to prevent the purchaser from exercising

---

2   Cf. LPA 1925, s. 45 (2), p. 309, ante, which applies only to leaseholds.
3   LPA 1925, s. 77 (1) (A). Special indemnity rules apply where land subject to a rentcharge created *after* the Act by virtue of s. 2 (3) (a) and (b) (i.e. a 'family' rentcharge) is conveyed for a consideration in money or money's worth: s. 11. In effect the LPA 1925, s. 77 is reversed by s. 11, which implies a covenant by the *vendor* to pay the rent. This covenant is not implied when the rentcharge is overreached by the conveyance; see s. 11 (1) (b). Nor does s. 11 apply to any such rentcharge created prior to the Act; for there could be no guarantee that the vendor of the land so affected would himself have the benefit of a covenant to pay the rentcharge.
4   See further Law. Com. No. 68, paras. 14—15.

this right would, it is thought, be ineffective. If the owner of the land subject to the rentcharge of £50 wishes to divide it between different parts on the occasion of the sale of each lot, he himself should take advantage of s. 4 (2), which enables him to obtain a legal apportionment in anticipation of a sub-division of the land.

A sale of land subject to a second or equitably apportioned rentcharge created before the Act of 1977 presents special problems for the conveyancer.

(a) Pitfalls to avoid

These situations need watching carefully. The vendor must disclose in the contract the existence of the overriding rentcharge. By analogy with cases concerning leaseholds, it would be an objection to the title if the contract, though stating that the property was subject to a certain rent, failed to disclose it was only an apportioned part[5]. A purchaser of land subject to an improved rent will need to be satisfied that the overriding rentcharge has been duly paid and the covenants observed; this can be governed by a condition requiring him to assume such matters. The possibility of B, the rentcharge owner, proceeding against him in the event of its non-payment renders it necessary for him to be satisfied that the indemnities given by A against this contingency are adequate for his protection[6]. Strictly this is a matter upon which the purchaser should satisfy himself before exchanging contracts. A vendor who is unable to produce a copy or abstract of the deed creating the overriding rentcharge should ensure that the contract excludes the purchaser's statutory right of production[7].

(b) Apportioned rentcharges

Where the rent has been informally apportioned, a purchaser is entitled to an abstract or copy of the deeds effecting previous apportionments. Using the example given above, suppose that A conveyed one plot to C at an apportioned rent of £5. By statute certain indemnity covenants would be implied on the part of both A (provided he conveyed as beneficial owner) and C. On a subsequent conveyance of another plot to D at a further apportioned part of £5, the benefit of the covenants by A and C would statutorily pass to, and be capable of enforcement by, D[8]. Accordingly D, or any later purchaser of that plot, needs to see the A-C conveyance to be satisfied that the apportionment was properly made. The owner (call him O) of the last of the ten houses to be sold is in a particularly difficult position. His property will have been conveyed subject to the entire rentcharge of £50, leaving him with the task of collecting £5 from each of the other nine owners. It is usually understood that the obligation to collect 'runs with the deed' i.e. the person possessing the deed creating the rentcharge. Usually this is the last owner of the plot. Sometimes there is an express covenant for collection of the apportioned rents but enforcement is difficult.

(c) Statutory legal apportionment

Section 4 (1) of the Rentcharges Act 1977, provides that the owner of land affected by a rentcharge which also affects land not in his ownership (e.g. C, D and O) may apply to the Secretary of State for the Environment for an order apportioning the rentcharge between his land and the remaining land. A

---

5   E.g. *Re Lloyds Bank Ltd and Lillington's Contract* [1912] 1 Ch 601, see p. 45, ante.
6   For the nature of these indemnities, see Easton, loc. cit., 82–86; Walford, 99–101.
7   See the LPA 1925, s. 45 (1), proviso (ii).
8   LPA 1925, s. 77 (1) (B), (5). Powers of entry and distress are implied by s. 190 (2).

request for a legal apportionment is likely to be made by a person such as O, who collects a number of equitably apportioned rents. If O's application is successful, his land is legally released from such part of the rentcharge as is not apportioned to his land[9]. The apportionment is binding upon B, the rent-charge owner, who thereafter is unable to call upon O to pay more than the apportioned rent of £5. The application may not always succeed. The rent owner (B) can object to the apportionment on the ground that it would provide insufficient security for any part of the rentcharge: s. 5 (5) (a). When the amount apportioned to O's land does not exceed £5[10], the Secretary of State must, if B so requests, order the applicant to redeem the apportioned rent-charge, unless to do so would cause O financial hardship: s. 7 (2), (3).

One obvious consequence of O's application proving successful is that B will look to one of the other nine house owners to pay the £45, the balance of the rent. His choice may be quite capricious. Understandably the person nomi-nated will resent having to assume the role of rent collector[11], and he in turn will undoubtedly initiate apportionment proceedings under s. 4 (1). As a result the Department of the Environment is in danger of finding itself having over several years to deal with a trickle of applications relating to the same rent-charge; whereas it would clearly be simpler and less costly to be able to dispose of several applications relating to the same rentcharge more or less simulta-neously. Yet the Act imposes no duty on the Secretary of State[12] to involve or even notify the other payers that an application for apportionment has been received. Nevertheless, the form of application does request details of the names and addresses of the other payers, so that the Department can encourage the other rent payers to join in the application. It is understood that this is done wherever possible.

All permitted rentcharges are apportionable under s. 4 except for the statu-tory rentcharges falling within group (iii) on page 344: s. 4 (3) (a).

5. Sale of rentcharges

Rentcharges, being legal interests, form a separate species of real property and are capable of being transferred. Unlike the sale of a lease, there are no statu-tory provisions regulating the title to be deduced on the sale of a rentcharge. It appears to be standard practice[13] to commence the title with the deed creating the rent, which does not, of course, establish the title of the person creating it. In the case of a recently created rentcharge the purchaser is well advised to stipulate for the title of the land out of which it issues to be deduced prior to its creation.

Certain points should be remembered when preparing the contract. Second rents, being invariably subject to a right of retention in the event of the payers being compelled to pay the overriding rent, should always be described as such, otherwise the purchaser will assume he is purchasing first rents not affected by

---

9   Section 7 (4). The apportionment procedure is regulated by ss. 4 (4) – (6), 5 and 6
    (relating to appeals), and the Rentcharges Regulations 1978, S.I. 1978 No. 16.
10 This figure can be altered by regulation: s. 7 (6).
11 He cannot legally refuse to pay the £45, since the rentcharge binds each part of the land
    affected by it.
12 For the Law Commission's reasons for not advocating such a duty, see paras. 74–82 of
    their Report. Their proposal that redemption and apportionment procedures should be
    administered by District Councils was not adopted by Parliament.
13 Walford, 94.

any such restriction. The land upon which the rent is charged should be accurately described in the contract[14], and where several rents are described in one lot, care should be taken not to misstate the amounts of the respective rents[15]. Failure in either respect may entitle the purchaser to rescind for misdescription.

It was held in *Grant v Edmondson*[16] that the benefit of a covenant to pay did not run with a rentcharge created before 1926. It is arguable that a post-1925 covenant to pay will run by virtue of s. 78 of the Law of Property Act 1925[17], but the present lack of authority renders it desirable for the purchaser to take an express assignment of the benefit of all the landowner's covenants. This assignment would be effective to pass the right to sue for arrears of rent outstanding at the date of the conveyance[18]. Whether or not the benefit of the covenant has passed, the purchaser can always maintain an action of debt for arrears against the terre-tenant, i.e., the freeholder for the time being[19].

14   *Cox v Coventon* (1862) 31 Beav 378.
15   *Lee v Rayson* [1917] 1 Ch 613 (sale of leasehold ground rents).
16   [1931] 1 Ch 1, CA; see Easton, op. cit., 97–98.
17   See the LPA 1925, s. 205 (1), (ix) ('land' includes 'rent'). See note 19, p. 344, ante.
18   Cf. *London and County (A & D) Ltd v Wilfred Sportsman Ltd* [1971] Ch 764, [1970] 2 All ER 600, CA (arrears of rent due under lease passing on sale of reversion by virtue of the LPA 1925, s. 141 (1)).
19   *Thomas v Sylvester* (1873) LR 8 QB 368.

Chapter 12

Deducing title III: registered land

A Introduction

As we saw in the first chapter, one of the principal objects of registered conveyancing is to abolish the repeated investigation of title each time a property is sold. The effect of a person being registered as proprietor of freehold land with an absolute title is to vest the fee simple in him, subject to the various matters set out in the Land Registration Act 1925[1]. This vesting is backed by the State guarantee. A purchaser is not concerned to know about the past history of the property; an investigation of the title does not assist him in deciding whether the title is good or defective[2]. His principal concern is the state of the vendor's title at the time of the sale, which, subject to various qualifications previously noted[3], he can ascertain by inspecting the vendor's register of title. The leading authority on registered conveyancing, whilst glossing over the defects in the system (of which overriding interests are the most notorious), has summarised the basic position in these term[4].

> ' A purchaser can at once safely accept the title offered. Subject to the possibility of rectification . . . there is no risk of an imperfect title such as would cause trouble when he comes to sell or mortgage land under the unregistered system being foisted on him.'

This must be read subject to the purchaser's need to check that the title offered accords with the title contracted to be sold. To this extent a purchaser must always investigate his vendor's title, even on a sale of registered land. For example in *Faruqi v English Real Estate Ltd*[5] a purchaser contracted to buy at an auction land which was sold 'subject to the entries on the register of title'. On later inspecting these he discovered that the land was subject to restrictive covenants imposed by an old deed, no copy or abstract of which had been produced to the Registry on first registration. The vendor could not provide any details of the covenants, and the purchaser was held entitled to recover his deposit.

---

1 LRA 1925, ss. 5, 20. References in this chapter to the Act are to be taken as references to the Land Registration Act 1925, unless otherwise indicated.
2 The position is otherwise in the case of titles less than absolute; see p. 352, post.
3 Pages 38–40, ante.
4 R & R (3rd edn), 10.
5 [1979] 1 WLR 963; *Re Stone and Saville's Contract* [1963] 1 All ER 353 (failure to disclose restrictive covenants).

The absence of any need to investigate the title (save as just mentioned) does not absolve a vendor from having to establish his title by the production of proper evidence. His obligations are defined by the Act, obligations which vary according to the type of title involved.

B   Freehold land

1.   Absolute titles

The vendor's obligations on a sale or other disposition of registered land are contained in s. 110 of the Act. Certain documents must be supplied to the purchaser (other than a lessee or chargee), *notwithstanding any stipulation to the contrary*; others must be furnished *in the absence of* any contrary agreement. Save for documents falling within either of these categories, s. 110 (3) enacts that it is not 'necessary for the vendor to furnish the purchaser with any abstract or other written evidence of title, or any copy or abstract of' the land or charge certificate.

(a) Documents that must be supplied (s. 110 (1))
The vendor is obliged to supply:

   (i)   an authority to inspect the register;
 (ii)   a copy of the subsisting entries on the register;
(iii)   a copy of the filed plan;
(iv)   copies or abstracts of documents noted on the register.

(i) *Authority to inspect.* The vendor's register of title is private[6]. The purchaser cannot inspect the register, obtain copies, or apply for an official search of the register to be made, without the proprietor's permission. The authority to inspect consists of a letter, signed by the proprietor or his solicitor and addressed to the Registrar, in the following form[7] —

> I, A.B., of etc., (the proprietor) hereby authorise the bearer to apply at any time to the Registrar for information as to the entries in the register of title.

The practice is to authorise the purchaser, or more usually his solicitor, by name, which renders the authority non-transferable. Therefore, unless a bearer authority is provided, it is essential that the purchaser ensures that the vendor is willing to authorise the making of a search of the register on behalf of a mortgagee who is separately represented[8].

(ii) *Copy of subsisting entries.* The vendor can discharge this obligation by preparing his own copies from the land certificate. It is preferable, however, to obtain office copies prepared by the Registry; these are admissible in evidence

---

6   LRA 1925, s. 112. See p. 36, ante.
7   LRR 1925, r. 289 (1); Schedule, Form 80. An authority 'to the like effect' is permissible and several variations are encountered in practice. The production can be dispensed with in certain circumstances with regard to official searches. See Chap. 14, post.
8   The obligations imposed by s. 110 do not extend to the purchaser's mortgagee. In fact only one search need be made; the mortgagee's search affords protection for both the transfer and the mortgage. See generally about searches, pp. 404–406, post.

to the same extent as the originals and a person suffering loss by reason of any inaccuracy is entitled to be indemnified under the Act[9]. Office copy entries are frequently sent to the purchaser's solicitor along with the draft contract, rather than after exchange of contracts.

(iii) *Copy of the filed plan.* This is necessary because registered land is always described by reference to a plan.

(iv) *Copies or abstracts of documents noted on the register.* Where, for instance, the charges register refers to a deed or transfer that imposes restrictive covenants without reproducing the covenants verbatim, the purchaser is entitled to a copy or abstract of the deed. As between vendor and purchaser any abstract filed in the Registry, or copy of, or extract from, a deed referred to on the register, must be assumed to be correct and to contain all material parts of the original document[10], production of which the purchaser is not entitled to require. This does not relieve the purchaser of the necessity of inspecting the abstract or copy.

The vendor's obligations do not extend to providing copies of charges or incumbrances to be discharged or overridden at or prior to completion, e.g. a mortgage, or to matters not affecting the land to be dealt with, e.g. on a sale of part of the registered property. He must, of course, supply a copy or abstract of any mortgage subject to which the property is sold. Parliament has laid the expense of obtaining the necessary documents at the purchaser's door where the purchase price is £1,000 or less[11], but in practice the fees are so small that even in such cases the vendor usually bears the cost.

(b) Copies to be supplied in the absence of contrary agreement (s. 110 (2))
The vendor must at his own expense furnish copies, abstracts and evidence (if any) in respect of appurtenant rights and interests as to which the register is not conclusive. The register is conclusive as to appurtenant rights, particulars of which appear as part of the description of the property. It is not conclusive if the Registrar has merely entered a note that the proprietor claims that an appurtenant right exists, e.g. by prescription[12].

Evidence of matters excepted from the effect of registration must be produced. These include (i) overriding interests and (ii) matters excepted on registration with a possessory or qualified title. As to the former it has been said[13] that it is seldom necessary or profitable to pursue this subject beyond the register, considering that overriding interests are matters on which abstracts of title under the unregistered system cannot be relied on for complete information, and that it is the practice to note on the register at the time of first registration any appearing in the abstracts that seem to be of importance. It is clear, however, that a vendor who is aware of some overriding interest not mentioned on the register should disclose it in the contract and, apart from any excluding provision, must satisfy the purchaser by proper evidence of its nature.

---

9   LRA 1925, s. 113. LSC 12 (1) (b) (i) stipulates that copy entries and the filed plan shall be office copies.
10   LRA 1925, s. 110 (4).
11   LRA 1925, s. 110 (1), proviso (a).
12   LRR 1925, r. 254 (1), (2), p. 473, post.
13   Brickdale, 259. And see p. 45, ante.

Special stipulations can be inserted in the contract restricting or excluding the purchaser's rights in relation to matters mentioned in this section. In any case his right is limited to such abstracts and evidence as he would have been entitled to if the land had not been registered.

(c) Sub-sales

Particular difficulty may be encountered in complying with these obligations in the case of a sub-sale or resale. Suppose A transfers part of his land to B who contracts to sell that land to C before the Registry have completed B's registration. Being a sale of part of A's land, a new register has to be opened for B's title, but B cannot fulfil his statutory duty of supplying C with copy entries of a non-existent register. Instead B supplies an office copy of A's register, and C applies for an official certificate of search, which will reveal the existence of the A-B transfer and will also indicate whether it is in order and whether or not it contains restrictive covenants or easements affecting C's land. C can then ascertain from B the precise terms of B's transfer and ultimately complete his own transaction in the normal way, after having made a second official search to secure the statutory protection for his transfer[14].

2.   Titles less than absolute

Where land is registered with a possessory or qualified title, the vendor must supply copy entries and an authority to inspect the register in the normal way. In relation to the estates and interests excepted from the effect of registration, the purchaser can call for the same evidence of title as he would have been entitled to had the land not been registered[15]. Since the State indemnity does not extend to matters excluded from registration, he needs to ascertain to what extent the title might be upset by some claim arising under any excepted estate. However, the vendor is free to contract out of this additional statutory obligation altogether, and it is common practice to preclude a purchaser from calling for evidence of excluded matters. But the vendor must expressly so provide in the contract[16]. The discussion in the two following paragraphs proceeds on the basis there is no contrary stipulation.

In the case of a possessory title, the title prior to first registration should be deduced in the normal unregistered manner so as to show that the title will not be disturbed. Thereafter the abstract will consist of a copy of the subsisting entries (as required by s. 110 (1) of the Act), save that as regards any incumbrance subsisting at the date of first registration the ordinary abstract should be continued to the date when it was discharged or to the date of the sale. A purchaser of a possessory title should consider the possibility of the title being converted into absolute[17].

Where the title is qualified, the nature of the vendor's obligations will depend on the kind of qualification involved[18]. For instance, if it excludes estates and interests arising under a certain document, the abstract should

14   See Registered Land Practice Note No. 17.
15   LRA 1925, s. 110 (2). For the effect of registration with a possessory or qualified title, see pp. 30–31, ante.
16   See e.g. 18 Ency F & P, 657, Forms 3:B:20C and E. LSC 12 (1) (b) merely adopts the statutory obligations. Similarly Con Law CS 6 (3).
17   Page 32, ante.
18   See R & R, 319.

commence with the document and then trace the title to those interests down to the time of the present sale.

3. Building estates

The advantages of registration of title are particularly demonstrated in the case of building estates. On a sale of property on a registered building estate, the developer's obligations as to title remain the same; however the normal procedure has been adapted under special arrangements[19] devised by the Registry to ensure that individual sales-off proceed smoothly.

(a) Approved lay-out plan

The developer may obtain official approval of his estate lay-out plan. This plan indicates each individual plot and the extent of its boundaries. This approved plan has two main advantages. First it enables negotiations between vendor and purchaser to proceed without an office copy of the filed plan in a manner to be described. Secondly the purchaser, when applying for an official search of the register, need only refer to the plot number on the plan instead of having to provide a separate plan. This procedure can only operate effectively provided no departure from the approved plan is undertaken without the Registry's knowledge. Failure to notify the Registry promptly of any alteration may result in the cancellation of applications for the registration of transfers based upon the old plan.

(b) Dispensing with filed plan—Form 102

The transfer of newly developed properties on a building estate to individual purchasers poses problems not normally encountered in the usual vendor-purchaser transaction involving a single property. The developer's solicitor may be faced with the task of supplying numerous office copies of the filed plan which, for practical reasons, is never likely to show land recently removed from the title. The Registry is faced with the difficulty of producing plans copied from an original which is constantly in use for recording transfers of part. The purchaser's solicitor, when confronted with a filed plan covering a large area of land, may be unable to ascertain that his client's land is within the vendor's title.

Where the lay-out plan has been officially approved, the purchaser's solicitor can, prior to exchanging contracts, apply to the Registry for a certificate of official inspection of a filed plan[20]. This document (known as Form 102) certifies that the purchaser's plot is comprised within the vendor's title and states whether or not the plot is affected by any colour or other reference shown on the plan and mentioned in the entries on the register. The theory is that the purchaser can dispense with an inspection of the filed plan, for the certificate furnishes him with the required information. It does not confer any priority for the subsequent registration of the transfer, but its accuracy is guaranteed under s. 83 (3) of the Act[1] so that a purchaser suffering loss through an error in the certificate is entitled to be indemnified in respect thereof.

---

19 For fuller details, see Registered Land Practice Notes 39 and 51, and Practice leaflet No. 7. See also R & R, 331–38.
20 Land Registration (Official Searches) Rules 1981, S.I. 1981 No. 1135, r. 12 (1)–(3).
1   Ibid., r. 12 (3). For s. 83 (3), see p. 90, ante.

That this procedure[2] has undoubted merits cannot be denied. Yet allegations have been made that it is not always self-sufficient, for the purchaser needs to inspect the plan to discover, e.g. the extent of restrictive covenants or the existence of rights of way[3]. This is a valid criticism, and a purchaser desiring maximum protection should insist upon a copy of the filed plan, for there is nothing in the relevant Rules to relieve the vendor of his statutory obligation to supply an office copy of this plan.

One defect has been acknowledged. Form 102 does not show the extent of the vendor's title. The purchaser cannot satisfy himself that the vendor has power to grant the easements provided for in the contract, such as rights of way or drainage. However it is possible when applying for the certificate to ask the Registry to confirm that the proposed rights are within the vendor's title. Vendors' solicitors can make arrangements for this information to be automatically included within the certificate[4].

(c) Approved transfers

The Registry is willing to approve a standard form of transfer for the estate, thereby enabling attention to be drawn to unusual features in the lay-out plan or the proposed contents. Approval of the transfer facilitates the proof of easements. A written assurance will be given by the Registry to the vendor that easements granted in the standard form will be registered as appurtenant to purchasers' individual titles. A purchaser relying upon this assurance is relieved of the duty of investigating the vendor's power to grant the easements[5].

(d) Building estates in non-compulsory areas

Although the Land Registration Act 1966, forbids voluntary registration of title within non-compulsory areas, the Registrar has exercised the discretion given to him by s. 1 (2) to permit it for building estates which, when developed, will contain at least twenty houses, flats or maisonettes, provided certain conditions are fulfilled[6]. The developer must lodge with his application for first registration a certificate in Form 168 C which incorporates various undertakings by the developer. In particular he agrees not to depart from the approved estate lay-out plan when constructing roads and erecting houses and boundary structures. Any changes must be notified to the Registry before any alteration occurs on the site. The Registrar reserves the right to suspend the registration of transfers of individual plots in the event of unauthorised deviations from the lay-out plan. The developer is also required to submit for official approval the draft form of standard transfer which must be adopted on each subsequent sale, subject only to essential variations (e.g. special rights rendered necessary by the character of the lay-out).

Once registered, the procedure already outlined in paragraphs (a) — (c) may be adopted on the subsequent transfer of plots to individual purchasers.

---

2   It was first put on a statutory basis in 1969, though it had been in operation for some years prior to this. See Ruoff, 'New Official Search Procedures' (1969) 66 LS Gaz 651, 653, claiming 'tremendous success' for the procedure.
3   See the correspondence in (1969), 66 LS Gaz 93, 227.
4   See Practice Note 39.
5   This will have been done by the Land Registry.
6   See Practice leaflet No.12.

4.   The title shown procedure[7]

The Registry has introduced a procedure, known as the title shown procedure, for adoption on the sale and subsequent first registration of the title to individual properties on large building estates. It is confined to *un*registered land within an area of compulsory registration. The prospective vendor deduces his title to the Registrar in the normal way. If he is satisfied as to the title, a letter is written to the vendor's solicitor stating the terms upon which an absolute title will be granted to subsequent purchasers. This letter is not just a mere opinion as to title. If copied and issued to prospective purchasers, it can be relied upon by them and the normal deduction and investigation of title can be dispensed with; the purchaser knows that the title is acceptable to the Registrar. There must, of course, be a conveyance to the purchaser. All proper searches must be undertaken, and a normal application for first registration submitted to the Registry. The contract for sale should provide for the adoption of this procedure.

This procedure is used when an established estate is being disposed of, as when a vendor offers to sell the freehold reversion to existing lessees. The Registry is only willing to operate the scheme in relation to estates comprising at least fifty houses, where the vendor's title is derived from a single conveyance in his favour. In the case of new development, a builder who has acquired his land prior to the introduction of compulsory registration can achieve the same result by registering his title voluntarily once the area has been made one of compulsory registration, notwithstanding the Act of 1966[8].

C   Leasehold titles

1.   The vendor's obligations

(a) Grant of lease
The Land Registration Act 1925, does not purport to alter the basic principles laid down by the Law of Property Act 1925[9], governing the investigation of title on the grant or sale of an existing lease. The obligations laid down by s. 110 only apply in favour of a purchaser *other than a lessee* or chargee. Therefore on the grant of a lease the lessee is not entitled to any office copy entries of the lessor's registered freehold title, and the desirability of contracting for such a right remains the same as in unregistered conveyancing. If the lessee investigates the freehold title or the lease is created out of a registered absolute title, the lessee can apply for registration with an absolute leasehold title[10].

(b) Sale of existing registered lease
Here the assignee ranks as a purchaser in relation to the leasehold title and is entitled to an authority to inspect the register, office copy entries and a copy of the filed plan. The vendor must also supply a copy or abstract of the lease which in effect constitutes the root of title as in unregistered conveyancing. This is

7   See further R & R, 238–44. For the special procedure applicable on the sale of
.   unregistered council houses pursuant to the Housing Act 1980, see s. 20 (2)–(4).
8   The Act does not prohibit voluntary registration *within* compulsory areas. Should this step
    not be taken, the individual sales-off will lead to first registration of title.
9   Section 44 (2)–(4), pp. 304–305, ante.
10   See further p. 459, post.

necessary because the property register contains merely brief particulars of the lease, such as the date, parties, term and rent. The Registry does not retain the original lease; at the most a copy is held there, and then not always[11].

Apart from any contractual stipulation to the contrary[12], the assignee cannot investigate the freehold title. On the sale of land registered with an *absolute* leasehold title, the purchaser need not concern himself with the superior title; the title is guaranteed even against defects affecting the freehold title and all restrictions affecting the reversion are entered on the lessee's title[13].

(c) Grant of underlease

The position on the *grant of an underlease* is rather obscure. In unregistered conveyancing the proposed underlessee is not barred by statute from investigating his own lessor's title[14], but he cannot call for the freehold reversion. The Land Registration Act 1925, does not define 'lessee', though 'lease' is defined to include 'undelease'[15]. Section 110 does not extend to a 'lessee'. Assuming that 'lessee' includes 'underlessee' the rights of an underlessee of registered land are more restricted than those of his unregistered counterpart, because he has no statutory right under s. 110 to call for information as to the lessee's registered title. It has been suggested that the grant of an underlease should be treated as a 'disposition of registered land' and the underlessee a 'purchaser' for the purposes of s. 110[16], an interpretation not without its own more fundamental objections[17].

(d) Titles less than absolute

In the case of a qualified or possessory leasehold, similar considerations to those previously mentioned in relation to the corresponding freehold titles apply, subject to the normal restrictions affecting superior titles.

(e) Non-registrable leases

On the sale of a lease for a term not exceeding twenty-one years (such a lease cannot, it will be recalled, be substantively registered), title must be deduced in the normal unregistered manner. To this extent, until some alteration is made to the present provisions regulating such leases, registration of title will never entirely supplant the unregistered system with its deducing and investigation of title.

---

11 An assignee of a lease applying for first registration is not required to supply a copy of the lease, though an original lessee so applying is. The Registry is not prepared, save in exceptional cases, to supply an office copy of any filed copy lease. See Practice Note 37.
12 LSC 8 (2) (a) (p. 306, ante) applies to all registered leasehold titles, except those that are absolute. On the sale of property registered with a good leasehold title, it may therefore be essential to exclude the operation of this condition.
13 See section 2, post.
14 Page 304, ante.
15 LRA 1925, s. 3 (x).
16 Potter, 304–5, adopted at 3 K & E, 321. R & R, 443 state that the normal law applies without considering the difficulty.
17 This would entitle the underlessee to investigate the freehold title, if the interpretation given by Simonds J (see note 19, post) to the word 'register' were to be applied to s. 110 (1). The new covenant for quiet enjoyment advocated by the Law Commission (pp. 314–316, ante) will, once implemented, improve the position of a lessee and an underlessee on the grant of a lease or underlease. See p. 357, post.

2.   Notice of superior title

As in unregistered conveyancing[18] an intending lessee or purchaser of registered leasehold property may be deemed to have notice of matters affecting a superior title, even though he has no means of ascertaining what they are. The problem exists in relation to good leasehold titles. By virtue of s. 50 (2) of the Act, on notice of a restrictive covenant (other than one between landlord and tenant) being entered on the register, the proprietor and the persons deriving title under him are deemed to be affected with notice of it. In *White v Bijou Mansions Ltd*[19] Simonds J, held that this provision extended to a purchaser of leasehold property without actual knowledge of the existence of the covenants affecting the registered freehold title. Consequently restrictive covenants noted against a registered freehold title are binding upon a lessee or a purchaser from him notwithstanding that he is not permitted by statute to inspect the register of the freehold title.

The lessee's position will be much improved if and when the proposed codification of our Landlord and Tenant Law reaches the statute book. For the purposes of the extended covenant for quiet enjoyment put forward by the Law Commission[20], a lessee will not be affected with notice under the Act of any incumbrance or entry appearing on any register of title other than his own, whether it be the register of the freehold title or any superior leasehold title. As we have seen the landlord will not be under any legal duty to provide an intending lessee with office copies of his title, the intention being that he will do this voluntarily in order to minimise any potential liability under the covenant.

The difficulty does not arise with absolute leasehold titles. Not only has the Registrar (at some time) approved the freehold title, but also on first registration a note will have been made on the lessee's title of all restrictive covenants appearing on the register of the superior title[1].

Restrictive covenants made between a lessor and a lessee cannot be noted on the register of title[2]. An underlessee is therefore bound by such covenants in the headlease if he has actual or constructive notice of them.

3.   Miscellaneous matters

A purchaser of a registered leasehold will be concerned to check that the rent is not in arrear and the covenants duly performed. He is entitled to the same evidence by way of proof as in unregistered conveyancing[3]. Where the lease contains a covenant against alienation without consent, the Registrar does not need to call for evidence of compliance before registering the transferee. Registration of an unlicensed transaction vests the legal title in the transferee but the entry on the transferor's title, excepting from the effect of registration all rights arising under an unlicensed transaction[4], ensures that the transferee cannot claim any indemnity if his title is upset by the lessor.

18   If the freehold title is unregistered, the position of a lessee whose title is registered is the same vis-à-vis the freehold as if the lease were not registered.
19   [1937] Ch 610, [1937] 3 All ER 269; on appeal [1938] Ch 351, [1938] 1 All ER 546.
20   Law Com. No. 67, paras. 57–58; Draft Bill cl. 5 (4) (b). See further pp. 314–316, ante.
 1   See R & R, 82–83.
 2   LRA 1925, s. 50 (1).
 3   LPA 1925, s. 45 (2), p. 309, ante.
 4   LRR 1925, r. 45.

D   Transmission on death

1.   Death of sole proprietor

On the death of a sole proprietor beneficially entitled, his personal representative can apply to be registered on production of the grant and the land certificate[5]. Without being registered himself, he can assent to the property vesting in the beneficiary, or can transfer it to a purchaser for value, leaving the beneficiary or purchaser to seek substantive registration. However a purchaser from the personal representative cannot be compelled to accept a title in this way[6]. Section 110 (5) of the Act enacts that a vendor selling on the basis of his entitlement to be registered cannot by contractual stipulation prevent the purchaser from insisting that the vendor first procures his own registration as proprietor. The purchaser can therefore require the personal representative to seek registration. This is, in fact, an unnecessary step, especially as the Registrar is not entitled to call for information concerning the reason why any transfer is made and must assume that the personal representative is acting correctly and within his powers[7].

Opinions differ as to whether the assent or transfer should contain an acknowledgment for production of the grant of probate or letters of administration in order to obviate any difficulty in lodging the grant at the Registry. However the point would appear to be academic in view of the Registry's willingness to accept in lieu of the original grant an official copy (obtainable from the Probate Registry) or even a plain copy (such as photographic copy), if certified by a solicitor as being a correct copy of the original grant[8].

(a)   Endorsement of notice of assent

Though there appears to be no express provision in the Act excluding the operation of s. 36 (6) of the Administration of Estates Act 1925[9], it is generally agreed that in relation to registered land an assentee who registers his title cannot be prejudiced by a failure to have notice of his assent endorsed on the grant of probate. His registration as proprietor vests the legal title in him and a subsequent disposition of the land by the personal representative in favour of a purchaser cannot deprive him of his title[10]. Indeed it would be contrary to the whole tenor of the Act if it were possible for a registered proprietor not guilty of any fraud to suffer rectification at the instance of some person whose alleged title only arose by virtue of some dealing effected after the assentee's registration. In any event a subsequent purchaser would not normally be able to claim the protection of s. 36 (6). His official certificate of search would reveal the existence of the assentee's registration with the result that a denial of any previous assent, given in the transfer to the purchaser, could not operate as 'sufficient evidence' of its correctness. For this reason it is not considered

---

5   LRR 1925, r. 168 (1).
6   It is suggested that such a purchaser would be difficult. See R & R, 599.
7   LRR 1925, r. 170 (1)–(5).
8   See Practice leaflet No. 6; R & R, 594; 19 Ency F & P, 1082 n. 6. Cf. Potter, 69–70; Emmet, 468.
9   See p. 336, ante.
10   R & R, 595 (referring to endorsement as a needless precaution); 3 K & E, 279. Were the subsequent purchaser to be registered as proprietor in error, the assentee could seek rectification under the LRA 1925, s. 82 (1) (e). It is perhaps advisable to endorse notice of an assent for record purposes.

necessary to incorporate in a transfer of registered land from a personal representative any statement that he has not given or made any previous assent or transfer[11].

(b) Effect of registration of personal representative

On registration, the personal representative holds the land upon the trusts and for the purposes upon and subject to which the same is applicable by law and subject to minor interests binding upon the deceased; but, save as to these matters, he is as regards any registered dealings in the same position as if he had acquired the land under a transfer for value[12]. An assentee, being a mere volunteer, is bound by all minor interests subject to which the deceased held the land.

2. Death of joint owner

On the death of one of two or more joint proprietors, his name will be deleted from the register on production of satisfactory proof of death[13] and the land certificate. This may also necessitate the removal of the restriction sometimes registered against joint proprietors[14].

E   Settlements

1. The curtain principle

As regards registered land the Settled Land Act 1925, takes effect subject to the provisions of the Land Registration Act 1925[15], but the latter Act in no way alters the substantive law governing settlements. It merely adapts the Settled Land Act machinery to the scheme of registered conveyancing. The mode of creation remains unchanged, except that a vesting deed affecting registered land must be in the statutory form[16]. The prescribed form contains all the details required by the Settled Land Act 1925, s. 5, and also includes a request for the entry of an appropriate restriction (the significance of which is considered in the next section). Registration of the proper person as proprietor is determined by the general law.

The curtain principle is preserved by the register of title and the beneficial interests are kept off the title. This principle is maintained in two ways. A purchaser is debarred from calling for production of any settlement filed in the Registry; he is not entitled to any copy or abstract of it nor is he affected with notice of its contents[17]. Secondly the beneficial interests arising under the

---

11 Normally a previous unregistered assent will not affect a subsequent registered purchaser of land included within the assent. But an interesting question arises whether an unregistered assentee in actual occupation can enforce his equitable interest under the will against the subsequent proprietor by virtue of s. 70 (1) (g) of the Act. His failure to endorse the probate coupled with the purchaser's reliance on the statement (if made) of no previous assent would seem to deprive the assentee of his 'rights' under the general law so as to make para. (g) inapplicable. But this view may not prevail now after the *Boland* case; see Chap. 3, ante.
12 LRA 1925, s. 43, a most obscurely drafted section; see R & R, 599; 3 K & E, 274.
13 LRR 1925, r. 172.
14 See p. 362, post.
15 SLA 1925, s. 119 (3).
16 LRR 1925, rr. 99–101; Forms 21–24.
17 LRA 1925, ss. 88 (1), 110 (1) (b).

settlement take effect as minor interests. They require protection on the register, as will be explained, but the beneficial limitations are never revealed by it and all dealings with the equitable interests take place off the register (being recorded in the Minor Interests Index)[18].

Protection of beneficial interests

The beneficiaries' rights are protected by means of an entry in the proprietorship register of a *restriction* which binds the proprietor during his life[19]. The Rules prescibe three different restrictions according to the circumstances[20]. The form (Form 9) for use when the tenant for life is registered as proprietor is as follows:

> No disposition by the proprietor of the land under which capital money arises is to be registered unless the money is paid to AB and CD (the trustees of the settlement of whom there must be two and not more than four individuals, or a trust corporation) or into court.
>
> Except under an order of the Registrar, no disposition is to be registered unless authorised by the Settled Land Act 1925.

Whilst it is clearly not the Registrar's duty to ensure that the appropriate restriction is entered, the Act deals with the question of this responsibility somewhat haphazardly. It may be the person applying for registration[1], or the deceased's personal representatives at the request of the statutory owners[2], or the trustees of the settlement[3] — all depending on the circumstances. As successive situations occur it may be necessary for an application to be made to vary the form of the restriction to meet the new circumstances.

2.   Changes of ownership

(a) Sale of settled land

The existence of the restriction in the proprietorship register warns a purchaser that he is dealing with settled land and notifies him of the need to pay the purchase money to the appropriate persons. Though the restrictions forbid registration of any disposition not authorised by the Settled Land Act 1925, this is to be read as referring to the statutory powers as extended by the settlement[4]. The register does not reveal these extended powers and a purchaser's only means of discovering them is to inspect the vesting instrument (which will set them out), which he can do by virtue of his authority to inspect the register.

(b) Death of life tenant

If the settlement continues the trustees of the settlement, as special personal representatives, will execute a vesting assent in favour of the succeeding life tenant by means of a document in the prescribed form. This contains an

---

18   LRA 1925, s. 102 (2). See note 8, p. 14, ante.
19   LRA 1925, s. 86 (3).
20   LRR 1925, r. 58.
 1   LRR 1925, r. 56. What if the applicant is unaware that the land is settled because of an inadvertent settlement; see *Binions v Evans* [1972] 2 All ER 70, [1973] CLJ 123 (R.J. Smith), [1978] Conv 229 (P.W. Smith). Occupation will not avail as against subsequent transferees as there can only be a minor interest. See LRA 1925, s. 86 (2) esp. '. . . not otherwise therein'.
 2   LRR 1925, r. 171 (1).
 3   LRA 1925, s.87 (6).
 4   LRR 1925, r. 58 (2).

application for entry of the appropriate restriction[5]. If the settlement terminates the deceased's general personal representatives, as in unregistered conveyancing, will execute an ordinary assent in favour of the person absolutely entitled. No deed of discharge is required[6]. The assent and the grant of probate (or copy) should be lodged at the Registry. The Registrar acts on the assent without question, registers the assentee as proprietor and automatically deletes the existing restriction[7].

3. Appointment of new trustees

New or additional trustees are appointed by deed in the manner prescribed by the Settled Land Act 1925. No deed of declaration is required. Its place is taken by an application to the Registry to modify the existing restriction by substituting the names of the new and continuing trustees in place of the previous ones[8]. This application should be signed by the life tenant, the previous trustees and the new and continuing ones, or by their respective solicitors. In the case of a deceased trustee his death certificate requires production.

4. Termination of settlement

A deed of discharge executed by the trustees is required on all occasions when it is necessary in unregistered conveyancing[9]. When lodged at the Registry, the Registrar is entitled to act upon it in the same way as would a purchaser of unregistered land. He must assume that the settlement has determined; accordingly he will cancel the restriction protecting the minor interests[10]. Termination of the settlement on the death of a life tenant has been considered.

F Trusts

1. Trusts for sale

Whenever registered land is transfered to joint owners, they hold on trust for sale under the general law. They are registered as proprietors[11] subject to an obligatory restriction which the Registrar automatically enters save in one situation[12]. No useful purpose is served by declaring the beneficial interests in the transfer, for this is lodged at the Registry and never sees the light of day although this is a common practice especially when the transfer is executed on first registration in lieu of an unregistered form of conveyance[13]. A deed of trust

---

5   LRR 1925, r. 170 (3), Form 57.
6   The position is the same as in unregistered conveyancing; SLA 1925, s. 110 (5), p. 319, ante.
7   Often in practice the assent includes a request for its removal, but this is unnecessary: R & R, 372.
8   LRR 1925, r. 235 (2), prescribing Form 77.
9   LRA 1925, s. 87 (4); LRR 1925, r. 106. See the SLA 1925, s. 17, pp. 319–320, ante.
10 LRA 1925, s. 87 (4).
11 LRA 1925, s. 94 (1). If there are more than four, the first four named will be registered: ibid., s. 95; Trustee Act 1925, s. 34.
12 LRA 1925, s. 58 (3).
13 LRR 1925, r. 72. For difficulties see *Pink v Lawrence* (1978) 36 P & CR 98, CA; *Robinson v Robinson* (1976) 241 Estates Gazette 153; (1977) 41 Conv (NS) 78–79, 365–366; [1979] Conv 5–7; R & R, 321.

or some written memorandum evidencing the beneficial interests is highly desirable in each case. If one of the proprietors refuses to join in a proposed transfer, an order for sale must be sought under s. 30 of the Law of Property Act 1925[14].

(a) The obligatory restriction

Except where the proprietors are entitled jointly in equity so that the survivor can give a valid receipt for capital money, the Registrar is obliged to enter a compulsory restriction, the modern form[15] of which reads:

> No disposition by one proprietor of the land (being the survivor of joint tenants and not being a trust corporation) under which capital money arises is to be registered except under an order of the Registrar or of the court.

This restriction is entered whenever the proprietors hold as tenants in common in equity, or for persons other than themselves. Its existence reminds a purchaser of the need to comply with s. 27 (2) of the Law of Property Act 1925. A sole surviving trustee cannot therefore pass a good title; if he proposes to sell, a new trustee must first be appointed. No application for entry of the restriction need be made. Every application for registration contains a question whether the survivor of joint proprietors can give a valid receipt, and the Registrar decides whether or not to enter the restriction, according to the reply given to that question. If the consent of some third person has to be obtained, a restriction to that effect is also entered.

(b) Law of Property (Joint Tenants) Act 1964

This Act does not apply to registered land[16]. The powers of a sole surviving trustee of registered land to pass a good title depend on the presence or absence of the restriction. Even if the survivor is not solely and beneficially entitled, a transferee for value prima facie[17] takes free from the interests of the beneficiaries should no restriction be entered.

(c) Single trustee for sale

The obligatory restriction procedure operates effectively in cases where it is apparent that there must be a trust for sale, either because one is expressly created, or because property is transferred to joint proprietors. However, as previously noted[18], a sole owner may strictly be a trustee for sale, in which case he ought to apply for entry of a restriction. But in practice he will usually be quite ignorant of his fiduciary character. In the absence of any protective entry against the title, a purchaser from a single trustee for sale will prima facie take free from the beneficiaries' interests in equity unless, perhaps, he has notice of them at the time of the transfer[19]. Moreover, if supported by actual occupation, a beneficiary's interest is capable of enforcement as an overriding interest under s. 70 (1) (g) of the Act, notwithstanding that it takes effect behind a trust for

---

14   See pp. 321–322, ante.
15   The form of restriction prescribed by the LRR 1925, r. 213 is no longer used, R & R, 380.
16   Section 3.
17   LRA 1925, s. 20 (1). But see para. (c) as to the possible effect of the purchaser's notice of the beneficiary's occupation.
18   Page 327, ante.
19   See *Peffer v Rigg* [1978] 3 All ER 745, doubted p. 72, ante. See also *Lyus v Prowsa Developments* (1982) 126 Sol Jo 102.

sale[20]. Additionally, the beneficiary himself can apply for entry of a restriction, provided the land certificate is produced at the Registry, otherwise he may lodge a caution[1]. Compared with his unregistered counterpart, a beneficiary under a trust for sale where there is only one trustee is much more favourably placed[2].

2. Dealings affecting equitable interests

Subsequent events affecting the equitable interests may render necessary cancellation of an existing restriction or require the entry of one for the first time. The need to cancel arises where a sole survivor, originally entitled in equity to an undivided share, becomes solely and beneficially entitled (e.g. under the will of his deceased co-proprietor). The Act declares that the obligatory restriction cannot be withdrawn[3], but this must be deemed subject to the proviso that the land remains subject to a trust for sale. To obtain cancellation of the restriction, the equitable title should strictly be produced to the Registrar, though in practice a statutory declaration by the survivor setting out the details is acceptable[4].

On severance of a joint tenancy in equity, a restriction should be entered to ensure that the survivor cannot make title by himself. The application can be made either by the registered proprietors or by the person effecting the severance, or in the case of bankruptcy, by the trustee or even the Registrar acting on his own initiative.

Subsequent dealings with the equitable interests, such as a sale by one of several equitable tenants in common to another or to a third person, operate behind the curtain and do not appear on the register. They need not result in any alteration in the legal title, though a registered proprietor ceasing to have any beneficial interest may prefer to retire from the trust. In this event the Registrar must give effect on the register to any express or implied vesting of the trust property in the continuing trustees[5].

20 *Williams & Glyn's Bank Ltd v Boland* [1979] 2 All ER 697, CA; affd. [1980] 2 All ER 408, HL. Similarly a beneficiary under a bare trust: *Hodgson v Marks* [1971] Ch 892, [1971] 2 All ER 684, CA.
1 *Elias v Mitchell* [1972] Ch 652, [1972] 2 All ER 153.
2 Who cannot register a land charge under the LCA 1972 (cf. *Taylor v Taylor* [1968] 1 All ER 843, CA), and whose occupation may not suffice to fix a purchaser with constructive notice of his rights, at least if the vendor is also in occupation: *Caunce v Caunce* [1969] 1 All ER 722, post. Whether this is still the case after the *Boland* case is now an open question.
3 LRA 1925, s. 58 (4).
4 LRR 1925, r. 214; R & R, 382.
5 LRA 1925, s. 47 (1). For the vesting of trust property on the retirement of a trustee, see the Trustee Act 1925, s. 40 (2).

Chapter 13

Investigation and acceptance of title

A Investigation of title

It is the purchaser's task to investigate the title which the vendor has deduced. Basically this involves three things:

(i) perusing the abstract and raising requisitions on title;
(ii) comparing the abstract with the original documents;
(iii) searching in the appropriate registers.

The first two of these processes are the concern of this chapter; the subject of official searches and the related topic of notice will be considered in the next chapter.

1. Perusal of the abstract

A study of the abstract or copy documents enables the purchaser's solicitor to ascertain whether the vendor is able to convey what he is contractually bound to convey. The solicitor cannot be completely satisfied on this until the deeds have been examined and the results of all necessary searches are to hand. In theory the examination of the deeds should be undertaken after perusal of the abstract and before the purchaser's solicitor asks his questions (requisitions), but in practice this is usually done on completion of the transaction.

The purchaser's solicitor is concerned to see that a good title is shown in accordance with the contract. He should satisfy himself on the following matters: that the abstract commences with the proper root of title; that particular documents are in law capable of having their supposed effect (which entails consideration of whether the executing parties had power to buy, convey[1], or otherwise deal with the property); that there are no subsisting incumbrances save for those mentioned in the contract; that all abstracted mortgages have been duly discharged; and that all documents are in order as to stamping, execution[2], registration, or other formal requirements. The identity of the property must be carefully checked[3]. It is often helpful to make an epitome or pedigree of the devolution of the title, so that an overall picture can be obtained at a glance.

Where the title is registered, it can readily be appreciated how much simpler this task is, particularly in relation to absolute titles. The purchaser is not

---

1 He should be watchful for conveyances in breach of trust.
2 Especially when executed under a power of attorney. See further pp. 436–440, post.
3 *Re Bramwell's Contract, Bramwell v Ballard's Securities Investments* [1969] 1 WLR 1659.

concerned with the devolution of the title. He must still ensure that the office copy entries do not reveal anything inconsistent with the description of the property in the contract. Requisitions may still have to be raised[4], but on the whole they tend to be the exception rather than the rule.

The simplification of our land law and the reduction in the period of investigation of title has, happily, greatly reduced, compared with one hundred years ago, the likelihood of the practitioner encountering a thoroughly bad title. Nevertheless the investigation of title is just as vital to the purchaser today. In the event of the title being defective, he is much more favourably placed if he discovers the defect before, rather than after, completion. Thus he may well be entitled to rescind the contract should the vendor be unable to remedy a defect discovered prior to completion, but thereafter he cannot as a general rule reopen the transaction. He cannot, for instance, recover the purchase money because he finds that the title is defective. What his remedies are in such situations is considered in Chapters 23 and 24.

2. Requisitions on title

Queries about or objections to the title, discovered by perusing the abstract, are brought to the vendor's attention by means of requisitions on title. They are technically more than mere questions, for they require the vendor to remove the defect or the doubt revealed by the abstract—hence their name.

(a) Nature of requisitions

The matters on which requisitions are in practice raised are legion. They may concern flaws or defects in the title[5], or inconsistencies between the contract description of the property and that deduced. The proper course here is to state the defect or objection and either ask how the vendor proposes to rectify it or state the purchaser's requirements. Over the years conveyancing practice has extended the categories of acceptable requisitions. Often they do no more than remind the vendor of matters on which the purchaser requires to be satisfied, e.g. the obtaining of a licence to assign, the discharge of an existing mortgage, the production of receipts on completion and the observance of covenants. Other requisitions may be concerned with the evidence of facts, the existence of official certificates of search or the clarification of mistakes in the abstract.

In the past use of standard form printed requisitions, obtainable from law stationers, tended to widen the scope of requisitions so as to include planning inquiries and non-title matters of a general nature. Printed requisitions have in large measure been superceded by preliminary inquiries, since the general non-title matters previously raised by way of requisition are now covered by preliminary inquiries and therefore resolved before exchange of contracts. Such matters need not be repeated later as so called requisitions. It is, however, customary to seek confirmation that if the preliminary inquiries were repeated as requisitions, the replies would be the same, a practice which, though judicially approved[6], has been criticised[7] on the grounds that it duplicates work and lets in many improper requisitions by the back door. A short form of printed requisitions is available for use when preliminary inquiries have been answered. This form deals with routine matters: the production of receipts

4 Page 370, post.
5 For typical illustrations, see 18 Ency F & P, 783–804.
6 *Goody v Baring* [1956] 2 All ER 11 at 16–17, per Danckwerts J.
7 (1959) 23 Conv (NS) 153–54; cf. Emmet, 160–161; Farrand, 115.

(e.g. for rates), the discharge of subsisting mortgages, completion and the mode of payment of the purchase money. Requisitions founded on the abstract or the contract must, of course, be added.

Improper or unnecessary requisitions. The purchaser should not raise requisitions which infer that relevant matter might have been suppressed from the abstract[8]. He is precluded by statute from making requisitions to the earlier title[9], but as we have seen he is not debarred from proving aliunde that the title is defective. One salutary point to remember is that most formal contracts contain a clause enabling the vendor to rescind the contract in certain circumstances if he is unable or unwilling to comply with a particular requisition[10]. This factor ought to suffice to confine the purchaser's requisitions to matters of substance upon which he is likely to insist if an unsatisfactory answer is given.

(b) Time for making requisitions

Where the contract is silent on this point, requisitions must be delivered within a reasonable time. This is clearly unsatisfactory, so a fixed period is provided for in the standard Conditions of Sale[11], as follows:

requisitions: to be sent within eleven working days after delivery of the abstract; *observations upon vendor's replies:* to be sent within six working days after delivery of those replies.

The National Conditions of Sale require the purchaser to raise his requisitions on the abstract as delivered, whether it is perfect or imperfect (i.e. incomplete). Time does not run in respect of any requisition that could not have been made on an imperfect abstract until the vendor has delivered the remainder of the abstract to complete the title[12].

(c) Time of the essence

The standard Conditions of Sale provide that time is of the essence in respect of the delivery of requisitions, notwithstanding that the abstract was not sent in due time. Subject to those requisitions raised in time, the purchaser is deemed to have accepted the title[13]. He cannot therefore resist an action for specific performance on the ground of an objection to title raised out of time[14] though

---

8   *Re Ford and Hill* (1879) 10 Ch D 365, p. 368, post. A request for confirmation that the property is not subject to any existing mortgage technically falls within this category; but on a sale of residential property some solicitors tend to raise this point when the abstract indicates that it is free from mortgage.

9   LPA 1925, s. 45 (1), p. 289, ante.

10   See p. 370, post.

11   NCS 9 (3). Cf. LSC 15 (2) (3) where the times are respectively six and four working days. Time is also made of the essence.

12   NCS 9 (5). Cf. old LSC 10 (3), deeming the abstract to be perfect, though in fact imperfect. This condition was somewhat harshly criticised in *Ogilvy v Hope-Davies* [1976] 1 All ER 683 by Graham J, whose own interpretation of it is capable of giving rise to absurdities. See at 686–87, where he indicates that a seriously deficient abstract cannot be considered as an adequate abstract at all. In effect, therefore, the purchaser could simply sit back and do nothing, as the time for raising requisitions would not have started to run. See further (1976) 126 NLJ 352. The position is not clarified under LSC 15 which specifically deals with the question of an incomplete abstract.

13   NCS 9 (5). See *Sinclair-Hill v Sothcott* (1973) 26 P & CR 490.

14   *Oakden v Pike* (1865) 34 LJ Ch 620. For a recent example see *Re Martins Bank Ltd's Contract, Thomas v Williams* (1969) 21 P & CR 221.

equity may refuse to decree specific performance if the title is clearly bad. A contractual provision that objections not made within the specific period are deemed to be waived and the title accepted has been construed as equivalent to making time of the essence[15].

The existence of the essential time clause for raising requisitions must not be overlooked by a solicitor acting for a purchaser whose mortgagee is separately represented. He may need the assistance of the vendor's solicitor to reply to the mortgagee's requisitions. Unless these are submitted within the contractual time limit, the vendor's solicitor can decline to reply, so causing difficulties for the purchaser, though usually he will do so by way of courtesy. It is clearly prudent for the purchaser's solicitor, before the time limit expires, to seek an extension for any requisitions raised by the mortgagee. This is normally granted in practice.

(d) Requisitions not subject to a time limit
A clause making time of the essence does not prevent the raising of requisitions out of time in three cases:

(i) *Objections going to the root of the title.* The purchaser can object that the vendor has no title at any time before completion; this is a fundamental objection importing that the vendor has broken or has no means of performing his contract, and the matter ceases to be simply one of objection and answer[16]. Apart from situations where the vendor has no title, e.g. because he has no power to sell[17], it is difficult to state with accuracy when an objection can be said to go to the root of the title for this purpose. It is not thought that it extends to an objection that the title is defective on account of some adverse third party right, such as a restrictive covenant or easement[18]. Requisitions on such matters are morely likely to fall within exception (ii).

(ii) *Defects not discoverable on perusal of the abstract*[19]. The purchaser is not bound by the time limits in respect of requisitions on matters discovered aliunde as a result of his own inquiries[20] or searches (e.g. the search in the land charges register), or on inspection of the deeds. He ought, however, to raise his requisitions on such matters within a reasonable time of their discovery[1]. It is customary for the purchaser's solicitor, when raising requisitions, to reserve the

---

15 *Oakden v Pike* (1865) 34 LJ Ch 620. This seems to be the true basis of this decision. It is not authority, it is submitted, for the view that the time for submission of requisitions is always of the essence, even without express mention; cf. 1 Dart, 173; Walford, 47–48.
16 *Want v Stallibrass* (1873) LR 8 Exch 175 at 181, per Kelly CB.
17 *Want v Stallibrass,* ante; *Saxby v Thomas* (1890) 63 LT 695 (vendor declining to obtain necessary consents); revsd. on other grounds (1891) 64 LT 65, CA. Cf. *Rosenberg v Cook* (1881) 8 QBD 162, CA (vendor having possessory title only; objection out of time not sustained).
18 See *McFadden v Pye* (1978) 93 DLR (3d) 198 (undisclosed easement restricting intended building operations not going to the root). Cf. Emmet, 163, suggesting the contrary; but the cases cited in support are both examples of defects not discoverable from the abstract.
19 *Warde v Dixon* (1858) 28 LJ Ch 315. This right is apparently reserved by LSC 15 (4). As to the NCS, see note 1, post.
20 *Re Cox and Neve's Contract* [1891] 2 Ch 109 (belated requisition as to undisclosed restrictive covenant upheld).
 1 Ibid., at 119, per North J. This rule continues to apply to contracts governed by the NCS, notwithstanding the new cl. 9(5), note 13, ante, the wording of which does not cover matters discovered aliunde.

right to make additional requisitions arising out of the usual searches and inspection of the deeds. The traditional reply, 'Noted subject to contract', does not entitle the vendor to refuse to answer any requisitions so arising.

(iii) *Matters of conveyance*[2]. Requisitions on such matters are strictly unnecessary, but they are often made simply as reminders. If they are raised they are not subject to any time limit[3], unless the Conditions of Sale are, exceptionally, expressed to include such matters. Perhaps the commonest example of a matter of conveyance is the discharge of a subsisting mortgage, provided (as will usually be the case) the vendor can discharge it as a matter of right. This will not be so when the legal date for redemption has not passed[4]. Technically, the purchaser is entitled to have the mortgage discharged by the time of completion; in practice his solicitor accepts an undertaking from the vendor's solicitor to do this after completion and to forward the mortgage deed duly vacated[5].

3. Vendor's replies

(a) Extent of vendor's duty

It has been said that the vendor is bound to answer all *specific* questions put to him in respect of the property or the title, unless this prima facie obligation is expressly negatived by the contract[6]. Inquiries of a general nature may strictly be ignored. In *Re Ford and Hill*[7] the vendors were held entitled to refuse to answer a requisition asking:

> ' Is there to the knowledge of the vendors or their solicitors any settlement, deed, fact, omission, or any incumbrance affecting the property not disclosed by the abstract?'

Where necessary a solicitor should always confirm the accuracy of his answers before replying to the requisitions. It has been suggested that a reply 'not so far as we are aware' should not be accepted if what is being sought is the *vendor's* confirmation[8]. A reply which accords with the general conveyancing practice does not give rise to any action by the vendor against his solicitor even though the answer enables the purchaser to resile from the contract[9]. Answers to requisitions submitted out of time should not be given without preserving the vendor's rights under the contract, otherwise he may be held to have waived them[10]. Simply to state that the replies are given 'as a matter of courtesy' may suffice for this purpose. But there is no hard and fast rule. In one case [11] where

---

2 See p. 280, ante.
3 *Re Scott and Eave's Contract* (1902) 86 LT 617.
4 Because e.g. it has been postponed, as in *Twentieth Century Banking Corpn Ltd v Wilkinson* [1977] Ch 99, [1976] 3 All ER 361.
5 For undertakings to discharge mortgages, see p. 423, post.
6 Emmet, 160, italics added.
7 (1878) 10 Ch D 365, CA. There is some uncertainty as to the limits of this decision; Emmet, loc. cit.
8 Emmet, 161.
9 *Simmons v Pennington & Son* [1955] 1 All ER 240, CA.
10 *Cutts v Thodey* (1842) 13 Sim 206. See also *Ogilvy v Hope-Davies* [1976] 3 All ER 683 (abstract delivered piecemeal; waiver of time limit inferred from request that purchaser raise his requisitions all at the same time). One consequence of a waiver might be to invalidate a notice to complete (see p. 414, post) served by the vendor if the purchaser delays completion. See further Emmet, 163.
11 *Luck v White* (1973) 26 P & CR 89.

the purchaser had already accepted the title before exchange of contracts, the vendor's solicitor's replies to out-of-time requisitions raised by a mortgagee were held not to constitute a waiver of the time stipulation. He was merely responding to the purchaser's solicitor's request for assistance in a transaction with a third party.

(b) Failure to reply

No time limit is specified in the National Conditions of Sale for answering requisitions, but procrastination by the vendor can prove fatal[12]. Should he delay the purchaser may serve a notice requiring an answer within a specific time (i.e. making time of the essence), failing which the purchaser can rescind the contract. In *Re Stone and Saville's Contract*[13] it was held that a notice to complete served by the vendor on the purchaser at a time when requisitions going to the root of the title remained unanswered entitled the purchaser to rescind at once, without first having to serve his own notice.

(c) Inaccurate replies

Little appears to have been said[14] about the standard of care that should be exercised when replying to requisitions, or about the purchaser's rights in the event of a reply proving to be erroneous. If he discovers the inaccuracy before completion, the purchaser should be able to re-open the question, whether it goes to the root of the title or not, even though the time for raising observations or replies has elapsed. The vendor can hardly rely upon his contractual rights where he has misled the purchaser. It is perhaps more likely that the error will only be discovered after completion. Whatever rights a purchaser may have, it seems he must be content with damages; he cannot have the transaction set aside, even if the reply is fraudulent. A statutory action for damages may lie if the false reply involves the concealment of any instrument or incumbrance material to the title; however, success requires proof of the defendant's intent to defraud[15]. An action in deceit may possibly lie[16] but this, though seemingly wider in scope than the statutory remedy, also requires a fraudulent intent. In the absence of fraud, the circumstance may be such as to give rise to an action on the covenants for title. However, as with preliminary inquiries[17], it would appear that a duty of care is owed when replying to requisitions, a duty which is owed separately by the vendor or his solicitor depending on the nature of the requisition raised. The purchaser could, therefore, sue for damages in respect of a negligent reply to a requisition if he could show that he had suffered financial loss resulting therefrom.

---

12   Cf. LSC 15 (2) which puts a four day time limit on the vendor. By clause 15 (5) time is of the essence thereby enabling the purchaser to rescind in the event of delay.

13   [1963] 1 All ER 353, CA.

14   For the fullest treatment, see Farrand, 116–117.

15   See LPA 1925, s. 183 (2), p. 299, ante; *District Bank Ltd v Luigi Grill Ltd* [1943] Ch 78, [1943] 1 All ER 136, where Lord Clauson assumed with considerable reservation (see [1943] 1 All ER at 139) that a failure to disclose the payment of rent in advance when answering requisitions came within s. 183. Maybe the section adds nothing to the liability incurred by the original omission from the abstract: Farrand, loc. cit.

16   *Gray v Fowler* (1873) LR 8 Exch 249 at 282, per Blackburn J, who suggested that a purchaser might recover damages in deceit for loss resulting from being induced to act on the vendor's representation, known by the vendor to be false, that the abstract was perfect.

17   In one respect there may be a difference. It does not seem open for the vendor's solicitor to give the replies 'without responsibility'. See *Wilson v Bloomfield* (1979) 123 Sol Jo 860 p. 189, ante.

(d) Observation on replies

Having considered the vendor's replies, the purchaser has a further period in which to submit any observations, should he still not be satisfied[18]. If as a result of a requisition a supplementary abstract is delivered, a question on that abstract constitutes an original requisition which the purchaser should raise within the appropriate time limit[19]. The vendor's offer of an indemnity may amount to a sufficient answer to the purchaser's objection[20].

The purchaser should always consider his position carefully before raising further observations. A purchaser who discovers a fundamental defect in the vendor's title may be entitled to repudiate the contract even before the completion date, provided he acts promptly. He will be deemed to have waived his right if, for instance, he seeks explanations or demands the getting in of outstanding interests[1].

(e) Rescission by vendor

It has for many years been the practice to insert in formal contracts a clause entitling the vendor to rescind the contract if the purchaser raises or persists in any objection to the title which the vendor is on reasonable grounds unable or unwilling to remove. The clause may take various forms and a detailed consideration of this right must await a later chapter[2]. Suffice it to say for the present that unless the clause is suitably drafted the vendor loses his right to rescind if he attempts to answer the requisition by, for example, supplying an abstract which purports to meet the objection[3]. The National Conditions of Sale cater for this difficulty by permitting rescission notwithstanding any intermediate negotiation or litigation[4]. The reference to litigation enables the vendor to rescind even after the commencement of proceedings by the purchaser for the recovery of his deposit (provided judgment has not been given[5]), but the court will normally award to the purchaser the costs of the proceedings up to the time of receipt of the rescission notice[6].

4. Registered land

Where the title to the property is registered there will be less need to raise requisitions on title, for registration will have eliminated any flaws or technical defects in the vendor's title. Some authorities suggest that a purchaser who tries to invent a requisition upon title properly so called is attempting the impossible[7]. Statements of this nature are based on a misconception of the true function of a requisition. Whether the title to the land is registered or unregistered, the purchaser must satisfy himself that the title deduced accords with the

---

18   See LSC 15 (3); NCS 9 (3).
19   *Re Ossemsley's Estates Ltd* [1937] 3 All ER 774.
20   *Re Heaysman's and Tweedy's Contract* (1893) 69 LT 89, CA; *Manning v Turner* [1956] 3 All ER 641 (insurance to cover contingent estate duty liability).
1   *Elliott and H. Elliott (Builders) Ltd v Pierson* [1948] Ch 452 at 456, [1948] 1 All ER 939 at 942, per Harman J. See further pp. 609−611, post.
2   See Chap. 23, post.
3   *Tanner v Smith* (1840) 10 Sim 410; cf. *Shoreditch Vestry v Hughes* (1864) 17 CBNS 137.
4   NCS 10 (1). Cf. LSC 16 which gives a purchaser a right to rescind in certain circumstances. See [1980] Conv 404, 410 (Wilkinson); [1981] Conv 6.
5   *Re Arbib and Class's Contract* [1891] 1 Ch 601.
6   *Isaacs v Towell* [1898] 2 Ch 285 (condition silent as to intermediate litigation).
7   R & R, 320; and see 18 Ency F & P, 174.

title contracted to be conveyed. Thus it is quite proper, to raise objections about restrictive covenants entered in the charges register, though not disclosed by the contract[8].

It may be necessary to raise requisitions about, for example, overriding interests (as to which the register of title is not conclusive), subsisting tenancies, identity, and cautions, though normally matters of this nature are resolved by pre-contract inquiries since the office copy entries are normally forwarded with the draft contract. In the case of a possessory or qualified title, requisitions may have to be raised upon the earlier title, or the defect, as the case may be, unless the raising of requisitions is precluded by the contract. The purchaser should ensure that the vendor complies with any restriction affecting his powers of disposition. Thus the existence of a restriction in Form 62[9] may necessitate the appointment of another trustee. The vendor's attention should be directed to this, though strictly it is a matter of conveyance.

5.   Examination of original documents

It is the duty of the vendor to verify the contents of the abstract and certain aspects of this duty were considered in Chapter 10. Verification takes place when the purchaser examines the abstract against the original documents in the vendor's possession. This section is concerned with two additional matters: (a) the object of examination and (b) the time when it should be undertaken.

(a) Object
Since the abstract does not constitute the vendor's evidence of title[10], it is essential to compare it with the actual deeds and documents in his possession. Indeed it has been said that the real proof of title only begins on verification and the most careful scrutiny of the abstract may be completely worthless if the purchaser's solicitor is lax in examining the evidence in its support[11]. The object of this examination may be said to be fourfold[12] — to ascertain:

(i)   that what has been abstracted is correctly abstracted;
(ii) that what is omitted from the abstract is immaterial;
(iii) that all documents are perfect respecting execution, attestation, and stamps;
(iv) that there are no memoranda endorsed on the deeds, nor any circumstances attending the mode of execution or attestation calculated to arouse suspicion.

When the abstract comprises photographic copies of the relevant documents the task of examination is greatly facilitated. The above four points will not necessarily be applicable in every case. But the purchaser's solicitor ought never to dispense with an examination of the original deeds. An inspection may, for example, reveal that part of a deed, or a memorandum endorsed on it, has inadvertently been omitted from the copy. Much of what appears in the next

---

8   See p. 149, ante.
9   Page 362, ante.
10 But see p. 302, ante, as to examined abstracts.
11 1 Williams, V & P, 180. Yet, somewhat surprisingly, the survey of conveyancing procedures contained in The Law Society's Report of Evidence to the Royal Commission on Legal Services did not mention this examination of the original deeds; see sec. XII, pp. 101–102, paras. 3.14–3.22.
12 1 Dart, 425.

paragraph, which is concerned primarily with the position when an abstract in traditional form has been supplied, is also relevant in situations where photographic copies have been provided.

The description of the property sold should always be carefully checked (especially where the abstract refers to it as 'the before abstracted premises'), and the wording of covenants watched. It is important to look for possible memoranda which are often endorsed on the back of a deed. Those most likely to be encountered in practice are those relating to restrictive covenants, the grant of easements, sales-off, the appointment of new trustees, and in the case of a grant of probate, assents affecting the deceased's property. Besides examining all abstracted deeds, search certificates and other certificates produced as evidence of abstracted facts should be inspected. It would also seem prudent to inspect any other documents and papers in the packet of deeds relating to the period of title which the purchaser has investigated; in this way information relating to some third party right might come to light or the existence of a material document omitted from the abstract discovered. He need not concern himself with title deeds dated prior to the time fixed for the commencement of the title, for he is not deemed to be affected with notice of any matter or thing relating to the earlier title unless he actually investigates such title[13]. Nevertheless he is not precluded from taking objection to the title if he does inspect a deed prior to the root of title and thereby discovers a defect in the title[14].

That the examination of the abstract against the deeds is a very vital part of the transaction has already been stressed. Unfortunately, even before the advent of photocopies, the verification of the abstract was all too frequently performed in a rather cursory fashion, or by some inexperienced person. Nowadays, particularly where photographic copies have been supplied, the examination is a very perfunctory affair. When completion takes place 'through the post'[15] it may sometimes be dispensed with altogether — a practice which clearly bears the stamp of professional negligence, but which some practitioners happily adopt, seemingly as a means of simplifying conveyancing procedures and reducing costs. In other cases the thoroughness of the examination will vary, depending on the circumstances. A verbatim check of an abstract in traditional form is most desirable whenever the original deeds are not to be handed over on completion, e.g. on a sale-off, for the abstract will be used as the purchaser's principal documentary evidence of title on future sales[16]. On the purchase of a typical suburban house, the title to which has been deduced several times before, it may be sufficient for an experienced practitioner merely to check that the vital parts of the abstracted deeds (e.g. date, stamp duty, parties, descriptions and execution) have been correctly abstracted[17]. When an abstract has been examined, a note to this effect is usually written in the outer margin, unless the original deeds are to be handed over on completion.

---

13   LPA 1925, s. 44 (8), p. 284, ante.
14   *Smith v Robinson* (1879) 13 Ch D 148 (discovery of counterpart lease in bundle of deeds when examining abstract).
15   See further Chap. 15, post. The vendor's solicitor will normally be asked to act as the purchaser's solicitor's agent on completion.
16   Page 302, ante.
17   All the abstracted deeds should be so checked, even those purporting to have been examined on a previous occasion. A solicitor should never rely on an examination conducted by someone else, though sometimes he has no alternative, as where the vendor

(b) Time

The former practice was to examine the deeds before raising requisitions. Technically this is the correct procedure, for requisitions should strictly relate to those queries which a purchaser is not able to resolve on verification of the abstract. Nowadays it is the almost invariable practice to leave the inspection of deeds until the time of actual completion, a procedure which does not meet with the approval of the Council of The Law Society[18]. Doubtless the increasing pressures of business life, coupled with the belief that the inspection of deeds is unlikely to reveal anything adverse especially if the title has frequently been examined on previous sales within a comparatively short period of time, have encouraged solicitors to adopt this time-saving practice. The discovery on completion of a serious defect is bound to result in delay to the annoyance and inconvenience of both parties, and this possibility ought perhaps to be a sufficient condemnation of the procedure. In practice, however, an inspection at this late stage does not seemingly operate to the parties' detriment, largely because so few major defects are in fact discovered, though it is conceivable that defects might well be overlooked, which would not have been missed had more time been available to consider the matter. The practice, often adopted in the case of trivial defects, of completing subject to the vendor's solicitor's undertaking not to account to his client for the purchase money until the defect is rectified, is open to serious objection.

It would not appear to be too late to raise an objection on completion, notwithstanding that the time for raising requisitions has elapsed. A defect only discoverable by inspection of the deeds would rank normally as a defect not discoverable on the face of the abstract itself and in respect of such defects the usual time clause does not apply. Some support for this view is afforded by the recent decision in *Pagebar Properties Ltd v Derby Investment Holdings Ltd*[19], where a purchaser was held to be entitled to object to the existence of a lease which his solicitor did not discover until he examined the deeds on completion. However, according to the Council of The Law Society[20], a solicitor may be guilty of negligence if, as a result of a belated examination of the deeds, he is out of time with his requisitions.

(c) Registered land

Under s. 113 of the Land Registration Act 1925, office copies of and extracts from the register of title are admissible in evidence to the same extent as the originals. A purchaser is entitled to compensation for loss resulting from any inaccuracy in them. Since the accuracy of office copies supplied by the vendor is guaranteed, verification against the actual register or the land certificate is technically unnecessary, provided the purchaser makes an official search[1] of

does not possess the deeds of the earlier title. In such a situation the solicitor ought to locate the whereabouts of the deeds and examine his 'marked' abstract against them. In practice this is not normally done; see p. 302, ante.

18   Law Society's Digest, Third Cumulative Supplement, Opinion No. 95 (a); Emmet, 164.
19   [1973] 1 All ER 65.
20   See note 18, ante. It is significant that in the *Pagebar* case Goulding J seems to have accepted that the purchaser could object only if there was no fault on his part (see at 70). It is, perhaps, arguable that a failure to examine the deeds within the period allowed for raising requisitions constitutes fault, and so bars the purchaser's objection. The purchaser was not at fault in the *Pagebar* case; his solicitor had, prior to exchange of contracts, inspected counterparts of the leases which were stated by the contract to affect the property.
1   See p. 404, post. For s. 113, see p. 351, ante.

the register prior to completion to ensure that the entries are up to date. Nevertheless a brief comparison of the copy entries with the land, or charge, certificate is normally undertaken on completion.

6.   Investigation of title by mortgagee

A mortgagee should investigate the mortgagor's title in the same way as if he were a purchaser. The possibility of the mortgagee having to exercise his power of sale on the mortgagor's default renders it necessary for him to ensure that he is lending on a good marketable security. It is common practice for an institutional lender to instruct the purchaser's solicitor to act with the result that there is no separate investigation on the mortgagee's behalf. Two matters of particular concern to an intending mortgagee must be mentioned.

(a)   Tenancies created before completion
Most purchases of residential property are made with the assistance of a mortgage. If prior to completion the purchaser is allowed into possession of the property and he purports to grant a legal tenancy of part (or the whole) to a third party, the tenancy will bind the mortgagee. At the time of its creation the purchaser has no legal estate to support the grant but at law a tenancy by estoppel arises; under the doctrine of feeding the estoppel, the tenancy becomes a legal tenancy on the purchaser's acquisition of the legal estate on completion. Though the conveyance to, and the mortgage by, the purchaser usually take effect virtually simultaneously there are in law two separate transactions. The conveyance precedes the mortgage; the tenancy is fed as from the moment of the conveyance so that the tenancy becomes binding on the mortgagee[2]. The tenancy must be capable of existing as a legal estate; an informal tenancy cannot be fed and will not bind the mortgagee unless it has been registered as an estate contract[3]. Where the land is registered, the mortgagee is bound if the tenant is in occupation at the time of the mortgage, irrespective of whether he holds under a legal or an equitable lease; his rights constitute an overriding interest[4].

Only by inspecting the property immediately before completing can a mortgagee ensure that no tenant is in occupation — clearly an impracticable procedure. It is common practice for the mortgagee's solicitor to obtain confirmation that the purchaser has not created or agreed to create any tenancies, but the purchaser's false reply will not bind the tenant unless in some way he was a party to the representation[5]. The possibility of the mortgagee's being bound can, in theory, be averted by a direct mortgage from the vendor to the mortgagee, followed by a conveyance to the purchaser subject to the mortgage[6]. However this seemingly neat but, for the vendor and purchaser, rather bewildering procedure is not a solution that is ever adopted in practice by institutional lenders, who are content to rely on inquiries made of the prospective mortgagor.

2   *Church of England Building Society v Piskor* [1954] Ch 553 [1954] 2 All ER 85, CA. See also (1977) 41 Conv (NS) 197 (P.W. Smith) considering *Jessamine Investment Co v Schwartz* [1976] 3 All ER 521 CA.
3   *Coventry Permanent Economic Building Society v Jones* [1951] 2 All ER 901. See *Midland Bank Trust Co Ltd v Green* [1981] 1 All ER 153, HL.
4   *Grace Rymer Investments Ltd v Waite* [1958] Ch 831, [1958] 2 All ER 777, CA; LRA 1925, s. 70 (1) (g).
5   See *Piskor's* case at 561 and 89, respectively, per Lord Evershed MR.
6   For a precedent see 14 Ency F & P, 388, Form 3:91; Emmet, 846–47.

(b) Priority
Whilst there can be only one legal fee simple estate in a particular plot of land
at any one point of time, several mortgages may affect the mortgagor's title at
the same time and the mortgagee needs to preserve his priority both as regards
existing and subsequent mortgages. It is not proposed to consider here the rules
governing the priority of mortgages[7]. Suffice it to say for present purposes that
although in large measure the question of priority is governed by registration
under the Land Charges Act 1972, there may still occur today situations when
it is necesary to apply the old rules of priority, as where the contest is between an
equitable mortgage protected by a deposit of the deeds (which is not registrable
as a land charge[8]) and a subsequent legal mortgage. On general principles the
mortgagee ought to be fixed with constructive notice of all facts which he would
have discovered upon the usual investigation of title[9], and he should be bound
by any prior (unregistrable) equitable mortgage if he refrains from investigating the title. However in determining questions of priority between competing
mortgaees the courts have sometimes by-passed the rules of notice in favour of a
doctrine of 'gross negligence'.
Hudston v Viney[10] serves as an illustration:

> In 1908 legal mortgagees of a freehold house accepted as a sufficient root
> of title a deed of 1888 by which the property was conveyed to the mort-
> gagor. They did not call for any abstract of title nor make any further
> investigation. In 1889 the mortgagor had created an equitable charge on
> the property, of which the mortgagees were unaware.

Eve J held that they took free from the equitable charge. Although they
had been negligent in not investigating the title, their carelessness was not
sufficiently gross to disentitle them to the protection of the legal estate. Had
the principle of notice been applied, the mortgagees ought, it seems, to have
been bound. Eve J appears to have assumed that this situation was no different
from those cases where the concept of gross negligence had been applied to
deprive a prior mortgagee of his priority[11]. In this he apparently had the
support of the earlier Court of Appeal decision in *Oliver v Hinton*[12], where a
purchaser of a legal estate who did not investigate the title and accepted an
inadequate excuse for the non-production of the deeds was held bound by a
prior equitable charge because of her gross negligence. Perhaps this decision is
best explained on the basis that a purchaser whose negligence is so gross as to
justify the court in concluding that there had been fraud in the equitable sense
is not a bona fide purchaser and so not entitled to equity's protection, irrespective of the question of notice[13]. So understood the case does not conflict[14] with
the ordinary rules of notice, but it provides no support for Eve J's, decision in

7 See M & W, 958—76.
8 Unless the argument that it requires registration as an estate contract is sound; see p. 386, post.
9 *Earl of Gainsborough v Watcombe Terra Cotta Clay Co Ltd* (1885) 54 LJ Ch 991; *Berwick & Co v Price* [1905] 1 Ch 632 at 638, per Joyce J.
10 [1921] 1 Ch 98.
11 E.g. *Clarke v Palmer* (1882) 21 Ch D 124 (postponement of legal mortgagee failing to ask for deeds). Nowadays he would be postponed on account of non-registration.
12 [1899] 2 Ch 264, CA; *Hewitt v Loosemore* (1851) 9 Hare 449.
13 At 275, per Sir F.H. Jeune. P. Lindley MR (at 273), expressly refrained from basing his judgment upon constructive notice.
14 Cf. M & W, 964, esp. n. 75.

Hudston v Viney[15] which, it is submitted, was wrongly decided. The absence of gross negligence merely went to the question of the mortgagees' good faith, leaving the separate question of notice to be determined by ordinary principles.

B   Acceptance of the title

The culmination of these processes of deducing, investigation and verification is the acceptance of the title by the purchaser. Except where there is an express acceptance (which is rare), or the purchaser is contractually bound to accept the vendor's title, a final acceptance does not in practice occur until completion of the transaction. In whatever manner acceptance takes place (and this will be considered shortly), it only relates to the title shown by the abstract. The purchaser can still raise objections not arising on the abstract[16], or on matters of conveyance. The purchaser's conduct may amount to a waiver of defects disclosed by the abstract, or of irremovable objections of which he has knowledge. In each case the question is whether the facts establish an intention to waive[17]. No intention to waive will be inferred if the purchaser continues to insist upon his objections or acts without prejudice to his right to require a good title[18].

(a) Conduct amounting to acceptance

(i) *Failure to send requisitions.* Certain old cases establish that a failure to raise requisitions or request an abstract constitutes a waiver of the right to investigate the title[19]. This matter is nowadays governed by the Conditions of Sale. The purchaser is deemed to have accepted the title, except for requisitions and observations that are delivered within the appropriate time limits[20].

(ii) *Delivery of draft conveyance.* A purchaser's solicitor normally submits a draft conveyance for approval by the vendor's solicitor at the same time as he delivers his requisitions. The Law Society's Conditions expressly provide that delivery of the draft or of the engrossment does not prejudice outstanding requisitions[1]. Even in the absence of such a clause, submission of a draft document for approval does not of itself operate as a waiver[2], and in any case it is common practice to make its submission 'subject to the vendor's replies to requisitions being satisfactory'.

(iii) *Taking possession.* Entry into possession does not under the standard Conditions of Sale operate as an acceptance of title or waiver of the right to raise requisitions[3], neither does the purchaser's possession under an express condition in the contract[4]. If the contract is silent on the question of waiver, the position is not absolutely clear; taking possession, though not by itself

15 [1921] 1 Ch 98.
16 *Bown v Stenson* (1857) 24 Beav 631; *Becker v Partridge* [1966] 2 QB 155, [1966] 2 All ER 266, CA.
17 *Flexman v Corbett* [1930] 1 Ch 672 at 682–83, per Maugham J.
18 *Burroughs v Oakley* (1819) 3 Swan 159, an important case on waiver.
20 Page 366, ante.
1 Condition 17 (3). See also Con Law CS 19 (1) (c). The NCS are silent on this point.
2 *Burroughs v Oakley* (1819) 3 Swan 159.
3 NCS 8 (3); LSC 18 (3).
4 *Stevens v Guppy* (1828) 3 Russ 171.

conclusive of an acceptance, will have this effect if coupled with other circumstances. For example, a purchaser who makes structural alterations to the property after receiving notice of an adverse incumbrance not disclosed in the contract will be held to have waived his right to object to the title on that account[5].

(b) Receipt of abstract prior to exchange of contracts

Reference has already been made[6] to the growing practice of forwarding the abstract of title with the draft contract. When this happens the purchaser's solicitor usually investigates the title before exchange of contracts, adding any 'requisitions' to his preliminary inquiries. In the absence of any requirement in the contract he is not obliged to do so. A solicitor who declines to investigate the title at this stage is well advised to preserve his client's rights to object to defects discovered by the post-contract examination. Perhaps he ought also to obtain his client's prior authority to adopt this course of action, certainly if he has any reason to suspect there might be difficulties with the title. It does not follow, however, that a purchaser whose solicitor exchanges contracts without expressly preserving the right to raise objections will be deemed thereby to have accepted the title. The terms of the contract must be considered. Thus, Condition 12 (3) of The Law Society's Conditions states that the purchaser is not fixed with notice of any matter contained in an abstract delivered pre-contract, unless the property is expressly sold subject to it. Apart from specific provisions of this type, the contractual term regulating the raising of requisitions is itself a prima facie denial of any acceptance[7], though this can be rebutted by clear evidence, e.g. from the correspondence passing between the solicitors, that the purchaser has accepted the title.

(c) Purchase subject to specific defect

A purchaser who discovers a defect in the title may elect to purchase the property subject to that defect. The vendor cannot resist specific performance on the ground that he has contracted to give a good title; such a term, being for the purchaser's benefit alone, can be waived by him[8].

---

5   *Re Gloag and Miller's Contract* (1883) 23 Ch D 320 (purchaser's knowledge of restrictive covenants). The mere taking of possession *with knowledge of* the incumbrance would bar his right to object if it were an irremovable defect, but not in the case of a removable defect such as a mortgage: ibid., at 327–28, per Fry J.
6   See p. 277, ante.
7   *Luck v White* (1973) 26 P & CR 89 at 93, per Goulding J. See particularly LSC 15 (2) (requisition to be raised within six days of contract date when abstract delivered before contract).
8   *Bennett v Fowler* (1840) 2 Beav 302 at 304, per Lord Langdale MR; *Valley Ready Mix Ltd v Utah Finance and Development (NZ) Ltd* [1974] 1 NZLR 123 (purchaser accepting title subject to undisclosed tenancy).

Chapter 14

Searches for incumbrances

A Introduction

One final step must be undertaken before completion, the search for registered land charges, or where the title is registered, the search for adverse entries on the register of title. In addition a search may be necessary in the Companies Register if the vendor is a limited company. A second search for local land charges is rarely made, as the responsibility for charges registered after the contract is normally made to fall on the purchaser[1].

There is no guarantee that the purchaser's investigation of title will disclose all incumbrances affecting the land. Indeed the complexities of our land law are such that the vendor himself may not be aware of them all. Discovery of an incumbrance aliunde prior to completion may entitle the purchaser to rescind the contract. Once completion has taken place, the question of its enforceability becomes vital. Whether or not the purchaser of a legal estate takes subject to a third party right depends on two principal considerations: notice and the nature of the right. Irrespective of notice he takes subject to existing *legal* estates and interests. These confer rights in rem enforceable against the whole world, though Parliament has made a limited encroachment upon this basic principle[2]. As to *equitable* interests, a bona fide purchaser for value of the legal estate takes free from any equitable interest of which he has no notice. This doctrine of notice has been severely curtailed by the system of registration under the Land Charges Act 1972, but by no means eclipsed. There are some equitable interests which do not fall within the ambit of the Act, and the number of such interests appears to be increasing, as recent decisions show[3]. The courts' continued willingness to apply the doctrine of notice is unfortunate; for, despite the drawbacks of the system of registration, the Act does provide a simple criterion for determining the question of enforceability.

Exceptionally a legal owner may be postponed to a *later* incumbrancer (legal or equitable) on the ground of fraud, estoppel, or gross negligence in relation to

---

1 Page 201, ante.
2 See e.g. the AEA 1925, s. 36 (6) (divesting of legal estate vested in beneficiary by assent), p. 336, ante, and the LPA 1925, s. 88 (1) (effect of conveyance by mortgagee), p. 339, ante.
3 See *E.R. Ives Investment Ltd v High* [1967] 2 QB 379, [1967] 1 All ER 504, CA (estoppel interest); *Shiloh Spinners Ltd v Harding* [1973] AC 691, [1973] 1 All ER 90, HL (equitable right of re-entry). See further p. 389, post.

the title deeds, a possibility most likely to occur within the field of mortgages when a prior mortgagee may be postponed to a subsequent mortgagee[4].

The doctrine of notice plays virtually no part in the system of land registration. A purchaser for value takes subject to all overriding interests and to all minor interests duly protected on the register, whether he knows of them or not[5]. He does, however, take free from the rights of a person in actual occupation of the land if inquiry is made of such person and the rights are not disclosed[6].

B   The purchaser without notice

Equity's jurisdiction has always stopped short of the purchaser of a legal estate, whose conscience is not affected by notice of an equitable right. In the words of James LJ, the plea of purchase for valuable consideration without notice is an absolute, unqualified, unanswerable defence, and an unanswerable plea to the jurisdiction of the Court of Chancery[7]. Various aspects of this defence require closer examination.

1.   Purchaser for value

In legal terminology a purchaser is a person who acquires an interest in land otherwise than by operation of law and includes a lessee or mortgagee. 'Value' means any consideration in money, money's worth (such as securities, other land, the discharge of an existing debt[8]) or marriage, provided it is a *future* marriage. A donee, and a devisee under a will, though technically purchasers, never come within the scope of the equitable doctrine since they give no value. They take subject to prior equitable interests, even those of which they have no notice. A squatter is similarly bound[9]; he is not a purchaser, acquiring his title by operation of law.

Equity only protects the purchaser for value if he is bona fide. Fraud or sharp practice deprives him of his special privileges. Fraud in the legal sense is not necessary. Negligence so gross as to justify a court of equity in concluding that there had been fraud in an artificial sense of the word suffices, such as omitting to make any investigation of the title of the property[10].

2.   Legal estate

Subject to the question of conscience, equity always accords due preference to the legal title whenever the contest is between a legal owner and an equitable owner. Where the rival claimants are both equitable owners, equity adopts the rule *qui prior est tempore, potior est iure*. The purchaser of an equitable interest is normally bound by a prior equitable interest, with or without notice,

---

4   See *Snell's Principles of Equity* (27th edn) pp. 56–57. See also *Walker v Linom* [1907] 2 Ch 104 (trustees failing to obtain title deeds postponed to subsequent equitable incumbrancer).

5   See *Parkash v Irani Finance Ltd* [1970] Ch 101, [1969] 1 All ER 930, p. 406, post. *Williams and Glyn's Bank Ltd v Boland* [1980] 2 All ER 408. But see *Peffer v Rigg* [1978] 3 All ER 745, and *Lyus v Prowsa Developments Ltd* (1982) 126 Sol Jo 102, p. 73, ante.

6   LRA 1925, s. 70 (1) (g).

7   *Pilcher v Rawlins* (1872) 7 Ch App 259 at 269.

8   *Thorndike v Hunt* (1859) 3 De G & J 563.

9   *Re Nisbet and Pott's Contract* [1906] 1 Ch 386, CA (restrictive covenant).

10   See *Oliver v Hinton* [1899] 2 QB 264, CA, discussed on p. 375, ante.

though he takes free from a mere equity of which he is unaware. This rule is subject to qualifications some of which arose for consideration in the recent case of *McCarthy and Stone Ltd v Julian S. Hodge and Co Ltd*[11].

> V contracted to sell land to P. V then created an equitable mortgage in favour of B who subsequently obtained a legal mortgage on the land. P registered his contract after the equitable mortgage but before the legal mortgage. P sought a declaration that his interest was free from B's mortgage, which the court granted.

B could not rely on the non-registration of the contract at the time of his equitable mortgage because he was held not to be a purchaser of a legal estate. His rights therefore depended on the general law. B claimed priority on the basis of the equitable doctrine enshrined in *Bailey v Barnes*[12] that a subsequent equitable incumbrancer who gets in the legal title takes precedence over the prior incumbrancer. Foster J held that although the wider equitable principle had survived the abolition of the doctrine as it applied to mortgages[13], it did not avail B who had constructive notice of P's rights. He also held that B could not rely on the doctrine of better right to call for the legal estate[14] by virtue of the declaration of trust in the equitable mortgage. V, having already become a trustee for P under the contract for sale, could not later declare himself a trustee for B.

3.   Without notice

Notice may be actual, constructive or imputed.

(a) Actual notice

This arises where the existence of the equitable interest is within the purchaser's own knowledge. Apparently a purchaser is not bound to attend to vague rumours or to statements by mere strangers; to be binding the notice should proceed from some person interested in the property[15]. This expression of the rule is perhaps too narrow; a purchaser would seem under a duty to investigate information emanating from a reasonable source, otherwise he might be fixed with constructive notice of matters he would have discovered on inquiry. Registration of any instrument or matter under the Land Charges Act 1972, is deemed to constitute actual notice thereof[16].

(b) Constructive notice

In their concern to ensure that too many purchasers of a legal estate did not escape through the net, the Chancery judges developed a complicated doctrine of constructive notice. Apart from this doctrine, a purchaser would have had every incentive to refrain from making inquiries, for the less he knew the better.

---

11   [1971] 2 All ER 973, noted at (1971) 35 Conv (NS) 357; *Rice v Rice* (1853) 2 Drew 73 (unpaid vendor's lien postponed to later equitable mortgage). See also *Re Sharp* [1980] 1 All ER 198, at 204 where Browne-Wilkinson J suggested that a purchaser of a legal estate would take free from an irrevocable licence if he did not have *express* notice of it.
12   [1894] 1 Ch 25.
13   See the LPA 1925, s. 94 (3).
14   *Taylor v London and County Bank Co* [1901] 2 Ch 231; *Assaf v Fuwa* [1955] AC 215, PC. See [1955] CLJ 32.
15   *Barnhart v Greenshields* (1853) 9 Moo PCC 18 at 36, per Lord Kingsdown.
16   LPA 1925, s. 198, p. 396, post, save for the purposes of the LPA 1969.

Constructive notice is the knowledge which the courts impute to a person upon a presumption so strong of the existence of the knowledge that it cannot be allowed to be rebutted, either from his knowing something which ought to have put him to further inquiry or from his wilfully abstaining from inquiry, to avoid notice[17]. Clothed as it now is in statutory form the rule reads thus. A purchaser shall not be prejudicially affected by notice of any instrument, matter or fact unless it is within his own knowledge, or would have come to his knowledge if such inquiries and inspections had been made as ought reasonably to have been made by him[18]. Clearly a purchaser is not affected with notice of a matter which he could not have discovered by making reasonable inquiries. Constructive notice may arise in three main ways.

(i) *Failure to make proper investigation of title.* This has already been considered in Chapter 10.

(ii) *Notice from the possession of deeds.* A purchaser (including a mortgagee) is bound to inquire for the title deeds and should insist on their production. If he does not do so, or accepts an unsatisfactory explanation for their non-production, he will take subject to the rights of the person having their custody. An explanation that the deeds were deposited at a bank for safe custody has been held to be insufficient to protect a purchaser[19].

Notice of a deed forming part of the title is notice of its contents[20]. Where a vendor in good faith informed the purchaser that an original deed had been lost and produced what purported to be a true copy, the purchaser was held bound by restrictive covenants not disclosed by the copy[1]. A purchaser is not deemed to have constructive notice of a deed's contents unless that deed necessarily affects the title[2].

(iii) *Failure to inspect property.* Every prudent purchaser should inspect the property. Normally he does this, though frequently he will fail to appreciate the legal significance of what he sees. Where the vendor is not in possession, the purchaser should inquire of the occupant, otherwise he will take subject to his rights. Occupation by a tenant fixes a purchaser of the land with notice of all the tenant's rights, including e.g. an option to purchase the freehold[3], but not with notice of the lessor's title or rights[4]. But what if the vendor resides on the property and another person is in sole occupation of part or shares the occupation with him? In *Caunce v Caunce*[5] it was held that a mortgagee of land in a husband's name but in which his wife had an equitable interest did not have notice of her interest by reason of her occupation there. Stamp J formulated the proposition that where the vendor is himself in occupation[6], the purchaser is

---

17 *Hunt v Luck* [1901] 1 Ch 45 at 52, per Farwell J; affd. [1902] 1 Ch 428, CA. The doctrine does not require any fraudulent intent on the purchaser's part; his negligence suffices to make it applicable.
18 LPA 1925, s. 199 (1) (ii) (a).
19 *Maxfield v Buton* (1873) LR 17 Eq 15.
20 *Peto v Hammond* (1861) 30 Beav 495.
1 *Hooper v Bromet* (1903) 89 LT 37; varied (1904) 90 LT 234, CA.
2 *Re Alms Corn Charity, Charity Comrs v Bode* [1901] 2 Ch 750.
3 *Daniels v Davison* (1809) 16 Ves 249.
4 *Hunt v Luck* [1902] 1 Ch 428, CA.
5 [1969] 1 All ER 722.
6 Aliter if the vendor is not living in the house (see at 728).

not affected with notice of the equitable interest of any other person who may be resident there and whose presence is wholly consistent with the title offered. This was considered to be a welcome decision for conveyancers[7]. To hold otherwise would render it necessary to make inquiries of every adult occupier, inquiries embarrassing to ask, intolerable to have to answer and perhaps in the end result uninformative.

To what extent this case can now be relied upon is a matter of doubt in view of the decisions of *Hodgson v Marks*[8] and *Williams and Glyn's Bank Ltd v Boland*[9]. Russell LJ in the first of these cases, whilst not quarrelling with the actual decision in *Caunce v Caunce* (which in his view could be supported on the ground that the wife's occupation could rightly be taken as that of her husband), was not prepared to accept statements tending to lay down a general proposition that inquiries could be dispensed with if the vendor was himself in occupation. A purchaser must pay heed to anyone in occupation if he is to be sure of getting a good title, and the law will protect the occupier (except so far as his rights require registration) even though the purchaser has no ready opportunity of finding out. In the *Boland* case the Court of Appeal were prepared to consider that occupation may constitute notice[10]. The House of Lords however confined their decision to registered land[11] but there are suggestions of disapproval of *Caunce* in the judgments[12]. It is considered that *Caunce* can no longer be regarded as correctly decided but the decision is still technically open. The argument that such a view would lead to an impossible burden of inquiry was dismissed as not a real problem[13] on the very dubious ground that conveyancing is generally conducted on the basis of good faith with something of a long stop in the shape of covenants for title.

Purchasers and their advisers are now left in a state of uncertainty as to the extent of the inquiries that should be made. Pending clarification of the position purchasers ought to err on the side of caution, making more rather than less inquiries, inconvenient though this may be[13a].

(c) Imputed notice
Actual or constructive notice possessed by the purchaser's agent is imputed to the purchaser. This rule is of particular importance in conveyancing transactions since the majority of vendors and purchasers employ a solicitor. The agent's notice is imputted to the principal only if it is acquired in the same transaction[14]. Knowledge obtained in a previous transaction does not suffice. Where the same solicitor acts for both parties, notice which he acquires in that

---

7   M & W, 447. Perhaps 'quasi matrimony' as opposed to matrimony ought to be considered the more likely 'blot' on the title.
8   [1971] Ch 892, [1971] 2 All ER 684, CA, p. 51, ante, where the problem is considered in relation to registered land. Though strictly an authority on registered land his comments are directly applicable to the problem of constructive notice as it affects a purchaser of unregistered land: see pp. 931 and 688, respectively.
9   [1980] 2 All ER 408, HL, affirming the Court of Appeal [1979] 2 All ER 697.
10   Ibid at 705, 708 and 714.
11   [1980] 2 All ER 408.
12   At 413, per Lord Wilberforce, and 418, per Lord Scarman.
13   See note 8, ante, at 932 and 688, respectively, a view which contrasts markedly with Russell LJ's comments in *National Provincial Bank Ltd v Hastings Car Mart Ltd* [1964] Ch 665 at 700–701, [1964] 1 All ER 688 at 704, CA. See also *Williams & Glyn's Bank Ltd v Boland* [1980] 2 All ER 408 at 415.
13a   See the inquiries before contract in this regard, p. 182, ante.
14   LPA 1925, s. 199 (1) (ii) (b). And see the LPA 1969, ss. 24 (4). 25 (11).

transaction as the vendor's agent is imputed to the purchaser[15] unless the solicitor agrees to conceal it from the purchaser[16].

4.   Successors in title

If A, a purchaser without notice of an equitable interest, later conveys to B, B can shelter behind A's lack of notice and take free from that interest, irrespective of his own notice. This consequence is not because of any special indulgence towards the successor, rather the need to protect A, the original purchaser without notice, so as not to 'clog the sale of estates'[17]. In effect A's lack of notice enables him to deal with his land unincumbered by the equitable interest[18]. There appears to be no authority to the effect that a volunteer from A, e.g. A's devisee, also takes free from the equitable interest but it would seem to follow on principle since he succeeds to A's unincumbered estate. It is thought, however, that a squatter would be bound; he is not a successor in title of the former dispossessed owner and equity's reason for protecting the successor is inapplicable in the case of a squatter.

One important qualification exists to this rule. A man cannot profit from his own wrong. A trustee selling trust property in breach of trust to a purchaser without notice continues to hold the property subject to the trusts if he later acquires the property[19]. This exception does not in terms cover the situation where V conveys land subject to an enforceable equitable interest to P, a purchaser without notice, and later reacquires it from P, for V is not a trustee for the equitable owner. Yet V ought on principle to be bound, for he cannot purge his own conscience by conveying to a purchaser without notice.

C   System of registration of charges

1.   Scheme of Land Charges Act 1972[20]

The scheme of the Land Charges Act 1972, is to compel[1] the owner of a registrable interest to protect his rights by registering it in an appropriate register maintained at a central Registry and open to public inspection. The Act achieves its objective indirectly by providing that failure to register avoids the interest in certain circumstances. A purchaser who takes a conveyance of land without searching the register takes subject to all registered interests, for registration constitutes *actual* notice[2]. Hence the importance of the search for incumbrances.

---

15   *Kennedy v Green* (1834) 3 My & K 699; *Mayer v Charters* (1918) 34 TLR 589.
16   *Sharpe v Foy* (1868) 4 Ch App 35.
17   *Lowther v Carlton* (1741) 2 Atk 242, per Lord Hardwicke.
18   *Wilkes v Spooner* [1911] 2 KB 473 at 484, CA, per Vaughan Williams LJ; *Kitney v MEPC Ltd* [1978] 1 All ER 595 at 605, CA, per Goff LJ.
19   *Re Stapleford Colliery Co, Barrow's Case* (1880) 14 Ch D 432 at 445, per Jessel MR, applied in *Gordon v Holland* (1913) 108 LT 385, PC (repurchase by partner from purchaser without notice of property originally sold in breach of partnership agreement).
20   Replacing the LCA 1925. References to 'the Act' appearing in the remainder of this chapter are to be taken as references to the LCA 1972, unless the context otherwise requires.
 1   But he owes no duty to the other party to register: *Wright v Dean* [1948] Ch 686, [1948] 2 All ER 415 (lessee's failure to register option no bar to recovery of damages from lessor). See *Midland Bank Trust Co Ltd v Green* [1981] 1 All ER 153, HL, revsg [1979] 3 All ER 28, post.
 2   LPA 1925, s. 198, p. 396, post.

It is tempting to interpret the Act as operating within the equitable doctrine of notice; it simply provides a statutory procedure for giving notice by way of registration. The Act does more than this. It extends the scope of the equitable rule by embracing some *legal* interests and in some cases confers protection on a mere *equitable* owner. It does not, however, apply to all equitable interests and those outside the Act continue to be governed by the equitable rule. Some commentators prefer therefore to treat the Act as establishing a separate system[3].

A system of registration is workable only so long as registered interests are readily discoverable. Since the time it first came into operation the Land Charges Act 1925, has suffered from one fundamental defect, and the Act of 1972, being merely a consolidating measure, makes no attempt to remedy it. Charges are registered not against the burdened land but against the estate owner. A purchaser can only make an effective search if he knows the names of all estate owners since 1925. This knowledge he is invariably denied, for the vendor need only deduce title for a period of fifteen years. In consequence a purchaser may be bound by a charge the existence of which he has no practical means of discovering.

The Law Commission considered, but rejected on the ground of impracticability, various possible alternatives[4]. Only the extension of the system of registration of title will eliminate the problem, and even then not completely so long as certain leasehold estates are incapable of registration. The Commission's temporary solution, given legislative effect by the Law of Property Act 1969[5], was to introduce a statutory right to compensation in certain cases.

Under s. 1(1) of the Act five separate registers are maintained in the Land Charges Register as follows[6]:

(a)   a register of land charges;
(b)   a register of pending actions;
(c)   a register of writs and orders affecting land;
(d)   a register of deeds of arrangement affecting land;
(e)   a register of annuities[7].

There is also kept at the Registry a register of agricultural charges required to be registered under the Agricultural Credits Act 1928[8].

2.   Register of land charges

Land charges comprise by far the most important category of registrable interests. They are divided into six classes, A, B, C, D, E, and F which was added to the original list by the Matrimonial Homes Act 1967. These six classes comprehend charges on or obligations affecting land[9], other than local land charges which are regulated by the Local Land Charges Act 1975. To constitute a land charge within the Act, there must be a charge on *land* which in general terms is defined[10] to mean corporeal land or incorporeal hereditaments. It does not

3   M & W 144.
4   Report on Land Charges Affecting Unregistered Land, Law Com. No. 18, paras. 17–27.
5   Section 25, p. 396, post.
6   See further 'Computerised Land Charges', published by H.M. Land Registry.
7   Cf. s. 1 (1) of the LCA 1925, where the register of land charges appeared at the bottom of the list.
8   These relate to charges in favour of a bank on farming stock and other agricultural assets; they do not directly affect the land.
9   LCA 1972, s. 2 (1).
10   LCA 1972, s. 17 (1).

include the proceeds of sale of land. Thus a charge on an undivided share of land is not a registrable land charge[11].

Our attention must now be turned to the individual classes which are defined in s. 2 of the Act. Unfortunately, uncertainty exists as to the precise scope of some of the classes. This is a major defect of the Act. It is highly desirable that a solicitor, who has to apply the Act in day to day conveyancing transactions, should be able to tell at a glance what obligations require registration, and the importance of giving to the section a plain and ordinary interpretation has recently been stressed[12].

(a) Class A: s. 2 (2)

This category consists of financial charges on land created pursuant to the application of some person under the provisions of a statute. It covers, for example, a charge obtained by a landlord in respect of compensation paid to a tenant for improvements to business premises[13].

(b) Class B: s. 2 (3)

This group comprises charges (not being local land charges) similar to those within Class A, save that they are imposed automatically by statute. Most of the charges which would qualify for inclusion within this Class are in fact excluded because they constitute local land charges and are therefore registrable in a local registry. The central Registry in Plymouth attracts few class B registrations. An example occurs under the Legal Aid Act 1974, which creates a charge in favour of The Law Society on property recovered or preserved for an assisted litigant[14].

(c) Class C: s. 2 (4)

The following constitute Class C land charges: a puisne mortgage, a limited owners' charge, a general equitable charge and an estate contract. Where the charge was created before 1 January 1926, it can only be registered if it is acquired under a document made on or after that date[15].

C (i) *Puisne mortgage.* This is any *legal* mortgage not being a mortgage protected by a deposit of documents relating to the legal estate affected. If a mortgagee has the title deeds, their non-production by the mortgagor will give notice of the mortgage to persons subsequently dealing with the land; protection by registration is unnecessary. It is not clear whether *all* the documents relating to the estate must be deposited with the mortgagee. Perhaps it suffices if the conveyance or other document vesting the estate in the mortgagor is handed over[16], though it would appear preferable to require the mortgagee to hold all the deeds relevant to the mortgaged estate.

11 *Re Rayleigh Weir Stadium* [1954] 2 All ER 283. See also *Georgiades v Edward Wolfe and Co Ltd* [1965] Ch 487, [1964] 3 All ER 433 (charge on deposit and proceeds of sale of land not registrable); *Taylor v Taylor* [1968] 1 All ER 843. Cf. the position under the LRA 1925, p. 69, ante.

12 *Shiloh Spinners Ltd v Harding* [1973] AC 691, [1973] 1 All ER 90 at 99, HL, per Lord Wilberforce. His observations were directed at s. 10 of the LCA 1925, now replaced by s. 2.

13 Landlord and Tenant Act 1927, s. 12 and Sch. 1, para. (7). For other examples, see the LCA 1972, Sch. 2; Emmet, 658.

14 Section 9, see *Hanlon v Law Society* [1981] AC 124, [1980] 2 All ER 199, HL.

15 LCA 1925, s. 2 (8), but a puisne mortgage created before that date may be registered before any transfer of the mortgage is made: s. 3 (3).

16 Williams, *Title*, 693, M & W, 901; cf. Emmet, 874.

C (ii) *Limited owner's charge.* This is defined as any equitable charge acquired by a tenant for life or statutory owner under the Finance Act 1975, or other statute, by reason of his discharge of capital transfer tax or other liabilities. Such a charge arises where a life tenant discharges capital transfer tax[17] payable on the death of the previous life tenant out of his own pocket instead of resorting to the settled property.

C (iii) *General equitable charge.* This is a comprehensive class of *equitable* charge *not included in any other class of land charge.* By definition it *excludes*:

(a)   an equitable charge protected by a deposit of deeds relating to the legal estate affected;

(b)   a charge arising or affecting an interest under a trust for sale or settlement;

(c)   a charge given by way of indemnity against rents equitably apportioned or charged on land.

The following appear to be registrable within this class: equitable charges of a legal estate, a vendor's lien for unpaid purchase money[18], annuities charged on land created after 1925[19], an equitable rentcharge. Strictly speaking an equitable mortgage would seem to fall within the next class, C (iv), as a contract to create a legal mortgage. This view, if sound, would, in relation to equitable mortgages protected by a deposit of deeds, appear to be contrary to the general policy of the 1925 property legislation which is to exclude from registration all mortgages secured by a deposit of deeds. Perhaps an equitable mortgage is now so well established as a conveyancing device in its own right that the courts will not insist that its enforceability depends on registration where it is accompanied by the deeds[20]. An equitable mortgage not protected by any deposit is registrable, not as a C (iii), but as a C (iv) land charge because of the express exclusion from Class C (iii) of any charge included in another class[1]. In practice, a purchaser having notice of the existence of an equitable mortgage (either from non-production of the deeds or registration as a C (iii) land charge), will insist upon its discharge, rather than rely on its being void against him for non-registration as a C (iv)[2].

C (iv) *Estate contract.* An estate contract is defined as:

' a contract by an estate owner or by a person entitled at the date of the contract to have a legal estate conveyed to him to convey or create a legal estate, including a contract conferring either expressly or by statutory implication a valid option to purchase, a right of pre-emption or any other like right.'

In addition to the rights included by express reference, this definition embraces (inter alia) a contract for the sale of land, an agreement for a lease,

---

17   See Finance Act 1975, s. 28 (4).
18   See *Uziell-Hamilton v Keen* (1971) 22 P & CR 655.
19   For annuities created before the Act.
20   See M & W, 970—971; Fisher and Lightwood, *Law of Mortgage* (9th edn), p. 52, Rowley, 'Conveyancing and Equitable Charges' (1962) 26 Conv (NS) 445, 446—49. The Report of the Committee on Land Charges (the Roxburgh Committee) 1956, Cmd. 9825, para. 16, recommended legislation to make it clear that such mortgages were not registrable.
1   *Shiloh Spinners Ltd v Harding* [1971] 2 All ER 307 at 316, CA, per Russell LJ; rvsd. [1973] AC 691, [1973] 1 All ER 90, HL.
2   Rowley, loc. cit.

an option to renew a lease[3], an equitable mortgage, a boundary agreement if there is a contract to convey land but not an agreement which merely confirms existing boundaries[4], and a contract to grant a legal easement[5]. A notice to treat is not registrable[6]. Writing is not essential to registrability of the contract[7].

The ambit of this class of charge has been judicially considered on several occasions. It is not confined to cases where a contracting party is to receive the legal estate; a contract between A and B whereby A contracts to convey a legal estate to B's nominee suffices[8], but not a contract whereby A agrees that B has power to accept offers to purchase made by third parties[9]. Provided the grantor possesses some estate in the land affected (estate ownership of *other* land does not suffice), it is immaterial that at the time of the contract he does not own the estate the subject of the contract. In a somewhat controversial decision the Court of Appeal held in *Sharp v Coates*[10] that a contract by a yearly tenant to grant a term of years if he became entitled to the freehold reversion constituted an estate contract which was unenforceable for non-registration against a purchaser of the freehold. A contract to convey unspecified land which may be acquired in the future is not registrable; there must be identifiable land affected by the contract to facilitate registration of the relevant particulars[11].

Registration of sub-contracts. Suppose A contracts to convey land to B and before completion B contracts to sell the same land to C. The B — C contract is within the definition of an estate contract, since B is 'a person entitled at the date of the contract to have a legal estate conveyed to him'. However, certainty ends here. Registration by C of his contract against B's name is ineffective[12]. Registration is required to be in the name of the estate owner (i.e. legal estate owner[13]) and this is A, not B, unless this can be said to be a situation where the context requires an extended meaning to be given to 'estate owner' so as to include an equitable owner[14]. It is generally accepted that C can register

3   *Beesly v Hallwood Estates Ltd* [1960] 2 All ER 314; affd. on other grounds [1961] Ch 105, [1961] 1 All ER 90, CA; *Taylor Fashions Ltd v Liverpool Victoria Trustees Co Ltd* [1981] 1 All ER 897. There are now problems over rights of pre-emption notwithstanding the express reference thereto. See *Pritchard v Briggs* [1980] Ch 388, [1980] 1 All ER 294, CA, ante. As to a contract to enter into a contract for sale of land, see *Daulia Ltd v Four Millbank Nominees Ltd* [1978] Ch 231, [1978] 2 All ER 557, CA. As to conditional contracts see [1974] CLJ 211–214 (R.J. Smith).
4   *Neilson v Poole* (1969) 20 P & CR 909, p. 516, post.
5   See the Roxburgh Committee, loc. cit.; *Gale on Easements* (14th edn) p. 72. In *E.R. Ives Investment Ltd v High* [1967] 2 QB 379 at 403, [1967] 1 All ER 504 at 513, CA, Winn LJ, accepted as correct counsel's submission that an agreement for a right of way should have been registered as an estate contract.
6   *Capital Investments Ltd v Wednesfield Urban District Council* [1965] Ch 774, [1964] 1 All ER 655.
7   LCA 1972, s. 3 (5); *Universal Permanent Building Society v Cooke* [1952] Ch 95 at 104, [1951] 2 All ER 893 at 898, CA, per Jenkins LJ; *Mens v Wilson* (1973) 231 Estates Gazette 843; *Jones v Morgan* (1973) 231 Estates Gazette 1167. The contract must be enforceable.
8   *Turley v Mackay* [1944] Ch 37, [1943] 2 All ER 1.
9   *Thomas v Rose* [1968] 3 All ER 765.
10 [1949] 1 KB 285, [1948] 2 All ER 871, CA; *Barrett v Hilton Developments Ltd* [1975] Ch 237, [1974] 3 All ER 944, CA. .
11 *Thomas v Rose* [1968] 3 All ER 765 at 769, per Megarry J.
12 *Barrett v Hilton Developments Ltd*, ante.
13 LCA 1972, ss. 3 (1), 17 (1), post.
14 As is argued by Adams, 'A Fly in the Ointment: Estate Contracts and the Land Charges' Computer' (1971) 35 Conv (NS) 155, where the problems are considered; see also (1937) 2 Conv (NS) 101. In *Holland New Homes Ltd v A.J. Wait & Co Ltd* (1971) 221 Estates

against A once he is aware of A's identity, though in practice he may not discover this until B delivers an abstract of title some weeks or months later, by
which time C's registration could be too late. Yet it is illogical that a contract
between B and C should require registration against A, a person who is not
bound by the contract. It seems clear that even though C registers his contract
against A, he cannot enforce it against a purchaser from A if B has failed to
register his own contract against A. These difficulties highlight again the
inherent weakness of a scheme requiring registration against names, rather
than against land[15].

(d) Class D: s. 2 (5)
This class comprises three groups.

D (i) *Charge for capital transfer tax.*   The Commissioners for Inland Revenue
may register a charge for such taxes[16]. They rarely do so. A charge can only be
registered in respect of freehold land[17].

D (ii) *Restrictive covenant.* This is described as a covenant or agreement
restrictive of the user of land, other than one made between lessor and lessee[18],
or entered into before 1926. Restrictive obligations imposed by a local authority are normally registered as local land charges[19]. A covenant to observe and
perform existing restrictive covenants by way of indemnity does not require
registration.

The application of the registration provisions to restrictive covenants arising
under building schemes is obscure. If the Act is relevant, total enforceability
by the purchasers and their successors inter se cannot be achieved unless the
common vendor registers the covenants against each purchaser. There is much
to be said for the view that a building scheme is outside the Act as it creates
reciprocity of obligation between the purchasers[20]. This argument at least has
the merit that the common vendor cannot destroy the scheme, in whole or in
part, by failing to register.

D (iii) *Equitable easement.* Like some of the other Classes, this category, has
been criticised on the grounds of vagueness. The Roxburgh Committee[1] even
suggested its abolition, but the Law Commission recommended a reprieve,
especially as D (iii) registrations ran at an annual rate of 2,500–3,500[2]. For the
purposes of the Act an equitable easement is:

Gazette 148, CA, the court treated a registration against the sub-vendor as effective and
for reasons not here relevant declined to vacate the entry. This decision was not considered
in the *Barrett* case.

15 See further Emmet, 656–657, discussing the *Barrett* case from the point of view of a third
purchaser after registration of the estate contract. Unless successors in title can rely on a
clear search, the effectiveness of the land charges system will be further questioned.
16 LCA 1972, s. 2 (5) as amended by Finance Act 1975, Sch. 12, para. 18 (3).
17 See generally Finance Act 1975, Sch. 4, paras. 20, 21 concerning the charge and
successors in title and Diamond *Capital Transfer Tax*, pp. 323–326.
18 Including other land not in the lease *Dartstone Ltd v Cleveland Petroleum Co Ltd* [1969] 3
All ER 668.
19 Local Land Charges Act 1975, s. 1. The exception as between lessor and lessee is
preserved, ibid., s. 2 (a).
20 (1928) 78 Law Jo 39; contra, Emmet, 624–625. Recent decisions on mutual benefits and
burdens, especially *E.R. Ives Investment Ltd v High* [1967] 2 QB 379, [1967] 1 All ER 504,
CA, perhaps add some weight to this argument.
1   Cmd. 9825, para. 16.
2   Law Com. No. 18, para. 65. This figure for the year ending 31 March 1981 was 1,550.

' an easement, right or privilege over or affecting land created or arising on or after 1 January 1926, and being merely an equitable interest.'

This class clearly covers the *grant* of an easement for life, or for a determinable period, e.g. a right of way until a road is adopted. A *contract* to grant a legal easement requires registration as an estate contract[3]. The words 'right or privilege' should be construed eiusdem generis with 'easement', and confined to incorporeal rights or rights similar in their general incidents to incorporeal rights[4]. Interests which confer a right to possession appear to be excluded. According to Lord Denning, MR[5], an equitable easement is some proprietary interest in land such as would before 1926 have been recognised as capable of being conveyed or created *at law*, but which since 1925 only takes effect as an equitable interest. Consequently rights arising in equity by reason of 'mutual benefit and burden', or arising out of acquiescence, or by reason of a contractual licence are not registrable within Class D (iii); such rights are creatures of equity, having no counterpart at law.

The ambit of Class D (iii) has recently been considered in *Shiloh Spinners Ltd v Harding*[6], where the House of Lords, reversing the Court of Appeal, held that an equitable right of re-entry[7] on breach of covenant was not a registrable land charge. Their Lordships rejected the argument, which had found favour with the majority of the appellate court, that all equitable claims affecting land must be either registrable as land charges, or capable of being overreached and transferred to the proceeds of sale under s. 2 of the Law of Property Act 1925. Furthermore, the right of re-entry did not fall within the category of an 'easement, right or privilege'. According to Lord Wilberforce[8], to include it in the description of 'equitable easement' offended a sense of elegance and accuracy, and there existed a difference of quality, not merely of degree, between a right to use or draw profit from another's land, and a right to take his land away altogether. Their Lordship's desire to give the Land Charges Act 1972, (as it now is) a straightforward interpretation is most laudable, but any extension of the doctrine of notice must, surely, be viewed with considerable misgivings.

(e) Class E: s. 2 (6)

Annuities created before 1926 but not then registered in the existing register of annuities[9] are registrable as Class E annuities.

3 Note 5 p. 387, ante. Whether it also requires registration within Class D (iii) is uncertain; cf. Gale, loc. cit. And see note 7, post.
4 *Lewisham Borough Council v Maloney* [1948] 1 KB 50, [1947] 2 All ER 36, CA (requisitioning authority's right to possession not a D (iii)).
5 *E.R. Ives Investment Ltd v High* [1967] 2 QB 379 at 395, [1967] 1 All ER 504 at 508, CA, applied by Cross J, obiter, in *Poster v Slough Estates Ltd* [1969] 1 Ch 495, [1968] 3 All ER 257 (right of entry to remove fixtures not registrable). See Davidge, 'Equitable Easements' (1937) 59 LQR 259.
6 [1973] AC 691, [1973] 1 All ER 90, HL, [1971] 2 All ER 307, CA.
7 The right was held not to come within the LPA 1925, s. 1 (2) (e). In the Court of Appeal, Russell LJ held that the right fell within both Class D (iii) and Class C (iv), thus lending some judicial support to the view that duplication among the various classes of s. 2 may exist; see [1971] 2 All ER 307 at 316. The House of Lords summarily dismissed the contention that a right of re-entry, which is penal in character, was a 'like right' within the definition of an estate contract. See further (1971) CLJ 258 (P.B. Fairest).
8 [1973] 1 All ER 90 at 98.
9 See p. 391, post.

(f)   Class F: s. 2 (7)

The Matrimonial Homes Act 1967[10], gives a spouse having no legal estate in the matrimonial home certain statutory rights of occupation during the subsistence of the marriage. These rights constitute a charge on the property, which is registrable as a Class F land charge. Ownership of an equitable interest in the property does not preclude registration of the charge[11] but registration does not give the charge priority over an existing mortgage[12], nor is it enforceable against the other spouse's trustee in bankruptcy[13]. Unlike the majority of land charges which are created by some transaction entered into by the estate owner affecting his land, so that he should in theory be aware of the likelihood of the charge being registered against him, a Class F charge arises by virtue of the statute and the non-owning spouse may register it without notifying the estate owner. As we have already seen[14], this situation can create difficulties for the estate owner should he subsequently contract to sell the property in ignorance of the registration[15].

3.   The other registers

(a)   Register of pending actions

Pending land actions and bankruptcy petitions are registrable in the register of pending actions[16]. A pending land action means[17] any action or proceeding pending in court relating to land or any interest in or charge on land. A summons claiming a declaration of entitlement to a share in the proceeds of sale of a house[18] is not registrable as there are no proceedings affecting an interest in land[19]. Registration of a bankruptcy petition, which is usually sought by the registrar of the court where the petition is filed, is essentially a temporary measure pending registration of the receiving order. It is registered against the bankrupt, whether or not he is known to own any land.

(b)   Register of writs and orders

The following are registrable in this register[20]—

10   Sections 1 (1), (2) (1), as amended by the Matrimonial Homes and Property Act 1981.
11   Matrimonial Proceedings and Property Act 1970, s. 38. See also Matrimonial Homes and Property Act 1981, s. 1.
12   Matrimonial Homes Act 1967, s. 2 (8). The spouse has a right to pay the mortgage instalments: s. 1 (5); but see *Hastings and Thanet Building Society v Goddard* [1970] 3 All ER 954, CA. See further Matrimonial Homes Act 1967, s. 7A added by the Matrimonial Homes and Property Act 1981, s. 2, which strengthens the position of the non-owning spouse as against the mortgagee.
13   Section 2 (5). For contracts for sale of property subject to such a charge, see p. 150, ante.
14   See *Watts v Waller* [1973] 1 QB 153, [1972] 3 All ER 257; *Wroth v Tyler* [1974] Ch 30, [1973] 1 All ER 897, pp. 154–155, ante.
15   Registration should not be used to freeze the assets of the owning spouse: *Barnett v Hassett* [1982] 1 All ER 80; *S v S* (1980) 10 Fam Law 153.
16   LCA 1972, s. 5 (1), replacing the LCA 1925, s. 2 (1).
17   LCA 1972, s. 17 (1).
18   *Taylor v Taylor* [1968] 1 All ER 843, CA; *Heywood v BDC Properties Ltd (No. 2)* [1964] 2 All ER 702, CA. But an application under the Matrimonial Causes Act 1973 is: *Whittingham v Whittingham* [1978] 3 All ER 805, CA. See also *Allen v Greenhi Builders Ltd* [1978] 3 All 1163 (claim to easement registrable).
19   Proceedings to forfeit a lease because of a breach of repair have been held registrable (*Selim Ltd v Brickenhall Engineering Ltd* [1981] 3 All ER 210). However although Megarry VC said in this case it was essential to protect purchasers one can conceive of problems for example if there is a mortgage and no registration followed by forfeiture of the mortgagor's estate. Presumably relief would be granted.
20   LCA 1972, s. 6 (1), replacing the LCA 1925, s. 6 (1).

(a)   any writ or order affecting land issued for the purpose of enforcing a judgment or recognisance;

(b)   an order appointing a receiver or sequestrator of land;

(c)   a receiving order in bankruptcy, whether or not it is known to affect land.

A court order charging the land of a judgment debtor with the payment of the money due falls within (a)[1].

(c) Register of deeds of arrangement

As an alternative to bankruptcy an insolvent debtor may make an arrangement with his creditors whereby he is released from their claims, though unable to discharge them in full. This arrangement often takes the form of a transfer of the debtor's property to a trustee for the benefit of his creditors. If the transfer (known as a deed of arrangement) affects land it should be registered[2].

It should be noted that any registration effected under ss. 5, 6 or 7 of the Act automatically lapses after five years but it may be renewed from time to time for a further period of five years[3].

(d) Register of annuities

This register exists for certain annuities and rentcharges registered under the Judgments Act 1855, which were transferred to the new register of annuities established by the Act of 1925. No new entries have been possible in this register since 1 January 1926, and in time it will be closed when all entries in it have been duly vacated[4]. Annuities created after 1925, and those created before 1926 but not registered until afterwards, are registrable (if at all) as Class C (iii) or Class E land charges respectively.

4.   Interests outside the registration system

Not all equitable interests are embraced by the Land Charges Act 1972.

(a) Interests that are overreached

Registration is inapplicable to interests arising under a settlement or trust for sale. These are not intended to be enforceable against a purchaser of the land, being transferred to the proceeds of sale on a conveyance in the prescribed manner.

(b) Equitable interests expressly excluded by Act

The following interests, all expressly excluded, continue to be governed by the rules of notice: actual, constructive and imputed:

(i)   pre-1926 equitable easements,

(ii)   pre-1926 restrictive covenants,

(iii)   restrictive covenants (whenever made) between lessor and lessee.

---

1   Charging Orders Act 1979, s. 2. Any interest in land can be charged including an interest under a trust for sale; see *National Westminster Bank Ltd v Stockman* [1981] 1 All ER 800, thereby reversing the effect of *Irani Finance Ltd v Singh* [1971] Ch 59, [1970] 3 All ER 199 under the Administration of Justice Act 1956.

2   LCA 1972, s. 7 (1), replacing the LCA 1925, s. 8 (1), (2). Deeds of arrangement also require registration under the Deeds of Arrangement Act 1914.

3   LCA 1972, s. 8, replacing the LCA 1925, ss. 2 (8), 6 (3), 8(4).

4   LCA 1972, s. 1 (4), Sch. 1, replacing the LCA 1925, s. 4.

Covenants affecting leasehold land are usually contained in the lease which every prudent purchaser will inspect, thus obtaining actual notice[5]. It has been held that a covenant given by a lessor to his lessee and affecting the lessor's adjoining land is not registrable on the ground that the benefit is annexed to the leasehold interest in the demised land[6]. This is perhaps an unfortunate decision. Unless the restriction is brought on to the title of the adjoining land, which is unlikely, a purchaser of that land will not discover its existence and will therefore take free from it unless he also purchases the freehold reversion of the demised land. The only sure way that the lessee can give the purchaser notice of his rights is to have a memorandum of the covenants endorsed on the deeds relating to the adjoining land, but he has no statutory right to require this[7].

(c) Sale followed by compulsory registration of title
Section 14 (3) of the Act renders it unnecessary to register any land charge created by a conveyance or other instrument which leads to compulsory first registration of title under s. 123 of the Land Registration Act 1925[8]. Such charges will be entered on the register of title on first registration. The exemption applies only to charges affecting the estate conveyed, and not to, for example, other unregistered land already owned by the purchaser.

(d) Equitable interests arising under a bare trust
Where X holds a fee simple estate in trust for Y absolutely, there is neither a trust for sale nor a settlement, so that the overreaching provisions of the property legislation of 1925 are inapplicable, nor does Y's equitable fee simple constitute a charge or obligation affecting land so as to make it registrable as a Class C or D land charge. The enforceability of his interest against a purchaser for value from X is governed by the ordinary rules of notice. His occupation of the land would normally be sufficient to fix the purchaser with constructive notice, but the extent to which this is so when X is also in occupation is uncertain[9].

(e) Mere equities
A purchaser for value of *any* interest (legal or equitable) takes free from a mere equity of which he has no notice. A mere equity is an equitable right falling short of an equitable interest. Essentially it is a right to equitable relief, such as a right to have a deed set aside for fraud or rectified for mistake[10].

(f) Estoppel interest[11] and contractual licences
Equity will always restrain a legal owner from exercising his legal rights if it would be unconscionable[12] on his part to do so. Illustrations of this principle

5   For the position of an underlessee and a purchaser from him, see p. 309, ante.
6   *Dartstone Ltd v Cleveland Petroleum Co Ltd* [1969] 3 All ER 668.
7   Cf. LPA 1925, s. 200, which does not apply to a lessee.
8   This exemption which was first introduced by the LR & LCA 1971, s. 9, only applies to charges created by an instrument executed on or after 27 July 1971, (the date when s. 9 came into operation). See also p. 476, post.
9   See pp. 381–382, ante.
10   Cf. the position of registered land however if the person is in occupation: he will have an overriding interest within LRA 1925, s. 70 (1) (g):- *Blacklocks v JB Developments (Godalming) Ltd* [1981] 3 All ER 392. The learned judge also considered the position would be the same if the title was unregistered, ibid., at 400.
11   Crane, 'Estoppel Interests in Land' (1967) 31 Conv (NS) 332; *Snell's Equity* (27th edn), pp. 565–566.
12   See e.g. *Binions v Evans* [1972] Ch 359 at 368, [1972] 2 All ER 70 at 76, CA, per Lord Denning MR.

have occurred in several well known recent cases, where X has expended money on Y's land (or even on his own land) in the expectation created or encouraged by Y that he (X) will be allowed to enjoy the fruits of that expenditure and equity has refused to allow Y to defeat X's expectation[13]. It is for the court to decide in each case how X's rights are to be satisfied[14]; sometimes the court orders a conveyance[15], sometimes an injunction which has the effect of creating a permanent right over land[16], sometimes compensation only. So viewed X's rights amount to an equity (and it is variously described by the judges as an equity arising out of acquiescence or an equity by estoppel) as distinct from an equitable interest. It is therefore unenforceable against a purchaser for value of *any* interest in the land affected.

The problem of notice was considered for the first time in the *Ives* case where both Lord Denning MR and Danckwerts LJ held that the defendant's equity arising out of acquiescence, a right of way over the plaintiff's yard, was not capable of registration as a land charge[17]. With respect it is difficult to see how it could have been registered. The defendant's rights were inchoate until litigated. It was not until the court had decided how to satisfy the equity, that it was known whether his rights were capable of binding the purchaser. The old rules of notice apply to this species of equitable right.

We have already had occasion to consider the uncertainties surrounding contractual licences to occupy[18]. If and so far as the occupier's rights under such a licence partake of a proprietary nature, their enforceability depends not on registration[19] but on the ordinary rules of notice.

D Effect of registration and non-registration

1. Manner of registration

Applications for registration under the Act should be made on, and furnish the particulars required by, the prescribed forms[20]. In the case of land charges form K1 requires the following information: the chargee's name and address, the type of charge, details of the instrument of creation[1], and the names and

---

13 E.g. *Inwards v Baker* [1965] 2 QB 29, [1965] 1 All ER 446, CA (son building own bungalow on father's land); *E.R. Ives Investment Ltd v High* [1967] 2 QB 379, [1967] 1 All ER 504, CA (erection of garage without proper access except over adjacent yard); *Hussey v Palmer* [1972] 3 All ER 744, CA (mother-in-law paying for extension to house owned by son-in-law). *Western Fish v Penwith District Council* [1981] 2 All ER 204, CA; *Taylor Fashions Ltd v Liverpool Victoria Trustees* [1981] 1 All ER 897; *Re Sharpe (a bankrupt)* [1980] 1 All ER 198.

14 *Inwards v Baker* [1965] 2 QB 29, at 37, [1965] 1 All ER 446 at 449, CA, per Lord Denning MR.

15 *Dillwyn v Llewelyn* (1862) 4 De GF & J 517; *Pascoe v Turner* [1979] 2 All ER 945, CA.

16 *Ward v Kirkland* [1967] Ch 194, [1966] 1 All ER 609 (drainage right); *Crabb v Arun District Council* [1976] Ch 179, [1975] 3 All ER 865 (right of way).

17 See note 13, ante. Winn LJ held that the agreement for the right of way was void for non-registration, but the statute had no impact on the estoppel created by the conduct of the plaintiff's predecessor. See also *Taylor Fashions case* note 13, ante.

18 See p. 150, ante. See *Re Sharpe (a bankrupt)* [1980] 1 All ER 198, where it is suggested that express notice may be required to defeat the licence; sed quaere.

19 Page 389, ante.

20 LCA 1972, s. 1 (2); Land Charges Rules 1974, and 'Computerized Land Charges Department' published by H.M. Land Registry.

1 Where the charge is not created by an instrument short particulars of its effect must be given: LCA 1972, s. 3 (5).

address of the estate owner[2], a short description of the land affected and the county (including the former county). Applications not made by a practising solicitor must be supported by a statutory declaration by the applicant. A person contemplating registration of a charge should consider the desirability of first lodging a priority notice[3].

Registration of a land charge must be in the name of the estate owner, that is the *legal* owner, whose estate is intended to be affected[4]. Surprisingly no guidance is given as to what is meant by 'name' in this context. Does it mean the name on the birth certificate, the name appearing in the title deeds, or the name by which a person is commonly known? In the recent case of *Diligent Finance Co Ltd v Alleyne*[5] it was held that in the absence of evidence to the contrary the proper name was assumed to be the name in which the conveyancing documents were taken. Consequently a spouse's registration of a Class F charge against her husband's name, Erskine Alleyne[6], was unenforceable against a later mortgagee who had obtained a clear certificate of search against the name of Erskine Owen Alleyne, the name appearing in the title deeds. The court did not have occasion to consider what contrary evidence might displace the assumption that was made. This case establishes a satisfactory working rule for land charges created by a written document, when registration against the grantor's name appearing therein ought normally to suffice, but it clearly highlights the difficulties facing a spouse seeking to register a Class F charge which arises under a statute. Most likely the spouse will never have seen the deeds of the property and consequently has no means of knowing that the name by which the other spouse is known is at variance with the one given in the deeds. A registration in an incorrect name may not always be invalid; for as Russell LJ, observed in *Oak Co-operative Building Society v Blackburn*[7], yet another case which demonstrates the problems that may arise under a system of registration against names, registration in a version of a person's name is valid against someone who makes no search, or who searches in the wrong name.

Ideally, registration should be effected immediately after creation of the interest concerned. Registration against a subsequent estate owner is valid unless the charge has become void against him (or a predecessor) for want of registration. Registration against one of two or more joint owners is ineffective[8].

(a) Registrar's duties
The applicant is under no obligation to establish the validity of his charge nor is the Registrar concerned to inquire into the accuracy or validity of the application. It would seem to be within his power to reject an application which on its face is outside the Act. Registration can thus be obtained of a matter which is not properly registrable, such as a covenant between lessor or lessee, or an estate contract when no binding contract exists. Non-registrable matters are

2 As to the problems when the estate owner sought to be registered against is no longer the estate owner on account of death or bankruptcy see [1979] Conv 249 (A.M. Pritchard).
3 Page 399, post.
4 LCA 1972, s. 3 (1), and s. 17 (1) which applies the meaning assigned to the same expression by the LPA 1925, s. 205 (1) (v).
5 (1972), 23 P & CR 346.
6 This was the name by which he was known to his wife.
7 [1968] Ch 730 at 743, [1968] 2 All ER 117 at 122 CA. In this case the estate owner's true name was Francis David Blackburn, registration was effected in the name of Frank David Blackburn and a search certificate was requested in the name of Francis Davis Blackburn.
8 *Snape v Snape* (1959) 173 Estates Gazette 679.

sometimes registered in an endeavour to provide a purchaser who obtains a search certificate with actual knowledge, though there is a feeling that such a use of the Act is improper and, for solicitors, unprofessional. It is uncertain whether the court has an inherent jurisdiction to remove a land charge registered in bad faith[9].

(b) Recording entries in the Registry
Prior to the advent of the computer-age, an alphabetical index was kept of all entries made in the registers maintained at the Registry[10]. The legislative changes foreshadowing the use of a computer in place of the manual index now require[11] the Registrar to keep an index (which includes any device or combination of devices serving the purpose of an index) whereby all entries can readily be traced. Now that the computer has taken over all data is recorded on paper tape to be fed into the computer and processed by it.

(c) Cancellation of entries
As we have seen[12] some registrations automatically lapse after five years unless renewed. In the case of land charges an application for cancellation, (Form K11), signed by the chargee or his solicitor must be sent to the Registry. Sufficient evidence of the chargee's title must be supplied unless he is the person on whose behalf the registration was made and is entitled to the benefit of entry[13]. Many entries remain uncancelled notwithstanding the discharge of the interest protected. These entries commonly create problems on a subsequent transaction. Apparently a purchaser whose search certificate discloses an entry relating to a discharged incumbrance such as a mortgage cannot require the vendor to cancel the entry. Production of the discharged mortgage is adequate notice that the charge is no longer subsisting. If the vendor has created the incumbrance he should hand over on completion the necessary form for removal of the entry[14] (unless the purchaser is to take subject to the charge).

Registration of a land charge may also be vacated pursuant to a court order[15]. Where a dispute exists relative to an entry, vacation can normally be obtained only after the court has determined the merits of the case[16]. However, since registration, particularly of an estate contract, can constitute a weapon of considerable nuisance value, a speedier remedy by way of summary application exists in cases where there are no substantial grounds for supporting the registration[17].

---

9 *Rutherford v Rutherford* [1970] 3 All ER 422 at 424, per Foster J. See further *Heywood v B.D.C. Properties Ltd (No. 2)* [1964] 1 All ER 180; *Calgary and Edmonton v Dobinson* [1974] 1 All ER 484 and *Northern Developments (Holdings) Ltd v UDT Securities Ltd* [1977] 1 All ER 747.

10 This index contained about three million cards, bound in volumes, holding up to 300 cards.

11 LCA 1972, s. 1 (1), (7), replacing the LCA 1925, s. 1 (2), as substituted by s. 5 (1) of the LR & LCA 1971.

12 Page 391, ante.

13 Land Charges Rules 1974, S.I. 1974 No. 1286, r. 10 (Form 13 should be used for cancellation of the Class F charge: ibid., r. 11).

14 See Law Society's Digest (Third Supplement), Opinion Nos. 136 and 139.

15 LCA 1972, s. 1 (6), replacing the LCA 1925, s. 10 (8).

16 *Re Engall's Agreement* [1953] 2 All ER 503.

17 *Heywood v B.D.C. Properties Ltd* [1963] 2 All ER 1063, CA; *The Rawlplug Co Ltd v Kamvale Properties Ltd* (1968) 20 P & CR 32 at 39, per Megarry J. See the cases noted at note 9, supra.

2.   Actual notice

Subject to ss. 24 (1) and 25 (2) of the Law of Property Act 1969[18], registration constitutes

> '*actual* notice of such instrument or matter . . . to all persons and for all purposes connected with the land affected . . . so long as the registration continues in force.'[19]

Registration does not confer any validity; it gives notice of the existence of a claim whose validity is determined under the general law. A purchaser would not be deemed to have notice of a matter which, though registered, was not properly registrable, but its disclosure on his search certificate would give him actual knowledge.

Undisclosed land charges
As we saw in Chapter 10, a purchaser is bound by a registered charge, even one registered against an estate owner whose name he could not discover on an investigation of the title for the full statutory period. If an undisclosed registered land charge comes to light after completion, the Law of Property Act 1969, entitles him to claim compensation from the Registrar (nominated as the Crown's representative) for loss sustained thereby provided (i) he had no actual knowledge of the charge on the completion date—and in considering his knowledge the fact of registration is to be discounted, and (ii) he investigated the 'relevant title', that is the title which he could have required under an open contract[20]. The Act excludes any right to compensation in respect of land charges registered against titles which he is statutorily precluded from investigating. It might be thought harsh that the purchaser should continue to be bound by the incumbrance, especially as his loss stems from a defective system established by Parliament. However it was preferable to uphold the principle that registration affords complete protection[1] to the chargee who ought not to be deprived of his vested interests if he has done all that is required of him. The Law Commission felt that recourse to these compensation provisions would be rare[2]. No case was known where loss had been sustained by a purchaser 'caught' by an old land charge; but the possibility will be increased now that the length of title has been reduced from thirty years to fifteen.

For the purposes of the Limitation Act 1980, an action to recover compensation under the section is deemed to accrue when the land charge comes to the purchaser's notice[3]. The measure of compensation is left to be assessed according to general principles. Basically the purchaser should recover the difference between what he paid for the land and its value as affected by the charge. He can also claim the costs of obtaining compensation, and any expenditure incurred for the purpose of securing that the estate is no longer affected by the charge or affected to a less extent[4], e.g. the costs of an application under s. 84

18   And certain other provisions; see LPA 1925, s. 94 (2), and s. 96 (2), as amended by the LP (Am) A 1926, Schedule.
19   LPA 1925, s. 198 (1).
20   Section 25 (1), (2). Registered land charge means any matter or instrument other than a local land charge registered under the LCA 1972: sub-s. (10). See note 14, p. 285, ante, on the meaning of 'relevant title'.
1   Save in the exceptional cases where the LCA 1972, s. 10 (4) applies, p. 402, post.
2   Law Com. No. 18, paras. 32, 38.
3   LPA 1969, s. 25 (5) as amended by the Limitation Act 1980, Sch. 2, para. 9.
4   Section 25 (4).

of the Law of Property Act 1925, for the modification or discharge of restrictive covenants. The Registrar is empowered to amend the register to facilitate the disclosure of any land charge that has given rise to a compensation claim.

3.   The consequences of non-registration

Section 199 (1) (i) of the Law of Property Act 1925, enacts that a purchaser is not prejudicially affected by notice of any instrument or matter capable of registration, which is void against him by reason of non-registration. The precise effect of non-registration varies according to the particular matter in question.

(a)   Avoidance of land charges

Unless registered in the appropriate register before the completion of the purchase, a land charge becomes void against a purchaser of *any* interest in the land affected[5]. But in the case of a land charge falling within Class C (iv) or Class D, non-registration avoids it only against a purchaser of a *legal estate for money or money's worth*[6]. Registration must be effected before completion of the purchase, but a last minute registration may be ineffective if the purchaser is protected by a clear certificate of search[7].

Registration is the sole criterion for determining the question of enforceability. The purchaser's *actual* knowledge is irrelevant. In one case the purchaser was held to take free from an unregistered interest notwithstanding that the conveyance of the land was expressed to be subject to the interest[8]. This rule has been criticised on the ground that it operates unduly harshly against the incumbrancer in possession who fails to register[9] and puts him at a disadvantage as compared with the occupier whose equitable interest is not capable of registration. Failure to register is immaterial as between the original parties to the transaction.

(b)   Avoidance of other matters

A *pending law action, writ or order* (other than a receiving order), *deed of arrangement* and *annuity* are all void against a purchaser unless they are for the time being duly registered, save that non-registration avoids a pending land action only if the purchaser is without express notice[10]. A *bankruptcy petition* and a *receiving order* are void against a purchaser of a legal estate in good faith for money or money's worth without notice of an available act of bankruptcy unless they are for the time being duly registered[11]. The title of the trustee in bankruptcy is only avoided against such a purchaser if neither the petition nor the receiving order is registered at the date of the conveyance[12].

---

5   LCA 1972, s. 4 (2), (5), (8), replacing the LCA 1925, s. 13 (1) − (3).
6   LCA 1972, s. 4 (6), as amended by the Finance Act 1975, Sch. 12, para. 18 (5): note 13, p. 398, post.
7   See p. 401, post.
8   *Hollington Bros Ltd v Rhodes* [1951] 2 All ER 578, CA; *Midland Bank Trust Co Ltd v Green* [1981] 1 All ER 153, HL.
9   M & W, 1049; Law Com. No. 18, paras. 51−53. Cf. LRA 1925, s. 70 (1) (g).
10   LCA 1972, ss. 5 (7), 6 (4), 7 (2), Sch. 1, para. 4, replacing the LCA 1925, ss. 3 (1), 5, 7 (1), 9.
11   LCA 1972, ss. 5 (8), 6 (5), replacing the LCA 1925, ss. 3 (1), 7 (1).
12   LCA 1972, s. 6 (6), replacing the LCA 1925, ss. 3 (3), 7 (2).

(c) Meaning of 'purchaser'
This word is defined to mean 'any person (including a mortgagee or lessee) who for valuable consideration takes *any* interest in land, or in a charge on land'[13]. A lessee's covenant to pay a rent of £30 per annum constitutes valuable consideration[14]. Failure to register avoids the land charge or other matter against a purchaser of even an equitable interest, save in those cases where he must be a purchaser of a legal estate[15]. In these cases also, he must purchase for 'money or money's worth', an expression narrower than 'valuable consideration' because it does not comprehend a future marriage.

(d) Extent of avoidance
Once a land charge becomes void against a purchaser for non-registration, it remains unenforceable against his successors in title whether or not for value. A purported registration after the land has vested in a purchaser who took free of the charge because of its non-registration does not operate to revive the avoided charge against a later purchaser[16]. A subsequent registration may nevertheless be effective against a purchaser of a different estate. Suppose B conveys freehold land to A, subject to restrictive covenants imposed by that conveyance. A mortgages the land to C. B's failure to register the covenants before completion of the mortgage makes them void against C and C's successors in title, such as a purchaser to whom C sells the land in exercise of his statutory power of sale. But D, a purchaser from A, is bound provided the covenants are registered before completion of the A−D purchase, because D derives title from A, not C.

(e) Lack of registration not fatal
In certain cases, failure to register does not avoid the interest against a successor in title.

(i) A donee, devisee, squatter, or other person not ranking as a purchaser for valuable consideration is bound, even in the absence of registration or notice, as is a purchaser of an equitable interest in the case of a Class C (iv) or Class D land charge.

(ii) Although the definition of 'purchaser' in the Land Charges Act 1972, does not incorporate the words 'in good faith'[17] the courts will not permit a sham transaction to be used to defeat a non-registered interest. Examples might occur where a husband sells the matrimonial home to a relative at a nominal

13   LCA 1972, s. 17 (1). See *Midland Bank Trust Co Ltd v Green*, ante, (sale of land at great undervalue to defeat unregistered option upheld). See also the Finance Act 1975, s. 51 (1) and Sch. 12, para. 18 (5) for a special definition of 'purchaser' with regard to DI charges.
14   *Vartoukian v Daejan Properties Ltd* (1969) 20 P & CR 983. It does not appear to have been appreciated that since the unregistered interest was an estate contract, the court should strictly have directed its attention to the question whether the covenant amounted to money or money's worth.
15   I.e. under LCA 1972, ss. 4 (6), 5 (8), 6 (5). *McCarthy and Stone Ltd v Julian S. Hodge & Co Ltd* [1971] 2 All ER 973 (unregistered estate contract not void against equitable mortgagee).
16   Though a literal interpretation of the LCA 1972, s. 4 (5) − (9) perhaps leads to the opposite conclusion, it is not thought that the rule under the Act differs from that operating under the equitable rules of notice, see p. 383, ante. See further [1979] Conv 249 (A.M. Pritchard) and Emmet, 657.
17   Section 17 (1). Cf. LPA 1925, s. 205 (1) (xxi), from which it follows that the LPA 1925, s. 199 (1) (i) p. 397, ante only applies in favour of a purchaser in good faith. Good faith is required for the purposes of the LCA 1972, ss. 5 (8), 6 (5), so that the omission from s. 17 (1) must be taken to be deliberate, though inconsistent with the LPA 1925. See also *Midland Bank Trust Co Ltd v Green*, ante.

price in an attempt to defeat his wife's statutory rights of occupation[18], or where a person conveys land to a company controlled by him in breach of an existing contract for sale[19].

(iii) In *E. R. Ives Investment Ltd v High*[20], Winn LJ held that an equitable interest such as an equitable easement void for want of registration may still be enforceable against a successor in title, if he is estopped by his conduct from denying the grantee's right of enjoyment. The Act has no impact on an estoppel, which is not registrable.

(iv) The right to compensation on the compulsory purchase of land is not pre-judiced by non-registration[1].

4. Indirect action[2]

The consequence of failure to register has the effect of depriving the person with the registrable interest of the right to enforce it against the land. However lack of registration may not be fatal. It may be possible to procure indirect enforcement. For example in the case of a restrictive covenant the original covenantor could be sued and then he could follow the chain of indemnity covenants down to the person currently in possession. Another alternative is to support a covenant by a right of re-entry. It is now established[3] that on the breach of a covenant the right of re-entry can still be enforced despite non-registration of the covenant.

Even if this is not the case the original grantor or covenantor will be liable for damages for breach of contract, conspiracy or inducing a breach of contract as the case may be[4].

5. Priority notices

A person intending to register a contemplated charge may give a priority notice before the registration is to take effect[5]. A priority notice should be lodged in a situation like that discussed on p. 398. Unless this procedure is adopted B (the vendor) cannot register the covenants before completion of the mortgage to C if, as is usual, the conveyance and mortgage are completed simultaneously. The covenants will therefore become void against C and his successors. The

---

18 *Miles v Bull* [1969] 1 QB 258 at 261–62, [1968] 3 All ER 632 at 635–36, per Megarry J, citing as an example *Ferris v Weaven* [1952] 2 All ER 233 (sale of house to brother for £30 (which was never paid) in an attempt to defeat deserted wife's equity). These cases should be regarded as exceptional in view of the House of Lords' decision in *Midland Bank Trust Co Ltd v Green*, supra.

19 Cf. *Jones v Lipman* [1962] 1 All ER 442.

20 [1967] 2 QB 379, [1967] 1 All ER 504, CA.

1 *Blamires v Bradford Corpn* [1964] Ch 585, [1964] 2 All ER 603 (unregistered estate contract).

2 See (1977) 41 Conv (NS) 318 (R.J. Smith).

3 *Shiloh Spinners v Harding* [1973] AC 691, [1973] 1 All ER 90, HL (held that the right of re-entry was enforceable for breach of a covenant void for want of registration). The right of re-entry was held equitable. However if it is annexed to a rentcharge it will be legal. A rentcharge created to enforce·covenants is an 'estate rentcharge' within the Rentcharges Act 1977 and is still capable of creation.

4 See e.g. *Midland Bank Trust Co Ltd v Green (No. 3)* [1979] Ch 496, [1979] 2 All ER 193 and the associated litigation at [1981] 1 All ER 153; [1979] 3 All ER 28; [1978] 3 All ER 555.

5 LCA 1972, s. 11 (1), (3), (6) (b), (replacing the LP(Am) A 1926, s. 4 (1)) and the Land Charges Rules 1974.

successful operation of this procedure involves strict observance of the prescribed time limits. B must lodge his priority notice at the Registry at least
fifteen working days before completion[6]. After completion an application for
substantive registration pursuant to the notice must be presented within thirty
working days after the notice was entered on the register. Registration then
takes effect as if it had been made at the time when the covenants were created,
i.e. on completion of the B−A conveyance. Since this precedes momentarily
the A−C mortgage, the covenants are deemed to be registered before completion of the mortgage. The existence of the priority notice will be revealed on
any official search certificate made by the mortgagee, so he has notice of the
intended registration. The National Conditions of Sale provide that where
restrictive covenants are to be created on the sale the purchaser shall inform the
vendor if he intends to execute a mortgage contemporaneously with the conveyance, in order to allow the vendor to give a priority notice[7].

Priority notices are not limited to restrictive covenants. They apply to any
contemplated charge, instrument or other matter (including a vendor's lien)
and are commonly used prior to registration of equitable easements.

E   Searches for incumbrances

1.   Purpose and mode of search

The primary object of a search is to discover the existence of any registered
entry affecting the land which the purchaser is acquiring. If some incumbrance
not disclosed on investigation of the title is discovered, he will call upon the
vendor to cancel the entry or secure its discharge if he can. A search certificate
that reveals no entries may mean that a registrable interest of which the purchaser is aware has not been registered and so is, or will become, void for want
of registration.

A search can be effected in one of four ways: (i) a personal search at the
Registry[8], (ii) a search by telephone, (iii) a search by telex or (iv) a written
requisition for a search to be made by the Registrar who issues a certificate of
the result[9]. The first three tend to be used in emergency only.

(a) Application for official search
The application must be made on the prescribed form, the Forms K15 and
K16, which require, in addition to the Christian names and surnames of the
persons to be searched against, the relevant county or counties, the period of
years sought to be searched against and, if possible[10], a brief description of the
land affected. It is common practice on the grant of a mortgage for the mortgagee's solicitor to require a search to be made against the prospective borrower
in order to verify that no bankruptcy proceedings have been instituted against
him. In this case, Form K16 is used.

---

6 A minimum period of fifteen days before completion is essential to ensure disclosure by the
   purchaser's search.
7 NCS 19 (4).
8 LCA 1972, s. 9, replacing the LCA 1925, s. 16 (as amended).
9 See generally *Computerized Land Charges Department* published by H.M. Land Registry.
10 See Adams, 'A Fly in the Ointment: Estate Contracts and the Land Charges' Computer'
   (1971) 35 Conv (NS) 155, for some problems, and [1979] Conv 249−257 (A.M. Pritchard).

(b) Result of official search

The Registrar is statutorily required to issue a certificate setting out the result of the search[11].

If there are no entries which affect the property, Form K17 is issued which states that there are no subsisting entries. If entries are revealed then Form K18 is used which sets out the entries. In cases of doubt[12] the Land Registry tend to play safe and the certificate may state: 'No subsisting entries clearly affecting but the following entries which may or may not relate thereto appear'. Conversely if there are more than 25 entries and a short description of the land has been supplied the certificate will be edited accordingly and this fact will be stated on it[13]. Office copies of any entry can be obtained[14].

(c) Against whom to search

Strictly, a search should be made against the name of every person appearing as an estate owner during the period of investigation covered by the abstract, including, of course, the vendor. The names referred to in the application for the search should correspond exactly with the name appearing on the title. Where there is a change of name or a variation in the spelling of an estate owner's name, it is a wise precaution to search each different name of variation. In practice it is customary not to search against a person in respect of whom a search was made on the occasion of some previous transaction. Whilst the abstract will normally reveal what prior searches have been made, only a photocopy of the certificate will indicate whether the application therefor contained the correct particulars for the certificate to be conclusive. Unless these can be verified, it may be dangerous to rely on a certificate obtained by someone else. The new procedure facilitates the making of searches against previous owners.

2.   Advantages of official search certificate

(a) Priority over late registrations

A purchaser who obtains an official certificate of the result of a search is not affected by any entry made in the register after the date of the certificate and before completion of the purchase, unless made pursuant to a priority notice entered on the register on or before the date of the certificate, *provided the purchase is completed before the expiration of the fifteenth day (excluding days when the Registry is not open to the public) of the certificate's date*[15].

---

11   LCA 1972, s. 10 (3) (a), replacing the LCA 1925, s. 17 (2A) as inserted by the LR & LCA 1971, s. 5 (5). He is also empowered to take other appropriate steps to communicate the result to the applicant (e.g. by telephone).

12   Because e.g. of a slight discrepancy in the names; see *Oak Co-operative Building Society v Blackburn* [1968] Ch 730, [1968] 2 All ER 117, CA.

13   A similar procedure is taken with the county description of the property. There is a clear potential for error in this both in the failure to specify the correct old and new counties and in the failure to give a description of the land (addresses change).

14   This can be an expensive exercise. A search against a bank, a local authority (or 'Fielding' in Blackpool) will reveal many entries. In practice the vendor's solicitor endorses the certificate as to the status of the charges, see further, post.

15   LCA 1972, s. 11 (5), (6) (a), replacing the LP (Am) A 1926, s. 4 (2) and Land Charges Rules 1974, r. 4 (priority notices). Originally s. 4 (2) afforded a mere two days' protection but this was increased to fourteen days by the Land Charges Rules 1940, S.I. 1940 No. 1998. The extra day was added by the Rules of 1972 in anticipation of the new methods of searching under the computer. The search certificate will reflect the state of the records when business closes on the preceding working day, and the certificate will be

Protection lasts for fifteen working days or until earlier completion. The certificate confers no protection in relation to incumbrances registered within the fifteen days' period but after completion of the purchase[16]. Should the period of protection expire before completion takes place, a fresh application must be made; dating the conveyance with some date falling within the protection period, a common but misconceived practice, is not sufficient[17]. The view has been expressed that as the section merely speaks of completion of the purchase, the making of a contract preceded by a search is not protected in the same way as the conveyance[18].

(b) Conclusiveness

Unless a purchaser can rely upon the certificate of search, the system of official searches would break down. Consequently it is provided that the certificate, according to its tenor, shall be conclusive, affirmatively or negatively, as the case may be[19]. If any entry is overlooked and a clear certificate is issued in error, the purchaser is entitled to assume that no charge is registered. He takes free from the registered charge and, though this point has not yet been decided, his successor in title also takes free, notwithstanding that his own search might disclose the entry, on the ground that he acquires his predecessor's unincumbered estate. To this extent actual registration does not prevail against an inaccurate certificate and the loss is made to fall upon the chargee who loses his incumbrance. A purchaser can, however, only rely on s. 10 (4) if his application gives no reasonable scope for misunderstanding so that the blame for the non-disclosure of the relevant entry rests fairly and squarely on the Registry officials[20]. Should the purchaser not search against the correct name of the estate owner, a clear search certificate which he may receive is not conclusive, even against an incumbrancer who has himself registered his charge in but a version of the estate owner's full name[1]. Where the result of a search is given over the telephone or by teleprinter, the confirmatory printed certificate, not the telephone or teleprinter reply, is conclusive as to the information disclosed. Section 10 (6) of the Act[2] exempts (fraud apart) any officer, clerk or person employed in the Registry from liability for loss suffered by reason of (a) any discrepancy between the particulars shown in the result of the search certificate and those given by the applicant in his requisition, or (b) the communication of the result of a search otherwise than by issuing a certificate (e.g. by telephone). As to exemption (a) it is to be recalled that the certificate is a separate document printed by the computer[3]. If, therefore, a search is requested against the name of XY and the result of the certificate shows no entries against XZ, no action

so dated. The one day extension compensates purchasers for the loss of one day by reason of the back-dating of the certificate. The computer search shows the date of the commencement of the period and its expiry.

16   This is an important consideration when determining the priority of two registrable mortgages created by a mortgagor within the space of a few days.
17   See further, p. 434, post.
18   Emmet, 671.
19   LCA 1972, s. 10 (4), replacing the LCA 1925, s. 17 (3).
20   *Du Sautoy v Symes* [1967] Ch 1146 at 1168, [1967] 1 All ER 25 at 37, per Cross J (insufficiently clear description of land).
 1   *Oak Co-operative Building Society v Blackburn* [1968] Ch 730, [1968] 2 All ER 117, CA, note 7, p. 394, ante.
 2   Replacing s. 5 (7) of the LR & LCA 1971.
 3   See p. 405, ante.

will be against the Registry officials for loss caused by this discrepancy[4]. It will be necessary to effect a second search against XY. Should the purchaser's solicitor complete the purchase without noticing the difference, the purchaser will be bound by any charge registered against XY. He cannot rely upon s. 10 (4) to give him a clear title because the search certificate which he has received is not conclusive as to XY.

3.   Erroneous certificates[5]

A solicitor or other person obtaining an official search certificate is not answerable for any loss arising from error in the certificate, neither is any trustee or executor for whom the solicitor is acting[6]. Criminal liability attaches to any Registry official who is wilfully negligent in the making of any certificate or is party to any act of fraud or collusion affecting it[7].

As to the rights of a chargee who loses his charge because of an inaccurate certificate, Salmon and Cross LJJ held in *Ministry of Housing and Local Government v Sharp*[8] that s. 17 (2) of the Land Charges Act 1925[9] did not impose an absolute duty on the Registrar to issue an accurate certificate, though they inclined to the view, expressed obiter[10], that the chargee might be able to maintain an action of negligence against him. Lord Denning MR dissented, holding that the section imposed an absolute obligation, breach of which was actionable irrespective of negligence[11]. Perhaps the present difference between the two views is slight, for an inaccurate certificate will ordinarily raise a strong prima facie case of negligence. Clearly the divergence of opinion is fundamental now the computer is operational since the computer might produce an erroneous certificate without negligence on anybody's part. The Crown cannot be sued for the Registry's mistakes[12]. Even assuming the aggrieved incumbrancer can sue for damages, this remedy is a poor substitute for the loss of his interest. For example, financial relief may be totally inadequate compensation for loss of a right to restrain by injunction breach of a restrictive covenant.

It is a matter of some regret that Parliament did not take the opportunity to deal with the problem in the Land Registration and Land Charges Act 1971. It would seem essential to give the incumbrancer a statutory right to compensation in all cases where the operation of s. 10 (4) of the Land Charges Act 1972 will render his interest unenforceable against the purchaser. To deprive him of his vested interests when he has complied with the statutory requirement of registration is a serious consequence; to do so without compensation seems morally indefensible[13].

4   Accordingly it is advisable to keep a copy of the search application form.
5   According to the Chief Land Registrar, during 1970–71 official certificates covering 3,425,000 names were issued, in respect of which only 83 errors were reported by solicitors: (1971) 68 LS Gaz 221.
6   LCA 1972, s. 12, replacing the LCA 1925, s. 17 (7)–(9).
7   LCA 1972, s. 10 (5), replacing the LCA 1925, s. 17 (5).
8   [1970] 2 QB 223, [1970] 1 All ER 1009, CA. The case concerned an inaccurate local land charges certificate but the Court treated the liabilities of the Registrar and a local registrar on the same footing.
9   See now the LCA 1972, s. 10 (3) (a), p. 401, ante.
10   The claim against the local registrar was not framed in negligence.
11   At 275 and 1024, respectively, per Salmon LJ.
12   Crown Proceedings Act 1947, s. 23 (3) (f).
13   The Registrar does in appropriate circumstances accept responsibility for mistakes made in the Registry. The Law Commission did not consider the problem to be of sufficient

F   Potential traps

The present system has a large number of potential pitfalls requiring great care to be taken in the matter of the searches. First there is the problem of ascertaining the complete names (and versions) of all estate owners back to 1926. The search now must cover the correct period of years and be attributed to the correct county and former county. The system of relying on the vendor's solicitor certifying charges do not relate as opposed to obtaining office copy entries is something which works quite well in practice but which has a great potential for disaster[14]. The changing description of land can also now cause potential problems. All the above matters may potentially invalidate the supposed conclusive search.

G   Registered land searches

1.   Official searches

The copy of the subsisting entries in the vendor's register of title, upon which the purchaser conducted his investigation of the title[15], may be out of date by the time he comes to complete. The Land Registration (Official Searches) Rules 1981[16], enable the purchaser to obtain free of charge an official certificate of search which not only reveals any adverse entry made subsequently to the date of the office copy entries, but also confers priority over late entries, in much the same way as the official certificate under the Land Charges Act 1972. The prescribed forms of application are form 94A or 94B[17], depending on whether the whole, or part only, of the land comprised in the title is being purchased. The applicant must indicate the date of commencement of the search, being either the day after the issue of an office copy of the subsisting entries or the last date when the land certificate was officially examined with the register. Since the register of title is private, an authority to inspect the register must be obtained[18]. A plan showing the extent of the land involved is also required if the transaction does not relate to the whole of the land within the proprietor's title, except where the Registry have approved an estate layout plan when only the plot number need be given.

Meaning of purchaser
The forms described above are for use by a purchaser, defined by r. 2 (1) to mean any person (including a lessee or chargee) who in good faith and for valuable consideration acquires or intends to acquire a legal estate in land. Any other person (e.g. an assentee, or chargee who merely intends to protect his security by a notice of deposit) can for the fee of £2 apply for an official certificate on form 94C, but the certificate confers on the applicant no priority

urgency to warrant any positive recommendation; Law Com. No. 18, paras. 49–50. But the problem needs to be looked at again in the light of the introduction of a computerised system.

14   It is often assumed erroneously that a charge will only be imposed on purchase and therefore entries subsequent to the date of acquisition can be duly certified. This is not the case.

15   See p. 350, ante.

16   S.I. 1981, No. 1135.

17   Rule 3 (1) and Sch. 1.

18   Although the solicitor acting for an applicant need not lodge it so long as he states in the form that he has it.

in respect of subsequent registrations (r. 9 (2)). Thus a person about to enter into a contract cannot apply for a certificate of search conferring priority for his contract[19].

2. Effect of official certificate

If the application is in order an official certificate of search is issued giving the result of the search as at the the time and date of its delivery. It may reveal the following:

(i)   entries affecting the land made in the register since the date specified in the application;

(ii)   applications for registration pending but not completed[20];

(iii) unexpired official certificates of search.

If the application is delivered after 11.00 hours on one day and before or at 11.00 hours on the next day it is deemed to have been delivered immediately before 11.00 hours on the second day[1]. This eliminates the difficulties that would otherwise result from the receipt of conflicting applications on the same day. A search certificate will always give priority over, say, an application to lodge a caution received by the Registry by the same post, because the application for the search is deemed to have been delivered first. By virtue of rule 5 where a purchaser obtains an official search, any entry made in the register during the priority period is postponed to a subsequent application to register the instrument affecting the purchase, provided the application is in order and it is delivered to the proper district registry *within the priority period*. In effect the purchaser takes free from the subsequent entry[2] but — and this is important — not only must completion have taken place, in addition his application for substantive registration must be received at the Registry within the period[3]. The period lasts for 30 working days and runs from the date when the application for the search is deemed to be delivered at the Registry[4], not from the date of the certificate. The expiration date of the period is stamped on the certificate, but it has no legal effect and an error does not give rise to a claim for indemnity.

Under rule 5 an official search made on behalf of an intending mortgagee automatically ensures protection for the transfer upon which the mortgage is dependent. Where on a purchase and mortgage the same solicitor acts for both the purchaser and the mortgagee, only one search on behalf of the mortgagee need be obtained. Should different solicitors be acting it is conceived that it is still the responsibility of the purchaser's solicitor to search on his client's behalf, rather than to leave the task to another.

19 A rule criticised by Robinson, 'Priorities of Interests in Registered Land-II' (1971) 35 Conv (NS) 168, 175, n. 47.

20 See (1965), 62 LS Gaz 507, refuting suggestions in *Strand Securities Ltd v Caswell* [1965] Ch 958 at 987, [1965] 1 All ER 820 at 831, CA, per Russell LJ, that the certificate does not confer protection in relation to pending applications. See also *Smith v Morrison* [1974] 1 All ER 957.

 1 Rule 2 (3). LRR 1925, r. 85 does not apply. In the case of two searches deemed to have been delivered at the same time priority is agreed between the applicants. Failing agreement, it is determined in accordance with LRR 1925, r. 298 (Rule 6 (2)).

 2 The system of priority notices introduced by the LP (Am) A 1926, s. 4 (1), p. 399, ante, has no counterpart under the LRA 1925. Rule 13 of the 1969 Rules revokes the LRR 1925, r. 88, which permitted lodgment of a priority notice against dealings.

 3 See further p. 452, post.

 4 Rule 2 (1).

3.   Erroneous certificates

A solicitor or other person is not answerable for loss that may arise from an error in an official certificate of search obtained by him, and this protection extends to any fiduciary owner for whom he acts[5]. The Land Registration Act 1925, contains no provision similar to s. 10 (4) of the Land Charges Act 1972, which makes the certificate conclusive according to its tenor. In *Parkash v Irani Finance Ltd*[6] Plowman J held that a purchaser of registered land took subject to a caution which his certificate of search failed to disclose. This was so even though s. 59 (6) of the Act of 1925 does not say in terms that a purchaser is affected by notice of matters protected by caution, for this is implicit in the scheme of the Act and in the subsection itself[7]. A similar decision would have been reached had it been a notice or a pending application for substantive registration that had been omitted from the certificate. The purchaser's remedy is to claim an indemnity under s. 83 (3) of the Act.

4.   Other modes of searching

(a) Personal search
A personal search can be undertaken at the Registry where on payment of a fee of £1, the applicant is shown the register, all documents referred to on it and any pending applications[8]. Compared with an official search, a personal search suffers from the following main disadvantages: (i) it confers no priority in respect of subsequent entries, (ii) it does not exempt a solicitor from responsibility for error and (iii) the applicant is limited to making pencil notes or extracts only[9].

(b) Searches by telephone or teleprinter
The Rules[10] permit a person having authority to inspect by his *solicitor* to request and obtain the result of a search by telephone or teleprinter. This mode of searching is used in an emergency. Like a personal search, the search possesses none of the advantages of an official search, nor does it rank as an official search within s. 83 (3) of the main Act so that no indemnity can be obtained in respect of errors in the search. In either case the request must be followed up by a normal application in form 94A or 94B, and the full benefits apply to the certificate of the result of this search.

(c) Search in Land Charges Register
Notwithstanding a dictum to the contrary by Lord Evershed MR in *City Permanent Building Society v Miller*[11], a purchaser of registered land need not make a search in the Land Charges Registry. The Land Registration Act 1925, provides its own machinery for the protection of matters which in the case of unregistered land require registration under the Land Charges Act 1972, and the enforceability of any such matter affecting a registered title is determined

5   LRR 1925, r. 295.
6   [1970] Ch 101, [1969] 1 All ER 930.
7   Per Plowman J at 110 and 935, respectively. It is expressly so stated in relation to notices: LRA 1925, ss. 48 (1), 50 (2), p. 67, ante.
8   See R & R, 682.
9   LRR 1925, r. 291.
10   Rules 7 and 8, and Sch. 2.
11   [1952] Ch 840 at 849, [1952] 1 All ER 621 at 625 CA; cf. *Webb v Pollmount Ltd* [1966] Ch 584 at 603, [1966] 1 All ER 481 at 489, per Ungoed-Thomas J. See R & R, 698–701.

solely by whether it is duly protected by notice, caution or inhibition under the former Act. Furthermore the Act expressly exempts a purchaser from any obligation to make a search in the Land Charges Registry[12], though in passing it should be observed that a purchaser of a qualified or possessory title ought to make such a search in respect of estates excepted from the effect of registration.

H   Search in the companies register

1.   Registration of financial charges: unregistered land

Prior to 1 January 1970, a land charge for *securing money created by a company* could be protected by registration under s. 95 of the Companies Act 1948, as an alternative to registration under the Land Charges Act 1925[13]. This was rather inconvenient for purchasers buying land from a company since it was essential to search in the register of companies maintained under the Act of 1948 in addition to the usual search in the Land Charges Registry. As no official search procedure was available at the companies registry, the company search (which was normally effected by a firm of law agents who confirmed the result of the search in writing) conferred no priority nor was it conclusive as to its contents. The Land Charges Act 1972, s. 3 (7), replacing s. 26 of the Law of Property Act 1969, partially remedies the position by requiring all land charges for securing money (other than floating charges[14]) created on or after 1 January 1970, to be registered (where necessary[15]) at the Land Charges Registry. However s. 3 (7) does not dispense with the need to make a company search altogether; such a search should still be made to discover the existence of (i) pre-1970 financial charges, and (ii) floating charges whenever created.

Section 3 (7) in no way abrogates the need for registration at the companies registry for the purposes of s. 95 of the Companies Act 1948[16] and this duality of registration produces at least one anomaly. A purchaser, not being a mortgagee, takes subject to a mortgage duly registered as a C (i) or C (iii) land charge, whereas a mortgagee (who ranks as a creditor within s. 95) is not bound if the mortgage, though registered as a land charge, is not also registered under s. 95.

On a purchase of land from a company, the purchaser should ascertain that no winding up proceedings are pending. In a winding up by the court a disposition of the company's property after commencement of the winding up is void unless the court otherwise directs[17]. A search of the *London Gazette* (again performed by London agents) will reveal the existence of any winding up petition.

---

12   LRA 1925, ss. 61 (6), 110 (7). On the simultaneous purchase and mortgage of registered land, the mortgagee will frequently effect a search against the purchaser-mortgagor in the land charges register for bankruptcy entries; see p. 400, ante.

13   Section 10 (5). See *Property Discount Corpn v Lyon Group Ltd* [1981] 1 All ER 379 (estate owner agreed to grant a lease to L who agreed to charge the same to P. P registered the charge in the Companies Registry against L but not in the Land Charges Registry. *Held* registration effective although not against the estate owner. See *Barrett v Hilton Developments Ltd* [1975] Ch 237, [1974] 3 All ER 944. See further T. Flanagan and D.M. Hare, 'Company Charges Relating to Land' [1982] Conv 43.

14   See section 3 below.

15   Thus a legal mortgage created by a company and secured by a deposit of deeds does not require registration as a land charge as it is excluded under the general law, p. 385, ante.

16   Section 95 avoids (inter alia) a charge on land against the liquidator and any creditor of the company unless particulars thereof are registered within 21 days of its creation.

17   Companies Act 1948, s. 227. For the commencement of the winding up, see s. 229.

2.   Registered land

A charge affecting registered land created by a company is treated no differently from one created by an individual. It does not bind a purchaser unless it is
properly protected under the Land Registration Act 1925, irrespective of its
registration under the Companies Act 1948. A company search, in so far as it is
made to discover registered charges, is unnecessary, but in practice many
solicitors make a search and there would appear to be valid reasons for so
doing[18].

3.   Floating charges

A floating charge is a charge

'presently affecting all the items expressed to be included in it but not
specifically affecting any item until the happening of an event which
causes the security to crystallise as regards all the items'[19].

It floats over the company's assets, enabling the company to deal with them
in the ordinary course of business. It becomes a fixed charge on the occurrence
of an event causing it to crystallise, e.g. liquidation, or the appointment of a
receiver.

A floating charge affecting unregistered land continues to be registrable
under s. 95 of the Companies Act 1948, not in the land charges register[20].
Strictly speaking a floating charge should be abstracted, for the purchaser
requires to know the events on which it will crystallise. Though the company
can convey the land without the chargee's concurrence, the purchaser is
entitled to evidence of non-crystallisation. The practice varies as to the kind of
evidence produced. Some practitioners are happy to accept a certificate to that
effect signed by an officer of the company, whereas others insist, and perhaps
more correctly, on a certificate from the chargee. The purchaser must bear the
expenses of obtaining the certificate[1]. If the charge has crystallised the mortgagee must join in to release the property.

A floating charge affecting registered land requires protection on the
register by means of a notice or a caution and unless it is so protected a purchaser is not bound even though it is registered in the companies register.
Apparently the Registrar will cancel the entry of the charge on production of a
certificate of non-crystallisation, signed by the company's solicitor[2].

---

18   E.g. to discover winding up proceedings. See the correspondence at (1970) 67 LS Gaz 107.
     Cf. R & R, 646–647, 688–689; (1977) 74 LS Gaz 132, 192.
19   *Evans v Rival Granite Quarries Ltd* [1910] 2 KB 979 at 1000, CA, per Buckley, LJ.
20   Its very nature makes this highly impracticable, for a fresh registration would be necessary
     on every change in the company's landed assets. But this is the very problem facing the
     mortgagee where the company later acquires registered land.
1   LPA 1925, s. 45 (4) (b), p. 303, ante.
2   R & R, 544; 18 Ency F & P 735, Form 3:B:17.

Chapter 15

Completing the transaction

A Introduction

The stage has now been set for forging the final link in the chain of procedures
— completion, an expression which, according to Stable J, usually refers to the
complete conveyance of the estate and final settlement of the business[1]. For the
parties this normally signifies cash for the vendor and keys (i.e. possession) for
the purchaser. From the legal standpoint, the vital element is the passing of the
legal estate[2]. Not even payment of the whole of the purchase price coupled with
possession of the premises constitutes completion, in the absence of any conveyance of the legal estate[3].

Needless to say, before proceeding to complete, the purchaser's solicitor
should satisfy himself that his searches have not expired, that there are no outstanding requisitions and that he has the balance of the purchase money. In
some respects completion can be the most frustrating and harassing part of the
whole transaction. Solicitors and their clients work for completion to take place
on the specified day, only to learn of some delay a few days beforehand. As we
have already had occasion to observe, in transactions involving residential property there is frequently a chain of vendors and purchasers; A is selling to B who
is selling to C, C to D — and so on. C's failure to complete on time may affect the
other people in the chain. As B is dependent on the money coming from C, he
cannot complete with A, though he may be able to avoid the impasse by obtaining a temporary loan from his bank. Similarly, unless C is able to find accommodation elsewhere, his failure to give vacant possession of his own house will
delay completion of his sale to D. Delay of only two or three days' duration may
suffice to create endless complications.

B Place of completion

Formal contracts normally provide for completion to take place at the offices
of the vendor's solicitor, or at those of the mortgagee's solicitor, if any[4]. If the

1 *Killner v France* [1946] 2 All ER 83 at 86. Cf. *Lewis v South Wales Rly Co* (1852) 22 LJ
   Ch 209.
2 This should be read subject to the peculiar effect of the law relating to escrows,
   pp. 430–432, post, and as regards registered land, to the LRA 1925, ss. 19 (1), 22 (1),
   p. 457, post.
3 *Killner v France* [1946] 2 All ER 83.
4 See LSC 21 (1). Cf. NCS 5 (4) (completion at such office or place as vendor's solicitor shall
   reasonably require).

purchaser's solicitor's offices are some distance away from the vendor's solicitor's offices, it is necessary for the former to instruct a local solicitor to attend completion on his behalf, unless he is prepared to attend personally. It is increasingly the case that completion is effected through the post. The purchaser's solicitor sends the balance[4a] of the purchase money and receives the deeds in exchange. The abstract is examined by the vendor's solicitor as agent for the purchaser's solicitor. Bearing in mind the theoretical importance of the examination of documents[5], this procedure cannot be recommended. Nor should a vendor's solicitor allow himself to be placed in a situation where the duty to his own client may conflict with his agent's responsibility to the other solicitor. The practice appears to be on the increase with sales of registered land where, however, less danger is involved.

The alternative venue caters for cases where the deeds are in the possession of a mortgagee who is separately represented[6]. It is generally felt that the rule is cumbersome and expensive, especially when the solicitors for the vendor and purchaser both practise in the same provincial town, and completion takes place, say, in London where the existing mortgagee's solicitor is. In practice the vendor's solicitor asks the mortgagee's solicitor to act as his agent, but prudence demands that a separate firm be instructed on the purchaser's behalf. Nevertheless both sides incur additional expense in the form of agency fees. A more sensible procedure, sometimes adopted, is to send the deeds to some firm in the same town as the vendor's solicitor, or better still to allow him to hold them from the inception of the transaction, but many mortgagees are reluctant to do this. The district office of the Land Registry has been suggested as a convenient venue for the completion of registered land transactions[7], but this is never done in practice.

If the contract is entirely silent on the venue, it may be that the vendor can insist on completion anywhere in the country[8], though judicial authority is lacking.

C   Date of completion[9]

1.   Formal contracts

Where a date has been agreed by the parties, it is expressly inserted in the contract, often with varying degrees of precision. Usually a specific date appears; sometimes expressions like 'on or before', or, less frequently, 'on or about', a certain date are to be found. Occasionally the appropriate clause in the contract appears, somewhat ludicrously, as: 'The date fixed for completion is the   day of   198– .' If the parties have not agreed any date, a common practice, of doubtful validity, is to insert a date one month after exchange of contracts.

4a   It is treated as being paid on the day it arrives at the vendor's solicitors: NCS 5 (5) (ii).
5   Page 371, ante.
6   It will be recalled that building societies and insurance companies operate a panel of 'approved' solicitors, the latter's being the more restrictive. Even building societies have been subjected to heavy criticism from the profession for their continued operation of the panel system; see the correspondence in (1964) 61 LS Gaz 135, 207, 275.
7   Williams, *Sale of Land*, p. 80, note (s).
8   Walford, 24.
9   See C.T. Emery 'The Date Fixed for Completion' [1978] Conv 144.

(a) 'On or before'

The reason for the use of this expression is patent; the parties have fixed their latest date but are hoping to effect completion earlier. It is equally obvious that adoption of the formula achieves nothing. One party cannot complete before the specified date without the other's concurrence, and the parties are free to arrange an earlier completion without resort to any special term. Solicitors are best advised to avoid adopting the expression[10]. Similar considerations apply to the phrase 'on or about', for the agreement of both parties is required to determine a definite date.

(b) No date mentioned

Failure by the parties to agree a date does not mean there is no effective completion date. The matter will be governed by a general condition of the contract. Thus Condition 5 (1) of the National Conditions provides that in the absence of an express date completion shall be on the 26th working day after the date of the contract or delivery of the abstract of the title (whichever is the later). With The Law Society's Conditions, a similar period is calculated from the date of the contract; see Condition 21 (1). This wording is somewhat unfortunate since solicitors seem notoriously reluctant to date contracts[10a]. The moral for the parties, especially if they want a speedy completion, is to ensure that their agreed date is inserted in the contract. If they have agreed a date which constitutes a term of the contract, its omission therefrom enables either party to plead that there is no written memorandum sufficient for the purposes of the Law of Property Act 1925, s. 40[11].

The application of a general condition is not by implication excluded even where the contract suggests that the parties contemplated the insertion of an agreed date. In one case[12] where the contract provided for completion 'on the day of   1959', it was held there was no inconsistency between the general condition and the passage left blank so as to oust the operation of the former. But suppose the contract provides for completion 'on the day of August 198 – ' and when calculating the period under the relevant general condition, the date is sometime in September. An inconsistency does result; neither the general nor the special condition can operate, so that the date will have to be determined as on an open contract.

2.   Open contracts

Where the contract fixes no completion date, e.g. where the written memorandum consists of a cheque and receipt sufficient for s. 40, or the contract results from the exercise of an option to purchase contained in a lease[13], it is well established that completion takes place within a reasonable time, measured by the legal business which has to be performed in connection with investigating the title and preparing the necessary conveyancing documents[14]. This is a question of fact.

10 See p. 413, post, on the question whether the expression makes time of the essence of the contract.
10a NCS 1 (7) deals with this difficulty by defining the date of the contract in certain instances.
11 *Johnson v Humphrey* [1946] 1 All ER 460; *Hawkins v Price* [1947] Ch 645, [1947] 1 All ER 649. Cf. *Gavaghan v Edwards* [1961] 2 QB 220, [1961] 2 All ER 477, CA (parties agreeing completion date after signing contract; solicitor acting for both parties entitled to create additional memorandum recording agreed date).
12 *Smith v Mansi* [1962] 3 All ER 857. See also *Lee Parker v Izzet* (1971) 22 P & CR 1098.
13 *Green v Sevin* (1879) 13 Ch D 589.
14 *Johnson v Humphrey* [1946] 1 All ER 460 at 463, per Roxburgh J.

3.   Delay in completion

(a) Differing attitudes of law and equity to time clauses
In practice the cherished hopes of vendor and purchaser that completion will take place on the agreed date are not always realised. To understand the consequences of delay and the rights of the parties in that event it is essential to understand the differing attitudes of law and equity to time clauses.

The common law always regarded the completion date as an essential part of the contract and held the parties to their bargain. A party who failed to complete on the appointed day was therefore in fundamental breach of contract.

True to character equity, refraining from following the harsh rule of law, exercised a jurisdiction akin to that of relieving forfeitures, or of permitting the redemption of mortgages after the contractual date had passed[15]. To use a time-hallowed expression, time was not prima facie of the essence of the contract. Courts of equity decreed specific performance of a contract, notwithstanding that the suitor had failed to observe the time stipulation and further, by way of ancillary relief, restrained proceedings at law brought by the other party. Yet equity only adopted this attitude if the time clause could be disregarded without injustice to the parties, not where it was contrary to the express wishes of the parties, or inequitable to hold the time limit as non-essential. Equity's rule has now been clothed, somewhat inartistically, in the following form[16].

> 'Stipulations in a contract, as to time or otherwise, which according to rules of equity are not deemed to be or to have become of the essence of the contract, are also construed and have effect at law in accordance with the same rules.'

It was considered by some that this provision had the effect of making the contractual date for completion a date which could safely be ignored as the obligation was to complete on that date or within a reasonable time thereafter[17]. It is now established by the House of Lords decision in *Raineri v Miles*[18] that failure to complete on the date fixed for completion (whether time is of the essence or not) constitutes a breach of contract[19] entitling the injured party to damages. Further remedies may be available if time is of the essence as appears hereafter.

(b) Time of the essence
Here the rule is strict. The party at fault is thereby debarred from enforcing the contract whilst the other party is free to pursue his remedies for breach of

---

15   *Stickney v Keeble* [1915] AC 386 at 401, HL, per Lord Atkinson. The judgment of Lord Parker contains a helpful survey of the legal and equitable positions: see at 415–16 and 80–81, respectively. See also *United Scientific Holdings Ltd v Burnley Borough Council* [1978] AC 904, [1977] 2 All ER 62, HL.

16   LPA 1925, s. 41, replacing s. 25 (7) of the Judicature Act 1873.

17   See *Re Sandwell Park Colliery* [1929] 1 Ch 277 at 282, per Maughan J; *Babacomp Ltd v Rightside Properties Ltd* [1973] 3 All ER 873 at 875, per Goff J; affd. [1974] 1 All ER 142 at 144, per Russell LJ; *Woods v Mackenzie Hill* [1975] 2 All ER 170 at 172, per Megarry J; Emmet, 264 and the previous edition of this book.

18   [1980] 2 All ER 145. See also *Oakacre Ltd v Claire Cleaners (Holdings) Ltd* [1981] 3 All ER 667 (writ issued before completion date). *Held*: damages recoverable because specific performance was initially claimed and that was not premature in that regard, relying on *Hasham v Zenab* [1960] AC 316.

19   Unless caused by some difficulty over the title, ibid., p. 158, per Lord Edmund-Davies.

contract on the very next day, if he so chooses. According to Lord Romilly MR, in *Parkin v Thorold*[20] time is regarded as essential to the contract in two situations: (i) where the parties make it so in the contract, and (ii) by necessary implication.

(i) *Act of the parties.* This may be done by providing in specific terms that time is of the essence. Alternatively such an intention may be gathered from other terms of the contract, as in *Barclay v Messenger*[1] where the agreement provided that if the purchaser should fail to pay the balance purchase moneys on a given date, the agreement should become null and void. Sir George Jessel MR said[2] he did not know how making time of the essence could have been more strongly expressed than that. The problem becomes one of construing the contract, which may incorporate provisions negativing any intention to make time of the essence. Thus a stipulation for the payment of interest in the event of delay contemplates a possible postponement of completion[3]. Suggestions have been made that the use of the 'on or before' formula may make time of the essence[4]. It is thought that this is not so. Not only is there judicial authority against the view[5], but the dictum cited in its support does not establish the proposition, when read in its context[6].

(ii) *Necessary implication.* As to this head, Lord Romilly said:

' The implication that time [is] of the essence of the contract is derived from the circumstance of the case, such as where the property sold is required for some immediate purpose, such as trade or manufacture, or where the property is of a determinable character, as an estate for life.'

Other judges have spoken of a third category, where time is deemed of the essence by virtue of the surrounding circumstances[7], but this situation is clearly covered by Lord Romilly's second head. Time has been held to be of the essence in respect of transactions involving mines[8], wasting properties such as a short

---

20 (1852) 16 Beav 59 at 65. See G. Boughen Graham, 'Stipulations as to Time' (1954) 18 Conv (NS) 452.
1 (1874) 43 LJ Ch 449.
2 (1874) 43 LJ Ch 449 at 455. See also *Harold Wood Brick Co Ltd v Ferris* [1935] 2 KB 198, CA.
3 *Webb v Hughes* (1870) LR 10 Eq 281; *Patrick v Milner* (1877) 2 CPD 342. This is so although a provision for interest might equally be treated as consistent with a possible waiver of the time clause. Cf. *Harold Wood Brick Co Ltd v Ferris* [1935] 2 KB 198, CA, where an interest provision was held not to be fatal.
4 (1956), 20 Conv (NS) 347; Farrand, 176. See p. 411, ante.
5 *James Macara Ltd v Barclay* [1945] 1 KB 148 at 156, [1944] 2 All ER 589 at 593, CA, per Uthwatt J delivering the opinion of the court.
6 *Patrick v Milner* (1877) 2 CPD 342 at 348, per Grove J. The context makes it clear that the reason why time might otherwise have been of the essence was not because of the words 'on or before', but simply because the sale concerned a reversionary interest where time is prima facie of the essence (see per Lopes J, at p. 350). But see *Raineri v Miles* [1980] 2 All ER 145 at 160, per Lord Frazer. Lord Edmund-Davies (at 155) considered it arguable that the surrounding circumstances may have made time of the essence; see [1980] Conv 238–242.
7 *Roberts v Berry* (1853) 3 De GM & G 284 at 292, per Turner LJ; *Stickney v Keeble* [1915] AC 386 at 416, HL, per Lord Parker; *Raineri v Miles*, supra, per Lord Edmund-Davies.
8 *MacBryde v Weekes* (1856) 22 Beav 533.

leasehold[9], property used for trade purposes[10], the sale of a shop as a going concern[11]. In each case delay might prejudice the parties; equity refused to intervene, leaving the aggrieved person to pursue his legal remedies unhindered. There is authority for saying that time is essential on the purchase of a house required for immediate residence on the day possession is agreed to be given[12]. However, it must not be taken as laying down any general principle applicable to present-day contracts involving residential property. In the absence of any express clause, it would need very special circumstances to make time of the essence in a contract for the sale of an ordinary private house with vacant possession[13]. Following *Hudson v Temple*[14] time would seem to be of the essence in a contract for the assignment of a leasehold house held on a short lease.

The rule that time may be of the essence by implication is ousted if express contractual provisions indicate to the contrary. In *Ellis v Lawrence*[15] General Conditions of Sale, regulating the payment of interest and the service of a contractual notice to complete in the event of delay, were held to show that time was not of the essence in a contract for the sale of premises on which the vendor conducted an ironmongery business.

(c) Making time of the essence

Where time is not originally of the essence, delay does not justify the aggrieved party in declining to proceed with the contract. Until an unreasonable delay has elapsed delay does not constitute a breach of contract entitling the innocent party to treat the contract as discharged, so that if the vendor cannot complete on the agreed date but can do so one week later, the purchaser must complete or risk proceedings for specific performance. If the party not in default wishes to terminate the contract, he must first serve on the other party a notice that he will consider the contract at an end, if it is not completed by a certain date. The effect of such a notice is to make time of the essence of the contract; it enables ·the party serving it to treat the contract as discharged by the other's non-performance, should completion be delayed beyond the required date[16]. It

9   *Hudson v Temple* (1860) 30 LJ Ch 251 (leasehold house and shop held on a 30 years' lease, of which 26 were unexpired). Though time was expressly made of the essence, Lord Romilly MR said that the character of the property would of itself make it so in equity (see at 254), How long has the unexpired residue to be before time ceases to be of the essence?
10   *Woods v Tomlinson* [1964] NZLR 399 (timber felling).
11   *Smith v Hamilton* [1951] Ch 174 at 179, [1950] 2 All ER 928 at 932, per Harman J; *Lock v Bell* [1931] 1 Ch 35, (licensed premises). Time was held to be essential though the contract provided for completion 'on or about' a certain date. According to Maugham J, the vendor must afford the purchaser 'the necessary latitude', i.e. a further date had to be mutually agreed upon before the purchaser could be said to be in breach. On this basis it is difficult to see how time could be said to have been originally of the essence. See also *Bernard v Williams* (1928) 139 LT 22.
12   *Tilley v Thomas* (1867) 3 Ch App 61, cited without disapproval by Lord Atkinson in *Stickney v Keeble* [1915] AC 386 at 402–3, HL.
13   *Smith v Hamilton* [1951] Ch 174 at 179, [1950] 2 All ER 928 at 932, per Harman J. Nevertheless the circumstances relied upon by the court in *Tilley's* case in support of their decision seem to differ little from those existing in many house sales today. In *Jamshed Khodaram Irani v Burjorji Dhunjibhai* (1915) 32 TLR 156 at 157, PC, Lord Haldane regarded *Tilley's* case as an illustration where equity inferred an intention that time was of the essence from what had passed between the parties before signing contracts.
14   (1860) 30 LJ Ch 251, note 9, ante.
15   (1969) 210 Estates Gazette 215; *Patrick v Milner* (1877) 2 CPD 342.
16   The view is put forward in Farrand, 178–180 that the concept of 'making' time of the essence is logically incorrect and that once unreasonable delay has occurred there is no need to serve a notice. Logically this seems entirely correct; time cannot be unilaterally

must be emphasised that giving this notice is the first step towards terminating the contract, i.e. *rescission*; it is inappropriate if specific performance is desired, though in practice it is frequently used in terrorem, as an inducement to the defaulting party to complete without court proceedings[17].

(i) *No contractual provision.* In the absence of any special term regulating the service of the notice, if an unnecessary delay is created by one party, the other has a right to limit a reasonable time within which the contract shall be completed by the other[18]. Two important propositions emerge. First a notice can only be served after there has been such delay on the part of a contracting party as to render it fair that, if steps are not immediately taken to complete, the person giving the notice should be relieved from his contract[19]. Secondly the notice must limit a reasonable time. The difficulties in the way of the person serving the notice are apparent. He has to embark on a guessing game. How long should he wait before serving his notice? Clearly he cannot serve it on the day after completion should have been effected, but this is all that can be said with certainty. How long is a reasonable notice? Reasonableness must be determined at the date when the notice is given and consideration must be had to what then remains to be done to complete[20]. There is some authority for saying that the purchaser's ability to raise the money is a relevant factor[1], though on principle the purchaser's financial arrangements ought not to be the vendor's concern. Notices giving as little as fourteen days have been upheld[2]; others giving as long as six weeks declared invalid[3]. It all depends . . . !

(ii) *General Conditions of Sale.* Both the standard form Conditions of Sale[4] regulate the service of a notice to complete in more or less similar terms. They

made of the essence. The service of the notice should as it is said therein have a twofold effect: (a) avoiding a problem of a breach already on the definition of unreasonable delay (b) operating in future to show what date will be considered unreasonable. However as the writer concedes it is too late to talk of other than making time of the essence; see *United Scientific Holdings v Burnley Borough Council* [1978] AC 904, [1977] 2 All ER 62, HL, and the *Raineri* case at 159 per Lord Fraser.

17 Boughen Graham, op. cit., p. 467. Further the notice under the standard Conditions of Sale LSC 23 and NCS 22 have the express effect of making time of the essence.
18 *Taylor v Brown* (1839) 2 Beav 180 at 183, per Lord Langdale MR. See generally [1980] Conv 19–26 (Angela Sydenham).
19 *Green v Sevin* (1879) 13 Ch D 589 at 599, per Fry J. Dicta suggesting that time can be made of the essence by a notice served at any time appear to be incorrect; see, for instance, Malins V-C, in *McMurray v Spicer* (1868) LR 5 Eq 527 at 542, and in *Webb v Hughes* (1870) LR 10 Eq 281 at 286.
20 *Crawford v Toogood* (1879) 13 Ch D 153 at 158, per Fry J. This is not the sole consideration; see *Stickney v Keeble* [1915] AC 386 at 419, HL, per Lord Parker.
1 *Re Barr's Contract, Moorwell Holdings Ltd v Barr* [1956] Ch 551 at 558, [1956] 2 All ER 853 at 857, per Danckwerts J (express clause providing for at least 28 days' notice interpreted as requiring such time as was reasonable). See also *Green v Sevin* (1879) 13 Ch D 589 at 601, where Fry J held a three weeks' notice insufficient, partly on the ground that it was somewhat short time for raising the purchase money. A more realistic approach was adopted by Buckley J in *Re Roger Malcolm Developments Ltd's Contract* (1960) 176 Estates Gazette 1237, noted at (1961) 25 Conv (NS) 260–61 ('. . . there ought not to be imputed to the vendors any knowledge that the purchasers might be in difficulties because of unfortunate occurrences happening at that time in the building society world'). See also *Ajit v Sammy* [1967] AC 255, PC (purchaser had no money and no prospect of raising any; six days' notice held sufficient).
2 *Nott v Riccard* (1856) 22 Beav 307; *Finkielkraut v Monohan* [1949] 2 All ER 234; *Ajit v Sammy* [1967] AC 255, PC, note 1, ante.
3 *Pegg v Wisden* (1852) 16 Beav 239. See also *Inns v D Miles Griffiths Piercy & Co* (1980) 255 Estates Gazette 623.
4 NCS 22, LSC 23.

enable *either* party *at any time* on or after the completion date to serve a written notice requiring the other party to complete the transaction in accordance with the condition now under discussion. This notice need not specify a date for compliance, for on service of an effective notice it becomes a term of the contract in respect of which time is of the essence that the party to whom it is given shall complete within twenty eight days after service[5]. This condition eliminates both of the uncertainties applicable to open contracts; the notice can be served irrespective of unreasonable delay and a fixed contractual period is substituted for the vague period of reasonable notice[6].

A notice is not effective unless the party giving it is at the time of service himself ready, able and willing to complete[7]. The significance of this qualification seems not to be fully appreciated in practice. Notices have been held to be ineffective when served by a vendor whose title was still subject to an adverse third party claim[8], and by a purchaser who was refusing to complete until the vendor procured a landlord's licence to assign[9]. The latest edition of the National Conditions merely requires the server to be 'ready and willing to fulfil his own outstanding' contractual obligations. Despite the absence of reference to any 'ability' to complete, it is not thought that his position is in any way improved. The expression 'ready and willing' has been judicially explained as implying 'not only the disposition but the capacity to do the act'[10].

(d) Consequences of default

Failure to abide by a time clause where time is of the essence (whether originally so or by virtue of a notice to complete) amounts to a breach of contract which is no different from breach of any other fundamental term. The party not in default may elect to treat the contract as terminated by the breach and he can pursue his normal contractual remedies. These are more fully considered in Part VI of this book[11]. One example will suffice as an illustration for present purposes. In *Finkielkraut v Monohan*[12] a vendor, having served a notice to complete, found himself unable to complete on the prescribed day. His action for specific performance was dismissed; moreover his own default discharged the

5   This provides an additional remedy consequent upon the original breach; it does not substitute a new contractual date for completion: *Raineri v Miles*, supra, approving *Woods v Mackenzie Hill Ltd* [1975] 2 All ER 170 on this point. In the case of the Law Society Conditions the period is 21 days.

6   See *Cumberland Court (Brighton) Ltd v Taylor* [1964] Ch 29, [1963] 2 All ER 536 (decided on the similarly worded NCS 22 (17th edn)).

7   LSC 23 (3); NSC 22 (1).

8   *Horton v Kurzke* [1971] 2 All ER 577.

9   *Re Davies's Agreement, Davies v Fagarazzi* (1969) 21 P & CR 328.

10   *De Medina v Norman* (1842) 11 LJ Ex 320 at 322, per Lord Abinger CB. See now the recent case of *Pagebar Properties Ltd v Derby Investment Holdings Ltd* [1973] 1 All ER 65, where it was held that a vendor was not entitled to serve a notice under NSC 22 at a time when he was in breach of his own obligation to disclose existing tenancies. See also *Clearbrook Property Holdings v Verrier* [1973] 3 All ER 614 (oral extension alleged); *Cole v Rose* [1978] 3 All ER 1121. (Outstanding mortgage not covered by undertaking). This latter case has been subjected to criticism: [1978] Conv 326–328; [1979] Conv 161–163; but the criticism appears more at large than specific LCS 23 (3) (b) is specifically drafted to deal with the problem by stating a vendor is ready to complete notwithstanding outstanding mortgages if the sum due on completion will be sufficient to discharge them.

11   See particularly in relation to delay, pp. 611–612, post. In *Talley v Wolsey-Neech* (1978) 38 P & CR 45, CA, it was held that a vendor rescinding under the former LSC 19 (4) (c) (liquidated damages on resale at loss) could not also claim outstanding interest. The new condition 23 (5) (b) has reversed this.

12   [1949] 2 All ER 234.

purchaser from the contract, entitling him to recover his deposit without it being necessary for the purchaser to serve his own notice.

Alternatively the party not at fault may treat the contract as still subsisting. This is what is meant by 'waiver' of time being of the essence[13]. The taking of possession on the completion date (when time was originally of the essence)[14], a continuance of negotiations by considering the procuring of an indemnity to cure a defect in title[15], and the acceptance of the abstract and subsequent raising of requisitions[16] have been held to amount to conduct from which it could be inferred there was no intention to treat the contract as determined. Subsequent negotiations expressly made without prejudice to a party's notice of abandonment do not effect a waiver[17]. A waiver of time being of the essence does not preclude the service of a further notice making time of the essence for the second time[18].

Waiver so-called must be distinguished from an extension of time and nothing more, which merely substitutes the extended time for the original time and does not destroy the essential character of the time[19]. Here the court enforces the later date just as it would the original date provided there is an extension to a definite date. An agreement by the parties made *before* time elapses, that time is no longer essential, effects not a waiver but a variation of the contract.

D Payment of purchase price

1. Mode of payment

In theory the only safe mode of payment is by cash. The dangers of accepting a cheque for the balance due on completion are obvious. The cheque might be dishonoured after the vendor's solicitor has parted with the deeds. To accept a cheque in these circumstances without his client's authority is clearly negligent[20]. Despite pressure from the profession, the Council of The Law Society has refused to sanction the use of cheques on completion[1]. Payment by banker's draft[2] is accepted and in practice no objection is taken to a building society's cheque.

---

13 *The Rawlplug Co Ltd v Kamvale Properties Ltd* (1968) 20 P & CR 32 at 37, per Megarry J. Cf. *Buckland v Farmer and Moody* [1978] 3 All ER 929, CA (a case on solicitors' negligence in respect of a conveyancing transaction alleging failure to inform the plaintiffs that the vendors had waived the time limit on a notice to complete. *Held*: extensions did not alter the effect of the notice making time of the essence).
14 *Ellis v Lawrence* (1969) 210 Estates Gazette 215.
15 *King v Wilson* (1843) 6 Beav 124.
16 *Hipwell v Knight* (1835) 1 Y & C Ex 401. Cf. *The Rawlplug Co Ltd v Kamvale Properties Ltd* (1968) 20 P & CR 32 (negotiations for making *new* contract indicated that previous contract treated as discharged).
17 *Tilley v Thomas* (1867) 3 Ch App 61.
18 *Webb v Hughes* (1870) LR 10 Eq 281 at 286, per Malins V-C. See LSC 23 (8) providing for a further notice with ten days instead of 21.
19 *Barclay v Messenger* (1874) 43 LJ Ch 449 at 456, per Jessel MR; *Tropical Traders Ltd v Goonan* (1964) 111 CLR 41; *Buckland v Farmer and Moody*, supra.
20 *Pape v Westacott* [1894] 1 QB 272.
 1 See (1969) 66 LS Gaz 406.
 2 Technically an order for the payment of money, drawn by one banker on another, but otherwise resembling an ordinary cheque.

2.   Apportionments

When calculating the balance due, the deposit must be brought into account. Often various allowances have to be made. For instance, if the vendor has not discharged the general rates for the financial year, he allows the purchaser a proportion to cover the period of his ownership from the previous 1 April to the completion date. Income receivable after completion is retained by the purchaser in full, for he has already allowed the vendor on completion the proportion covering the vendor's period of entitlement. As we have previously observed, under the general law[3] income (e.g. rents) and outgoings (e.g. rates, a rentcharge issuing out of the property) are usually apportioned as at the contractual date of completion. The National Conditions provide for apportionments to be made as at the date of *actual* completion in certain instances as follows:

(i)   where the vendor elects to take income in lieu of charging interest;

(ii)   on a sale to a sitting tenant;

(iii) where the purchaser elects to have them so apportioned because (a) completion is delayed on account of the vendor' failure to obtain a landlord's licence to assign, or (b) the vendor remains in beneficial occupation after the completion date[4].

The Law Society's Conditions are of similar effect[5] but provide for apportionment as at the date of actual completion where the property is sold with entire vacant possession (irrespective of whether the vendor retains actual occupation). This clause is not limited solely to residential property.

Apportionments are calculated by the vendor's solicitor a few days before actual completion and incorporated into a Completion Statement sent to the purchaser's solicitor; he then has an opportunity to check the figures and obtain any extra money from his client. On completion he should inspect all receipts for the current year's outgoings to verify their discharge by the vendor.

3.   Charging interest

The purchaser's delay in completing prima facie entitles the vendor to charge interest on the balance of the purchase money. This he can do in the absence of any stipulation in the contract[6]. It has been the practice over the years to make express provision for the payment of interest. In the past several different clauses have been in vogue[7]; practitioners today are most familiar with the standard conditions in The National and The Law Society's Conditions of Sale, Conditions 7 and 22 respectively.

(a) National Conditions
These conditions may be summarised as follows:
(i) Unless the delay is attributable to the vendor's act or default[8], the purchaser must pay interest on the balance of the purchase money at the rate of interest

---

3   Page 259, ante.
4   See NCS 5 (1) – (3). It seems that under (iii) (b) the purchaser can make his election although the vendor has only occupied for part of the intervening period.
5   See LSC 19.
6   *Esdaile v Stephenson* (1822) 1 Sim & St 122 at 123, per Leach V-C.
7   See the various examples considered in Williams, *Title*, p. 497.
8   Including that of his mortgagee or SLA trustee.

prescribed by the General Conditions⁹ unless a different rate is specified in the Special Conditions.
(ii) Instead of claiming interest the vendor may elect in writing to take the rents and profits. This option constitutes a valuable right where the property consists of a block of flats or multiple dwellings producing considerable revenue. One important limitation must be observed. Wilberforce J held in *Re Hewitt's Contract*¹⁰ that the right to income is linked with the right to interest; if the vendor would be debarred from claiming interest (e.g. because the delay was attributable to his own default) he cannot elect to take the income. This construction of the General Conditions puts the vendor in a position inferior to that he would enjoy under an open contract where he is at least permitted to retain the interim rents and profits should his delay disentitle him to interest.
(iii) As an alternative to paying interest the purchaser can deposit the balance at a bank, provided the delay is not attributable to his own default and he gives written notice thereof to the vendor. In this event the vendor must take the accruing interest and cannot opt for the rents and profits. This provision is unlikely to avail most house purchasers who will normally be dependent on a mortgage advance, or have their capital tied up in their existing property.

(b) Law Society Conditions
The 1980 Conditions have introduced a new radically different condition¹¹ which gives either party the right to claim interest on the default of the other party causing a delay in completion. As an alternative, compensation can be claimed. This provision has been criticised as being capable of attack on the grounds of it being a penalty¹². In addition to the above a vendor can elect to take the income in lieu¹²ᵃ.

(c) Meaning of default
As we have just seen a vendor cannot charge interest if the delay is attributable to his default. According to Bowen LJ¹³, in an often repeated dictum:

' Default is a purely relative term, just like negligence. It means nothing more, nothing less, than not doing what is reasonable under the circumstances — not doing something which you ought to do, having regard to the relations which you occupy towards the other persons interested in the transaction.'

Formerly the practice was to qualify default on the vendor's part by adding 'wilful', a word which it has been said is difficult to define¹⁴. Examples of conduct held to amount to wilful default are not wanting, but decided cases¹⁵ are of

9   See para. 4 of the construction clause.
10 [1963] 3 All ER 419 (a decision on NCS 6 (17th edn) which is reproduced in the 18th and 19th edns).
11 LSC 22.
12 [1980] Conv 404 at 412–413 (H.W. Wilkinson).
12a This will only be done in the case of a sale without vacant possession as the vendor is not generally entitled to the income until after the date for completion: LSC 19 (1). In this case the vendor can therefore apparently take the income (if any) *and* interest. This would be the opposite of *Re Hewitt*, supra.
13 *Re Young and Harston's Contract* (1885) 31 Ch D 168 at 174, CA. But see the critical comments of Wilberforce J in *Re Hewitt's Contract* [1963] 3 All ER 419 at 423.
14 *Re London Corpn and Tubb's Contract* [1894] 2 Ch 524 at 530, CA, per Lopes LJ. Less timorous judges have attempted a definition; see e.g. Bowen LJ, in *Re Young and Harston's Contract* (1885) 31 Ch D 168 at 174, CA.
15 *Re Young and Harston's Contract* (1885) 31 Ch D 168, CA (vendor's departure abroad two days before completion without executing the conveyance); *Re Pelly and Jacobs Contract* (1899) 80 LT 45 (refusal to deliver abstract due to misinterpretation of contract). It will not be necessary to show more where the condition refers to default simpliciter.

limited assistance for it is a question of fact depending on the circumstances of each case. Happily neither of the forms in general use introduce this concept of wilfulness, though it may be found in the Conditions of Sale of some local law societies. In *Re Hewitt's Contract*[16] vendors who had simply underestimated the time necessary to complete were held responsible for the delay since the circumstances occasioning it were foreseeable. A purchaser may still be liable for interest although completion is delayed though remedying a defect in title, at least where there is no want of reasonable care on the vendor's part in not discovering and not providing for the defect in the contract[17]. Default, once proved, must be shown to have caused the delay[18].

(d) Purchaser in possession before completion

The rights of a purchaser in this situation have already been discussed[19]. Nothing need be added, save to state the obvious, that it is the taking of possession that determines his liability for interest, payment of which is quite independent of any default of his part.

(e) No operative conditions

Under an open contract the purchaser must pay interest from the time that he could prudently take possession, that is, from the time when a good title is shown[20]. From that time he is also entitled to the rent and profits including an occupation rent should the vendor retain possession. Where the vendor is responsible for the delay in completion and the interest would exceed the amount of the income, the purchaser can require the vendor to take the rents and profits in lieu of interest[1]. If the purchaser is not himself at fault, he can avoid the payment of interest and still retain the revenue by depositing the money at a bank, or, if the money is already there, by giving notice that it is lying idle[2].

4.   Receipt for payment

The balance of the purchase money, adjusted to take account of any apportionments, interest and rent, is handed over on completion in return for the deeds of the property and, where appropriate, the keys. A receipt is invariably embodied in the conveyance and under s. 67 of the Law of Property Act 1925, this is a sufficient discharge without any further receipt being endorsed on the deed—as was the practice prior to 1881. By virtue of s. 69 of the Act, a receipt in the deed is sufficient authority for payment to the solicitor producing it; consequently the money can safely be paid to the vendor's solicitor in the vendor's absence. The producing solicitor must be acting for the person signing the receipt; possession of the deed at his offices is not equivalent to its production[3].

16   [1963] 3 All ER 419.
17   *Re London Corpn and Tubb's Contract* [1894] 2 Ch 524, CA; *Re Woods and Lewis's Contract* [1898] 2 Ch 211, CA. The LSC no longer exclude the vendor's right to interest where the delay is attributable to his default in deducing title; cf. LSC 7 (2) (a) (1953 edn).
18   *Re London Corpn and Tubb's Contract* [1894] 2 Ch 524, CA.
19   See p. 265, ante.
20   *Re Keeble and Stillwell's Fletton Brick Co* (1898) 78 LT 383; see *Bennett v Stone* [1903] 1 Ch 509 at 524, CA, per Cozens-Hardy MR, for a useful survey of the position.
1   *Esdaile v Stephenson* (1822) 2 Sim & St 122; *Re Hewitt's Contract* [1963] 3 All ER 419 at 423, per Wilberforce J.
2   *Regent's Canal Co v Ware* (1857) 23 Beav 575; *Dyson v Hornby* (1851) 4 De G & Sim 481.
3   *Day v Woolwich Equitable Building Society* (1889) 40 Ch D 491, a decision on the Conveyancing Act 1881, s. 56.

Doubts have been expressed whether the protection afforded by s. 69 extends to members of the solicitor's firm, such as his managing or articled clerk, or to the London or provincial agent acting for the vendor's solicitor[4]. Suffice it to say that in practice the section causes no problems. There are similar provisions applicable to solicitors of trustee-vendors[5].

5. Vendor's lien

If the vendor completes without having received the total purchase money, he has an equitable lien, arising by operation of law, on the land for the unpaid balance[6]. This lien is more than a mere equity; it creates a charge upon and interest in the property sold, in the same manner as if it had been expressly created[7]. The lien arises immediately there is a binding contract for sale and is discharged on completion to the extent that the purchase money is paid[8]. The vendor may waive or abandon his lien, expressly or impliedly from the circumstances of the case. It has been held that no lien arises where the vendor takes a legal mortgage on the property for the amount unpaid[9]. The mere taking of a personal security like a promissory note does not prima facie exclude the lien; it depends whether the court infers from the circumstances whether the vendor intends to rely on the security of the estate, or the purchaser's personal credit[10].

(a) Enforcement of lien

A lien does not give any right to possession; it confers a right of action for foreclosure[11] or for an order for the sale of the property[12]. It is enforceable against the purchaser though the conveyance to him contains a receipt clause for all the money[13], against volunteers, and sometimes against a subsequent purchaser.

The Law of Property Act 1925, s. 68, provides that a receipt for consideration money in the body of a deed or endorsed thereon is, in favour of a subsequent purchaser without notice that all the money has not been paid, sufficient (but not conclusive) evidence of the payment of the whole. Nevertheless, as the section itself envisages, the enforceability of a vendor's lien ultimately rests on the doctrine of notice rather than on a purchaser's reliance upon a receipt

4   Law Society's Digest, Opinions Nos. 163 & 164 favour a restricted operation of the section. Cf. Williams V & P, 743. In *Day v Woolwich Equitable Building Society* (1889) 40 Ch D 491 no significance was attached to the fact that payment was made, not to the solicitor, but to his clerk.
5   Trustee Act 1925, s. 23 (3).
6   *Mackreth v Symmons* (1808) 15 Ves 329; *Capital Finance Co Ltd v Stokes* [1969] 1 Ch 261 at 278, [1968] 3 All ER 625 at 629, CA, per Harman LJ.
7   *Re Stucley, Stucley v Kekewich* [1906] 1 Ch 67 at 83, CA, per Cozens-Hardy LJ.
8   *Re Birmingham, Savage v Stannard* [1959] Ch 523, [1958] 3 All ER 625; *London and Cheshire Insurance Co Ltd v Laplagrene Property Co Ltd* [1971] Ch 499 at 514, [1971] 1 All ER 766 at 779, per Brightman J.
9   *Capital Finance Co Ltd v Stokes* [1969] 1Ch 261, [1968] 3 All ER 625, CA; *Burston Finance Ltd v Speirway Ltd* [1974] 3 All ER 735. A person who provides purchase money will *not* generally be subrogated to a vendors lien: *Orakpo v Manson Investments Ltd* [1978] AC 95, [1977] 3 All ER 1, HL.
10   *Winter v Lord Anson* (1827) 3 Russ 488 at 491, per Lord Lyndhurst LC (purchaser's bond conditioned for payment of balance did not negative existence of lien); *Hughes v Kearney* (1803) 1 Sch & L 132 (promissory note).
11   *Hughes v Griffin* [1969] 1 All ER 460 at 461, CA, per Harman LJ. This is equivalent to seeking cancellation of the contract by the court; see *Lysaght v Edwards* (1876) 2 Ch D 499 at 506, per Jessel MR; *Baker v Williams* (1893) 62 LJ Ch 315.
12   *Williams v Aylesbury and Buckingham Rail Co* (1873) 28 LT 547.
13   *Winter v Lord Anson* (1827) 3 Russ 488.

clause. The prima facie sufficiency of the receipt appears to be displaced if the vendor, having parted with the deeds on completion, registers the lien as a Class C (iii) land charge, for this will give the purchaser actual notice[14]. Similarly if he retains the deeds their non-availability[15] will constitute constructive notice of the vendor's rights.

(b) Registered land

The application of s. 68 to sales of registered land was considered by Brightman J in *London and Cheshire Insurance Co Ltd v Laplagrene Property Co Ltd*[16]:

> ' A, a limited company, transferred registered freehold property to B, who was in due course registered as proprietor. The transfer contained the usual receipt clause for the consideration which, however, was never paid. On the same day as the transfer B leased the property back to A who remained in occupation. Later B charged the property to C and it became necessary to determine whether A's lien was enforceable against C.

It was conceded that A, being in occupation, could enforce his lien against C as an overriding interest under s. 70 (1) (g) of the Land Registration Act 1925, notwithstanding that such a 'right' was not vested in him qua tenant[17]. Brightman J held that A did not lose his overriding interest when he vacated the property on a date subsequent to C's charge. It was argued, however, that A could not assert his lien because of the receipt clause in the transfer. On this point the learned judge decided that for the purposes of s. 68 it was not necessary for C to see the actual deed (and in practice purchasers seldom inspect previous transfers of the land); it sufficed if he saw an accurate record of the deed and a suitable entry in the proprietorship register was adequate even though the register was itself not a deed. Nevertheless he held that the entry 'Price paid £ —' in the register simply meant 'cost price'; it did not purport to record the receipt of the purchase money. Consequently C could not rely on s. 68[18].

14   LPA 1925, s. 198, p. 396, ante. Conversely non-registration would entitle the subsequent purchaser to take free, even if he had actual knowledge (e.g. because of the absence of a receipt clause) that the whole price had not been paid. This does not seem to be what s. 68 intended. Further, it is uncertain to what extent a vendor's lien is affected by the peculiar effect of the law of escrows, as illustrated in *Thompson v McCullough* [1947] KB 447, [1947] 1 All ER 265, CA, discussed p. 432, post. The court held that in the absence of evidence to the contrary, the conveyance was delivered by the vendor as an escrow pending payment of the balance of the purchase money and it did not operate to pass the legal estate to the purchaser until payment of the remainder. If the purchaser defaults in payment of the balance the vendor is technically in a position to convey to another purchaser, but not before the court has released him from the obligations attaching to the delivery of the escrow (see p. 431, post). Further if non-payment of the price in full prevents the legal title passing to the purchaser, the lien cannot strictly be registered against him for he is not an estate owner within the LCA 1972, s. 3 (1), p. 394, ante.

15   In this situation the lien is not registrable as a land charge.

16   [1971] Ch 499, [1971] 1 All ER 767; noted at (1971) 35 Conv (NS) 188.

17   See *Webb v Pollmount Ltd* [1966] Ch 584, [1966] 1 All ER 481, p. 49, ante.

18   This view, with respect, appears technically sound (cf. (1971) 35 Conv (NS) 191). The decision may have the effect of depriving a purchaser of the benefits of s. 68, but this seems to be no great loss in view of the section's apparent irrelevance to the question of the lien's enforceability. In any case the prima facie sufficiency of the receipt under s. 68 would have been displaced because A being in occupation, C had constructive notice of his rights: see pp. 511 and 777, respectively.

In the normal situation the unpaid vendor will not be in occupation. To be enforceable his lien requires protection on the register by entry of a notice or caution against the purchaser's title. In the absence of such protection (or occupation), a later purchaser takes free from the lien, irrespective of s. 68.

One further point should be considered in passing. Since no legal title vests in the purchaser on a sale of registered land until he is registered as proprietor, the question is sometimes raised whether he is technically safe in handing over the purchase money on completion. The better view would seem to be that if he obtains a clear certificate of search and applies for registration within the protection period, he may with practical safety pay the purchase money in exchange for a duly executed transfer and the land or charge certificate[19]. This is the procedure adopted in practice. Neither of the standard sets of Conditions of Sale see the need to make any special provision for completion of sales of registered land[20].

E Title deeds

1. Collection on completion

Unless the purchaser is acquiring part only of the land in the vendor's title his solicitor will on completion collect all the deeds, documents, searches and other relevant papers relating to the title, having first examined the deeds[1], often rather hurriedly, against the abstract of title. It is customary for the vendor's solicitor to obtain the signature of the purchaser's solicitor to a schedule of the deeds and documents received by the latter.

If the title is registered, a purchaser acquiring the whole of the vendor's interest receives the land (or charge) certificate which is subsequently forwarded to the Land Registry for registration purposes. On a transfer of part, the certificate is not handed over; it is the vendor's duty to deposit it at the Registry for completion of the purchaser's registration[2].

Discharge of mortgages

Where the property purchased is subject to a mortgage to be discharged by the vendor out of the money provided by the purchaser, the vendor's solicitor (or the mortgagee's solicitor if the mortgagee is separately represented) retains the mortgage so that a vacating receipt can in due course be endorsed and executed by the mortgagee. Strictly speaking a purchaser is perfectly entitled to require the mortgage deed, duly discharged, to be handed over on completion. Unfortunately most institutional mortgages are reluctant to vacate the mortgage until actual receipt of the redemption money. As it is inconvenient in practice for the vendor to discharge the mortgage prior to completion by means of a temporary loan from his bank, the practice has developed whereby the vendor's solicitor gives his undertaking to repay the mortgage and to forward the discharged deed to the purchaser's solicitor. The Council of The Law Society have expressed the opinion[3] that this practice facilitates conveyancing and should be

---

19 Brickdale, 38; contra Williams, *Sale of Land*, p. 80, note (s).
20 Cf. 3 K & E, 346–47, 373.
 1 See p. 371, ante.
 2 LRA 1925, ss. 64 (1), 110 (6). See generally pp. 451–453, post.
 3 See (1970) 67 LS Gaz 753. Their opinion is limited to the discharge of building society mortgages. As regards other mortgages, presumably their previous opinion (see (1949) 46

accepted by purchasers' solicitors so long as building societies refuse to change their practice[4]. The Council's recommended form of under-taking has been subjected to criticism on the ground that it does not require the deed to be sent to the purchaser's solicitor within any specified period, but only as soon as it is received from the society, though it is somewhat unrealistic to expect a solicitor to undertake to do something over which he has no control.

This practice of giving undertakings is universal and in the vast majority of cases operates smoothly. Nevertheless theoretical hazards exist and occasionally they materialise[5]. The present attitude of institutional lenders would appear to be unnecessarily cautious; for there can be no real objection from a mortgagee's point of view to sealing receipts in advance of repayment, especially as the money will on completion be received by the mortgagee's solicitor.

Care should be taken to ensure that the date of the receipt is not later than that of the purchaser's conveyance, otherwise it may operate as a transfer of the mortgage, instead of its intended discharge[6].

A mortgage of registered land is vacated in the manner provided for by the Land Registration Rules 1925, i.e. by the mortgagee signing an instrument known as Form 53[7]. The Chief Land Registrar can act upon other sufficient proof of satisfaction of the mortgage; a normal vacating receipt endorsed on the mortgage is an adequate alternative to Form 53 and, apparently, many building societies prefer this alternative. In this event the charge certificate is retained and an undertaking given as before; if Form 53 is employed the charge certificate is handed to the purchaser (or his mortgagee) with an undertaking to forward the form duly executed in due course. It is not obligatory to wait until the appropriate document is received before applying to the Registry for registration of the purchaser as proprietor; the Registry automatically stands the case over to await receipt of the discharge or charge certificate vacated[8].

2. Acknowledgment for production of deeds[9]

(a) Circumstances necessitating acknowledgment

Where the purchaser buys part only of the vendor's land, he cannot, for obvious reasons, take the vendor's deeds on completion. The Law of Property Act 1925, s. 45 (9), entitles a vendor to retain documents of title where (i) he retains any part of the land to which the documents relate, or (ii) the document consists of a trust instrument or other instrument creating a trust which is still subsisting, or an instrument relating to the appointment or discharge of a trustee of a

---

LS Gaz 230) still holds good, namely that a purchaser's solicitor should obtain his client's authority to accept an undertaking to discharge, otherwise he may be liable in negligence if the mortgage is not vacated.

4 See (1971) 35 Conv (NS) 3, and the correspondence at (1971) 68 LS Gaz 76, 165, 264; (1973) 70 LS Gaz 1346, 1360 (J.E. Adams) and (1980) 77 LS Gaz 259. And see generally, Emmet, 308–309 and 2nd Supplement.
5 See the instance considered at (1971) 35 Conv (NS) 306.
6 Under the LPA 1925, s. 115 (2). See *Cumberland Court (Brighton) Ltd v Taylor* [1964] Ch 29, [1963] 2 All ER 536. A building society receipt in the form of the Building Societies Act 1962, 6th Sch. cannot operate as a transfer; it does not name the payer.
7 Rule 151. After the usual heading Form 53 states that: 'I, AB, of . . . hereby admit that the charge dated . . . and registered . . . , of which I am the proprietor has been discharged.' The proprietor's signature must be attested. In the case of a building society, it should be under the society's seal and countersigned by the secretary. See also p. 466, post.
8 R & R, 542. This practice is in no way affected by the Land Registration (Official Searches) Rules 1981, p. 404, ante.
9 See Emmet, 711–717.

subsisting trust. Thus a personal representative can retain the grant of probate when disposing of the deceased's landed property. The statutory entitlement can be varied by contract. A vendor is entitled to retain documents showing title to, and extinguishment of, an easement formerly appurtenant to the land sold over the servient land retained by him[10].

Where land is vested in a local authority by virtue of a vesting declaration, a person retaining possession of any document relating to the title to the land is deemed to have given to the authority an acknowledgment in writing for its production[11].

(b) Obligations imposed by statutory acknowledgment

A vendor who retains documents may give to the purchaser an acknowledgment in writing of the purchaser's right to their production and to delivery of copies. Such an acknowledgment has effect as provided by s. 64 of the Law of Property Act 1925[12]. It does not confer any right to damages for loss or destruction of or injury to the documents (sub-s. (6)); it merely gives a right to specific performance of the obligations at the expense of the person requesting the same. Consequently there is usually coupled with the acknowledgment an undertaking to keep the documents safe, whole, uncancelled and undefaced unless prevented from so doing by fire, or other inevitable accident (sub-s. (9)). An action for damages lies for breach of this undertaking, but since destruction does not affect title, merely its proof, damages will apparently be limited to the cost of executing the necessary statutory declarations and exhibits[13]. The acknowledgment and undertaking may be the subject of a separate document, in which case it is usually in writing (thereby being exempt from stamp duty), rather than under seal, but normally they are contained in the conveyance to the purchaser in some such form as:

> The vendor hereby acknowledges the right of the purchaser to the production of the documents referred to in the schedule[14] hereto (the possession of which is retained by the vendor) and to delivery of copies thereof and hereby undertakes for the safe custody of the same.

It has become customary for fiduciary vendors (personal representatives, trustees and mortgagees) not to enter into the undertaking for safe custody. This practice, though without apparent legal foundation[15], has in fact received statutory recognition[16], and upon an enfranchisement of leaseholds under the

---

10   *Re Lehmann and Walker's Contract* [1906] 2 Ch 640.
11   Compulsory Purchase (Vesting Declarations) Act 1981, s. 14.
12   The full obligation is contained in sub-s. (4). Note that it does not give any right to take one's own copies, and there is an exemption for fire and other inevitable accident (sub-s. (2)).
13   Williams, *Title*, 799, note (18). Cf. *Barrett v Brahms* (1967) 111 Sol Jo 35. X requested verified copies of Y's deeds so that X could prove his own title at the Land Registry and get it registered. Y's deeds had been lost. Held: an inquiry as to damages should be ordered, but no direction as to the assessment of the quantum should be made until after X's application to the Registry.
14   Where the acknowledgment relates to a single document, its particulars are included within the body of the clause.
15   See Farrand, 305; cf. 1 W & C (13th edn), 144. Yet a fiduciary owner who subsequently acquires the possession of deeds comes under the obligations of sub-s. 9 if a previous owner has given the undertaking. A purchaser cannot require an undertaking from a fiduciary vendor under LSC 17(5).
16   See note 11, ante.

Leasehold Reform Act 1967, a landlord cannot be required to enter into an undertaking[17].

In merely refering to 'documents', the section introduces some uncertainty as to what it covers. Clearly it relates to deeds affecting the land conveyed, and to probates and letter of administration now that they may be endorsed with notice of assents and conveyances[18]. It is not considered necessary, nor is it the practice, to include planning permissions or certificates of search in an acknowledgment. Illogically, although a vendor must hand over all deeds in his possession, authority exists for saying that a purchaser is not entitled to an acknowledgment for documents dated prior to the date fixed for commencement of the title[19].

(c) When effective

The statutory acknowledgment and undertaking are only effective when given by the person retaining the deeds 'to another'. An executor's acknowledgment for production of the probate contained in an assent whereby he vests the property in himself beneficially is valueless[20]. A subsequent purchaser should endeavour to obtain one in the conveyance to him. Failing this, he would seem to have an equitable right to its production[1]. Equally worthless is an acknowledgment by a mortgagor-vendor in a conveyance of part of the mortgaged property. Normally the mortgagee holds the deeds; he is therefore the proper person to give the acknowledgment, the obligations of which will devolve upon the mortgagor when the deeds come into his possession. The mortgagee will not undertake for their safe custody, and it is uncertain whether, apart from express stipulation, the purchaser can insist on the vendor's covenanting to give the undertaking when the deeds come into his possession[2].

(d) Enforceability

The statutory obligations only bind the person having possession or control of the deeds so long as they are in his possession or control. The duties imposed by the undertaking are similarly imposed on the possessor only[3].

The benefit of the acknowledgment runs with the land under sub-s. (3) in favour of any successor (other than a lessee at a rent), whether of the whole or part of the original purchaser's land. If A conveys part of his land to B who later conveys a smaller portion to C, the benefit of A's acknowledgment to B will pass to C who will, however, require an acknowledgment from B for the A – B conveyance. There is no corresponding provision for the running of the benefit of the undertaking; it is thought that it runs under s. 78 of the Law of Property Act 1925[4].

---

17   Section 10 (6).
18   *Re Miller and Pickersgill's Contract* [1931] 1 Ch 511. See p. 336, ante.
19   Emmet, 712, citing *Re Guest and Worth* (unreported).
20   But see *Rowley Holmes & Co v Barber* [1977] 1 All ER 801 and Emmet, 2nd Supplement referring to p. 467 of main text.
1   According to 1 Dart V & P 483 every person who has an interest in land has an equitable right to the production of all deeds affirmatively proving his title, but not to those which do not. For cases on the subject, see *Fain v Ayers* (1826) 2 Sim & St 533; *Re Jenkins and Commercial Electric Theatre Co's Contract* [1917] WN 49.
2   Under LSC 17 (5) a non-fiduciary vendor can be required to covenant. A mortgagee cannot be compelled even to given an acknowledgement; if he refuses, the vendor must give a covenant for production: *Re Pursell and Deakin's Contract* [1893] WN 152.
3   LPA 1925, s. 64 (2), (9).
4   Farrand, 304; Walford, 209. Title deeds to real estate devolved on the heir prior to 1926

(e) Registered land

Generally no acknowledgment or undertaking is required, for the land certificate is sufficient proof of title without reference to the vendor's earlier title. However an acknowledgment and undertaking (if appropriate) appear desirable[5] on:

(i)   a transfer of part of the transferor's *possessory* title, in which case an acknowledgment for pre-registration documents should be given (or on a transfer of the whole, they should be handed over);

(ii)   a transfer (by way of assignment) of part of leasehold property, when an acknowledgment for the lease is required.

It does not seem necessary, as we have already seen[6], for an assent or transfer by a personal representative to contain any acknowledgment for production of the grant of representation.

3. Endorsements on deeds

The Law of Property Act 1925, s. 200, provides that on a sale of part of the land comprised in the vendor's title, the purchaser is entitled, notwithstanding any contrary stipulation, to require a memorandum to be endorsed on some deed relating to the common title and retained by the vendor, giving notice of restrictive covenants or easements created by the conveyance to him and affecting land retained by the vendor. The purchaser has the right to select which deed shall bear the endorsement; usually the conveyance to the vendor is chosen. The endorsement does not affect the validity of the rights granted, nor obviate the need to register restrictive covenants. The existence of an endorsement is of advantage when title is later deduced by the vendor to his retained land. The section does not apply to a lessee or mortgagee, nor to dispositions of registered land.

It should be observed that the provision does not assist a purchaser where the vendor conveys part of his land without granting rights affecting his retained land. It is, however, common practice to endorse a memorandum of a sale-off, a procedure which is clearly desirable for it considerably reduces the risk of the sale being overlooked on a subsequent sale of the retained land[7]. A purchaser desirous of having notice endorsed ought to raise the matter by way of requisition; the vendor's solicitor rarely refuses to comply with the request.

F The purchase deed[8]

1. Introduction

The remaining document which the purchaser's solicitor takes up on completion is the grant to the purchaser, whether it be a conveyance, transfer, lease,

---

(*Atkinson v Baker* (1791) 4 Term Rep 229) and so come within the definition of 'land' in the LPA 1925, s. 205 (1) (ix); the requirement of s. 78 (covenant relating to any *land* of the covenantee) is satisfied.

5   R & R, 327–328 where the requirement is stated to be 'mere verbiage'. Cf. Emmet, 715.

6   Page 358, ante.

7   *Re Sea View Gardens, Claridge v Tingey* [1966] 3 All ER 935; *Epps v Esso Petroleum Co Ltd* [1973] 2 All ER 465 p. 85, ante, illustrate some problems that can result from failure to endorse notice of a sale-off. And see (1971) 68 LS Gaz 91. For endorsements on grants of representation, see p. 336, ante.

8   For the form and contents of a typical conveyance, see Chap. 18.

assignment or other assurance. This document has previously been executed by the vendor and possibly by the purchaser, whose solicitor has to satisfy himself that the vendor's execution is in order. This may entail comparing the vendor's signature with that on the conveyance to him[9]. He has presumably checked his own client's execution (if any), for it is more than likely that it has been done in his presence. The advisability of acquainting a party to a deed, especially the purchaser, with its contents and effect need hardly be stressed, though this may not be without its problems[10].

A party to a deed having more than one capacity (e.g. a trustee-vendor who in a combined document appoints a new trustee, both of whom then convey to the purchaser[11]) does not have to execute it twice. The better view seems to be that, unless the document indicates he has executed in one capacity only, then he is estopped from denying that the one execution covers both capacities[12]. Execution in each capacity eliminates any doubt. The purchaser's execution of a conveyance of an unincumbered fee simple is unnecessary, and the prescribed forms of transfer for registered land make no provision for the purchaser's execution—one can be added if desired[13]. It is usual for the purchaser to execute the conveyance or transfer where e.g. it contains covenants by him with the vendor, or a clause in which joint purchasers declare their entitlement in equity. The purchaser's non-execution of the deed cannot prejudice the vendor; a party who takes the benefit of a deed is bound by it, as are his successors[14]. He can be sued upon covenants which he has entered into although he no longer claims any benefit under the deed, having disposed of his interest in the land[15].

2. Requirements for valid execution[16]

As long ago as 1584 in *Goddard's Case*[17] it was stated:

> ' There are three things of the essence and substance of a deed, that is to say, writing on paper or parchment, sealing and delivery . . . The order of making a deed is, first to write it, then to seal it, and after to deliver it, and therefore it is not necessary that the sealing or delivery be mentioned in the writing, forasmuch as they are to be done after . . . and when a deed is delivered, it takes effect by the delivery, and not from the day of

9   The author recalls an occasion when there was a marked disparity between the vendor's two signatures, attributable to his intervening illness. The purchaser's solicitor refused to complete without a statutory declaration setting out the circumstances. See also [1978] Conv 249 discussing *Re Beaney* [1978] 2 All ER 595.
10   Page 533, post.
11   See 19 Ency F & P, 991, Form 7:D:3. The Law of Property (Joint Tenants) Act 1964, p. 328, ante, does not dispense with the need for such an appointment where the equitable interests are held by tenants in common.
12   *Young v Schuler* (1883) 11 QBD 651, CA (evidence admitted that agent's single signature of guarantee was both for principal and on own behalf) is not inconsistent with the view in the text, since his 'p.p.' signature prima facie indicated he had signed for his principal only.
13   LRR 1925, r. 98, referring to Forms 19 and 20 although the printed stationers forms do, see further, post.
14   Co. Litt. 231a; *May v Belville* [1905] 2 Ch 605. Thus a mortgagee who does not normally execute the mortgage is bound by a proviso for reduction of the interest rate on punctual payment. Cf. LPA 1925, s. 65, p. 526, post.
15   *Burnett v Lynch* (1826) 5 B & C 589.
16   See (1980) 43 MLR 415 (David C. Hoath).
17   (1584) 2 Co Rep 4b, at 5a.

the deed. And therefore be the deed without a date, or of a false or impossible date, yet the deed is good.'

At common law, signature was not of the essence of due execution. However, with the spread of education, the signature became important for the authentication of documents, and is now obligatory under the Law of Property Act 1925, s. 73, for deeds executed after 1925. To be validly executed, a deed must be signed, sealed and delivered, a requirement applying alike to registered and unregistered conveyancing. What does this entail?

(a) Signed
There appears to be no reported case as to the meaning of 'signed' for the purposes of s. 73. Presumably the word will receive the same liberal construction as has been adopted in other statutes where it appears, so that a name stamped by means of an engraved facsimile of the ordinary signature suffices[18]. Yet it has been objected that in modern English when a document is required to be 'signed' by someone, that means he must write his name with his own hand upon it[19]. Section 73 permits a person to 'place his mark' (usually the sign of a cross) instead of signing. If a transfer of registered land incorporates a plan, the plan must also be signed by the transferor and by or on behalf of the transferee[20].

(b) Sealed
The modern practice is to attach a wax or wafer seal to the deed, as a reminder of the days when the seal amounted to a wax impression of a man's crest, coat-of-arms or initials. This little red wafer (½ inch in diameter) can hardly be said to authenticate the document, yet it suffices. One seal will do for several parties provided it professes to be the seal of each[1]; usually there are as many seals as executing parties. It was once customary for the executing party to place his finger or thumb on the wafer (as a token adoption of it as his seal) and to utter the words: 'I deliver this as my act and deed.' It may be questionable how many solicitors today ensure that their clients perform this ritual. Non-observance of this touching ceremony does not invalidate the deed; if a person signs a document bearing a wafer seal with the intention of executing the document as a deed, that is sufficient recognition of the seal to constitute due execution[2]. The seal may consist of a mark affixed to the document, provided there is some kind of impression, e.g. one caused by the end of a ruler, assuming it is intended to replace the seal. In *Re Smith, Oswell v Shepherd*[3] a document stated to be

---

18 *Bennett v Brumfitt* (1867) LR 3 CP 28 (document signed for purposes of the
    Parliamentary Voters Act 1843); applied in *Goodman v J Eban Ltd* [1954] 1 QB 550,
    [1954] 1 All ER 763, CA.
19 *Goodman v J Eban Ltd* [1954] 1 QB 550 at 561, [1954] 1 All ER 763 at 768, CA, per
    Denning LJ.
20 LRR 1925, r. 79.
 1 *Cooch v Goodman* (1842) 2 QB 580 at 598, per Denman CJ.
 2 *Stromdale and Ball Ltd v Burden* [1952] Ch 223 at 230, [1952] 1 All ER 59 at 62, per
    Danckwerts J. Earlier judicial pronouncements do not go as far. During the passage of the
    Powers of Attorney Bill through the Lords, Lord Wilberforce referred to sealing as a
    'completely fictitious matter' and expressed the hope (not to be realised) that in relation to
    the execution of powers of attorney it might be possible to dispense with such mumbo-
    jumbo; see H.L. Debates, 25 February 1971, Vol. 315, col. 1213.
 3 (1892) 67 LT 64, CA; *National Provincial Bank of England v Jackson* (1886) 33 Ch D 1,
    CA. Cf. *Linton v Royal Bank of Canada* (1967) 60 DLR (2d) 398 (guarantee expressed to

'sealed with my seal' but bearing no trace of any seal was held, in the absence of supporting evidence, not to have been duly executed. A circular line enclosing the letters 'L.S.' (locus sigilli, the place of the seal) has been hold to be a seal, when the circle was signed over[4].

(c) Delivered

This requirement is equally as vital as the other two elements of execution, yet its legal significance is generally not appreciated. Until delivery a document is inoperative. Delivery does not mean 'handed over' to the other side; it means delivered in the old legal sense, namely, an act done so as to evince an intention to be bound[5]. Relative to the mode of delivery, Blackburn J said in *Xenos v Wickham*[6]:

> ' No particular technical form of words or acts is necessary to render an instrument the deed of the party sealing it. The mere affixing of the seal does not render it a deed; but as soon as there are acts or words sufficient to show that it is intended by the party to be executed as his deed presently binding on him it is sufficient. The most apt and expressive mode of indicating such an intention is to hand it over, saying: 'I deliver this as my deed;' but any other words or acts that sufficiently show that it was intended to be finally executed will do as well. And it is clear on the authorities, as well as the reason of the thing, that the deed is binding on the obligor before it comes into the custody of the obligee, nay even before he knows of it . . .'

Delivery is unilateral. It may be absolute or conditional: if absolute the deed becomes immediately effective to pass the property, if conditional the delivery (and consequently the document) does not become effective until the condition is fulfilled.

(d) Escrows

A deed may be delivered on condition that it is not to be operative until some event happens or some condition is performed. Such a document is termed an escrow. It does not become a binding deed unless and until the condition is satisfied[7]. Delivery as an escrow is a matter of intention, primarily of the grantor, secondarily of the grantee, to be gathered from their oral or written statements. In the absence of evidence on the question of intention, the court will assume that execution was absolute[8], unless the circumstances raise an inference of an escrow, as in a transaction effected by way of lease and counter-

be 'signed, sealed and delivered' and bearing the word 'seal' beside the space provided for signature held to be a deed so that the subsequent addition of a paper wafer did not materially alter the deed and discharge the guarantor).

4 *First National Securities Ltd v Jones* [1978] Ch 109, [1978] 2 All ER 221, CA. The Court of Appeal explained *Re Balkis Consolidated Co Ltd* (1888) 58 LT 300 on the basis that the judge therein did not decide the issue as to the adequacy of the seal.

5 *Vincent v Premo Enterprises (Voucher Sales) Ltd* [1969] 2 QB 609 at 619, [1969] 2 All ER 941 at 944, CA, per Lord Denning MR.

6 (1866) LR 2 HLC 296 at 312. *Sheppard's Touchstone*, Vol. 1, p. 57. See Yale, 'The Delivery of a Deed' (1970) 28 CLJ 52.

7 *Vincent v Primo Enterprises (Voucher Sales) Ltd* [1969] 2 QB 609, [1969] 2 All ER 941, CA (condition fulfilled at date of hearing).

8 *D'Silva v Lister House Development Ltd* [1971] Ch 17, [1970] 1 All ER 858; *Re Vanstone, Vanstone v Vanstone* [1955] NZLR 1079 (deed executed by eight out of nine parties binding on signatories, notwithstanding non-execution by remaining party).

part where it is readily inferred that the lease is delivered by the lessor as an escrow conditional upon the lessee's execution of the counterpart[9].

As soon as the condition is fulfilled, the document takes effect *as from the date*[10] *of the original delivery*, so that in the case of a conveyance of unregistered land, the legal estate is passed retrospectively as at that date[11]. No redelivery is required. An escrow cannot be revoked by the grantor and remains effective notwithstanding his intervening death[12]. If the condition is never performed the document never becomes binding; in the event of unreasonable delay in the performance of the condition, the court has power to release the grantor from his obligation[13]. A document under seal which is handed to a third person (e.g. the grantor's agent) subject to an overriding power in the grantor to recall the deed cannot be an escrow; it is an undelivered deed[14].

This doctrine of relation back only applies for the purposes of title; it does not confer any right to intermediate rents nor operate to validate a notice to quit served when the fee simple was not vested in the landlord[15]. Its effect is clearly demonstrated by the case of *Hooper v Ramsbottom*[16].

> A executed a conveyance to B as an escrow to take effect on payment of the residue of the purchase money and left the deeds with his (A's) solicitor. Later A obtained the deeds from the solicitor and deposited them with C to secure an overdraft. It was held that on tender of the balance B was entitled to the estate free from C's rights. He had priority because the performance of the condition threw the commencement of his title back to the time of delivery of the escrow.

Another instructive case is *Beesly v Hallwood Estates Ltd*[17].

> X, Ltd., thinking that an option to renew exercised by their tenant, Y, was binding on them, executed a further lease of the property in Y's favour. At about the same time Y executed a counterpart lease. Later X, Ltd. discovered the option was unenforceable for want of registration and refused to continue.

The Court of Appeal held that the company had delivered the lease as an escrow, conditional upon Y's execution of the counterpart, which Y had done. Fulfilment of this condition made the company's lease fully binding. The decision would have been the same had X, Ltd. attempted to resile after sealing the lease but *before* Y had executed her counterpart, for having delivered it, it was not recallable by them, but not, of course, if Y never executed the counterpart at all.

9   *Beesly v Hallwood Estates Ltd* [1961] Ch 105, [1961] 1 All ER 90, CA.
10   See *Alan Estates Ltd v W.G. Stores Ltd* [1981] 3 All ER 481, CA, [1981] Conv 321. Cf. *Terrapin International v IRC* [1976] 2 All ER 461.
11   *Foundling Hospital (Governors and Guardians) v Crane* [1911] 2 KB 367 at 376, CA, per Farwell LJ. This doctrine has no application to a transfer of registered land in view of the LRA 1925, s. 19 (1), p. 451, post, except in the case of a transfer pursuant to LRR 1925, r. 72 on first registration.
12   *Perryman's Case* (1599) 5 Co Rep 84a; *Graham v Graham* (1791) 1 Ves 272.
13   *Beesly v Hallwood Estates Ltd* [1961] Ch 105 at 118, [1961] 1 All ER 90 at 94, CA, per Harman LJ.
14   *Foundling Hospital (Governors and Guardians) v Crane* [1911] 2 KB 367 at 375, CA, per Vaughan Williams LJ.
15   *Thompson v McCullough* [1947] KB 446, [1947] 1 All ER 265, CA.
16   (1815) 6 Taunt. 12. It is far from clear how this retrospective vesting of the legal title affects the scheme of registration and the making of searches under the LCA 1972.
17   [1961] Ch 105, [1961] 1 All ER 90, CA.

In the typical vendor-purchaser transaction involving unregistered land, the vendor is taken to deliver the conveyance as an escrow conditional upon payment by the purchaser of the balance of the purchase money[18]. The decision in *Thompson v McCullough*[19] shows that in the absence of evidence to the contrary the courts will infer delivery as an escrow, even though the vendor has not expressly delivered it as such. If the vendor allows part of the purchase price to remain unpaid on completion, the purchaser, it seems, does not obtain the legal estate, unless the vendor has agreed to allow that part to remain outstanding on mortgage, even though the purchaser has the title deeds including the (as yet) ineffective conveyance signed by the vendor[20]. There is another possibility. The vendor may have delivered the conveyance unconditionally when he signed it, but this alternative can readily be discounted. It can hardly be his intention to pass the legal estate, and so enable the purchaser to deal with the property as full legal owner, before payment of the price in full.

A solicitor cannot on completion deliver the conveyance on the vendor's behalf without his client's authority under seal[1], which there never is in practice. It has, however, been suggested that for a vendor's complete security, he should execute in favour of his solicitor a power of attorney enabling him to deliver the conveyance on completion. This would obviate any possibility of the purchaser's acquiring the legal title by tendering the purchase money, at a time when the vendor was unwilling to complete[2].

Not only is the law relating to delivery of deeds misunderstood, it is unrealistic, completely ignored in practice and likely to produce unexpected consequences. Recently Cross LJ has indicated a possible modification of the law by the introduction of some adoptive demonstration, in addition to the affixing of the seal, so as to indicate whether the deed has been delivered absolutely or conditionally[3]. Clearly some change in the law is urgently required.

(e) Attestation of execution

At common law attestation was unnecessary for a deed's validity, but the custom has long been to execute deeds in the presence of a witness and to indicate in an attestation clause signed by the witness that this formality has been observed. Section 75 of the Law of Property Act 1925, recognises the practice without making it compulsory by entitling the purchaser at his own expense to have the execution of the deed attested by his appointee, including

---

18   In *Kingston v Ambrian Investments Ltd* [1975] 1 All ER 120, CA, it was held that the condition of the escrow was effective. Rejecting the defendants' contention that the payment should be made promptly Lord Denning MR, at 125, said the condition should be satisfied within a reasonable time; Buckley LJ did not so consider it but contemplated service of a notice making time of the essence. This was approved of in *Glessing v Green* [1975] 2 All ER 696, CA. In both that and the *Kingston* case there was no antecedent contract and the possibility of service of a notice in such a case has been rightly criticised, see Emmet, 652; Farrand, 318.

19   [1947] KB 447, [1947] 1 All ER 265, CA.

20   It therefore behoves a mortgagee to ascertain that all the purchase money has been paid, or, if not, to obtain the vendor's express waiver of the non-fulfilment of the condition.

1   *Re Seymour, Fielding v Seymour* [1913] 1 Ch 475 at 481, per Joyce J.

2   1 Ency F & P, 325−26, note 15, where a precedent of such a power is given. For powers of attorney generally, see pp. 436−440, post. One impractical method of avoiding the difficulty is to have the vendor attend completion to execute the deed.

3   *Vincent v Premo Enterprises (Sales Vouchers) Ltd* [1969] 2 QB 609 at 623, [1969] 2 All ER 941 at 948, CA. He considered it more realistic to rely on physical movement or legal control of the deed after sealing. See also (1969) 33 Conv (NS) 227; (1970) 34 Conv (NS) 145−47, where the present state of the law is shown to be hopeless.

his solicitor. The right is rarely resorted to but is a useful provision for the few suspected cases of fraud or forgery. Registered land transfers and charges are required by statute to be executed in the presence of an attesting witness[4], as are some other special documents[5]. A party to a deed cannot also be a witness[6], but there is no rule of law preventing a wife from attesting her husband's execution, or vice versa; nevertheless many solicitors when forwarding execution instructions to a client still request the attesting witness to be some person other than the spouse. Evidently the Chief Land Registrar takes no objection to an attesting spouse[7].

(f) Execution by corporations

Before 1926 execution of a deed by a corporation had to comply with the requirements of its articles of association[8]. A purchaser was not obliged on completion to require evidence of facts as to due execution (e.g. by requiring production of the articles) since formalities regarding the use of the seal were presumed, albeit rebuttably, to have been observed[9]. Yet inspection was prudent, for the corporation was not bound by a forgery. As an alternative to any other legitimate mode of execution, the Law of Property Act 1925, s. 74 (1) now provides:

'In favour of a purchaser a deed shall be deemed to have been duly executed by a corporation aggregate if its seal be affixed thereto in the presence of and attested by its clerk, secretary or other permanent officer or his deputy, and a member of the board of directors, council or other governing body of the corporation, and where a seal purporting to be the seal of a corporation has been affixed to a deed, attested by persons purporting to be persons holding such offices as aforesaid, the deed shall be deemed to have been executed in accordance with the requirements of this section, and to have taken effect accordingly.'

This section has been held to have a substantive effect. In a recent case Buckley J held that a lease sealed and attested in accordance with s. 74 (1) effectively bound the lessor-company; it was immaterial that the seal was affixed without the authority of a resolution of the board of directors[10]. This produces the absurd result that a company will be bound by a deed executed even against the decision of its board, and requires that a company cannot safely seal a deed until after the passing of an appropriate resolution. Despite doubts expressed in certain quarters there is ample authority for the view that a corporation can deliver a deed as an escrow[11].

4 LRR 1925, rr. 98, 115 and 139, and the forms therein referred to.
5 E.g. certain powers of attorney under the Powers of Attorney Act 1971, ss. 1 (2), 9 (3). See also the LPA 1925, s. 74 (1), considered in para. (f), post.
6 *Seal v Claridge* (1881) 7 QBD 516 esp. at 519, CA, per Lord Selbourne LC.
7 R & R, 271. Presumably the legal oneness of the spouses influenced the tradition, yet even wills, required by statute to be attested (Wills Act 1837, s. 9), are not invalidated because the testator's spouse witnesses the will, though any gift to the spouse lapses (s. 15).
8 Nowadays articles of association incorporating art. 113, Sch. 1, Table A, of the Companies Act 1948, provide for the affixing of the seal by authority of the directors in the presence of a director and the secretary (or second director).
9 *Parker v Judkin* [1931] 1 Ch 475, CA.
10 *D'Silva v Lister House Development Ltd* [1971] Ch 17, [1970] 1 All ER 858. A subsequent confirmatory resolution was alleged to have been passed in error.
11 See e.g. *Beesly's* case, discussed on p. 431, ante; cf. *Gartside v Silkstone and Dodworth Coal and Iron Co* (1882) 21 Ch D 762 at 768, per Fry J.

Where the title is registered, the Land Registry requires satisfying that a deed not executed in accordance with s. 74 (1) was executed in the manner prescribed by the articles[12]. This seems to be an unnecessary precaution in view of the presumption previously mentioned.

3.   Date of deed

It is the invariable practice to date the conveyance or other transfer deed though, as *Goddard's* case[13] shows, the date is not of the substance. The prescribed forms of transfer of registered land provide for the dating of the document[14]. If two documents bear the same date, e.g. the conveyance to and mortgage by the purchaser, the court presumes they have been executed in such order as to give effect to the parties' manifest intention[15].

The date usually inserted in the purchase deed is that of the day of actual completion in the erroneous belief that this is when a conveyance of unregistered land operates to vest the legal estate in the purchaser. There is, however, an abundance of ancient authority to the effect that a deed takes effect from the time of delivery, not from its date[16]. The date is only prima facie evidence of the true time of execution; as soon as the contrary appears, the apparent date is to be utterly disregarded[17]. Wright J once said that it is such weak evidence that a court ought not to act upon it[18]. Theory dictates that the conveyance should be dated when it was delivered by the vendor. This is when the legal estate passes to the purchaser in unregistered conveyancing, albeit in most cases retrospectively as a result of the delivery originally being conditional[19]. But the theory is ignored in practice.

Backdating

When completion is delayed, a solicitor sometimes finds that his land charges search certificate has expired by the time the parties are ready to complete. Rather than delay completion until a second search certificate is to hand[20], some earlier date is inserted in the deed in an endeavour to obtain for the purchaser the benefit of the Land Charges Act 1972, s. 11 (5)[1]. It is submitted that this practice is totally ineffective to achieve the desired result. The section gives protection provided *the purchase is completed* before the expiration of 15 working days from the date of the certificate. Merely dating the conveyance with some date falling within the protection period cannot alter the fact, where this is the case, that completion is effected after expiration of that period. The purchaser will, therefore, be bound by any third party interest registered

12   R & R, 271.
13   (1584) 2 Co Rep 4b, p. 428, ante.
14   See the LRR 1925, Schedule, Forms 19, 23, 24, 33, 34.
15   *Gartside v Silkstone and Dodworth Iron and Coal and Iron Co* (1882) 21 Ch D 762 at 767–68, per Fry J.
16   *Clayton's Case* (1585) 5 Co Rep 1a; *Halter v Ashe* (1696) 3 Lev 438 (lease for life to hold from date of lease: lease commenced from time of delivery).
17   *Browne v Burton* (1847) 17 LJQB 49 at 50, per Patterson J. Cf. *Roberts v Church Comrs for England* [1972] 1 QB 278 at 283, [1971] 3 All ER 703 at 705, CA, per Russell LJ. The date of a deed is taken as the relevant date for stamping requirements, p. 442, post.
18   *Re Slater, ex p Slater* (1897) 76 LT 529 at 530.
19   Page 430, ante.
20   A solicitor can always make a personal search by telephone and obtain the result the same day. This method is not without disadvantages (see p. 402, ante), but it is preferable to backdating.
1   Page 401, ante.

before completion of the purchase. Further where the deed has been back-dated, it seems possible that it could be held to be a forgery within the Forgery and Counterfeiting Act 1981, on the ground that it bore a false date[2], even though the date is not ordinarily material[3] to the operation of the deed, nor is it relevant to s. 11 (5) which, as we have just seen, speaks of the date of completion.

The practice of backdating should disappear now a telephone or teleprinter search can be made. A solicitor who discovers at the last moment that his existing certificate has expired will be able to requisition a search by telephone or teleprinter. But an element of risk will remain even when completing on the basis of an informal search, for the result of this search will not be conclusive[4] and there will exist the possibility of error or misunderstanding arising in the making of the requisition for, or the communicating of the result of, the search. These difficulties can be avoided by adopting the simple expendiency of obtaining a second certificate prior to the expiry of the previous one.

Ante-dating with a view to obtaining protection against intervening incumbrances does not arise with registered titles. Protection is determined, not by the completion date, but by the date of lodgement of the transfer for registration.

4. Alterations in deeds

Alterations in or additions to a deed are rebuttably presumed to have been made before execution[5]. If proved to have been made afterwards, their effect on the parties' rights depends on their materiality. A non-material alteration does not affect a deed's validity, such as, adding the names of tenants occupying the property conveyed[6], or altering the Christian names of one of the parties[7]. A material alteration is one which varies the rights, liabilities or legal position of the parties, or varies the document's legal effect[8]; it avoids the deed but only to a limited degree and not retrospectively. A party making (or authorising) an alteration cannot enforce any term of the deed against a non-consenting party[9]. A material alteration by the purchaser does not operate to divest the title, otherwise this would be a facile way of getting rid of onerous estates[10], and a party bound by a deed cannot evade his liabilities thereunder by

2 See s. 9 (1) (g) making an instrument false if it purports to have been made on a date when it was not so made.
3 Cf. *R v Ritson* (1869) LR 1 CCR 200 (lease of land executed after but dated earlier than conveyance of fee so as to defraud freeholder), and *R v Wells* [1939] 2 All ER 169, CCA (date of settlement falsified to avoid effect of pending legislation), in both of which the date was held to be material and the deed a forgery. A forged deed is null and void, and passes no legal estate: *Re Cooper, Cooper v Vesey* (1882) 20 Ch D 611, CA (execution of mortgages by son impersonating deceased father).
4 See p. 402, ante. These informal means of searching are only available to persons maintaining a credit account at the Registry: LCA 1972, s. 10 (1).
5 *Re Spollon and Long's Contract* [1936] Ch 713, [1936] 2 All ER 711, the reason being, according to Co. Litt. 225b, that a deed cannot be altered after execution without fraud or wrong and the presumption is against these.
6 *Adsett v Hives* (1863) 33 Beav 52, unless the names are essential to identify the property conveyed.
7 *Re Howgate and Osborn's Contract* [1902] 1 Ch 451, where Kekewich J concluded that the original names were merely a misdescription so that the conveyance had always been to A, B and C, though C was wrongly calld D. Aliter if C and D were two different people and C had fraudulently been substituted for D.
8 See *Norton on Deeds*, (2nd edn) p. 44.
9 *Ellesmere Brewery Co v Cooper* [1896] 1 QB 75.
10 *Doe d. Lewis v Bingham* (1821) 4 B & Ald 672 at 678, per Best J.

materially altering it. If the deed is incorrect, the proper course is to seek rectification. The effect of alterations by strangers is obscure.

If a mistake or omission is discovered in an instrument delivered for registration, it can only be corrected in accordance with the Rules. Minor clerical errors can be corrected by the Chief Land Registrar under r. 13. Where a material alteration has to be made after the document has been lodged for registration, it can be withdrawn and returned for amendment and re-execution[11], otherwise, if registration has been effected, a deed of rectification is required.

G   Powers of attorney

A person (the donor of the power) can generally speaking authorise an attorney (the donee of the power) to perform any act which the donor of the power can do. Powers of this nature are now governed by the Powers of Attorney Act 1971, which gives effect to the recommendations in the Law Commission's Report on the topic[12]. The Act replaces and extends the previous legislation on the subject contained in the Law of Property Act 1925, and the Trustee Act 1925. The Act came into operation on 1 October 1971.

1.   Form of power

The power may be a wide one, including dealing with property by sale or lease, with power to execute deeds giving effect to such dealings, or it may be limited to the execution or delivery of a particular document. In an endeavour to encourage greater standardisation of powers of attorney, the Act provides a simple statutory form which, if adopted, confers on the donee a general power 'to do on behalf of the donor anything which he can lawfully do by an attorney'[13]. If a more limited power is intended it will be necessary to spell out the specific powers which it is sought to confer, remembering always that a power is strictly construed according to its terms[14]. The statutory form cannot be used to delegate the donor's functions which he possesses in some fiduciary capacity, e.g. as trustee[15]. It is considered preferable in these cases for the power to refer specifically to the particular trusts concerned. In relation to transactions effected with an attorney prior to the Act's operation, it will continue to be necessary for a later purchaser to satisfy himself that the transaction was authorised by the power.

Section 1 of the Act requires all powers, whether in the statutory form or not, to be by deed, signed and sealed by the donor[16]. The section introduces a welcome innovation by enabling the execution of the power by a third person by direction and in the presence of the donor, provided two other persons are

11   LRR 1925, r. 86.
12   Law Com No. 30. See Liddle 'The Powers of Attorney Act 1971' (1971) 68 LS Gaz 434.
13   Powers of Attorney Act 1971, s. 10 (1), and Sch. 1. A form 'to the like effect but expressed to be made under [the] Act' confers the same general power.
14   See e.g. *Re Dowson and Jenkins's Contract* [1904] 2 Ch 219, CA.
15   Notwithstanding this in practice general powers of attorney are frequently proffered in the case of co-owners notwithstanding the fact that the legal estate is clearly held in a fiduciary capacity, see (1977) 41 Conv (NS) 369–372; [1978] Conv 8–9, 85; [1980] Conv 191 (P.W. Smith). A similar problem can arise if the trustees appoint the same donee, see [1978] Conv 85; [1980] Conv 191 at 194.
16   The Act omits any reference to delivery. Does this mean that an instrument creating a power is not technically a deed?

present as witnesses and they attest the instrument. Thus a person who is physically incapable of executing a legal document can now appoint an attorney.

Once created the contents of the power may be proved by means of a photographic copy duly certified by a solicitor or stockbroker as a true and complete copy of the original[17]. This will facilitate the verification of title to land. Where a conveyance is executed by an attorney, the power becomes a document of title; the attorney can retain the original, handing the certified copy to the purchaser. If the purchaser later splits up his land and conveys plots to X and Y, he can make certified photo-copies of the certified photo-copy and these are to be accepted by X and Y as equivalent to the original power[18]. The advantages of the photo-copying process have finally been recognised by the legislature; if the first copy is accurate, a photo-copy of that copy must equally be accurate.

2. Appointment of attorney by trustee

The maxim *delegatus non potest delegare* restricts the appointment of agents by a trustee, though various statutory encroachments were made upon this principle by the Trustee Act 1925. Section 9 of the Act of 1971 replaces the former power to delegate during absence abroad[19] by a much wider provision which applies to any trust whenever created. This enables a trustee (and other fiduciary owners such as a tenant for life) by power of attorney to delegate for a period not exceeding twelve months the exercise of all or any of the trusts, powers and discretions vested in him. The trustee cannot delegate to his sole co-trustee not being a trust corporation. The instrument creating the power must be executed in the presence of an attesting witness, and various notices of its making must be given, although non-compliance does not invalidate the title of a person dealing with the attorney. The donor of the power remains liable for the donee's acts or defaults in the same manner as if they were his own.

3. Execution of deeds by attorney

Section 7 (1) of the Act permits an attorney when executing a deed to sign with his own name and under his own seal, except in cases where an instrument has to be executed in the name of the estate owner. If he adopts this procedure, the deed should state that he executes as attorney, i.e. he signs his own name, adding 'as attorney on behalf of B' (the donor). He may sign with the donor's name, in which case the form is 'B by his attorney A'.

An attorney can execute a deed on behalf of a corporation. As an alternative to the method prescribed by s. 7, he can adopt the procedure permitted by the Law of Property Act 1925, which allows him to sign in the corporation's name in the presence of at least one witness and to affix his own seal[20].

---

17 Section 3 (1). The reasons for limiting the class of persons qualified to certify are contained in Law Com. No. 30, para. 7. A special procedure must be observed where the original document consists of two or more pages: see s. 3 (1) (b) (ii).

18 Section 3 (2). Prior to the Act a power of attorney relating to land had to be filed at the Central Office of the Supreme Court unless it only related to one transaction and was to be handed over on completion. By virtue of s. 4 (1) of the Evidence and Powers of Attorney Act 1940, an office copy of a filed power is sufficient evidence of its contents. Section 2 of the Act of 1971 abolishes the need to file a power, but the right to search for or obtain office copies of powers filed before the commencement of the Act is expressly preserved.

19 See the Trustee Act 1925, s. 25.

20 Section 7 (2) expressly preserves the alternative modes of execution under the LPA 1925, s. 74 (3), and (4) (which applies where a corporation is attorney).

4.   Protection of attorney and purchasers

At common law a power of attorney was revoked by the donor's death, insanity, marriage or bankruptcy[1], and by its very nature was revocable by him at any time unless coupled with an interest[2]. For a purchaser the inherent danger in taking a conveyance from an attorney was the revocability of the power. The Law of Property Act 1925, contained several provisions for the protection of both the attorney and the purchaser dealing with him. The Law Commission considered these difficult to construe and unsatisfactory in result. Their suggested simplification of the law is now embodied in s. 4 and 5 of the Act. These new provisions apply to all powers whenever created but do not determine the validity of transactions effected before the commencement of the Act, which will continue to be governed by the law as laid down by the Act of 1925[3].

The following paragraphs relate soley to the position under the new Act. It is necessary to distinguish between (a) powers given by way of security, and (b) other powers.

(a) Security powers

Under s. 4 (1) where a power is expressed to be irrevocable and is given to secure a proprietary interest of the donee[4], then so long as the donee has the interest the power cannot be revoked either by the donor without his consent or by the donor's death, incapacity or bankruptcy. Where the power is given to the donee and his successors in title, the latter are deemed to be donees so that a transfer of the secured interest does not terminate the power (sub-s. (2)). Section 4 will apply, for example, to an irrevocable power of attorney contained in an equitable mortgage whereby the mortgagee (the donee of the power) is empowered to convey the legal estate if the mortgagor (the donor) defaults under the terms of the mortgage.

A third party who deals with the donee of the power has no means of knowing that the power has not been revoked with his concurrence. Section 5 (3) deals with this situation and protects any person dealing with the attorney (not merely a purchaser) who is, in effect, entitled to assume that the power is still fully operational unless he knows that it has been revoked with the attorney's concurrence. In the absence of such knowledge his title will always be good despite the revocation of the power. The wording of this subsection needs watching carefully. It only applies where a power is *expressed to be* irrevocable *and to be* given by way of security[5]. What the power says rather than what it does seems to be vital here. If it is expressed to be by way of security even though it was not in fact so given[6], a person dealing with the attorney is protected unless he knows that it was not so given. Conversely the subsection cannot apply where the power is in fact given by way of security, *but it does not say so*. In such a case

1   See *Tingley v Muller* [1917] 2 Ch 144 at 183, CA, per Bray J.
2   *Walsh v Whitcomb* (1797) 2 Esp 565.
3   Sections 124, 126–28, as to which see Emmet (15th edn), 246–50; Law Com. No. 30, paras. 29–31.
4   Or the performance of an obligation owed to him – which will not usually occur in a conveyancing context.
5   Cf. the wording of s. 4 (1): 'Where a power . . . is expressed to be irrevocable and is given to secure . . .'
6   Section 5 (3). This has provoked the not unjustificable comment that the provision may encourage abuse of the Act by the dressing-up of ordinary powers as security powers in order to obtain the wider protection of s. 5 (3). See (1971) 68 LS Gaz 437, 524; cf. ibid., 482.

the third party would not seem to get a good title if the secured interest has ended or if the power has been revoked with the donee's concurrence[7].

(b) Other powers
In relation to other powers s. 5 (2) of the Act provides that when a power has been revoked and a person, without knowledge of the revocation, deals with the attorney, the transaction between them shall, in favour of that person, be as valid as if the power had been in existence. The validity of the transaction is preserved in the absence of the third party's knowledge of revocation, but under sub-s. (5) knowledge of the occurrence of an event (such as death) which has the effect of revoking the power is equivalent to knowledge of revocation, notwithstanding that the third party was unaware that the event had that effect. If the third party has knowledge, he does not, of course, obtain any title to the property. Again it should be noted that sub-s. (2) applies in favour of any person dealing with the donee, not merely a purchaser.

The validity of the third party's title depends on his absence of knowledge of revocation but how is a purchaser from him to be satisfied that he had no such knowledge? Section 5 (4) gives the answer by providing that it is to be *conclusively presumed* in favour of a *purchaser* that the third party did not know that the power had been revoked if (i) the transaction between the donee and the third party was completed within a year from when the power came into operation[8] or (ii) if outside that period, the third party makes a statutory declaration, before or within three months of the completion of the purchase, that he did not know of the revocation. Unless the case falls within (i) it clearly behoves the purchaser to obtain at his own expense the desired declaration at the time of the purchase. Indeed it would seem advantageous for the third party himself to make an appropriate declaration immediately after the transaction between himself and the attorney. Such a declaration would seem to be within s. 5 (4) since it will have been made before the completion of any subsequent purchase, and the Act does not specify any period prior to completion within which it has to be made[9]. Unless the third party is able in this way to anticipate a future sale, the Act appears to leave unresolved the problem of what happens in a case falling outside situation (i) above where the third party dies and his personal representative conveys to a purchaser. He cannot declare as to the state of the deceased's knowledge and unless it can be established that the power had not in fact been revoked (e.g. by a declaration to that effect by the donor), he may have difficulty in satisfying a purchaser of the soundness of the title.

(c) Registered land
Where the land is registered and the transaction between the attorney and the person dealing with him is not completed within twelve months from when the power came into operation, the latter must furnish[10] the Registrar with a

7   He would seem entitled to the benefit of s. 5 (2), post, under which the validity of the transaction with the donee is preserved if he is without knowledge of the revocation. Many powers of attorney given in equitable mortgages (if based on existing precedents) fall foul of s. 5 (3) because they are not *expressed* as security powers.
8   This will be the date of the power unless it otherwise provides.
9   The fact that it was made at a time when no sale was contemplated appears to be irrelevant. This interpretation disposes of the difficulties that are said to arise from the failure of s. 5 (2) to provide how the third party can establish his ignorance of any revocation of the power; see (1971) 68 LS Gaz 437–38.
10   LRR 1925, r. 82 (3), (4), as substituted by the Land Registration (Powers of Attorney) Rules 1971, S.I. 1971 No. 1197.

statutory declaration that at the time of completion he did not know of the
revocation of the power or of any event which had that effect. In the case of a
security power he must declare that he did not know that the power was not
given by way of security and did not know that it had been revoked with the
donee's consent. Production of the appropriate declaration is vital if the third
party is to be registered as proprietor even in cases where the transaction with
the attorney results in a first compulsory registration of title. The power, or a
copy, must accompany every application for registration[11].

On a subsequent sale of the land by the third party, it would not seem essential for the purchaser to obtain a statutory declaration under s. 5 (4) of the Act,
as might be the case (depending on the circumstances) if the land were
unregistered, for, where necessary, an appropriate declaration will already
have been made by the third party as a pre-requisite to his own registration,
and presumably the Registrar will not require a second declaration to the same
effect before registering the purchaser.

(d) Protection of attorney
Section 5 (1) of the Act regulates the position of the attorney. If he acts in
ignorance that the power has been revoked, he does not incur any liability
either to the donor or to any other person, but under s. 5 (5) he is deemed to
know of the revocation if he knows of an act having that effect.

H   Post completion matters

One obvious task for both solicitors to perform after completion is to report to
their respective clients. In the case of the vendor's solicitor, this will include
accounting to the vendor for the purchase money after deduction of costs and
disbursements. However in most house sales, the purchase money received on
completion will be utilised in part by the solicitor for other purposes—in
discharge of the vendor's mortgage, or towards the price of another property
which the vendor is purchasing. There are still other important matters to be
attended to, especially by the purchaser's solicitor, before the practitioner can
regard the transaction as closed.

1.   Registration of title

If the transaction is the first conveyance on sale, lease, or assignment on sale
after the introduction of compulsory registration of title in the area where the
property is situated, an application for registration of the grantee as proprietor
may have to be submitted to the appropriate district land registry within the
prescribed period. Where the title is already registered, the transfer must be
completed by registration of the transferee as the proprietor. Until the appropriate entry is made the legal estate remains vested in the transferor[12]. It is the
responsibility of the purchaser's solicitor to effect registration. Compulsory first
registration and the registration of transfers are considered more fully in the
next chapter.

11   LRR 1925, r. 82 (1).
12   LRA 1925, ss. 19 (1), 22 (1). See pp. 451–454, and 462, post.

2.   Notification of change of ownership

On a sale or other disposition of leasehold property it may be necessary to give notice of the assignment to the lessor (or his solicitor) under a covenant in the lease or by virtue of a statutory requirement[13]. This obligation must not be confused with the licence to assign which should be procured before the assignment is completed. Strictly speaking it is the vendor's responsibility to give the notice and pay any registration fee, subject to any contractual stipulation to the contrary. Even in the absence of any such clause it is in practice more convenient for the purchaser to give the notice, especially when the covenant also requires production of the assignment to the lessor for registration purposes. In the case of registered leasehold property, production of the transfer or a copy, or the land (or charge) certificate after registration, operates as sufficient compliance with a covenant requiring production[14].

3.   Undertakings

It is not uncommon for a vendor's solicitor on completion to enter into a written undertaking to do, or refrain from doing, certain acts, e.g. to discharge an existing mortgage, to procure the cancellation of registered land charges. A solicitor should not give a personal undertaking unless he is in a position to perform it personally, though undertakings to use one's best endeavours to bring about a given result are commonly given and accepted. The breach of an undertaking by a solicitor is a serious matter. Depending on the facts of each case, it may be enforced against him personally[15]. The court has jurisdiction to compel a solicitor, who is an officer of the court, to implement his undertaking[16]. Failure to obey the court's order is punishable by committal for contempt. Where the undertaking does not fix a period within which the act is to be performed nor provide for it to be done forthwith, it is first necessary to obtain a court order fixing a time limit.

4.   Registration and cancellation of land charges

One important point that is sometimes overlooked is the registration of land charges created by the conveyance or lease, such as restrictive covenants in favour of the vendor[17], or an option to purchase conferred upon a lessee. A purchaser's solicitor who has registered the contract as an estate contract should as a matter of good conveyancing practice effect its cancellation after completion[18] if only to avoid possible queries about the registration on a subsequent sale of the property. Under Condition 16 (2) (b) of The Law Society's

---

13   Landlord and Tenant Act 1927, s. 19 (1) (b). The covenant often extends to notifying a superior lessor of the grant, or assignment, of an underlease. See *Portman v J. Lyons & Co Ltd* [1937] Ch 584, [1936] 3 All ER 819.

14   LRR 1925, r. 91 (1).

15   See generally Emmet, 308.

16   See *Re A Solicitor* [1966] 3 All ER 52; *Geoffrey Silver and Drake v Baines* [1971] 1 QB 396; and *Re Mallows* (1960) 176 Estates Gazette 1117 (failure to procure cancellation of land charges). The basis of this jurisdiction is not the enforcing of legal rights, but the enforcing of honourable conduct by the courts' own officers: per Pennycuick J in *Re A Solicitor* (supra), at 55.

17   Restrictive covenants created on a sale of registered land are automatically entered on the charges register by the Registrar without any special application, p. 477, post. And see also p. 392, ante.

18   Law Society's Digest, 3rd Cumulative Supplement, Opinion No. 940 (b).

Conditions of Sale, the purchaser must at his own expense procure the cancellation of a registered estate contract where the contract is rescinded by the vendor under a contractual provision.

5.   Stamping documents

A document liable to the payment of stamp duty should be presented for stamping within thirty days of its execution, which for present purposes is taken to be the date of the deed. In theory the Stamp Act 1891, requires instruments to be stamped before execution, but permits conveyances on sale, leases, mortgages and settlements to be stamped after execution[19]. A document that is presented late for stamping can only be stamped on payment of the unpaid duty with interest, a fixed penalty of £10 and a further penalty equal to the amount of the unpaid duty. The Commissioners of Inland Revenue are empowered to mitigate or remit any penalty.

An improperly stamped document is not admissible in evidence, but it will be received in evidence on a solicitor's undertaking to pay the duty and penalties except where the document cannot be legally stamped after execution[20]. A purchaser is entitled to have every deed forming a link in the chain of title properly stamped[1]. When investigating title, a purchaser's solicitor should check the stamp duty on all abstracted documents and to this extent it is necessary to be aware of heads of charge and rates of duty that have since been abolished or reduced. A condition of sale framed so as to preclude any objection as to the absence or insufficiency of stamp upon any instrument executed after 16 May 1888, is void[2]. A document adequately stamped for its principal object is treated as duly stamped for everything accessory to that object[3]. A conveyance does not require an extra stamp because it contains an acknowledgment for production of documents.

(a)   Rates of duty
Full details of rates of duty must be sought in a standard work on stamp duties. A few points may usefully be mentioned in relation to the more common conveyancing transactions encountered in practice.

(i)   *Conveyances on sale.*   A conveyance on sale is exempt from duty where the consideration is £25,000 or under, and attracts duty at the rate of £0.5 per cent where it exceeds £25,000 and does not exceed £30,000, £1 per cent where it exceeds £30,000 but does not exceed £35,000, £1.5 per cent where it exceeds £35,000 but does not exceed £40,000 and £2 per cent above that[4], being the normal rate. These are in fact special rates which only apply if the conveyance contains a 'certificate for value' clause to the effect that the transaction does not form part of a larger transaction or series of transactions in respect of which the aggregate amount of the consideration exceeds £20,000 [or £25,000 or £30,000][5]. In the case of a conveyance to a sub-purchaser, duty is levied on the

19   Stamp Act 1891, s. 15 (1), (2).
20   Stamp Act 1891, s. 14. It is unprofessional to take the point per se.
1   See *Whiting to Loomes* (1881) 17 Ch D 10 (discharged mortgage).
2   Stamp Act 1891, s. 117.
3   *Limmer Asphalte Paving Co v I.R. Comrs* (1872) LR 7 Exch 211.
4   Finance Act 1980, s. 95.
5   See Finance Act 1963, s. 55 (1); Finance Act 1974, Schedule 11, para, 4. The practice of 'altering' the purchase price to a lower figure by 'finding' fixtures and fittings is to be discouraged.

consideration moving from the sub-purchaser, not on the original purchase price[6]. Duties which vary according to the amount of the consideration are termed ad valorem duties.

(ii) *Leases.* The duties payable on the grant of a lease are rather complicated, being determined in the main by the length of the term and the amount of the annual rent[7]. Duty is also payable on any premium at the ordinary rate applicable to conveyances on sale, but provided the rent does not exceed £250 the premium attracts the reduced rates of duty if below the appropriate figure[8].

(iii) *Mortgages.* Mortgages are no longer subject to stamp duty; the head of charge under which duty was formerly leviable was abolished by the Finance Act 1971, s. 64, as from 1 August 1971.

(iv) *Voluntary dispositions*[9]. A conveyance of property without consideration or for some consideration (excluding marriage) conferring a substantial benefit on the grantee by reason e.g. of its inadequacy, constitutes a voluntary disposition and is chargeable with the same duty as a conveyance on sale. The value of the property has to be adjudicated by the Commissioners of Inland Revenue and the deed will bear a special adjudication stamp indicating that the deed is properly stamped. The reduced rates for conveyances on sale also apply provided there is incorporated a suitably amended certificate for value clause. Adjudication is obligatory for voluntary dispositions, but any person may require the Commissioners to state whether a particular instrument is liable to duty and, if so, to what amount[10].

(v) *Documents subject to a fixed duty of 50p.* Certain deeds encountered in practice attract a fixed duty of 50p. The most common are as follows: an appointment of new trustees, an assent under seal, a deed of exchange of land (for if no consideration passes it is not a conveyance on sale), a deed of grant of an easement unless for consideration, a power of attorney and a conveyance made in consideration of marriage.

(b) Sale agreements and building agreements
On the sale of new residential property it is a common practice to effect the transaction by means of a contract for the sale of the land followed by a conveyance, and a separate contract for the erection of a house on the land[11]. The stamp duty position in this situation is rather confused. The Board of Inland Revenue have issued a statement of their present policy[12], but their views have no legal force. Briefly the Board's attitude is as follows:

(i)   The concurrent existence of a contract for the erection of a house will not prima facie increase the stamp duty chargeable on the conveyance

6 Stamp Act 1891, s. 58 (4).
7 For the present rates, see the Finance Act 1980, s. 94.
8 Finance Act 1980, s. 95 (2). The certificate of value has reference to the consideration other than rent.
9 See the Finance (1909–10) Act 1910, s. 74.
10 Stamp Act 1891, s. 12 (1).
11 Often the vendor and the builder were separate companies.
12 See Emmet, 1204. The Law Society recommend adjudication in these instances; (1957) 54 LS Gaz 450–51.

provided the purchaser is entitled to a conveyance in consideration only of the price of the site[13].

(ii)   If at the date of the contract for the sale of the land a house has been wholly or partially erected by the vendor (or his agent or nominee), the value of the house at that time is treated as part of the consideration and liable to ad valorem duty.

(iii)   If the purchaser is not entitled to a conveyance of the land until a house has been erected by the vendor, the full price of the house forms part of the consideration for the conveyance.

(iv)   If in (iii) the purchaser obtains a conveyance *before* completion of the house, the value of the house at the time of completion attracts ad valorem duty.

(v)   Where the house is to be erected by the purchaser or someone employed by him, duty is leviable only on the consideration for the land.

(c) Production of documents to Commissioners

Irrespective of whether stamp duty is leviable, certain documents must be produced within thirty days of execution to the Commissioners of Inland Revenue; such documents are a conveyance on sale of the fee simple, a grant of a lease for at least seven years or the transfer on sale of any such lease. In addition the transferee or lessee must furnish the Commissioners with a statement of certain particulars regarding the instrument[14]. A document produced in accordance with the statutory provisions is stamped with a special stamp (a 'Particulars Delivered' or 'P.D.' stamp as it is commonly called) denoting it has been produced. Without this stamp (where required) the document is not deemed duly stamped and therefore may not be received in evidence. Failure to comply with the Act also renders the grantee liable on summary conviction to a fine not exceeding £50.

I   Merger of contract in conveyance

On completion of the transaction the contract is said to merge in the conveyance. The conveyance puts an end to the contractual obligations which are thereby satisfied. After completion the purchaser cannot bring an action on the contract. Unless he is able to establish grounds for rescission or rectification, or prove the existence of some collateral warranty, his only remedy is to sue on the covenants for title.

The doctrine of merger is not absolute. It does not apply to cases where the contractual obligation is of such a kind that it cannot have been the parties' intention that it should be extinguished by the conveyance[15]. It therefore becomes necessary to construe the contract to see whether it was intended to survive the execution of the conveyance[16] and to what extent. Neither of the standard form Conditions of Sale throws any light on the question of which of the General Conditions is intended to remain in force after completion. In cases of dispute resort must be had to general principles. No merger was held to have occurred in respect of these contractual terms—for vacant possession on

---

13   See *Kimbers & Co v IRC* [1936] 1 KB 132.
14   Finance Act 1931, s. 28, Sch. 2, as amended by the Land Commission Act 1967, s. 87, Sch. 14, 15. The appropriate form is labelled 'Stamps L (A) 451'.
15   *Clarke v Ramuz* [1891] 2 QB 456 at 461, CA, per Bowen LJ.
16   See *Palmer v Johnson* (1884) 13 QBD 351 at 357, per Bowen LJ, CA.

completion[17], for compensation for misdescription[18], for the erection and completion of a house in a proper manner[19]. In these cases an action for damages was maintainable after completion.

An instructive case is *Feldman v Mansell*[20] which, unfortunately, is not reported in the major reports. A contract for the sale of freehold land contained a provision that

> ' the purchaser shall be supplied with copies of [certain] leases and shall be deemed to purchase with full knowledge of the purport and effect thereof'.

After completion the purchaser discovered that one of the copies was inaccurate. Paull J held that there was an obligation to provide a true copy, which had not been performed. The purchaser had lost the right to claim a reduction in the price or to refuse to complete, and loss of this right was not affected by the conveyance. He was therefore entitled to damages for breach of contract.

The doctrine of merger applies to sales of registered land[1] though it is uncertain whether the contract merges on completion of the transaction or on subsequent registration. Perhaps the former is the better view, support for which may be derived from s. 110 (6) of the Land Registration Act 1925. This subsection requires the vendor, on a sale of the entirety of the land within his title, to deliver the land (or charge) certificate to the purchaser on completion of the purchase, in order to enable the purchaser to be registered as the new proprietor. Although the Act clearly envisages that the purchaser will subsequently apply for registration, this does not form part of the parties' contractual obligations. In theory, the purchaser may elect to enter into possession by virtue of his unregistered transfer, without proceeding to acquire the legal estate by registration[2].

17 *Hissett v Reading Roofing Co Ltd* [1970] 1 All ER 122; *Topfell Ltd v Galley Properties Ltd* [1979] 2 All ER 388 (vacant possession of ground floor not possible because of statutory restriction limiting occupation of property to one household).
18 *Palmer v Johnson* (1884) 13 QBD 351, CA.
19 *Lawrence v Cassel* [1930] 2 KB 83; *Hancock v B W Brazier (Anerley) Ltd* [1966] 2 All ER 901, CA.
20 (1962) 106 Sol Jo 591. A much fuller report appears in (1962) 184 Estates Gazette 331. See also *Eagon v Dent* [1965] 3 All ER 334 (assignment failing to incorporate contractual indemnity).
 1 *Knight Sugar Co Ltd v Alberta Railway and Irrigation Co* [1938] 1 All ER 266, PC (a decision on a colonial statute similar to the LRA 1925); noted at (1938) 2 Conv (NS) 262.
 2 Cf. *Montgomery and Rennie v Continental Bags (NZ) Ltd* [1972] NZLR 884, where a mistake as to the identity of the land transferred was discovered after completion, but before registration. It was held that no merger took place until registration of the purchaser as the new proprietor, and the purchaser was entitled to rescind the contract and recover the purchase money paid under it. However it appears that under the Torrens system of land registration (which operates in New Zealand), it is the transferor's duty to procure registration: see at 892.

Chapter 16

Registered titles: first registration and registration of dealings

A Freehold titles

1. Compulsory first registration

Section 123 of the Land Registration Act 1925 provides for the registration of title on every conveyance on sale of freehold land within an area in which registration of title has been declared compulsory. The first section of this chapter is concerned mainly with the procedural details involved in first registration. The legal effects of registration and the meaning of conveyance 'on sale' have already been considered[1].

(a) The application
The application for first registration should be made within two months of the date of the conveyance, or of any authorised extension, otherwise the conveyance becomes void as regards the grant of the legal estate in the land. The consequences of this avoidance are discussed later in this chapter.

(i) *Title applied for.* The purchaser normally seeks registration with an absolute title. Where the title is based upon adverse possession, or the title deeds have been lost or destroyed, a possessory title should be sought, though the Registrar is empowered to issue an absolute title, if satisfied as to the soundness of the applicant's title. No application can be made for a qualified title.

(ii) *Form of application.* The application must be made on a prescribed form appropriate to the particular case[2]. The operative part of the form (Form 1B) used by solicitors to obtain registration on behalf of a purchaser reads:

> ' We A.B., of etc., solicitors, hereby apply for the registration of Y, of etc., (hereinafter called the applicant) as proprietor, with absolute [or possessory] title of the freehold land described above assured by the accompanying conveyance dated . . . made between (1) X (2) the applicant.'

The application also contains a lengthy certificate, for signature by the solicitor, as to the soundness of the title, including the existence of incumbrances

---

1 See Chapter 2.
2 LRR 1925, r. 19. See R & R, 190–191. See Appendix B for a list of the more common Land Registry Forms in daily use. References in this chapter to 'the Act', or to 'the Rules', are references to the LRA 1925, and the LRR 1925, respectively unless otherwise stated.

and the capacity in which the land is vested in the applicant. The solicitor will already have approved the title on his client's behalf, so signing this certificate should create no additional complications[3]. Where the applicants are joint proprietors, it is essential to state whether the survivor has power to give a valid receipt for purchase money arising on a future sale; if not the obligatory restriction in Form 62 will be entered on the register[4]. In the case of other limited owners, an application should be made for entry of the appropriate restriction or information given to enable the proper restriction to be entered.

A special form of application (Form 1E) is available for use when a limited company seeks first registration. In theory a copy of the memorandum and articles of association and a certified copy of the certificate of incorporation should be lodged[5], but in practice the Registrar accepts in lieu the solicitor's confirmation of due incorporation and of the company's power to hold, sell, mortgage and otherwise deal with land. Any charge created by the company must be certified as not contravening the provisions of the memorandum and articles.

(iii) *Accompanying documents.* All deeds[6] and documents in the applicant's possession must be forwarded with the application, including preliminary inquiries, requisitions and replies, the contract for sale, search certificates, opinions of counsel on the title. Abstracts should be marked as having been verified in the usual way. In addition a certified copy of the conveyance to the applicant, and of any mortgage created by him, must be supplied. A list in triplicate of all documents lodged is required; one copy is returned as a receipt for the application, another returned on completion of registration showing what documents have been kept in the Registry, and the third is retained there for record purposes. An application for a possessory title must be supported by adequate statutory declarations[7].

(iv) *Form of conveyance.* It should be observed that on a sale of freehold land leading to compulsory first registration it is permissible for the purchaser to take a transfer in the normal Land Registry form, as if the title were already registered, instead of a conveyance in the usual unregistered form[8]. If advantage is taken of this facility, it will be necessary to modify the statutory form in certain respects[9]. The statutory form merely refers to 'the land comprised in the title above mentioned', a meaningless phrase where the title is as yet unregistered. Consequently the transfer must contain a satisfactory description of the land conveyed; a reference to the description contained in

3 Although the attitude to the certificate can be somewhat cavalier, a large number of them are not completed or even signed.
4 See p. 362, ante.
5 LRR 1925, r. 259.
6 This requirement is sometimes overlooked. The Land Registry is not limited to the title shown from the root of title. In practice it makes little difference but these are two immediate examples: (a) the entry of incumbrances is made by reference to the original deed creating them; accordingly that should be lodged, and (b) the presence of existing legal interests (especially rentcharges) requires the Land Registry to see all documents. See R & R, 202–3.
7 LRR 1925, r. 37, referring to Form 4. And see R & R, 651–656.
8 LRR 1925, r. 72. See Practice Leaflet No. 5 (First Registration of Title to Land).
9 For a precedent see Hallett, 1107–8. The usual form of Land transfer (Form 19) is set out on p. 494, post.

some previous deed forming part of the title deduced suffices, provided no part of the land comprised in that earlier deed has subsequently been sold-off.

(v) *Death of applicant*. An application does not abate in the event of the applicant's death before completion of registration; it may be continued by any person entitled to apply for registration who desires to adopt it[10], e.g. the deceased's personal representatives. It seems that an application can be pursued in the name of the purchaser, even though he dies before submission of any application; registration of the deceased applicant as first proprietor would not be a nullity[11].

(b) Examination of title and completion of registration

On receipt of the application and all relevant documents at the proper district registry, it is entered in a list of pending applications[12]. This list sets out the title number allotted to the property and contains a short verbal description of it. This is merely a temporary expediency, and the entry is removed from this list as soon as the location of the land has been marked on the public index map[13]. The application is also entered in a book[14] (known in the Registry as the 'day list') which contains a complete record by reference to title numbers of all current applications, both for first registration and for dealings with existing registered titles. This list is kept in the form of a series of card indexes, each card being filed by its title number in numerical order, thus facilitating easy reference. The card relating to any particular application is not removed from this list until registration has been completed.

This is followed by the examination of title by the Registry officials and the raising of requisitions if the title is not in order[15]. The Registrar may grant an absolute title, notwithstanding the title is open to objection, if satisfied that the proprietor's possession is unlikely to be disturbed. In the case of a serious defect in the title, only a qualified or possessory title will be granted.

When the Registrar has approved the title and determined what class of title to grant, the registration is regarded as completed as of the day on which the application was delivered[16]. A land certificate is then issued to the proprietor, the form and contents of which have previously been considered in Chapter 2[17]. Where the purchase is accompanied by a mortgage, a charge certificate is issued to the mortgagee and the land certificate is retained at the Registry until

10 LRR 1925, r. 305.
11 Unless for some reason the conveyance to the purchaser fails to vest the legal title in him so that first registration has a curative effect by virtue of s. 5 of the Act. In this event the earliest time that there can be any vesting is the day on which the application is delivered (LRR 1925, r. 42). If the purchaser has died before this date, it is difficult to see how a title can vest in a deceased person.
12 LRR 1925, r. 10. See Ruoff, 'Official Search by a Prospective Lessee of Registered Land' (1965), 62 LS Gaz 507. Explanatory Leaflet No. 9, issued by H.M. Land Registry, contains a list of counties, county boroughs and London boroughs with the district land registries which serve them.
13 Page 14, ante.
14 LRR 1925, r. 24.
15 See generally LRA 1925, s. 13; LRR 1925, rr. 25–27. In certain cases the Registrar may rely on the solicitor's certificate given in the application form, without conducting his own investigation of title: ibid., r. 29. See (1976) 40 Conv (NS) 122 (C.T. Emery); [1980] Conv 7, 165.
16 LRR 1925, r. 42.
17 See pp. 37–41, ante. The recording of easements and covenants existing at the time of first registration is dealt with at pp. 472–477, post.

the mortgage is discharged[18]. When the purchaser and his mortgagee are separately represented the purchaser's solicitor has no opportunity of verifying the filed plan and the entries in the charge certificate to see whether they correctly reflect his client's title. He can, however, apply for office copies of the plan and entries to be issued to him on completion of the registration; this request should be lodged with the application for registration which in this situation is submitted by the mortgagee's solicitor[19].

Before returning all original deeds not retained in the Registry to the applicant's solicitors, the Registry, as a means of protection against fraud or mistake, places its official stamp on the conveyance to the purchaser. The only way to eliminate fraud completely would be for the Registry to stamp all the deeds[20], but this it is unable to do because of staffing difficulties. This omission is unlikely to promote widespread fraudulent conduct on the part of registered proprietors seeking to deal with their land on the basis that it is still unregistered, at least not where the land is in an area of compulsory registration. A search in the public index map will always reveal whether or not the title to a particular piece of land has been registered[1].

(c) Dealings by person entitled to be registered

A person having the right to apply for first registration may deal with the land before he is himself registered in the same way as if he were the registered proprietor[2]. No dealing (other than a lease) can be accepted for registration until an application has been made for first registration, but where the dealing takes the form of a sub-sale, the sub-purchaser is deemed to be the applicant for first registration. Where a conveyance leading to first registration is followed immediately by a mortgage, the mortgagee's solicitor applies on behalf of the purchaser-mortgagor for first registration of the estate on which the mortgage has been created.

(d) Effect of failure to register

As previously noticed in Chapter 2[3], the Land Registration Act 1925, s. 123, provides a sanction against non-registration; on the expiration of two months from the date of the conveyance (or of any authorised extension) the conveyance becomes 'void so far as regards the grant or conveyance of the legal estate in the freehold . . . comprised in the conveyance'. This not very happily drafted section raises several interesting problems[4].

Section 123 is not a punitive measure, seeking to deprive a purchaser of his rights acquired by purchase; it operates rather as a potent inducement for him to register. Failure to seek registration within the prescribed period does not avoid the conveyance in toto. The purchaser loses the legal estate, but the deed

---

18   LRA 1925, s. 65.
19   See Registered Land Practice Note 54. See para. (c) below.
20   The LRA 1925, s. 16 envisages the stamping of all the deeds but empowers the Registrar to dispense with this if he is satisfied that without such marking the fact of registration cannot be concealed from a person dealing with the land. See R & R, 236.
 1   The risk of fraud would appear to be much greater in the case of land in a non-compulsory area registered voluntarily prior to the coming into operation of the LRA 1966 (see p. 23, ante). It is not the general practice to search the public index map on a purchase of land in a non-compulsory area.
 2   LRA 1925, s. 123 (2); LRR 1925, rr. 72, 73.
 3   Page 19, ante.
 4   See further the author's 'Compulsory Registration of Title—The Effect of Failure to Register' (1968) 32 Conv (NS) 391.

remains effective for other purposes, such as the enforcement of covenants. Rather surprisingly, the section does not state in whom the legal title vests on avoidance. The general consensus of opinion is that it revests in the vendor. Not that he holds it for his own use and benefit, for having received the purchase money he becomes a bare trustee of the legal estate for the benefit of the purchaser in equity. The suggestion that a recital in the conveyance of the vendor's seisin would create an estoppel which, on being fed, would return the legal estate to the purchaser appears unsound[5]; it is unlikely that any estoppel would be held to arise in the face of the statutory provision.

(i) *Acquisition of legal estate again.* It is understood that the Chief Land Registrar is always willing to make an extension order if some quite ordinary but reasonable excuse for the delay in submission of the application is given by the applicant's solicitor and the proper fee is paid. The request for such an order should accompany the application for first registration; it need not be made in advance of it[6]. An extension order granted after the default has occurred does not itself revest the legal title in the purchaser; it simply ensures that the Registrar will consider the application in the normal way. The subsequent registration operates to vest the legal title in him, without any reconveyance from the vendor[7]. If no order is forthcoming, a purchaser who seeks registration must first acquire the legal title again. This should present no problem, for he can call upon the vendor-trustee to vest it in him under the well known rule in *Saunders v Vautier*[8].

What is more surprising, and doubtless unintended by Parliament, is that s. 123 can be used to evade the requirements of compulsory registration. A purchaser (P1) may elect not to register his title. By remaining in possession for 12 years (plus two months), he can acquire the legal title by adverse possession. ·This acquisition does not require registration as it does not result from a conveyance on sale. Thereafter he can make title to a purchaser (P2)[9], though he will have to substantiate his position with suitable statutory declarations. Even before expiration of the limitation period P1 can assign the equitable interest existing under the implied trust to P2, whose possession for the remainder of the period results in his acquisition of the legal title which, again, does not require registration. A subsequent conveyance after the expiration of the limitation period by the original vendor (who obtains the legal estate under s. 123) to P3 cannot, it seems, operate to defeat the interest of P1 (or P2), even if P3 is registered as the first proprietor. Assuming P1 is in actual occupation of the land, his rights constitute an overriding interest; P3's registration takes effect subject to these rights[10], including the right to have the legal title vested in P1.

---

5   Farrand, 140. For recitals creating estoppels, see p. 507, post.
6   Practice Leaflet No. 5; R & R, 179.
7   LRA 1925, ss. 5, 69 (2).
8   (1841), 4 Beav 115; affd. Cr & Ph 240. There appears to be no breach of the vendor's implied covenant (if any) for further assurance (see p. 632, post), so the purchaser cannot sue on the covenant.
9   *Re Cussons Ltd* (1904) 73 LJ Ch 296; see also *Bridges v Mees* [1957] Ch 475, [1957] 2 All ER 577. The conveyance from P1 to P2 will occasion a compulsory registration.
10 LRA 1925, s. 70 (1) (g), p. 49, ante. P3's registration would still be subject to P1's equitable rights even though the limitation period had not then expired. His occupation would constitute constructive notice of his equitable interest under the trust and so prevent the conveyance to P3 operating to defeat it.

Practical objections to these modes of acquisition make any wholesale evasion of s. 123 unlikely. It is nevertheless apparent that some amendment to the section is required to prevent possible abuse.

2.   Transfers

(a) Application for registration

Unlike unregistered conveyancing, completion (in the sense in which this word is used in the preceding chapter) of a sale of registered land does not result in the legal estate vesting in the purchaser. Section 19 (1) of the Land Registration Act 1925, provides that:

> 'The transfer of the registered estate in the land or part thereof shall be completed by the registrar entering on the register the transferee as the proprietor of the estate transferred, but until such entry is made the transferor shall be deemed to remain proprietor of the registered estate . . .'

It is the purchaser's responsibility to seek registration.

(i) *Documents to be lodged.*   The application should be made on printed Form A4 which is the appropriate form for use for every kind of application affecting the *whole* of the land comprised in a title; on a transfer of part of a registered estate, Form A5 should be used. Care should be taken to ensure the form is completed correctly; any error or omission merely produces a requisition from the Registry, so delaying the registration process. In the case of a transfer to joint tenants or a limited company, special certificates, similar to those required on a first registration, have to be given[11].

The application must be accompanied by the following documents (where relevant): (i) the land (or charge) certificate[12], (ii) a discharge (Form 53) in respect of the transferor's mortgage, (iii) the transfer and, if it imposes restrictive covenants, a certified copy of the transfer, (iv) the mortgage created by the transferee, (v) a certified copy of the mortgage and (vi) a remittance to cover the Land Registry fees[13]. It is no longer obligatory to lodge the official search certificate with the application[14].

(ii) *Form of transfer.* The forms specified in the schedule to the Land Registration Rules 1925, are to be used in all matters to which they refer, or are capable of being applied or adapted, with such alterations and additions as are necessary or desired and the Registrar allows[15]. He can decline to enter in the register any instrument improper in form or substance or not clearly expressed[16]. In practice the Registrar permits alterations and additions to a considerable extent, provided no document other than that produced has to be

---

11   Page 447, ante.
12   If the land certificate has been placed on deposit at the Registry, the deposit number must be quoted.
13   See the Land Registration Fee Order 1981, S.I. 1981 No. 54.
14   This requirement, introduced by the Land Registration Rules 1930, SR & O 1930 No. 211, r. 1 (c), was abolished by the Land Registration (Official Searches) Rules 1969, S.I. 1969 No. 1179. Previously many solicitors omitted to lodge the certificate with a consequent loss of priority for their clients.
15   LRR 1925, r. 74.
16   LRR 1925, r. 78

perused and the general principles on which the register is maintained are not violated[17]. Thus trusts are not normally allowed to be mentioned, nor references to unregistered documents.

(iii) *Lodgment at the Registry.* On receipt of the application at the Registry, it is entered in the 'day list' in the order in which it is received[18]. Where two or more instruments or applications relating to the same land are delivered at the same time by the same person, they rank for priority purposes in such order as may be directed by or inferred from the instruments or applications[19].

(b) Time for application
Unlike applications for first registration of title, no sanction is imposed to compel the transferee to seek registration within a stated time, or even at all. The transferee may in theory rely on his equitable title. His actual occupation of the property ensures that his equitable interest will, as an overriding interest, bind any third person to whom the transferor purports to dispose of the property. No useful purpose is served by not registering. A purchaser from an unregistered transferee has a statutory right to require him to procure registration[20] and in practice no mortgagee would allow the transferee to remain unregistered.

The application should be forwarded to the Registry as soon as possible after completion, and in any event within the period of protection conferred by the official certificate of search[1]. It is absolutely vital that the application is received by the Registry within the priority period. It is the responsibility of the purchaser's solicitor (or that of his mortgagee) to ensure that this is done. Any delay in submitting may result in the purchaser's registration taking effect subject to some third party right only protected on the register after the date of the purchaser's search or even after completion of the purchase[2]. The application need not be delayed because a discharge of a registered charge (Form 53) signed by the mortgagee has not been received; the mortgagee's solicitor's undertaking to discharge the mortgage should be forwarded with the application which is treated as in order if the discharge is subsequently lodged. Similarly, priority is not prejudiced merely because the Registry raises some requisition, provided the requisition is satisfactorily complied with within one month. When a deed requires adjudication for stamp duty purposes, it should, if priority is to be preserved, be sent first to the Registry with a certified copy and a request for the original's immediate return. The Registry will return the deed and hold over the application until adjudication is completed and the deed re-lodged at the Registry.

17   R & R, 321. As to the necessity of transferees to execute the transfer see *Robinson v Robinson* (1976) 241 Estates Gazette 153. Cf. *Pink v Lawrence* (1978) 36 P & CR 98, [1979] Conv 5.
18   LRR 1925, r. 83 (1); see p. 448, ante. If the form and application is accepted and entered in the day list, that is conclusive evidence that the form is sufficient; *Smith v Morrison* [1974] 1 All ER 95.
19   LRR 1925, r. 84.
20   LRA 1925, s. 110 (5).
 1   A fairly high percentage fail to be lodged in time. It was thought erroneous that an overlapping search (as opposed to an extension) preserved the applicant's position but this is not the case. See R & R, 677. The increase of the period to 30 days should reduce this problem.
 2   See further, p. 405, ante; and *Watts v Waller* [1973] 1 QB 153, [1972] 3 All ER 257, CA (completion of transaction before expiry of search but application lodged after expiry. W's Class F registered after search took priority on application to register).

(c) Completion of registration

When the transferee has been entered as the new proprietor, the land certificate, amended and brought up to date, is returned to him (or his solicitor), unless he has obtained a mortgage, in which case it is retained in the Registry. On a transfer of part of the land comprised in a registered title, that land is removed from the vendor's title and a new land certificate is issued to the purchaser with a new title number. A note is made on the vendor's property register that the land edged green on the filed plan has been removed from his title and registered under the purchaser's new number shown in green on the plan. The vendor's amended certificate is then returned to him, unless it is deposited in the Registry, as is usually the case on the development of a building estate where transfers of part are frequently made.

(d) Effect of registration

Section 20 (1) of the Land Registration Act 1925, enacts that a transfer of an absolute freehold title for valuable consideration operates on registration to confer on the transferee an estate in fee simple together with appurtenant rights[3], but subject to (i) the incumbrances and other entries on the register and (ii) overriding interests affecting the land. The transfer operates in like manner as if the transferor

' were (subject to any entry on the register to the contrary) entitled to the registered land in fee simple in possession for his own benefit.'[4]

Registration is therefore effective to vest the legal title in the transferee even though the transferor was not himself entitled to be registered as proprietor because, for example, he had been inadvertently registered as proprietor of land already registered in another's name[5]. This does not necessarily give the transferee a title free from the rights of the proprietor who had been registered first, for if the latter is in occupation he will have an overriding interest[5a].

(i) *Position of transferee before registration.* Registration operates to vest in the transferee the legal estate which until then has remained in the transferor. Though s. 19 (1) of the Act suggests that the legal title does not vest in him until the Registrar usually enters his name on the register, registration takes effect as of the date on which the application is delivered at the Registry, for this is when registration is deemed to be completed[6]. The date of registration is given in the particulars recorded in the proprietorship register. Until registration the purchaser would appear to be in a position analogous to that of a beneficiary under a bare trust, having a right to obtain the legal title by applying for registration. In the meantime his equitable interest constitutes a minor interest and if he is in actual occupation his rights rank as an overriding interest. The absence of any legal estate until registration precludes the exercise of any right dependent upon the existence of a legal title for its validity. Thus he cannot

3   Including rights and interests which would, under the LPA 1925, have been transferred had the land not been registered, e.g. under s. 62. The transfer itself is deemed to imply the general words; see the LRA 1925, s. 19 (3).

4   Cf. s. 5 of the Act (effect of first registration with an absolute title) which also operates to cure defects in the vendor's title despite the absence of words similar to those quoted in the text. See p. 25, ante.

5   This situation gives rise to a case for rectification under the LRA 1925, s. 82 (1) (e).

5a   Cf. *Blacklocks v J B Developments (Godalming) Ltd* [1981] 3 All ER 392, p. 72, ante.

6   LRR 1925, r. 83 (2); *Strand Securities Ltd v Caswell* [1965] Ch 958 at 978, [1965] 2 All ER 820 at 825, CA, per Lord Denning MR.

serve a valid notice to quit[7]. However this fundamental defect in the scheme of registration is largely mitigated by s. 37 of the Act, which permits a person entitled to be registered as proprietor to dispose of or charge the land in the prescribed manner, and the disposition or charge takes effect as if he were registered as proprietor[8]. Apart from this provision it would be impossible for a purchaser to raise money on the security of his property until he had been registered as proprietor.

(ii) *Death of transferee prior to registration.* If the transferee dies before the registration is complete, it is clear that the Registrar cannot register as proprietor a deceased person. The deceased's equitable interest will pass to his personal representatives, entitling them to continue with the application[9] and it seems perfectly proper for the Registrar to register them as proprietors, once they have substantiated their own title by production of the grant of representation.

It may be debateable whether the death of the transferor before the transferee's registration prevents the transfer operating as the instrument of a living proprietor[10], but in any event the transferee's subsequent registration is effective under s. 20 (1) to vest the legal title in him.

(e) Status of Land Registry transfer
Nowhere in the Land Registration Act 1925, nor in the Rules, is the precise function of the transfer expressly stated. A disposition by way of sale must be 'in the prescribed manner', that is, made by an instrument in the scheduled form[11]. Being under seal it is clearly a deed[12]; equally clearly it passes no legal estate, for this passes on registration[13]. It constitutes an authority to the Registrar to enter the transferee's name on the register as proprietor, though by itself it is insufficient without the land certificate. Yet without a transfer the purchaser cannot obtain the legal title (except by adverse possession) and to this extent it plays just as important a role as does the conveyance in unregistered conveyancing.

A transfer creates rights and obligations enforceable by the parties and a person not a party to a transfer can enforce a covenant made with him[14]. It also seems effective to confer an equitable interest, at least where the transferor is a beneficial owner and the transfer is for value. In one case[15] X executed a

7 *Smith v Express Dairy Co Ltd* [1954] JPL 45.
8 This does not mean that s. 37 operates to vest a legal title in the second transferee or the chargee immediately, even in a case where the subsequent disposition is not one capable of registration. Suppose V transfers to P who, prior to his own registration, creates a short term lease in favour of T. T cannot obtain a legal lease until P is registered as proprietor, notwithstanding the words in s. 37 (2) that the disposition in T's favour takes effect as if P 'were registered as proprietor'. See *Grace Rymer Investments Ltd v Waite* [1958] Ch 831, [1958] 2 All ER 777, CA, where a similar argument based on s. 27 (3) (p. 466, post) was rejected; see per Evershed MR, at 850, and 783, respectively.
9 LRR 1925, r. 305, p. 448, ante.
10 Cf. *Cope v Keene* (1968) 118 CLR 1 at 7, per Kitto J.
11 LRA 1925, s. 18 (1); LRR 1925, r. 98.
12 *Chelsea and Walham Green Building Society v Armstrong* [1951] Ch 853, [1951] 2 All ER 250.
13 LRA 1925, s. 19 (1). The contrary view expressed in 3 K & E, 139, cannot be supported.
14 *Chelsea and Walham Green Building Society v Armstrong* [1951] Ch 853, [1951] 2 All ER 250 (transfer of equity of redemption incorporating covenant by transferee to pay mortgage debt). Vaisey J considered the transfer was analogous to a deed-poll, rather than a deed inter partes.
15 *Pilewska v Haduch* (1962), 184 Estates Gazette 11.

transfer of property in favour of himself and Y. This was held to confer on Y an equitable interest in half the proceeds of sale, entitling Y to be registered as joint proprietor with X. Therefore, despite the absence of a specifically enforceable contract for sale, an executed transfer will vest a good equitable title in the purchaser[16].

Most commentators agree that a transfer ranks as a 'conveyance' within the Law of Property Act 1925, s. 205 (1) (ii), a view doubted by one learned author[17]. Sufficient uncertainty appears to exist on the point for a recent statute to enact expressly that any reference therein to a conveyance includes a reference to a transfer of registered land[18]. Nevertheless it is submitted that a Land Registry transfer should constitute a 'conveyance' inasmuch as it confers an equitable interest[19].

(f) Voluntary transfers

Registration of a transfer made without valuable consideration has the same effect as a disposition for value, save for the important qualification that the donee takes the legal estate subject to any minor interests subject to which the transferor held the same[20], even though they are not protected on the register. For instance the donee takes the land subject to the right of the donor's trustee in bankruptcy to upset the transaction in certain circumstances[1]. 'Valuable consideration' includes marriage but not a nominal consideration in money[2].

It must be remembered that equity will not perfect an imperfect gift. The problem of incomplete gifts of registered land does not appear to have been considered by the English courts. It has arisen several times in Commonwealth jurisdictions, where the following test has been adopted[3]—has the intending donor by his acts placed the donee in such a position that under the relevant statute the latter has a right to have the transfer registered, a right which the donor or his personal representative cannot defeat? To establish such a right, delivery of both an executed transfer[4] and the land certificate to the donee are essential[5]. An executed but undelivered transfer probably vests no equitable title in the donee[6].

---

16 In the case of a transfer pursuant to LRR 72 (supra) it will presumably also convey the legal estate; see p. 447, ante.

17 Farrand, 216—7; Brickdale, 100; R & R, 565; 3 K & E 137, take the opposite view.

18 Land Commission Act 1967, s. 99 (5). It may also be significant that certain provisions in the LPA 1925, relating to 'conveyances' have been specifically incorporated into the LRA 1925, e.g. s. 19 (3) (general words), s. 38 (1) (execution).

19 See Potter, 78, adopted by 3 K & E, 137. The argument (see Farrand, 217) that *Borman v Griffith* [1930] 1 Ch 493 (agreement for lease not a 'conveyance') demolishes this conclusion appears unsound. This was a decision on the Conveyancing Act 1881, s. 2 (v) which confined the definition of 'conveyance' to instruments made by deed, which the informal lease clearly was not.

20 LRA 1925, s. 20 (4).

1 Bankruptcy Act 1914, s. 42.

2 LRA 1925, s. 3 (xxxi).

3 Per Dixon J in *Brunker v Perpetual Trustee Co* (1937) 57 CLR 555 at 602. And see the analogous English decisions involving share transfers: *Milroy v Lord* (1862) 4 De GF & J 264; *Re Rose, Rose v IRC* [1952] Ch 499, [1952] 1 All ER 1217, CA.

4 In this context 'delivery' is used in its non-technical meaning of handing over physical possession.

5 The donee requires the land certificate for production purposes: LRA 1925, s. 64 (1) (a); *Scoones v Galvin and Public Trustee* [1934] NZLR 1004 (donor retained certificate; gift imperfect): *Cope v Keene* (1968) 118 CLR 1. It is conceived that the Registrar cannot compel production of the outstanding land certificate under the LRA 1925, s. 64 (2) in order to perfect the gift.

6 Cf. *Macedo v Stroud* [1922] 2 AC 330 at 338, PC, per Viscount Haldane.

B   Leasehold titles

The benefits of the system of land registration, designed as it is to facilitate the transfer of interests in land, are not so great in relation to leases as they are to freeholds, for a lease has a limited life-span and it may contain terms which reduce the chances of dealing with it. Nevertheless this is no justification for the haphazard and illogical manner in which the Act deals with leases. There are perplexing anomalies and inconsistencies capable, it has been said[7], of stimulating the academic student of the subject. Members of the Bench[8] and practising solicitors have alike been misled by the vast jungle of statutory regulation.

For the purposes of the Act, leases fall into one of three categories:

(1)   leases capable of substantive registration;
(2)   leases not capable of substantive registration, but requiring to be protected by entry of a notice in the charges register of the lessor's superior title (sometimes termed 'noted' leases);
(3)   leases which require neither registration nor notation because they take effect as overriding interests.

Unfortunately the position becomes somewhat blurred because leases falling within the first two groups, which are not properly protected in the prescribed manner, may still rank as overriding interests under s. 70 (1) (g) by virtue of the lessee's occupation. Similarly the grant of a lease of *registered* land (often termed a dispositionary lease) may possess a dual character. It not only creates a new estate in land which may result in an application for first registration, it is also a disposition or dealing with registered land[9]. It is particularly important to remember this in practice, when dealing with the grant of a lease of registered land in a compulsory area for a term exceeding 21 years but not exceeding 40 years[10].

1.   First registration

(a) Leases capable of substantive registration
An important distinction must be observed between situations where the reversionary title is registered and where it is unregistered. Substantive registration is necessary in the following cases, if the lessee is to obtain a legal estate:

(1)   the grant of a lease of *unregistered* land in a compulsory area for a term of not less than 40 years;
(2)   the assignment on sale of *unregistered* land in a compulsory area for a term having at least 40 years to run;
(3)   the grant of a lease of land *already registered* for a term of more than 21 years *irrespective of where the land is situated*.

(i) *Reversionary title unregistered*. Transactions (1) and (2) fall within s. 123 (1) of the Act. Failure to register results in a divesting of the legal

7   R & R, 440, claiming that such difficulties have not hampered the Registry's practical dealings with leases.
8   The Chief Land Registrar's article (see note 12, p. 448, ante) was prompted by certain misunderstandings expressed by the Court of Appeal in *Strand Securities Ltd v Caswell* [1965] Ch 958, [1965] 1 All ER 820, CA.
9   LRA 1925, s. 18 (1) (e), (5), hence the use of the expression 'dispositionary' lease.
10   Such a lease falls outside the compulsory provisions of s. 123 of the Act but is caught by s. 19; see p. 457, post.

estate[11]. As between the lessor and the unregistered lessee, the latter seems to hold, not under an equitable lease, but under a legal periodic tenancy arising by virtue of his entry into possession coupled with the payment and acceptance of rent[12]. Even though the lease is unregistered, the lessee's rights will rank as an overriding interest if he is in occupation or in receipt of the rents and profits. The grant of a lease of unregistered land within a compulsory area for a term of more than 21 years[13] but less than 40 *may* be registered on a voluntary basis. The Land Registration Act 1966, does not preclude the voluntary registration of titles within a compulsory area. At present considerable confusion is caused by these differing periods of 40 years and 21 years and the removal of this distinction would be a helpful step towards simplification[14].

(ii) *Reversionary title registered (transaction (3))*. The registered proprietor of freehold land may grant a lease of the registered land for any term of years absolute for any purpose in any form which sufficiently refers to the registered land[15]. This requires a reference to the title number of the superior estate and there must be an identifying plan if part only of the superior estate is subject to the lease. Such a lease ranks as a disposition of registered land. If granted for more than 21 years it requires completion by substantive registration of the lessee as proprietor of the new term[16]. Presumably the lessor holds the leasehold term in trust for the lessee until registration. The lessee must therefore register his title to obtain a legal estate. The rights of a lessee of an unregistered dispositionary lease constitute an overriding interest if he is himself in occupation or is in receipt of the rents and profits, but not where he allows another sole occupation on a rent free basis[17].

The obligation to register a dispositionary lease cannot, it seems, be affected by the somewhat contradictory provision in s. 8 (1) (a) that the applicant for registration of a leasehold interest must be an estate owner holding under a lease for a term of which more than 21 years are unexpired. Taken literally this requirement would preclude any application to register a dispositionary lease on the simple ground that the applicant, not having any legal title, is not an estate owner[18]. The Registrar is prepared in certain circumstances to permit the registration of a dispositionary lease granted for more than 21 years notwithstanding that at the time of application less than 21 years remain unexpired[19]. The time limits and penalties imposed by s. 123 do not apply to

11 *British Maritime Trust Ltd v Upson* [1931] WN 7 (sub-lease by unregistered lessee; sublessee held to have no legal interest).
12 *Bishop of Bangor v Parry* [1891] 2 QB 277 (lease avoided by Charitable Trusts Amendment Act 1855); (1968) 32 Conv (NS) 391, 404—6. For the consequences of failure to register after an assignment of an existing term, see R & R, 177; (1968) 32 Conv (NS) at 406—9.
13 A lease granted for less than 21 years is incapable of substantive registration: LRA 1925, s. 8 (1) (a); see p. 458, post.
14 The Law Commission provisionally recommend that the 40 years' period in s. 123 be reduced to 21 years, so that the dividing line between registrable and unregistrable leases is drawn at 21 years for all purposes: Published Working Paper No. 32, para. 33.
15 LRA 1925, ss. 18 (1), (e), 21 (1) (d) (grant of sub-lease by leaseholder).
16 LRA 1925, ss. 19 (1), 22 (1). A dispositionary lease granted for a term not exceeding 21 years cannot be registered: ibid., ss. 19 (2) (a), 22 (2) (a). But its effect may be devastating, see *Freer v Unwins Ltd* [1976] Ch 288, [1976] 1 All ER 634 p. 8, ante.
17 *Strand Securities Ltd v Caswell* [1965] Ch 958, [1965] 1 All ER 820, CA.
18 See LRA 1925, s. 3 (iv). This must be an occasion where the context demands displacement of the statutory definition.
19 See R & R, 449.

the grant of a dispositionary lease, not even to a lease of land within a compulsory area for a term exceeding 40 years. The avoiding provisions of the section are inapplicable to situations where the lessee cannot, by virtue of s. 19 (1), obtain any legal title until registration.

On registration of a dispositionary lease, notice of the lease must be entered on the lessor's register of title[20]. The noting of leases on the superior title will be considered later in this chapter. One point requires consideration here. According to the official view[1] notation is an essential element in completion of the registration process, and so a prerequisite for obtaining the legal title. Consequently, if by an oversight the Registry omit to enter notice, the lessee only holds an equitable title. It is considered that this view is not warranted by the Act. The vital thing in the completion process is the entry on the register of the lessee as proprietor of the leasehold estate[2] and it is difficult to see why the entry of something which operates by way of notice only (see s. 52 (2) of the Act) should be held to be so fundamental to the process of substantive registration.[3]

(b) Leases incapable of substantive registration

The following leases cannot be the subject of an application for substantive registration:

(1)   a lease originally granted for a term of 21 years or less at a rent without taking a fine (i.e. premium);

(2)   a lease granted for the same term as in (1) but at a premium;

(3)   a lease with only 21 years (or less) to run at the time of application for registration[4];

(4)   a lease containing an absolute prohibition against alienation inter vivos;

(5)   an equitable lease;

(6)   a mortgage term where there is a subsisting right of redemption.

Leaving aside the mortgage term which is considered later in this chapter in the section dealing with mortgages, these leases may take effect either as overriding interests or as minor interests, depending on the circumstances. A lease for 21 years or less ranks as an overriding interest under s. 70 (1) (k) if granted at a rent without taking a fine[5]. It takes effect as if it were a registered disposition[6] and exists as a legal estate if it is for a term of years absolute. Where, however, a premium is paid it is anomalously excluded from para. (k)[7].

Leases falling within groups (2), (3), (4) and (5) rank as minor interests and require protection by entry of a notice in the charges register of the superior

---

20   LRA 1925, s. 19 (2).

1   R & R, 447.

2   LRA 1925, s. 19 (1), (2).

3   Cf. Law Com. Working Paper No. 32 para. 22 where entry of a notice is not regarded as part of the process of substantive registration. If the mere omission of notice prevents the acquisition of any legal title, this may affect the rights of the parties inter se and clearly governs the nature of subsequent dealings by the lessee. The lessee can seek rectification of the register and, if he suffers loss, is entitled to be indemnified: LRA 1925, ss. 82 (1) (b), (h), 83 (2).

4   LRA 1925, s. 8 (1) (a), but see p. 457, note 19, ante.

5   Page 457, ante. R & R, 110 describe these as 'occupation leases' but there is in fact no such requirement. There is a danger here combined with LRA 1925, s. 18 (3) (power to grant such a lease to take effect in possession or within one year of the date thereof).

6   LRA 1925, s. 19 (2), p. 461, post.

7   The Law Commission have suggested the abolition of this distinction so that all legal leases for 21 years or less will constitute overriding interests within para. (k); see Working Paper No. 32, para. 46.

title. Being minor interests they take effect only in equity[8], and if not noted they are unenforceable against a subsequent purchaser of the superior title. Despite lack of notice on the register, these leases may, in effect, be protected as over-riding interests under s. 70 (1) (g) by virtue of the lessee's occupation, and additionally in the case of an inalienable lease under para. (k)[9]. It will be remembered that a lease cannot at the same time be both a minor interest and an overriding interest[10].

This present division of non-registrable leases into overriding and minor interests can produce consequences that may not be readily appreciated. For example, under the general law a term of years absolute for (say) fourteen years granted by deed *at a fine or premium* may exist as a legal estate. Under the Land Registration Act 1925, it ranks as a minor interest and must therefore be equitable. It is excluded from s. 70 (1) (k), as we have just seen. Even where the lessee is in actual occupation and so able to claim the protection of s. 70 (1) (g) (assuming no notice of the lease is entered on the register), his rights still remain equitable[11]. This difference between short term leases granted with or without a premium will, happily, disappear if the Law Commission's provisional recommendations[12] find their way into the statute book.

(c) Application for substantive registration

The procedure on application is much the same as that for freehold titles. The appropriate form must be selected, depending on the particular case and the title requested[13]. A certified copy of the lease must be supplied by an applicant who is an original lessee; in other cases the lease must be produced if it is in the applicant's possession or control.

(i) *Title applied for.* Where the freehold title out of which the leasehold estate is created is itself registered with an absolute title, or where the lessee can deduce the unregistered freehold title to the Registrar, application for registration with an absolute leasehold title may be made; otherwise the applicant will normally have to be content with a good leasehold title. However the lessee, not generally being in a position to investigate the superior title, may not have sufficient information to enable him to apply for an absolute title and at present there is no power for the Registrar to grant an absolute title on an application for a good leasehold title[14]. Where only a possessory title is sought he may grant a good leasehold title without the applicant's consent.

(ii) *Notices and advertisements.* On an application to register a lease of land already registered, notice must be given to the proprietor of the freehold (and of any superior leasehold) estate. If no valid objection is made within seven days, or the proprietor consents in writing, the lease is noted against the free-hold and superior leasehold titles[15]. The lessor's deposit of his land certificate at

---

8   LRA 1925, ss. 2 (1), 101 (2), (3).
9   See further R & R, 110.
10   See LRA 1925, s. 3 (xv), p. 65, ante.
11   It cannot be treated as a registered disposition under s. 19 (2) which expressly does not apply to leases required to be noted on the register.
12   See note 7, p. 458, ante.
13   See further Appendix B, Forms 2B, 3B, 2E, 3E, and 2F.
14   The Law Commission provisionally recommend an alteration to this rule: Working Paper No. 32, para. 52.
15   LRR 1925, r. 46 (1), (2).

the Registry signifies consent, in which event no notice is served. Before registration is completed with absolute or good leasehold title, an advertisement, calling for objections, must be inserted in the *Gazette*. Provision has been made for dispensing with the advertisement in most cases[16].

(d) Completion of registration

On substantive registration of a leasehold estate a new title is opened with its own title number. A land certificate is issued to the lessee, containing short particulars of the lease — the date, parties, term and rent. The various provisions of the lease, such as the covenants, do not appear on the register. The lease constitutes an integral part of the title; it is returned with the certificate and a note of registration is endorsed on the lease.

The effect of registration according to the particular type of leasehold title granted has already been considered[17]. On first registration of a dispositionary lease the legal title is deemed to have vested on the date the completed application is received at the Registry[18], subject as is variously stated in the Act.

(e) Entry of notice of lease on lessor's title

Save as hereafter appears, notice of every dispositionary lease must be entered on the register of the freehold title or the superior leasehold title[19]. This obligation applies alike to those leases which require substantive registration and those which are incapable of registration. In the first case entry of the notice is done automatically at the time of registration[20]; in the second the lessee must make an application in the prescribed manner for its entry[1]. No entry can, of course, be made if the freehold title is unregistered; it will be the Registry's responsibility to enter notice of a registered lease in the charges register at the time of first registration of the freehold title.

Substantive registration of a leasehold title does not of itself bring the fact that a lease has been granted on to the register of the reversionary title. This is the purpose of the notice and in its absence a subsequent purchaser of the freehold reversion will take free from the leasehold interest[2], save where the lessee's rights are protected as an overriding interest by virtue of s. 70 (1) (g) of the Act. It operates by way of notice only and does not confer validity on any lease otherwise invalid[3]. It gives notice, not merely of the existence of the lease, but also of its contents[4]. It is not, therefore, necessary to apply for entry of a separate notice protecting an option to renew, or to purchase the freehold reversion[5], though the Registry do this automatically.

16   LRR 1925, rr. 31, 33; R & R, 230.
17   Pages 28–31, ante.
18   LRR 1925, r. 83 (2). On first registration of a lease of land formerly unregistered, the legal title will already be vested in the lessee under the grant, except where s. 123 has operated to divest the legal title.
19   LRA 1925, ss. 19 (2), 22 (2).
20   LRR 1925, r. 46, subject to production of the lessor's land certificate where necessary; see LRA 1925, s. 64 (1) (c), post.
1   LRA 1925, s. 48.
2   LRA 1925, s. 20 (1).
3   LRA 1925, s. 52 (2).
4   A certified copy of the lease (LRR 1925, r. 186 (2)) is filed in the Registry so becoming part of the register. See R & R, 460. It will not validate an option therein already void for want of registration: *Kitney v MEPC Ltd* [1978] 1 All ER 595, CA, p. 25, ante.
5   The option may also constitute an overriding interest within s. 70 (1) (g): *Webb v Pollmount Ltd* [1966] Ch 584, [1966] 1 All ER 481, p. 49, ante.

Section 19 (2) (a) of the Act expressly provides that entry of a notice is not required in the case of a lease granted for a term not exceeding 21 years at a rent without taking a fine. Entry of a notice is unnecessary since the lease ranks as an overriding interest[6]. As we have already seen[7] the use of the word 'granted' imports the creation of a legal lease. By virtue of s. 19 (2) it takes effect 'as if it were a registered disposition immediately on being granted.' It is therefore deemed to be completed and the lessee acquires a legal estate at once, presumably for the class of title enjoyed by the lessor. Where a non-registrable lease is created by a lessor not himself registered as proprietor but entitled to be so registered, then the effect of its creation is governed by s. 37 of the Act[8].

(f) Production of the lessor's land certificate
Section 64 (1) (a) of the Land Registration Act 1925, requires production of the land certificate to the Registrar 'on every entry in the register of a disposition' by the registered proprietor. In *Strand Securities Ltd v Caswell*[9] the Court of Appeal held that this paragraph did not apply to an application to register a new leasehold title. The court declared as erroneous the Registrar's established practice of requiring the lessor's certificate before treating as complete the lessee's application for first registration of his lease. A lessee has no right under the general law to call for his lessor's land certificate[10] and consequently the Registrar should not be entitled to insist on its production. Though the *Strand* case was concerned with a lease at a rack rent, the tenor of the judgments clearly indicates that the decision is of general application.

Section 64 (1) (c) also requires production of an outstanding land certificate on entry of a notice, *except* notice of a lease at a rent without taking a fine. In the *Strand* case the lease fell within this exception so it was not necessary to consider whether the Registrar could have demanded production for notation purposes. However, even had the lease been granted at a premium, it would have been illogical to hold production unnecessary for the purposes of paragraph (a) and yet essential for (c).

In practice the parties normally make arrangements before completion of the lease for the deposit of the lessor's certificate at the Registry and cases of non-cooperation are rare. If, of course, the superior title is subject to a registered charge, the lessor's land certificate will be held on deposit in the Registry and the necessary entry can be made against the lessor's title[11]. The Law Commission have given consideration[12] to this whole question and though their conclusions are only tentative they require mention here. In their view the lessor's land certificate should be produced by the *lessor* at the Registry on any application for first registration of a lease. To ensure that the lessee is not prejudiced by the lessor's failure or delay in producing it, the lessee's application is to be deemed complete when he has duly lodged all necessary documents under his control. Enforcement of the lessor's duty of production should rest with the

---

6   Section 70 (1) (k). Though not required for its protection, entry of a notice is permitted by s. 70 (3), in which case the lease ceases to be an overriding interest.
7   *City Permanent Building Society v Miller* [1952] Ch 840, [1952] 2 All ER 621, p. 55, ante.
8   See note 8, p. 454, ante.
9   [1965] Ch 958, [1965] 1 All ER 820, CA. See R & R, 478–79.
10   LRA 1925, s. 110 (6) does not apply as between lessor and lessee.
11   LRA 1925, s. 65. The Registrar can compel production of the charge certificate (LRR 1925, r. 266), at least where the lease has been granted with the chargee's consent.
12   For a summary of their provisional conclusions, see Working Paper No. 32, para. 69.

Registrar. The desirability of noting the lease on the lessor's land certificate seems[13] to be the sole reason advanced for requiring its production and it is questionable whether this is adequate justification to warrant the procedure. There appears to be no valid reason why the Registrar cannot automatically enter notice of the lease on the freeholder's register of title kept at the Registry without production of the lessor's certificate, as soon as the seven days required by r. 46[14] have elapsed without objection from the lessor — as is the present position for leases granted without a premium. The lessee is adequately protected and if the lessor wishes to have his land certificate made to correspond with the entries in the register, he can produce this voluntarily.

(g) Proposals for reform

The main proposals of the Law Commission affecting leases have been referred to in the preceding pages. Although at the moment they represent nothing more than provisional recommendations, they at least suggest the general pattern of law reform in this field. The proposed division of leases into two main categories of registrable and overriding (rather than three as at present) must surely be implemented. Such an amendment should do much to reduce the complexity of the law, particularly if it is coupled with a provision which excludes from the list of overriding interests any lease requiring substantive registration or protection by entry on the register[15]. Unfortunately some leases will not be embraced by this dual division and these must still rank as minor interests. A registrable lease where the lessee simply relies upon his equitable title without seeking substantive registration would fall into this category, as would an agreement for a lease. The latter will constitute an important group but the suggested amendment to the list of overriding interests should at least ensure that equitable leases cannot fall within more than one category.

2.   Transfers of registered leases

Although a particular form of transfer is prescribed for an assignment of lease-hold property, it is the practice to adopt the statutory form for freehold transfers[16]. Covenants for indemnity, similar to those operative in unregistered conveyancing, are automatically implied[17]; these can be varied or negatived as desired. Registration of the transfer is effected in much the same way as a transfer of freehold land. The appropriate application form is Form A4. No legal title vests in the assignee until he is registered as the proprietor, though this will be deemed to have vested retrospectively as of the date when his application was received by the Registry. Section 23 of the Land Registration Act 1925, deals with the effect of registration[18]. Under sub-s. (1) a disposition for valuable consideration of a leasehold registered with an absolute title is deemed, on registration, to vest in the transferee the estate transferred together with all implied or expressed rights and privileges attached to the estate, but subject to (i) the implied and express covenants and obligations incident to the estate, (ii) the incumbrances and other entries on the register and (iii)

13   Working Paper No. 32, para. 64.
14   Page 459, ante.
15   See p. 64, ante.
16   Form 19, as opposed to Form 32 prescribed by r. 115.
17   LRA 1925, s. 24, p. 637, post.
18   Cf. the effect of first registration; see pp. 28–29, ante. See also pp. 451–452, ante, relating to the effect of registration of a disposition of freehold land.

overriding interests affecting the estate. The transfer operates as if the transferor were absolutely entitled to the estate for his own benefit. The transfer of a good leasehold title has the same effect by virtue of s. 23 (2), save that the disposition does not prejudice the enforcement of any right or interest affecting or in derogation of the lessor's title to grant the lease. Where the disposition is not for value then in both cases the transferee holds the estate subject to minor interests which were binding on the transferor; see sub-s. (5).

An assignment of *part* of the land comprised in a registered leasehold title necessitates an application for first registration. Such a transaction normally results in an informal or equitable apportionment of the rent (i.e. without the consent of the lessor). Particulars of the apportionment and any modification of the implied covenants are entered on the register of title.

It should also be remembered that on an assignment of a lease which is incapable of substantive registration the title must be deduced in accordance with the normal conveyancing practice for unregistered titles.

3. Determination of leases

The Registrar is required to notify in the prescribed manner on the register the determination of a lease, on satisfactory proof of its termination[19]. An application for this purpose must be made and the procedure differs slightly according to whether the lease is registered or merely noted.

(a) Registered lease
The following documents and evidence must be produced at the Registry:

(1) the lease and counterpart lease,
(2) the land certificate of the leasehold title,
(3) the land certificate of the superior title, if registered, and if unregistered, adequate evidence of the lessor's title (e.g. a marked abstract),
(4) evidence of the determination.

The leasehold title is closed and the notice of the lease on the freehold title (if itself registered) is cancelled.

(b) Noted lease
Notice of the lease is cancelled on production of:

(1) the lease and counterpart,
(2) the lessor's land certificate[20],
(3) an application (Form 92) for cancellation of the notice,
(4) sufficient evidence of the leasehold title to establish the applicant's title, where there have been dealings with the lease,
(5) evidence of the determination.

(c) Evidence of determination[1]
The nature of such evidence depends on the reason for determination. In the case of *merger*, the Registrar may treat a lease as merged where the title to the lease and the superior estate have become vested in the same person in the same

---

19 LRA 1925, s. 46.
20 Normally the application will be made by the lessor or some person entitled to be registered as proprietor of the superior title.
1 LRR 1925, rr. 200–8; R & R, 464–472.

capacity, as where the freehold estate is transferred to the registered tenant. The application to close the leasehold title can be incorporated in the application for registration of the ex-tenant as proprietor of the freehold. In the case of a *surrender*, the deed of surrender must be produced; a surrender by operation of law, e.g. by vacating the premises and handing over the keys, must be supported by a statutory declaration of the facts. A lease determined by *effluxion of time*[2] will only be cancelled if the Registrar is satisfied that it has not been statutorily extended, e.g. under the Landlord and Tenant Act 1954.

C   Mortgages and charges

A registered proprietor may by deed charge his land with the payment of any principal sum of money either with or without interest; in addition he can, subject to any entry to the contrary on the register, mortgage by deed or otherwise his land in any manner which would have been permissible if the land had not been registered and with like effect[3]. A mortgage of registered land can thus take one of several forms:

(1)   a legal mortgage completed by the registration of the lender as proprietor of the charge, known as a registered charge;

(2)   a lien created by a deposit of the land certificate with the lender;

(3)   any mortgage by deed or otherwise which would have been permissible had the title not been registered.

Of these differing methods, the creation of a registered charge is that most frequently encountered in practice.

1.   Registered charges

(a) Form of charge

A charge of registered land may be in any form, provided it adequately identifies the land comprised in it[4], and for this purpose a description by reference to the title number suffices, though usually the address of the property is included. The Rules prescribe a simple form of charge by way of legal mortgage[5] for use, if desired. This is in similar form to that of a transfer to which is added a statement of the principal and interest and dates of payment[6]. Special stipulations may be added, and certain covenants on the part of the mortgagor are automatically implied (unless there is a contrary entry on the register), including a covenant for payment of principal and interest[7].

In practice institutional lenders prefer to employ their ordinary form of mortgage, adapted to meet the special requirements of registered titles. The substantive provisions of the Act and the Rules apply alike to whichever form of mortgage is used.

---

2   Production of the lease and leasehold land certificate is dispensed with in cases where the applicant cannot obtain them.

3   LRA 1925, ss. 25 (1), 106 (1). See also s. 66, p. 467, post.

4   LRA 1925, s. 25 (2).

5   See LRA 1925, s. 27 (1).

6   LRR 1925, r. 139, prescribing Form 45.

7   LRA 1925, s. 28 (1) (a).

(b) Completion by registration
An application for registration must be submitted in the same manner as for a transfer. The land certificate, the charge and a certified copy must be lodged at the Registry. Where the mortgage is in conjunction with a transfer of the property to the borrower, a single application suffices for both transactions[8]. The creation of a registered charge ranks as a disposition of registered land and requires completion by the Registrar entering in the mortgagor's charges register the name of the mortgagee as the proprietor of the mortgage together with particulars of it[9]. This constitutes registration of the mortgage as a registered charge. The mortgage, it is to be observed, is not registered as a separate title, but the mortgagee is issued with a charge certificate which contains a copy of the filed plan and of the subsisting entries on the register. The original mortgage deed is bound up with the certificate. The proprietor's land certificate is retained at the Registry until cancellation of the charge[10].

In the case of a second mortgage a modified charge certificate is issued, containing an epitome of the entires, but without a plan. Production of the prior charge certificate is unnecessary and that of the land certificate impossible.

Charges by limited companies. When a mortgage is created by a company, a certificate of registration under s. 95 of the Companies Act 1948, should be lodged with the application, otherwise a note is made on the register that the charge is subject to the provisions of that section[11]. A certificate that the charge does not contravene the company's memorandum or articles of association is also required to ensure compliance with the restriction, normally entered on registration of a company as proprietor of land, that except under the Registrar's order no charge by a company is to be registered unless a duly signed certificate of non-contravention is furnished[12].

Since a registered charge must be a charge on specific land, a floating charge (which is a charge on all the company's property for the time being) cannot be registered. It can be protected on the register by means of a notice (if the land certificate is produced), or by a caution.

(c) Effect of registration
Registration confers on the mortgagee the legal interest in the charge. As a disposition of the land by the registered proprietor, it takes effect subject to overriding interests and to minor interests protected on the register[13]. Thus the mortgagee takes subject to a tenancy, under which the tenant enters into immediate occupation, created by the mortgagor before completion of the purchase and mortgage[14]. If the mortgagor is registered with a good leasehold,

8   See p. 451, ante, for a list of the documents to be lodged. If the mortgagee is separately represented, his solicitor submits the application.
9   LRA 1925, s. 26 (1). For the form of the entries, reference should be made to the illustration on pp. 42–43, ante.
10 LRA 1925, s. 65.
11 LRR 1925, r. 145. Section 95 of the Companies Act 1948, enacts that a charge on land created by a company shall be void against the company's liquidator unless it is registered with the registrar of companies within 21 days of creation.
12 See LRR 1925, rr. 121 (4), 259. The certificate must be signed by the company's secretary, solicitor or director.
13 LRA 1925, ss. 18 (4), 20 (1).
14 *Woolwich Equitable Building Society v Marshall* [1952] Ch 1, [1951] 2 All ER 769; *Grace Rymer Investments Ltd v Waite* [1958] Ch 831, [1958] 2 All ER 777, CA. This result is in

qualified or possessory title, the charge takes effect subject to the provisions of the Act affecting land registered with such a title[15].

Though the mortgagee cannot obtain a legal interest before registration, this does not mean that the mortgage deed is wholly ineffective until then[16]. Section 27 (3) provides that the mortgage takes effect from the date of its delivery, so that pending registration the provisions of the mortgage are fully operative as between the parties. This subsection does not, however, enable the mortgagee to exercise the powers conferred by law on the owner of a legal mortgage — only a registered proprietor has these[17]. A registered chargee can transfer the charge to another, a power which cannot be negatived by the mortgage provisions[18].

(d) Further charges

Special rules regulate the priority of further advances on the security of registered land. Where a prior mortgagee is under an *obligation* noted on the register to make further advances, a subsequent registered chargee takes subject to any further advances, even though his charge is registered before the prior mortgagee makes the further advance[19]. In cases where the mortgage merely secures further advances, the prior mortgagee does not obtain priority in respect of further advances made by him after notification from the Registry of the prospective entry on the register of another charge[20].

(e) Discharge of registered charge

The provisions in the Law of Property Act 1925, governing the discharge of mortgages do not apply to registered charges[1]. The discharge of a registered charge can only be effected by a discharge entered on the register. The Rules prescribe a suitable form (Form 53) which consists of a simple admission by the mortgagee that the charge of which he is the proprietor has been discharged. Use of this form is not obligatory; the Registrar has a wide discretion to accept other evidence of repayment[2], such as an acknowledgement of receipt of all moneys outstanding endorsed on the mortgage deed.

The charge certificate, together with Form 53 (or other satisfactory evidence) must be delivered to the Registry. The entry relating to the mortgage in the charges register is deleted, and the charge certificate is cancelled,

no way affected by LRA 1925, s. 27 (3). Cf. *City Permanent Building Society v Miller* [1952] Ch 840, [1952] 2 All ER 621, CA (equitable tenancy not binding since tenant's occupation commenced after registration of mortgage). Where the mortgage excludes the tenant's power of leasing, a tenancy created after the mortgage will not bind the mortgagee, even though the tenant enters into occupation before the mortgagee's registration is effected.
15 LRA 1925, s. 26 (3).
16 See *Grace Rymer Investments Ltd v Waite* [1958] Ch 831 at 850, [1958] 2 All ER 777 at 783–84, CA, per Lord Evershed MR.
17 *Lever Finance Ltd v Trustee of Property of Needleman* [1956] Ch 375, [1956] 2 All ER 378 (appointment of receiver). See the LRA 1925, s. 34 (1). Quaere whether a proposed chargee could transfer the charge under LRA 1925, s. 37. Cf. R & R 522, 535; Hayton, *Registered Land*, (3rd edn) p. 128.
18 LRA 1925, ss. 25 (3) (i), 33.
19 LRA 1925, s.30 (3), as added by LP (Am) A 1926, s. 5. Section 94 of the LPA 1925, does not apply to registered charges (see sub-s. (4) thereof).
20 LRA 1925, s. 30 (1), (2). A mortgage in favour of a bank to secure an overdraft is a common example of a charge to secure further advances. The honouring of each cheque by the bank constitutes a further advance.
1 LPA 1925, s. 115 (10).
2 LRR 1925, r. 151.

whereupon the charge is deemed to have ceased and any term or sub-term granted by the mortgage is extinguished and merges in the registered estate without any surrender[3]. The land certificate is brought up to date and returned, on request, to the proprietor or his solicitor, though in practice the land certificate often remains at the Registry since discharge of the existing charge is part of a transaction culminating in the issue of a new charge certificate to the purchaser's mortgagee.

A discharge of a building society mortgage may be either in Form 53 or by way of an endorsed receipt in accordance with the Building Societies Act 1962, s. 37 (1). The Rules require Form 53, where used, to be executed under the society's seal and countersigned by the secretary[4], but the Registrar accepts the form if it is countersigned by a person acting under the authority of the board of directors, the mode prescribed for statutory receipts under s. 37 (1).

2.   Mortgage cautions

A mortgage made by deed could formerly be protected by a caution in a special form[5]. The land certificate, mortgage deed and certified copy had to be lodged at the Registry. This mortgage caution was similar in effect to a caution against dealings, except that it could not be warned off by notice to the mortgagee, and any subsequent disposition of the registered land was subject to the rights protected by the caution[6]. Mortgage cautions were virtually obsolescent. However in *Barclays Bank Ltd v Taylor*[7] it was suggested that this procedure had to be adopted and the practice of taking the land certificate and protecting the charge by caution was ineffective. However its anachronism 'has now been sunk'[8].

3.   Deposit of land certificate

(a) Procedure for creation
By virtue of s. 66 of the Act, a registered proprietor may create a lien on the registered land by deposit of the land certificate with the chargee, provided there is no entry to the contrary on the register, such as a bankruptcy inhibition or creditor's notice. This lien which takes effect subject to overriding interests and interests already registered or protected on the register is equivalent to a lien created in the case of unregistered land by the deposit of documents of title by an owner entitled to the land for his own benefit.

There must be a deposit of the land certificate with the lender; therefore the existence of a prior registered charge precludes the creation of this lien as the land certificate will already be in the Registry. It does not seem necessary to deposit other relevant title deeds, e.g. the lease in the case of a leasehold title, though this is highly desirable[9].

(b) Nature of protection
The depositee may give written notice of the deposit to the Registrar who acknowledges its receipt and enters notice of the deposit in the proprietor's

3   LRA 1925, s. 35; LRR 1925, r. 267.
4   Rule 152 (2).
5   LRA 1925, s. 106 (1) (2); LRR 1925, r. 223, prescribing Form 64.
6   LRR 1925, r. 225.
7   [1973] Ch 63, [1972] 2 All ER 752, CA.
8   R & R, 123. See Administration of Justice Act 1977, s. 26 (1) which has abolished the old method and provides for protection by notice, caution or any other prescribed method.
9   See further R & R, 549.

charges register[10]. This notice (not the applicant's notice) operates as a caution[11], thus entitling him to oppose any application to register a disposition or transmission of which he is notified. The depositee is in fact in a superior position than an ordinary cautioner. No disposition or transmission or any other entry for which production of the land certificate is required can be registered without his surrendering the certificate. If he consents to a particular transaction, he can deposit the certificate at the Registry with directions for its return to him[12].

The lien arises by virtue of the deposit without the necessity to execute a memorandum. Where, as is frequently the case, the deposit is accompanied by a memorandum of deposit, it is the memorandum, not the deposit, that creates the equitable charge[13]. In *Re White Rose Cottage*[14] the Court of Appeal held that a notice of deposit under r. 239 is permissible, even though the deposit itself does not constitute the security because there is an accompanying memorandum. They did, however, suggest that the correct course in his situation was to apply for entry of notice of the memorandum under s. 49 (1) (c)[15], or (per Lord Denning MR[16]) for a caution under s. 54.

(c) Withdrawal of notice
The notice may be withdrawn on a written request signed personally by the person entitled to the lien or his successor in title[17]. In the case of a limited company, the signature of a responsible official (e.g. a director) is accepted. In all cases the land certificate must accompany the written request.

(d) Notice of intended deposit
Where a purchaser not yet registered as proprietor borrows money on this form of security, he may give to the Registrar notice of intended deposit. The notice is signed by the intending proprietor indicating the person with whom the deposit is to be made and to whom the land certificate should be sent after entry of the notice[18]. In practice the lender's solicitor will attend completion of the purchase, collect the necessary documents and forward to the Registry the application for registration together with the notice signed by the purchaser. A notice of intended deposit operates in the same way as a notice of deposit and is similarly withdrawn.

4.   Generally

A mortgage may be protected by means of a caution, entry of which does not require production of the land certificate. Alternatively, but only if the land

10   LRR 1925, r. 239. The notice is usually given on Form 85A, which is submitted in duplicate. The Registrar returns the copy by way of acknowledgment. The form printed on the reverse side can be used to request withdrawal of the notice.
11   Under LRA 1926, s. 54. For cautions generally see pp. 69–71, ante.
12   LRR 1925, r. 244.
13   *Re White Rose Cottage* [1965] Ch 940 at 955, [1965] 1 All ER 11 at 18, CA, per Harman LJ.
14   [1965] Ch 940, [1965] 1 All ER 11, CA.
15   Per Lord Denning MR, at 949 and 14; per Harman LJ, at 955 and 18. Sed quaere. Section 49 (1) (c) permits entry of a notice in respect of land charges, but according to the better view, a memorandum of charge secured by a deposit of documents is not capable of registration as a land charge under the LCA 1972; see p. 386, ante.
16   At 949–50 and 14, respectively.
17   LRR 1925, r. 246. See note 10, ante.
18   LRR 1925, rr. 241, 242. This procedure also applies to an intended deposit on first registration.

certificate is lodged at the Registry, entry of a notice under s. 49 may be sought, provided the mortgage is effected by a written memorandum unaccompanied by any deposit of the land certificate with the mortgagee. If there is a deposit, the special procedure of r. 239 may be used, or an ordinary caution under s. 54 but not, it seems, entry of a notice[19].

D   Settlements and trusts for sale

These have already been considered in Chapter 12 and no further comment is necessary.

E   Rentcharges[20]

1.   The need to register

Rentcharges are included in the definition of 'land' for the purposes of the Act. The title to a rentcharge can therefore be registered in its own right, independently of the land out of which it issues, provided it is capable of subsisting as a legal interest[1]. It is necessary to distinguish between a rentcharge created out of unregistered land and one reserved out of land already registered. In the first case, registration of the rentcharge is never compulsory even where the land is in a compulsory area and the rentcharge is created as part of a transaction resulting in first registration of the title of the land[2]. Registration is voluntary and nothing in the Land Registration Act 1966 prohibits the voluntary application for registration of a rentcharge affecting land in a compulsory area. In the second case the creation of a rentcharge constitutes a disposition of registered land and it must be completed by registration if the rentcharge owner is to acquire a legal interest[3].

2.   Application for substantive registration

The procedure varies according to whether the land out of which the rent issues is unregistered or registered.

(a) Unregistered land
If registration is desired, an application must be made, using the official form appropriate to the circumstances of the case[4]. A separate application is necessary even though the rentcharge is granted as part of the consideration for a conveyance of land which itself results in an application by the purchaser (the grantor of the rentcharge) for first (i.e. compulsory) registration of the land. These documents must be lodged with the application — (1) the deed creating

19 See note 15, p. 468, ante. LRA 1925, s. 106 (2) as amended by Administration of Justice Act 1977, s. 26 (1).
20 See Ruoff, *Rentcharges in Registered Conveyancing*, for a full treatment of this topic. See also Practice Leaflet No. 9 (First Registration of the Title to Rentcharges), and R & R, Chap. 28.
 1 LRA 1925, ss. 2 (1), 3 (viii), (ix).
 2 LRA 1925, s. 120 (1) proviso. Section 123 (1) does not apply to the grant of a rentcharge. Only an 'estate rentcharge' within the Rentcharges Act 1977 can now be created.
 3 LRA 1925, ss. 18 (1) (b), (d), 19 (2).
 4 Form 1F should be used when registration is sought by an individual (other than a company) immediately after the grant or sale of the rentcharge.

the rentcharge (this will be the duplicate conveyance where the rentcharge is created on a sale of the land), (2) a certified copy, (3) an examined abstract covering the period of investigation of title, (4) any other original deeds[5] and documents relating to the rentcharge title and (5) the invariable list in triplicate of documents delivered. In addition satisfactory evidence of the identity of the burdened land must be supplied, but this is usually provided by the plan drawn on the rentcharge deed or simply the address of the property if in a built-up area.

(i) *Title granted.* Of the four classes of title, three apply to a rentcharge: absolute, qualified and possessory. Registration with these titles has the same effect as first registration of a freehold estate in land, subject to modifications necessary to account for the differences in the natures of the interests. To receive an absolute title, the applicant should, in the case of a newly created rentcharge, deduce title to the land out of which it issues for at least fifteen years commencing with a good root of title. On an application for registration after the sale of an existing rentcharge, the grantor's title to make the grant, together with a fifteen years' title to the rentcharge must be deduced[6]. Possessory and qualified rentcharge title are rarely encountered[7].

(ii) *Certificate of title.* On completion of the registration the rentowner receives a rentcharge certificate, with its own number. The entry in the property register appears as follows:

> PERPETUAL YEARLY RENTCHARGE of £15 payable half yearly on 25 March and 29 September created by a Conveyance dated 16 January 1972 and made between (1) AB (2) CD. The registered rentcharge is charged upon and issues out of the FREEHOLD land shown and edged with red on the plan of the above title filed at the Registry known as . . .

The deed of creation becomes an essential part of the register of title by virtue of the reference to it in the property register. Any power of absolute re-entry granted by the deed in cases of default automatically vests in the registered owner without express mention on his title[8]. The rentcharge deed is issued with the certificate, and the copy is filed in the Registry.

Where the rentcharge is a second rentcharge, i.e. where the land out of which it issues is, together with other land, subject to a previously created (or overriding) rentcharge, the property register contains short particulars of the overriding rent and of any indemnities given against payment of it.

(b) Registered land

Subject to any contrary entry in the register, a registered properietor may grant a rentcharge in possession in any form which sufficiently refers to the registered land which is charged; he may also transfer the land (or part of it) subject to the reservation there out of a rentcharge[9]. Some differences in the procedure for registration must be noted, according to whether the rentcharge is created (i)

---

5   There will, of course, be deeds relating to the devolution of the rentcharge, where registration is sought after successive sales of the rent.
6   R & R, 200. See also pp. 347–348, ante.
7   See further Ruoff, op. cit., pp. 8–11.
8   See LRA 1925, s. 5; LRR 1925, r. 251. An absolute right of re-entry annexed to a legal rentcharge is itself a legal interest: LPA 1925, s. 1 (2) (e).
9   LRA 1925, s. 18 (1) (b), (d), (2).

on a transfer of the registered land or (ii) by a deed of grant[10]. In either case the application should be submitted within the period of protection afforded by the official certificate of search.

(i) *Creation on transfer.* The application for registration should strictly be made by the owner of the newly created rentcharge; in practice it is more convenient for the transferee to do so when he applies to be registered as proprietor of the land. An application[11] in printed Form A4 (or A5) should be submitted together with the land certificate, the transfer and two certified copies (one for binding in the rentcharge certificate and the other in the land certificate). The transferee is registered as proprietor of the land in the normal way, while the rent is automatically noted in the charges register as an incumbrance. The transferor is registered as the proprietor of the rentcharge under a separate title and issued with a rentcharge certificate[12]. The rentcharge thereupon takes effect as a legal interest. If the land itself is registered with an absolute title, the rentowner's title will be registered as absolute. Only a qualified title will be granted if the land is registered with less than an absolute title[13].

The entry in the transferee's charges register is in the following form:

C. CHARGES REGISTER TITLE NUMBER LT 1234	
1.	3 May 1971 — The land is subject to a perpetual yearly rentcharge of £12 created by a Transfer dated 19 April 1971 by AB to CD.	Title to rentcharge registered under LT 1235. Copy transfer in certificate.

Express mention of the covenants, powers and remedies for the protection and recovery of the rentcharge need not be made. The reference to the transfer brings them on to the register and gives notice of their existence to subsequent purchasers.

(ii) *Creation on grant.* Here the creation is unconnected with any transfer of the land. The grantee must submit his own application for first registration (usually Form 1F, or 1H in the case of a corporation), together with the deed of grant, and two certified copies. In addition s. 64 (1) (a) of the Act requires production of the land certificate at the Registry (if outstanding). Normally the grantee will rank as a purchaser for the purposes of the Act[14]; as such, and unlike a lessee on the grant of a registrable lease, he can call upon the grantor to

10 The difference between these two situations is as follows. In (i) V sells the land to P and reserves in his own favour the rentcharge as part (or the whole) of the consideration for the transfer; in (ii) V grants to P a rentcharge out of the land which V still owns.
11 This should give clear directions for the issue of the new rentcharge certificate to the rentowner.
12 LRR 1925, rr. 107 (2), 108.
13 Ruoff, op. cit., p. 62.
14 LRA 1925, s. 3 (xxi).

produce his land certificate for the completion of the registration[15]. Once registered, the rentcharge takes effect as a legal rentcharge and it is noted as an incumbrance against the grantor's title[16]. If the grantee does not apply for registration of the rentcharge, it operates only in equity. In constitutes a minor interest and requires protection by entry of a notice or caution.

3. Transfer of rentcharges

There appears to be no express provision empowering the rentowner to deal with his registered rentcharge, and in fact none is necessary, seeing that the statutory definition of 'land' embraces rentcharges and the proprietor can transfer the land in the prescribed manner. The transfer must be completed by registration which operates to vest the legal title (retrospectively) in the transferee. If the transfer assigns the benefit of the covenant to pay the rent[17], no note of this assignment is made on the register, unless specifically requested by the transferee, because registration automatically vests in him 'all rights, privileges and appurtenances'[18].

F   Easements[19]

The various provisions in the Land Registration Act 1925, and the Rules relating to easements are not entirely consistent and free from ambiguity. It is essential to distinguish between (i) easements existing at the time of first registration, and (ii) easements created afterwards by or in favour of a registered proprietor. In both cases two plots of land are inevitably involved, but it does not follow that the titles to both are registered, which adds to the difficulties.

1.   Easements existing at first registration

(a) Adverse easements
Here we are considering easements which adversely affect the *servient* land. Where at the time of first registration any easement created by an instrument and appearing on the title adversely affects the land, the Registrar must enter a note thereof on the register[20]. This is a mandatory requirement[1], of somewhat limited application. It does not extend to easements arising by virtue of the Law of Property Act 1925, s. 62, nor to prescriptive easements. The omission of

---

15   LRA 1925, s. 110 (6).
16   Ruoff, op. cit., p. 60, maintains that notation is necessary for the creation of a legal
      rentcharge; but see p. 458, ante.
17   See p. 348, ante.
18   LRA 1925, s. 20 (1). Is the benefit of a positive covenant a 'right, privilege or
      appurtenance' within the meaning of sub-s. (1), as amplified by r. 251, which refers to
      rights, etc., capable of passing under the LPA 1925, s. 62? Apart from s. 20 (1) the
      assignment in the transfer would be effective to vest the benefit in the transferee, at least in
      equity.
19   The Law Commission is currently looking at the whole question of appurtenant rights
      (including easements and covenants); see Published Working Paper No. 36. Any changes
      in the substantive law will undoubtedly entail changes in the present law governing the
      enforceability and mode of protection of easements and covenants affecting registered
      land. Covenants are considered in the next section.
20   LRA 1925, s. 70 (2).
1   *Re Dances Way, West Town, Hayling Island* [1962] Ch 490, at 510, [1962] 2 All ER 42 at
      51, CA, per Diplock LJ. Section 70 (2) is not qualified by r. 41 which gives a discretionary
      power to enter easements not appearing on the title: per Diplock LJ.

such easements from the register of the servient title will not normally prejudice
the dominant owner; if they exist as legal easements under the general law, they
constitute overriding interests and registration of the servient owner as proprietor takes effect subject to overriding interests[2]. The Registrar is empowered to
enter notice of the burden of these easements if admitted or proved to his satisfaction, but an easement not created by an instrument cannot be noted against
the title to the servient land if the proprietor shows sufficient cause to the
contrary, after notice served on him[3].

The entry must, so far as practicable and convenient, be made either by
reference to the instrument of creation or by setting out an extract therefrom[4].
Once noted against the servient title, the easement ceases to be an overriding
interest. The Registrar may cancel the entry of any easement on the application
of the servient proprietor, if it appears it was wrongly made[5].

(b) Appurtenant easements

First registration with an absolute title vests in the proprietor all easements,
rights, privileges and appurtenances appertaining or reputed to appertain to
the land without these being expressly mentioned on his register of title[6]. The
benefit of an easement may be entered as appurtenant to the registered estate,
if capable of subsisting as a legal easement[7]. It is entered in the property register
as part of the description of the land. Registration guarantees its validity and
confers on the proprietor a title to the easement of the same kind as the title to
the dominant land.

An application by the dominant owner for entry of an appurtenant easement
is entirely optional, even where the servient land is unregistered, and a
purchaser of registered land with appurtenant, but unregistered, easements
cannot compel the vendor under s. 110 (5) of the Act to procure registration of
himself as proprietor of those easements[8].

2.   Easement created after first registration

The creation of an easement by a registered proprietor constitutes a disposition
of the registered land and must be completed by registration in the same way as
a transfer of corporeal land[9], if the grantee is to have a legal easement. What is
meant by 'completed by registration' in this context is not certain. Clearly it
does not mean substantive registration as this is not possible with easements.
Though the wording of the relevant proviso is ambiguous, registration is commonly thought to entail the entry of notice against the title of the servient land
and (if the dominant land is also registered) registration of the easement as
appurtenant to the dominant land[10]. An implied easement arising under s. 62
of the Law of Property Act 1925, is not regarded as an easement created by a
registered disposition[11].

2   LRA 1925, s. 5.
3   LRA 1925, s. 70 (3); LRR 1925, rr. 41, 197. The entry of trivial rights is not necessary:
r. 199, e.g. rights of way over roads found to be adopted on first registration.
4   LRR 1925, r. 41 (2).
5   *Re Dances Way, West Town, Hayling Island* [1962] Ch 490, [1962] 2 All ER 42, CA.
6   LRA 1925, ss. 5, 72, p. 24, ante.
7   LRR 1925, r. 257; see also rr. 251−56.
8   *Re Evans's Contract, Evans v Deed* [1970] 1 All ER 1236. For s. 110 (5), see p. 452, ante.
9   See LRA 1925, ss. 18 (1) (c), 19 (2), 21 (1) (b), 22 (2).
10 LRA 1925, s. 19 (2), proviso (c). See R & R, 98, 345; 17 Ency F & P, 199. Cf. Potter, 273;
3 K & E, 58.
11 3 K & E, 58.

(i) *Servient title registered.* Where the easement is created on a transfer of part of the land within a registered title, the Registrar makes the relevant entries as a matter of course. Where a proprietor creates an easement by deed of grant independently of any transfer of the land, the grantee (whether or not his own land is registered) must apply for notice to be entered against the servient title. He must therefore ensure that the servient owner lodges the land certificate at the Registry to enable the required entry to be made[12]. Entry of the notice forms an integral part of the registration process. The absence of this notice prevents the acquisition of any legal easement and operates to defeat the easement on a subsequent registered transfer for value of the servient land[13]. If the grantee's title is also registered, it seems that he must register the easement as appurtenant to his own title.

(ii) *Only dominant title registered.* Where only the dominant land is registered, the grantee may apply to have the easement entered as appurtenant to his title, and should do so if he wishes its validity to be guaranteed. It will be necessary to deduce to the Registrar the title to the unregistered servient land. Should there be doubts as to the grantor's title, a note is entered on the grantee's register of title to the effect that the deed purported to grant the right. However application for entry of an appurtenant easement is not obligatory. As the servient land is not registered, the grant of the easement does not constitute a disposition by a registered proprietor so that the necessity for 'completion by registration' does not arise. When the servient land is subsequently registered, the easement will automatically be registered against the servient title as part of the registration process[14].

3.   Easements created otherwise than by express grant

(a) Implied easements

Easements may be acquired on registration under the rule in *Wheeldon v Burrows*[15], or by virtue of s. 62 of the Law of Property Act 1925, in the same way as if the land were not registered[16]. There is no need to note these against the servient title, and they take effect as overriding interests[17]. They may be noted as appurtenant to the dominant title, on an application by the owner stating the nature of the right and furnishing evidence of its existence, but not until the Registrar has given notice to the proprietor of the servient land. If the Registrar is satisfied as to the existence of the right he enters notice of it as a burden on the register of the servient land[18].

(b) Prescription

The rules somewhat obscurely provide that an easement acquired by prescription[19], capable of taking effect at law, 'shall take effect at law also' and if it

12   Where he ranks as a purchaser (see s. 3 (xxi) he can compel production of the land certificate (if outstanding) under s. 110 (6)).
13   LRA 1925, s. 20 (1). Being a mere equitable easement, it cannot rank as an overriding interest under s. 70 (1) (a), p. 47, ante.
14   LRA 1925, s. 70 (2), p. 472, ante.
15   (1879) 4 QBD 494, CA.
16   LRA 1925, s. 20 (1). The general words implied in conveyances under the LPA 1925, apply to dispositions of a registered estate: LRA 1925, s. 19 (3).
17   LRR 1925, r. 258.
18   LRR 1925, rr. 252, 253; R & R, 219. Once entered on the register these easements cease to be overriding: see LRA 1925, s. 3 (xvi).
19   It will be recalled that a right claimed under the Prescription Act 1832, is inchoate till litigated; see M & W, 851.

is an overriding interest, the Registrar may enter notice of it against the servient title[20]. He can himself determine the validity or otherwise of the claim, but he must, before entering notice on the register, notify the servient owner who can show cause why it should not be made. A prescriptive easement may be registered as part of the description of the dominant land. This operates to guarantee its validity; consequently, unless the court has previously determined the matter, the Registrar will only make the entry if satisfied of its acquisition.

4. Equitable easements

An equitable easement may arise through lack of form (i.e. absence of a grant under seal), because it is not equivalent to a fee simple or term of years absolute (e.g. a right of way granted over a road until adoption by the highway authority), or because, being granted by a registered proprietor, the disposition is not completed by registration. They are not overriding interests, and consequently require protection on the register to be enforceable against later purchasers of the servient land. Equitable easements created by an instrument are automatically noted against the servient title on first registration. In other cases notice may be entered[1] on production of the land certificate of the servient title; if the proprietor does not concur only a caution can be entered.

G   Covenants

1. Positive covenants

As a general rule only the covenantor and his estate can be rendered liable for breach of positive covenants. Consequently the land registration system does not require that their existence should be revealed on the register[2]. To assist practitioners in their task of deciding upon the necessity for indemnity covenants, the Registrar has, as a special concession, permitted a limited reference to these covenants on the register[3]. In the case of positive covenants (including express covenants of indemnity) *created after* first registration, the following note is made in the proprietorship register:

> ' NOTE: The transfer to the proprietor contains a purchaser's personal covenant (copy of covenant in land certificate).'

The covenants themselves are set out verbatim on a separate sheet entitled 'Personal Covenants'. This is sewn into the land certificate but does not form part of the register of title. No reference is made in the register of the existence of positive covenants created prior to first registration[4].

---

20 LRR 1925, r. 250 (2), referring to s. 70 (3), p. 473, ante.
 1 Under the LRA 1925, s. 49 (1) (c).
 2 See note 19, p. 472, ante.
 3 Registered Land Practice Note 21; R & R, 313–315. Since transfers are retained in the Registry, it is impossible to tell whether any previous transfer contained an indemnity covenant.
 4 An exception is in the case of a rentcharge deed which creates both positive and negative covenants. Usually the whole deed is issued in the land certificate. The presence of the right of re-entry can also make the covenants indirectly enforceable.

2.   Restrictive covenants

(a) First registration

All restrictive covenants (other than those between lessor and lessee) appearing to the Registrar to be existing at the time of first registration are noted in the charges register of the new title. The covenants are either set out in a schedule attached to the register, or a copy of the deed creating them is bound up in the certificate[5]. In some circumstances the Registrar may feel that the applicant has been unable to disclose all possible restrictions, e.g. on a purchase of land from a squatter or where the deeds have been lost or destroyed. To minimise the risk of an indemnity becoming payable under the Act, the Registrar places a 'protective' entry on the title to the effect that the land is subject to such restrictive covenants as may have been imposed thereon before a specified date, so far as they are subsisting and capable of being enforced[6].

One point is often overlooked by solicitors when making an application for first registration. The Registrar can be requested to omit from the register any restrictive covenant that is void for non-registration as a land charge. This request must be supported by an official certificate of search against the correct name of the covenantor, which does not disclose the registration of the restriction as a land charge. However entry of a previously avoided covenant does not revive it, as the next paragraph will show.

(i) *Effect of notice.* Entry of the notice fixes the proprietor and those deriving title under him with notice of the covenant as an incumbrance on the land, but only if and so far as it is otherwise valid[7]. Entry of a notice in no way guarantees or establishes the enforceability of the covenant; this question must be determined by general principles of land law. Thus in one case a positive covenant was noted on the register; it was held that the entry did not make it enforceable against a purchaser from the covenantor who had omitted to take an indemnity covenant from the purchaser[8]. A lessee is deemed to have notice of restrictive covenants entered against the freehold title, even though he has no right, apart from contract, to investigate the superior title[9].

(ii) *Registration under Land Charges Act 1972.* Prior to the passing of the Land Registration and Land Charges Act 1971, it was considered necessary to register as land charges restrictive covenants created by a conveyance leading to compulsory first registration of title, notwithstanding that the covenants would be entered on the purchaser's register of title as part of the registration process. Failure to register them as land charges would, it was felt, avoid the covenants against the purchaser's mortgagee. Section 9 of that Act relieved practitioners of this minor irritant by excluding from the operation of the Land Charges Act 1925[10], all land charges (not merely restrictive covenants) created by instruments caught by the provisions for compulsory registration of title and

5   See further Registered Land Practice Note 31.
6   See R & R, 209–10. A vendor should deal with this by way of a special condition in the contract; see *Faruqi v English Real Estates Ltd* [1979] 1 WLR 963.
7   LRA 1925, ss. 50 (2), 52 (1).
8   *Cator v Newton and Bates* [1940] 1 KB 415, [1939] 4 All ER 457, CA; *Willie v St. John* [1910] 1 Ch 325.
9   *White v Bijou Mansions Ltd* [1937] Ch 610, [1937] 3 All ER 269; affd. [1938] Ch 351, [1938] 1 All ER 846, CA, p. 357, ante.
10 Section 9 added a new section, s. 23A, to the LCA 1925; see now the LCA 1972, s. 14 (3), p. 392, ante.

affecting the land to be registered. Registration of the covenants as land charges is, therefore, now unnecessary. This provision only applied to instruments executed on or after 27 July 1971[11], consequently in relation to covenants created before this date a failure to register might still be material if the mortgagee seeks to dispose of the property free from the covenants.

(b) Covenants created on subsequent dealing

A registered proprietor is statutorily empowered[12] to impose restrictive covenants binding upon registered land, either in a transfer of the land or by a separate deed of covenant. On a transfer of part, the Registrar automatically makes the appropriate entry in the covenantor's charges register whether the parties expressly apply for it or not, even in cases where the covenants are imposed on the vendor's retained land. Covenants created by a separate deed of covenant require production of the land certificate at the Registry before notice can be entered. There appears to be no express prohibition preventing a covenantee unable to secure production of the certificate from lodging a caution against dealings.

3. Entry of the benefit of covenants

The provisions in the Act and the Rules relating to the benefit of restrictive covenants are most unsatisfactory and the practice at the Registry tends to be unhelpful. It is apparently not possible[13], save in very exceptional cases, to state on the register that land has the benefit of restrictive covenants, the reason being that they may not always remain enforceable. Yet surely the test ought to be whether they are enforceable at the time of application. There would seem to be many more cases than the Registry is prepared to admit, where a proprietor can readily establish that his land is benefited, e.g. on a transfer of part where covenants are imposed for the benefit of the vendor's retained land. In such a case a note of the benefit should be made in the vendor's property register. Indeed s. 40 (3) provides that entries *shall be made* on the register of all obligations acquired by the proprietor for the benefit of the registered estate[14].

For similar reasons the Registry also refuses to make any entry that a transfer assigns the benefit of existing covenants, a practice which would also seem to be unwarranted by the Act. The question whether the benefit of covenants not annexed to the land has passed to a successor of the covenantee can be of considerable importance. The fact that the transfer assigning the benefit is retained in the Registry should be adequate justification for noting that the transfer purported to assign them to the proprietor. This information is recorded on the transfer of a rentcharge[15] and the same procedure should, it is

11 The date when s. 9 came into operation.
12 LRA 1925, s. 40.
13 R & R, 347–348, 717–718. Consider whether this can be justified now following *Federated Homes Ltd v Mill Lodge Properties Ltd* [1980] 1 All ER 371, CA.
14 Cf. R & R, 718 where it is stated that there is nothing in the Act or Rules authorising the Registrar to make any entry of the benefit of restrictive covenants. This is plainly inconsistent with s. 40 (3) and r. 3 (2) (c) which provides for the entry in the property register of such notes as have to be entered relating to inter alia covenants for the benefit of the land. Neither of these provisions is even considered by R & R in relation to the problem under discussion. The argument in Brickdale, 328, that r. 3 (2) does not authorise the entry of equitable interests because the rule applies only to legal rights within r. 252 appears unsound.
15 If specifically requested by the transferee; see p. 472, ante.

submitted, be adopted in relation to the transfer of the benefit of other covenants, whether negative or positive (such as an option in gross). At the most the entry would only provide notice. There could be no claim for an indemnity, should it be that the proprietor was unable to enforce the covenants since, unlike easements, covenants cannot be registered as appurtenant to the 'dominant' land. In relation to matters which might adversely affect a registered estate, the Registry is always anxious to ensure that the register conveys as much information as a perusal of title deeds would reveal. It is unfortunate that a similar policy is not adopted for appurtenant rights.

4.   Release and discharge

Any release or modification of restrictive covenants should be noted on the register[16]. Where the covenant is discharged or modified by an order under the Law of Property Act 1925, s. 84, or the court refuses to grant an injunction to enforce the same, the entry is either cancelled, or reference is made to the order and a copy is filed at the Registry[17].

H   Transmissions of registered land

The title to registered land may alter consequent upon some event other than a registered disposition. This is known as a transmission, an expression nowhere defined in the Act or Rules. A transmission can occur in three situations:

(1)   on death, by registration of a personal representative or beneficiary;
(2)   on bankruptcy, by registration of the official receiver or trustee in bankruptcy;
(3)   on liquidation of a company, by registering the resolution or order appointing the liquidator.

These situations have already been discussed in earlier parts of this book[18], and nothing further need be added here, save to mention that in each case the land certificate must be produced at the Registry before the transmission can be registered[19].

16   LRR 1925, r. 212.
17   LRA 1925, s. 50 (3).
18   Pages 271–272, and 273, ante (bankruptcy and liquidation), pp. 358–359 (death).
19   LRA 1925, s. 64 (1) (b).

Part Five

Conveyancing documents

Chapter 17

Drafting and construction of deeds generally

A Forms of conveyance past and present

Section 51 (1) of the Law of Property Act 1925, enacts that:

 ' All lands and all interests therein lie in grant and are incapable of being conveyed by livery or livery of seisin, or by feoffment, or by bargain and sale and a conveyance of an interest in land may operate to pass the possession or right to possession thereof, without actual entry, but subject to all prior rights thereto.'

This provision conceals a wealth of legal history pertaining to the mode of land transfer over the centuries and a brief survey of the different forms of conveyance may not be amiss though rarely will the average practitioner ever encounter these ancient forms.

At common law the 'most ancient method of conveyance, the most solemn and public'[1] was the *feoffment with livery of seisin*. Originally a feoffment took the form of a public and oral delivery by the grantor (the feoffor) to the grantee (the feoffee) of actual seisin. This entailed the entry on the land by both parties (or their attorneys) and a symbolic handing to the feoffee of some twig, or clod of earth, accompanied by suitable words explaining the purpose of the ceremony. Subsequently it became the practice to evidence the transaction in writing, called a charter of feoffment. A written document was made essential by the Statute of Frauds 1677, but it was not until the Real Property Act 1845, that a deed was required. In addition s. 2 of this Act also enabled a conveyance of land to be effected by a *deed of grant* without livery. Hitherto a deed of grant had been the appropriate mode of transfer for incorporeal rights only, such as rents, reversions, advowsons. These were said to lie in grant; not being the object of the senses, they could not lie in livery.

The disadvantages of the ancient mode of transfer by livery of seisin, particularly the publicity and the need for the parties' presence on or near the land, were such that long before 1845 other forms of land transfer had been devised and were in operation. One such method recognised by the common law was the *lease and release*. X leased land to Y for one year; no feoffment was required because the lease created mere personal property. The following day X released his reversion to Y by a deed of release, thus vesting the freehold estate in Y without any livery of seisin. The drawback to this simple device was the need for Y's actual entry on the land before the release took effect, for the

---

1   2 *Blackstone's Commentaries*, 310.

release was only operative in favour of a lessee who had an actual term of years and at common law he had no estate prior to entry, only an interesse termini[2].

After the passing of the Statute of Uses 1535, this particular disadvantage could be avoided by creating a term by means of an assurance taking effect by virtue of the Statute. X bargained and sold (i.e. contracted to sell) land to Y for one year. In equity this operated to create a use in Y's favour, which the Statute executed, giving Y a legal term. Actual entry was unnecessary for the Statute enacted that the cestui que use should be deemed 'in lawful possession' for the equivalent legal estate. Having a legal term, the release by X of his reversion became immediately effective without Y's entry[3]. This mode of transfer became the classical form of assurance[4] of land until it was rendered virtually obsolete by the Real Property Act 1845, which, as we have seen, enabled land to be conveyed by a simple grant.

Section 51 (1) of the Law of Property Act 1925, abolishes these ancient forms of conveyance. Now all land lies in grant only. Section 52 (1) of the same Act further provides that, save for certain statutory exceptions, all conveyances of land or of any interest therein are void for the purpose of conveyancing or creating a legal estate unless made by deed. The requirements for a valid deed have been fully considered in Chapter 15. As we have already noticed[5], a transfer of registered land does not vest in the transferee any legal title, which only passes on registration.

Cases where a deed is not required

Exceptionally a legal estate may pass or be created without any deed and s. 52 (2) of the Act provides for seven such occasions which must briefly be considered.

(a) Assents by personal representatives
This exception has previously been encountered[6] and needs no further comment.

(b) Certain disclaimers
The most important example within this group occurs in the Bankruptcy Act 1914, s. 54, which enables a trustee in bankruptcy to disclaim onerous property forming part of the bankrupt's estate, e.g. land burdened with onerous covenants. The disclaimer which must be in writing operates to determine the rights and liabilities of the bankrupt in respect of the property, but not so as to affect

2   This constituted a legal proprietary interest in the land (but not an estate), conferring a right to take possession. It was assignable but did not entitle the lessee to sue on a covenant for quiet enjoyment or for damages for trespass: *Wallis v Hands* [1893] 2 Ch 75. The doctrine was abolished by the LPA 1925, s. 149 (1).
3   In equity an oral bargain and sale of freehold land created a use in favour of the purchaser, which vested the legal estate in him by virtue of the Statute of Uses. It was immediately appreciated that this Statute, if left unamended, would have facilitated oral and secret transfers of land. In consequence the Statute of Enrolments 1535, was passed which enacted that no bargain and sale of *freehold* land was effectual unless made by deed and duly enrolled within six months. The bargain and sale enrolled never became a popular mode of transfer; the deed was open to inspection and it was not possible to declare uses on it. The Statute of Enrolments did not apply to leases, hence the popularity of the lease and release.
4   M & W, 166.
5   Page 491, ante.
6   Page 332, ante.

the position of third persons[7]. The trustee cannot generally disclaim a lease without leave of the court[8].

(c) Implied surrenders

A surrender occurs when the owner of a smaller estate or interest in land yields up his interest to the person entitled to the immediate estate in remainder or in reversion, as where a tenant surrenders his lease to the landlord prior to the time of its determination. The effect of this surrender is to pass to the landlord the tenant's estate which thereupon merges with the freehold reversion. An express surrender must be by deed but a surrender by operation of law, or implied surrender as it is frequently termed, takes effect without any deed. Delivery of possession by the tenant which is accepted by the landlord effects an implied surrender[9]; so does the tenant's acceptance of a new lease to commence during the currency of an existing lease.

(d) Short term leases

By virtue of s. 54 (2) of the Act a legal lease may be created by parol, or by writing not under seal, provided it takes effect in possession for a term not exceeding three years at the best rent reasonably obtainable without taking a fine. This provision includes periodic tenancies, notwithstanding that they may endure for more than three years[10], but not a lease for fourteen years determinable by the tenant at the end of any year[11]. The assignment of a lease created informally must, however, be by deed to vest the legal estate in the assignee.

(e) Receipts not required by law to be under seal

This refers to the statutory receipt endorsed on a mortgage under s. 115 of the Law of Property Act 1925, which is effective to discharge the mortgage and extinguish the mortgagee's interest without any reconveyance or surrender.

(f) Court vesting orders

A vesting order made by the court for the purpose of conveyancing or creating a legal estate operates to vest that estate in the same manner as if it had been a conveyance executed by the estate owner[12].

(g) Conveyances taking effect by operation of law

Within this category come probates and letters of administration, and the appointment of a trustee in bankruptcy under the Bankruptcy Act 1914.

Reverters under the School Sites Act 1841

Such reverters do not pass the legal estate automatically[13] when the site ceases to be used for the purpose for which it was conveyed.

---

7   See e.g. *Re Bastable, ex p. The Trustee* [1901] 2 KB 518, CA, p. 271, ante. See further in relation to bankruptcy, pp. 48–49, and 269–273, ante.
8   Bankruptcy Act 1914, s. 54 (3); see *Metroplis Estates Co Ltd v Wilde* [1940] 2 KB 536, [1940] 3 All ER 522, CA.
9   *Dodd v Acklom* (1843) 6 Man & G 672 (return of keys).
10   *Hammond v Farrow* [1940] 2 KB 332 (yearly tenancy).
11   *Kushner v Law Society* [1952] 1 KB 264, [1952] 1 All ER 404.
12   LPA 1925, s. 9 (1). For an example of the court's power to make a vesting order, see ibid., s. 30 (refusal of trustees for sale to exercise duties).
13   *Re Clayton's Deed Poll* [1980] Ch 99, [1979] 2 All ER 1133.

B   Drafting the conveyance

1.   Responsibility for drafting

In the main it is the purchaser's responsibility to prepare at his own expense the conveyance for execution by the necessary parties. A draft is first prepared in duplicate and submitted, usually at the same time as the requisitions on title, to the vendor's solicitor for approval. When the draft has been agreed and any amendments made by the vendor's solicitor accepted, it is engrossed and after execution by the purchaser (where necessary) is tendered to the vendor for his execution. The time for delivery of the draft and the engrossment are normally regulated by the contract[14], though the relevant time limits are frequently ignored. Although submission of the draft conveyance or the engrossment does not generally constitute an acceptance of the title[15], it is common practice to tender these documents without prejudice to any outstanding requisitions. Should the vendor require the execution of a duplicate conveyance (e.g. because the conveyance imposes restrictive covenants for his benefit or reserves easements in his favour) he must expressly stipulate for this in the contract[16], failing which he cannot require the purchaser to prepare a duplicate at his own expense. Nor can he cast on the purchaser the costs of procuring the concurrence and execution of other parties, e.g. mortgagees, whose concurrence is necessary to vest a good title in the purchaser[17].

It is the general practice on the grant of a lease for the lease to be drafted by the lessor's solicitor; the lessor retains the freehold reversion in the property and it is for him to indicate what he is willing to grant and upon what terms. On the creation of a mortgage the mortgage deed is drafted and engrossed by the mortgagee's solicitor, but at the mortgagor's expense.

2.   Form of deed

The nature and form of the conveyance are for the purchaser, or rather his solicitor, to decide, and this is very much a matter of the draftsman's individual preference. The deed should give effect to the contract and it is clearly advisable to have that document, the answers to preliminary inquiries (for these might amplify the contract) and the abstract of title before him when drafting the deed. The draftsman should preferably be the person who has investigated the title. The aim should always be to frame a document which will in the future form a good root of title. The fact that the draft is approved on behalf of the vendor must not be used as an excuse for sloppy draftsmanship. The purchaser's solicitor cannot expect the vendor's solicitor to perform his task for him; he must therefore see that the draft gives his client everything to which he is entitled.

The drafting of a conveyance relating to the average dwellinghouse presents no difficulties, though even here attention must always be paid to the description

---

14   NCS 19 (3); LSC 17 (1) (2), requiring delivery of the draft six and twelve working days respectively before completion and the engrossment within three and five working days of the return of the draft approved.

15   See p. 376, ante.

16   In these circumstances the execution of a duplicate is preferable to obtaining an acknowledgment from the purchaser for production of the conveyance which may not be effective under the LPA 1925, s. 64, since it is not given by a person who retains possession of documents; see p. 426, ante.

17   *Re Sander and Walford's Contract* (1900) 83 LT 316; see also the LPA 1925, s. 42 (2).

of the property. Drafting a lease or tenancy agreement, or a conveyance creating covenants, granting easements, or involving some complicated commercial transaction, may not be so straightforward. In every situation the draftsman must ensure that the document gives full effect to his client's rights, as governed by the contract, and in a way most beneficial to him, especially in relation to fiscal matters. In practice constant use is made of the many standard conveyancing precedents, though the very plethora of these may tend towards his undoing. Whenever a precedent is adopted, care must be exercised to ensure that all aspects of the transaction in question are provided for, otherwise the precedent must be suitably adapted[18]. At least one precedent book issues a warning of the dangers of using within the same draft bits from different collections of precedents[19].

3. Vendor's right to submit draft

Section 48 (1) of the Law of Property Act 1925, entitles a vendor to furnish a form of instrument from which the draft is to be prepared and to charge a reasonable fee therefor, provided the right has been reserved in the contract. Advantage is frequently taken of this power on the grant of a lease or underlease[20], on the creation of a rentcharge, or on the sale of land forming part of a housing estate. In these situations the contract usually provides that the conveyance or lease shall be in the form of the draft annexed to the contract. This puts the purchaser of freehold land at a disadvantage in that he is compelled to accept a form of conveyance before having had an opportunity to investigate the title, and he ought perhaps to reserve his right to object to any part of the form (such as references to incumbrances alleged to affect the property) which an examination of the title discloses as being improper or unnecessary. In addition his solicitor must check the proposed draft very carefully and make any objections to its form before exchange of contracts. Experience suggests that the document supplied is often drafted more with the developer in mind than the purchaser. In particular covenants may be couched in language too wide for the protection of the developer's legitimate interests, and provisions which may relate to the majority of plots on the estate may not be applicable to the purchaser's particular plot[1]. It is, alas, on the development of building estates that conveyancing practice may be seen at its worst. Not only are charges made for supplying plans and draft documents, often out of all proportion to the cost of their production, but many (though by no means all) developers' solicitors adopt a take-it-or-leave-it attitude without permitting any meaningful variations to their hallowed drafts or attempting to justify their form. Regrettably some practitioners, faced with this prevalent practice and pressed by clients who are not interested in legal niceties or trivia, bow to the inevitable and meekly accept the forms supplied. Neither attitude has anything to commend it, and such practices do nothing to enhance the conveyancer's reputation.

---

18 For an example of the dangerous use of precedents see *Re Leverhulme (No 2)* [1943] 2 All ER 274, and *Re Brocklehurst* [1978] Fam 14, [1978] 1 All ER 767, CA.

19 1 Prideaux's Precedents, 21. See generally pp. 11–22 on hints on drafting.

20 This is expressly provided for by NCS 19 (1).

1 For example clauses purporting to reserve rights in respect of overhanging eaves and protruding foundations will be irrelevant to a corner plot which is not overhung by any adjacent house.

4.   Approval of draft by vendor

Since the form of the conveyance is for the purchaser to determine, it is idle for the vendor to raise objections as to form save where it involves a matter of substance affecting him[2]. The draft should not be altered merely because the vendor's solicitor would have adopted a different form. The rule has sensibly been expressed as follows[3]: no alterations should be made except those necessary to correct clerical errors, to protect one's own client and to make the draft work. Basically the vendor's solicitor needs to ensure that the draft does not give the purchaser more, nor the vendor less, than his entitlement under the contract. Particular problems may arise when the purchaser seeks to convey the land by a description different from that given in the contract. These are considered in the following chapter[4]. Technically it is not the vendor's responsibility to alter the draft in favour of the purchaser where, for instance, it omits some matter contained in the contract for the purchaser's own benefit, for the vendor is entitled to assume that the purchaser has decided to rely on his contractual rights[5]. In reality the omission is more likely to be the result of an oversight, and it is worthwhile remembering that a failure to correct the position before completion may give rise to a subsequent claim against the vendor for rectification of the conveyance.

5.   Statutory forms of conveyance

Special forms of conveyance are authorised by enactments relating to the acquisition of land under compulsory powers[6] and by various other statutes[7]. The Law of Property Act 1925, provides specimen forms of conveyances and other instruments[8]. These are merely illustrative of the working of the Act and are not intended to be compulsory. On a transfer of registered land the use of the prescribed forms is mandatory[9], though necessary additions are permitted. Leases and charges of registered land commonly follow the form adopted in unregistered conveyancing.

C   Wording of conveyancing documents

Lawyers are conservative creatures and of all lawyers conveyancers tend to be the most conservative. Nowhere is this most displayed than in legal documents, often criticised as tautological and generally unintelligible to the lay public[10]. Lawyers are accused of being so wrapped up in the language of their profession that they have eschewed any kind of prose style that might commend itself to those outside the magic circle of the law. Unfortunately the man in the street is tempted to think that it is all part of a legal conspiracy to preserve the lawyer's monopoly. Yet the spread of compulsory registration of title and the increased

2   See *Cooper v Cartwright* (1860) John 679 at 685, per Page-Wood V-C.
3   1 Prideaux's Precedents, 21, adding that to pass a draft without alteration is not a sign of weakness, rather the reverse, which is salutary advice.
4   Page 506, post.
5   Subject to the doctrine of merger (see p. 444, ante) but in the situation under consideration this would not appear to be the vendor's concern.
6   Lands Clauses Consolidation Act 1845, s. 81, Sch. A, B.
7   E.g. the School Sites Act 1841, s. 10.
8   Section 206 (1), Sch. 5.
9   LRR 1925, rr. 98, 114; p. 451, ante.
10   See *Cresswell v Potter* [1978] 1 WLR 255 at 260, per Megarry J.

use of relatively simple forms has spurred some practitioners to abandon the traditional methods of draftmanship, and to prepare documents meaningful to those who execute them[11]. On the other hand there are many who feel that certainty cannot be sacrificed on the altar of simplicity, and at least one major book of conveyancing precedents has been published within the past decade which still adheres to the traditional methods and phraseology[12].

The draftsman is free to choose his own form and draft it according to his own particular tastes. If he adopts the modern idiom, he should make sure that his document gives full effect to the parties' intentions, and satisfy himself that his simplified version covers all eventualities likely to occur. Should he be of the old school of thought, he ought at least to consider whether many of his time-hallowed expressions are really necessary, such as: 'messuage or dwelling-house', 'delineated and described', 'covenants conditions and agreements', 'in the County of Leicester' (instead of 'Leicestershire'). The slavish adoption of a precedent form, even one of ancient lineage, without considering whether its language accords with modern conditions, cannot be recommended. Thus, whilst it may be important in a particular grant to indicate whether a right of way is to be vehicular, or on foot, or both[13], it is rather absurd today to grant a right of way 'with or without horses, carts, carriages'[14]. It would be a step in the right direction if figures were used instead of words when mentioning dates, and if some attempt were made to introduce punctuation[15]. The absence of punctuation can be as frustrating for the conveyancer as it is incomprehensible to his client. Thus if a deed states that the vendors of a recited conveyance were Henry James Martin Charles Arthur Vernon Bruce and William Thornton of the one part, it is impossible to tell without looking at the original deed the correct names of the individual vendors, or even how many there were. Indeed it has been fairly pointed out[16] that punctuation is resorted to in a disguised manner, for capital letters are frequently used to introduce new sentences without being preceded by full stops. Even for the practitioner who cannot see his way to reject the traditional form and language of yesterday, there is considerable room for improvement in the drafting of documents so as to make them more intelligible to his client.

D   Construction of deeds

Not only is the conveyancer required to draft deeds, he may also be called upon to interpret documents drafted by others. A brief introduction to the 'basic rules of construction' is therefore necessary[17]. Particular problems of construction relating to some specific matters are also considered in the following chapter[18].

11   See Parker, *Modern Conveyancing Precedents* (1964).
12   Hallett's *Conveyancing Precedents*. See also *Precedents for the Conveyancer* published in conjunction with the *Conveyancer and Property Lawyer*.
13   See further p. 520, post.
14   1 Prideaux's Precedents, 433, Form 6.
15   Punctuation is freely used in Prideaux's Precedents, but not in Hallett, nor in the Ency F & P.
16   Parker, op. cit., p. 7.
17   For a fuller understanding of this important topic, see *Norton on Deeds* (2nd edn); Odgers, *The Construction of Deeds and Statutes* (5th edn).
18   Pages 506–509, post (parcels clause); p. 520, post (easements).

1.   The intention of the parties

When construing a deed the aim is always to discover the intention of the parties as expressed in the document. The question to be asked is: 'What is the meaning of what the parties have said?' not 'What did the parties mean to say?'[19]. For the purposes of interpretation the parties' expressed meaning is equivalent to their intention[20] and the court will give effect to that meaning, rather than to their presumed intention, even though to do so may defeat their real intention or produce some consequence which they did not have in mind[1]. In arriving at the true meaning the deed must be construed as a whole. As was said in an ancient case, every part of a deed must be compared with the other and one entire sense made thereof[2]. Where the transaction between the parties is effected by two or more documents they should be construed together. In *Plumrose Ltd v Real and Leasehold Estates Investment Society Ltd*[3], two leases were read together where one was described as supplemental to the other in order to determine whether the supplementary lease incorporated a covenant for renewal.

2.   Ordinary meaning

In determining the meaning of the words used, the rule of construction, as enunciated by Lord Wensleydale in *Grey v Pearson*[4], is that the grammatical and ordinary sense of the words is to be adhered to unless that would lead to some absurdity, or some repugnance or inconsistency with the rest of the deed, in which case the grammatical and ordinary meaning may be modified so as to avoid that result. Prima facie the ordinary meaning of a word is that which the ordinary usage of society applies to it, what may be said to be the popular sense, but this meaning will be displaced if the context shows that the words were not intended to be used in their ordinary meaning. Thus a reservation of 'minerals' prima facie includes every substance which can be got from underneath the surface of the earth for profit, but when the word appears in a reservation of 'mines and minerals, sand, quarries of stone, brickearth and gravel pits', there is a clear indication that the draftsman was using 'minerals' in a special limited sense[5].

It is assumed that technical terms, whether scientific or legal, are employed in their technical sense but, again, the technical meaning will give way to the popular meaning if an intention to this effect is evinced on the face of the instrument.

Section 61 of the Law of Property Act 1925, provides that (unless the context otherwise requires) in deeds, contracts and other instruments executed

19 Norton, op. cit., p. 50.
20 *Shore v Wilson* (1842) 9 Cl & F 355 at 525, HL, per Coleridge J.
1 For a recent example see *Re Hopkin's Lease, Caerphilly Concrete Products Ltd v Owen* [1972] 1 All ER 248, CA (perpetually renewable lease). But see *Burnett (Marjorie) v Barclay* (1980) 125 Sol Jo 199.
2 *Throckmerton v Tracy* (1555) 1 Plow 145 at 161, per Staunford J.
3 [1969] 3 All ER 1441.
4 (1857) 6 HL Cas 61 at 106.
5 See *Hext v Gill* (1872) 7 Ch App 699 at 712, per Mellish LJ; *Tucker v Linger* (1882) 21 Ch D 18, CA (flint excluded); *Earl of Lonsdale v A-G* (1982) Times, 19 January (oil and natural gas not included).
6 Prima facie at common law 'month' meant lunar month: *Phipps & Co (Northampton and Towcester Breweries) Ltd v Rogers* [1925] 1 KB 14.

after 31 December 1925, 'month' means calendar month[6], 'person' includes a corporation, the singular includes the plural and the masculine the feminine, and vice versa.

3. Admissibility of extrinsic evidence

The general rule is that extrinsic evidence is not admissible to add to, vary or contradict the terms of a deed. Its construction cannot be controlled by the parties' previous negotiations, their conduct subsequent to the deed's execution, or the terms of the contract[7]. In one old case a deed conveyed a messuage 'with the appurtenances thereunto belonging'. On the question whether it operated to pass an adjoining garden occupied with the house, evidence that the conditions of sale expressly excluded the garden was held to be inadmissible as the word 'appurtenances' in the deed sufficed to pass the garden[8]. It is not even permissible to have recourse to the draft conveyance. In *City and Westminster Properties (1934) Ltd v Mudd*[9] the question arose whether a clause in a lease which restricted the use of the demised premises to showrooms, workrooms and offices only, prevented the lessee using them as a residence. Harman J held that he could not call in aid the fact that express words of prohibition as to residence had originally appeared in the draft, but were later deleted and omitted from the lease as executed.

The rule given in the preceding paragraph is subject to several well recognised exceptions. First, extrinsic evidence is allowed to explain the meaning of the words used or to resolve a latent ambiguity. Thus to determine the meaning of 'repair' in a repairing covenant it is necessary to have regard to the age, character and condition of the building at the time of the lease[10]. The recent case of *White v Taylor (No. 2)*[11] affords an illustration of the use of extrinsic evidence to elucidate an ambiguity in the parcels clause of a conveyance. Land was conveyed together with such rights of common of pasture for sheep on a certain Down as appertained or belonged to the land conveyed. This wording rendered it necessary to decide what (if any) sheep rights existed at the time of the grant. Buckley J held that the formula was sufficient to cover equitable rights and to see what rights were comprised within it he was entitled to look at the contracts for sale which specifically conferred on the purchasers sheep rights enforceable in equity.

Second, it is permissible to look at the surrounding circumstances existing at the time of the deed in order to place the court, as far as possible, in the position of the parties[12]. Frequent recourse is had to this rule when construing the grant of an easement or interpreting the scope of covenants. Thus the nature of the demised premises is a very relevant consideration in the construction of a user clause affecting the property[13].

Finally extrinsic evidence is always admissible to show that a deed is not binding on the ground of, for example, fraud, or that on account of some mutual

7   See *Leggott v Barrett* (1880) 15 Ch D 306 at 309, 311, CA, per James and Brett LJJ.
8   *Doe d. Norton v Webster* (1840) 12 Ad & El 442; *Barton v Dawes* (1850) 10 CB 261.
9   [1959] Ch 129, [1958] 2 All ER 733. Cf. *White v Taylor (No. 2)* [1969] 1 Ch 160, [1968] 1 All ER 1015, considered, post.
10 *Proudfoot v Hart* (1890) 25 QBD 42, CA; *Brew Bros Ltd v Snax (Ross) Ltd* [1970] 1 QB 612, [1970] 1 All ER 588, CA.
11 [1969] 1 Ch 160, [1968] 1 All ER 1015.
12 *Baird v Fortune* (1861) 5 LT 2, HL; *Roe v Siddons* (1888) 22 QBD 224 at 233, CA, per Lord Esher MR.
13 *Levermore v Jobey* [1956] 2 All ER 362, CA; *City and Westminster Properties (1934) Ltd v Mudd* [1959] Ch 129, [1958] 2 All ER 733.

mistake the deed does not record the real contract between the parties. The introduction of extrinsic evidence in these and similar circumstances does not really constitute an exception to the basic rule since the evidence is not adduced for the purposes of construing the deed. Again, evidence may be given of a collateral contract not to enforce a certain clause in the deed. This was the basis of the actual decision in *Mudd's* case[14], where the lessor's action for forfeiture of the lease for breach of covenant was dismissed on the ground that the lessee had executed the lease in reliance on a promise by the lessor's agent that the lessor would not enforce the covenant as to user against him personally.

4.   Miscellaneous rules

A passing mention must also be made of a few specific rules of interpretation that the courts have recourse to when resolving problems of construction.

(a) Contra proferentem
In cases of doubt or uncertainty a deed is construed against the grantor in favour of the grantee. This rule is sometimes utilised in disputes as to the effect of an exception or reservation in a conveyance[15].

(b) Expressum facit cessare tacitum
An express provision automatically ousts the implication of any provision to like effect. For example, at common law the use of the word 'demise' in a lease of land automatically implied in the lessee's favour a covenant for quiet enjoyment, but where the lessor enters into an express covenant for quiet enjoyment there is no room for the implied covenant[16].

(c) Falsa demonstratio non nocet
A false description contained in a document does not normally prejudice its intended effect. Thus where land is conveyed by a composite description part of which is true and part inaccurate, then, provided the true part describes the land with sufficient certainty, the false part will be rejected. Further consideration is given to the operation of this rule in Chapter 18.

(d) Certum est quod certum reddi potest
Whilst no draftsman should leave the interpretation of his document to inference, a lack of precision or certainty in it may not necessarily defeat the document since what is capable of being rendered certain is to be treated as certain. Examples of the application of this maxim have been encountered in Chapter 5 when discussing the contents of the memorandum for the purposes of the Law of Property Act 1925, s. 40[17].

5.   Effect of recitals on construction of deed

The construction of a deed may be assisted by the recitals i.e. those clauses, introduced by the word 'whereas', which explain the purpose of the deed or set

---

14   [1959] Ch 129, [1958] 2 All ER 733, p. 489, ante.
15   For a recent example see *St Edmundsbury and Ipswich Diocesan Board of Finance v Clark (No 2)* [1975] 1 All ER 772, CA.
16   See *Miller v Emcer Products Ltd* [1956] Ch 304, [1956] 1 All ER 237, CA.
17   Pages 105–107, ante. See also *Owen v Thomas* (1834) 3 My & K 353; *Shardlow v Cotterell* (1881) 20 Ch D 90.

out the grantor's title to make the grant. Since the recitals constitute merely a subordinate part of the deed and are not even an essential part of it[18], they cannot control the operative part of the deed (i.e. that part which carries out the object of the instrument) where the operative part uses language which admits of no doubt[19]. Thus land described with certainty in the parcels clause of the conveyance cannot be cut down or extended by recitals showing that something less, or more, was intended to pass. Similarly the operation of a covenant for title is not limited by the fact that a defect in the title appears in a recital[20].

Where the operative part of the deed is ambiguous or doubtfully expressed, recourse may be had to the recitals to discover the true meaning of the deed. Not that the recitals must be looked at to the exclusion of other subsidiary parts of the deed, since any question of construction renders it essential to refer to the whole of the instrument, but it is more likely that the recitals leading up to the operative part will furnish the key to its true construction than the other subsidiary clauses[1]. For example, the interpretation of a conveyance of land described in general terms may be assisted by a recital expressed in specific terms which reveals that only certain specific property was intended to pass[2]. It is also permissible to resort to the recitals to resolve some uncertainty or ambiguity arising in a covenant. Thus in one case[3] a covenant to pay an annuity was preceded by a recital that the annuity was to be payable out of the covenantor's salary; it was held that the liability to pay determined when the salary ceased.

If both the recitals and the operative part of a deed are clear and unambiguous, but they are inconsistent with each other, the operative part prevails[4].

6. Correction of errors

Since a deed is construed to give effect to the parties' expressed intentions as appearing from the whole of its contents, the court will make any corrections which a perusal of the document shows to be necessary[5]. Incorrect grammar and spelling may be corrected, repugnant words rejected and words that have obviously been left in by mistake ignored. Words omitted by inadvertence may even be supplied, but not where this will alter the legal effect of the deed[6]. In short the normal run-of-the-mill typographical error which is frequently encountered in practice will not be allowed to defeat the intentions of the parties[7]. If through some mutual mistake the deed fails to carry out the contract

---

18 *Earl of Bath and Earl of Montague's Case* (1693) 3 Cas in Ch 55 at 101, per Holt CJ.
19 *Bailey v Lloyd* (1829) 5 Russ 330 at 344, per Leach MR; see also Lord Esher MR's, three rules enunciated in *Re Moon, ex p Dawes* (1886) 17 QBD 275 at 286, CA.
20 *Page v Midland Rail Co* [1894] 1 Ch 11, p. 627, post.
1 *Orr v Mitchell* [1893] AC 238 at 254, HL, per Lord Macnaghten.
2 *Jenner v Jenner* (1866) LR 1 Eq 361; see also p. 508, post.
3 *Hesse v Albert* (1828) 3 Man & Ry KB 406. For other examples see *Field v Hopkins* (1890) 44 Ch D 524, CA; *Crouch v Crouch* [1912] 1 KB 378.
4 See the third of Lord Esher's rules propounded in *Re Moon, ex p. Dawes*, note 19, ante.
5 See *Gwyn v Neath Canal Co* (1868) LR 3 Exch 209 at 215, per Kelly CB.
6 *Re Ethel and Mitchells and Butlers' Contract* [1901] 1 Ch 945 ('in fee' not read as 'in fee simple' so that only life estate passed).
7 The author recalls a case where a conveyance recited a deed of 30 September 1961 and contained an acknowledgment by the vendor for production of 'the said conveyance' of 30 September 1962. The mortgagee's solicitor insisted on the execution of a separate

between the parties, then the proper course is to execute a confirmatory deed; should there be a dispute between the parties, proceedings for rectification[8] will be necessary.

acknowledgment for the deed of 1961. This would appear to have been completely unnecessary. There was clearly a typing error and the reference to 'the said conveyance' showed that the parties intended the acknowledgment to relate to the deed previously referred to. No possibility of doubt existed as to which 'said' deed was intended, since the conveyance did not refer to any other deeds.

8   See Chapter 25, post.

Chapter 18

Form and contents of conveyance

A Introduction

A conveyance is divided into a number of constituent parts as follows:

1. the commencement, including the date and the parties;
2. the recitals;
3. the testatum, commencing with the words 'Now this deed witnesseth . . .' and ending with 'hereby conveys unto the purchaser';
4. the parcels;
5. the habendum[1] ('To hold' etc.);
6. the testimonium, linking the contents of the deed with the signatures and seals.

Other clauses may have to be added, depending on the nature of the transaction, arranged after the habendum in the following order: declaration of trusts, powers (e.g. power of re-entry for non-payment of a rentcharge) and covenants. Taking the conveyance which appears in abstract form on page 294 as an illustration of a conveyance of freehold land, the deed itself would be in some form similar to that shown below.

> THIS CONVEYANCE is made the 21st day of May 1981[2] BETWEEN ABEL SMALL of 'Fairhaven' Mead Road Oadby in the County of Leicester (hereinafter called 'the vendor') of the one part and DAVID LARGE of 32 Church Lane in the City of Leicester (hereinafter called 'the purchaser') of the other part
> WHEREAS the vendor is seised of the property hereinafter described for an estate in fee simple in possession subject as hereinafter appears and has agreed with the purchaser for the sale to him of the said property for a like estate at the price of £24,000
> NOW THIS DEED WITNESSETH as follows:
> 1. In pursuance of the said agreement and in consideration of the sum of £24,000 paid to the vendor by the purchaser (the receipt whereof the vendor hereby acknowledges) the vendor as beneficial owner HEREBY

---

1 That part of the deed which precedes the habendum is technically called 'the premises', an expression which has come to mean in popular language simply land or buildings. See *Gardiner v Sevenoaks RDC* [1950] 2 All ER 84 at 85, per Lord Goddard CJ.
2 In most conveyances the dates and the other figures (save for house numbers) would, following the traditional practice, be expressed in words, not numbers.

CONVEYS unto the purchaser ALL THAT [parcels[3]] TO HOLD unto the purchaser in fee simple SUBJECT to the covenants on the part of the grantee and the conditions contained in the Conveyance[4]

2. With the object and intent of affording to the vendor a full and sufficient indemnity in respect of the said covenants and conditions but not further or otherwise the purchaser hereby covenants with the vendor to observe and perform the said covenants and conditions and to indemnify the vendor against all actions claims demands and liability in respect thereof

3. It is hereby certified that the transaction hereby effected does not form part of a larger transaction or of a series of transactions in respect of which the amount or value or the aggregate amount or value of the consideration exceeds £25,000

IN WITNESS whereof the parties hereto have hereunto set their respective hands and seals the day and year first before written
SIGNED, etc.

By way of comparison a transfer of the same land would, if the title were registered, be in the following form.

H.M. LAND REGISTRY
LAND REGISTRATION ACTS 1925 TO 1966
TRANSFER OF WHOLE[5]

County: Leicester
Title Number: LT12345
Property: 'Fairhaven', Mead Road, Oadby
Date: 21 May 1981

1. In consideration of twenty four thousand pounds (£24,000) the receipt whereof is hereby acknowledged I, ABEL SMALL, of 'Fairhaven', Mead Road, Oadby, Bank Manager[6], as beneficial owner hereby transfer to DAVID LARGE of 32 Church Lane, Leicester, Schoolmaster, the land comprised in the title above mentioned

2. [Covenant for indemnity as before, but suitably amended[7]]

3. [Certificate for value clause]
Signed, etc.

This chapter looks principally at the contents of a conveyance of freehold land, and of a transfer of registered land. From time to time reference will also be made to other types of documents which operate to vest a legal estate in the grantee.

---

3   The description of the property will be identical with that given in the abstract, except that the words 'the before abstracted Conveyance' will be replaced by 'a Conveyance'.

4   Frequently there is added a qualifying phrase such as 'so far as the same are still subsisting and are capable of being enforced'. For the significance of these words see 19 Ency F & P 884, n. 12, but it is doubtful whether their omission from the deed can operate (as is tentatively suggested) to revive covenants that have ceased to be enforceable.

5   These words appear in the form promulgated by the Chief Land Registrar under the LRA 1925, s. 127; they are not part of the statutory form prescribed by the LRR 1925, r. 98, Schedule, Form 19.

6   As to the need to add the descriptions of the parties, see p. 496, post.

7   It will be necessary to replace 'the said covenants and conditions' by some expression such as 'the covenants and conditions referred to in entry no. — of the charges register of the above mentioned title'.

B Description of document

It is customary today to describe a document affecting unregistered land according to the nature of the transaction effected, e.g. as a conveyance, lease, assignment, assent, deed of appointment, mortgage, and so on, or it may simply be styled 'This deed'[8]. At one time a deed made between two or more parties (a deed inter partes) was termed an indenture. Originally it was written (engrossed) in two parts on the same piece of parchment and each part was cut off in an indented line, so that each copy fitted the other and so could be identified. Later it became the practice merely to engross one copy and to indent the document by cutting the top of the first page or sheet in a wavy line. In contrast a deed poll, i.e. a document made by one party only, was so named because the top was polled or shaved. A deed between parties now has the effect of an indenture though not indented or expressed to be an indenture[9].

A transfer of registered land bears no descriptive title, but is required by way of a heading to contain a reference to the county and district (or London borough), the title number and the property. It has been judicially stated that a registered land transfer is in form analogous to a deed poll, rather than a deed inter partes[10].

C Date of deed

As we have seen[11] it is the practice to date the deed with the date of actual completion, though strictly speaking it should be dated with the date of its delivery. Since a vendor must be taken in the normal case to have executed the conveyance as an escrow, it would not seem improper to insert the date when the condition is fulfilled, which is ordinarily the date of completion.

D Parties

1. Mode of description

(a) Name

The surname and Christian or fore names should appear in full. Where the name of a party differs from that given in an earlier deed, it is advisable to draw attention to the discrepancy by means of a simple statement when reciting the earlier deed that the vendor was therein called by such and such a name. The purpose of the parenthetical phrase introduced by the words 'hereinafter called' is obvious; it saves unnecessary repetition of the parties' names in the body of the deed. On the grant of a lease, it is common practice to incorporate within the description words of definition to include the reversioner for the time being and the lessee's successors in title[12].

The need to ensure accuracy when naming the parties cannot be too highly stressed. A wrong name or spelling may give rise to subsequent inconvenience.

---

8   LPA 1925, s. 57.
9   LPA 1925, s. 56 (2).
10   *Chelsea and Walham Green Building Society v Armstrong* [1951] Ch 853 at 857–58, [1951] 2 All ER 250 at 252–53, per Vaisey J, p. 454, ante.
11   Page 434, ante.
12   As to the effect of such a definition on the transfer of an option to purchase, see p. 557, post.

In particular it should be remembered that the name in the deed will, in the absence of contrary evidence, be taken as the estate owner's proper name for the registration of land charges[13].

(b) Address and description

There is no statutory provision requiring the addition of a party's address and occupation in a conveyance of unregistered land; they are given simply for identification purposes. Traditionally a woman is described, not by her occupation, but by her status as 'spinster', 'widow', or 'the wife of —' (sometimes 'married woman'), as the case may be. It is doubtful whether inclusion of the occupation serves any useful purpose and the practice of stating this is fast becoming obsolete[14].

In the case of registered land, a marginal note to the form of transfer published by H.M. Stationery Office directs that the postal address and descriptions of both the transferor and the transferee should be inserted in the document. The inclusion of the transferee's description would appear to be necessary in view of the fact that the proprietorship register is required[15] to contain the name, address and description of the proprietor, though sometimes the description is omitted. In addition the proprietor must furnish the Register with an address for service of notices[16]. However this requirement is satisfied, not by stating the transferee's address in the transfer, for this will often be his former address, but by completing the appropriate question in the form of application leading to registration.

(c) Parts of a deed

In a deed inter partes the various persons who join therein for differing purposes or representing different interests are expressed to be of a separate part—the vendor 'of the one part' and the purchaser 'of the other part'. The party of the 'one' (or 'first', 'second', as the case may be) part may comprise more than one person; they may be joint tenants, who are considered as one person in law as regards estate ownership. A person who executes a deed in more than one capacity (e.g. a vendor life tenant who is also one of the trustees of the settlement) will be a party to the conveyance in more than one part.

It will be noticed that the form of a registered land transfer differs from that of a conveyance. There is no reference to the parties at the beginning of the document; they are mentioned as required. It is also expressed in the first person: 'I XY of   hereby transfer', though this personal element is readily abandoned whenever the transfer contains additional clauses, in which XY usually appears as 'the transferor', or 'the vendor'.

2.   Who are necessary parties

In a straightforward case the only parties are the vendor and the purchaser, lessor and lessee, mortgagor and mortgagee. There may only be a single party to the document, as where an executor assents to the vesting of land in himself as sole beneficiary. The circumstances of a particular case may render it necessary to join other people as parties in order to give effect to the transaction between the two main parties.

13   *Diligent Finance Co Ltd v Alleyne* (1972) 23 P & CR 346, p. 394, ante.
14   It is not necessary to give the estate owner's occupation when applying for an official certificate of search.
15   LRR 1925, r. 6.
16   LRA 1925, s. 79.

(a) Collateral purposes

There are many occasions when the execution of the conveyance by some third party is essential. The following examples are not intended to be exhaustive. On the sale of land by a life tenant the trustees of the settlement should join in to receive the purchase money. The existence of a mortgage which is not to be redeemed on or before completion requires the mortgagee to join in the deed to release the land conveyed from the charge, if the purchaser is to take free from it. On a sale of land by trustees the required consent (if any) of a beneficiary can be signified by his executing the deed.

(b) Equitable owners

Any equitable owner whose interest will not be overreached by the conveyance must join in to vest his interest in the purchaser. Seldom is this likely to occur. A vendor who is not beneficially entitled in equity usually has power by his conveyance to overreach equitable interests because he is selling under the Settled Land Act 1925, or under his statutory power as personal representative or mortgagee, or, in the case of joint vendors, in execution of a trust for sale. In other cases the purchaser can require[17] the vendor to overreach the equitable interest by means of an ad hoc settlement or trust for sale[18]. Yet it may be simpler in some instances, e.g. where A holds in trust for B, for the purchaser to accept a conveyance made with B's concurrence rather than insist on the cumbersome overreaching procedure.

(c) Purchaser's nominee

In the absence of any agreement to the contrary[19] a purchaser can require the vendor to convey the land to such person or persons as he may direct, save where this would be to the prejudice of the vendor because, for example, the purchaser has agreed to enter into personal covenants and the personality of the covenantor is fundamental to the transaction[20].

On a sub-sale, the conveyance is usually made direct to the sub-purchaser, so as to save the expense of a second conveyance and (where applicable) double stamp duty[1]. The original purchaser is a necessary party to this deed if (i) he has resold at a higher price, in which case he must join in to acknowledge receipt of the increase, or (ii) he has contracted to assume some personal liability and the vendor is unwilling to accept the sub-purchaser as covenantor.

(d) Persons acquiring other interests

At common law no person could sue on a covenant made with him in a deed inter partes unless he was a party to that deed, and this was the case even if he executed the deed[2]. By virtue of s. 56 of the Law of Property Act 1925, a person may take an immediate or other interest in land or the benefit of any condition, covenant or agreement respecting land[3], although he is not named as a party to

17 LPA 1925, s. 42 (1), p. 164, ante.
18 SLA 1925, s. 21; LPA 1925, s. 2 (2).
19 See LSC 17 (6) which entitles the vendor to decline to convey to someone else on reasonable grounds. A restrictive clause of this nature was first introduced to avoid possible liability for the payment of betterment levy under the Land Commission Act 1967. Now that the levy has been abolished there seems little point in having such a condition. It is still retained, however, in the 1980 Revision.
20 For the position on a sale of leaseholds, see *Curtis Moffat Ltd v Wheeler* [1929] 2 Ch 224.
1 See p. 442, ante.
2 *Norton on Deeds* (2nd edn), p. 28.
3 Such as an option to purchase: *Stromdale and Ball Ltd v Burden* [1952] Ch 223, [1952] 1 All ER 59.

the conveyance. Since considerable divergence of judicial opinion exists as to the precise scope of s. 56[4], it is advisable to make any such interested person a party to the instrument whenever possible. His failure to execute the deed does not, it seems, affect his right to enforce the covenant or take the interest granted. Circumstances may render it impracticable to join the interested parties because they are too numerous, as when the purchaser enters into restrictive covenants expressed to be made with the vendor and with his assigns, owners for the time being of land adjacent to that conveyed[5].

Unlike a deed inter partes, a deed poll could always be sued upon by a person with whom the covenant was made. Where a transfer of registered land contained a covenant by the transferee with a building society for the repayment to them of money due under a mortgage to which the land transferred was subject, it was held that the society could sue on the covenant, since the transfer was analogous to a deed poll[6].

E   Recitals

Recitals, though not a necessary part of any deed[7], are commonly inserted in conveyances. They are introduced by the word 'whereas', and fall into two main classes: (1) narrative recitals which set out the vendor's or grantor's title to make the assurance, and (2) introductory recitals which explain the purpose or operation of the deed. They are also used to state matters of fact, which by virtue of various statutory provisions[8] are to be accepted as evidence of the matter stated. No document or matter which is irrelevant to the deed in question, or which may cast doubts on the validity of the title should be recited. It is not considered good draftsmanship to recite the contract as a document[9], though it is the practice to refer to the fact of agreement. Frequently the only recital in a straightforward conveyance of a dwellinghouse is the one appearing in the precedent on page 493. There are, however, many transactions apart from sales where it is desirable to incorporate appropriate recitals, as a reference to any standard precedent book will show. A deed expressed to be supplemental to a previous instrument is read and has effect as if it contained a full recital of the previous deed[10].

1.   Narrative recitals

The general rule as to narrative recitals is that they should be limited to such matters as are necessary to explain the operative part of the conveyance[11]. A recital of the steps by which the vendor became entitled to convey is generally unnecessary. A simple recital of the vendor's seisin suffices. Recitals are commonly encountered on a sale by personal representatives. Thus a conveyance by

---

4   See p. 537, post.
5   *Re Ecclesiastical Comrs for England's Conveyance* [1936] Ch 430. But see *Robinson v Robinson* [1976] 241 Estates Gazette 153; *Pink v Lawrence* (1978) 36 P & CR 98 discussed at [1979] Conv 5.
6   *Chelsea and Walham Green Building Society v Armstrong* [1951] Ch 853, [1951] 2 All ER 250.
7   See note 18, p. 491, ante.
8   Page 501, post.
9   1 Dart, 475.
10 LPA 1925, s. 58.
11 18 Ency F & P, 288.

executors usually recites: (i) the seisin of the testator at the time of his death, (ii) the date of his will, his death and the grant of probate to the vendors, (iii) a statement that no previous assent or conveyance has been given[12] and (iv) the agreement for sale[13].

Recitals are not generally incorporated in the grant of a lease. The practice on the assignment of a lease varies. Traditionally it has been the custom to recite the lease (including a verbatim description of the demised property taken from the lease) followed by a recital of the assignment to the vendor. Where several transactions have intervened between the lease and the vendor's assignment, these intermediate dealings are recited generally by means of some blanket clause such as: 'by virtue of divers mesne assurance acts in the law and events and ultimately by . . .' Then follows the vendor's assignment. Some draftsmen, preferring not to bring the history on to the title and anxious to keep the assignment to manageable proportions, merely recite that the vendor is possessed of the property assigned for a legal estate for the residue of the term granted by the lease[14].

The case of *Re Duce and Boots Cash Chemists (Southern) Ltd's Contract*[15] reveals the dangers of inserting recitals in an assent. It is safer to adopt a general practice of not having recitals in an assent unless absolutely necessary[16]. A precedent of an assent is given on p. 565.

Form of recital of seisin
The once familiar recital of the conveyance to the vendor has largely fallen into desuetude, being replaced by the commonplace recital of seisin. The precise wording of this recital differs according to the draftsman and the various precedent books do not agree on any uniform wording, though the import is basically the same in each case. A typical recital where the land is not conveyed free from incumbrances may read:

' WHEREAS the vendor is seised of the property hereinafter described for an estate in fee simple in possession subject as hereinafter mentioned but otherwise free from incumbrances and . . .'

Some draftsmen feel that if the vendor is the beneficial owner, the recital should say so by adding words such as 'for his own sole benefit'[17]; others prefer a recital that the vendor is 'the estate owner in respect of the fee simple in possession of the property hereinafter described'. Opinions are divided on the question whether it is correct to state that the vendor is seised 'free from incumbrances', notwithstanding that the land is conveyed subject to, for example, easements or restrictive covenants. The meaning to be attributed to the word 'incumbrance' in this context is uncertain. Neither the statutory definition in the Law of Property Act 1925[18], nor the decision of Danckwerts J

12 For the purposes of the AEA 1925, s. 36 (6), p. 336, ante.
13 19 Ency F & P, 1075, Form 7:5:1. It is preferable to omit reference to the will appointing the vendors as executors. Cf. Hallett, 239, Form 27, where the statement of no prior assent appears in the operative part of the deed.
14 Compare, for example, the precedent in Hallet, 321, Form 81, with 19 Ency F & P, 1464, Form 8:A:3.
15 [1937] Ch 642, [1937] 3 All ER 788.
16 See 8 Ency F & P, 772, Form 2:12 (assent of property subject to mortgage where mortgagee takes new covenant from beneficiary and releases testator's estate).
17 Hallett, 192, Form 2.
18 Section 205 (1) (vii) which, without being exhaustive, refers to financial charges secured on land.

in *District Bank Ltd v Webb*[19] that a lease would not normally be treated as an incumbrance is to be regarded as conclusive. In a conveyancing context the word often has an extended meaning. The view has been expressed[20] that a vendor's solicitor should not permit his client to execute a conveyance containing an unqualified recital of seisin free from incumbrances, if he holds subject to an interest the existence of which would mean that a vendor selling under an open contract could not show a good title to an unincumbered fee simple estate, the reason being that an unqualified recital may operate as an absolute warranty of title wider than that imported by the usual covenants for title. It may even be that a purchaser has no right to insist on the inclusion of the phrase 'but otherwise free from incumbrances' for this conflicts with the usual contractual provision[1] that the land is sold subject to any easements, liabilities, and other rights affecting the same. A vendor who contracts to convey an unincumbered fee simple cannot object to an unqualified recital.

A recital of seisin may be omitted altogether when the conveyance is to be endorsed on the previous conveyance, or the title is to be registered on completion. According to one view[2] there is no necessity to recite the vendor's seisin at all where it appears on the abstract (in the form of the conveyance to him). However it is usual to incorporate the recital. Not only does it become sufficient evidence of its truth after 20 years[3] but solicitors investigating title feel happier where the document forming the root of title contains such a recital[4].

2.   Introductory recitals

Besides indicating the intended operation of the conveyance or other instrument, for example, to give effect to an agreement for sale or for the grant of a right of way, introductory recitals also explain the reason for joining the various parties. A typical illustration arises where a mortgagee joins in a conveyance of land by the mortgagor. After reciting seisin of the vendor subject to the mortgage, and the state of the mortgage debt, there is usually a recital to this effect:

> ' The vendor has agreed with the purchaser for the sale to him of the said property at the price of £ — and it has been agreed that the sum of £ — part of the said purchase price shall be paid to the mortgagee in part discharge of the principal money owing to him under the mortgage and that the mortgagee shall join in these presents in manner hereinafter appearing.'

3.   Recitals in land registry transfers

Recitals in a registered land transfer are generally regarded as unnecessary and inconsistent with the principles on which the register is maintained[5]. They are missing from the statutory forms set out in the Schedule to the Land Registration Rules 1925. Certainly narrative recitals giving details of the devolution of the title have no place in a transfer, but in as much as the general law governing the effect of recitals applies equally to those contained in a registered land transfer, it may be desirable to incorporate a recital for some

---

19   [1958] 1 All ER 126, p. 502, post. But see note 5, page 146, ante.
20   Emmet, 502.
 1   NCS 14; LCS 5 (2) (b), p. 147, ante.
 2   19 Ency F & P, 857, note 1; Williams V & P, 649.
 3   Page 501, post.
 4   Hallett, 191, note 1.
 5   Ruoff, *Concise Land Registration Practice* (2nd edn), p. 86; Hallett, 1318, note 1.

collateral purpose[6]. For instance, they may be used to explain why a particular party executed the transfer or to show that, although no monetary consideration passed between the parties, the transfer was not a deed of gift. Where recitals are incorporated the parties should be set out after the usual heading as in an ordinary conveyance.

4. Effect of recitals

(a) Recitals as evidence

By virtue of the Law of Property Act 1925, s. 45 (6) recitals contained in any instrument 20 years old at the date of the contract are to be taken as sufficient evidence of the truth of the facts recited, unless proved to be inaccurate. The Law Commission[7] felt on balance that this rule should be retained notwithstanding the reduction in the period of investigation of title from 30 years to 15. An example of the operation of this provision occurred in *Re Marsh and Earl Granville*[8] where a recital that trustees had caused property to be put up for sale 'in pursuance of the trust for sale conferred on them' was held to be sufficient evidence of the non-exercise of a power of revocation which the settlor had reserved. A recital in a deed of appointment of a new trustee of land as to the reasons for a vacancy (e.g. that a trustee refuses or is unfit to act) must be accepted by a purchaser as *conclusive* evidence of the matter stated[9].

(b) Estoppel

A recital in a deed may operate by way of estoppel against (but not for) the party making it in any action upon that deed but not in any collateral proceedings[10]. This is a doctrine whereby falsehood is made to have the effect of truth and the courts are not disposed to extend the rule[11]. The estoppel binds the party making the statement and his successors in title and operates in favour of the other party and his successors[12]. Where A purports to convey land to which he has no title to B in a conveyance containing a recital of A's alleged seisin, A is estopped from denying that he had the title; if A subsequently acquires title to that land, the estoppel is said to be fed and the estate automatically vests in B without the need for any confirmatory conveyance from A[13]. The estoppel binds any person, even a purchaser for value without notice, to whom A conveys the land after his acquisition of a good title.

No estoppel is created by a general recital, or by a recital which merely infers the vendor's seisin without saying so expressly[14]. There must be a recital of a

---

6 3 K & E, 125—26, adopting much the same view as that originally expressed by Potter, 79—81. For precedents of transfers incorporating recitals, see 3 K & E, 420, 428, Forms XVI and XXII.

7 Interim Report on Root of Title to Freehold Land, Law Com. No. 9, paras. 42—45. See further pp. 283—284, ante.

8 (1883) 24 Ch D 11 (decided on the Vendor and Purchaser Act 1874, s. 2).

9 Trustee Act 1925, s. 38; SLA 1925, s. 35 (3).

10 *Carter v Carter* (1857) 3 K & J 617.

11 *Onward Building Society v Smithson* [1893] 1 Ch 1 at 13—14, CA, per Lindley LJ.

12 *Palmer v Ekins* (1728) 2 Ld Raym 1550; *Poulton v Moore* [1915] 1 KB 400, CA. The benefit does not pass to a volunteer: *General Finance, Mortgage, and Discount Co v Liberator Permament Benefit Building Society* (1878) 10 Ch D 15 at 24, per Jessel MR.

13 *Poulton v Moore* [1915] 1 KB 400 at 414—15, CA, per Phillimore LJ. And see *Cumberland Court (Brighton) Ltd v Taylor* [1964] Ch 29, [1963] 2 All ER 536. Even in the absence of a recital of seisin, equity will compel A to make good the conveyance to B, if A later acquires title; see p. 628, post.

14 *Onward Building Society v Smithson* [1893] 1 Ch 1, CA; *Heath v Crealock* (1874) 10 Ch App 22 (recital that vendor 'well entitled' to certain property inadequate).

particular fact[15] expressed in precise and unambiguous terms, as the case of *District Bank Ltd v Webb*[16] shows.

> A and B granted a legal lease of property to A and C. Later A and B conveyed the land to D; the deed recited that they were 'seised in unincumbered fee simple in possession.' D mortgaged the land to a bank which was claiming possession from A, B and D. A and B, who were living in the property under the lease (C no longer claiming any beneficial interest in it), sought to resist the bank's claim, relying on the lease. The bank contended that the recital in the deed precluded their setting up the existence of the lease.

Danckwerts J held that the lease had priority to the mortgage and rejected the bank's claim. The recital was not sufficiently clear and unambiguous to found an estoppel. The lease did not constitute an incumbrance in this situation and the expression 'in possession' did not mean vacant possession but merely described an estate not in reversion. In the absence of a recital, no estoppel is created by the operative words of a conveyance[17], or by the giving of convenants for title[18]. The existence of an estoppel may be negatived by the deed itself, for example, where the truth appears elsewhere in the instrument[19].

(c) Creation of covenant
No technical words are required to create a covenant and a recital that shows an intention that one of the parties shall do or not do a thing will operate as a covenant unless the deed expresses a contrary intention. If in a deed of exchange of land by adjoining owners for the purpose of straightening a common boundary it is recited that one party has agreed to erect and maintain a boundary fence, then in the absence of any covenant appearing in the operative part of the deed, the recital itself consitutes a covenant on his part[20]. The rule expressed by the maxim *expressum facit cessare tacitum* prevents the recital operating as such if the deed contains an express covenant to erect and maintain a fence.

(d) Construction
Recitals may assist in the construction of the operative part of the deed; this was considered in the previous chapter.

F The consideration

After the recitals comes the operative part of the deed introduced by the words 'NOW THIS DEED WITNESSETH as follows'. The requirement in s. 5 of the Stamp Act 1891, that all the facts and circumstances affecting the liability of any instrument to stamp duty must be fully and truly set forth makes it essential

15 *Bensley v Burden* (1830) 8 LJOS Ch 85 at 87, per Lord Lyndhurst LC.
16 [1958] 1 All ER 126.
17 See p. 504, post.
18 *General Finance, Mortgage, and Discount Co v Liberator Permament Benefit Building Society* (1878) 10 Ch D 15.
19 Co. Litt. 352b; *Right d. Jefferys v Bucknell* (1831) 2 B & Ad 278 at 281, per Lord Tenterden CJ. Cf. *Morton v Woods* (1869) LR 4 QB 293.
20 For examples, see *Re Weston, Davies v Tagart* [1900] 2 Ch 164 (agreement in separation deed by spouses to live apart); *Buckland v Buckland* [1900] 2 Ch 534.

to state the consideration (if any) in the deed. This explains the reason for the words, 'in consideration of the sum of £ — paid by the purchaser to the vendor'. This phrase may, or may not, depending on the draftsman, be preceded by the expression 'In pursuance of the said agreement', this being a reference to the agreement for sale which has previously been mentioned in the recitals[1]. In a registered land transfer the statement of consideration appears immediately after the usual heading and the date. The consideration may take forms other than the payment of money, such as the creation of a rentcharge, or the performance of covenants by the purchaser. An assignment of leasehold property may be made in consideration of the assignee's taking upon himself the rent and covenants in the lease. In a deed of gift it is common practice to state that the deed is made in consideration of the natural love and affection which the donor has for the donee.

G   Receipt clause

Prior to 1882 the vendor was accustomed to endorse a separate receipt for the purchase money on the conveyance, a practice which is no longer necessary because a receipt in the body of the deed now operates as a sufficient discharge to the person making payment without any further receipt being endorsed[2]. It will be recalled that special considerations apply to the receipt of capital money arising on the sale of settled land or land held on trust for sale. To overreach the beneficial interests it must be paid to, or applied by the direction of, not fewer than two trustees of the settlement, or two trustees for sale, or (in either case) to a trust corporation. A sole personal representative is empowered to give a valid receipt for the proceeds of sale[3]. The written receipt of a mortgagee is a sufficient discharge for money arising under the power of sale, and a person paying the same to him is not concerned to inquire whether any money remains due under the mortgage[4].

1.   Statutory effects of receipt clause

To operate as a sufficient discharge there must be a receipt, that is, an acknowledgment by the vendor that he has received the money. A statement that the consideration has been paid to the vendor, or that a building lease was granted in consideration of moneys already expended by the lessee[5] does not suffice. As between the vendor and the purchaser the receipt acts as a *sufficient* discharge; it is not conclusive evidence of payment. The equitable rule is thus preserved that evidence of non-payment is admissible. The vendor retains his equitable lien for unpaid purchase money, notwithstanding that the conveyance contains an acknowledgment of its receipt[6], unless there are circumstances which negative the existence of a lien.

---

1   See the precedent on p. 493, ante. Some draftsmen prefer the following form: 'NOW THIS DEED made in consideration of the sum of £ — paid . . . to the vendor (the receipt . . . acknowledges) WITNESSETH as follows . . .'
2   LPA 1925, s. 67 (1), (2).
3   See p. 336, ante.
4   LPA, s. 107 (1).
5   *Renner v Tolley* (1893) 63 LT 815.
6   *Winter v Lord Anson* (1827) 3 Russ 488; see p. 421, ante. At common law a receipt in a deed operated to estop the person who had given it from asserting non-payment: *Baker v Dewey* (1823) 1 B & C 704. The equitable rule now prevails.

As against a subsequent purchaser without notice of non-payment, s. 68 (1) of the Law of Property Act 1925, enacts that the receipt is sufficient evidence that the money has been paid. The difficulties surrounding this provision have already been discussed[7]. In addition under s. 69 of the same Act production by the vendor's solicitor of a deed containing a receipt for the consideration operates as sufficient authority for the purchaser to pay the money to that solicitor. This also has been considered previously[8].

2. Registered land transfers

The forms of transfer prescribed by the Land Registration Rules 1925, contain no receipt clause. Yet it is the practice to insert such a clause and the printed forms published by H.M. Stationery Office include an acknowledgment by the vendor of his receipt of the money. It would seem necessary to incorporate a receipt clause if it is desired to take advantage of ss. 67−69. The argument that its inclusion is possibly superfluous appears unsound[9].

H   Words of grant

These words tell what the vendor or grantor does and in a normal conveyance they are comprehended within the words: 'the vendor as beneficial owner[10] HEREBY CONVEYS unto the purchaser . . .' In days of old when multiplicity of language was the order of the day the usual expression was 'grant, bargain, sell, alien, convey, release and confirm'. Today no technical words of grant are necessary. Any word suffices to pass the legal estate if the intention is to pass it[11]. 'Conveys' is usually employed in conveyances of freehold land, 'demises' on the grant of a lease, and 'assigns' on the sale of an existing leasehold estate. In the case of registered titles the word 'transfer' is employed. The use of the word 'grant' is not necessary to convey land[12], nor does its use imply any covenant, save where otherwise provided by statute[13].

I   Parcels clause

1. Introduction

The parcels clause which is commonly introduced by the words 'ALL THAT . . .' contains a physical description of the land which is the subject of the

7   Page 421, ante.

8   Pages 420−421, ante.

9   Farrand, 249−250, citing *Rimmer v Webster* [1902] 2 Ch 163 at 173−74, per Farwell J. But the learned judge held, not that the statutory form of transfer which stated the fact of payment without acknowledging its receipt brought into play the forerunner of s. 68, but that it would suffice to create an estoppel. For a recent case where s. 68 was considered in relation to a transfer of registered land, see *London and Cheshire Insurance Co Ltd v Laplagrene Property Co Ltd* [1971] Ch 499, [1971] 1 All ER 766, discussed at p. 422, ante. There is the real problem of the purchaser never seeing the transfer. The vital issue will be the vendor's lien.

10 The significance of this, and expressions such as 'as trustee', 'as mortgagee', etc., is considered in Chapter 24.

11 *Re Stirrup's Contract* [1961] 1 All ER 805 at 809, per Wilberforce J.

12 LPA 1925, s. 51 (2). The Real Property Act 1845, s. 2, enabled land in possession to be conveyed by grant (see p. 481, ante) and that word was normally used in conveyances thereafter.

13 LPA 1925, s. 59 (2). Examples of statutes which otherwise provide are the Queen Anne's Bounty Act 1838, s. 22, and the Lands Clauses Consolidation Act 1845, s. 132.

conveyance. Doctrinally, of course, the deed operates to vest in the purchaser, not the land, but an estate in the land delimited by the parcels clause; it is the province of the habendum clause[14] to describe the quantum or size of estate which the grantee is to acquire. Also included within the parcels are easements and other rights which are granted to the purchaser, and exceptions and reservations in favour of the vendor.

The need to strive for complete accuracy when describing the land to be conveyed cannot be stressed too frequently, though, alas, the parcels clause does not always receive the attention that its importance warrants. One recent judicial observation castigates modern conveyances for being all too often indefinite and contradictory in their parcels[15]. It is clearly impracticable on the grounds of expense alone to expect every purchaser to have a detailed survey undertaken so as to check that the actual boundaries of the plot correspond with the description given in the muniments of title. To this extent the system of land registration, which describes every registered title by reference to an officially (and expertly) prepared plan, solves many, but not all[16], of the problems that may arise from inadequately drafted parcels. Every purchaser's solicitor should at the very least check with his client that the description of the land in the contract and the conveyance corresponds with the land which the purchaser thinks he is buying, that any plan by reference to which the land is conveyed is accurate and does not conflict with the verbal description, and that the plan annexed to the conveyance or other deed is not at variance with the contract plan[17]. The taking of these elementary precautions at the appropriate stages should reveal in most cases the existence of any discrepancy between what the purchaser thinks he is purchasing and what the vendor intends to sell, so reducing the risk of litigation between the parties. Once the contract has been signed, a purchaer will not normally have any redress if he discovers that he is not getting what he thought he was purchasing, save where the contract itself contains a misdescription as to quantity or quality. It is also equally essential for the vendor's solicitor when drafting the contract to ensure that the description of the property in the particulars is accurate and accords with what the vendor intends to sell[18]. Special care should be exercised when drafting parcels and delineating boundaries on a sub-division of land into smaller plots, or on the development of a building estate.

2. Mode of description

The aim of the description should be to enable the purchaser to identify on the spot the extent of the land which it embraces and where the boundaries lie[19]. If this counsel of perfection were to be strictly observed the parcels clause of many modern conveyances would be considerably longer than they often are. On a conveyance of land leading to first registration of title, it is essential to ensure that the deed contains sufficient particulars of the land, by plan or otherwise, to enable the property to be fully identified on the ordnance map or the

---

14 Page 531, post.
15 *Neilson v Poole* (1969) 20 P & CR 909 at 915, per Megarry J. See also *Willson v Greene* [1971] 1 All ER 1098 at 1103, per Foster J, for another instance of parcels judicially branded as vague.
16 See p. 516, post.
17 As occurred in *Willson v Greene* [1971] 1 All ER 1098.
18 See e.g. *Lloyd v Stanbury* [1971] 2 All ER 267. See further p. 143, ante.
19 Cf. *Eastwood v Ashton* [1915] AC 900 at 912, per Lord Parker.

Registry's general map[20]. The form of description may vary according to the type of property conveyed. It may be sufficient to describe a dwellinghouse with clearly defined boundaries in some such form as:

> ' ALL THAT dwellinghouse known as   together with the land forming the site thereof and occupied therewith.'

This mode of description, often employed on the sale of terraced houses, is clearly inadequate where uncertainty may exist as to the extent of the land occupied with the property[1]. The description of a plot of land on a building estate is often partly verbal, and partly visual, the former including a reference to the intended address of the property, a statement of the plot area and (sometimes) the dimensions of its boundaries. This description will normally be adopted on subsequent sales, but care must be exercised on each occasion to bring it up-to-date where necessary. A more detailed description may be essential in a conveyance of industrial property or agricultural land, though in practice long verbal descriptions can be avoided by using an accurate plan[2]. It may be convenient to place a lengthy or involved description in a schedule at the end of the conveyance. For instance, on a sale of agricultural land, it may be desired to give the name or ordnance survey map number and the area of particular fields included in the conveyance, and it is clearly preferable to tabulate this information in schedule form.

In practice the description of the parcels frequently corresponds with that in the contract which in turn often repeats that appearing in the conveyance to the vendor[3]. There is no absolute rule that a vendor can insist on a repetition of the exact words employed in the contract and refuse to convey by any other description. The true rule appears to be that the purchaser is entitled to insert in the conveyance such a description as will clearly identify the land intended to be conveyed. Where the contract description is misleading, inadequate or obsolete, he can insert his own accurate description according to its condition at the date of the conveyance[4]. This appears to be the extent of the purchaser's right. If the description in the contract is of itself completely adequate to identify the land sold the vendor cannot, it seems, be compelled to convey, or to give covenants for title, by reference to a description different from that contained in the contract[5]. The right of a purchaser to supplement a verbal description by a plan raises problems for consideration in a later section of this chapter.

3.   Construction of parcels

Problems of construction arise when a conveyance adopts more than one mode of description and it has to be determined which of two conflicting descriptions is to prevail, or where the parcels are vague so that it becomes necessary to look outside the deed to ascertain the extent of the land conveyed. The dangers of a

20   See LRR 1925, rr. 20 (iii), 50−54.
1   See e.g. *Leachman v L. & K. Richardson Ltd* [1969] 3 All ER 20.
2   For examples of different forms of parcels clauses, see 15 Ency F & P, 590−602; Hallett, 181−86.
3   See *Wallington v Townsend* [1939] Ch 588, [1939] 2 All ER 225 (note 9, p. 143, ante for the dangers of this practice).
4   *Re Sansom and Narbeth's Contract* [1910] 1 Ch 741 at 749, per Swinfen Eady J, adopting a passage from 1 Williams V & P (1st edn), 557; see now 4th edn Vol. I, 651.
5   Williams V & P, 651.

multiple description were considered by Lord Sumner in *Eastwood v Ashton*[6], a leading case on the construction of the parcels. He said:

' As long as only one species of description is resorted to in describing parcels no harm is done, and often good, by copious enumeration of particulars all belonging to that species. If the description is by name, certainty is increased by naming every close which has a separate name; if by metes and bounds, by setting out every bound; if by admeasurement, by stating not only acres and roods, but also poles. To do this is always troublesome and often impracticable, but at least it is not a cause of uncertainty. If, however, several different species of description are adopted, risk of uncertainty at once arises, for if one is full, accurate, and adequate, any others are otiose if right, and misleading if wrong.'

In this case the House of Lords had to decide whether a small strip of land some 150 feet long by 36 feet wide was included in a conveyance of a farm containing over 84 acres. The parcels were described by reference to four matters: (i) the name of the farm, (ii) its acreage, (iii) the names of the occupants and (iv) a plan drawn to scale and indorsed on the deed. Their Lordships held that the description by reference to the plan, which showed that the strip of land was included, must prevail. It was the only certain and unambiguous description; the remaining descriptions could only be rendered certain by extrinsic evidence. The description by name was too vague and by itself gave no indication whether any particular plot of land was comprised within the farm. The description by area could be disregarded; it was merely approximate (i.e. stated to be 'or thereabouts') and could be satisfied either with or without the inclusion of the small strip of land. The reference to occupation[7] was in fact erroneous since the person named as the occupant of the part which included the disputed strip had sub-let to others who were in occupation.

(a) Falsa demonstratio non nocet

A description of the land conveyed, sufficient of itself to render certain what is intended to be conveyed, will prevail and the addition of a wrong name or of an erroneous statement as to quantity, occupancy, locality, or an erroneous enumeration of particulars will be ignored[8]. If V conveys to P his freehold property known as 'Blackacre' stated to be in the County of Leicester, the court will give effect to the grant notwithstanding that the property is in fact located in Derbyshire; the erroneous description is rejected as a 'false demonstration'. This rule which applies alike to deeds and wills[9] is often expressed in the terms of the latin maxim *falsa demonstratio non nocet* — a false description does not vitiate. The order in which the conflicting descriptions occur is not decisive. The court can reject a false statement even though it precedes the true description, but the maxim cannot be applied unless and until the court has decided

6 [1915] AC 900 at 915–16, HL.
7 A description by occupation is one so inconclusive and liable to error that it will readily yield to any more accurate and convincing description: per Lord Wrenbury, at 919. For a case where the words 'in the occupation of the purchaser' were held to be the only description capable of determining whether a disputed plot of land passed, see *Gresty v Meacock* (1961) 180 Estates Gazette 653, CA.
8 *Cowen v Truefitt Ltd* [1898] 2 Ch 551 at 554, per Romer J; affd. on other grounds, [1899] 2 Ch 309, CA.
9 Many of the reported cases relate to the construction of wills; see *Hardwick v Hardwick* (1873) LR 16 Eq 168 (location and occupation wrongly described); *Portman v Mill* (1839) 8 LJ Ch 161 (erroneous statement of area disregarded).

which of two or more conflicting descriptions ought to be considered as the true one[10].

Where the grant is expressed in *general* terms coupled with a particular description, the latter is not rejected as a false description but is treated as restricting the generality of the grant. Thus in *Homer v Homer*[11], a testator devised to X all his land 'situate at G in the occupation of S'. It was held that the devise did not pass land at G occupied by J. Similarly where general words of description in the parcels refer to a schedule containing a definite and specific enumeration of particulars, and the enumeration omits something which might otherwise be covered by the general description, the designation by schedule is read as restrictive of the general description and only the property mentioned in the schedule will pass[12]. The court does not readily infer an error or falsehood[13]; consequently any doubt as to whether words are a false demonstration or words of restriction will be resolved in favour of the latter.

(b) Recitals explaining parcels
The court, if still unable to determine from the parcels the extent of the land comprised within the conveyance, will endeavour to ascertain the parties' intentions by looking at the remainder of the deed, and in particular at the recitals. For instance where a recital shows an intention to convey specific property (e.g. all V's land in the County of Leicester) and the parcels describe the property in terms sufficiently general to include other property not within the recital (e.g. all V's land and V has land in an adjoining county), the recital operates to limit the grant and only the specific property passes[14]. But, as we have seen[15], a recital cannot control the operative words of the conveyance if they are clear and unambiguous. Therefore parcels described with certainty are not extended, or cut down, by a recital showing that more, or less, was intended to be conveyed[16].

Recitals may assist the court in deciding which of two (or more) possible constructions that may be given to the parcels is the correct one. In *Eastwood v Ashton*[17] the conveyance recited that the land intended to be assured was described as lot 4 in the particulars of sale at a certain public auction. Since there was an ambiguity in the parcels, their Lordships were entitled to have recourse to the recital to see what lands were described as lot 4 and this revealed that the disputed strip was intended to be conveyed to the purchaser. Where there is doubt between two possible constructions, the operative part should be construed so as to give effect to that intention[18].

(c) Extrinsic evidence
It is a question of fact whether a particular plot of land is or is not included within the description in the parcels. Should uncertainty still exist after looking at the parcels and the remainder of the deed, recourse may be had to extrinsic

10 *Eastwood v Ashton* [1915] AC 900 at 912–13, per Lord Parker.
11 (1878) 8 Ch D 758, CA.
12 *Re Brocket, Dawes v Miller* [1908] 1 Ch 185 at 196, per Joyce J; cf. *Re McManus, ex p Jardine* (1875) 10 Ch App 322.
13 *Morrell v Fisher* (1849) 4 Exch 591 at 606, per Alderson B.
14 *Jenner v Jenner* (1866) LR 1 Eq 361; *Re Earl of Durham, Earl Grey v Earl of Durham* (1887) 57 LT 164.
15 Page 491, ante.
16 *Re Medley, ex p Glyn* (1840) 1 Mont D & De G 29.
17 [1915] AC 900, HL, p. 507, ante.
18 At 920, per Lord Wrenbury.

evidence to identify the land. Where land is conveyed by reference to its name together with the land occupied with it, evidence may be given to establish that a disputed strip of land has previously been recognised as part by former owners. The acts of parties, contemporaneous or even later in date, may be admissible in proper circumstances to construe a deed the meaning of which, without such evidence, is doubtful[19]. In particular evidence of what a common vendor has done in subsequent conveyances is relevant, at least if it amounts to an admission against the interests of himself and his successors in title[20]. Thus if the vendor of plot A subsequently conveys the adjoining plot B in a form which resolves against his interests some doubtful dimension or boundary, this is an admissible aid to the construction of the conveyance of plot A[1]. Where the line of a boundary is unidentifiable because of the vagueness of the parcels, the court may accept a boundary marked out on the land and agreed to by the parties prior to the contract[2]. Unless the conveyance contains a full recital of the agreement for sale[3], the contract itself cannot normally be resorted to for construction purposes since it is superseded by the conveyance on completion.

It should always be remembered, however, that extrinsic evidence can only be resorted to in cases of doubt and uncertainty. It is not admissible to vary or contradict the terms of the instrument[4].

4. Plans

(a) Use of plans
It is common practice on a sub-division of land or on the development of a building estate to describe the land by the additional means of a plan, or map. Established property is often conveyed by reference to a plan on an earlier deed. Unfortunately the preparation of the plan is sometimes marked by a total disregard for the demands of accuracy. Plans, not drawn to scale, are hastily prepared or copied by a junior member of the staff, using totally unsuitable drawing implements. If an annexed plan is to have any meaningful significance, and in particular if it is intended to control the verbal[5] description, it should be prepared by a surveyor[6], drawn to a sufficiently large scale to enable measurements to be arrived at with some degree of accuracy, and contain adequate information as to dimensions to identify clearly the boundaries of the land conveyed[6a]. Care should also be taken to ensure that no conflict exists between the plan and the verbal description. The case of *Hopgood v Brown*[7]

19 *Watcham v A-G of the East African Protectorate* [1919] AC 533, PC. The extent to which this case is good law is doubtful, but see *L Schuler AG v Wickman Machine Tool Sales Ltd* [1974] AC 235, [1973] 2 All ER 39, HL; the observations of Megarry J in *Neilson v Poole* (1969) 20 P & CR 909 at 914–15 and in *St. Edmundsbury Diocesan Board of Finance v Clark (No 2)* [1973] 3 All ER 902 at 915–16.

20 *Neilson v Poole* (1969) 20 P & CR 909; *Smout v Farquharson* (1971) 220 Estates Gazette 1595 (common vendor's continued use of disputed strip).

1 An example cited by Megarry J in *Neilson v Poole* (1969) 20 P & CR 909 at 913.

2 *Wilson v Greene* [1971] 1 All ER 1098; *Scarfe v Adams* [1981] 1 All ER 843 (auction particulars admissible).

3 As in *Eastwood v Ashton* [1915] AC 900.

4 See p. 489, ante.

5 In this context 'verbal' signifies the written description of the property in the deed as opposed to the plan.

6 The consent of the Controller of H.M. Stationery Office is required for the reproduction of part of an ordnance survey map. Solicitors can obtain a licence to make copies on payment of an annual fee; see Emmet, 435.

6a See *Scarfe v Adams* [1981] 1 All ER 843, CA.

7 [1955] 1 All ER 550, CA.

demonstrates the problems that can arise when there is a discrepancy between
the plan and the actual boundaries apparent on inspection of the site.

> In 1932 two adjoining plots of land, plot A and plot B, were conveyed to
> the same purchaser by separate conveyances expressed in similar terms.
> In neither case were any measurements given of the common boundary
> between the plots but on the deed plans it appeared as a straight line. Plot
> A was the subject of various transactions and ultimately it became vested
> in the plaintiff. In each conveyance the same description was adopted as
> was used on the first conveyance of plot A. In the meantime the defen-
> dant who owned plot B had built a garage on his land which encroached
> upon plot A, making the boundary between the plots appear to be in two
> straight lines forming an obtuse angle. The plaintiff sued for the trespass
> in respect of the garage.

A majority of the Court of Appeal held that the repetition in the subsequent
conveyances of plot A of the same parcels as appeared in the 1932 deed showed
that what was conveyed on each occasion was precisely the same plot as was conveyed in 1932, and the construction of the plaintiff's conveyance was not
affected by the defendant's alteration of the boundary. The garage was held to
be an encroachment but the plaintiff's claim was dismissed on other grounds.

Reference should be made in the parcels clause to any plan drawn on or
bound up inside the deed. A plan forming part of a conveyance but not referred
to in it may be looked at to identify the land conveyed, provided the description
of the parcels, read in the light of the other admissible evidence, still leaves it
uncertain as to what is included[8], but not where there is no ambiguity or doubt.
It is apparently good conveyancing practice to have the plan signed by the
parties executing the deed[9] but, save in the case of a plan used on a transfer of
registered land when signature of the plan is required[10], this procedure does not
seem to be widely adopted by practitioners.

(b) Construction

A properly incorporated plan forms part of the description of the property and
must be considered when determining the extent and effect of the grant. The
parcels may indicate that the plan is to rank as the primary description. In the
absence of words suggesting otherwise the plan is prima facie regarded as being
an alternative visual description, not intended to contradict the verbal description, and the court will endeavour to give effect to both. In *Truckell v Stock*[11]
the question arose whether the conveyance of a house passed to the purchaser
the eaves and footings projecting beyond the area of the land as depicted on the
deed plan. The court refused to recognise any inconsistency between the plan
which indicated the boundary at ground level and the verbal description
referring to a 'dwellinghouse', which was taken to mean all parts of the house
including the protruding eaves and footings (but not the intervening column of
air). In the event of a conflict, however, it becomes necessary to decide which

---

8   *Leachman v L. & K. Richardson Ltd* [1969] 3 All ER 20, distinguishing the contrary
    opinion, relied on by *Norton on Deeds* (2nd edn) p. 238, in *Wyse v Leahy* (1875) IR 9 CL
    384.
9   Law Society's Digest, Opinion No. 157.
10 LRR 1925, rr. 79, 113.
11 [1957] 1 All ER 74, CA. See also *Grigsby v Melville* [1973] 3 All ER 455, CA (conveyance
    of house passed underground cellar though existing access to cellar exclusively via the
    adjoining premises retained by vendor).

prevails—the plan or the verbal description. The court may resolve the problem by applying the rule of *falsa demonstratio non nocet*[12], or the deed itself may point one way or the other.

(i) *Plan prevails.* The conveyance may describe the property as 'more particularly delineated [or described] on the plan drawn hereon and thereon edged red'. Such words tend to show that in case of conflict or uncertainty the plan is to prevail[13]. Even without any guiding phrase, the plan will prevail if it is clear and unambiguous, whereas the verbal description is vague and requires extrinsic evidence to render it certain[14].

(ii) *Plan not prevailing.* The verbal description has been held to prevail when the plan was drawn on so small a scale that the boundaries could not be ascertained with sufficient precision[15]. The plan may also be displaced by a clear and complete verbal description[16]. One method often adopted on the development of building estates is to state that the plan is for 'the purposes of identification only and not by way of limitation or enlargement.' Formerly it was thought that phrases of this nature confined the use of the plan to ascertaining the situation of the land; it could not control the parcels nor assist in identifying the precise boundaries[17]. However, the Court of Appeal have held sensibly that the wording does not prevent the use of a plan limited by those words to define boundaries if the verbal description is unclear[18]. From a purchaser's standpoint, the use of a plan for identification only is not objectionable if the plot can be recognised as such on inspection and its boundaries are clearly defined or its measurements given in the verbal description. Yet there seems to be a general reluctance to state the measurements with the result that it is impossible to locate the exact boundaries from the verbal description. Moreover the introduction of the qualifying words is sometimes taken as conferring permission upon the developer to alter the boundaries after exchange of contracts. However all may not always be lost for the purchaser who discovers after completion that his plot has been reduced in size. In *Wilson v Greene*[19] Foster J held that where the parcels are approximate a boundary marked out and agreed by the parties supersedes a plan which is for identification only.

The qualifying phrase 'for the purposes of identification only' should not be linked with the expression 'more particularly delineated on the plan'. As Megarry J observed in *Neilson v Poole*[20], when used together they tend to be mutually stultifying and do not give the plan any predominance over the verbal

12 Page 490, ante. *Llewellyn v Earl of Jersey* (1843) 11 M & W 183.
13 *Neilson v Poole* (1969) 20 P & CR 909 at 916, per Megarry J. See e.g. *Wallington v Townsend* [1939] Ch 588, [1939] 2 All ER 225.
14 See e.g. *Eastwood v Ashton* [1915] AC 900 at 912, HL, per Lord Parker, though in this case the property was also more particularly described in a plan.
15 *Taylor v Parry* (1840) 1 Man & G 604. See *Scarfe v Adams* [1981] 1 All ER 843, CA.
16 *Willis v Watney* (1881) 51 LJ Ch 181 (yard not coloured on plan held to pass because parcels referred to 'yards'); cf. *Smith v Sun Garage (Kingsdown) Ltd* (1961) 179 Estates Gazette 89.
17 *Neilson v Poole* (1969) 20 P & CR 909 at 916, per Megarry J.
18 *Wigginton and Milner Ltd v Winster Engineering Ltd* [1978] 3 All ER 436. For problems in the case of registered land see [1979] Conv 316—319, 398—399.
19 [1971] 1 All ER 1098, following *Webb v Nightingale* (1957) 169 Estates Gazette 330, CA; *Sharwood Properties (Ealing) Ltd v Maclellan* (1971) 219 Estates Gazette 830 (boundary fixed by common vendor and defendant's predecessor).
20 (1969) 20 P & CR 909 at 916.

description. The frequency with which one encounters this combination of expressions suggests that many draftsmen are using them solely out of habit, unaware of their legal significance.

(c) Purchaser's entitlement to plan

The question sometimes arises whether the purchaser is entitled to have the land conveyed by reference to a plan, in a case where the vendor has contracted to sell by means of a verbal description. It is the vendor's duty to convey the property under a description which is a sufficient and satisfactory identification of the land sold. If he can do this without a plan the purchaser cannot insist on a plan in the conveyance, for this would involve the vendor in unnecessary expense in having the accuracy of the plan checked by his own surveyor. In *Re Sharman and Meade's Contract*[1] the vendor's proposed description ran:

> ' All that piece or parcel of land situate . . . in . . . Brighton bounded on the west by Norfolk Square, on the north by No. 28 Norfolk Square, on the east by No. 30 Norfolk Square and on the south by No. 26 Norfolk Square together with the . . . dwellinghouse erected thereon . . . and known as No. 27 Norfolk Square.'

Farwell J rejected the purchaser's claim that he was entitled to a plan. As the proposed plan was intended to be for identification purposes only, it did not add anything to the verbal description which was perfectly adequate without it. In the earlier case of *Re Sansom and Narbeth's Contract*[2], Swinfen Eady J is reported as saying that in ordinary simple cases the purchaser is entitled to a conveyance by reference to a plan as part of the rule that he is entitled to have the conveyance in his own form, but this observation must be read subject to his previous remark that the plan must assist the description.

On the question of the sufficiency or otherwise of the verbal description, each case must depend on its particular facts. Where the description in the contract fails to identify the boundaries (e.g. by measurements) and there are insufficient physical features on the land itself to enable them to be located, the purchaser would seem to be within his rights to insist upon a plan. In this situation the vendor cannot insist on the insertion in the conveyance of such restrictive words as 'for the purposes of identification only'[3].

The vendor cannot refuse to convey by reference to a plan if the property is so described in the contract, and it seems he cannot object to one prepared by the purchaser should the latter show that the contract plan is inaccurate. Conversely, it is thought that the purchaser must accept the introduction of qualifying words in the conveyance if the land was so described in the particulars of sale, unless the verbal description is itself vague and meaningless without the plan, though it is arguable that by not raising the point before signing the contract he has lost his right to object later.

5. Boundaries

The necessity for a landowner to know the exact boundaries of his land is all too obvious in these days of land scarcity and high density development, when a

---

1 [1936] Ch 755, [1936] 2 All ER 1547.
2 [1910] 1 Ch 741 at 749–50, explained by Farwell J in *Re Sharman and Meade's Contract* [1936] Ch 755, [1936] 2 All ER 1547. The two decisions are not easy to reconcile.
3 *Re Sparrow and James' Contract* (1902) [1910] 2 Ch 60.

matter of a few feet can be of vital importance to the householder contemplating an extension to his property. The courts are not infrequently asked to adjudicate upon boundary disputes (often of a comparatively trivial nature) and in many of these instances litigation could have been avoided had the deeds delineated the boundaries with greater precision. On a new estate development the opportunity should be taken, not only of indicating clearly the plot boundaries, but also of defining the ownership of boundary walls and fences. Such is the general difficulty of defining boundaries that the Conditions of Sale commonly absolve a vendor from having to establish the exact boundary line[4]. Where the relevant deeds do not resolve the problem, recourse may be had to certain legal presumptions to ascertain the exact boundary limits.

(a) Walls fences and hedges[5]

(i) *Walls and fences.* A boundary wall built exclusively on the land of one person belongs to him and an adjoining owner has no rights in respect of it unless he can prove an easement of support. A demise of a building bounded by an outside wall prima facie includes both sides of the wall[6]. Prior to 1926 a wall which straddled the boundary was presumed, in the absence of evidence to the contrary, to belong to the adjoining owners as tenants in common, along with the land on which it was built. Such a wall was known as a party wall[7], and each owner enjoyed mutual rights of support. Now by virtue of s. 38 of the Law of Property Act 1925, which substitutes vertical severance for the former tenancy in common, each adjoining owner becomes sole owner of his respective section, but without prejudice to his rights over the rest of the structure. The majority of party walls and other structures used in common are now governed by s. 38[8]. An agreement and declaration, commonly inserted in post-1925 conveyances, that dividing walls and fences are deemed to be party walls and fences suffices to bring s. 38 into operation, for such a clause created a tenancy in common in the wall before 1926[9]. The usual form of declaration[10] provides for the adjoining owners to contribute equally to the cost of repairs, but does not impose any duty to repair. This may be a serious omission, for s. 38 does not create any new liabilities. At common law a duty to support did not involve any obligation to repair[11], though one co-tenant was entitled to repair the other's half of the wall (but at his own expense[12]) so far as was reasonably necessary for the enjoyment of his own rights in the wall[13]. A right to have a wall or fence maintained by one's neighbour may, however, arise by prescription at common law and the

---

4   NCS 13 (2), p. 144, ante.
5   See Powell-Smith, *Law of Boundaries and Fences*, (2nd edn).
6   *Goldfoot v Welch* [1914] 1 Ch 213; *Re Webb's Lease, Sandom v Webb* [1951] Ch 808, [1951] 2 All ER 131, CA (no right for landlord to maintain hoarding).
7   The term 'party wall' might be used in one of four different senses; see *Watson v Gray* (1880) 14 Ch D 192 at 194–95, per Fry J. It was most commonly used to denote the type of party wall discussed in the text.
8   In Inner London a special code contained in the London Building Acts (Amendment) Act 1939, Pt. VI, regulates the rights of adjoining owners in relation to party structures, to the exclusion of their common law rights. See Wright, 'Party Walls in London' (1954) 18 Conv (NS) 347. The Law Commission have suggested a possible extension of this code, suitably amended, throughout the country: Law Com. Working Paper No. 36, para. 50.
9   *Watson v Gray* (1880) 14 Ch D 192.
10   See e.g. 18 Ency F & P, 431.
11   *Sack v Jones* [1925] Ch 235.
12   See *Leigh v Dickeson* (1884) 15 QBD 60, CA.
13   *Jones v Pritchard* [1908] 1 Ch 630 at 638, per Parker J.

right is of such a nature as to be capable of passing under s. 62 of the Law of Property Act 1925[14].

On the development of a building estate it is common practice for conveyances of individual plots to impose on each purchaser an obligation to erect and maintain one or more dividing fences (appropriately marked, often by a 'T' mark, on the deed plan)[15]. In such cases the fence will mark the boundary and will be deemed to belong to the party responsible for its repair, although it is perhaps preferable for the deed to indicate which fences are included in the grant. The covenant to repair is not enforceable by the neighbouring owner. Alternatively dividing fences may be declared to be party fences, repairable at the joint expense of each neighbour. The difficulties surrounding this alternative have been noticed. One party can enforce the obligation to contribute against the other but not, as a matter of contract, against a successor in title, for the burden of a positive covenant does not run at law[16]. The common belief that a fence belongs to the owner of the land on whose side the posts and rails are placed is without legal foundation.

(ii) *Hedges and ditches.* Where two plots of land are separated by a hedge or bank and ditch the boundary prima facie runs along the edge of the ditch away from the hedge or bank. The person who made the ditch is presumed to have dug it at the extremity of his land and thrown the soil on his own land to form the bank. This has been described as a convenient rule of common sense which, nevertheless, rests on rather slender foundations; it assumes what may not be true, that when the ditch was dug there was no common ownership of the two pieces of land[17]. The presumption does not apply where the title deeds show the actual boundary. In particular if the parcels describe the boundaries by reference to the ordnance survey map, the boundary is presumed to run down the centre of the hedge or ditch in accordance with the universal practice of the ordnance survey when making up their maps[18]. Therefore, where land is conveyed by reference to the ordnance survey map and the boundaries do not extend to the centre of any hedges, the parcels should clearly state the exact line of the boundary. The hedge and ditch presumption, where applicable, can be rebutted but apparent acts of ownership by the adjoining owner, such as cleaning the ditch, are not sufficient[19].

(b) Highways
A person owning land adjoining a public or private road is presumed to own also the soil of one-half of the road co-extensive with his land (*usque ad medium filum viae*). This is not a mere conveyancing presumption. It is a rule of

---

14   *Lawrence v Jenkins* (1873) LR 8 QB 274; *Jones v Price* [1965] 2 QB 618, [1965] 2 All ER 625, CA; *Crow v Wood* [1971] 1 QB 77, [1970] 3 All ER 425, CA; *Egerton v Harding* [1975] QB 62, [1974] 3 All ER 689, CA. For the operation of s. 62, see pp. 527–530, post.

15   For a full discussion of the various possibilities, see Adams, 'Ownership of Fences – The Conveyancer's Choice' (1971) 68 LS Gaz 275, 375.

16   It is arguable that the successor may be bound on the principle of mutual benefits and burdens; see *Halsall v Brizell* [1957] Ch 169, [1957] 1 All ER 371.

17   *Fischer v Winch* [1939] 1 KB 666 at 669–70, [1939] 2 All ER 144 at 145, CA, per Sir Wilfrid Greene MR. It is doubtful whether the presumption applies to a natural ditch: *Marshall v Taylor* [1895] 1 Ch 641, CA.

18   *Fischer v Winch* [1939] 1 KB 666, [1939] 2 All ER 144, CA. See also *Davey v Harrow Corpn* [1958] 1 QB 60, [1957] 2 All ER 305, CA.

19   *Henniker v Howard* (1904) 90 LT 157.

construction that a house includes a moiety of the road in which it is situated[20]. A conveyance or lease of land operates prima facie to pass one half in width of an adjacent road, including one which is only a private road[1]. The presumption is rebuttable, but not simply by showing that the land is described as containing an area which can be satisfied without including half of the road, or that the land is described as bounded by the road, or is edged in colour on the deed plan but the road is uncoloured[2]. It may, however, be rebutted by express negative words in the conveyance, by showing that the site of the road was not vested in the vendor, or by evidence of surrounding circumstances leading to the inference that no part of the road was intended to pass[3].

The presumption is readily rebutted on the sale of plots forming part of a building estate, for the developer needs to retain ownership of the soil of the intended roads for the purposes of construction and subsequent dedication to the public[4]. It has even been doubted whether the presumption applies at all to a building estate[5]. There is no reason why a conveyance of individual building plots (with or without houses already erected thereon) should not state expressly the intention of the parties by e.g. including within the land conveyed the appropriate area of road and reserving to the developers a right of way over it. Unless the conveyance vests the soil of the intended road in individual purchasers, the developers will retain a legal estate in the soil of the estate roads long after they have developed the estate[6]. The owner of land which includes the site of a road still retains ownership of the sub-soil, even after its dedication to the public, for the effect of dedication is simply to vest in the highway authority a fee simple estate in the surface of the road and so much above and below as may be necessary for it to carry out its statutory duties[7].

A similar presumption applies on the conveyance of land abutting on a non-tidal river so as to pass to the grantee the bed of the river up to the medial line and with it the right to fish in the water above that half of the bed[8]. The presumption does not operate to pass islands in mid-stream; the presumed boundary is drawn between the island and the shore[9].

(c) Projections
On the conveyance of property part of which overhangs the vendor's adjoining land, the purchaser should ensure that the vendor grants to him a right to

---

20 *Central London Rly Co v City of London Land Tax Comrs* [1911] 1 Ch 467 at 474, CA, per Cozens-Hardy, MR; affd. sub nom *City of London Land Tax Comrs v Central London Rly Co* [1913] AC 364. For a discussion of the origins of this rule see Cozens-Hardy MR, loc. cit.
1 *Lang v House* (1961) 178 Estates Gazette 801.
2 *Norton on Deeds* (2nd edn), p. 252; *Dwyer v Rich* (1871) IR 6 CL 144 at 149, per Fitzgerald J.
3 For examples, see *Pryor v Petre* [1894] 2 Ch 11, CA; *Mappin Bros v Liberty & Co Ltd* [1903] 1 Ch 118.
4 *Leigh v Jack* (1879) 5 Ex D 264; *Giles v County Building Constructors (Hertford) Ltd* (1971) 22 P & CR 278.
5 *Leigh v Jack* (1879) 5 Ex D 264 at 274, per Cotton LJ.
6 This produces an absurd result in cases where the developer is a limited company which is subsequently dissolved; under the Companies Act 1948, s. 354, the sub-soil will vest in the Crown as bona vacantia.
7 *Tithe Redemption Commission v Runcorn UDC* [1954] Ch 383, [1954] 1 All ER 653, CA. See *Royco Homes Ltd v Eatonwill Construction Ltd* [1979] Ch 276, [1978] 2 All ER 821.
8 See *Hesketh v Willis Cruisers Ltd* (1968) 19 P & CR 573, CA; *Rice v Dodds* (1969) 213 Estates Gazette 759.
9 *Great Torrington Commons Conservators v Moore Stevens* [1903] 1 Ch 347.

maintain the projections (usually overhanging eaves and protruding footings) over the vendor's land together with a right of entry for the purposes of maintenance[10]. Failure to make express provision for these matters may not be fatal, though it may give rise to future difficulties. In *Truckell v Stock*[11] the footings and eaves protruded beyond the area shown by the deed plan but it was held that the reference in the parcels to a 'dwellinghouse' showed that the parties intended all its parts including projections to pass. In the earlier case of *Corbett v Hill*[12] a vendor conveyed land which was overhung by certain first floor rooms of the house next door owned by himself; the court held that these rooms remained part of his house but the column of air above and below the protrusion passed to the purchaser. Where a house is built flush with the plot boundary no reservation of a right of access over the adjoining land for the purposes of inspecting and maintaining the flank wall will be implied[13].

(d) Boundary agreements

The parties to a boundary dispute may settle their differences by entering into a boundary agreement. This can take one of two forms[14]. It may constitute a contract to convey land as where they agree that in return for a concession by A in one place, straightening the boundary, B will make a concession in another place. Such an agreement should be registered as a land charge, and if unregistered the agreement is statutorily avoided against a subsequent purchaser. However it is unlikely that he would be allowed by equity to revoke the agreement without giving up the land his predecessor had acquired. Indeed revocation may not even be open to a subsequent purchaser since he would seem to be estopped from denying that the boundaries were otherwise than as set out in the agreement[15]. Alternatively the agreement may do nothing more than identify on the ground what is described in words or delineated in plans. This is not registrable as there is no contract to convey. Boundary agreements are usually of an informal nature, and the courts tend to regard them as falling into the second category unless there is clear evidence that the agreement is intended to convey land.

6. Registered land

(a) Description of registered land

According to s. 76 of the Land Registration Act 1925, registered land may be described on the register of title in one of three different ways, regard being had

---

10   Thése rights, if constituting legal easements, will bind a purchaser of the retained land without express mention in his conveyance.

11   [1957] 1 All ER 74, CA; *Fox v Clarke* (1874) LR 9 QB 565.

12   (1870) LR 9 Eq 671 Cf. *Laybourn v Gridley* [1892] 2 Ch 53, where a conveyance of land was held to pass the overhanging part of the adjoining premises retained by the vendor. This case may perhaps be explained on the ground that the parcels showed that the deed plan was to prevail (see North J, at 58), but this can hardly have been what the vendor intended. In *Grigsby v Melville* [1973] 1 All ER 385; affd. [1973] 3 All ER 455 (note 11, p. 510, ante). Brightman J (at 390) described *Laybourn v Gridley* as 'a fairly extreme case' and suggested that it might be decided differently today. And see (1957) 21 Conv (NS) 164.

13   *Kwiatkowski v Cox* (1969) 213 Estates Gazette 34. Had the plaintiff's conveyance preceded the defendant's it seems unlikely that he could have established an implied grant of an easement. See also *Ward v Kirkland* [1967] Ch 194, [1966] 1 All ER 609.

14   *Neilson v Poole* (1969) 20 P & CR 909 at 918–20, per Megarry J.

15   *Hopgood v Brown* [1955] 1 All ER 550, CA.

to ready identification of parcels, correct descriptions of boundaries and, so far as may be, uniformity of practice. Only one of the three permissible methods is used in practice, namely the verbal description used in conjunction with the filed plan (which is preferred to the general map)[16], thus:

> The freehold land shown and edged with red on the plan of the above Title filed at the Registry registered on   known as 'Fairhaven', Mead Road, Oadby.

The description of every registered title by means of an accurate and expertly prepared plan based on the ordnance survey map achieves one of the principal objectives of the system of registered conveyancing, that of certainty, and enables the system to score over the unregistered system in a vital respect[17]. But the advantages of the filed plan should not be over-emphasised. In particular the plan which is drawn to a scale of 1/1250 (104.166 feet to 1 inch)[18], does little more than indicate the location of the land. It is too small to show short distances or record kinks in an otherwise straight boundary, and no measurements or dimensions appear on the plan. The Registry will always consider a request for a plan on a larger scale and will provide an enlargement when, for example, there are small buildings, such as a washhouse or garage, physically separated from the main plot, which would not be clearly visible on the normal size plan[19]. Furthermore criticism is sometimes made of the Registry's plans because they are not as informative as the best plans used in unregistered conveyancing, and information recorded on deed plans, of assistance in determining the ownership of boundary structures, is not reproduced on the register of title or the field plan and is therefore lost on first registration. This information can, however, be readily obtained by consulting the pre-registration deeds[20]. It is the Registry's practice to make an entry on the register of any declaration as to the ownership of boundary structures contained in a transfer of registered land[1].

On a transfer of the whole of the land comprised within a registered title the prescribed form of transfer describes the property simply as 'the land comprised in the title above referred to.' On a sale of part the wording is

> ' the land shown and edged with red on the accompanying plan and known as   being part of the land comprised in the title above referred to.'[2]

---

16   See p. 40, ante.
17   See R & R, 43. The Chief Land Registrar estimates that approximately one plan in eight used in unregistered conveyancing transactions is seriously defective. The advantage of the filed plan is not put forward so boldly in the current edition of R & R. Cf. p. 43 as opposed to p. 46 of the 3rd edition. Similarly the old advantage of registration (6) at p. 10 of the 3rd edition has now disappeared (p. 10). In so far as this represents a more cautious assessment of registration of title it is to be welcomed.
18   For farms and smallholdings, the scale is a mere 1/2500. The Registry have announced that as from January 1969, metric measurements will gradually replace measurements based on the imperial system, but not so as to result in any wholesale substitution of the new measurements on existing plans. See Land Registry Practice Leaflet for Solicitors No. 11; R & R, 49–51.
19   R & R, 44.
20   Though some would argue that if the theory of the registered system is that the land certificate replaces the title deeds, the register of title ought to record all information that a perusal of the deeds would reveal relative to the title. But see pp. 38–40, ante.
1   R & R, 52 which sets out the occasions when 'T' marks shown on a pre-registration deed plan will be reproduced on the filed plan.
2   LRR 1925, r. 98, prescribing Form 20. A particular verbal description which is desired to be entered on the register may be added in a schedule.

The plan, which must be signed by the transferor and by or on behalf of the transferee, may be dispensed with where the property can be clearly defined by means of a verbal reference to the filed plan[3]. Occasionally the Registrar will permit the parties' own professionally drawn plan to be used as an adjunct to or even in place of the filed plan[4].

(b) Boundaries

(i) *General boundaries.* The filed plan merely indicates the general boundaries of the registered land; it does not profess to determine whether it includes a hedge or part of an adjoining road, or runs along the centre of a wall or fence, and this rule applies irrespective of whether the plan includes or excludes the whole or part of a wall, fence, ditch or road[5]. In the absence of assistance from the transfer or conveyance leading to first registration, recourse must be had to the general presumption to ascertain the exact line of the boundary. It is arguable that the general boundaries rule allows the hedge and ditch presumption to apply, notwithstanding that the ordnance survey map which is the basis of every filed plan runs the boundary line through the centre of the hedge[6]. Sometimes the filed plan shows the boundaries by dotted lines, in which case a note is added that they have been plotted from the deed plan and are liable to revision on survey. This is a common occurrence on building estates when individual plots are transferred before the erection of the fences. The Registry is reluctant to plot the boundaries from the survey or site pegs, for not infrequently these do not coincide with the fences subsequently erected.

(ii) *Fixed boundaries.* A procedure, virtually unused in practice, does exist[7] for defining the exact boundaries, so that the filed plan shows the precise position of the boundaries. Notice of an intention to fix the boundary must be given to owners and occupiers of adjoining land; their titles, if unregistered, require investigation and the applicant must produce a plan sufficiently clear to show the fixed boundary. Once fixed a note to that effect is added to the applicant's property register. Since an error made in drawing a plan with general boundaries and producing financial loss can be compensated, the ultimate gain in fixing boundaries has been said to be negligible[8].

(iii) *Inconsistencies.* Though happily such occurrences are rare, it does occasionally happen that a discrepancy exists between the verbal description contained in the property register and the filed plan or between the latter and a plan on the transfer. Conflicts falling within the first category are decided by the Registrar[9]. In *Lee v Barrey*[10]:

3   LRR 1925, r. 79.
4   See Registered Land Practice Notes 6, 45, 46; R & R, 44.
5   LRR 1925, r. 278 (1), (2), (4). It is not the Registry's practice to include the half in width of an adjoining road. The Law Commission favour the retention of this general boundaries rule: Law Com. Published Working Paper No. 45, para. 22.
6   See p. 514, ante.
7   LRR 1925, rr. 276, 277.
8   R & R, 59. Nevertheless the Law Commission are of the provisional opinion that the procedure should continue to be available; loc. cit., para. 36.
9   LRR 1925, r. 285. According to the LRA 1925, s. 76, the plan operates to assist the identification of the land, suggesting that in cases of conflict the verbal description should prevail. See [1979] Conv 316–319, 398–99.
10   [1957] Ch 251, [1957] 1 All ER 191, CA.

the defendant proprietor built a house within the boundaries indicated by the filed plan (which showed a straight boundary), though according to the transfer plan (which showed an angled boundary) part of the house was built on the plaintiff's adjacent plot. *Held*: the transfer plan prevailed, and therefore the defendant had trespassed on the plaintiff's land.

Not only did the filed plan indicate no more than the general boundaries, it also showed them as dotted lines, subject to revision on survey. In such circumstances the plan in the land certificate did not override the transfer plan which accurately recorded the bargain between the common vendor and the defendant. This case was suggested[11] as indicating a breakdown in the operation of the machinery of registered conveyancing; the land certificate was not as reliable as it was made out to be and a prudent purchaser ought to examine the plan on the previous transfer. The Chief Land Registrar has sought to allay these fears by acknowledging that the Registry neglected to apply its own procedure to the transaction in that case. The following extract from the relevant Practice Note[12] outlines the normal practice:

' . . . where the conveyance or transfer plan shows boundaries which do not agree with those actually existing on the ground, the Registry will consider the need to have either the deed plan or the boundaries altered so that the two correspond and thus give effect to the intentions of the parties . . . Where there are no physical features defining the boundaries of the land the conveyance or transfer plan will always be treated as the governing factor and the existence of survey pegs which do not conform with the boundaries shown on the deed plan will be ignored by the Registry.'

7.   Easements[13]

(a) Existing easements

An easement passes automatically without express mention on a conveyance of the dominant land to which it is appurtenant, and a failure to mention it in the parcels in no way prejudices the purchaser[14]. In practice it is customary to mention existing easements, introducing them by the words 'TOGETHER WITH'. Some practitioners merely incorporate them by reference to the deed of creation, whereas others prefer to set them out in extenso, on the basis that the parcels in the conveyance should adopt the description of the property given in the previous conveyance. No useful purpose is served by setting out rights of way previously granted over roads which have subsequently been taken over and adopted by the highway authority.

The burden of a legal easement binds the servient land and is enforceable against any subsequent owner or occupier thereof, irrespective of notice. The enforceability of equitable easements is governed either by registration or notice[15].

11   (1957) 21 Conv (NS) 162–63. R & R, 57.
12   Note 27. The defendant in *Lee v Barrey* was compensated for the loss of the land; see R & R, 57.
13   Easements are at present being considered by the Law Commission; see Published Working Paper No. 36, which does not, of course, represent the Commission's concluded views.
14   This was the rule at common law. It is conceived that an equitable easement, like a legal easement, enures for the benefit of the dominant land and passes automatically with it; see *Gale on Easements* (14th edn), p. 69.
15   See p. 388, ante.

(b) Easements created on sale
Where the conveyance to the purchaser creates easements in his favour[16], they may be set out in the parcels, similarly introduced by 'TOGETHER WITH', or alternatively, and preferably if they are lengthy, they may be set out in full in a subsequent clause of the deed[17] or in a schedule — which is the invariable practice in a transfer of registered land. Easements are commonly granted on the sale or lease of land forming part of a building estate[18].

Easements may also be created by a deed of grant independently of the conveyance of land. In the case of registered land the grant must be completed by registration, otherwise the easement operates merely in equity[19]. It should also be remembered that the effect of a conveyance may be to pass to the grantee as an easement some right or privilege not previously existing as such, either by virtue of the general words implied by s. 62 of the Law of Property Act 1925[20], or under the rule in *Wheeldon v Burrows*[1].

(c) Points to consider when granting easements[2]
It is outside the scope of this book to discuss in detail the acquistion of easements. It is, however, necessary to draw attention to certain considerations which should be borne in mind when drafting a deed which creates easements. These factors apply alike to grants and reservations. The following comments are confined principally to rights of way, these being the class of easement most frequently encountered, though many of the problems also affect other easements. Strictly speaking these matters arise for consideration at the contract stage, at least if that document purports to define the exact terms of the grant or reservation, but they can properly be discussed in this chapter since the conveyance gives effect to, and supersedes, the contract.

(i) *Extent.* Two separate points arise here: (1) the persons entitled to the benefit of the easement and (2) the scope or quality of their enjoyment. On the first point, an easement is appurtenant to the dominant land and on its subdivision into several lots the benefit of the easement will prima facie pass to the grantee of each part, possibly to the detriment of the servient land. This is an important consideration when granting to a purchaser a right to use existing drains under the grantor's land, since an increase in use may overload the grantor's pipes[3]. A typical grant[4] of a right of way is expressed in favour of

> ' the grantee his successors in title the owners and occupiers for the time being of [the dominant land] or any part thereof and his or their respective servants and licensees.'

16   The vendor can also create or reserve (this being the technical expression) easements in favour of himself; see p. 524, post.
17   In which case the parcels clause should merely state 'together with the rights and easements mentioned in clause   hereof'.
18   See further pp. 353–354, post.
19   Page 473, ante.
20   Page 527, post.
 1   (1879) 12 Ch D 31, 49, CA, per Thesiger LJ. For the operation of this rule see M & W, 830–835; Emmet, 562–565.
 2   See Bodkin, 'Easements and Uncertainty' (1971) 35 Conv (NS) 324.
 3   Where A grants to B a right to lay and maintain a drain in A's adjacent land with a right to the free and uninterrupted passage and running of water and soil through it, A cannot grant to C a right to connect into B's drain. The drain belongs to B (notwithstanding it is laid in A's land) and the effect of the grant is to give B an exclusive right to its use: *Simmons v Midford* [1969] 2 Ch 415, [1969] 2 All ER 1269.
 4   7 Ency F & P, 663, Form 1. This form will not do if it is intended to limit the right to successors of the whole of the dominant land.

Words in the grant mentioning people other than the grantee are not generally regarded as exhaustive but as illustrative[5].

On the question of scope of user, consideration should be given to the possibility of a change in the use of the dominant land. Prima facie the scope or extent of an easement is governed by the construction of the words used. For example the grant of a right of way 'at all times and for all purposes' is not restricted to the mode of user required at the time of the grant[6]. However the right of way cannot be used so as to interfere with or cause a nuisance to others entitled to the same right; the easement is construed as a grant for all the purposes within the parties' reasonable contemplation at the time of the grant[7]. Clear words are necessary to limit the exercise of the right of way in connection with the use of the dominant land at the time of the conveyance[8]. The grant of a right of a way 'as at present enjoyed' has been held to refer simply to the means of locomotion, i.e. on foot or with vehicles, not to the purposes for which the dominant land was being used at the relevant time[9]. Similarly the grant of a right of way simpliciter will be construed as a right to pass with vehicles as well as on foot, but the surrounding circumstances may operate to cut down the extent of the grant; for example the way referred to may not have been suitable for vehicular usage at the time of the grant[10]. A right of way restricted to vehicular traffic confers no right of way for pedestrians[11].

(ii) *Identification of dominant land.* The grant of an easement does not fail simply because the deed of creation fails to specify the dominant land. Consequently the older view, exemplified by *Ackroyd v Smith*[12] that the grant of a right of way for all purposes without referring to any land for the benefit of which the right was to be exercised could at the most only create a personal licence, no longer represents the law. As a matter of good conveyancing practice, however, it is highly desirable to identify the dominant land, thereby removing the element of doubt and reducing the likelihood of litigation. Adequate identification can be achieved by delineating the dominant land on the deed plan (if any) or by naming the owner or occupier of identified dominant land for the benefit of which the easement is created[13]. Where the grant fails to specify the dominant land extrinsic evidence is admissible to identify it, and when construing the deed the court is entitled to have evidence of all material facts at the time of its execution so as to place the court in the situation of the parties[14]. Difficulties in adducing such evidence will obviously arise in

---

5   *Hammond v Prentice Bros Ltd* [1920] 1 Ch 201 at 216, per Eve J.
6   *White v Grand Hotel, Eastbourne Ltd* [1913] 1 Ch 113, CA (house turned into hotel); *Jelbert v Davis* [1968] 1 All ER 1182, CA (agricultural land changed to caravan site); cf. the rule for prescriptive easements: *RPC Holdings Ltd v Rogers* [1953] 1 All ER 1029.
7   *Jelbert v Davis* [1968] 1 All ER 1182, CA.
8   E.g. a right of way 'for all purposes connected with the use and enjoyment of [the grantee's premises] as a private residence but not for any other purpose whatsoever'; see 7 Ency F & P, 667, Form 3.
9   *Hurt v Bowmer* [1937] 1 All ER 797.
10 See *Todrick v Western National Omnibus Co Ltd* [1934] Ch 190; on appeal [1934] Ch 561, CA; cf. *Keefe v Amor* [1965] 1 QB 334, [1964] 2 All ER 517, CA (right of way not limited by existing physical features); *St Edmundsbury and Ipswich Diocesan Board of Finance v Clark (No 2)* [1975] 1 All ER 772, approving Emmet, 572.
11 *Barry v Fenton* [1952] NZLR 990.
12 (1850) 10 CB 164.
13 *The Shannon Ltd v Venner Ltd* [1965] Ch 682 at 692, [1965] 1 All ER 590 at 594, CA, per Danckwerts LJ.
14 *Johnstone v Holdway* [1963] 1 QB 601, [1963] 1 All ER 432, CA.

litigation between persons who are not the original grantor and grantee, which is another reason why express identification is advisable. In the absence of any identification, there may be a presumption in favour of the land conveyed but it is rebutted if the surrounding circumstances point to a different conclusion[15]. In *The Shannon Ltd v Venner Ltd*[16] the facts were these:

> In 1927 V conveyed certain land to P. In 1930 V conveyed to P adjoining land described as to the north of land recently sold by V to P together with a right of way for P and its successors in title to use V's drive. The conveyance of 1930 did not identify the dominant land.

The Court of Appeal held that the easement was appurtenant to the whole of P's land, including the land acquired in 1927 upon which P had built a factory. On the construction of the deed of grant, the reference to the adjoining land recently sold to P, taken in conjunction with the facts that no physical division existed between the two plots and that a proposed extension of P's factory was known to V[17], pointed to the conclusion that the dominant tenement was the whole of P's land.

On the other hand, it is clear that a grantee cannot use a right of way for access to another piece of land owned by him[18]. If the dominant tenement is not clearly identified it may be possible to argue that the right of way is appurtenant to the larger plot[19].

(iii) *Application of perpetuity rule.* The grant of an easement to arise in the future is subject to the rule against perpetuities. In *Dunn v Blackdown Properties Ltd*[20] the grant of a right to use sewers and drains 'now passing or hereafter to pass' under a private road was held to be void for perpetuity, there being no sewers or drains existing at the date of the grant. The grant was not saved by s. 162 (1) (d) of the Law of Property Act 1925, which exempts from the rule rights granted over or under land for the purposes of (inter alia) constructing and repairing drains; this provision pre-supposes the existence of a right not itself void and merely preserves ancillary rights which may be exercisable from time to time in the indefinite future and which might otherwise fail. However the grant in *Dunn's* case would, it seems, have been valid if at the date of the grant there had been an existing sewer under the road[1]. For the draftsman this decision demonstrates the need to ensure that the grant of any future easement is limited to take effect only within the perpetuity period. For this purpose the period of 80 years permitted by the Perpetuities and Accumulations Act 1964, may be selected as an alternative to the common law period of

---

15   *The Shannon Ltd v Venner Ltd* [1965] Ch 682, [1965] 1 All ER 590, CA.
16   [1965] Ch 682, [1965] 1 All ER 590, CA.
17   Evidence of P's future intentions regarding the use of the land which explained the form which the conveyance of 1930 took was also held admissible as throwing light upon the circumstances in which it came to be executed.
18   *Harris v Flower* (1904) 74 LJ Ch 127; *Bracewell v Appleby* [1975] Ch 408, [1975] 1 All ER 993 (injunction refused however); *Nickerson v Barraclough* [1981] 2 All ER 369.
19   Emmet, 573.
20   [1961] Ch 433, [1961] 2 All ER 62, applied in *Newham v Lawson* (1971) 22 P & CR 852, note 6, p. 523, post. See 'Grants of Easements and the Rule against Perpetuities' (1964) 61 LS Gaz 59. See also *Nickerson v Barraclough* [1981] 2 All ER 369 at 374, per Brightman LJ, identifying in all probability the cause of the difficulties in that case.
1   [1961] Ch 433 at 440, [1961] 2 All ER 62 at 66, per Cross J. This has been doubted: (1962) 106 Sol Jo 147.

21 years or a 'royal lives' clause. If the grant is not so limited, it is no longer void ab initio (as at common law); under s. 3 of the Act it is not avoided until it becomes established that the vesting must occur outside the 'wait and see' period. Thus the grant today of a right similar to that arising in *Dunn's* case would entitle the grantee and his successors to use any drain *constructed* within 21 years of the death of the survivor of the original parties to the grant[2] and it would seem immaterial that the grantee (or a successor) does not in fact exercise his right within such period. The grant only becomes void if no drain is constructed during the period.

The Act of 1964 is not retrospective. Consequently it will remain necessary for many years to come to apply the ruling in *Dunn v Blackdown Properties Ltd*[3] to all future easements, not merely rights of drainage, created before 16 July 1964, the date of commencement of the Act. One disturbing implication of the decision is that it prima facie invalidates many easements drafted on the basis of precedents then current, which did not when using the 'now or hereafter' formula restrict their operation to the perpetuity period and which hitherto had been considered good. However when advising upon the validity of what appears to be a pre-Act future easement, the practitioner should remember that things may not always be what at first sight they seem to be. Various possibilities should be considered. First, it is a question of construction of the particular grant whether it confers an immediate right or a right to arise in the future. The law favours early vesting and where possible the grant will be treated as an immediate one, e.g. a right of way along a defined route over which the grantor covenants to construct a road at some future specified time[4]. Again, depending on the circumstances (e.g. whether any drain or road has been constructed), the owner of the dominant land may be able to enforce the easement against the original grantor as a matter of contract (irrespective of the perpetuity rule) if the servient land is still vested in that grantor[5]. Second, in cases where the invalidity of the grant has not been appreciated and the grantee or his successor has in fact exercised his right, an easement may have arisen by prescription[6] unless in the case of rights of drainage the user is 'clam'. Finally, the dominant owner, whether original grantee or successor, would appear to have an action against the original grantor or his estate (for what it is worth) for breach of the implied covenants for title, at least if he conveyed as beneficial owner; if the servient land is still vested in the grantor, the covenant for further assurance entitles the dominant owner to a fresh grant of a valid easement in order 'further or more perfectly' to assure the subject-matter of the conveyance[7].

---

2   At comon law lives in being had no significance in commercial transactions, but the lives of the grantor and the grantee are, somewhat illogically, expressly made relevant to the statutory 'wait and see' period by s. 3 (4), 5 (a) (b) (v); see M & W, 221. If both original parties are limited companies, the wait and see period is 21 years (s. 3 (4) (b)).

3   [1961] Ch 433, [1961] 2 All ER 62.

4   See (1964) 61 LS Gaz 59; Emmet, 580–581. Contra it seems if the right only arises '*when* an intended road shall have been made and which *thereafter* shall always be kept open as a road' (a case encountered by one of the authors). See also *Dunn v Blackdown Properties Ltd* [1961] Ch 433 at 441, [1961] 2 All ER 62 at 67, per Cross J.

5   *South Eastern Rly Co v Associated Portland Cement Manufacturers (1900) Ltd* [1910] 1 Ch 12, CA.

6   As occurred in *Newham v Lawson* (1971) 22 P & CR 852 (grant of right of light for church not erected at time of grant void for perpetuity, but prescriptive right acquired by virtue of 100 years' enjoyment of light since erection).

7   Covenants for title are considered in Chapter 24 and the covenant for further assurance at

(iv) *Repairs to rights of way.* In the absence of any express agreement regulating the responsibility for repairs, neither the grantor nor the grantee is under any legal obligation to repair. The grantee can effect such repairs as are necessary and he has a right of entry on the servient land for this purpose[8]. The owner of the right of way cannot recover damages for physical damage to the servient land caused by another person entitled to use the right of way, unless the damage is such as to cause a substantial interference with his right[9]. Where the grant of an easement is coupled with a covenant by the grantee to repair or contribute towards maintenance costs, it should be remembered that the burden of the covenant, being positive, does not run so as to bind the grantee's successors, but any successor wishing to take the benefit of the easement will be obliged to accept the burden of repair[10]. Authority exists for the proposition that the benefit of the grantor's covenant to repair passes with the easement, though it is uncertain to what extent this represents the law in England[11]. The benefit may be expressly assigned on a conveyance of the dominant land.

8.   Exceptions and Reservations

(a) Nature

The parcels clause not only describes the land intended to be conveyed to the grantee, it also delimits what is not to pass to him. The vendor may wish to retain for himself a specified part — certain fields from the conveyance of a farm, or the underlying mines and minerals. What the vendor retains is termed an *exception*. An exception of mines and minerals results in the surface and the subjacent minerals becoming separate tenements severed in title[12]. The grantor retains all his original rights in relation to the property excepted together with all incidents necessary for its enjoyment. He can, for example, construct a tunnel through excepted minerals for the transporting of other minerals belonging to him in adjacent lands[13].

Exceptions and reservations, though commonly bracketed together as if similar in nature, are in truth essentially different and should not be confused. An exception always refers to something in esse; it forms part of the land granted, at least before the conveyance takes effect. A *reservation* refers to some newly created right; it is not, therefore, in esse prior to the conveyance. Strictly the term 'reservation' is only properly admitted of services rendered by a tenant to his landlord or lord of the manor, such as the payment of rent or provision of a beast (or heriot)[14]. The term has now acquired a wider meaning and

---

p. 632, post. Normally no action will be possible against an intermediate vendor of the dominant land because he will not in general be responsible for the acts of the original grantor; see p. 624, post.

8   For a useful discussion, see *Jones v Pritchard* [1908] 1 Ch 630 at 637–39, per Parker J. The owner of a right of drainage who allows his pipes to fall into disrepair so that water escapes on to the servient land is liable for any damage caused, ibid. See also *Stokes v Mixconcrete (Holdings) Ltd* (1978) 38 P & CR 488, CA.

9   *Weston v Lawrence Weaver Ltd* [1961] 1 QB 402, [1961] 1 All ER 478 (churning up and destroying surface of private road; claim failed).

10   *Halsall v Brizell* [1957] Ch 169, [1957] 1 All ER 371.

11   *Gaw v Coras Iompair Eireann* [1953] IR 232; cf. *Grant v Edmondson* [1931] 1 Ch 1, CA (rentcharge), p. 348, ante.

12   *Duke of Hamilton v Graham* (1871) LR 2 Sc & Div 166; see also LPA s. 205 (1) (ix) ('land' includes mines and minerals whether or not held apart from the surface).

13   *Duke of Hamilton v Graham* (1871) LR 2 Sc & Div 166; *Ramsey v Blair* (1876) 1 App Cas 701 at 704, HL, per Lord Hatherley.

14   See *Mason v Clarke* [1954] 1 QB 460 at 467, [1954] 1 All ER 189 at 192, CA, per Denning

today it more usually connotes some incorporeal right over the land granted of which the grantor desires to have the benefit, such as a right of way, or sporting rights. At common law such a reservation, unlike a reservation proper, operated as a re-grant of the right by the grantee whose execution of the deed was necessary to give effect to the right[15].

Exceptions and reservations are normally introduced within the parcels by the words 'Excepting and reserving'. Exceptions correctly form part of the parcels, whereas reservations should strictly appear immediately after the habendum (i.e. 'To hold') clause. The expression 'reserving' is appropriate only to the creation of new rights. It is not technically correct on a subsequent transaction to repeat verbatim the exceptions and reservations appearing in the previous conveyance, for this may have the unintended effect of creating new rights in favour of the subsequent vendor, at least if he owns adjacent land. The correct procedure is to refer to them in the habendum, prefaced by the words 'subject to the exceptions and reservations . . .' Should the 'excepting and reserving' formula be adopted, the court will not as a matter of construction recognise the creation of new rights if it is clear that the parties merely intended a reference to existing rights[16]. The use of an incorrect introductory expression will not preclude the court from giving effect to the parties' intentions. In one case the court upheld a right of way in favour of the grantee's successors in title, notwithstanding that in the deed of creation the right was introduced by the words 'save and except'[17]. But the mere reservation of a right to win minerals will not be construed as an exception thereof, unless an intention to that effect clearly appears[18].

(b) Vendor's entitlement

The right of the vendor to have an exception or reservation in his favour stems from the contract. A vendor intending to reserve a right of way over the land granted cannot insist on the conveyance incorporating the reservation if he has failed to provide for such a right in the contract[19]. Where the owner of two adjoining properties conveys one of them there is no *implied* reservation of any rights over the land sold, save for easements for necessity and reciprocal rights of support, though the court will imply the appropriate reservation if the circumstances of the case raise a necessary inference that the common intention of the parties was to reserve some easement in favour of the grantor[20]. A conveyance which fails to give effect to a reservation provided for in the contract operates as an extinguishment of the intended right, and the vendor's only remedy is to seek rectification of the conveyance[1]. It hardly needs to be stressed that the vendor's solicitor must ensure that the words of the reservation inserted

LJ; revsd. on another point [1955] AC 778, [1955] 1 All ER 914, HL. See *Grigsby v Melville* [1973] 3 All ER 445, CA (general words of exception and reservation in conveyance did not reserve cellar under property sold).
15 But see now the LPA 1925, s. 65 (1), p. 526, post.
16 *Re Dances Way, West Town, Hayling Island* [1962] Ch 490, [1962] 2 All ER 42, CA.
17 *British Railways Board v Glass* [1965] Ch 538, [1964] 3 All ER 418, CA; *A-G for New South Wales v Dickson* [1904] AC 273, PC ('reserving' held to operate as exception).
18 *Duke of Sutherland v Heathcote* [1892] 1 Ch 475, CA.
19 *Simpson v Gilley* (1922) 92 LJ Ch 194.
20 *Re Webb's Lease, Sandom v Webb* [1951] Ch 808 at 823, [1951] 2 All ER 131 at 141, CA, per Jenkins LJ. A right of light is not an easement of necessity: *Ray v Hazeldine* [1904] 2 Ch 17. See also *Nickerson v Barraclough* [1981] 2 All ER 369, CA.
1 *Teebay v Manchester, Sheffield and Lincolnshire Rly Co* (1883) 24 Ch D 572.

in the conveyance are ample enough to give his client what he wants[2]. The vendor should retain documentary evidence of his title to the exception or reservation and the contract should stipulate for the conveyance to be executed in duplicate.

(c) Execution of conveyance

At common law the reservation of an easement or profit operated as a regrant by the purchaser. Consequently, unlike an exception, the purchaser's execution of the deed was essential to make the reservation effective at law[3]. The deed did, however, create an equitable easement enforceable against the purchaser and his successors who were bound because the conveyance itself gave notice of the attempted reservation[4]. The need for the purchaser's execution has now been abolished by s. 65 (1) of the Law of Property Act 1925, which provides that

' a reservation of a legal estate shall operate at law without any execution of the conveyance by the grantee . . . or *any regrant* by him, so as to create the legal estate reserved and so as to vest the same in possession' [in the grantor].

The implication of the expression 'without . . . any regrant' has not been fully appreciated until recently, for it had been generally understood that a reservation still operated as a regrant. For example in *Johnstone v Holdway*[5]:

X held land in trust for Y. By a conveyance X as trustee and Y as beneficial owner conveyed part of the land to Z. This deed contained a reservation of a right of way in favour of Y over the land conveyed to Z.

The Court of Appeal, without referring to s. 65 (1), held that the reservation operated as a regrant by Z. Since Z had the legal estate in the servient land, the conveyance was effective to vest in Y a legal easement, notwithstanding that Y merely held an equitable title in the dominant land. In two cases[6] Megarry J held that s. 65 (1) effected a change in the substantive law, so that a reservation of a legal easement now operates without any regrant by the purchaser.

In the first case *Johnstone v Holdway*[7] was not cited to the learned judge but it was in the second case and the learned judge disposed of it with some skill[8]. Unfortunately the Court of Appeal[9] disapproved of this view (although

---

2   For a case of ineffective drafting, see *Cordell v Second Clanfield Properties Ltd* [1969] 2 Ch 9, [1968] 3 All ER 746.

3   After 1881 a reservation was effective at law without the grantee's execution if advantage was taken of the Conveyancing Act 1881, s. 62, which, in effect, made the Statute of Uses 1535, applicable to reservations.

4   *May v Belleville* [1905] 2 Ch 605.

5   [1963] 1 QB 601, [1963] 1 All ER 432, CA.

6   *Cordell v Second Clanfield Properties Ltd* [1969] 2 Ch 9, [1968] 3 All ER 746; *St. Edmundsbury and Ipswich Diocesan Board of Finance v Clark (No 2)* [1973] 3 All ER 902.

7   [1963] 1 QB 601, [1963] 1 All ER 432, but other dicta were which he did follow, see *Bulstrode v Lambert* [1953] 2 All ER 728 at 731, per Upjohn J; *Mason v Clarke* [1954] 1 QB 460 at 467, [1954] 1 All ER 189 at 191, CA, per Denning LJ; revsd. on another point [1955] AC 778, [1955] 1 All ER 914, HL. In neither instance were the words of s. 65 (1) quoted.

8   By following his decision in *Cordell*, not following M & W, 826 (see 4th edn, 830), he explained the *Johnstone* case as being mistakenly made.

9   [1975] 1 All ER 772. The tenor of the judgment leaves it open to doubt whether it is 'right but repulsive' as opposed to 'wrong but romantic'.

affirming the decision). The Court decided that the *Johnstone*[10] case was not decided by a mistake and was therefore binding on them. It is rightly said that the roles of author and judge are 'discrete'[11] but the result is that the section had merely the effect of obviating the necessity for the purchaser to execute the conveyance. This has the unfortunate result that a purchaser in this situation is the 'grantor' for the purposes of construing any ambiguity in an express reservation in favour of the vendor.

(d) Perpetuity

One distinction still remains. An exception relates to something in esse; the vendor retains property already vested in him, consequently the rule against perpetuities is inapplicable. A reservation creates some *new* right, and as we have seen the grant of a *future* easement is caught by the rule. Despite the provision that a reservation operates without any regrant, the rule continues to apply to reservations which are only to arise at some indefinite future time.

9. General words

Prior to 1882 it was customary to insert in a conveyance a long list of general words enumerating the constituent elements of the property conveyed, such as the various buildings, yards, sewers, trees, easements, etc. Often such words had no practical effect, save to add to legal fees by increasing the length of the deed; sometimes, and it was for such occasions that the words were included, they operated to pass reputed rights and quasi-easements, which did not pass automatically like appurtenant easements. Nowadays general words are statutorily implied in the absence of a contrary intention. By virtue of s. 62 (2) of the Law of Property Act 1925[12], a conveyance of land *with houses or other buildings thereon* is deemed to include and operates to convey with the land, houses or other buildings:

> '. . . all outhouses, erections, fixtures, cellars, areas, courts, courtyards, cisterns, sewers, gutters, drains, ways, passages, lights, watercourses, liberties, privileges, easements, rights, and advantages whatsoever, appertaining or reputed to appertain to the land, houses or other buildings conveyed, or any of them, or any part thereof, or, at the time of conveyance, demised, occupied, or enjoyed with, or reputed or known as part or parcel of or appurtenant to, the land, houses, or other buildings conveyed, or any of them, or any part thereof.'

Any such matter as is referred to in the subsection is prima facie deemed to be included within the parcels, and so passes to the purchaser. For the purposes of the section 'conveyance' includes a written tenancy agreement for a term not exceeding three years[13] but not an agreement for a lease for seven years[14]. The section applies to registered land[15]. It does not operate to convey chattels, so

---

10   [1963] 1 QB 601, [1963] 1 All ER 432.
11   *Raineri v Miles* [1980] 2 All ER 145 at 156, per Lord Edmund-Davies. The result is that the 3rd edition of M & W is now right but the 4th is wrong.
12   Sub-s. (1) deals with a conveyance of *land* and sub-s. (3) with the conveyance of a *manor*. Section 62 replaces the Conveyancing Act 1881, s. 6.
13   *Wright v Macadam* [1949] 2 KB 744, [1949] 2 All ER 565, CA. But an oral tenancy is not a 'conveyance': *Rye v Rye* [1962] AC 496, [1962] 1 All ER 146, HL.
14   *Borman v Griffith* [1930] 1 Ch 493. And see the LPA 1925, s. 205 (1) (ii).
15   LRA 1925, ss. 19 (3), 22 (3), p. 453, ante.

that greenhouses resting on the land by their own weight without being secured cannot constitute 'erections' and do not pass without express mention[16]; nor does the section pass other land not included in the parcels, even though it has previously been enjoyed with the land conveyed. As is well known the section operates to transform into legal easements reputed rights, or rights which merely existed as liberites or privileges whose enjoyment had previously been permissive or precarious. According to Ungoed-Thomas J, in *Ward v Kirkland*[17], s. 62 is directed to whether the privilege is enjoyed in practice irrespective of permission or the form which permission takes, though it is submitted that it does not apply where the user has been objected to continually. For a detailed consideration of the working of s. 62, reference should be made to standard real property textbooks[18]. The following matters require some discussion here.

(a) Rights known to the law

The section only applies to a right or advantage capable of existing at law as an easement. Therefore the following cannot pass: a right to wind and air coming in an undefined channel[19], a right to protection from the weather[20], a right to use a passage if and when it is not inconvenient to the servient owner and his tenants[1], or the right to the performance of personal services[2].

(b) Title of the vendor

The statute does not pass by implication any right which the vendor is not capable of granting expressly[3]. This is an important and obvious restriction which is not always fully appreciated. If the owner of Blackacre grants to the owner of the adjoining land, Whiteacre, a licence to cross Blackacre, a subsequent conveyance of Whiteacre does not operate to convert this advantage into an easement for the benefit of the purchaser. The servient land (Blackacre) is not owned by the vendor who has no power, express or implied, to grant rights over it. In effect the operation of s. 62 is confined to cases where there is a severance of land in common ownership, or where a lessor sells to, or renews the lease of, his tenant[4].

(c) Diversity of occupation

Authority exists for the proposition that s. 62 does not apply unless there was diversity of occupation prior to the conveyance to the purchaser[5]. For example,

---

16 *H. E. Dibble Ltd v Moore* [1970] 2 QB 181, [1969] 3 All ER 1465, CA.
17 [1967] Ch 194 at 230, [1966] 1 All ER 609 at 620 (right to enter land to repair wall).
18 See M & W, 835–841; Jackson, 'Easements and General Words' (1966) 30 Conv (NS) 340. See also (1977) 41 Conv (NS) 415 (C. Harpum); [1978] Conv 449 (P.W. Smith); [1979] Conv 113 (C. Harpum); [1979] Conv 311 (P.W. Smith).
19 *Webb v Bird* (1861) 13 CBNS 841.
20 *Phipps v Pears* [1965] 1 QB 76, [1964] 2 All ER 35, CA.
1 *Green v Ascho Horticultural Ltd* [1966] 2 All ER 232.
2 *Regis Property Co Ltd v Redman* [1956] 2 QB 612, [1956] 2 All ER 335, CA (supplying hot water and central heating).
3 LPA 1925, s. 62 (5); *Quicke v Chapman* [1903] 1 Ch 659; *Gale on Easements* (14th edn), p. 124. See *Nickerson v Barraclough* [1981] 2 All ER 369, CA.
4 See also *Goldberg v Edwards* [1950] Ch 247, CA (privilege afforded to tenant allowed into possession before grant of formal lease converted into easement).
5 *Long v Gowlett* [1923] 2 Ch 177 (right to enter land to clear mill-stream and repair its bank not passing under general words). See also *Sovmots Investments Ltd v Secretary of State for the Environment* [1979] AC 144, [1977] 2 All ER 385, where there are dicta

if the owner and occupier of two adjoining properties, Blackacre and Whiteacre, crosses Blackacre to reach Whiteacre, a conveyance of Whiteacre will not pass any right over Blackacre under the section, for that right was not enjoyed with Whiteacre (the quasi-dominant land) but was attributable to the vendor's own occupation of Blackacre (the servient land)[6]. Though obiter support for this view can be found in Ungoed-Thomas J's judgment in *Ward v Kirkland*[7] it is generally considered[8] that the necessity for diversity of occupation constitutes an unwarranted gloss on the statute, not the least because of the difficulty of satisfactorily distinguishing *Broomfield v Williams*[9], where the Court of Appeal held that the general words operated to pass to a purchaser of a house a right of light over the vendor's adjacent land, despite the fact that the vendor had previously lived in the house.

(d) Contrary intention

Section 62 applies only if and so far as a contrary intention is not expressed in the conveyance[10]. A statement on the deed plan which shows the vendor's adjacent land as 'building land' does not suffice to prevent the acquisition of a right of light over that land[11], nor does the express grant of a limited easement operate as a contrary intention to exclude wider rights passing under the general words[12]. The vendor's right to have a contrary intention inserted in the conveyance depends on the terms of the contract. The necessity for a solicitor, when he is drafting the contract, to consider carefully the possible relevance and implications of s. 62, has been considered in an earlier chapter[13]. The vendor can insist on the insertion in the conveyance of appropriate words modifying or excluding the operation of the section whenever the general words will give the purchaser more than his entitlement under the contract[14]. An omission of such a clause through some mutual mistake may lead to rectification of the conveyance[15].

The contract may be silent on the question of the purchaser's rights. According to the older view[16], the purchaser was entitled in this event only to existing easements appurtenant to the land sold, and such quasi-easements as were necessary or intended by the parties. However in *Borman v Griffith*[17]

---

supporting this contention, but see further Jackson, op. cit., P.W. Smith, op. cit. The weight of academic authority is against this view.

6   *Long v Gowlett* [1923] 2 Ch 177 at 200–1, per Sargant J.
7   [1967] Ch 196 at 230, [1966] 1 All ER 609 at 618, where there was separate occupation at the appropriate time.
8   Jackson, op. cit., 346–48.
9   [1897] 1 Ch 602, CA. In *Long v Gowlett* [1923] 2 Ch 177 at 202, Sargant J was compelled to accept the binding force of the earlier decision as regards any easement on the same footing as light, i.e. one that is continuous and apparent. Merely to state that this case is different because it relates to an easement of light does not, with respect, deal with the question, see [1977] 2 All ER 385 at 398, per Lord Edmund-Davies.
10   Section 62 (4).
11   *Broomfield v Williams* [1897] 1 Ch 602, CA; *Pollard v Gare* [1901] 1 Ch 834.
12   *Hansford v Jago* [1921] 1 Ch 322; *Gregg v Richards* [1926] Ch 521, CA.
13   Page 161, ante.
14   *Re Walmsley and Shaw's Contract* [1917] 1 Ch 93.
15   *Clarke v Barnes* [1929] 2 Ch 368, p. 651, post; cf. *Slack v Hancock* (1912) 107 LT 14 (rectification refused).
16   *Bolton v Bolton* (1879) 11 Ch D 968 at 970, per Fry J; *Re Walmsley and Shaw's Contract* [1917] 1 Ch 93 at 98, per Eve J; 1 Williams V & P, 658.
17   [1930] 1 Ch 493 at 498–99.

Maugham J appears to have enlarged the scope of the rule by holding that the purchaser can claim the same rights as if specific performance had been decreed in his favour of a pre-1882 conveyance without mention of easements. In other words he is entitled by the contract to all such rights as would pass under the rule in *Wheeldon v Burrows*[18], that is, all continuous and apparent quasi-easements that are necessary to the reasonable enjoyment of the land conveyed[19] and are in fact enjoyed at the time of the conveyance.

10.   The 'all estate' clause

Section 63 (1) of the Law of Property Act 1925, provides that every conveyance is effectual to pass 'all the estate, right, title, claim and demand'[20] which the conveying parties have, or have power to convey, in the property. This provision (which replaces the Conveyancing Act 1881, s. 63) renders it unnecessary to insert an express clause of similar import, as was the practice prior to 1882, to ensure that there passes to the purchaser any outstanding estate vested in the vendor and not expressly mentioned in the conveyance. The section does not apply if there is a contrary intention and has effect subject to the terms and provisions in the deed itself (sub-s. (2)). Thus the grant of a lease does not operate to pass the lessor's freehold estate, despite the absence of any expressed contrary intention, for the habendum clause clearly demonstrates that the lessee is to acquire a term of years.

Section 63 operates to pass to the grantee every estate or interest held by the grantor in the land, although not expressly mentioned in the conveyance, or not vested in him in the capacity in which he is made a party to the deed[1]. A conveyance of the fee simple may, therefore, pass to the purchaser an outstanding term of years vested in the vendor, which has not merged with the freehold[2]. In *Re Stirrup's Contract*[3] Wilberforce J held that an assent under seal executed by personal representatives was effective because of s. 63 to pass the legal estate vested in them, though technically they had no power to execute an assent, since the title had not devolved on them as required by s. 36 (1) of the Administration of Estates Act 1925. Similarly the section ensures that a conveyance by an executor-beneficiary as 'beneficial owner' vests in the purchaser both the legal and equitable titles in the property, notwithstanding that he has not executed any assent in his own favour[4].

---

18   (1879) 12 Ch D 31, CA. This reasoning is not without its difficulties (see M & W, 839), but it is accepted by Emmet, 570. Strictly the rule in *Wheeldon v Burrows* applies on the *grant* of land, see M & W, 833.

19   It is uncertain whether this requirement is synonymous with, or alternative to, the first requirement, or perhaps even additional to it (see e.g. Maugham J in *Borman v Griffith* [1930] 1 Ch 493 at 499).

20   See *Hill v Booth* [1930] 1 Ch 381, CA ('demand' does not cover unpaid balance of premium reserved on grant of lease).

1   *Drew v Earl of Norbury* (1846) 3 Jo & Lat 267 at 284, per Lord St. Leonards; *Taylor v London and County Banking Co* [1901] 2 Ch 231 at 255, CA, per Stirling LJ. In *Cedar Holdings Ltd v Green* [1981] Ch 129, [1979] 3 All ER 117, CA, it was held that the section could not be relied on so as to read a purported legal charge as a charge of the equitable interest in the proceeds of sale, relying on *Irani Finance v Singh* [1971] Ch 59. [1970] 3 All ER 199. However, Lord Wilberforce in *Williams and Glyn's Bank Ltd v Boland* [1980] 2 All ER 408 at 415, stated he considered the decision to be wrongly decided.

2   *Burton v Barclay* (1831) 7 Bing 745; see also *Thelluson v Liddard* [1900] 2 Ch 635.

3   [1961] 1 All ER 805, p. 332, ante. 'Conveyance' includes an assent: LPA s. 205 (1) (ii). Cf. *Hanbury v Bateman* [1920] 1 Ch 313.

4   The apparently contradictory opinion expressed in *Faussett v Carpenter* (1831) 2 Dowl &

In relation to registered land, there is no provision in the Land Registration Act 1925, exactly corresponding to s. 63. However the all estate clause would appear to be implied, though whether for any effective purpose is extremely doubtful[5], by the wide words of ss. 20 (1) and 23 (1) of that Act, which provide that registration confers on the proprietor the legal estate together with 'the appropriate rights and interests which would, under the Law of Property Act 1925, have been transferred if the land had not been registered.'

J   Habendum clause

The habendum determines the size or quantum of the estate to be acquired by the grantee. In the normal conveyance it often appears in this form: 'TO HOLD'[6] unto the purchaser in fee simple'. In a lease it is usually drafted in some such form as 'TO HOLD unto the lessee for the term of — years from the date hereof', and in an assignment of an existing leasehold term as 'TO HOLD unto the purchaser for all the residue now unexpired of the term created by the lease'. A term of years commencing *from* a specified date is generally reckoned as exclusive of that day, whereas a term to start *on* a certain day includes that day[7]. Though the term may be expressed to run from some date anterior to the date of the lease, the lessee's actual interest therein only takes effect from the date of delivery (taken to be the date of the deed). Thus in *Roberts v Church Comrs for England*[8] a lease dated 29 October 1952, which granted a term of 21¼ years from 25 March 1950, was held not to create a long tenancy (i.e. one for a term exceeding 21 years) for the purposes of s. 3 (1) of the Leasehold Reform Act 1967; consequently the tenant was not entitled under the Act to acquire the freehold. No habendum clause appears in the prescribed forms of registered land transfers[9]. The size of the estate acquired by the transferee is indicated, if only indirectly. The transfer relates to 'the land comprised in the title above mentioned' and this is a sufficient reference to the register of title which contains particulars of the registered estate.

The habendum is strictly a non-essential part of the deed even at common law. In the absence of any habendum, the grantee took the quantum of estate mentioned in the premises (i.e. that part of the deed preceding the habendum)[10] otherwise he took a mere life estate. It might be thought there is even less need today for the habendum in the normal conveyance of freehold land, since it is enacted that the deed operates to pass the fee simple or other the grantor's whole interest without any words of limitation unless a contrary intention appears[11]. Nevertheless it is still the general practice to retain the expression 'in fee simple' in the habendum. Indeed this appears to be a highly desirable practice, for the omission of these three words may well render

Cl 232 is thought to be wrong; see the dicta cited in note 1, ante; *Norton on Deeds* (2nd edn) p. 304.

5   See Potter, 91—92.
6   Originally the clause commenced 'To have (habendum) and to hold (tenendum)', the purpose of the latter being to signify the tenure by which the estate was to be held, e.g. *tenendum in libero socagio*; see 2 *Blackstone's Commentaries*, 298—99.
7   *Meggeson v Groves* [1917] 1 Ch 158, *Clayton's Case* (1585) 5 Co Rep 1a.
8   [1972] 1 QB 278, [1971] 3 All ER 703, CA; *Bradshaw v Pawley* [1979] 3 All ER 273 at 276—77, per Megarry VC.
9   See LRR 1925, Schedule, Forms 19, 32.
10   *Goodtitle d. Dodwell v Gibbs* (1826) 5 B & C 709.
11   LPA 1925, s. 60 (1). As to rentcharges, see M & W, 795.

nugatory the implied statutory covenants for title[12]. The habendum is the proper place to refer to existing exceptions and reservations, restrictive covenants and other liabilities and incumbrances subject to which the property is conveyed. The object of qualifying the habendum in this way is to limit the operation of the vendor's covenants for title. The purchaser is entitled to a conveyance expressed to be subject only to such restrictive covenants and other adverse rights as are mentioned in the contract[13]. The omission of some adverse interest or incumbrance from the habendum does not affect the question of its enforceability which is determined by general principles, but it may render the vendor liable on his covenants for title.

Over the years various rules have been laid down by the courts to resolve conflicts between the premises and the habendum. These are of little practical importance today and only one need be mentioned. The habendum cannot be read so as to enlarge the description of the parcels; consequently land not included in the parcels does not pass though it is named in the habendum[14]. This rule does not prevent the passing of land or appurtenant rights referred to only in the habendum, which are deemed to be included within the parcels by virtue of the general words and so pass to the grantee in any event.

K   Reddendum clause

On the grant of a lease the habendum is followed by the reddendum clause which specifies the amount of the rent and the time when it is payable[15].

L   Declaration of trusts

Prior to 1926 the habendum was commonly followed by a declaration of uses operating by virtue of the Statute of Uses 1535, but nowadays this position is often filled by the usual joint tenancy clause, declaring how joint purchasers are to hold the property in equity and enlarging the powers of the trustees for sale. Considerable diversity of opinion exists as to the usefulness of this clause. Some maintain that the declaration of beneficial trusts should be contained in a separate document and kept off the legal title altogether[16] which is certainly the proper procedure where the beneficiaries and the trustees are different persons. Nevertheless the practice of declaring the beneficial interests in the conveyance in the normal purchase by husband and wife is so widespread that it is conceived that no real harm can ensue. When acting in connection with a joint purchase, a solicitor should always obtain full instructions as to the nature and extent of the beneficial interests, particularly on the purchase by spouses of a matrimonial home[17]. It should not even be assumed, merely because the conveyance is being taken in joint names, that the legal owners are to be the persons entitled in equity[18]. In a transaction involving spouses, proper consideration

---

12   1 K & E, 537; p. 627, post.
13   *Re Wallis and Barnard's Contract* [1899] 2 Ch 515.
14   *Sheppard's Touchstone*, 75; *Norton on Deeds* (2nd edn), pp. 311–12.
15   See further, p. 554, post.
16   See the comments of Buckley J in *Wilson v Wilson* [1969] 3 All ER 945 at 948.
17   See *Cowcher v Cowcher* [1972] 1 All ER 943 at 959, per Bagnall J. See (1977) 41 Conv (NS) 243 (S.M. Bandali).
18   This was the mistake made in *Wilson v Wilson* [1969] 3 All ER 945 (purchaser requesting brother to join in transaction solely to facilitate obtaining of mortgage by purchaser). See

must be given to the capital transfer tax consequences of the purchase. In particular it may be preferable for them to hold as beneficial tenants in common rather than as joint tenants (as is usually the case)[19].

1.   Express or implied trust for sale

Whenever land is conveyed to two or more people there must always be a trust for sale. Often an express trust for sale is created, the conveyance containing a declaration that:

> ' the purchasers shall hold the said property upon trust to sell the same with power to postpone the sale thereof and shall hold the net proceeds of sale and other money applicable as capital and the net rent and profits thereof until sale upon trust for themselves as joint tenants.'

It is generally agreed that the device of a trust for sale (whether express or implied) introduces a large degree of unreality into joint purchases, especially of the matrimonial home[20]. Many a solicitor has experienced acute embarrassment when endeavouring to explain the significance of an express trust for sale to bewildered clients. Until recently certain fiscal benefits existed which made it advantageous for joint purchasers of expensive property to rely on the statutory trust for sale arising under ss. 34 (2) and 36 (1) of the Law of Property Act 1925[1].

In the absence of an express trust for sale it is the practice to indicate the beneficial holding by saying 'TO HOLD unto the purchasers in fee simple as beneficial joint tenants' or 'as beneficial tenants in common in equal shares'. A conveyance containing a declaration of the spouses' beneficial entitlement is conclusive and the courts will not go behind the declaration save in cases of fraud, mistake[2] or where clear evidence exists that the parties have altered their equitable rights[3].

2.   Enlarging the trustees' powers

As trustees for sale the purchasers have vested in them all the powers conferred by statute on a tenant for life and on trustees of a settlement[4]. Wide though these powers are they do not authorise a mortgage of the property in order to

also *Peffer v Rigg* [1978] 3 All ER 745; *Joyce v Barker Bros* (1980) Times, 26 February (conveyance stating the purchasers were both tenants in common and joint tenants. Held the first expression i.e. joint tenants prevailed applying *Slingsby's Case* (1587) 5 Co Rep 18b). See Emmet, 325.

19   For a discussion see (1970) 120 LJ 775, 795.
20   See (1966) 82 LQR 34.
 1   See generally Prichard, 'Co-ownership, Estate Duty and Additional Powers' (1972) 36 Conv (NS) 182.
 2   Cf. *Wilson v Wilson* [1969] 3 All ER 945, note 18, ante; *Re Colebrook's Conveyances, Taylor v Taylor* [1973] 1 All ER 132 (father and son; conveyance rectified by inserting 'tenants in common' for 'joint tenants' as parties intended at time of conveyance to hold as tenants in common). See *Joyce v Barker Bros* note 18, ante.
 3   *Re John's Assignment Trusts, Niven v Niven* [1970] 2 All ER 210; *Pettitt v Pettitt* [1970] AC 777 at 813, [1969] 2 All ER 385 at 405, per Lord Upjohn (though the statement that it concludes the question 'for all time' appears too wide). As to the necessity for the purchasers to execute the conveyance, see *Robinson v Robinson* (1976) 241 Estates Gazette 153; *Pink v Lawrence* (1978) 36 P & CR 98, CA; [1979] Conv 5. See also *Godwin v Bedwell* (1982) Times, 10 March, CA.
 4   LPA 1925, s. 28 (1). *Re Svenson-Taylors Settlement* [1974] 3 All ER 397 (no power to mortgage land to purchase additional land). See further Emmet, 809, 810.

raise the purchase money. To overcome possible objections from mortgages it has become established practice to incorporate a declaration that:

> ' the purchasers or other the trustees for the time being of this deed shall have full power to mortgage charge lease or otherwise dispose of all or any part of the property hereby conveyed with all the powers in that behalf of an absolute owner.'

However where the trustees are also the persons absolutely and beneficially entitled, they can deal with the property in any way they like and it is generally considered that a specific extension of their powers as trustees is otiose[5]. It is otherwise where the trustees do not comprise all those beneficially entitled.

Perpetuity rule
Section 8 of the Perpetuities and Accumulations Act 1964, appears to render it unnecessary to limit the exercise of the trustees' powers to the perpetuity period, as had been the hitherto recommended practice consequent upon the ruling in *Re Allott, Hanmer v Allott*[6]. It is now enacted that the rule against perpetuities shall not invalidate a power conferred on trustees

> ' to sell, lease, exchange or otherwise dispose of any property for full consideration, or to do any other act in the administration (as opposed to the distribution) of any property.'

Some commentators still advocate the need for an express limitation on the ground that it is doubtful whether s. 8 covers a power to mortgage[7]. Whether or not this point is valid, and whether or not as a matter of law the perpetuity rule ever applied to powers conferred on trustees for sale[8], an express limitation of the exercise of the power to mortgage within a specified period can do no harm.

3. Registered land

On a transfer of registered land to joint proprietors it is common practice to utilise Form 19, adding the words 'as beneficial joint tenants' or 'as beneficial tenants in common'. These words are for the sole benefit of the purchasers and obviate the need for a separate document declaring the beneficial entitlement. The Registrar is not affected with notice of trusts and references thereto are excluded from the register as far as possible[9]. The beneficial interests are protected by registration of the obligatory restriction in Form 62, where necessary[10]. It has forcefully been denied that any extension of the trustees' powers is necessary in the case of registered land transactions, for on registration joint

---

5   Hallett, 300; 18 Ency F & P, 117. Yet the possibility still remains of a severance in equity followed by a disposal of the equitable interest to some third party. The view propounded by Lord Denning MR, that as between spouses there can be no severance of an equitable joint tenancy so long as one of them is in possession, though morally defensible, is not good law; see *Bedson v Bedson* [1965] 2 QB 666 at 678, [1965] 3 All ER 307 at 311–12, CA; contra, Russell LJ at 690 and 319, respectively.
6   [1924] 2 Ch 498 (trustees' leasing power declared invalid).
7   Is a mortgage a disposal 'for full consideration'? Is it any other administrative act? See 19 Ency F & P, 971.
8   See Farrand, 302, arguing that the rule does not apply to statutory powers, and express additional powers operate with like effect as the statutory powers (SLA 1925, s. 109 (2)).
9   LRA 1925, s. 74.
10 Page 562, ante.

proprietors have all the powers of a sole proprietor unless the register contains some restriction curtailing their powers[11] (and Form 62 relates only to the payment of capital money). It is felt that this view over-simplifies the position. The absence of any qualifying restriction ensures that on a subsequent sale by the trustees a purchaser (at least if unaware of any breach of trust) will obtain a good title. Yet it has been persuasively shown[12] that such absence cannot exonerate the trustee-proprietors vis-à-vis the beneficiaries from a breach of trust if they do in fact exceed their powers. The better view seems to indicate that no difference should be made in this respect between transfers and conveyances. The Registrar does not take objection to a transfer including an express enlargement of the trustees' powers.

M   Covenants

1.   Nature of covenants

The practitioner is frequently called upon to draft a deed which imposes covenants on one or both of the parties. Whether any, and if so what, particular covenants are necessary depends on the nature of the transaction. Express covenants are invariably created on the sale of a new house on a building estate, or on the grant of a formal lease. On the conveyance of land subject to existing covenants the need for an indemnity covenant must be considered. The right of either party to impose covenants depends largely on the contract which should, wherever possible, set out the actual words of the covenants to be inserted in the deed. Care should be taken to ensure that the conveyance gives effect to all the terms of the contract, for on completion the contract merges in the conveyance, save for those terms that are expressly or impliedly to remain effective thereafter[13]. In the conveyance itself lengthy covenants are commonly set out in a schedule. It is not proposed to traverse in detail ground already familiar to the reader but to concentrate particularly on matters of concern to the draftsman. However, as it is essential to have a proper understanding of the rules regulating the enforceability of covenants affecting land, it will be helpful to state the basic rules in outline[14]. The entire subject of covenants is at present under review by the Law Commission and it may well be that in the not too distant future the mode of creation and the enforcement of covenants will be considerably simplified.

(a) Rules governing enforceability

As between the contracting parties all covenants are enforceable (assuming they are not void for uncertainty or contrary to public policy or statutory provision). In certain circumstances a covenant relating to land may be enforceable by and against successors in title of the original parties, depending on the nature of the covenant i.e whether it is positive or negative. Where a landlord-tenant relationship exists, that is, where there is privity of estate, both position and negative covenants which touch and concern the land are enforceable, irrespective of whether privity of contract exists between the parties. As to covenants affecting freehold land the position can be summarised as follows.

11   R & R, 377; 19 Ency F & P, 972, note 3.
12   Farrand, 301–302. Cf. Emmet, 802.
13   For the doctrine of merger, see p. 444, ante.
14   See further M & W, 742, et seq; Emmet, 599 et seq.

(i) *Positive covenants*. The *burden* of a positive covenant does not run at law[15]. The *benefit* may pass at law to the covenantee's successors if (1) the covenant touches and concerns land owned by the covenantee, (2) the original parties have shown an intention that the benefit should run with the land, and (3) the suing successor owns the same legal estate in the land as the covenantee originally possessed, though this requirement has been held to have been modified by statute[16].

(ii) *Negative covenants*. In equity both the benefit and burden may pass. Under the doctrine of *Tulk v Moxhay*[17] a successor with notice is *bound* by a negative or restrictive covenant, provided it was made for the protection of land retained by the covenantee and there existed a clear intention to bind the covenantor's land. Equity never enforces, even at the instance of the original covenantee, a purely personal covenant against the covenantor's assign[18]. The *benefit* of the covenant is enforceable by the covenantee's successor if the covenant touches and concerns land originally retained by the covenantee and now vested in him (in whole or part) and the benefit of the covenant has been vested in him by assignment, or is annexed to the land, or is enforceable under a building scheme.

(b) Words of creation
No technical words are necessary for the making of a covenant, provided the words used indicate an agreement to do or refrain from doing something. The usual expression in a conveyance is that the purchaser 'hereby covenants with the vendor that . . .' In the absence of express words of obligation a covenant will arise by construction where the deed shows an intention that a party is to be bound. The words 'provided' or 'on condition that' have been held to create a covenant but in each case it is necessary to look at the whole of the instrument to ascertain the parties' intention[19]. Similarly a covenant arises where, for instance, a purchaser is granted a right to enter adjoining land for certain purposes, 'the purchaser making good all damage caused thereby'. A recital may operate as a covenant. The normal rules for the construction of documents apply to covenants, so that the words of the covenant are taken most strongly against the covenantor.

It is not, however, sufficient to convey land subject to restrictions contained in a schedule to the deed without imposing on the purchaser a covenant to observe them. As between the vendor and the purchaser, the latter is under an equitable obligation to observe them, but no covenant in the strict sense exists and a purported assignment of the benefit of the restrictions is totally ineffective[20]. Non-execution of the deed by the purchaser-covenantor prevents

15   *Austerberry v Oldham Corpn* (1885) 29 Ch D 750, CA. Cf. *Halsall v Brizell* [1957] Ch 169, [1957] 1 All ER 371 (successor bound on principle of mutual benefits and burdens). There are statutory exceptions, see e.g. Housing Act 1974, s. 126.
16   LPA 1925, s. 78, as interpreted by *Smith and Snipes Hall Farm v River Douglas Catchment Board* [1949] 2 KB 500, [1949] 2 All ER 179, CA. For the meaning of touch and concern, see Tucker LJ, at 506 and 183, respectively. On the question whether an express assignment of the benefit is necessary, see p. 543, post.
17   (1848) 2 Ph 774.
18   *Formby v Barker* [1903] 2 Ch 539, CA (vendor imposing restrictions in conveyance disposing of all his land).
19   *Sheppard's Touchstone*, 162; *Brookes v Drysdale* (1877) 3 CPD 52; cf. *Geery v Reason* (1628) Cro Car 128.
20   *Re Rutherford's Conveyance, Goadby v Bartlett* [1938] Ch 396, [1938] 1 All ER 495.

liability at law arising, though he and the persons claiming title under him are bound in equity[1].

(c) Covenanting parties

(i) *Covenantee.* Usually the covenantee is a party to the deed creating the covenant, but he need not be. At common law in an indenture inter partes the covenantee had to be named as a party to it in order to take the benefit of the covenant[2]. Section 56 (1) of the Law of Property Act 1925, replacing s. 5 of the Law of Property Act 1845, enacts that:

> ' A person may take . . . the benefit of any . . . covenant or agreement over or respecting land or other property, although he may not be named as a party to the conveyance or other instrument.'[3]

Though the scope of this enactment has been the subject of differing views, it now seems to be accepted that there must be *actual words of covenant with* the intended covenantees; they must, therefore, be in existence and named in the deed, or at least be capable of being identified. A vague indication that they are to have the benefit is inadequate[4]. A covenant by A with C (a non-party to the instrument of creation) suffices[5] but not a covenant by A with B (a party) for the benefit of C (a non-party). A draftsman intending to take advantage of s. 56 should use some such words as:

> ' The purchaser hereby covenants as a separate covenant with the owners or occupiers for the time being of the land adjoining or adjacent to the land hereby conveyed[6] [or of the land coloured brown on the plan annexed hereto] . . .'

The section operates to make existing owners of the designated land original covenantees just as much as if they were expressed to be parties in the instrument.

Another relevant provision is s. 78 (1) of the Law of Property Act 1925, which enacts that a covenant relating to land of the covenantee is deemed to be made with the covenantee and his successors in title and the persons deriving title under him or them, and has effect as if such successors and other persons were expressed. The Court of Appeal held in *Smith and Snipes Hall Farm v River Douglas Catchment Board*[7] that this section extended the scope of the common law rule and the reference to 'persons deriving title' indicated that the benefit of a positive covenant which touched and concerned the land passed to and could be enforced by the covenantee's *lessee*.

(ii) *Covenantor.* For obvious reasons the covenantor must be a party to the instrument. By virtue of s. 79 (1) of the Law of Property Act 1925, a covenant

1 Ibid., at 404 and 501, respectively, per Simonds J.
2 The rule did not apply to an indenture not inter partes: *Cooker v Child* (1673) 2 Lev 74 (covenant in charterparty enforceable by person not named as a party).
3 See generally, *Beswick v Beswick* [1968] AC 58, [1967] 2 All ER 1197, HL, where Lord Hodson described s. 56 as a 'remarkable' section: see at pp. 79 and 1206, respectively.
4 See *White v Bijou Mansions Ltd* [1937] Ch 610 at 625, [1937] 3 All ER 269 at 277, per Simonds J; affd. [1938] Ch 351, [1938] 1 All ER 546, CA; *Beswick v Beswick* [1968] AC 58 at 106, [1967] 2 All ER 1197 at 1224, per Lord Upjohn.
5 See *Stromdale and Ball Ltd v Burden* [1952] Ch 223, [1952] 1 All ER 59.
6 See *Re Ecclesiastical Comrs. for England's Conveyance* [1936] Ch 430.
7 [1949] 2 KB 500, [1949] 2 All ER 179, CA; followed in *Williams v Unit Construction Co Ltd* (1951), (1955) 19 Conv (NS) 261, CA.

made by A with B, relating to A's land, is deemed to be made by A on behalf of himself, his successors in title and persons deriving title under him and has effect as if such successors and other persons were expressed, unless a contrary intention appears. This provision has been on the statute book nigh on 60 years, yet considerable uncertainty exists as to its precise effect[8]. At the least it operates to show a prima facie intention that the covenant shall run with the covenantor's land, for he is deemed to covenant on behalf of himself and his successors. Prior to the Act words of similar import were expressly required if it was intended to bind the covenantor's land, and not merely the covenantor personally[9]. Notwithstanding the wide interpretation given to the corresponding s. 78, it is not thought that s. 79 extends the class of covenants capable of running with the land. It does not, for instance, alter the fundamental common law rule that the burden of a positive covenant does not run with freehold land[10]. On the question of a contrary intention, an express exclusion of s. 79 is not necessary. The wording and context of the instrument, or the covenant itself, may contain a sufficient contrary intention[11].

(d) Joint and several covenants

A covenant *by* two or more persons is generally framed as a joint and several covenant. The covenantee can elect how he will sue upon the covenant. He can sue both or all covenantors together, or he may sue just one of them, charging the entire liability on that particular covenantor. This form of liability may be indicated by other expressions, e.g. 'A and B covenant for themselves and each of them'. The covenant operates as a several covenant where joint covenantors limit their liability to their own acts or defaults.

At common law a single covenant could not be made *with* covenantees jointly and severally; it had to be one or the other. Now by virtue of s. 81 (1) of the Law of Property Act 1925, a covenant made after the Act with two or more jointly is to be construed as being made with each of them.

2. Creation of new restrictive covenants

The main task of the draftsman is to ensure that the covenants are enforceable not only by and against the original parties, but their successors also. He should eschew any desire to frame the covenant in broad general terms, for fear it should be held void for uncertainty[12]. Special points arise on the creation of restrictive covenants, and these apply alike to transactions affecting registered

---

8 See for example notes 20 and 1, p. 540, post.

9 See *Re Fawcett and Holmes Contract* (1889) 42 Ch D 150, CA; *Powell v Hemsley* [1909] 1 Ch 680 at 689, per Eve J: affd. [1909] 2 Ch 252, CA.

10 See this problem discussed in M & W, 723, 764; Emmet, 604. At law the benefit of a positive covenant affecting freehold land was capable of passing to a limited category of persons, which s. 78 has extended, whereas the burden of such a covenant passed to no one. But see *Federated Homes Ltd v Mill Lodge Properties Ltd* [1980] 1 All ER 371, CA, (1981) 97 LQR 32 (G.H. Newson). It seems difficult to see how the wording in s. 78 can have a substantive effect but not that in s. 79. Whilst 'different considerations' apply to the section (ibid, p. 380) that does not seem to be a satisfactory explanation. Of course to give a substantive effect to s. 79 would be to make positive covenants run and thereby cure a major defect in the present law.

11 *Re Royal Victoria Pavilion, Ramsgate* [1961] Ch 581, [1961] 3 All ER 83 (covenant to 'procure' certain state of affairs).

12 See e.g. *Brigg v Thornton* [1904] 1 Ch 386, CA; *National Trust v Midlands Electricity Board* [1952] Ch 380, [1952] 1 All ER 298.

and unregistered land. A typical covenant by a purchaser to observe new restrictions might be as follows[13]:

' For the benefit and protection of the land of the vendor coloured brown on the plan annexed hereto and each and every part thereof and so as to bind so far as may be the land hereby conveyed into whosesoever hands the same may come the purchaser hereby covenants with the vendor that the purchaser and the persons deriving title under him will at all times hereafter observe[14] the restrictions set out in the Schedule hereto but so that the purchaser shall not be liable for any breach of such restriction occurring on or in respect of the land hereby conveyed after he shall have parted with all interest therein.'

(a) Annexation[15]

A covenant which is annexed to land automatically passes on a subsequent conveyance of that land, without express mention and even though the purchaser is unaware of its existence[16]. Annexation is essentially a question of the construction of the instrument of creation. Annexation, if intended (and the draftsman should direct his mind to this question), should be made apparent in the conveyance itself. Such intention is shown by stating that the covenant is for the benefit of land of the covenantee (as in the above example) or that it is made with the vendor in his capacity as owner of the benefited land. For the avoidance of doubt the land to be benefited should be defined in the deed itself. This can be achieved by identifying such land by reference to the deed plan, or by naming the vendor's estate. If it is intended to annex the covenant to particular parts of the land so as to enable a purchaser of part to sue for breach, words like 'each and every' part must be added. In *Russell v Archdale*[17] certain covenants were stated to benefit 'the vendor's adjoining and neighbouring land'. These words were held sufficient to annex the covenants to the *whole* of the neighbouring land, but not to individual parts of it. In all cases it is essential to consider the intentions of the covenantee-vendor, in particular whether he proposes to preserve the benefited land as a continuing entity or to dispose of it in lots for development. A purported annexation of covenants to the entirety of the vendor's retained land is ineffective if they do not in fact touch and concern the whole; the court will not sever the covenant and treat it as annexed to such parts as may be benefited[18].

The law in this area has, apparently, been radically altered by the decision of the Court of Appeal is *Federated Homes Ltd v Mill Lodge Properties Ltd*[19] in which the Court have given a very wide meaning to section 78 and have thereby

---

13   Adapted from 19 Ency F & P, 887, Form 7:A:20.
14   If the schedule contains positive covenants, it should read 'observe and perform the restrictions and stipulations'. Negative and positive covenants should not be lumped indiscriminately in one schedule, but rather set out in different ones. See *Shepherd Homes Ltd v Sandham* (No. 2) [1971] 2 All ER 1267 (single positive covenant embracing three negative obligations).
15   See [1972B] CLJ 157 (H.W.R. Wade).
16   *Rogers v Hosegood* [1900] 2 Ch 388, CA; *Lawrence v South County Freeholds Ltd* [1939] Ch 656 at 680, [1939] 2 All ER 503 at 523, per Simonds J ('a hidden treasure which may be discovered in the hour of need').
17   [1964] Ch 38, [1962] 2 All ER 305 (where there was also an express assignment of the benefit).
18   *Re Ballard's Conveyance* [1937] Ch 473, [1937] 2 All ER 691.
19   [1980] 1 All ER 371. For a criticism see (1981) 97 LQR 32 (G.H. Newson).

eliminated most of the difficulties over annexation by having the benefit annexed by that section.

(b) Binding successors in title
Prima facie the intention to make the covenants run with the covenantor's land is imported by s. 79 of the Law of Property Act 1925. Consequently the words in the specimen clause 'so as to bind the land hereby conveyed into whosesoever hands the same may come' are strictly unnecessary[20]. Nevertheless their inclusion is considered desirable (and it is the general practice to bind successors expressly) because they establish beyond doubt that the covenants are not merely personal to the covenantor.

(c) Limiting covenantor's personal liability
The covenantor's liability for breach of covenant does not terminate on conveyance of the land to a purchaser. By virtue of s. 79 he is deemed to covenant for himself and his successors in title. He therefore assumes a personal or vicarious liability for the actions of his successors[1]. Hence the need for an indemnity covenant. His liability may be *expressly* limited to the duration of his interest in the land, but unless the contract so provides the covenantor-purchaser is not entitled to a qualified covenant[2]. The wording in the precedent clause ensures that he will remain liable for breaches of covenant committed by his lessee. The covenantor's liability can, of course, be made to terminate on his parting with possession of the land.

(d) Existence of building scheme
It is the invariable practice today on the development of a residential building estate to impose on individual purchasers a host of detailed restrictions, apparently designed to preserve the amenities of the estate. These restrictions can be of little practical value if they are only enforceable by the developer, for on completion of the estate he will have no real interest in their continued observance and, unless he retains adjacent land capable of being benefited by the covenants, he cannot enforce them against subsequent purchasers. The existence of a building scheme enables individual purchasers and their successors to enforce the restrictions inter se. Nevertheless the purchaser of existing property forming part of a housing estate may often find himself unable to sue a neighbour who has infringed the restrictions for two main reasons. There seems a general reluctance on the part of builders (or their legal advisers) of houses in the lower or middle price ranges to impose building schemes. For a scheme to exist it is imperative (inter alia) that the developer laid out the estate in plots subject to restrictions intended by him to be for the benefit of all lots sold[3]. This intention is commonly lacking, the covenants being imposed by the developer

---

20 But see *Shepherd Homes Ltd v Sandham (No 2)* [1971] 2 All ER 1267 at 1270–71, per Megarry J.
1   See *Powell v Hemsley* [1909] 1 Ch 680 at 689, per Eve J; affd. [1909] 2 Ch 252, CA. Contra M & W, 753; *Sefton v Tophams Ltd* [1967] AC 50 at 81, [1966] 3 All ER 1039 at 1053, per Lord Wilberforce (where, however, the covenant was not to cause or permit).
2   *Pollock v Rabbits* (1882) 21 Ch D 466, CA.
3   Alternatively, such intention may be inferred from the execution of a deed of mutual covenants: *Baxter v Four Oaks Properties Ltd* [1965] Ch 816, [1965] 1 All ER 906. For the essentials of a building scheme, see Parker J, in *Elliston v Reacher* [1908] 2 Ch 374 at 384; affd. [1908] 2 Ch 665, CA. Recent decisions suggest that the courts are anxious to find the existence of a scheme, whenever possible; see *Re Dolphin's Conveyance, Birmingham Corpn v Boden* [1970] 2 All ER 664; *Eagling v Gardner* [1970] 2 All ER 838; *Brunner v Greenslade* [1970] 3 All ER 833.

for his own benefit so as to maintain the value of his unsold plots. In addition the existence of a scheme is a question of fact, often difficult of ascertainment many years after completion of the estate, which is usually when the court becomes seised of the problem. There is no valid reason why the existence of a scheme should not be made apparent in the conveyance itself. Evidence of an intention to create a scheme can be shown by a suitably drafted recital[4], and a simple proviso that nothing shall be deemed to imply the existence of a scheme suffices to negative any intention to create one. In the case of registered land it is essential to disclose the existence of a scheme in the transfer and to require the Registrar to enter notice of it on the title.

Clearly it is the duty of the solicitor acting for the purchaser of a new house on a building estate to ascertain before exchange of contracts whether it is intended to impose a scheme and to see that the draft conveyance provides accordingly. Unfortunately the complexity of the subject and the refusal of many builders' solicitors to permit alterations to their draft conveyances[5] is frequently a sufficient inducement for a purchaser's solicitor not to persist with his endeavours to produce a solution satisfactory to his client. If no scheme is intended, a purchaser can object to any attempt by the vendor to annex the benefit of the restrictions to individual parts of his retained land, for this produces the Gilbertian situation[6] that a later purchaser of part (and his successors in title) can enforce the covenants against an earlier purchaser, without the latter having any corresponding right to enforce them against the later purchaser.

(e) Registration of restrictive covenants

By way of reminder, restrictive covenants affecting unregistered land should be registered as class D (ii) land charges, otherwise they become unenforceable against a later purchaser of the burdened land[7]. It is thought that this vital precaution is not infrequently ignored in practice. In the case of registered land, restrictive covenants created on a transfer of land are automatically entered on the register of title as part of the registration process. In other cases application for entry of a notice must be made.

3.   Assignment of benefit of covenants

(a) Negative covenants

In the absence of any annexation of the benefit of restrictive covenants to the covenantee's land (in which event the benefit passes automatically), the covenantee may expressly assign the benefit to a purchaser of the benefited land[8]. This rule is of special significance in relation to the enforcement of restrictive covenants. The benefit should always be expressly assigned in the conveyance of the benefited land. A subsequent separate assignment of the benefit is ineffectual, at least where the covenantee has disposed of the whole of his retained

4   See e.g. 19 Ency F & P, 906, Form 7:A:27.
5   It will be recalled that on the conveyance of a house on a building estate the vendor normally requires the conveyance to be in the form of a specimen draft document annexed to the contract; see p. 536, ante.
6   *Re Jeff's Transfer, Rogers v Astley (No. 2)* [1966] 1 All ER 937 at 942, per Stamp J. This can be avoided if the later purchasers enter into a separate covenant with the owners of plots previously sold, so as to attract the provisions of the LPA 1925, s. 56.
7   As to the registration of restrictive covenants arising under a building scheme, see p. 348, ante.
8   A purely personal covenant cannot be assigned: *Formby v Barker* [1903] 2 Ch 539, CA.

land[9]. Once he has parted with his interest in the land, the covenantee ceases to be entitled to enforce the covenant in equity and he cannot confer any greater rights on his assignee than he himself possesses[10]. As a matter of construction of the original covenant, an assignment of the benefit may be prohibited but in the absence of clear words excluding assignment, express assignability is assumed[11]. In particular annexation of a covenant to the entirety of an estate does not of itself preclude an express assignment of the benefit to a subsequent purchaser of part of the estate[12]. The weight of modern authority is against the view, expressed in some older authorities, that an express assignment operates to annex the benefit of the covenant to the land, so that thereafter it passes automatically. Consequently a suing successor can only enforce the covenants if he establishes a complete chain of assignments[13]. The proper place for the assignment of the benefit of covenants is in the parcels clause in some such wording[14] as follows:

' and together with the full benefit of the covenants contained in the said conveyance with power in the name of the vendor but at the cost in all respects and sole risk of the purchaser and the persons deriving title under him to sue upon and enforce the said covenants.'

The position where a transfer of registered land purports to assign the benefit of restrictive covenants has been considered elsewhere[15]. The Registry's reluctance to note on the register that the transfer assigns the benefit will not, it seems, prevent the benefit passing, at least in equity, but renders it more difficult to ascertain whether the benefit has been assigned. However an office copy of the transfer (which is lodged in the Registry) can be obtained by any person entitled to inspect it[16].

The benefit of restrictive covenants may also pass by operation of law, for example, on the death of the covenantee[17]. Strictly speaking his personal representatives should expressly assign the benefit of the covenants to the devisee in whose favour they execute an assent of the benefited land. Should they fail to do so, they become bare trustees of the benefit for the beneficiary. He can himself sue in equity to enforce the restrictions without making the personal representatives parties to the action[18] and an assignment by him of the benefit of the

9 *Re Union of London and Smith's Bank Conveyance, Miles v Easter* [1933] Ch 611, CA. A later assignment suffices to enable the successor to sue the original covenantor who is bound *at law*.
10 Ibid., at 633 and 366, respectively, per Romer LJ. It is not thought that a subsequent assignment is effectual, even if the covenantee still retains part of the benefited land: ibid., at 632 and 366.
11 *Stilwell v Blackman* [1968] Ch 508 at 526, [1967] 3 All ER 514 at 520, per Ungoed-Thomas J.
12 *Stilwell v Blackman* [1968] Ch 508, [1967] 3 All ER 514; *Russell v Archdale* [1964] Ch 38, [1962] 2 All ER 305 (where the point was not argued, the action being at law against the original covenator).
13 *Re Pinewood Estate, Farnborough* [1958] Ch 280, [1957] 2 All ER 517; *Stilwell v Blackman* [1968] Ch 508 at 526, [1967] 3 All ER 514 at 520, per Ungoed-Thomas J. Contra, *Renals v Cowlishaw* (1878) 9 Ch D 125 at 130, 131, per Hall V-C; *Rogers v Hosegood* [1900] 2 Ch 388 at 408, per Collins LJ.
14 Taken from the conveyance before the court in *Stilwell v Blackman* [1968] Ch 508, [1967] 3 All ER 514, adopting 19 Ency F & P, Form 7:A:19.
15 Page 477, ante.
16 LRR 1925, r. 296; cf. r. 287 which applies to documents referred to in the register. But see R & R, 306.
17 *Ives v Brown* [1919] 2 Ch 314.
18 *Earl of Leicester v Wells-next-the-Sea UDC* [1972] 3 All ER 77.

covenants to a purchaser of the benefited land is effective in equity to vest the benefit in the purchaser[19].

(b) Positive covenants
The need to assign the benefit of *positive* covenants also arises on occasions. It appears that the benefit of a positive covenant which touches and concerns the land passes automatically at law with the benefited land without express assignment; but direct authority on this point is lacking and caution perhaps requires an express assignment of the benefit every time[20]. Two specific cases deserve mention. The benefit of a covenant to pay a rentcharge does not run with the rentcharge[1] and a conveyance thereof should expressly assign the benefit of the grantor's covenant to pay. Secondly an option to purchase the freehold reversion, granted by a landlord to his tenant, does not pass automatically with the demised premises. It is good conveyancing practice to include in an assignment of the lease an express transfer of the benefit of the option (assuming the purchaser is to have the benefit of it). Yet failure to assign the benefit may not be fatal. Not only is the option separately assignable (provided it is not merely personal to the lessee), but the assignment of the lease may itself operate to transfer the option without express mention, if the lease contains the conventional definition clause of 'lessee' as including his successors in title[2].

4. Indemnity covenants

Existing covenants subject to which the land is sold should be introduced within the operative part of the deed in the habendum. The covenantor's continuing liability for breach of covenant renders it essential for a vendor to obtain an indemnity covenant from the purchaser whenever the vendor is—

(i) the original covenantor who will remain liable on the covenants after the conveyance, or
(ii) a successor in title who has entered into an indemnity covenant with the covenantor, or some intermediate predecessor in title.

The need is the same whether the covenants are negative or positive, and even if in the case of the former the restrictions will be unenforceable in equity against the purchaser for want of registration[3]. In some cases an indemnity is implied by statute. These will be considered later.

19 *Newton Abbot Co-operative Society Ltd v Williamson and Treadgold Ltd* [1952] Ch 286, [1952] 1 All ER 279.
20 See p. 536, ante. It is thought that the position is the same as in equity. In *Smith and Snipes Hall Farm v River Douglas Catchment Board* [1949] 2 KB 500, [1949] 2 All ER 179, CA, there was an express assignment of the benefit by the covenantee to his freehold successor but not (it seems) by the latter to his tenant who merely held an oral tenancy.
1 *Grant v Edmondson* [1931] 1 Ch 1, CA, p. 348, ante.
2 *Griffith v Pelton* [1958] Ch 205, [1957] 3 All ER 75, CA; *Re Button's Lease, Inman v Button* [1964] Ch 263; [1963] 3 All ER 708 (where it was left open whether the option passed automatically on the assignment of the lease, or by virtue of a subsequent separate assignment of the option itself). Cf. [1957] CLJ 148 at 150, where it is argued that it should be the terms of the assignment, rather than the lease, that determine whether the option passes. See further Barnsley, *Land Options*, pp. 54–59.
3 The possibility of an action at law for damages still exists; cf. *Wright v Dean* [1948] Ch 686, [1948] 2 All ER 415 (option void for non-registration; grantor liable for damages).

(a) Express indemnity covenant

The vendor's right to an indemnity covenant is regulated by the contract, if either the National Conditions or The Law Society's Conditions apply,[4] provided the property is expressed in the contract to be sold subject to the covenants. Even failing any contractual stipulation, the court will require the purchaser to enter into a suitable indemnity[5]. The precedent on page 493 includes a typical indemnity covenant. It is standard practice to preface the covenant with the words: 'With the object and intent of affording the vendor a full indemnity but not otherwise.' This limitation makes it clear that the covenant is to operate by way of indemnity only and is not intended to enable the vendor himself to enforce the original covenants[6]. If he requires the purchaser to observe the original restrictions for the benefit of his own retained land, clear provision for this must be made in the contract and in the conveyance.

The original covenantor (V) cannot insist upon an indemnity on a subsequent sale if his liability is expressly limited to the duration of his ownership of the burdened land. The implications of this limitation of liability are not always fully appreciated. Not infrequently an indemnity covenant is (unnecessarily) obtained, or given, when V conveys to a purchaser (P1). However the mere existence of P1's covenant of indemnity with V does not entitle P1 to insist upon an indemnity on a sale to P2. There is no possibility of P1's having to indemnify V in respect of breaches of covenant committed by P2, since the covenantee is precluded from suing V after V has parted with his interest in the land.

(b) Implied indemnity covenants

An indemnity covenant may be statutorily implied in certain circumstances, the two circumstances most likely to be encountered being (i) the conveyance of land subject to an existing rentcharge, and (ii) the assignment of land comprised within a lease. In these instances, provided the transfer is for valuable consideration, the purchaser impliedly covenants to pay the rentcharge, or rent, and to observe and perform all the covenants, agreements and conditions contained in the document creating the rentcharge, or in the lease[7]. An express indemnity is required when the transaction is not for value, e.g. on an assent of leasehold property to a beneficiary[8]. No indemnity covenant is implied, and one should be stipulated for, on a conveyance of a freehold (or leasehold) reversion. Condition 18 (3) of the National Conditions of Sale, if applicable, regulates the vendor's rights in this situation by providing that the purchaser shall keep the vendor indemnified against all claims by the tenant for compensation or otherwise. This clause extends to all claims arising out of the landlord-tenant relationship, as the decision in *Eagon v Dent*[9] illustrates.

---

4   NCS 19 (6); LSC 17 (4).
5   *Moxhay v Inderwick* (1847) 1 De G & Sm 708.
6   See *Re Poole and Clarke's Contract* [1904] 2 Ch 173, CA. Even if the covenant is not so framed it will still be construed as an indemnity only: *Reckitt v Cody* [1920] 2 Ch 452. LSC 17 (4) requires the purchaser to covenant to indemnify the vendor; cf. NCS 19 (6) (covenant to observe and perform, and to indemnify).
7   LPA 1925, s. 77 (1) (A), (C), Sch. 2, Parts VII, IX. The indemnity relates to positive and negative covenants.
8   As to the personal representatives' right to require an indemnity, see AEA 1925, s. 36 (10); Hallett, 82.
9   [1965] 3 All ER 334. LSC 5 (2) (c) specifically relates to a situation like this by requiring the purchaser to indemnify the vendor against claims arising in respect of a contract void against the purchaser for non-registration.

L granted T an underlease which conferred an option to renew. T failed to register the option. L assigned the leasehold reversion to A who declined to renew T's lease. T sued L for breach of covenant[10]. L was held entitled by virtue of condition 18 (3) to an indemnity from A in respect of T's claim. The assignment to A contained no express indemnity covenant but it was conceded that the contractual provision did not merge in the assignment.

5.   Covenants for title

These are fully discussed in Chapter 24.

6.   Proposals for reform

In their report on Restrictive Covenants in 1967[11] the Law Commission put forward twelve propositions designed to simplify to a considerable degree the creation and enforcement of restrictive covenants. These recommendations remain unimplemented, for since then the Commission have embarked on a more ambitious project by considering the possible assimilation of covenants and easements along lines more akin to the latter. Their earlier propositions have not all been readopted in their Working Paper[12] on the subject. As their latest proposals do not represent their concluded opinions, it would be improper to do more than mention briefly some possible future developments which, if adopted, will effect far reaching changes in the existing law. Restrictive covenants (which will constitute one class of a new interest in land to be termed a Land Obligation) will only be effectively created if the deed of creation expressly identifies the dominant land. Happily, the distinction between annexation and assignment seems likely to disappear[12a], for once created the benefit (and the burden) will automatically pass to any successor having an interest in the dominant (or servient) land. Indemnity covenants will become unnecessary, for the contractual relationship between the original parties will terminate when either parts with his land. Finally a land obligation corresponding to a restrictive covenant will be capable of being legal in nature so that its enforceability will not, so far as unregistered land is concerned, be dependent on registration as a land charge[13].

N   Acknowledgment for production of deeds

Where on completion the vendor retains possession of deeds and documents relating to the land conveyed, the conveyance will incorporate an acknowledgment by him of the purchaser's right to the production and delivery of copies of the documents retained. Sometimes he will also enter into an undertaking for their safe custody. The occasions when the vendor is entitled to retain the deeds, and the obligations which he assumes by giving an acknowledgment and undertaking have already been considered[14].

10   T's claim was maintainable despite his failure to register the option: *Wright v Dean* [1948] Ch 686, [1948] 2 All ER 415.
11   Law Com. No. 11.
12   Published Working Paper No. 36, 'Appurtenant Rights'.
12a   The Federated case above may well have achieved this already.
13   The Working Paper does not profess to deal with the effect of any reformulation of the law on existing rights.
14   Pages 424–427, ante.

O   Certificate for value

The purpose of the certificate for value clause has already been explained[15]. This clause is usually in the following form:

> It is hereby certified that the transaction hereby effected does not form part of a larger transaction or of a series of transactions in respect of which the amount or value or the aggregate amount of value of the consideration exceeds £25,000 [or £30,000 or £35,000 or £40,000].

P   Testimonium and execution

The testimonium links the contents of the deed with the parties' seals and signatures, as follows:

> IN WITNESS whereof the parties hereto have hereunto set their respective hands and seals the day and year first before written

Underneath towards the left hand side of the page appears the attestation clause and the executing party signs his name on the right hand side, thus—

SIGNED SEALED AND DELIVERED
by the said ABEL SMITH in   Abel Smith (Seal)
the presence of:

The requirements of a valid execution and the necessity for any attestation have already been considered in Chapter 15[16]. Any schedules appended to the deed are sandwiched between the testimonium and the attestation clause. A registered land transfer contains no testimonium and the signatures and seals appear immediately after the certificate for value clause (if any), except where there are schedules to the transfer, which are also placed before the attestation clause.

15   Page 442, ante.
16   Pages 428–433, ante.

Chapter 19

Documents for particular transactions

A Introduction

A cursory glance at any book of conveyancing precedents will soon indicate the vast number of different transactions for which the conveyancer may be required to draft a suitable document. The aim of this chapter is not to furnish the reader with a selection of simple precedents, but to consider mainly (though not exclusively) the contents of conveyances and other documents relating to some of the transactions to which we have had occasion to refer in the preceding chapters and to draw attention to particular problems for which special provision should be made in the deed. This chapter concentrates upon the contents of deeds relating to unregistered land. However, though we have seen that the form of a transfer of registered land is much simpler than that of a conveyance, especially in relation to the description of the land transferred and the absence of any need to have recitals, any special provisions which a particular transaction renders necessary must be incorporated in a transfer of registered land just as in a conveyance of unregistered land.

A precedent of a simple conveyance of freehold land by a beneficial owner appears on page 493. This form, suitably amended, can be used for straightforward transactions by vendors who are only limited owners. One point in particular should be remembered. When the vendor is not a beneficial owner, the conveyance should make reference to the authority, statutory or otherwise, which enables him to convey free from the rights of the beneficiaries. Thus in a conveyance in execution of an express trust for sale, the vendors should be expressed to convey 'as trustees in execution of the said [or the before recited] trust for sale'. Similarly a conveyance by a mortgagee under his statutory power of sale[1] will recite the mortgage and the agreement of sale, and continue in some such form as follows:

NOW THIS DEED WITNESSETH as follows:
1. In pursuance of the said agreement and in consideration of £-paid by the purchaser to the vendor (the receipt whereof the vendor hereby acknowledges) the vendor as mortgagee in exercise of the power of sale conferred on him by the Law of Property Act 1925 HEREBY CONVEYS unto the purchaser ALL THAT [parcels] TO HOLD unto the purchaser in fee simple discharged[2] from all right of redemption and claims under the before recited mortgage.

1 See 19 Ency F & P, 1340, Form 7:K:26; Hallett, 273, Form 52.
2 It is customary to insert the words 'discharged etc.,' since they occur in the statutory form

Any incumbrances subject to which the property is conveyed are introduced by the usual words 'SUBJECT to' which appear in the habendum immediately after 'in fee simple', and the words 'discharged, etc.,' come at the end of the clause after the incumbrances. Where the land is subject to restrictive covenants, the purchaser need not enter into any indemnity covenant[3] with the mortgagee; since the latter will not have given any such covenant to the mortgagor, he does not require to be protected by a similar covenant from the purchaser.

In the following pages it is proposed to enlarge upon the contents of the documents listed below:

> A conveyance of a new house on a building estate
> A conveyance creating a rentcharge
> Conveyances of the freehold reversion
> A lease, and other documents relating to leasehold land
> A conveyance, or lease, of a flat
> An assent.

B   Conveyance of new house on building estate

The conveyancer is frequently involved in the drafting or approval of conveyances of new residential property. In practice the reader will encounter a wide variety of such conveyances, some more complex in their provisions than others. In keeping with the general policy of this chapter, it is proposed to draw attention to those matters for which it is normally necessary to provide in a straightforward conveyance of a new house, rather than to comment upon a specific precedent. Some points have already been touched upon in the preceding chapter, but the following discussion affords an opportunity to bring together several topics previously considered in isolation.

1.   Parcels clause

Nothing further need be said about the description of the property, save to stress the point made in Chapter 18 that it is vital to ensure that the description is accurate and that any plan which is intended to control the parcels faithfully represents the actual boundaries of the plot[4].

2.   Easements and reservations

It is usually essential for the conveyance to grant and reserve rights of way and use of sewers and other services. At the time of the conveyance the estate roads are probably still under construction and the site of these roads is still vested in the vendor. The purchaser should be granted a right of way for all purposes connected with the use of the land conveyed[5] with or without vehicles along the

---

of conveyance by a mortgagee (see the LPA 1925, Sch. 5, Form No. 4), but their inclusion does not seem essential in view of s. 88 (1) (b) of the Act.

3   See pp. 543–544, ante.
4   See pp. 504–508, ante.
5   It is preferable to specify the dominant land but if this is not done extrinsic evidence is admissible to identify it; p. 521, ante.

estate roads (an expression which will require amplification in the actual deed) or along a road or roads suitably indicated on the deed plan or named in the deed. Where the land conveyed includes a section of the road fronting it[6], there should be a reservation in favour of the vendor and his successors in title of a similar right of way over the purchaser's section.

In addition to this right of way there is a grant of a right, frequently expressed (as in the case of the right of way) to be in common with the vendor and all others entitled to use the like rights, to connect with and to use the sewers, drains, watercourses, pipes, cables, wires and other services 'now laid or hereafter to be laid' in, under or over the vendor's adjacent land. The use of the 'now or hereafter' formula renders it essential to see that the easement is limited to take effect within the perpetuity period[7]. There will be a reservation of a similar right to use the sewers, etc., under the purchaser's land.

Where part of the building erected on the purchaser's plot overhangs the adjacent land the conveyance should grant adequate rights to maintain footings, foundations, eaves and gutters in, under or over the adjacent land, and to enter that land for the purposes of maintenance and repair on condition that any resulting damage to the adjacent land or buildings is made good by the purchaser.

3.   Covenants

As we have already observed[8], it is the invariable practice on any residential development to subject individual purchasers to numerous detailed restrictions. The following are only illustrative of the many that find their way into present day conveyances: not to use otherwise than as a single private dwelling; not to create nuisances or annoyance; not to add to or alter the existing buildings without the vendor's written consent; not to display advertisements (other than for sale or to let notices); not to station caravans and other vehicles (other than private cars) on the land; not to plant poplars and certain other trees within specified distances of adjacent buildings. These and similar restrictions which can do much to preserve the amenities of a building estate serve a useful purpose if imposed so as to create a building scheme[9], thereby enabling one owner to enforce the restrictions against his neighbour. If this is the intention it should be so stated in the conveyance. Alas, all too frequently the restrictions are imposed solely for the protection of the vendor's unsold land. Whilst the vendor clearly has a legitimate interest to protect, it is to be regretted that so many practitioners representing builders are reluctant to consider the wider implications of estate development. In the absence of an enforceable building scheme these restrictions become virtually obsolete once the estate has been completed and the vendor has disposed of the entirety of his interest in the land. Ultimately it is the law that is brought into disrepute, for a house owner may feel justly aggrieved when he is told that the law is powerless to help him take action against a neighbour who is in breach of covenant. He may well question the reason for imposing the restrictions in the first place and is hardly likely to be satisfied when told they were imposed for the vendor's benefit.

Little need be said about a purchaser's positive covenants. A covenant to maintain one or more boundary fences[10] is often encountered. On some estate

6   See p. 514, ante.
7   See p. 522, ante.
8   Page 535, ante.
9   For building schemes, see pp. 540–541, ante.
10   As to which, see p. 514, ante.

developments the vendor lays out the front garden with trees, shrubs and flowering plants, and the purchaser is commonly required to maintain and replace these when necessary.

The only obligation usually entered into by the vendor is the covenant to construct the road upon which the property abuts to the satisfaction of the local highway authority. The wording of this covenant needs watching. Unless the vendor also covenants to repair and maintain the road until its adoption[11], the liability for maintenance pending adoption falls on the individual purchasers.

4.　Other clauses

Attention needs to be drawn to some miscellaneous clauses frequently encountered. It is advisable to regulate the rights of adjoining owners as regards walls, fences, spouts, pipes, drains and similar matters used and enjoyed in common. The difficulties created by the standard form declaration that these are to be maintained and repaired at the joint expense of the persons entitled to use them have previously been considered[12]. It is standard practice for the vendor to reserve the right[13] to modify, waive or release the restrictions affecting any land forming part of the development and to prevent the purchaser's acquisition of any right of light or air which will restrict or interfere with the use of the vendor's adjoining land for building or other purposes. Such a clause would appear to be ineffective to prevent the acquisition of a right of light over land not owned by the vendor at the time but subsequently acquired by him, though frequently the clause professes to extend to land 'now or hereafter' belonging to the vendor.

The conveyance will also contain an acknowledgment for production of deeds and (where appropriate) a certificate for value clause[14].

C　Conveyance creating rentcharge

As we saw in Chapter 11[15], it was a common feature of residential development in certain parts of the country to create a perpetual yearly rentcharge on the conveyance of each house. In addition to restrictive covenants of the type considered in the previous section, the conveyance would impose certain positive covenants intended for the protection of the vendor's rentcharge[16]. The ones encountered most often are — to pay the rentcharge; to build; to keep in good repair; to insure; to permit inspection. A rentcharge can still be created to enforce covenants under the Rentcharges Act 1977.

It will immediately be appreciated that these are positive covenants, the burden of which does not run with the land so as to bind subsequent owners[17]. The rights of the rentcharge owner are therefore bolstered by reserving in the conveyance a right of re-entry if the rent is unpaid for (usually) one year, or if

11　See pp. 200–201, ante.
12　Page 513, ante.
13　Even in cases where no building scheme is created.
14　See pp. 545–546, ante. A transfer of registered land will not, of course, contain any acknowledgment for production, p. 427, ante.
15　See p. 342, ante.
16　For a precedent, see 19 Ency F & P, 1365, form 7:L:2.
17　But an action of debt for the amount of the rent lies against the freeholder for the time being, whether he is the original purchaser or a successor in title: *Thomas v Sylvester* (1873) LR 8 QB 368, p. 348, ante. The right of re-entry is also a powerful weapon.

there is a breach of any of the other covenants imposed for the security of the rentcharge[18]. In either of these events the vendor may, in the language of a typical re-entry clause,

' . . . enter the land or any part thereof in the name of the whole and to have and repossess the same as if this deed had not been made.'

In other words the clause entitles the rentowner to determine the purchaser's fee simple estate in the land[19]. A right of re-entry annexed to a legal rentcharge ranks as a legal interest[20]. As it is binding upon successors in title of the original purchaser, the threat of forfeiture operates as a potent inducement to pay the rent and perform the covenants. For the avoidance of doubt this right of re-entry is generally expressed to be in addition to the statutory remedies[1] for recovery of rentcharges by way of distress, receipt of income and leasing the land to trustees. Although the right of re-entry may arise at some future uncertain date, it is not necessary to limit its exercise to the perpetuity period. Section 11 (1) of the Perpetuities and Accumulations Act 1964, provides[2] that the rule against perpetuities does not apply to a right of re-entry for non-payment of a rentcharge. The better view[3] is that this statutory exemption also applies to any right of re-entry for breach of some ancillary covenant such as the covenant to repair.

Where the rentcharge was created on the sale of a house forming part of a building estate, the vendor would retain the title deeds (other than the conveyance to the purchaser) and would give the usual statutory acknowledgment for their production. Where it was created on the sale of a single house, the vendor would normally hand over on completion the deeds relating to the property, in which event the conveyance would incorporate an express acknowledgment and undertaking by the purchaser in respect of those deeds[4]. Alternatively the contract might provide[5] for the vendor to retain the deeds and he would enter into the statutory acknowledgment for production. Whenever a rentcharge was created the conveyance would be executed in duplicate; the

---

18 The power of re-entry should not be made to extend to breaches of the negative covenants imposed for the benefit of the vendor's adjoining land. Restrictive covenants cannot be, it is said, annexed to a rentcharge (*Torbay Hotels Ltd v Jenkins* [1927] 2 Ch 225 at 239, per Clauson J), so that a rentowner, not owning any adjacent land, cannot enforce restrictive covenants against a successor in title of the servient land. However this may not be the case now after the Law of Property Act 1925, s. 78 (a rentcharge is included in the definition of the word 'land' (s. 205 (1) (ix)). In any event the benefit of the right of re-entry is freely assignable and does not depend on the covenant for its enforceability: *Shiloh Spinners v Harding* [1973] AC 691, [1973] 1 All ER 90, HL.
19 The owner of the servient land can, it seems, apply for relief under the LPA 1925, s. 146 which applies to the grant of a fee farm rent (see sub-s. (5) (a)), assuming 'fee farm rent' includes a rentcharge.
20 LPA 1925, s. 1 (2) (e).
1   See the LPA 1925, s. 121.
2   The section only applies to rentcharges created on or after 16 July 1964 (see s. 15 (5) of the Act). The rule probably applied to rentcharges created prior to this date but the position is not absolutely clear; see M & W, 797.
3   See 25 Halsbury's Statutes (3rd edn) 15; cf. 19 Ency F & P, 1367, note 13 where the point is considered to be open.
4   The vendor requires an acknowledgment from the purchaser to enable him to establish his title to the land out of which the rentcharge issues. An express acknowledgment is desirable as the purchaser does not seem to be a person who 'retains' deeds as required by the LPA 1925, s. 64; see p. 425, ante.
5   See p. 344, ante.

duplicate conveyance retained by the vendor constitutes his documentary evidence of its creation.

D   Conveyances of freehold reversion

1.   Sale to stranger

On a sale of freehold land subject to an existing lease, the conveyance normally contains a recital of the vendor's seisin subject to the lease and the habendum will read as follows: 'TO HOLD unto the purchaser is fee simple subject to but with the benefit of the before recited lease.' There is no need to incorporate an express assignment of the benefit of the rent reserved by, and the lessee's covenants contained in, the lease[6]; these pass automatically by virtue of s. 141 of the Law of Property Act 1925, a provision which also operates to vest in the purchaser the right to sue and re-enter (assuming there is a forfeiture clause) for rent in arrear at the time of the conveyance[7]. It is no longer necessary to qualify the reference to the lease in the habendum by words such as 'if and so far as subsisting'. The decision in *Davenport v Smith*[8] to the effect that a conveyance omitting such qualifying words operated as a waiver of existing breaches of covenant, thereby precluding the purchaser from exercising his right of re-entry, was overruled by the Court of Appeal in *London and County (A & D) Ltd v Wilfred Sportsman Ltd*[9].

2.   Sale to lessee

Where the purchaser of the freehold reversion is the lessee himself, his solicitor should consider the need for including in the conveyance a formal declaration that the lessee's leasehold term shall merge and be extinguished in the fee simple estate. Merger depends on the intention, expressed or implied, of the parties[10]. Where merger is capable of taking place, an appropriate declaration by the purchaser is desirable, if such be the intention, for it obviates any requisitions on title on this point when the purchaser comes to sell his property. In the absence of any expressed intention, the court considers what is most advantageous for the party owning the two estates[11]. There can be no merger if the leasehold estate is subject to incumbrances, e.g. a mortgage, or if he holds the two estates in different capacities. A declaration of merger should not be included if it is intended to preserve the enforceability of restrictive covenants entered into by the lessor in the lease in respect of the lessor's adjoining land[12]. In some precedents[13] the vendor is expressed to convey the property 'to the intent that' the lease shall merge. However a vendor would seem entitled to object to this formula since he cannot tell whether merger is possible without investigating the lessee's title, and it is preferable for the declaration of merger

---

6   Cf. 19 Ency F & P, 1262, Form 7:J:1.
7   *London and County (A &D) Ltd v Wilfred Sportsman Ltd* [1971] Ch 764, [1970] 2 All ER 600, CA.
8   [1921] 2 Ch 270.
9   [1971] Ch 764, [1970] 2 All ER 600.
10   See the LPA 1925, s. 185, which applies the equitable rule to all cases of merger. The rule at law was independent of intention.
11   *Ingle v Vaughan Jenkins* [1900] 2 Ch 368.
12   *Golden Lion Hotel (Hunstanton) Ltd v Carter* [1965] 3 All ER 506, CA (covenants destroyed).
13   E.g. 19 Ency F & P, 1266, Form 7:J:4.

to be contained in a separate clause[14]. It is considered that merger cannot affect a charge of the leasehold estate[15]. However that does not appear to be the case if the titles are registered[16]. The reason for this is that a merger in that case requires closure of the leasehold title which would destroy the chargee's security.

Where the lessee purchases in exercise of an option in his favour, it is the practice to treat the conveyance as being in pursuance of an ordinary agreement for sale, in which case there is no need to recite the option. Special problems arise where the conveyance takes effect under the Leasehold Reform Act 1967, and the reader is referred to specialist books on this aspect[17].

E   Documents relating to leasehold land

1.   Form of lease

The form of a lease differs in some important respects from that of a conveyance, as the following precedent shows:

> THIS LEASE made the   day of   197– BETWEEN
> AB of (etc.) (hereinafter called 'the landlord' which expression shall where the context so admits include the person for the time being entitled to the reversion immediately expectant on the determination of the term hereby granted) and XY of (etc.) (hereinafter called 'the tenant' which expression shall where the context so admits include his successors in title) WITNESSETH as follows:
> 1. In consideration of the rent and the tenant's covenants hereinafter reserved and contained the landlord HEREBY DEMISES unto the tenant ALL THAT [parcels] TO HOLD unto the tenant from the   day of   for a term of   years YIELDING AND PAYING therefor during the said term the rent of £   by equal quarterly payments on the usual quarter days[18] the first of such payments to be made on the   day of   next
> [Then follow the covenants by the parties and the other provisions of the lease.]

The following miscellaneous points should be noted. Recitals are not normally included in leases, though exceptionally they may be desirable where e.g. it is intended to create a letting scheme enabling each tenant to enforce the common regulations against other tenants of adjoining properties[19]. Where there is consideration other than the rent and lessee's covenants, such as the payment of a premium, the deed should so state. The word 'demise' is generally used as the operative word of grant. The landlord is not expressed to demise in any stated capacity. The reason for this is that the statutory covenants for title implied by s. 76 of the Law of Property in a conveyance by a person who

14   See Hallett, 315, Form 77.
15   See Emmet, 928.
16   R & R, 465.
17   See Hill and Redman's *Law of Landlord and Tenant* (17th edn), Woodfall *Landlord and Tenant* (27th edn), and Emmet.
18   These being 24 March, 24 June, 29 September and 25 December. In some districts the usual quarter days differ from the four just listed and a lease of land in such an area should preferably specify the local quarter days.
19   See Hallett, 519, Form 9.

conveys and is expressed to convey in a certain capacity do not apply to 'a demise by way of lease at a rent'[20]. The quantum of the lessee's estate is indicated by the habendum clause. It should be remembered that a lease takes effect from the date of its delivery, notwithstanding that the term is expressed to commence from some earlier date[1]. The words 'Yielding and Paying' introduce the reddendum clause which specifies the amount of the rent and the time when it is payable. The rent, which need not consist in the payment of money, must be certain, but this requirement is satisfied if it can be rendered certain by calculation. It is common to provide in leases of business or industrial premises for the rent to be re-assessed from time to time by a surveyor or according to some agreed formula stated in the lease. The words 'yielding and paying' import a covenant by the lessee to pay the rent in the unlikely absence of an express covenant to pay.

The grant of a lease of registered land normally follows the form of a lease of unregistered land, save that the deed must contain the usual heading and the parcels clause must sufficiently refer in the prescribed manner to the registered land[2].

Leases which are capable of taking effect at law though in writing only[3] are usually drafted in the form of tenancy agreements, in which 'the landlord lets and the tenant takes' the demised premises and the obligations assumed by the parties appear simply as agreements and not as covenants as in the case of a lease under seal. Where, as sometimes occurs, an agreement under hand only is used for a letting which exceeds three years, the agreement is not effective to create a legal lease but it operates in equity to vest an equitable lease in the tenant[4].

2.   Contents of lease

Considerable variation exists in the precise contents of a formal lease, depending on the length of the term and the type of property demised. Thus the provisions of a lease of an agricultural holding will differ from those of a lease of an office block or factory. Similarly the obligations imposed on a lessee of residential property may well vary according to whether the lease is granted at a rack rent, i.e. a rent representing the full annual value of the land and buildings, or at a nominal (or ground) rent, i.e. a rent representing the annual value of the land only, plus a premium. Leases of this second kind are normally for a long term of years, e.g. 99 or 999 years, and are frequently encountered in certain parts of the country. Some clauses are, as is to be expected, common to most leases, such as the lessee's covenant to pay rent, the lessor's covenant for quiet enjoyment and the proviso for re-entry. It is not intended to consider particular precedents nor to recount at length what may or may not constitute a breach of particular covenants, for this is adequately discussed in real property text books[5]. Attention will be directed to a few common clauses with a view to

20   LPA 1925, s. 76 (5). But see note 20, p. 620, post.
1   See p. 531, ante.
2   LRA 1925, s. 18 (1) (e) p. 451, ante, s. 76 (p. 516, ante). In practice these specific requirements are ignored where the lease takes effect as an overriding interest under the LRA 1925, s. 70 (1) (k), p. 55, ante.
3   See p. 483, ante.
4   *Walsh v Lonsdale* (1882) 21 Ch D 9, CA. See further on the implications of this equitable lease, M & W, 625–629; see also *Warmington v Miller* [1973] QB 877, [1973] 2 All ER 372.
5   See M & W, 689–704; Cheshire, 394–409.

considering some matters that have drafting implications. It may, however, be helpful to list those provisions which are most frequently to be found in leases.

Covenants by the lessee
To pay the rent reserved
To pay rates and taxes
To repair
Not to make alterations without the landlord's consent
To insure (sometimes in a named insurance office) and to apply the insurance moneys in rebuilding
Not to assign, underlet or part with possession
To register assignments and underleases with the lessor
To permit the landlord to enter to view the state of the property
To use as a private residence, or for certain specified trades
To yield up the premises on the determination of the term.

Covenants by the lessor
For quiet enjoyment
To repair the outside of the premises
To insure and re-instate[6] (in cases where there is no insurance covenant by the lessee)[7].

Provisos
Power of re-entry
For the sooner determination of the term on giving notice.

(a) Covenant to repair
In long leases and leases at a premium the obligation to do all repairs is cast on the lessee, whereas in short leases the lessor frequently assumes responsibility for external repairs. Furthermore in leases of residential property for less than seven years the landlord is statutorily[8] made liable for the repair of the structure and exterior of the house, and for the maintenance of installations for the supply of water, gas, electricity, and for sanitation. Where this obligation applies, the tenant is sometimes required to covenant to do repairs except in so far as the liability therefor is cast on the landlord by statute[9].

The obligations imposed by the covenant depend on the parties' intention, ascertained from the wording of the covenant and taking into account the age and character of the property and the locality where it is situated. The covenant is variously phrased as a duty 'well and sufficiently to repair', or to keep in 'good repair' or 'tenantable repair'. It may well be[10] that these different expressions add nothing to the basic obligation to repair, which involves the restoration by renewal or replacement of subsidiary parts of the premises[11]. A tenant's ordinary repairing covenant does not require him to eliminate an

6 See *Mumford Hotels Ltd v Wheler* [1964] Ch 117, [1963] 3 All ER 250, CA.
7 It is not usual to insert a tenant's covenant to insure in leases for less than seven years.
8 See the Housing Act 1961, ss. 31, 32. See also *Brikon Investments Ltd v Seaford* [1981] 2 All ER 783.
9 A landlord is also under an implied obligation to take reasonable care of the common parts: *Liverpool City Council v Irwin* [1977] AC 239, [1976] 2 All ER 39.
10 See *Anstruther-Gough-Calthorpe v McOscar* [1924] 1 KB 716 at 729, CA, per Strutton LJ; but see per Atkin LJ, at 731.
11 *Lurcott v Wakeley and Wheeler* [1911] 1 KB 905 at 924, CA, per Buckley LJ; *Brew Bros Ltd v Snax (Ross) Ltd* [1970] 1 QB 612, [1970] 1 All ER 587, CA. See also *Smedley v Chumley and Hawkers* (1981) 126 Sol Jo 33, CA.

inherent defect even though it affects a subsidiary part only of the premises[12], but he is bound to replace a building which is destroyed e.g. by fire[13].

The covenant may be qualified by inserting words such as 'fair wear and tear excepted'. This exception exempts the tenant from liability for disrepair resulting from the reasonable use of the premises coupled with the ordinary operation of natural forces. But if further damage is likely to flow from the wear and tear, he must do such repairs as are necessary to stop that further damage[14].

(b) Covenant for quiet enjoyment

The landlord's covenant for quiet enjoyment ensures that the tenant shall:

> ' peaceably hold and enjoy the demised premises during the said term without any lawful interruption by the lessor or any person claiming under or in trust for him.'

This covenant replaces the covenants for title which a vendor enters into on a conveyance of freehold land[15]. It entitles the lessee to be put into possession and to enjoy the property free from disturbance by the exercise of adverse rights over the property or over adjacent land occupied by the landlord or someone for whom he is responsible[16]. It is not the practice to extend the operation of the covenant to interruption by a person claiming by title paramount, so that an underlessee has no claim under the covenant against his immediate landlord on eviction by the superior lessor who has exercised a right of re-entry for breach of covenant in the head lease[17]. It is also customary to preface the covenant by words such as:

> ' The tenant paying the rent hereby reserved and performing and observing the covenants on his part and the conditions herein contained, the tenant shall peaceably hold . . .'

These words can safely be omitted as they do not make the operation of the landlord's covenant conditional upon performance by the tenant of his obligations[18].

(c) Proviso for re-entry

Most leases contain a proviso for re-entry[19] by the lessor if the rent is in arrear for twenty-one days or on breach of covenant. In a lease at a rack-rent the

---

12 *Collins v Flynn* [1963] 2 All ER 1068 (inadequate foundations). This case has been doubted however in *Ravenseft Properties Ltd v Davstone (Holding) Ltd* [1980] QB 12, [1979] 1 All ER 929, where Forbes J propounded the test as being one of degree and rejected the idea that inherent vice could never come within the ambit of a repair covenant.

13 *Bullock v Dommitt* (1796) 6 Term Rep 650; *Redmond v Dainton* [1920] 2 KB 256 (bomb). Although in an extreme case the tenant may be able to rely on the doctrine of frustration: *National Carriers Ltd v Panalpina (Northern) Ltd* [1981] AC 675, [1981] 1 All ER 161, HL.

14 *Regis Property Co Ltd v Dudley* [1959] AC 370, [1958] 3 All ER 491, HL.

15 See Chap. 24. The mere relation of landlord and tenant suffices at common law to imply a covenant for quiet enjoyment in the absence of any express covenant: *Budd-Scott v Daniell* [1902] 2 KB 351.

16 See e.g. *Sanderson v Berwick-upon-Tweed Corpn* (1884) 13 QBD 547 (tenant of the neighbouring farm causing damage by flooding drains).

17 *Kelly v Rogers* [1892] 2 QB 910, CA; *Jones v Lavington* [1903] 1 KB 253, CA (enforcement of restrictive covenants by freeholder).

18 *Edge v Boileau* (1885) 16 QBD 117.

19 There are various statutory restrictions and conditions precedent to the exercise of this right; see LPA 1925, s. 146 (1); Protection From Eviction Act 1977.

proviso commonly embraces the lessee's bankruptcy or winding up, but the inclusion of this extended proviso cannot be recommended in a long lease at a ground rent, since the tenant is likely to borrow money on mortgage and mortgagees frequently refuse to lend on the security of such leases on the ground that relief against forfeiture cannot be granted[20]. Where a proviso for re-entry for bankruptcy exists, an assignee of the lease is not exposed to forfeiture on account of the original lessee's bankruptcy[21].

At common law the landlord cannot re-enter for non-payment of rent without first making a formal demand therefor. To dispense with the need to comply with the technical formalities which this entails[1] the words 'whether formally demanded or not' should be inserted in the proviso.

(d) Clauses granting options[2]

Several points arise for consideration when drafting a lease which grants an option to purchase, or to renew. In the case of an *option to purchase the freehold reversion*, it is necessary to ascertain precisely who is to be entitled to exercise the option. Prima facie the benefit of an option is assignable[3]. If therefore the option is intended to be personal to the original lessee, the lease should say so expressly. Furthermore a clause in the lease whereby 'lessee' is defined to include his executors, administrations and assigns appears to have a restrictive effect and limits possible assignees of the option to persons who are assignees of the term[4]. It will not generally be necessary to limit the exercise of the option to the perpetuity period, save where it is conferred on some third party, since the rule against perpetuities no longer applies if (i) the option is exerciseable only by the lessee and his successors in title, and (ii) it ceases to be exerciseable at or before the expiration of one year after the determination of the lease[5].

The grant of a right to *renew the lease* is frequently made subject to the due performance by the tenant of his obligations under the lease, a condition that is construed most strictly against him[6]. The lessor's obligation is usually expressed as being to grant a further term of—years 'containing the like covenants and provisos as are herein contained *except this clause for renewal'*. The inclusion of the italicised words is desirable to exclude any possibility that the covenant confers a perpetual right of renewal. Were the clause to read 'including this present covenant for renewal', it would create a perpetually renewable lease which takes effect as a demise for 2,000 years[7]. Some renewal clauses add a proviso whereby the option becomes null and void unless it is duly registered as

---

20 LPA 1925, s. 146 (9). For such a case see *Malliard Property Co Ltd v Jack Segal Ltd* [1978] 1 All ER 1219 (holding such a clause when breached required a notice under s. 146 to be served enable forfeiture to take place).

21 *Smith v Gnonow* [1891] 2 QB 394. Conversely the disclaimer by an assignee on liquidation does not destroy the original tenant's liability: *Warmford Investments Ltd v Duckworth* [1979] Ch 127, [1978] 2 All ER 517. It is otherwise if the original tenant disclaims.

1 *Doe d. Wheeldon v Paul* (1829) 3 C & P 613; Cheshire, 438.

2 See generally Barnsley *Land Options*.

3 *Re Button's Lease, Inman v Button* [1964] Ch 263, [1963] 3 All ER 708.

4 *Griffith v Pelton* [1958] Ch 205 at 227, [1956] 3 All ER 75 at 85, CA, per Jenkins LJ.

5 Perpetuities and Accumulations Act 1964, s. 9 (1). The Act does not affect options granted prior to 16 July 1964, which continue to be subject to the rule: *Woodall v Clifton* [1905] 2 Ch 257 at 259–66, per Warrington J.

6 See *Finch v Underwood* (1876) 2 Ch D 310, CA; *West Country Cleaners (Falmouth) Ltd v Saly* [1966] 3 All ER 210 (trivial breach of tenant's decorating covenants sufficient to render option unenforceable).

7 LPA 1922, Sch. 15, para. 5; *Parkus v Greenwood* [1950] Ch 644, [1950] 1 All ER 436, CA; *Re Hopkins's Lease, Caerphilly Concrete Products Ltd v Owen* [1972] 1 All ER 248, CA. Cf. *Marjorie Burnett Ltd v Barclay* (1980) 125 Sol Jo 199.

a land charge or protected on the register of title within a specified period. In the absence of this provision a landlord who sells the freehold reversion may be held liable to the tenant for breach of contract if the tenant has failed to register and the purchaser of the reversion declines to grant a renewal[8].

Whether the option is one for purchase or for renewal, the draftsman should ensure that the clause clearly defines the time limits within which the option is to be exercised[9], and contains a formula for determining the price or the rent and effective machinery for working out that formula (e.g. by arbitration). Should no formula for quantifying the rent be laid down, as where the option is for renewal 'at a rent to be agreed'[10], the option will be void for uncertainty. But the courts are reluctant to strike down on the grounds of uncertainty contractual provisions intended to have legal effect, as the case of *Brown v Gould*[11] demonstrates. Here the renewed lease was to be at a rent 'to be fixed having regard to the market value of the premises at the time of exercising the option'. Megarry J declined to declare the option void for uncertainty. The clause was not devoid of any meaning nor was it capable of a variety of meanings so as to make it impossible to say which was intended. Furthermore he held that the failure to provide any machinery for working out the agreed formula was not fatal, for if the parties were to disagree as to the rent payable the court itself had jurisdiction to resolve the dispute by determining the rent.

In addition the terms of an option to purchase should preferably regulate the lessor's obligations as to title[12] and be so drafted as to ensure that service of the notice exercising the option does not terminate the lease. This can be achieved by making the landlord's obligation to sell conditional upon receipt of the purchase price and interest, with the result that no contract for sale comes into existence until payment is actually made[13].

3. Grant of underlease

In certain parts of the country it is relatively common for a housing estate to be developed by way of lease and underlease. The freeholder, F, demises the land to D, the developer, for (say) 999 years at an annual rent of £500. D builds 50 houses on the land and sub-demises individual properties for a term of 990 years at a premium (representing the cost of the house) plus a yearly rent of £20. It is essential that the underlease confers adequate protection for each 'purchaser' in the event of D's failure to perform the covenants in the head lease and the consequent risk of forfeiture proceedings by F. It should contain a covenant by D to pay the rent of £500 and perform the covenants so far as they relate to the remainder of the land comprised in the head lease. This is a purely

8   Cf. *Wright v Dean* [1948] Ch 686, [1948] 2 All ER 415. He may be entitled to an indemnity from the purchaser of the reversion under the contract for sale; see *Eagon v Dent* [1965] 3 All ER 334, p. 544, ante. The purchaser of the reversion may be estopped in some circumstances from denying its enforceability: *Taylor Fashions Ltd v Liverpool Victoria Trustees* [1981] 1 All ER 897.
9   See *Wheatley v Burrell Enterprises* (1963) 186 Estates Gazette 259 (option exercisable on giving 3 months' written notice; held: notice given must be such as would expire during term so that notice given less than a month before expiration was ineffective).
10 *King's Motors (Oxford) Ltd v Lax* [1969] 3 All ER 665.
11 [1972] Ch 53, [1971] 2 All ER 1505; *Smith v Morgan* [1971] 2 All ER 1500 (right of pre-emption 'at a figure to be agreed upon' upheld). Cf. *Sudbrook Trading Estate Ltd v Eggleton* [1981] 3 All ER 105, CA.
12 See 2 Prideaux's Precedents, 121, Form 30.
13 11 Ency F & P, 344, Form 2:57; cf. *Cockwell v Romford Sanitary Steam Laundry Ltd* [1939] 4 All ER 370, CA, note 19, p. 162, ante.

collateral covenant which does not touch and concern the land demised by the underlease; it does not bind an assignee of the head lease[14]. The benefit of the covenant is, however, annexed to the demised land and is enforceable against the original underlessor by a purchaser of the sub-lease notwithstanding that the benefit has not been expressly assigned to him[15]. The underlessor's covenant is not merely for indemnity; it constitutes a covenant to perform the obligations in the head lease and is enforceable by the underlessee irrespective of whether the head lessor is seeking to enforce the covenant[16].

In practical terms the underlessor's covenant may be worthless should he default in payment of the rent, for in theory any one of the underlessees may find himself faced with a demand for £500. It is, therefore, usual to confer additional remedies[17] on each underlessee. Until he is fully re-imbursed all money, loss or damage, paid or sustained he is empowered: (i) to retain the rent reserved by his own underlease, (ii) to receive or collect the rents reserved by the underleases already granted or thereafter to be granted, and (iii) to enter upon the remainder of the land still occupied by the underlessor and to receive and distrain for the rents and profits. The efficacy of these various rights is suspect, to say the least. Remedy (iii) will probably be valueless, for the undeveloped or partly developed sections of the estate are not likely to be income-producing, and the power of collection in (ii) may prove worthless since there is no means of enforcing payment from a defaulter. However, irrespective of any express powers, an underlessee who pays the head rent under threat of forfeiture is entitled in equity to a contribution from his co-underlessees since he has borne a burden for the benefit of others amongst all of whom exists community of interest[18].

Whether the term created by the sub-lease is for a short or a long period, the underlessor must ensure that in relation to the property underleased the sub-lessee is under an obligation to observe covenants at least as stringent as those in the head lease (other than that for payment of rent). Where the underlease repeats verbatim the relevant covenants appearing in the head lease an indemnity covenant should, in addition, be taken from the underlessee. Without such a covenant the underlessor cannot recover the costs of proceedings for relief against forfeiture incurred by him as a result of the underlessee's default[19].

4. Assigment of existing lease

An assignment of an existing leasehold term is similar in form to a conveyance of freehold land, subject to such alterations as are dictated by the difference in

14 *Dewar v Goodman* [1909] AC 72, HL.
15 LPA 1925, s. 189 (2).
16 *Ayling v Wade* [1961] 2 QB 228, [1961] 2 All ER 399, CA (underlessor's failure to repair). The court distinguished *Harris v Boots Cash Chemists (Southern) Ltd* [1904] 2 Ch 376, and *Reckitt v Cody* [1920] 2 Ch 452 (note 6, p. 544, ante) where similar covenants were construed as indemnity covenants only, on the ground that the vendor had parted with all interest in the land sold and was not concerned about the continued performance of the covenants save for the possibility of being sued by the convenantee.
17 For a precedent, see 11 Ency F & P, 330, Form 2:46.
18 See *Whitham v Bullock* [1939] 2 KB 81 at 88, [1939] 2 All ER 310 at 316, CA, per Clauson LJ; cf. *Johnson v Wild* (1890) 44 Ch D 146 (assignee of part paying entirety of rent not entitled to contribution from underlessee of part).
19 *Clare v Dobson* [1911] 1 KB 35. A mere covenant to perform the covenants in the head lease implies an obligation to indemnify: *Hornby v Cardwell* (1881) 8 QBD 329, CA.

the tenure of the land transferred. As we have had occasion to observe, considerable variation exists in practice in the mode of reciting the vendor's estate ownership[20]. Where the lease contains a covenant against assignment, whether absolute or qualified, it is generally considered prudent to recite that the lessor's consent has been duly obtained. The operative part of the deed will be in some such form as this:

> ' . . . the vendor as beneficial owner HEREBY ASSIGNS unto the purchaser ALL AND SINGULAR the property comprised in the lease[1] TO HOLD unto the purchaser for all the residue now unexpired of the term of years created by the lease SUBJECT henceforth to the rent reserved by and to the lessee's covenants and the conditions contained in the lease.'

In the case of an assignment for value an express covenant for indemnity is unnecessary in view of the implied statutory covenant[2]. Where part only of the property comprised in a lease is assigned, the rent reserved thereby is usually apportioned informally, that is, without the consent of the lessor, between the land assigned to the purchaser and that retained by the vendor. The lessor is not bound by this informal apportionment and he can distrain on any part of the land for the whole rent[3]. The position between the vendor and purchaser is largely regulated by statute which implies in an assignment for value mutual covenants by the parties to pay the apportioned part of the rent and perform the covenants in respect of the land vested in each of them[4]. Advantage is sometimes taken of the statutory power whereby each party charges his land with the payment of money which may become payable under his implied covenant[5]. The existence of a charge on the land enables the court to order a sale in appropriate circumstances.

F   Sale of flats

1.   The problems involved

The building of flats for sale or to be held on a long lease has considerably increased over the past decade. Whilst the complexities of the problems that arise are outside the scope of this book[6] the reader should at least be aware of some of the ways in which the difficulties are tackled in practice. The comfort and enjoyment of any flat is largely dependent on the maintenance and repair of the rest of the building, the continuance of services (e.g. heating and lifts) and the upkeep of amenities such as gardens and access roads. To be satisfactory to a prospective flat owner (whether he is a purchaser from the

---

20   Page 499, ante.
1   This wording is adopted where the property has already been fully described in the recital of the lease. Alternatively a full description of the property may be given in the parcels clause or in a schedule.
2   LPA 1925, s. 77 (1) (C).
3   As to the rights inter se of the assignees of part, see *Whitham v Bullock* [1939] 2 KB 81, [1939] 2 All ER 310, CA.
4   LPA 1925, s. 77 (1) (D). The vendor's covenant is implied only where he assigns 'as beneficial owner'.
5   LPA 1925, s. 77 (7). The incorporation of these mutual charges cannot be insisted upon unless the contract so provides.
6   See further George, *The Sale of Flats* (4th edn).

developer or a person buying from an existing flat owner) the scheme of development must provide for the effective enforcement of these obligations on two fronts. First, the owners of individual units must be able to enforce their obligations inter se; secondly, responsibility for the maintenance of the common parts of the building (such as the entrance, passages and stairs) and the provision of the services must continue to remain vested in some interested person or body, be it the developer himself or some third party, after all the flats have been transferred to the individual owners.

The present law governing the enforceability of positive covenants has tended to hamper the disposal of freehold flats notwithstanding the apparent preference of purchasers for this form of ownership[7]. Some of the difficulties can be readily appreciated by considering the simplest form of flat development, the horizontal division of a single house into two self-contained flats (sometimes known as maisonettes), each having a separate entrance from ground floor level. On a sale of, for example, the lower flat, the common vendor will extract suitable repairing covenants from the purchaser for the benefit of the upper flat. But since the burden of a positive covenant does not run with freehold land the vendor (or a purchaser from him of the upper flat) cannot enforce these covenants against a later purchaser of the lower flat. Various devices have been adopted in an endeavour to make the covenants enforceable against the second purchaser. One such method uses the device of mutual covenants. Thus the conveyance of the lower flat[8] contains mutual covenants by the vendor and the purchaser that each of them will procure that his successor in title enters into a covenant with the owner for the time being of the other flat to observe and perform the covenants intended for the protection of the other flat. However, this scheme is not foolproof. The purchaser of the lower flat may convey his flat without ensuring that his successor gives the required covenant, though this omission renders him liable to an action for damages at the suit of the other flat owner. In the case of a house divided into only two flats, the inability of one flat owner to sue the other directly may not be unduly prejudicial, for he has an implied right of entry[9] into the other flat to effect repairs necessary to preserve the express, or implied[10], right of support in his favour. But the absence of any right to sue an adjoining flat owner may well be a serious drawback in the case of a block of flats containing a large number of individual units.

Since the burden of positive covenants does not run with the land save as between landlord and tenant, it has been the general practice of flat developers to grant long leases of their flats at a nominal rent instead of conveying the freehold outright. This mode of disposal has in fact been encouraged by building societies and other mortgagees, who have generally been reluctant to advance on the security of freehold flats. However, as we have already noted, one of the principal concerns of the flat owner is the need to be able to enforce the positive obligations against other flat owners and the ensuing problems are basically the same whether the flats are freehold or leasehold. Of course where the developer himself holds a leasehold estate in the land, the disposal of individual flats must

---

7 See the Report of the Committee on Positive Covenants Affecting Land (the Wilberforce Committee) 1965, Cmnd. 2719, para. 8 (i).

8 For a precedent, see 19 Ency F & P, 926, Form 7:A:36.

9 *Bond v Nottingham Corpn* [1940] Ch 429 at 438–39, [1940] 2 All ER 12 at 18, CA, per Sir Wilfrid Greene MR.

10 See *Richards v Rose* (1853) 9 Exch 218; *Shubrook v Tufnell* (1882) 46 LT 886. It is usual to grant express rights of entry and of support.

be by the leasehold method. Leases are also generally used when the development requires the provision of lifts and other services or where it justifies the
creation of a management company to maintain the common parts and super-
vise the various services provided[11]. Whichever method is adopted the
draftsman must be alive to the problems involved. The same is true of the
purchaser's adviser, and even more so, in as much as the draft conveyance or
lease will have been prepared in the first instance by the developer's solicitor,
and perhaps drafted with the developer's interests in view rather than the
purchaser's.

2.　Parcels clause

The precise boundaries of the flat should be defined, and this requires stating
which walls, floors and ceilings are included in the grant. The conveyance or
lease will also grant to each flat owner various easements over the remainder of
the block for the benefit of the part granted, the most important of these being
rights of access, support and protection from other parts of the building and a
right of entry for the purpose of effecting repairs. There will be a reservation of
reciprocal rights in and over the flat transferred for the benefit of the other flat
owners. The grant and reservation of these various rights are best set out in
separate schedules.

3.　Covenants by the flat owner

(a) Negative covenants
Each flat owner should be required to covenant to observe various restrictions
designed to preserve the comfortable enjoyment of each unit as a residence.
The exact nature of these will vary but usually they include covenants
against—making alterations, using the flat otherwise than as a residence for
one family, causing nuisances, obstructing common access ways and inter-
fering with the support and protection afforded by the flat to other parts of the
building. The imposition of a scheme analogous to a building scheme[12] ensures
that these covenants are enforceable inter se, an essential requirement when
people are living in close proximity.

(b) Positive covenants
In addition each flat owner normally enters into a number of positive covenants, again intended for the benefit of the other flat owners, though in reality
they may amount only to 'paper' covenants because of the difficulty of their
enforcement inter se. These will include covenants to repair, to insure and to
contribute in accordance with some agreed formula[13] to the cost of maintaining

---

11　See George, op. cit., p. 15, adding that in other cases there is little to choose between the
　　freehold or leasehold method. The Wilberforce Committee recommended two statutory
　　schemes for voluntary adoption in appropriate cases. The Law Commission in their
　　Working Paper on Appurtenant Rights provisionally advocate the imposition of certain
　　minimum statutory obligations attaching to the parts of a building in multiple occupation
　　(e.g. rights of entry for repair, and of contribution). They made no recommendation on
　　the important question of the maintenance of the structure, feeling that tailor-made
　　arrangements regulating such matters would be preferable to any inflexible statutory
　　obligation. See Paper No. 36, paras. 73–81, Propositions 1 and 2.
12　See p. 540, ante.
13　The contribution may be divided equally amongst the owners or determined according to
　　the rateable value of their respective flats. It is advisable to enumerate in a schedule those
　　expenses to which the flat owners must contribute.

the common parts and providing the services. The existence of a landlord-tenant relationship in the case of a leasehold flat enables the lessor (or his successor in title) to enforce against an assignee of an original lessee all positive covenants which touch and concern the land. The main disadvantage affecting freehold flats is the inability of the vendor to maintain any action for breach of a positive covenant against a successor in title of the original purchaser, unless that successor has covenanted with him to perform the covenants. Compliance can, however, be secured indirectly in two main ways. First, the creation of a rentcharge coupled with a right of re-entry for breach of covenant induces performance of the covenants by the owner for the time being so as to avoid a possible forfeiture. Secondly, by making the right to enjoy the easements granted by the conveyance conditional upon performance of the covenants, a flat owner can, on the principle applied in *Halsall v Brizell*[14], be restrained from exercising those rights except on the terms that he abides by the obligations imposed by the deed.

Unlike the developer or lessor an individual flat owner cannot generally enforce positive covenants directly against another flat owner, and it makes no difference whether the flat is freehold or leasehold. Suppose V conveys flat No. 1 to A and later conveys flat No. 2 to B, both conveyances containing covenants by A and B to keep their respective flats in good repair. Should B fail to perform his covenant and as a result A suffers damage, A may be able to sue B if B covenanted with V and also with the owners for the time being of the other flats (therefore including A)[15]. But A cannot sue a person, C, who buys the flat from B, since the burden of B's covenant does not pass to C, unless the original V−B conveyance required B to procure[16] a suitable covenant from C with V and the other flat owners and C in fact gave the covenant. So long as V is prepared to enforce the covenants against any defaulting flat owner A's position is relatively secure, but there is no guarantee that V or his successor will always intervene. Where the flat owners have been granted long leases, their position can be improved by the inclusion in each lease of a covenant by the lessor to enforce, at a lessee's request and expense, the covenants entered into by the other lessees[17].

4.   Developer's responsibilities

The vendor or lessor should covenant to maintain the main structure and the common parts, to provide any agreed services, and to abide by the flat scheme by requiring every purchaser or lessee from him to covenant to observe the common restrictions. The continued performance of these obligations after completion of the development is another major practical difficulty facing the flat owner. Several different schemes regulating the maintenance and management of the flats have been devised; broadly speaking they fall into three main categories.

14   [1957] Ch 169, [1957] 1 All ER 371, note 16, p. 514, ante.
15   By virtue of the LPA 1925, s. 56, p. 537, ante. The benefit of this covenant passes to A's successor under s. 78 of the same Act, thereby enabling him to sue B. Similarly B could sue A if A were in breach, provided V had assigned to B the benefit of A's covenant to repair..
16   See p. 560, ante.
17   See George, op. cit., p. 97. In the absence of such a covenant the common lessor is under no obligation to enforce the other lessees' covenants: *Malzy v Eichholz* [1916] 2 KB 308, CA.

(a) Developer's continuing responsibility

The developer himself may remain responsible for the continued management, though the actual maintenance will be in the hands of a manager or agent employed by him. In general the developer's interest in receiving the rents or the rentcharges should suffice to ensure the fulfilment of his management obligations. Yet the danger is always present that he may lose interest especially if the march of inflation reduces the value of his receivable rents, or he may dispose of his interest to an unsatisfactory assignee who, in the case of a freehold flat scheme, would not be bound by the positive covenants entered into by the developer[18].

(b) Flat owners' management company

These disadvantages can be avoided if the flat owners themselves are responsible for management. The developer conveys his freehold interest in the common parts and the benefit of the individual owners' covenants to a management company consisting of all the flat owners. The difficulties of this method tend to be of a human rather than a legal nature. The flat owners may be inexperienced in property management, disputes between them may arise and the effective running of the company may well be left to the interested few. Legal complications may arise when a flat owner transfers his interest to a purchaser, for, unless suitable provisions have been inserted in the original conveyance or lease[19], it seems that the purchaser cannot be compelled to become a member of the company against his will.

(c) Concurrent lease

Some practitioners favour the device of a concurrent lease to an independent management company[20]. This scheme requires that leases are granted to the flat owners. After the grant of the last of these leases, the developer grants a concurrent lease to a management company (preferably an established property company, but sometimes, and less satisfactorily, a company formed for the sole purpose of managing the block). A concurrent lease is a lease granted by the reversioner during the continuance of a prior lease and for a term which commences before the expiration of the prior lease. The effect of such a lease is to vest the benefit and the burden of the flat leases in the concurrent lessee who therefore becomes responsible for the management of the flats. The lease is frequently granted at a rent equal to the value of the receivable rents under the flat leases, less a profit rental of £X per flat, this difference representing the concurrent lessee's remuneration for taking over the developer's responsibilities. The actual cost of maintenance is borne by the flat lessees whose contributions are payable to the concurrent lessee by virtue of the lease in his favour.

G Assents

A simple assent of freehold land by a sole executor in favour of the devisee may be as follows:

---

18 But see George, op. cit., pp. 94–95, for a way of circumventing this difficulty.
19 See George, op. cit., pp. 175–176.
20 Andrae-Jones 'A Concurrent Lease to Secure Flat Maintenance' (1962) 26 Conv (NS) 348.
    For a precedent of such a lease, see ibid., 723; George, op. cit., 165–167, 337–341.

I AB of [etc.] as the personal representative of XY late of [etc.] do this
day of   197– hereby as such personal representative
assent to the vesting in CD of [etc.] of ALL THAT [parcels] for an estate
in fee simple[1] and I acknowledge the right of the said CD to production of
the will of the said XY and to delivery of copies thereof[2].

An assent in this form is usually executed under hand only[3] and does not
attract stamp duty. Alternatively it may be an inter partes document between
AB of the one part and CD of the other part. This form is frequently adopted
when the assent is by deed because, for example, the beneficiary enters into an
indemnity covenant to observe restrictive covenants created by the testator.
The dangers of inserting recitals in an assent have already been stressed[4], and
unless absolutely vital it is the general practice to omit all recitals.

It is commonplace[5] to incorporate in an assent a statement that the personal
representative has not given or made any previous assent or conveyance in
respect of a legal estate affecting the land. This appears to be a misguided
practice, for such a statement in favour of an assentee serves no useful purpose.
It affords him no protection against either a prior purchaser or a prior
assentee[6], and it is of no assistance to a purchaser *from the beneficiary* for the
statement is of value only when inserted in a conveyance of the legal estate *by
the personal representative* to a purchaser.

An assent by a personal representative in his own favour will not, of course,
contain any acknowledgment for production of the probate. The statutory
acknowledgment is only effective when given 'to another'[7]. A purchaser from
the beneficiary should ensure that an acknowledgment is included in the
conveyance to him.

Where the will creates a trust for sale, it becomes necessary to decide whether
the assent should be made upon the trust for sale contained in the will, or upon
an independent trust for sale created by the assent[8]. Adoption of the former
method results in the abstracting of the will on any sale in execution of the trust
in order to establish that the property is subject to a trust for sale. The main disadvantage of the latter scheme is that the appointment of new trustees of the
will and of the assent must be by separate instruments. Furthermore it is not
always appreciated that the same persons must be appointed as new trustees of
both the will and the assent[9].

1 Or 'for all the estate and interest of the said XY at the time of his death'. The wording in
   the text is preferable. And see p. 281, ante.
2 This follows the statutory form (see the LPA 1925, Sch. 5, Form No. 8) with the addition
   of an acknowledgment for production.
3 An assent in writing suffices to pass a legal estate: LPA 1925, s. 52 (2) (a); AEA 1925,
   s. 36 (4).
4 Pages 335, and 499, ante. In some cases recitals may be necessary, e.g. to take advantage
   of the Law of Property (Joint Tenants) Act 1964; see (1977) 41 Conv (NS) 423 (P.W.
   Smith).
5 See e.g. Hallett, 101, Form 2; 3 Prideaux's Precedents, 906, form V.
6 See the AEA 1925, s. 36 (6), p. 336, ante. The statement only operates as sufficient
   evidence in favour of a purchaser, who does not include an assentee: see sub-s. (11). Notice
   of the assent should be endorsed on the grant of representation.
7 LPA 1925, s. 64 (1), p. 425, ante. Consider *Rowley Holmes Co v Barber* [1977] 1 All ER
   801.
8 Executors apparently have power to create an independent trust for sale; see the LPA
   1925, Sch. 5, Form No. 9.
9 Trustee Act 1925, s. 35 (1); LPA 1925, s. 24 (1). The respective merits of the two methods
   are considered in Hallett, 110–13.

Part Six

Remedies

Chapter 20

The rights of the parties on breach of contract: an introduction

The vast majority of vendor-purchaser transactions proceed smoothly to completion without any major dispute arising between the parties. Sometimes, however, the contract is never completed; sometimes it is completed only after litigation between the parties and occasionally it may be necessary to have recourse to the courts after completion of the transaction. Part VI of this book deals with the various rights of the parties on a breach of the contract. A variety of factors determine what these rights are: which party is in default, why the contract has been broken, and whether a particular remedy is available under the general law or only exercisable by virtue of some contractual provision. There is also an important distinction to be drawn between the rights of the parties whilst the contract is still executory and their position after completion. It will be helpful to give a brief survey of the principal remedies available to the parties, prior to a detailed consideration of these remedies in the subsequent pages.

A   Remedies under uncompleted contract

On breach by one party to a contract for the sale or other disposition of an interest in land, the injured party may wish to pursue one of three main remedies: specific performance, an action for damages, or rescission.

1.   Specific performance

This is a remedy peculiar to contracts relating to land and is not generally applicable to other contracts. The plaintiff seeks a decree from the court ordering the other party to perform the contract specifically.

2.   Damages

Here the injured party seeks compensation for the loss occasioned by the breach.

3.   Rescission

Strictly speaking this is not a judicial remedy; it is a unilateral right[1] whereby one party can in certain circumstances set it aside and be restored to his former

---

1   *Re Stone and Saville's Contract* [1962] 2 All ER 114 at 121, per Buckley J; affd. [1963] 1 All ER 353, CA.

position as if the contract had not been made. This, it will be observed, is the exact reverse of specific performance. Rescission brings the contract to an end and thereafter the parties cannot revive it except by something amounting to a new agreement[2]. Rescission can be exercised without recourse to the courts but in practice their aid is frequently sought to uphold or enforce the plaintiff's right, or to obtain consequential relief. The right to rescind may arise under the general law or by virtue of some stipulation in the contract.

These three remedies are discussed in Chapters 21, 22 and 23. A plaintiff may seek more that one remedy in the same action. A claim for specific performance may be linked with an alternative claim for damages or rescission[3]. He must elect at the hearing which remedy he intends to pursue and judgment for one will bar the others.

4.   Forfeiture of deposit

As we saw in Chapter 9[4] the deposit acts as a guarantee of performance. On breach by the purchaser, the vendor may be entitled to forfeit the purchaser's deposit. A vendor who elects to forfeit the deposit is really exercising his right to rescind the contract. Compared with the purchaser the vendor is in a much superior position. Forfeiture of the deposit frequently enables him to obtain adequate compensation (and often more) without the assistance of the court, save where the purchaser disputes his right to forfeit; whereas the purchaser can only recover the deposit he has paid, assuming he is entitled to its repayment, by means of legal proceedings, should the vendor refuse to return it voluntarily.

5.   Vendor and purchaser summons

A statutory procedure exists for the settling of disputes between vendor and purchaser that may arise during the course of the transaction. Under the Law of Property Act 1925, s. 49 (1):

> ' A vendor or purchaser of any interest in land . . . may apply in a summary way to the court in respect of any requisitions or objections, or any claim for compensation or any other question arising out of or connected with the contract (not being a question affecting the existence or validity of the contract), and the court may make such order upon the application as to the court may appear just . . .'

This procedure enables either party to obtain a decision upon some particular point, without having to commence an action for specific performance. For example, the summons may ask the court to declare whether the vendor has sufficiently answered a requisition, whether he has a right to rescind under the contract, or whether he has discharged his obligation to show a good title in accordance with the contract. There is no jurisdiction to determine the existence or validity of the contract. The court can make such order as it thinks appropriate in the circumstances. It may be for the return of the deposit with interest and costs (including costs of the summons), should the court declare

2   Per Buckley J, loc. cit.
3   *Farrant v Olver* (1922) 127 LT 145; *Lowe v Hope* [1970] Ch 94, [1969] 3 All ER 605.
4   See further pp. 250–254, ante, and p. 576, post.

that the vendor has failed to show a good title[5], and the costs can be ordered to be a charge on the vendor's interest in the property[6].

In contrast with former days, this procedure is infrequently used today, doubtless because of the spread of land registration and the comparative simplicity of the present day title to unregistered land. In February 1970, a specially expedited procedure for the hearing of these summonses was cancelled only three years after its introduction on account of there being too few cases to justify it[7].

B   Post-completion remedies

Once the contract is executed and the legal title vested in the purchaser, the parties' remedies in the event of a dispute are somewhat restricted. Usually it is the purchaser who wishes to sue and in the main he is confined to his action (if any) on the covenants for title. The following remedies briefly mentioned in this section may be available to the parties, depending on the circumstances. Chapters 24 and 25 deal with post-completion rights in greater detail.

1.   Covenants for title

The doctrine of merger, whereby on completion the contract is superseded by the conveyance, ensures that the purchaser's only mode of redress if his title proves to be defective is an action for damages on the covenants for title implied in the conveyance. Fraud apart, he cannot recover the purchase price even though the conveyance turns out to be worthless[8]. Notwithstanding completion a purchaser can, however, still maintain an action for damages for breach of contract if he establishes a breach of some collateral warranty, such as a failure to build a house in a proper and workmanlike manner[9], or breach of a contractual term that has survived completion e.g. a clause which provides for compensation for errors in the contract[10]. Similarly completion of the transaction is no bar to the vendor's right to sue for any unpaid purchase money, or to enforce his seller's lien.

2.   Setting the transaction aside

The right to set aside the transaction on account of some vitiating factor, such as fraud or common mistake of a fundamental nature, survives completion and the court can, on sustaining the plaintiff's plea, set aside the conveyance or declare it to be void, and may order it to be delivered up and cancelled. Usually it is the purchaser who will institute such proceedings, but a vendor or grantor may also be desirous of having the deed set aside on account of e.g. undue

---

5   *Re Hargreaves and Thompson's Contract* (1886) 32 Ch D 454, CA; cf. *Re Davis and Cavey* (1888) 40 Ch D 601.
6   *Re Higgins and Percival* (1888) 57 LJ Ch 807.
7   See the *Practice Directions* at [1967] 1 All ER 656, and [1970] 1 All ER 671. Recent instances of the use of this procedure occurred in *Faruqi v English Real Estates* [1979] 1 WLR 963 and *MEPC Ltd v Christian-Edwards* [1981] AC 205, [1979] 3 All ER 752, HL.
8   *Clare v Lamb* (1875) LR 10 CP 334.
9   See p. 173, ante.
10   *Palmer v Johnson* (1884) 13 QBD 351, CA, p. 444, post. For the doctrine of merger, see p. 444, ante.

influence, or because he was mistaken as to the nature of the document which he executed. The setting aside of a transaction after completion is commonly termed rescission[11].

3.   Rectification

Where the conveyance does not correctly give effect to the terms of the contract, either party may seek equity's aid to rectify it so as to make it accord with their real intention. Equally it may be that the written contract fails to express what the parties orally agreed. In no sense is this a remedy which can only be sought after completion, but it is considered in Chapter 25 for the sake of convenience.

C   Effect of breach of contract

Before proceeding to discuss particular remedies, it is essential to give some consideration to the precise legal effect of a breach of contract on the parties' position. It will be remembered that a breach of contract can assume a variety of forms. It may be a failure to perform some fundamental term of the contract; it may consist of a renunciation of performance by words or conduct[12] before the time for performance arrives.

1.   Innocent party put to election

The following example may help to illustrate the various possibilities. Suppose that after the making of a contract for sale of land by V to P, V notifies P that he has decided not to proceed with the transaction. P is entitled to treat this repudiation as terminating the contract. If he adopts this course, not only is he discharged from further liability to perform his obligations under the contract, but he can immediately enforce the appropriate remedy. If he elects to treat the contract as discharged, he may either sue for damages i.e. seek to be put in the same position so far as money can do this as if the contract had been fully performed, or, alternatively, he may be content to seek restitution to the pre-contract position i.e. to rescind in the sense explained on page 570. This right of a party discharged by breach to rescind is well established. Thus in the case of *Flight v Booth*[13], a purchaser was held entitled at law to rescind the contract and recover his deposit as money had and received on account of a material misdescription contained in the contract.

It must be stressed that the defendant's (i.e. V's) repudiation does not per se operate to discharge the contract. There must be acceptance of the repudiation by P. But he is not obliged to adopt this attitude. He has an option and he may prefer not to do so. If he elects to ignore the repudiation, the contract remains subsisting for the benefit of the parties both of whom continue to be bound by their respective obligations, and P must await the completion date before pursuing his remedies if V still refuses to perform the contract. Moreover the party in default can avail himself of any defence to an action for a breach of

---

11   But see p. 640, post.
12   As where the vendor puts it out of his power to perform the contract by conveying to a third party: *Lovelock v Franklyn* (1846) 8 QB 371; *Goffin v Houlder* (1920) 90 LJ Ch 488.
13   (1834) 1 Bing NC 370, p. 601, post.

contract occasioned by his ultimate non-performance just as if his previous default had never occurred[14].

This rule that the innocent party can keep the contract alive may produce some startling consequences if pushed to its logical conclusion. For example, can he insist on performing his part of the contract, despite the known repudiation by the other party, and ultimately recover the full contract price, rather than merely claiming damages for the breach? In *White and Carter (Councils) Ltd v McGregor*[15] a bare majority of the House of Lords on an appeal from Scotland answered this question in the affirmative. On the basis of this decision it has been suggested[16] that, despite the purchaser's repudiation, the vendor could perform his part of the contract by executing the conveyance unconditionally[17], so vesting the legal estate (in the case of unregistered land) in the purchaser. The vendor could then sue for the full price or exercise his equitable lien, and he need not be limited to damages for loss of profit nor have to resort to equity for a decree of specific performance.

The *White* decision has not on the whole been well received. It is difficult to reconcile with the principle of mitigation, for the innocent party is aggravating the damages. Recently, in *Hounslow London Borough v Twickenham Gardens Developments Ltd*[18] Megarry J had occasion to make some observations on the implications of the majority decision and he clearly felt considerable disquiet at its possible unqualified application. In particular it appears that the doctrine does not apply where the innocent party cannot complete the contract himself without the other party doing, allowing or accepting something[19]. This limitation might well operate in the situation mentioned in the preceding paragraph, at least if the purchaser repudiates before forwarding the conveyance for the vendor's execution[20].

2. Trivial breach

Not every breach of contract entitles the innocent party to treat the contract as discharged, but only one that goes to the root of the consideration. Various expressions have been used to describe the governing principle; in the main there must be a breach of an essential obligation. Breach of a non-essential term gives rise to an action for damages but does not entitle the injured party to treat the contract as discharged[1]. If he does he may find himself in breach of contract, as happened in *Cornwall v Henson*[2] where the purchaser's failure to pay the last of twelve equal instalments of the purchase price did not constitute a repudiation of the contract, and the vendor was held liable to pay damages to the purchaser for having let the land to a tenant in the meantime.

---

14 *Avery v Bowden* (1855) 5 E & B 714.
15 [1962] AC 413, [1961] 3 All ER 1178, HL (continued display of advertisements after cancellation of contract by promoter).
16 Farrand, 206.
17 See p. 430, ante.
18 [1971] Ch 233, [1970] 3 All ER 326.
19 *White and Carter (Councils) Ltd v McGregor* [1962] AC 413 at 428–29, [1961] 3 All ER 1178 at 1181–82, per Lord Reid.
20 It is not open to the purchaser to disclaim the conveyance, so causing the legal title to revest in the vendor, as this doctrine does not apply as between vendor and purchaser; see p. 459, post.
1 E.g. failure to complete on the date fixed for completion where time is not of the essence: see *Raineri v Miles* [1980] 2 All ER 145, HL.
2 [1900] 2 Ch 298, CA.

3. Meaning of the word 'rescission'

It was once considered that rescission of a contract for sale of land following a breach of contract terminated the contract ab initio with the result that the innocent party could not obtain damages[3]. However it is now clear that rescission of a contract for breach does not so operate. This is different, of course, from rescission for fraud or misrepresentation. In this case the contract is void ab initio[4]. There may be other meanings to rescission[5]. The use of the word in this Part of the book will vary according to the occasion.

---

3 Williams V & P, 993, 1004, 1006. *Lowe v Hope* [1970] Ch 94, [1969] 3 All ER 605 at
   607–608 per Pennycuick J and *Horsler v Zorro* [1975] Ch 302, [1975] 1 All ER 584.
4 See Albery 'The Cyprian Williams' Great Heresy' (1975) 91 LQR 337; *Buckland v Farmer
   and Moody* [1978] 3 All ER 929 at 939, 943 per Buckley and Goff LJJ; *Johnson v Agnew*
   [1980] AC 367, [1979] 1 All ER 883 at 889, HL, per Lord Wilberforce.
5 See Emmet, 257.

Chapter 21
Specific performance

A General nature of remedy

1. Introduction

Land has a special character of its own, and in the eyes of equity a purchaser ought not to have to be content simply with the common law remedy of damages for breach of a contract for the sale or leasing of land. Damages do not constitute adequate compensation for him. The main part of the doctrine of specific performance is that the purchaser is actually to get the land[1]. Nevertheless this remedy is available to a vendor, even though his claim is essentially monetary[2]. In practice a vendor is usually content to forfeit the deposit and resell the property. In some situations a decree of specific performance is of no avail to him, as where the purchaser has no funds to pay for the property. A contract for a loan, whether secured or unsecured, is not specifically enforceable[3]; equity regards the award of damages for breach of this type of contract as a sufficient remedy. This rule does not prevent specific performance being decreed of a contract for the purchase of land, one of whose terms provides for part of the purchase price to remain outstanding on mortgage, for the contract is in substance and in fact one for the sale and purchase of land[4].

As we have already noticed[5], a claim for specific performance can be linked in one action with an alternative claim for damages for breach of contract, or for rescission. Specific performance may be counterclaimed by a purchaser in a vendor's action for damages, and vice versa. If no counterclaim is made and damages are awarded, the defendant cannot, in the case of breach of an essential stipulation, subsequently enforce the contract specifically.

---

1 *Re Scott and Alvarez's Contract* [1895] 2 Ch 603 at 615, CA, per Rigby LJ.
2 *Adderley v Dixon* (1824) 1 Sim & St 607.
3 *Rogers v Challis* (1859) 27 Beav 175, unless, it seems, the money has actually been advanced on the strength of the borrower's promise to execute a mortgage: *Hermann v Hodges* (1873) LR 16 Eq 18.
4 *Starkey v Barton* [1909] 1 Ch 284. Cf. *Loan Investment Corpn of Australasia v Bonner* [1970] NZLR 724, PC (specific performance refused of composite agreement to sell land and lend money as the provision for a loan formed a principle part of the transaction).
5 Page 570, ante. For the plaintiff's right to apply for summary judgment on the ground that the defendant has no defence to the action, see RSC Ord. 86; *Bigg v Boyd Gibbins Ltd* [1971] 2 All ER 183, CA.

2.   Breach of contract unnecessary

This equitable remedy is fundamentally different from the action at law for damages, where a breach of the contract is a condition precedent to the right to sue. An award of specific performance is not necessarily dependent upon a breach of contract by the defendant, though a breach is usually requisite to induce the court to interfere[6]. In *Marks v Lilley*[7]:

> Completion of a contract for the sale of land did not take place on the contractual day. Sometime later, but without first serving a notice making time of the essence, the purchaser issued a writ for specific performance. *Held*, the plaintiff's action was justified. His equitable right to specific performance had accrued by the time that the writ was issued, notwithstanding that the vendor was not in breach because no notice making time of the essence had been served.

A writ for specific performance can be validly issued before the contractual date for completion has arrived[8], though the court will not compel performance before the proper day. A vendor seeking specific performance is under no obligation to mitigate his loss by re-selling, even when the purchaser refuses to complete, for this would require him to take action which would preclude him from performing his contract with the purchaser[9].

3.   Discretionary remedy

Specific performance has been described as 'special and extraordinary in character'[10]. It lies in the discretion of the court to grant or withhold the relief claimed. The discretion is not exercised capriciously or arbitrarily, but according to fixed and settled principles of equity. As long ago as 1804, it was said that in an unobjectionable case it would be decreed as much of course as damages were granted at law[11].

As a condition precedent to any claim for specific performance, the plaintiff must establish two basic requirements. First, there must be a concluded contract, the terms of which are sufficiently certain for the court to order their performance. Specific performance cannot be decreed of negotiations subject to contract for the grant of a lease[12], or of an agreement for a lease making no mention of the date of commencement of the term[13]. Moreover the contract must be capable of being specifically performed. Equity does nothing in vain and will not make any decree if in the meantime the vendor has conveyed the property to a third person, unless that transaction was merely a sham and the

6   *Marks v Lilley* [1959] 2 All ER 647 at 648, per Vaisey J adopting a passage from Williams, *Contract of Sale of Land*, p. 132.
7   [1959] 2 All ER 647.
8   *Manchester Diocesan Council for Education v Commercial and General Investments Ltd* [1969] 3 All ER 1593, following *Hasham v Zenab* [1960] AC 316, PC (vendor tearing up contract within minutes of signing it); *Oakacre Ltd v Claire Cleaners (Holdings) Ltd* [1981] 3 All ER 667.
9   *Ellis v Lawrence* (1969) 210 Estates Gazette 215.
10   36 Halsbury's Laws (3rd edn), 263; *Hope v Walter* [1900] 1 Ch 257 at 259, per Lindley, MR.
11   *Hall v Warren* (1804) 9 Ves 605, at 608, per Grant MR.
12   *D'Silva v Lister House Development Ltd* [1971] Ch 17, [1970] 1 All ER 858. See further p. 127, ante.
13   *Harvey v Pratt* [1965] 2 All ER 786, CA. And see *Pallant v Morgan* [1953] Ch 43, [1952] 2 All ER 951. Specific performance will not be ordered if it will put the defendant in breach of his obligations; see *Warmington v Miller* [1973] QB 877, [1973] 2 All ER 372, CA.

vendor has it in his power to compel the third person to convey to the purchaser[14]. Secondly the plaintiff must himself be able and willing to perform his part of the contract. Thus, as has already been seen, a vendor who by notice makes time of the essence as regards the date for completion is not entitled to an order for specific performance if unable to complete on the day fixed[15]. It is for this reason also that equity will not assist a vendor who cannot show a good contractual title[16].

4. Mutuality

It is commonly stated that to be specifically enforceable the contract must be mutual, that is, the court will refuse the remedy to one party where it could not be claimed by the other[17]. This was the traditional reason for refusing a decree at the instance of a minor[18], though nowadays his statutory inability to hold a legal estate renders any award impossible. However this mutuality rule has been shown[19] to be subject to so many exceptions as to cast doubts upon its validity. It is perhaps preferable to regard mutuality, not as a prerequisite for equity's intervention, but as 'a consideration generally material'[20].

One significant exception arises under the Law of Property Act 1925, s. 40. A party who has not signed a written memorandum or contract can maintain an action for specific performance against a party who has signed, but (in the absence of sufficient acts of part performance) a party who has signed cannot succeed against a defendant who has not signed. This follows from the wording of the section itself which merely requires the signature of the defendant or his agent[1].

B Refusal of specific performance

1. Defences available at law

The grounds upon which equity refuses a decree of specific performance fall into well established categories. The court will not enforce a contract where the defendant raises a defence which would be a complete answer to a claim at law, as where the contract is void for mistake[2], or illegal, or voidable for misrepresentation. Equity sometimes goes further and may refuse a decree where the mistake or misrepresentation[3] is not of such a nature as to entitle the plaintiff to rescind the contract. As to mistake Kay J expressed the rule in the following terms[4]:

14 *Jones v Lipman* [1962] 1 All ER 442 (conveyance to company controlled by vendor).
15 *Finkielkraut v Monohan* [1949] 2 All ER 234, p. 416, ante.
16 See pp. 608–611, post.
17 Williams, *Title*, p. 751; *Snell's Equity* (27th edn), pp. 582–583. The plea does not deprive the court of jurisdiction; it merely goes towards consideration of its discretion: *Price v Strange* [1978] Ch 337, [1977] 3 All ER 371, CA.
18 *Flight v Bolland* (1828) 4 Russ 298.
19 Ames, 'Mutuality in Specific Performance' (1903) 3 Col LR 1.
20 *Salisbury v Hatcher* (1842) 2 Y & C Ch Cas 54 at 63, per Knight Bruce V-C.
 1 For s. 40, see pp. 101–112, ante. According to Leach MR, in *Flight v Bolland* (1828) 4 Russ 298 at 301, this is not even an exception because by bringing his action, the plaintiff makes the remedy mutual.
 2 *Jones v Clifford* (1876) 3 Ch D 779 (sale of land already owned by purchaser).
 3 See *Holliday v Lockwood* [1917] 2 Ch 47.
 4 *Goddard v Jeffreys* (1881) 30 WR 269 at 270.

'Speaking generally . . . the purchaser may escape from his bargain on
the ground of mistake, if it was a mistake to which the vendors
contributed[5]; that is, if he was misled by the vendors; but if he was not
misled by any act of the vendors, if the mistake was entirely his own, then
the court ought not to let him off his bargain on the ground of a mistake
made by himself solely, unless the case is one of considerable harshness
and hardship.'

For example in *Tamplin v James*[6], the purchaser bid for a public house at an
auction under the mistaken impression that the lot included land at the rear.
There was no misdescription or ambiguity in the particulars of sale and, there
being no 'hardship amounting to injustice'[7], specific performance was decreed.

There are various defences to a claim for specific performance, which are not
generally available at law, these being: delay, misdescription, hardship,
inequitable conduct, and doubtfulness of the vendor's title.

2.   Delay

Delay defeats equity. The plaintiff must pursue his remedy promptly.
Although a claim for specific performance of a contract for the sale of land is
not subject to the normal six years' limitation period[8], yet in practice a much
shorter period operates to bar the plaintiff's claim. In general a delay of one
year is fatal[9], or even less where time is of the essence[10]. Delay in the prosecution
of proceedings once instituted may disentitle a plaintiff to relief[11].

In one important respect laches is no bar, that is where the purchaser takes
possession of the land under the contract. In *Williams v Greatrex*[12] a delay of
ten years did not debar a purchaser in possession from successfully claiming a
decree. He had not been sleeping on his rights, but relying on his equitable title
without thinking it necessary to perfect his legal title. There must, however, be
acquiescence by the vendor in the purchaser's continued possession throughout
the period.

3.   Misdescription

Where there is a substantial misdescription of the property in the contract, the
purchaser has a choice of action. He can resist the vendor's claim for specific
performance, and himself rescind the contract. Alternatively he can call upon
the vendor to convey what he has got, subject to a reduction in the purchase

5   See e.g. *Denny v Hancock* (1870) 6 Ch App 1.
6   (1880) 15 Ch D 215, CA; *Van Praagh v Everidge* [1902] 2 Ch 266 (purchaser buying wrong
    lot); revsd. on other grounds [1903] 1 Ch 434, CA. Cf. *Malins v Freeman* (1837) 2 Keen
    25. For hardship, see p. 579, post.
7   Per James LJ, at 221.
8   Limitation Act 1980, s. 36.
9   *Watson v Reid* (1830) 1 Russ & M 236. It is not an invariable rule, however in *Lazard Bros
    & Co Ltd v Fairfield Properties Co (Mayfair) Ltd* (1977) 121 Sol Jo 793 an order for
    specific performance was made notwithstanding two years' delay. Does such delay go to
    jurisdiction or exercise of discretion? If the latter, a plaintiff could sue for specific
    performance outside the limitation periods and thereafter seek damages in lieu.
10 *Glasbrook v Richardson* (1874) 23 WR 51 (sale of leasehold colliery; delay of fourteen
    weeks fatal).
11 *Lamshed v Lamshed* (1963) 109 CLR 440 (nearly five years' delay in bringing action to
    trial); cf. *Du Sautoy v Symes* [1967] Ch 1146, [1967] 1 All ER 25.
12 [1956] 3 All ER 705, CA. This had been a long established exception in the case of leases:
    Clarke v Moore (1844) 1 Jo & Lat 723.

price. This is known as specific performance with abatement. In the case of a slight misdescription, either the vendor or the purchaser can enforce the contract, subject to compensation. Misdescription is more fully discussed in the chapter on rescission[13].

4.   Hardship

Being a discretionary remedy, equity may refuse to grant specific performance if to do so would work hardship on the defendant. Hardship is often pleaded in connection with some other factor, such as mistake[14] or misrepresentation, but it appears to be a sufficient defence by itself. In one case no decree was ordered on a sale of land without any definite means of access[15]. It will not be granted where it would subject the purchaser to forfeiture[16], or expose him to civil or criminal proceedings[17], or require him to embark upon uncertain litigation[18].

The excessiveness or inadequacy of the consideration is not of itself a sufficient ground to refuse relief[19], though it may be evidence of fraud, or undue influence if the parties stand in a fiduciary relationship. The court will not withhold specific performance merely because the transaction turns out unfavourably to the party against whom it is sought, or because the defendant entered into the agreement without proper legal advice[20]. In *Haywood v Cope*[1] specific performance of a lease was decreed notwithstanding that the lessee was ignorant of mining matters and unable to appreciate that the mine was uneconomic. The fact that the purchaser is entirely impecunious because his financial arrangements have broken down has been held an insufficient ground of hardship to refuse performance against him[2]. The hardship must have existed at the time of the contract; a subsequent change of circumstances causing hardship in the completion of the contract is no defence. Hardship must not be confused with impossibility. No decree will be made if supervening events render performance impossible, as where the vendor has in the meantime conveyed the property to a third person[3].

---

13   Pages 599–605, post. See also [1981] CLJ 47 (Harpum).
14   See *Tamplin v James* (1880) 15 Ch D 215 CA, p. 578, ante.
15   *Denne v Light* (1857) 8 De GM & G 774.
16   See *Dowson v Solomon* (1859) 1 Drew & Sm 1; *Becker v Partridge* [1966] 2 QB 155, [1966] 2 All ER 266, CA, p. 305, ante. In such cases the purchaser may be entitled to rescind the contract.
17   *Pegler v White* (1864) 33 Beav 403; *Hope v Walter* [1900] 1 Ch 257, CA (property used as brothel; liability to prosecution under Criminal Law Amendment Act 1885).
18   *Wroth v Tyler* [1974] Ch 30, [1973] All ER 897 (proceedings necessary to terminate wife's statutory rights of occupation).
19   *Western v Russell* (1814) 3 Ves & B 187; *Fragomeni v Fogliani* (1968) 42 ALJR 263 (purchaser mistaken as to price to which committing himself when signing contract). The rule was once otherwise; see 2 Williams V & P, 830, note (s). See also *Mountford v Scott* [1975] Ch 258, [1975] 1 All ER 198, CA.
20   *Langham v Donnelly* (1962) 181 Estates Gazette 405, unless the agreement can be attacked on the ground that it is unconscionable.
1   (1858) 25 Beav 140.
2   *Nicholas v Ingram* [1958] NZLR 972.
3   *Denton v Stewart* (1786) 1 Cox Eq Cas 258; *Beeston v Stutely* (1858) 27 LJ Ch 156 (agreement for lease; refusal of existing lessee to surrender term).

Hardship on third parties ·

The court will not decree specific performance of a contract which would, if enforced, operate to the prejudice of third parties[4], or would involve a breach of trust[5] or breach of an existing contract with a third party[6]. This defence can be raised even by the party in default. For this reason it has been suggested that in these cases the court refuses to intervene, not on the ground of hardship, but because equity will not act inconsistently with its own principles so as to defeat a prior equity[7].

5. Inequitable conduct

He who comes to equity must come with clean hands. In the exercise of its discretion the court will consider all the circumstances of the case, including the conduct of all parties, and their mental and physical condition. When the court's aid is sought by way of specific performance, the principles of ethics have a more extensive sway than when a contract is sought to be rescinded[8]. It will not assist a plaintiff if there is evidence of fraud, duress, undue influence, misrepresentation, non-disclosure, or if the transaction is otherwise unconscionable[9]. A plaintiff who has committed a breach of an essential term of the contract cannot obtain specific performance, but this principle does not extend to non-essential or trivial breaches[10]. In the absence of any legal duty of disclosure[11], mere silence is no bar to specific performance, even in relation to material matters like the identity of the other contracting party[12] or the value or fitness of the property, which if known to the defendant, would have induced him not to enter into the contract. In the case of *Haywood v Cope*[13], already mentioned, the lessor had himself worked the colliery previously and found it to be unproductive, but his failure to communicate this fact did not disentitle him to a decree. This is simply another aspect of the caveat emptor rule that has been encountered before.

Illegal conduct

As we have already seen, equity follows the law and refuses to enforce an illegal contract. Specific performance will not be decreed of an agreement for a lease of property to be used for immoral purposes[14]. Where a purchaser buys land,

---

4 *Thomas v Dering* (1837) 1 Keen 729 (sale by life tenant harmful to remainderman).
5 *Rede v Oakes* (1865) 4 De GJ & Sm 505; *Jacobs v Bills* [1967] NZLR 249.
6 *Willmott v Barber* (1880) 15 Ch D 96 (contract to assign lease containing covenant not to assign). It is immaterial that the prior contract has not been registered as a land charge, or protected on the register of title.
7 2 Williams V & P, 1052.
8 Kerr, *Fraud and Mistake* (7th edn), p. 562.
9 See *Conlon v Murray* [1958] NI 17 (suspicious circumstances arising from extraordinary haste in rushing through transaction); *Knupp v Bell* (1968) 67 DLR (2d) 256 (inequality of parties resulting in improvident sale by senile woman). See also the observations of Evershed J, in *Hawkins v Price* [1947] Ch 645 at 660.
10 *Dyster v Randall & Sons* [1926] Ch 932 (failure to submit plans for approval no bar).
11 For the effect of non-disclosure, see pp. 608–611, post. And see *Beyfus v Lodge* [1925] Ch 350.
12 *Dyster v Randall & Sons* [1926] Ch 932 (purchaser an undischarged bankrupt); *Champagne v Pratley* (1961) 180 Estates Gazette 153 (estate agent posing as schoolmaster; specific performance decreed).
13 Page 579, ante; cf. *Hill v Harris* [1965] 2 QB 601, [1965] 2 All ER 358, CA, p. 170, ante.
14 *Upfill v Wright* [1911] 1 KB 506 at 512, per Bucknill J. For illegality generally, see Treitel, *The Law of Contract* (5th edn) Chap. 11.

intending to use it for an illegal purpose but without disclosing this to the vendor, the vendor can compel specific performance and the purchaser cannot allege his own unlawful intent as a defence[15]. A purchaser who intends using land for a purpose not authorised under the town and country planning legislation is not, it seems, debarred from claiming this remedy unless, perhaps, both parties know of the proposed unauthorised use and that the purchaser has no intention of seeking permission[16].

6. Defective title

Where the vendor is unable to make a title i t accordance with the contract, the purchaser can not only resist specific performance, he may also be entitled to rescind the contract. Rescission is considered in Chapter 23. A purchaser cannot resist specific performance on the ground of some defect which he is contractually bound to accept. One exception to this principle exists. The court will not enforce the contract if the title is clearly bad and will expose the purchaser to immediate eviction. The essence of the doctrine of specific performance is that the purchaser is actually to get the land; it is therefore inapplicable in any case where he cannot get the land in any substantial sense, not even a good holding title[17]. The parties are therefore left to their remedies at law.

(a) Doubtful title

The court will not require a purchaser to complete a contract if the vendor's title is doubtful, that is, one not shown to be good or bad. The title may be considered doubtful because it depends upon the construction of a will[18], or of some ill-drafted document, or on facts which are difficult to establish. Thus a purchaser will not be compelled to accept a title depending on the fact that the vendor had no notice of an equitable incumbrance[19]. The court will, however, endeavour to resolve the doubt one way or the other, if possible. It will determine questions of law, including the construction of documents not requiring extrinsic evidence, but not questions of fact, or of mixed law and fact, though in these cases the vendor is given an opportunity of resolving the doubt at his own cost[20]. A purchaser cannot set up the doubtfulness of the vendor's title as a defence if the doubt relates to some matter to which he is by the contract precluded from objecting[1].

---

15 *Doe d Roberts v Roberts* (1819) 2 B & Ald 367; 2 Williams V & P, 841.
16 *Best v Glenville* [1960] 3 All ER 478 at 481, CA, per Ormrod LJ. And see *Williams v Greatrex* [1956] 3 All ER 705 (erection of buildings without statutory licence no bar).
17 *Re Scott and Alvarez's Contract, Scott v Alvarez* [1895] 2 Ch 603 at 613, CA, per Lindley LJ (condition restricting objections to intermediate title), p. 158, ante; *Warren v Richardson* (1830) 1 You 1 (conduct amounting to waiver of objections).
18 *Wilson v Thomas* [1958] 1 All ER 871 (sale of reversionary interest; latent ambiguity in description of beneficiary in will). See generally *Mullings v Trinder* (1870) LR 10 Eq 449.
19 *Nottingham Patent Brick and Tile Co v Butler* (1885) 15 QBD 261, CA, p. 150, ante; *Re Handman and Wilcox's Contract* [1902] 1 Ch 599, CA.
20 The various authorities are carefully considered by Roxburgh J in *Wilson v Thomas* [1958] 1 All ER 871.
1 Cf. *Wilson v Thomas* [1958] 1 All ER 871, where the special condition was held not to preclude the objection taken. See also *Faruqi v English Real Estates Ltd* [1979] 1 WLR 963 (failure to disclose absence of documents referred to in the Register); *MEPC Ltd v Christian-Edwards* [1981] AC 205, [1979] 3 All ER 752, HL (ancient contract no defect).

(b)   Inquiry into title

In every suit for specific performance, the purchaser has a right to have an inquiry directed as to whether the vendor can make a good title to the property in accordance with the contract. The underlying reason for this rule is simply that a court of equity will not call upon a purchaser to perform the contract specifically unless the vendor has such a title as the purchaser is willing, or can be compelled, to accept. A vendor may succeed at the hearing in establishing a prima facie case of specific performance (thus signifying that the purchaser's defence has been rejected); yet the purchaser can require the vendor to establish his title and if this is not done to the court's satisfaction, the purchaser is not obliged to take the property. The vital question of costs is sufficient to dissuade a purchaser from making a frivolous demand for an inquiry, and today, the title to land being far less complicated than previously, inquiries into title are not as frequently encountered. Reference to this inquiry into title, if requested, is incorporated in the judgment for specific performance[2]. The purchaser can waive his right, e.g. by admitting or not denying the vendor's title in his defence to the vendor's claim. The inquiry takes place in the judge's chambers[3] and the result is embodied in a certificate.

A purchaser requests an inquiry at his own risk. If he does so in his own action and the certificate upholds the title, he must pay the vendor's costs of the proceedings. Even if the certificate is against the title, he is in something of a dilemma. He must either accept the title as shown, despite the defects, and pay the costs of the inquiry, or allow his action to be dismissed without costs. In the latter event, he can recover damages for breach of contract (i.e. the vendor's inability to make title), but these[4] will not include the costs of his action for specific performance. He is more favourably placed if the vendor takes proceedings and it transpires he cannot make title. Here the purchaser can rescind the contract with leave of the court and recover his deposit and costs, including the costs of the action and the inquiry into title[5].

7.   Consequences of refusal of decree

(a)   Damages

Equity's refusal to grant a decree leaves the parties to their common law remedies. A purchaser may successfully resist specific performance; yet his failure to complete may constitute a breach of contract, in respect of which the vendor can claim damages or forfeit the deposit — provided the purchaser is not himself entitled to rescind the contract. *Wood v Scarth*[6] is an instructive case. The defendant agreed to let a public house to the plaintiff, intending to charge a premium in addition to the annual rent. Unfortunately his clerk omitted to advise the plaintiff of the premium. The mistake was held to be sufficiently serious for a court of equity to decline to grant specific performance, but the contract was still binding at law and in subsequent proceedings[7] the plaintiff recovered damages for breach of contract.

2   See 3 *Seton's Judgments and Orders* (7th edn) p. 2158. A vendor cannot ask for an inquiry into his own title: *Bradley v Munton* (1852) 15 Beav 460.
3   Occasionally where there is no issue between the parties except as to title, the court may determine the question at the hearing of the action; see *Wilson v Thomas* [1958] 1 All ER 871.
4   As to the measure of damages, see pp. 587–589, post.
5   See generally, Walford, 77–78, and cases there cited.
6   (1855) 2 K & J 33.
7   (1858) 1 F & F 293.

Furthermore, under its general jurisdiction to give complete and final relief, the court can award damages in addition to or in substitution for specific performance[8]. This power is not confined to cases where the plaintiff establishes a prima facie case for specific performance[9]. If the contract is merely oral, though supported by sufficient acts of part performance, the court will not award damages in any case where it is unable to decree specific performance[10]. The subject of damages is dealt with in the following chapter.

(b) Return of deposit

The harshness of the rule which entitled the vendor to forfeit the purchaser's deposit if he did not complete the purchase, notwithstanding that he had successfully resisted the vendor's claim for specific performance[11], has now been mitigated by s. 49 (2) of the Law of Property Act 1925. This provision enables the court, if it thinks fit, to order the repayment of any deposit where it refuses to grant specific performance. The courts have a complete discretion under the section so as to be able to do justice between the parties[12]. It has been observed that there is no power to order return of less than the whole; it must be all or nothing[13]. The section is confined to deposits and does not extend to part payments. The suggestion has also been made that the court's jurisdiction is ousted where the vendor has a lawful right to retain the deposit, not as forfeited, but as liquidated damages, or in reduction or on account of damages[14].

C Enforcement of order

1. Form of order

The judgment generally commences with a declaration that the court orders and adjudges the agreement 'to be specifically performed and carried into execution'. Then follow directions, varying according to the circumstances, for

---

8 See the Supreme Court Act 1981, s. 50; *Cooper v Morgan* [1909] 1 Ch 261; *Scott v Bradley* [1971] Ch 850, [1971] 1 All ER 583 (specific performance and damages for delay in completing contract). Equity's power to award damages was first granted by the Chancery Amendment Act 1858. Prior to this Act equity exercised jurisdiction to award compensation as ancillary to a decree of specific performance, but never independently: *Newham v May* (1824) 13 Price 749; *Joliffe v Baker* (1883) 11 QBD 255 at 267. For an example of the exercise of this power to award compensation, see p. 601, post. See generally [1981] Conv 286 (Ingham and Wakefield).

9 *Elmore v Pirrie* (1887) 57 LT 333; White and Tudor, *Leading Cases in Equity* (9th edn), pp. 399–402.

10 *Lavery v Purcell* (1888) 39 Ch D 508. The equitable doctrine of part performance cannot be used to obtain damages on a contract at law: per Chitty J at 518. See also *Stimson v Gray* [1929] 1 Ch 629.

11 See *Scott and Alvarez's Contract* [1895] 2 Ch 603, CA, p. 158, ante; *Beyfus v Lodge* [1925] Ch 350.

12 *Universal Corpn v Five Ways Properties Ltd* [1979] 1 All ER 552; applying *Schindler v Pigault* (1975) 30 P & CR 328. Cf. *Cole v Rose* [1978] 3 All ER 1121. As to the actual exercise of the discretion see *Charles Hunt Ltd v Palmer* [1931] 2 Ch 287 (misleading representation in contract); *James Macara Ltd v Barclay* [1944] 2 All ER 31 (failure to give vacant possession): affd. on other grounds [1945] KB 148, [1944] 2 All ER 589, CA; *Finkielkraut v Monohan* [1949] 2 All ER 234, p. 416, ante.

13 Per Vaisey J, in *James Macara Ltd v Barclay* [1944] 2 All ER 31 at 32.

14 1 Williams V & P, 31.

the payment of interest, the taking of accounts, the inquiry into the vendor's title (unless this has been accepted or the right to a reference waived), the preparation and execution of the conveyance to be settled by the judge, and for the simultaneous delivery at a time and place to be appointed of the executed conveyance and the other title deeds in exchange for the purchase money, interest and costs[15]. If the purchaser is in possession of the property, he is put to his election to give up possession or to pay the balance due into court[16].

2. Mode of enforcement

Having obtained his decree, the plaintiff must then obtain an order fixing a time and place for completion of the contract, though this must await the outcome of the inquiry (if any) into the title. Where the vendor obtains a decree but the certificate is adverse to the title, the purchaser should apply to the court to be discharged from the contract[17].

Failure by the defendant to comply with the order results in his being in contempt of court and he can be proceeded against on that basis. The plaintiff's subsequent rights vary according to whether he is the vendor or the purchaser. Where the purchaser defaults, the vendor can apply to the court for an order for the termination of the contract and for forfeiture of the deposit[18]. If the contract reserves an express power of resale, he should apply for liberty to exercise this power[19], so that he can thereby recover any deficiency in price to which the contract may entitle him on resale at a loss. There are other courses open to the vendor which may, however, prove to be less effective. He can levy an execution on the purchaser's goods, apply for a charging order on his land[20] or apply for a writ of sequestration.

On default by the vendor, the purchaser is in a stronger position, for he can apply to the court for an order vesting the land in him or for the appointment of a third person to convey it to him[1].

---

15 See the form of the order in *Palmer v Lark and Clark* [1945] Ch 182, [1945] 1 All ER 355. As to delay in prosecution of the order see *Easton v Brown* [1981] 3 All ER 278.
16 *Greenwood v Turner* [1891] 2 Ch 144; *Maskell v Ivory* [1970] Ch 502, [1970] 1 All ER 488.
17 *Halkett v Earl of Dudley* [1907] 1 Ch 590 at 601, per Parker J. The purchaser's application may be refused if the vendor has managed to perfect his title by that time.
18 *Hall v Burnell* [1911] 2 Ch 551.
19 See *Shuttleworth v Clews* [1910] 1 Ch 176; see further p. 611, post.
20 Under the Charging Orders Act 1979. The order for payment of the price is a final judgment on which a bankruptcy notice can be founded: *Re A Debtor (No 837 of 1912)* [1912] 3 KB 242, CA.
1 Trustee Act 1925, ss. 48–50. The procedure by way of vesting order is the more convenient; see *Jones v Davies* (1940) 84 Sol Jo 334.

Chapter 22

Damages

A Introduction

Breach of a contract for the sale or purchase of land gives rise to a right of action at common law for damages. The breach may take different forms, with varying consequences. Breach of a term of vital importance, such as the vendor's inability to show a good title in accordance with the contract, entitles the innocent party to treat himself as discharged from the contract. He may elect to rescind the contract; alternatively he can choose to affirm it and sue for damages for its breach. Breach of a non-essential term merely gives rise to an action for damages. The breach may also take the form of a repudiation of the contract by one of the parties before the time for performance has arrived. This may result from an express refusal to proceed with the contract, or it may be inferred from one party's conduct as, for instance, where the vendor puts it out of his power to perform the contract by conveying it to another[1]. Again the innocent party is put to his election.

Damages are not confined solely to cases where the contract is not performed. A purchaser, for instance, may seek damages after completion but, because of the rule that on conveyance the contract and any remedies under it become merged in the conveyance, damages are not normally recoverable after completion. There are exceptions to this rule, and damages may be obtained in the event of:

(i)   a fraudulent misrepresentation inducing the contract, and now by virtue of the Misrepresentation Act 1967, damages may be recoverable in certain circumstances notwithstanding that the misrepresentation is not made fraudulently[2];

(ii) a breach of a collateral warranty[3];

(iii) a breach of some contractual term which has not merged in the conveyance[4].

In addition the normal remedy for breach of the statutory covenants for title sounds in damages; covenants for title are considered in Chapter 24.

---

1   *Goffin v Houlder* (1920) 90 LJ Ch 488 (sale of property during currency of option).
2   Section 2 (1), (2), p. 593, post.
3   See p. 172, ante.
4   See p. 444, ante.

B   Damages recoverable by vendor

In relation to damages contracts for the sale of land are no different from other contracts; the general common law rule applies, subject as regards a purchaser to one important qualification to be considered later. The injured party is entitled to be placed in the same position as if the contract had been performed, so far as money can do this, provided the damage suffered is not too remote. The normal contractual rule formulated in *Hadley v Baxendale*[5] governs the question of remoteness. Only such damages are recoverable as may fairly and reasonably be considered as arising naturally, i.e. according to the usual course of things, from the breach, or such as may reasonably be supposed to have been within the contemplation of both parties when they made the contract as the probable result of it.

The vendor's damages are measured by the amount of the loss actually sustained. He is not entitled to recover the purchase price as damages, save where the conveyance has been executed and the legal title vested in the purchaser; he cannot have both the land and its value. Consequently he is limited to recovering the difference in value, if any, between the contract price and the value of the property at the time of the breach[6]. This later value is determined by the price obtained, or obtainable, on a resale within a reasonable time of the breach, but excluding any inflated price which the property might fetch by nursing it[7]. In assessing damages credit must be given for any deposit that has been paid[8], so that where the loss is covered by the amount of the deposit a vendor is often content to rescind the contract and forfeit the deposit (which he can also do notwithstanding that he manages to re-sell at the same or a higher price, so not sustaining any loss). The vendor is not entitled to recover in addition to damages his expenses incurred in connection with the abortive sale (e.g. legal fees). However, as an alternative to suing for damages for loss of profit, he may elect to claim for wasted expenditure and recovery is not limited to post-contract expenses[9], but he cannot forfeit the deposit and also recover his expenses[10]. Should the vendor resell the property at a lower figure, he can claim the expenses of the resale in addition to the difference in price but again the deposit paid by the defendant (i.e. the defaulting purchaser) must be brought into account[11].

To succeed in a claim for damages for non-performance the vendor must show that he can give a good title and that he is ready and willing to complete, otherwise he cannot establish a breach of contract by the purchaser since he himself is unable to perfom what is a condition precedent to performance by the other party. Thus in *Noble v Edwardes*[12], where time was of the essence of the contract, the vendor was denied damages on the ground that he could not make a good title on the completion date.

5   (1854) 9 Exch 341. See further p. 589, post.
6   *Laird v Pym* (1841) 7 M & W 474; *Watkins v Watkins* (1849) 12 LTOS 353. This is not an absolute basis for assessment: *Johnson v Agnew* [1979] 1 All ER 883 at 896, per Lord Wilberforce.
7   *Keck v Faber, Jellett and Keeble* (1915) 60 Sol Jo 253.
8   *Ockenden v Henley* (1858) EB & E 485; *Shuttleworth v Clews* [1907] 1 Ch 176.
9   *Anglia Television Ltd v Reed* [1972] 1 QB 60, [1971] 3 All ER 690, CA, p. 591, post.
10   In *Essex v Daniell* (1875) LR 10 CP 538 recovery of expenses was allowed apparently on the basis of a contractual provision. The case is thought to be wrongly decided by 2 Williams V & P, 1017, note (q); cf. Williams, *Title*, p. 558.
11   *Ockenden v Henley* (1858) EB & E 485.
12   (1877) 5 Ch D 378, CA, especially at 393, per James LJ; *Bellamy v Debenham* [1891] 1 Ch 412, CA (vendor unable to convey mines and minerals).

C Damages recoverable by purchaser

1. The rule in Bain v Fothergill[13]

A purchaser's right to damages is subject to one important qualification. Where non-performance of the contract results from the vendor's inability to make a good title, the only damages recoverable are the expenses incurred by the purchaser in investigating the title. He cannot recover damages for loss of the bargain. This is known as the rule in *Bain v Fothergill*[14], where the House of Lords affirmed a principle first established one hundred years earlier by the decision in *Flureau v Thornhill*[15]. The reasons advanced in *Flureau v Thornhill* in support of the rule are hardly convincing and it has been left to later judges to supply a satisfactory rationale. In his dissenting judgment in *Sikes v Wild*[16], Cockburn CJ somewhat reluctantly justified the rule in the following terms:

> ' The immunity is in itself an anomaly. It probably had its origin in the difficulty in which, in the complicated and highly artificial state of our law relating to real property, an owner of real estate having contracted to sell is too frequently placed from not being able to make out a title such as a purchaser would be bound or willing to take. The hardship which would be imposed on a bona fide vendor if, upon some legal flaw appearing in his title, he were held liable in all the consequences which would attach upon a breach of contract relating to personalty, and the difficulty which might be thrown in the way of bringing real property into the market if the full liability attached in such a case, have probably, by an understanding and usage among those engaged in the transfer of estates, led to this exception to the general law.'

It is questionable whether the exception would have been allowed to blossom had it first taken root at a time like today when the making of title to land is considerably easier than it was formerly. Indeed it is doubtful whether the rule should be permitted to survive, now that the alleged justification for its existence has largely disappeared. In the meantime, anomalous though the rule is, it is to be taken as operating as an impled term or condition[17] in every contract for the sale or leasing of land. The rule applies whenever a vendor is unable, without fault on his part, to make a good title; it is not limited to cases where the title is found to be subject to some long-forgotten or obscure incumbrance, as the frequent references in the judgments to the complexities of our land law as the basis for the rule might perhaps suggest.

It has been applied in the following cases: where one partner in good faith contracted to sell partnership property without the concurrence of his co-partner who repudiated the contract[18], where a lessor was unable to implement his contract because of restrictive covenants, created by his predecessors, affecting the user of the land[19], and where a vendor of leasehold property failed, despite reasonable endeavours, to obtain the lessor's required consent to

13 See (1977) 41 Conv (NS) (Sydenham) and [1978] Conv 338 (Emery).
14 (1874) LR 7 HL 158.
15 (1776) 2 Wm Bl 1078.
16 (1861) 1 B & S 587 at 596; on appeal (1863) 4 B & S 421; *Engell v Fitch* (1869) LR 4 QB 659 at 666, per Kelly CB; *Bain v Fothergill* (1874) LR 7 HL 158 at 210–11, per Lord Hatherley.
17 *Sikes v Wild* (1861) 1 B & S 587 at 594, per Blackburn J; on appeal (1863) 4 B & S 421.
18 *Keen v Mear* [1920] 2 Ch 574. Cf. *Watts v Spence* [1976] Ch 165, [1975] 2 All ER 528; p. 589, post.
19 *J. W. Cafés Ltd v Brownlow Trust Ltd* [1950] 1 All ER 894.

the proposed assignment[20], although in a later case substantial damages were recovered when the vendor actually induced the lessor to withhold his consent[1]. It is immaterial that the vendor could have discovered the existence of the defect or incumbrance with reasonable diligence and so have made provision for it in the contract. He can, it seems, shelter behind the rule where the sale goes off because of some irremovable incumbrance such as a restrictive covenant which he himself has previously created and in good faith omitted to disclose in the contract. Not even the vendor's knowledge when making the contract that his title is defective entitles the purchaser to substantial damages if the vendor bona fide believes he can perfect the title prior to completion[2]. Knowledge by the vendor that he had no means of curing the defect would be evidence of bad faith, enabling the purchaser to recover damages in tort for deceit[3]. Where the rule operates a purchaser is limited to the recovery of his deposit plus interest, and the expenses incurred in investigating the title[4]. This will cover his solicitor's conveyancing costs and, it has been held, the amount of an insurance premium paid on the strength of the contract[5].

2. Recovery of substantial damages

As the rule in *Bain v Fothergill* is anomalous, the courts will not extend it to cases in which the reasons on which it is based do not operate[6]. The vendor cannot rely on the rule where the breach is occasioned, not because of some defect in title, but by his own default in failing to take all proper steps to complete. In *Engell v Fitch*[7] vendor-mortgagees failed to give vacant possession as provided by the contract because of their unwillingness to incur expense in ejecting the mortgagor; the purchaser was held entitled to damages for loss of the bargain. In *Re Daniel, Daniel v Vassall*[8], mortgagees refused to release the property sold from their mortgage which the vendor was financially unable to redeem. In *Malhota v Choudhury*[9] the rule was not applied when the defendant was unable to show that he had taken any reasonable steps to obtain his wife's consent to the sale. The property was in their joint names but he alone was contractually bound[10]. Though innocent of wilful default or bad faith, the vendor was held liable for general damages. It follows from these cases that a vendor is liable for full damages if, having a good title, he wrongfully conveys the property to another[11], or simply refuses to proceed with the transaction. These

20   *Bain v Fothergill* (1874) LR 7 HL 158 (mining royalty).
 1   *Day v Singleton* [1899] 2 Ch 320, CA.
 2   *Sikes v Wild* (1863) 4 B & S 421 (land incumbered with annuity which annuitant orally agreed to transfer to other property but later changed her mind).
 3   *Bain v Fothergill* (1874) LR 7 HL 158 at 207, per Lord Chelmsford; *J. W. Cafés Ltd v Brownlow Trust Ltd* [1950] 1 All ER 894 at 897, per Lord Goddard CJ.
 4   *Keen v Mear* [1920] 2 Ch 574.
 5   *Keen v Mear* [1920] 2 Ch 574.
 6   See *Wroth v Tyler* [1973], 1 All ER 897 (statutory charge under the Matrimonial Homes Act 1967, s. 2 (1), p. 390, ante, held not to fall within the spirit and intendment of the rule).
 7   (1869) LR 4 QB 659; *Braybrooks v Whaley* [1919] 1 KB 435 (failure by mortgagees to apply to court as required by emergency legislation).
 8   [1917] 2 Ch 405; *Thomas v Kensington* [1942] 2 KB 181, [1942] 2 All ER 263 (plaintiff's knowledge of mortgage when making contract held to be immaterial).
 9   [1980] Ch 52, [1979] 1 All ER 186 CA.
10   For difficulties of co-owners see [1980] Conv 191 (P.W. Smith). In the instant case the damages were not assessed at the breach; see p. 590, post.
11   *Ridley v De Geerts* [1945] 2 All ER 654, CA, p. 590, post; *Chugal Properties Ltd v Levine* (1971) 17 DLR (3d) 667.

are instances where for one reason or another the contract is never performed. Substantial damages are also recoverable by a purchaser where, though the contract is performed, there has been delay in completion (not in consequence of some defect in title)[12], or the vendor fails to give vacant possession in accordance with the contract[13].

To be entitled to damages the purchaser must establish his own ability to perform the contract, and strictly speaking he should prove a tender of both the conveyance for execution and the balance of the purchase money. In one case where the purchaser claimed damages for delay in completion, she was denied damages for the period between the completion date and the date when her solicitor sent the engrossment to the vendor's solicitor[14]. In practice it suffices if the purchaser pleads that he is ready and willing to complete[15].

It has been held that the rule does not apply to a claim for damages for misrepresentation[16]. To this extent the actual effect of the rule today is much reduced.

(a) Measure of damages
The damages recoverable will in the first instance be dependent on the nature of the vendor's breach of contract. Where the contract remains unperformed, the purchaser retains his money, but does not obtain the property; the breach, however, entitles him to be placed in the same position, so far as money can do this, as if it had been conveyed to him, subject only to this, that the purchaser is always entitled to the return of his deposit and interest thereon in respect of loss of its use[17]. He can recover damages for loss of bargain, as it is termed, that is, the difference (if any) between the purchase price of the property and its market value at the date of the breach. A resale of the property at an increased price will be accepted as prima facie evidence of its market value[18].

Loss of the bargain is loss which can be said to result from the vendor's breach of contract in the ordinary course of events; it falls within the first limb of the rule in *Hadley v Baxendale*[19]. Loss of prospective profits to be obtained from developing the property attracts the operation of the second limb of the rule; such additional loss is also recoverable if the damages are

'such as may reasonably have been supposed to have been in the contemplation of both parties, at the time they made the contract, as the probable result of the breach.'

In *Cottrill v Steyning and Littlehampton Building Society*[20], the vendor was aware of the purchaser's intention to develop the land, and damages were

12 *Jones v Gardiner* [1902] 1 Ch 191.
13 *Beard v Porter* [1948] 1 KB 321, [1947] 2 All ER 407, CA, p. 592, post.
14 *Phillips v Lamdin* [1949] 2 KB 33, [1949] 1 All ER 770, p. 592, post.
15 *Lovelock v Franklyn* (1846) 8 QB 371.
16 *Watts v Spence* [1976] Ch 165, [1975] 2 All ER 528 (represented that he was the owner); see also *Errington v Martell-Wilson* (1980) 130 NLJ 545 (representation that vendor had title by entering into the contract); see further [1981] Conv 167.
17 The deposit is an earnest of the performance of the contract to which the innocent party is entitled. Interest at 6 per cent was allowed in *Lloyd v Stanbury* [1971] 2 All ER 267; see (1971) 217 Estates Gazette 22, at 25.
18 *Engell v Fitch* (1869) LR 4 QB 659. But see *Wroth v Tyler* [1974] Ch 30, [1973] 1 All ER 897 (damages in lieu of specific performance assessed at date of hearing, not at date of breach); *Johnson v Agnew* [1980] AC 367, [1979] 1 All ER 883, HL.
19 (1854) 9 Exch 341, at 354, p. 586, ante.
20 [1966] 2 All ER 295; *Jacques v Millar* (1876) 6 Ch D 153.

assessed by reference to the profits which both parties contemplated he would make, whereas in *Diamond v Campbell-Jones*[1] the vendor was ignorant of the purchaser's development projects and Buckley J held that the fact that the property was ripe for conversion was insufficient to impute such knowledge to him.

In these inflationary times property could increase in value considerably after the breach of contract leaving an innocent party out of pocket by the time the issue came to trial. As a result it was held[2] that the court initially could award damages in lieu of specific performance assessed at the date of the hearing. This produced a different result to a claim for damages at common law. However, it is now established that the position is the same at common law[3]. The plaintiff can effectively obtain a later date by claiming specific performance and then electing at the trial for damages[4].

(b) Conveyancing and other expenses

Damages awarded to a disappointed purchaser are not intended to place him in a better position than if the contract had been performed. Consequently he cannot have in addition to general damages his conveyancing expenses[5], for he would have had to incur these had the property been conveyed to him. In *Ridley v De Geerts*[6] the Court of Appeal rejected an argument that there should be *deducted* from the purchaser's damages the cost (including stamp duty) which he would have paid had the transaction been completed, though the court did indicate that in some cases they would be a proper deduction. Notwithstanding this decision which must be confined to its special facts, it would seem on principle to be proper to deduct from the damages recoverable all expenses (e.g. land registration fees) that would otherwise have been paid[7].

Where the purchaser cannot show he has suffered any loss of profit, damages are at large. This enables the court to award the purchaser his out-of-pocket expenses which he would not have been put to had the contract never been made. The damages are awarded to restore as far as possible the status quo ante. This is neatly illustrated by the case of *Lloyd v Stanbury*[8]:

> V contracted to sell to P a farm on which P intended, to the knowledge of V, to carry out poultry farming. It was a term of the contract that P was to

1 [1961] Ch 22, [1960] 1 All ER 583.
2 *Wroth Tyler* [1974] Ch 30, [1973] 1 All ER 897.
3 *Johnson v Agnew* [1980] AC 367, [1979] 1 All ER 883, HL. Conversely the court have moved the date back if the plaintiff has delayed in prosecuting the order: *Malhotra v Choudbury* [1980] Ch 52, [1979] 1 All ER 186, CA.
4 See *Domb v Isoz* [1980] 1 All ER 942, CA, where it was also stated that a purchase of another property was not inconsistent with a claim for specific performance.
5 *Re Daniel, Daniel v Vassall* [1917] 2 Ch 405, *Anglia Television, Ltd v Reed* [1972] 1 QB 60, [1971] 3 All ER 690, CA. The cases of *Engell v Fitch* (1869) LR 4 QB 659 and *Godwin v Francis* (1870) LR 5 CP 295, where both damages and expenses were awarded (though the purchaser's entitlement to the latter was not disputed) must be regarded as wrongly decided.
6 [1945] 2 All ER 654, CA. The market was active and the purchaser could have re-sold immediately at a profit. There is also the suggestion that the vendor had acted in a high-handed manner by repudiating the contract within a very few days of making it.
7 Compare the rule in tort that damages for loss of earnings should take into account the tax that the plaintiff would have paid: *British Transport Commission v Gourley* [1956] AC 185, [1955] 3 All ER 796. See also *Diamond v Campbell-Jones* [1961] Ch 22, [1960] 1 All ER 583 (damages paid gross since liable to attract tax as part of profits or gains of purchaser's business).
8 [1971] 2 All ER 267.

provide a caravan for V's use until completion of a bungalow which V was having built. P went into occupation of the farm, but subsequently differences arose between the parties, V repudiated the contract and P vacated the farm. P claimed damages for breach of contract. There was no evidence that the value of the farm was greater than the purchase price.

Besides his conveyancing costs and the deposit (less sums paid by way of an occupation rent), the plaintiff recovered the cost of various expenses incurred doing acts which were within the parties' contemplation, including: (i) the removal and installation charges in relation to the caravan, and (ii) expenses for the removal of the purchaser's furniture. Item (i) was allowed since it was an act required to be done by the contract and was performed in anticipatory implementation of it. The removal expenses were recoverable because the vendor knew the purchaser desired an early completion and the contract was arranged on that basis. Brightman J also awarded £250 for loss of earnings. This was a proper head of recoverable damage in as much as the vendor knew that the purchaser's purpose in buying was to re-establish his earning potential, which the vendor's breach of contract had delayed. The learned judge rejected a claim for the cost of improvements to the farm[9]; it is not usually to be regarded as in the contemplation of the parties that the buyer will spend money on improving the property before it is conveyed to him, as distinct from expenditure necessary for its preservation.

Brightman J's, decision in *Lloyd v Stanbury* on the question of recovery of pre-contract expenditure was approved by the Court of Appeal in *Anglia Television Ltd v Reed*[10], where Lord Denning MR, stated the rule in these terms[11]. Expenses preliminary to the contract may be claimed provided they are 'likely to be such as would reasonably be in the contemplation of the parties as likely to be wasted if the contract was broken'. The purchaser can recover his legal fees, including costs incurred prior to exchange of contracts[12]; and he would also be entitled on the basis of Lord Denning's dictum to claim the cost of having the property surveyed[13].

(c) Failure to obtain vacant possession

The vendor's contractual obligation to give vacant possession (where applicable) does not merge with the conveyance[14]; consequently the purchaser is entitled to damages if vacant possession is not given. Since the right to vacant possession not only includes possession free from any claim of right by the vendor or a third party, but also comprises the right to actual unimpeded physical enjoyment, he can recover damages if the premises are full of

9 These rejected items were the installation of a fire circuit and a telephone, the erection of a television aerial, and the construction of a roadway across part of the land.
10 [1972] 1 QB 60, [1971] 3 All ER 690, CA (actor repudiating television contract). This decision raises a number of important questions relating to contract damages, which are outside the scope of this book. See (1972) 35 MLR 423.
11 [1972] 1 QB 60 at 64, [1971] 3 All ER 690 at 692.
12 This was established in *Wallington v Townsend* [1939] Ch 588, [1939] 2 All ER 225.
13 This expense is one that ought reasonably to be within the vendor's contemplation as likely to be incurred by the purchaser. Other pre-contract expenses which purchasers, in the first flush of enthusiasm after buying a house, sometimes imprudently incur, such as the cost of buying curtains, carpets and similar items, will not normally be recoverable.
14 Page 444, ante.

rubbish[15], provided the rubbish constitutes an impediment which substantially prevents or interferes with the enjoyment of the right of possession of a substantial part of the property[16]. In *Beard v Porter*[17] the presence of a sitting tenant (who had retracted his promise to quit) prevented the vendor from being able to give vacant possession and the purchaser was obliged to purchase a second house. He was entitled to recover (i) the difference in value between the purchase price and the value of the house subject to the tenancy, (ii) payments made for lodgings, and (iii) solicitors' charges and stamp duty incurred in buying the second house.[18].

It will be observed that the failure to give vacant possession resulted from a defect in title (the tenancy). It seems, therefore, that the rule in *Bain v Fothergill* does not preclude the recovery of substantial damages where the contract is completed, at least when the purchaser sues for breach of some independent obligation such as the vendor's undertaking to give vacant possession. Normally the existence of the tenancy would cause the sale to go off[19], in which event the purchaser could only recover his conveyancing costs.

(d) Delay in completion

In *Phillips v Lamdin*[20] Croom-Johnson J held that delay in completion caused by the vendor's wilful default entitled the purchaser to damages for loss of earnings and expenses. The learned judge considered there was no difference in this respect between contracts for the sale of land and contracts for the sale of goods (where damages for delay are available). This decision received approval in the House of Lords in *Raineri v Miles*[1]. However the question of merger did not arise in the case as the writ was issued claiming specific performance and damages on the day of completion. Therefore the question of whether damages under this head can be claimed after completion is a moot one[2]. The proper course of action in the event of delay, assuming the purchaser wants the property, is to sue for specific performance with the addition of a claim for damages[3]. Damages are not recoverable in respect of any period when the delay

15 *Cumberland Consolidated Holdings Ltd v Ireland* [1946] KB 264, [1946] 1 All ER 284, CA (hardened sacks of cement in warehouse cellars); *Wroth v Tyler* [1973] 1 All ER 897 (spouse).
16 Per Lord Greene MR, at 271, 287 respectively.
17 [1948] 1 KB 321, [1947] 2 All ER 407, CA.
18 Evershed LJ dissented as to item (iii) on the ground that they were expenses forming part of the cost of the second purchase and not flowing from the vendor's breach. Somervell LJ, seems to have considered they were recoverable only to the extent to which the second house was of similar value to the first (see at 327, 408, respectively). No point was taken as to that, but the stamp duty payable on the second purchase suggests a price around £3,000, whereas the first house cost £2,500. See also *Topfell Ltd v Galley Properties Ltd* [1979] 2 All ER 388 (breach of vacant possession obligation on sale of house subject to a tenancy of part because of a Housing Act notice limiting occupation to one household). In *Strutt v Whitnell* [1975] 2 All ER 510, CA, it was held a purchaser did not have to mitigate his loss by selling the property back to the vendor.
19 In *Beard v Porter* [1948] 1 KB 321, [1947] 2 All ER 407, CA, the contract provided for vacant possession to be given some four months *after* completion, which is most unusual.
20 [1949] 2 KB 33, [1949] 1 All ER 770.
1   [1980] 2 All ER 145.
2   See the arguments of counsel in *Phillips v Lamdin*, supra. The argument was not mentioned in *Oakacre Ltd v Claire Cleaners (Holdings) Ltd* [1981] 3 All ER 667, where the writ was issued before completion.
3   *Jaques v Millar* (1877) 6 Ch D 153; *Scott v Bradley* [1971] Ch 850, [1971] 1 All ER 583; *Jones v Gardiner* [1902] 1 Ch 191, which Croom-Johnson J professed to follow, but in that

is attributable to the vendor's difficulties in making title[4]. Alternatively the purchaser may elect to claim interest from the vendor under General Condition 22 of the Law Society's Conditions of Sale, if applicable[5].

(e) Misrepresentation

(i) *Fraud.* A person induced by fraud to enter into a contract is put to his election. If he discovers the fraud prior to completion he may rescind the contract, or proceed to completion (i.e. affirm the contract) and claim damages in an action of deceit at law; where the fraud is not detected until after completion, he can sue to set aside the conveyance[6], or, again, he can sue for damages for deceit. It is not proposed to consider the constituent elements of the tort of deceit, with which the reader will already be familiar. We are concerned here with the measure of damages, assuming there is an actionable fraudulent misrepresentation. An action for fraud is an action in tort, not an action for breach of contract. The plaintiff-purchaser is entitled to be put in the same position in which he would have been had the representation *not been made*. He cannot claim to be put in the position he would have been in if the representation were true, i.e. he cannot recover damages for loss of the bargain (which would be the contractual measure of damages). Prima facie the damages recoverable are the difference between the price paid and the amount which he would have paid had he known the actual circumstances[7], this being taken to represent the actual value of the property at the time of the sale.

The purchaser can recover all non-remote consequential loss, for the vendor is bound to make reparation for all the actual damage directly flowing from the fraud[8]. The damage will be regarded as too remote in any case where the purchaser has not behaved with reasonable prudence[9] or common sense, or has been the author of his own misfortune[10]. In *Doyle v Olby (Ironmongers) Ltd*[11] the plaintiff was induced by the defendants' fraud to take an assignment of a leasehold shop and the ironmongery business carried on there, which he continued to run at a loss for three years before being able to sell. He was held entitled to damages for all his loss brought about by that representation[12] based on a comparison of his position before it was made to him with his position afterwards.

case completion took place *after* issue of the writ (not before, as in *Phillips v Lamdin* [1949] 2 KB 33, [1949] 1 All ER 770) and without prejudice to the purchaser's rights.
4   *Jones v Gardiner* [1902] 1 Ch 191 especially at 195, per Byrne J. But see *Beard v Porter* [1948] 1 KB 321, [1947] 2 All ER 407, CA, discussed on p. 592, ante.
5   Page 419, ante. That condition also expressly provides for a claim thereunder not to be merged in the conveyance.
6   See pp. 640–642, post.
7   *London County Freehold and Leasehold Properties Ltd v Berkeley Property and Investment Co Ltd* [1936] 2 All ER 1039 at 1047–48 , CA, per Slesser LJ, p. 184, ante; *Hepting v Schaaf* (1964) 43 DLR (2d) 168 (fraudulent statement that property contained rentable suite).
8   *Doyle v Olby (Ironmongers) Ltd* [1969] 2 QB 158 at 167, [1969] 2 All ER 119 at 122, CA, per Lord Denning MR.
9   Cf. *Hamer v James* (1886) 2 TLR 852, CA (special damage occurring after discovery of fraud, when plaintiff might have rescinded, not recoverable).
10   *Doyle v Olby (Ironmongers) Ltd* [1969] 2 QB 158 at 168, [1969] 2 All ER 119 at 123, CA, per Winn LJ.
11   [1969] 2 QB 158, [1969] 2 All ER 122, CA. For a discussion of some of the difficulties raised by this decision, see (1969) 32 MLR 556.
12   For a detailed breakdown of the assessment of the damages, reference should be made to the judgment of Winn LJ, at 169–70 and 124–25, respectively.

(ii) *Innocent misrepresentation*. Prior to the Misrepresentation Act 1967, the distinction between fraudulent and innocent misrepresentation was vital. In the absence of fraud, not only was recission not possible after completion[13], but damages were not even recoverable, either directly[14], or indirectly, e.g. by claiming specific performance with abatement[15], unless the purchaser could establish breach of some collateral warranty[16]. The Act of 1967, the provisions of which were considered in Chapter 8, has now largely rendered this difference academic. It will be recalled that s. 2 (2) of the Act gives the court a discretion where rescission is claimed for a non-fraudulent misrepresentation 'to declare the contract subsisting and to award damages in lieu of rescission'. The court is given some guidance in determining how to operate this new power; it must be

> ' equitable to do so, having regard to the nature of the misrepresentation and the loss that would be caused by it if the contract were upheld, as well as to the loss that rescission would cause to the other party.'

The court has therefore to balance the competing interests of the vendor and the purchaser. It is conceived that the court may well exercise its discretion where the misrepresentation relates to some relatively unimportant matter or, possibly, where (as is often the case with transactions involving land) the vendor has himself entered into another contract on the strength of the one which the purchaser seeks to rescind[17]. Subsection (2) does not confer any *right* to damages, nor does it enable the court to order rescission *and* award damages; these may, however, be recoverable under subsection (1) for what may loosely be termed a negligent misrepresentation. Attention has already been drawn to some of the problems that s. 2 of the Act appears to create[18] and no further discussion of these is called for here. As to the measure of damages under s. 2 (2), about which the Act is silent, it has been observed[19] that they are really sui .generis, being neither tortious nor contractual, and it remains to be seen what measure the courts will apply.

13   See p. 184, ante. Section 1 of the Act abolishes this rule.
14   *Joliffe v Baker* (1883) 11 QBD 255 (innocent error in acreage; no provision for compensation); *Lawrence v Hull* (1924) 41 TLR 75.
15   *Gilchester Properties Ltd v Gomm* [1948] 1 All ER 493, p. 185, ante.
16   E.g. *De Lassalle v Guidford* [1901] 2 KB 215, CA., p. 172, ante.
17   But see pp. 656–658, post.
18   Pages 184–185, ante.
19   See Treitel, *The Law of Contract* (5th edn), p. 267, who favours the tortious measure which seems to be the relevant measure for actions under s. 2 (1) of the Act. But see *Watts v Spence* [1967] Ch 165, [1975] 2 All ER 528 (damages for loss of bargain awarded).

Chapter 23
Rescission

A Introduction

As we have seen in Chapter 20[1] a contracting party may in certain circumstances be entitled to set the contract aside for all purposes and to be restored as far as possible to the state of affairs which existed before the making of the contract, in other words to rescind the contract ab initio. Even prior to 1875 rescission was available both at law and in equity. At common law a contract could be rescinded on the ground of fraud or on account of some breach of contract going to the root of the transaction[2]. Money paid under a rescinded contract (such as a deposit) was recoverable by an action for money had and received. However, rescission at law was only possible provided both parties could be put in statu quo as before the contract. This requirement was very strictly interpreted with the result that at law a purchaser or tenant who had entered into occupation of the property could not rescind[3]. On the other hand equity, by virtue of its superior machinery, particularly in relation to the taking of accounts and the making of allowances, was able to give relief by way of rescission wherever by the exercise of its powers it could do what was practically just, although not able to restore the parties precisely to their pre-contract position[4]. Additionally equity permitted rescission in circumstances unknown to the common law, notably for innocent misrepresentation; moreover it was possible only in equity to bring an action to enforce rescission by a judgment. Consequently rescission has come to be regarded as essentially an equitable remedy.

A right to rescind, or to sue for rescission, and to be restored to the pre-contract position may arise for any of the following reasons:

1. misrepresentation;
2. misdescription;
3. mistake;
4. defective title;
5. failure to complete;
6. by virtue of some provision in the contract.

This is not intended to be an exhaustive list of circumstances justifying rescission, but it does represent the main situations that are likely to be of

---

1 Page 569, ante.
2 See e.g. *Simmons v Heseltine* (1858) 5 CBNS 554; *Phillips v Caldcleugh* (1868) LR 4 QB 159.
3 *Hunt v Silk* (1804) 5 East 449; *Blackburn v Smith* (1848) 2 Exch 783.
4 *Erlanger v New Sombrero Phosphate Co* (1878) 3 App Cas 1218 at 1278, per Lord Blackburn.

concern to the conveyancer[5]. The following pages deal with the rights of the parties to rescind whilst the contract is still executory. Rescission after completion is considered in Chapter 25. It should also be noted that the right to rescind may be barred on several grounds; these also are more fully discussed in the same chapter[6]. Before embarking on a consideration for the topics listed in the preceding paragraph it is necessary to look in greater detail at the individual rights of the vendor or the purchaser once a right of rescission has been validly exercised. Of the above examples items 4 and 5 can be considered to be examples of rescission for breach whereas the remainder are instances of rescission ab initio.

B   Effect of breach

We have already seen[7] that rescission can have more than one meaning. It is now clearly established[8] that, contrary to earlier views[9], rescission for breach of contract does not prevent a claim for damages consequent upon that breach.

1.   Position of the vendor

Where the vendor rescinds for the purchaser's breach, he is entitled to his costs of deducing title[10] and to recover possession of the land if the purchaser has been allowed into occupation. The purchaser must account for rents and profits actually received by him[11], but somewhat illogically the vendor cannot charge him with an occupation rent[12].

(a) Forfeiture of deposit
It is well established that a vendor who elects to rescind is entitled to forfeit the deposit, irrespective of any express provision in the contract to this effect, for a deposit, besides being part payment of the price, is an earnest or guarantee of the fulfilment of the contract[13]. Once forfeited the purchaser cannot later recover the deposit on the ground that the vendor's title is discovered to have been defective[14]. The vendor is not entitled to retain other sums paid on account of the purchase price, nor can he claim payment of any outstanding part of the deposit, for having elected to bring the contract to an end by rescission, he cannot insist on the performance of the contract in relation to the

---

5   Non-disclosure could be added to the list but it is considered that this is adequately comprehended within the heading of defective title.
6   See pp. 653−658, post.
7   Chap 20, ante.
8   *Buckland v Farmer and Moody* [1978] 3 All ER 929, CA; *Johnson v Agnew* [1980] AC 367, [1979] 1 All ER 883, HL, overriding *Henty v Schroder* (1879) 12 Ch D 666; *Barber v Wolfe* [1945] Ch 187, [1945] 1 All ER 399; *Capital and Suburban Properties Ltd v Swycher* [1976] Ch 319, [1976] 1 All ER 881; and *Horsler v Zorro* [1975] Ch 302, [1957] 1 All ER 584. Before the *Johnson* case innocent parties had to be careful how they 'terminated' the contract for breach. An alternative was to sue for specific performance and then for damages in lieu. See *Biggin v Minton* [1977] 2 All ER 647; and [1979] Conv 293, (1979) 42 MLR 696.
9   See the previous edition of the book and the authorities relied on.
10   *Barber v Wolfe* [1945] Ch 187, [1945] 1 All ER 399.
11   *King v King* (1833) 1 My & K 442; *Clark v Wallis* (1866) 35 Beav 460.
12   *Barber v Wolfe* [1945] Ch 187, [1945] 1 All ER 399.
13   *Hall v Burnell* [1911] 2 Ch 551; see p. 250, ante. The contract may show an intention to exclude forfeiture: *Palmer v Temple* (1839) 9 Ad & El 508 (stipulation that party making default to pay £1,000 as liquidated damages).
14   *Soper v Arnold* (1889) 14 App Cas 429, HL.

deposit[15]. The vendor's right of forfeiture is now subject to the court's discretion to order its return in cases where it refuses an award of specific performance[16].

(b) Right of resale
The vendor is restored to his former position as owner of the property free from the contract. He can therefore resell the property without recourse to the courts and independently of any special clause in the contract. This point is well illustrated by *Howe v Smith*[17]:

> After protracted delays by P in completing the purchase, V resold the property for the same price. P claimed specific performance.

It was held that P's delay was a complete answer to his claim and justified V in rescinding the contract and forfeiting the deposit. On the facts V was held to have resold as owner under his absolute title, without relying on the contractual power to resell on default. Standard form contracts invariably contain an express power of resale in certain cases, so the vendor may find he can pursue alternative remedies though not necessarily with the same results[18].

(c) Damages
It is clear that damages can now be recovered after rescission following a breach of contract accepted by the innocent party[19]. Equally it is clear that an innocent party can sue for specific performance and at a later stage elect for damages. However if damages are elected for immediately specific performance cannot thereafter be claimed as the contract is at an end save for the question of damages[20].

A vendor in a position to forfeit the purchaser's deposit will not normally be interested in seeking damages, unless the loss on the resale exceeds the amount of the deposit. It is clear now that the deposit can be forfeited *and* damages claimed[1].

2. Position of the purchaser

On rescission of the contract by the purchaser he is entitled to recover his deposit with interest, and his legal expenses incurred in investigating the title. He is also entitled to a lien on the land for the deposit[2], which is enforceable in the same manner as the vendor's lien for unpaid purchase money[3]. On the other

---

15 *Lowe v Hope* [1970] Ch 94, [1969] 3 All ER 605; but see *Dewar v Mintoft* [1912] 2 KB 373 (part of deposit recovered as damages); *Buckland v Farmer and Moody*, ante; and Emmet, 2nd Supplement, 265.
16 LPA 1925, s. 49 (2), p. 583, ante.
17 (1884) 27 Ch D 89, CA.
18 See p. 611, post.
19 See note 8, ante.
20 *Johnson v Agnew* [1980] AC 367, [1979] 1 All ER 883, HL. The court will not terminate an order for specific performance and substitute a claim for damages if it is unjust to the other party. On similar grounds if there has been delay in prosecuting the order that may affect the measure of damages: *Malhotra v Choudhury* [1980] Ch 52, [1979] 1 All ER 186, CA.
 1 *Johnson v Agnew* and *Buckland v Farmer and Moody*, supra. The case of *Lowe v Hope* [1970] Ch 94, [1969] 3 All ER 605 seems to be of doubtful authority now and there seems no reason why damages representing a shortfall in the deposit cannot be claimed. Conversely repayment of a large deposit may be awarded; *Universal Corpn v Five Ways Properties Ltd* [1979] 1 All ER 552 at 556, per Buckley LJ.
 2 *Whitbread & Co v Watt* [1902] 1 Ch 835.
 3 See p. 421, ante. It should be registered as a land charge.

hand he cannot retain any advantage under the contract; he must account for rents received and is chargeable with an occupation rent if he has enjoyed personal possession[4]. It is perhaps worth noting in passing that where the vendor's breach of contract consists of a failure to deduce a good title, the purchaser can achieve nothing more by electing to sue for damages instead of rescinding ab initio if possible, for the rule in *Bain v Fothergill*[5] precludes him from recovering as damages anything more than his deposit with interest and conveyancing costs.

C   Misrepresentation

A purchaser acquires a prima facie right to rescind the contract if he has been induced to enter into it by a false representation made by the vendor, who intends him to act on it. The reader will already be familiar with the basic elements of misrepresentation[6], and it is not intended to do more here than to draw attention to one or two particular aspects. There must be a statement of fact; this excludes representations of law, opinion and future intention, though a statement of future conduct may amount to a statement of present intention and thus a misrepresentation of fact if at the time of making the statement the vendor had no such intention. An expression of opinion may also involve an implied assertion that the speaker knows nothing leading to the contrary conclusion. In *Smith v Land and House Property Corpn*[7] the description of a tenant who was considerably in arrear with his rent as 'most desirable' was held an actionable misrepresentation. No action lies in respect of 'puffing'. Words are not essential for a representation; conduct may suffice as where a vendor disguised defects in his house by papering over cracks in the walls[8]. No right to rescind arises if the purchaser knew at the time of making the contract that the representation was untrue, or if he did not rely on it because he commissioned an independent survey or report. In the absence of evidence of non-reliance, inducement to enter into the contract will be readily inferred if it is a material representation calculated to induce the purchaser to contract[9].

The purchaser is invariably the party seeking rescission for misrepresentation. A contract for the sale of land is not uberrimae fidei. Although the purchaser is under no duty to disclose information which could influence the price, statements made by him and intended to induce the vendor to believe in the existence of a non-existing fact which might affect the price may suffice for the court to refuse to award the purchaser specific performance[10], and in extreme cases may warrant setting the contract aside for fraud[11], or even an account of the profits made may be awarded[12].

---

4   *Allen v Smith* [1924] 2 Ch 308.
5   (1874) LR 7 HL 158, pp. 587–588, ante.
6   See further Treitel, *The Law of Contract* (5th edn) Chap. 9. See also the discussion in Chap. 7, pp. 184–188, ante.
7   (1884) 28 Ch D 718, CA; *Holliwell v Seacombe* [1906] 1 Ch 426 ('valueable freehold land immediately ripe for development' subject to restrictive covenants); *Laurence v Lexcourt Holdings Ltd* [1978] 2 All ER 810 (premises described as 'offices' when restricted planning permission only was available).
8   *Ridge v Crawley* (1959) 173 Estates Gazette 959.
9   *Redgrave v Hurd* (1881) 20 Ch D 1 at 21, CA, per Jessel MR.
10   *Walters v Morgan* (1861) 3 De GF & J 718. And see p. 580, ante.
11   *Coaks v Boswell* (1886) 11 App Cas 232 at 236, HL, per Lord Selbourne.
12   *English v Dedham Vale Properties Ltd* [1978] 1 All ER 382.

At law a misrepresentation gave rise to a right to rescind the contract only if it was made fraudulently, that is, with knowledge of its falsity or in reckless disregard whether it was true of false. In equity, however, rescission was available in respect of an innocent misrepresentation. The Misrepresentation Act 1967, leaves a purchaser's right to rescind for misrepresentation prior to completion basically unaltered, save that s. 2 (2) of the Act[13] gives the court a discretion to award damages in lieu of rescission in cases where a person is entitled to rescind a contract by reason of a non-fraudulent misrepresentation. The subsection does not empower the court to award damages as an alternative to rescission where it is sought on the grounds of the vendor's failure to make a good title, or because of a substantial misdescription.

D   Misdescription

1.   Nature of misdescription

An error or misstatement appearing in the contract and relating to the property to be sold amounts to a misdescription. Mistakes as to the area of the property, or the nature of the vendor's interest[14], or the net annual rental of the property[15], or the terms of restrictive covenants affecting the property[16] all constitute misdescriptions. Representations made as to the quality of the land may also be misdescriptions. In *Re Puckett and Smith's Contract*[17], for instance, the misdescription took the form of a statement in the particulars of sale that the land possessed a 'valuable prospective building element' whereas an underground culvert crossed the land, creating a substantial drawback to the use of the land for building purposes. Similarly, in a more recent case the particulars of sale of a house purchased at auction contained a full description of its accommodation. Part of the property was in fact subject to an undisclosed closing order. The purchaser was held entitled to rescind the contract on the ground of misdescription; rooms which were the subject-matter of a closing order could not properly be described as 'accommodation'[18]. Like misrepresentation, there must be a statement which purports to be of fact; on the other hand laudatory expressions extolling the virtues of the property, not uncommonly encountered in sales by public auction, will be treated as mere 'puff'. Descriptions like 'fertile and improvable'[19] and 'valuable and extensive . . . very suitable for development'[20] have been treated as falling within this category.

13   Page 185, ante. As to the changes made in relation to rescission after completion, see s. 1 (b) of the Act, discussed at p. 644, post.
14   *Turner v West Bromwich Union Guardians* (1860) 3 LT 662 (copyhold land described as freehold); *Re Russ and Brown's Contract* [1934] Ch 34, (land sold as leasehold held by underlease); p. 145, ante.
15   *Palmer v Johnson* (1884) 13 QBD 351, CA; *Re Englefield Holdings Ltd and Sinclair's Contract* [1962] 3 All ER 503.
16   *Flight v Booth* (1834) 1 Bing NC 370.
17   [1902] 2 Ch 258, CA.
18   *Registered Holdings Ltd v Kadri* (1972) 222 Estates Gazette 621.
19   *Dimmock v Hallet* (1866) 2 Ch App 21. Cf. *Registered Holdings Ltd v Kadri* (1972) 222 Estates Gazette 621, note 18, ante (property described at auction as 'nice house' held to be an actionable misrepresentation).
20   *Watson v Burton* [1956] 3 All ER 929 at 931, per Wynn-Parry J (misstatement of area).

Some writers[1] do not differentiate between misrepresentation and mis-description; yet they are quite distinct and give rise to different remedies. The essence of a misdescription is that it is contained in the contract itself, usually in the particulars of sale. In results in a breach of contract *at law*; the vendor is unable to convey what he has contracted to convey and common law remedies are available in respect of the breach. A misrepresentation induces the contract, without causing any breach of it (save where it is later incorporated as a term), and, prior to the Misrepresentation Act 1967, relief for an innocent misrepresentation could only be obtained *in equity* by way of rescission.

2.   Rights of the parties

It has long been the practice for vendors to safeguard their position by expressly regulating in the contract the rights of the purchaser in the event of misdescription. Consequently only a brief survey need be given of the parties' rights under the general law. These depend on the nature of the misdescription, a difference being taken according to whether it is substantial or slight.

(a) Substantial misdescription
At law the purchaser can rescind the contract and recover his deposit in an action for money had and received. Even in the absence of fraud a misdescription in a material and substantial point results in the contract being 'avoided altogether'[2]. The meaning of 'substantial' in this context will be considered in the following section. Nor will equity decree specific performance against the purchaser, for the court will not compel him to take something different from what he has agreed to buy.

(b) Slight misdescription
An insubstantial error innocently made does not entitle the purchaser to rescind the contract at law and he must be content with damages[3], whereas equity will enforce the contract at the instance of the vendor, subject to his allowing the purchaser compensation[4].

(c) Specific performance with abatement[5]
As an alternative to rescission at law, the purchaser may seek the assistance of equity for a decree of specific performance with a reduction in the purchase price by way of compensation for the deficiency. This jurisdiction is based upon the principle of equitable estoppel; a vendor representing and contracting to sell an estate cannot afterwards assert that he has not got what he has contracted to sell, and the purchaser can call upon him to convey what he actually has[6]. The limits of this jurisdiction are perhaps somewhat ill-defined. Generally it is immaterial whether the misdescription is slight or substantial, though equity will not intervene where the error is so great as to 'affect the

1   E.g. Walford, 222.
2   *Flight v Booth* (1834) 1 Bing NC 370 at 377, per Tindal CJ; *Jones v Edney* (1812) 3 Camp 285 (tied public house described as free).
3   *Belworth v Hassall* (1815) 4 Camp 140 (contract for sale of unexpired term of eight years, though only seven years seven months remained).
4   *McQueen v Farquhar* (1805) 11 Ves 467.
5   For a detailed analysis of this topic see C. Harpum, 'Specific Performance with Compensation as a Purchaser's remedy—A study in Contract and Equity' [1981] CLJ 47.
6   See *Mortlock v Buller* (1804) 10 Ves 292 at 315—16, per Lord Eldon LC.

whole foundation and substance of the contract'[7]. Specific performance with abatement has been allowed where there was a deficiency of 28 acres out of a total of 217[8], and where a vendor purporting to sell the fee simple was only a life tenant[9]. It has been refused where the amount of the compensation was difficult to assess[10], and where it would cause great hardship on the vendor to enforce the contract against him[11]. In these case the purchaser must elect to rescind the contract or submit to its performance on payment of the full price.

3. Contractual restrictions of purchaser's rights

The brief survey given in the preceding section demonstrates the weakness of the vendor's position under the general law. Clauses designed to ameliorate his lot by excluding the purchaser's right of rescission, with or without compensation, have been in vogue for over 150 years. Various clauses have been employed in the past and, though in some respects decided cases are no more than decisions on the construction of the particular condition before the court, these cases do assist the formulation of general principles applicable to the clauses in the standard form contracts today. To these we must now turn.

Condition 17 (1) of the National Conditions of Sale is in the following terms (so far as is here relevant):

> ' no error, misstatement or omission[12] . . . in the sale plan or the Special Conditions[13], shall annul the sale, nor (save where the error, misstatement or omission is in a written answer and relates to a matter materially affecting the description or value of the property) shall any damages be payable or compensation allowed by either party in respect thereof.'

(a) 'no error . . . shall annul the sale . . .'

To prevent rescission by the purchaser was the vendor's chief concern and this has always been the intention of clauses dealing with misdescription. Yet, notwithstanding the apparently unequivocal language of the condition, the courts have steadfastly refused to enforce this provision. In the course of his judgment in *Re Fawcett and Holmes' Contract*[14], where the court had to consider a condition that errors of description should not annul the sale but were to be the subject of compensation, Lord Esher MR, observed that such a condition was inapplicable to three sets of circumstances: (i) to fraudulent misdescriptions, (ii) to misdescriptions in respect of which compensation could not be assessed, and (iii) to cases within the rule of *Flight v Booth*[15], a rule easy to understand, but difficult to apply. This third situation is particularly relevant in this

---

7   *Re Terry and White's Contract* (1886) 32 Ch D 14 at 22, CA, per Lord Esher MR. Cf. Farwell J, in *Rudd v Lascelles* [1900] 1 Ch 815 at 819, who would confine relief to cases where the actual subject-matter is substantially the same as that stated in the contract.
8   *Hill v Buckley* (1811) 17 Ves 394. A rateable abatement of price will probably leave both parties in nearly the same relative situation in which they would have stood if the true quantity had been originally known: per Grant MR, at 401.
9   *Barnes v Wood* (1869) LR 8 Eq 424; *Burrow v Scammel* (1881) 19 Ch D 175.
10 *Rudd v Lascelles* [1900] 1 Ch 815 (restrictive covenants).
11 *Earl of Durham v Legard* (1865) 34 Beav 611; *Rudd v Lascelles* [1900] 1 Ch 815.
12 These words are not applicable to a misrepresentation inducing the contract: *Bellotti v Chequers Development Ltd* [1936] 1 All ER 89 (inaccurate representation of size of garden not incorporated in contract).
13 This includes the particulars of sale: Construction clause, para. 3.
14 (1889) 42 Ch D 150 at 156, CA.
15 (1834) 1 Bing NC 370.

context. A vendor is precluded from resorting to the condition because a sufficiently serious misdescription vitiates the whole contract, including the condition[16].

For the rule to apply there must, according to Tindal CJ, in *Flight v Booth*[17], be a misdescription 'in a material and substantial point' so far affecting the transaction that the purchaser could be considered 'as not having purchased the thing which was really the subject of the sale'. In each case the question depends on the view of the court as to the importance of the error[18]. The court is bound to consider every incident differentiating the property offered from that actually bought and if the sum of these incidents really alters the subject-matter, the purchaser can rescind[19]. In *Jacobs v Revell*[20] the purchaser was held entitled to rescind when it was discovered that the vendor did not have a good title to approximately one acre out of five. In *Re Fawcett and Holmes' Contract*[1] the purchaser was held to have got substantially what he bargained for, although 339 square yards of the 1372 square yards which he had contracted to buy had been sold-off by a previous owner. In *Flight v Booth*[2] the misdescription took the form of a substantial discrepancy between the restrictive covenants affecting the property and those actually revealed in the particulars. The purpose to which the purchaser proposes to put the land is also a relevant consideration. In *Re Puckett and Smith's Contract*[3] the existence of the underground culvert was a serious drawback to the use of the land for building purposes, whereas in *Re Brewer and Hankin's Contract*[4] the land was acquired for residential purposes so that the existence of an undisclosed sewer made very little difference and the purchaser was obliged to accept compensation.

(b) 'nor shall any damages be payable or compensation allowed'
This stipulation precludes the purchaser from obtaining specific performance with compensation, whether the error is trivial or serious (save in so far as the contract might provide for limited compensation). He cannot insist on something which is expressly excluded by the contract[5]. The vendor can enforce the contract, subject to his allowing compensation, but it is generally considered that he can only obtain specific performance in the case of slight errors[6]. In *Curtis v French*[7] the condition was held to debar the purchaser's claim for damages for breach of the term to give vacant possession on completion. This decision has been criticised on the ground that the statement regarding vacant possession was not a representation of fact but an express promise intended to

---

16 *Re Terry and White's Contract* (1886) 32 Ch D 14 at 29, CA, per Lindley LJ.
17 (1834) 1 Bing NC 370 at 377.
18 *Re Fawcett and Holmes' Contract* (1889) 42 Ch D 150 at 157, CA, per Lord Esher MR.
19 *Lee v Rayson* [1917] 1 Ch 613 at 619, per Eve J.
20 [1900] 2 Ch 858; *Watson v Burton* [1956] 3 All ER 929 (40 per cent over-statement).
1   (1889) 42 Ch D 150, CA.
2   (1834) 1 Bing NC 370; cf. *Re Courcier and Harrold's Contract* [1923] 1 Ch 565.
3   [1902] 2 Ch 258, CA, p. 599, ante.
4   (1899) 80 LT 127, CA; *Re Belcham and Gawley's Contract* [1930] 1 Ch 56.
5   *Cordingley v Cheeseborough* (1862) 4 De GF & J 379; *Re Terry and White's Contract* (1886) 32 Ch D 14, CA.
6   But see the not very satisfactory decision in *Whittemore v Whittemore* (1869) LR 8 Eq 603 (deficiency of 180 square yards out of 753; contract enforced by *vendor* subject to compensation).
7   [1929] 1 Ch 253 (statutory tenant in occupation); cf. *Beard v Porter* [1948] 1 KB 321, [1947] 2 All ER 407, CA; p. 592, ante.

be binding[8]. It is extremely doubtful whether this case can be regarded as sound authority for a general proposition that a vendor unable to give vacant possession can plead a no-compensation clause as a defence to the purchaser's action for damages.

(c) 'save where the error . . . relates to a matter materially affecting the description or value'
This parenthetical saving clause purports to entitle either party to claim compensation in respect of material errors, but its limitations must be noted. It does not enable a vendor to enforce specific performance subject to compensation if the rule in *Flight v Booth*[9] applies, though the cases establish that the courts are more inclined to decree specific performance in cases where the condition allows compensation than in cases where it is excluded altogether. Nor does it entitle a vendor to a decree where the error is to his disadvantage[10], e.g. where the actual area is greater than that stated in the contract, for it would be manifestly unjust for the court to enforce the contract against the purchaser at an enhanced price which he might be unable to pay. In effect, therefore, this provision gives the purchaser a contractual right to compensation if the error materially affects the property's description or value (but not otherwise), and it seems that an error may fall within this saving clause and yet not be sufficiently substantial to justify rescission[11]. This contractual right does not merge with the conveyance on completion and an action may lie in respect of errors not discovered until after completion[12]. It has been held further that the clause is an unfair contractual term in so far as it purports to restrict liability in respect of a pre-contract inquiry[13].

(d) Vendor's power to rescind
The purchaser's right to rescind or claim compensation is subject to the vendor's overriding contractual power under General Condition 10 (1) to rescind on account of the purchaser's refusal to withdraw a requisition. Contractual clauses of this nature will be considered later in this chapter, but their application to the present situation warrants a brief mention here. The vendor's entitlement to exercise this contractual right to rescind, which defeats the purchaser's claim to compensation for misdescription, was upheld in *Re Terry and White's Contract*[14] and *Ashburner v Sewell*[15]. However, the wording

8 Williams, *The Contract of Sale of Land*, p. 129, note (x); Walford, 178–79. The purchaser could have rescinded but he sought damages in an attempt to recover loss of profit on resale. But to what extent could he have obtained substantial damages, bearing in mind the failure to give vacant possession was due to a defect of title? See pp. 587–588, ante.
9 (1834) 1 Bing NC 370, where there was a clause providing for compensation; cf. *Re Fawcett and Holmes' Contract* (1889) 42 Ch D 150, CA.
10 See *Price v North* (1837) 2 Y & C Ex 620.
11 See *St. Pier Ltd v Shirley* (1961) 179 Estates Gazette 837 where the contract failed to exclude a cellar vested in an adjacent owner; this constituted an omission within NCS (17th edn) cl. 14 (1) (in this respect the same as the present condition) and Pennycuick J ordered the purchase price of £6,600 to be reduced by £250.
12 *Palmer v Johnson* (1884) 13 QBD 351, CA. The purchaser may, depending on the circumstances, have an alternative claim on the implied covenants for title.
13 *Walker v Boyle* [1982] 1 All ER 634, applying Misrepresentation Act 1967, s. 3 as amended by the Unfair Contract Terms Act, 1977. See further p. 605, post, discussing the modification in the 20th edition of the NCS attempting to deal with this decision.
14 (1886) 32 Ch D 14, CA (deficiency in area). The purchaser's claim was also rejected on the ground that compensation was excluded by the contract.
15 [1891] 3 Ch 405 (undisclosed right of way).

of Condition 10 (1) raises doubts whether the right extends to all cases where the purchaser might seek compensation for misdescription. The vendor's right to rescind arises if the purchaser persists in any objection to the title, and a requisition as to deficiency is more likely to be treated as an objection on a matter appearing on the particulars[16] rather than one on the title. Of course, if the purchaser gets in first and validly rescinds for misdescription, it is too late for the vendor to attempt to rescind under Condition 10 (1)[17].

(e) The Law Society's Conditions of Sale
The effect of General Condition 7 of The Law Society's Conditions is essentially the same as Condition 17 (1); any error or misstatement in the contract is not to annul the sale, but either vendor or purchaser may require compensation if the error materially affects the description of the property, but this provision does not affect the purchaser's right to rescind where the compensation cannot be assessed. It is expressly stated by Condition 7 (4) that the vendor cannot compel the purchaser to accept (with or without compensation) property which differs substantially from that agreed to be sold, if the purchaser would be prejudiced by the difference. This is partial recognition of the purchaser's general right to rescind if the case comes within the *Flight v Booth* principle. It is doubtful whether the additional qualification adds anything significant; sufficient prejudice will normally exist because a substantial difference will prevent the purchaser obtaining what he contracted to buy. In so far as the qualification purports to limit the purchaser's right of rescission under the general law, it will probably be disregarded by the courts. It was, however, treated by Wynn-Parry J in *Watson v Burton*[18] as a valid pre-requisite to the purchaser's right to rescind, and on the facts he found that the purchaser was prejudiced.

Condition 7 (4) enables the vendor to resist specific performance even with compensation if he is prejudiced by a substantial error. Perhaps this does no more than give contractual force to the equitable rule applicable under an open contract that the court will not enforce the contract against the vendor if this will cause him hardship.

(f) Misrepresentation Act 1967
It will have been noticed that in the standard form contracts the same clause that deals with misdescription also restricts the purchaser's rights in respect of misrepresentation[19]. As we saw in Chapter 7[20], s. 3 of the Misrepresentation Act 1967, provides that a contractual provision which excludes or restricts the liabilities or remedies of the contracting parties for misrepresentation 'shall be of no effect' except to the extent to which it satisfies the test of reasonableness[21]. Prima facie it would seem that s. 3 makes the whole clause of no effect, including those provisions which regulate the parties' rights with regard to misdescription. Nevertheless it is conceived that the court would enforce that part relating to misdescription on the basis that it was fair and reasonable. Alternatively the court might sever the various parts of the Condition, leaving the compensation provisions outside the operation of s. 3.

16 See *Re Terry and White's Contract* (1886) 32 Ch D 14, CA (where the vendor's right to annul the sale was upheld on somewhat different wording). Cf. LSC 16 (1) (failure to withdraw any requisitions or objection). See pp. 612–616, post.
17 *Holliwell v Seacombe* [1906] 1 Ch 426, a case on misrepresentation.
18 [1956] 3 All ER 929 (decided on a similar provision in the 1953 edn). See note 20, p. 602, ante.
19 See p. 187, ante, for a discussion of NCS 17 (1) in relation to misrepresentation.
20 See p. 186, ante.
21 NCS 17 (1) failed the test in *Walker v Boyle* [1982] 1 All ER 634.

New NCS 17 (2)
As a result of the decision in *Walker v Boyle*, above, this Condition was introduced providing that the vendor cannot rely on Condition 17 in the case of
fraudulent or reckless mis-statements. This appears to be based on an obiter
dictum of Dillon J therein to the effect that the decision could be otherwise if
the misrepresentation was 'trifling'[22]. It seems doubtful whether this new clause
will be upheld[1].

Incorporated misrepresentations. A misrepresentation inducing a contract
may become in effect a misdescription if it is later incorporated into the
contract as a term, thus tending to obscure the differences between the two.
Prior to the Act there was some authority (though the point was not free from
doubt) for the view that in such circumstances the right to rescind for the misrepresentation did not survive its incorporation into the contract; in other
words the purchaser might be confined to his remedy of damages for breach of
contract. Now under s. 1 of the Act, the purchaser's right to rescind for misrepresentation is preserved, notwithstanding that it has become a term. This
new statutory rule does not apparently deprive the purchaser of his right to
claim damages for breach of the term, but he cannot do both. He is put to his
election. If he rescinds for misrepresentation, the contract is set aside for all
purposes and damages cannot be claimed[2], though the court may in effect
reverse his decision, for under s. 2 (2) of the Act it can exercise its discretion to
declare the contract subsisting and award damages in lieu of rescission.

E   Mistake

The reader will already be familiar with the intricacies and controversies
surrounding the law of mistake in contract. For a detailed exposition of the law
on this complicated topic, reference should be made to text-books on the law of
contract[3]. This present section purports to be nothing more than a brief
attempt to remind the reader of some of the basic principles. At the outside it is
necessary to appreciate the differing attitudes of law and equity to the problem
of mistake. At law mistake, if operative, makes the contract void ab initio. It
prevents any real consensus existing between the parties; there is no contract.
This differentiates mistake from other vitiating factors like fraud, misrepresentation or duress, which make a contract voidable, not void. Strictly
speaking, therefore, it is inappropriate to speak of rescinding a contract void
for mistake, though the expression is commonly used to denote the process of
setting the alleged contract aside, whereby each party restores what he has
received and recovers what he gave. Since the contract is void, no title can be
acquired under it and this can operate to the detriment of a third party[4].
  On the other hand equity is prepared to afford relief in cases where the
mistake does not fall within the narrow confines of the common law. Relief may
take one of three forms: (i) a refusal of specific performance, the effect of which

22   At 644.
 1   An innocent misrepresentation need not always be trifling. Further, as appears from
     p. 644, the judge considered an innocent misrepresentation to be a bar to specific
     performance. Two other obiter dicta are worthy of note. First the clause apparently
     extended to all oral mis-statements howsoever made. This has been catered for in NCS
     17 (2) but it would appear to be the end of the new LSC (5) in this regard. Secondly, the
     judge stated the disclaimer at the top of the pre-contract inquiries (p. 187, ante) did not
     prevent the statements being representations of fact (ibid., at 641).
 2   Page 596, ante. See Treitel, op. cit., 280–281; cf. Farrand, 56–57.
 3   See Trietel, op. cit., Chap. 8.
 4   See e.g. *Cundy v Lindsay* (1878) 3 App Cas 459, HL.

is to leave the parties to their common law rights; (ii) recission which, being a form of equitable relief, may be granted unconditionally or on terms; (iii) rectification of a written document to accord with the true terms agreed between the parties[5]. Of these three only rescission will be considered here.

1.   Mistake at law

According to Lord Atkin in *Bell v Lever Bros Ltd*[6], mistake, if it operates at all, does so to negative or nullify consent and he instanced three particular forms of mistake which it will be convenient to adopt for present purposes, these being mistake as to: (i) the existence of the subject-matter of the contract, (ii) the identity of the contracting parties, and (iii) the quality of the subject-matter.

(a) Existence of subject-matter

Within this category come cases where, unknown to both parties, the subject-matter of the contract has ceased to exist at the date of the contract, or where (in a conveyancing context) the land is already owned by the purchaser — cases of res extincta, or res sua[7]. Here the parties have contracted on the basis of a fundamental assumption which is false. For example a contract for the sale of a life interest is void if the life tenant is already dead[8], and notwithstanding completion of the transaction the conveyance will be set aside and the purchaser is entitled to recover the price as money paid under a mistake of fact. The same appears to be true where prior to the contract the land has been completely swept away by a flood[9], or a house totally destroyed by fire[10], though in this latter instance the same reasoning employed to save the contract from frustration where destruction succeeds the making of the contract is perhaps equally applicable to preserve the contract where the destruction precedes the contract[11]. Several cases establish that a contract is void both at law and in equity where the purchaser or tenant is already the owner or lessee of the subject-matter of the contract[12]. A mistake of private rights is for these purposes regarded as a mistake of fact, not law. Where, however, unknown to both parties the title is not in the vendor but in some third party, there is a valid contract, albeit unenforceable by the vendor, and the purchaser is entitled to recover damages for the vendor's breach of contract[13].

A mistake by one party as to the subject-matter does not avoid the contract. Thus if a purchaser bids for one lot at an auction, thinking that it is another,

5   See pp. 649–653, post.
6   [1932] AC 161 at 217, HL.
7   Perhaps the true basis of the decision in these cases is not so much the fact of a common mistake as the absence of any contractual subject-matter. Cf. *Amalgamated Investments and Property Co Ltd v John Walker & Sons Ltd* [1976] 3 All ER 509, CA.
8   *Strickland v Turner* (1852) 7 Exch 209; *Scott v Coulson* [1903] 2 Ch 249.
9   *Hitchcock v Giddings* (1817) 4 Price 135 at 141, per Richards CB.
10   2 Williams V & P, 772.
11   See p. 263, ante.
12   *Cooper v Phibbs* (1867) LR 2 HL 149 (agreement for lease of fishery) regarded by Lord Atkin in *Bell v Lever Bros Ltd* [1932] AC 161 at 218, as a contract void at law, though the tenant filed a petition in Chancery for delivery up of the agreement and consequential relief; *Jones v Clifford* (1876) 3 Ch D 779. Cf. *Bligh v Martin* [1968] 1 All ER 1157 (lessee already owning freehold of part of land leased to him; no rescission); see p. 645, post.
13   As to the measure of damages, see p. 587, ante. The purchaser may choose to waive the objection to the title and complete the purchase. He may think it worthwhile to do this to enter into occupation, taking his chance of it ripening into a title acquired by adverse possession. If the want of title is not discovered until after completion, he can only sue on the covenants for title.

the contract will normally be enforced against him, his mistake being no defence to the vendor's action for specific performance[14]. The minds of the parties are not strictly ad idem, but the purchaser is not allowed to give evidence of the state of his mind. It is imperative that contracts should be observed wherever possible and the purchaser (or the vendor) is not to be freed from his bargain when to all outward appearances he has agreed on the same terms on the same subject-matters[15]. The contract is therefore valid at law, but there may be circumstances sufficient in equity to justify a refusal of specific performance.

(b) Identity

It is clear that a mistake as to the identity of the other contracting party operates to avoid the contract if personal considerations are fundamental to its formation. The defence has been difficult to establish in relation to contracts relating to land. It has been raised unsuccessfully by vendors in several cases where the apparent purchaser has been an agent for some undisclosed principal[16]. In *Sowler v Potter*[17] a lease was held void for mistake on the ground that the tenant, who had been convicted of permitting disorderly conduct in a café, applied for and obtained the lease in an assumed name, but it is generally agreed that this decision cannot be supported on the ground of mistake though the lease was clearly voidable on account of fraud.

Equity adopts a similar attitude on the question of identity. In *Dyster v Randall & Sons*[18], Lawrence J enforced a contract at the instance of a purchaser who was an undischarged bankrupt, although the contract had been made on his behalf by an agent who knew that the vendor would not have contracted with the undisclosed principal; the contract was not one where personal considerations formed a material ingredient. However, in the exercise of its discretionary jurisdiction, equity is more willing than the common law to take account of personal attributes. Thus it has been said that where a lease is concerned the tenant's solvency must necessarily be of primary importance and his insolvency may be a ground for refusing specific performance[19].

(c) Quality

According to Lord Atkin[20] a mistake as to the quality of the subject-matter only avoids the contract at law if it makes the actual subject-matter something essentially different from what it is supposed to be. The cases suggest that rarely will mistake as to quality be regarded at law as so fundamental as to avoid the contract. In *Solle v Butcher*[1] the parties mistakenly thought that a flat was free from rent control; the lease they entered into on this assumption was upheld at law, though relief was given in equity. It follows that a mistake by one party as to quality or as to some element affecting the value of the land, such as the presence of subjacent minerals, will not affect the contract at law, even though he would not have entered into the contract had he been aware of the true facts.

---

14 *Van Praagh v Everidge* [1902] 2 Ch 266; revsd. [1903] 1 Ch 434, CA, on the ground there was no memorandum to satisfy the Statute of Frauds; *Tamplin v James* (1880) 15 Ch D 215, p. 578, ante.
15 See Blackburn J's, classical explanation in *Smith v Hughes* (1871) LR 6 QB 597 at 607.
16 See e.g. *Smith v Wheatcroft* (1878) 9 Ch D 223; *Nash v Dix* (1898) 78 LT 445 (where the purchaser was held not to be an agent but a person buying for resale); *Dyster v Randall & Sons* [1926] Ch 932.
17 [1940] 1 KB 271, [1939] 4 All ER 478.
18 [1926] Ch 932.
19 *Dyster v Randall & Sons* [1926] Ch 932 at 939, per Lawrence J, citing *O'Herlihy v Hedges* (1803) 1 Sch & Lef 123.
20 *Bell v Lever Bros Ltd* [1932] AC 161 at 218.
1 [1950] 1 KB 671, [1949] 2 All ER 1107, CA.

The vendor's contribution to the mistake may be a sufficient ground for equity to refuse to enforce the contract against the purchaser. If the mistake finds its way into the contract, so becoming a term, as where there is an error as to quantity, there is misdescription which, as we have seen, may entitle the purchaser to rescind, but this is quite different from avoiding the contract for mistake.

2.   Mistake in equity

In cases of res extincta or res sua equity follows the law and treats the contract as a nullity. In the exercise of its jurisdiction to set aside the contract equity goes further than the common law and may impose terms on the parties[2]. Equity may also intervene where the contract is valid at law. The rule enunciated by Denning LJ, in *Solle v Butcher*[3] is as follows:

> ' A contract is also liable in equity to be set aside if the parties were under a common misapprehension either as to the facts, or as to their relative respective rights, provided that the misapprehension was fundamental and that the party seeking to set it aside was not himself at fault.'

The limits of this equitable jurisdiction are uncertain. Indeed the jurisdiction itself has been hotly disputed and it has since been invoked on two occasions only, by Goff J, in *Grist v Bailey*[4]:

> ' Property thought by both parties to be subject to a statutory tenancy was sold for £850. The value of the property if sold with vacant possession was £2250. In fact the property was occupied by a person (the son of the previous statutory tenant) who did not claim the protection of the Rent Acts. On discovery of the true position the vendor refused to complete. The purchaser sued for specific performance and the vendor counterclaimed for rescission.'

Goff J held there was a fundamental common mistake, insufficient to avoid the contract at law, but within the equitable principle laid down by Denning LJ. He dismissed the plaintiff's action and ordered rescission of the contract, but on terms that the vendor entered into a fresh contract at a proper vacant possession price. On the need for an absence of fault the learned judge, though unsure of what this requirement comprehended, felt there must be some degree of blameworthiness beyond the mere fault of having made a mistake[5]. Perhaps it does no more than ensure that the party seeking to take advantage of the mistake comes to equity with clean hands. Rescission in equity on the ground of mistake is a discretionary remedy and is subject to the usual bars[6].

F   Defective title

It is the vendor's duty to show a good title to the property in accordance with the contract. Failure in this respect constitutes a breach of contract which may, depending on the nature of the failure and any express contractual provisions,

---

2   See e.g. *Cooper v Phibbs* (1867) LR 2 HL 149.
3   [1950] 1 KB 671 at 693, [1949] 2 All ER 1107 at 1120, CA.
4   [1967] Ch 532, [1966] 2 All ER 875. See also *Laurence v Lexcourt Holdings Ltd* [1978] 2 All ER 810, (parties under mistaken impression that premises had unrestricted use permission as offices — rescission ordered).
5   [1967] Ch 532 at 542, [1966] 2 All ER 875 at 880–881.
6   See pp. 653–658, post.

entitle the purchaser to rescind the contract and recover the deposit and his costs of investigating the title. As we have seen[7] the vendor's title is defective if he cannot convey, or compel another to convey, the estate contracted to be sold. He must also show that he can convey free from all incumbrances, save those mentioned in the contract. Non-disclosure of a latent defect in title[8], such as a restrictive covenant or rentcharge, renders the title defective. The purchaser's remedies in respect of non-disclosure are basically the same as for misdescription; he can, therefore, rescind the contract if the non-disclosure relates to a substantial defect[9]. It should also not be forgotten that the purchaser's right to rescind may be affected by the contract. Thus General Condition 17 (1) of the National Conditions of Sale extends to omissions from the contract, though as we saw in the section on 'Misdescription'[10] this condition does not preclude rescission where the non-disclosure is such as to prevent the purchaser getting substantially what he contracted to buy.

1.   Nature of purchaser's right

The purchaser's right of rescission on discovery of a fundamental defect in the vendor's title is well established. In the oft-quoted words of Sir John Romilly MR[11],

'. . . when a person sells property which he is neither able to convey himself nor has the power to compel a conveyance of it from any other person, the purchaser, as soon as he finds that to be the case, may say, "I will have nothing to do with it".'

Considerable controversy rages over the nature of this right. In *Halkett v Earl of Dudley*[12], Parker J expressed the view that this right is no more than an equitable right, arising out of want of mutuality, which merely bars any relief being subsequently given to the vendor by way of specific performance. This statement of principle has been adopted in at least two subsequent first instance decisions[13]. If this is merely an equitable right of repudiation, to be distinguished from the common law right of rescission, the consequences are as follows. The contract remains subsisting at law. Should the vendor subsequently acquire title before the contractual date for completion, he can recover damages for breach of contract if the purchaser fails to complete[14]. Moreover, as Sargant J held in *Proctor v Pugh*[15], where the purchaser repudiated the contract on the ground of non-disclosure of restrictive covenants, the vendor is still free to exercise his own contractual right to rescind.

7   Pages 279–280, ante.
8   For the vendor's duty of disclosure, see pp. 146–150, ante.
9   *Phillips v Caldcleugh* (1869) LR 4 QB 159 (failure to disclose restrictive covenants); *Carlish v Salt* [1906] 1 Ch 335 (party wall notice).
10   Page 601, ante.
11   *Forrer v Nash* (1865) 35 Beav 167 at 170; *Re Hucklesby and Atkinson's Contract* (1910) 102 LT 214 at 217, per Eve J.
12   [1907] 1 Ch 590 at 596.
13   *Proctor v Pugh* [1921] 2 Ch 256; *Elliott and H Elliott (Builders) Ltd v Pierson* [1948] Ch 452, [1948] 1 All ER 939.
14   *Halkett v Earl of Dudley* [1907] 1 Ch 590 at 596, per Parker J; contra *Brewer v Broadwood* (1882) 22 Ch D 105, note 17, post.
15   [1921] 2 Ch 256.

Notwithstanding this body of authority, this view has been subjected to considerable criticism, notably by T. Cyprian Williams[16] who maintained that the purchaser's right to rescind on account of a substantial defect of title was a right enjoyed at law. Several cases support this opinion[17]. In *Re Atkinson and Horsell's Contract*[18], Fletcher-Moulton LJ spoke of the vendor's failure to make such a title as he was contractually bound to make as constituting 'a total breach of the contract which [the purchaser] is entitled to take advantage of by insisting on the common law right of rescission'. It has been held that a purchaser, on discovering a vendor has no title, can terminate the contract both at law and equity immediately without waiting for the contractual completion date[19]. This would appear to be confined to irremovable defects and 'so on'[20]. It should also be noted that the vendor could not make title at the date fixed for completion also.

Rescission at law puts an end to the contract; consequently the vendor cannot recover damages for breach of contract[21], nor can he himself enforce a contractual stipulation conferring on him a right of rescission.

2.   Exercise of right

Whatever the true nature of the purchaser's right, he must exercise it categorically and expeditiously. There must be a definite repudiation in unequivocal terms. When he rescinds the purchaser is not inviting the vendor to agree to any course of action; he is exercising a unilateral right[22]. The clearest way of intimating this is for him to say, 'I rescind'. An offer to cancel by consent does not suffice[1]. He must not delay exercising his right, otherwise he will be held to have elected to treat the contract as subsisting. Waiver will be inferred if he calls upon the vendor to perfect his title by getting in outstanding interests or requiring the concurrence of third parties who can complete the title[2]. Registration of the contract as a land charge is sufficient affirmation to

16   1 V & P, 203–5. In *Proctor v Pugh* [1921] 2 Ch 256, Sargant J referred to these criticisms, but rejected them without consideration. This prompted Harman J's comment in *Elliott and H Elliott (Builders) Ltd v Pierson* [1948] Ch 452 at 456, [1948] 1 All ER 939 at 942, that notwithstanding Mr Williams' counter-attack the field remained in the possession of the judiciary.

17   See e.g. *Phillips v Caldcleugh* (1968) LR 4 QB 159, note 9, ante; *Weston v Savage* (1879) 10 Ch D 736, especially at 741, per Hall V-C; *Brewer v Broadwood* (1882) 22 Ch D 105 (purchaser's rescission good defence to vendor's action for damages).

18   [1912] 2 Ch 1 at 12–13, CA; *Re Stone and Saville's Contract* [1963] 1 All ER 353 at 355, CA, per Lord Denning MR.

19   *Pips (Leisure Productions) Ltd v Walton* (1981) 260 Estates Gazette 601 (V contracted to sell the 5½-year residue of a 21-year lease. The lease was forfeited before completion although V stated he was not aware of any breach of covenant. P terminated the contract four months after the completion date on discovery of possession. *Held* (1) time was of the essence; (2) in any event P could terminate as soon as he discovered V had no title without waiting for completion).

20   Ibid. at 604.

21   See note 17, ante; *Bellamy v Debenham* [1891] 1 Ch 412, CA, where the court refused to award damages to a vendor who only perfected his title *after* the date for completion; see the judgment of Kay LJ, at 423, who expressed the opinion that the contract having been validly rescinded, no claim for specific performance or damages could possibly be sustained.

22   *Re Stone and Saville's Contract* [1962] 2 All ER 114 at 121, per Buckley J; affd. [1963] 1 All ER 353, CA.

1   *Re Atkinson and Horsell's Contract* [1912] 2 Ch 1, CA; *Re Hailes and Hutchinson's Contract* [1920] 1 Ch 233.

2   *Murrell v Goodyear* (1860) 1 De GF & J 432.

bar rescission[3]. The issue of a vendor and purchaser summons, asking for a declaration that a requisition has not been answered and for return of the deposit, is not inconsistent with an allegation that the contract has been rescinded[4]. The purchaser should, however, beware of acting too precipitously. The abstract may disclose a prima facie defect in title because, e.g. it is incomplete, but if the purchaser repudiates before giving the vendor a reasonable opportunity of showing there is no defect, he does so at his own risk. The cases establishing the purchaser's right to rescind do not apply where the vendor has a complete title or the power to make a complete title *at the date of the contract* and the only default of which the vendor is guilty is in not having satisfied the purchaser by showing this title[5].

Where the purchaser elects to proceed with the contract, the vendor can obtain specific performance if he subsequently cures the defect[6], and he can exercise the usual contractual right of rescission if the purchaser persists in his objection to the title[7]. Should the defect not be cured by the contractual date for completion, the purchaser is not obliged to wait indefinitely for the vendor to perfect his title. Clearly he cannot rescind immediately because time is not generally of the essence of the contract; he is entitled to serve the usual notice to complete and he can rescind on its expiry if the title is still imperfect. Yet even at this late stage the vendor seems able to exercise his own contractual right of rescission (if any), unless on the facts he is held to have waived his right[8].

G Failure to complete: rescission for breach

Failure to complete on the *contractual* date may or may not constitute a fundamental breach of contract entitling the injured party to rescind. Where time is of the essence of the contract he may, as has been seen in a previous chapter[9], rescind the contract on the very next day if he wishes, and the normal consequences will flow from that rescission. If time is not of the essence he may be able to pursue alternative remedies. For instance, protracted delay by the purchaser may amount to a repudiation of the contract, entitling the vendor to rescind without any further action on his (the vendor's) part, i.e. without serving the usual notice to complete. Since rescission terminates the contract he is at liberty to resell under his own absolute title and to forfeit the deposit[10]; in addition he can recover any deficiency resulting from the sale either as damages or under a clause in the contract.

In practice most injured parties will prefer to act more expeditiously by serving a notice making time of the essence of the contract. Various aspects relating to notices to complete have already been discussed[11]; here it is

---

3   *Elliott and H Elliott (Builders) Ltd v Pierson* [1948] Ch 452, [1948] 1 All ER 939. See also *Aquis Estates Ltd v Minton* [1975] 3 All ER 1043, CA (continued exercise of contractual rights a bar).
4   *Re Stone and Saville's Contract* [1963] 1 All ER 353, CA.
5   *Re Hucklesby and Atkinson's Contract* (1910) 102 LT 214 at 217, per Eve J (sub-vendor failing to abstract contract between legal owner and himself).
6   It is sufficient if he acquires a title by the date of the certificate as to title: *Eyston v Simonds* (1842) 1 Y & C Ch Cas 608.
7   *Re Deighton and Harris's Contract* [1898] 1 Ch 458, CA.
8   *Bowman v Hyland* (1878) 8 Ch D 588, p. 616, post.
9   Page 412, ante.
10   *Howe v Smith* (1884) 27 Ch D 89, CA, p. 597, ante.
11   Pages 414–416, ante.

necessary to consider in greater detail the consequences of non-compliance with a valid notice to complete. Where the contract provides for service of a notice, the parties' rights are governed by the relevant condition.

1.   Purchaser in default

Both the standard form Conditions of Sale[12] provide in the event of the purchaser's default for (i) forfeiture of the deposit, (ii) resale of the property if the vendor chooses, and (iii) recovery of any loss occasioned by a resale within a stated period, including costs and expenses incidental thereto[13], but after giving credit for the deposit[14]. The Standard Conditions do not provide for the retention by the vendor of any surplus on a resale but he appears to have such a right in the absence of any such power[15]. The various rights given to the vendor are expressed to be without prejudice to any other right or remedy available to him. The existence of this contractual right to resell does not debar a resale under the general law[16].

2.   Default by vendor

The National Conditions make no provision regulating the purchaser's rights in the event of the vendor's failure to comply with the notice. His rights must therefore be governed by the general law, i.e. the open contract position. He can accept the repudiatory breach and claim damages. Alternatively he can sue for specific performance and for damages for any loss arising from the delay.

Condition 23 (7) of The Law Society's Conditions, whilst preserving the purchaser's legal and equitable remedies, entitles him on the vendor's default to serve a further written notice requiring repayment of the deposit forthwith. By so doing he abandons his right to specific performance[17] without affecting any claim for damages. It has been stated[18] that this right will be useful to a purchaser who no longer wishes to purchase that particular property and wants to be free from the contract so as to be able to buy another house. However, the clause does not entitle him to interest or costs, both of which he can recover by rescinding the contract and suing for the return of his deposit—and there is nothing in Condition 23 (7) to deny him this course of action. At the least this clause should facilitate a speedy return of the deposit, without recourse to legal proceedings, to a purchaser willing to forgo interest and costs.

12   NCS 22 (3); LSC 23 (5), (6).
13   LSC 23 (6) permits the recovery of the expenses of any attempted resale, and requires the ultimate resale to be *contracted* within one year from the 'contractual completion date' being the date for completion fixed in the contract. Cf. NCS 22 (3) which requires the resale to be within 12 months of the expiration of the notice to complete. This is perhaps not free from ambiguity and seems to require completion to be within this period—which reduces the time.
14   This would be so even in the absence of this term: *Ockenden v Henly* (1858) EB & E 485 (express provision for forfeiture of deposit).
15   *Ex p Hunter* (1801) 6 Ves 94 at 97, per Eldon LC; Williams, *Title*, 703. Cf. LSC (1973) 19 (4) (c).
16   *Howe v Smith* (1884) 27 Ch D 89, CA.
17   But see p. 415, ante, where the point is made that service of a notice to complete is strictly an inappropriate and unnecessary step to take if specific performance is desired. The purchaser can sue for specific performance as soon as the contractual date for completion has passed; see p. 576, ante.
18   (1970) 67 LS Gaz R 741.

H Contractual rights of rescission

A party to a contract may be entitled to rescind by virtue of some express stipulation in the contract. Of the various provisions found in formal contracts today which confer such a right, the one most frequently encountered is that which enables the vendor to rescind if the purchaser insists on any objection or requisition which the vendor is unable or unwilling to comply with or remove. No such right exists under an open contract.

1. Rescission on requisition being pressed

Condition 10 of the National Conditions of Sale is in the following terms[19]:

(1) If the purchaser shall persist in any objection to the title which the vendor shall be unable or unwilling, on reasonable grounds, to remove, and shall not withdraw the same within ten working days of being required so to do, the vendor may, subject to the purchaser's rights under Law of Property Act 1925, ss. 42 and 125, by notice in writing to the purchaser or his solicitor, and notwithstanding any intermediate negotiation or litigation, rescind the contract.

(2) Upon such rescission the vendor shall return the deposit, but without interest, costs of investigating title or other compensation or payment, and the purchaser shall return the abstract and other papers furnished to him.

The purpose of this and similar clauses, which have a long ancestry, is obvious. It confers on the vendor a lawful right to terminate the contract on terms most advantageous to himself, i.e. on repayment of nothing more than the deposit and other money paid, if it appears from the purchaser's requisitions that he may not be able to convey what he has contracted to convey, or can only do so after incurring considerable expense. In days when titles to land were more complicated than they are today, this was an extremely valuable right. What is more, by resorting to this power the vendor can deny the purchaser the exercise of rights to which he might otherwise have recourse.

(a) Exercise of right
The exact circumstances in which the vendor can rescind depend on the precise terms of the contract. The following points in relation to Condition 10 set out above should be noted.

(i) *'objection to the title'*. This does not cover any requirement which is a matter of conveyance[20], nor will it enable the vendor to rescind if the purchaser takes objection to an erroneous description as to quantity[1]. In this respect the wording of the corresponding Condition 16 (1) of The Law Society's Conditions of Sale is wider; it speaks of 'any requisition or objection'. At one time it was queried whether the condition could properly extend to objections as to

19 See also LSC 16 which is similar in effect. This condition has introduced a right for the *purchaser* to withdraw after the service of the notice to withdraw by the *vendor*.
20 *Kitchen v Palmer* (1877) 46 LJ Ch 611 (purchaser requiring vendor to get in outstanding estate). *Leominster Properties Ltd v Broadway Finance Ltd* (1981) 42 P & CR 372 (discharge of mortgage).
1 See *Re Terry and White's Contract* (1886) 32 Ch D 14 at 24–25, CA per Lord Esher MR, p. 603, ante.

conveyance even though expressed[2], but there is no doubt that the courts will now give effect to it[3].

(ii) *'shall not withdraw'*. Unlike some clauses where the right arose on the making of an unwelcome requisition[4], the purchaser is entitled to a locus poenitentiae; he has an opportunity to consider whether to accept what might be a doubtful title or suffer rescission at some financial loss. The purchaser must 'persist' in his objection before a withdrawal notice can be served; this requires the vendor at least to attempt to answer the requisitions.

(iii) *'subject to the purchaser's rights'* under LPA 1925, ss. 42 (8) and 125 (3). The vendor cannot rescind on the ground that the purchaser insists upon his statutory rights to have any outstanding legal estate got in[5] or the production of a post 1925 power of attorney affecting the title[6].

(iv) *'notwithstanding any intermediate negotiation or litigation'*. A vendor exercising his contractual right must do so within a reasonable time, though not necessarily before the agreed completion date[7]. He may, however, be deemed to have waived his right by doing acts inconsistent with its exercise by, for example, attempting to comply with the requisition or by suing for specific performance. The introduction of these words into the contract safeguards the vendor's position generally, but does not afford complete protection. A denial by the vendor of the existence of any defect does not constitute 'negotiation', which imports some communication between the parties as to how an admitted defect can be removed[8]. The right to rescind notwithstanding 'previous litigation' cannot be exercised after judgment[9] or whilst the vendor's own action for specific performance is still proceeding[10].

(v) *'rescind'*. A notice of rescission signed 'without prejudice' is ineffective[11]. The vendor must repay the deposit but without interest or expenses (both of which the purchaser could have claimed had he rescinded). The purchaser must return the abstract and other papers and (under The Law Society's Conditions only) procure at the purchaser's expense the cancellation of any registered estate contract. A condition as to compensation does not preclude the vendor putting into force his contractual right to rescind[12].

(b) Limitations
The reservation of this right of rescission has been attacked as a violation of one of the first principles of the law of contract[13]. Though the right is sometimes expressed in unqualified language, the courts have consistently refused to

2   *Hardman v Child* (1885) 28 Ch D 712 at 718, per Pearson J.
3   *Re Deighton and Harris's Contract* [1898] 1 Ch 458, CA (outstanding legal estate).
4   *Re Starr-Bowkett Building Society and Sibun's Contract* (1889) 42 Ch D 386, CA.
5   See p. 164, ante.
6   See p. 290, ante.
7   *Shoreditch Vestry v Hughes* (1864) 17 CBNS 137; cf. *Bowman v Hyland* (1878) 8 Ch D 588.
8   *Gardom v Lee* (1865) 6 H & C 651.
9   *Re Arbib and Class's Contract* [1891] 1 Ch 601, CA; cf. *Isaacs v Towell* [1898] 2 Ch 285.
10 *Public Trustee v Pearlberg* [1940] 2 KB 1, [1940] 2 All ER 270, CA.
11 *Re Weston and Thomas's Contract* [1907] 1 Ch 244.
12 *Ashburner v Sewell* [1891] 3 Ch 405 (non-disclosure of right of way).
13 Williams, *The Contract of Sale of Land*, xi. See Farrand, 119–121.

countenance any improper use of the power. In *Re Dames and Wood*[14] Lindley LJ, said:

> ' The power so reserved to the vendor must be exercised with reference to the object with which it was inserted, an object perfectly well known to everybody who has any experience in real property transactions. The vendor cannot say, "I will not complete and will throw up the contract for sale"; he must exercise the power bona fide for the purpose for which it was made part of the contract.'

The language used by judges in the cases is not always easy to reconcile, but the underlying principles are now well established. The difficulty often lies in determining whether the facts of a particular case bring it within the limitations imposed by the courts. The vendor's inability to rely on the clause leaves the way open for the purchaser to pursue his remedies. He may, for instance, rescind and recover his deposit with interest and costs or alternatively he may seek specific performance.

The following restrictions on the exercise of the right exist.

(i) *Unreasonable exercise.* It is variously stated that the vendor must not act capriciously or arbitrarily, expressions which mean no more than that he must not act without reasonable cause[15]. This requirement is expressly embodied in the standard Conditions of Sale. He cannot use the power as a facile mode of terminating the contract simply because he has decided not to sell, or has received a higher offer from a third party[16]. The requisition to which he takes umbrage must be one of some substance in the sense that compliance will involve him in considerable expense, or even litigation. In *Re Weston and Thomas's Contract*[17] the vendor's purported rescission, following the purchaser's insistence on the discharge of a contingent liability in respect of succession duty, was held unreasonable because neither difficulty, delay nor expense was involved in assessing and commuting the duty.

(ii) *Recklessness.* Recklessness in entering into the contract precludes the exercise of the right. A vendor is under a duty to his purchaser to satisfy himself before signing the contract that he can convey the property[18]. In this context 'recklessness' connotes

> ' an unacceptable indifference to the situation of a purchaser who is allowed to enter into a contract with the expectation of obtaining a title which the vendor has no reasonable anticipation of being able to deliver.'[19]

Such conduct does not, therefore, involve any element of fraud or dishonesty. Recklessness may exist in the making of some untrue statement of fact about the property, without having any or at the most only insubstantial grounds for believing it is true. In *Re Jackson and Haden's Contract*[20]:

---

14   (1885) 29 Ch D 626 at 634, CA; see also *Selkirk v Romer Investments Ltd* [1963] 3 All ER 994 at 999, PC, per Viscount Radcliffe.
15   *Quinion v Horne* [1906] 1 Ch 596 at 604, per Farwell J.
16   *Smith v Wallace* [1895] 1 Ch 385.
17   [1907] 1 Ch 244; *Quinion v Horne* [1906] 1 Ch 596.
18   *Baines v Tweddle* [1959] Ch 679 at 695, [1959] 2 All ER 724 at 732, CA, per Romer LJ.
19   *Selkirk v Romar Investments Ltd* [1963] 2 All ER 994 at 999, PC, per Viscount Radcliffe.
20   [1906] 1 Ch 412, CA; *Nelthorpe v Holgate* (1844) 1 Coll 203.

V, knowing that he had not title to the subjacent minerals, contracted to sell to P his land by a description wide enough to include the minerals. *Held*: V was guilty of a misdescription and was debarred from relying on his right to rescind. P was entitled to specific performance with compensation.

In the more recent case of *Baines v Tweddle*[1] a vendor contracted to sell mortgaged property free from incumbrances without first inquiring whether the mortgagees would join in the conveyance to release the land. He was held unable to rescind on learning of the mortgagees' refusal to concur. A vendor is not denied his right of rescission where he makes an untrue statement under a genuine belief that it is true and there exists some substantial ground for his belief[2]. For instance, if in *Baines v Tweddle*[3] the vendor had, before signing the contract, received some assurance from the mortgagees that they would join in the conveyance and they had later changed their mind, he could have relied on the clause. The court also considered, but did not answer, the interesting question whether the vendor would have been entitled to rescind had he been erroneously informed by his solicitor that the mortgagees would concur. Is he only to be affected by his own personal default, or do the general principles of agency apply? The doctrine of imputed notice is one of general application in a conveyancing context and it may be argued that as a matter of policy a purchaser should not be prejudiced by the default of the vendor's solicitor, for the vendor will normally be able to recover from his solicitor any loss resulting from his inability to rely on Condition 10.

(iii) *No title*. The case of *Bowman v Hyland*[4] establishes that a vendor who has no title at all to the property cannot shelter behind the normal rescission clause for it is not framed with reference to this particular situation[5]. An objection that the vendor has no title at all is one going to the root of the contract and it has recently been queried whether such objections come within the scope of the condition. In *Baines v Tweddle*[6], Pearce LJ doubted whether the standard condition applied 'where the defect in title is, in view of all the circumstances, so radical and extensive'. This suggests further judicial restrictions on the exercise of his right. However, there is clear authority that provided he can show title to part of the land agreed to be sold, he is not debarred from exercising his right if the purchaser objects that he has no title to the remainder[7].

(iv) *Contract already at an end*. It follows from general principles that the vendor loses his right to rescind if the purchaser has already validly rescinded the contract on the ground of, for instance, misrepresentation[8] or mis-

1 [1959] Ch 679, [1959] 2 All ER 724; CA; *Re Des Reaux and Setchfield's Contract* [1926] Ch 178 (vendor knowing of lack of title when making contract but hoping to make it good with concurrence of third party).
2 *Duddell v Simpson* (1866) 2 Ch App 102; *Merrett v Schuster* [1920] 2 Ch 240.
3 See Lord Evershed MR, [1959] Ch 679 at 689–90, [1959] 2 All ER 724 at 728.
4 (1878) 8 Ch D 588. The vendor contracted to sell freehold land, but in fact merely possessed the fag-end of a long term of years which expired shortly after making the contract.
5 Where the title is vested in a third party, 'the matter is not one capable of being complied with as between vendor and purchaser': per Hall V-C, at 590.
6 [1959] Ch 679 at 698, [1959] 2 All ER 724 at 734; see also at 687–88 and 727 respectively, per Lord Evershed MR.
7 *Heppenstall v Hose* (1884) 51 LT 589 (vendor no title to 1½ acres out of 5).
8 *Holliwell v Seacombe* [1906] 1 Ch 426.

description. Once rescinded the entire contract falls and with it the clause for rescission[9].

2.   Other contractual rights

The provisions of Condition 10 (2) are made to apply in two other situations which have already been encountered in different parts of the book. First, in the case of leasehold property the vendor's inability to procure any necessary licence to assign entitles him to rescind and return the deposit[10]. Second the purchaser can rescind where the Special Conditions state that the property is sold on the footing of a specified authorised use and it is discovered before actual completion that the specified use is not an authorised use for the purposes of the planning legislation[11]. When a purchaser does exercise his contractual right to rescind it is on the terms of Condition 10 (2), and he is entitled to the return of his deposit but no more.

3.   Purchaser's short right to rescind

Both sets of standard conditions[12] have an optional condition (which requires express incorporation by the Special Conditions) entitling the purchaser to rescind the contract if the property is affected by any matter which falls within the ambit of the conditions[13]. It is doubtful whether this will facilitate early exchange of contracts on this basis because of the risk of the use of this clause, especially in a chain of transactions. It remains to be seen how popular this clause will be.

---

9   Cf. *Proctor v Pugh* [1921] 2 Ch 256, p. 609, ante. Sargant J was particularly concerned (see at 268) that if the rule as stated by him were otherwise it would render the vendor's rescission clause almost inoperative, for once the purchaser took a good objection to the title the vendor could not resort to the clause. With respect the learned judge does not appear to have appreciated that a purchaser often waives his right by requesting the vendor to cure the defect and in this situation the clause remains fully operative.

10   NCS 11 (5); cf. LSC 8 (3) (c) which permits rescission by either party. See p. 314, ante.

11   NCS 15 (3), Chap. 8, ante.

12   NCS 3; LSC 4.

13   Any matter which materially affects the value of the property (NCS); a financial charge, statutory prohibition or matter affecting the purchase price (LSC).

Chapter 24

Covenants for title

A Nature and purpose of covenants for title

On completion the transaction between the vendor and purchaser is at an end
and can only be re-opened within certain well-defined limits. The finality of
the conveyance was explained in *Allen v Richardson*[1] by Malins V-C., in these
terms:

> ' I do not think there is a more important principle than that a purchaser
> investigating a title must know that when he accepts the title, takes the
> conveyance, pays his purchase money and is put into possession, there is
> an end to all as between him and the vendor on that purchase. If it were
> otherwise, what would be the consequence. A man sells an estate
> generally because he wants the money; if this were not the rule, he must
> keep the money at his banker's, and there never would be an end to the
> question . . .'

The difficulties of making title to land are such that a purchaser can never be
absolutely sure that he will obtain a perfect title. The possibility of an adverse
claim arising after completion may be remote, but it can never be discounted
altogether even on the transfer of a registered absolute freehold title. The discovery of such a claim does not entitle the purchaser to recovery of the purchase
money, fraud apart[2], and in the absence of any express warranty of ownership
given by the vendor (and such warranties are nowadays never encountered in
practice), the purchaser's remedy is to sue for breach of the implied covenants
for title[3].

1. Historical development[4]

The origins of covenants for title lie in the mists of antiquity. On a grant of land
under the feudal system, the lord was required to warrant his tenant's title to
the land, and a clause of the Statute De Bigamis 1276, implied a limited warranty from the use of certain words in a feoffment. Express warranties became

---

1   (1879) 13 Ch D 524 at 541; *Clare v Lamb* (1875) LR 10 CP 334 at 338–39, per Grove J.
2   *Early v Garrett* (1829) 9 B & C 928.
3   *Clare v Lamb* (1875) LR 10 CP 334; *Soper v Arnold* (1887) 37 Ch D 96 at 101–2, CA, per
    Cotton LJ; affd. *Soper v Arnold* (1889) 14 App Cas 429, HL. Cf. *Cripps v Reade* (1796) 6
    Term Rep 606 (price recoverable where no conveyance taken). For the purchaser's rights if
    the contract is still executory, see pp. 608–611, ante.
4   See Holdsworth, *History of English Law*, Vol. iii, pp. 159–63, 230–1.

customary after the Statute Quia Emptores 1290, which prohibited further subinfeudation on the grant of fee simple estates with the result that there was no longer any lord-tenant relationship between the grantor and the grantee. This express warranty was often extended by a promise to grant lands of equal value in exchange if the grantee was evicted by someone having a superior title. By the seventeenth century, the old law of warranty had been replaced by express covenants for title which in course of time became more and more involved. Ultimately the concept of compensation in specie was ignored.

2. Implication of statutory covenants for title today[5]

Statutory covenants for title have been implied in conveyances since 1881 by the use of special words. The present position is regulated, in relation to unregistered conveyancing, by the Law of Property Act 1925, s. 76 and Sch. 2[6]. The appropriate expressions are: 'as beneficial owner', 'as settlor', 'as trustee', 'as mortgagee', 'as personal representative' or 'under an order of the court'. The comprehensiveness of the various covenants differs greatly according to the capacity in which the vendor is expressed to convey, and depends also on whether the land is freehold or leasehold. Where the covenants are given *by* more than one vendor, they are implied 'by each person who conveys', i.e. they are several covenants, whereas covenants made *with* more than one covenantee are made *with them jointly*[7].

(a) Conveyance of freehold land by beneficial owner
The widest covenants are implied on the part of a vendor 'who conveys and is expressed to convey as beneficial owner'. Provided the conveyance is for valuable consideration[8], s. 76 (1) (A)[9] and Part I of Sch. 2 imply covenants for—

(i)   Good right to convey[10]
(ii) Quiet enjoyment
(iii) Freedom from incumbrances
(iv) Further assurance

It is customary to think in terms of four separate and distinct covenants. In reality they are essentially parts of one entire covenant[11]; the section speaks of implying *a* covenant. Further, the better view is that obligation (iii) does not form an independent covenant but is strictly part of (ii)[12]. These beneficial owner covenants do not constitute an *absolute* warranty of title. They are controlled by the introductory words, which limit the vendor's liability to defects

---

5   See Russell, 'Covenants for Title: Implication' (1968), 32 Conv (NS) 123; [1979] Conv 93 (C.K. Liddle).
6   Replacing with amendments the Conveyancing Act 1881, s. 7, which in turn adopted in general terms the standard covenants then in vogue. For registered conveyancing, see pp. 634–637, post.
7   LPA 1925, s. 76 (1).
8   This expression includes marriage but not a nominal consideration in money: LPA 1925, s. 205 (1) (xxi).
9   See also s. 76 (2) (conveyance by direction of a person expressed to direct as beneficial owner).
10 Pre-1882 conveyances sometimes contained an express covenant for title, i.e. that the vendor was lawfully and rightfully seised of the estate, but such a covenant was of the same general import and effect as the covenant for good right to convey: per Lord Ellenborough in *Howell v Richards* (1809), 11 East 633 at 642.
11 *David v Sabin* [1893] 1 Ch 523 at 531, CA, per Lindley MR.
12 This point is elaborated on p. 629, post.

arising since the last transaction for value. This important qualification will be considered in greater detail later in the chapter.

(b) Conveyance of freehold land by fiduciary owner[13]

Where a person conveys 'as trustee', 'mortgagee', 'personal representative', or under an order of the court, a single covenant is implied that the grantor has not himself incumbered the land. The implication of this covenant is not dependent on the transaction being for value; it may be implied in an assent by a personal representative. On a sale of settled land, the vendor should convey 'as trustee', for he is a trustee both of the legal estate and in relation to the exercise of the statutory powers[14]. Evidently the former practice was for him to convey 'as beneficial owner'[15].

Joint tenants traditionally convey 'as trustees' (not as trustees for sale, an expression sometimes encountered in practice), though this has been questioned in cases where they are beneficially entitled in equity. On a conveyance to a sub-purchaser (i.e. where A contracts to sell to B who contracts to sell to C and A conveys to C, with B joining in the conveyance) it is not uncommon for B (the original purchaser) to convey 'as trustee', but the more usual practice is for both A and B to convey as 'beneficial owner'[16]. On a conveyance of land to a tenant under the Leasehold Reform Act 1967, the landlord need only convey 'as trustee', notwithstanding that he is a beneficial owner[17].

(c) Conveyance by way of settlement

The use of the expression 'as settlor' in a conveyance by way of settlement imports a limited covenant for further assurance[18].

(d) Transfer of leasehold land by beneficial owner

On an assignment of an existing leasehold term by a beneficial owner, there are implied the four covenants outlined in paragraph (a) above, and by virtue of s. 76 (1) (B) two additional ones, namely—

(i)   that the lease is valid and subsisting;
(ii) that the rent has been paid and the covenants in the lease duly performed[19].

These six covenants are only implied on an assignment for valuable consideration and never on the *grant* of a lease, or sub-lease[20]. The mere relationship of landlord and tenant automatically implies a qualified covenant by the lessor for quiet enjoyment[1], and it is common practice to incorporate an express

---

13   LPA 1925, s. 76 (1) (F); Sch. 2, Part VI; p. 633, post.
14   SLA 1925, ss. 16 (1), 107 (1).
15   See *Re Ray* [1896] 1 Ch 468 at 472, CA, per Lindley LJ. This would appear to be the proper mode where the vendor is absolutely and beneficially entitled, save only for equitable interests that will be overreached by the conveyance.
16   See Hallett, 227; cf. 19 Ency F & P, 953, Form 7:B:1. It may not always be proper for the vendor (A) to convey 'as beneficial owner', e.g. where he has already received the purchase money and has delivered possession to B; see (1962) 106 Sol Jo 132.
17   Section 10 (1).
18   LPA 1925, s. 76 (1) (E); Sch. 2, Part V.
19   See *Middlegate Properties Ltd v Bilbao* (1972) 24 P & CR 329.
20   LPA 1925, s. 76 (5), though use of the correct expression would imply the covenants in a lease at a premium but no rent.
1   *Markham v Paget* [1908] 1 Ch 697.

covenant in the lease. It is uncertain whether the purchaser's indemnity in respect of the covenants in the lease constitutes value for present purposes[2]. Although a lease may be voidable at the date of the assignment by virtue of the non-performance of the repairing covenant in the lease, a purchaser cannot maintain an action against his vendor for breach of covenant (i) above where the defect has been cured by the lessor's subsequent acceptance of rent from the purchaser[3].

Though not strictly relevant to a consideration of covenants for title, it should be remembered that on an assignment for value of leasehold property, covenants are implied by the purchaser to pay the rent, to observe and perform the covenants and to indemnify the assignor. Similar covenants are implied on the sale of freehold land subject to an existing rentcharge[4].

(e) Transfer of leasehold land by fiduciary owner

The same covenant as that considered in paragraph (b) is implied. This follows because the word 'conveyance' is wide enough to cover an assignment of lease-hold property. The two additional covenants implied by s. 76 (1) (B) do not apply, but perhaps the fiduciary vendor's limited covenant extends to some acts which would otherwise be within the special leasehold covenants[5].

(f) Mortgage of land

A mortgagor who 'as beneficial owner' demises or charges land by way of mort-gage enters into the four beneficial owner covenants, but with this important difference — the covenants are absolute, not qualified, i.e. the covenants are *not* limited, as in the case of a vendor's beneficial owner covenants, to defects arising since the last transaction for value[6]. It will be observed on looking at any building society mortgage that joint mortgagors regularly enter into these covenants even though their technical capacity is that of trustees. Where the property mortgaged is freehold subject to a rentcharge, or leasehold, there is an additional covenant to pay the rent and perform the covenants during the con-tinuance of the security[7].

(g) No covenants for title

The use of one of the specific capacities operates as a kind of magic formula, implying the relevant covenants. If the grantor is not expressed to convey in one of those categories, no covenant is, by virtue of the section, implied in the con-veyance[8]. Use of an incorrect expression, such as, trustees for sale, absolute owner, mortgagor, is ineffective to imply any covenants. It is not customary to enter into covenants for title on a voluntary conveyance, or where the vendor only has a possessory title; in this latter case the vendor contracts to convey only such title as he has, if any. It has been suggested that no covenants for title need be given on a compulsory acquisition, but there is some authority against this view[9].

---

2   Cf. *Vartoukian v Daejan Properties Ltd* (1969) 20 P & CR 983 (covenant to pay rent of £30 valuable consideration for the purposes of the LCA 1972). See note 14, p. 398, ante.
3   *Butler v Mountview Estates Ltd* [1951] 2 KB 563, [1951] 1 All ER 693.
4   See LPA 1925, s. 77 (1) (A), (C), Sch. 2, Parts VII, IX.
5   See p. 633, post.
6   LPA 1925, s. 76 (1) (C); Sch. 2, Part III.
7   LPA 1925, s. 76 (1) (D); Sch. 2, Part IV.
8   LPA 1925, s. 76 (4).
9   The opinion expressed in 34 Halsbury's Laws (3rd edn), 352, can no longer be sustained, it

3.   Conveys and is expressed to convey

Section 76 implies the appropriate covenant by a person *'who conveys and is expressed to convey'* in a stated capacity. Do these words require that the vendor must actually possess the capacity in which he is expressed to convey? Much controversy and conflict of opinion, judicial and otherwise, rages around this question. The phraseology adopted by the parliamentary draftsman appears to have been quite deliberate, and in marked contrast to the wording of s. 77, where covenants are implied on the part of a person who conveys *or* is expressed to convey as beneficial owner[10]. Starting with dicta in *Fay v Miller Wilkins & Co*[11], judicial opinion during the past four decades has certainly favoured an interpretation which requires the vendor to possess the actual capacity in which he is expressed to convey, failing which no covenants are implied. The most recent observations have been made by Megarry J in *Re Robertson's Application*[12], a case concerning a tenant's application to acquire the freehold under the Leasehold Reform Act 1967, where the identity of the landlord was unknown. After referring to section 10 of the Act[13], he continued:

> ' In such a case it may perhaps suffice if in the conveyance the owner is merely expressed to convey "as trustee". Yet by the Law of Property Act 1925, section 76 (1) (F), the appropriate covenant is implied by the use of this phrase only if the grantor in fact "conveys" as trustee, as well as being expressed to convey thus: see *Fay v Miller Wilkins & Co*. If he is in fact a beneficial owner it may be said that he will not in fact be conveying as trustee and so the covenant will not be implied merely by expressing that he conveys "as trustee". If this is so, the covenant should be imposed by inserting words of covenant in the conveyance[14], and not by merely relying on the statutory implication.'

This modern trend of judicial opinion is inconsistent with several pre-1926 decisions which proceed on the basis that the vendor's actual capacity is irrelevant, though the point seems to have been assumed rather than specifically argued. For instance, in *Eastwood v Ashton*[15] the House of Lords awarded damages for breach of the covenants in a case where the vendor had ceased to be owner of part of the land because he had allowed a stranger to acquire title to it by adverse possession. Similarly in *Wise v Whitburn*[16] a breach of the fiduciary owner's limited covenant was held to have occurred

---

seems, in view of *Re King, Robinson v Gray* [1962] 2 All ER 66, especially at 82, per Buckley J (executor vendor required on compulsory acquisition of leasehold premises to give the covenant implied by s. 76 (1) (F), p. 620, ante; revsd. in part on other grounds, [1963] 2 QB 459, [1963] 1 All ER 781, CA).

10   Sub-s. (1) (B) (ii), (D) (ii). See Russell, op. cit., p. 124, who points out that the three Conveyancing Bills in 1880–81 adopted the formula 'is expressed to convey as beneficial owner'. The words 'conveys and' were only added at the eleventh hour.

11   [1941] Ch 360 at 363, 366, [1941] 2 All ER 18 at 23, 26, CA, per Lord Greene MR, and Clauson LJ respectively. It may well be that this conclusion forms part of the ratio of this case: *Pilkington v Wood* [1953] Ch 770 at 777, [1953] 2 All ER 810 at 813, per Harman J.

12   [1969] 1 All ER 257 at 258. Cf. M & W, 603, note 60, where the learned authors state that the actual interest of the vendor should be irrelevant. And see Emmet, 520, Farrand, 263.

13   This section sets out the rights conveyed to the tenant. The landlord gives only the limited covenant: see p. 633, post.

14   Megarry J approved a form of conveyance incorporating such a clause which at the worst would be 'mere surplusage' (at 259).

15   [1915] AC 900.

16   [1924] 1 Ch 460. See also *David v Sabin* [1893] 1 Ch 523 (life tenant conveyancing 'as beneficial owner'); *Parker v Judkin* [1931] 1 Ch 475.

when executors, after assenting to the vesting of leasehold property in a life tenant, purported to assign it after her death to a purchaser 'as personal representatives'.

If the modern interpretation is subsequently upheld (for none of the earlier decisions were apparently cited in the more recent cases), it will have unfortunate repercussions. Prior to the Act of 1881 the vendor's actual capacity was irrelevant because he entered into express covenants, so that what was intended simply as a form of statutory shorthand to reduce the length of conveyances has effected a substantive alteration in the law[17]. Furthermore under this view the covenants afford no protection when it is perhaps most needed, that is where the so-called beneficial owner has previously disposed of his whole estate in the land, in which event he is not even an owner and can convey nothing[18]. Should the conveyance fail to give effect to the contract because the covenant which the vendor contracted to give has not in fact been implied, the purchaser should not overlook the possibility of seeking rectification of the conveyance. This remedy might mitigate the harshness of a strict interpretation of s. 76, but remembering the old adage that prevention is better than cure, it is surely preferable to adopt a construction which avoids these difficulties.

4. Variations

Any implied covenant may be varied or extended with the like incidents, effects and consequences as if such variations or extensions were directed to be implied by the section[19]. The need for some suitable variation is clearly essential on the sale by a beneficial owner of leasehold property which, in breach of covenant, is in a state of disrepair. His implied covenant is in the nature of a warranty that the covenants have been duly performed and he thus renders himself liable to the purchaser, even though the latter is aware of the breach of covenant[20]. Limitation of the vendor's covenant for title in this situation is now expressly provided for by the standard Conditions of Sale[1]. Where the conveyance fails to give effect to some contractual variation of the normal covenant for title, a claim for rectification of the conveyance will lie[2].

B   Enforceability of covenants

1. Burden

Even the covenant for title given by a vendor conveying 'as beneficial owner' does not constitute an absolute warranty of title. He assumes liability for the acts or omissions of himself and of certain other people for whom he is made responsible. The liability extends to the acts or omissions of—

---

17   This is, of course, not unknown. See the LPA 1925, s. 78, (p. 537, ante) as interpreted by *Smith and Snipes Hall Farm Ltd v River Douglas Catchment Board* [1949] 2 KB 500, [1949] 2 All ER 179, CA.

18   (1882) 2 LQR 511; cf. *Eastwood v Ashton* [1915] AC 900.

19   LPA 1925, s. 76 (7).

20   *Butler v Mountview Estates Ltd* [1951] 2 KB 563, [1951] 1 All ER 693.

 1   NCS 11 (7); LSC 8 (4). The LS Condition operates notwithstanding there is a special condition requiring sale as 'beneficial owner' thereby negativing the argument that in such a case the condition became inoperative. See (1974) 38 Conv (NS) 312.

 2   *Stait v Fenner* [1912] 2 Ch 504; *Butler v Mountview Estates Ltd* [1951] 2 KB 563, [1951] 1 All ER 693.

(i)   the vendor himself,
(ii)   any person through whom he claims otherwise than for value (and for this purpose 'value' does *not* include marriage[3]),
(iii) any person claiming by, through or under the vendor, or some person within (ii),
(iv)   any person claiming in trust for the vendor[4].

Groups (ii) and (iii) require further explanation.

(a) Liability for predecessors

A vendor conveying 'as beneficial owner' is not rendered liable for the acts or omissions of any person from whom he purchased the land for value. Lindley LJ explained the position in the following terms[5]:

> ' The covenant by a vendor in fee is not understood as extending to acts done previously to the last preceding sale. On each sale the title is investigated, and conveyancers are content with a series of covenants for title each of which covers the time which has elapsed since the last conveyance from a vendor in fee.'

Suppose A conveys land to B who later conveys it to C, the conveyances being for value and both vendors conveying 'as beneficial owner'. The burden of A's covenant does not pass to B. Moreover B is not liable on his own covenants given to C in respect of any incumbrance created by A which causes disturbance to C, since B derives title through A by virtue of a purchase for value[6]. But B is liable for the acts or omissions of a person through whom he derives title *otherwise than by purchase for value*. If in the above illustration A had devised the property to B, B would be liable for any incumbrance created by A. If this were not so, C would be without remedy; no action could be maintained against A's estate because A, having died, has not entered into any covenant. B would similarly be liable if he had acquired the land from A by way of gift or marriage settlement.

(b) Liability for persons deriving title under him

A covenantor is liable for the acts or omissions of persons claiming from him a *derivative* interest, such as his lessee, or mortgagee. In *David v Sabin*[7]:

> A leased land to B who mortgaged the land to M by demise. B surrendered his lease to A for value without disclosing the mortgage to M, which remained unaffected by the surrender. Later A conveyed the land to B in fee 'as beneficial owner', and B conveyed to C. *Held*: the creation of the mortgage term by B was an incumbrance 'made by a person rightfully claiming through' A within the covenant for quiet enjoyment and freedom from incumbrances and C was entitled to damages[8].

---

3 See the LPA 1925, Sch. 2, Part I. Cf. note 8, p. 619, ante.
4 Per Lindley LJ in *David v Sabin* [1893] 1 Ch 523 at 532, CA.
5 *David v Sabin* [1893] 1 Ch 523 at 534, CA.
6 This is not to say that C has no remedy. It will be seen that the *benefit* of A's covenant passes to C, enabling C to sue A.
7 [1893] 1 Ch 523, CA.
8 It was also held that there was a breach of A's covenant for good right to convey; the grant of the lease to B, which was still outstanding for M's benefit, was an act done by A within that covenant.

It should be noted that the covenantor is not liable for the acts of his successors in title. Thus had A originally conveyed (and not merely leased) the land to B who had created the mortgage term, and B had then conveyed to C without disclosing the mortgage, A would not have been liable to C for the incumbrance created by B. B would be liable for his own act.

2.   Benefit

The benefit of the implied covenant is annexed and incident to, and passes with, the estate of the implied covenantee[9]. If A conveys land to B, and then B to C, C obtains the benefit of any covenant which A gave B, and C can enforce the covenant against A. A purchaser may, therefore, receive the benefit of a chain of covenants for title which previous vendors entered into at the time of their respective conveyances. In theory this affords partial relief against the principle, already noted, that covenants for title do not constitute an absolute warranty of title. Yet in practice the protection afforded by this chain of covenants is rather illusory; previous vendors in the chain may have died, or merely given a fiduciary owner covenant, or the right of action may be time barred because more than twelve years have elapsed since the date of their respective conveyances[10]. In effect the purchaser may frequently find that he is limited to suing on the covenant given by his own vendor.

The benefit of the implied covenant is enforceable by every person in whom the covenantee's estate is, for the whole or any part thereof, from time to time vested. Therefore on a sub-division of land, a purchaser of part obtains the benefit of the covenant given by the vendor of the entirety. Where a man by fraud procures a conveyance of land to him with the usual covenants for title, and then conveys to a purchaser for value without notice of the fraud, the benefit of the original vendor's covenant still passes to that purchaser, and the original vendor cannot plead the fraud as a defence to an action brought against him by the innocent purchaser[11].

(a) Mortgages

The extent to which a mortgagee receives the benefit of covenants implied on the occasion of previous transactions affecting the land is uncertain[12]. If V 'as beneficial owner' conveys land to P who mortgages it to M, it seems that M does not take the benefit of V's implied covenant with P. The mortgage takes effect as a demise. There is nothing in s. 76 (6), which in this respect merely confirms the common law rule, to extend the benefit of covenants for title to persons deriving title under the covenantee, such as his lessee or mortgagee, as distinct from successors in title to his estate. M's inability to sue V (or any earlier covenantor) would not seem to be unduly prejudicial (save where the mortgagor's covenant is worthless on account of his insolvency), for the covenant for title given by P to M is *absolute*[13] with the result that P assumes responsibility for the acts and omissions of his predecessors, including those through whom he claims by purchase for value. It has been argued[14], however, that M acquires the benefit of V's covenant by virtue of the Law of Property Act 1925, s. 78 (1).

---

9   LPA 1925, s. 76 (6).
10   For the running of time, see pp. 628 and 631, post.
11   *David v Sabin* [1893] 1 Ch 523, CA.
12   See Prichard 'Mortgages and Covenants for Title' (1964) 28 Conv (NS) 205.
13   Page 621, ante.
14   Farrand, 267.

This conclusion may be satisfactory so far as a mortgagee is concerned; unfortunately it also results in the benefit passing to a lessee, which seems contrary to the spirit of s. 76. No statutory covenant for title is implied on the demise of land at a rent. Consequently the anomalous position is reached that the lessee, though unable to enforce any statutory covenant for title against his own lessor, may be able by virtue of s. 78 (1) to bring an action against some predecessor in title of the lessor and this notwithstanding that the lessee has no statutory right to investigate the superior title[15]. This, it is conceived, cannot be correct.

It is generally assumed that on a conveyance of land by a mortgagee in exercise of his power of sale, the purchaser obtains the benefit of the mortgagor's absolute covenant[16]. Though strictly speaking the purchaser obtains a larger interest than the mortgagee possessed, the conveyance by the latter operates to convey the estate in like manner as if it had been executed by the mortgagor[17], and this would appear sufficient to entitle the purchaser to the benefit of the mortgagor's covenant with the mortgagee.

(b) Burden of proof

Some limitations on the effectiveness of a chain of covenants have already been noted. There is a further hurdle to bar the progress of a purchaser seeking to enforce a covenant for title — the burden of proof. Thus in the illustration on page 625, C may have the benefit of covenants given by A and B, but the onus is on him to establish whether it is A, or B, who is liable, a task that may be well nigh impossible if the origin of the adverse claim is uncertain[18].

C   Particular covenants

1.   Good right to convey

The first section of the covenant implied in a conveyance for valuable consideration by a person who conveys and is expressed to convey as beneficial owner, reads as follows:

> ' That, notwithstanding anything by the person who so conveys or any one through whom he derives title otherwise than by purchase for value, made, done, executed, or omitted, or knowingly suffered, the person who so conveys has . . . full power to convey the subject-matter expressed to be conveyed, subject as, if so expressed, and in the manner in which, it is expressed to be conveyed . . .'

This covenant is a covenant for title. It constitutes an assurance that neither the vendor nor any person for whom he is responsible has done or omitted to do any act which will prevent the purchaser acquiring 'the subject-matter expressed to be conveyed'. Herein lies one justification for the continued use of

---

15 LPA 1925, s. 44 (2), p. 304, ante. The argument based on s. 78 (1) is not without its attractions, but the whole tenor of the LPA 1925, restricting as it does a lessee's rights in relation to the superior title, appears to militate against it, at least as regards matters of title.

16 2 Williams V & P, 1076.

17 LPA 1925, ss. 9 (1) (e), 88 (1).

18 *Stoney v Eastbourne Rural Council* [1927] 1 Ch 367 (no evidence when right of way dedicated to public). The potential liability on covenants is well illustrated by this case in that the property had been in the vendor's family from 1782.

technical words of limitation. A conveyance of land to a purchaser to hold 'in fee simple' signifies that it purports to deal with a fee simple estate. The covenant for title operates as a warranty that the vendor has such an estate in the land, though this is subject to an important qualification to be considered shortly. In the absence of such words there passes the fee simple or other the whole interest which the vendor has power to convey[19]. In other words the 'subject-matter expressed to be conveyed' is such interest as he actually has, if any. If he has no title, the purchaser cannot sue on the covenant for the simple reason that the vendor has not covenanted that he has any title. Nor can the purchaser sue in respect of any defect or incumbrance subject to which the property is expressed to be conveyed, these for obvious reasons being outside the scope of the covenant. Where the property is not expressed in the conveyance to be conveyed subject to a specific defect or incumbrance, a purchaser is not debarred from suing on the covenant in respect thereof merely because he has knowledge of it, even if the defect appears on the face of the conveyance itself.[20].

(a) Breach of covenant

A breach of the covenant occurs if the land conveyed remains subject to any outstanding estate, interest, mortgage, charge or claim, to which the conveyance is not expressly made subject[1], such as an undisclosed right of way[2] or other easement. The vendor is liable if he has previously conveyed or leased part of the land which he subsequently purports to convey to the purchaser[3]. The covenant also extends to 'omissions'. In *Eastwood v Ashton*[4]:

> V conveyed land to P. At the date of the conveyance an adverse title to a strip of land had been acquired by adjoining owners. V's failure to prevent acquisition of this adverse title constituted an omission within the covenant, for which he was liable.

But a vendor is not guilty of an omission within the covenant because he fails to perfect his title by getting in some incumbrance which was created by a previous vendor and of which he is unaware[5]. As previously mentioned the onus of proof lies on the covenantee. He must establish that the act or omission creating the defect is that of the vendor (or of someone for whom he is responsible). If, therefore, it is uncertain when adverse possession first commenced, or when a right of way became dedicated to the public[6], the plaintiff's claim will fail. He cannot show that his vendor is in breach.

There is no breach of the covenant where the purchaser is evicted by *a title paramount*. This is a vital qualification. The covenant is not a complete

---

19 See the LPA 1925, s. 60 (1), p. 531, ante.
20 *Page v Midland Rly Co* [1894] 1 Ch 11, CA (defect disclosed by recital); *Great Western Rly Co v Fisher* [1905] 1 Ch 316.
1 2 Williams V & P, 1078.
2 *Turner v Moon* [1901] 2 Ch 825; *David v Sabin* [1893] 1 Ch 523, CA (outstanding mortgage).
3 *May v Platt* [1900] 1 Ch 616; *Conodate Investments Ltd v Bentley Quarry Engineering Co Ltd* (1970) 216 Estates Gazette 1407. Cf. *Butler v Broadhead* [1974] 2 All ER 401 (innocent double conveyance; purchaser unable to recover from its vendor company after dissolution).
4 [1915] AC 900, HL. For the suggestion that 'omitted' was an error for 'committed', see Russell, op. cit., pp. 268–9.
5 *David v Sabin* [1893] 1 Ch 523 at 529, per Romer J; at 534, per Lindley LJ, CA. He would, however, be liable for its creation if it was the act of someone for whom he was responsible.
6 *Stoney v Eastbourne Rural Council* [1927] 1 Ch 367. Difficult problems arise where the defect is an easement acquired by prescription; see Prichard, op. cit., p. 206, note 6.

warranty that the vendor has a title, rather that he has done no act to affect or derogate from his title[7]. As Lord Eldon once explained, the vendor is to be taken as selling his land in the plight that he received it and not in any degree made worse by him[8]. A purchaser cannot, therefore, sue his vendor on the covenant if the latter never had any title at all, or if his interest ceases before completion otherwise than as result of his own act or default[9]. The purchaser may be able to sue a previous vendor through whose act or omission the title was lost. Suppose A conveys land to B, and later purports to convey the same land to C. C conveys it to D. On eviction by B, D cannot sue C, but he gets the benefit of A's covenant with C and can maintain an action against A because the conveyance to B is a breach of A's implied covenant with C. However, it is not difficult to visualise circumstances when the purchaser may be completely without remedy. It seems that the vendor incurs no liability under the statutory covenants where, for instance, the conveyance includes land which never belonged to the vendor or his predecessors but is vested in some adjacent owner under an independent title, or land wrongfully occupied by the vendor and in respect of which no title has been acquired under the Limitation Act 1980[10]. If the vendor knows he has no title, the purchaser may be entitled to have the conveyance set aside for fraud or recover damages in an action in tort or misrepresentation[11].

Where a vendor with no title purports to convey land to a purchaser, equity will compel him to make good his contract with the purchaser if he later acquires title to the land[12]. He cannot plead that the contract has been discharged by performance, because the conveyance is defective. If in the illustration given in the preceding paragraph B (the true owner) devises the land to C, equity will require C to convey it to D, irrespective of any covenant for further assurance. Moreover, a recital of C's seisin in the first C-D conveyance may work an estoppel[13] and operate to vest the land in D without any further conveyance, as soon as C acquires the title.

(b) Limitation

Breach of this covenant occurs and is complete at the time of execution of the conveyance[14]. It is not a continuing breach. Time begins to run in the covenantor's favour as from that date, not from the time when the covenantee first learns of the breach.

7   *Thackeray v Wood* (1865) 6 B & S 766 at 773, per Erle CJ.
8   *Browning v Wright* (1799) 2 Bos & P 13 at 22. The then Chief Justice continued (at 23): 'What is the common course of business in such a case? An abstract is laid before the purchaser's counsel, and though to a certain extent he relies on the vendor's covenants, still his chief attention is directed to ascertaining what is the estate, and how far it is supported by the title. The purchaser, therefore, not being misled by the vendor, makes up his mind whether he shall complete his bargain or not . . .' This can only be a satisfactory explanation if the abstract reveals the non-existence of the vendor's title. In most cases it does not, for if it did, the purchaser would presumably not complete. This rule is simply another illustration of the principle of caveat emptor.
9   *Stannard v Forbes* (1837) 6 Ad & El 572 (assignment of leasehold term known by vendor to have determined on death of third party).
10   *Thackeray v Wood* (1865) 6 B & S 766 at 768, per Martin B arguendo. See also Sweetman 'Good Right to Convey' (1954) 18 Conv (NS) 362; 1 Williams V & P, 665.
11   See *Watts v Spence* [1975] 2 All ER 528; *Errington v Martell-Wilson* (1980) 130 NLJ 545, [1981] Conv 167.
12   *Smith v Osborne* (1857) 6 HL Cas 375 at 390, per Lord Cranworth LC; *Re Bridgwater's Settlement, Partridge v Ward* [1910] 2 Ch 342.
13   For recitals as estoppels, see p. 501, ante.
14   *Turner v Moon* [1901] 2 Ch 825. Cf. Kelly CB's dissenting judgment in *Spoor v Green* (1874) LR 9 Exch 99 at 116.

(c) Measure of damages

The measure of damages, assessed as at the date of the conveyance, is the difference between the value of the property as purported to be conveyed and its value as the vendor had power to convey it[15]. In the absence of evidence to the contrary, the price actually paid is taken to be the value as purported to be conveyed. Thus, depending on particular circumstances, the purchaser can recover money paid to a third party in order to enjoy the land in the actual state in which he was entitled by the contract to enjoy it[16], or the amount by which the adverse interest diminishes the value of the property, or even the full purchase price if he suffers total eviction[17]. Though there is an absence of authority on the point, the costs of subsequent improvements to the property do not seem recoverable on a breach of the covenant for good right to convey[18].

2. Quiet enjoyment free from incumbrances

This part of the covenant reads:

> '. . . and that, notwithstanding anything as aforesaid, the subject-matter shall remain to and be quietly entered upon, received and held, occupied, enjoyed, and taken, by the person to whom the conveyance is expressed to be made, and any person deriving title under him, and the benefit thereof shall be received and taken accordingly, without any lawful interruption or disturbance by the person who so conveys . . .
>
> And that, freed and discharged from, or otherwise by the person who so conveys sufficiently indemnified against, all such estates, incumbrances, claims and demands, other than those subject to which the conveyance is expressly made, as, either before or after the date of the conveyance, have been or shall be made, occasioned, or suffered by that person . . .'

This is a covenant against disturbance and for indemnity in that event. The words 'And that, freed and discharged from' are sometimes interpreted as creating a separate covenant that the estate is free from incumbrances[19]. The better view[20] is that both parts constitute a single obligation. The vendor covenants that the land will be quietly enjoyed free from incumbrances and, in effect, he undertakes to indemnify the purchaser in the event of his enjoyment being disturbed by the enforcement of some incumbrance. In addition to assuming responsibility for the acts of predecessors in title through whom he claims otherwise than by purchase for value, the covenantor is liable for lawful disturbance caused by a person claiming through[1], under or in trust for him. He is not responsible for unauthorised wrongful or negligent acts of persons

15 *Turner v Moon* [1901] 2 Ch 825.
16 *Great Western Rly Co v Fisher* [1905] 1 Ch 316 (compensation paid for blocking up right of way).
17 *Jenkins v Jones* (1882) 9 QBD 128, CA.
18 2 Dart, 676; 2 Williams V & P, 1090. But see p. 631, post, and compare the position under the Sale of Goods Act 1979, ss. 12, 53 (2): *Mason v Burningham* [1949] 2 KB 545, [1949] 2 All ER 134, CA (cost of overhauling stolen typewriter recoverable).
19 See, e.g., Joyce J in *Turner v Moon* [1901] 2 Ch 825 at 828. So to interpret this part of the covenant is to add little, if anything, to the covenant for good right to convey.
20 2 Williams V & P, 1080; Farrand, 258, Williams, *Title*, 755, [1979] Conv 93 (C.K. Liddle). For the contrary view see Russell 'The Principal Covenants for Title' (1970) 34 Conv (NS) 178, 187.
 1 This is limited to persons with a derivative title only, pp. 624–625, ante.

claiming under him[2]. Again it will be noticed that the covenantee cannot complain of any disturbance, claim or demand resulting from an incumbrance subject to which the conveyance is expressly made. No action lies where the liability is imposed, not as a result of the vendor's conduct, but by statute or under the common law[3]. As with the previous covenant, no protection is afforded in cases of disturbance by title paramount.

(a) Breach of the covenant

The covenantee must prove that he has actually been disturbed in his possession, or his enjoyment interrupted by the enforcement of some adverse claim. The mere existence of some incumbrance effects no breach of this covenant, though it may give rise to liability under the covenant for good right to convey. In *Howard v Maitland*[4] it was held that a court decree declaring that land in Epping Forest, including land previously conveyed by the defendant to the plaintiff, was subject to a general right of common was not actionable because there had been no entry on the land nor any disturbance of the plaintiff's possession. A breach of the covenant is established on proof of the existence of some adverse right of way, a threat of eviction by some person to whom the vendor conveyed the land prior to its purported conveyance to the plaintiff[5], a decree or judgment against the purchaser recognising the existence of some third party claim[6], or the discharge by the purchaser of some mortgage or charge affecting the land. In *Stock v Meakin*[7] the vendor was held liable to indemnify the purchaser in respect of private street works expenses, though the final apportionment was not made until after completion. The expenses were an 'incumbrance, claim or demand suffered' by the vendor, notwithstanding they were incurred without any default on his part. In relation to charges in favour of local authorities, it must be remembered that the Conditions of Sale will normally regulate the respective rights of the parties in relation to the discharge of expenses due to a local authority[8]. It has been suggested[9] that service of an enforcement notice on the purchaser consequent upon a contravention of the town and country planning legislation by the vendor is a 'claim or demand' occasioned by the vendor so as to render him liable for breach of the implied statutory covenant, but again the terms of the contract between the parties cannot be ignored.

The covenant for quiet enjoyment cannot enlarge the scope of the conveyance to the purchaser. He cannot complain that acts lawfully done by the vendor on his adjoining land amount to a breach of the covenant merely because such acts cause him inconvenience, without affecting his title or possession to the land. This rule applies whether the adjoining land was owned by the vendor at the time of the conveyance or acquired subsequently, except that

---

2   See *Williams v Gabriel* [1906] 1 KB 155 (a landlord and tenant case). The covenant for quiet enjoyment given by a vendor is very similar to that implied on the grant of a lease.
3   *Chivers & Sons Ltd v Air Ministry* [1955] Ch 585, [1955] 2 All ER 607, CA (liability to repair church chancel).
4   (1883) 11 QBD 695, CA.
5   *Conodate Investments Ltd v Bentley Quarry Engineering Co Ltd* (1970) 216 Estates Gazette 1407.
6   *Howard v Maitland* (1883) 11 QBD 695 at 700, per Brett MR. The vendor was not a party to the suit in Chancery establishing the right of common.
7   [1900] 1 Ch 683, CA. Aliter if the expenses are not a charge upon the land: *Egg v Blayney* (1888) 21 QBD 107.
8   See NCS 16; LSC 3.
9   Emmet, 523.

in the former case the vendor may be liable, not upon the covenant, but upon the principle of non-derogation from grant[10].

(b) Measure of damages

This covenant is broken when the purchaser's quiet enjoyment is actually disturbed. For the purposes of the Limitation Act 1980, time begins to run from the occasion of the breach and, the covenant being a continuing one, a fresh cause of action accrues on every disturbance. The measure of damages is also referable to the date of the breach. It follows that where the interruption takes the form of eviction, the covenantee can recover the value of the property at the date of the breach, including any increase in value since conveyance due to a general rise in land prices. In *Bunny v Hopkinson*[11] it was held that the purchaser could recover the value of improvements, in that case the cost of erecting houses on the land. Sir John Romilly MR, rejected an argument that so to hold would impose on the covenantor an unlimited liability depending on what the covenantee might later erect on the land. The land had in fact been purchased for building purposes, so the erection of houses was within the contemplation of the parties. However, it seems that the value of improvements are recoverable, even though they may not be within the covenantor's contemplation at the time of the conveyance[12]. The covenantee can recover any loss which is the natural consequence of the breach, such as expenses involved in moving into other premises, or the cost of defending an action brought against him by an adverse claimant, provided he notifies the covenantor of the action to obtain his instructions as to the course to be adopted[13].

Where there is no eviction but, for example, the interruption takes the form of the exercise of a right of way, the Court of Appeal held in *Child v Stenning*[14] that the measure of damages is not the permanent injury to the land[15] but only the damage actually sustained at the commencement of the action. The court refused to accept as evidence of damage the diminution in the value of the land for building purposes. Subsequent cases have not always adhered to this principle. In *Sutton v Baillie*[16], Cave J awarded damages to a purchaser for depreciation in the value of the land by reason of the existence of rights of way. In *Turner v Moon*[17], Joyce J reached a similar decision in effect; but since the

10   See *Davis v Town Properties Investment Corpn Ltd* [1903] 1 Ch 797, CA; *Harmer v Jumbil (Nigeria) Tin Areas Ltd* [1921] 1 Ch 200, CA (both landlord-tenant cases). Cf. *Tebb v Cave* [1900] 1 Ch 642, doubted in *Davis's* case. See generally [1978] Conv 418 (M.J. Russell).
11   (1859) 27 Beav 565.
12   *Rolph v Crouch* (1867) LR 3 Exch 44 (cost of conservatory recovered). Cf. *Lewis v Campbell* (1819) 8 Taunt 715. Since the benefit of the covenant passes to the covenantee's successors in title, it would be improper to limit the damages to those recoverable under the normal contractual rule.
13   *Rolph v Crouch* (1867) LR 3 Exch 44. See generally, 2 Williams V & P, 1089–91.
14   (1879) 11 Ch D 82 (an action for breach of the covenant for quiet enjoyment contained in a lease).
15   This could not be ascertained since it was uncertain to what extent, if at all, the incumbrancer might choose to exercise his right in the future: per Jessel MR, at 85.
16   (1891) 65 LT 528. It is sometimes said (in reliance on certain observations of Jessel MR in *Child v Stenning* (1879) 11 Ch D 82 at 85) that the difference between the two cases lies in the fact that in a conveyance by a beneficial owner there is in addition to the covenant for quiet enjoyment of a covenant for good right to convey: see *McGregor on Damages* (13th edn), para. 719. Nevertheless there is nothing in the report of *Sutton v Baillie* to suggest that damages were awarded otherwise than for breach of the covenant for quiet enjoyment.
17   [1901] 2 Ch 825, especially at 829, see p. 629, ante.

learned judge equated the covenant for freedom from incumbrances with that for good right to convey, rather than treating it as part of the covenant for quiet enjoyment, the correctness of his decision on this point may be doubted. Nevertheless, it would seem preferable to allow the recovery of permanent injury, including diminution in the value of the land, if such injury can be shown to have been suffered at the time the writ is served.

3.   Further assurance

This covenant imposes on the vendor an obligation to 'execute and do all such lawful assurances and things for further or more perfectly assuring the subject-matter of the conveyance' to the grantee, provided the outstanding estate is vested in him, or in some person for whom he assumed responsibility. If V conveys to P a plot of land to which V has no title, but subsequently he acquires title thereto, whether for value or not, P can call upon V to convey it to him[18]. The cost of the deed of further assurance must be borne by P, but this apart he cannot be required to compensate V in any way. If V refuses to execute the necessary deed, P can sue for specific performance. The covenant can be enforced against V's trustee in bankruptcy[19], or his successors in title, including a purchaser with notice of the covenant[20]. The purchaser can enforce the covenant notwithstanding that the legal title may have automatically vested in him under the doctrine of estoppel[1]. Indeed a conveyance from the vendor is highly desirable in order to perfect the paper title. It appears from certain old cases that the deed of further assurance should not itself contain additional covenants for title[2].

A purchaser can rely on the covenant to require the vendor to discharge an undisclosed mortgage affecting the property[3], or, it seems, to regrant a valid future easement where the vendor's original grant was void for perpetuity[4]. There is ancient authority for saying that the covenant obliges the covenantor to execute a duplicate if the original has been accidentally destroyed by the purchaser[5] or handed over to a later purchaser of part of the land sold[6]. It is, however, open to question whether the implied covenant extends to situations like these, where the original conveyance is fully effective to vest the legal title in the purchaser and the need for a duplicate or confirmatory assurance stems solely from some act or neglect on the part of the purchaser, occurring after the original grant[7].

---

18   For cases where equity will compel execution of a conveyance in the absence of this covenant, see p. 628, ante. This covenant would be relied on if the purchaser failed to register his title within the two months period as required by LRA 1925, s. 123, with the consequent avoiding of the conveyance.

19   *Re Phelps, ex p Fripp* (1846) 1 De G 293.

20   The burden of the covenant, though not running with the land, constitutes a covenant to convey which equity will specifically enforce. See 2 Williams V & P, 1085.

1   Page 501, ante.

2   34 Halsbury's Laws (3rd edn) 377, note (c), citing *Coles v Kinder* (1620) Cro Jac 571; 2 Williams V & P, 1087.

3   *Re Jones, Farrington v Forrester* [1893] 2 Ch 461.

4   See p. 523, ante. Disposal of the servient land would render the vendor liable to an action of damages at the purchaser's instance.

5   *Bennett v Ingoldsby* (1676) Cas *Temp* Finch 262.

6   *Napper v Lord Allington* (1700) 1 Eq Cas Abr 166; 2 Dart, 673.

7   Cf. the rule that the covenant for quiet enjoyment is not broken when the disturbance is the natural consequence of the covenantee's own act or default; see *Norton on Deeds* (2nd edn), p. 617.

4.   Covenant given by fiduciary vendor

A vendor who conveys and is expressed to convey as trustee, mortgagee or personal representative covenants that he has:

> ' . . . not executed, or done, or knowingly suffered, or been party or privy to, any deed or thing whereby . . . the subject-matter of the conveyance . . . is or maybe impeached, charged, affected, or incumbered in title, estate or otherwise, or whereby . . . [he] is in anywise hindered from conveying the subject-matter of the conveyance . . . in the manner in which it is expressed to be conveyed.'

This is a somewhat limited covenant in comparison with the beneficial owner covenants just discussed. It is expressly limited to the covenantor's own acts only[8]. The restricted operation of this covenant is often advocated as a sufficient reason why beneficial co-owners (as is the usual case where the vendors are husband and wife) should convey, not as trustees, but as beneficial owners. The covenant is broken by the vendor's creation of some adverse incumbrance, or by a previous conveyance or assent by him[9] of the property. The covenantor's obligations are limited to anything 'executed, or done, or knowingly suffered'; the word 'omitted' is significantly absent. The word 'suffer' has been widely interpreted in different contexts but it does not cover the failure to prevent the acquisition of an adverse title by a squatter. In *Eastwood v Ashton*[10] the House of Lords held that such failure was an 'omission' within the covenant for good right to convey[11]. Liability also arises if the covenantor has been 'party or privy' to a deed creating an incumbrance. In this context 'privy' means, not knowledge, but participation in some act by which the parties will be bound[12]. The covenant therefore catches a mortgagee who, in exercise of his power of sale, conveys the mortgaged property to a purchaser without disclosing the existence of a right of way which the mortgagor created by a deed to which the mortgagee was a party[13].

This covenant applies alike to freehold and leasehold land. As previously noted, an assignment of leasehold land by a vendor 'as personal representative' (for example) implies no covenant that the lease is in full force or that the covenants in the lease have been observed and performed[14]. However, the fiduciary owner's implied covenant overlaps to some extent this special leasehold covenant, for it extends to acts whereby the subject-matter of the assignment 'is or may be impeached', but again there is no protection in respect of omissions such as a failure to repair.

---

8   LPA 1925, s. 76 (1) (F).

9   *Wise v Whitburn* [1924] 1 Ch 460, p. 622, ante.

10   [1915] AC 900 p. 627, ante. See particularly Lord Parker at 913. Compare on the meaning of 'suffer' Luxmoore J in *Barton v Reed* [1932] 1 Ch 362 at 375.

11   At first instance Sargant J held (see [1913] 2 Ch 39 at 54) that the vendor, by allowing the squatter to erect and maintain a boundary fence on his land, 'suffered' something to continue by which his title and power to convey were lost.

12   *Woodhouse v Jenkins* (1838) 9 Bing 431 at 441, per Tindal CJ.

13   Cf. *Clifford v Hoare* (1874) LR 9 CP 362, where the claim against the mortgagee only failed because there was no substantial interference with the plaintiff's interest.

14   Page 621, ante.

D   Registered conveyancing[15]

Neither the Land Registration Act 1925, nor the Rules made thereunder deal with covenants for title in a satisfactory manner, due largely to the wholesale application of the provisions of the Law of Property Act 1925, to the somewhat different statutory rules governing the transfer of registered land. Rule 76 of the Land Registration Rules 1925, states that:

> ' For the purposes of introducing the covenants implied under sections 76 and 77 of the Law of Property Act 1925, a person may, in a registered disposition, be expressed to execute, transfer, or charge as beneficial owner, as settlor, [etc.] . . . but no reference to covenants implied under section 76 aforesaid shall be entered in the register.'

This provision would appear to justify the view that the general law relating to covenants for title applies to registered land, subject only to express modifications made by the Act or the Rules, yet such a conclusion may not be entirely free from doubt[16]. It is the usual practice to incorporate the covenants. The form commonly used by solicitors and obtainable from H.M. Stationery Office includes the expression 'as beneficial owner'[17]. However, to what extent are covenants for title necessary on a sale of registered land, and, if implied, what measure of protection do they afford?

1.   Freehold land

It is generally agreed that the implied covenants for title serve a valid purpose where the title is qualified or possessory, as protection may be necessary in respect of rights or interests subsisting prior to or excepted from registration. Yet these are likely to be the very situations when a beneficial owner is reluctant to enter into full beneficial owner covenants. On the other hand where an absolute title is transferred, it is sometimes stated that covenants for title can rarely be required[18]. Indeed under s. 16 (3) of the Land Transfer Act 1897, a vendor of land registered with an absolute title could not be required to enter into any covenant for title in the absence of a special stipulation, a provision significally omitted from the Act of 1925. Yet an absolute title is not indefeasible. In the event of the register being rectified against the proprietor of an absolute title he is entitled to be indemnified only if he suffers loss[19] and his eviction or disturbance of possession may not always constitute loss for the purposes of the Act. The existence of covenants for title may enable a purchaser to obtain redress from his vendor in circumstances where the Act affords no assistance, for example, where he suffers rectification in order to give effect to an overriding interest[20]. To what extent a purchaser can sue on the implied covenants in any particular case is another question, governed largely by Rule 77.

15   See R & R, 283–304, [1982] Conv 145 (M.J. Russell).
16   For example, it has been argued that LRR 1925, r. 76 relates more to a question of form than of substance: Farrand, 268–269. See also p. 454, ante, on the question whether a transfer of registered land is a 'conveyance' within the LPA 1925, s. 205 (1).
17   A marginal note reads: 'If desired or otherwise as the case may be'. Curiously enough the forms of transfer prescribed by r. 98 omit any reference to the vendor's capacity.
18   2 Williams V & P, 1160; 3 K & E, 127; R & R, 362; cf. Hallett, 1248. See also *Re King, Robinson v Gray* [1962] 2 All ER 66 at 82, per Buckley J.
19   Page 89, ante.
20   See *Re Chowood's Registered Land* [1933] Ch 574, (squatter's adverse title); *Re Boyle's Claim* [1961] 1 All ER 629 (neighbour's trespassing garage).

(a) Rule 77
The wording of this rule should be noted carefully. It provides that any implied covenant for title takes effect *as though the disposition was expressly made subject to —*

(a)   all charges and other interests appearing or protected on the register at the time of the execution of the disposition[1] and affecting the covenantor's title;
(b)   any overriding interests of which the purchaser has notice and subject to which it would have taken effect, had the land been unregistered.

The benefit of any implied covenant runs with the land and can be enforced by the proprietor for the time being of that land[2]. The Registrar can also enforce on behalf of the Crown any implied covenant which a person indemnified under the Act could have enforced in relation to the matter in respect of which indemnity has been paid[3]. The italicised words are important. The covenants for title take effect subject as the property is expressed in the conveyance[4]. In registered conveyancing it is not customary to refer to adverse incumbrances in the transfer[5], nor do the prescribed forms of transfer provide for their express mention; any reference to third party rights is unnecessary in view of s. 20 (1) of the Land Registration Act 1925. Nevertheless r. 77 preserves the unregistered conveyancing position by deeming the transfer to be made expressly subject to interests and charges appearing or protected on the register, thus precluding any action by the purchaser.

(b) Overriding interests
Rule 77 (1) (b) prevents recourse to the covenants for title in respect of overriding interests of which the purchaser has notice. Paragraph (b) has, not without justification, been criticised as being an ill-drafted and misconceived rule[6]. It gives rise to several problems. In unregistered conveyancing cases such as *Great Western Rly Co v Fisher*[7] demonstrate that mere notice of an incumbrance is immaterial to the enforcement of the covenants. It is not clear why a different rule should operate in registered conveyancing. Perhaps the rule is intended to relate to cases where the existence of the overriding interest is disclosed to the purchaser in the contract; in unregistered conveyancing the vendor would be entitled to have the property conveyed expressly subject to that interest, so excluding the operation of any covenant for title. Again

1   This is significant. It does not preclude an action on the covenant in respect of, e.g. restrictive covenants entered on the register after execution of the transfer but before the purchaser's registration as proprietor, though with the protection of a clear official certificate of search, he would take free from such restrictions provided he lodged his application in time (see p. 405, ante).
2   Rule 77 (2). Though this is not clearly stated, it is assumed that the benefit passes to a propietor of part; cf. LPA 1925, s. 76 (6), p. 625, ante.
3   LRA 1925, s. 83 (10).
4   Page 627, ante.
5   Save where on first registration a transfer is used instead of the normal conveyance (p. 447, ante); see Hallett, 1108.
6   See (1970) 34 Conv (NS) 129.
7   [1905] 1 Ch 316, p. 627, ante. In their discussion of overriding interests and covenants for title in Published Working Paper No. 36, para. 28, the Law Commission merely say that it is 'logical' that the purchaser's notice should prevent any action on the covenants, without considering why the rule should have been held to be otherwise in unregistered conveyancing.

r. 77 (1) preserves the position under the general law by deeming the disposition to take effect as though it were expressly made subject to known overriding interests. But the rule goes further. No limitation is placed on the word 'notice' which must extend to notice acquired aliunde[8]. If a case similar to *Fisher's* case but involving registered land were to occur today, no action could be maintained even though the contract was silent about the right of way. Furthermore the additional requirement in (b) that the disposition would have taken effect subject to that interest had the land been unregistered is at present meaningless in relation to certain overriding interests, such as an estate contract or an equitable lease, which may be protected as overriding interests under s. 70 (1) (g) of the Land Registration Act 1925, as being rights of a person in actual occupation of the land. Yet in unregistered conveyancing the enforcement of such interests is determined by their registration as land charges[9], and the Land Charges Act 1972, has no application to registered titles. This difficulty, it is conceived, would disappear if a rule were adopted that an interest capable of protection on the register of title, but not protected in the appropriate manner, could not also rank as an overriding interest.

It would seem a clear inference from r. 77 (1) (b) that a purchaser can obtain redress upon the implied covenants for title in respect of overriding interests of which he has *no notice*. Hitherto it has been assumed that on the transfer of an absolute title the normal implied covenants for title serve some useful purpose within defined limits; nevertheless this assumption is open to serious doubt. Opinion on this vexed issue is at variance, but there is much to commend the view, first advocated by Professor Potter and since adopted by some later commentators[10], that the mere insertion of the words 'as beneficial owner', or as the case may be, so as to imply the statutory covenants, affords no protection even against overriding interests of which the purchaser has no notice. In unregistered conveyancing the covenants for title operate where the conveyance fails to convey what it purports to convey; thus a purchaser sues, for example, because the land is subject to an undisclosed right of way *not* expressed in the conveyance as affecting the land. But on a sale of registered land the vendor can only transfer what he actually possesses by virtue of the Land Registration Act 1925, which is a freehold estate subject (inter alia) to overriding interests, if any, whether disclosed or not[11]. There is no discrepancy between what the purchaser actually gets and what the transfer purports to give to him, and so there is nothing upon which the covenants can bite.

The reader may be pardoned for thinking that this was not the Act's intention. Rules 76 and 77, coupled with the omission from the Act of 1925 of any provision similar to s. 16 (3) of the Land Transfer Act 1897, mentioned on page 634, point to the conclusion that the covenants for title, if introduced,

8   Presumably occupation will be noticé thereby preventing any claim for a right within paragraph (g).
9   Not being so registered, there would be nothing in r. 77 to bar an action on the appropriate covenant for title.
10   Potter, 69; Potter 'Covenants for Title and Overriding Interests' (1942) 58 LQR 356; Emmet, 525–526; Farrand, 270–272; R & R, 288–291; 17 Ency F & P, 194–95; 3 K & E, 127–28; (1941) 57 LQR 564; [1981] Conv 32 (P.H. Kenny); Hayton 67–77.
11   Sections 5 (b), 20 (1) (b). It will not be forgotten that it is not the transfer that vests the legal title in the transferee, but the subsequent registration. It is on this basis that it is contended that the covenant for further assurance is unnecessary (R & R, 287). However suppose the vendor is not registered as proprietor. In such a case if there are difficulties over registration could not the purchaser require the vendor to procure his registration? The covenant would also be useful on first registration (see note 18, p. 632, ante).

apply to overriding interests of which the purchaser has no notice[12]. Nevertheless in view of the uncertainty some precedent books urge the insertion in the transfer of express covenants for title extending to undisclosed overriding interests[13], a recommendation which appears to be ignored in practice. Irrespective of this thorny problem, there may still exist exceptional circumstances[14] justifying the incorporation of the statutory covenants by means of the appropriate expressions.

2. Leasehold titles

On an *assignment* of registered leasehold property certain covenants on the part of both transferor and transferee are implied by s. 24 of the Land Registration Act 1925, unless the transfer indicates to the contrary (in which event an entry negativing their implication is made on the register[15]). These covenants do not operate on the grant of a lease or underlease. The transferee's covenants implied by sub-s. (1) (b), to pay the rent and perform the covenants, differ little from the indemnity covenant implied in an assignment for valuable consideration by virtue of s. 77 (1) (C) of the Law of Property Act 1925[16]. Closer attention must be paid to the transferor's covenants, for, though these are somewhat similar to those implied by s. 76 (1) (B)[17] of the same Act, there are several important differences. The Land Registration Act 1925, s. 24 (1) (a) implies a covenant on the part of the transferor with the transferee that—

> 'notwithstanding anything by such transferor done, omitted or knowingly suffered, the rent, covenants and conditions reserved and contained by and in the registered lease, and on the part of the lessee to be paid, performed, and observed, have been so paid, performed, and observed up to the date of the transfer; . . .'

The following points are to be observed.

1. The s. 24 covenant is not as wide as its unregistered counterpart. It implies no covenant that the lease is valid and subsisting, and limits the covenantor's liability to his own acts or omissions.

2. There is no express provision for the running of the benefit of the covenant[18].

---

12 This is the interpretation favoured by the Law Commission, on the ground that there is no specific provision in the LRR 1925 dealing with unknown overriding interests: see Published Working Paper No. 36, para. 31. The Commission did not consider the argument discussed in the text, but they admitted to the possibility of having over-simplified the statutory provisions in arriving at their suggested interpretation.
13 Hallett, 1248 note (t); 3 K & E, 128, 408, where a precedent of a suitable clause is given, though its necessity is queried. Express stipulation for such a clause would be required in the contract.
14 E.g., boundary disputes: Hallett, 1248 note 1 (c); and see *Re Boyle's Claim* [1961] 1 All ER 620, where the transferee's claim to indemnity might now be barred by the LRA 1925, s. 83 (5) (a), as substituted by the LR & LCA 1971, s. 3 (1), p. 91, ante.
15 LRR 1925, r. 115. It is the entry on the register giving effect to the statement in the transfer that operates to negative their implication.
16 See p. 544, ante.
17 See p. 620, ante.
18 Cf. LPA 1925, s. 76 (6), though perhaps the benefit of the covenant in s. 24 (1) (a) runs under the LPA 1925, s. 78.

3. Under s. 24 the covenant is implied irrespective of whether the assignment is for value and—this is most important—it is *not* dependent on the transferor's capacity as beneficial owner[19]. This obviously constitutes a trap for the unwary, for as previously noted the normal assignment of leasehold property by a fiduciary owner implies the limited covenant against personal incumbrance only (s. 76 (1) (F)), not the wider leasehold covenant under s. 76 (1) (B) which is given by a beneficial owner[20]. Where the transferor is, e.g. a trustee or personal representative, the practitioner must not overlook the fact that the s. 24 covenant will be automatically implied, unless it is expressly excluded or modified, and for this to be forced on a purchaser there must be express provision in the contract[1]. The Law Commission tentatively suggest[2] the repeal of s. 24, thus leaving the parties to incorporate the Law of Property Act 1925, covenants by the use of the appropriate statutory formula.

For the sake of completeness mention may perhaps be made of s. 24 (2), though like sub-s. (1) (b) the covenants implied by sub-s. (2) are not strictly covenants for title. In effect s. 24 (2) automatically implies in a transfer of part of the land held under a registered lease covenants on the part of both parties to pay the apportioned rent and perform the covenants so far as they affect the part transferred, or retained, as the case may be. These can be varied, or excluded altogether where it is intended to rely on the covenants implied under s. 77 of the Law of Property Act 1925[3].

E Effectiveness of covenants today

The protection afforded by the usual covenants for title is still basically the same as it was before they were put on a statutory basis in 1881, yet it is impossible to resist the conclusion that today they do not play so vital a part in a purchaser's armoury as they did of yore. The title to land is considerably less complicated than it was before the Property legislation of 1925 and happily recourse to the covenants seems less frequent than formerly. Since 1925 fewer than six major cases involving covenants for title appear to have been reported. This may not necessarily be too significant for one authority suggests that whether or not a case falls within the covenant is clear and the claim is usually settled or compromised[4]. One would also like to think that the decrease in the number of claims is partly attributable to improved standards of conveyancing.

Nevertheless there is perhaps a tendency to treat the covenants as a kind of panacea for most post-completion ills and it has been said that more value is attached to them than they are worth[5]. Practitioners are sometimes tempted to refrain from pursuing possible defects on the basis that if anything goes wrong,

---

19 In practice the transferor is expressed to transfer 'as beneficial owner' (if such he be) in order to obtain the full beneficial owner covenants implied by the LPA 1925, s. 76 (1) (A).
20 Page 620, ante.
 1 Cf. *Re King, Robinson v Gray* [1962] 2 All ER 66 (s. 24 (1) (a) negatived on compulsory acquisition of leasehold property from executor vendor); revsd. in part on other grounds, [1963] Ch 459, [1963] 1 All ER 781, CA.
 2 Law Com. Published Working Paper No. 32, para. 61.
 3 LRR 1925, r. 117. Where reliance is placed on s. 77, the transfer must make express reference to that section or to the relevant parts of the LPA 1925, Sch. 2; LRR 1925, r. 77 (4).
 4 2 K & E, 826.
 5 34 Halsbury's Laws (3rd edn), 369, note (e).

there are always the covenants for title on which to fall back. Fortunately matters do not often go wrong. If they do, a purchaser may find himself without redress for various reasons. The most important qualification is that the vendor's covenant does not amount to an absolute warranty of title. Obvious injustice is caused to a purchaser who is unable to obtain compensation because his vendor never had any title to the land[6]. Equally, injustice results if the loss is made to fall on the vendor when the defect is not caused by his own act or default. Fortunately the gradual extension of the system of land registration with its built-in indemnity schemes should alleviate many of the hardships caused by this particular limitation. One plea can perhaps be made. It is not too much to hope that an early opportunity will be taken to simplify the language of the covenants and at the same time to resolve the controversy over the words 'convey and is expressed to convey'.

6   In theory he can sue a previous vendor who was responsible for the defect, but in practice this right is often worthless.

Chapter 25

Miscellaneous post-completion remedies[1]

The finality of the transactions once it has been completed was mentioned at the commencement of the previous chapter. Nevertheless it may still be possible to have the conveyance set aside after completion on the ground of fraud, innocent misrepresentation or mistake. This is commonly termed rescission, but it has been pointed out that rescission in this sense is substantially different from the rescission which can be effected out of court, e.g. for misrepresentation. A court order is required to set aside an executed transaction.

A Fraud

1. Fraudulent representations

At law to establish fraud the plaintiff had to show that the false representation inducing him to enter into the contract was made by the other party knowingly, or without belief in its truth, or recklessly, not caring whether it was true or false. The party deceived could either avoid the contract, subject to the normal limitations, or affirm it and sue to recover damages in an action of deceit. Completion of the transaction was no bar to avoiding the transaction at law, provided the parties could be restored to their former position, and the purchaser could recover the purchase price in an action for money had and received. Equity exercised a concurrent jurisdiction to grant relief against fraud (but without being able originally to award damages) and it also had an exclusive jurisdiction to compel the delivery up and cancellation of documents procured by fraud.

(a) Effect of fraud
A contract induced by fraud is voidable at the instance of the party defrauded, but it is not void. Consequently a conveyance giving effect to the contract operates to vest the legal title in the purchaser. In *Feret v Hill*[2], for instance,

> T procured the grant of a lease of premises from L by falsely representating he intended to carry on there his business as a perfumier. Having obtained possession he converted them into a brothel and was forcibly evicted by L. T's action of ejectment to recover possession was upheld.

---

1 For a more detailed analysis of this topic reference should be made to the standard text books on Contract and Equity.
2 (1854) 15 CB 207.

The lease was effective to vest a legal estate in T and with it the right to lawful possession and, though it was liable to be set aside for fraud, T was in the meantime entitled at law to regain possession from L who had wrongfully expelled him[3].

The right to rescind a contract of fraud does not run with the land conveyed. Where A by fraud induces B to buy land and B assigns the benefit of the contract to C who later takes a conveyance direct from A, C has no right to rescind as against A. Although B may communicate the information to C, the representation is made to B who buys on the strength of it and the effect of the misrepresentation is spent when A makes the contract with B[4]. However, a purchaser's right to set aside a conveyance for, e.g. undue influence, is an interest of such a nature as to be devisable by will and passes under a general devise of real property[5].

(b) Extent of jurisdiction

The jurisdiction to set side a conveyance for fraud is not confined to cases of affirmative fraud where one party fraudulently makes an express statement which induces the other to enter into the contract[6]. According to Grant MR in *Edwards v M'Leay*[7] equity will intervene if 'the vendor knows and conceals a fact material to the validity of the title'. In this case he failed to disclose a known defect of title affecting part of the land, which was material to the enjoyment of the remainder. This principle was applied in a case where a lessor failed to disclose to his lessee that he had no title to part of the land comprised within the lease, as the lessor well knew[8]. Perhaps the most striking illustration of equity's intervention occurs in *Hart v Swaine*[9].

> V agreed to sell to P a field containing 4 acres, the land being described in the contract as freehold. There was nothing in the abstract furnished to P to indicate the land was other than freehold. V must have been aware that not all the land was freehold because on the occasion of his purchase some years earlier, the land had been described as partly copyhold but V had the whole property conveyed to him as freehold. In fact all 4 acres were copyhold and on discovering this after completion P sought to have the conveyance set aside.

Fry J upheld the purchaser's claim. Even assuming the vendor had made the representation believing it to be true[10], he had, in order to secure a benefit for

3   This was not a case where the plaintiff was seeking the court's assistance to enforce an unlawful agreement, which the court will not do; see *Upfill v Wright* [1911] 1 KB 506 (flat knowingly let for immoral purpose; landlord unable to recover rent).

4   *Gross v Lewis Hillman Ltd* [1970] Ch 445, [1969] 3 All ER 1476, CA. The position may well be different if A repeats the misrepresentation to C or if, knowing that B was transferring the benefit of the contract to C and also repeating A's fraudulent statements, A stands by and allows C to complete the purchase without disillusioning C, per Cross LJ, at 461 and 1483, respectively. If B is aware of their falsity when repeating the misrepresentations, C has a cause of action against B.

5   *Gresley v Mousley* (1862) 4 De G & J 78.

6   See, e.g. *Bousfield v Seymour* (1960) 175 Estates Gazette 593 (fraudulent misrepresentation by vendor of intention to effect repairs).

7   (1815) Coop G 308, at 312; affd. (1818) 2 Swan 287. There appears in this case to have been an express representation of title. Cf. Farrand, 70–71.

8   *Mostyn v The West Mostyn Coal and Iron Co Ltd* (1876) 1 CPD 145.

9   (1877) 7 Ch D 42.

10 He alleged that events subsequent to his own purchase, particularly the fact that no

himself, asserted that to be true which had turned out to be false, and according to the learned judge he had 'in the view of a Court of Law committed a fraud'[11]. It is not easy to follow the reasoning of this case, though the actual decision is generally accepted as correct[12]. It is perhaps best explained as an illustration of misrepresentation amounting to fraud[13]. It does not lay down any general proposition that a purchaser can, in the absence of deceit, have the transaction set aside after completion if the title turns out to be bad[14].

Cases like *Hart v Swaine*[15] give warning of the care to be exercised by the vendor when instructing his solicitor to draft the contract. Any deliberate failure to disclose a material defect of title may justify rescission after completion, so may a material representation incorporated in the contract, made recklessly with indifference as to its truth or falsity. To enter into a contract knowing that he has no title does not amount to fraud unless he has no intention of acquiring one or no reasonable belief in his ability to do so[16], and it is perfectly proper for a vendor to contract to convey such title as he has, if any[17].

2.   Equitable fraud

Equity's understanding of fraud was much wider than that recognised at law and its courts were prepared to set aside transactions not induced by any fraudulent representation, but nevertheless procured by the exercise by one party of influence over the mind of the other[18]. This equitable doctrine applies alike to contracts and conveyances for value as it does to voluntary settlements and gifts inter vivos.

(a) Occasions where undue influence exists
There are two main groups of cases in which equity will set aside a transaction for undue influence.

(i) *Presumed influence*. The first situation arises in cases where a fiduciary or confidential relationship exists between the parties. The mere existence of the relationship suffices to raise a presumption of undue influence and the onus is on the person seeking to uphold the conveyance to establish it was not in fact exercised. This presumption can be rebutted by showing that the transaction was the spontaneous act of the grantor or donor resulting from a free exercise of his will[19]. Proof of independent advice from a competent person usually suffices. In the case of a conveyance for value, it must be shown that the full price was paid. The presumption arises whenever two persons stand in such a relationship that confidence is necessarily reposed by the one and the influence

demand for payment of any quit-rent had been made, had led him to conclude that no part of the land was copyhold.

11   Per Fry J, at 47.
12   See *Jolliffe v Baker* (1883) 11 QBD 255 at 259–60, per Watkin Williams J; *Brownlie v Campbell* (1880) 5 App Cas 925 at 938, HL, per Lord Selbourne LC.
13   *Soper v Arnold* (1887) 37 Ch D 96 at 102, CA, per Cotton LJ; affd. (1889) 14 App Cas 429.
14   Per Cotton LJ, loc. cit.
15   (1877) 7 Ch D 42.
16   *Bain v Fothergill* (1874) LR 7 HL 158 at 207, per Lord Chelmsford.
17   See p. 158, ante.
18   A contract induced by duress in the shape of actual force or threats of personal violence is voidable at law.
19   *Allcard v Skinner* (1887) 36 Ch D 145 at 171, CA, per Cotton LJ.

which naturally flows out of that confidence is held by the other[20]. It has been held to exist between parent and child, fiancés, trustee and beneficiary, religious advisor and disciple, but not as between spouses. It is not however confined to certain particular kinds of relationship. In *Tufton v Sperni*[1],

> A and B were members of a committee formed for the promotion of a Moslem cultural centre. A conveyed his house to B for use as the centre at a price of £10,500 which was roughly double its market value.

The Court of Appeal set the transaction aside. A fiduciary relationship existed between the parties; they had joined together to further a charitable or altruistic objective and the purchaser had reposed confidence in the vendor which was abused. Transactions between solicitor and client are subject to the rule. A sale by a client to his solicitor will be upheld if the client was fully informed, received competent independent advice and was paid a fair price[2]. Although the relationship of solicitor and client has in a strict sense terminated, the same principles apply so long as the confidence naturally arising from that relationship is proved, or may be presumed, to continue[3]. A presumption of undue influence also exists when a solicitor sells to his client. Similarly a guarantee given by a father in favour of his son's bank has been set aside[4].

(ii) *Actual influence*. In the absence of any fiduciary relationship, equity will set aside a conveyance if actual or express undue influence can be established. The onus of proof lies with the person seeking to upset the deed. To succeed there must be evidence of unfair and improper conduct, or some coercion from outside, some overreaching or some form of cheating[5]. For example in *Ellis v Barker*[6] the court set aside a conveyance of property executed under pressure of a threat of preventing the grantor from being accepted as a tenant of a farm (this being a condition precedent to his taking a benefit under his father's will).

(b) Unconscionable bargains

The mere fact that a simpleton makes an improvident or even ruinous bargain with a person astute and unscrupulous enough to take advantage of his simplicity does not of itself entitle the victim to relief, at all events where the transaction has been completed[7]. Nevertheless equity maintains a wary eye on all transactions tainted by unfair dealing and may set aside a conveyance where there is inequality of position between the parties coupled with inadequacy of consideration, unless the party seeking to uphold the transaction can prove that it was fair and reasonable[8]. Instances of equity's intervention are not lacking, though most of the cases were decided upwards of a century ago[9].

20 *Tate v Williamson* (1866) 2 Ch App 55 at 60, per Lord Chelmsford LC.
1 [1952] 2 TLR 516, CA.
2 *Wright v Carter* [1903] 1 Ch 27, CA.
3 *Demerara Bauxite Co Ltd v Hubbard* [1923] AC 673, PC. For mortgages by a client to his solicitor see *Cockburn v Edwards* (1881) 18 Ch D 449, CA.
4 *Lloyds Bank Ltd v Bundy* [1975] QB 326, [1974] 3 All ER 757, CA; Cf. *Re Brocklehurst, Hall v Roberts*, [1978] Fam 14, [1978] 1 All ER 767, CA.
5 *Allcard v Skinner* (1887) 36 Ch D 145 at 181, CA, per Lindley LJ.
6 (1871) 7 Ch App 104; *Trevett v Sear* (1963) 186 Estates Gazette 879; *Fuller v De Ritter* (1963) Times, 9 April.
7 *Tufton v Sperni* [1952] 2 TLR 516 at 526, CA, per Jenkins LJ.
8 See *Fry v Lane* (1888) 40 Ch D 312 at 321–22, per Kay J. For acquisitions of reversions at an undervalue, see now the LPA 1925, s. 174 (1), replacing the Sales of Reversions Act 1867.
9 *Longmate v Ledger* (1860) 2 Giff 157; *Clark v Malpas* (1862) 4 De GF & J 401; see also

B   Innocent misrepresentation

Prior to the Misrepresentation Act 1967, no ground existed at law or in equity for setting aside an executed transaction for an innocent misrepresentation or an innocent concealment of some defect of title. This rule applied equally to conveyances[10], as it did to leases[11]. Two basic considerations seemed to lie at the foundation of this rule: the existence of an opportunity for the purchaser to investigate the title between contract and conveyance, and the overriding need for finality in land transactions[12]. It is true that the normal investigation of title would not reveal structural defects but the principle of caveat emptor warns every purchaser of the advisability of having the property surveyed before he makes the contract. The man who chooses to buy his house in reliance on the vendor's innocent representations and without adequate survey, like one who does not fully investigate the title, must know he is taking a risk[13]. Perhaps in ideal situations he ought not to be entitled to complain if he voluntarily accepts that risk. But in days of housing scarcity a cautious purchaser or tenant may find that in the meantime the property has been sold or let to some other interested, but not as fussy, party, so he is often compelled to take a chance to ensure that he and his family have a roof over their heads.

The repeated criticism of the rule, particularly in relation to its application to contracts for the sale of goods, eventually bore fruit and s. 1 (b) of the Act permits rescission of any contract on the ground of innocent misrepresentation notwithstanding its performance, but subject to the usual bars[14]. The Law Reform Committee had previously recommended retention of the rule for contracts affecting land (save for leases not exceeding three years)[15] and the Bill as originally presented in the House of Lords included this exception. It was deleted at the Committee stage in the Lords, but not before considerable misgivings had been voiced as to the wisdom of a rule of general application[16]. It remains to be seen whether these fears prove to be unfounded in relation to land transactions.

C   Mistake

Mistake can affect a transaction involving land in three different ways. First, as we saw in Chapter 23, it may affect the formation of the contract; this section is concerned primarily with the rights of the parties where relief is sought *after* completion of the purchase. Second, a party to a transaction may allege that he executed a document under the mistaken impression that it was a document of

---

Gardner v Simmonds (1958) 172 Estates Gazette 809. For a more recent application see *Cresswell v Potter* [1978] 1 WLR 255n; *Backhouse v Backhouse* [1978] 1 All ER 1158, and (1979) 123 Sol Jo 193 (P.W. Smith).

10   *Wilde v Gibson* (1848) 1 HL Cas 605 (non-fraudulent concealment of right of way).

11   *Legge v Croker* (1811) 1 Ball & B 506; *Angel v Jay* [1911] 1 KB 666.

12   *Wilde v Gibson* (1848) HL Cas 605 at 633, per Lord Campbell ('There would be no safety for the transactions of mankind . . .'); *Allen v Richardson* (1879) 13 Ch D 524 at 541, per Malins V-C.

13   See the Law Reform Committee, 10th Report (Innocent Misrepresentation), Cmnd. 1782, para. 6.

14   The section does not appear to cover mere non-disclosure.

15   See para. 7.

16   In particular Lord Upjohn expressed the view that its removal might give rise to 'very grave injustice': see H.L. Debates, 17 May 1966, Vol. 274, cols. 943, 944. Both The Law Society and the Royal Institution of Chartered Surveyors favoured retention of the original clause.

a totally different kind, i.e. he raises the plea of non est factum. Thirdly, the executed written document, be it contract or conveyance, may contain a mistake by failing to embody the parties' true agreement, so giving rise to a claim for rectification.

1.   Mistake affecting formation

(a)   Total failure of consideration

Prior to *Solle v Butcher*[17] relief on account of common mistake could only be obtained after completion of a contract involving land on the narrow ground of a total failure of consideration. In effect this limited rescission to cases of res sua or res extincta, cases like *Bingham v Bingham*[18] where the purchaser was conveyed land which unknown to both parties he already owned, or like *Strickland v Turner*[19] where an assignment of an annuity was executed in ignorance of the fact that the annuitant had died before the making of the agreement for sale. In such cases the conveyance was devoid of legal effect since the vendor had nothing to sell or convey, and the purchaser could recover the purchase price in an action at law without equity's intervention. If the purchaser desired some form of relief not available at law, proceedings had to be commenced in equity[20].

Though there are dicta suggesting otherwise[1], rescission after completion was not available in the absence of a total failure of consideration. In *Re Tyrell, Tyrell v Woodhouse*[2], Cozens-Hardy J declined to be the first judge to give a decision contrary to this rule, when holding that the post-completion discovery that the land conveyed was subject to a reversionary lease (the existence of which was unknown to both parties) was no ground for setting the conveyance aside. Again rescission was not available in a recent case where the tenant already owned one-tenth of the land comprised within the tenancy agreement; Pennycuick J declined to dissect the agreement and to declare it void as to part only of the land included in it[3]. The same principle has been affirmed by the High Court of Australia in *Svanosio v McNamara*[4], where the plaintiff discovered after completion that the hotel he had bought was erected partly on land to which the vendor unknowingly had no title. His action to set aside the conveyance for common mistake was dismissed. A purchaser is not necessarily without remedy in a situation like this. He may have a contractual right to claim compensation[5]. Alternatively he may be able to sue on the covenants for title. Yet these will not always afford him protection[6], for the vendor covenants, not that he has a title, but that he has done nothing to cause the defect. If he never had any title to the missing land, then apart from any contractual rights the purchaser has no remedy[7].

---

17   [1950] 1 KB 671, [1949] 2 All ER 1107, CA.
18   (1748) 1 Ves Sen 126.
19   (1852) 7 Exch 208.
20   *Cooper v Phibbs* (1867) LR 2 HL 149.
 1   *Debenham v Sawbridge* [1901] 2 Ch 98 at 109, per Byrne J.
 2   (1900) 82 LT 675; *Debenham v Sawbridge* [1901] 2 Ch 98 (discovery after completion that part of house conveyed belonged to third party: rescission denied).
 3   *Bligh v Martin* [1968] 1 All ER 1157.
 4   (1956) 96 CLR 186. See also *Montgomery and Rennie v Continental Bags (NZ) Ltd* [1972] NZLR 884, note 2, p. 445, ante.
 5   *Palmer v Johnson* (1884) 13 QBD 351, CA, note 12, p. 603, ante.
 6   See p. 627, ante.
 7   It is dangerous to try to extract any wider equitable principle in relation to mistake from a

(b) Solle v Butcher

In *Solle v Butcher*[8] the Court of Appeal set aside an executed lease because the parties had made a fundamental mistake as to whether reconstruction of a flat, the subject of the letting, had taken it out of the Rent Restriction Acts. There was no total failure of consideration. The basis of equity's jurisdiction to intervene, even after completion, is the existence of some common fundamental misapprehension as to the facts or the parties' respective rights, which goes to the root of the contract. It remains to be seen how extensive this principle is and in particular whether it will be held to apply generally to completed contracts for the sale of land. *Solle v Butcher* concerned the grant of a seven years' lease, something very different from a sale of freehold land with its built-in protection afforded by the investigation of title. It was adopted by Goff J in *Grist v Bailey*[9], though in this case the mistake was discovered before completion of the conveyance.

Prima facie the rule as stated by Denning LJ in *Solle v Butcher*[10] appears wide enough to cover cases where the parties make a fundamental mistake as to quantity, but it is far from clear that he was purporting to lay down a rule intended to apply to conveyances of land[11]. In the Australian case of *Svanosio v McNamara*[12] the court took the view that *Solle v Butcher* did not extend to completed contracts for the sale of land. To allow the purchaser a remedy after completion in such circumstances would run counter to the hallowed principle that the purchaser must stand or fall by his investigation of the title and any loss sustained recovered under the covenants for title. However, the limitations of these covenants have already been exposed[13] and many will argue that there can be little justification today for denying all remedy to the purchaser. In some jurisdictions the principle has already been established that an error as to quantity justifies rescission even after completion if it is so substantial that in essence it alters the quality of the subject-matter of the contract (an error in substantialibus as it is termed), notwithstanding there is no total failure of consideration[14].

line of nineteenth century cases (discussed pp. 651–653, post) where the court in a rectification suit gave the defendant the option of submitting to rectification or cancelling the contract. For example in *Paget v Marshall* (1884) 28 Ch D 255, a lessor when negotiating for a lease of a block of property made it clear to the intending tenant that he proposed to retain certain rooms for his own use. When making a formal written offer to the tenant he omitted to mention this reservation and by error the lease included these rooms. Bacon V-C said (at 266) that the contract ought to have been annulled because of the lessor's 'plain and palpable' mistake, though he considered that justice could be done by putting the defendant to his election. The learned judge appears to have assumed that because equity could refuse to decree specific performance of the contract against a mistaken party (see p. 578, ante) the court had a similar jurisdiction to set aside an executed contract, notwithstanding there was no total failure of consideration, or even no common mistake. The authorities do not support such an extensive proposition.

8   [1950] 1 KB 671, [1949] 2 All ER 1107, CA.
9   [1967] Ch 532, [1966] 2 All ER 875, p. 608, ante. It must remain a matter of conjecture whether he would so readily have applied *Solle v Butcher* had the true position come to light after completion. See also *Amalgamated Investments and Property Co Ltd v John Walker & Sons Ltd* [1976] 3 All ER 509, CA; and *Laurence v Lexcourt Holdings Ltd* [1978] 2 All ER 810.
10   [1950] 1 KB 671 at 693, [1949] 2 All ER 1107 at 1120, CA, p. 608, ante.
11   See his observations at 692 and 1121, respectively.
12   (1956) 96 CLR 186, at 198, 210.
13   See p. 627, ante.
14   *Hyrsky v Smith* (1969) 5 DLR (3d) 385 (vendor having title to only half of land conveyed; rescission allowed after four years); *Marwood v Charter Credit Corpn* (1970) 12 DLR (3d) 765; on appeal (1971) 20 DLR (3d) 563.

2.   Non est factum

A party to a deed who alleges that he was induced to execute something different in character from what he thought he was signing may be entitled to raise the plea of *scriptum predictum non est factum suum*. He thereby seeks to have the deed set aside on the ground that it is void against him as not being his deed, and being void it is ineffectual to pass the estate or interest which it purports to transfer. This plea originated in the late sixteenth century for the protection of blind and illiterate people but it was subsequently extended in a far from satisfactory manner to written contracts generally, irrespective of the disability of the signatory. Fortunately the recent decision of the House of Lords in *Saunders v Anglia Building Society*[15] has clarified the law, rendering a detailed consideration of the earlier cases unnecessary. The facts were these:

> X, a widow aged 78, was induced to execute a deed in the belief that it was a deed of gift of her leasehold house to her nephew, Y, whereas in fact it was an assignment of the house to Z. Z mortgaged the property to a building society. X did not read the assignment; her glasses were broken at the time and she was content to trust Y who witnessed her signature to the deed. Later Z defaulted in payment of the mortgage instalments and the society commenced possession proceedings. X pleaded that the deed to Z was void so that the society acquired no rights under the mortgage deed.

As against Z the assignment was voidable as having been induced by fraud and it was held to be void against him. Their lordships upheld the Court of Appeal's decision that X was not entitled to raise the plea of non est factum against the building society. The House took the opportunity of considering the previous decisions on this topic and the law as stated by them appears to be as follows.

(a) Applicability

The plea of non est factum is not confined to the blind and illiterate. Though it must be kept within narrow limits, it may in exceptional circumstances be available to a person of full capacity. To eliminate the plea altogether in these circumstances would deprive the courts of what may be an instrument of justice[16].

(b) Burden of proof

The onus of establishing non est factum lies on the party seeking to disown his signature. It requires clear and positive evidence. In the *Saunders'* case, the plaintiff had fallen far short of making the clear and satisfactory case which is required of those who seek to have a legal act declared void and of establishing a sufficient discrepancy between her intention and her act[17]. Her evidence indicated that she would have executed the deed in Z's favour, even if the transaction had been fully explained to her.

---

15   [1971] AC 1004, [1970] 3 All ER 961. The original plaintiff (the widow) died during the course of the litigation and the proceedings were continued by her executrix.

16   [1971] AC 1004 at 1026, [1970] 3 All ER 961 at 972, per Lord Wilberforce. In the Court of Appeal Lord Denning MR had rejected the widow's claim on the ground that the doctrine did not apply to persons of full age and understanding who could read and write: see *Gallie v Lee* [1969] 2 Ch 17 at 31–32, [1969] 1 All ER 1062 at 1072.

17   Per Lord Wilberforce at 1027 and 973, respectively.

(c) Availability

A plaintiff is not entitled to relief if (i) he has failed to exercise reasonable care when signing the document or (ii) the actual document is not fundamentally different from the document as the signer believed it to be[18]. The two separate limbs of this rule require further treatment.

(i) *Negligence.* Common prudence dictates that every person should exercise care when signing a document, though commercial life sees this trite advice constantly ignored. Yet, surprisingly, it was the law before the *Saunders'* case that negligence on the part of the person signing did not prevent his relying on the plea[19]. This oft-criticised rule has now been buried and the correct rule, as expressed by Lord Wilberforce, is as follows[20]:

> '. . . a person who signs a document, and parts with it so that it may come into other hands, has a responsibility, that of the normal man of prudence, to take care what he signs, which, if neglected, prevents him from denying his liability under the document according to its tenor.'

It therefore affords no assistance to the man who does not read the document before signing it because he was too busy or too lazy or because of the trust he placed in another[1]. What amounts to reasonable care will depend on the circumstances of the case[2], including the nature of the document which it is thought is being signed. The same standard of care ought not to be expected of an elderly spinster who might be none the wiser if she read the document as of a business executive. The word 'negligence' in this context does not involve the proposition that want of care is irrelevant unless there can be found a specific duty to the opposite party to take care[3].

(ii) *Fundamental difference.* There must be a difference which is 'radical', or 'fundamental' or 'very substantial'—various expressions were used by their lordships—between what the plaintiff signed and what he thought he was signing, or in Lord Hodson's words[4] a difference in some particular 'which goes to the substance of the whole consideration or to the root of the matter'. The House of Lords disapproved of the distinction formerly drawn between a difference in character or class (which was sufficient to raise the plea) and a difference only in contents (which did not suffice). The plaintiff's mistake in the *Saunders'* case was not sufficiently fundamental; she intended to divest herself of her leasehold property by transferring it to another albeit by way of gift rather than by an assignment ostensibly for value[5]. A sufficient difference

---

18 Per Lord Pearson at 1034 and 979, respectively.
19 *Carlisle and Cumberland Banking Co v Bragg* [1911] 1 KB 489.
20 [1971] AC 1004 at 1027, [1970] 3 All ER 961 at 973. He did, however, suggest that special rules may apply to negotiable instruments.
1   See e.g. *United Dominions Trust v Western* [1976] QB 513, [1975] 3 All ER 1017; Marston (1976) CLJ 218.
2   Per Viscount Dilhorne at 1023 and 969, respectively.
3   Per Lord Hodson at 1019 and 966, respectively.
4   At 1019 and 965, respectively.
5   For some of the earlier authorities, reference may be made to *Foster v MacKinnon* (1869) LR 4 CP 704 (bill of exchange indorsed as guarantee: plea succeeded); *Bagot v Chapman* [1907] 2 Ch 222 (mortgage described as power of attorney: plea upheld); *Howatson v Webb* [1908] 1 Ch 1 (conveyance described as mortgage: plea defeated because it was a mere mistake as to contents).

would seem to exist for the purpose of this rule where a man is induced to execute a conveyance under the impression he is granting a lease for seven years, but perhaps not vice versa.

A mistake of identity may or may not be fundamental depending on the circumstances. In the case of a deed an error of personality is not necessarily so vital as in the case of a contract, which requires consensus[6]. The mistake as to the identity of the transferee in the *Saunders'* case (i.e. Z in place of Y) was considered not to make the deed totally different from what she intended to sign. A mistake as to the legal effect of a document cannot give rise to a plea of non est factum.

(d) Illiterate persons

The House of Lords were not directly concerned with the position of illiterate or blind people, but it seems that signers within this category must establish the same basic requirements. Because of the nature of their disability they will more readily be able to raise the plea successfully, but even they must still act responsibly and carefully according to their circumstances when putting their signature to legal documents[7]. If no third party has become involved relief may be obtained on the ground of fraud, without it being necessary to rely on the plea.

3. Rectification

(a) The jurisdiction to rectify

It is a fundamental rule of English law that extrinsic evidence is not admissible to vary or contradict the terms of a written document. To this basic proposition an important exception exists. Where owing to some error of drafting a written document fails to record accurately the terms of the parties' true agreement, equity will rectify the document to make it accord with their agreement. This jurisdiction to rectify must not be confused with the courts' inherent power to correct obvious errors as a matter of construction of a document[8]. Normally rectification must be specifically claimed in the pleadings, but the court may accede to rectification at the instance of a defendant, despite the absence of any counterclaim, if the result would otherwise be to award to the plaintiff what was plainly contrary to the parties' bargain[9].

Equity assumes jurisdiction in a proper case to rectify conveyances, leases, voluntary deeds, contracts and other written instruments. After considerable uncertainty on the point[10] it is now clear that a plaintiff can in the same action claim rectification of a written contract for the sale of land and specific performance of the contract as rectified. It is no bar to rectification that a mistake in the written agreement has been repeated in the conveyance[11]. The granting of relief in these circumstances seems at first sight to run foul of the Law of Property Act 1925, s. 40, for the court is specifically performing a written agreement with a parol variation. The truth of the matter is that after rectification

---

6 Per Lord Hodson at 1019 and 965, respectively.
7 Per Lord Wilberforce at 1027 and 971, respectively.
8 Page 491, ante. See e.g. *Re Alexander's Settlement, Jennings v Alexander* [1910] 2 Ch 225.
9 *Butler v Mountview Estates Ltd* [1951] 2 KB 563, [1951] 1 All ER 693, note 20, p. 656, post.
10 See the various authorities collected and discussed by Lawrence J in *Craddock Bros Ltd v Hunt* [1922] 2 Ch 809; affd. [1923] 2 Ch 136, CA.
11 *Craddock Bros Ltd v Hunt* [1923] 2 Ch 136, CA.

the written agreement does not continue to exist with a parol variation; it is read as if it has been originally drawn in its rectified form and it is the amended written document of which specific performance is decreed[12].

(b) Conditions for rectification
In *Craddock Bros Ltd v Hunt*[13], Warrington LJ said:

> ' The jurisdiction of courts of equity in this respect [i.e. as to rectification] is to bring the written document executed in pursuance of an antecedent agreement into conformity with that agreement. The conditions to its exercise are that there must be an antecedent contract and the common intention of embodying or giving effect to the whole of that contract by the writing, and there must be clear evidence that the document by common mistake failed to embody such contract and either contained provisions not agreed upon or omitted something that was agreed upon, or otherwise departed from its terms.'

(i) *Prior agreement*. As this dictum reveals, it was once thought that the court could only rectify a document so as to make it accord with a complete antecedent concluded oral contract. This view is no longer accepted. In *Joscelyne v Nissen*[14] the Court of Appeal held that a concluded binding agreement is not essential; a claim to rectification can be based on an antecedent expressed accord reached during negotiations and adhered to in intention by the parties. Rectification can therefore be obtained when a formal contract fails to incorporate some term agreed in a 'subject to contract' document.

(ii) *Intention to embody in writing*. The parties must intend the written document to contain all the terms of their agreement, a requirement not difficult to establish in relation to contracts affecting land. The requisite intention was not present in *City and Westminster Properties (1934) Ltd v Mudd*[15]. It will be recalled that in this case premises were let solely for business purposes, though both parties intended that the tenant should be permitted to live there. The tenant's claim for rectification of the lease by including an express proviso allowing him to reside there was rejected; there was no common intention to insert such a provision in the document, the landlords in particular having no desire to attract the provisions of the Rent Acts.

(iii) *Common mistake*. The plaintiff must establish by convincing proof[16] that by some common mistake in drafting the subsequent written document does not accurately express their prior agreement. He must prove the existence of a mistake. Rectification will not be ordered merely because the parties desire to introduce additional terms, or because one of the parties intended to incorporate a particular term but failed to do so[17]. Moreover, the plaintiff must establish that the alleged intention continued concurrently in the minds of both

---

12 *Craddock Bros Ltd v Hunt* [1923] 2 Ch 136 at 151–52, CA, per Lord Sterndale MR.
    Often there will be accompanying acts of part performance (e.g. possession) to take the case out of the statute.
13 [1923] 2 Ch 136 at 159, CA.
14 [1970] 2 QB 86, [1970] 1 All ER 1213, CA. And see note 7, post.
15 [1959] Ch 129, [1958] 2 All ER 733.
16 The standard of proof is the civil standard nevertheless: *Thomas Bates & Son v Wyndham's (Lingerie) Ltd* [1981] 1 All ER 1077, CA.
17 But see the cases discussed in paragraph (iv), post.

parties down to the time of the signing of the contract or the execution of the deed[18]. Rectification will be ordered if there is a common intention and (a) one party believes the document carries out that intention albeit erroneously (b) the other party knows it does not carry out the common intention by reason of a mistake of the other party, (c) that party fails to bring the mistake to the attention of the other party and (d) that mistake would benefit the defendant or adversely affect the plaintiff[19].

The plaintiff must give 'convincing proof' of the mistake. In *Joscelyne v Nissen*[20] the Court of Appeal eschewed the use of the old fashioned epithet 'irrefragable' and thought it best not to import from the criminal law the phrase 'beyond all reasonable doubt'. The court, though reluctant to do so, may act on the parol evidence of the plaintiff[1]. Rectification is commonly granted where a conveyance or other deed fails to give effect to the terms of the written contract. Here the plaintiff may be able to succeed merely on proof of the disparity, whereas a more onerous burden of proof will usually rest on the shoulders of one seeking to show that a written contract does not accord with an antecedent oral bargain[2]. A conveyance may be rectified where, for instance, by mutual mistake parcels are omitted from the deed[3], or the vendor's covenants for title are wider than those provided for by the contract[4], or the statutory general words operate to pass to the purchaser an implied right of way contrary to terms of the contract[5], or a lease mistakenly includes an option to renew[6]. A recent example is furnished by *Wilson v Wilson*[6a]:

> Land was transferred to A and B. B joined in the transaction solely to enable A to obtain a mortgage. There was never any intention that B should acquire a beneficial interest in the property and he paid nothing towards the purchase price or mortgage instalments. Owing to an oversight the transfer contained the usual declaration that they held as joint tenants in equity. The court ordered rectification by striking out that part of the deed which declared the beneficial interests. The learned judge held that he had jurisdiction to make the order, notwithstanding the vendor was not a party to the proceedings.

(iv) *Unilateral mistake.* Equitable relief by way of rectification is founded upon the common intention of both parties. Where only one party is mistaken

---

18 *Fowler v Fowler* (1859) 4 De G & J 250. A change of mind after signing contracts cannot, of course, assist a vendor or purchaser resisting rectification of the conveyance.

19 *Thomas Bates & Son Ltd v Wyndham's (Lingerie) Ltd*, supra, applying a dictum of Russell LJ from *Riverlate Properties Ltd v Paul* [1974] 2 All ER 656.

20 [1970] 2 QB 86 at 98, [1970] 1 All ER 1213 at 1222, CA, per Russell LJ.

1 *Smith v Iliffe* (1875) LR 20 Eq 666; *Bonhote v Henderson* [1895] 1 Ch 742; affd. [1895] 2 Ch 202, CA.

2 See *Lloyd v Stanbury* [1971] 2 All ER 267 (no convincing proof of vendor's intention to exclude disputed plot from contract: rectification refused); *Re Butlin's Settlement Trust* [1976] Ch 251, [1976] 2 All ER 1083, CA (error in settlement rectified at instance of settlor).

3 *White v White* (1872) LR 15 Eq 247; *Beale v Kyte* [1907] 1 Ch 564 (too much land conveyed).

4 *Stait v Fenner* [1912] 2 Ch 504; *Butler v Mountview Estates Ltd* [1951] 2 KB 563, [1951] 1 All ER 693.

5 *Clarke v Barnes* [1929] 2 Ch 368.

6 *Kent v Hartley* (1966) 200 Estates Gazette 1027.

6a [1969] 3 All ER 945; *Re Colebrook's Conveyances, Taylor v Taylor* [1973] 1 All ER 132 ('tenants in common' inserted for 'joint tenants'). It will be observed that in both these cases rectification was based on an arrangement between relatives falling short of any concluded contract. But see *Joyce v Barker Bros* (1980) Times, 26 February.

there can be no rectification. To this general rule there are two, possibly three, exceptions. It will be ordered if one party is mistaken and the other fraudulent. Since constructive fraud suffices, most of the reported decisions illustrating this exception concern the rectification of marriage or family settlements. In *Lovesy v Smith*[7] rectification was ordered where a solicitor failed to explain to his fiancée clauses in his favour in a marriage settlement drafted by him and executed by her. Closely allied to this exception, indeed it may amount to nothing more than a specific illustration of its operation, is the rule that a party cannot resist rectification if he knows that a document contains a mistake to his advantage but does nothing to correct it. It is not clear whether this rule is based on fraud and so requires proof of dishonesty, or whether it rests upon a species of equitable estoppel in which case it is not essential to establish any particular degree of obliquity on the defendant's part[8].

This principle provides a ready explanation for a much discussed trilogy of nineteenth century cases, though the cases themselves were decided on different grounds. They appear to establish that equity may put a defendant on terms to submit to rectification or have the contract annulled, even though the plaintiff seeking rectification cannot show either a common mistake or actual fraud. This jurisdiction seems to have originated with Lord Romilly MR's, judgment in *Garrard v Frankel*[9] where —

> L agreed to lease premises to T at a yearly rent of £230. A lease was subsequently executed in which the rent was erroneously stated to be £130. Lord Romilly considered that T was aware of the mistake when she executed the lease and intended to take advantage of it, but he shrank from branding her conduct as fraudulent.

He refused to rectify the lease at L's instance, but gave T the option of taking the lease as rectified or of rejecting it altogether. A similar order was made in *Harris v Pepperell*[10], where Lord Romilly expressed the view that mutuality of mistake did not apply as between vendor and purchaser, and by Bacon V-C in *Paget v Marshall*[11]. These cases have been subjected to considerable adverse criticism. In *May v Platt*[12] Fry J considered that they could only be supported on the ground that the defendant's conduct was treated as equivalent to fraud, otherwise there was no jurisdiction to grant the relief that was ordered. Yet if fraud were established, the plaintiff's claim should have succeeded and he ought not to have been subjected to the risk of losing the bargain altogether. There are indications in these cases that the court, in adopting a compromise solution, was swayed by the plaintiff's contribution to the defendant's position[13], a factor that should not be ignored.

---

7   (1880) 15 Ch D 655. With true Victorian melodrama the report states that the settlement was signed by the plaintiff on the morning of the wedding day, 'she having been called down to execute it while making her wedding toilet'.

8   See *A. Roberts & Co Ltd v Leicestershire County Council* [1961] Ch 555 at 570–71, per Pennycuick J; *Snell's Equity* (27th edn), p. 614.

9   (1862) 30 Beav 445.

10   (1867) LR 5 Eq 1 (purchaser using own deed plan, not the vendor's which included more land than the vendor intended to sell). In *Bloomer v Spittle* (1872) LR 13 Eq 427, the same judge put the defendant to his election in a case where he found a common mistake but refused to grant rectification because of the plaintiff's laches. But if laches barred the claim, why was judgment not given for the defendant?

11   (1884) 28 Ch D 255, note 7, p. 645, ante.

12   [1900] 1 Ch 616 at 623; *Blay v Pollard and Morris* [1930] 1 KB 628 at 633, CA, per Scrutton LJ; see also 2 Williams V & P, 784–91.

13   In *Harris v Pepperrell* (1867) LR 5 Eq 1, at 5, the vendor's conduct in not causing the

In *Riverlate Properties Ltd v Paul*[14] these cases were strongly disapproved and the precise status of them seems uncertain[15]. Despite the criticisms, they have been heralded as examples of equity's flexibility in using equitable remedies to do justice between the parties, and they were cited with apparent approval by Denning LJ in *Solle v Butcher*[16]. It is, however, arguable that since in each case the defendant appears to have been aware of the mistake which he did nothing to correct, a court, if confronted with the same situation today, would be justified in finding for the plaintiff on the basis of the second exception considered on page 652.

(c) Effect of order

Rectification relates back to the time when the document was executed and it is to be read as if it had been originally drawn in its rectified form. The execution of a fresh document is unnecessary. The court order operates to pass any outstanding legal estate[17]. It is the practice to indorse a copy of the order on the deed or other instrument. The court will give effect to any consequential rights following rectifications, such as the implied reservation of a right of way[18].

D   Loss of right to rescind

The right to have a transaction set aside may be barred on one or more of the several grounds. These apply alike whether rescission is sought before or after completion. If the right of rescission has been lost, the injured party must have recourse to any alternative remedy available to him, such as an action for damages in deceit[19], or an action on the covenants for title implied in his conveyance. In this section the following bars[20] to relief are considered:

1. Impossibility of restitutio in integrum
2. Affirmation
3. Lapse of time
4. Intervention of third party rights.

1.   Restitutio in integrum impossible

It has always been a condition of rescission both at law and in equity that the parties should be put in statu quo and if this cannot be achieved rescission is not available. However, as McCardie J once remarked, the expression restitutio in integrum is somewhat vague and must be applied with care[1]. As we have already seen[2] equity by the exercise of its wider powers was able to uphold the right of an aggrieved party to rescind in a much wider variety of cases than

deed plan to be examined to see if it was correct was termed 'gross negligence'; *Garrard v Frankel* (1862) 30 Beav 445 at 459.
14   [1974] 2 All ER 656, CA.
15   See Hanbury, 714; Treitel, 233.
16   [1950] 1 KB 671 at 696, [1949] 2 All ER 1107 at 1122, CA; *Devald v Zigeuner* (1958) 16 DLR (2d) 285.
17   *White v White* (1872) LR 15 Eq 247.
18   *Rice v Dodds* (1969) 213 Estates Gazette 759.
19   *Clarke v Dickson* (1858) EB & E 148. See p. 593, ante.
20   These bars do not apply where rescission is sought on the ground of mistake operative at law, e.g. in cases of res sua or where non est factum is successfully pleaded.
1   *Armstrong v Jackson* [1917] 2 KB 822 at 828.
2   Page 595, ante.

those which the common law would recognise as admitting of rescission. In effect rescission is possible if the court can restore the parties *substantially* to the status quo. Thus occupation by the purchaser is no bar because he can be required to pay rent for his period of occupation, neither is deterioration of the property for this can be the subject of compensation. Restitution may be impossible if the plaintiff has disposed of the property or it has ceased to exist e.g. where the purchaser of a mine has worked it out[3]. In one case the purchaser of a business conducted on leasehold premises, who in order to cut his losses was obliged to close the shop and abandon the premises, was held entitled to rescind for fraud notwithstanding that the landlord had in the meantime re-entered the premises[4].

A contract cannot be rescinded in part and still be good for the remainder. One reason for refusing rescission here is that the parties cannot be restored to their status quo. In *Thorpe v Facey*[5] it was held that a single contract for the purchase of four separate plots of land could not be rescinded by a vendor on account of the purchaser's failure to complete, because a conveyance of one of the plots had already been taken. Perhaps a better explanation for this rule is simply that the vendor having affirmed the contract as to part cannot disaffirm it as to the balance. If the rule were otherwise the court would be re-making the bargain for the parties.

Rectification

Authority exists for saying that the equitable jurisdiction to compel a defendant to submit to rectification or cancel the contract will only be exercised if he can be restored to his former position should he elect to cancel[6]. This seems an obvious requirement; if the rule were otherwise cancellation might operate to his detriment, leaving him with no genuine choice. Apart from this the impossibility of restoring the status quo is no bar to a claim for rectification.

2.   Affirmation

A contract cannot be rescinded once the injured party, with knowledge of all material facts, elects to affirm the transaction. Affirmation may be inferred from conduct, or from words, or simply from a failure to repudiate. A tenant induced to take a lease by fraudulent misrepresentation cannot rescind if he remains in possession and continues to pay rent after discovering the truth[7]. Nor can a plaintiff rescind who has continued to carry on at a profit a business the purchase of which he seeks to set aside[8]. The acts and conduct relied upon as evidence of affirmation must be such as are more consistent, on a reasonable

3   *Lagunas Nitrate Co v Lagunas Syndicate* [1899] 2 Ch 392, CA.
4   *Alati v Kruger* (1955) 94 CLR 216. Apparently the court considered the lease (which was originally granted for three years with the option of a further two) to be practically worthless, for the purchaser was not even required to compensate the vendor for its loss.
5   [1949] Ch 649, [1949] 2 All ER 393. The vendor's alternative claim for damages also failed. The purchaser's failure to complete did not constitute a repudiation of the contract, and the vendor had not served any notice making time of the essence.
6   *Harris v Pepperrell* (1867) LR 2 Eq 1 at 4, per Romilly MR, citing *Earl of Bradford v Earl of Romney* (1862) 30 Beav 431.
7   Cf. *Kennard v Ashman* (1894) 10 TLR 213; affd. 10 TLR 447.
8   *Seddon v North Eastern Salt Co Ltd* [1905] 1 Ch 326. If he elects not to rescind, he is precluded from recovering special damage occurring after discovery of the fraud: *Hamer v James* (1886) 2 TLR 852, CA.

view of them, with that than with any other theory[9]. Thus a purchaser has been held entitled to rescind a contract for substantial misdescription notwithstanding that he had paid the balance of the deposit and asked for repairs to be done after he became aware of the misstatement, for his conduct was consistent with his intention to try in the first instance to negotiate a reduction in the price[10].

3. Lapse of time

The remedy of rescission is regarded as essentially an equitable one and equity requires its suitors to act with promptness. Delay of itself does not bar the claim, but it is a factor which the court cannot disregard. Coupled with other circumstances it may defeat the plaintiff. It may be taken as evidence of affirmation, or in the interval an innocent third party may have acquired an interest in the property, or the subject-matter of the contract may have changed, preventing substantial restoration to the status quo.

Running of time
Some uncertainty surrounds the rules determining when time begins to run. To some extent they depend on the reason why the plaintiff seeks to have the transaction set aside.

(i) *Fraud.* It is clear that the defrauded party is not affected by mere lapse of time so long as he remains in ignorance of the fraud[11]. Time runs from discovery of the fraud and thereafter if the plaintiff delays his claim for more than six years, equity will (apart from any other reason) act by analogy to the Limitation Act 1980, and refuse to grant relief[12].

(ii) *Innocent misrepresentation.* It might be thought that the same rule would apply alike to fraudulent and innocent misrepresentation but apparently this is not so. In *Leaf v International Galleries*[13], a case concerning the purchase of a painting induced by an innocent misrepresentation, the Court of Appeal dismissed the purchaser's claim for rescission on the ground of lapse of time, notwithstanding he had instituted proceedings immediately on learning the truth. He had accepted the picture and had had ample opportunity for examination in the first few days after buying it — reasoning which could equally be applied to a case of fraud though it must be remembered that of all forms of conduct fraud is the one least likely to attract the court's sympathy. Since the Misrepresentation Act 1967, puts contracts for the sale of land on the same footing in relation to innocent misrepresentation as other contracts, it would be difficult to maintain that a different rule governing the running of time should apply to

9 *Watson v Burton* [1956] 3 All ER 929 at 937, per Wynn-Parry J adopting a passage from 26 Halsbury's Laws (3rd edn) 884–85. See *Aquis Estates Ltd v Minton* [1975] 3 All ER 1043, CA.
10 *Watson v Burton* [1956] 3 All ER 929. The sale was by auction at which the plaintiff paid only a nominal deposit. See also *Laurence v Lexcourt Holdings Ltd* [1978] 2 All ER 810 (tenant not prejudiced by negotiations over lease. When these failed they gave reasonable notice and vacated).
11 *Rolfe v Gregory* (1865) 4 De J & S 576 at 579, per Lord Westbury; *Oliver v Court* (1820) 8 Price 127 (lapse of 12 years); *Gresley v Mousley* (1862) 4 De G & J 78 (conveyance set aside for undue influence 22 years later); Limitation Act 1980, s. 32.
12 *Armstrong v Jackson* [1917] 2 KB 822 at 830–31, per McCardie J.
13 [1950] 2 KB 86, [1950] 1 All ER 693, CA (five years' delay). The court assumed that rescission was available in the case of an executed contract for the sale of goods.

contracts relating to land, although it by no means follows that a purchaser of land can verify or disprove the truth of a representation as easily as the Court in *Leaf's* case thought was possible in the case of a painting. Perhaps the length of time in bringing proceedings might be a relevant consideration for the court in deciding whether to award damages in lieu of rescission[14].

(iii) *Mistake*. The cases involving rectification of documents are contradictory. In *Bloomer v Spittle*[15] Lord Romilly MR held that time ran from the execution of the conveyance sought to be rectified and he refused rectification after a delay of four years on the ground that it was the purchaser's bounden duty to look at his conveyance to see what he had obtained[16]. However, this decision was questioned in *Beale v Kyte*[17] by Neville J who said obiter that time runs from when the plaintiff's attention is first called to the error. Lord Romilly obviously felt that since the purchaser has the means of discovering the mistake at his disposal, he ought not to be heard to say that he did not check. Perhaps this reasoning is far too idealistic in a day and age when most purchasers never see their title deeds[18].

As to other forms of mistake, authority is lacking as to whether time runs from the making of the contract or the discovery of the mistake, though in *Beale v Kyte*[19] Neville J expressed the rule in terms wide enough to cover all cases of mistake.

In view of the confused and uncertain state of the law, it may perhaps be argued that save in cases of fraud it is more in keeping with equitable principles not to lay down a hard and fast rule, but to allow the court to do justice in each particular case. Irrespective of when the plaintiff commences proceedings, should hardship result to a vendor of land having to submit to rescission long after completion of the contract, the court can in the exercise of its discretion refuse to grant it. If the purchaser delays a long time after ascertaining the truth, it will be open for the court to infer affirmation.

4.   Third party rights

Equity will not allow rescission to the prejudice of a third party who has acquired an interest in the property for value and without notice of the equitable right. The right to have a transaction set aside or a contract or deed rectified is a mere equity (not an equitable interest) and it becomes unenforceable against a purchaser of *any* interest (i.e. legal or equitable)[20].

---

14   But not if the rule is that loss of the right to rescind bars any discretionary award of damages, p. 185, ante.
15   (1872) LR 13 Eq 427.
16   (1872) LR Eq 427 at 431, reasoning which accords very closely with that of Jenkins LJ in *Leaf v International Galleries* [1950] 2 KB 86 at 92, [1950] 1 All ER 693 at 696, CA.
17   [1907] 1 Ch 564. Laches was not pleaded.
18   It is not the practice to provide clients with copies of the deeds they execute and it is doubtful whether the client would discover the mistake even if instructed to check. Most clients would raise the objection that this is what they employed their solicitor to do. Trietel, *The Law of Contract* (5th edn), p. 237 favours the time of making the mistake by analogy with the rule for innocent misrepresentation; contra Snell, op. cit., p. 618.
19   [1907] 1 Ch 564 at 566. Further support for this view may be derived from Romer J in *Rees v De Bernardy* [1896] 2 Ch 437 at 445.
20   In *Butler v Mountview Estates Ltd* [1951] 2 KB 563, [1951] 1 All ER 693 (where rectification took the form of limiting the vendor's liability on the implied covenants for title) the plaintiff purchaser had resold the land and rectification was limited so as not to affect the purchasers if they had purchased without notice; *Smith v Jones* [1954] 2 All ER 823.

Where a purchaser of land has disposed of it for value to another he is no longer able to return the land to the vendor. In this situation the intervention of the third party interest makes restoration to the status quo impossible. It does not follow that the existence of a third party right always has this effect, as is shown by cases where a vendor or grantor seeks rescission. In *Sturge v Sturge*[1]:

> X obtained rescission of a conveyance of land to his younger brothers on the ground of equitable fraud, notwithstanding that they had conveyed much of the land to purchasers. X elected to take the purchase money in lieu of land which had been sold and he agreed to confirm the conveyances to the purchasers.

Rescission and the Misrepresentation Act 1967

Reference has already been made[2] to the division of opinion during the early stages of the Misrepresentation Bill on the question whether rescission of a contract for the sale of land induced by an innocent misrepresentation should be allowed after completion. The Law Reform Committee in their report on Innocent Misrepresentation[3] had plumped for finality in conveyancing transactions, and gave as their reasons for not recommending a change in the law the following explanation:

> ' The vendor will often have spent the proceeds of sale on the purchase of another house and so be unable to repay them. The purchase of a house is commonly linked with the raising of a mortgage and perhaps a sequence of other transactions. Rescission of one sale may thus start a chain reaction.'

It seems to have been accepted that there may not be many occasions involving land transactions where a clear-cut case of rescission after completion can arise[4]. In particular, it is said[5], the existence of a mortgage will make it difficult or impossible to restore the parties to their original positions. This conclusion appears to be open to serious doubt. Suppose V conveys property to P, the contract being induced by an actionable innocent misrepresentation. P mortgages the property to M. An institutional lender will not normally object to a premature repayment and there seems no reason why the court cannot order V to repay direct to M so much of the purchase money as is necessary to redeem the mortgage, and on its discharge P can reconvey the property to V free from the charge. The fact that V has invested the money received from P in the purchase of another house should not be a bar to relief[6], for he can raise the cash by reselling the house. This seems to be the extent of the chain reaction which the Law Reform Committee feared might result. The existence of a mortgage or the likelihood of hardship being caused to a vendor in having to resell his newly-acquired property may well be factors to be considered by the court in determining whether to award damages in lieu of rescission. And a strict application of the principle of restitutio in integrum in these situations

1   (1849) 12 Beav 229.
2   Page 644, ante.
3   10th Report, Cmnd. 1782, para. 6.
4   See H.L. Debates, 18 October 1966, Vol. 277, col. 52.
5   (1967) 64 LS Gaz 404, (1967) 117 NLJ 413.
6   It can hardly be argued that V could resist rescission because he had used the money to buy stocks and shares. Why should it be material that he bought a house instead?

may on one possible interpretation of the Act[7] deprive the court of its discretionary power to award damages.

E Terms on which relief granted

The underlying principle in the granting of relief is the substantial restoration of the parties to their original position. Basically this entails, where rescission is sought after completion, repayment of the purchase price to the purchaser and revesting the legal estate in the vendor. The court will set aside the transaction and order the purchaser to reconvey the property to the vendor[8] at the latter's expense, or declare that the conveyance is inoperative and order a memorandum of the judgment to be endorsed on the deed[9]. Where rescission is sought on the ground of mistake, as in *Cooper v Phibbs*[10], no reconveyance is necessary since the original conveyance, being completely nugatory, passes no legal title to the plaintiff. Equity will, however, make a decree setting aside the transaction and will impose such terms as it considers necessary to do justice between the parties.

A purchaser who successfully rescinds is entitled to repayment of the purchase money with interest, and to his expenses incurred in consequence of the purchase. He must account for all rents and profits which he has received, and if he has been in occupation he is charged with an occupation rent[11]. He is entitled to an allowance in respect of substantial repairs and improvements, provided they are undertaken before he discovers that the transaction is voidable[12]. The purchaser must compensate the vendor in respect of depreciation caused by his acts, e.g. by a partial working of mines[13]. There may be circumstances when the purchaser is denied relief because he cannot obtain repayment of the purchase money from the vendor. In *Debenham v Sawbridge*[14] land had been sold by the court and the vendor, a trustee, had never received the money which had been paid into court and distributed among the beneficiaries. Byrne J considered this to be one reason for rejecting the purchaser's claim for rescission.

The allowances received and given by a purchaser are much the same when it is not he but the vendor or grantor who is entitled to have the transaction set aside. As is to be expected, the purchaser is responsible for the vendor's expenses, and he is chargeable with any depreciation caused by acts of waste or, it seems, mere deterioration[15].

---

7 Page 185, ante.
8 *Edwards v M'Leay* (1818) 2 Swan 287; *Sturge v Sturge* (1849) 12 Beav 229. The suggestion in Farrand, 60, that on rescission after completion under the Misrepresentation Act 1967, the legal estate reverts by operation of law seems unsound.
9 See *Hart v Swaine* (1877) 7 Ch D 42, p. 643, ante.
10 (1867) LR 2 HL 149.
11 *Donovan v Fricker* (1821) Jac 165; *Bousfield v Seymour* (1960) 175 Estates Gazette 593.
12 *Trevelyan v White* (1839) 1 Beav 588; *Edwards v M'Leay* (1818) 2 Swan 287 at 289, per Eldon LC.
13 A complete working out of the mine may preclude rescission altogether, p. 654, ante.
14 [1901] 2 Ch 98.
15 *Ex p Bennett* (1805) 10 Ves 381; *Gresley v Mousley* (1862) 4 De G & J 78 (sale to solicitor who granted mining leases set aside).

F   Disclaimer

1.   Right of disclaimer

Previously in this chapter we have been mainly concerned with situations where because of some vitiating element in a transaction a party to a conveyance seeks to have it set aside and thereby undo the bargain he has made. There is another way whereby a grantee of land can divest himself (otherwise than by disposition) of a legal estate in land—by disclaimer. Disclaimer is not a remedy like rescission; it is simply a right which can be exercised independently of court proceedings to renounce an estate or interest under a deed. Suppose A conveys land to B by way of gift[16]. Delivery of the deed by A is effective to vest the legal estate in B, without B's execution of the deed, and even without his knowledge[17]. But no man is obliged to accept any assurance of land made to him without his consent, so that B has a right to refuse to accept the gift, or, in other words, to disclaim. Until he disclaims the legal estate remains vested in him.

Disclaimer need not be by deed; an estate may be disclaimed by conduct without any express declaration[18]. On disclaimer the deed becomes void and the legal estate which passed under it revests in the grantor (or his personal representatives) by operation of law[19].

2.   Loss of right to disclaim

The grantee cannot disclaim once he has unequivocally signified his acceptance of the grant. Acceptance may be express. It may be inferred from conduct, by acting as owner of the property in demanding rents or advertising the property for sale[20], by taking up residence there, or perhaps by merely accepting the title deeds of the property.

Disclaimer by purchasers

Though direct authority is lacking, it is clear from general principles that this doctrine of disclaimer has no application between vendor and purchaser. The rule at law has always been that acceptance of the grant is implied until disagreement is signified[1]. In the case of a purchaser prior acceptance has already been expressly given by entering into a binding contract to purchase the estate, so that an attempted disclaimer of the conveyance would be inoperative[2], even where the legal estate had become vested in him as a result of the vendor's unconditional delivery of the conveyance without payment of the balance of the purchase money[3].

---

16   See e.g. *Hughes v Griffin* [1969] 1 All ER 460, CA, where A executed a conveyance of land in favour of his nephew, B, expressed to be in consideration of £1,500 acknowledged to have been received by A. A later forgave the debt. B knew nothing of all this until A handed the deeds to him some eight years later.
17   See p. 430, ante.
18   *Re Birchall, Birchall v Ashton* (1889) 40 Ch D 436 (disclaimer by trustee).
19   See generally *Sheppard's Touchstone* (7th edn), p. 285; *Mallot v Weston* [1903] 2 Ch 494 at 501, per Byrne J.
20   *Bence v Gilpin* (1868) LR 3 Exch 76.
1   *Thompson v Leach* (1690) 2 Vent 198 at 203, per Ventris J.
2   See 12 Halsbury's Laws (4th edn) 550, para. 1371, citing *Bence v Gilpin* (1868) LR 3 Exch 76, where however assent was inferred from subsequent acts of ownership.
3   See p. 432, ante.

Appendices

List of areas where registration of title compulsory as at 30 January 1982

County (including Greater London)	Areas of compulsory registration
Avon	The districts of Bath, Bristol and Kingswood.
Bedfordshire	The districts of Luton, North Bedfordshire and South Bedfordshire.
Berkshire	The whole county.
Buckinghamshire	The district of Beaconsfield.
Cambridgeshire	The districts of Cambridge and Peterborough.
Cheshire	The whole county.
Cleveland	The whole county.
Cumbria	The district of Barrow-in-Furness.
Derbyshire	The districts of Bolsover, Chesterfield, Derby, Erewash and South Derbyshire.
Devon	The districts of East Devon, Exeter, Plymouth, South Hams, Teignbridge and Torbay.
Dorset	The districts of Bournemouth, Christchurch, Poole, Weymouth and Portland, and Wimborne.
Durham	The districts of Chester-le-Street, Darlington, Durham, Easington and Sedgefield.
Dyfed	The district of Llanelli.
East Sussex	The whole county.
Essex	The districts of Basildon, Brentwood, Epping Forest, Harlow, Southend-on-Sea and Thurrock.
Gloucestershire	The district of Gloucester.
Greater London	The whole administrative area.
Greater Manchester	The whole county.
Gwent	The districts of Islwyn and Newport.
Hampshire	The districts of Eastleigh, Fareham, Gosport, Havant, Portsmouth, New Forest and Southampton.
Hereford and Worcester	The districts of Bromsgrove, Hereford and Worcester.

County (including Greater London)	Areas of compulsory registration
Hertfordshire	The districts of Broxbourne, East Hertfordshire, Hertsmere, St. Albans, Stevenage, Three Rivers, Watford and Welwyn Hatfield.
Humberside	The districts of Cleethorpes, Grimsby, Kingston upon Hull, North Wolds and Scunthorpe.
Kent	The whole county.
Lancashire	The districts of Blackburn, Blackpool, Burnley, Fylde, Preston and Rossendale.
Leicestershire	The districts of Blaby, Charnwood, Hinckley and Bosworth, Leicester, North West Leicestershire, and Oadby and Wigston.
Lincolnshire	The district of Lincoln.
Merseyside	The whole county.
Mid Glamorgan	The districts of Ogwr, Rhondda and Taff-Ely.
Norfolk	The district of Norwich.
Northamptonshire	The districts of Kettering and Northampton.
Northumberland	The districts of Blyth Valley and Wansbeck.
North Yorkshire	The district of York.
Nottinghamshire	The districts of Ashfield, Broxtowe, Gedling, Mansfield, Nottingham and Rushcliffe.
Oxfordshire	The districts of Oxford, South Oxfordshire and Vale of White Horse.
South Glamorgan	The whole county.
South Yorkshire	The whole county.
Staffordshire	The districts of Cannock Chase, Lichfield, Newcastle-under-Lyme, Stoke-on-Trent and Tamworth.
Suffolk	The district of Ipswich.
Surrey	The whole county.
Tyne and Wear	The whole county.
Warwickshire	The districts of North Warwickshire, Nuneaton, Rugby and Warwick.
West Glamorgan	The whole county.
West Midlands	The whole county.
West Sussex	The districts of Adur, Arun, Crawley, Mid Sussex and Worthing.
West Yorkshire	The whole county.

For full details reference should be made to the Registration of Title Order 1977, S.I. 1977 No. 828.

Appendix B

Land Registry forms in common use[1]

Form no.	Description
1A	Application by owners for first registration of freehold land—no solicitor acting.
1B	Application by solicitors for first registration of a purchaser (other than a corporation) of freehold land within one year of purchase.
2B	Application by solicitors for first registration with good leasehold title of a recent purchaser[2] (other than a corporation).
3B	Application by solicitors for first registration with good leasehold title of an original lessee (other than a corporation).
1E	Application by solicitors for first registration of a corporation as a recent purchaser[2] of freehold land.
2E	Application by solicitors for first registration with good leasehold title of a corporation after a recent purchase.[2]
3E	Application by solicitors for first registration with good leasehold title of a corporation as an original lessee.
1F	Application by solicitors for first registration of a rentcharge on behalf of a purchaser or original grantee (other than a corporation) within one year of the sale or grant.
2F	Application by solicitors for first registration with absolute leasehold title of a recent purchaser[2] (other than a corporation[3]).
3F	Application by solicitors for first registration with absolute leasehold title of an original lessee (other than a corporation[4]).
6	Application for conversion of title made ten or fifteen years after date of first registration.

1   Some of the forms in the list are statutory forms (with or without modifications); others
    have been promulgated by the Chief Land Registrar under the power conferred upon him
    by the LRA 1925, s. 127. Not all the forms listed exist as printed forms obtainable from
    H.M. Stationary Office.
2   The expression 'recent purchaser' or 'recent purchase' indicates that the application for
    registration is made within a year of the purchase. Where the application is not so made, a
    different form must be used, form 1C, 1C (Co.), 2C, 2C (Co.), 1G, depending on the
    circumstances.
3   Where the applicant is a company or other corporation the appropriate form is form
    2F (Co.).
4   Where the applicant is a company or other corporation the appropriate form is form
    3F (Co.).

Form no.	Description
7	Application for conversion of good leasehold into absolute leasehold.
9	Restriction where life tenant is registered as proprietor.
10	Restriction where statutory owners or trustees holding on trust for sale are entered as proprietors.
14	Statutory declaration in support of a caution.
19	Transfer of freehold land (whole).
19R1	Transfer of registered rentcharge.
20	Transfer of freehold land (part).
20R1	Transfer of part of land within a registered title in consideration (or partly in consideration) of a rentcharge.
21	Transfer (in lieu of vesting instrument) to life tenant.
31	Transfer of whole in exercise of power of sale contained in registered charge.
33	Transfer of leasehold land being part of that originally demised, where the rent has already been apportioned.
43	Transfer of land imposing restrictive covenants.
44	Exchange of land.
45	Charge[5].
53	Discharge of registered charge.
54	Transfer of registered charge.
56	Assent of land in favour of beneficiary.
59	Application for entry of notice of some right, interest or claim.
62	Entry restraining a disposition by a survivor of joint tenants.
63	Caution against dealings with registered land.
70	Notice warning-off caution.
71	Application to withdraw caution.
75	Application to register restriction.
77	Application to withdraw or modify restriction.
78	Land certificate.
80	Authority to inspect register of title.
82	Application to register transmission on death of sole proprietor.
83	Application to register the death of a joint proprietor.
84	Application to register notice of lease.
85A	Notice of deposit of land certificate.
85B	Notice of intended deposit of land certificate on first registration.
85C	Notice of intended deposit of land certificate on a dealing.
86	Application to withdraw notice of deposit.
94A	Application by purchaser for official search of register in respect of the whole of the land in a title.
94B	Application by purchaser for official search of register in respect of part of the land in a title.
94C	Application by person other than purchaser for official search of register.
94D	Official certificate of the result of search.

5   Four different charge forms exist, each relating to a different situation, e.g. form 45B is a charge of part of the land comprised within a registered title.

Form no.	Description
96	Application for official search of index map and parcels index.
99	Application for registration of notice under the Matrimonial Homes Act 1967.
101	Application for certificate of inspection of filed plan.
102	Certificate of inspection of filed plan.
A4	Application for registration of dealing with registered land (whole).
A5	Application for registration of dealing with registered land (part).
A44	Application for office copies of documents.

The National Conditions of Sale (20th edition)[1]

Construction of the conditions

In these conditions, where the context admits—

(1) The 'vendor' and the 'purchaser' include the persons deriving title under them respectively

(2) 'Purchase money' includes any sum to be paid for chattels, fittings or other separate items

(3) References to the 'Special Conditions' include references to the particulars of sale and to the provisions of the contract which is made by reference to the conditions

(4) The 'prescribed rate' means the agreed rate of interest or, if none, then the rate of interest prescribed from time to time under Land Compensation Act 1961, s. 32

(5) 'Solicitor' includes a barrister who is employed by a corporate body to carry out conveyancing on its behalf and is acting in the course of his employment

(6) 'Working day' means a day on which clearing banks in the City of London are (or would be but for a strike, lock-out, or other stoppage, affecting particular banks or banks generally) open during banking hours. Except in condition 19 (4), in which 'working day' means a day when the Land Registry is open to the public

(7) 'Designated bank' means a bank designated by the Chief Registrar under Building Societies Act 1962, s. 59

(8) The 'Planning Acts' means the enactments from time to time in force relating to town and country planning

(9) On a sale by private treaty references to the 'auctioneer' shall be read as references to the vendor's agent

(10) On a sale in lots, the conditions apply to each lot

(11) 'Abstract of title' means in relation to registered land such documents as the vendor is required by Land Registration Act 1925, s. 110, to furnish.

---

1   Reproduced by kind permission of The Solicitors' Law Stationery Society, Limited.

The conditions

1.   The sale: by auction: by private treaty

(1) Paragraphs (2) to (5) of this condition apply on a sale by auction and paragraphs (6) and (7) on a sale by private treaty

(2) Unless otherwise provided in the Special Conditions, the sale of the property and of each lot is subject to a reserve price and to a right for the vendor or any one person on behalf of the vendor to bid up to that price

(3) The auctioneer may refuse any bid and no person shall at any bid advance less than the amount fixed for that purpose by the auctioneer

(4) If any dispute arises respecting a bid, the auctioneer may determine the dispute or the property may, at the vendor's option, either be put up again at the last undisputed bid, or be withdrawn

(5) Subject to the foregoing provisions of this condition, the highest bidder shall be the purchaser and shall forthwith complete and sign the contract, the date of which shall be the date of the auction

(6) Where there is a draft contract, or an arrangement subject to contract, or a negotiation in which there are one or more outstanding items or suspensory matters (which prevent there being as yet a concluded agreement of a contractual nature), a solicitor, who holds a document signed by his client in the form of a contract of sale in writing and embodying this condition, shall (unless the other party or his solicitor is informed to the contrary) have the authority of his client to conclude, by formal exchange of contracts, or by post, or by telex or other telegraphic means, or by telephone, and in any case with or without involving solicitors' undertakings, a binding contract in the terms of the document which his client has signed

(7) The date of the contract shall be—

  (i)   the date, if any, which is agreed and put on the contract, but if none, then
  (ii) on an exchange of contracts by post (unless the parties' solicitors otherwise agree), the date on which the last part of the contract is posted, or
  (iii) in any other case, the date on which, consistently with this condition, a binding contract is concluded.

2.   Deposit

(1) Unless the Special Conditions otherwise provide, the purchaser shall on the date of the contract pay a deposit of 10 per cent of the purchase price, on a sale by auction, to the auctioneer, or on a sale by private treaty, to the vendor's solicitor and, in either case, as stakeholder

(2) In case a cheque taken for the deposit (having been presented, and whether or not it has been re-presented) has not been honoured then and on that account the vendor may elect—

either   (i)   to treat the contract as discharged by breach thereof on the purchaser's part
or   (ii) to enforce payment of the deposit as a deposit, by suing on the cheque or otherwise.

3.   Purchaser's short right to rescind

(1) This condition shall have effect if the Special Conditions so provide, but not otherwise

(2) If the property is affected by any matter to which this condition applies, then the purchaser may by notice in writing (hereinafter referred to as a 'Condition 3 Notice') given to the vendor or his solicitor and expressly referring to this condition and the matter in question, and notwithstanding any intermediate negotiation, rescind the contract on the same terms as if the purchaser had persisted in an objection to the title which the vendor was unable to remove

(3) A Condition 3 Notice shall not be given after the expiration of 16 working days from the date of the contract, time being of the essence of this condition

(4) This condition applies to any matter materially affecting the value of the property, other than —

  (i)   a matter which was not yet in existence or subsisting at the date of the contract

  (ii) a specific matter to which the sale was expressly made subject, or

(iii) a matter of which the purchaser had at the date of the contract express notice or actual knowledge, not being notice or knowledge imputed to the purchaser by statute solely by reason of a registration of such matter, or notice or knowledge which the purchaser is only deemed to have had by the conditions

(5) This condition and condition 15 are additional to each other.

4.   Chattels, etc., and separate items

If the sale includes chattels, fittings or other separate items, the vendor warrants that he is entitled to sell the same free from any charge, lien, burden, or adverse claim.

5.   Date and manner of completion

(1) The completion date shall be the date specified for the purpose in the contract or, if none, the 26th working day after the date of the contract or the date of delivery of the abstract of title, whichever be the later

(2) Unless the Special Conditions otherwise provide, in respect of the completion date time shall not be of the essence of the contract, but this provision shall operate subject and without prejudice to —

  (i)   the provisions of condition 22 and

  (ii) the rights of either party to recover from the other damages for delay in fulfilling his obligations under the contract

(3) The purchaser's obligations to pay money due on completion shall be discharged by one or more of the following methods —

  (i)   authorisation in writing to release a deposit held for the purposes of the contract by a stakeholder

  (ii) banker's draft issued by a designated bank

(iii) cheque drawn on and guaranteed by a designated bank

(iv) telegraphic or other direct transfer (as requested or agreed to by the vendor's solicitor) to a particular bank or branch for the credit of a specified account

(v) legal tender

(vi) any other method requested or agreed to by the vendor's solicitor

(4) Completion shall be carried out, either formally at such office or place as the vendor's solicitor shall reasonably require, or (if the parties' solicitors so arrange) by post, or by means of solicitors' undertakings concerning the holding of documents or otherwise. Provided that on a sale with vacant possession of the whole or part of the property, if the conveyance or transfer will not, by overreaching or otherwise, discharge the property from interests (if any) of persons in, or who may be in, actual occupation of the property or such part of it, then (subject always to the rights of the purchaser under Law of Property Act 1925, s. 42 (1)), the purchaser may, by giving reasonable notice, require that on, or immediately before the time of, completion possession of the property or part be handed over to the purchaser or his representative at the property

(5) The date of actual completion shall be the day on which, the contract being completed in other respects, the purchaser has discharged consistently with the provisions of this condition the obligations of the purchaser to pay the money due on completion Provided that —

(i) for the purposes only of conditions 6, 7 and 8, if but for this proviso the date of actual completion would be the last working day of a week (starting on Sunday) and the purchaser is unable or unwilling to complete before 2.15 p.m. on that day, then the date of actual completion shall be taken to be the first working day thereafter

(ii) a remittance sent by post or delivered by hand shall be treated as being made on the day on which it reaches the vendor's solicitor's office, unless that day is not a working day in which case the remittance shall be treated as being made on the first working day thereafter.

6. Rents, outgoings and apportionments

The purchase being completed (whether on the completion date or subsequently), the income and outgoings shall be apportioned as follows (the day itself in each case being apportioned to the vendor): —

(1) In a case in which proviso (i) to condition 7 (1) applies apportionment shall be made as at the date of actual completion

(2) In a case in which the purchaser is in possession of the whole of the property as lessee or tenant at a rent apportionment shall be made as at the date of actual completion unless proviso (ii) to condition 7 (1) applies, when apportionment shall be made as at the date of the purchaser's notice under that proviso

(3) In any other case apportionment shall be made as from the completion date Provided nevertheless that, if delay is attributable to the vendor's failure to obtain the reversioner's licence, where necessary, or if the vendor remains in beneficial occupation of the property after the completion date, the purchaser may by notice in writing before actual completion elect that apportionment shall be made as at the date of actual completion

(4) Rates shall be apportioned according to the period for which they are intended to provide and rents (whether payable in advance or in arrear) according to the period in respect of which they have been paid or are payable; and apportionment of yearly items (whether or not the same are payable by equal quarterly, monthly or other instalments) shall be according to the relevant number of days relatively to the number of days in the full year

(5) Service charges under leases, in the absence of known or readily ascertainable amounts, shall be apportioned according to the best estimate available at the time of completion and, unless otherwise agreed, the vendor and the purchaser shall be and remain mutually bound after completion to account for and pay or allow to each other, within 15 working days after being informed of the actual amounts as ascertained, any balances or excesses due.

7.   Interest

(1) If the purchase shall not be completed on the completion date then (subject to the provisions of paragraph (2) of this condition) the purchaser shall pay interest on the remainder of his purchase money at the prescribed rate from that date until the purchase shall actually be completed Provided nevertheless—

  (i)   That (without prejudice to the operation of proviso (ii) to this paragraph) the vendor may by notice in writing before actual completion elect to take the income of the property (less outgoings) up to the date of actual completion instead of interest as aforesaid
 (ii)   That, if the delay arises from any cause other than the neglect or default of the purchaser, and if the purchaser (not being in occupation of the property in circumstances to which condition 8 applies) places the remainder of his purchase money (at his own risk) at interest on a deposit account in England or Wales with any designated bank, and gives written notice thereof to the vendor or his solicitor, then in lieu of the interest or income payable to or receivable by the vendor as aforesaid, the vendor shall from the time of such notice be entitled to such interest only as is produced by such deposit
(iii)   That the vendor shall in no case be or become entitled in respect of the same period of time both to be paid interest and to enjoy income of the property, or to be paid interest more than once on the same sum of money

(2) The purchaser shall not be liable to pay interest under paragraph (1) of this condition—
  (i)   so long as, or to the extent that, delay in completion is attributable to any act or default of the vendor or his mortgagee or Settled Land Act trustees
 (ii)   in case the property is to be constructed or converted by the vendor, so long as the construction or conversion is unfinished.

8.   Occupation pending completion

(1) If the purchaser (not being already in occupation as lessee or tenant at a rent) is let into occupation of the property before the actual completion of the purchase, then, as from the date of his going into occupation and until actual completion, or until upon discharge or rescission of the contract he ceases to occupy the property, the purchaser shall—

  (i)   be the licensee and not the tenant of the vendor

 (ii)   pay interest on the remainder of the purchase money at the prescribed rate

(iii)   keep the property in as good repair and condition as it was in when he went into occupation

(iv)   pay, or otherwise indemnify the vendor against, all outgoings and expenses (including the cost of insurance) in respect of the property, the purchaser at the same time taking or being credited with the income of the property (if any)

 (v)   not carry out any development within the meaning of the Planning Acts

(2) Upon discharge or rescission of the contract, or upon the expiration of 7 working days' or longer notice given by the vendor or his solicitor to the purchaser or his solicitor in that behalf, the purchaser shall forthwith give up the property in such repair and condition as aforesaid

(3) A purchaser going into occupation before completion shall not be deemed thereby to have accepted the vendor's title

(4) Where the purchaser is allowed access to the property for the purpose only of carrying out works or installations, the purchaser shall not be treated as being let into occupation within the meaning of this condition.

9. Abstract, requisitions and observations

(1) The vendor shall deliver the abstract of title not later than 11 working days after the date of the contract but, subject and without prejudice as mentioned in condition 5 (2), that time limit shall not be of the essence of the contract

(2) Subject always to the rights of the purchaser under Law of Property Act 1925, s. 42 (1), the vendor may be required by the purchaser to deal with requisitions and observations concerning persons who are or may be in occupation or actual occupation of the property, so as to satisfy the purchaser that the title is not, and that the purchaser will not be, prejudicially affected by any interests or claims of such persons

(3) The purchaser shall deliver in writing his requisitions within 11 working days after delivery of the abstract, and his observations on the replies to the requisitions within 6 working days after delivery of the replies.

(4) In respect of the delivery of requisitions and observations, time shall be of the essence of the contract, notwithstanding that the abstract may not have been delivered within due time

(5) The purchaser shall deliver his requisitions and observations on the abstract as delivered, whether it is a perfect or an imperfect abstract, but for the purposes of any requisitions, or observations which could not be raised or made on the information contained in an imperfect abstract, time under paragraph (3) of this condition shall not start to run against the purchaser, until the vendor has delivered the further abstract or information on which the requisitions or observations arise

(6) Subject to his requisitions and observations, the purchaser shall be deemed to have accepted the title.

10.   Vendor's right to rescind

(1) If the purchaser shall persist in any objection to the title which the vendor shall be unable or unwilling, on reasonable grounds, to remove, and shall not withdraw the same within, 10 working days of being required so to do, the vendor may, subject to the purchaser's rights under Law of Property Act 1925, ss. 42 and 125, by notice in writing to the purchaser or his solicitor, and not-withstanding any intermediate negotiation or litigation, rescind the contract

(2) Upon such rescission the vendor shall return the deposit, but without interest, costs of investigating title or other compensation or payment, and the purchaser shall return the abstract and other papers furnished to him.

11.   Existing leaseholds

(1) Where the interest sold is leasehold for the residue of an existing term the following provisions of this condition shall apply

(2) The lease or underlease or a copy thereof having been made available, the purchaser (whether he has inspected the same or not) shall be deemed to have bought with full notice of the contents thereof

(3) On production of a receipt for the last payment due for rent under the lease or underlease, the purchaser shall assume without proof that the person giving the receipt, though not the original lessor, is the reversioner expectant on the said lease or underlease or his duly authorised agent

(4) No objection shall be taken on account of the covenants in an underlease not corresponding with the covenants in any superior lease

(5) The sale is subject to the reversioner's licence being obtained, where necessary. The purchaser supplying such information and references, if any, as may reasonably be required of him, the vendor will use his best endeavours to obtain such licence and will pay the fee for the same. But if the licence cannot be obtained, the vendor may rescind the contract on the same terms as if the purchaser had persisted in an objection to the title which the vendor was unable to remove

(6) Where the property comprises part only of the property comprised in a lease or underlease, the rent, covenants and conditions shall, if the purchaser so requires, be legally apportioned at his expense, but completion shall not be delayed on that account and in the meantime the apportionment by the auctioneer shall be accepted, or the property may at the option of the vendor be sub-demised for the residue of the term, less one day, at a rent apportioned by the auctioneer and subject to the purchaser executing a counterpart containing covenants and provisions corresponding to those contained in the lease or underlease aforesaid

(7) Any statutory covenant to be implied in the conveyance on the part of a vendor shall be so limited as not to affect him with liability for a subsisting breach of any covenant or condition concerning the state or condition of the property, of which state and condition the purchaser is by paragraph (3) of condition 13 deemed to have full notice, and where Land Registration Act 1925, s. 24, applies the purchaser, if required, will join in requesting that an appropriate entry be made in the register.

12.   Vendor's duty to produce documents

(1) If an abstracted document refers to any plan material to the description of the property, or to any covenants contained in a document earlier in date than the document with which the title commences, and such plan or earlier document is in the possession or power of the vendor or his trustees or mortgagee, the vendor shall supply a copy thereof with the abstract

(2) If the property is sold subject to restrictive covenants, the deed imposing those covenants or a copy thereof having been made available, the purchaser (whether he has inspected the same or not) shall be deemed to have purchased with full knowledge thereof

(3) The vendor shall not be required to procure the production of any document not in his possession or not in the possession of his mortgagee or trustees, and of which the vendor cannot obtain production, or to trace or state who has the possession of the same.

13.   Identity: boundaries: condition of property

(1) The purchaser shall admit the identity of the property with that comprised in the muniments offered by the vendor as the title thereto upon the evidence afforded by the descriptions contained in such muniments, and of a statutory declaration, to be made (if required) at the purchaser's expense, that the property has been enjoyed according to the title for at least 12 years

(2) The vendor shall not be bound to show any title to boundaries, fences, ditches, hedges or walls, or to distinguish parts of the property held under different titles further than he may be able to do from information in his possession

(3) The purchaser shall be deemed to buy with full notice in all respects of the actual state and condition of the property and, save where it is to be constructed or converted by the vendor, shall take the property as it is.

14.   Property sold subject to easements, etc.

Without prejudice to the duty of the vendor to disclose all latent easements and latent liabilities known to the vendor to affect the property, the property is sold subject to any rights of way and water, rights of common, and other rights, easements, quasi-easements, liabilities and public rights affecting the same.

15.   Town and country planning

(1) In this condition, where the context admits, references to 'authorised use' are references to 'established use', or to use for which permission has been granted under the Planning Acts, or to use for which permission is not required under those Acts, as the case may be

(2) The purchaser shall be entitled to deliver, with his requisitions in respect of the title, requisitions concerning the authorised use of the property for the purposes of the Planning Acts. The vendor in reply shall give all such relevant information as may be in his possession or power

(3) Where the property is in the Special Conditions expressed to be sold on the footing of an authorised use which is specified, then if it appears before actual

completion of the purchase that the specified use is not an authorised use of the property for the purposes of the Planning Acts, the purchaser may by notice in writing rescind the contract, and thereupon paragraph (2) of condition 10 shall apply. But, subject to the foregoing provisions of this condition, the purchaser shall be deemed to have accepted that the specified use is an authorised use of the property for the purposes of the Planning Acts

(4) Save as mentioned in the Special Conditions, the property is not to the knowledge of the vendor subject to any charge, notice, order, restriction, agreement or other matter arising under the Planning Acts, but (without prejudice to any right of the purchaser to rescind the contract under paragraph (3) of this condition) the property is sold subject to any such charges, notices, orders, restrictions, agreements and matters affecting the interest sold

(5) Subject as hereinbefore provided, and without prejudice to the obligations of the vendor to supply information as aforesaid, the purchaser shall be deemed to buy with knowledge in all respects of the authorised use of the property for the purposes of the Planning Acts.

16.   Requirements by local authority

(1) If after the date of the contract any requirement in respect of the property be made against the vendor by any local authority, the purchaser shall comply with the same at his own expense, and indemnify the vendor in respect thereof: in so far as the purchaser shall fail to comply with such requirement, the vendor may comply with the same wholly or in part and any money so expended by the vendor shall be repaid by the purchaser on completion

(2) The vendor shall upon receiving notice of any such requirement forthwith inform the purchaser thereof.

17.   Errors, mis-statements or omissions

(1) Without prejudice to any express right of either party, or to any right of the purchaser in reliance on Law of Property Act 1969, s. 24, to rescind the contract before completion and subject to the provisions of paragraph (2) of this condition, no error, mis-statement or omission in any preliminary answer concerning the property, or in the sale plan or the Special Conditions, shall annul the sale, nor (save where the error, mis-statement or omission relates to a matter materially affecting the description or value of the property) shall any damages be payable, or compensation allowed by either party, in respect thereof

(2) Paragraph (1) of this condition shall not apply to any error, mis-statement or omission which is recklessly or fraudulently made, or to any matter or thing by which the purchaser is prevented from getting substantially what he contracted to buy

(3) In this condition a 'preliminary answer' means and includes any statement made by or on behalf of the vendor to the purchaser or his agents or advisers, whether in answer to formal preliminary enquiries or otherwise, before the purchaser entered into the contract.

18.   Leases and tenancies

(1) Abstracts or copies of the leases or agreements (if in writing) under which the tenants hold having been made available, the purchaser (whether he has

inspected the same or not) shall be deemed to have notice of and shall take subject to the terms of all the existing tenancies and the rights of the tenants, whether arising during the continuance or after the expiration thereof, and such notice shall not be affected by any partial or incomplete statement in the Special Conditions with reference to the tenancies, and no objection shall be taken on account of there not being an agreement in writing with any tenant

(2) Where a lease or tenancy affects the property sold and other property, the property sold will be conveyed with the benefit of the apportioned rent (if any) mentioned in the Special Conditions or (if not so mentioned) fixed by the auctioneer, and no objection shall be taken on the ground that the consent of the tenant has not been obtained to the apportionment and the purchaser shall not require the rent to be legally apportioned

(3) The purchaser shall keep the vendor indemnified against all claims by the tenant for compensation or otherwise, except in respect of a tenancy which expires or is determined on or before the completion date or in respect of an obligation which ought to have been discharged before the date of the contract

(4) Land in the occupation of the vendor is sold subject to the right (hereby reserved to him) to be paid a fair price for tillages, off-going and other allowances as if he were an outgoing tenant who had entered into occupation of the land after 1st March 1944, and as if the purchaser were the landlord, and in case of dispute such price shall be fixed by the valuation of a valuer, to be nominated in case the parties differ by the President of the Royal Institution of Chartered Surveyors.

19. Preparation of conveyance: priority notices: indemnities

(1) Where the interest sold is leasehold for a team of years to be granted by the vendor, the lease or underlease and counterpart shall be prepared by the vendor's solicitor in accordance (as nearly as the circumstances admit) with a form or draft annexed to the contract or otherwise sufficiently identified by the signatures of the parties or their solicitors

(2) In any other case the conveyance shall be prepared by the purchaser or his solicitor and the following provisions of this condition shall apply

(3) The draft conveyance shall be delivered at the office of the vendor's solicitor at least 6 working days before the completion date and the engrossment for execution by the vendor and other necessary parties (if any) shall be left at the said office within 3 working days after the draft has been returned to the purchaser approved on behalf of the vendor and other necessary parties (if any)

(4) Where the property is unregistered land not in an area of compulsory registration and the conveyance is to contain restrictive covenants, and the purchaser intends contemporaneously with the conveyance to execute a mortgage or conveyance to a third party, he shall inform the vendor of his intention and, if necessary, allow the vendor to give a priority notice for the registration of the intended covenants at least 15 working days before the contract is completed

(5) Where the property is sold subject to legal incumbrances, the purchaser shall covenant to indemnify the vendor against actions and claims in respect of them; and the purchaser will not make any claim on account of increased expense caused by the concurrence of any legal incumbrancer

(6) Where the property is sold subject to stipulations, or restrictive or other covenants, and breach thereof would expose the vendor to liability, the purchaser shall covenant to observe and perform the same and to indemnify the vendor against actions and claims in respect thereof

(7) Paragraphs (5) and (6) of this condition shall have effect without prejudice to the provisions of Law of Property Act 1925, s. 77, and Land Registration Act 1925, s. 24, where such provisions respectively are applicable, and in respect of matters covered by a covenant implied under either of those sections no express covenant shall be required.

20.   Severance of properties formerly in common ownership

Where the property and any adjacent or neighbouring property have hitherto been in common ownership, the purchaser shall not become entitled to any right to light or air over or in respect of any adjacent or neighbouring property which is retained by the vendor and the conveyance shall, if the vendor so requires, reserve to him such easements and rights as would become appurtenant to such last-mentioned property by implication of law, if the vendor had sold it to another purchaser at the same time as he has sold the property to the purchaser.

21.   Insurance

(1) With respect to any policy of insurance maintained by the vendor in respect of damage to or destruction of the property, the vendor shall not (save pursuant to an obligation to a third party) be bound to keep such insurance on foot or to give notice to the purchaser of any premium being or becoming due

(2) The purchaser shall be entitled to inspect the policy at any time

(3) The vendor shall, if required, by and at the expense of the purchaser obtain or consent to an endorsement of notice of the purchaser's interest on the policy, and in such case the vendor (keeping the policy on foot) may require the purchaser to pay on completion a proportionate part of the premium from the date of the contract.

22.   Special notice to complete

(1) At any time on or after the completion date, either party, being ready and willing to fulfil his own outstanding obligations under the contract, may (without prejudice to any other right or remedy available to him) give to the other party or his solicitor notice in writing requiring completion of the contract in conformity with this condition

(2) Upon service of such notice as aforesaid it shall become and be a term of the contract, in respect of which time shall be of the essence thereof, that the party to whom the notice is given shall complete the contract within 16 working days after service of the notice (exclusive of the day of service): but this condition shall operate without prejudice to any right of either party to rescind the contract in the meantime

(3) In case the purchaser refuses or fails to complete in conformity with this condition, then (without prejudice to any other right or remedy available to the vendor) the purchaser's deposit may be forfeited (unless the court otherwise directs) and, if the vendor resells the property within 12 months of the

expiration of the said period of 16 working days, he shall be entitled (upon crediting the deposit) to recover from the purchaser hereunder the amount of any loss occasioned to the vendor by expenses of or incidental to such resale, or by diminution in the price.

Appendix D

The Law Society's General Conditions of Sale (1980 edition)[1]

1. Definitions

In these conditions—

(a) 'the contract rate' means the annual rate of interest specified in a special condition or, if none is so specified, four per centum above Bank of England minimum lending rate from time to time in force

(b) 'contractual completion date' has the meaning given in condition 21

(c) 'conveyance' includes an assignment and a transfer under the Land Registration Acts

(d) 'lease' includes underlease

(e) 'working day' means any day from Monday to Friday (inclusive) other than—

      (i)   Christmas Day, Good Friday and any statutory bank holiday, and

      (ii)   any other day specified in a special condition as not a working day

(f) a reference to a statute includes any amendment or re-enactment thereof.

2. Service and delivery

(1) Section 196 of the Law of Property Act 1925 applies to any notice served under the contract, save that—

(a) a notice shall also be sufficiently served on a party if served on that party's solicitors

(b) any reference to a registered letter shall include a prepaid first class ordinary letter

(c) if the time at which a letter containing a notice would in the ordinary course be delivered is not on a working day, the notice shall be deemed to be served on the next following working day

(d) any notice shall also be sufficiently served if sent by telex or by telegraphic facsimile transmission to the party to be served, and that service shall be deemed to be made on the day of transmission if transmitted before 4 p.m. on a working day, but otherwise on the next following working day.

(2) Sub-condition (1) applies to the delivery of documents as it applies to the service of notices.

3. Matters affecting the property

(1) In this condition—

1   Reproduced by kind permission of The Law Society.

(a) 'competent authority' means a local authority or other body exercising powers under statute or Royal Charter

(b) 'requirement' includes (whether or not subject to confirmation) any notice, order or proposal

(c) 'relevant matter' means any matter specified in sub-condition (2) whenever arising

(2) The property is sold subject to—

(a) all matters registrable by any competent authority pursuant to statute

(b) all requirements of any competent authority

(c) all matters disclosed or reasonably to be expected to be disclosed by searches and as a result of enquiries formal or informal, and whether made in person, by writing or orally by or for the purchaser or which a prudent purchaser ought to make

(d) all notices served by or on behalf of a reversioner, a tenant or sub-tenant, or the owner or occupier of any adjoining or neighbouring property.

(3) (a) Notwithstanding sub-condition (2), the vendor warrants that he has informed the purchaser of the contents of any written communication received by, or known to, the vendor on or before the working day preceding the date of the contract relating to any relevant matter. Failure to give such information before the contract is made shall be deemed to be an omission in a statement in the course of the negotiations leading to the contract, but shall give rise to no right to compensation to the extent that the purchaser has a claim for damages against a competent authority

(b) In the event of any conflict or variation between information in fact received from any competent authority relating to any relevant matter and any statement made by the vendor in respect of the same matter, the purchaser shall rely on the information received from the competent authority to the exclusion of that given by the vendor.

(c) The vendor shall forthwith inform the purchaser of the contents of any written communication received by him after the working day preceding the date of the contract and before the day of actual completion which if received on or before the former day would have fallen within paragraph (a).

(4) The purchaser (subject to any right or remedy arising from sub-condition (3)) will indemnify the vendor in respect of any liability under any requirement of a competent authority (whether made before or after the date of the contract), including the reasonable cost to the vendor of compliance after reasonable notice of the purchaser of the vendor's intention to comply, such sum to be payable on demand. The provision of this sub-condition shall prevail in the event of conflict with any other general condition.

4. Opportunity to rescind

(1) This condition only applies if a special condition so provides and is without prejudice to the provisions of condition 3.

(2) Within such period as is specified in a special condition or, if none is so specified, within four weeks from the date of the contract (as to which, in either case, time shall be of the essence), the purchaser shall be entitled to rescind this contract by service of notice on the vendor specifying a matter to which this condition applies affecting the property.

(3) This condition applies to any of the following matters of which the purchaser had no knowledge on or before the working day preceding the date of the contract —

(a) a financial charge which the vendor cannot, or has not at the purchaser's written request agreed to discharge on or before completion

(b) a statutory provision prohibiting, restricting or imposing adverse conditions upon the use or the continued use of the property for such purpose as a special condition declares that the purchaser intends to use it after completion, or, in the absence of such declaration, the purpose for which the vendor used it immediately before the date of the contract

(c) a matter which is likely materially to reduce the price which a willing purchaser could otherwise reasonably be expected to pay for the vendor's interest in the property in the open market at the date of the contract.

(4) For the purposes of this condition, the purchaser's knowledge —

(a) includes everything in writing received in the course of the transaction leading to the contract by a person acting on his behalf from the vendor, a person acting on the vendor's behalf, or a competent authority (as defined in condition 3 (1) (a))

(b) does not include anything solely because a statute deems that registration of a matter constituted actual notice of it.

5.   **Easements, reservations, rights and liabilities**

(1) The vendor warrants that he has disclosed to the purchaser the existence of all easements, rights, privileges and liabilities affecting the property, of which the vendor knows or ought to know, other than the existence of those known to the purchaser at the date of the contract.

(2) Without prejudice to the generality of sub-condition (1) —

(a) the purchaser shall purchase with full notice of the actual state and condition of the property and shall take it as it stands, save where it is to be constructed or converted by the vendor

(b) the property is sold, and will if the vendor so requires be conveyed, subject to all rights of way, water, light, drainage and other easements, rights, privileges and liabilities affecting the same

(c) where the property is subject to an estate contract, void against a purchaser for want of registration, but the purchaser has been supplied prior to the date of the contract with full details thereof, the purchaser shall indemnify the vendor against all claims, demands and liability howsoever arising in respect thereof.

(3) (a) In this sub-condition 'the retained land' means land retained by the vendor —

    (i)   adjoining the property, or

    (ii) near to the property and designated as retained land in a special condition.

(b) The conveyance of the property shall contain such reservations in favour of the retained land and the grant of such rights over the retained land as would have been implied had the vendor conveyed both the property and the retained land by simultaneous conveyances to different purchasers.

6. Tenancies

(1) This condition applies if the property is sold subject to any lease or tenancy and shall have effect notwithstanding any partial, incomplete or inaccurate reference to any lease or tenancy in the special conditions or the particulars of the property.

(2) Copies or full particulars of all leases or tenancies not vested in the purchaser having been furnished to him, he shall be deemed to purchase with full knowledge thereof and shall take the property subject to the rights of the tenants thereunder or by reason thereof.

(3) The vendor gives no warranty as to the amount of rent lawfully recoverable from any tenant, as to the effect of any legislation in relation to any lease or tenancy or as to the compliance with any legislation affecting the same.

(4) The vendor shall inform the purchaser of any change in the disclosed terms and conditions of any lease or tenancy.

(5) If a lease or tenancy subject to which the property is sold terminates for any reason, the vendor shall inform the purchaser and, on being indemnified by the purchaser against all consequential loss, expenditure or liability, shall act as the purchaser directs.

7. Errors, omissions and misstatements

(1) No error, omission or misstatement herein or in any plan furnished or any statement made in the course of the negotiations leading to the contract shall annul the sale or entitle the purchaser to be discharged from the purchase.

(2) Any such error, omission or misstatement shown to be material shall entitle the purchaser or the vendor, as the case may be, to proper compensation, provided that the purchaser shall not in any event be entitled to compensation for matters falling within conditions 5 (2) or 6 (3).

(3) No immaterial error, omission or misstatement (including a mistake in any plan furnished for identification only) shall entitle either party to compensation.

(4) Sub-condition (1) shall not apply where compensation for any error, omission or misstatement shown to be material cannot be assessed nor enable either party to compel the other to accept or convey property differing substantially (in quantity, quality tenure or otherwise) from the property agreed to be sold if the other party would be prejudiced by the difference.

(5) The purchaser acknowledges that in making the contract he has not relied on any statement made to him save one made or confirmed in writing.

8. Leaseholds

(1) This condition applies if the property is leasehold.

(2) (a) In all cases the immediate title to the property shall begin with the lease. Where the lease, unless registered with absolute title, is dated not more than fifteen years before the date of the contract and was granted for a term exceeding twenty-one years, the freehold title and all other titles superior to the

lease shall be deduced for a period beginning not less than fifteen years prior to the date of the contract and ending on the date of the lease.

(*b*) A copy of the lease and a copy of, sufficient extract from, or abstract of, all superior leases the contents of which are known to the vendor having been supplied or made available to the purchaser, he shall be deemed to purchase with full notice of the contents thereof, whether or not he has inspected the same.

(3) Where any consent to assign is necessary—

(*a*) the vendor shall forthwith at his own cost apply for and use his best endeavours to obtain such consent

(*b*) the purchaser shall forthwith supply such information and references as may reasonably be required by the reversioner before granting such consent

(*c*) if any such consent is not granted at least five working days before contractual completion date, or is subject to any condition to which the purchaser reasonably objects, either party may rescind the contract by notice to the other.

(4) Where there is any breach of the terms of the lease as to the state and condition of the property, any statutory implied covenant on the part of the vendor shall not extend to the said breach and the assignment shall so provide. In the case of registered land the transfer shall incorporate a request by both parties to note such modification on the register. This sub-condition applies notwithstanding that a special condition provides for the vendor to convey as beneficial owner.

(5) Where the property is sold subject to an apportioned rent specified as such in a special condition, the purchaser shall not require the consent of the reversioner to be obtained, or the rent to be otherwise legally apportioned.

(6) The purchaser shall assume that any receipt for the last payment due for rent under the lease before actual completion was given by the person then entitled to such rent or his duly authorised agent.

9.   Deposit

The purchaser shall on or before entering into the contract pay to the vendor's solicitors as stakeholders such a sum as will, together with any preliminary deposit paid to the vendor or his agent, amount to ten per centum of the purchase money (excluding any separate price to be paid for chattels, fixtures or fittings). Save in the case of a sale by auction, such deposit shall be paid either by banker's draft or by a cheque drawn upon a solicitors' bank account. In the event that the said draft or cheque is dishonoured upon first presentation, the vendor shall have the right by notice to the purchaser within seven working days thereafter to elect to treat such dishonour as a fundamental breach of the purchaser's obligations under the contract.

10.   Optional methods of exchange

(1) Exchange of contracts may be effected by post and if so effected the contract shall be made when the last part is posted.

(2) The solicitors to the parties may agree by telephone or telex that the contract be immediately effective and thereupon the solicitors holding a part of the contract signed by their client shall hold it irrevocably to the order of the other party.

11.   Insurance

(1) If the property is destroyed or damaged prior to actual completion and the proceeds of any insurance policy effected by or for the purchaser are reduced by reason of the existence of any policy effected by or for the vendor, the purchase price shall be abated by the amount of such reduction.

(2) Sub-condition (1) shall not apply where the proceeds of the vendor's policy are applied towards the reinstatement of the property pursuant to any statutory or contractual obligation.

(3) This condition takes effect in substitution for section 47 of the Law of Property Act 1925.

(4) The vendor shall be under no duty to the purchaser to maintain any insurance on the property, save where the property is leasehold and the vendor has an obligation to insure.

12.   Abstract of title

(1) Forthwith upon exchange of contracts the vendor shall deliver to the purchaser —
(a) where the title is not registered, an abstract of the title to the property or an epitome of the title together with photocopies of the relevant documents:
(b) where the title is registered —
    (i)   the documents, particulars and information specified in section 110 of the Land Registration Act 1925, save that copies of the entries on the register, the filed plan and any documents noted on the register and filed in the registry shall be office copies, and
    (ii) such additional authorities to inspect the register as the purchaser shall reasonably require for any sub-purchaser or prospective mortgagee or lessee.

(2) Where the title is not registered, the vendor shall at his own expense produce the relevant documents of title or an abstract, epitome of title or copy thereof (bearing in each case original markings of examination of all relevant documents of title or of examined abstracts thereof).

(3) Where before the date of the contract any abstract, epitome or document has been delivered to the purchaser, he shall not, save as provided by conditions 6 (2) or 8 (2) (b), or by the particulars or the special conditions, be deemed to have had notice before the date of the contract of any matter of title thereby disclosed.

13.   Identity and boundaries

(1) The vendor shall produce such evidence as may be reasonably necessary to establish the identity and extent of the property, but shall not be required to define exact boundaries, or the ownership of fences, ditches, hedges or walls, nor, beyond the evidence afforded by the information in his possession, separately to identify parts of the property held under different titles.

(2) If reasonably required by the purchaser because of the insufficiency of the evidence produced under sub-condition (1), the vendor shall at his own expense provide and hand over on completion a statutory declaration as to the relevant facts, in a form agreed by the purchaser, such agreement not to be unreasonably withheld.

14.   Mortgages in favour of friendly and other societies

Where the title includes a mortgage or legal charge in favour of trustees on behalf of a friendly society, a building society or a society registered under the Industrial and Provident Societies Acts, the purchaser shall assume that any receipt given on the discharge of any such mortgage or legal charge and apparently duly executed was in fact duly executed by all proper persons and is valid.

15.   Requisitions

(1) In this condition 'abstract' means all of the documents particulars and information required to be delivered by the vendor under condition 12.

(2) Subject to sub-condition (4), the purchaser shall deliver any requisitions or objections relating to the title, evidence of title or the abstract, in writing within six working days of receipt of the abstract (or, in the case of an abstract delivered before the date of the contract, within six working days of the date of contract). Within four working days of such delivery the vendor shall deliver his replies in writing.

(3) The purchaser shall deliver any observations on any of the vendor's replies in writing within four working days of their receipt.

(4) Where —
(a) some but not all parts of the abstract have been delivered, or
(b) defects in title are not disclosed by such parts of the abstract as have been delivered, then in respect only of the undelivered parts or undisclosed defects (as the case may be) the abstract shall be deemed to be received for the purpose of sub-condition (2) at the time or respective times when any previously undelivered part is delivered.

(5) Time shall be of the essence of the contract for the purposes of this condition.

16.   Rescission

(1) If the vendor is unable, or on some reasonable ground unwilling, to satisfy any requisition or objection made by the purchaser, the vendor may give the purchaser notice (specifying the reason for his inability or the ground of his unwillingness) to withdraw the same. If the purchaser does not withdraw the same within seven working days of service, either party may thereafter, notwithstanding any intermediate negotiation or litigation, rescind the contract by notice to the other.

(2) Upon rescission under any power given by these conditions or any special condition —
(a) the vendor shall repay to the purchaser any sums paid by way of deposit or otherwise under the contract, with interest on such sums at the contract rate from four working days after rescission until payment,
(b) the purchaser shall forthwith return all documents delivered to him by the vendor and at his own expense procure the cancellation of any entry relating to the contract in any register.

17. Preparation of conveyance

(1) The purchaser shall deliver the draft conveyance at least twelve working days before contractual completion date, and within four working days of such delivery the vendor shall deliver it back approved or revised.

(2) The purchaser shall deliver the engrossment of the conveyance (first executed by him, where requisite) at least five working days before contractual completion date.

(3) The purchaser shall not, by delivering the draft conveyance or the engrossment, be deemed to accept the vendor's title or to waive any right to raise or maintain requisitions.

(4) Save to the extent that a covenant for indemnity will be implied by statute, the purchaser shall in the conveyance covenant to indemnify the vendor and his estate (and any estate of which the vendor is personal representative or trustee) against all actions, claims and liability for any breach of any covenant, stipulation, provision or other matter subject to which the property is sold and in respect of which the vendor or any such estate will remain liable after completion.

(5) The vendor shall give an acknowledgment for production and, unless in a fiduciary capacity, an undertaking for safe custody of documents of title retained by him. Where any such document is retained by a mortgagee, trustee or personal representative, the vendor shall procure that such person shall give an acknowledgment for production and the vendor, unless in a fiduciary capacity, shall covenant that if and when he receives any such document he will, at the cost of the person requiring it, give an undertaking for safe custody.

(6) The vendor shall be entitled on reasonable grounds to decline to convey the property to any person other than the purchaser, by more than one conveyance, at more than the contract price or at a price divided between different parts of the property.

18. Possession before completion

(1) This condition applies if the vendor authorises the purchaser to occupy the property before actual completion, except—
(a) where the purchaser is already lawfully in possession of any part of the property, or
(b) where the property is a dwellinghouse and the authority for the occupation is only for the purpose of effecting works of decoration, repair or improvement agreed by the vendor, or
(c) where the property is an agricultural holding as defined in the Agricultural Holdings Act 1948.

(2) The purchaser occupies the property as licensee and not as tenant. The purchaser may not transfer his licence or authorise any other person save members of his immediate family to occupy any part of the property.

(3) The purchaser shall not, by taking such occupation, be deemed to accept the vendor's title or to waive any right to raise or maintain requisitions.

(4) While the purchaser is in occupation of the whole or any part of the property under this condition, he shall—

(*a*) pay and indemnify the vendor against all outgoings, the cost of repairs and any other expenses in respect of the property and pay to the vendor interest at the contract rate on the amount of the purchase money (less any deposit paid)
(*b*) be entitled to receive any rents and profits from any part of the property not occupied by him
(*c*) insure the property in a sum not less than the purchase price against all risks in respect of which premises of the like nature are normally insured.

(5) The purchaser's licence to occupy the property shall end —
(*a*) forthwith upon the termination of the contract or
(*b*) upon the expiry of seven days' notice given by either party to the other, and thereupon the purchaser shall give up occupation of the property and leave the same in as good repair as it was in when he went into occupation.

19.   Apportionments

(1) In this condition —
(*a*) 'the apportionment day' means —
    (i)   if the property is sold with vacant possession of the whole, the date of actual completion
    (ii) in any other case, contractual completion date
(*b*) 'payment period' means one of the periods for which a sum payable periodically is payable, whether or not such periods are of equal length.

(2) On completion the income and outgoings of the property shall, subject to sub-condition (5) and condition 22 (4) and any adjustment required by condition 18 (4) be apportioned as at the apportionment day.

(3) For the purposes of apportionment only, it shall be assumed —
(*a*) that the vendor remains owner of the property until the end of the apportionment day, and
(*b*) that the sum to be apportioned —
    (i)   accrues from day to day
    (ii) is payable throughout the relevant period at the same rate as on the apportionment day

(4) Sums payable periodically shall be apportioned by charging or allowing —
(*a*) for any payment period entirely attributable to one party, the whole of the instalment payable therefor
(*b*) for any part of a payment period, a proportion on an annual basis.

(5) A sum shall not be apportioned if —
(*a*) the purchaser cannot, by virtue only of becoming the owner of the property, either enforce payment of it or be obliged to pay it, or
(*b*) it is an outgoing paid in advance, unless the vendor cannot obtain repayment and the purchaser benefits therefrom or is given credit therefor against a sum that would otherwise be his liability.

(6) (*a*) This sub-condition applies, where the property is leasehold, to any sum due under the lease by the tenant to the landlord or vice versa in respect of any period falling wholly or partly prior to the appointment day, the amount of which is not notified to either party before actual completion.
(*b*) A sum to which this sub-condition applies shall forthwith upon such notification be apportioned as if it had been so notified before actual completion, and thereupon the vendor shall make any appropriate payment to the purchaser or vice versa.

20.   Endorsement of memorandum

Where the vendor does not hand over all the documents of his title, he shall at completion endorse a memorandum of the sale to the purchaser on the last such document in each relevant title and thereupon produce the endorsed documents for inspection.

21.   Completion

(1) Contractual completion date shall be as stated in the special conditions but if not so stated shall be the first working day after the expiration of five weeks from the date of the contract. Completion shall take place at the office of the vendor's solicitors or, if required by the vendor at least five working days prior to actual completion, at the office of the vendor's mortgagee or his solicitors.

(2) The vendor shall not be obliged to accept payment of the money due on completion other than by one or more of the following methods—
(a) legal tender
(b) a banker's draft drawn by and upon a member of the Committee of London Clearing Bankers, a trustee saving bank or National Girobank
(c) an unconditional authority to release any deposit held by a stakeholder
(d) otherwise as the vendor shall have agreed before actual completion.

(3) If the parties agree that completion shall be effected through the post, completion shall take place when, on contractual completion date or a subsequent working day—
(a) the money due on completion is paid to the vendor, and
(b) the vendor's solicitors hold to the order of the purchaser all the documents to which he is entitled on completion.

(4) For the purposes of this condition money is paid when the vendor receives payment by a method specified in sub-condition (2). Where the parties have agreed upon a direct credit to a bank account at a specified branch, payment is made when that branch receives the credit.

(5) (a) This sub-condition applies if the money due on completion is not paid by such time on the day of actual completion as is specified in the special conditions or if none is so specified by 2.30 p.m. on that day.
(b) For the purposes of condition 22 only, completion shall be deemed to be postponed by reason of the purchaser's delay from the day of actual completion until the next working day.
(c) The purchaser shall not as a result of the deemed postponement of completion be liable to make any payment to the vendor unless the vendor gives him notice claiming such payment at or within five working days after completion (as to which period time shall be of the essence of the contract). Payment shall be due five working days after receipt of such notice.

22.   Compensation for late completion

(1) For the purposes of this condition—
(a) 'delay' means failure to perform or lateness in performing any obligation of the contract which causes or contributes to lateness in completion
(b) a party is 'in default' if and to the extent that the period, or the aggregate of the periods, of his delay exceeds the period, or the aggregate of the periods, of delay of the other party

(*c*) 'the period of default' means the length of the excess defined in paragraph (*b*).

(2) If the sale shall be completed after contractual completion date, the party in default (if any) shall be liable to compensate the other for loss occasioned to the other by reason of that default.

(3) Before actual completion, the party entitled to compensation may, by notice to the other party, opt to be paid or allowed on completion a sum equal to interest at the contract rate on the amount of the purchase money (less any deposit paid) for the period of default, as liquidated damages in settlement of his claim for compensation.

(4) If the vendor is entitled to compensation, he may, before actual completion, by notice to the purchaser, opt to take the net income of the property for the period of default in lieu of such compensation.

(5) The right to recover any compensation under this condition shall not be prejudiced by completion of the sale, whether before or after the commencement of proceedings.

23.   Completion notice

(1) This condition applies unless a special condition provides that time is of the essence in respect of contractual completion date.

(2) In this condition 'completion notice' means a notice served in accordance with sub-condition (3).

(3) If the sale shall not be completed on contractual completion date, either party being then himself ready, able and willing to complete may after that date serve on the other party notice to complete the transaction in accordance with this condition. A party shall be deemed to be ready, able and willing to complete—
(*a*) if he could be so but for some default or omission of the other party
(*b*) notwithstanding that any mortgage on the property is unredeemed when the completion notice is served if the aggregate of all sums necessary to redeem all such mortgages (to the extent that they relate to the property) does not exceed the sum payable on completion.

(4) Upon service of a completion notice it shall become a term of the contract that the transaction shall be completed within twenty-one days of service and in respect of such period time shall be of the essence of the contract.

(5) If the purchaser does not comply with a completion notice—
(*a*) the purchaser shall forthwith return all documents delivered to him by the vendor and at his own expense procure the cancellation of any entry relating to the contract in any register.
(*b*) without prejudice to any other rights or remedies available to him, the vendor may—
     (i)   forfeit and retain any deposit paid and/or
     (ii)   resell the property by auction, tender or private treaty.

(6) If on any such re-sale contracted within one year after contractual completion date the vendor incurs a loss the purchaser shall pay to the vendor liquidated damages. The amount payable shall be the aggregate of such loss,

all costs and expenses reasonably incurred in any such re-sale and any attempted re-sale and interest at the contract rate on such part of the purchase money as is from time to time outstanding (giving credit for all sums received under any re-sale contract on account of the re-sale price) after contractual completion date.

(7) If the vendor does not comply with a completion notice, the purchaser, without prejudice to any other rights or remedies available to him, may give notice to the vendor forthwith to pay to the purchaser any sums paid by way of deposit or otherwise under the contract and interest on such sums at the contract rate from four working days after service of the notice until payment. On compliance with such notice the purchaser shall not be entitled to specific performance of the contract, but shall forthwith return all documents delivered to him by the vendor and at the expense of the vendor procure the cancellation of any entry relating to the contract in any register.

(8) Where after service of a completion notice the time for completion shall have been extended by agreement or implication, either party may again invoke the provisions of this condition which shall then take effect with the substitution of 'ten days' for 'twenty-one days' in sub-condition (4).

24. Chattels

The property in any chattels agreed to be sold shall pass to the purchaser on actual completion.

25. Auctions

(1) This condition applies if the property is sold by auction.

(2) The sale is subject to a reserve price for the property and, when the property is sold in lots, for each lot.

(3) The vendor reserves the right —
(a) to divide the property into lots and to sub-divide, re-arrange or consolidate any lots
(b) to bid personally or by his agent up to any reserve price
(c) without disclosing any reserve price, to withdraw from the sale any property or lot at any time before it has been sold, whether or not the sale has begun.

(4) The auctioneer may —
(a) refuse to accept a bid
(b) in the case of a dispute as to any bid, forthwith determine the dispute or again put up the property or lot at the last undisputed bid.

(5) The purchaser shall forthwith complete and sign the contract and pay the deposit in accordance with condition 9.

Index

National Conditions of Sale—*continued*
omissions, 676
preparation of conveyance, 677
priority notices, 677
purchaser's right to rescind, 670
rents, outgoings and apportionments, 671
requisitions, 675
severance of properties in common ownership, 678
special notice to complete, 678
town and country planning, 675
vendor's duty to produce documents, 675
right to rescind, 674
**National House Builders' Registration
Council**
common law remedies, effect of scheme, 80
exclusions, 179
persons protected by scheme, 179
protection afforded by scheme, 177
scheme compared with statutory obligation,
180
Negligence
availability of *non est factum*, 647
vendor's liability for negligent work, 170
New towns
local land charges, 193
Non-rectification. *See* Rectification
Notice
actual, 380
constituted by registration, 396
application to register lease of land already
registered, 459
assent, of, death of sole proprietor, 358
completion—
by certain date, of, 414
statutory time limit as to planning permission, 220
constructive, 380
creditor's, vendor's title against, 270
deducing title as to leaseholds, 307
deposit of land certificate—
by intending proprietor, 468
of, 467
floating charge on registered land, 408
imputed, 382
lease, of, on lessor's title, 460
light obstruction, local and charges, 194
planning control—
enforcement, 226–228
continuing force of, 230
rights of appeal, 228
priority, before registration, 399
National Conditions of Sale, 676
protection of minor interests by, 67–69
effect of entry, 68
production of land certificate, 67
proposals for reform, 75
purchaser without, 379
actual notice, 380
constructive notice, 380
imputed, 382
restrictive covenants, of, entry of, 476
service of Law Society's Conditions of Sale,
680

Notice—*continued*
special, to complete, National Conditions of
Sale, 678
superior title, of, registered leasehold
property, 357
treat, to, under compulsory purchase order,
245
unprotected minor interest, of 72
withdrawal of land certificate, 468
written, by planning authority, 215
Occupation
actual, meaning, 51
date of, 52
diversity of, rights not conveyed, 528
meaning, 49
pending completion—
Law Society's Conditions of Sale, 687
National Conditions of Sale, 673
Occupier
beneficial interest, claiming, 57 *et seq.*
intending, consent to mortgage, 61
overriding interests, 58, 59
refusal to vacate, 58
rights, 49 *et seq.*
failure to disclose, 53
inquiry into, 53
Option
agreement, protection against gazumping,
242
purchase of freehold reversion, 557
purchase, to, 243
registration of, 257
right of pre-emption, 256
renewal of lease, 557
Order
avoidance by non-registration, 397
civil aviation, local land charges, 193
compulsory purchase—
local land charges, 193
notice to treat, 245
court vesting, deed of conveyance not
required, 483
development, planning permission, 212
new town, local land charges, 193
opencast coal mining, local land charges,
193
rectification, for, effect of, 654
register of, 390
specific performance, for, 583
Overriding interests
beneficiary under a trust for sale, 54
disclosure of, on sale, 149
effect of entry on register, 56
general nature and characteristics, 44, 45
inquiry as to occupier's rights, 53, 54
Law Commission's proposals to reduce, 64
matrimonial home, 50, 51, 57 *et seq.*
mines and minerals, 56
mortgage, 57 *et seq.*, 60, 62, 63
need for reform of, 63
occupation—
actual, meaning, 51

Sale—*continued*
  sub-sale—*continued*
    registered land, 352
  tenants, to, special conditions, 161
  trust for, deducing title, 320 *et seq.*
Schedule
  deed of conveyance, appended to, 546
Search
  additional inquiries, 183, 197
  builders' liability in respect of new houses,
    173
  caveat emptor, extent of rule, 169
  certificates of, inclusion in abstract, 297
  collateral warranty, 172
  company register—
    floating charges, 408
    registered land, 408
    unregistered land, 407
  effectiveness of inquiries, 183
  excluding liability, 186
  general inquiries, 181
    explanation, 167
  incumbrances, for, 378 *et seq.*
    potential traps, 404
    purpose and mode, 400
  land charges, 201
    registered, explanation, 202
  Land Charges Register, in, 406
  leasehold inquiries, 182
    property, 172
  leases, 173
  legal unfitness, 169
  liability—
    incorrect replies to additional inquiries,
      for, 197
    road charges, for, 198
  local land charges. *See* Local land charges
  Misrepresentation Act 1967, under, 185
    purchaser's rights, 185
  National House Builder's Registration Coun-
    cil scheme, 177 *et seq.*
  official—
    application for, 400
    certificate—
      effect of, 405
      erroneous, 406
      under Land Registration (Official
        Searches) Rules 1969 . . . 404
    result of, 401
    search certificate—
      advantages of, 401
      erroneous, 403
  personal, 406
  persons included in, 401
  public index map, 203
  purchaser, inquiries as to planning, 232
  replies—
    fraudulent, 184
    inaccurate, 184
  sales by public auction, 243
  standard form, 181
  statutory liability, new houses, 174
  survey, independent, used for, 168

Search—*continued*
  telephone, by, 406
  teleprinter, by, 406
  tortious liability, 188
  vendor's implied, exclusion of, 173
Settlements
  beneficial interests, protection of, 360
  covenants for title, 620
  curtain principle, title, as to, 359
  death of life tenant, 360
  deducing title—
    settled land, of, 316
    vesting deed, 317
  devolution of settled land, 318
  equitable interest affecting registered land,
    66
  protection of beneficial interests, 360
  purchaser, protection of, 318
  sale of settled land, title, 360
  termination of, 319, 361
Severability
  invalid conditions of planning permission,
    225
Signature
  written memorandum, 109–112
Simplification
  existing procedures, of, 9
Solicitor
  acting for both parties, 133n., 137, 239
  deposit, holding of, 251
  employment of own, 165
  signature of written memorandum by, 112
  vendor's, as agent or stakeholder, 252
Specific performance .
  breach of contract not necessary, 576
  discretionary remedy, 576
  enforcement of, mode of, 584
    order, 584
  form of order, 583
  general explanation, 575
  illegal conduct, 580
  misdescription, 600
  mutuality, 577
  refusal—
    consequences of, 582
    damages, 576
    defective title, 581
    defences available at law, 577
    delay, 578
    hardship, 579
    inequitable conduct, 580
    misdescription, 578
Stakeholder
  deposit, holding of, 251
  loss of deposit, 253
Stamp duty
  building agreements, 443
  Commissioners of Inland Revenue, produc-
    tion of documents to, 444
  fixed rate of 50p, 443
  rates of, 442
  sale agreements, 443
  time limit for presentation, 442